NATIONAL STANDARDS
FOR CIVICS AND GOVERNMENT

I. What are civic life, politics, and government?

A. What is civic life? What is politics? What is government? Why are government and politics necessary? What purposes should government serve?

B. What are the essential characteristics of limited and unlimited government?

C. What are the nature and purposes of constitutions?

D. What are alternative ways of organizing constitutional governments?

II. What are the foundations of the American political system?

A. What is the American idea of constitutional government?

B. What are the distinctive characteristics of American society?

C. What is American political culture?

D. What values and principles are basic to American constitutional democracy?

III. How does the government established by the Constitution embody the purposes, values, and principles of American democracy?

A. How are power and responsibility distributed, shared, and limited in the government established by the United States Constitution?

B. How is the national government organized and what does it do?

C. How are state and local governments organized and what do they do?

D. What is the place of law in the American constitutional system?

E. How does the American political system provide for choice and opportunities for participation?

IV. What is the relationship of the United States to other nations and to world affairs?

A. How is the world organized politically?

B. How do the domestic politics and constitutional principles of the United States affect its relations with the world?

C. How has the United States influenced other nations, and how have other nations influenced American politics and society?

V. What are the roles of the citizen in American democracy?

A. What is citizenship?

B. What are the rights of citizens?

C. What are the responsibilities of citizens?

D. What civic dispositions or traits of private and public character are important to the preservation and improvement of American constitutional democracy?

E. How can citizens take part in civic life?

National Standards for Civics and Government ©1994, 2003
Center for Civic Education. All Rights Reserved. Reprinted with permission.

HOLT McDOUGAL

CIVICS
IN PRACTICE

PRINCIPLES OF GOVERNMENT AND ECONOMICS

Gregory I. Massing

Developed in Partnership with

 Center for
Civic Education™

Charles Quigley
John Hale
Dick Kean
Maria Gallo
Michael Fischer
Kaci Patterson
Robert Leming
Kari Coppinger
Theresa Richard
Mark Stritzel
Mark Gage

HOLT McDOUGAL
a division of Houghton Mifflin Harcourt

AUTHOR
Gregory I. Massing

Gregory Massing is a graduate of the Virginia School of Law. He was law review editor and in the top one percent of his graduating class and has the unique combination of experience for this particular course—legal and constitutional scholarship with real-life applications. His undergraduate degree in economics from the University of California, Berkeley, where he was a Phi Beta Kappa, allows him to write about economics concepts and applications for the mainstream classroom. Massing served for more than a decade as a prosecutor in Massachusetts, as both an assistant attorney general and an assistant district attorney. Today he serves as General Counsel for the Executive Office of Public Safety and Security, the Massachusetts cabinet department charged with oversight of matters involving law enforcement, criminal justice, and public safety. He also teaches a course in constitutional criminal procedure as an adjunct professor at Boston College Law School.

2011 Printing

 Center for Civic Education, We the People: The Citizen & the Constitution, PROJECT Citizen Project Citizen, FOUNDATIONS of DEMOCRACY Foundations of Democracy, and NATIONAL STANDARDS FOR CIVICS AND GOVERNMENT National Standards for Civics and Government are trademarks of The Center for Civic Education.

 World Almanac is a trademark of World Almanac Education Group, Inc., registered in the United States of America and/or other jurisdictions.

Printed in the United States of America

ISBN-13: 978-0-547-31836-3
ISBN-10: 0-547-31836-7

5 6 7 8 9 10 11 12 1678 17 16 15 14 13 12
4500357353

Reviewers

Special Consultants

Service Learning
Michael Fischer
Director, We the People:
Project Citizen
Center for Civic Education
Calabasas, California

Media Literacy
Tessa Jolls
President and CEO
Center for Media Literacy
Santa Monica, California

Elizabeth Thoman
Founder
Center for Media Literacy
Santa Monica, California

Economics/Personal Finance
Mary Suiter
Director
Center for Entrepreneurship
and Economic Education
University of Missouri–St. Louis
St. Louis, Missouri

Barbara Flowers
Associate Director
Center for Entrepreneurship
and Economic Education
University of Missouri–St. Louis
St. Louis, Missouri

Constitutional Law
Dr. Delbert A. Taebel
Professor Emeritus
University of Texas at Arlington
Arlington, Texas

Academic Reviewers

John Fliter, Ph.D.
Associate Professor,
Political Science
Kansas State University
Manhattan, Kansas

William Parle, Ph.D.
Associate Professor
Head, Department
of Political Science
Oklahoma State University
Stillwater, Oklahoma

Andrew Washburn
Center for the Constitution
James Madison's Montpelier
Montpelier Station, Virginia

Educational Reviewers

Katherine A. DeForge
Social Studies Chair
Marcellus Central Schools
Marcellus, New York

Pat Feichter
State Coordinator
Project Citizen
Center for Civic Education
Elk Grove, Illinois

Stan Harris
State Coordinator
We the People Programs
Boonville, Indiana

Dee Runaas
Law-related Education Coordinator
State Bar of Wisconsin
Madison, Wisconsin

Cynthia Stroud
Social Studies Consultant
and Teacher Evaluator
Greenville, South Carolina

Joseph E. Webb
Project Citizen State Coordinator
Adjunct Professor
East Carolina University
Jacksonville, North Carolina

Field Test Reviewers

Meredith Aby
Jefferson High School
Bloomington, Minnesota

Timothy Arnold
University High School
Newark, New Jersey

Cameron Brooks
Gaffney High School
Gaffney, South Carolina

Tom Daniels
Cameron High School
Cameron, Wisconsin

Eric Eyong
Corliss High School
Chicago, Illinois

Jason Gray
Goodrich High School
Goodrich, Michigan

Michelle LeeMaster
Hinkley High School
Aurora, Colorado

Monte Linebarger
Martin Luther King, Jr.
Senior High School
Lithonia, Georgia

Denny Pelley
Speedway High School
Speedway, Indiana

Nancy Riebau
Hinkley High School
Aurora, Colorado

Ozni Torres
Hubbard High School
Chicago, Illinois

Doreen Waishek
The English High School
Jamaica Plain, Massachusetts

Steve Williams
Glen Rose High School
Malvern, Arkansas

Contents

UNIT 1 | A Tradition of Democracy 1

CHAPTER 1 We the People 2

CHAPTER 2 Foundations of Government 26

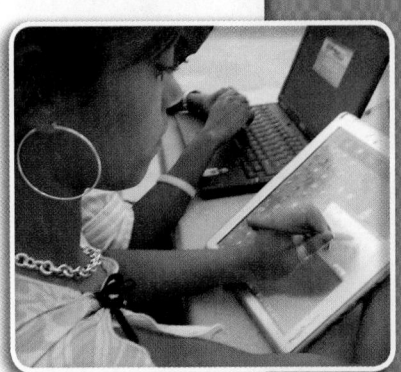

■ ■ ■ ■

Features

Center for Civic Education

Center for Civic Education
The Center for Civic Education is dedicated to helping students become effective and responsible citizens by encouraging participation in state or local government. The **Students Take Action** and the **Law 101** features in your textbook were developed in conjunction with the Center for Civic Education.

STUDENTS TAKE ACTION — PROJECT Citizen

Read about students who have played a role in their communities through this program.

LAW 101 — FOUNDATIONS of DEMOCRACY

This feature focuses on legal issues that affect your everyday life.

PRIMARY SOURCES

*Important documents help develop your
understanding of civics.*

HISTORIC DOCUMENTS

*Examine key documents that have shaped
U.S. history and government.*

POLITICAL CARTOONS

Interpret political cartoons to learn about civics and economics.

Daryl Cagle, Cagle Cartoons

MEDIA INVESTIGATION

Use photos, illustrations, political cartoons, and more to understand key concepts.

Focus On

Meet the people who have influenced U.S. government and the economy.

Examine key facts and concepts quickly and easily with graphics.

✳ Interactive

Charts, Graphics, Maps, and Time Lines

Analyze information presented visually to learn more about civics and economics.

FOCUS ON WRITING

Use writing skills to study and reflect on the concepts of civics and economics.

FOCUS ON SPEAKING

Discover how speaking skills advance your study and understanding of civics.

Reading Skills

Learn reading skills that will help you better understand your civics lessons.

Civics Skills

Learn, practice, and apply the skills you need to analyze civics and economics.

How to Make This Book Work for You

Studying civics will be easy for you using this textbook. Take a few minutes to become familiar with the easy-to-use structure and special features of this civics book. See how this textbook will make civics come alive for you!

CHAPTER

Each chapter begins with a chapter opener introduction that lists the sections of the chapter as well as the National Standards for Civics and Government covered in the chapter.

Reading Skills

lessons at the beginning of each chapter teach you important skills to help you read the textbook more successfully.

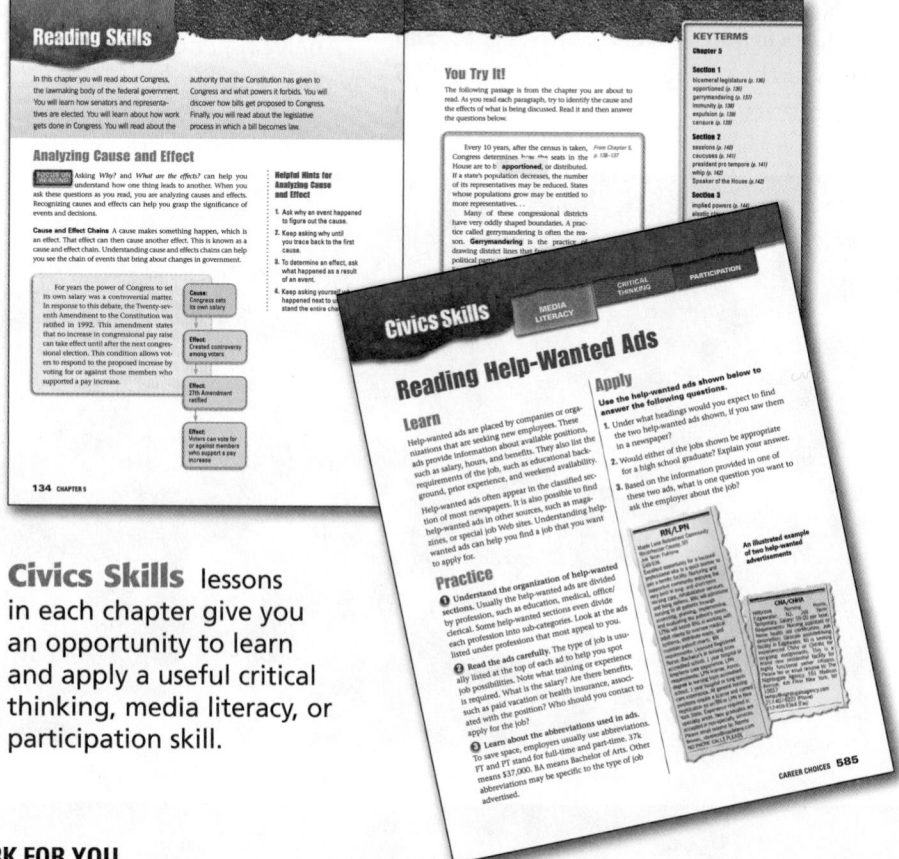

Civics Skills lessons in each chapter give you an opportunity to learn and apply a useful critical thinking, media literacy, or participation skill.

SECTION

Each section in the textbook includes many helpful features.

The Main Idea provides the overarching idea of each section.

Reading Focus questions serve as your guide as you read through the section.

Key Terms are introduced at the beginning of each section and are clearly marked throughout the section.

Taking Notes provides a graphic organizer that will help you read and take notes on the important ideas in the section.

Civics in Practice introduces the information in each section and relates that information to your life.

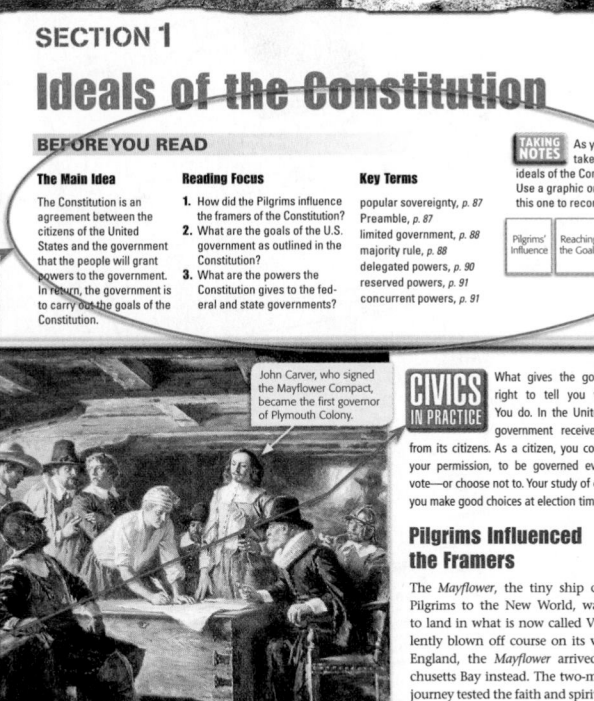

SECTION 1
Ideals of the Constitution

BEFORE YOU READ

The Main Idea

The Constitution is an agreement between the citizens of the United States and the government that the people will grant powers to the government. In return, the government is to carry out the goals of the Constitution.

Reading Focus

1. How did the Pilgrims influence the framers of the Constitution?
2. What are the goals of the U.S. government as outlined in the Constitution?
3. What are the powers the Constitution gives to the federal and state governments?

Key Terms

popular sovereignty, p. 87
Preamble, p. 87
limited government, p. 88
majority rule, p. 88
delegated powers, p. 90
reserved powers, p. 91
concurrent powers, p. 91

TAKING NOTES As you read, take notes on the ideals of the Constitution. Use a graphic organizer like this one to record your notes.

Pilgrims' Influence | Reaching the Goals | Federal and State Governments

John Carver, who signed the Mayflower Compact, became the first governor of Plymouth Colony.

This painting shows some of the Pilgrims signing the Mayflower Compact.

CIVICS IN PRACTICE What gives the government the right to tell you what to do? You do. In the United States, the government receives its powers from its citizens. As a citizen, you consent, or give your permission, to be governed every time you vote—or choose not to. Your study of civics will help you make good choices at election time.

Pilgrims Influenced the Framers

The *Mayflower*, the tiny ship carrying the Pilgrims to the New World, was supposed to land in what is now called Virginia. Violently blown off course on its voyage from England, the *Mayflower* arrived in Massachusetts Bay instead. The two-month ocean journey tested the faith and spirits of the religious Pilgrims aboard.

Pilgrims Agree to Be Governed

William Bradford, who would soon be governor of the Massachusetts Colony, observed the day before their landing, some passengers were "not well affected to concord." That is, they were arguing. Colonists realized that before they got

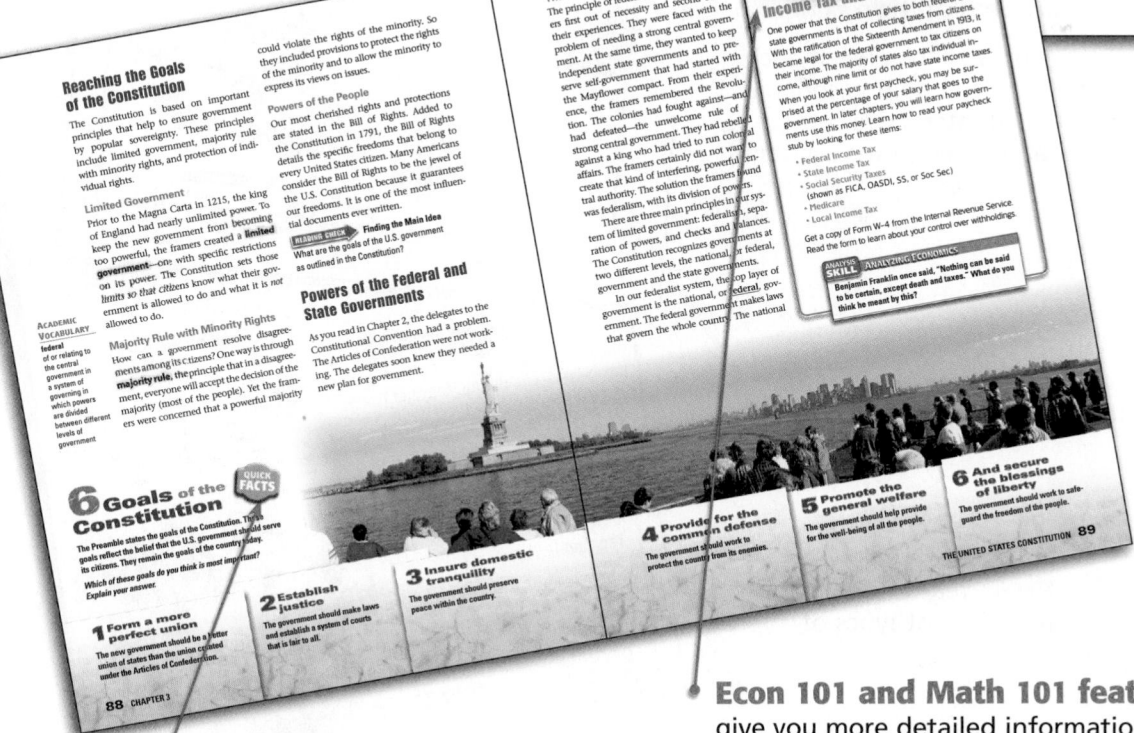

Quick Facts features display important facts in an easy-to-read way.

Econ 101 and Math 101 features give you more detailed information about interesting economic and math topics related to civics.

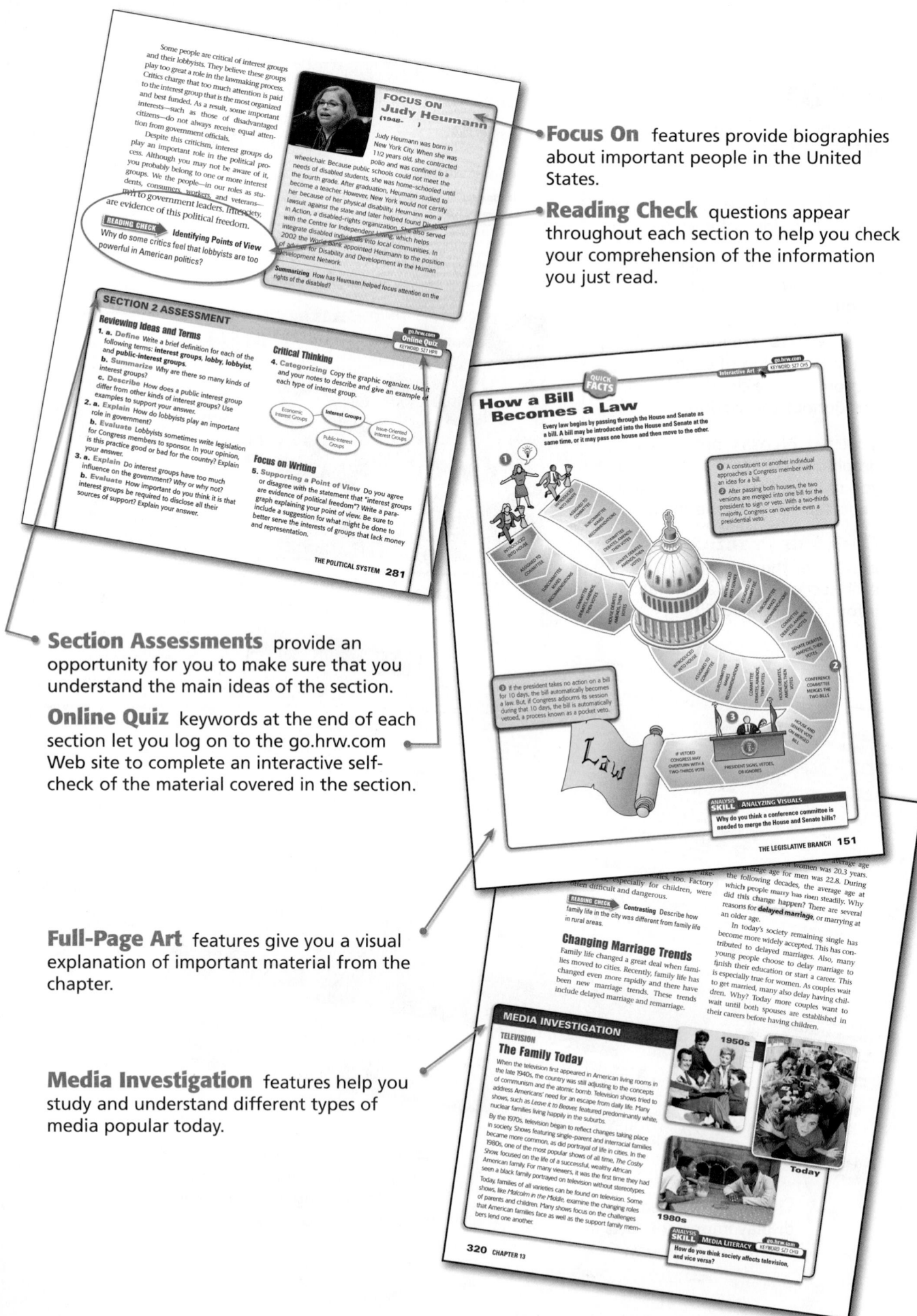

Some people are critical of interest groups and their lobbyists. They believe these groups play too great a role in the lawmaking process. Critics charge that too much attention is paid to the interest group that is the most organized and best funded. As a result, some important interests—such as those of disadvantaged citizens—do not always receive equal attention from government officials.

Despite this criticism, interest groups do play an important role in the political process. Although you may not be aware of it, you probably belong to one or more interest groups. We the people—in our roles as students, consumers, workers, and veterans—turn to government leaders. In essence, they are evidence of this political freedom.

READING CHECK **Identifying Points of View** Why do some critics feel that lobbyists are too powerful in American politics?

FOCUS ON
Judy Heumann
(1948–)

Judy Heumann was born in New York City. When she was 1 1/2 years old, she contracted polio and was confined to a wheelchair. Because public schools could not meet the needs of disabled students, she was home-schooled until the fourth grade. After graduation, Heumann studied to become a teacher. However, New York would not certify her because of her physical disability. Heumann won a lawsuit against the state and later helped found Disabled in Action, a disabled-rights organization. She also served with the Centre for Independent Living, which helps integrate disabled individuals into local communities. In 2002 the World Bank appointed Heumann to the position of adviser for Disability and Development in the Human Development Network.

Summarizing How has Heumann helped focus attention on the rights of the disabled?

SECTION 2 ASSESSMENT

Reviewing Ideas and Terms

1. **a. Define** Write a brief definition for each of the following terms: **interest groups, lobby, lobbyist,** and **public-interest groups.**
   b. Summarize Why are there so many kinds of interest groups?
   c. Describe How does a public interest group differ from other kinds of interest groups? Use examples to support your answer.

2. **a. Explain** How do lobbyists play an important role in government?
   b. Evaluate Lobbyists sometimes write legislation for Congress members to sponsor. In your opinion, is this practice good or bad for the country? Explain your answer.

3. **a. Explain** Do interest groups have too much influence on the government? Why or why not?
   b. Evaluate How important do you think it is that interest groups be required to disclose all their sources of support? Explain your answer.

Critical Thinking

4. **Categorizing** Copy the graphic organizer. Use it and your notes to describe and give an example of each type of interest group.

Economic Interest Groups — Interest Groups — Issue-Oriented Interest Groups — Public-Interest Groups

Focus on Writing

5. **Supporting a Point of View** Do you agree or disagree with the statement that "interest groups are evidence of political freedom"? Write a paragraph explaining your point of view. Be sure to include a suggestion for what might be done to better serve the interests of groups that lack money and representation.

go.hrw.com
Online Quiz
KEYWORD: SZ7 HP8

THE POLITICAL SYSTEM **281**

Focus On features provide biographies about important people in the United States.

Reading Check questions appear throughout each section to help you check your comprehension of the information you just read.

Section Assessments provide an opportunity for you to make sure that you understand the main ideas of the section.

Online Quiz keywords at the end of each section let you log on to the go.hrw.com Web site to complete an interactive self-check of the material covered in the section.

Full-Page Art features give you a visual explanation of important material from the chapter.

Media Investigation features help you study and understand different types of media popular today.

QUICK FACTS

How a Bill Becomes a Law

Every law begins by passing through the House and Senate as a bill. A bill may be introduced into the House and Senate at the same time, or it may pass one house and then move to the other.

Interactive Art
go.hrw.com
KEYWORD: SZ7 CH5

1 A constituent or another individual approaches a Congress member with an idea for a bill.

2 After passing both houses, the two versions are merged into one bill for the president to sign or veto. With a two-thirds majority, Congress can override even a presidential veto.

3 If the president takes no action on a bill for 10 days, the bill automatically becomes a law. But, if Congress adjourns its session during that 10 days, the bill is automatically vetoed, a process known as a pocket veto.

Law

IF VETOED CONGRESS MAY OVERTURN WITH A TWO-THIRDS VOTE

PRESIDENT SIGNS, VETOES, OR IGNORES

ANALYSIS SKILL **ANALYZING VISUALS** Why do you think a conference committee is needed to merge the House and Senate bills?

THE LEGISLATIVE BRANCH **151**

---

too. Especially for children, Factory often difficult and dangerous.

READING CHECK **Contrasting** Describe how family life in the city was different from family life in rural areas.

Changing Marriage Trends

Family life changed a great deal when families moved to cities. Recently, family life has changed even more rapidly and there have been new marriage trends. These trends include delayed marriage and remarriage.

...women was 20.3 years. ...average age for men was 22.8. During the following decades, the average age at which people marry has risen steadily. Why did this change happen? There are several reasons for **delayed marriage,** or marrying at an older age.

In today's society remaining single has become more widely accepted. This has contributed to delayed marriages. Also, many young people choose to delay marriage to finish their education or start a career. This is especially true for women. As couples wait to get married, many also delay having children. Why? Today more couples want to wait until both spouses are established in their careers before having children.

MEDIA INVESTIGATION

TELEVISION
The Family Today

When the television first appeared in American living rooms in the late 1940s, the country was still adjusting to the concepts of communism and the atomic bomb. Television shows tried to address Americans' need for an escape from daily life. Many shows, such as *Leave It to Beaver,* featured predominantly white, nuclear families living happily in the suburbs.

By the 1970s, television began to reflect changes taking place in society. Shows featuring single-parent and interracial families became more common, as did portrayal of life in cities. In the 1980s, one of the most popular shows of all time, *The Cosby Show,* focused on the life of a successful, wealthy African American family. For many viewers, it was the first time they had seen a black family portrayed on television without stereotypes.

Today, families of all varieties can be found on television. Some shows, like *Malcolm in the Middle,* examine the changing roles of parents and children. Many shows focus on the challenges that American families face as well as the support family members lend one another.

1950s

1980s

Today

ANALYSIS SKILL **MEDIA LITERACY** go.hrw.com KEYWORD: SZ7 CH3 How do you think society affects television, and vice versa?

320 CHAPTER 13

CHAPTER REVIEW

Each chapter ends with a review that assesses your knowledge
of the main ideas presented in the chapter.

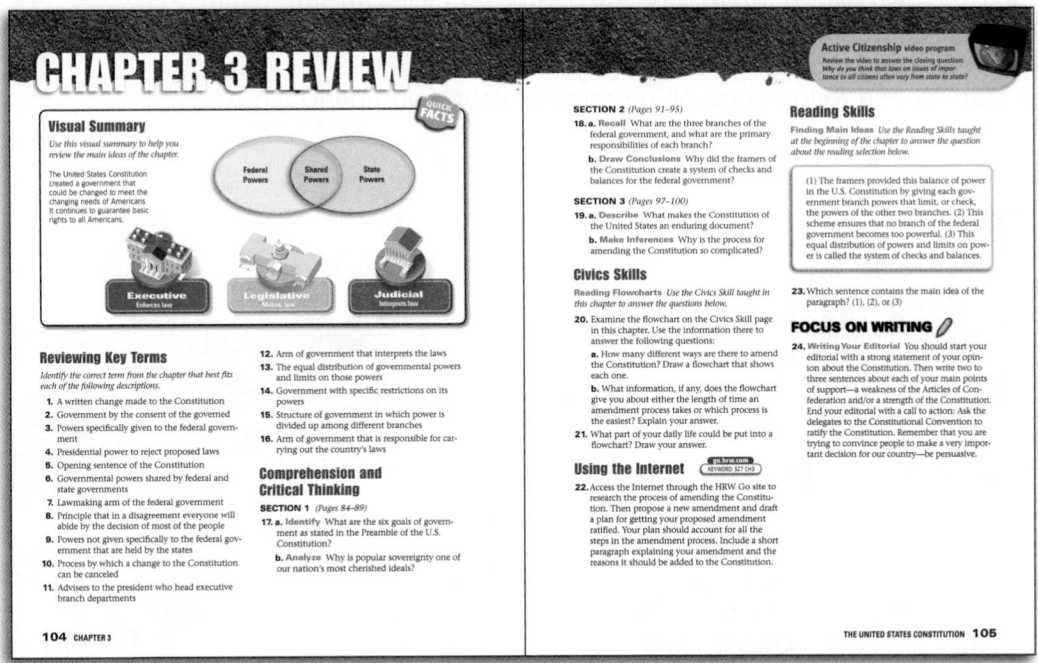

A **Visual Summary** begins each chapter
review and provides a visual review of the
chapter's main ideas.

Using the Internet activities in each
chapter review provide a link to exciting
activities that you can create using the
Internet.

Reading Skills questions help you make
sure that you understand the reading skill
taught at the beginning of the chapter.

Civics Skills review questions check your
understanding of the civics skill that you
learned in the chapter.

REFERENCES

The Reference section in the
back of the book provides useful
information.

The **Supreme Court
Decisions** section includes
the background to important
Supreme Court cases in U.S.
history along with the Court's
decision and the significance of
each case.

Historic Documents shed
light on key events from
American history and provide
important primary source
accounts.

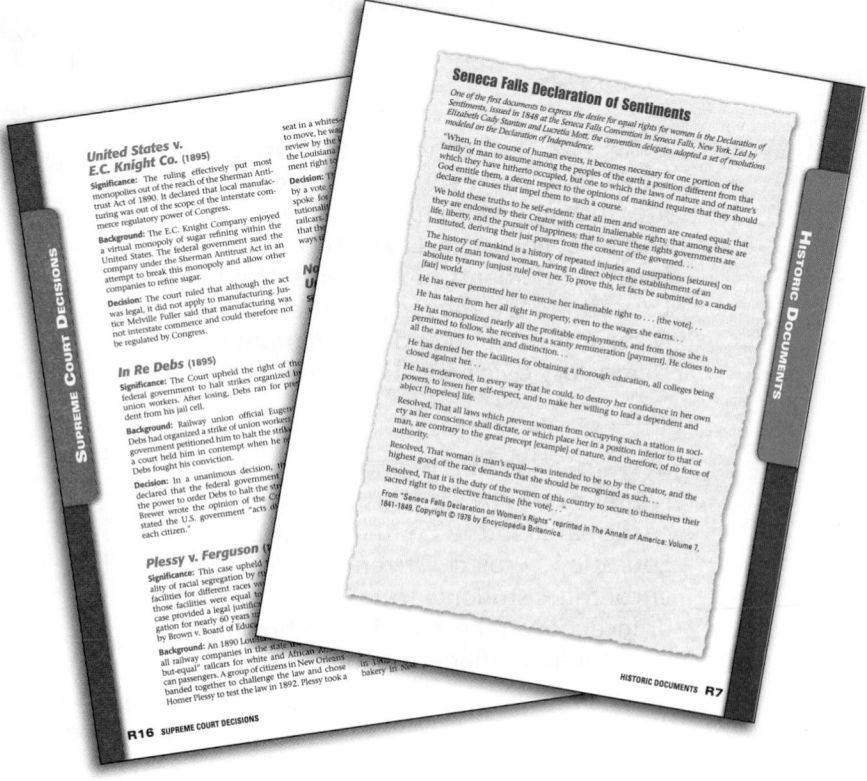

SPECIAL FEATURES

Throughout Holt *Civics in Practice*, you will find special features that will help you understand more about your roles in your country and community. Many of these features were developed with our partners, the Center for Civic Education and the World Almanac Education Group. In addition, the Personal Finance Handbook, which provides real-world problems and solutions involving money management, will help you plan for and follow through on some of your own financial goals.

Center for Civic Education

The Center for Civic Education is an organization dedicated to helping students become informed and active citizens. The Center's programs will help you increase your understanding of the constitutional basis of our democracy and the basic values and principles on which our country was founded. These programs can help you to become an effective and responsible citizen. Your textbook includes two features developed in conjunction with the Center for Civic Education:

Law 101 This feature focuses on legal issues that affect you in your everyday life, such as government regulations and juvenile justice. Law 101 brings together elements of the Center for Civic Education's *We the People: The Citizen & the Constitution* and *Foundations of Democracy* civic education texts.

Students Take Action This feature relates stories of students who have participated in the Center for Civic Education's Project Citizen program, which encourages students to take part in state or local government and learn how to monitor and influence public policy.

The World Almanac and Book of Facts has been one of America's best sources of information about the United States and the world for almost 140 years—since 1868! In your textbook you will find a special reference section containing information about U.S. presidents, all 50 states, the U.S Constitution, and the branches of the American government. All of this information is contained in colorful, easy-to-read pages that give you quick access to the information.

Personal Finance Handbook

The Personal Finance Handbook teaches you the basics of dealing with money. You will learn how to earn and save money as well as how to protect and budget your earnings. The Personal Finance Handbook even introduces you to the fundamentals of borrowing, investing, and paying taxes.

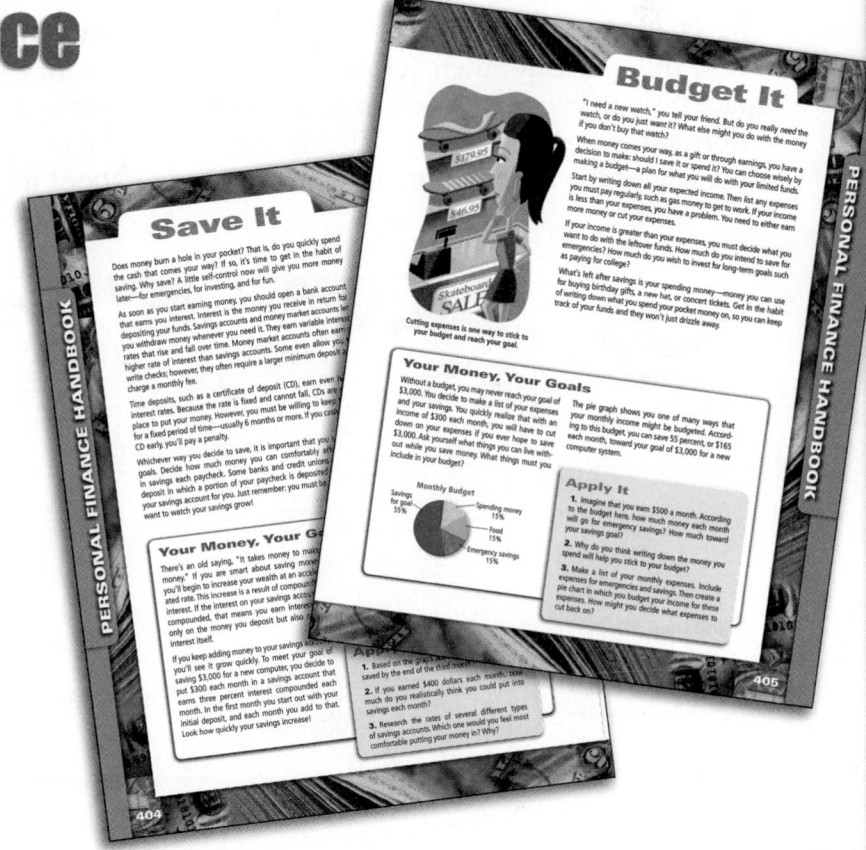

Become an Active Reader

by Dr. Kylene Beers

Did you ever think you would begin reading your civics book by reading about *reading?* Actually, it makes better sense than you might think. You probably would make sure you learned some soccer skills and strategies before playing in a game. Similarly, you need to learn some reading skills and strategies before reading your civics book. In other words, you need to make sure you know whatever you need to know in order to read this book successfully.

Tip #1
Read Everything on the Page!

This book is filled with information that will help you understand what you are reading. If you do not study that information, however, it might as well not be there. Be sure to study everything on the page.

Boldfaced Words

Important words you should remember are highlighted and defined on the page where they appear. They will help you understand important concepts.

Charts, Photos, and Artwork

These things are not there just to take up space or look good! Study them and read the information beside them. It will help you understand the information in the chapter.

Tip #2
Use the Reading Skills Pages in Your Textbook

Good readers use a number of skills and strategies to make sure they understand what they are reading. At the beginning of each chapter you will find help with important reading skills and strategies.

Reading Skills

These lessons provide you with the skills and strategies necessary to understand the chapter. Then they provide you with an opportunity to practice your new skill.

Key Terms and Academic Vocabulary

Before you read the chapter, review these words and think about them. Have you read the word before? What do you already know about it? Watch for these words and their meanings as you read the chapter.

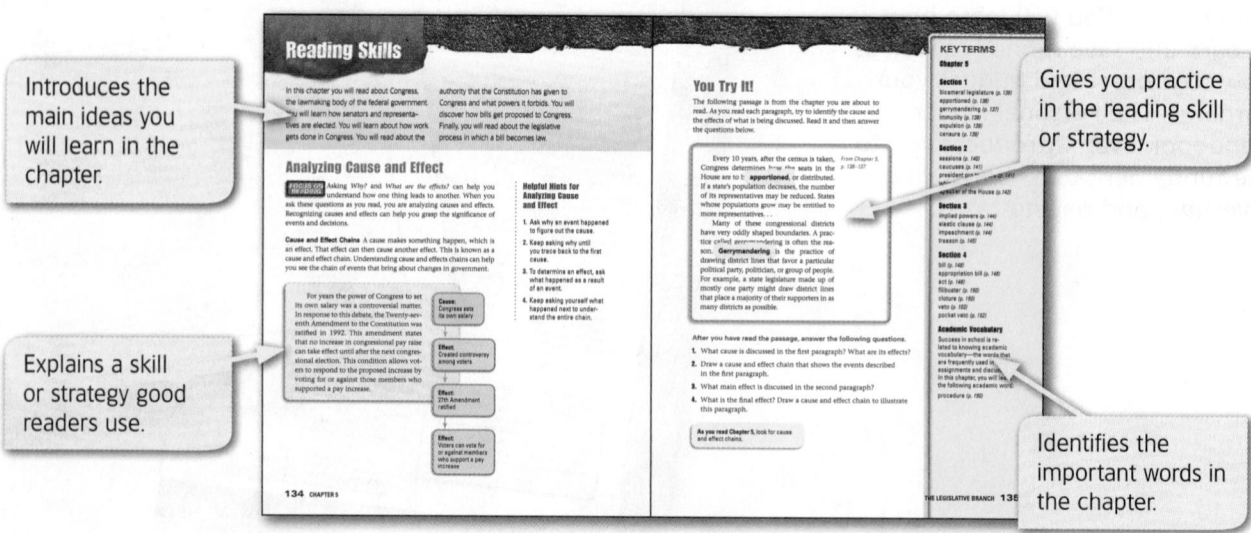

Introduces the main ideas you will learn in the chapter.

Explains a skill or strategy good readers use.

Gives you practice in the reading skill or strategy.

Identifies the important words in the chapter.

Tip #3
Read Like a Skilled Reader

You will never get better at reading your civics book—or any book for that matter—unless you spend some time thinking about how to be a better reader.

Skilled readers do the following:

- They preview what they are supposed to read before they actually begin reading.
- They divide their notebook paper into two columns. They title one column "Notes from the Chapter" and the other column "Questions or Comments I Have."
- They take notes in both columns as they read.
- They read like **active readers**. The Active Reading list below shows you what that means.

- They use clues in the text to help them figure out where the text is going. The best clues are called signal words.

  Chronological Order Signal Words: *first, second, third, before, after, later, next, following that, earlier, finally*

  Cause-and-Effect Signal Words: *because of, due to, as a result of, the reason for, therefore, consequently*

  Comparison/Contrast Signal Words: *likewise, also, as well as, similarly, on the other hand*

Active Reading

Successful readers are **active readers**. These readers know that it is up to them to figure out what the text means. Here are some steps you can take to become an active, and successful, reader.

Predict what will happen next based on what has already happened. When your predictions do not match what happens in the text, re-read the confusing parts.

Question what is happening as you read. Constantly ask yourself why things have happened, what things mean, and what caused certain events.

Summarize what you are reading frequently. Do not try to summarize the entire chapter! Read a bit and then summarize it. Then read on.

Connect what is happening in the part you are reading to what you have already read.

Clarify your understanding. Stop occasionally to ask yourself whether you are confused by anything. You may need to re-read to clarify, or you may need to read further and collect more information before you can understand the text.

Visualize what is happening in the text. Try to see the events or places in your mind by drawing maps, making charts, or jotting down notes about what you are reading.

Tip #4

Pay Attention to Vocabulary

It is no fun to read something when you do not know what the words mean, but you cannot learn new words if you only use or read the words you already know. In this book, we know we have probably used some words you do not know, but we have followed a pattern when we have used more difficult words.

Key Terms

At the beginning of each section you will find a list of key terms that you will need to know. Be on the lookout for those words as you read through the section.

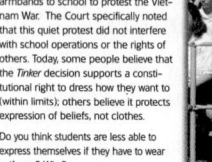

American Civil Liberties

Are Public School Uniforms Constitutional?

In his 1996 State of the Union address, President Bill Clinton said, "If it means that teenagers will stop killing each other over designer jackets, then our public schools should be able to require their students to wear school uniforms."

After President Clinton's speech, public schools began to require uniforms in order to improve discipline and reduce gang violence. However, critics of the idea, including many teens, argue that students have the right to express themselves through their dress.

The closest Supreme Court case related to this issue is *Tinker v. Des Moines*. There the Court ruled that students had the right to wear black armbands to school to protest the Vietnam War. The Court specifically noted that this quiet protest did not interfere with school operations or the rights of others. Today, some people believe that the *Tinker* decision supports a constitutional right to dress how they want (within limits); others believe it protects expression of beliefs, not clothes.

Do you think students are less able to express themselves if they have to wear uniforms? Why?

Interpreting the Constitution

The Constitution does not attempt to cover every possible situation. It sets broad guidelines for governing. A number of changes in the federal government have come about simply through custom and tradition. For example, the Constitution does not call for regular meetings of the executive branch. However, President George Washington brought these leaders together regularly to serve as his advisers. They are known as the president's **cabinet**. Since those early days, meetings between the president and the cabinet have been an accepted practice.

Such traditions are seldom written down or passed into law. For this reason, they are sometimes referred to as the "unwritten Constitution."

...these leaders together...serve as his advisers. They are known as the president's **cabinet**. Since those early days, meetings between the president and the cab...been an accepted practi...

Nineteenth Amendment
Ratified 1920 Gave women the right to vote

Twenty-Sixth Amendment
Ratified 1971 Changed the voting age from 21 to 18

BALLOTS

THE UNITED STATES CONSTITUTION

MEDIA INVESTIGATION

RADIO
War of the Worlds

On Sunday, October 30, 1938, millions of Americans sat listening to their radios. Listeners expecting to hear the broadcast of the Mercury Theater's weekly radio play received a shocking surprise. Invaders from Mars, it seemed, had landed in New Jersey and were heading for New York City!

In the early 1900s millions of Americans turned to radio broadcasts for entertainment. One popular program was Orson Welles' Mercury Theater on the Air, which dramatized well-known novels and plays. When the group decided to present H. G. Wells' science fiction novel, *The War of the Worlds*, they performed it as a real-life news program. So realistic was their presentation that thousands of listeners believed New York was under attack by aliens. Panicked listeners called police stations, hid in basements, and looked for ways to protect themselves.

Most listeners, however, knew there was no Martian invasion. *The War of the Worlds* taught many Americans to think critically about the media—and not to believe everything they hear.

Orson Welles' broadcast of *The War of the Worlds* convinced many Americans that they were under attack by Martians.

ANALYSIS SKILL | **MEDIA LITERACY** | go.hrw.com KEYWORD SZ7 CH4

Draw Conclusions Why might some people have believed that the invasion was real?

allow you to work with others and make the most of your peers' skills and ideas.

READING CHECK **Finding the Main Idea** How do we learn from experience?

Learning to Think Critically

The most important skill we learn is how to think. Thinking is a **complex** process. It involves considering options, forming opinions, and making judgments.

How We Think

There are several ways to think. One way, called **insight**, is thinking that seems to come from your heart more than your mind. Sometimes you do not have direct experience with a problem, but you have the ability to see the details of a problem and understand it. Your insight comes from your experiences with other similar situations.

Another type of thinking is **creativity**. Creativity is the ability to find new ways to think about or do things. Everyone can think creatively. Whenever you solve a problem, you have used your creativity.

You have other thinking abilities as well. You can question and weigh information. You can draw conclusions and make predictions.

Critical Thinking

If someone told you that there is a car that drives itself, would you believe it? It seems possible, but you would probably want proof. Maybe you would like to read or hear more about it. Perhaps you would like to see this car for yourself, or better yet, take a ride in it before you decide whether it is real.

The thinking that we do to reach decisions and to solve problems is called **critical thinking**. Critical thinking involves several steps.

352 CHAPTER 14

ACADEMIC VOCABULARY

complex: difficult, not simple

ACADEMIC VOCABULARY

complex: difficult, not simple

Academic Vocabulary

When we use a word that is important in all classes, not just social studies, we define it in the margin under the heading Academic Vocabulary. You will run into these academic words in other textbooks, so you should learn what they mean while reading this book.

Academic Vocabulary

in *Civics in Practice*

As you read this textbook, you will be more successful if you know or learn the meaning of the academic vocabulary words on this page. These words are important in all of your classes, not just in civics. You will see these words in other textbooks, so you should learn what they mean while reading this book.

Academic Words

acquire	to get
affect	to change or influence
agreement	a decision reached by two or more people or groups
aspects	parts
authority	power, right to rule
complex	difficult, not simple
consequences	the effects of a particular event or events
contract	a binding legal agreement
develop	create
development	creation
distinct	separate
efficiently	productive and not wasteful
established	set up or created
execute	to perform, carry out
explicitly	fully revealed without vagueness
facilitate	to bring about
factors	causes
features	characteristics
federal	a system of governing where the powers of government are divided between the national government and the state governments
functions	use or purpose

impact	effect, result
implement	to put in place
incentive	something that leads people to follow a certain course of action
influence	change, or have an effect on
logical	reasoned, well thought out
methods	ways of doing something
neutral	unbiased, not favoring either side in a conflict
policy	rule, course of action
primary	main, most important
principle	a basic belief, rule, or law
procedure	a series of steps by which a task is completed
process	a series of steps by which a task is accomplished
purpose	the reason something is done
role	a part or function
strategies	plans for fighting a battle or a war
structure	the way something is set up or organized
traditional	customary, time-honored
values	ideas that people hold dear and try to live by

Critical Thinking

Throughout your textbook, you will be asked to think critically about issues that affect your role as an American. The development of critical-thinking skills is essential to effective citizenship. The following critical-thinking skills are reviewed in each section assessment and chapter review in this textbook.

1. **Analyzing Information** is the process of breaking a concept down into sections and then examining the relationships between those parts. Analyzing enables you to better understand the information as a whole.

2. **Sequencing** is the process of placing events in their chronological order to better understand the relationships between those events.

3. **Categorizing** is the process of grouping things together by the characteristics they have in common. Putting things or events into categories makes it easier to see similarities and differences.

4. **Identifying Cause and Effect** is one way to interpret the relationships between events. A cause is a circumstance that leads to an action. The outcome of that action is an effect.

5. **Comparing and Contrasting** is the process of examining events, situations, or points of view for their similarities and differences.

6. **Finding the Main Idea** is the process of combining and sifting through information to determine the idea that is most important.

7. **Summarizing** is the process of taking a large amount of information and boiling it down into a short and clear statement.

8. **Making Generalizations and Predictions** is the process of interpreting information to form general statements and to guess what will happen next. A generalization is a broad statement that holds true for a variety of events or situations. A prediction is an educated guess about an outcome.

9. **Drawing Inferences and Conclusions** is forming possible explanations for an event, situation, or problem. When you make inferences, you take the information you know to be true and make an educated guess about what else you think may be true about that situation. A conclusion is a statement that can be made based on what you already know.

10. **Identifying Points of View** is the process of identifying factors that influence the outlook of an individual or a group. A person's point of view includes beliefs and attitudes that are shaped by factors such as age, gender, religion, race, and economic status.

11. **Supporting a Point of View** is a process that involves choosing a viewpoint on a particular event or issue and then arguing persuasively for that position.

12. **Evaluating** is the process of assessing the significance, or overall importance, of something. You should base your judgment on standards that others will understand and that they are likely to share.

Standardized Test-Taking Strategies

Throughout your school career, you probably will be asked to take standardized tests. These tests are designed to demonstrate the information and skills you have learned. In most cases the best way to prepare for these tests is to pay close attention in class.

Tips for Answering
Multiple-Choice Questions

1. If there is a written or visual piece accompanying the question, study it carefully.

2. Read the question for its general intent. Then re-read it carefully, looking for words that give clues.

3. Read all of the possible answer choices, even if the first one seems like the correct answer. There may be a better choice.

4. Re-read the question and your answer to be sure that you made the best choice and that you marked it correctly on the answer sheet.

Tips for Answering
Short-Answer Questions

1. Read the passage in its entirety, paying close attention to the main ideas. Jot down or underline information you think is important.

2. If you cannot answer a question, skip it and come back later.

3. Be sure you understand what each question is asking you to do, for example, compare, contrast, interpret, discuss, or summarize.

4. Organize your thoughts on a separate sheet of paper. Write a general topic statement with which to begin.

5. When writing your answer, be precise but brief. Be sure to refer to details from the passage in your answer.

Tips for Answering
Essay Questions

1. Read the question carefully.

2. Decide what kind of essay you are being asked to write: persuasive, classificatory, compare/contrast, or how-to.

3. Pay attention to key words, such as *compare, contrast, describe, advantages, disadvantages, classify,* and *speculate.* They will give you clues as to the structure that your essay should follow.

4. Organize your thoughts on a separate sheet of paper. Develop a general topic sentence that expresses your main idea. Then create an outline to help you organize the points that support your topic sentence.

5. Write your composition using complete sentences. Be sure to use correct grammar, spelling, and punctuation.

6. Be sure to proofread your essay once you have finished writing.

Scavenger Hunt

Holt *Civics in Practice* contains a great deal of information about American government, citizenship, and economics. Before you begin your journey through the book, take a minute to familiarize yourself with its contents. This will help make your journey easier.

1 How many units and chapters are in the book? Where did you find this information?

2 Where in *Civics in Practice* do you find the atlas? Where is the Historic Documents section located?

3 According to the Table of Contents, what are the section titles for Chapter 24?

4 What are the key terms for Chapter 11, Section 2?

5 Where in *Civics in Practice* do you find a detailed discussion of the Supreme Court?

6 *Civics in Practice* was created to help you learn all of the material covered by the National Standards for Civics and Government. Where do you find a complete list of these standards?

7 Where do you find questions to help you review the entire chapter?

8 What is the subject of the Visual Summary on page 650?

9 Where do you look to find a list of all of the Students Take Action features in the book?

10 Where are the two-page reading skills activities for each chapter located?

UNIT 1
A TRADITION OF DEMOCRACY

ARE YOU

DOING ALL YOU CAN ?

This World War II poster
from 1942 reminds Americans
to do all they can to meet
their responsibilities as
U.S. citizens.

1

CHAPTER 1
WE THE PEOPLE

SECTION 1
Civics in Our Lives

SECTION 2
Who Are U.S. Citizens?

SECTION 3
The American People Today

NATIONAL STANDARDS®
FOR CIVICS AND GOVERNMENT

I.   What are civic life, politics, and government?

    A. What purposes should government serve?

II. What are the foundations of the American political system?

    B. What are the distinctive characteristics of American society?

III. How does the government established by the Constitution embody the purposes, values, and principles of American democracy?

    E. How does the American political system provide for choice and opportunities for participation?

V.   What are the roles of the citizen in American democracy?

    A. What is citizenship?

    B. What are the rights of citizens?

    C. What are the responsibilities of citizens?

    D. What civic dispositions or traits of private and public character are important to the preservation and improvement of American constitutional democracy?

    E. How can citizens take part in civic life?

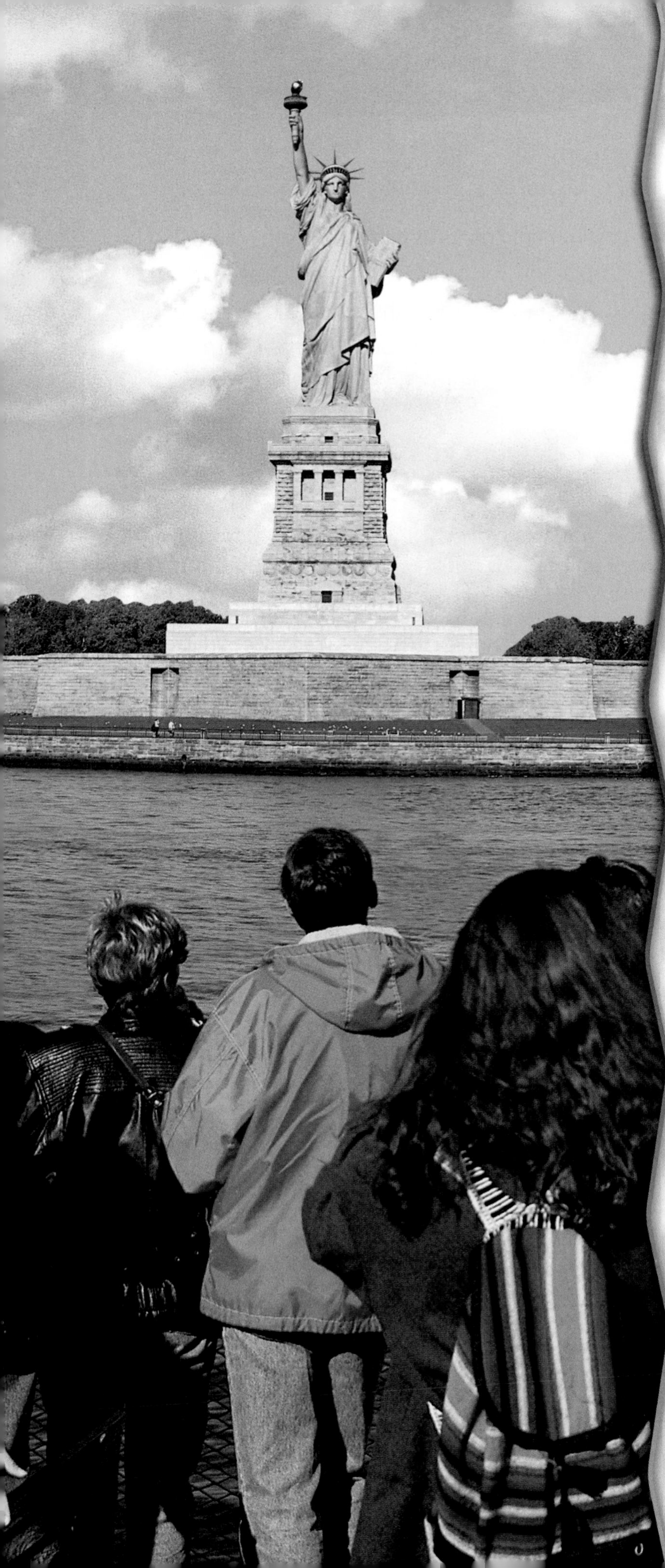

WHY CIVICS Matters

The United States is a model of freedom, democracy, and economic strength for the rest of the world. Our continued success as a world leader depends on whether citizens like you take an active part in our government and institutions.

PROJECT ★Citizen

STUDENTS TAKE ACTION

CHANGING ADS You look at lots of magazine ads every day. If you found out that some ads were illegal or potentially harmful, what could you do? Think of some solutions for taking action as you read this chapter.

FOCUS ON WRITING

WRITING A LETTER In this chapter, you will be reading about what it means to be an American citizen. Imagine that an American citizen named Fran is talking on line to a new friend in Turkey. After you read this chapter, you'll write an e-mail message from Fran to this new friend. You'll tell the friend about American ideals, American citizens, and American citizenship.

Reading Skills

In this chapter you will read about the rights, privileges, and responsibilities of being an American citizen. You will learn that the United States is a diverse nation filled with immigrants from many countries and learn how the government counts its citizens. As you read the chapter, you will come across new terms used in studying civics. Look at the words and sentences surrounding new words. See if you can learn their meanings from clues right in the passage.

Using Context Clues

FOCUS ON READING When you are reading your textbook, you may often come across a word you do not know. If that word is not listed as a key term, how do you find out what it means?

Using Context Clues *Context* means surroundings. Authors often include clues to the meaning of a difficult word in its context. You just have to know how and where to look.

Clue	How It Works	Example	Explanation
Direct Definition	Includes a definition in the same or a nearby sentence	We are primarily immigrants—*people who came here from other lands*—or descendants of immigrants.	The phrase *people who came here from other lands* defines *immigrants*.
Restatement	Uses different words to say the same thing	Most of them went to live in urban areas, or *cities*.	The word *cities* is another way to say *urban*.
Comparisons or Contrasts	Compares or contrasts the unfamiliar word with a familiar one	*As the population continued to grow rapidly and people moved to the cities,* urban areas became crowded.	The phrase *As the population continued to grow rapidly and people moved to the cities* indicates that urban areas are the same as cities.

Helpful Hints for Identifying Context Clues

1. Look at the words and sentences around a new word.

2. See if the words and sentences give you clues about the word's meaning.

3. Look for a word or phrase nearby that has a similar meaning.

You Try It!

The following sentences are from the chapter you are about to read. Read them and then answer the questions below.

1. The United States has been an inspiration to other nations because of its basic values: equality, liberty, and justice for all people. These values are the foundation of many of your important rights and freedoms. *From Chapter 1 p. 8*

2. The law gives preference to three groups of people: (1) husbands, wives, and children of U.S. citizens; (2) people who have valuable job skills; and (3) aliens. Aliens are permanent residents of the United States who are still citizens of another country. *p. 14*

3. Farmworkers and their families began a migration, a movement of large numbers of people from region to region, to the cities. The 1830 census showed that urban areas were growing faster than rural areas. *p. 20*

Answer the questions about the sentences you read.

1. In example 1, what does the term *values* mean? What clues did you find in the example to figure that out?

2. In example 2, where do you find the meaning of *aliens*? What does this word mean?

3. From example 3, what do you think an urban area is? What clues did you find to figure that out?

> **As you read Chapter 1,** remember that sometimes you need to read entire passages to understand unfamiliar words. Don't stop when you come to a word you don't know. Read on!

KEY TERMS

CHAPTER 1

Section 1
civics *(p. 6)*
citizen *(p. 6)*
government *(p. 7)*

Section 2
immigrants *(p. 12)*
quota *(p. 14)*
aliens *(p. 14)*
native-born *(p. 15)*
naturalization *(p. 15)*
refugees *(p. 16)*

Section 3
census *(p. 17)*
demographics *(p. 18)*
birthrate *(p. 19)*
death rate *(p. 19)*
migration *(p. 20)*

Academic Vocabulary

Success in school is related to knowing academic vocabulary—words that are frequently used in school assignments and discussions. In this chapter you will learn the following academic word:

values *(p. 8)*

Civics in Our Lives

BEFORE YOU READ

The Main Idea

As a U.S. citizen, it is your duty to help preserve freedom and to ensure justice and equality for yourself and all Americans.

Reading Focus

1. Why do we study civics?
2. What are the values that form the basis of the American way of life?
3. What are the roles and qualities of a good citizen?

Key Terms

civics, *p. 6*
citizen, *p. 6*
government, *p. 7*

TAKING NOTES As you read, take notes on how civics affects our lives. Use a chart like the one below to organize your notes.

Studying Civics	
American Values	
Qualities of a Good Citizen	

Every Fourth of July Americans come together to celebrate their rights and freedoms as American citizens.

CIVICS IN PRACTICE Government "by the people" does not mean government by the uninformed. Good government requires educated citizens. In fact, the main reason for public education is to help young people become more effective citizens. Remember, everything the government does affects you directly or indirectly. It is important for you to be aware of the issues we face as a nation.

Why Study Civics?

What is civics and why do you study it? **Civics** is the study of citizenship and government. It is the study of what it means to be a citizen. A **citizen** is a legally recognized member of a country. The word *civics* comes from the Latin *civis*, which means "citizen." The concept of the citizen originated in Greece around 590 BC, and was later adopted by the Romans.

Being a Citizen

What it means to be a citizen has changed since the Roman Republic. Romans used the term to distinguish the people who lived in the city of Rome from people born in the territories that Rome had conquered.

Civics, the Economy,
and You

Your daily life is affected by your community, the economy, and the government. Government provides services and structure for communities.

Economy

Government

Community

If a man or boy was a citizen (women had some rights but could not be citizens), he had many privileges. Roman citizens had the right to vote and had a say in the way their country was run. Citizens had duties, too, such as paying taxes, attending assembly meetings, and serving in the Roman army.

Citizens today have rights and responsibilities that differ from country to country. For example, many countries allow their citizens to vote, but some do not. Most nations require their citizens to pay taxes, just as Rome did. Some countries, such as Israel, require all citizens—men and women—to serve in the military. The rights and duties of citizens depend on their country's type of government. A **government** is the organizations, institutions, and individuals who exercise political authority over a group of people.

Being an American Citizen

Under the American system of government, citizens have many rights and responsibilities. Your civics course will help you understand those rights and responsibilities. You will discover that being a U.S. citizen means more than just enjoying the rights that the American system provides.

Citizenship includes being a productive and active member of society. Americans participate in society in many ways. For example, most Americans belong to a family, go to school for several years, and work with other people. Americans are also members of their local communities—villages, towns, and cities. And in the United States, you are a citizen of both your country and the state in which you live. Being an effective American citizen means fulfilling your duties and responsibilities as a member of each of these various groups and communities.

You need training in order to become a good athlete or a good musician. Likewise, you need training in order to become a good citizen. What kind of training? First, you must understand the purpose of government. Next, you need to know how the government works, on the national, state, and local levels. You must also understand how the U.S. economic system works and how government and economy interact. Then you are ready to explore ways to fulfill your role as a citizen.

Some people complain about the government. Other people get involved—in large or small ways—so they can make their government better. Right now, governments across the United States and in your community are making decisions that will affect how much money you might earn, the roads you travel on, the cost of your doctors' visits, and the protections you have under the law.

READING CHECK **Supporting a Point of View**
Why is studying civics important?

American Values

The United States has been an inspiration to other nations because of its basic **values**: equality, liberty, and justice for all people. These values are the foundation of many of your important rights and freedoms. In fact, new nations often look to the United States, its values, and its system of government as a model in creating their own governments.

As American citizens, we are all guaranteed the same rights and freedoms, which are protected by the U.S. Constitution and our laws. These laws, our system of government, and the American way of life are based on the ideals of equality, liberty, and justice.

Equality

The Declaration of Independence states, "We hold these truths to be self-evident, that all men are created equal, that they are endowed by their Creator with certain unalienable Rights . . ." What does this mean? It means

Equality of Access

Rosa Parks (1913–2005), the woman in the photo, sparked the modern civil rights movement when she refused to give up her seat on a segregated bus in Montgomery, Alabama. Today laws provide equal access in all areas of society for all Americans.

How do people today benefit from equal access to transportation?

that, ideally, all people are equal under the law. The rights of each citizen are equal to those of every other citizen. No one has the right to act as though his or her liberties are more important than those of others.

Equality means that each citizen has the same right to enjoy the many benefits granted to all citizens. Everyone has the right to seek an education or choose a job or career. U.S. law guarantees that any citizen qualified for a job has an equal opportunity to secure it.

Liberty

Can you imagine what your future might be if you did not have the freedom to get an education? What if you were not able to take a job that you wanted or start a business? What if you could not speak or write certain things without fear of punishment? Would you like to live in a place where the government told you where you had to live, or that you could not travel from one place to another within your own country? How would you feel if you could not practice religion? What if the government could put you in jail for no reason and hold you indefinitely without a trial?

Our rights seem normal to us—and some people probably take them for granted—but millions of people around the world do not have these basic freedoms. However, the people who created our government gave us a system that guarantees these rights.

Justice

Do you believe all citizens have certain rights that no one can take away? Do you think that laws should protect those rights? Our government has given power to the police to prevent others from violating our rights. But if those rights are infringed, or violated, our government has given the courts the power to punish those responsible.

Your rights and freedoms cannot be taken away from you, as long as you follow the laws of your community, state, and country. But as an American citizen, you must be willing to do your share to protect this freedom. Your rights and freedoms have been handed down from one generation of Americans to the next for more than 200 years. Throughout our history, citizens have fought and died for the freedoms we enjoy. If thousands of Americans gave their lives to preserve our rights and freedoms, then we must all do our part to protect those rights. This is called our "civic duty."

READING CHECK Analyzing Information What values are important to Americans?

Qualities of a Good Citizen

Imagine a society in which people did not take their civic duties seriously. For instance, what if people stayed home and did not vote? What would happen if people never expressed their opinions to their representatives in government? We cannot have government "by the people," as Abraham Lincoln said, unless the people participate.

Voting in Elections

A basic principle of American government is that public officeholders should respond to citizens' wishes. That is why most of the important positions in government are elected. Voters elect candidates who they think will best represent their views. If elected officials do not respond to the voters, people can vote them out in the next election. In this way, people govern themselves through the officials they elect.

Voting is one of the most important of a citizen's responsibilities. But you can also help in other ways to choose the men and women who will govern. You can work for a political party, for example. Anyone who answers telephones or stuffs envelopes for a political party is playing a part in the U.S. political system.

Expressing Your Opinion

It is also your responsibility as a citizen to tell officials what you need or how you disagree with government actions or policies. For example, you can write or call public officials or send letters to editors of newspapers.

Being an Effective Citizen

How can you be an effective citizen? Here are 10 characteristics of a good citizen. You can probably think of others. Good citizens

1. are responsible family members,
2. respect and obey the law,
3. respect the rights and property of others,
4. are loyal to and proud of their country,
5. take part in and improve life in their communities,
6. take an active part in their government,
7. use natural resources wisely,
8. are informed on key issues and willing to take a stand on these issues,
9. believe in equal opportunity for all people, and
10. respect individual differences, points of view, and ways of life that are different from their own.

READING CHECK **Drawing Inferences and Conclusions** What are some similarities among the characteristics of a good citizen?

go.hrw.com
Online Quiz
KEYWORD: SZ7 HP1

SECTION 1 ASSESSMENT

Reviewing Ideas and Terms

1. a. Define Write a brief definition for the terms **civics**, **citizen**, and **government**.
  b. Explain Why is it important to study civics?
  c. Elaborate What are ways in which American citizens participate in our society?
2. a. Recall What are three fundamental American values?
  b. Evaluate Which of those three values do you think is most important to American society? Give reasons and examples to support your answer.
3. a. Summarize How does the U.S. system of government ensure that officials are responsible to the people?
  b. Predict What would happen to an office holder who never responded to voters in his district?

Critical Thinking

4. Categorizing Using your notes and the graphic organizer, identify the roles and qualities of a good U.S. citizen.

U.S. Citizens	
Roles	Qualities

Focus on Writing

5. Analyzing Information Imagine that you head a committee to encourage good citizenship in your community. Create a chart showing five goals you want your committee to achieve and suggestions for achieving each goal.

SECTION 2

Who Are U.S. Citizens?

BEFORE YOU READ

The Main Idea

Throughout history, immigrants have brought their languages, ideas, beliefs, hopes, and customs to the United States. Their ways of life are constantly mixing with and influencing the culture of Americans who came before.

Reading Focus

1. Who are "Americans," and from where did they come?
2. What changes have occurred in U.S. immigration policy since the early 1800s?
3. How does a person become a U.S. citizen?

Key Terms

immigrants, *p. 12*
quota, *p. 14*
aliens, *p. 14*
native-born, *p. 15*
naturalization, *p. 15*
refugees, *p. 16*

TAKING NOTES As you read, take notes on U.S. citizens. Use a diagram like the one below to organize your notes on who Americans are and where they come from, the U.S. immigration policy, and becoming a U.S. citizen.

U.S. Citizens

CIVICS IN PRACTICE The United States is a nation of immigrants. With the exception of Native Americans, all of us can trace our family's roots to another country. Some families have been here longer than others. Some families continue to speak other languages and treasure customs from their homelands.

Americans Are from Everywhere

The heritage of freedom and equality in what is now the United States was formed bit by bit. Over time, groups from various parts of the world have settled here, contributing to American society. From their countries of origin, people have brought their different languages, ideas, beliefs, customs, hopes, and dreams. Today all Americans can be proud of the rich and varied heritage we share.

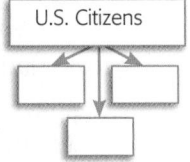

Today's Americans come from every nation on Earth.

Traditionally, people called the United States a "melting pot." **Immigrants**—people who came here from other countries—entered the nation—the pot—and adopted American customs and blended into American society.

That picture of America is not quite accurate. Many immigrants practice their traditions and customs after they move to the United States. That is why both New York City and San Francisco have neighborhoods called Chinatown. In cities throughout the United States, you can visit areas called Little Italy or Little Korea, where other countries' ways of life are preserved.

Some people say America is more like a "salad bowl." In a salad, foods do not melt together, they are a mixture of separate and distinct flavors.

A More Accurate Picture

So which image is correct? Actually, some combination of the two would be more accurate.

People who come here as adults often keep the customs they grew up with in their native countries. However, their children and grandchildren, raised in the United States, often blend into what we think of as typical American ways of life. An immigrant from Bolivia describes his adopted culture:

"Now, I live in the U.S. and I feel so much pride for being American ... I identify myself with the U.S. culture; flag, history, traditions and goals.

America the Beautiful gave me the opportunity to excel; from the jungles of the Amazon, where there was nothing, to ... the American dream: home, life satisfaction, and dreams. All these, thanks to America ... patriotic, diverse, democratic, religious, [home to] free enterprise, and moral. That is the America that I want, that I love and I will defend."

—Oscar Arredondo, quoted on
The New Americans Web page, PBS.org

Other immigrants practice both old ways and new ones. Ivy, an immigrant from Peru whose father brought her and her family here from South America, explained it this way:

"My father never wanted us to live among other Latinos [Hispanics] because he wanted us to learn the American culture among Americans—to act, to speak and think like them. But we kept our language and culture at home so that ... we would never forget who we were and where we had come from. I have been back to visit Peru several times and it will always be the country of my birth, but the U.S. is my home and my country and thanks to my parents, I can speak two languages and have better opportunities."

—Ivy, immigrant from Peru, quoted on
The New Americans Web page, PBS.org

Early Americans

Many scientists believe that the first people to settle in North America came here from Asia between 12,000 and 40,000 years ago. These early groups were the ancestors of modern-day American Indians and were the first Americans.

TIME LINE

Patterns of Migration

20,000 BC
The first people in North America migrate into what is now Canada from Asia over the Bering land bridge, which formed during the last ice age.

1492
Columbus sails to the Caribbean islands and brings the wealth of the New World back to Spain.

1620
Pilgrims travel from England on the Mayflower and settle near Cape Cod, Massachusetts.

Religious Tolerance

Can you imagine what it would be like if the government could order you to go to church, or if it could outlaw the temple or mosque you attended? Thanks to the experience of early colonists, you do not have to worry about situations like these.

Many early colonists settled in America to escape persecution in their home countries. Sometimes these new settlements were tolerant of other religions; sometimes they were as intolerant as the places the colonists had fled.

Years later, the founding fathers debated the role of religion in the new country. Some, like Patrick Henry, argued for a national church to provide a moral base. Others, like Thomas Jefferson, recalled the intolerance of some early settlements and strongly opposed having a state religion.

When the Constitution was adopted, this debate was still not fully resolved. With the passage of the Bill of Rights, the First Amendment prohibited the government from interfering in your religious freedom.

1. What role did religion play in the arrival of early American colonists?
2. Why do you think some colonial settlements were successful in supporting religious liberty while others were not?

Eventually, Europeans began to arrive in the Americas. In 1492 Christopher Columbus sailed to the Caribbean islands and claimed lands for Spain. Columbus and his crews were the first Europeans to build settlements in the Americas.

The Immigrants

Europeans soon learned that the Americas possessed vast natural resources. It had plenty of room for newcomers from crowded regions of Europe.

Spanish settlers soon spread across the Caribbean, Mexico, Central and South America, and present-day Florida, Texas, California, and the southwestern United States. People from the British Isles settled America's original thirteen colonies. Other Europeans also came to North America. Germans settled in Pennsylvania, the Dutch along

The first wave of modern immigration to the United States brings people from Britain, Ireland, and Germany.

Most immigrants today come from Spanish-speaking countries. America remains a nation that relies on immigration.

1850

1900

Southern and eastern Europeans enter the United States in large numbers.

Today

ANALYSIS SKILL **READING TIME LINES**

Sequence When was the Pilgrims' landing?

the Hudson River, Swedes along the Delaware River, and the French in New York, Massachusetts, and South Carolina.

Many Africans came to the Americas, but unlike most other immigrants, most Africans had been captured and brought here as slaves. They and their children were forced to live in bondage for many years.

READING CHECK ▶ **Categorizing** What groups settled in the Americas, and in what region did each group settle?

Immigration Policy

News about America spread quickly. For newcomers willing to work hard, America held the promise of a good life. It had abundant space, rich resources, and one precious resource: freedom. Over time, the British colonies grew, and beginning in 1775 they fought the American Revolution. This newly independent country became the United States of America. It was founded on a strong belief in human equality and the right to basic liberties.

FOCUS ON
George Washington
(1732-1799)

George Washington was not an immigrant. But like many Americans, Washington's ancestors had come from another country. He was the great-grandson of British settlers in the American colonies.

Washington had an elementary school education, but he had a gift for mathematics. At 16, Washington was hired by Lord Fairfax, head of a powerful Virginia family, to survey Fairfax's property in the American wilderness.

In 1789, Washington was elected the first president of the United States. Washington's cautious, balanced, and strong leadership as president served as a model for future presidents. Washington helped build the foundations of a national government that has continued for more than two centuries.

Draw Conclusions Why do you think that George Washington was a cautious president?

The United States attracted people from around the world. Europeans came by the tens of thousands, mainly to the East Coast of the United States. In the mid-1800s thousands of Chinese arrived on the West Coast.

These new immigrants worked in factories and farms across the country. Businesses welcomed the new laborers to their expanding enterprises. But not everyone was happy about the flood of immigrants. The newcomers were willing to work for low wages. That angered many American workers. Americans and immigrants clashed over religion and culture as well.

In the 1880s the U.S. Congress passed laws limiting immigration. For example, the Chinese Exclusion Act of 1882 halted Chinese immigration to the United States. Other laws prevented Chinese Americans from becoming citizens or owning property.

Congress passed a broader set of laws in the 1920s. The laws established a **quota**, or a specific number, of immigrants from certain countries or regions who were allowed to enter the country each year. The annual quotas have changed from time to time since then.

Today, the Immigration Act of 1990 sets a total annual quota of immigrants at 675,000, starting in 1995. The law gives preference to three groups of people: (1) husbands, wives, and children of U.S. citizens; (2) people who have valuable job skills; and (3) aliens. **Aliens** are permanent residents of the United States who are still citizens of another country.

READING CHECK ▶ **Analyzing** How has U.S. immigration policy changed over time?

Becoming a U.S. Citizen

Over the years, millions of immigrants have become U.S. citizens. Some citizens belong to families that have lived in the United States for many generations. Other Americans were born in foreign countries. All citizens, regardless of their heritage, have the same legal rights and responsibilities.

Citizenship by Birth

Are you **native-born**? That is, were you born in the United States? According to the 2000 census, almost 90 percent of Americans were native-born, while more than 10 percent were foreign-born.

If you were born in any U.S. state or territory, you are an American citizen. If one or both of your parents was a U.S. citizen, then you are a citizen, too. What if you were born here, but neither of your parents was a U.S. citizen? In most cases, you are a citizen.

Citizenship by Naturalization

If you are not a citizen by birth, it is still possible to gain U.S. citizenship. The legal process by which an alien may become a citizen is called **naturalization**.

Naturalized citizens have the same rights and duties as native-born Americans. For example, when a parent is naturalized, his or her children automatically become citizens as well. The only exception is that naturalized citizens cannot become president or vice president of the United States.

Legal Aliens

The 2000 census counted about 18.7 million legal aliens living in this country.

New U.S. citizens take their oath.

The Pathway to Citizenship

Naturalization is the legal process through which immigrants become U.S. citizens. To qualify, a person must be at least 18 years old and have a background check showing "good moral character," which includes no criminal record. Normally, completing the process takes between 7 and 11 years.

THE STEPS

1 Apply for a permanent residency visa

Many people visit the United States to travel, work, or go to school. To remain in the country, they must have a permanent residency visa. To get one, they need family or a job in the country.

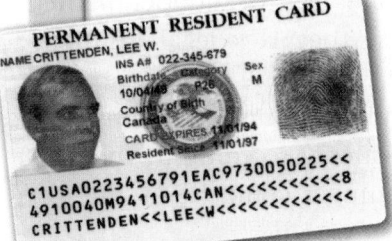

PERMANENT RESIDENT CARD

NAME CRITTENDEN, LEE W.
INS A# 022-345-679
Birthdate   Category   Sex
10/04/69   P26   M
Country of Birth
Canada
CARD EXPIRES 11/01/94
Resident Since 11/01/97

C1USA0223456791EAC9730050225<<
4910040M9411014CAN<<<<<<<<<<<<<8
CRITTENDEN<<LEE<W<<<<<<<<<<<<<<<

A green card

THE TIME IT TAKES

✓ *Receiving a green card may take more than five years.*

✓ *After receiving a green card, a permanent resident must hold it for five years before applying for citizenship.*

✓ *Permanent residents must have been on U.S. soil for two-and-a-half years when they apply.*

✓ *Traveling to another country means starting the two-and-a-half years over.*

2 Apply for citizenship
Permanent residents submit a form with photographs and other documents.

3 Get fingerprinted
Permanent residents receive an appointment letter to appear and have their fingerprints taken.

4 Be interviewed and pass tests on civics, U.S. history, and English
Applicants may be rejected for many reasons, including test scores and background check.

5 Take the Oath of Allegiance to the United States

"I hereby declare, on oath, that I absolutely and entirely give up and reject all loyalty and faithfulness to any foreign prince, ruler, state, or sovereignty of whom or which I have heretofore been a subject or citizen; that I will support and defend the Constitution and laws of the United States of America against all enemies, foreign and domestic… that I will bear arms on behalf of the United States when required by law… and that I take this obligation freely without any mental reservation or purpose of evasion; so help me God."

A legal alien is a citizen of another country who has received permission to enter the United States. Most aliens come to the United States to visit or to attend school. Aliens enjoy many of the benefits of American citizenship. Yet they cannot serve on juries, vote, or hold public office. Unlike U.S. citizens, aliens must carry an identification card, called a green card, at all times.

Illegal Immigrants

Some people come to this country illegally. Many come seeking jobs or better education and health care for their children. Illegal aliens are called undocumented residents because they lack legal immigration documents. No one knows exactly how many undocumented residents live in the United States. According to the government, the number could be as high as 8 million.

Life is often difficult for illegal aliens. They often have to work for low wages under poor conditions. Many become migrant workers, moving from farm to farm picking crops. They constantly face capture and deportation.

The Immigration Reform and Control Act of 1986 legalized undocumented residents who met certain requirements in an attempt to reduce the flow of illegal immigration. To discourage illegal immigration from Mexico, Congress and several states have allocated funds to build a series of high fences along the Mexican border. Yet the flow of illegal aliens remains high.

Refugees

Today's immigration quotas do not include **refugees**, people who are trying to escape dangers in their home countries. Refugees come to the United States from countries all around the world. Refugees are usually fleeing persecution, wars, political conflicts, and other crisis situations in their countries. The president works with Congress to set yearly quotas for the number of refugees allowed to enter the United States.

READING CHECK **Categorizing** Describe the types of residents in the United States and how their rights and obligations vary.

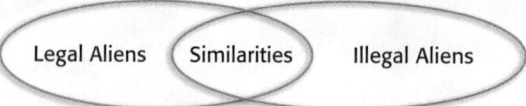

go.hrw.com
Online Quiz
KEYWORD: SZ7 HP1

SECTION 2 ASSESSMENT

Reviewing Ideas and Terms

1. a. Define Write a brief definition for the term **immigrant**.
b. Explain Describe early European settlement of the Americas.
c. Evaluate Which description of the United States—a melting pot or a salad bowl—do you think is more accurate? Explain your answer.
2. a. Define Write a brief definition for the terms **quota** and **aliens**.
b. Analyze Why were most immigrants eager to come to the United States?
3. a. Define Write a brief definition for the terms **native-born**, **naturalization**, and **refugees**.
b. Compare and Contrast What rights do U.S. citizens have that documented aliens do not have?

Critical Thinking

4. Comparing and Contrasting Use your notes and the graphic organizer to identify the similarities and differences between legal and illegal aliens.

Legal Aliens   Similarities   Illegal Aliens

Focus on Writing

5. Identifying Points of View Imagine that you have just become a naturalized citizen of the United States. Write a letter to a friend in the country in which you were born, explaining why and how you became a U.S. citizen.

SECTION 3
The American People Today

BEFORE YOU READ

The Main Idea

The U.S. population continues to grow and change today.

Reading Focus

1. Why is the census important?
2. In what ways does population grow and change?
3. What has changed about the American population over the years?
4. For what reasons have Americans moved and settled in new areas over the course of U.S. history?

Key Terms

census, p. 17
demographics, p. 18
birthrate, p. 19
death rate, p. 19
migration, p. 20

 **TAKING NOTES** As you read, take notes on the American population today. Use a diagram like the one below to organize your notes.

Census	→	
Population Growth	→	
Population Changes	→	

Take a good look at this woman. She was created by a computer from a mix of several races. What you see is a remarkable preview of . . .

THE NEW FACE OF AMERICA

Today's American population is a mix of people from all over the world.

CIVICS IN PRACTICE Have you ever received a gift meant for someone younger? Maybe a distant relative forgot that you'd grown up? As you get older, you change. A country changes too. The United States of today is not the United States of 1789. One way to keep track of changes in the nation is by taking a census. A census periodically gathers information and provides a picture of the population. In that way what we do with national resources matches the nation's needs.

The Census

In ancient times, kings, emperors, and pharaohs counted their people. Usually, rulers counted the men so that they could tax them or force them to join the army.

In modern times, many countries take a **census**, an official, periodic counting of a population. The United States conducts a census every 10 years. The last nationwide census occurred in 2000. It measured the official U.S. population at 281.4 million, up 13.2 percent from 1990. That was the largest census-to-census increase in the nation's history.

MATH 101

Percentages and Population Growth

In the years since the United States became a nation, its population has steadily increased. The 1990 census reported 248,709,873 people living in the United States—a 6,300 percent jump from the 3,929,214 people reported during the first U.S. census in 1790, only 200 years earlier.

U.S. Population, 1900-2000

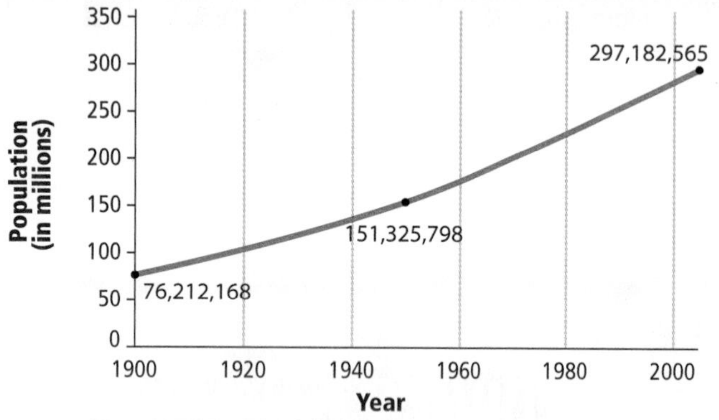

Population (in millions) vs. Year

- 1900: 76,212,168
- 1950: 151,325,798
- 2000: 297,182,565

Source: U.S. Census Bureau

ANALYSIS SKILL — ANALYZING GRAPHS

In 1950 the U.S. population was about 150 million people. By 2000 the population had expanded to almost twice that number. Use the graph above to find the percent by which the population grew from 1950 to 2000.

The Census Counts People

Census information is used for many purposes, but mainly to find out how many people live in each state. Population determines how many representatives each state gets to send to Congress. A census tracks the number of people who live in an area. It also shows the rate at which a population is growing or shrinking. Our country's population has continued to grow, but the rate of growth changes from year to year.

By using census information, we can make predictions about how a country's population will grow or shrink. In fact, our country's population is expected to increase to close to 310 million people by 2010.

The Census Tracks Characteristics

Today's census also collects demographic information as well. **Demographics** is the study of the characteristics of human populations. For example, a census might provide information on people's ethnic backgrounds, the number of children in each family, or even how many pets a family owns.

The U.S. Census information is published in print and posted on the Internet so that everyone may see it and use it. Information gathered by the census helps the government, businesses, and even individuals plan for the future.

READING CHECK **Making Predictions** How might businesses, government, and individuals use census information to plan for the future?

Population Growth

The United States did not stop growing with the 2000 census. In fact, by 2005, the Census Bureau projected that the U.S. population had grown to 295.5 million, and it will not stop there. By 2010, the U.S. population may be close to 310 million people. Typically, countries grow in three ways: by natural increase, by adding territory, or through immigration.

Natural Increase in Population

A population increases naturally when the birthrate is greater than the death rate. The **birthrate** refers to the annual number of live births per 1,000 members of a population. The **death rate** refers to the annual number of deaths per 1,000 members of a country's population.

The first U.S. Census, taken in 1790, found fewer than 4 million people living in the original thirteen states. Then, in 1830 the number of Americans more than tripled, to almost 13 million. Why? In early America, the birthrate was very high—perhaps five or more children per family. Most people lived on farms, and children worked with other family members on the farm. These large families led to a natural increase in population.

Adding Territory

In its first century, the United States expanded across the continent. These new lands held vast natural resources, allowing existing populations to grow and expand.

Also during the 1800s, the United States gained huge sections of territory from Mexico, including present-day Texas and California and much of the Southwest. The people of Native American, Spanish, and mixed heritage who lived on those lands became an important part of the U.S. population.

Immigration

Since 1820, more than 60 million immigrants from all over the world have come to the United States. Those immigrants and their descendants make up most of America's population.

READING CHECK ▶ **Analyzing Information** What are three ways a population can grow?

Population Changes

The structure of the American family, the roles of men and women, and families' ways of life continue to change, as they have throughout our history. Information collected in the U.S. Census helps us track these changing demographics.

Changing Households

American households have changed in several ways. An increase in divorces has created more one-parent households, many of them headed by women. Some couples are deciding to have fewer children or are waiting to have children. Some people today choose not to marry at all. In addition, people live longer today and are better able to live by themselves in their old age. These factors have caused the size of U.S. households to shrink since 1970.

Changing Women's Roles

If you were a woman in 1950 who wanted to be a construction worker, police officer, bank president, or pilot, your options were limited. Today? These careers—and more—are open to women. The majority of women today work outside the home. That is a big demographic shift. Another change is that more women than men now enter college and graduate. After graduation, more women are entering the workforce than ever before.

An Older Population

The American population is getting older. The U.S. Census counted about 65,000 centenarians—people who are 100 years old or older—in 2000. That number is expected to rise to more than 380,000 by 2030. In 1900, only 4 percent of Americans were 65 or older. In 2000 that number rose to 13 percent and is expected to rise to 20 percent by 2030. People are living longer because of their healthier lifestyles and better medical care.

These changing demographics present a huge challenge for the future: A shrinking proportion of younger wage earners will be faced with helping support a rising proportion of older Americans in need.

A More Diverse Population

Our population is not only older but also more diverse. Early census forms gave

LAW 101

Learning English: What's the Best Way?

Have you ever tried to communicate with someone who does not speak the same language as you? What if that person were your teacher? Would it be hard to learn from him or her? That is what school is like for millions of students in the United States who do not speak English. What is the best way for those students to learn to read and write English while also studying other subjects?

Why it Matters Some educators support bilingual education—teaching students subjects such as math and social studies in their first language while they are also learning English. But critics of this method say that it takes too long for students to learn English well enough to enter mainstream, or regular, classes. These educators generally support immersion, in which students take all subjects in English. Recently, some states have voted to cut funding for bilingual programs. Instead, voters supported placing students in "sheltered immersion" programs (in which most subjects are taught in English) for one year before joining mainstream classes.

Bilingual programs in schools across the United States help students learn to speak English.

ANALYSIS SKILL **EVALUATING THE LAW**

go.hrw.com
KEYWORD: SZ7 CH1

What might be the advantages and disadvantages of both bilingual and immersion programs?

---

people few choices for identifying their race or ethnic background.

In recent years, the number of Americans of mixed heritage has grown. So in the 2000 Census, the federal government made new categories available for people to select. The new categories reflect demographic changes, as people from various ethnic groups identify themselves as having mixed heritage.

> **READING CHECK** **Making Predictions** What challenges might result from demographic changes occurring in the United States today?

A Population on the Move

At its birth, the United States was mostly a nation of farmers. There were a few cities,

such as Boston, New York, and Philadelphia, but they were quite small by today's standards. Merchants, sailors, bankers, and many wealthy Americans lived in these cities. However, most Americans lived in the rolling hills and flat plains of the eastern seacoast, rich with dark, fertile farmland.

Migration to the Cities

The rise of American industry in the early 1800s brought thousands of new factory jobs to growing cities. Farm workers and their families began a **migration**, a movement of large numbers of people from region to region, to the cities.

The 1830 census showed that urban areas were growing faster than rural areas. With each census, the proportion of Americans living in or near cities continued to grow. By the late 1800s, urban overcrowding had become a major national problem. Disease, crime, fires, noise, and choking factory smoke plagued the cities. Nevertheless, by 1920 the country's urban population exceeded its rural population.

The Drive to the Suburbs

Until the early 1900s, Americans generally stayed close to home. Then came one of America's favorite inventions: the automobile. As car sales soared in the 1920s, the nation's demographics began to change. After World War II, interstate highways were built. As a result, Americans did not have to live where they worked. They could move out of the cities and into surrounding areas, known as suburbs. People moved to the suburbs in search of larger homes, better schools, and quiet neighborhoods. Today more people live in suburbs than in cities.

According to the 2000 census, more than 80 percent of Americans live in metropolitan areas, or regions made up of cities and their suburbs. More than half of U.S. residents now live in areas with populations of 1 million people or more.

Migration to the Sunbelt

For most of our history, the nation's largest populations lived in the Northeast and Midwest. Then starting in the 1950s, industries and people began to move out of the colder northern cities to the warmer southern states. This part of the country, with its milder climate and lots of sunshine, is called the Sunbelt, and it includes states from North Carolina and Florida in the east to southern California in the west. Because of the population shift to the Sunbelt, cities in the South and West are growing. For example, according to the 2000 census, Las Vegas, Nevada, is one of the fastest growing cities in the United States. Despite this population trend, however, New York City remains the country's most populous city.

READING CHECK **Making Generalizations and Predictions** If better jobs and opportunities arose in the Northeast and Midwest, what changes in demographics might occur?

go.hrw.com
Online Quiz
KEYWORD: SZ7 HP1

SECTION 3 ASSESSMENT

Reviewing Ideas and Terms

1. a. Define Write a brief definition for the terms **census** and **demographics**.
  b. Explain Why is the census important to the nation?
2. a. Define Write a brief definition for the terms **birthrate** and **death rate**.
  b. Describe What are three ways in which a country may grow in population?
3. a. Summarize What are four ways in which the American population is changing?
  b. Predict How might U.S. society be different if the makeup of its population changes?
4. a. Define Write a brief definition for the term **migration**.

b. Explain Describe the effects of climate and technology on American migration patterns.

Critical Thinking

5. Identifying Cause and Effect Using your notes and a graphic organizer like the one below, identify the population changes that have taken place in recent years.

Population Changes in the United States

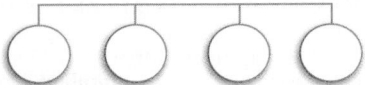

Focus on Writing

6. Summarizing Imagine that it is the year 2020 and you are a history textbook author. Describe for your readers the U.S. population in the year 2009.

Conducting Internet Research

Learn

The Internet's size makes it a great reference source. However, that size can also make it difficult to find the information you need. Having the skill to use the Internet efficiently increases its usefulness. Be aware, though, that there is a lot of inappropriate and inaccurate information on the Internet.

Practice

1 **Use a search engine.** These are Web sites that search the whole Internet for a word or a phrase that you type in. The word you type is called a search term. Knowing how to use search terms can help you search more efficiently.

2 **Click on a hyperlink.** Read the search results, a list of Web pages containing your search term. Each page on the list is shown as a hyperlink. Clicking on a link will take you to a Web page.

3 **Study the Web page.** Your search term should appear somewhere on the Web site. To find out where, you can read carefully or use the "Find" feature to search the page for the word. Printing out a Web page may make it easier to read.

4 **Return to your search results.** If one Web page does not have the information you want, hit the "Back" button to return to your search results. Try the next hyperlink on the list and keep looking.

Apply

Use the search results shown below to answer the following questions:

1. Which hyperlink would you click for news about immigration?

2. Which Web site is probably the most useful for learning about American immigration?

3. How are the Web sites listed at the top and right sides different from the Web sites in the main list?

WEB*STER*

| immigration | | Search | Advanced Search Preferences |

Web Images Groups News Local **more »**

Web   **immigration** [definition]

News results for **immigration** - View today's top stories   *Advertisements*

Immigration Smuggler Arrested - NYTimes.com - 2 hours ago   **Immigration** Law
                                                                                Just Apply through an Online Form &
US Citizenship and Immigration Service   Hire Lawyers for Less than $1 a Day
InfoPass eliminates waiting in line for **immigration** information; ... Notice to   www.411-immigrationlaw.com
Individuals Granted **Immigration** Benefits by Immigration Judges Read more. ...

The Department of **Immigration** and Indigenous Affairs   **Immigration**
Official Australian Government migration and **immigration** website, with   Free immigration law info from the
information and application forms for migration and temporary entry toAustralia, ...   experts at the Law Encyclopedia.
                                                                                www.TheLawEncyclopedia.com
Citizenship and **Immigration** Canada | Citoyenneté et **Immigration** Canada
Citizenship and **Immigration** Canada / Citoyenneté et **Immigration** Canada.
Welcome/Bienvenue. English Français Canada. Important Notices, Avis importants.

STUDENTS TAKE ACTION

Righting a Wrong

Every week when students at Twinfield Union School in Plainfield, Vermont, opened national news magazines, they saw advertisements for cigarettes. These were student editions of the magazines—designed especially for teens in middle and high schools. One group of Twinfield eighth-graders decided that cigarette ads were not appropriate and that they were going to do something about it.

Community Connection As part of their work with Project Citizen, the students from Twinfield contacted Vermont attorney general William Sorrel to express their concern that cigarette ads were being placed in magazines for young people. The attorney general was surprised to hear this news but grateful that the students had contacted him. As the students had discovered through research into the issue, under a previous agreement, cigarette companies are not allowed to advertise to teens.

Taking Action The attorney general of Vermont shared the information provided by Twinfield's students with attorneys general in other states. Together, they complained to the tobacco companies. The companies agreed to remove their ads from student editions of magazines. "I never thought at this age I could actually affect something nationwide," said Maegan Mears, one of the students. "I hope to continue to make a difference, now that I know I can." Vermont's attorney general also expressed his appreciation for the Twinfield students' actions: "Without their involvement," he said, "we would not have known what was going into these student editions. This is a wonderful example of what can be accomplished through active citizen participation."

Students from Twinfield Union School took action to stop cigarette advertisements in student magazines.

go.hrw.com
Project Citizen
KEYWORD: SZ7 CH1

SERVICE LEARNING

1. Why did this group of eighth-graders try to get cigarette advertisements removed from some magazines?
2. How did the Twinfield students make a difference for teens nationwide?

Visual Summary

Use this visual summary to help you review the main ideas of the chapter.

Reviewing Key Terms

Identify the correct term from the chapter that best fits each of the following descriptions.

1. The study of what it means to be a citizen
2. A legally recognized member of a country
3. The organizations, institutions, and people who exercise political authority over a group of people
4. People who come to a country from other countries
5. Specific number of immigrants from certain countries allowed to enter the country in a year
6. Permanent residents of the United States who are citizens of another country
7. Person born in the United States
8. Legal process by which an alien may become a citizen
9. People who are trying to escape dangers in their home countries
10. Official periodic counting of a population

11. The study of the characteristics of human populations
12. Annual number of live births per 1,000 members of a population
13. Annual number of deaths per 1,000 members of a population
14. Movement of large numbers of people from region to region

Comprehension and Critical Thinking

SECTION 1 *(Pages 6–10)*

15. **a. Explain** What is civics, and what does it have to do with being a good citizen? Give examples to support your answer.

    b. Analyze What principles and ideals form the foundation of the American system of government?

    c. Elaborate How do the qualities of a good citizen reflect and support American values? Give examples.

Active Citizenship video program
Review the video to answer the following question:
What are some advantages of not offering bilingual education in school? What are some disadvantages?

SECTION 2 *(Pages 11–16)*

16. a. Explain How has U.S. immigration policy changed since the early 1800s?

b. Analyze What benefits do people derive from being a citizen of the United States?

c. Evaluate Do you think the steps to citizenship should be made easier or harder? Give reasons for your answer.

SECTION 3 *(Pages 17–21)*

17. a. Identify What are three ways that the populations of countries increase?

b. Explain What are three ways in which the population of the United States is changing?

c. Analyze Why do you think that a serious natural disaster, such as a flood, a famine, or an earthquake, might lend to a migration?

Civics Skills

Conducting Internet Research *Use the Civics Skill taught in this chapter to answer the question below.*

18. Use a search engine to search the Internet for information on one of the topics in this chapter, such as what it means to be a citizen, the ideals of freedom and equality, immigration and citizenship, and demographic changes in the American population. Use the information you find to create an illustrated brochure or poster that answers the following questions about your topic:

a. What is different today from what existed in this country in the 1700s?

b. What may be different from today in the year 2025?

Reading Skills

Using Context Clues *Use the Reading Skill taught in this chapter to answer the question about the reading selection below.*

> This part of the country, with its milder climate and lots of sunshine, is called the Sunbelt. *(p. 21)*

19. According to the reading selection above, what is the best definition of *Sunbelt*?

a. a region of the country that grows most of the nation's wheat

b. a region of the country receiving a high amount of sunshine

c. a region of the country made up of states that have older industrial areas

d. a region of the country that is experiencing population decline

Using the Internet

go.hrw.com
KEYWORD: SZ7 CH1

20. Tracking Trends Did you know the first American census was taken in 1790? A lot has changed since then, but the U.S. Census Bureau continues its work by conducting a nationwide census every 10 years. Enter the activity keyword to research population shifts, growth, and population diversity in the United States. Then use information from the 2000 census to create a thematic map, graph, or chart that illustrates trends in one of the above areas.

FOCUS ON WRITING

21. Writing Your Letter First, review your notes and decide what is important to tell Fran's friend about American values and American ideals. Then tell the person what it means to be an American citizen, including the rights and the responsibilities of citizenship. End with an explanation of how America's population is changing and how you can be a part of the future.

FOUNDATIONS OF GOVERNMENT

SECTION 1
Why Americans
Have Governments

SECTION 2
The First Government

SECTION 3
A New Constitution

NATIONAL STANDARDS®
FOR CIVICS AND GOVERNMENT

I. What are civic life, politics, and government?

   A. What is government? What purposes should government serve?

   B. What are the essential characteristics of limited and unlimited government?

   C. What are the nature and purposes of constitutions?

II. What are the foundations of the American political system?

   A. What is the American idea of constitutional government?

   B. What are the distinctive characteristics of American society?

   D. What values and principles are basic to American constitutional democracy?

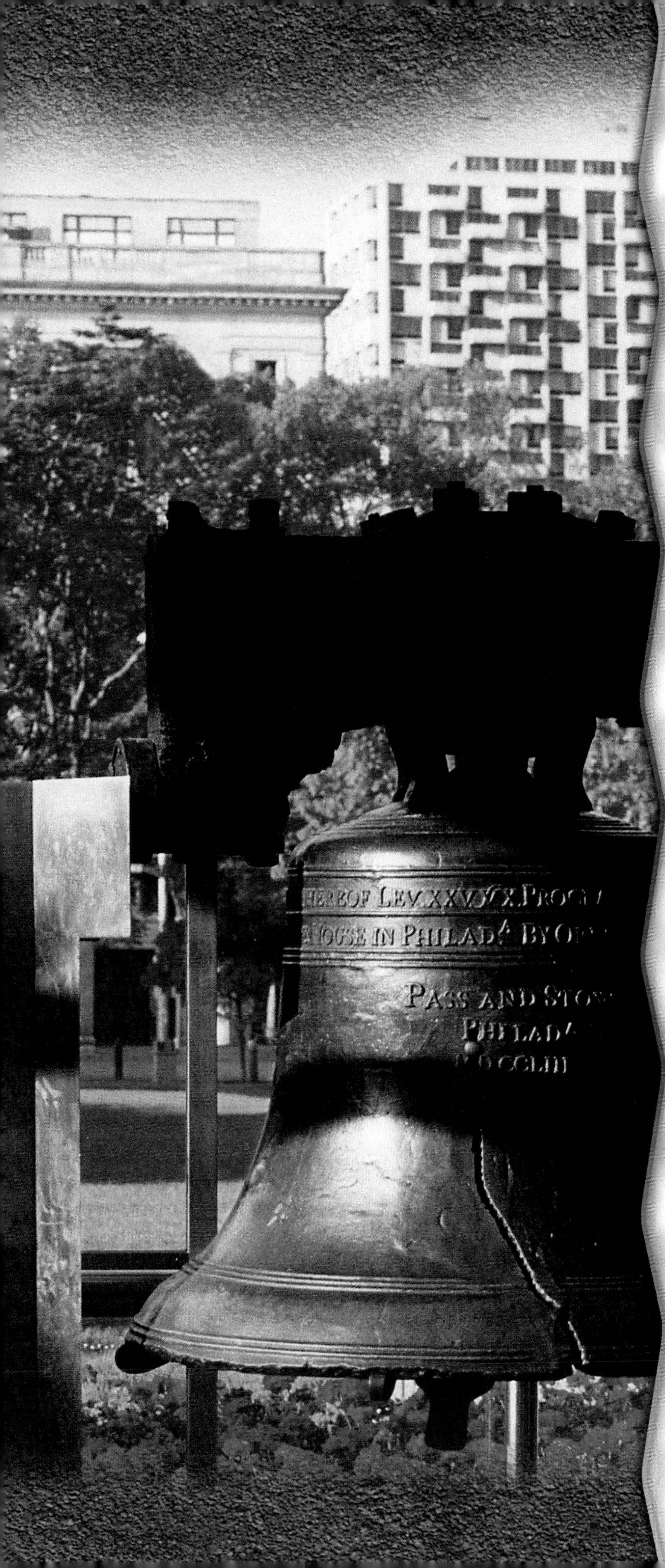

Active Citizenship Video Program
Watch the video to learn how young citizens
are working to protect their communities.

WHY CIVICS Matters

Our government is based on ideals of freedom and liberty. In 1776 the Declaration of Independence was signed in the building we call Independence Hall. Tradition holds that the Liberty Bell rang to summon people to hear the first public reading of the Declaration. The freedoms you enjoy today began with those acts more than 230 years ago.

PROJECT Citizen

STUDENTS TAKE ACTION

SAFE NEIGHBORHOODS? What if you and your friends found out that the man in the ice cream truck was selling toy guns to young children? As you read this chapter, remember that you can play a part in making your street safe. How could you do it?

FOCUS ON WRITING

A PAMPHLET Everyone in the United States benefits from our government. However, many people don't know the origins and purposes of our government as well as they should. In this chapter you will read about the foundations of our government and the rights it guarantees to citizens. Then you'll create a four-page pamphlet to share this information with your fellow citizens.

Reading Skills

In this chapter you will read about the different types and functions of government around the world. You will learn why the American colonies fought Great Britain for the right to govern themselves and about the ideals set forth in the Declaration of Independence. You will learn how American leaders wrote a new plan of government for the United States. Finally, you will read how this plan created a stronger national government and Congress.

Chronological Order

FOCUS ON READING History, just like our lives, can be seen as a series of events in time. To understand history and events, we often need to see how they are related in time.

Understanding Chronological Order The word **chronological** means "related to time." Sometimes, events discussed in this Civics book are discussed in **sequence**, in the order in which they happened. To understand sequencing better, you can use a chain to take notes about events in the order in which they happened.

Sequence Chain

1775—The colonists grew more angry about additional British taxation.

↓

1776—The Declaration of Independence is written and adopted.

↓

1781—The Articles of Confederation are adopted.

↓

1787—The United States Constitution was adopted and submitted to the states for ratification.

Helpful Hints for Sequencing Events

Writers sometimes signal chronological order, or sequence, by using words or phrases like these:

first, before, then, later, soon, after, before long, next, eventually, finally

You Try It!

Practice using the chronological note-taking format discussed on the previous page by using the steps outlined below the passage.

> The Declaration of Independence [1776] was not a plan or a blueprint to provide a government for the new country. The Declaration was the colonists' statement of grievances against the king. It listed their reasons for creating their own new government. The next step came in 1777, when the Continental Congress adopted a plan of government—the Articles of Confederation. The Articles were approved in 1781 by the 13 states. The new government went into effect. When the Revolutionary War ended in 1783, the former colonies of Great Britain had won. They were now a confederation called "The United States of America."
>
> *From Chapter 2, p. 35*

Refer to the passage to answer the following questions.

1. What step came between the Declaration of Independence and the approval of the Articles of Confederation?

2. Read the passage above again, pausing to stop and jot notes about dates and events. How many dates and events should you have in your notes?

3. Make a sequence chain based on the information in your notes.

Why Americans Have Governments

BEFORE YOU READ

The Main Idea

Government plays an essential role in every country. A country's government affects the lives of its people. Often, it affects people around the world.

Reading Focus

1. What are two main types of government?
2. What are the purposes of government?
3. How does the U.S. government guarantee freedom to its citizens?

Key Terms

monarch, p. 30
dictator, p. 30
democracy, p. 31
direct democracy, p. 31
representative democracy, p. 31
republic, p. 31
constitution, p. 32

 **TAKING NOTES** As you read, take notes on why Americans have governments. Use a chart like this one to record your notes.

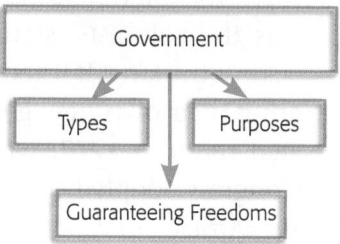

 The U.S. government is more than just buildings and people. It is the system of laws and authority that acts on your behalf to protect your rights and your freedoms. Governments provide society with laws so that everyone knows what is expected and what is not acceptable from citizens. In the United States, every citizen has a voice in making the laws. That's what makes America and its government different from many other countries.

Types of Governments

Every country in the world has a government. However, these governments vary widely. Governments differ in the way their leaders are chosen and in the amount of power held by the people. Each country's government has been shaped by the **traditional** beliefs of its people and by their history. Governments generally fall into two different types: nondemocratic and democratic governments.

ACADEMIC VOCABULARY
traditional customary, time-honored

Nondemocratic Governments

In a nondemocratic government, citizens do not have the power to rule. The following are several types of nondemocratic governments:

Monarchies A **monarch** is a person, such as a king or queen, who reigns over a kingdom or an empire. Today, European countries such as the United Kingdom and Sweden have monarchs with limited powers who serve as ceremonial heads of state. The actual power of government lies elsewhere. Saudi Arabia's monarch controls the government. In the past, some European monarchs held all power and often ruled by force. They were called absolute monarchs.

Dictatorships A **dictator** is a person who rules with complete and absolute power. An absolute monarch may be a dictator, but dictators often take power by force. An oligarchy

POLITICAL CARTOON
A History of Protest

Throughout history, groups of Americans have dissented—disagreed with and protested against—government policies. For example, protests played an important role in the civil rights movement. The Constitution protects people's right to assemble and speak out against the government and other groups, as long as they do so in a peaceful manner.

Mike Keefe THE DENVER POST 2003 www.caglecartoons.com

THAT'S ALWAYS BEEN MY PHILOSOPHY, TOO!

DISSENT IS UNPATRIOTIC

Saddam Hussein, the dictator of Iraq in 2003, suppressed dissent in his own country and approved of punishing protesters.

The man here is carrying a sign with a peace symbol on it to protest the U.S. invasion of Iraq in 2003.

ANALYSIS SKILL **ANALYZING POLITICAL CARTOONS**

Make Inferences What is the cartoonist trying to say about those who wish to suppress peaceful protest?

is a type of dictatorship in which all power is concentrated in a small group of people. Dictatorships are authoritarian, which means that the rulers answer only to themselves, not to the people they rule. Some dictatorships are also totalitarian, which means that the rulers try to control every aspect of citizens' lives, including their religious, cultural, political, and personal activities.

Theocracy A theocracy is a government controlled by one or more religious leaders who claim to rule on behalf of God or the gods worshipped in their country. Citizens may elect a theocratic government, but the rulers respond to divine guidance and not to the wishes of the people.

Democratic Governments

Other countries have democratic governments. In a **democracy** the people of a nation either rule directly or they elect officials who act on their behalf. The word *democracy* comes from an ancient Greek term meaning "rule of the people."

There are two forms of democracy. In a **direct democracy**, all voters in a community meet in one place to make laws and decide what actions to take. Historically, direct democracies have been suited only to small communities. In a **representative democracy** the people elect representatives to carry on the work of government for them. The people consent to be ruled by their elected leaders. This system of government is called a **republic**. The United States is a republic.

READING CHECK **Summarizing** What are two main types of governments, and what are their characteristics?

Purposes of Government

Could we manage our own affairs without our government? Who would provide basic services, such as public roads or fire departments? What are the basic purposes of government?

Helping People Cooperate

Whenever groups of people have lived in a community, they have found it necessary and useful to have rules and work together. They have formed a government.

TELEVISION NEWS
East Coast Blackout

On August 14, 2003, a power outage cut electricity to about 50 million people in an area stretching from east of New York City, north to Toronto, Canada, and west to Detroit, Michigan. The outage began at about 4 p.m. Immediately, television news programs began carrying the breaking story.

LIVE

WCBS

BREAKING NEWS
CONNECTICUT, NEW JERSEY
ALSO INVOLVED IN BLACKOUT

CNN

NAS ▲ 13.73

Governments provide safety services, such as traffic lights on streets and roads. When the power goes out, government also provides traffic control by police officers.

ANALYSIS SKILL   ANALYZING MEDIA   go.hrw.com KEYWORD: SZ7 CH2

How do television news programs keep people around the country informed about disasters? What are television's limitations?

Government provides a way for people to unite, solve problems, and cooperate. Even traditional forms of government, such as in a small clan or tribe, helped to make life safer and easier.

Providing Services

Over the years, government at all levels has grown more complex. Yet its basic purposes have remained the same. Governments provide expensive or important services to large groups of people who might otherwise have to do without the service. For example, by establishing schools, the government makes it possible for all children to receive a good education.

The federal government also protects people from attacks by foreign countries. Other governments provide police to protect lives and property and fire departments to protect homes and businesses.

Because of government, we can travel highways that stretch from border to border. We have a system of money that makes it easy for us to buy and sell things and to know the price of these things. Trash is collected, and health laws are enforced to protect us. We can go to public libraries. Government provides these and many more services.

Providing Laws

The basic plan under which Americans live is contained in a **constitution**, or a written plan of government. Americans have used constitutions to establish national and state governments. A constitution sets forth the purposes of the government and describes how the government is to be organized.

Governments also provide laws for society. Laws must be constitutional to be valid. Laws are recorded so that people can know and obey them. Laws are passed by the government to guide and protect all of us.

READING CHECK **Summarizing** What purposes do laws and constitutions serve in governments?

Guaranteeing Freedom

The government of the United States has a fourth purpose—to guarantee the freedoms of its citizens. Remember, a democratic country's government helps put into practice the ideals of the people—that is, the things in which they believe. The United States was founded on the belief that the people should rule themselves. Americans also believe that each person is important and that no one should be denied his or her rights. What are these rights? The Declaration of Independence describes these rights as "life, liberty, and the pursuit of happiness."

To safeguard each citizen's liberty, the laws of the United States guarantee certain freedoms, including freedoms of speech, the press, and religion. These freedoms can never be taken away from any U.S. citizen by the government. Nor can these rights be restricted, except to keep people from using these freedoms to violate the rights of others.

For example, having free speech and a free press does not mean we are free to tell lies or write false statements about another person. Each citizen has the right to have his or her reputation protected.

Most Americans believe that if any citizen is denied his or her rights, the liberty of all citizens is endangered. Thus, the U.S. government passed and enforces laws that guarantee equal rights for all citizens. For example, U.S. laws require that all Americans have equal access to education and employment, and have the right to vote.

The U.S. Constitution and all state constitutions set out rights and freedoms that are guaranteed to all individuals. But those rights and freedoms do not take care of themselves. You, and all citizens like you, must take an active role in protecting and preserving those rights and freedoms.

READING CHECK **Analyzing Information** What are some of the freedoms guaranteed by U.S. laws?

go.hrw.com
Online Quiz
KEYWORD: SZ7 HP2

SECTION 1 ASSESSMENT

Reviewing Ideas and Terms

1. a. Define Write a brief definition for the terms **monarch, dictator, democracy, direct democracy, representative democracy**, and **republic**.
b. Explain Why are governments important? Give examples to support your answer.
c. Evaluate What are two basic types of government, and what are advantages and disadvantages of each type?
2. a. Define Write a brief definition for the term **constitution**.
b. Summarize What are three purposes of government?
c. Elaborate How does having a constitution help a government fulfill its purposes for citizens? Give examples to support your answer.
3. a. Summarize How does the U.S. system of government guarantee each citizen's freedoms?
b. Elaborate Why is it necessary to restrict rights in some instances?

Critical Thinking

4. Categorizing Copy the chart below. Use it and your notes to identify three purposes of government in our society and to state how government fulfills each purpose.

The Purposes of Government		

Focus on Writing

5. Supporting a Point of View Write a three-paragraph essay explaining what you think are the most important functions of your local (city or town) government. Be sure to explain how these functions affect members of your community.

The First Government

BEFORE YOU READ

The Main Idea

The American ideals that people should rule themselves and that government should protect human rights are clearly set forth in the Declaration of Independence.

Reading Focus

1. Why is the Declaration of Independence so important?
2. What were the Articles of Confederation, and what were their weaknesses?
3. What was the effect of a weak national government on the United States?

Key Terms

human rights, *p. 34*
confederation, *p. 36*
sovereignty, *p. 36*

 **TAKING NOTES** As you read, take notes on the beginnings of government in the United States. Use a chart like this one to record your notes.

Declaration of Independence	Articles of Confederation

 **CIVICS IN PRACTICE** Why does a football team need a head coach? Someone has to be in charge of the whole team. After winning their independence, each of the 13 states acted independently, making its own laws. The national government was weak. Something had to change, or the new nation could fail. The United States in which you live today, with the freedoms and opportunities you have, might not exist.

The Declaration of Independence

In 1775, angry about new taxes and actions of the British Parliament, the American colonies went to war with Great Britain. The next year the Continental Congress—representatives from the 13 colonies—met in Philadelphia. At this meeting, the delegates appointed a committee to draw up a Declaration of Independence. Thomas Jefferson wrote most of the Declaration of Independence. The Continental Congress approved it on July 4, 1776.

The Declaration and Human Rights

The Declaration of Independence lists the reasons the colonies decided to separate from Great Britain and to form an independent country. For example, colonists objected to being taxed without their consent. The colonists believed that the power of government comes from the consent of the governed—the people of the country. If any government ignores the will of those people, the people have a legitimate right to change the government.

Thus, the Declaration of Independence is much more than a document to justify independence. It is also a statement of American ideals. It explains to the world in clear language that the purpose of government is to protect **human rights**, which are the basic rights to which all people are entitled.

The Declaration clearly states these rights. "We hold these truths to be self-evident, that all men are created equal, that they are endowed by their Creator with certain unalienable Rights, that among these are Life, Liberty, and the pursuit of Happiness." This passage is one of the most famous in American writing.

Declaration of Independence

This painting, "Declaration of Independence" by John Trumbull, is fictional. It does not show either the introduction of the draft of the Declaration of Independence on June 28, 1776, or the adoption of the Declaration on July 4, 1776. Trumbull's intention was to portray the images of the men who were the authors of the Declaration.

The man in the red vest is Thomas Jefferson, the principal author of the Declaration of Independence. In 1800 Jefferson was elected as third president of the United States.

The man seated at the table is John Hancock, a popular and respected leader of the American Revolution. His signature is one of the most recognizable on the Declaration of Independence.

Ideals of American Government

Over the years this language from the Declaration of Independence has come to mean that all Americans are equal under the law. Every person has an equal right to life, liberty, and the pursuit of happiness. The signers of the Declaration realized that these ideals would be difficult to achieve. Yet they believed such ideals were worth, as the Declaration states, "our lives, our fortunes, and our sacred honor."

The Declaration of Independence is considered one of the greatest documents in our country's history. Although it was written more than 225 years ago, it remains a lasting symbol of American freedom.

READING CHECK **Finding the Main Idea** What was the purpose and significance of the Declaration of Independence?

The Articles of Confederation

The Declaration of Independence was not a plan or a blueprint to provide a government for the new country. The Declaration was the colonists' statement of grievances against the king. It listed their reasons for creating their own new government. The next step came in 1777, when the Continental Congress adopted a plan of government—the Articles of Confederation. The Articles were approved in 1781 by the 13 states. The new government went into effect. When the Revolutionary War ended in 1783, the former colonies of Great Britain had won. They were now a confederation called The United States of America.

The Thirteen Colonies

The thirteen original colonies were founded in the years from 1607 (Virginia) to 1732 (Georgia). After the Revolutionary War, these colonies became the original United States of America.

- Virginia 1607
- Massachusetts 1620
- New Hampshire 1623
- Maryland 1634
- Connecticut c. 1635
- Rhode Island 1636
- Delaware 1638
- North Carolina 1653
- South Carolina 1663
- New Jersey 1664
- New York 1664
- Pennsylvania 1682
- Georgia 1732

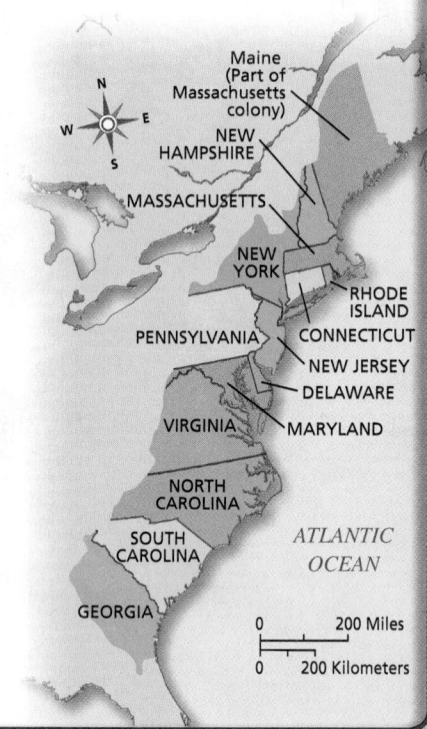

Government under the Articles

A **confederation** is a loose association, rather than a firm union, of states. The Articles of Confederation set up a "firm league of friendship" among the 13 states. Each state was to have equal powers and in most ways was to be independent of the other states. The central, or national, government had very limited powers. The majority of people in the 13 states feared that a strong central government, such as the one they were fighting, might limit the freedom of the separate states. As a result, under the Articles of Confederation, the national government consisted of a lawmaking body called Congress. Each state had one vote in Congress, regardless of the number of people living in the state.

The writers of the Articles wanted to preserve the states' **sovereignty**, or absolute power. Thus, the Articles gave the power to enforce national laws to the states, rather than to the national government. The Articles also did not establish a national court system.

During the Revolutionary War, the new states had problems working together to achieve victory. After the war, many Americans experienced difficult times. Property had been destroyed. Trade with other countries had slowed. American businesses suffered. Moreover, the war left the country deeply in debt. The Articles of Confederation had not given the new government the powers it needed to solve all these problems.

The Need for Change

The Articles of Confederation succeeded in establishing a new country. However, the residents of each state still tended to think of themselves as citizens of their particular state rather than as Americans. Under the Articles many of the states continued to have only limited contact with each other. This made it difficult for them to agree on the common interests and goals for the government.

The weaknesses of the national government became clear as the young country began to face new problems. The states quarreled over boundary lines. They became involved in disputes over trade. The national government was powerless to end these disagreements or to prevent new ones from arising. In addition to domestic troubles, the country looked weak to other nations. Many leaders began to favor strengthening the national government. As a result, in 1787 Congress asked the states to send representatives to a meeting where revisions to the Articles could be discussed.

READING CHECK **Analyzing Information** What type of government did the Articles create?

Weaknesses of the Articles

The national government had several weaknesses under the Articles of Confederation. For example, Congress had trouble passing laws because a vote of 9 of the 13 states was needed to pass important measures. Getting 9 states to agree to any change was difficult. The Quick Facts in the next column explains some of the other weaknesses.

As a result of these weaknesses, states acted more like small, separate nations than as members of a confederation. The states often refused to obey the laws of Congress. Relations between the states and Congress worsened.

READING CHECK ▶ **Analyzing Information** What were some of the weaknesses of the national government under the Articles of Confederation?

Weaknesses of the Articles of Confederation

The overall weakness of the Articles of Confederation was in the structure of the relationship between the state governments and the national government. Problems included:

- Without a president or an executive branch, there were no officials to ensure that the laws passed by Congress were carried out.

- Without national courts, there was no means of interpreting laws or judging those who broke them.

- Without money, Congress could not pay the country's debts or carry on any government activities that might be needed. Congress also could not pay the soldiers who had fought in the Revolutionary War. These limitations harmed relations with foreign nations and endangered America's national security.

go.hrw.com
Online Quiz
KEYWORD: SZ7 HP2

SECTION 2 ASSESSMENT

Reviewing Ideas and Terms

1. a. Define Write a brief definition for the term **human rights**.

b. Explain What was the importance of the Declaration of Independence to the people of the 13 colonies? Give examples to support your answer.

c. Elaborate You read that the Declaration of Independence is more than a document to justify independence from Great Britain. Why is the Declaration of Independence still considered one of the most important documents in American history?

2. a. Define Write a brief definition for each of the following terms: **confederation** and **sovereignty**.

b. Elaborate How did the fact that the Articles of Confederation protected states' sovereignty limit the success of the new nation? Give examples to support your answer.

3. a. Summarize What was the overall problem with the Articles of Confederation? Give four specific examples that illustrate the problem.

b. Evaluate With the improvements in transportation and communication, would the original Articles of Confederation work for all 50 states today? Explain your reasoning.

Critical Thinking

4. Summarizing Use your notes and a graphic organizer like this one to summarize each of the weaknesses of the Articles of Confederation.

Weaknesses of the Articles of Confederation

Focus on Writing

5. Analyzing Information Imagine that you are a farmer living in Virginia in the 1780s. In a letter to the editor of your local newspaper, describe the effect of the Articles of Confederation on your life and community. Recommend what action must be taken to improve your situation.

The Declaration of Independence

EXPLORING THE DOCUMENT Thomas Jefferson wrote the first draft of the Declaration in a little more than two weeks. **How is the Declaration's idea about why governments are formed still important to our country today?**

Vocabulary

impel force

endowed provided

usurpations wrongful seizures of power

evinces clearly displays

despotism unlimited power

tyranny oppressive power exerted by a government or ruler

candid fair

EXPLORING THE DOCUMENT Here the Declaration lists the charges that the colonists had against King George III. **How does the language in the list appeal to people's emotions?**

In Congress, July 4, 1776
The unanimous Declaration of the thirteen united States of America,

When in the Course of human events, it becomes necessary for one people to dissolve the political bands which have connected them with another, and to assume among the Powers of the earth, the separate and equal station to which the Laws of Nature and of Nature's God entitle them, a decent respect to the opinions of mankind requires that they should declare the causes which **impel** them to the separation.

We hold these truths to be self-evident, that all men are created equal, that they are **endowed** by their Creator with certain unalienable Rights, that among these are Life, Liberty, and the pursuit of Happiness. That to secure these rights, Governments are instituted among Men, deriving their just powers from the consent of the governed, That whenever any Form of Government becomes destructive of these ends, it is the Right of the People to alter or to abolish it, and to institute new Government, laying its foundation on such principles and organizing its powers in such form, as to them shall seem most likely to effect their Safety and Happiness. Prudence, indeed, will dictate that Governments long established should not be changed for light and transient causes; and accordingly all experience hath shown, that mankind are more disposed to suffer, while evils are sufferable, than to right themselves by abolishing the forms to which they are accustomed. But when a long train of abuses and **usurpations**, pursuing invariably the same Object **evinces** a design to reduce them under absolute **Despotism**, it is their right, it is their duty, to throw off such Government, and to provide new Guards for their future security.—Such has been the patient sufferance of these Colonies; and such is now the necessity which constrains them to alter their former Systems of Government. The history of the present King of Great Britain is a history of repeated injuries and usurpations, all having in direct object the establishment of an absolute **Tyranny** over these States. To prove this, let Facts be submitted to a **candid** world.

He has refused his Assent to Laws, the most wholesome and necessary for the public good.

He has forbidden his Governors to pass Laws of immediate and pressing importance, unless suspended in their operation till his Assent should be obtained; and when so suspended, he has utterly neglected to attend to them.

He has refused to pass other Laws for the accommodation of large districts of people, unless those people would **relinquish** the right of Representation in the Legislature, a right **inestimable** to them and **formidable** to tyrants only.

He has called together legislative bodies at places unusual, uncomfortable, and distant from the depository of their Public Records, for the sole purpose of fatiguing them into compliance with his measures.

He has dissolved Representative Houses repeatedly, for opposing with manly firmness his invasions on the rights of the people.

He has refused for a long time, after such dissolutions, to cause others to be elected; whereby the Legislative Powers, incapable of **Annihilation**, have returned to the People at large for their exercise; the State remaining in the mean time exposed to all the dangers of invasion from without, and **convulsions** within.

He has endeavored to prevent the population of these States; for that purpose obstructing the Laws of **Naturalization of Foreigners**; refusing to pass others to encourage their migration hither, and raising the conditions of new **Appropriations of Lands**.

He has obstructed the Administration of Justice, by refusing his Assent to Laws for establishing Judiciary Powers.

He has made Judges dependent on his Will alone, for the **tenure** of their offices, and the amount and payment of their salaries.

He has erected **a multitude of** New Offices, and sent hither swarms of Officers to harass our people, and eat out their substance.

He has kept among us, in times of peace, Standing Armies without the Consent of our legislature.

He has affected to render the Military independent of and superior to the Civil Power.

He has combined with others to subject us to a jurisdiction foreign to our constitution, and unacknowledged by our laws; giving his Assent to their Acts of pretended legislation:

For **quartering** large bodies of armed troops among us:

For protecting them, by a mock Trial, from Punishment for any Murders which they should commit on the Inhabitants of these States:

For cutting off our Trade with all parts of the world:

For imposing taxes on us without our Consent:

For depriving us in many cases, of the benefits of Trial by Jury:

Mum Bett, a Massachusetts slave, believed that the words "all men are created equal" should apply to her and other enslaved Africans. She successfully sued for her freedom in 1781.

arbitrary not based on law

render make

abdicated given up

foreign mercenaries soldiers hired to fight for a country not their own

perfidy violation of trust

insurrections rebellions

petitioned for redress asked formally for a correction of wrongs

unwarrantable jurisdiction unjustified authority

magnanimity generous spirit

conjured urgently called upon

consanguinity common ancestry

acquiesce consent to

EXPLORING THE DOCUMENT Here the Declaration calls the king a tyrant. **What do you think *tyrant* means in this passage?**

For transporting us beyond Seas to be tried for pretended offences:

For abolishing the free System of English Laws in a neighboring Province, establishing therein an **Arbitrary** government, and enlarging its Boundaries so as to **render** it at once an example and fit instrument for introducing the same absolute rule into these Colonies:

For taking away our Charters, abolishing our most valuable Laws, and altering fundamentally the Forms of our Governments:

For suspending our own Legislature, and declaring themselves invested with Power to legislate for us in all cases whatsoever.

He has **abdicated** Government here, by declaring us out of his Protection and waging War against us.

He has plundered our seas, ravaged our Coasts, burnt our towns, and destroyed the lives of our people.

He is at this time transporting large armies of **foreign mercenaries** to complete the works of death, desolation and tyranny, already begun with circumstances of Cruelty & **perfidy** scarcely paralleled in the most barbarous ages, and totally unworthy the Head of a civilized nation.

He has constrained our fellow Citizens taken Captive on the high Seas to bear Arms against their Country, to become the executioners of their friends and Brethren, or to fall themselves by their Hands.

He has excited domestic **insurrections** amongst us, and has endeavored to bring on the inhabitants of our frontiers, the merciless Indian Savages, whose known rule of warfare, is an undistinguished destruction of all ages, sexes and conditions.

In every stage of these Oppressions We have **Petitioned for Redress** in the most humble terms: Our repeated Petitions have been answered only by repeated injury. A Prince, whose character is thus marked by every act which may define a Tyrant, is unfit to be the ruler of a free People.

Nor have We been wanting in attention to our British brethren. We have warned them from time to time of attempts by their legislature to extend an **unwarrantable jurisdiction** over us. We have reminded them of the circumstances of our emigration and settlement here. We have appealed to their native justice and **magnanimity**, and we have **conjured** them by the ties of our common kindred to disavow these usurpations, which, would inevitably interrupt our connections and correspondence. They too have been deaf to the voice of justice and of **consanguinity**. We must, therefore, **acquiesce** in the necessity, which denounces our Separation, and hold them, as we hold the rest of mankind, Enemies in War, in Peace Friends.

We, therefore, the Representatives of the united States of America, in General Congress, Assembled, appealing to the Supreme Judge of the world for the **rectitude** of our intentions, do, in the Name, and by Authority of the good People of these Colonies, solemnly publish and declare, That these United Colonies are, and of Right ought to be Free and Independent States; that they are Absolved from all Allegiance to the British Crown, and that all political connection between them and the State of Great Britain, is and ought to be totally dissolved; and that as Free and Independent States, they have full Power to levy War, conclude Peace, contract Alliances, establish Commerce, and to do all other Acts and Things which Independent States may of right do. And for the support of this Declaration, with a firm reliance on the Protection of Divine Providence, we mutually pledge to each other our Lives, our Fortunes and our sacred Honor.

Vocabulary

rectitude rightness

EXPLORING THE DOCUMENT Here is where the document declares the independence of the colonies. **Whose authority does the Congress use to declare independence?**

John Hancock	Benjamin Harrison	Lewis Morris
Button Gwinnett	Thomas Nelson, Jr.	Richard Stockton
Lyman Hall	Francis Lightfoot Lee	John Witherspoon
George Walton	Carter Braxton	Francis Hopkinson
William Hooper	Robert Morris	John Hart
Joseph Hewes	Benjamin Rush	Abraham Clark
John Penn	Benjamin Franklin	Josiah Bartlett
Edward Rutledge	John Morton	William Whipple
Thomas Heyward, Jr.	George Clymer	Samuel Adams
Thomas Lynch, Jr.	James Smith	John Adams
Arthur Middleton	George Taylor	Robert Treat Paine
Samuel Chase	James Wilson	Elbridge Gerry
William Paca	George Ross	Stephen Hopkins
Thomas Stone	Caesar Rodney	William Ellery
Charles Carroll of Carrollton	George Read	Roger Sherman
	Thomas McKean	Samuel Huntington
George Wythe	William Floyd	William Williams
Richard Henry Lee	Philip Livingston	Oliver Wolcott
Thomas Jefferson	Francis Lewis	Matthew Thornton

EXPLORING THE DOCUMENT The Congress adopted the final draft of the Declaration of Independence on July 4, 1776. A formal copy, written on parchment paper, was signed on August 2, 1776. **From whom did the Declaration's signers receive their authority to declare independence?**

EXPLORING THE DOCUMENT The following is part of a passage that the Congress removed from Jefferson's original draft: "He has waged cruel war against human nature itself, violating its most sacred rights of life and liberty in the persons of a distant people who never offended him, captivating and carrying them into slavery in another hemisphere, or to incur miserable death in their transportation thither." **Why do you think the Congress deleted this passage?**

Civics Skills

MEDIA
LITERACY

CRITICAL
THINKING

PARTICIPATION

Learning from Fine Art

Learn

Although most of history happened before the Internet, television, and photography, we can still see the past in paintings, drawings, and sculpture. Fine art can be "read" as if it were a letter from the artist who made it.

You can understand art in two ways—literally and symbolically. In the literal view, things are just as they appear. The uniform shown is what Washington wore when he posed for the painting. In the symbolic view, things are what they represent. The uniform also symbolizes his role as commander in chief.

Practice

❶ **Determine the subject.** The piece to the right is titled *The Washington Family*, which tells us that we are looking at the family of George Washington.

❷ **Notice small details.** Even a family portrait can be full of small but important symbols. Notice that Martha Washington is pointing to a map with her fan. She is actually pointing to the future site of the White House.

❸ **Determine the point of view.** A piece of art expresses an artist's feelings and ideas. The time and place of its creation, the kind of life the artist led, and how the artist felt about the subject all may affect the point of view.

❹ **Use outside knowledge.** We know that Washington owned slaves. We also know that William Lee was Washington's valet and was freed in his will. Most historians believe that William Lee is the man standing against the wall.

Apply

Granger Collection, New York

Answer the following questions with details from the painting.

1. What seems to be the artist's point of view about George Washington?

2. Why do you think the artist included William Lee in *The Washington Family*? How does this part of the painting make you feel?

3. George Washington did not have any children. The children shown are his step-grandchildren. For what literal and symbolic reasons might they have been included?

4. What small details do you notice in the painting? What do they tell you about the subject?

5. What does this painting tell you about George Washington?

A New Constitution

BEFORE YOU READ

The Main Idea

The framers of the U.S. Constitution drew upon a history of democratic ideals while developing a document that would establish a new, stronger federal government.

Reading Focus

1. What historical principles of government influenced the delegates to the Constitutional Convention?
2. How did the U.S. government become stronger under the Constitution?
3. When was the Constitution ratified?

Key Terms

Parliament, *p. 44*
federalism, *p. 46*
compromise, *p. 46*
ratification, *p. 47*
Federalists, *p. 47*
Antifederalists, *p. 47*

TAKING NOTES As you read, take notes on how the Constitutional Convention made government stronger and how the Constitution was ratified. Use a chart like this one to record your notes.

Constitution Strengthens Government	Ratification

The U.S. Constitution

This cartoon shows the steps from the Articles of Confederation to the Constitution of the United States.

STEPS IN THE ESTABLISHMENT OF A MORE STABLE GOVERNMENT

The FEDERAL CONSTITUTION

PHILADELPHIA CONVENTION 1787

ANNAPOLIS CONVENTION 1786

MT. VERNON CONVENTION 1785

ARTICLES OF CONFEDERATION

In 1787, delegates from 12 states met in Philadelphia, Pennsylvania, to follow up on the Annapolis Convention. These delegates ended up writing the U.S. Constitution.

In 1786, 5 of the 13 states met at Annapolis, Maryland, to discuss commercial problems and the weaknesses of the national government.

In 1785, delegates from Maryland and Virginia met at Mt. Vernon, Virginia, to discuss navigation conflicts.

CIVICS IN PRACTICE

By 1787 people in the new United States realized that the Articles of Confederation needed to be fixed. The states called a convention where the delegates wrote a completely new plan for government. The new plan became the Constitution. That Constitution, with a few amendments, describes the relationship between the national government and you as a citizen of the United States.

The Constitutional Convention and History

The delegates who attended the Constitutional Convention wrote a constitution that has endured for more than 220 years. It is the world's oldest written constitution still governing a country today. These delegates were familiar with history, and they had learned many important lessons from the past. The delegates wanted Americans to enjoy all of the rights the English people had fought for and won during past centuries.

FOCUS ON
James Madison
(1751 – 1836)

In 1772, after completing his studies at what is now Princeton University, 21-year-old James Madison returned to his native Virginia, unsure of his career plans. Though he had studied law, what interested him most was political philosophy. With the emergence of a new nation, Madison was afforded the opportunity to pursue those interests. He played a central role in framing the Constitution, and, as a contributor to the *Federalist Papers,* helped secure its ratification. Elected to the first Congress under the new government, Madison helped draft the Bill of Rights. Later, as secretary of state under Thomas Jefferson, and then, as president himself, Madison further pursued balance between a strong national government and individual liberty.

Summarize Why might Madison be called the Father of the Constitution?

British Principles Influence the Delegates

The delegates turned to their British heritage and adopted many principles of government from England. The delegates took principles from:

Magna Carta In 1215, English nobles forced King John to sign the Magna Carta, which means "Great Charter." The Magna Carta guaranteed that free people could not be arrested, put in prison, or forced to leave their nation unless they were given a trial by a jury of their peers. It guaranteed that the citizens of England were to be judged according to English law only. Magna Carta also protected the rights of Parliament against the monarch.

English Bill of Rights The delegates to the Convention in 1787 also wished to guarantee Americans the rights contained in the English Bill of Rights of 1689. One of these rights was the right to petition, or request, the government to improve or to change laws. Another was the right to a fair punishment if a citizen were to be found guilty of a crime.

Parliamentary Government The Convention delegates also carefully studied the example of parliamentary government in England. **Parliament**, the lawmaking body of Great Britain, is bicameral. That is, it consists of two parts, or houses—the House of Lords, appointed by the monarch, and the House of Commons, elected by the people. Each house can check the work of the other house. Today, however, the House of Lords holds less power than it once did.

The head of the British government is the prime minister. The prime minister is usually chosen from the political party that holds the most seats in the House of Commons. The prime minister chooses the top administrative officials in the government. Both the prime minister and his or her appointees can be replaced if the prime minister loses a majority vote in Parliament. A new election is held and voters choose a new government.

Delegates Hold Their Meetings in Secret

The delegates to the Convention wanted to be able to discuss their ideas about government freely. For this reason, many delegates wanted to hold their meetings in secret. Also, some delegates feared that if they spoke publicly on an issue, they would be pressured by outsiders. Taking a public stand might also make it more difficult for delegates to change their minds after debate and discussion.

Some delegates favored open public debate and criticized the idea of secrecy. Yet without secrecy, agreement on difficult issues might not have been possible. The delegates voted to hold their meetings in secret.

Today we know what took place during the Convention because James Madison kept a journal of the proceedings. Because of the role Madison played in the proceedings, he is sometimes called the Father of the Constitution.

The Origins of the Constitution

The U.S. Constitution created a republican form of government based on the consent of the people. Its framers blended ideas and examples from the American colonies and England to write this lasting document.

King John signing Magna Carta

MAGNA CARTA, 1215

England's Magna Carta was the first document to check the power of the king by declaring that people could not be deprived of lives, liberty, or property "except by the lawful judgment of [their] peers, or by the law of the land." This idea is continued in the Fifth Amendment to the Constitution.

BRITISH PARLIAMENT, 1295
The two-chambered structure of the British Parliament was retained in the U.S. Constitution at Article I, Section 1.

THE MAYFLOWER COMPACT, 1620
The *Mayflower* sailed to the colonies from England. At the end of the journey, 41 men signed the Mayflower Compact, the first document to establish self-government in the colonies.

THE ENGLISH BILL OF RIGHTS, 1689
To strengthen the protections of Magna Carta, the English Bill of Rights established freedom from taxation without representation, freedom from cruel and unusual punishment, the right to bear arms, and many other rights that would eventually be included in the U.S. Constitution.

THE ENLIGHTENMENT, 1700s
Eighteenth-century philosophers, such as John Locke, Thomas Hobbes, and Jean-Jacques Rousseau, influenced the framers of the Constitution. Locke argued that government exists only by the "consent of the governed." This idea is echoed in the Preamble, which begins, "We the people..."

VIRGINIA STATUTE FOR RELIGIOUS FREEDOM, 1786
Thomas Jefferson wrote the Virginia Statute for Religious Freedom, which vigorously argued that government has no right to impose, coerce, or interfere with religious practice. This same principle is expressed in the First Amendment to the Constitution.

Thomas Jefferson

England

American Colonies

ANALYSIS SKILL   ANALYZING INFORMATION

Which of the ideas listed here do you consider most important? Why?

Writing the Constitution

The framers of the Constitution agreed that the central government needed greater power. At the same time, the framers agreed that the states should keep the powers needed to govern their own affairs. To achieve this balance, the framers established a system of government known as **federalism**, or a federal system.

Federalism divides a government's powers between the national government, which governs the whole country, and state governments, which govern each state. This system is much different from a unitary system, in which the national government possesses all legal power. Local governments have no independent power under either system.

The delegates discussed many ideas and proposals for organizing the federal system. They eventually settled many differences of opinion by a series of compromises. A **compromise** is an agreement in which each side gives up part of its demands in order to reach a solution to a problem.

The most serious disagreement arose over the question of representation in the new national legislature, or lawmaking body. The larger states favored a legislature in which representation would be based on the size of a state's population. The smaller states wanted each state to have an equal number of representatives in the legislature.

Finally, both sides agreed to a compromise. Their agreement provided for a bicameral lawmaking body called Congress. In one house, the Senate, the states were to have equal representation. In the other house, the House of Representatives, each state was to be represented according to the size of its population. This agreement became known as the Great Compromise.

READING CHECK ▶ **Evaluating** How was the Great Compromise an effective agreement?

Government Becomes Stronger

The framers increased the powers of the national government under the Constitution. Congress was given the powers to coin and print money, raise armed forces, regulate trade among the states and with foreign nations, and set taxes. Provision was also made for a president to carry out the country's laws. The framers also created the Supreme Court to interpret the laws made by Congress.

The Constitution Is Completed

By September 1787 the delegates had completed their work. Probably no delegate was satisfied with each and every part of the document. For example, Benjamin Franklin did not approve of parts of the Constitution. Nevertheless, he believed that the framers had written

The Constitution Strengthens the National Government

QUICK FACTS

Strengths of the Constitution	Weaknesses of the Articles of Confederation
✔ most power held by national government	• most power held by states
✔ three branches of government	• one branch of government
✔ legislative branch has many powers	• legislative branch has few powers
✔ executive branch led by president	• no executive branch
✔ judicial system an equal branch	• no judicial system
✔ firm system of checks and balances	• no system of checks and balances

The Sixth Amendment: Right to a Jury Trial

Imagine that you are accused of a crime. Instead of having a trial, you are thrown into a pond to see if you will float or sink! In some places, this was once a way of determining guilt (floating) or innocence (sinking).

Our right to a jury trial comes from the English Magna Carta. In this document from the year 1215, King John agreed that "No freeman shall be taken, imprisoned . . . or in any other way destroyed . . . except by the lawful judgment of his peers, or by the law of the land." For the first time, a person could not be jailed at the whim of the king or by a biased judge.

This English right spread to the American colonies. After the Revolutionary War, the right to a jury trial was established permanently in the Bill of Rights: The Sixth Amendment provides that "In all criminal prosecutions, the accused shall enjoy the right to a speedy and public trial by an impartial jury . . ."

In order for juries to be fair, or impartial, they must include a cross-section of people from the community. It is unconstitutional for a prosecutor to keep people off of a jury because of their race, gender, or national origin.

1. Why is trial by jury a fair way of deciding guilt or innocence?

2. What must lawyers consider when selecting members of a jury?

The right to a trial by jury is almost 800 years old.

---

the best constitution possible. For this reason, he urged the delegates to sign the document.

Most of the delegates shared Franklin's belief. On September 17 the Constitution was signed by 39 of the 42 framers present. After a farewell dinner, the delegates left for home.

Approving the Constitution

The work of the members of the Constitutional Convention was not over when they left Philadelphia. The Constitution now had to be sent to the states for **ratification**, or approval. Before the Constitution could go into effect, it had to be ratified by 9 of the 13 states. Each state set up a special convention of delegates to vote on the Constitution.

People quickly took sides over whether or not to adopt the Constitution. Some people strongly supported the new plan of government. Others were opposed to it. The public was swamped with pamphlets, letters to newspapers, and speeches representing both sides of the debate.

Federalists, Antifederalists, and Ratification

Supporters of the Constitution, who favored a strong national government, were called **Federalists**. The Federalists argued that a strong national government was needed to keep the country united. Alexander Hamilton, John Jay, and James Madison were leading Federalists. They published a series of articles known as the *Federalist Papers* to help increase support for the Constitution.

People who opposed the new Constitution and the federal system of government were called **Antifederalists**. They feared that a constitution that established such a strong national government defeated the purpose of the Revolutionary War. The Antifederalists believed that the proposed Constitution would protect neither the states' power nor the people's freedom.

READING CHECK **Contrasting** About what issues did Federalists and Antifederalists disagree?

The Constitution Is Ratified

Gradually, Federalists gained support. However, many citizens were upset that the Constitution did not contain a list of the rights of the people. Some states suggested that such a list, or bill, of rights be added if the new Constitution was ratified.

Most of the states ratified the Constitution in 1787 and 1788. The required ninth state ratified it in June 1788, and the new U.S. government began to operate in March 1789. Two states, North Carolina and Rhode Island, did not approve the Constitution until after it went into effect. On April 30, 1789, George Washington was sworn in as the first president of the United States. The country's new government was under way.

READING CHECK **Analyzing Information** What did some citizens think was missing from the new Constitution?

Our Nation's Origins

In 1777 the Continental Congress adopted a design for the first flag. The Congress left no record to show why it chose the red, white, and blue colors for the flag. The 13 stars represent the 13 colonies and are arranged in a circle so that no colony would be seen as being above another.

go.hrw.com
Online Quiz
KEYWORD: SZ7 HP2

SECTION 3 ASSESSMENT

Reviewing Ideas and Terms

1. a. Define Write a brief definition for the terms **Parliament**, **federalism**, and **compromise**.

b. Explain How are the three principles of government the framers adopted from English government relevant to citizens today? Give details to support your answer.

2. a. Define Write a brief definition for the terms **ratification**, **Federalists**, and **Antifederalists**.

b. Elaborate Identify three ways in which the Constitution strengthened the national government and explain why these changes were important to the new country.

3. a. Finding the Main Idea Briefly describe the ratification of the U.S. Constitution.

b. Draw Conclusions Why do you think that several states wanted a bill of people's rights added to the Constitution?

Critical Thinking

4. Finding Main Ideas Copy the graphic organizer. Use it to show some of the Constitution's main ideas, its influences, and a compromise that allowed for its passage.

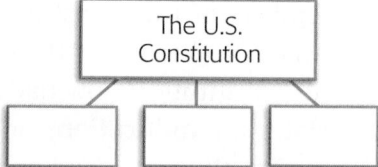

Focus on Writing

5. Contrasting Write a speech that supports ratification of the Constitution. Compare the Constitution to the Articles of Confederation and explain how the Constitution will strengthen the national government. Consider:

- taxes
- interstate and international trade
- the power of the national government

STUDENTS TAKE ACTION

Keeping Students Safe

Around the country, many students keep an eye out for neighborhood ice cream trucks. Students in Modesto, California, however, are thinking about something other than ice cream. Ice cream trucks in their town have also been selling BB guns and toy guns, and concerned students are studying this issue. By working cooperatively with government officials and educating community members, this Project Citizen class is making sure that people are hearing their message.

Community Connection When a young student in Modesto was shot in the eye with a pellet fired from a toy gun that was bought from an ice cream truck, older students took notice. The extent of the problem became clear when three students were suspended from school and a second student was injured in BB gun incidents. Student Leela Lowe, who was the second person shot, said, "When they sell the guns, kids just buy them like they are nothing. They just shoot people."

Taking Action Now students in Nicholas Kellner's and Patty McLean's classes are researching the problem as part of the Project Citizen program and are working on a policy to help prevent future accidents. These students are trying to develop different ways to stop ice cream trucks from selling toy guns. The Modesto students have held a student public awareness assembly within their school and reached out to the community through local public television and newspapers. They have also organized a protest and planned a meeting with the city council. They hope their actions will get more people involved in creating solutions to the toy gun problem.

Students in Modesto, California, want to stop the sale of toy guns from ice cream trucks.

go.hrw.com
Project Citizen
KEYWORD: SZ7 CH2

SERVICE LEARNING

1. Why do the Modesto students think that selling toy guns from ice cream trucks is a problem?
2. If you were a student in Modesto, what are some of the ways you could address the issue of toy gun sales?

CHAPTER 2 REVIEW

Visual Summary

Use the visual summary to help you review the main ideas of the chapter.

Governments provide services and structure to society. The U.S. government embodies our national ideals.

Reviewing Key Terms

For each term or name below, write a sentence explaining its significance to the foundations of American government.

1. monarch
2. dictator
3. democracy
4. direct democracy
5. representative democracy
6. republic
7. constitution
8. human rights
9. confederation
10. sovereignty
11. Parliament
12. federalism
13. compromise
14. ratification
15. Federalists
16. Antifederalists

Comprehension and Critical Thinking

SECTION 1 *(Pages 30–33)*

17. **a. Describe** What are two main types of government, and which type better protects and reflects the wishes of its citizens? Explain your answer.

    b. Explain What are three purposes of government? Use examples from the United States to illustrate your answer.

    c. Elaborate How does the U.S. government guarantee the freedoms of U.S. citizens? Give examples to support your answer.

SECTION 2 *(Pages 34–37)*

18. **a. Describe** What were the key purposes of the Declaration of Independence?

    b. Elaborate What were the Articles of Confederation and why did they need to be changed?

SECTION 3 *(Pages 43–48)*

19. a. Identify In what ways did the colonists' English political heritage influence American ideas about government and individual rights?

b. Explain What was the outcome of the Constitutional Convention?

c. Elaborate What were the arguments of the Federalists and Antifederalists?

Civics Skills

Learning from Fine Art *Review the painting on the Civics Skills page in this chapter, then answer the questions below.*

Granger Collection, New York

20. To what aspect of Washington's life does his uniform refer?

   a. His military career

   b. His ownership of a plantation

   c. His time spent as a surveyor

   d. His presidency

21. To what aspect of his life do the official papers on which Washington's arm rests refer?

   a. His military career

   b. His ownership of a plantation

   c. His time spent as a surveyor

   c. His presidency

22. The children in the painting are Washington's stepgrandchildren. What might they symbolize?

   a. Other children Washington had known at Mount Vernon

   b. The future generations of America

   c. Washington's own childhood

   d. The new nation of the United States

Reading Skills

Chronological Order *Use the Reading Skill taught in this chapter to answer the question below.*

23. Organize the following events chronologically according to the chapter.

   a. *Federalist Papers* are published.

   b. Constitution is ratified.

   c. Articles of Confederation is ratified.

   d. Constitutional Convention meets in Philadelphia.

Using the Internet

24. Access the Internet through the HRW Go site to research the Constitutional Convention. Then imagine you are one of the delegates. Create a series of journal entries outlining what you thought and how you voted. Make sure you reflect on the different plans for government and give your own view on which plans would have been best for the nation.

FOCUS ON WRITING

25. Creating a Pamphlet Use the information you have gathered about the foundations of the U.S. government. Use that information to create your pamphlet. On the first page, write a title for your pamphlet and a phrase or sentence that will get the attention of your audience. On each of the following pages, you can use this format: (1) a heading and sentence at the top of the page identifying the topic of the page, and (2) the list of most important points for that topic. At the end of page four, write one sentence that summarizes the importance of the Constitution to the government and to citizens.

FOUNDATIONS®
of DEMOCRACY

Fourth Amendment Protection in Today's Electronic World

When the authors of the Bill of Rights wrote the Fourth Amendment, they were thinking of the violations of privacy they had suffered as colonists—specifically, how British officers had been allowed to search inside any building where they suspected smuggled goods might be hidden. The writers of the amendment could not have foreseen that when they protected "persons, houses, papers, and effects against unreasonable searches," one day those words would be interpreted to also include e-mail, instant messages, and cellular phone calls.

Why it Matters Technology has changed greatly since the late 1700s, requiring the courts to revisit the Fourth Amendment throughout the years to see how it currently applies. In 1928, for example, Roy Olmstead was imprisoned for selling liquor during Prohibition, when alcohol was illegal. Federal law enforcement agents had wiretapped Olmstead's telephone lines without a search warrant to prove his guilt. Olmstead sued the government in *Olmstead* v. *United States*, claiming that wiretaps violated his right to privacy. The Supreme Court upheld wiretaps as legal since there was no physical entrance of the suspect's home or office. However, in a 1967 case, *Katz* v. *United States*, the Court reversed this decision, ruling that a wiretap is a search that requires a warrant.

Telephones are not the only form of technology involved in Fourth Amendment debates in the digital age. In 1986 Congress passed the Electronic Communications Privacy Act to protect the transmission of e-mails and instant messaging. However, the law provides less protection for messages stored on computers.

The debate over how to apply the Fourth Amendment continues in the 21st century. For example, when the USA PATRIOT Act of 2001 was passed in response to the terrorist attacks of September 11, it expanded the government's ability to monitor certain individuals' phone calls and e-mails without a warrant. In 2005, Congress voted to reauthorize the act, portions of which had been set to expire, only after several new clauses intended to protect Americans' civil liberties had been added. Even years later, however, debate continues over whether the privacy limits of the act should be expanded or further limited.

Your right to privacy extends to your e-mails and cellular phone calls in most—but not all—cases.

ANALYSIS SKILL EVALUATING THE LAW

go.hrw.com
KEYWORD: SZ7 CH2

1. Do you think the government should be allowed to read people's e-mails without a search warrant? How might this help with national-security concerns? How could it affect your privacy?
2. Do you think the authors of the Fourth Amendment would write it differently today? Explain your opinion.

THE UNITED STATES CONSTITUTION

An Uncle Sam mechanical bank

The Constitution of the United States

Preamble
The short and dignified preamble explains the goals of the new government under the Constitution.

We the People of the United States, in Order to form a more perfect Union, establish Justice, insure domestic Tranquility, provide for the common defense, promote the general Welfare, and secure the Blessings of Liberty to ourselves and our Posterity, do ordain and establish this Constitution for the United States of America.

Note: The parts of the Constitution that have been lined through are no longer in force or no longer apply because of later amendments. The titles of the sections and articles are added for easier reference.

Article I The Legislature

Section 1. Congress

All legislative Powers herein granted shall be vested in a Congress of the United States, which shall consist of a Senate and House of Representatives.

Section 2. The House of Representatives

1. Elections The House of Representatives shall be composed of Members chosen every second Year by the People of the several States, and the Electors in each State shall have the Qualifications requisite for Electors of the most numerous Branch of the State Legislature.

2. Qualifications No Person shall be a Representative who shall not have attained to the Age of twenty five Years, and been seven Years a Citizen of the United States, and who shall not, when elected, be an Inhabitant of that State in which he shall be chosen.

3. Number of Representatives Representatives and direct Taxes shall be apportioned among the several States which may be included within this Union, according to their respective Numbers, which shall be determined by adding to the whole Number of free Persons, including **those bound to Service**[1] for a Term of Years, and excluding Indians not taxed, three fifths of **all other Persons**.[2] The actual **Enumeration**[3] shall be made within three Years after the first Meeting of the Congress of the United States, and within every subsequent Term of ten Years, in such Manner as they shall by Law direct. The Number of Representatives shall not exceed one for every thirty Thousand, but each State shall have at Least one Representative; and until such enumeration shall be made, the State of New Hampshire shall be entitled to choose three, Massachusetts eight, Rhode-Island and Providence Plantations one, Connecticut five, New-York six, New Jersey four, Pennsylvania eight, Delaware one, Maryland six, Virginia ten, North Carolina five, South Carolina five, and Georgia three.

4. Vacancies When vacancies happen in the Representation from any State, the Executive Authority thereof shall issue Writs of Election to fill such Vacancies.

5. Officers and Impeachment The House of Representatives shall choose their Speaker and other Officers; and shall have the sole Power of impeachment.

Legislative Branch

Article I explains how the legislative branch, called Congress, is organized. The chief purpose of the legislative branch is to make laws. Congress is made up of the Senate and the House of Representatives.

The House of Representatives

The number of members each state has in the House is based on the population of the individual state. In 1929 Congress permanently fixed the size of the House at 435 members.

Vocabulary

[1] **those bound to Service** indentured servants

[2] **all other Persons** slaves

[3] **Enumeration** census or official population count

Section 3. The Senate

1. Number of Senators The Senate of the United States shall be composed of two Senators from each State, ~~chosen by the Legislature thereof,~~ for six Years; and each Senator shall have one Vote.

2. Classifying Terms Immediately after they shall be assembled in Consequence of the first Election, they shall be divided as equally as may be into three Classes. The Seats of the Senators of the first Class shall be vacated at the Expiration of the second Year, of the second Class at the Expiration of the fourth Year, and of the third Class at the Expiration of the sixth Year, so that one third may be chosen every second Year; ~~and if Vacancies happen by Resignation, or otherwise, during the Recess of the Legislature of any State, the Executive thereof may make temporary Appointments until the next Meeting of the Legislature, which shall then fill such Vacancies.~~

3. Qualifications No Person shall be a Senator who shall not have attained to the Age of thirty Years, and been nine Years a Citizen of the United States, and who shall not, when elected, be an Inhabitant of that State for which he shall be chosen.

4. Role of Vice President The Vice President of the United States shall be President of the Senate, but shall have no Vote, unless they be equally divided.

5. Officers The Senate shall choose their other Officers, and also a President **pro tempore,**[4] in the Absence of the Vice President, or when he shall exercise the Office of President of the United States.

6. Impeachment Trials The Senate shall have the sole Power to try all **Impeachments.**[5] When sitting for that Purpose, they shall be on Oath or Affirmation. When the President of the United States is tried, the Chief Justice shall preside: And no Person shall be convicted without the Concurrence of two thirds of the Members present.

7. Punishment for Impeachment Judgment in Cases of Impeachment shall not extend further than to removal from Office, and disqualification to hold and enjoy any Office of honor, Trust or Profit under the United States: but the Party convicted shall nevertheless be liable and subject to Indictment, Trial, Judgment and Punishment, according to Law.

The Vice President

The only duty that the Constitution assigns to the vice president is to preside over meetings of the Senate. Modern presidents have usually given their vice presidents more responsibilities.

EXPLORING THE DOCUMENT If the House of Representatives charges a government official with wrongdoing, the Senate acts as a court to decide if the official is guilty. **How does the power of impeachment represent part of the system of checks and balances?**

Vocabulary

[4] **pro tempore** temporarily

[5] **Impeachments** official accusations of federal wrongdoing

Federal Office Terms and Requirements — QUICK FACTS

Position	Term	Minimum Age	Residency	Citizenship
President	4 years	35	14 years in the U.S.	natural-born
Vice President	4 years	35	14 years in the U.S.	natural-born
Supreme Court Justice	unlimited	none	none	none
Senator	6 years	30	state in which elected	9 years
Representative	2 years	25	state in which elected	7 years

Section 4. Congressional Elections

1. Regulations The Times, Places and Manner of holding Elections for Senators and Representatives, shall be prescribed in each State by the Legislature thereof; but the Congress may at any time by Law make or alter such Regulations, except as to the Places of choosing Senators.

2. Sessions ~~The Congress shall assemble at least once in every Year, and such Meeting shall be on the first Monday in December, unless they shall by Law appoint a different Day.~~

Section 5. Rules/Procedures

1. Quorum Each House shall be the Judge of the Elections, Returns and Qualifications of its own Members, and a Majority of each shall constitute a **Quorum**[6] to do Business; but a smaller Number may **adjourn**[7] from day to day, and may be authorized to compel the Attendance of absent Members, in such Manner, and under such Penalties as each House may provide.

2. Rules and Conduct Each House may determine the Rules of its Proceedings, punish its Members for disorderly Behaviour, and, with the Concurrence of two thirds, expel a Member.

3. Records Each House shall keep a Journal of its Proceedings, and from time to time publish the same, excepting such Parts as may in their Judgment require Secrecy; and the Yeas and Nays of the Members of either House on any question shall, at the Desire of one fifth of those Present, be entered on the Journal.

4. Adjournment Neither House, during the Session of Congress, shall, without the Consent of the other, adjourn for more than three days, nor to any other Place than that in which the two Houses shall be sitting.

Section 6. Payment

1. Salary The Senators and Representatives shall receive a Compensation for their Services, to be ascertained by Law, and paid out of the Treasury of the United States. They shall in all Cases, except Treason, Felony and Breach of the Peace, be privileged from Arrest during their Attendance at the Session of their respective Houses, and in going to and returning from the same; and for any Speech or Debate in either House, they shall not be questioned in any other Place.

2. Restrictions No Senator or Representative shall, during the Time for which he was elected, be appointed to any civil Office under the Authority of the United States, which shall have been created, or the **Emoluments**[8] whereof shall have been increased during such time; and no Person holding any Office under the United States, shall be a Member of either House during his **Continuance**[9] in Office.

Vocabulary

[6] **Quorum** the minimum number of people needed to conduct business

[7] **adjourn** to stop indefinitely

[8] **Emoluments** salary

[9] **Continuance** term

EXPLORING THE DOCUMENT The framers felt that because members of the House are elected every two years, representatives would listen to the public and seek its approval before passing taxes. **How does Section 7 address the colonial demand of "no taxation without representation"?**

EXPLORING THE DOCUMENT The veto power of the president is one of the important checks and balances in the Constitution. **Why do you think the framers included the ability of Congress to override a veto?**

Section 7. [How a Bill Becomes a Law]

1. Tax Bills All **Bills**¹⁰ for raising Revenue shall originate in the House of Representatives; but the Senate may propose or concur with Amendments as on other Bills.

2. Lawmaking Every Bill which shall have passed the House of Representatives and the Senate, shall, before it become a Law, be presented to the President of the United States: If he approve he shall sign it, but if not he shall return it, with his Objections to that House in which it shall have originated, who shall enter the Objections at large on their Journal, and proceed to reconsider it. If after such Reconsideration two thirds of that House shall agree to pass the Bill, it shall be sent, together with the Objections, to the other House, by which it shall likewise be reconsidered, and if approved by two thirds of that House, it shall become a Law. But in all such Cases the Votes of both Houses shall be determined by yeas and Nays, and the Names of the Persons voting for and against the Bill shall be entered on the Journal of each House respectively. If any Bill shall not be returned by the President within ten Days (Sundays excepted) after it shall have been presented to him, the Same shall be a Law, in like Manner as if he had signed it, unless the Congress by their Adjournment prevent its Return, in which Case it shall not be a Law.

3. Role of the President Every Order, Resolution, or Vote to which the Concurrence of the Senate and House of Representatives may be necessary (except on a question of Adjournment) shall be presented to the President of the United States; and before the Same shall take Effect, shall be approved by him, or being disapproved by him, shall be repassed by two thirds of the Senate and House of Representatives, according to the Rules and Limitations prescribed in the Case of a Bill.

How a Bill Becomes a Law

❶ A member of the House or the Senate introduces a bill and refers it to a committee.

❷ The House or Senate Committee may approve, rewrite, or kill the bill.

❸ The House or the Senate debates and votes on its version of the bill.

❹ House and Senate conference committee members work out the differences between the two versions.

❺ Both houses of Congress pass the revised bill.

Section 8.

Powers Granted to Congress

1. Taxation The Congress shall have Power To lay and collect Taxes, **Duties**,[11] **Imposts**[12] and **Excises**,[13] to pay the Debts and provide for the common Defense and general Welfare of the United States; but all Duties, Imposts and Excises shall be uniform throughout the United States;

2. Credit To borrow Money on the credit of the United States;

3. Commerce To regulate Commerce with foreign Nations, and among the several States, and with the Indian Tribes;

4. Naturalization and Bankruptcy To establish an uniform **Rule of Naturalization**,[14] and uniform Laws on the subject of Bankruptcies throughout the United States;

5. Money To coin Money, regulate the Value thereof, and of foreign Coin, and fix the Standard of Weights and Measures;

6. Counterfeiting To provide for the Punishment of counterfeiting the **Securities**[15] and current Coin of the United States;

7. Post Office To establish Post Offices and post Roads;

8. Patents and Copyrights To promote the Progress of Science and useful Arts, by securing for limited Times to Authors and Inventors the exclusive Right to their respective Writings and Discoveries;

9. Courts To constitute Tribunals inferior to the supreme Court;

10. International Law To define and punish Piracies and Felonies committed on the high Seas, and Offences against the Law of Nations;

LINKING TO TODAY

Native Americans and the Commerce Clause

The commerce clause gives Congress the power to "regulate Commerce with . . . the Indian Tribes." The clause has been interpreted to mean that the states cannot tax or interfere with businesses on Indian reservations, but that the federal government can. It also allows American Indian nations to develop their own governments and laws. These laws, however, can be challenged in federal court. Although reservation land usually belongs to the government of the Indian group, it is administered by the U.S. government.

Drawing Conclusions How would you describe the status of American Indian nations under the commerce clause?

Vocabulary

[11] **Duties** tariffs

[12] **Imposts** taxes

[13] **Excises** internal taxes on the manufacture, sale, or consumption of a commodity

[14] **Rule of Naturalization** a law by which a foreign-born person becomes a citizen

[15] **Securities** bonds

6 The president signs or vetoes the bill.

7 Two-thirds majority vote of Congress is needed to approve a vetoed bill. Bill becomes a law.

ANALYSIS SKILL ANALYZING INFORMATION

Why do you think the framers created this complex system for adopting laws?

Vocabulary

[16] **Letters of Marque and Reprisal** documents issued by governments allowing merchant ships to arm themselves and attack ships of an enemy nation

11. War To declare War, grant **Letters of Marque and Reprisal**,[16] and make Rules concerning Captures on Land and Water;

12. Army To raise and support Armies, but no Appropriation of Money to that Use shall be for a longer Term than two Years;

13. Navy To provide and maintain a Navy;

14. Regulation of the Military To make Rules for the Government and Regulation of the land and naval Forces;

15. Militia To provide for calling forth the Militia to execute the Laws of the Union, suppress Insurrections and repel Invasions;

16. Regulation of the Militia To provide for organizing, arming, and disciplining, the Militia, and for governing such Part of them as may be employed in the Service of the United States, reserving to the States respectively, the Appointment of the Officers, and the Authority of training the Militia according to the discipline prescribed by Congress;

17. District of Columbia To exercise exclusive Legislation in all Cases whatsoever, over such District (not exceeding ten Miles square) as may, by Cession of particular States, and the Acceptance of Congress, become the Seat of the Government of the United States, and to exercise like Authority over all Places purchased by the Consent of the Legislature of the State in which the Same shall be, for the Erection of Forts, Magazines, Arsenals, dock-Yards, and other needful Buildings;—And

18. Necessary and Proper Clause To make all Laws which shall be necessary and proper for carrying into Execution the foregoing Powers, and all other Powers vested by this Constitution in the Government of the United States, or in any Department or Officer thereof.

The Elastic Clause

The framers of the Constitution wanted a national government that was strong enough to be effective. This section lists the powers given to Congress. The last portion of Section 8 contains the so-called elastic clause.

The Elastic Clause

The elastic clause has been stretched (like elastic) to allow Congress to meet changing circumstances.

Section 9. Powers Denied Congress

1. Slave Trade The Migration or Importation of such Persons as any of the States now existing shall think proper to admit, shall not be prohibited by the Congress prior to the Year one thousand eight hundred and eight, but a Tax or duty may be imposed on such Importation, not exceeding ten dollars for each Person.

2. Habeas Corpus The Privilege of the **Writ of Habeas Corpus**[17] shall not be suspended, unless when in Cases of Rebellion or Invasion the public Safety may require it.

3. Illegal Punishment No **Bill of Attainder**[18] or **ex post facto Law**[19] shall be passed.

4. Direct Taxes No **Capitation**,[20] or other direct, Tax shall be laid, unless in Proportion to the Census or enumeration herein before directed to be taken.

5. Export Taxes No Tax or Duty shall be laid on Articles exported from any State.

6. No Favorites No Preference shall be given by any Regulation of Commerce or Revenue to the Ports of one State over those of another; nor shall Vessels bound to, or from, one State, be obliged to enter, clear, or pay Duties in another.

7. Public Money No Money shall be drawn from the Treasury, but in Consequence of Appropriations made by Law; and a regular Statement and Account of the Receipts and Expenditures of all public Money shall be published from time to time.

8. Titles of Nobility No Title of Nobility shall be granted by the United States: And no Person holding any Office of Profit or Trust under them, shall, without the Consent of the Congress, accept of any present, Emolument, Office, or Title, of any kind whatever, from any King, Prince, or foreign State.

Section 10. Powers Denied the States

1. Restrictions No State shall enter into any Treaty, Alliance, or Confederation; grant Letters of Marque and Reprisal; coin Money; emit Bills of Credit; make any Thing but gold and silver Coin a Tender in Payment of Debts; pass any Bill of Attainder, ex post facto Law, or Law impairing the Obligation of Contracts, or grant any Title of Nobility.

2. Import and Export Taxes No State shall, without the Consent of the Congress, lay any Imposts or Duties on Imports or Exports, except what may be absolutely necessary for executing it's inspection Laws: and the net Produce of all Duties and Imposts, laid by any State on Imports or Exports, shall be for the Use of the Treasury of the United States; and all such Laws shall be subject to the Revision and Control of the Congress.

3. Peacetime and War Restraints No State shall, without the Consent of Congress, lay any Duty of Tonnage, keep Troops, or Ships of War in time of Peace, enter into any Agreement or Compact with another State, or with a foreign Power, or engage in War, unless actually invaded, or in such imminent Danger as will not admit of delay.

EXPLORING THE DOCUMENT Although Congress has implied powers, there are also limits to its powers. Section 9 lists powers that are denied to the federal government. Several of the clauses protect the people of the United States from unjust treatment. **In what ways does the Constitution limit the powers of the federal government?**

Vocabulary

[17] **Writ of Habeas Corpus** a court order that requires the government to bring a prisoner to court and explain why he or she is being held

[18] **Bill of Attainder** a law declaring that a person is guilty of a particular crime

[19] **ex post facto Law** a law that is made effective prior to the date that it was passed and therefore punishes people for acts that were not illegal at the time

[20] **Capitation** a direct uniform tax imposed on each head, or person

Executive Branch

The president is the chief of the executive branch. It is the job of the president to enforce the laws. The framers wanted the president's and vice president's terms of office and manner of selection to be different from those of members of Congress. They decided on four-year terms, but they had a difficult time agreeing on how to select the president and vice president. The framers finally set up an electoral system, which varies greatly from our electoral process today.

Presidential Elections

In 1845 Congress set the Tuesday following the first Monday in November of every fourth year as the general election date for selecting presidential electors.

Article II   The Executive

Section 1.   The Presidency

1. Terms of Office   The executive Power shall be vested in a President of the United States of America. He shall hold his Office during the Term of four Years, and, together with the Vice President, chosen for the same Term, be elected, as follows:

2. Electoral College   Each State shall appoint, in such Manner as the Legislature thereof may direct, a Number of Electors, equal to the whole Number of Senators and Representatives to which the State may be entitled in the Congress: but no Senator or Representative, or Person holding an Office of Trust or Profit under the United States, shall be appointed an Elector.

3. Former Method of Electing President   ~~The Electors shall meet in their respective States, and vote by Ballot for two Persons, of whom one at least shall not be an Inhabitant of the same State with themselves. And they shall make a List of all the Persons voted for, and of the Number of Votes for each; which List they shall sign and certify, and transmit sealed to the Seat of the Government of the United States, directed to the President of the Senate. The President of the Senate shall, in the Presence of the Senate and House of Representatives, open all the Certificates, and the Votes shall~~

The Electoral College

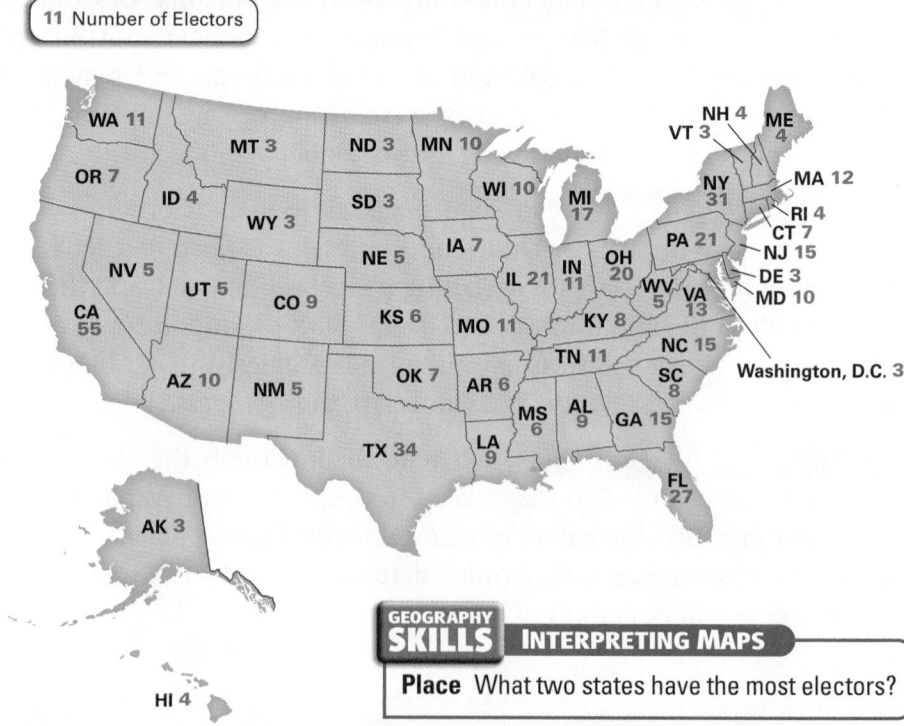

11 Number of Electors

WA 11 · OR 7 · MT 3 · ID 4 · WY 3 · ND 3 · MN 10 · SD 3 · WI 10 · NH 4 · VT 3 · ME 4 · NY 31 · MA 12 · MI 17 · RI 4 · CT 7 · NV 5 · UT 5 · CO 9 · NE 5 · IA 7 · IL 21 · IN 11 · OH 20 · PA 21 · NJ 15 · DE 3 · CA 55 · KS 6 · MO 11 · KY 8 · WV 5 · VA 13 · MD 10 · AZ 10 · NM 5 · OK 7 · AR 6 · TN 11 · NC 15 · SC 8 · Washington, D.C. 3 · MS 6 · AL 9 · GA 15 · TX 34 · LA 9 · FL 27 · AK 3 · HI 4

GEOGRAPHY SKILLS   INTERPRETING MAPS

Place What two states have the most electors?

then be counted. ~~The Person having the greatest Number of Votes shall be the President, if such Number be a Majority of the whole Number of Electors appointed; and if there be more than one who have such Majority, and have an equal Number of Votes, then the House of Representatives shall immediately choose by Ballot one of them for President; and if no Person have a Majority, then from the five highest on the List the said House shall in like Manner choose the President. But in choosing the President, the Votes shall be taken by States, the Representation from each State having one Vote; A quorum for this purpose shall consist of a Member or Members from two thirds of the States, and a Majority of all the States shall be necessary to a Choice. In every Case, after the Choice of the President, the Person having the greatest Number of Votes of the Electors shall be the Vice President. But if there should remain two or more who have equal Votes, the Senate shall choose from them by Ballot the Vice President.~~

4. Election Day The Congress may determine the Time of choosing the Electors, and the Day on which they shall give their Votes; which Day shall be the same throughout the United States.

5. Qualifications No Person except a natural born Citizen, ~~or a Citizen of the United States, at the time of the Adoption of this Constitution~~, shall be eligible to the Office of President; neither shall any Person be eligible to that Office who shall not have attained to the Age of thirty five Years, and been fourteen Years a Resident within the United States.

6. Succession In Case of the Removal of the President from Office, or of his Death, Resignation, or Inability to discharge the Powers and Duties of the said Office, the Same shall devolve on the Vice President, and the Congress may by Law provide for the Case of Removal, Death, Resignation or Inability, both of the President and Vice President, declaring what Officer shall then act as President, and such Officer shall act accordingly, until the Disability be removed, or a President shall be elected.

7. Salary The President shall, at stated Times, receive for his Services, a Compensation, which shall neither be increased nor diminished during the Period for which he shall have been elected, and he shall not receive within that Period any other Emolument from the United States, or any of them.

8. Oath of Office Before he enter on the Execution of his Office, he shall take the following Oath or Affirmation:—"I do solemnly swear (or affirm) that I will faithfully execute the Office of President of the United States, and will to the best of my Ability, preserve, protect and defend the Constitution of the United States."

EXPLORING THE DOCUMENT The youngest elected president was John F. Kennedy; he was 43 years old when he was inaugurated. (Theodore Roosevelt was 42 when he assumed office after the assassination of McKinley.) **What is the minimum required age for the office of president?**

Presidential Salary

In 1999 Congress voted to set future presidents' salaries at $400,000 per year. The president also receives an annual expense account. The president must pay taxes only on the salary.

Section 2. Powers of Presidency

1. Military Powers The President shall be Commander in Chief of the Army and Navy of the United States, and of the Militia of the several States, when called into the actual Service of the United States; he may require the Opinion, in writing, of the principal Officer in each of the executive Departments, upon any Subject relating to the Duties of their respective Offices, and he shall have Power to grant **Reprieves**[21] and **Pardons**[22] for Offences against the United States, except in Cases of Impeachment.

2. Treaties and Appointments He shall have Power, by and with the Advice and Consent of the Senate, to make Treaties, provided two thirds of the Senators present concur; and he shall nominate, and by and with the Advice and Consent of the Senate, shall appoint Ambassadors, other public Ministers and Consuls, Judges of the supreme Court, and all other Officers of the United States, whose Appointments are not herein otherwise provided for, and which shall be established by Law: but the Congress may by Law vest the Appointment of such inferior Officers, as they think proper, in the President alone, in the Courts of Law, or in the Heads of Departments.

3. Vacancies The President shall have Power to fill up all Vacancies that may happen during the Recess of the Senate, by granting Commissions which shall expire at the End of their next Session.

Section 3. Presidential Duties

He shall from time to time give to the Congress Information of the State of the Union, and recommend to their Consideration such Measures as he shall judge necessary and expedient; he may, on extraordinary Occasions, convene both Houses, or either of them, and in Case of Disagreement between them, with Respect to the Time of Adjournment, he may adjourn them to such Time as he shall think proper; he shall receive Ambassadors and other public Ministers; he shall take Care that the Laws be faithfully executed, and shall Commission all the Officers of the United States.

Section 4. Impeachment

The President, Vice President and all civil Officers of the United States, shall be removed from Office on Impeachment for, and Conviction of, Treason, Bribery, or other high Crimes and Misdemeanors.

Article III   The Judiciary

Section 1.   Federal Courts and Judges

The judicial Power of the United States shall be vested in one supreme Court, and in such inferior Courts as the Congress may from time to time ordain and establish. The Judges, both of the supreme and inferior Courts, shall hold their Offices during good Behavior, and shall, at stated Times, receive for their Services a Compensation, which shall not be diminished during their Continuance in Office.

Section 2.   Authority of the Courts

1. General Authority   The judicial Power shall extend to all Cases, in Law and Equity, arising under this Constitution, the Laws of the United States, and Treaties made, or which shall be made, under their Authority;—to all Cases affecting Ambassadors, other public Ministers and Consuls;—to all Cases of admiralty and maritime Jurisdiction;—to Controversies to which the United States shall be a Party;—to Controversies between two or more States —between a State and Citizens of another State; —between Citizens of different States;—between Citizens of the same State claiming Lands under Grants of different States, and between a State, or the Citizens thereof, and foreign States, Citizens or Subjects.

2. Supreme Authority   In all Cases affecting Ambassadors, other public Ministers and Consuls, and those in which a State shall be Party, the supreme Court shall have original Jurisdiction. In all the other Cases before mentioned, the supreme Court shall have appellate Jurisdiction, both as to Law and Fact, with such Exceptions, and under such Regulations as the Congress shall make.

Federal Judicial System   QUICK FACTS

Supreme Court

Reviews cases appealed from lower federal courts and highest state courts

Courts of Appeals

Review appeals from district courts

District Courts

Hold trials

Judicial Branch

The Articles of Confederation did not set up a federal court system. One of the first points that the framers of the Constitution agreed upon was to set up a national judiciary. In the Judiciary Act of 1789, Congress provided for the establishment of lower courts, such as district courts, circuit courts of appeals, and various other federal courts. The judicial system provides a check on the legislative branch: it can declare a law unconstitutional.

3. Trial by Jury The Trial of all Crimes, except in Cases of Impeachment, shall be by Jury; and such Trial shall be held in the State where the said Crimes shall have been committed; but when not committed within any State, the Trial shall be at such Place or Places as the Congress may by Law have directed.

Section 3. Treason

1. Definition Treason against the United States, shall consist only in levying War against them, or in adhering to their Enemies, giving them Aid and Comfort. No Person shall be convicted of Treason unless on the Testimony of two Witnesses to the same overt Act, or on Confession in open Court.

2. Punishment The Congress shall have Power to declare the Punishment of Treason, but no Attainder of Treason shall work **Corruption of Blood**,[23] or Forfeiture except during the Life of the Person attainted.

The States

States must honor the laws, records, and court decisions of other states. A person cannot escape a legal obligation by moving from one state to another.

Article IV   Relations among States

Section 1.   State Acts and Records

Full Faith and Credit shall be given in each State to the public Acts, Records, and judicial Proceedings of every other State. And the Congress may by general Laws prescribe the Manner in which such Acts, Records and Proceedings shall be proved, and the Effect thereof.

Section 2.   Rights of Citizens

1. Citizenship The Citizens of each State shall be entitled to all Privileges and Immunities of Citizens in the several States.

2. Extradition A Person charged in any State with Treason, Felony, or other Crime, who shall flee from Justice, and be found in another State, shall on Demand of the executive Authority of the State from which he fled, be delivered up, to be removed to the State having Jurisdiction of the Crime.

3. Fugitive Slaves ~~No Person held to Service or Labour in one State, under the Laws thereof, escaping into another, shall, in Consequence of any Law or Regulation therein, be discharged from such Service or Labour, but shall be delivered up on Claim of the Party to whom such Service or Labour may be due.~~

EXPLORING THE DOCUMENT The framers wanted to ensure that citizens could determine how state governments would operate. **How does the need to respect the laws of each state support the principle of popular sovereignty?**

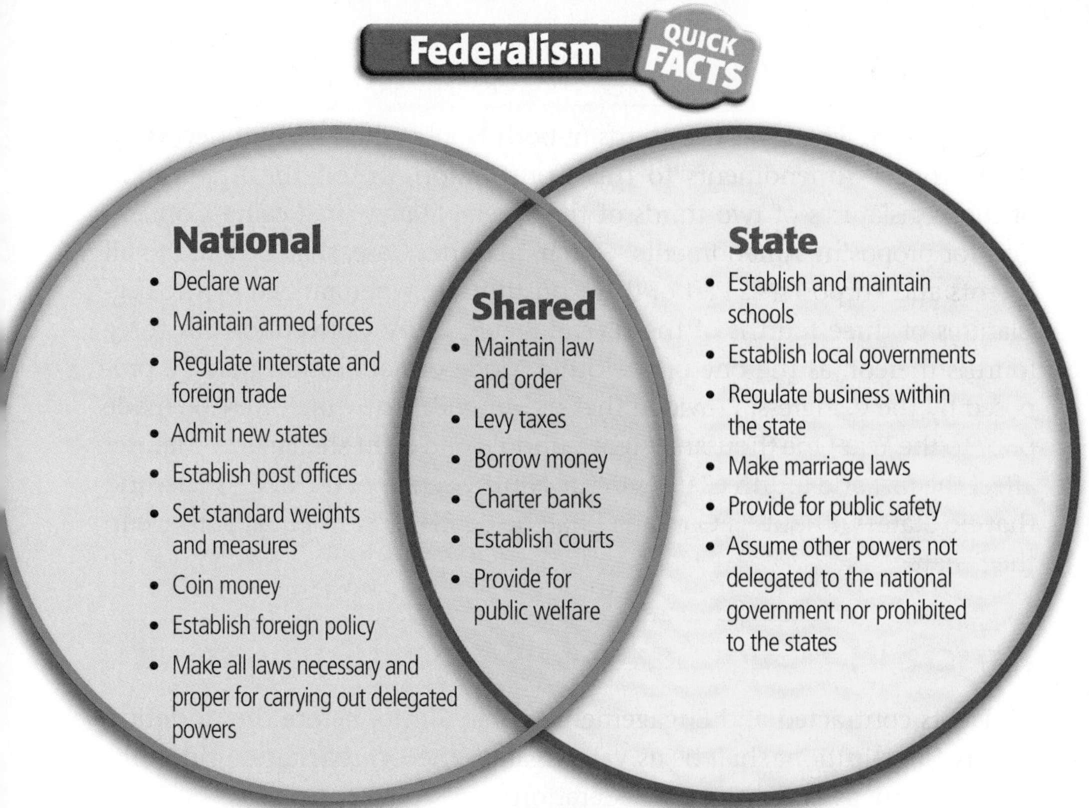

Federalism QUICK FACTS

National
- Declare war
- Maintain armed forces
- Regulate interstate and foreign trade
- Admit new states
- Establish post offices
- Set standard weights and measures
- Coin money
- Establish foreign policy
- Make all laws necessary and proper for carrying out delegated powers

Shared
- Maintain law and order
- Levy taxes
- Borrow money
- Charter banks
- Establish courts
- Provide for public welfare

State
- Establish and maintain schools
- Establish local governments
- Regulate business within the state
- Make marriage laws
- Provide for public safety
- Assume other powers not delegated to the national government nor prohibited to the states

ANALYSIS SKILL **ANALYZING INFORMATION**

Why does the power to declare war belong only to the national government?

Section 3. New States

1. Admission New States may be admitted by the Congress into this Union; but no new State shall be formed or erected within the Jurisdiction of any other State; nor any State be formed by the Junction of two or more States, or Parts of States, without the Consent of the Legislatures of the States concerned as well as of the Congress.

2. Congressional Authority The Congress shall have Power to dispose of and make all needful Rules and Regulations respecting the Territory or other Property belonging to the United States; and nothing in this Constitution shall be so construed as to Prejudice any Claims of the United States, or of any particular State.

Section 4. Guarantees to the States

The United States shall guarantee to every State in this Union a Republican Form of Government, and shall protect each of them against Invasion; and on Application of the Legislature, or of the Executive (when the Legislature cannot be convened), against domestic Violence.

EXPLORING THE DOCUMENT In a republic, voters elect representatives to act in their best interest. **How does Article IV protect the practice of republicanism in the United States?**

EXPLORING THE DOCUMENT America's founders may not have realized how long the Constitution would last, but they did set up a system for changing or adding to it. They did not want to make it easy to change the Constitution. **By what methods may the Constitution be amended? Under what sorts of circumstances do you think an amendment might be necessary?**

National Supremacy

One of the biggest problems facing the delegates to the Constitutional Convention was the question of what would happen if a state law and a federal law conflicted. Which law would be followed? Who would decide? The second clause of Article VI answers those questions. When a federal law and a state law disagree, the federal law overrides the state law. The Constitution and other federal laws are the "supreme Law of the Land." This clause is often called the supremacy clause.

Article V Amending the Constitution

The Congress, whenever two thirds of both Houses shall deem it necessary, shall propose Amendments to this Constitution, or, on the Application of the Legislatures of two thirds of the several States, shall call a Convention for proposing Amendments, which, in either Case, shall be valid to all Intents and Purposes, as Part of this Constitution, when ratified by the Legislatures of three fourths of the several States, or by Conventions in three fourths thereof, as the one or the other Mode of Ratification may be proposed by the Congress; Provided that no Amendment which may be made prior to the Year One thousand eight hundred and eight shall in any Manner affect the first and fourth Clauses in the Ninth Section of the first Article; and that no State, without its Consent, shall be deprived of its equal Suffrage in the Senate.

Article VI Supremacy of National Government

All Debts contracted and Engagements entered into, before the Adoption of this Constitution, shall be as valid against the United States under this Constitution, as under the Confederation.

This Constitution, and the Laws of the United States which shall be made in Pursuance thereof; and all Treaties made, or which shall be made, under the Authority of the United States, shall be the supreme Law of the Land; and the Judges in every State shall be bound thereby, any Thing in the Constitution or Laws of any State to the Contrary notwithstanding.

The Senators and Representatives before mentioned, and the Members of the several State Legislatures, and all executive and judicial Officers, both of the United States and of the several States, shall be bound by Oath or Affirmation, to support this Constitution; but no religious Test shall ever be required as a Qualification to any Office or public Trust under the United States.

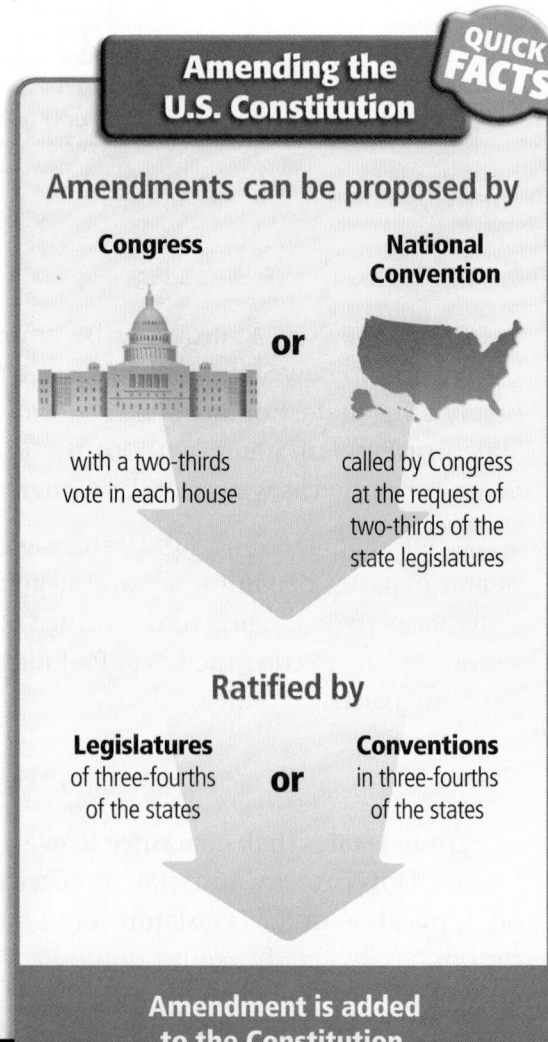

QUICK FACTS

Amending the U.S. Constitution

Amendments can be proposed by

Congress
with a two-thirds vote in each house

or

National Convention
called by Congress at the request of two-thirds of the state legislatures

Ratified by

Legislatures
of three-fourths of the states

or

Conventions
in three-fourths of the states

Amendment is added to the Constitution

Article VII Ratification

The Ratification of the Conventions of nine States, shall be sufficient for the Establishment of this Constitution between the States so ratifying the Same.

Done in Convention by the Unanimous Consent of the States present the Seventeenth Day of September in the Year of our Lord one thousand seven hundred and Eighty seven and of the Independence of the United States of America the Twelfth In witness whereof We have hereunto subscribed our Names,

George Washington—
President and deputy from Virginia

Ratification

The Articles of Confederation called for all 13 states to approve any revision to the Articles. The Constitution required that 9 out of the 13 states would be needed to ratify the Constitution. The first state to ratify was Delaware, on December 7, 1787. Almost two-and-a-half years later, on May 29, 1790, Rhode Island became the last state to ratify the Constitution.

Delaware

George Read
Gunning Bedford Jr.
John Dickinson
Richard Bassett
Jacob Broom

Maryland

James McHenry
Daniel of
  St. Thomas Jenifer
Daniel Carroll

Virginia

John Blair
James Madison Jr.

North Carolina

William Blount
Richard Dobbs Spaight
Hugh Williamson

South Carolina

John Rutledge
Charles Cotesworth
  Pinckney
Charles Pinckney
Pierce Butler

Georgia

William Few
Abraham Baldwin

New Hampshire

John Langdon
Nicholas Gilman

Massachusetts

Nathaniel Gorham
Rufus King

Connecticut

William Samuel Johnson
Roger Sherman

New York

Alexander Hamilton

New Jersey

William Livingston
David Brearley
William Paterson
Jonathan Dayton

Pennsylvania

Benjamin Franklin
Thomas Mifflin
Robert Morris
George Clymer
Thomas FitzSimons
Jared Ingersoll
James Wilson
Gouverneur Morris

Attest:
William Jackson,
Secretary

Constitutional Amendments

Note: The first 10 amendments to the Constitution were ratified on December 15, 1791, and form what is known as the Bill of Rights.

Amendments 1–10. The Bill of Rights

Amendment I

Congress shall make no law respecting an establishment of religion, or prohibiting the free exercise thereof; or abridging the freedom of speech, or of the press; or the right of the people peaceably to assemble, and to petition the Government for a redress of grievances.

Amendment II

A well regulated Militia, being necessary to the security of a free State, the right of the people to keep and bear Arms, shall not be infringed.

Amendment III

No Soldier shall, in time of peace be **quartered**[24] in any house, without the consent of the Owner, nor in time of war, but in a manner to be prescribed by law.

Amendment IV

The right of the people to be secure in their persons, houses, papers, and effects, against unreasonable searches and seizures, shall not be violated, and no **Warrants**[25] shall issue, but upon probable cause, supported by Oath or affirmation, and particularly describing the place to be searched, and the persons or things to be seized.

Amendment V

No person shall be held to answer for a capital, or otherwise **infamous**[26] crime, unless on a presentment or **indictment**[27] of a Grand Jury, except in

Bill of Rights

One of the conditions set by several states for ratifying the Constitution was the inclusion of a bill of rights. Many people feared that a stronger central government might take away basic rights of the people that had been guaranteed in state constitutions.

EXPLORING THE DOCUMENT The First Amendment forbids Congress from making any "law respecting an establishment of religion" or restraining the freedom to practice religion as one chooses. **Why is freedom of religion an important right?**

Rights of the Accused

The Fifth, Sixth, and Seventh Amendments describe the procedures that courts must follow when trying people accused of crimes.

Vocabulary

[24] **quartered** housed

[25] **Warrants** written orders authorizing a person to make an arrest, a seizure, or a search

[26] **infamous** disgraceful

[27] **indictment** the act of charging with a crime

Fundamental Liberties

Freedom of Religion

Freedom of Speech

cases arising in the land or naval forces, or in the Militia, when in actual service in time of War or public danger; nor shall any person be subject for the same offence to be twice put in jeopardy of life or limb; nor shall be compelled in any criminal case to be a witness against himself, nor be deprived of life, liberty, or property, without due process of law; nor shall private property be taken for public use, without just compensation.

Amendment VI

In all criminal prosecutions, the accused shall enjoy the right to a speedy and public trial, by an impartial jury of the State and district wherein the crime shall have been committed, which district shall have been previously **ascertained**[28] by law, and to be informed of the nature and cause of the accusation; to be confronted with the witnesses against him; to have compulsory process for obtaining witnesses in his favor, and to have the Assistance of Counsel for his defence.

Amendment VII

In suits at common law, where the value in controversy shall exceed twenty dollars, the right of trial by jury shall be preserved, and no fact tried by a jury, shall be otherwise reexamined in any Court of the United States, than according to the rules of the common law.

Amendment VIII

Excessive bail shall not be required, nor excessive fines imposed, nor cruel and unusual punishments inflicted.

Amendment IX

The enumeration in the Constitution, of certain rights, shall not be construed to deny or disparage others retained by the people.

Amendment X

The powers not delegated to the United States by the Constitution, nor prohibited by it to the States, are reserved to the States respectively, or to the people.

Trials

The Sixth Amendment makes several guarantees, including a prompt trial and a trial by a jury chosen from the state and district in which the crime was committed.

Vocabulary

[28] **ascertained** found out

EXPLORING THE DOCUMENT The Ninth and Tenth Amendments were added because not every right of the people or of the states could be listed in the Constitution. **How do the Ninth and Tenth Amendments limit the power of the federal government?**

Washington Star-News
NIGHT FINAL LATE STOCKS SPORTS
ON TV AT 9 TONIGHT
Nixon Resigning

Freedom of Assembly

MR. PRESIDENT HOW LONG MUST WOMEN WAIT FOR LIBERTY

Freedom to Petition the Government

ANALYSIS SKILL **ANALYZING INFORMATION**

Which amendment guarantees these fundamental freedoms?

Freedom of the Press

Amendments to the U.S. Constitution

The Constitution has been amended only 27 times since it was ratified more than 200 years ago. Amendments help the structure of the government change along with the values of the nation's people. Read the time line below to learn how each amendment changed the government.

1870
Amendment 15
Prohibits national and state governments from denying the vote based on race

1791
Bill of Rights
Amendments 1–10

1865
Amendment 13
Bans slavery

| 1790 | 1820 | 1870 |

1795
Amendment 11
Protects the states from lawsuits filed by citizens of other states or countries

1804
Amendment 12
Requires separate ballots for the offices of president and vice president

1868
Amendment 14
Defines citizenship and citizens' rights

Amendments 11–27

Amendment XI

Passed by Congress March 4, 1794. Ratified February 7, 1795.

The Judicial power of the United States shall not be **construed**[29] to extend to any suit in law or equity, commenced or prosecuted against one of the United States by Citizens of another State, or by Citizens or Subjects of any Foreign State.

Amendment XII

Passed by Congress December 9, 1803. Ratified June 15, 1804.

The Electors shall meet in their respective states and vote by ballot for President and Vice-President, one of whom, at least, shall not be an inhabitant of the same state with themselves; they shall name in their ballots the person voted for as President, and in distinct ballots the person voted for as Vice-President, and they shall make distinct lists of all persons voted for as President, and of all persons voted for as Vice-President, and of the number of votes for each, which lists they shall sign and certify, and transmit sealed to the seat of the government of the United States, directed to the President of the Senate;—the President of the Senate shall, in the presence of the

Vocabulary

[29] **construed** explained or interpreted

President and Vice President

The Twelfth Amendment changed the election procedure for president and vice president.

1919
Amendment 18
Bans the making, selling, and shipping of alcoholic beverages

1920
Amendment 19
Extends the right to vote to women

1933
Amendment 21
Repeals Amendment 18

1961
Amendment 23
Gives citizens of Washington, D.C., the right to vote in presidential elections

1964
Amendment 24
Bans poll taxes

1971
Amendment 26
Gives 18-year-olds the right to vote in federal and state elections

1920

1970

2000

1913
Amendment 16
Allows Congress to tax incomes

Amendment 17
Establishes the direct election of U.S. senators

1933
Amendment 20
Changes the date for starting a new congressional term and inaugurating a new president

1951
Amendment 22
Limits terms a president can serve to two

1967
Amendment 25
Establishes procedures for presidential succession

1992
Amendment 27
Limits the ability of Congress to increase its pay

ANALYSIS SKILL **READING TIME LINES**

1. How are the Eighteenth and Twenty-first Amendments related?
2. Which amendments relate to the right to vote?

Senate and House of Representatives, open all the certificates and the votes shall then be counted;—The person having the greatest number of votes for President, shall be the President, if such number be a majority of the whole number of Electors appointed; and if no person have such majority, then from the persons having the highest numbers not exceeding three on the list of those voted for as President, the House of Representatives shall choose immediately, by ballot, the President. But in choosing the President, the votes shall be taken by states, the representation from each state having one vote; a quorum for this purpose shall consist of a member or members from two-thirds of the states, and a majority of all the states shall be necessary to a choice. ~~And if the House of Representatives shall not choose a President whenever the right of choice shall devolve upon them, before the fourth day of March next following, then the Vice-President shall act as President, as in case of the death or other constitutional disability of the President.~~—The person having the greatest number of votes as Vice-President, shall be the Vice-President, if such number be a majority of the whole number of Electors appointed, and if no person have a majority, then from the two highest numbers on the list, the Senate shall choose the Vice-President; a quorum for the purpose shall consist of two-thirds of the whole number of Senators, and a majority of the whole number shall be necessary to a choice. But no person constitutionally ineligible to the office of President shall be eligible to that of Vice-President of the United States.

Abolishing Slavery

Although some slaves had been freed during the Civil War, slavery was not abolished until the Thirteenth Amendment took effect.

Protecting the Rights of Citizens

In 1833 the Supreme Court ruled that the Bill of Rights limited the federal government but not the state governments. This ruling was interpreted to mean that states were able to keep African Americans from becoming state citizens and keep the Bill of Rights from protecting them. The Fourteenth Amendment defines citizenship and prevents states from interfering in the rights of citizens of the United States.

Vocabulary

[30] **involuntary servitude** being forced to work against one's will

Amendment XIII

Passed by Congress January 31, 1865. Ratified December 6, 1865.

1. Slavery Banned Neither slavery nor **involuntary servitude**,[30] except as a punishment for crime whereof the party shall have been duly convicted, shall exist within the United States, or any place subject to their jurisdiction.

2. Enforcement Congress shall have power to enforce this article by appropriate legislation.

Amendment XIV

Passed by Congress June 13, 1866. Ratified July 9, 1868.

1. Citizenship Defined All persons born or naturalized in the United States, and subject to the jurisdiction thereof, are citizens of the United States and of the State wherein they reside. No State shall make or enforce any law which shall abridge the privileges or immunities of citizens of the United States; nor shall any State deprive any person of life, liberty, or property, without due process of law; nor deny to any person within its jurisdiction the equal protection of the laws.

2. Voting Rights Representatives shall be apportioned among the several States according to their respective numbers, counting the whole number of persons in each State, excluding Indians not taxed. But when the right to vote at any election for the choice of electors for President and Vice-President of the United States, Representatives in Congress, the Executive and Judicial officers of a State, or the members of the Legislature thereof, is denied to any of the male inhabitants of such State, being twenty-one years of age, and citizens of the United States, or in any way abridged, except for participation in rebellion, or other crime, the basis of representation therein shall be reduced in the proportion which the number of such male citizens shall bear to the whole number of male citizens twenty-one years of age in such State.

3. Rebels Banned from Government No person shall be a Senator or Representative in Congress, or elector of President and Vice-President, or hold any office, civil or military, under the United States, or under any State, who, having previously taken an oath, as a member of Congress, or as an officer of the United States, or as a member of any State legislature, or as an executive or judicial officer of any State, to support the Constitution of the United States, shall have engaged in insurrection or rebellion against the same, or given aid or comfort to the enemies thereof. But Congress may by a vote of two-thirds of each House, remove such disability.

4. Payment of Debts The validity of the public debt of the United States, authorized by law, including debts incurred for payment of pensions and

The Reconstruction Amendments

The Thirteenth, Fourteenth, and Fifteenth Amendments are often called the Reconstruction Amendments. This is because they arose during Reconstruction, the period of American history following the Civil War. The country was reconstructing itself after that terrible conflict. A key aspect of Reconstruction was extending the rights of citizenship to former slaves.

The Thirteenth Amendment banned slavery. The Fourteenth Amendment required states to respect the freedoms listed in the Bill of Rights, thus preventing states from denying rights to African Americans. The Fifteenth Amendment gave African American men the right to vote.

African Americans participate in an election.

ANALYSIS SKILL **ANALYZING INFORMATION**

Why was the Thirteenth Amendment needed?

bounties for services in suppressing insurrection or rebellion, shall not be questioned. But neither the United States nor any State shall assume or pay any debt or obligation incurred in aid of insurrection or rebellion against the United States, ~~or any claim for the loss or emancipation of any slave~~; but all such debts, obligations and claims shall be held illegal and void.

5. Enforcement The Congress shall have the power to enforce, by appropriate legislation, the provisions of this article.

Amendment XV

Passed by Congress February 26, 1869. Ratified February 3, 1870.

1. Voting Rights The right of citizens of the United States to vote shall not be denied or abridged by the United States or by any State on account of race, color, or previous condition of servitude.

2. Enforcement The Congress shall have the power to enforce this article by appropriate legislation.

Amendment XVI

Passed by Congress July 2, 1909. Ratified February 3, 1913.

The Congress shall have power to lay and collect taxes on incomes, from whatever source derived, without apportionment among the several States, and without regard to any census or enumeration.

Amendment XVII

Passed by Congress May 13, 1912. Ratified April 8, 1913.

1. Senators Elected by Citizens The Senate of the United States shall be composed of two Senators from each State, elected by the people thereof, for six years; and each Senator shall have one vote. The electors in each State shall have the qualifications requisite for electors of the most numerous branch of the State legislatures.

2. Vacancies When vacancies happen in the representation of any State in the Senate, the executive authority of such State shall issue writs of election to fill such vacancies: *Provided*, That the legislature of any State may empower the executive thereof to make temporary appointments until the people fill the vacancies by election as the legislature may direct.

3. Future Elections This amendment shall not be so construed as to affect the election or term of any Senator chosen before it becomes valid as part of the Constitution.

Amendment XVIII

Passed by Congress December 18, 1917. Ratified January 16, 1919. Repealed by Amendment XXI.

1. Liquor Banned After one year from the ratification of this article the manufacture, sale, or transportation of intoxicating liquors within, the importation thereof into, or the exportation thereof from the United States and all territory subject to the jurisdiction thereof for beverage purposes is hereby prohibited.

2. Enforcement The Congress and the several States shall have concurrent power to enforce this article by appropriate legislation.

3. Ratification This article shall be inoperative unless it shall have been ratified as an amendment to the Constitution by the legislatures of the several States, as provided in the Constitution, within seven years from the date of the submission hereof to the States by the Congress.

EXPLORING THE DOCUMENT The Seventeenth Amendment requires that senators be elected directly by the people instead of by the state legislatures. **What principle of our government does the Seventeenth Amendment protect?**

Prohibition

Although many people believed that the Eighteenth Amendment was good for the health and welfare of the American people, it was repealed 14 years later.

Women Fight for the Vote

To become part of the Constitution, a proposed amendment must be ratified by three-fourths of the states. Here, suffragists witness Kentucky governor Edwin P. Morrow signing the Nineteenth Amendment in January 1920. By June of that year, enough states had ratified the amendment to make it part of the Constitution. American women, after generations of struggle, had finally won the right to vote.

ANALYSIS SKILL ANALYZING INFORMATION

What right did the Nineteenth Amendment grant?

Amendment XIX

Passed by Congress June 4, 1919. Ratified August 18, 1920.

1. Voting Rights The right of citizens of the United States to vote shall not be denied or abridged by the United States or by any State on account of sex.

2. Enforcement Congress shall have power to enforce this article by appropriate legislation.

Amendment XX

Passed by Congress March 2, 1932. Ratified January 23, 1933.

1. Presidential Terms The terms of the President and the Vice President shall end at noon on the 20th day of January, and the terms of Senators and Representatives at noon on the 3d day of January, of the years in which such terms would have ended if this article had not been ratified; and the terms of their successors shall then begin.

Women's Suffrage

Abigail Adams and others were disappointed that the Declaration of Independence and the Constitution did not specifically include women. It took many years and much campaigning before suffrage for women was finally achieved.

Taking Office

In the original Constitution, a newly elected president and Congress did not take office until March 4, which was four months after the November election. The officials who were leaving office were called lame ducks because they had little influence during those four months. The Twentieth Amendment changed the date that the new president and Congress take office. Members of Congress now take office during the first week of January, and the president takes office on January 20.

2. Meeting of Congress The Congress shall assemble at least once in every year, and such meeting shall begin at noon on the 3d day of January, unless they shall by law appoint a different day.

3. Succession of Vice President If, at the time fixed for the beginning of the term of the President, the President elect shall have died, the Vice President elect shall become President. If a President shall not have been chosen before the time fixed for the beginning of his term, or if the President elect shall have failed to qualify, then the Vice President elect shall act as President until a President shall have qualified; and the Congress may by law provide for the case wherein neither a President elect nor a Vice President shall have qualified, declaring who shall then act as President, or the manner in which one who is to act shall be selected, and such person shall act accordingly until a President or Vice President shall have qualified.

4. Succession by Vote of Congress The Congress may by law provide for the case of the death of any of the persons from whom the House of Representatives may choose a President whenever the right of choice shall have devolved upon them, and for the case of the death of any of the persons from whom the Senate may choose a Vice President whenever the right of choice shall have devolved upon them.

5. Ratification Sections 1 and 2 shall take effect on the 15th day of October following the ratification of this article.

6. Ratification This article shall be inoperative unless it shall have been ratified as an amendment to the Constitution by the legislatures of three-fourths of the several States within seven years from the date of its submission.

Amendment XXI

Passed by Congress February 20, 1933. Ratified December 5, 1933.

1. 18th Amendment Repealed The eighteenth article of amendment to the Constitution of the United States is hereby repealed.

2. Liquor Allowed by Law The transportation or importation into any State, Territory, or Possession of the United States for delivery or use therein of intoxicating liquors, in violation of the laws thereof, is hereby prohibited.

3. Ratification This article shall be inoperative unless it shall have been ratified as an amendment to the Constitution by conventions in the several States, as provided in the Constitution, within seven years from the date of the submission hereof to the States by the Congress.

Amendment XXII

Passed by Congress March 21, 1947. Ratified February 27, 1951.

1. Term Limits No person shall be elected to the office of the President more than twice, and no person who has held the office of President, or acted as President, for more than two years of a term to which some other person was elected President shall be elected to the office of President more than once. ~~But this Article shall not apply to any person holding the office of President when this Article was proposed by Congress, and shall not prevent any person who may be holding the office of President, or acting as President, during the term within which this Article becomes operative from holding the office of President or acting as President during the remainder of such term.~~

2. Ratification ~~This article shall be inoperative unless it shall have been ratified as an amendment to the Constitution by the legislatures of three-fourths of the several States within seven years from the date of its submission to the States by the Congress.~~

After Franklin D. Roosevelt was elected to four consecutive terms, limits were placed on the number of terms a president could serve.

Amendment XXIII

Passed by Congress June 16, 1960. Ratified March 29, 1961.

1. District of Columbia Represented The District constituting the seat of Government of the United States shall appoint in such manner as Congress may direct:

A number of electors of President and Vice President equal to the whole number of Senators and Representatives in Congress to which the District would be entitled if it were a State, but in no event more than the least populous State; they shall be in addition to those appointed by the States, but they shall be considered, for the purposes of the election of President and Vice President, to be electors appointed by a State; and they shall meet in the District and perform such duties as provided by the twelfth article of amendment.

2. Enforcement The Congress shall have power to enforce this article by appropriate legislation.

Voting Rights

Until the ratification of the Twenty-third Amendment, the people of Washington, D.C., could not vote in presidential elections.

Poll taxes were used to deny many poor Americans, including African Americans and Hispanic Americans, their right to vote. These taxes were made unconstitutional by the Twenty-fourth Amendment.

The American GI Forum

Says: BUY YOUR POLL TAX

1939 Poll Tax Receipt R. P 5 L 37
STATE OF TEXAS - COUNTY OF
PRECINCT NUMBER 3
WARD No.
GILLESPIE
DATE Oct. 21 19 39 N° 49
RECEIVED OF Mr. Emil Boaz
ADDRESS
STREET AND HOUSE NO. Luckenbach
R. F. D. BOX
LENGTH OF RESIDENCE
AGE STATE COUNTY CITY
YEARS YEARS YEARS YEARS
59 59 59 —
SEX: MALE FEMALE
RACE: WHITE COLORED
NATIVE-BORN CITIZEN NATURALIZED
OCCUPATION
PAID BY AGENT
STATE AND COUNTY OR FOREIGN COUNTRY BORN IN
THE SUM OF ONE AND 75/100 DOLLARS IN PAYMENT OF POLL TAX FOR THE YEAR SHOWN ABOVE, THE SAID TAXPAYER BEING DULY SWORN BY ME SAYS THAT THE ABOVE IS CORRECT ALL OF WHICH I CERTIFY.
BY Milton C. Kerst DEPUTY WM M PETMECKY
ASSESSOR AND COLLECTOR OF TAXES OF AFORESAID COUNTY

VOTE for FREEDOM
BALLOT BOX

ANALYSIS SKILL ANALYZING INFORMATION

How did poll taxes deny poor Americans the opportunity to vote?

Presidential Disability

The illness of President Eisenhower in the 1950s and the assassination of President Kennedy in 1963 were the events behind the Twenty-fifth Amendment. The Constitution did not provide a clear-cut method for a vice president to take over for a disabled president or upon the death of a president. This amendment provides for filling the office of the vice president if a vacancy occurs, and it provides a way for the vice president—or someone else in the line of succession—to take over if the president is unable to perform the duties of that office.

Amendment XXIV

Passed by Congress August 27, 1962. Ratified January 23, 1964.

1. Voting Rights The right of citizens of the United States to vote in any primary or other election for President or Vice President, for electors for President or Vice President, or for Senator or Representative in Congress, shall not be denied or abridged by the United States or any State by reason of failure to pay poll tax or other tax.

2. Enforcement The Congress shall have power to enforce this article by appropriate legislation.

Amendment XXV

Passed by Congress July 6, 1965. Ratified February 10, 1967.

1. Sucession of Vice President In case of the removal of the President from office or of his death or resignation, the Vice President shall become President.

2. Vacancy of Vice President Whenever there is a vacancy in the office of the Vice President, the President shall nominate a Vice President who shall take office upon confirmation by a majority vote of both Houses of Congress.

3. Written Declaration Whenever the President transmits to the President pro tempore of the Senate and the Speaker of the House of Representatives his written declaration that he is unable to discharge the powers and duties of his office, and until he transmits to them a written declaration to the contrary, such powers and duties shall be discharged by the Vice President as Acting President.

4. Removing the President Whenever the Vice President and a majority of either the principal officers of the executive departments or of such other body as Congress may by law provide, transmit to the President pro tempore of the Senate and the Speaker of the House of Representatives their written declaration that the President is unable to discharge the powers and duties of his office, the Vice President shall immediately assume the powers and duties of the office as Acting President.

Thereafter, when the President transmits to the President pro tempore of the Senate and the Speaker of the House of Representatives his written declaration that no inability exists, he shall resume the powers and duties of his office unless the Vice President and a majority of either the principal officers of the executive department or of such other body as Congress may by law provide, transmit within four days to the President pro tempore of the Senate and the Speaker of the House of Representatives their written declaration that the President is unable to discharge the powers and duties of his office. Thereupon Congress shall decide the issue, assembling within forty-eight hours for that purpose if not in session. If the Congress, within twenty-one days after receipt of the latter written declaration, or, if Congress is not in session, within twenty-one days after Congress is required to assemble, determines by two-thirds vote of both Houses that the President is unable to discharge the powers and duties of his office, the Vice President shall continue to discharge the same as Acting President; otherwise, the President shall resume the powers and duties of his office.

Amendment XXVI

Passed by Congress March 23, 1971. Ratified July 1, 1971.

1. Voting Rights The right of citizens of the United States, who are eighteen years of age or older, to vote shall not be denied or abridged by the United States or by any State on account of age.

2. Enforcement The Congress shall have power to enforce this article by appropriate legislation.

Amendment XXVII

Originally proposed September 25, 1789. Ratified May 7, 1992.

No law, varying the compensation for the services of the Senators and Representatives, shall take effect, until an election of representatives shall have intervened.

Expanded Suffrage

The Voting Rights Act of 1970 tried to set the voting age at 18. However, the Supreme Court ruled that the act set the voting age for national elections only, not for state or local elections. The Twenty-sixth Amendment gave 18-year-old citizens the right to vote in all elections.

CHAPTER 3
THE UNITED STATES CONSTITUTION

SECTION 1
Ideals of the Constitution

SECTION 2
The Three Branches of Government

SECTION 3
An Enduring Document

NATIONAL STANDARDS
FOR CIVICS AND GOVERNMENT

I. What are civic life, politics, and government?

   C. What are the nature and purposes of constitutions?

II. What are the foundations of the American political system?

   A. What is the American idea of constitutional government?

III. How does the government established by the Constitution embody the purposes, values, and principles of American democracy?

   A. How are power and responsibility distributed, shared, and limited in the government established by the United States Constitution?

   B. How is the national government organized and what does it do?

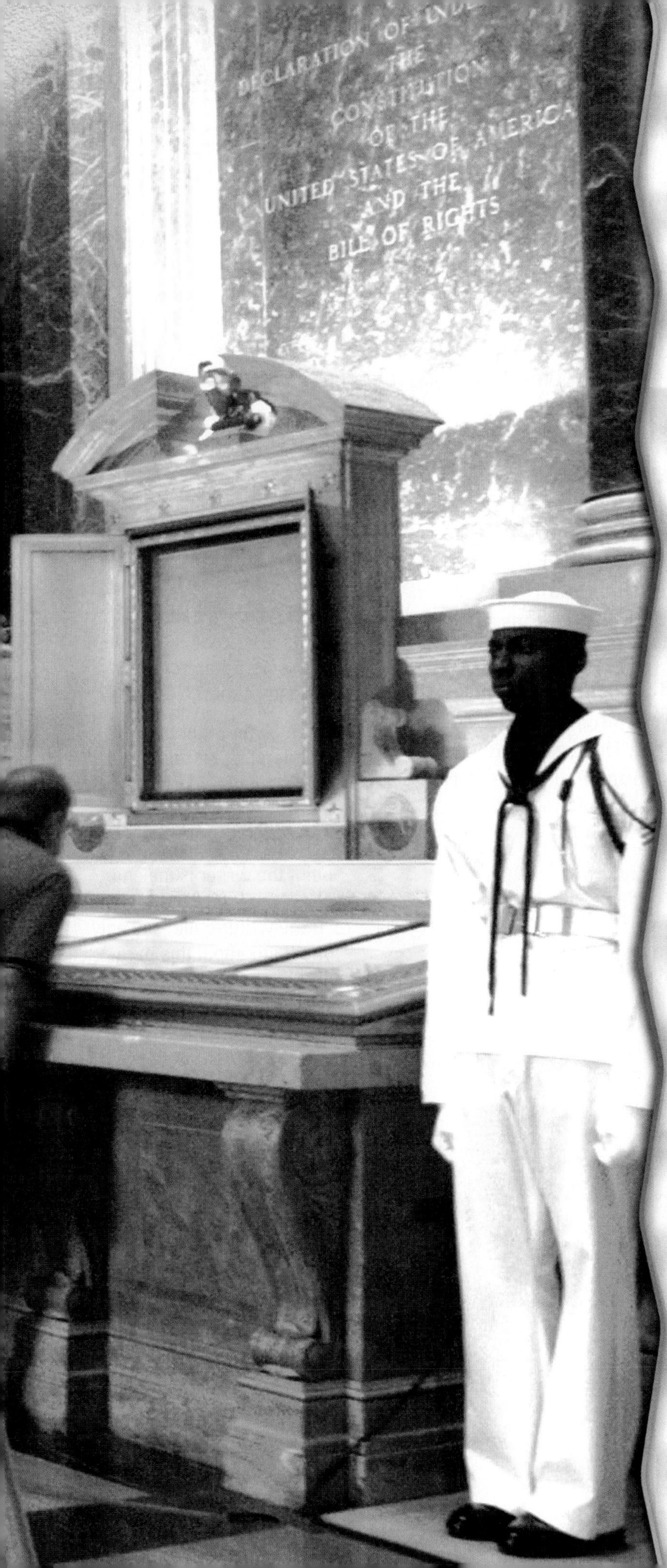

Active Citizenship video program
Watch the video to understand state laws about speed limits.

WHY CIVICS Matters

The United States Constitution created a government flexible enough to change with the times while still guaranteeing your basic rights and the rights of all Americans.

STUDENTS TAKE ACTION

PROTECTING COMMUNITY HEALTH

What would you do if you learned that houses in your community were filled with a gas that causes lung cancer? Think about a plan to protect people in your neighborhood from this health problem.

FOCUS ON WRITING

A NEWSPAPER EDITORIAL It is 1787 and you're writing an editorial for a local newspaper. You want to convince your readers that the new Constitution will be much better than the old Articles of Confederation. In this chapter you'll find the information you need to support your opinion.

Reading Skills

In this chapter you will read about the United States Constitution, the document that outlines the founding principles of our nation and our government. You will learn about the goals of the Constitution, the three branches of American government, and the role of the Constitution in your world today. As you read the chapter, look for the most important concepts and main ideas. Use organizers or take notes to help you remember them.

Finding Main Ideas

FOCUS ON READING When you are reading, it is not always necessary to remember every tiny detail of the text. Instead, what you want to remember are the main ideas, the most important concepts around which the text is based. Use the Reading Focus questions at the beginning of each section to help you get started.

Identifying Main Ideas Most paragraphs in civics books include main ideas. Sometimes the main idea is stated clearly in a single sentence. At other times, the main idea is suggested, not stated. However, that idea still shapes the paragraph's content and the meaning of all of the facts and details in it.

> The Revolutionary War began in 1775. Colonists known as Patriots chose to fight for independence. Loyalists—sometimes called Tories—were those who remained loyal to Great Britain. Historians estimate that 40 to 45 percent of Americans were Patriots, while 20 to 30 percent were Loyalists. The rest were neutral.

Topic: The paragraph is about Americans' loyalties during the war.

Facts and Details:
- Patriots wanted independence.
- Loyalists wanted to remain part of Great Britain.
- Some people stayed neutral.

Main Idea: Americans' loyalties were divided as the colonies prepared for the Revolutionary War.

Helpful Hints for Identifying Main Ideas

1. Read the paragraph. Ask yourself, "What is the topic of this paragraph—what is it mostly about?"

2. List the important facts and details that relate to that topic.

3. Ask yourself, "What seems to be the most important point the writer is making about the topic?" Or ask, "If the writer could say only one thing about this paragraph, what would it be?" This is the main idea of the paragraph.

You Try It!

The following passage is from the chapter you are about to read. Read it and then answer the questions below.

> In our federalist system, the top layer of government is the national, or federal, government. The federal government makes laws that govern the whole country. The national government is based in our nation's capital, Washington, D.C. It has offices and officials throughout the country and the world.
>
> The second layer is the state governments. Each state government has authority only over the people who live within that state. The state of California, for example, cannot pass a law governing the people of New York. Each state has its own capital, constitution, and state officials.

From Chapter 3, pp. 89–90

After you have read the passage, answer the following questions.

1. The main idea of the second paragraph is stated in a sentence. Which sentence expresses the main idea?

2. What is the first paragraph about? What facts and details are included in the paragraph? Based on your answers to these questions, what is the main idea of the first paragraph?

As you read Chapter 3, identify the main ideas of the paragraphs you are reading.

KEY TERMS

Chapter 3

Section 1
popular sovereignty *(p. 87)*
Preamble *(p. 87)*
limited government *(p. 88)*
majority rule *(p. 88)*
delegated powers *(p. 90)*
reserved powers *(p. 91)*
concurrent powers *(p. 91)*

Section 2
separation of powers *(p. 93)*
legislative branch *(p. 94)*
executive branch *(p. 94)*
judicial branch *(p. 94)*
checks and balances *(p. 96)*
veto *(p. 96)*
judicial review *(p. 97)*

Section 3
amendment *(p. 100)*
repeal *(p. 100)*
cabinet *(p. 101)*

Academic Vocabulary
Success in school is related to knowing academic vocabulary—the words that are frequently used in school assignments and discussions. In this chapter you will learn the following academic word:

federal *(p. 89)*

Ideals of the Constitution

BEFORE YOU READ

The Main Idea

The Constitution is an agreement between the citizens of the United States and the government that the people will grant powers to the government. In return, the government is to carry out the goals of the Constitution.

Reading Focus

1. How did the Pilgrims influence the framers of the Constitution?
2. What are the goals of the U.S. government as outlined in the Constitution?
3. What are the powers the Constitution gives to the federal and state governments?

Key Terms

popular sovereignty, p. 87
Preamble, p. 87
limited government, p. 88
majority rule, p. 88
delegated powers, p. 90
reserved powers, p. 91
concurrent powers, p. 91

TAKING NOTES As you read, take notes on the ideals of the Constitution. Use a graphic organizer like this one to record your notes.

Pilgrims' Influence	Reaching the Goals	Federal and State Governments

John Carver, who signed the Mayflower Compact, became the first governor of Plymouth Colony.

This painting shows some of the Pilgrims signing the Mayflower Compact.

What gives the government the right to tell you what to do? You do. In the United States, the government receives its powers from its citizens. As a citizen, you consent, or give your permission, to be governed every time you vote—or choose not to. Your study of civics will help you make good choices at election time.

Pilgrims Influenced the Framers

The *Mayflower*, the tiny ship carrying the Pilgrims to the New World, was supposed to land in what is now called Virginia. Violently blown off course on its voyage from England, the *Mayflower* arrived in Massachusetts Bay instead. The two-month ocean journey tested the faith and spirits of the religious Pilgrims aboard.

Pilgrims Agree to Be Governed

William Bradford, who would soon be governor of the Massachusetts Colony, observed that on the day before their landing, some of the passengers were "not well affected to unity and concord." That is, they were arguing. The colonists realized that before they got off their ship, they had better agree on some rules. The group decided that "there should be an association and agreement." Bradford noted "that we should combine together in one body, and to submit to such government and governors as we should by common consent agree to make and choose . . ."

This was a historic decision. In the 1600s most people were governed or ruled without their consent. These Pilgrims knew they needed some government, so they took the next step. They *willingly* gave their consent to be ruled by a government that they would create.

Mayflower Compact

The agreement that the Pilgrims signed on November 21, 1620, is known as the Mayflower Compact. The citizens of the new colony gave up some of their individual powers to the government they had created. At the same time, they agreed to submit to and obey the government they chose.

The Mayflower Compact includes some of the basic ideals upon which the United States was founded. For example, the Declaration of Independence states that governments should receive their powers from "the consent of the governed." Later, the framers of the Constitution began that document with the words "We the People" to show that the foundation of their new government was its citizens.

Government Power from the People

"We the People . . ." These three small words are heavy with meaning. Like a stone dropped in a pond, these opening words of the Constitution have rippled throughout time. The phrase has inspired generations of citizens around the world. But what does "We the People" mean?

The framers of the Constitution, following the ideas of the Mayflower Compact, chose these words to make it clear that the United States government gets its power from the American people. Government by **popular sovereignty**, or consent of the governed, is

one of our nation's most cherished ideals.

"We the People" appears in the Preamble of the Constitution. The **Preamble** is an introduction that explains why the U.S. Constitution was written. It outlines the principle of popular sovereignty when it states that the American people "do ordain [authorize] and establish this Constitution." Government, once established by the free choice of the people, then serves the people, who have supreme power.

READING CHECK **Summarizing** What did the Pilgrims do that later influenced the framers of the Constitution?

Reaching the Goals of the Constitution

The Constitution is based on important principles that help to ensure government by popular sovereignty. These principles include limited government, majority rule with minority rights, and protection of individual rights.

Limited Government

Prior to the Magna Carta in 1215, the king of England had nearly unlimited power. To keep the new government from becoming too powerful, the framers created a **limited government**—one with specific restrictions on its power. The Constitution sets those limits so that citizens know what their government is allowed to do and what it is *not* allowed to do.

Majority Rule with Minority Rights

How can a government resolve disagreements among its citizens? One way is through **majority rule**, the principle that in a disagreement, everyone will accept the decision of the majority (most of the people). Yet the framers were concerned that a powerful majority could violate the rights of the minority. So they included provisions to protect the rights of the minority and to allow the minority to express its views on issues.

Powers of the People

Our most cherished rights and protections are stated in the Bill of Rights. Added to the Constitution in 1791, the Bill of Rights details the specific freedoms that belong to every United States citizen. Many Americans consider the Bill of Rights to be the jewel of the U.S. Constitution because it guarantees our freedoms. It is one of the most influential documents ever written.

READING CHECK ➡ **Finding the Main Idea**
What are the goals of the U.S. government as outlined in the Constitution?

Powers of the Federal and State Governments

As you read in Chapter 2, the delegates to the Constitutional Convention had a problem. The Articles of Confederation were not working. The delegates soon knew they needed a new plan for government.

ACADEMIC VOCABULARY

federal
of or relating to the central government in a system of governing in which powers are divided between different levels of government

6 Goals of the Constitution
QUICK FACTS

The Preamble states the goals of the Constitution. These goals reflect the belief that the U.S. government should serve its citizens. They remain the goals of the country today.

Which of these goals do you think is most important? Explain your answer.

1 Form a more perfect union
The new government should be a better union of states than the union created under the Articles of Confederation.

2 Establish justice
The government should make laws and establish a system of courts that is fair to all.

3 Insure domestic tranquility
The government should preserve peace within the country.

The Federal System

The principle of federalism came to the framers first out of necessity and second out of their experiences. They were faced with the problem of needing a strong central government. At the same time, they wanted to keep independent state governments and to preserve self-government that had started with the Mayflower Compact.

From their experience, the framers remembered the Revolution. The colonies had fought against—and had defeated—the unwelcome rule of a strong central government. They had rebelled against a king who had tried to run colonial affairs. The framers certainly did not want to create that kind of interfering, powerful central authority. The solution the framers found was federalism, with its division of powers.

The federalist system created by the United States Consitution divides powers between two different levels, the national, or federal, government and the state governments. The top layer of government is the national, or **federal**, government. The federal government makes laws that govern the whole country. The national

ECON 101

Income Tax and Your Paycheck

One power that the Constitution gives to both federal and state governments is that of collecting taxes from citizens. With the ratification of the Sixteenth Amendment in 1913, it became legal for the federal government to tax citizens on their income. The majority of states also tax individual income, although nine limit or do not have state income taxes.

When you look at your first paycheck, you may be surprised at the percentage of your salary that goes to the government. In later chapters, you will learn how governments use this money. Learn how to read your paycheck stub by looking for these items:

- **Federal Income Tax**
- **State Income Tax**
- **Social Security Taxes**
  (shown as FICA, OASDI, SS, or Soc Sec)
- **Medicare**
- **Local Income Tax**

Get a copy of Form W-4 from the Internal Revenue Service. Read the form to learn about your control over withholdings.

ANALYSIS SKILL   **ANALYZING ECONOMICS**

Benjamin Franklin once said, "Nothing can be said to be certain, except death and taxes." What do you think he meant by this?

4 Provide for the common defense

The government should work to protect the country from its enemies.

5 Promote the general welfare

The government should help provide for the well-being of all the people.

6 And secure the blessings of liberty

The government should work to safeguard the freedom of the people.

FOUNDATIONS®
of DEMOCRACY

State Seat Belt Laws

In 1885 American inventor Edward J. Claghorn patented the first seat belt, to prevent people from falling out of horse-drawn carriages traveling on bumpy, unpaved roads. More than 120 years later, seat belt use is higher than ever, thanks in part to legislation requiring the restraints in 49 of the 50 states.

State of Virginia officials estimate that seat belt usage reduces the risk of death in auto accidents by 45 percent.

Why it Matters You're probably obeying a law every time you buckle your seat belt. Since the early 1980s, states have taken steps to make sure that their citizens—especially children—are buckled in while driving or riding. In some states, if police stop you for a violation, such as speeding, you can also be ticketed for not wearing a seat belt. In other states, the police can stop you and ticket you just for not being buckled in—these laws have been nicknamed "Click It or Ticket." In some states, everyone in the car must be wearing a belt, whether they're 3 or 93.

In general, the issue of public safety is left to the individual states to regulate. Some people argue that laws that make it illegal not to wear a seat belt violate personal civil liberties. But supporters of seat belt laws point to the fact that states have the responsibility to protect the lives and health of their citizens. One way to do that, they argue, is to require that all people wear their seat belts.

ANALYSIS SKILL EVALUATING THE LAW

go.hrw.com
KEYWORD: SZ7 CH3

1. Why do you think seat belt laws vary from state to state?
2. Do you think a driver's age should affect which passengers have to wear seat belts?

government is based in Washington, D.C. It has offices and officials throughout the country and the world.

The second layer is the state governments. Each state government has authority only over the people who live within that state. The state of California, for example, cannot pass a law governing the people of New York. Each state has its own capital, constitution, and state officials.

One of the strong points of our federal system is that the national government can focus on matters of wide, national concern, such as national defense and international trade. At the state level, each state has a different mix of people, traditions, needs, problems, and resources. Our federal system recognizes those differences and lets states solve local problems based on their own needs.

Federal Government Powers

The powers the Constitution specifically gives to the federal government are called **delegated powers**. For example, only the federal government has the power to print money and control trade with other nations. The federal government also has the power to provide for the country's defense.

Under the Articles of Confederation, the central government did not have some of these important powers. That was one of the drawbacks of the Articles. To overcome these problems, the Constitution delegated important powers to the federal government alone. This made the national government stronger. However, the framers also wanted to limit the power of the federal government, to keep it from becoming too powerful.

State Government Powers

The Constitution gives several important powers to the states alone, allowing them to manage their own affairs. For example, states conduct all elections, even for national offices. States alone are responsible for establishing schools. State governments also regulate trade within the states.

The states, or the people, have all the powers that the Constitution does not give specifically to the federal government. These powers are known as **reserved powers** because they are reserved, or set aside, for the states or the people. The state governments, for example, conduct elections, regulate trade within the state, and establish local governments.

Shared Powers

The federal and state governments also share many powers. These powers are known as **concurrent powers**. For example, both the federal and state governments can raise money through taxes. Both have the power to borrow money. The federal and state governments also share the power to establish courts, to create banks, to enforce laws, and to provide for the health and well-being of the American people.

States do pass laws. What happens when a state law disagrees with the Constitution or with a federal law? The state law is invalid. The framers of the Constitution made this clear by stating that the Constitution and the laws of the federal government shall be "the supreme law of the land."

The Constitution expresses our nation's commitment to individual freedoms, democracy, and equal justice under the law. The constitutional principle of federalism both grants government powers and limits them. In this way, each level of government can do its part to meet the constitutional commitments.

READING CHECK ▷ **Drawing Inferences and Conclusions** Explain why the Constitution sets out the powers granted to the federal and state governments.

SECTION 1 ASSESSMENT

Reviewing Ideas and Terms

1. a. Define Write a brief definition for the terms **popular sovereignty** and **Preamble**.
   b. Explain What did the Pilgrims do that later influenced the framers of the Constitution?
   c. Predict Is a government that states that it receives its power from the people likely to be more stable or less stable than a government that takes power by military force? Explain your reasoning.

2. a. Define Write a brief definition for the terms **limited government** and **majority rule**.
   b. Analyze Which of the six goals of the Constitution do you think is most important? Give reasons and examples to support your answer.

3. a. Define Write a brief definition for the terms **delegated powers, reserved powers**, and **concurrent powers**.
   b. Find the Main Idea Why is it important that the federal government and the state governments have separate as well as shared powers?

Critical Thinking

4. Comparing and Contrasting Use your notes and a graphic organizer like the one here to identify powers granted to federal and state governments and powers that they share.

Focus on Writing

5. Analyzing Information Write a poem or song that describes how the ideals of the Constitution affect your life today.

Federal Shared State

Historical Documents

Origins of the Republic

Some of the basic principles of government contained in the Declaration of Independence and the U.S. Constitution can be found in much earlier documents from Virginia.

Charters of the Virginia Company of London In 1607 the Virginia Company of London formed the colony of Jamestown in what is now Virginia. The company's charters included the ideas of government by consent of the governed and the right of people to enjoy the fruits of their labor.

In 1619 the company formed a General Assembly at Jamestown. The Jamestown colonists looked to the company charters for rules of government as well as for guarantees of fundamental rights and liberties.

Virginia Declaration of Rights, 1776 The people of Virginia drafted their constitution during the Revolutionary War. The Virginia Declaration of Rights accompanied this constitution. The Declaration of Rights stated that people's inherent rights came from nature rather than government. The declaration also stated that people possess fundamental rights such as the enjoyment of life, liberty, property, and the pursuit of happiness.

Virginia Statute of Religious Freedom In 1779 Thomas Jefferson drafted the Virginia Statute of Religious Freedom, which was based on the principle that church and state should be separated. This statute was written in reaction against the Virginia legislature's attempts to make taxpayers provide for churches.

Ties to the Constitution Although the Virginia documents established important rights and freedoms, the Declaration of Independence and U.S. Constitution guarantee freedoms that were left out of these earlier documents. For example, the Bill of Rights grants citizens freedom of speech, the right to assemble, the right to petition the government, the right to a trial by grand jury, and the right to legal representation—all privileges and rights not mentioned in the earlier documents. Nevertheless, the Virginia documents all embody the principle of government according to rules established in a written document. More importantly, perhaps, they contain ideas about the inherent rights of life, liberty, the pursuit of happiness, and government by consent of the governed—core values that have shaped U.S. politics for more than 200 years.

1. What is the significance of the General Assembly that met in Jamestown, Virginia, in 1619?

2. Why is Thomas Jefferson's Statute of Religious Freedom important today?

3. How might a fundamental or "inherent" right be defined?

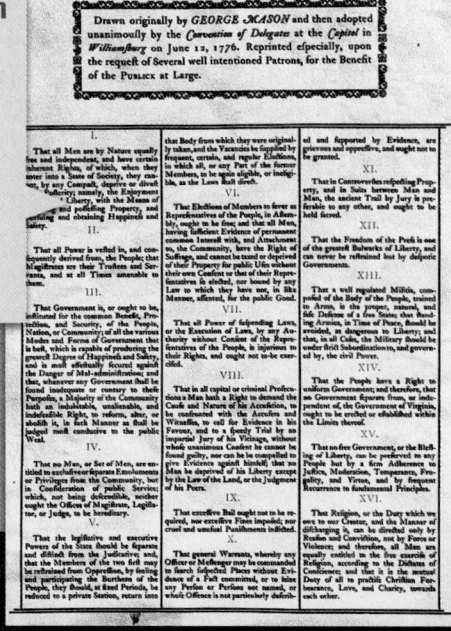

Virginia Declaration of Rights

The Declaration states that "all men are by nature equally free and independent." This idea is also included in the Declaration of Independence.

THE VIRGINIA DECLARATION of RIGHTS

Drawn originally by *GEORGE MASON* and then adopted unanimously by the *Convention of Delegates* at the *Capitol* in *Williamsburg* on June 12, 1776. Reprinted especially, upon the request of Several well intentioned Patrons, for the Benefit of the PUBLICK at Large.

SECTION 2

The Three Branches of Government

BEFORE YOU READ

The Main Idea

The Constitution prevents any person, or any part of the government, from taking too much power. It does this by creating three separate branches of the federal government and distributing power among them.

Reading Focus

1. Why does the Constitution provide for the separation of powers?
2. What are the main responsibilities of each of the three branches of government?
3. How does the system of checks and balances work?

Key Terms

separation of powers, *p. 93*
legislative branch, *p. 94*
executive branch, *p. 94*
judicial branch, *p. 94*
checks and balances, *p. 96*
veto, *p. 96*
judicial review, *p. 97*

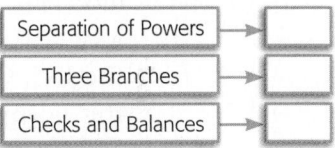 As you read, take notes on the U.S. government. Use a chart like this one to record your notes on the separation of powers, the three branches, and checks and balances.

Separation of Powers	→	
Three Branches	→	
Checks and Balances	→	

Members of both the Senate and the House of Representatives meet in the House chamber when the president gives his speech.

The nine justices of the U.S. Supreme Court are part of the judicial branch of our government.

The president is the head of the executive branch.

President George W. Bush addresses Congress, the Supreme Court, and other important officials in the annual State of the Union address.

CIVICS IN PRACTICE Why do we have three branches of government? Well, who would protect your rights if the power to make and enforce laws was put in the hands of only one person? What might happen to your freedom of speech or your right to privacy?

Separation of Powers

Having all government power in the same hands is, in James Madison's words, "the very definition of tyranny." The framers of the Constitution agreed with Madison. They could have created a central government with all government power concentrated in one group of people. Many people feared such an all-powerful government.

As a shield against tyranny, the framers created separate branches of the federal government. One branch would write the laws. Another would carry out the laws. A third branch would intepret the laws. This structure is called the **separation of powers**.

READING CHECK **Summarizing** Why did the framers separate the powers of government?

THE UNITED STATES CONSTITUTION 93

The Three Branches of Government

The concept of separation of powers had been written into many state constitutions already. For example, Georgia's constitution stated that, "the legislative, executive, and judiciary departments shall be separate and distinct, so that neither exercise the powers properly belonging to the other."

The Legislative Branch

"[I]n republican government, the legislative authority necessarily predominates [is supreme]," James Madison wrote in *Federalist* No. 51. The Constitution reflects this idea. Article I of the Constitution creates the U.S. Congress as the **legislative branch**, the lawmaking arm of the federal government. Congress's functions are described in greater detail in the Constitution than the functions of the other branches. Besides making laws, Congress controls the money for the national government. This gives Congress great power.

The first Congress went right to work in the spring of 1789. In 519 days, it passed laws that helped set up the entire government. It constructed a financial system, organized new departments of the government, wrote the Bill of Rights, dealt with debts from the Revolutionary War, and chose a permanent location for the nation's capital: Washington, D.C.

The Executive Branch

Once George Washington took office as the nation's first president, Congress had to figure out how he should be addressed. The Senate came up with "His Highness the President of the United States of America and Protector of the Same." Opponents in the House of Representatives laughed at the suggestion of this kingly title. So Congress decided on the more modest title we use today: "Mr. President."

The president is head of the **executive branch** of the government, established by Article II of the Constitution. The executive branch is responsible for executing, or carrying out, the country's laws. At first, the executive branch consisted of just the president and the vice president, as specified in the Constitution. Today the executive branch includes 15 executive departments, including the Department of State and the Department of the Treasury. The executive branch also includes thousands of agencies, divisions, commissions, and offices. The most recent addition to the executive branch was the Department of Homeland Security, created in 2002 to guard against terrorism.

The Judicial Branch

The Constitution described relatively little about the third branch of the government. The **judicial branch**, established in Article III, interprets the meaning of the laws passed by Congress and sets punishments for people who break the law.

The Constitution created the Supreme Court as the head of the judicial branch. It also set the limits of judicial power and created a process for appointing judges. Yet it left to Congress the enormous job of actually setting up the system of "lower" courts, those beneath the Supreme Court.

READING CHECK ▶ **Comparing and Contrasting** Compare the functions of the three branches of government.

Checks and Balances

When creating the three branches of government, the framers often looked to European philosophers for wisdom about human behavior and its effects on government. One such source was a 1748 work, *The Spirit of the Laws*, written by the French philosopher and judge Baron de Montesquieu. In it Montesquieu described how liberty could be threatened if one branch of government became too hungry for power. He argued for a balance of power among the branches of government.

3 Principles of Limited Government

QUICK FACTS

The genius of the U.S. Constitution is that it spreads the powers of government both within the national government and between the federal government and state governments.

1 Federalism

In our system of government, some powers of government belong only to the federal government, while others belong only to the state governments. Still other powers are shared by both levels of government.

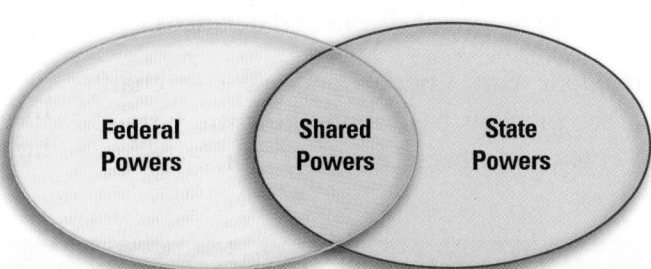

Federal Powers — Shared Powers — State Powers

2 Separation of Powers

The powers of government are divided among the executive, legislative, and judicial branches.

Executive
Enforces law

Legislative
Makes law

Judicial
Interprets law

3 Checks and Balances

Each of the three branches of government has ways to check, or limit, the powers of the other branches.

Legislative
- Can impeach and remove the president
- Can override veto
- Controls spending of money
- Senate can refuse to confirm presidential appointments and ratify treaties

Judicial
- Can declare executive acts unconstitutional
- Judges, appointed for life, are free from executive control

Executive
- Can veto acts of Congress
- Can call special session of Congress
- Can suggest laws and send messages to Congress

Judicial
- Judicial review: Can declare acts of Congress unconstitutional

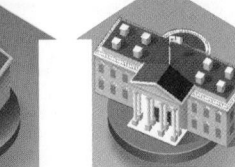
Executive
- Appoints federal judges
- Can grant reprieves and pardons for federal crimes

Legislative
- Can impeach and remove federal judges
- Establishes lower federal courts
- Can refuse to confirm judicial appointments

ANALYSIS SKILL **ANALYZING VISUALS**

1. How does the federal system limit the powers of government?
2. What checks does the executive branch have over the other two branches?

A Balance of Power

The framers provided this balance of power in the U.S. Constitution by giving each government branch powers that limit, or check, the powers of the other two branches. This scheme ensures that no branch of the federal government becomes too powerful. This equal distribution of powers and limits on power is called the system of **checks and balances**.

President Can Check Congress The chart on the previous page shows how the system of checks and balances works. For instance, while Congress has the power to make laws, the president has the power to **veto**, or reject, proposed laws. (The Latin word veto means "I forbid.") With this *veto* power, the president can check the lawmaking power of Congress.

Congress Can Check the President In turn, the Constitution gives Congress a check on the president's veto power. It allows Congress to override a presidential veto—that is, to pass the law despite the veto. Overriding a veto requires a two-thirds vote of both houses of Congress.

PRIMARY SOURCE

POLITICAL CARTOON
Checks and Balances

This cartoon deals with the principle of executive privilege, which asserts that the president has the right to withhold certain information from Congress.

In June 2007 President George W. Bush invoked executive privilege several times to withhold documents after congressional committees had requested them.

Many in Congress were frustrated by the president's actions because they felt that the claim of executive privilege upset the system of checks and balances set up in the Constitution.

ANALYSIS SKILL **ANALYZING POLITICAL CARTOONS**

What does this cartoon suggest about the president's attitude toward invoking executive privilege?

Checks, Balances, and the Judicial Branch

Although the Constitution says relatively little about the judicial branch, President Washington believed that setting up the judicial branch was "essential to the happiness of our country and to the stability of its political system." Congress went to work, passing a law that made the Supreme Court the head of the judicial branch. They set the number of Supreme Court justices at six, including a chief justice. Congress established the lower federal courts and designated their relationship to the state courts. Even when the judicial branch had been created, it was not clear how much power it would have in the checks and balances system. The Supreme Court defined the role of the judicial branch through one major ruling.

The Courts and Judicial Review

In an 1803 case called *Marbury* v. *Madison*, Chief Justice John Marshall established the principle of **judicial review**. According to this principle, it is up to the courts to review the acts of the other branches of government and decide whether the government has acted correctly.

As a result of *Marbury*, the Supreme Court can check the powers of the other branches. For example, it can decide if laws passed by Congress are constitutional and can strike down laws that are unconstitutional. The Supreme Court can also determine if an act of the president or members of the executive branch are constitutional. Later in this book you will learn more about how the branches of the federal government check and balance each other.

The Constitution embodies our American ideals of liberty and justice. No government—federal, state, or local—is supposed to act in violation of the Constitution. Sometimes, however, a legislative body passes a law that may or may not be constitutional. Such a law may be challenged in the judicial system. In some cases, that challenge may go all the way to the U.S. Supreme Court. It is the Supreme Court that enforces the Constitution as the highest law of the land.

READING CHECK ▶ **Evaluating** Why is the system of checks and balances important to government?

go.hrw.com
Online Quiz
KEYWORD: SZ7 HP3

SECTION 2 ASSESSMENT

Reviewing Ideas and Terms

1. a. Define Write a brief definition for the term **separation of powers**.
  b. Recall Why were the framers of the Constitution concerned about concentrating government power in one place?
  c. Describe What is the separation of powers under the U.S. Constitution?

2. a. Define Write a brief definition for the terms **legislative branch**, **executive branch**, and **judicial branch**.
  b. Explain When it comes to the country's laws, how is the legislative branch's responsibility different from the executive branch's responsibility?
  c. Predict What do you think would happen if a president tried to avoid carrying out a law because he or she thought that the law was unconstitutional?

3. a. Define Write a brief definition for the terms **checks and balances, veto,** and **judicial review**.
  b. Explain Does veto power enable the president to stop any law passed by Congress? Why or why not?
  c. Evaluate How important do you think it is that the Supreme Court can review laws passed by Congress and, if necessary, declare the laws unconstitutional? Explain your answer.

Critical Thinking

4. Categorizing Copy the graphic organizer. Use it to list the powers of each branch of the U.S. government.

Executive	Legislative	Judicial

Focus on Writing

5. Identifying Points of View Write a newspaper editorial explaining what might happen if the system of checks and balances were eliminated.

STUDENTS TAKE ACTION

Improving Community Health

In November of 2004, the City Council of Waterloo, Illinois, unanimously passed a resolution that said, in part, "that any home being sold in Waterloo should be tested with a short-term radon canister so that the quantity of radon in the home may be determined."

Community Connection Students from Waterloo Junior High had studied radon gas in their science classes. They learned that radon is the second-leading cause of lung cancer deaths in the United States. As part of the science classes, all eighth grade students were offered a free radon test canister to test for radon gas in their homes. Data collected by the students showed that 28 percent of the homes tested had radon levels above what is considered safe for human health.

Students from Waterloo Junior High School explain the results of their radon study to the city council.

Taking Action Disturbed by these results, students used what they had learned in civics class about local government. They called and met with local officials. Students also invited the local media to publish the results of the residential radon study. Then students presented their data to the city council, which passed the radon testing resolution. The next year, another Project Citizen class worked to get the county board of commissioners to pass a similar resolution at the county level. As a result of the efforts of Project Citizen classes, all new home construction permits in Waterloo, Illinois, are now required to include educational information about installation of passive radon-reduction systems.

go.hrw.com
Project Citizen
KEYWORD: SZ7 CH3

SERVICE LEARNING

1. How did the students at Waterloo Junior High use their knowledge of science to help the local community?
2. Why were good relationships with the city government and local media so important to the success of the Waterloo service-learning project?

An Enduring Document

BEFORE YOU READ

The Main Idea

The Constitution is an enduring document that has met the needs of a changing country for more than 200 years.

Reading Focus

1. How did the framers envision change when writing the Constitution?
2. What are two ways in which the Constitution may be changed?

Key Terms

amendment, *p. 100*
repeal, *p. 100*
cabinet, *p. 101*

TAKING NOTES As you read, use the graphic organizer below to take notes on the U.S. Constitution.

Amending the Constitution	Interpreting the Constitution	Congress and the Constitution

The framers of the Constitution of the United States knew that we the people might need to change the Constitution. Therefore, they included ways for us to amend the document.

The Constitution of the United States

CIVICS IN PRACTICE Our nation has changed greatly since 1787, when the Constitution was written. However, the framers of the Constitution planned a system of government that could adapt to meet changing conditions and changing needs. The U.S. Constitution is truly an enduring document.

Envisioning Change

The authors of the Constitution sat at wooden desks, dipping a quill pen into a bottle of ink to scratch notes on paper made of pressed animal skin. When they finally finished the document, it was copied on wooden printing presses. It took days or weeks for the copies to be delivered, on horseback or by carriage, to the 13 states.

The Constitution has traveled in time for more than two centuries to the legislators of the present. Today's lawmakers ride in cars and airplanes, talk on cellular phones, and get email on portable electronic devices. Their discussions in Congress appear instantly to millions of people worldwide on television and the Internet. Lawmakers wrestle with issues unimaginable to the nation's founders: What steps should the nation take to protect against nuclear terrorism? How should the government spend its *trillions* of dollars?

The framers realized that Americans might someday want or need to change the Constitution. Therefore, they included in the Constitution a process for making changes to it. The framers wrote the document to be adaptable to situations they could never have imagined.

READING CHECK ➤ **Drawing Inferences and Conclusions** What are some changes in modern times that the framers could not have foreseen?

Changing the Constitution

Altering the Constitution is difficult. The framers wanted the Constitution to endure the influence of politics and temporary changes of public opinion. The Constitution can be changed in two ways: formally by amendment and informally by government acts or by custom.

The Amendment Process

An **amendment** is a written change made to the Constitution. Article V of the Constitution outlines the process for making amendments. Proposed amendments must be approved by three-fourths of the states. The process can take a long time, and success is never certain. Lawmakers have succeeded in changing the document only 27 times, a small number considering how much the nation has grown and changed.

An amendment may be proposed in two ways:

- Congress can propose an amendment by a two-thirds vote in both houses.
- The legislatures of two-thirds of the states—34 out of 50—can ask Congress to call a national convention to propose an amendment.

After an amendment has been proposed, it must then be ratified, or approved, by the states. There are two ways an amendment may be ratified. The method of ratification must be described in each proposed amendment.

- The proposed amendment can be sent to the state legislatures for approval. All but one of the amendments to the Constitution were approved this way.
- The proposed amendment can be sent to state conventions for consideration.

After an amendment has been ratified by three-fourths (38) of the states, it becomes part of the written Constitution. If the people do not like the effects of an amendment, another amendment can be passed to **repeal**, or cancel, it. The most famous repeal occurred in 1933, when the Twenty-first Amendment was passed to repeal the Eighteenth Amendment, which had banned the production and sale of alcohol.

The Constitution Endures

QUICK FACTS

The framers of the Constitution recognized that as society changed, there had to be a way to make sure that the Constitution endured as the foundation of democracy. These amendments helped expand voting rights.

If the right to vote is expanded or extended today to include more citizens, to whom do you think the right to vote might be given?

Thirteenth, Fourteenth, and Fifteenth Amendments
Ratified 1865, 1868, and 1870 Passed as a result of the Civil War and gave African Americans full citizenship in the United States

Are Public School Uniforms Constitutional?

In his 1996 State of the Union address, President Bill Clinton said, "If it means that teenagers will stop killing each other over designer jackets, then our public schools should be able to require their students to wear school uniforms."

After President Clinton's speech, public schools began to require uniforms in order to improve discipline and reduce gang violence. However, critics of the idea, including many teens, argue that students have the right to express themselves through their dress.

The closest Supreme Court case related to this issue is *Tinker* v. *Des Moines*. There the Court ruled that students had the right to wear black armbands to school to protest the Vietnam War. The Court specifically noted that this quiet protest did not interfere with school operations or the rights of others. Today, some people believe that the *Tinker* decision supports a constitutional right to dress how they want to (within limits); others believe it protects expression of beliefs, not clothes.

Do you think students are less able to express themselves if they have to wear uniforms? Why?

long beach unified school district

A Uniform Success

Interpreting the Constitution

The Constitution does not attempt to cover every possible situation. It sets broad guidelines for governing. A number of changes in the federal government have come about simply through custom and tradition. For example, the Constitution does not call for regular meetings of the executive branch. However, President George Washington brought these leaders together regularly to serve as his advisers. They are known as the president's **cabinet**. Since those early days, meetings between the president and the cabinet have been an accepted practice.

Such traditions are seldom written down or passed into law. For this reason, they are sometimes referred to as the "unwritten Constitution."

MR. PRESIDENT WHAT WILL YOU DO FOR WOMAN SUFFRAGE

New York

Nineteenth Amendment
Ratified 1920 Gave women the right to vote

Twenty-Sixth Amendment
Ratified 1971 Changed the voting age from 21 to 18

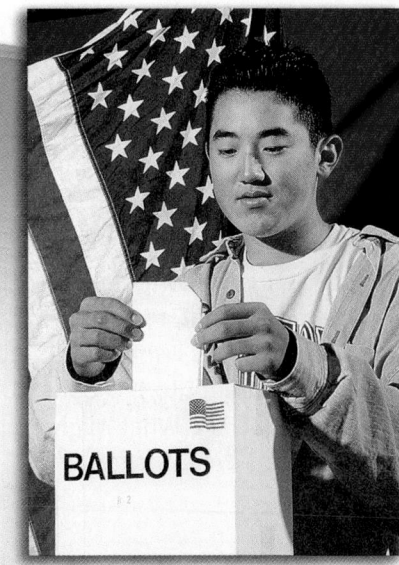

BALLOTS

FOCUS ON
John Marshall
(1755-1835)

John Marshall was a prominent Federalist. President John Adams appointed Marshall as chief justice of the Supreme Court in 1801. As chief justice, Marshall played a key role in cases such as *Marbury* v. *Madison*, which established the principle that the Court was an equal branch of government, and *McCulloch* v. *Maryland*, in which the Court declared that Congress had powers beyond those specifically listed in the Constitution. Marshall's actions and decisions made him one of the most influential Supreme Court justices in U.S. history.

Summarizing How did Marshall increase the power of the Supreme Court?

Congress and the Constitution

Congress often applies the Constitution to a particular issue in society. It does this by interpreting whether some passage, or clause, in the Constitution gives Congress the authority to pass a particular law.

For example, the Constitution says nothing about whether all workers should earn a minimum wage. However, the Constitution does give Congress the power to control trade among the states. Goods made by workers usually travel from one state to another. So Congress decided that the Constitution gives it the power to pass laws affecting working conditions nationwide, including wage rates. It then wrote laws establishing a minimum wage.

The Supreme Court has the power to decide if Congress has interpreted the Constitution correctly. The Court's interpretation is final. If the Supreme Court rules that a law is unconstitutional, the law is dead. If the Court upholds the law, it remains in effect.

If the Supreme Court declares an act of Congress unconstitutional, Congress may rewrite the law. If Congress overcomes the Court's objections, the new law will stand. For example, Congress may not pass bills of attainder (laws that punish a person without a jury trial) or ex post facto laws (which make an act a crime after the act has been committed). Congress also may not suspend the writ of habeas corpus (a court order requiring the government to bring a prisoner to court and explain why he or she is being held).

READING CHECK **Analyzing Information** How can the Constitution be changed?

go.hrw.com
Online Quiz
KEYWORD: SZ7 HP3

SECTION 3 ASSESSMENT

Reviewing Ideas and Terms

1. a. Explain Why is it important that the framers wrote the Constitution to include a process for changing the Constitution?
b. Elaborate How have changes in daily life since 1787 changed the problems that lawmakers deal with today?
2. a. Define Write a brief definition for the terms **amendment**, **repeal**, and **cabinet**.
b. Explain What are the two ways that an amendment to the Constitution may be proposed?
c. Predict What might happen if it were easier to amend the Constitution?

Critical Thinking

3. Categorizing Draw a graphic organizer like this one on your own sheet of paper. Then, use your notes to summarize the two ways in which the Constitution can be amended.

Amending the Constitution

Focus on Writing

4. Supporting a Point of View Imagine that you are a delegate to the Constitutional Convention in Philadelphia in 1787. Write a short speech that will convince the other delegates that it is important to make the Constitution an enduring document.

Reading Flowcharts

Learn

A flowchart is a diagram that presents information in a visual, easy-to-understand way. Its main purpose is to show the various steps that a process follows. Once you learn how to read a flowchart, you will be able to trace the movement of a process through time.

Practice

To read a flowchart:

1 Determine the subject. Read the title of the chart to determine its subject matter. Look at any major headings for an overview of the process shown in the flowchart.

2 Identify the beginning and end points. Study the arrows in the chart, noting their direction. They will tell you how the process begins and how it ends. A process on a flowchart may have more than one beginning and more than one end.

3 Study the middle stages. The middle stages show you movement through time by connecting all the stages in the order in which they take place. They also show you where the process may become stalled.

Apply

Examine the flowchart below. Then answer the following questions.

1. What are the two ways in which an amendment to the Constitution can be proposed?

2. Based on the information in the flowchart, is the following statement true or false? *"A majority of people must favor an amendment before it is added to the Constitution."* Explain your answer.

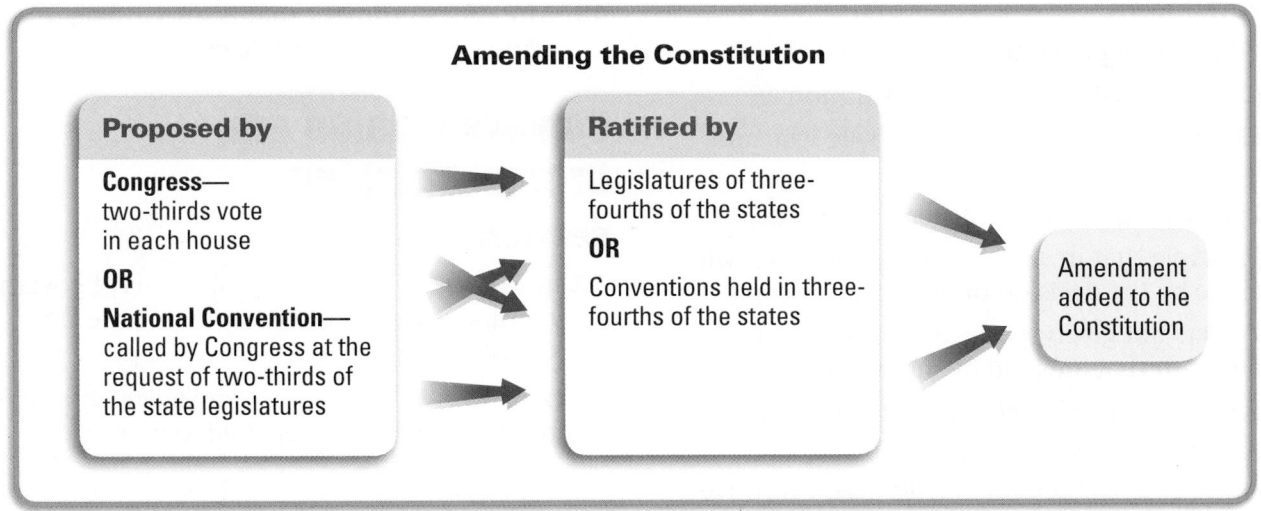

Amending the Constitution

Proposed by

Congress— two-thirds vote in each house

OR

National Convention— called by Congress at the request of two-thirds of the state legislatures

Ratified by

Legislatures of three-fourths of the states

OR

Conventions held in three-fourths of the states

Amendment added to the Constitution

QUICK FACTS

Visual Summary

Use this visual summary to help you review the main ideas of the chapter.

The U.S. Constitution created a government that could be changed to meet the changing needs of Americans. It continues to guarantee basic rights to all Americans.

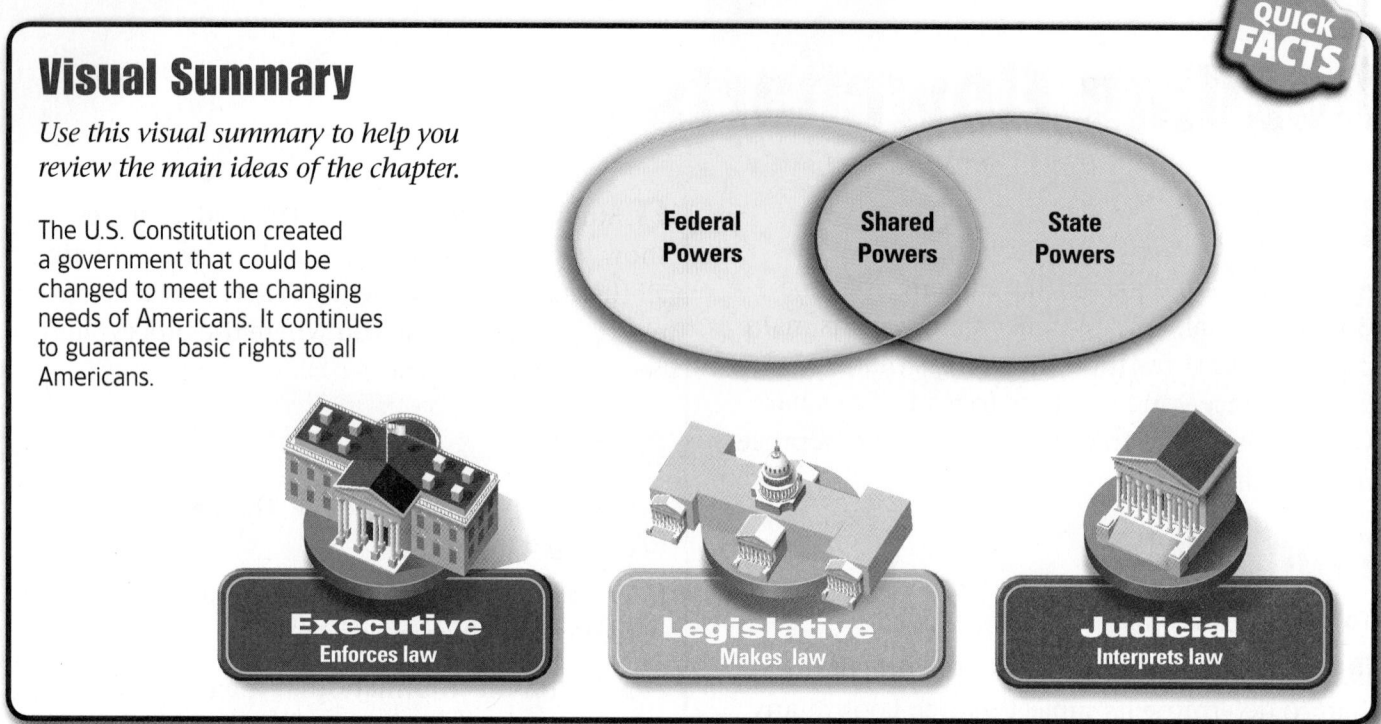

Federal Powers Shared Powers State Powers

Executive
Enforces law

Legislative
Makes law

Judicial
Interprets law

Reviewing Key Terms

Identify the correct term from the chapter that best fits each of the following descriptions.

1. A written change made to the Constitution
2. Government by the consent of the governed
3. Powers specifically given to the federal government
4. Presidential power to reject proposed laws
5. Opening sentence of the Constitution
6. Governmental powers shared by federal and state governments
7. Lawmaking arm of the federal government
8. Principle that in a disagreement everyone will abide by the decision of most of the people
9. Powers not given specifically to the federal government that are held by the states
10. Process by which a change to the Constitution can be canceled
11. Advisers to the president who head executive branch departments

12. Arm of government that interprets the laws
13. The equal distribution of governmental powers and limits on those powers
14. Government with specific restrictions on its powers
15. Structure of government in which power is divided up among different branches
16. Arm of government that is responsible for carrying out the country's laws

Comprehension and Critical Thinking

SECTION 1 *(Pages 86–91)*

17. a. **Identify** What are the six goals of government as stated in the Preamble of the U.S. Constitution?

    b. **Analyze** Why is popular sovereignty one of our nation's most cherished ideals?

Active Citizenship video program

Review the video to answer the closing question: *Why do you think that laws on issues of importance to all citizens often vary from state to state?*

SECTION 2 *(Pages 93–97)*

18. a. Recall What are the three branches of the federal government, and what are the primary responsibilities of each branch?

b. Draw Conclusions Why did the framers of the Constitution create a system of checks and balances for the federal government?

SECTION 3 *(Pages 99–102)*

19. a. Describe What makes the Constitution of the United States an enduring document?

b. Make Inferences Why is the process for amending the Constitution so complicated?

Civics Skills

Reading Flowcharts *Use the Civics Skill taught in this chapter to answer the questions below.*

20. Examine the flow chart on the Civics Skills page in this chapter. Use the information there to answer the following questions:

a. How many different ways are there to amend the Constitution? Draw a flowchart that shows each one.

b. What information, if any, does the flowchart give you about either the length of time an amendment process takes or which process is the easiest? Explain your answer.

21. What part of your daily life could be put into a flowchart? Draw your answer.

Using the Internet

go.hrw.com
KEYWORD: SZ7 CH3

22. Amending the Constitution Though the Constitution is the bedrock of the United States government, it is not exactly set in stone. Enter the activity keyword and research the process of amending the Constitution. Then propose a new amendment and draft a plan for getting your proposed amendment ratified. Your plan should account for all the steps in the amendment process. Include a short paragraph explaining your amendment and the reasons it should be added to the Constitution.

Reading Skills

Finding Main Ideas *Use the Reading Skill taught at the beginning of the chapter to answer the question about the reading selection below.*

(1) The framers provided this balance of power in the U.S. Constitution by giving each government branch powers that limit, or check, the powers of the other two branches. (2) This scheme ensures that no branch of the federal government becomes too powerful. (3) This equal distribution of powers and limits on power is called the system of checks and balances.

23. Which sentence contains the main idea of the paragraph? (1), (2), or (3)

FOCUS ON WRITING

24. Writing Your Editorial You should start your editorial with a strong statement of your opinion about the Constitution. Then write two to three sentences about each of your main points of support—a weakness of the Articles of Confederation and/or a strength of the Constitution. End your editorial with a call to action: Ask the delegates to the Constitutional Convention to ratify the Constitution. Remember that you are trying to convince people to make a very important decision for our country—be persuasive.

CHAPTER 4
RIGHTS AND RESPONSIBILITIES

NATIONAL STANDARDS®
FOR CIVICS AND GOVERNMENT

II. What are the foundations of the American
political system?

A. What is the American idea of constitutional
government?

B. What are the distinctive characteristics of
American society?

D. What values and principles are basic to
American constitutional democracy?

V. What are the roles of the citizen in American
democracy?

B. What are the rights of citizens?

C. What are the responsibilities of citizens?

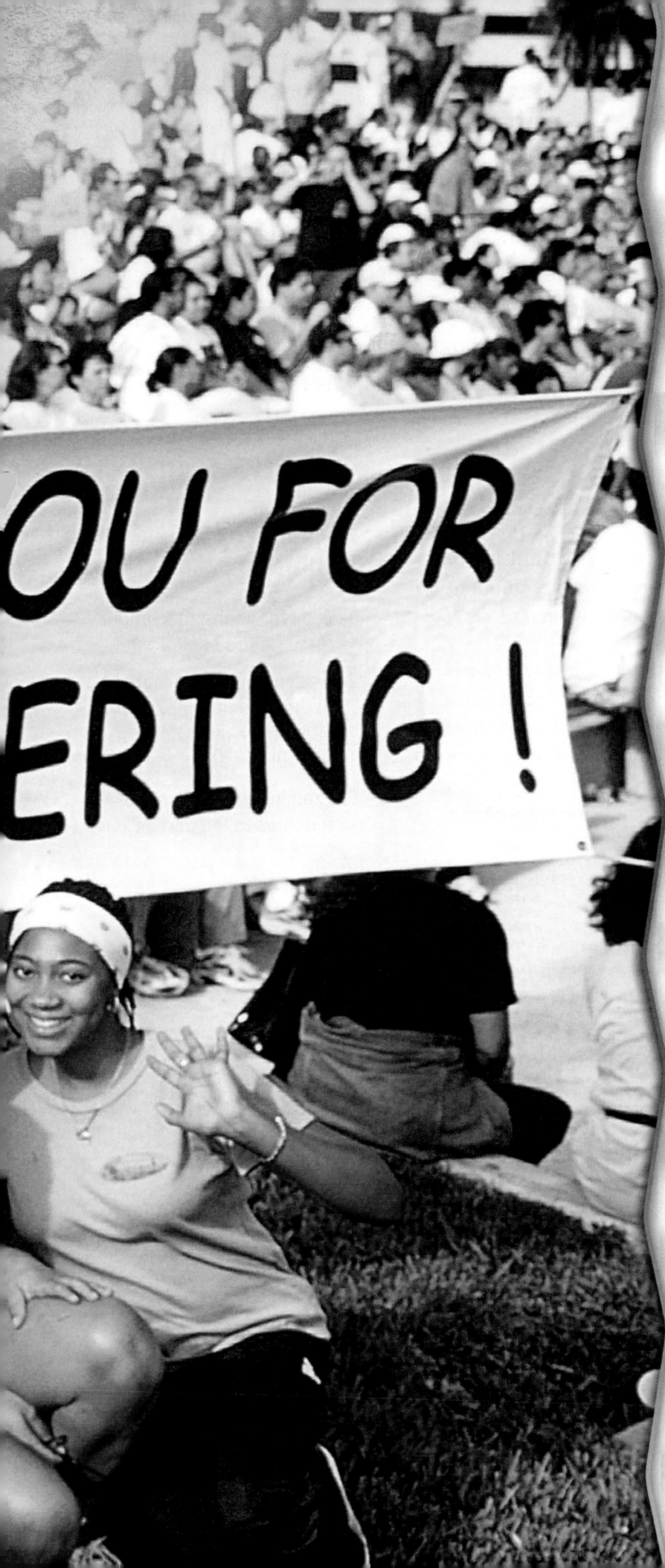

WHY CIVICS Matters

The first 10 amendments to the Constitution—the Bill of Rights— guarantee that you have certain rights. These are precious rights, and one of your responsibilities as a citizen is to make sure that future generations have the same freedoms.

STUDENTS TAKE ACTION

SCHOOL BUS SAFETY Riding a bus to school is not always fun. The experience is worse if you have to wait on a muddy sidewalk or walk on sidewalks that get slippery when they are wet. If these unpleasant and dangerous conditions were in your neighborhood, what steps might you take to correct the problems?

FOCUS ON WRITING

AN INTERVIEW You are a reporter for a city newspaper in 1789. Many people support the ratification of the Constitution, but they want to be sure it includes a Bill of Rights. One of those people is James Madison, and you have been assigned to interview him. As you read this chapter, you will write interview questions for your meeting with Madison.

Reading Skills

In this chapter you will read about the Bill of Rights and how it guarantees important rights for all Americans. You will learn how the Bill of Rights ensures that new rights can be added to the Constitution. You will read about later amendments that expanded the civil rights of all Americans and that along with these rights and freedoms come important duties and responsibilities for citizens. Finally, you will learn about the importance of voting, staying informed, and protecting the rights of all Americans.

Identifying Points of View

FOCUS ON READING To be an informed citizen, you must read and think about other people's opinions and beliefs. To evaluate different opinions, you need to understand people's points of view on a topic.

Point of View A point of view is a person's outlook or attitude. Each person's point of view is shaped by his or her background. Because people's backgrounds are different, their points of view are, too. You can usually determine a person's point of view by the attitude he or she takes toward a topic. Below is an excerpt from Abraham Lincoln's "House Divided" speech of 1858. As you read it, look for clues about Lincoln's point of view on slavery.

Helpful Hints for Identifying Points of View

1. Look for information about the person's background.

2. Ask yourself what factors in the person's background might have influenced his or her opinion about the topic.

3. Examine the opinion closely for clues to the person's point of view.

"'A house divided against itself cannot stand.' I believe this government cannot endure, permanently, half slave and half free. I do not expect the Union to be dissolved; I do not expect the house to fall; but I do expect it will cease to be divided. It will become all one thing, or all the other. Either the opponents of slavery will arrest the further spread of it . . . or its advocates will push it forward till it shall become alike lawful in all the states, old as well as new, North as well as South."

Lincoln's background:
At the time Lincoln gave this speech, he was a candidate for the U.S. Senate seat from Illinois. He was reacting to the Supreme Court's *Dred Scott* decision that said that African Americans could not be citizens and that the federal government could not ban slavery in U.S. territories. Lincoln was personally opposed to slavery.

+

Clues in the opinion
- Says the nation cannot survive being split between slave and free states
- Says that slavery will eventually be legal everywhere or banned everywhere in the United States

Lincoln's Point of View: It isn't possible to compromise on the issue of slavery. Everyone has to choose a side. This means trying to help the practice of slavery expand throughout the nation or else working to get rid of it entirely. Otherwise, disagreements over slavery will split the nation in two.

You Try It!

The following passage is a quote from President John F. Kennedy. Read it and then answer the questions below.

> "The right to vote in a free American election is the most powerful and precious right in the world —and it must not be denied on the grounds of race or color. It is a potent [powerful] key to achieving other rights of citizenship. For American history—both recent and past—clearly reveals that the power of the ballot has enabled those who achieve it to win other achievements as well, gain a full voice in the affairs of their state and nation, and to see their interests represented in the governmental bodies which affect their future. In a free society, those with the power to govern are necessarily responsive to those with the right to vote."
>
> —President John F. Kennedy,
> Special Message on Civil Rights, February 28, 1963

After you have read the passage, answer the following questions.

1. Which of the following statements best describes President Kennedy's point of view?

    a. The only way that people can influence their government is by writing to elected officials.

    b. You are not a citizen if you do not vote.

    c. Voting affects everyone's future.

    d. Government officials are more likely to respond to citizens if they know that citizens can vote them out of office.

2. Based on what you know about the Constitution, what amendment is President Kennedy probably referring to when he says that people of any race or color should not be denied the right to vote?

> **As you read Chapter 4,** think about the points of view that influenced the Bill of Rights.

KEY TERMS
Chapter 4

Section 1
Bill of Rights, *p. 110*
separation of church and state, *p. 112*
self-incrimination, *p. 115*
due process of law, *p. 115*
eminent domain, *p. 115*
bail, *p. 116*

Section 2
civil rights, *p. 118*
suffrage, *p. 119*
poll tax, *p. 122*

Section 3
draft, *p. 125*
rationed, *p. 125*
jury duty, *p. 125*

Academic Vocabulary
Success in school is related to knowing academic vocabulary—the words that are frequently used in school assignments and discussions. In this chapter, you will learn the following academic word:

principles *(p. 119)*

SECTION 1

The Bill of Rights

The Main Idea

The freedoms spelled out in the Bill of Rights—the freedoms of religion, speech, the press, and petition, and the right to a speedy and fair trial—are essential to our democratic system.

Reading Focus

1. Why was the Bill of Rights added to the Constitution?
2. How does the First Amendment protect personal freedoms?
3. What other rights does the Bill of Rights guarantee?

Key Terms

Bill of Rights, *p. 110*
separation of church and state, *p. 112*
self-incrimination, *p. 115*
due process of law, *p. 115*
eminent domain, *p. 115*
bail, *p. 116*

TAKING NOTES As you read, take notes on the freedoms guaranteed by the Bill of Rights. Use a diagram like this one to record your notes.

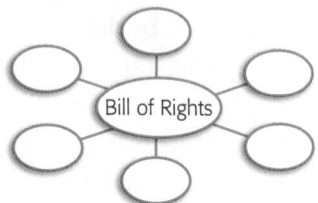

Bill of Rights

CIVICS IN PRACTICE We all know about the Bill of Rights—the first 10 amendments to the Constitution. However, did you know that the Bill of Rights was not in the original Constitution? It was added because people believed that rights like the freedoms of religion, speech, and of the press—which you still enjoy today—were too important to be left out of the Constitution.

Adding the Bill of Rights

Between 1787 and 1790 the 13 original states ratified the new Constitution. Many people, however, believed that the document did not go far enough in protecting individual rights. They wanted their rights spelled out in a bill, or list. The need for a Bill of Rights was expressed by Thomas Jefferson, among others.

"I will now add what I do not like. First the omission of a bill of rights providing clearly ... for freedom of religion, freedom of the press, protection against standing armies ... A bill of rights is what the people are entitled to ...and what no just government should refuse ..."

from Thomas Jefferson's letter to James Madison, December 20, 1787

Treasury Secretary Alexander Hamilton disagreed. He argued that the new nation did not need laws to stop the government from doing things that the Constitution gave it no power to do. Federalists like Hamilton argued that the states already had their own bills of rights. However, some states, including New York, did not have these protections.

Many people feared that some states might oppose the Constitution without a bill of rights. As a result, James Madison, one of the framers of the Constitution, proposed a list of amendments that focused on individual rights. In 1791 the states ratified 10 of these amendments. The **Bill of Rights**—the first 10 amendments to the U.S. Constitution—became a model used around the world to protect human freedoms.

READING CHECK **Analyzing Information** Why did some people oppose a bill of rights?

QUICK FACTS

The First Amendment

Added to the U.S. Constitution in 1791, the Bill of Rights clearly defines the rights and freedoms of Americans. Some of the most fundamental rights of U.S. citizens—freedom of religion, freedom of speech, freedom of the press, and others—are outlined in the First Amendment.

Congress shall make no law respecting an establishment of religion, or prohibiting the free exercise thereof; or abridging the freedom of speech, or of the press; or the right of the people peaceably to assemble, and to petition the Government for a redress of grievances.

Congress OF THE United States

Freedom of Religion

The First Amendment prohibits the government from establishing an official religion or from limiting the freedom of religion.

Freedom of the Press

The First Amendment prevents Congress from limiting the freedom of the press to publish information or ideas.

Freedom of Speech

The First Amendment protects Americans' right to express their ideas and points of view.

MR. PRESIDENT HOW LONG MUST WOMEN WAIT FOR LIBERTY

Freedom to Petition the Government

The First Amendment allows citizens the freedom to petition, or make requests of the government.

Freedom of Assembly

The First Amendment grants Americans the right to peaceably assemble, or hold meetings.

ANALYSIS SKILL ANALYZING VISUALS

Which of the freedoms granted in the First Amendment do you think is most important? Why?

POLITICAL CARTOON
The Bill of Rights

The Bill of Rights is considered one of the most important documents in U.S. history. In this political cartoon, some of the rights and freedoms in the Bill of Rights have been crossed out.

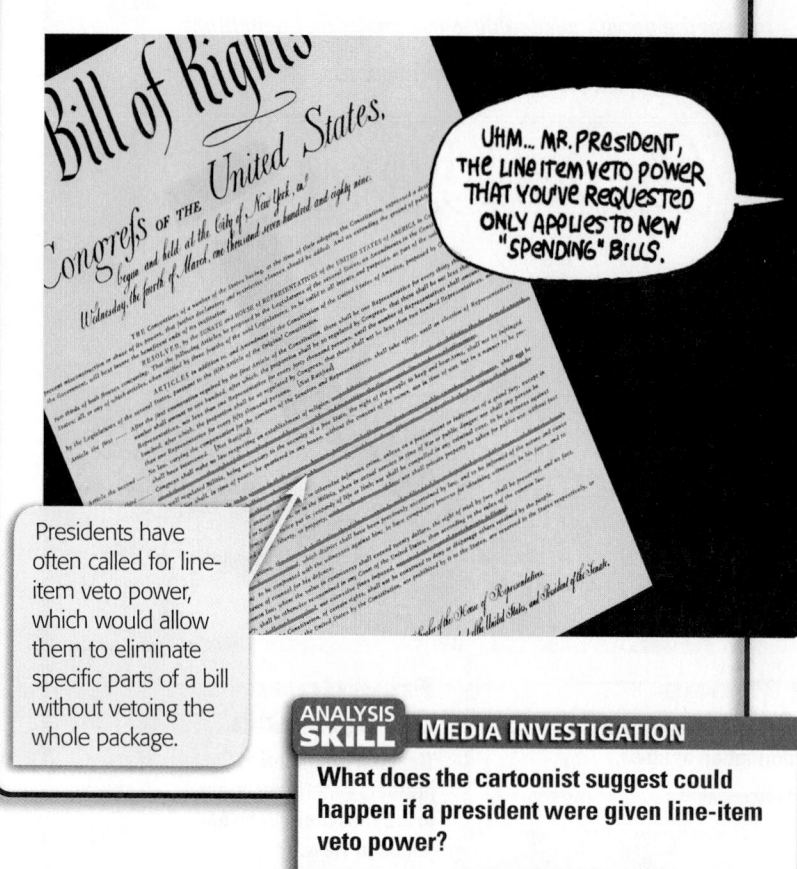

UHM... MR. PRESIDENT, THE LINE ITEM VETO POWER THAT YOU'VE REQUESTED ONLY APPLIES TO NEW "SPENDING" BILLS.

Presidents have often called for line-item veto power, which would allow them to eliminate specific parts of a bill without vetoing the whole package.

ANALYSIS SKILL **MEDIA INVESTIGATION**

What does the cartoonist suggest could happen if a president were given line-item veto power?

First Amendment Protects Personal Freedoms

Of the 10 amendments in the Bill of Rights, most people know the first one best. That's because the First Amendment directly touches our lives every day. It protects some of the most basic freedoms that we enjoy as Americans.

Freedom of Religion

"Congress shall make no law respecting an establishment of religion," the First Amendment begins. This means that Congress cannot establish an official national religion, nor can it favor one religion over another. At the time the Constitution was written, countries had official religions supported by the governments.

Jefferson and Madison held this freedom supreme. Therefore it is no surprise that the freedom of religion comes first in the First Amendment. Americans have the right to practice any religion, or to practice no religion at all.

Over time, the U.S. Supreme Court has interpreted this passage as requiring a **separation of church and state**. In other words, there should be a clear division between government and religion. Upholding this principle, Supreme Court decisions have banned school-sponsored prayers in public schools.

Freedom of Speech

"Congress shall make no law . . . abridging (limiting) the freedom of speech." This passage protects the right to express our ideas and opinions openly, as well as to listen to the speech of others. It means that we may talk freely to friends and neighbors or deliver a public speech. Free speech seems perfectly natural to us, but in some countries, free speech is severely limited.

One reason free speech is so important is that it allows us the freedom to criticize our government and government officials. People who live under a totalitarian government can be punished for criticizing their leaders.

There are limits to free-speech rights, however. You may not use your free speech rights in a way that could cause physical harm to others. For example, you do not have the right to yell "Fire!" in a crowded room just for fun. Yelling "Fire!" could cause a panic and get people hurt.

Courts have often attempted to define the limits to our freedom of speech. For example, the Supreme Court decision *Schenck* v. *United States* established what is known as the "clear and present danger rule." Under this rule, if an act of free speech can be closely linked to an unlawful action, the government has the right to prevent it.

Freedom of the Press

"Congress shall make no law . . . abridging the freedom . . . of the press." In colonial times, newspapers were forbidden to criticize the government or public officials—even if the criticisms were true. Because of this, the freedom of the press, or the right to express ideas in writing, was included in the First Amendment.

The courts have extended freedom of the press to include electronic as well as print media. This means that the press includes books, newspapers, and magazines published both on paper and on the Internet. Radio, television, and even online journals all are forms of protected free press.

The freedom of the press has limitations. Writers may not spread libel—rumors that damage a person's reputation. A person who has been libeled can sue for damages.

Freedom of Assembly

"Congress shall make no law . . . abridging . . . the right of the people peaceably to assemble." Another of the rights guaranteed by the First Amendment is the freedom to hold meetings. Americans have the right to meet to discuss problems, to protest government decisions, or to socialize. Of course, such meetings must be peaceful.

Freedom of Petition

"Congress shall make no law . . . abridging . . . the right of the people . . . to petition the Government for a redress of grievances." That means that you have the right to ask the government to address your concerns.

Freedom of petition gives you the right to contact your representatives and ask them to pass laws you favor or change laws you do not like. The right of petition helps government officials learn what citizens want to have done. It also helps to ensure that we have government "by the people."

READING CHECK **Summarizing** What basic freedoms does the First Amendment guarantee?

MEDIA INVESTIGATION

TABLOID
Freedom of the Press

The freedom of the press means that people may express their ideas—including ideas that may be untrue or unpopular—in writing without worrying that the government will stop or punish them. Tabloid newspapers, a type of newspaper that focuses on sensational news stories, use this freedom to write incredible stories.

In 1992, a newspaper published an amazing story about a boy, half human and half bat, two feet tall and weighing 65 pounds. According to reports, the boy—nicknamed Batboy—had been captured in a cave in West Virginia. Since then, the paper has reported that Batboy has been captured by and has escaped from various tormentors. According to one story, Batboy even fell in love.

Tabloid stories like this one may seem outrageous. However, under the First Amendment the press has the freedom to publish the stories they choose, providing that they do not intentionally spread libel. The freedom of the press is vital to democracy. With this freedom, people can express their opinions to each other and to the government. Without this freedom, we would not be free to express our ideas—no matter how incredible.

Tabloid newspapers like this one attract readers' attention with eye-grabbing headlines and photos.

ANALYSIS SKILL **MEDIA INVESTIGATION**

1. How is this newspaper constructed?
2. When you see the front page of a newspaper with a headline and photo similar to the one above, how do you react?
3. Why are newspapers like this published?

The Second Amendment

In 1639, fearful of attacks by Native Americans, the colony of Virginia passed a law requiring many colonists to carry a firearm or be fined. In the 1700s, as suspicion of the British military increased and the Revolutionary War broke out, colonists no longer needed to be told to bear arms. Without the right to bear arms, colonists like those in the painting at right, would not have been able to defend themselves against British troops.

By the time the Bill of Rights was drafted, Americans were convinced of the need for the militias mentioned in the Second Amendment to protect "the Security of a free state."

Today, the United States has a strong national military and no longer depends on such militias. However, many Americans continue to cherish the Second Amendment's promise of the right to "keep and bear Arms." Since 1934, Congress has more strictly monitored gun ownership, including the type of firearms a person can buy. Around 39 percent of American households own guns.

Why do you think the right to own a gun remains important to many Americans today?

Other Rights Guaranteed by the Bill of Rights

The Bill of Rights does more than grant the freedoms of religion, speech, and the press. The other amendments in the Bill of Rights protect citizens, guarantee rights for the accused, and establish the rights of states and citizens.

Protecting Citizens

The Second and Third Amendments are designed to protect citizens. The Second Amendment deals with state militias and the right to bear arms. The Third Amendment prevents the military from forcing citizens to house soldiers.

Second Amendment This amendment was probably created both to ensure that state militias would continue as an armed means of defense and to ensure that individual citizens had a right to own a firearm. Americans in the 1790s had a different attitude toward the military than many people have today. Big national armies were not trusted.

Although there had been a regular army in the war for independence, much of the fighting had been done by the state militias. These same militias also defended against attacks from Indians. These concerns led to the Second Amendment, which protects Americans' right to keep and bear arms—that is, to own and carry weapons.

Today, the language of the Second Amendment is frequently the source of heated debate. On one side of the debate are citizens who believe the amendment should be read to apply only to well-regulated militias. This would not prevent the government from regulating the possession of handguns. Opposing this view are citizens who believe that the amendment absolutely prevents the government from imposing any restrictions on the ownership of firearms. Both sides have historical support for their position. The meaning of the amendment continues to be debated today.

Third Amendment In colonial days, British soldiers could enter homes and force colonists to quarter them, or to give them housing and food. The framers ended this practice with the Third Amendment, which prohibits the quartering of soldiers without permission.

Rights of the Accused

Amendments four through eight of the Bill of Rights protect citizens from abuses in the criminal justice system. In some countries, the police and the courts can arrest their political enemies. They can conduct trials in which the accused person has few rights. Conviction is certain from the start. To protect against this, amendments four through eight establish codes of conduct for the police and the courts. These amendments are some of our most cherished legal protections.

Fourth Amendment The Fourth Amendment protects citizens from unreasonable searches and seizures. In many cases, a search is considered reasonable only if a judge issues a warrant authorizing it. A search warrant is a legal document that describes the place to be searched and the people or items to be seized. A search warrant can be issued only if there is good reason to believe that evidence of a crime will be found.

Under some circumstances, however, police officers are allowed to conduct searches without a warrant. To do so the officers must have probable cause to believe there is a danger to public safety or that criminal activity is involved. For example, police can search people or their cars for illegal drugs.

Fifth Amendment Before a person can be tried for a serious crime, such as murder, a grand jury must indict, or formally accuse, the individual of the crime. The grand jury decides if there is enough evidence to go to trial. This protects an accused person from hasty government action.

The Fifth Amendment also protects an accused person from **self-incrimination**, or having to testify against oneself. In addition, it protects people from double jeopardy, or being tried twice for the same crime.

Another Fifth Amendment protection states that no person can be denied life, liberty, or property without **due process of law**. This principle is tremendously important. It means that a person cannot be punished for a crime until the law has been fairly applied to his or her case. In other words, our government must act within the law.

The last clause of the Fifth Amendment establishes another basic protection. It reads, "nor shall private property be taken for public use, without just compensation." That is, the government cannot take private property without giving the owner fair payment for it.

This part of the Fifth Amendment protects a person's right to own private property, one of the principles upon which our economic system is based. However, it does give the government the right of **eminent domain**, the power to take private property for public use. Imagine that the government needs land to build a highway or a school. The right of eminent domain allows government officials to force property owners to sell their land to the government at what is determined to be a fair price.

Sixth and Seventh Amendments Do you watch crime shows on television? If so, you may have heard about the Sixth Amendment. It provides that a person accused of a crime has the right to a prompt and public trial decided by a jury. People accused of a crime must be informed of the charges against them. They have the right to hear and question all witnesses against them, and to have their own witnesses testify as well. They also have the right to an attorney. The Supreme Court has interpreted the Sixth Amendment to mean that if an accused person cannot afford a lawyer, the government will provide one for free.

The Seventh Amendment is less well known. It provides for a trial by jury in certain kinds of cases involving money or property.

Eighth Amendment To ensure that people accused of crimes appear for trial, judges can order them to pay bail. **Bail** is money or property that the accused gives the court to hold. Upon paying bail, the person is released from jail. The only way to get the money back is to show up for trial. The Eighth Amendment states that the courts cannot set excessive bail.

The Eighth Amendment also forbids cruel and unusual punishment. Punishments such as branding or whipping were once used in the United States. However, they are now considered cruel and unusual. Today the debate is whether the death penalty should be considered cruel and unusual.

Rights of States and Citizens

The authors of the Bill of Rights did not want to imply that citizens had *only* the rights set out in the Constitution and the first eight amendments. As a result, they wrote two amendments to ensure that Americans would enjoy other rights and freedoms not mentioned in the Bill of Rights.

Ninth Amendment This amendment implies that Americans enjoy basic rights not listed in the Constitution. These rights are open to interpretation, for they are not specifically defined.

The Supreme Court has sometimes used the Ninth Amendment to support people's claims to specific rights. These rights have included the right to political activity and the right to privacy.

Tenth Amendment The Tenth Amendment is a final guarantee of citizens' rights. It deals with powers not specifically given to the federal government by the Constitution nor forbidden to the states by the Constitution.

These powers belong either to the states or to the people. The Tenth Amendment thus gives states the power to act independently of the federal government to protect citizens' rights.

READING CHECK **Evaluating** Which of the rights of the accused is most important? Why?

---

go.hrw.com
Online Quiz
KEYWORD: SZ7 HP4

SECTION 1 ASSESSMENT

Reviewing Ideas and Terms

1. a. Define What is the **Bill of Rights**?
b. Explain Why did Americans want a bill of rights added to the Constitution?
c. Predict How might American citizens respond if the Bill of Rights were suspended? Explain your reasoning.
2. a. Define Write a brief definition for the term **separation of church and state**.
b. Analyze Why is freedom of speech so important to a democratic society?
c. Evaluate Which First Amendment freedom do you think is most important? Explain your reasoning.
3. a. Define Write a brief definition for the terms **self-incrimination, due process of law, eminent domain,** and **bail**.

b. Summarize What rights are protected by the Fifth Amendment?
c. Elaborate Should state laws offer stronger protection of individual rights than the Bill of Rights? Why or why not?

Critical Thinking

4. Summarizing
Use your notes and a web diagram like this one to describe the freedoms guaranteed by the First Amendment.

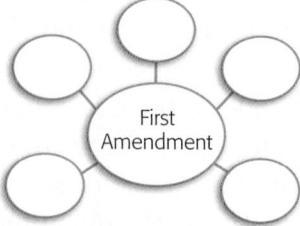

First Amendment

Focus on Writing

5. Supporting a Point of View Why did Americans feel the need to add the Ninth and Tenth Amendments? Write a short paragraph in support of these amendments.

Making an Oral Presentation

Learn

An oral presentation can be more than just a report or a talk you give to your class. Political speeches, graduation talks, class lectures, and business proposals are all forms of oral presentations. Even a job interview can be treated as an oral presentation. After all, you are using words to convince someone to hire you.

Creating and giving a good oral presentation—both inside and outside of school—are important skills. Through oral presentations, you are able to reach other people and maybe even change their minds about important issues. Follow the steps below to prepare and deliver an effective oral presentation.

Practice

❶ **Create a strong opener.** Give your audience a reason to pay attention to you. A thought-provoking beginning helps grab the audience's attention and sets the tone for the rest of your presentation.

❷ **Structure your presentation.** Too much information loses an audience. Focus on a few main points and support them with clear examples and visual aids.

❸ **Practice your presentation.** The best presentations do not sound memorized or rehearsed. To achieve a natural feel, practice ahead of time. During the presentation, use note cards, outlines, or brief notes to remember key points.

❹ **Be prepared for questions.** A good presentation makes an audience think. People may want to know more about what you have told them. Be prepared by thinking of likely questions and developing answers ahead of time.

Apply

1. You have been asked to give a presentation about the importance of the Bill of Rights. Write a strong opener for your presentation.

2. Look at the photograph below. Is the student pictured using good oral presentation techniques? Explain why or why not.

3. What visual aid might you use for an oral presentation about the different rights and freedoms guaranteed by the Bill of Rights?

Guaranteeing Other Rights

BEFORE YOU READ

The Main Idea

Other amendments to the Constitution expanded the civil rights of Americans.

Reading Focus

1. How did the Thirteenth and Fourteenth Amendments extend civil rights?
2. Which amendments extended Americans' voting rights?

Key Terms

civil rights, *p. 118*
suffrage, *p. 119*
poll tax, *p. 122*

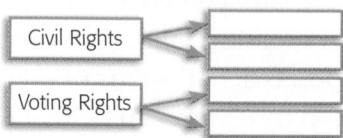 **TAKING NOTES** As you read, take notes on the amendments that extended civil rights and voting rights to Americans. Use a diagram like this one to organize your notes.

Civil Rights

Voting Rights

This Reconstruction-era painting shows African Americans voting after the passage of the Fifteenth Amendment.

CIVICS IN PRACTICE

The right to vote is one of the greatest privileges you have as a U.S. citizen. However, when the United States held its first presidential election in 1789, the only Americans who could vote were white, male property-owning citizens. As the nation grew, people's ideas about fairness changed. Over time, the Constitution has been changed to extend the right to vote to almost everyone 18 years old and older. The strength of the Constitution is that it can be changed when society's attitudes change.

Amendments Extend Civil Rights

Americans have certain rights simply by being members of society. Rights guaranteed to all U.S. citizens are called **civil rights**. The U.S. Constitution, particularly the Bill of Rights, is the foundation for civil rights in this country.

In the first decades of the country's history, the job of guarding people's civil rights was left largely to the individual states. It took the Civil War to trigger the addition of a series of new amendments to the Constitution that would extend civil rights in the United States.

HISTORIC DOCUMENT
The Fifth and the Fourteenth Amendments

In 1833 the Supreme Court ruled that the Bill of Rights applied to the federal government but not to state governments. As a result, many states denied citizenship and basic rights to African Americans. Following the Civil War, the Fourteenth Amendment was ratified, defining citizenship and preventing states from interfering in the rights of U.S. citizens.

> The Fifth Amendment calls for due process for all citizens.

"No person shall be . . . deprived of life, liberty, or property, without due process of law."

"All persons born or naturalized in the United States, and subject to the jurisdiction thereof, are citizens of the United States and of the State wherein they reside. No State shall make or enforce any law which shall abridge the privileges or immunities of citizens of the United States; nor shall any State deprive any person of life, liberty, or property, without due process of law . . ."

> The Fourteenth Amendment prevents states from denying basic civil rights granted in the Bill of Rights.

ANALYSIS SKILL **ANALYZING HISTORICAL DOCUMENTS**

How did the Fourteenth Amendment extend civil rights to African Americans?

Thirteenth Amendment

In 1863 President Abraham Lincoln issued the Emancipation Proclamation. The order banned slavery in the Confederate states. Yet, while it marked a great step in American history, the Emancipation Proclamation did not free all the slaves. For example, in the state of Delaware slavery remained legal because Delaware had not joined the Confederacy. The Thirteenth Amendment, ratified in 1865, outlawed slavery in all states and in all lands governed by the United States.

Fourteenth Amendment

Another key amendment is the Fourteenth Amendment, ratified in 1868. First, it granted full citizenship to African Americans. Second, it declared that no state could take away a citizen's "life, liberty, or property, without due process of law." That clause echoes the Fifth Amendment in the Bill of Rights, which prohibits such actions by the federal government. Finally, the Fourteenth Amendment guarantees every citizen within a state equal protection under the laws.

READING CHECK **Summarizing** Why did Congress pass the Thirteenth and Fourteenth Amendments?

Amendments Extend Voting Rights

Voting is one of the most basic **principles** of citizenship. However, in the British colonies, only free, white men who owned property could vote. Some states' constitutions expanded the right to vote to include any white man who paid taxes. However, in every state, the right to hold public office was limited. Only landowners could hold office.

Originally, the Constitution mentioned nothing about voting rights. As a result, many state and local laws prevented women, African Americans, poor people, and other groups from voting. Between 1870 and 1971, a series of six constitutional amendments extended **suffrage**, or the right to vote, to all U.S. citizens.

ACADEMIC VOCABULARY

principles: a basic belief, rule, or law

FOCUS ON
Hiram Revels
(1822–1901)

In 1870 Hiram Revels became the first African American member of the U.S. Congress. Revels was born in 1822 in Fayetteville, North Carolina. His heritage was a mixture of African and Croatan Indian. When his brother died, Revels became manager of the family barbershop.

Eventually, Revels left home to pursue an education. He became a minister in the African Methodist Episcopal Church. He preached in many states, settling in Baltimore, Maryland, where he became the principal of a school for African Americans. When the Civil War began in 1861, Revels supported the Union by organizing regiments of troops from Maryland and Missouri. He became a chaplain and the provost marshal of Vicksburg, a strategically important town in Mississippi.

After the war, Revels settled in Mississippi, where he continued to preach and earn the respect of local citizens, who eventually elected him to the state senate. In 1860 he filled the U.S. Senate seat vacated by Jefferson Davis, who had left a decade earlier to become president of the Confederacy. Following his term in office, Revels returned to public work in Mississippi.

Draw Conclusions How did the life of Hiram Revels reflect the changes brought by civil rights laws?

Fifteenth Amendment

The Fifteenth Amendment, ratified in 1870, stated that no one could be denied suffrage because of race or color. It was a step in the right direction. However, women still could not vote, so the amendment applied only to African American men.

Despite the Fifteenth Amendment, many former Confederate states passed laws to keep African Americans from voting. Some people who dared to challenge these laws suffered violence. It was not until the 1960s, after decades of divisive battles, that the U.S. Congress finally passed civil rights laws to guarantee voting rights for African Americans.

Seventeenth Amendment

Under Article I, Section 3 of the Constitution, citizens of each state did not elect their senators. Instead, each state's legislature elected that state's senators. This was the case until 1913 when the country adopted the Seventeenth Amendment, which called for the direct election of senators. Eligible voters of each state could now choose their senators directly. This amendment strengthened the principle of direct representation by making senators answerable to the voters and not to other politicians.

Nineteenth Amendment

Less than a century ago, many Americans, both men and women, believed that letting women vote would be dangerous. Some people argued that women were not wise enough to choose a candidate or smart enough to understand the issues. It took a long, bitter battle to challenge these opinions. Courageous women such as Susan B. Anthony, Carrie Chapman Catt, Lucretia Mott, and Elizabeth Cady Stanton led the women's suffrage movement that began in the mid-1800s.

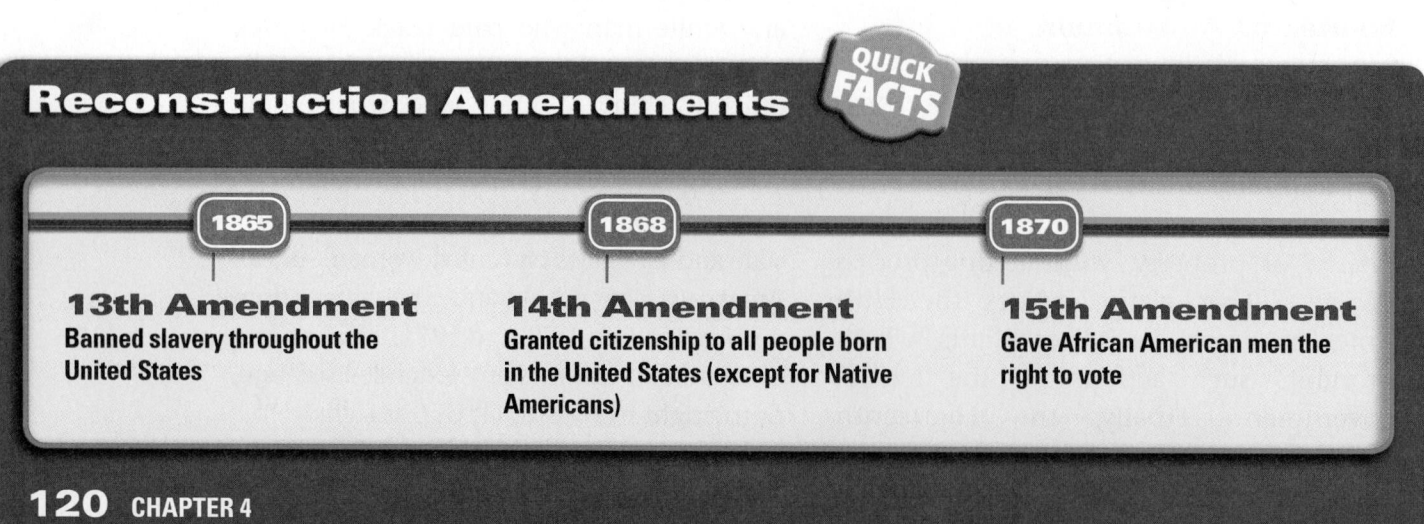

Reconstruction Amendments

QUICK FACTS

1865

13th Amendment
Banned slavery throughout the United States

1868

14th Amendment
Granted citizenship to all people born in the United States (except for Native Americans)

1870

15th Amendment
Gave African American men the right to vote

Expanding the Right to Vote

Over the years, six constitutional amendments have expanded voting rights to more Americans. African Americans, women, and young citizens have all earned the right to vote.

Men

Over time, states allowed men to vote regardless of property ownership. The Twenty-fourth Amendment outlawed poll taxes as a requirement for voting.

Young Americans

The Twenty-sixth Amendment granted citizens 18 years old and older the right to vote in all federal, state, and local elections.

African Americans

The Fifteenth Amendment provides voting rights for African Americans. It states that the right to vote cannot be denied based on race or color.

Women

Women received the right to vote with the ratification of the Nineteenth Amendment.

ANALYSIS SKILL **ANALYZING VISUALS**

Do you think voting rights might be expanded in the future? Why or why not?

Wyoming became the first state to give women the right to vote when it entered the Union in 1890. Gradually, other states passed women's suffrage laws. The battle for a national suffrage law finally succeeded in 1920 with the ratification of the Nineteenth Amendment, which gave all women the right to vote.

Twenty-third Amendment

Ratified in 1961, the Twenty-third Amendment gave citizens living in the District of Columbia—the district of the nation's capital—the right to vote for president and vice president. Residents there had not been able to vote in national elections since the late 1700s.

Twenty-fourth Amendment

Some states tried to keep some African Americans from voting by requiring citizens to pay a poll tax. A **poll tax** is a tax a person had to pay to register to vote. Because some Americans could not afford to pay the tax, they could not vote. In 1964 the Twenty-fourth Amendment banned the use of poll taxes as requirements for voting in national elections. In 1966 the Supreme Court also outlawed poll taxes in state elections.

Twenty-sixth Amendment

Many young men from the age of 18 fought in the Vietnam War. Many people at the time believed that if 18-year-olds are old enough to go to war, they are old enough to vote. As a result, the Twenty-sixth Amendment, ratified in 1971, lowered the voting age in all elections to 18.

As a result of the six amendments you have just read about, no one can be denied the right to vote because of their gender, the color of their skin, or their religion. No one has to own land or pay money in order to vote. Voting is one of our most important rights. Every citizen should exercise that right when he or she has the chance.

READING CHECK **Analyzing Information** How has the right to vote expanded over time?

SECTION 2 ASSESSMENT

Reviewing Ideas and Terms

1. a. Define Write a brief definition for the term **civil rights**.

b. Explain What was the basic purpose of the Thirteenth and Fourteenth Amendments?

c. Elaborate If you were asked to write an amendment protecting or guaranteeing a civil right today, what right would your amendment cover? Write your amendment in four or five sentences.

2. a. Define Write a brief definition for the terms **suffrage** and **poll tax**.

b. Sequencing Beginning with the ratification of the Constitution, list in order the groups of people to whom the right to vote has been given.

c. Evaluate Do you think that the right to vote should be extended to people ages 14 to 16? Why or why not?

Critical Thinking

3. Categorizing Copy the chart, then use your notes to fill in the information about amendments that have extended Americans' right to vote.

Extending Voting Rights		
Amendment	Year Ratified	Group Benefiting from Amendment
	1870	
Nineteenth	1920	
Twenty-third		
	1971	

Focus on Writing

4. Identifying Points of View Write a brief narrative from the perspective of a person who has just received the right to vote. Make sure that your narrative explains the importance of the right.

STUDENTS TAKE ACTION

Improving Safety at School

A Project Citizen class in Brownsville, Texas, had a simple idea to improve the area where their school buses loaded and unloaded. The area was so muddy that students often had to walk in the street. In the end, students' efforts made the area safer for everyone, especially students who were mobility impaired.

Community Connection The students in Martin Leal's class realized that many safety problems needed solving. For example, the school bus area had narrow, slippery sidewalks and no ramps. Students found that this was a violation of a federal law called the Americans with Disabilities Act (ADA). Additionally, a city law said that sidewalks should be slip-resistant.

Students with disabilities were not the only ones affected. The bus area was on a busy street where cars often drove too fast, endangering pedestrians. The project soon took the name "Watch Out for that Car!"

Taking Action Students interviewed classmates about problems with the bus area and created posters illustrating those problems. With help from the police, they also tracked the speed of cars in the area. In 30 minutes, they found 12 cars speeding. Students presented their concerns to the mayor, the city public works director, and the city commission of Brownsville.

City leaders quickly responded to the team's findings. Speed bumps now keep traffic slow, wide sidewalks and curbs follow ADA rules, and the bus area is located away from traffic. "Kids can help their community and make it safe," said Rogelio Garduza, one of the students involved in the project.

go.hrw.com
Project Citizen
KEYWORD: SZ7 CH4

SERVICE LEARNING

1. Why was it important for students to involve the police and local government in this project?
2. Are there any areas in or around your school or neighborhood that are safety concerns? What could be done about them?

Citizens' Duties and Responsibilities

BEFORE YOU READ

The Main Idea

Along with the rights and freedoms of U.S. citizenship come important duties and responsibilities.

Reading Focus

1. What are the duties of citizenship?
2. What are the responsibilities of citizenship?

Key Terms

draft, *p. 125*
rationed, *p. 125*
jury duty, *p. 125*

TAKING NOTES As you read, take notes on the duties and responsibilities of U.S. citizens. Use a diagram like this one to record your notes.

Duties	Responsibilities

These citizens are being sworn in to serve as jurors.

CIVICS IN PRACTICE You have probably heard the saying, "There's no free lunch." That just means that you cannot get something for nothing. In almost any kind of relationship, there is some give and take. When this country was founded, citizens gave up some of their individual powers to the government. In return, the government agreed to protect the rights of citizens.

But the government is you. You must play your part, too. In order to ensure that your rights and freedoms are protected, you have duties and responsibilities to the country. You must be an informed, active, and involved citizen.

Duties of Citizenship

In return for having the privileges of a citizen, there are a few duties that a citizen must do. These duties are crucial to making our democratic government work.

Obeying the Law

Of course, we must all obey the laws of our land. What would happen if people didn't? Our society would quickly collapse. To obey the laws, you have to know what the laws are. For example, if a police officer stops you for speeding, it probably will not help to claim that you did not know the speed limit. Why? It is your duty to find out what the speed limit is and to obey it.

Attending School

You have to go to school, at least until age 16. The United States highly values education. That is why we have free, public schools.

A democracy cannot function without educated citizens. People need good thinking skills so they can wisely choose their leaders. They must be able to read about and understand issues that affect us. Education also gives citizens the skills they need to join the workforce and help the economy grow.

Paying Taxes

If you work, you probably have to pay taxes. When you buy things, you probably have to pay taxes. Almost nobody escapes them. We might not love paying taxes, but we enjoy the services that our tax money buys. Taxes pay for police and fire protection and countless other services. When you drive down a paved street, go to school, or turn on an electric light, you are seeing the results of taxes you pay. Tax money also pays the huge costs of national security and defense.

Serving in the Armed Forces

Whenever America has been threatened, its citizens have come together to defend it. In the American Revolution, volunteers formed militias, or armies, to fight the British. Volunteers have fought in every war in U.S. history.

When the country has needed huge numbers of soldiers, it sometimes has had to establish a **draft**. Draft laws require men of certain ages and qualifications to serve in the military. Such laws have generally been put into effect during times of war.

The United States has not had a draft since 1973, during the Vietnam War. Since then, the armed forces have used only volunteers

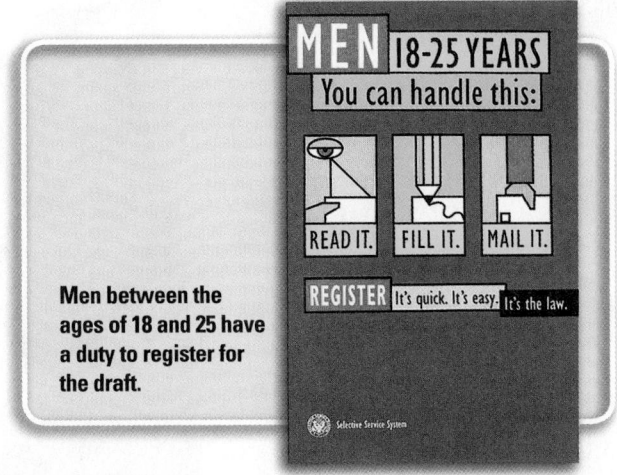

Men between the ages of 18 and 25 have a duty to register for the draft.

to fight wars. However, 18-year-old men must still register to serve in the military if they meet the qualifications for service. The registration process allows the government to keep track of the names and addresses of all men of draft age. Registration ensures that if a war or other crisis requires that the country quickly expand its armed forces, a draft could be launched again.

Although only some men must serve in the armed forces, other citizens have been called on to help protect the country. During World War II, Americans at home had to give up or cut back their use of various supplies needed for the troops overseas. Butter, sugar, beef, coffee, gasoline, and cloth were **rationed**, or limited by law to a certain amount per household.

Appearing in Court

Citizens must report to serve as members of a jury, if they are called to do so. This responsibility is called **jury duty**. Jury duty often involves sacrifice. Many citizens must take time off work to serve on a jury, and they are paid very small sums for their time. Why do we ask people to make this sacrifice? The Constitution guarantees citizens the right to a trial by jury of their peers—that is, their fellow citizens. Citizens must also testify in court if called as witnesses. For our system of justice to function, citizens must fulfill their duty to serve on juries and appear as witnesses.

READING CHECK **Summarizing** Describe five duties of American citizenship.

Being a Good Citizen
Part of being a good citizen means helping your community. These volunteers are helping to build homes in their community.

What are some ways you could help your community?

Responsibilities of Citizenship

The duties of citizenship are the things we *must* do. There are other things we *should* do as citizens. These tasks are not required by law, yet most Americans accept them as their responsibility. A few of them are listed below.

Voting

American editor and drama critic George Jean Nathan once said, "Bad officials are elected by good citizens who do not vote." If you do not vote, you leave the choice up to others—and you might not like the candidate they choose. Another way of putting this is the familiar phrase, "If you don't vote, don't complain about the results."

Many people throughout our history gave their lives so that all citizens could vote. That makes voting not only an honor, but also a responsibility. Our government is based on the consent, or the approval, of the governed. Therefore, we must let our legislators know when we approve or disapprove of their actions. We do that by voting for people whose views we support and who we believe to be good, honest candidates. The first step in voting is to know what you are voting on.

Being Informed

To cast your vote wisely, you must be well informed about candidates, current events, and key issues. That involves taking an interest in the programs and activities of the government. You also have a responsibility to tell your representatives what you think about topics of public concern.

Taking Part in Government

Some people watch a basketball game. Other people play the game. Being informed is just the start of participating in government. We also need people who will join political parties and help shape their positions on issues. We need citizens who will lead, who will educate others, and who will influence public opinion.

We especially need people willing to run for political office and serve wisely if elected. The quality of any democratic government depends on the quality of the people who serve in it.

Helping Your Community

One of the most important ways to be a responsible citizen is to take pride in your community. In addition, you should make sure that your community can take pride in you and your actions.

Have you ever volunteered to help your community? There are so many ways to help, from giving your time at the public library to participating in a walk for hunger. Citizens should volunteer to improve their communities. The government cannot be aware of every small problem, much less fix them all. Yet solving small problems is something volunteers can do in many ways. Think of how small acts of kindness—such as planting a tree, cheering up a sick person, or caring for a stray animal—make community life better.

Volunteering, just like voting, is a serious responsibility. It can also be a lot of fun. Almost everyone can find a way to help out in the community.

Respecting and Protecting Others' Rights

The lasting success and the strength of the United States depends on the protection of the rights of its citizens. You can play an important role in protecting these priceless rights. The first step is knowing your own rights as an American citizen. Then remember that the people around you share those same rights. By knowing what rights all people share, you can be sure to respect those rights. For example, it is essential that community members respect others' property. You should also know when people's rights are being violated. You have a responsibility to help protect the rights of others, just as you would want them to defend your rights.

All Americans must help defend human rights. Only then can the country truly have, in Abraham Lincoln's words, a "government of the people, by the people, and for the people." As one of the people, you have the responsibility to help make sure that our society works for everyone.

READING CHECK ▶ **Making Generalizations** How can individual citizens contribute to society?

SECTION 3 ASSESSMENT

Reviewing Ideas and Terms

1. a. Define Write a brief definition for the terms **draft**, **rationed**, and **jury duty**.

b. Explain Why do citizens owe certain duties to their country?

c. Predict What do you think would happen if only a very small group of people performed their civic duties? Explain your answer.

2. a. Recall What are four responsibilities that each citizen has to the country?

b. Analyze Why is voting often considered the most important responsibility a citizen has?

c. Elaborate What is one problem in your community that you think students might help solve? Write a short plan of action.

Critical Thinking

3. Summarizing Copy the graphic organizer. Use it and your notes to list the duties of citizenship.

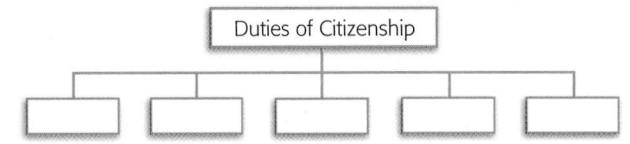

Duties of Citizenship

Focus on Writing

4. Categorizing Write a short paragraph identifying several actions you could take on a daily basis to help your community.

CHAPTER 4 REVIEW

Visual Summary

Use this visual summary to help you review the main ideas of the chapter.

The Constitution's Bill of Rights guarantees the rights and freedoms of all Americans. It is the responsibility of all Americans to protect those rights.

Review Key Terms

For each term below, write a sentence explaining its significance to citizens' rights and responsibilities.

1. Bill of Rights
2. separation of church and state
3. self-incrimination
4. due process of law
5. eminent domain
6. bail
7. civil rights
8. suffrage
9. poll tax
10. draft
11. rationed
12. jury duty

Comprehension and Critical Thinking

SECTION 1 *(Pages 110–116)*

13. **a. Recall** Why was the Bill of Rights added to the U.S. Constitution, and why was the Ninth Amendment included in the Bill of Rights?

    b. Analyze Which freedom in the Bill of Rights is most important? Why?

    c. Identify Cause and Effect Why did Americans want to ensure that accused persons had the right to trial by jury? What might happen to our system of justice if citizens refused to serve on juries?

SECTION 2 *(Pages 118–122)*

14. **a. Describe** How did the Thirteenth and Fourteenth Amendments extend the civil rights of Americans?

Active Citizenship video program
Review the video to answer the closing question:
*Why do you think students do not always have
control over their own privacy at school?*

b. Analyze How have voting rights been expanded through constitutional amendments?

c. Evaluate Would you support the Twenty-sixth Amendment if it were being voted on today? Why or why not?

SECTION 3 *(Pages 124–127)*

15. a. Recall What are the duties and responsibilities of citizenship?

b. Describe How might the country be affected if citizens failed to perform their duties and responsibilities?

c. Elaborate What are some ways you can help in your community?

Using the Internet

go.hrw.com
KEYWORD: SZ7 HP4

16. Understanding Citizenship U.S. citizenship is not all about rights and freedoms. It is also about duty and responsibility. Enter the activity keyword to research the rights and responsibilities of citizenship. Then choose one of the responsibilities outlined in the chapter and create an action plan to increase community awareness of this responsibility. Your plan should outline the responsibility on which you will focus and how you will raise awareness of it.

Civics Skills

Making An Oral Presentation *Use the steps below about making oral presentations to help you answer the following questions.*

1 Create a strong opener.

2 Structure your presentation.

3 Practice your presentation.

4 Be prepared for questions.

17. Imagine that you are preparing an oral presentation on the responsibilities and duties of American citizens. Write an opener that will capture your audience's attention.

18. What kind of visual aid could you use to enhance your presentation?

19. What types of questions might you expect to be asked after your presentation?

Reading Skills

Identifying Points of View *Read the selection below, then answer the question that follows.*

> *"*I do conceive that the constitution may be amended; that is to say, if all power is subject to abuse, that then it is possible the abuse of the powers of the general government may be guarded against in a more secure manner than is now done, while no one advantage, arising from the exercise of that power, shall be damaged or endangered by it. We have in this way something to gain, and, if we proceed with caution, nothing to lose; and in this case it is necessary to proceed with caution; for while we feel all these inducements to go into a revisal of the constitution, we must feel for the constitution itself, and make that revisal a moderate one.*"*

James Madison Proposes the Bill of Rights to the House of Representatives, June 8, 1789

20. What was Madison's point of view about the Bill of Rights?

a. The Bill of Rights was unnecessary, and he opposed it.

b. There was no good reason to adopt a Bill of Rights, but we should do it anyway.

c. The Constitution is flawed, and a Bill of Rights is absolutely necessary to protect our rights.

d. Power can be abused, so we should adopt some moderate changes to protect against that abuse.

FOCUS ON WRITING

21. Writing Your Interview Questions Review the notes you have taken about the Bill of Rights. Then, based on your notes, begin writing questions for your interview with James Madison. What will the readers of your newspaper want to learn more about? Write at least 10 interview questions that your readers will want to have answered.

FOUNDATIONS *of* DEMOCRACY

School Records and Your Rights

You probably hear a lot about the things you are not allowed to do at school. You can't skip classes, break the dress code, or prevent school officials from searching your locker. When it comes to your school records, however, you do have certain rights. A law called the Family Educational Rights and Privacy Act of 1974 (FERPA) protects your right to see your records, and, if necessary, ask the school to correct them.

Why it Matters Schools keep records on each student that can include information about grades, attendance, standardized test scores, health information (such as when you had your immunization shots), and disciplinary actions. Under FERPA, it is usually your parents who have the right to see or get a copy of your school records. In most states, the right to review your records transfers to you at the age of 18. In a few states, you have this right at age 14.

If you think there is an error in your record, you or your parents may request to have that information changed. If you cannot get the information corrected or removed, FERPA allows you to add a statement or additional information to your record to explain what you think is wrong with it.

FERPA also makes sure that schools do not share your records with anyone else—except certain school or government officials—without your permission. Schools may release basic directory information, such as your name, address, birth date, and when you attended school, without telling you. However, you have the right to ask your school to keep your directory information confidential. FERPA applies to any school that receives money from the federal government, including all public and many private schools.

Schools are required to protect your school records under the Family Educational Rights and Privacy Act of 1974.

go.hrw.com KEYWORD: SZ7 CH4

ANALYSIS SKILL **EVALUATING THE LAW**

1. Why is it important for you and your parents to know what is written in your school record?
2. Why do you think FERPA states that your records cannot be released to other people without your permission?

UNIT 2
THE FEDERAL GOVERNMENT

I WANT YOU
FOR U.S. ARMY
NEAREST RECRUITING STATION

The figure of Uncle Sam
is often used in posters
to represent the U.S.
federal government.

CHAPTER 5

THE LEGISLATIVE BRANCH

NATIONAL STANDARDS®
FOR CIVICS AND GOVERNMENT

I. What are the foundations of the American political system?

   A. What is the American idea of constitutional government?

II. How does the government established by the Constitution embody the purposes, values, and principles of American democracy?

   A. How are power and responsibility distributed, shared, and limited in the government established by the United States Constitution?

   B. How is the national government organized and what does it do?

   E. How does the American political system provide for choice and opportunities for participation?

©1994, 2003 Center for Civic Education. All Rights Reserved.

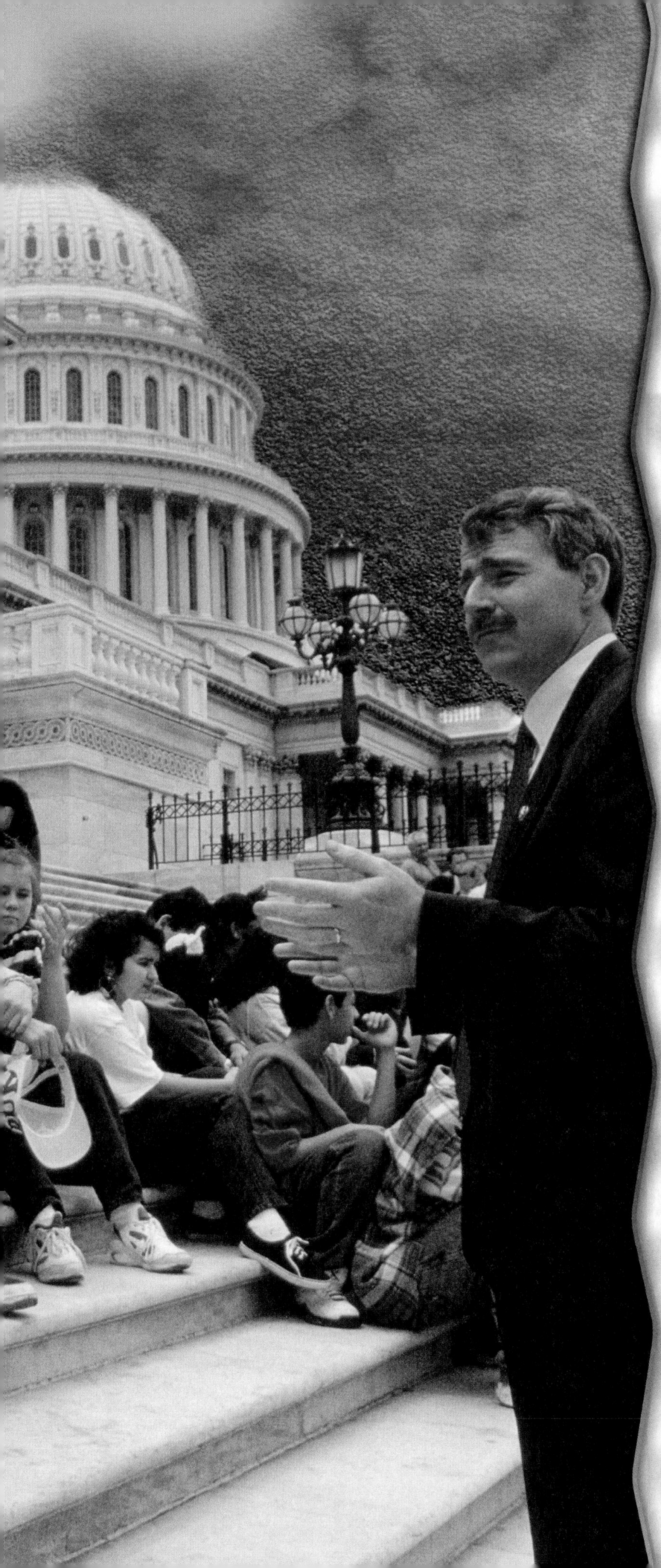

Active Citizenship video program
Watch the video to to learn how young
citizens can affect the legislative process.

WHY CIVICS Matters

The legislative branch is the part
of our government that represents
the voice of the people. As an active
citizen, it is up to you to make your
representatives listen.

STUDENTS TAKE ACTION

NO MORE BULLYING Many schools across
the nation have a problem with bullying.
Perhaps bullying is a problem in your school.
Maybe you or your friends have experienced
this problem personally. One of the purposes
of government is to pass laws that protect
people's rights and ensure their safety. How
would you get your elected representatives to
make a law to address the problem of bullying?

FOCUS ON SPEAKING

PERSUASIVE SPEECH You are a member
of the House of Representatives. You have
introduced a bill to protect students from
bullying, and now that bill is coming up
for debate. You must convince your fellow
representatives that this bill should become
a law. Prepare and give a speech persuading
Congress to pass a law that addresses the
problem of bullying in schools.

Reading Skills

In this chapter you will read about Congress, the lawmaking body of the federal government. You will learn how senators and representatives are elected. You will learn about how work gets done in Congress. You will read about the authority that the Constitution has given to Congress and what powers it forbids. You will discover how bills get proposed to Congress. Finally, you will read about the legislative process in which a bill becomes law.

Analyzing Cause and Effect

FOCUS ON READING Asking *Why?* and *What are the effects?* can help you understand how one thing leads to another. When you ask these questions as you read, you are analyzing causes and effects. Recognizing causes and effects can help you grasp the significance of events and decisions.

Cause and Effect Chains A cause makes something happen, which is an effect. That effect can then cause another effect. This is known as a cause and effect chain. Understanding cause and effects chains can help you see the chain of events that bring about changes in government.

Helpful Hints for Analyzing Cause and Effect

1. Ask why an event happened to figure out the cause.

2. Keep asking why until you trace back to the first cause.

3. To determine an effect, ask what happened as a result of an event.

4. Keep asking yourself what happened next to understand the entire chain.

For years the power of Congress to set its own salary was a controversial matter. In response to this debate, the Twenty-seventh Amendment to the Constitution was ratified in 1992. This amendment states that no increase in congressional pay raise can take effect until after the next congressional election. This condition allows voters to respond to the proposed increase by voting for or against those members who supported a pay increase.

Cause:
Congress sets its own salary

↓

Effect:
Created controversy among voters

↓

Effect:
27th Amendment ratified

↓

Effect:
Voters can vote for or against members who support a pay increase

You Try It!

The following passage is from the chapter you are about to read. As you read each paragraph, try to identify the cause and the effects of what is being discussed. Read it and then answer the questions below.

> Every 10 years, after the census is taken, Congress determines how the seats in the House are to be **apportioned**, or distributed. If a state's population decreases, the number of its representatives may be reduced. States whose populations grow may be entitled to more representatives . . .
>
> Many of these congressional districts have very oddly shaped boundaries. A practice called gerrymandering is often the reason. **Gerrymandering** is the practice of drawing district lines that favor a particular political party, politician, or group of people. For example, a state legislature made up of mostly one party might draw district lines that place a majority of their supporters in as many districts as possible.

From Chapter 5, pp. 136–137

After you have read the passage, answer the following questions.

1. What cause is discussed in the first paragraph? What are its effects?

2. Draw a cause and effect chain that shows the events described in the first paragraph.

3. What main effect is discussed in the second paragraph?

4. What is the final effect? Draw a cause and effect chain to illustrate this paragraph.

As you read Chapter 5, look for cause and effect chains.

Academic Vocabulary

Success in school is related to knowing academic vocabulary—the words that are frequently used in school assignments and discussions. In this chapter you will learn the following academic word:

procedure *(p. 150)*

The Senate and the House of Representatives

BEFORE YOU READ

The Main Idea

Congress is divided into two houses, the Senate and the House of Representatives, and its members have certain qualifications.

Focus Questions

1. What are the two houses of Congress?
2. What are the qualifications, salaries, and rules of conduct for members of Congress?

Key Terms

bicameral legislature, p. 136
apportioned, p. 136
gerrymandering, p. 137
immunity, p. 138
expulsion, p. 139
censure, p. 139

TAKING NOTES As you read, take notes on the Senate and the House of Representatives. Use a chart like this one to record your notes.

U.S. Congress	
Two Houses	Congress Members

When your town decides local issues, such as funding for a road or a new school tax, each voter has a say. This is direct democracy. On a national level, direct democracy would not be practical. Imagine a vote on every national issue. Instead, we choose men and women to vote for us. They represent us. These representatives are the members of Congress.

Two Houses of Congress

Congress is the lawmaking body of the federal government. The Constitution states that the Congress shall be composed of two houses—the Senate and the House of Representatives.

Why is Congress divided into two houses? The framers of the U.S. Constitution wanted to make sure that both small and large states would be fairly represented. So they created a **bicameral legislature**, a lawmaking body of two houses. Membership in the House of Representatives is based on state population. In the Senate, each state is represented equally. The system also allows each house to check the actions of the other.

The House of Representatives

According to the Constitution, the number of representatives each state can elect to the House is based on the state's population. Each state is entitled to at least one representative. Washington, D.C., Guam, American Samoa, and the Virgin Islands each have one nonvoting delegate in the House.

Today there are 435 members in the House. Why 435 members? In 1789, when the first Congress met, the Constitution allowed for 65 representatives in the House. Each state elected one representative for every 30,000 people in the state. However, as new states joined the Union and the population increased, membership in the House kept growing. Eventually, Congress had to limit the size of the House to 435 members.

Every 10 years, after the census is taken, Congress determines how the seats in the House are to be **apportioned**, or distributed. If a state's population decreases, the number of its representatives may be reduced. States whose populations grow may be entitled to more representatives.

Congressional Representation

Every 10 years, after a national census, Congress apportions representatives to the House based on population. California, with 53 representatives, has the most, while Montana and six other states have only 1 representative.

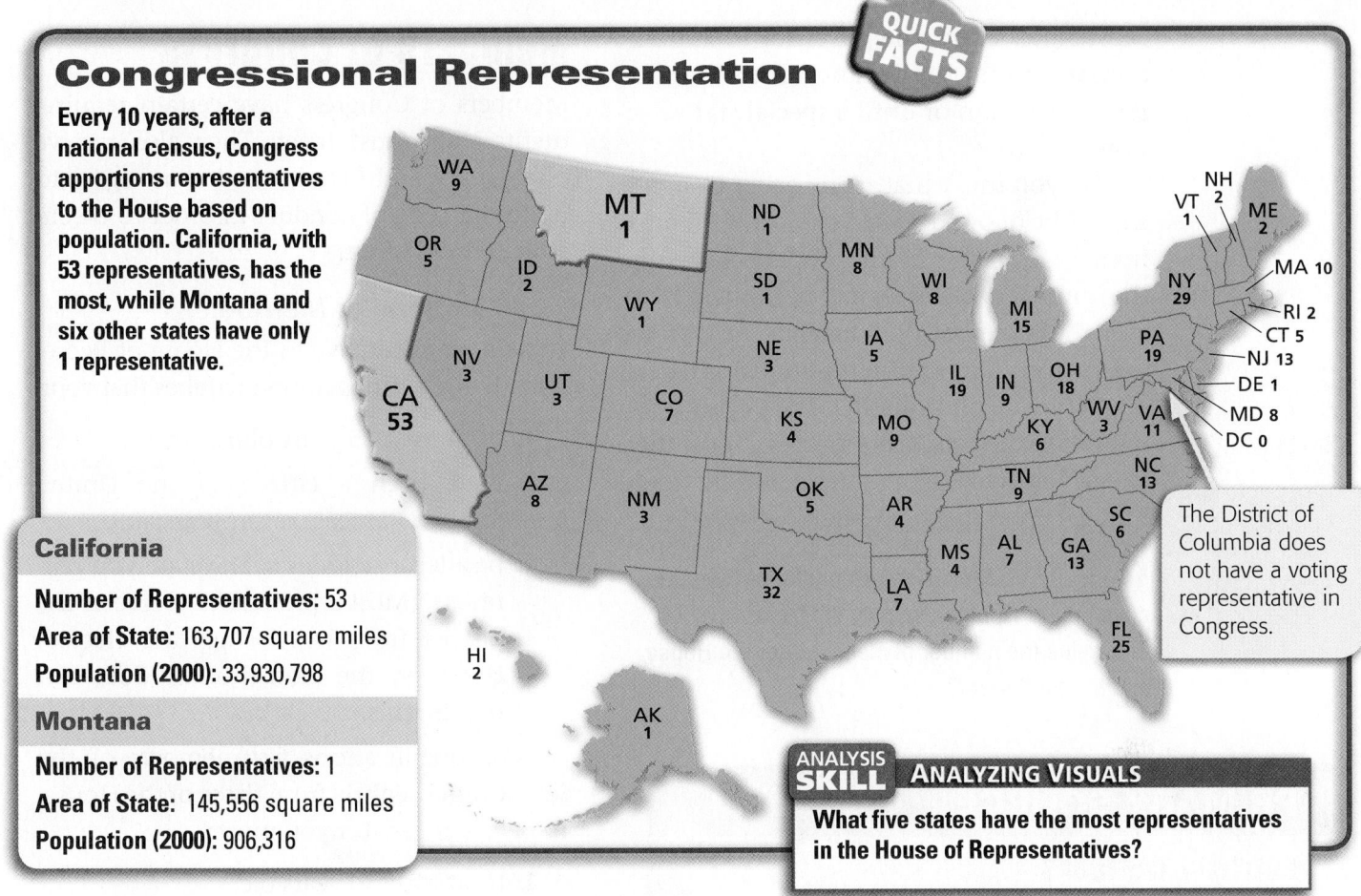

California

Number of Representatives: 53
Area of State: 163,707 square miles
Population (2000): 33,930,798

Montana

Number of Representatives: 1
Area of State: 145,556 square miles
Population (2000): 906,316

The District of Columbia does not have a voting representative in Congress.

ANALYSIS SKILL · ANALYZING VISUALS

What five states have the most representatives in the House of Representatives?

Voters elect their representative according to the congressional district in which they live. Each state's legislature is responsible for dividing the state into as many congressional districts as it has members in the House of Representatives. District boundaries must be drawn so that each district is almost equal in population.

Many of these congressional districts have very oddly shaped boundaries. A practice called gerrymandering is often the reason. **Gerrymandering** is the practice of drawing district lines that favor a particular political party, politician, or group of people. For example, a state legislature made up of mostly one party might draw district lines that place a majority of their supporters in as many districts as possible.

Elections for members of the House of Representatives are held in November of each even-numbered year. All representatives are elected for two-year terms. If a representative dies or resigns before the end of a term, the governor of the representative's home state is required to call a special election to fill the vacancy.

The Senate

The Senate is much smaller than the House of Representatives. No matter what its population, each state is represented by two senators. As a result, today's Senate has 100 members—two senators from each of the 50 states.

Senators are elected to Congress for six-year terms. Elections are held in November of each even-numbered year. However, only one-third of the Senate's membership comes up for election every two years. Organizing elections in this way ensures that at least two-thirds of the senators have prior experience. If a senator dies or resigns before the end of a term, someone must take his or her place.

Most states allow the governor to appoint a person to fill the vacancy until the next regular election or until a special state election is held.

Do you think that members of Congress should be allowed to serve for an unlimited number of terms? Many people believe that the number of terms should be limited. However, the Supreme Court disagrees. In 1995 the Court ruled that such term limits for federal offices are unconstitutional. The Constitution reserves to the people the right to choose their federal lawmakers, and term limits would infringe upon this right, the Court ruled.

READING CHECK **Analyzing Information** Why does the Constitution specify different ways to determine the number of members for the House and for the Senate?

PRIMARY SOURCE

POLITICAL CARTOONS
Term Limits

Term limits would restrict the number of terms a representative could serve in a particular office. While many states have term limits, there are none for members of Congress.

Career politicians fear that term limits might force them from office.

BOO!

ANALYSIS SKILL **ANALYZING POLITICAL CARTOONS**

What point do you think this cartoon is trying to make about term limits? Do you agree? Why or why not?

Members of Congress

Members of Congress have certain requirements they must meet. They also receive a set salary and benefits and must agree to uphold a code of conduct in order to be eligible to hold office.

Qualifications of Members

To be a representative in the House of Representatives, the Constitution requires that you:

1. be at least 25 years old;
2. have been a citizen of the United States for at least seven years; and
3. be a legal resident of the state you represent. (Most representatives live in the district from which they are elected. However, the Constitution does not require this.)

The qualifications for members of the Senate differ slightly from those of the House. To be a U.S. senator you must:

1. be at least 30 years old;
2. have been a citizen of the United States for at least nine years; and
3. be a legal resident of the state you represent.

Salary and Benefits

As of January 2006, each member of Congress receives a yearly salary of $165,200. Members of Congress have offices in the Capitol Building and receive an allowance to pay staff members. Members of Congress receive free trips to their home state, an allowance for local district offices, and a stationery allowance. In addition, they have the franking privilege—the right to mail official letters or packages free of charge.

Members of Congress also have **immunity**, or legal protection. Immunity means that when Congress is in session its members cannot be arrested in or on their way to or from a meeting in Congress. This protection ensures that Congress members are not unnecessarily kept from performing their duties.

Rules of Conduct

Both houses of Congress have the right to decide who shall be seated as members. Sometimes members of the Senate or the House question the qualifications of a newly elected member of Congress. For example, in 1996, Republican Representative Robert Dornan challenged the election of Democrat Loretta Sanchez. In such a case, the member may not be seated until an investigation of the charges is made. The House considered Dornan's challenge and eventually ruled that Sanchez was the winner.

The Supreme Court may review the actions of Congress in this regard. Congress seldom has refused to seat one of its members.

The House and Senate have passed codes of conduct for their members. These codes establish limits to the amount of outside income a member of Congress may earn and requires members to make a full disclosure of their financial holdings.

What would happen if a member of Congress violated the code of conduct? The Constitution allows both houses of Congress to discipline its members. A person who is accused of a serious offense might be expelled from office. **Expulsion** of a member means that the person must give up his or her seat in Congress. Expulsion from the Senate or House requires a vote of two-thirds of the senators or representatives.

Expulsion is rare. Only five House members have been expelled, the last one in 2002. In the Senate, 15 members have been expelled. The last senator expelled was Jesse D. Bright in 1862. He was expelled for supporting the Confederacy.

Less serious offenses may bring a vote of **censure**, or formal disapproval of a member's actions. A censured member must stand alone at the front of the House or Senate and listen as the charges against him or her are read.

Since 1789, the Senate has censured only 9 of its members, the last one in 1990. The House has censured 22 of its members.

READING CHECK ▶ **Summarizing** What are the qualifications for senators? For representatives?

go.hrw.com
Online Quiz
KEYWORD: SZ7 HP5

SECTION 1 ASSESSMENT

Reviewing Ideas and Terms

1. a. Define Write a brief definition for each of the following terms: **bicameral legislature, apportioned**, and **gerrymandering**.

b. Analyze Information If a senator dies or resigns before the end of a term of office, the seat must be occupied. Why do you think this law exists?

c. Make Predictions What might have happened if the House of Representatives had never been formed and only the Senate represented the people?

2. a. Define Write a brief definition for each of the following terms: **immunity, expulsion**, and **censure**.

b. Defend a Point of View Do you think members of Congress should be required to make a full disclosure of their financial holdings? Why or why not?

Critical Thinking

3. Comparing and Contrasting Use your notes and a graphic organizer like this one to identify the similarities and differences between the House of Representatives and the Senate.

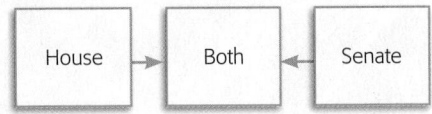

House → Both ← Senate

Focus on Writing

4. Supporting a Point of View Where do you stand on congressional term limits? Write a position statement agreeing or disagreeing with the Supreme Court's decision on the issue of congressional term limits.

SECTION 2

How Congress Is Organized

The Main Idea

Congress is organized in a way that allows its members to consider and pass legislation without each member having to do everything.

Reading Focus

1. What are the terms and sessions of Congress?
2. How is Congress organized?

Key Terms

sessions, *p. 140*
caucuses, *p. 141*
president pro tempore, *p. 141*
whip, *p. 142*
Speaker of the House, *p. 142*

 **TAKING NOTES** As you read, take notes on how Congress is organized. Use a graphic organizer like this one to record your notes about terms and sessions and the organization of Congress.

Vice President Joe Biden shakes hands with House Speaker Nancy Pelosi before President Obama addresses a joint session of Congress.

As vice president, Joe Biden is the president of the U.S. Senate. He cannot vote, however, unless it is to break a tie.

CIVICS IN PRACTICE What if you had to remember to breathe, digest, and circulate blood? Your body is organized so that everything works together to keep you going. Similarly, if every member of Congress had to deal with every legislative detail, government would grind to a halt. To avoid this, Congress divides the workload.

Terms and Sessions

Under the Twentieth Amendment, a term of Congress begins at noon on January 3 of every odd-numbered year. The first term of Congress was in 1789. The Congress whose term lasts from 2009 to 2011 is the 111th Congress. The Constitution requires Congress to meet at least once each year. So each term of Congress is divided into two **sessions**, one for each year of the term. Each session begins on January 3 (unless Congress chooses another date). When Congress finishes its legislative work, both houses adjourn and the session is ended. In unusual circumstances, the president may call one or both houses back into a special session after they have adjourned. Although each house usually meets by itself to conduct business, the two houses occasionally meet together in what is called a joint session.

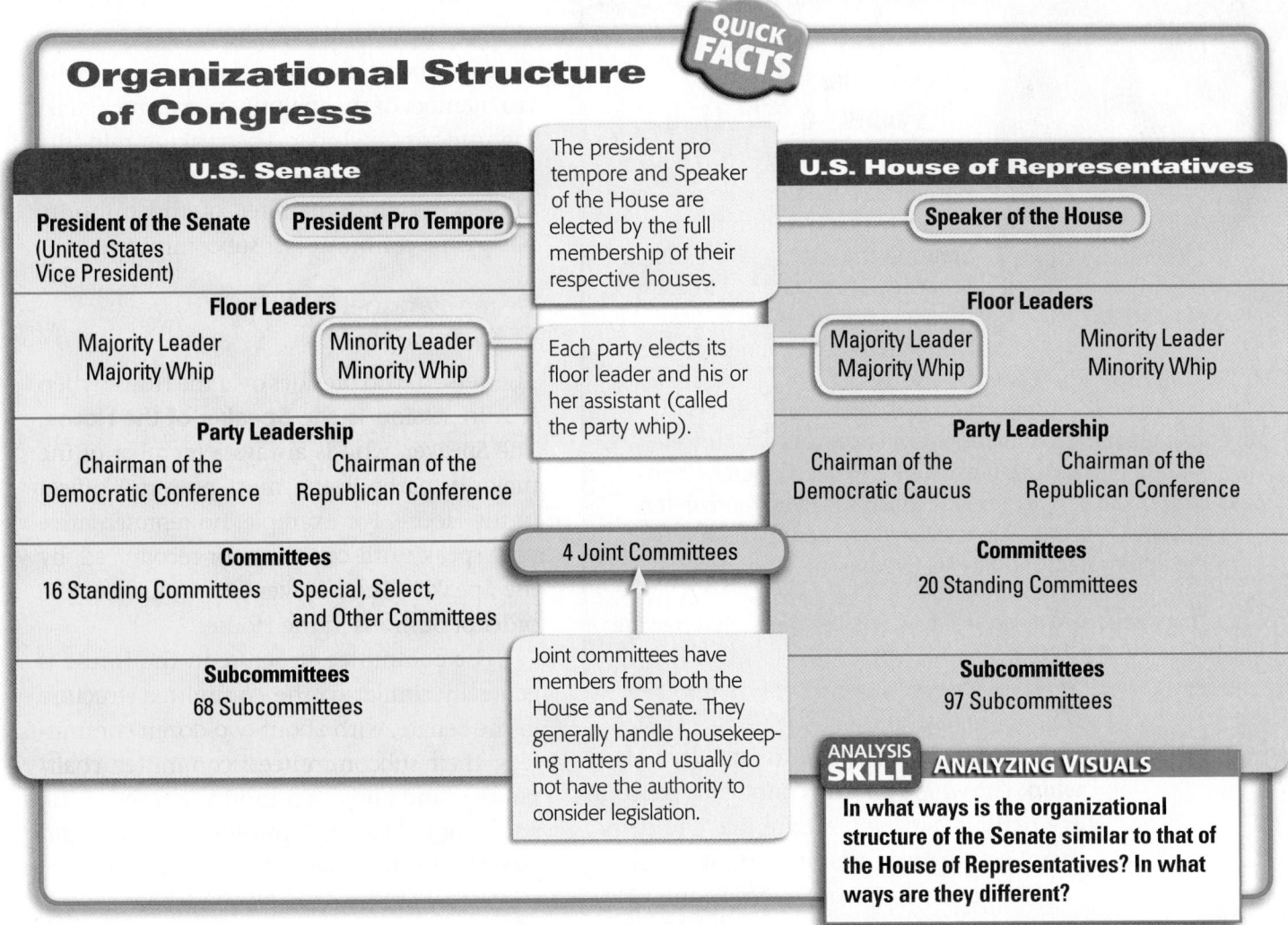

Organizational Structure of Congress

QUICK FACTS

U.S. Senate	U.S. House of Representatives
President of the Senate (United States Vice President) — **President Pro Tempore**	**Speaker of the House**
Floor Leaders	**Floor Leaders**
Majority Leader / Majority Whip — Minority Leader / Minority Whip	Majority Leader / Majority Whip — Minority Leader / Minority Whip
Party Leadership	**Party Leadership**
Chairman of the Democratic Conference — Chairman of the Republican Conference	Chairman of the Democratic Caucus — Chairman of the Republican Conference
Committees 16 Standing Committees — Special, Select, and Other Committees	**Committees** 20 Standing Committees
Subcommittees 68 Subcommittees	**Subcommittees** 97 Subcommittees

4 Joint Committees

The president pro tempore and Speaker of the House are elected by the full membership of their respective houses.

Each party elects its floor leader and his or her assistant (called the party whip).

Joint committees have members from both the House and Senate. They generally handle housekeeping matters and usually do not have the authority to consider legislation.

ANALYSIS SKILL **ANALYZING VISUALS**

In what ways is the organizational structure of the Senate similar to that of the House of Representatives? In what ways are they different?

For example, when the president delivers the State of the Union address each year, all the members of the House and the Senate meet in the House chamber to hear the speech.

READING CHECK **Contrasting** What is the difference between a regular session and a special session of Congress?

Organization of Congress

The Constitution has only three rules about how Congress should be organized. First, it directs the House of Representatives to select a presiding officer. Second, it names the vice president of the United States as president of the Senate. Third, it calls for the selection of a senator to preside in the vice president's absence.

Shortly after the first day of each term, the Republican and Democratic members in each house gather separately in private meetings. These private meetings are called party **caucuses**. At these caucuses, the Republican members of each house choose their own leaders, and the Democratic members do the same. The political party that has the most members in each house is known as the majority party. The political party that has fewer members is called the minority party.

Organization of the Senate

The vice president of the United States does not usually preside over the daily meetings of the Senate. Instead, the majority party elects one of its members to be the **president pro tempore**. *Pro tempore* is a Latin phrase meaning *for the time being*.

Each party has its floor leaders, known as the majority leader and the minority leader.

FOCUS ON
Ileana
Ros-Lehtinen
(1952-)

Born in Havana, Cuba, Ileana Ros-Lehtinen immigrated to the United States at the age of seven. U.S. Representative Lehtinen became the first Latina elected to the Florida House of Representatives in 1982. In 1989 Ros-Lehtinen also became the first Latina elected to the U.S. Congress, as well as the first Cuban American elected to Congress. As an advocate for human rights and democracy, Representative Ros-Lehtinen helped pass the Cuban Democracy Act, which seeks to improve the lives of Cuban citizens. She is also committed to the effort to preserve and protect the Florida Everglades.

Draw Conclusions Why do you think Ros-Lehtinen supported the Cuban Democracy Act?

Each party's floor leader is assisted by a party **whip**. The whip's job is to count votes, encourage party loyalty, and ensure that the party's members are present for important votes.

The Senate has about twenty committees that consider legislation and hold hearings. Each committee has one or more subcommittees that may consider legislation before it is taken up by the full committee. Each committee and subcommittee has a chairperson, who is a member of the majority party, and a ranking minority member. The ranking minority member is the highest ranking (and usually longest serving) member of the minority party on a committee or subcommittee.

Organization of the House of Representatives

The person who presides over the House when it is in session is the **Speaker of the House**. The Speaker, who is always a member of the majority party, is the most powerful officer in the House. For example, no representative may speak until called on, or recognized, by the Speaker. The Speaker also influences the order of business in the House.

The committee structure in the House is generally similar to the committee structure in the Senate, with about two dozen committees, their subcommittees, committee chairpersons, and ranking minority members. The names of the House committees are often different from the names of the Senate committees, but the basic organization is the same.

READING CHECK **Summarizing** How is each house of Congress organized?

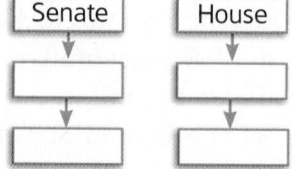

go.hrw.com
Online Quiz
KEYWORD: SZ7 HP5

SECTION 2 ASSESSMENT

Reviewing Ideas and Terms

1. a. Define Write a brief definition for the term **sessions**.
   b. Draw Inferences and Conclusions What do you think are some issues that might cause the president to call a joint session of Congress?
2. a. Define Write a brief definition for each of the following terms: **caucuses, president pro tempore, whip,** and **Speaker of the House.**
   b. Elaborate Why does the majority party have an advantage over the minority party under the committee system?

Critical Thinking

3. Analyzing Use your notes and a graphic organizer like the one here to explain the structure of the U.S. Senate and House of Representatives.

Senate	House
↓	↓
↓	↓

Focus on Writing

4. Evaluate What do you think might happen if both houses of Congress are controlled by the same political party?

SECTION 3

The Powers of Congress

BEFORE YOU READ

The Main Idea

The Constitution both defines and limits the powers of Congress.

Reading Focus

1. What types of powers are granted to Congress?
2. What are some of the limits on the powers of Congress?

Key Terms

implied powers, *p. 144*
elastic clause, *p. 144*
impeach, *p. 144*
treason, *p. 145*

  As you read, take notes on the powers and limits of Congress. Use a chart like this one to organize your notes.

Powers	Limits

As one of its delegated powers, Congress can authorize the printing and coining of money.

CIVICS IN PRACTICE Who decides how to spend the money in your house? In many families, it is a team discussion. Some bills must be paid now, while some can be paid later. It's that way in government. Congress collects money through taxes, decides how to spend it, and pays the bills. And these are only some of its powers.

Congressional Powers

Some of the powers of Congress have been expressly granted, or delegated, by the Constitution. Other powers are implied by the language of the Constitution. The Constitution also gives Congress impeachment power and specific special powers.

Delegated Powers

Article I, Section 8, of the Constitution lists the powers delegated to Congress. These powers can be grouped into five general categories.

Financing Government The Constitution grants Congress the power to finance the federal government. In order to pay for government programs and defense, Congress has the authority to raise and collect taxes, to borrow money, and to print and coin money.

Powers of Congress

Article I, Section 8 of the U.S. Constitution lists all the powers of Congress. The last power listed is "to make all laws which shall be necessary and proper" to execute all the other powers. Known as the elastic clause, this phrase gives the government the ability to expand to meet needs that the Founding Fathers could not have foreseen, such as the creation of a national system of highways.

Powers Granted in Article I, Section 8:

- Collect taxes
- Borrow money
- Coin money
- Punish counterfeiters
- Regulate trade
- Grant copyrights and patents
- Make immigration law
- Form the federal court system
- Punish piracy
- Declare war
- Fund and regulate armed forces
- Form and arm militias
- Establish a postal service
- Create Washington, D.C.

ANALYSIS SKILL · ANALYZING VISUALS

Do you think that the creation of a national system of highways was a "necessary and proper" act of Congress?

Regulating and Encouraging American Trade and Industry Congress helps businesses by regulating trade with foreign countries and among the states and by passing laws that protect the rights of inventors.

Defending the Country Congress has the power to declare war and to maintain armed forces.

Creating Lower Courts Congress has the power to pass certain laws. To ensure that these laws are upheld, Congress has set up a system of national courts.

Providing for Growth Congress can pass laws to regulate immigration and naturalization. Congress is also given the power to govern the country's territories and to provide for the admission of new states.

Implied Powers

The Constitution states that Congress has the power "to make all laws which shall be necessary and proper for carrying into execution [carrying out] the foregoing powers." This means Congress has been given the power to do any action relating to its delegated powers that it considers "necessary and proper." The powers that Congress has exercised under this clause are called **implied powers**.

For example, Congress established national military academies to train officers for the armed forces. The Constitution does not specifically give Congress this power. However, Congress argued that establishing the academies is "necessary and proper" to ensure the defense of the United States.

The necessary and proper clause allows Congress to stretch delegated powers to cover many other areas. Because of its flexibility, the necessary and proper clause is also called the **elastic clause**.

Impeachment Power

Congress has the power to impeach federal officials charged with serious crimes and bring them to trial. To **impeach** is to accuse an officeholder of misconduct.

Congress may remove these officials from office if they are found guilty of serious crimes such as treason. **Treason** is an act that betrays or endangers one's country.

The charges against an accused official must be drawn up in the House of Representatives. If a majority of representatives vote in favor of the list of charges, the official is impeached, or formally accused. The individual will then be put on trial. The procedure of drawing up and passing the list of charges in the House is called impeachment.

The trial on the impeachment charges is held in the Senate. During the impeachment trial, the Senate becomes a court. The vice president usually acts as the judge. However, if the president is impeached, the chief justice of the Supreme Court presides over the trial instead. Two-thirds of the Senate must find the official guilty before he or she can be dismissed from office.

Two presidents, Andrew Johnson and Bill Clinton, have been impeached. In 1868 President Johnson was found not guilty by only one vote. President Clinton was impeached in December 1998 on charges that he lied under oath and obstructed justice. The Senate found Clinton not guilty of both charges. In 1974 the threat of impeachment led President Richard M. Nixon to resign from office.

Special Powers

The Constitution gives each house of Congress certain special powers. For example, the House of Representatives must start all bills for raising revenue. The House also has the sole power to impeach public officials, and the House chooses the president if no presidential candidate receives enough electoral votes to be elected.

The Senate has four special powers.

1. All impeachment trials must be held in the Senate.

2. If no vice presidential candidate receives enough electoral votes to be elected, the Senate chooses the vice president.

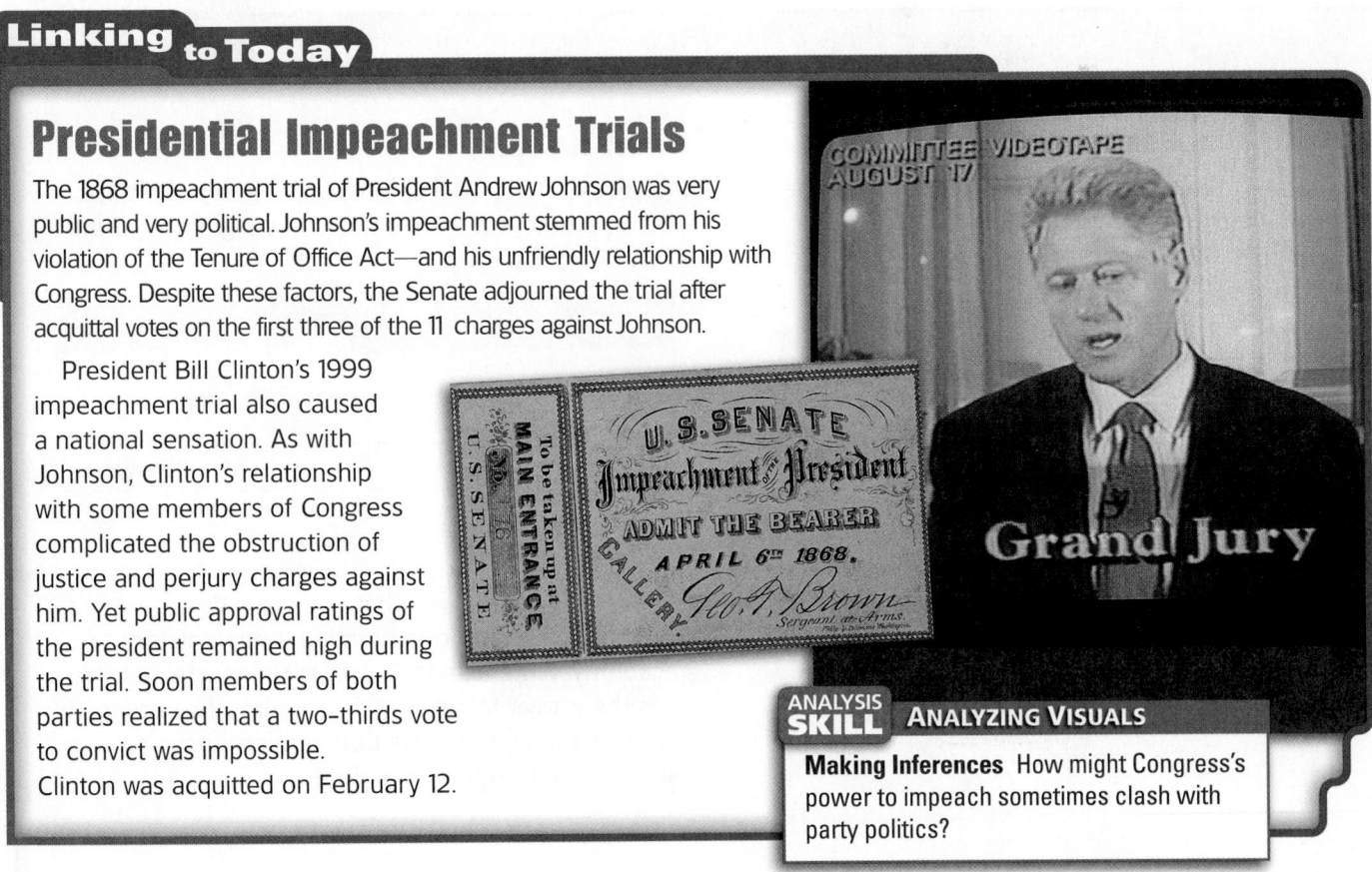

Linking to Today

Presidential Impeachment Trials

The 1868 impeachment trial of President Andrew Johnson was very public and very political. Johnson's impeachment stemmed from his violation of the Tenure of Office Act—and his unfriendly relationship with Congress. Despite these factors, the Senate adjourned the trial after acquittal votes on the first three of the 11 charges against Johnson.

President Bill Clinton's 1999 impeachment trial also caused a national sensation. As with Johnson, Clinton's relationship with some members of Congress complicated the obstruction of justice and perjury charges against him. Yet public approval ratings of the president remained high during the trial. Soon members of both parties realized that a two-thirds vote to convict was impossible. Clinton was acquitted on February 12.

ANALYSIS SKILL ANALYZING VISUALS

Making Inferences How might Congress's power to impeach sometimes clash with party politics?

3. All treaties, or written agreements, with foreign nations must be approved in the Senate by a two-thirds vote.

4. Certain high officials, such as Supreme Court justices, appointed by the president must be approved in the Senate by a majority vote.

The House is often the more active legislative body, while the Senate is said to be the more deliberative and cautious body.

READING CHECK **Supporting a Point of View** Which powers of Congress do you think are the most important? Explain your answer.

Limits on Powers

The Constitution places limits on the powers granted to Congress. For example, the Tenth Amendment reserves some powers for the state governments. These reserved powers include the states' authority to regulate and conduct elections, create and administer schools, and establish marriage laws. The Constitution also specifically forbids Congress from:

- Passing ex post facto laws—laws that apply to actions that occurred before the laws were passed
- Passing bills of attainder—laws that sentence people to prison without trial
- Suspending the writ of habeas corpus—removing the right to a court order, called a writ, requiring that a person be brought to court to determine if there is enough evidence to hold the person for trial
- Taxing exports
- Passing laws that violate the Bill of Rights
- Favoring trade of a state
- Granting titles of nobility
- Withdrawing money without a law

For further explanation of these restrictions, see the U.S. Constitution, pages 53–81.

READING CHECK **Analyzing Information** Why do you think the Constitution limits the powers of Congress?

go.hrw.com
Online Quiz
KEYWORD: SZ7 HP5

SECTION 3 ASSESSMENT

Reviewing Ideas and Terms

1. a. Define Write a brief definition for each of the following terms: **implied powers**, **elastic clause**, **impeach**, and **treason**.
b. Compare and Contrast How are the special powers granted to the Senate different than the special powers granted to the House of Representatives?
c. Elaborate Why do you think the Senate must approve of certain high officials appointed by the president?

2. a. Recall What types of powers are reserved to the states under the Tenth Amendment?
b. Analyze Information Why do you think Congress is prohibited from taxing exports?
c. Elaborate Why do you think Congress is specifically forbidden from some actions?

Critical Thinking

3. Categorizing Using your notes and a chart like the one here, categorize the powers granted to the U.S. Congress.

Special Powers	Limits on Powers

Focus on Writing

4. Evaluating Imagine that you are a Congress member who supports building a new military academy. Write a speech that explains why Congress has the power to set up this academy. Be sure to address the fact that the Constitution does not specify that Congress can do this.

Analyzing Advertisements

Learn

Advertisements are all around us—billboards on buses, bumper stickers on cars, and commercials on television or the radio. All of these advertisements have a common goal: to convince you to buy or support something. Manufacturers use advertisements to persuade you to buy their goods. Candidates running for office use ads to ask for your vote. To make a decision about whether to purchase a product or support a candidate, it is important to analyze advertisements carefully.

Practice

1 **Determine the message.** The purpose of an advertisement is to sell a product, service, or idea, whether a car, a movie, a slogan, or something else. When you view an advertisement, always identify what is being sold.

2 **Examine the information.** Advertisers often use facts and opinions to persuade us to support their product or idea. The facts might be statistics or evidence from research. Opinions might be quotes from people familiar with the product or idea. Determine what information can be proven.

3 **Identify techniques.** Advertisements use different methods to persuade us. Some advertisements appeal to our emotions or try to convince us that everyone supports the product or idea.

4 **Draw conclusions.** Carefully study the advertisement and the facts presented. Then, ask yourself whether you support the point of view of the advertisement.

Apply

Analyze the political advertisement below carefully. Use the example of an advertisement to answer the questions below.

1. What is the "product" in this advertisement? What techniques does the advertisement use to sway your opinion?

2. What facts does this advertisement present? What opinions does it present?

3. Did this advertisement win your support? Why or why not?

MARIA SANDOVAL

As governor, Maria Sandoval

• raised the minimum wage

• increased health care benefits

• increased funding to our schools

IMAGINE WHAT MARIA SANDOVAL COULD DO IN THE U.S. CONGRESS

The right choice for working Americans!

Political advertisement paid for by Maria Sandoval, candidate for U.S. Congress

Illustrated example of a political advertisement

SECTION 4

How a Bill Becomes a Law

BEFORE YOU READ

The Main Idea

To become a law, a bill goes through a multistage process involving both houses of Congress.

Reading Focus

1. How does a bill begin?
2. How do the House and the Senate consider a bill?
3. In what ways can the president act on the bill?

Key Terms

bill, *p. 148*
appropriation bill, *p. 148*
act, *p. 148*
filibuster, *p. 150*
cloture, *p. 150*
veto, *p. 152*
pocket veto, *p. 152*

 **TAKING NOTES** As you read, take notes on how a bill begins, how the House and Senate consider a bill, and what actions the president can take with a bill. Use a diagram like the one here to record your notes.

 If you asked your classmates what single change would improve your school, you might get 20 different ideas. If you asked every student in your school, you would get even more ideas. Some ideas would be better than others. Which idea would you try to put into effect? This is the job of Congress—its members have many ideas for legislation but must decide which ideas deserve to become laws.

How a Bill Begins

A **bill** is a proposed law. Getting a bill passed is a long and difficult process. This careful process helps ensure that the country's laws will be sound ones.

Congress Considers Legislation

Each year the Senate and the House of Representatives consider thousands of bills. A bill can be introduced in either house. The only exception to this rule is an **appropriation bill**, or bill approving the spending of money, which must begin in the House of Representatives. Both the House and Senate must pass the bill. Once passed, the bill can be signed by the president and become a law. A law is also known as an **act**.

Sources of Legislation

Where do the ideas for these bills begin, or originate? Ideas come from several sources, including U.S. citizens, organized groups, congressional committees, members of Congress, and the president.

When a large number of constituents, or citizens of a Congress member's district, requests a law, the Congress member usually listens. If the member of Congress agrees, he or she then introduces a bill that reflects the constituents' ideas.

Sometimes members of Congress introduce bills because certain groups ask them to do so. For example, businesspeople may want to limit competition from industries in other countries. Labor groups may call for laws establishing improved working conditions or higher hourly wages.

Bills can originate from members of Congress themselves. Congress members often become experts in certain fields. A representative who has experience with farming issues, for example, may introduce a bill to fund an agriculture program.

Perhaps the most influential person to introduce a bill is the president. Early in each session, the president appears before a joint

LAW 101

FOUNDATIONS®
of DEMOCRACY

Constitution and Citizenship Day

In 2004 Congress passed a law establishing September 17, the date the Constitution was signed in 1787, as Constitution and Citizenship Day. The law requires all schools that receive federal funds to hold an educational program of their choice about the Constitution for all students on that date.

Why it Matters This law did not pass through the usual process of introduction, readings, committee review, and floor debate. Instead, Senator Robert Byrd of West Virginia added it as a rider to a 2005 federal appropriations bill. A rider is an amendment to a funding bill and is used to pass legislation unrelated to the main bill. Opposing and defeating a rider can potentially jeopardize the passage of the original bill.

Most Americans agree that learning about the Constitution is important. Some people argued that in passing the rider, however, Congress used powers reserved to the states by requiring the teaching of a particular topic. Supporters of the rider point out that any schools that do not want to have Constitution Day programs do not have to take federal education funds.

Constitution Day gives students the opportunity to discuss the U.S. Constitution.

ANALYSIS SKILL **EVALUATING THE LAW** go.hrw.com KEYWORD: SZ7 CH5

Should members of Congress be allowed to attach riders to funding bills? Explain.

---

session of Congress to deliver the State of the Union address. In this speech the president recommends laws that he or she believes are needed to improve the country's well being. Members of Congress who agree with the president soon introduce many of these ideas as bills.

READING CHECK **Summarizing** What groups or individuals might come up with ideas for bills?

The House and the Senate Consider the Bill

Any member of either house can introduce a bill. When a bill is introduced, it is assigned letters and a number, such as HR1215. The letters HR indicate that the bill was introduced in the House of Representatives. The number 1215 indicates the bill's place among all the bills introduced in the House during the current session of Congress. After the bill is introduced, it is printed in the *Congressional Record*. The *Congressional Record* is a publication that covers the daily proceedings of Congress.

The Bill Is Sent to Committee

The bill is then sent to a standing committee. A standing committee is a permanent congressional committee that meets regularly.

THE LEGISLATIVE BRANCH **149**

Usually the subject of the bill determines which committee will study it. The committee may then refer the bill to a subcommittee for review. Sometimes, a bill is set aside and is never returned to the floor for action. This action effectively kills the bill. If the bill is not set aside, the committee holds hearings on the bill. At the hearings the committee calls witnesses to testify for and against the bill. These witnesses give committee members the information they need to recommend that the bill be accepted, rejected, or changed. After the hearings, the committee may pass the bill without changes, make changes and pass the bill, or vote to kill the bill.

The House Acts on the Bill

In the House, if the committee recommends the bill, it is officially reported out of committee. The bill is sent back to the House of Representatives and placed on the House calendar. The calendar is the schedule that lists the order in which bills have been reported out of committee. However, bills do not usually come to the floor in the same order in which they appear on the schedule. The Speaker of the House determines when or if a bill will reach the floor and where it will be debated.

Before the House begins debate on the bill, the House Rules Committee decides how much time will be given to debate the bill. The time to be spent in debate, or discussion, is divided evenly between supporters and opponents of the bill. House members may offer amendments to the bill, but the amendments must be relevant to the bill.

For the debate on some legislation, the House acts as a Committee of the Whole, which means that all the members act as one large committee. Amendments may be offered, but not always. Debate on each amendment is limited, and then a vote is taken on the amendment. When all discussion is finished and all amendments considered, the bill as a whole is voted on.

A quorum, or majority of the members, must be present in order to do business. When action has been completed on amendments, the House is ready to vote on the entire bill. In most cases, a majority is needed to pass a bill. If the bill is an important one, a roll-call vote is taken. Each member's name is called, and a record is made of his or her vote. If the bill passes the House, it is then sent to the Senate for consideration.

The Senate Acts on the Bill

Whether a bill is introduced in the Senate or is a bill that has been passed by the House, it goes through the same steps as a bill in the House. The bill is read and is sent to a committee. After committee hearings and any revisions, the bill is sent back to the Senate for a vote.

Unlike members of the House of Representatives, senators usually are not limited in their debate of a bill. In the Senate, speeches may last a long time. To prevent the Senate from taking a vote on a bill, some senators may threaten to talk for many hours, thereby "talking the bill to death." This method of delay is called a **filibuster**. Debate in the Senate, including filibusters, can be limited only if at least three-fifths of the full Senate vote to limit it. The legislative **procedure** for ending debate in the Senate and taking a vote is called **cloture**. After senators finish their debate on the bill, a vote is taken.

The Final Bill Is Sent to the President

When a bill passes the House and Senate in identical form, it is ready to be sent to the president. However, the two houses often pass different versions of the same bill. To reconcile any differences, the bill is sent to a conference committee. A conference committee is made up of an equal number of senators and representatives who work to reach a compromise on the bill. The compromise bill is sent back to both houses, which usually approve the work of the conference committee.

READING CHECK **Summarizing** Describe the process that a bill goes through in Congress.

ACADEMIC VOCABULARY

procedure: a series of steps by which a task is completed

How a Bill Becomes a Law

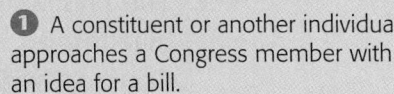

Every law begins by passing through the House and Senate as a bill. A bill may be introduced into the House and Senate at the same time, or it may pass one house and then move to the other.

1

INTRODUCED INTO SENATE

ASSIGNED TO COMMITTEE

SUBCOMMITTEE MAKES RECOMMENDATIONS

COMMITTEE DEBATES, AMENDS, THEN VOTES

SENATE DEBATES, AMENDS, THEN VOTES

INTRODUCED INTO HOUSE

ASSIGNED TO COMMITTEE

SUBCOMMITTEE MAKES RECOMMENDATIONS

COMMITTEE DEBATES, AMENDS, THEN VOTES

HOUSE DEBATES, AMENDS, THEN VOTES

1 A constituent or another individual approaches a Congress member with an idea for a bill.

2 After passing both houses, the two versions are merged into one bill for the president to sign or veto. With a two-thirds majority, Congress can override even a presidential veto.

INTRODUCED INTO SENATE

ASSIGNED TO COMMITTEE

SUBCOMMITTEE MAKES RECOMMENDATIONS

COMMITTEE DEBATES, AMENDS, THEN VOTES

SENATE DEBATES, AMENDS, THEN VOTES

INTRODUCED INTO HOUSE

ASSIGNED TO COMMITTEE

SUBCOMMITTEE MAKES RECOMMENDATIONS

COMMITTEE DEBATES, AMENDS, THEN VOTES

HOUSE DEBATES, AMENDS, THEN VOTES

2

CONFERENCE COMMITTEE MERGES THE TWO BILLS

HOUSE AND SENATE VOTE ON MERGED BILL

3 If the president takes no action on a bill for 10 days, the bill automatically becomes a law. But, if Congress adjourns its session during that 10 days, the bill is automatically vetoed, a process known as a pocket veto.

Law

3

IF VETOED CONGRESS MAY OVERTURN WITH A TWO-THIRDS VOTE

PRESIDENT SIGNS, VETOES, OR IGNORES

ANALYSIS SKILL **ANALYZING VISUALS**

Why do you think a conference committee is needed to merge the House and Senate bills?

The President Acts on the Bill

Once both houses have agreed upon and passed a final version of a bill, it is sent to the president for approval. The president then may take one of three possible actions on a bill from Congress.

1. The president may sign the bill and declare it to be a law.

2. The president may refuse to sign the bill. Instead, the bill is sent back to Congress with a message giving the president's reasons for rejecting it. This action is called a **veto**.

3. The president may choose to keep the bill for 10 days without signing or vetoing it. If Congress is in session during this 10-day period, the bill becomes a law without the president's signature. However, if Congress is not in session and the president does not sign the bill within 10 days, it does not become a law. Instead, the bill has been killed by a **pocket veto**. Presidents do not use the pocket veto often.

Congress has the power to pass a bill over a presidential veto by a two-thirds vote of both houses. However, it is usually difficult to obtain the necessary votes to override a presidential veto. If Congress thinks that there is strong public support for a bill, it may vote to override the president's veto.

Often the president is the nation's chief legislator, even though he or she is not a member of the legislative branch. A president generally has programs that he or she wants to pass, so the president can greatly influence the legislature's agenda. The president may offer legislation, and then request, suggest, or even demand that Congress pass it.

The long and involved process of making laws may seem slow. Yet it does provide a means of making necessary laws while at the same time preventing hasty legislation. The process ensures that bills signed into law are important and useful.

READING CHECK **Drawing Conclusions** Why is it important for the president to have final approval over congressional legislation?

go.hrw.com
Online Quiz
KEYWORD: SZ7 HP5

SECTION 4 ASSESSMENT

Reviewing Ideas and Terms

1. **a. Define** Write a brief definition for each of the following terms: **bill**, **appropriation bill**, and **act**.
   b. Summarize What are four sources of ideas for bills?

2. **a. Define** Write a brief definition for each of the following terms: **filibuster** and **cloture**.
   b. Draw Inferences and Conclusions Why is it necessary for a bill to be considered by a committee?
   c. Defend a Point of View Do you think the process of making laws is too long and involved? Explain your answer.

3. **a. Define** Write a brief definition for the terms **veto** and **pocket veto**.
   b. Summarize Explain the actions that the president can take on a bill.

Critical Thinking

4. **Sequencing** Using your notes and a graphic organizer like this one, identify the steps in the process of passing a bill into law.

Focus on Writing

5. **Sequencing** Imagine that you are a senator who has been invited to visit a school classroom. Write a presentation on how citizens can become involved in the process of recommending new laws.

STUDENTS TAKE ACTION

Writing a Law

"**A** student can make a difference in society," said Tucson, Arizona, student Mounir Koussa. Other students in Ms. Cheri Bludau's class also know that they have a voice in their community. In fact, they wrote a bill that is now Arizona state law.

Community Connection The Tucson students were concerned about bullying in schools. Some of the students had experienced bullying personally, and after the class researched the issue, all of the students learned how serious the effects of bullying can be. The class found out that students who are bullied are much more likely to miss school and develop other personal problems. What could these teens do about such a large challenge?

Bullying often takes place in the halls between classes.

Taking Action With the help of State Representative David Bradley and the support of other legislators, the students wrote a bill as part of their participation in the Project Citizen program. It would let students report bullying without having to reveal their names, require teachers and other school staff to report bullying, require all reports of bullying to be investigated, and discipline those found guilty of bullying. Bradley submitted the bill to the Arizona House of Representatives almost exactly as the students wrote it. Tashina Sosa, one of the involved students, described what happened next as "a very long process. It's like a never-ending thriller book." For the Tucson students, the book had a happy ending. The bill passed in both houses of the Arizona legislature. Then on June 30, 2005, Governor Janet Napolitano signed the bill into law.

go.hrw.com
Project Citizen
KEYWORD: SZ7 CH5

SERVICE LEARNING

1. How did the Tucson students and the state legislature work together to help the bill become a law?
2. What problem would you like a law passed to solve? Why?

QUICK FACTS

Visual Summary

Use the visual summary to help you review the main ideas of the chapter.

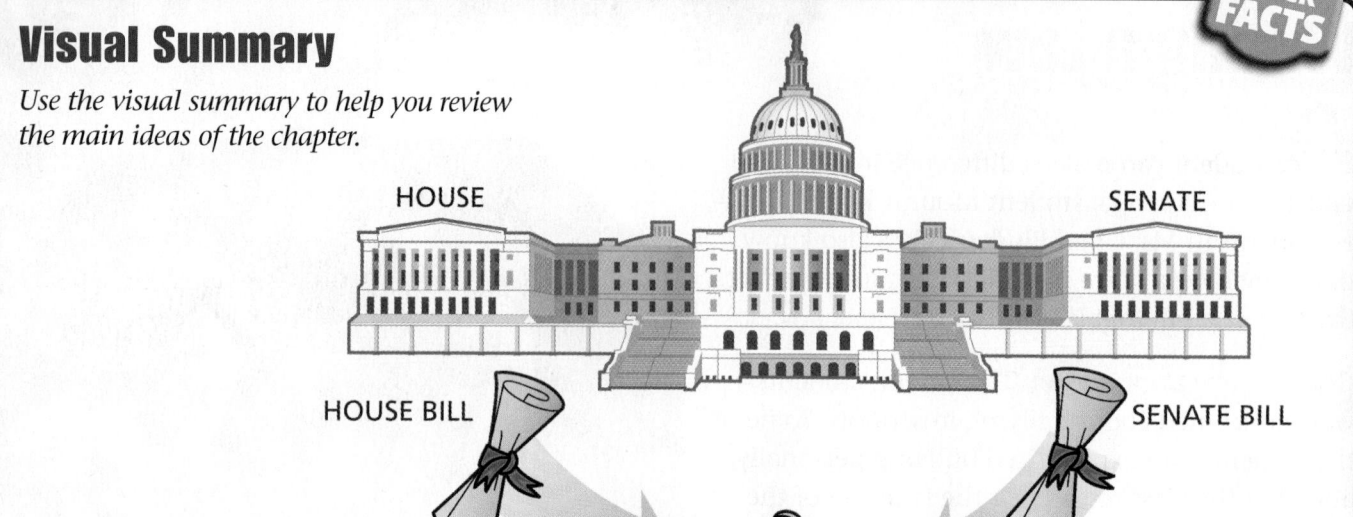

HOUSE

SENATE

HOUSE BILL

SENATE BILL

The legislative branch, made up of the Senate and the House of Representatives, has certain powers defined by the Constitution, including passing bills into law.

Law

Reviewing Key Terms

For each term below, write a sentence explaining its significance to the legislative branch of the U.S. government.

1. bicameral legislature
2. apportioned
3. gerrymandering
4. immunity
5. expulsion
6. censure
7. sessions
8. caucuses
9. president pro tempore
10. whip
11. Speaker of the House
12. implied powers
13. elastic clause
14. impeach
15. treason
16. bill
17. appropriation bill
18. act
19. filibuster
20. cloture
21. veto
22. pocket veto

Comprehension and Critical Thinking

SECTION 1 *(Pages 136–139)*

23. **a. Summarize** What is the difference between the way a state is represented in the House of Representatives and the way it is represented in the Senate?

    b. Supporting a Point of View Which part of Congress, the House or the Senate, do you think is more important? Explain your answer.

SECTION 2 *(Pages 140–142)*

24. **a. Recall** What are the jobs of the floor leader and the whip in the legislative process?

    b. Elaborate Why is most of the work of Congress done through committees?

Active Citizenship video program
Review the video to answer the closing question:
How can students in particular influence certain parts of the legislative process?

SECTION 3 *(Pages 143–146)*

25. a. Describe What is the difference between Congress's delegated and implied powers, and what does this have to do with the elastic clause?

b. Explain What special powers does each house of Congress have, and why do you think each house has separate powers?

SECTION 4 *(Pages 148–152)*

26. a. Recall How do bills become laws, and what can the president do with a bill passed by Congress?

b. Compare and Contrast What are the advantages and disadvantages of having Congress follow a lengthy and complex lawmaking process?

Civics Skills

Analyzing an Advertisement *Review the advertisement below. Then answer the question that follows.*

MARIA SANDOVAL

As governor, Maria Sandoval

• raised the minimum wage

• increased health care benefits

• increased funding to our schools

IMAGINE WHAT MARIA SANDOVAL COULD DO IN THE U.S. CONGRESS
The right choice for working Americans!
Political advertisement paid for by Maria Sandoval, candidate for U.S. Congress

27. What is the purpose of this ad?

a. To convince voters to support increased funding for schools

b. To encourage voters to elect Maria Sandoval to Congress

c. To convince voters to support Maria Sandoval for governor

d. To convince voters not to elect Maria Sandoval

28. What does the phrase "The right choice for working Americans" mean? Give reasons for your answer.

Reading Skills

Analyzing Causes and Effects *Use the Reading Skills taught in this chapter to answer the question about the reading selection below.*

> The framers of the Constitution wanted to make sure that both small and large states would be fairly represented. So they created a bicameral legislature, a lawmaking body of two houses. Membership in the House of Representatives is based on state population. In the Senate, each state is represented equally.

29. According to the passage above, what is a cause of the structure of the legislative branch of the U.S. government?

a. the House of Representatives

b. the Senate

c. small states and large states

d. the desire for fair representation

FOCUS ON SPEAKING

30. Writing a Persuasive Speech First, decide whether you will deliver your speech about your legislation that protects students from bullying at a committee hearing or on the floor of the House. Then write a three paragraph persuasive speech to your colleagues. Remember that you want the press and the public to know what you are proposing, too.

Using the Internet

go.hrw.com
KEYWORD: SZ7 CH5

31. Understanding Congress In each session, Congress makes decisions that affect not only national and world affairs, but also your life, your school, and your community. Who is making these decisions? Enter the activity keyword to compare and contrast the roles, requirements, and powers of both houses of Congress. Then create an illustrated diagram to present your information.

CHAPTER 6
THE EXECUTIVE BRANCH

NATIONAL STANDARDS®
FOR CIVICS AND GOVERNMENT

III. How does the government established by the Constitution embody the purposes, values, and principles of American democracy?

A. How are power and responsibility distributed, shared, and limited in the government established by the U.S. Constitution?

B. How is the national government organized, and what does it do?

©1994, 2003 Center for Civic Education. All Rights Reserved.

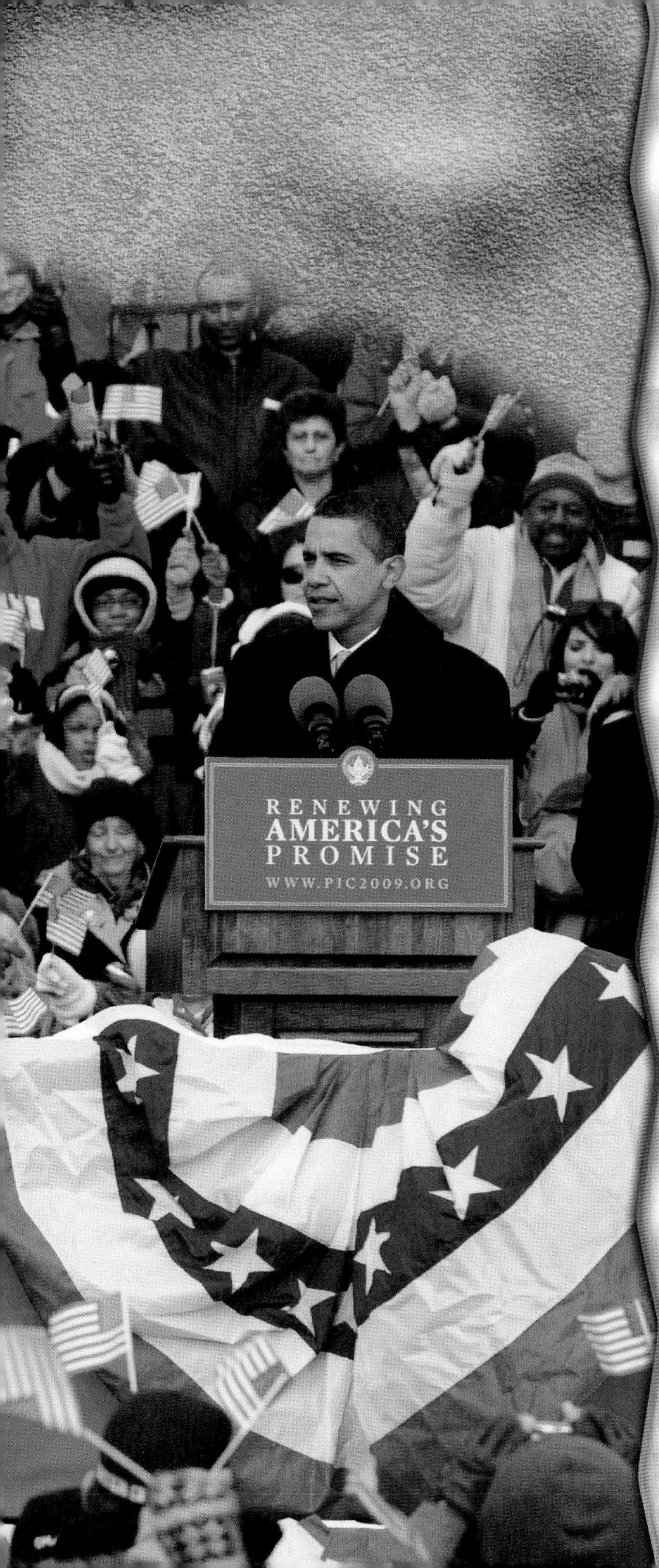

Active Citizenship video program

Watch the video to learn how young citizens can work for change at the local level.

WHY CIVICS Matters

On January 20, 2009, Barack Obama became the 44th president of the United States and the first African American to hold that office. More than 1 million people gathered in Washington, D.C., to attend his inauguration. En route to the inauguration, Obama conducted a whistle stop train tour, emulating the one taken by Abraham Lincoln in 1861.

STUDENTS TAKE ACTION

PROMOTING RECYCLING Many recycling centers in Massachusetts had closed because they were not making enough money. A group of students figured out ways to make recycling profitable again, and proposed changes that will put these recycling centers back in business. What can you do in your community to promote or expand recycling efforts?

FOCUS ON WRITING

A CHARACTER SKETCH What qualifications and characteristics must a man or woman have to hold the highest office in our country? As you read this chapter, take notes on the duties and responsibilities of the president. Think about the types of skills and knowledge a person must have to do the job well.

RENEWING AMERICA'S PROMISE

WWW.PIC2009.ORG

Reading Skills

In this chapter you will read about the executive branch of the federal government, which is responsible for carrying out the country's laws. You will learn about the qualifications and election of the president, who is the head of the executive branch. You will learn about the powers and roles of the president and the 15 executive departments. Finally, you will read about the independent agencies and other departments that assist the executive branch.

Supporting Facts and Details

 Main ideas and big ideas are just that, ideas. How do we know what those ideas really mean?

Understanding Ideas and Their Support A main idea or big idea may be a kind of summary statement, or it may be a statement of the author's opinion. Either way, a good reader looks to see what support—facts and various kinds of details—the writer provides. If the writer does not provide good support, the ideas may not be trustworthy. Notice how the passage below uses facts and details to support the main idea.

When George Washington became the nation's first president, no one knew what to call him. Vice President John Adams wanted to call him His Highness, the President of the United States and Protector of the Rights of the Same. The Senate supported the title, but the House of Representatives did not. Washington also wanted a simpler title. Leaders of the new government agreed to simply call their new president Mr. President. All U.S. presidents since then have gone by this title.

> The main idea is stated first.

> These sentences provide facts and anecdotes about the process of deciding a formal title for the president.

> The writer concludes with a fact that sums up the history of the president's title.

Helpful Hints for Identifying Supporting Facts and Details

1. Look for **facts and statistics**. Facts are statements that can be proved. Statistics are facts in number form.

2. Watch for **examples**, specific instances that illustrate the facts.

3. Recognize **anecdotes**, brief stories that help explain the facts.

4. Watch for **definitions**, explanations of unusual terms or words.

5. Look for **comments from experts or eyewitnesses**, statements that help support the reasons.

You Try It!

The following passage is from the chapter you are about to read. Read it and then answer the questions below.

Department of State

Foreign policy is the special responsibility of the Department of State. The secretary of state heads a large staff of officials who represent the United States around the world. Ambassadors are the highest-ranking U.S. representatives in foreign countries. The official residence and offices of an ambassador in a foreign country are called an embassy. A consul represents U.S. commercial interests in foreign countries.

From Chapter 6 p. 169

After you have read the passage, answer the following questions.

1. Which sentence best states the writer's main idea?

  a. A consul represents U.S. commercial interests in foreign countries.

  b. Ambassadors are the highest-ranking U.S. representatives in foreign countries.

  c. Foreign policy is the special responsibility of the Department of State.

2. Which method of support is not used to support the main idea?

  a. facts

  b. definitions

  c. anecdotes

3. Which sentence in this passage provides an example?

As you read Chapter 6, notice what kinds of supporting facts and details help you understand the big ideas.

KEY TERMS

Chapter 6

Section 1

presidential succession (p. 162)

Section 2

State of the Union Address (p. 164)
foreign policy (p. 165)
diplomacy (p. 166)
treaties (p. 166)
reprieve (p. 166)
pardon (p. 166)
commutation (p. 166)

Section 3

secretary (p. 168)
attorney general (p. 169)
ambassadors (p. 169)
embassy (p. 169)
consul (p. 169)
consulate (p. 169)
passports (p. 169)
visas (p. 169)
Joint Chiefs of Staff (p. 169)
Department of Homeland Security (p. 170)

Section 4

independent agencies (p. 171)
regulatory commission (p. 172)
bureaucracy (p. 173)

Academic Vocabulary

Success in school is related to knowing academic vocabulary—the words that are frequently used in school assignments and discussions. In this chapter, you will learn the following academic words:

role (p. 162)
neutral (p. 166)
distinct (p. 168)
established (p. 172)

The Presidency

BEFORE YOU READ

The Main Idea

The president and the vice president are required to have certain qualifications.

Reading Focus

1. What are the qualifications and terms of office for the presidency?
2. What are the duties of the vice president?
3. What are the rules of succession for the presidency?

Key Terms

presidential succession, p. 162

TAKING NOTES As you read, take notes on the qualifications to be president, the vice president's duties, and presidential succession. Use a chart like this one to record your notes.

President's Qualifications	Vice President's Duties	Presidential Succession

Barack Obama celebrated his victory in the 2008 presidential election with his supporters in Chicago's Grant Park. He is pictured here with his wife, Michelle, and their daughters, Sasha and Malia (left to right).

CIVICS IN PRACTICE The U.S. president is our highest elected official and is one of the most powerful persons in the world.

The Presidency

Who can become president? The Constitution sets forth only three qualifications that the president of the United States must meet. The president must

1. be a native-born U.S. citizen;
2. be at least 35 years of age; and
3. have been a resident of the United States for at least 14 years.

As stated by the U.S. Constitution, the president is elected to a four-year term. However, the Constitution did not originally specify how many terms the president could serve. In fact, many people urged George Washington to run for a third term. He refused to do so and thereby set the precedent of a two-term limit. No one broke this two-term tradition until Franklin D. Roosevelt was elected to a third term as president in 1940. In 1944 he won a fourth and final term. In 1951 the passage of the Twenty-second Amendment set a two-term limit to the presidency.

The president is paid a salary of $400,000 a year, plus a $50,000 nontaxable allowance, plus an annual allowance for travel costs. What kind of person has taken the job of president? So far, all the people who have been elected president have shared similar traits. Until 2008, all had been white men. Most have been Christian. Most presidents have attended college. Many have been lawyers, and most have held other state or national political offices before becoming president.

Recently, though, more women and members of minority groups have run for president. In 2004 African Americans Carol Moseley Braun and the Reverend Alfred C. "Al" Sharpton sought the Democratic Party's nomination. In 2008 Senator Barack Obama of Illinois made history when he became the first African American to be elected president of the United States, as the Democratic nominee. Also in 2008 Sarah Palin, a Republican, became the second woman to run for vice president on a major-party ticket.

READING CHECK **Summarizing** What qualifications does the Constitution require of the president of the United States?

The Vice Presidency

For much of the country's history, a vice president had very little to do. What are the responsibilities of the modern vice president? One very important responsibility is to serve as president if the president dies, leaves office, or is unable to fulfill his or her duties. Eight presidents have died while in office, and one president resigned. In each case, the vice president was sworn in as president. The vice president also serves a four-year term and must meet the same constitutional qualifications as the president. The vice president receives a salary of $208,100 a year, plus a $10,000 taxable expense allowance.

The vice president has only one other job defined in the Constitution—to preside over the Senate. However, the vice president is not a member of the Senate. He or she cannot take part in Senate debates and may vote only in the case of a tie.

In recent years, presidents have given their vice presidents more responsibilities than those described by the Constitution.

Linking to Today

Modern Vice Presidents

In the first three U.S. presidential elections, vice presidents had little responsibility, outside of breaking tie votes in the Senate. As Thomas Jefferson once described the position, "a more tranquil and unoffending station could not have been found."

In the last 100 years, as the job of president has become more complex, the relationship between the president and the vice president has changed. Vice presidents now attend cabinet meetings regularly, serve on the National Security Council, and take a visible role in domestic and foreign policy.

ANALYSIS SKILL **ANALYZING VISUALS**

In today's world, what are three ways a vice president might assist the president?

Presidents often send their vice presidents to represent the United States overseas. Vice presidents usually work closely with the president in order to be fully informed on the issues. For example, Vice President Dick Cheney had an important **role** on President Bush's team, becoming involved in developing policy and in gathering support for the president's programs.

ACADEMIC VOCABULARY
role: a part or function

> **READING CHECK** **Contrasting** How have vice presidential duties changed in recent years?

The Rules of Succession

If the president dies or resigns and is succeeded by the vice president, the Twenty-fifth Amendment to the Constitution provides that the new president nominates a new vice president. That nomination must be approved by a majority vote of both houses of Congress.

If both the president and the vice president die or leave office, the Twentieth Amendment gives Congress the power to set the order of **presidential succession**. The Speaker of the House of Representatives is first in line for the office, followed by the president pro tempore of the Senate and then the members of the president's cabinet in the order in which their departments were created.

> **READING CHECK** **Summarizing** What is the order of presidential succession?

FOCUS ON Abraham Lincoln (1809–1865)

Abraham Lincoln is one of the great symbols of American democracy. Lincoln did not have a formal education, but he taught himself at home. He became a lawyer and settled in Springfield, Illinois, where he began his political career. Lincoln was elected president in 1860. Lincoln once said, "A house divided against itself cannot stand." Lincoln led the nation through the Civil War, and in 1863, he issued the Emancipation Proclamation, which freed slaves in the rebelling states of the South. Following the war he supported the Thirteenth Amendment, which abolished slavery. At age 56, Lincoln's life was cut short by an assassin.

Make Inferences Why might Lincoln be considered one of the great symbols of American democracy?

go.hrw.com
Online Quiz
KEYWORD: SZ7 HP6

SECTION 1 ASSESSMENT

Reviewing Ideas and Terms

1. a. Recall What are the three qualifications a person must meet to become president of the United States?
   b. Summarize What characteristics have many presidents shared?
2. a. Summarize What are the roles of the vice president as defined by the Constitution?
   b. Draw Inferences and Conclusions Why do you think presidents, in recent years, have given vice presidents more responsibilities?
3. a. Define Write a brief definition for the term **presidential succession**.
   b. Summarize If the president dies or resigns, who succeeds to the job?

Critical Thinking

4. Sequencing Use a graphic organizer like this one to show the qualifications to be president, the duties of the vice president, and the order of presidential succession.

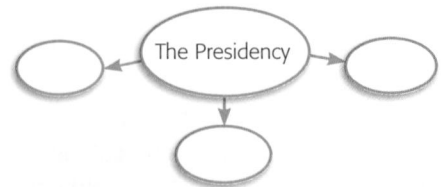

Focus on Writing

5. Making Generalizations and Predictions Write a two-paragraph essay describing the advantages and disadvantages of the Twenty-second Amendment.

STUDENTS TAKE ACTION

Promoting Recycling

"**I** like helping out with problems," said Caroline Doan, a student from Quabbin Regional Middle School in western Massachusetts. She and fellow Project Citizen students, supported by teachers Erin Stevens and Todd D. Stewart, have indeed worked hard to solve problems affecting recycling in their state. The class even received input on their ideas from a key representative of the state executive branch.

Community Connection While researching recycling efforts, the teens found that hundreds of bottle and can redemption centers had closed because they did not make enough money. The students determined that raising the handling fee would make centers more profitable. This move would also allow the centers to hire more employees to sort recyclable items, rather than asking consumers to do so.

Taking Action The students contacted public officials to answer questions and give them advice on their proposal. Lieutenant Governor Kerry Healey came to visit the students to answer questions about the issue. Following the lieutenant governor's advice, the students prepared a bill to increase the handling fee that drink distributors pay to redemption centers from 2.25 cents per bottle or can to 3 cents. After obtaining a sponsor in the state Senate, the class members went to the capital to present their bill. When the state House of Representatives filed its own similar bill, the students had support from the governor's office and both houses of the legislature.

Senator Stephen M. Brewer discusses recycling plans with Project Citizen students.

go.hrw.com
Project Citizen
KEYWORD: SZ7 CH6

SERVICE LEARNING

1. What specific environmental problem did the students identify in their community?
2. How did the students go about convincing the legislature to support their idea? How did support from the state executive branch help their cause?

SECTION 2

Powers and Roles of the President

BEFORE YOU READ

The Main Idea

The powers and roles of the U.S. president affect not only the citizens of the United States but also people throughout the world.

Reading Focus

1. What are some of the leadership roles of the president?
2. What powers does the president have?

Key Terms

State of the Union Address, p. 164
foreign policy, p. 165
diplomacy, p. 166
treaties, p. 166
reprieve, p. 166
pardon, p. 166
commutation, p. 166

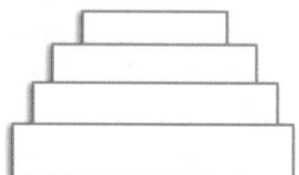 As you read, take notes on the powers of the president. Use a chart like this one to record your notes.

 Ancient kings had absolute, or total, power. What they wished became law. The framers of the Constitution wanted a strong president but not one with unlimited power. As commander in chief, for example, the president can send troops to trouble spots outside the country, but Congress must approve the action. The president can nominate a justice to the Supreme Court, but Congress must approve the appointment. In this manner, executive power is balanced by legislative power.

The President's Roles

The Constitution states that "the executive power shall be vested in [given to] a President of the United States of America." This power applies to several areas of the government, including the military and foreign policy.

Legislative Leader

The president recommends, or suggests, new laws to Congress. Every year the president delivers a **State of the Union Address** to Congress. Usually presented in late January, this televised speech sets forth the programs and policies that the president wants Congress to put into effect as laws. These programs and policies usually address the country's most pressing concerns. The president also sends Congress a budget proposing how the federal government should raise and spend money. In this budget, the president recommends laws and programs to help the economy. The legislature takes the president's budget plan into account at budget time.

The president also influences Congress by indicating what legislation he or she does not want. One powerful way for the president to do this is by using the veto. This tactic is so effective that just the threat of a presidential veto often discourages Congress from passing a bill. It takes a two-thirds vote of both houses of Congress to override a veto, or pass a bill after the president has vetoed it.

LAW 101

The Constitution and the Presidency

What do you want to be when you get older? Have you thought about becoming a teacher, a movie star, or the chief of police? Maybe you'd like to become president!

Why it Matters In the United States, you do not have to be born into a wealthy, famous, or powerful family to become president. Article 2, Section 1 of the Constitution lists only three requirements. The candidate must be at least 35 years old, must have been born in the United States, and must have lived in this country for at least 14 years.

Past presidents have had very varied backgrounds. Abraham Lincoln split fence posts and worked in a store before he became a lawyer and held elected office. Harry Truman was a farmer and a store owner. Woodrow Wilson was a college professor, and Ronald Reagan was an actor.

Ronald Reagan, U.S. president from 1981 to 1989, was a TV and movie actor before he went into politics.

ANALYSIS SKILL **EVALUATING THE LAW** go.hrw.com KEYWORD: SZ7 CH6

Do you think that being a natural-born citizen should still be a requirement for being president? Explain.

Commander in Chief

The president is the head, or commander in chief, of the U.S. armed forces. This means that all military officers, during war or in peacetime, ultimately answer to the president. The president is also in constant contact with U.S. military leaders and has the final say in planning how a war is to be fought.

Under the Constitution, only Congress can declare war. However, the president may send forces to any part of the world where U.S. interests are threatened. Presidents have sent troops into action in foreign lands many times in U.S. history, but this power is limited. Congress passed the War Powers Resolution in 1973. This act requires that the president recall troops sent abroad within 60 days,

unless Congress approves the action. The 60 days may be extended to 90 days if necessary to ensure the safe removal of U.S. troops.

Foreign Policy Leader

The president must give constant attention to U.S. foreign policy. **Foreign policy** is the government's plan for interacting with the other countries of the world. The actions of the United States affect nations everywhere, and the actions of many other countries may also strongly impact the United States. Because of this, the president tries to secure friendly relations with foreign countries while preserving national security.

The president appoints diplomats to represent the U.S. government in foreign countries.

The president also meets with leaders and representatives of other countries in the United States, in the officials' home nations, and at **neutral** locations. The art of interacting with foreign governments is called **diplomacy**. A president's visits to foreign countries builds international friendship and security, and promotes U.S. interests. And no matter where the president is, he or she has immediate access to a powerful and sophisticated communications system that provides the connections with other governments whenever necessary.

The U.S. government also makes written agreements, called **treaties**, with other countries. Many officials work to reach these agreements. The president, however, assumes the final responsibility for the agreements. All treaties must be made with the advice and consent of the Senate. The Senate must approve a treaty by a two-thirds vote before it becomes effective. The president then makes sure that the treaty is carried out.

ACADEMIC VOCABULARY
neutral: unbiased, not favoring either side in a conflict

READING CHECK **Evaluating** How can the president influence legislation, the military, and foreign policy?

More Presidential Powers

The Constitution also gives the president the power to appoint Supreme Court justices and other federal judges. Some presidents, such as President Bush in 2005, have the rare opportunity to name two justices in the same year. Under our system of checks and balances, these judicial appointments must be confirmed by a majority vote of the members of the Senate.

In addition, the president has the power to grant reprieves and pardons to those who have committed certain federal crimes. A **reprieve** postpones the carrying out of a person's sentence. If the president believes that a person has been wrongly convicted of a crime, received punishment that was too harsh, or has reformed, the president can issue a pardon. A **pardon** forgives a person for his or her crime and eliminates the punishment. The president also has the power of **commutation**, reducing a person's sentence.

READING CHECK **Contrasting** What is the difference between a pardon and a commutation?

go.hrw.com
Online Quiz
KEYWORD: SZ7 HP6

SECTION 2 ASSESSMENT

Reviewing Ideas and Terms

1. a. Define Write a brief definition for the following terms **State of the Union Address, foreign policy, diplomacy,** and **treaties**.
  b. Summarize What different military powers do the president and Congress have?
2. a. Define Write a brief definition for the terms **reprieve, pardon,** and **commutation**.
  b. Summarize What are some of the judicial powers held by the president?

Critical Thinking

3. Categorizing Copy the graphic organizer to the right. Use it to explain the duties that accompany each presidential role.

Presidential Role	Duty
Legislative leader	
Commander in chief	
Foreign-policy leader	
Chief of state	
Judicial powers	

Focus on Writing

4. Problem Solving Using the president's State of the Union Address as a model, write a State of the School Address. In your speech, identify some of the challenges facing your school, suggest possible solutions, and provide a plan to resolve them.

Civics Skills

Evaluating Internet Resources

Learn

The Internet provides a wealth of information. With the help of a search engine, you can learn about anything from the fall of the Roman Empire to the powers granted to the American president.

The Internet is a useful reference source that you can use anywhere there is a computer and online access. However, you need to be aware that not all Internet references are sources you can trust. Almost anyone can create a Web page and fill it with information. When using the Internet, you need to practice identifying reliable and unreliable sources of information.

Practice

1 **Determine the source.** Trusted Internet sources include online reference books, such as encyclopedias, and government Web pages. A good source always identifies a knowledgeable author or a known producer. While someone's personal Web site might provide interesting information, it might not be reliable.

2 **Pay attention to content.** A good Internet source will present the facts and not try to influence a reader toward a particular point of view. It also will present references for its information and links to relevant sites.

3 **Check the date.** Most Internet pages indicate at the bottom of the page when they have been updated. Use this date to make sure the Web site contains timely information.

4 **Think about quality.** If a page is messy or includes mistakes in grammar or spelling, the author may not be reliable. It is likely a personal Web site, which is a limited source of information.

Apply

Answer the following questions by looking at the Internet page.

1. Would you consider this page a good source of general information about the Department of Justice? What makes it a good source?

2. Of what use is the http://www.usdoj.gov link? What kind of information did you find there?

3. Look at the Web page below. What makes it reliable or unreliable? What are the questions you would raise about this site?

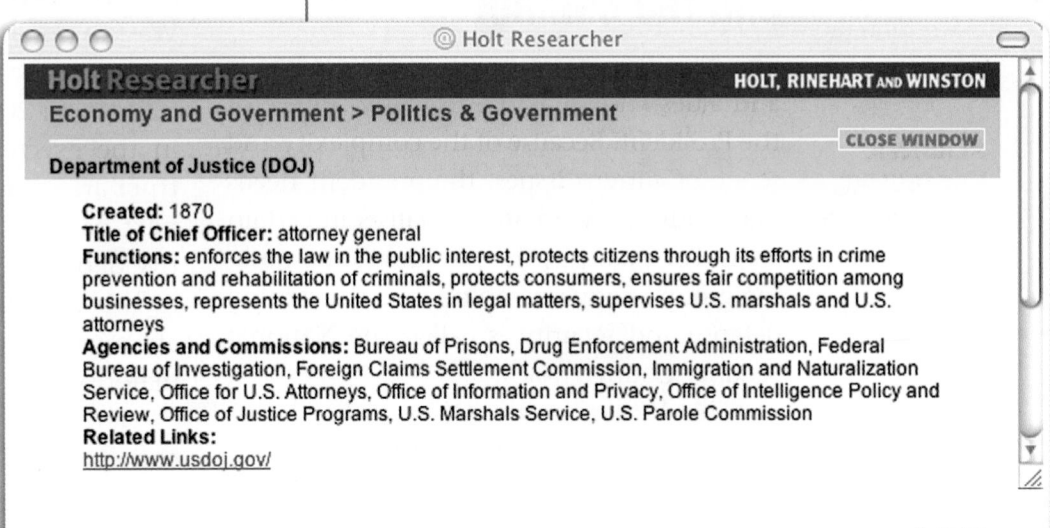

@ Holt Researcher

Holt Researcher   HOLT, RINEHART AND WINSTON

Economy and Government > Politics & Government

CLOSE WINDOW

Department of Justice (DOJ)

Created: 1870
Title of Chief Officer: attorney general
Functions: enforces the law in the public interest, protects citizens through its efforts in crime prevention and rehabilitation of criminals, protects consumers, ensures fair competition among businesses, represents the United States in legal matters, supervises U.S. marshals and U.S. attorneys
Agencies and Commissions: Bureau of Prisons, Drug Enforcement Administration, Federal Bureau of Investigation, Foreign Claims Settlement Commission, Immigration and Naturalization Service, Office for U.S. Attorneys, Office of Information and Privacy, Office of Intelligence Policy and Review, Office of Justice Programs, U.S. Marshals Service, U.S. Parole Commission
Related Links:
http://www.usdoj.gov/

SECTION 3

Executive Departments and the Cabinet

BEFORE YOU READ

The Main Idea

The executive branch of the U.S. government is divided into several departments, each of which has certain duties.

Reading Focus

1. What is the Executive Office of the President, and what is the cabinet?
2. What are the purposes of the Department of State and the Department of Defense?
3. What are the other executive departments in the federal government?

Key Terms

secretary, *p. 168*
attorney general, *p. 169*
ambassadors, *p. 169*
embassy, *p. 169*
consul, *p. 169*
consulate, *p. 169*
passports, *p. 169*
visas, *p. 169*
Joint Chiefs of Staff, *p. 169*
Department of Homeland Security, *p. 170*

TAKING NOTES As you read, take notes on the executive departments and their responsibilities. Use a chart like this one to record your notes.

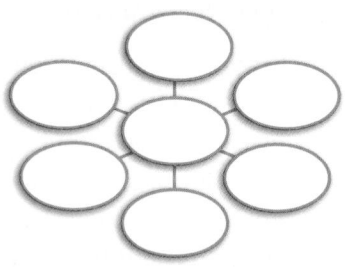

If you have a tough decision to make, it often helps to get advice from someone—a parent or a teacher—who might know more about the issue or who can provide a different point of view. Likewise, the president has people who can help with those tough decisions.

The Executive Office and the Cabinet

ACADEMIC VOCABULARY

distinct: separate

The president has a group of close advisers and aides known as the Executive Office of the President. Because of the complexity and scope of current issues, the president needs many advisers who are specialists in certain areas. For example, the president's top-ranking group of advisers on matters concerning defense and security is called the National Security Council (NSC).

The White House Office, which falls under the Executive Office of the President,

includes the president's closest personal and political advisers, and a press secretary who represents the president to the news media and to the public. This office also includes researchers, clerical staff, secretaries, and other assistants. They schedule appointments and write speeches, and help maintain good relationships with Congress and with other departments of the executive branch.

The executive branch under George Washington had five departments. The heads of these departments formed the president's cabinet. In 2005 there were 15 departments in the executive branch, each with a **distinct** area of responsibility. The chart on the next page shows the names of each executive department. The president appoints the members of the cabinet. However, the Senate must approve these appointments by a majority vote.

The title of most cabinet members is **secretary**. For example, the head of the

Cabinet members, plus the vice president, act as the president's official advisory group. The president appoints members of the cabinet and the Senate must confirm them.

Cabinet Departments			
Department of Agriculture	Department of the Interior	Department of Commerce	Department of Justice
Department of Defense	Department of Labor	Department of Education	Department of State
Department of Energy	Department of Transportation	Department of Health and Human Services	Department of the Treasury
Department of Homeland Security	Department of Veterans Affairs	Department of Housing and Urban Development	*The president may create new cabinet seats at any time.*

Department of State is called the secretary of state. The head of the Department of the Treasury is called the secretary of the treasury. The head of the Department of Justice, however, is known as the **attorney general**.

> **READING CHECK** **Recalling** Who makes up the president's cabinet?

Departments of State and Defense

Two very important departments are those of State and Defense. Both help maintain U.S. relations with the rest of the world.

Department of State

Foreign policy is the special responsibility of the Department of State. The secretary of state heads a large staff of officials who represent the United States around the world. **Ambassadors** are the highest-ranking U.S. representatives in foreign countries. The official residence and offices of an ambassador in a foreign country are called an **embassy**. A **consul** represents U.S. commercial interests in foreign countries. A U.S. consul's office, or **consulate**, can be found in most large foreign cities.

At home the Department of State's duties include keeping track of people traveling to and from the United States. One way it does this is by issuing documents known as passports and visas. **Passports** are formal documents that allow U.S. citizens to travel abroad. **Visas** allow foreigners to come to the United States.

Department of Defense

The Department of Defense is in charge of the nation's armed forces and operates hundreds of military bases in the United States and in other nations. Aside from military action, U.S. armed forces are used in relief efforts when other countries suffer from a natural disaster, such as the tsunami that devastated several southern Asian countries in 2004.

The secretary of defense is always a civilian. This ensures nonmilitary control over the armed forces. However, the secretary has military officers as assistants. The highest-ranking military officers of each of the armed forces form the **Joint Chiefs of Staff**. This group advises the president on military affairs.

> **READING CHECK** **Summarizing** What are the responsibilities of the Department of State and the Department of Defense?

Other Executive Departments

Congress has the power to reorganize and combine different executive departments as needed. Congress can also create new departments if necessary. For example, the **Department of Homeland Security** was established after the terrorist attacks of September 11, 2001. Its primary mission is to protect the nation against further terrorist attacks. The department also provides federal assistance when natural disasters occur in the United States, such as when Hurricanes Katrina and Rita struck New Orleans and the Gulf Coast in 2005.

Departments other than State and Defense play important roles in U.S. government. For example, the Treasury Department promotes conditions for economic prosperity and stability in the United States and in the rest of the world. Some of the major duties of the Treasury Department include managing federal finances; collecting taxes, duties and monies paid to and due to the government; producing postage stamps, currency and coinage; and investigating and prosecuting tax evaders, counterfeiters, and forgers.

The Department of Justice has the job of enforcing the laws of the United States. It helps to ensure public safety against foreign and domestic threats, and it is the government agency that works to prevent and control crime. It is also committed to ensuring the fair and impartial administration of justice for all Americans.

READING CHECK ▶ **Finding the Main Idea** Why was the Department of Homeland Security formed?

SECTION 3 ASSESSMENT

Reviewing Ideas and Terms

1. a. Define Write a brief definition for the terms **secretary** and **attorney general**.
   b. Draw Conclusions Why must the Senate approve the president's cabinet appointments?
2. a. Define Write a brief definition for the terms **ambassadors**, **embassy**, **consul**, **consulate**, **passports**, **visas**, and **Joint Chiefs of Staff**.
   b. Make Inferences Why do you think the Departments of War and the Navy were combined to form the Department of Defense?
3. a. Define Write a brief definition for the term **Department of Homeland Security**.
   b. Defend a Point of View What do you think is the most important executive department? Why?
   c. Draw Conclusions Could a modern president run government with five cabinet members, as George Washington did? Does a president today need 15 cabinet members? Explain.

Critical Thinking

4. Categorizing Copy the graphic organizer. Use it to describe the responsibilities of each of the five departments listed.

Department	Function
State	
Treasury	
Defense	
Justice	
Homeland Security	

Focus on Writing

5. Problem Solving Imagine that you are a newly appointed secretary to an executive department (of your choice). Your first duty is to write a memo to the president. In two paragraphs, describe the most pressing national issue facing your department and explain a plan to address it. Be sure to explain how your plan will affect citizens.

SECTION 4

Independent Agencies and Regulatory Commissions

BEFORE YOU READ

The Main Idea

The independent agencies and regulatory commissions of the U.S. government perform specialized duties.

Reading Focus

1. What are some examples of independent agencies, and what duties do they perform?
2. What are regulatory commissions, and who runs them?
3. What makes up the federal bureaucracy?

Key Terms

independent agencies, *p. 171*

regulatory commission, *p. 172*

bureaucracy, *p. 173*

TAKING NOTES As you read, take notes on the duties of federal independent agencies and regulatory commissions. Use a chart like this one to record your notes.

Agency or Commission	Duties

The space shuttle Discovery takes off on a mission to the International Space Station.

NASA, an independent agency, runs the U.S. space program.

 **CIVICS IN PRACTICE** The executive branch has many duties that do not fit any of the 15 executive departments. Independent agencies and regulatory commissions have been created to cover such areas.

Independent Agencies

Each of the more than 65 **independent agencies** in the government was created by Congress to perform a specialized job. For example, the U.S. Commission on Civil Rights collects information about discrimination against minorities. The National Aeronautics and Space Administration (NASA) runs the U.S. space program.

Several agencies assist the work of the entire government. For example, the Office of Personnel Management gives tests to people who want to apply for jobs with the federal government. The General Services Administration buys supplies for the federal government.

READING CHECK **Summarizing** Why are independent government agencies important?

POLITICAL CARTOON
Regulatory Agencies

Federal regulatory commissions and agencies are where many specific laws are made. These commissions and agencies perform important functions, but people sometimes complain that the rules and regulations from these agencies are too complex. This cartoon shows how "red tape" affected government efforts to help fight a natural disaster.

The term *red tape* is often used as a symbol for government paperwork. It refers to the practice of tying government documents with red cloth tape.

ANALYSIS SKILL **ANALYZING POLITICAL CARTOONS**

What is the cartoonist saying about the government's response to a natural disaster?

Regulatory Commissions

A **regulatory commission** is a type of independent agency that has the power to make rules and bring violators to court. The decisions of regulatory commissions often have the force of law.

Regulatory commissions are usually **established** because of a perceived need. For example, in 1971 the federal government determined that the financing and running of federal elections should be closely monitored. In response to this need, Congress passed the Federal Election Campaign Act. A regulatory commission called the Federal Election Commission (FEC) was created in 1974 to enforce this act. The FEC enforces election laws, provides financial information for campaigns, and controls public funding of presidential elections.

The Consumer Product Safety Commission is another example of a regulatory commission. It sets and enforces safety standards for consumer products and conducts safety research. The Securities and Exchange Commission helps enforce laws regulating the buying and selling of stocks and bonds. The National Labor Relations Board enforces federal labor laws. This board also works to prevent unfair labor practices among businesses.

The heads of the regulatory commissions are appointed by the president. These commissions are independent so that they have the freedom they need to do their jobs. As a result, they have a lot of power in their particular areas.

Because of this power, Congress wanted to help prevent the commissions from being too influenced by a single president and his or her political party. The heads of these commissions, therefore, serve long terms. As a result, a single president cannot appoint more than a few commission leaders. In addition, the Senate must approve all of these appointments.

Some people claim that the independence of the regulatory commissions makes

ACADEMIC VOCABULARY

established: set up or created

them too powerful. Many critics feel that these commissions over-regulate and interfere too much in our lives. Other people defend these commissions. They say that the commissions' regulations are needed to protect the public.

READING CHECK ▶ **Contrasting** What makes a regulatory commission different from other independent agencies?

The Federal Bureaucracy

All of the employees of these agencies, as well as those of the executive departments, make up the federal **bureaucracy**. Almost 3 million people work in the bureaucracy. They include administrators, lawyers, scientists, doctors, engineers, secretaries, and clerks. They work in Washington, D.C., in other cities throughout the United States, and in foreign countries.

As you can see, the federal bureaucracy is quite large and is involved in many areas of daily life. It makes many rules and regulations. Some people complain that the regulations are confusing, and often several different departments may be involved in regulating the same area. Sometimes people dealing with government agencies must fill

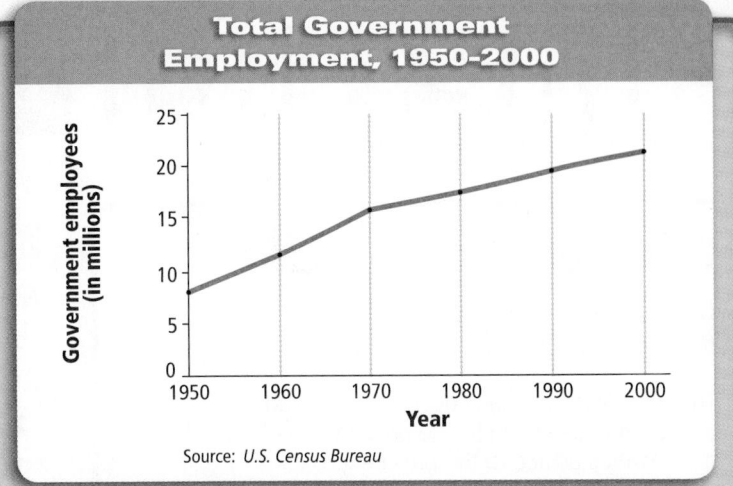

Total Government Employment, 1950–2000

Source: U.S. Census Bureau

The graph shows the number of people employed by government at all levels. The percentage of the population employed by government has not changed significantly.

When did total government employment first exceed 15 million?

out several forms or stand in long lines to see a government representative. And the government is not always efficient in working with the public. However, other people argue that the complexity of modern life requires many layers of oversight and management.

READING CHECK ▶ **Identifying Cause and Effect** What does the bureaucracy use to carry out activities, and what is often the result?

go.hrw.com
Online Quiz
KEYWORD: SZ7 HP6

SECTION 4 ASSESSMENT

Reviewing Ideas and Terms

1. a. Define Write a brief definition for the term **independent agencies**.
   b. Recall What independent agency collects information about discrimination?

2. a. Define Write a brief definition for the following term: **regulatory commission**.
   b. Summarize How has Congress tried to limit the influence of the president on regulatory commissions?

3. a. Define Write a brief definition for the term **bureaucracy**.
   b. Explain What are some criticisms of the federal bureaucracy?

Critical Thinking

4. Making Comparisons Copy the graphic organizer. Use it to show the similarities and differences between independent agencies and regulatory commissions.

Independent agencies — Similarities — Regulatory commissions

Focus on Writing

5. Supporting a Point of View Imagine that you are seeking federal loans to start a small business. Write a three-paragraph speech that either supports or criticizes the role of the federal bureaucracy.

Visual Summary

QUICK FACTS

Use the visual summary to help you review the main ideas of the chapter.

The president has many duties as the head of the executive branch. The president's cabinet provides advice to the president.

JUSTICE
STATE
INTERIOR
COMMERCE
DEFENSE
LABOR
TRANSPORTATION
EDUCATION
HEALTH AND HUMAN SERVICES
ENERGY
AGRICULTURE
HOMELAND SECURITY
VETERANS AFFAIRS
TREASURY
HOUSING AND URBAN DEVELOPMENT

Reviewing Key Terms

For each term below, write a sentence explaining its significance to the executive branch.

1. presidential succession
2. State of the Union Address
3. foreign policy
4. diplomacy
5. treaties
6. reprieve
7. pardon
8. commutation
9. secretary
10. attorney general
11. ambassadors
12. embassy
13. consul
14. consulate
15. passports
16. visas
17. Joint Chiefs of Staff
18. Department of Homeland Security
19. independent agencies
20. regulatory commission
21. bureaucracy

Comprehension and Critical Thinking

SECTION 1 *(Pages 160–162)*

22. **a. Describe** What is the vice president's role in government?

    b. Explain What limitation did the Twenty-second Amendment place on the terms of the presidency?

SECTION 2 *(Pages 164–166)*

23. **a. Recall** What is the purpose of the State of the Union Address?

Active Citizenship video program
Review the video to answer the closing question:
How can making changes in your community eventually affect larger groups of people?

b. Contrast What different military powers do the president and Congress have?

SECTION 3 *(Pages 168–170)*

24. a. Identify Who are the Joint Chiefs of Staff?

   b. Summarize How does the Executive Office of the President serve the president?

SECTION 4 *(Pages 171–173)*

25. a. Make Inferences Why are the independent agencies separate from the executive departments?

   b. Contrast What distinguishes a regulatory commission from other independent agencies?

Using the Internet

go.hrw.com
KEYWORD: SZ7 CH6

26. A Classified Ad Access the Internet through the HRW Go site to research the qualifications, daily job requirements, and personal qualities needed in a successful president. Then write a newspaper classified advertisement for the president of the United States. Be sure to include qualifications, a brief job description, salary, and benefits. Make it as realistic as possible by looking in a local newspaper for examples of what the ad might look like.

Civics Skills

Evaluating Internet Resources *Use the Web page shown below to answer the questions that follow.*

```
○ ○ ○                    @ Holt Researcher

Holt Researcher
Economy and Government > Politics & Government

Department of Justice (DOJ)

Created: 1870
Title of Chief Officer: attorney general
Functions: enforces the law in public interest, protects
citizens through its efforts in crime prevention and rehabilitation
of criminals, protects consumers, ensures fair competition among
businesses, represents the United States in legal matters, supervises
U.S. marshals and U.S. attorneys
Agencies and Comissions: Bureau of Prisons, Drug Enforcement
Administration, Federal Bureau of Investigation, Foreign Claims Settlement
Comission, Immigration and Naturalization Service, Office for U.S. Attorneys,
Office of Information and Privacy, Office of Intelligence Policy and Review,
Office of Justice Programs, U.S. Marshals Service, U.S. Parole Commission
Related Links: http://www.usdoj.gov/
```

27. Which of the following information can be found at this Web site?

  a. The name of the current attorney general

  b. The duties of the U.S. Marshals Service

  c. The name of the president who created the Department of Justice

  d. The general functions of the Department of Justice

28. Write two questions about the Department of Justice that you can answer reliably from this Web site.

Reading Skills

Supporting Facts and Details *Use the Reading Skills taught in this chapter to answer the question about the reading selection below.*

> Regulatory commissions are usually established because of a perceived need. For example, in 1971 the federal government determined that the financing and running of federal elections should be closely monitored. In response to this need, Congress passed the Federal Election Campaign Act. A regulatory commission called the Federal Election Commission (FEC) was created in 1974 to enforce this act. *(p. 172)*

29. What is the main idea of the selection?

  a. The federal government is worried about elections.

  b. Regulatory agencies are rarely established.

  c. Regulatory agencies are usually established to meet a need.

  d. Elections need to be supervised.

FOCUS ON WRITING

30. Writing a Character Sketch Write a paragraph describing a character that you think would be an ideal president. Be sure to describe the skills and traits a person must have to be a good president and how your character fulfills these roles.

THE JUDICIAL BRANCH

NATIONAL STANDARDS®
FOR CIVICS AND GOVERNMENT

III. How does the government established by the Constitution embody the purposes, values, and principles of American democracy?

A. How are power and responsibility distributed, shared, and limited in the government established by the U.S. Constitution?

D. What is the place of law in the American constitutional system?

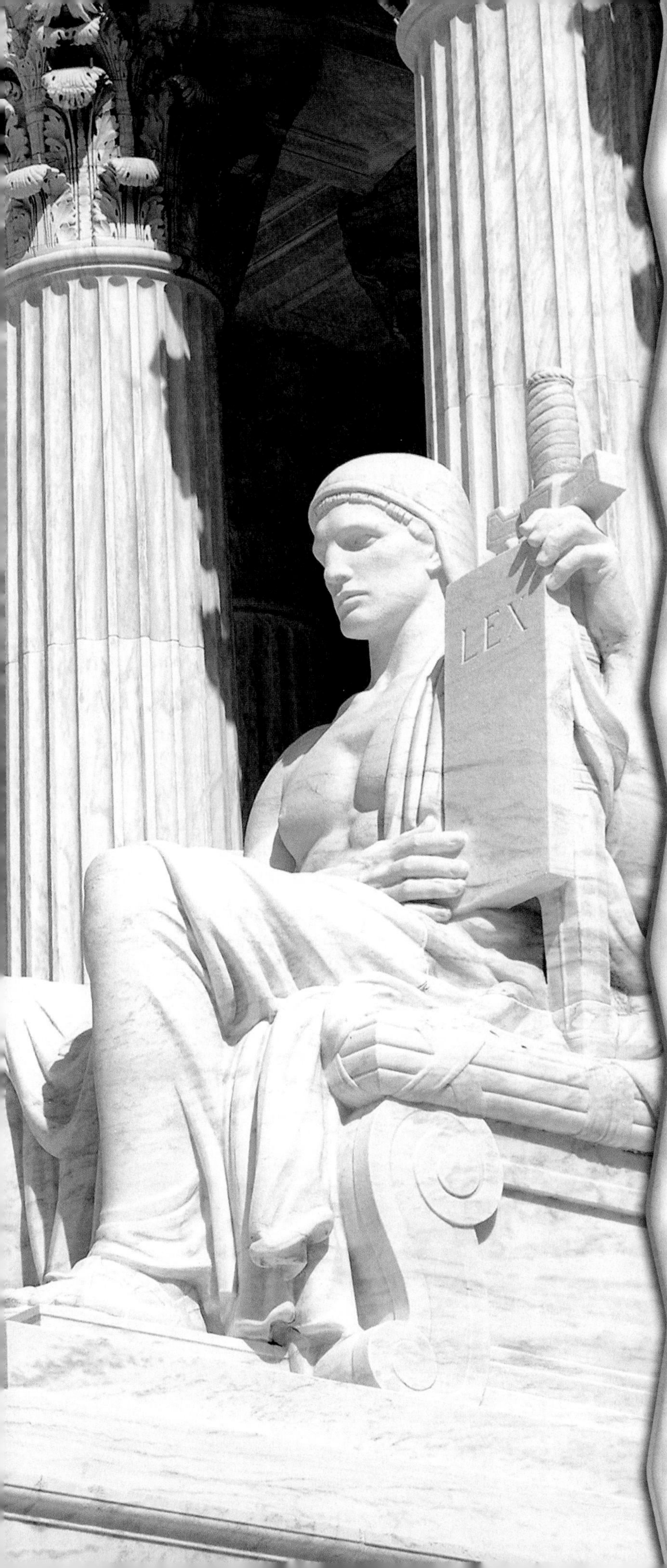

Active Citizenship Video Program
Watch the video to examine the impact the
judicial branch can have on young people's lives.

WHY CIVICS Matters

The actions of the U.S. government
and its citizens are governed by laws.
The government relies on a special set
of officials to interpret these laws and
to punish lawbreakers. These functions
are the responsibility of the judicial
branch of the federal government.

STUDENTS TAKE ACTION

ENCOURAGING SAFE EXERCISE Riding
a bike in Mexico, Missouri, has become safer
thanks to a group of students who worked with
their city to have bike trails and bike lanes built.
What can you do in your community to promote
safe exercise?

FOCUS ON SPEAKING

A RADIO NEWS BROADCAST All of the
cases that the Supreme Court hears start in
the lower courts. As you read this chapter, take
notes on the process a court case takes from
the original trial all the way to the Supreme
Court. Then you will prepare a radio news story
following a case through the judicial system.

Reading Skills

In this chapter you will read about the judicial branch of the federal government, which is guided by the ideal of equal justice for all. You will learn about the four kinds of law and how the U.S. court system uses them to settle disputes.

You will also read about the three main levels of federal courts. Finally, you will learn about the U.S. Supreme Court. You will learn how justices are appointed and how the other branches of government check the powers of the Court.

Distinguishing between Fact and Opinion

FOCUS ON READING People have many opinions about our government and political issues. To become an informed citizen, however, you need to be able to tell the difference between fact and opinion.

Identifying Facts and Opinions Something is a fact if there is a way to prove it or disprove it. For example, research can prove or disprove the following statement: "There are nine justices on the Supreme Court." But research cannot prove the following because it is one person's opinion or belief: "John Marshall was the greatest chief justice." Use the process below to decide whether a statement is fact or opinion.

Helpful Hints for Distinguishing between Fact and Opinion

1. Phrases such as "I believe," "I think," or "I feel" indicate an opinion.

2. Telling readers what *should* be done is another clue that an opinion is being given.

3. Judgment words such as **best**, **worst**, and **greatest** are often used in opinions.

4. Facts often include numbers, measurements, or other things that can be proved.

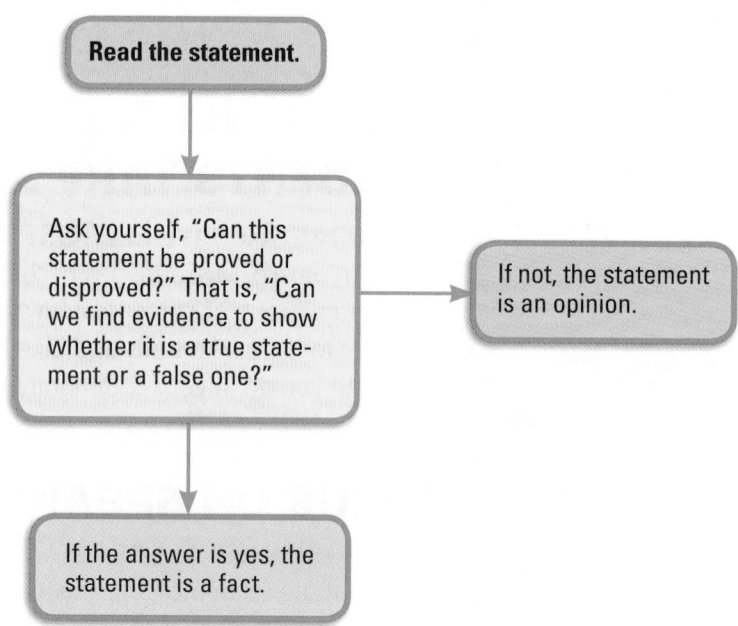

Read the statement.

Ask yourself, "Can this statement be proved or disproved?" That is, "Can we find evidence to show whether it is a true statement or a false one?"

If not, the statement is an opinion.

If the answer is yes, the statement is a fact.

You Try It!

The following passage tells about the influence of John Marshall on the Supreme Court. All the statements in this passage are facts. What makes them facts and not opinions?

The Power of Judicial Review

From Chapter 7, p.190

The Constitution does not explicitly give the judicial branch the power of judicial review. John Marshall established the power when he served as chief justice of the Supreme Court from 1801 to 1835. Marshall promoted the idea of judicial review for the first time in 1803 in the case of *Marbury* v. *Madison*.

. . . However, Chief Justice Marshall ruled that the act gave the Supreme Court powers that it had not been granted by the Constitution. Because the Constitution is the supreme law of the land, the Judiciary Act passed by Congress was declared unconstitutional. This was the first time the Supreme Court had declared an act of Congress unconstitutional and thus established the concept of judicial review.

Identify each of the following statements as a fact or an opinion, and then explain your choice.

1. John Marshall expanded the power of the Supreme Court by establishing the power of judicial review.

2. John Marshall served for 34 years as chief justice.

3. Most people believe John Marshall served too long as chief justice.

4. Scholars believe the *Marbury* v. *Madison* case changed the Supreme Court for the better.

Section 1

crime *(p. 181)*
criminal law *(p. 181)*
civil law *(p. 181)*
common law *(p. 182)*
precedent *(p. 183)*
constitutional law *(p. 183)*
appeal *(p. 183)*

Section 2

jurisdiction *(p. 185)*
district courts *(p.186)*
original jurisdiction *(p. 186)*
courts of appeals *(p. 187)*
appellate jurisdiction *(p. 187)*
justices *(p. 188)*

Section 3

judicial review *(p. 189)*
remand *(p. 190)*
opinion *(p. 190)*
concurring opinion *(p. 190)*
dissenting opinion *(p. 191)*

Academic Vocabulary

Success in school is related to knowing academic vocabulary—the words that are frequently used in school assignments and discussions. In this chapter you will learn the following academic words:

affect *(p. 183)*
authority *(p. 185)*
explicitly *(p. 190)*

As you read Chapter 7, look closely at statements about the judicial branch. Are they facts or opinions?

Equal Justice under the Law

BEFORE YOU READ

The Main Idea

The rights of all U.S. citizens are protected by laws and the courts.

Reading Focus

1. In what ways is the United States a nation of laws?
2. What are the four sources of law in the United States?
3. What roles do the courts play in the United States?

Key Terms

crime, *p. 181*
criminal law, *p. 181*
civil law, *p. 181*
common law, *p. 182*
precedent, *p. 183*
constitutional law, *p. 183*
appeal, *p. 183*

TAKING NOTES As you read, take notes on equal justice under the law. Use a chart like this one to record your notes.

Type of Law	Sources	Courts

CIVICS IN PRACTICE Carved in marble over the entrance of the Supreme Court building in Washington, D.C., is the motto "Equal Justice under Law." What does this motto mean to you? It means that you and all other citizens are considered equal and are protected by the rule of law. Laws define individual rights and freedoms. But where does your freedom end and another person's freedom begin? The judicial branch of the government—the court system—helps find the answer.

A Nation of Laws

Every society needs rules. Without rules, people might feel like they could do anything to anybody anytime they wanted. That is one reason why societies have laws. Laws are society's rules. Laws promote the common good. Laws protect you. Laws, such as traffic laws and laws against rape and murder, are aimed at protecting your personal and physical safety.

A criminal trial.

> The judge ensures that the law and proper court procedures are followed during the trial.

LeRoy E. Millette, Jr.
Judge

> The car is being used as evidence in the trial.

> The jury hears the case and decides the guilt or innocence of the defendant.

HISTORIC DOCUMENT
Hammurabi's Code

The Babylonian ruler Hammurabi is credited with putting together the earliest known written collection of laws. Written around 1780 BC, Hammurabi's Code was a collection of 282 laws that set down rules for both criminal and civil law, and informed citizens what was expected of them. There were laws on everything from trade, loans, and theft to marriage, injury, and murder. It contained some ideas that are still found in laws today. Specific crimes brought specific penalties.

196. If a man put out the eye of another man, his eye shall be put out.

197. If he break another man's bone, his bone shall be broken.

198. If he put out the eye of a freed man, or break the bone of a freed man, he shall pay one gold mina.

199. If a man put out the eye of a man's slave, or break the bone of a man's slave, he shall pay one-half of its value.

221. If a physician heal the broken bone or diseased soft part of a man, the patient shall pay the physician five shekels in money.

222. If he were a freed man he shall pay three shekels.

223. If he were a slave his owner shall pay the physician two shekels.

– Hammurabi, from the *Code of Hammurabi*, translated by L. W. King

ANALYSIS SKILL **ANALYZING PRIMARY SOURCES**

Why was it important that Hammurabi's code was written down?

Other laws protect your property, your freedom to speak and practice your religion, and your health. Laws set boundaries or limits on behavior. So while you may have the right to practice playing your electric guitar, that right is limited somewhat by your neighbor's right to the peaceful enjoyment of his or her property.

Criminal Law

There are two basic categories of laws, criminal law and civil law. When people talk about "breaking the law," they are usually referring to a crime. A **crime** is any behavior that is illegal because society, through its government, considers the behavior harmful to society. **Criminal law** refers to the group of laws that define what acts are crimes. Criminal law also describes how a person accused of a crime should be tried in court and how crimes should be punished.

Criminal laws are intended to protect society as a whole. For example, laws against assault, murder, and rape help protect you and other people from being harmed. Laws against stealing help protect your property and other people's property as well. You might think that a crime against another person does not affect you, but that is not true. If someone who breaks into your neighbor's house and steals something is not caught and punished, the criminal may steal again. The criminal might even break into your house next. And if criminals are not caught and punished, people may begin to think that it is okay to steal.

Civil Law

The other basic category of laws is civil law. **Civil law** is the group of laws that refer to disputes between people. If you have a dispute with someone and you cannot solve it privately, you may go to court to settle the matter. In court, the judge and maybe a jury will listen to the facts of the case. The judge will then apply the civil law and make a decision. Civil laws are used to settle a wide range of personal issues, such as contract disputes, divorce proceedings, and property boundaries.

READING CHECK **Finding the Main Idea** How do laws protect freedom?

Sources of Law

There are several sources of criminal and civil law in the United States. The four principal sources include statutory law, common law, administrative law, and constitutional law. All these laws must follow the principles set forth in the Constitution, which is the supreme law of the land.

Statutory Law

Laws that are passed by lawmaking bodies are known as statutes, or statutory laws. Congress and state and local governments pass these laws. Most criminal laws are statutory laws. Many civil laws are also statutes. For example, a state law that requires all public buildings to contain fire exits is a statutory law.

Statutory laws usually represent majority rule, or what the majority of citizens believe to be right or wrong. If citizens later change their position on the issue, the law can adapt to the country's needs. Every American citizen has the duty to know and obey these laws. One way to practice good citizenship is by obeying laws.

Common Law

No matter how hard the legislature tries, statutes cannot cover every type of wrongdoing. Judges and courts must often make decisions based on customs, traditions, and cases that have been decided before. This type of law is called common law. **Common law** is a type of law that comes from judges' decisions that rely on common sense and previous cases.

For example, before automobiles became a major form of transportation, there were no laws about driving them. So if an automobile ran into a horse and wagon, the driver of the automobile might argue that the case should be dismissed. No laws existed that regulated the speed of automobiles so, the driver might argue, he should not have to pay. Would the case be dismissed? Probably not. The judge might reply that there is an established principle that people cannot use their property to injure others. The judge would apply tradition and common sense in such a case.

In the previous example, the judge's decision might be remembered by another judge hearing a similar case. Eventually, most judges

---

American Civil Liberties

Serving on a Jury

Someday after you turn 18, you will probably receive a letter calling you to jury service. Performing this civic duty might be your only involvement with the judicial system—but it is a duty that carries great responsibility. In a criminal case, the jury decides if the defendant is guilty of the crime charged by the government. In a civil case, the jury decides if the defendant is liable, or responsible, for the damages named in the case, and if so, how much money to award.

As stated by the Sixth Amendment, the parties in a case are entitled to a jury selected from a fair cross-section of the community. Lawyers cannot exclude potential jurors on the basis of their gender or identifiable racial or ethnic group. There have been many cases that were appealed because of alleged discrimination during jury selection.

1. How could discrimination in jury selection affect a defendant in a criminal case?
2. Why would it matter to citizens if they were not called for jury duty because of their gender, race, or ethnicity?

might follow the same **precedent**, or earlier decision, when considering such cases. Over time, this rule would become a part of the country's customary, or common, law.

Administrative Law

Many of the laws that **affect** our daily lives are created by government agencies instead of legislatures. These laws, which are similar to statutory laws, are known as administrative laws. Administrative laws cover many areas of daily life, such as health, safety, education, and banking. For example, the Consumer Product Safety Commission (CPSC) uses administrative law when it rules that a particular toy is unsafe and must be taken off the market immediately.

Constitutional Law

The Constitution is the supreme law of the United States. **Constitutional law** is based on the Constitution and on Supreme Court decisions interpreting the Constitution. For example, the Sixth Amendment guarantees that a defendant in a criminal case has the right to the "assistance of counsel" for his or her defense. Because of the Supreme Court ruling in 1963 in the case of *Gideon* v. *Wainwright*, states are required to provide free legal aid to those defendants who cannot afford to pay for legal representation.

> **READING CHECK** **Summarizing** List and describe the sources of law that exist in the United States.

The Roles of the Courts

Courts use the four sources of law to settle disputes. Disputes may take different forms. Some disputes are between people; others are between people and the government; and still others are between governments. In a criminal case, the dispute is between society and an individual. Society is represented by an attorney for the government. In a civil dispute, both sides have attorneys or may represent themselves.

In criminal cases, the person accused of the crime has certain rights, including the right to an attorney, the right to confront the accuser, and the right to a jury trial. The accused is also always presumed to be innocent. It is up to the person bringing the charges to prove "beyond a reasonable doubt" that the accused is guilty of a crime. Finally, if a person is convicted of a crime, he or she has the right to appeal the decision. An **appeal** is the process by which the person asks a higher court to review the result of the trial. A higher court may find that the lower court has applied the law unfairly or inaccurately. A review of a decision helps to ensure that cases are decided fairly.

ACADEMIC VOCABULARY
affect: to change or influence

> **READING CHECK** **Evaluating** Why do you think the accused is considered innocent until proven guilty?

go.hrw.com
Online Quiz
KEYWORD: SZ7 HP7

SECTION 1 ASSESSMENT

Reviewing Ideas and Terms

1. **a. Define** Write a brief definition for each of the following terms: **crime**, **criminal law**, and **civil law**.
   b. Elaborate How does being a nation of laws both protect and limit freedom?
2. **a. Define** Write a brief definition for each of the following terms: **common law**, **precedent**, and **constitutional law**.
   b. Support a Point of View Do you think common law is more just or less just than administrative law? Explain your answer.
3. **a. Define** Write a brief definition for the term **appeal**.
   b. Explain What roles do courts play in society?

Critical Thinking

4. **Categorizing** Copy the graphic organizer. Use it and your notes to explain the four sources of law that govern Americans. Describe each type.

Four Sources of Law

Focus on Writing

5. **Problem Solving** Write a descriptive paragraph about life in a country in which there is no rule of law. How might life be improved by establishing a permanent legal system?

Analyzing a News Article

Learn

One way to learn about events that are taking place in the world is to read a news article. You can find articles in newspapers, magazines, or on the Internet. News articles provide us with easy access to information on current events or issues.

Ideally, news articles should present balanced information about a subject. Reporters should focus on the important facts related to the story. However, news stories are reported from the perspective of the journalist writing the story. Because much of our knowledge of current events comes from news articles, it is important to be able to analyze them critically. Use the steps below to learn how to analyze a news article.

Practice

1 **Determine how the story is framed**. Read or listen to the news story carefully. Identify the subject of the article, then identify the who, what, when, where, why, and how of the issue.

2 **Analyze the facts.** Articles should include evidence, such as statistics and quotes from people related to the issue, to back up the main idea.

Carefully analyze the information in the article to determine if it is fact or opinion.

3 **Identify the sources.** On what does the author base his or her information? Does the article cite reliable or anonymous sources? Questionable sources might make the information the author presents unreliable.

4 **Identify points of view.** News reporters, though they may try to be balanced, have a point of view. Ask yourself if the article presents more than one point of view. If not, the article may not be balanced.

Apply

Carefully examine the news article below, then answer the questions that follow.

1. What is this news article about? What facts does the author provide?

2. On what sources does the author base his or her information? What evidence do you find that the sources are either reliable or unreliable?

3. Do you think this article is balanced? What elements are someone's opinion?

July 20, 2005
BUSH NOMINATES ROBERTS TO SUPREME COURT

Republicans praise nominee as Dems vow thorough review

WASHINGTON (CNN) -- President Bush on Tuesday chose as his first Supreme Court nominee U.S. Circuit Judge John Roberts Jr., a conservative whose selection pleased Republicans and prompted Democrats to vow a thorough review in the Senate.

If confirmed by the Senate, Roberts would replace retiring Justice Sandra Day O'Connor, who gained a reputation as a moderate swing voter in her 24 terms on the nation's highest court.

Bush called the selection of a nominee to the high court "one of the most consequential decisions a president makes."

Bush's announcement, televised nationally in prime time Tuesday from the White House, ended nearly three weeks of fervent speculation about who would take O'Connor's pivotal place on the court.

A senior administration official told CNN that Bush interviewed Roberts Friday at the White House and made his final decision Tuesday morning. He called Roberts about 12:30 p.m. to offer him the appointment.

With Roberts standing at his side, Bush said the nominee "has devoted his entire professional life to the cause of justice and is widely admired for his intellect, his sound judgment and personal decency."

In a brief statement, Roberts said, "It is both an honor and very humbling to be nominated to serve on the Supreme Court."

Source: CNN.com

SECTION 2

The Federal Court System

BEFORE YOU READ

The Main Idea

The federal court system consists of three levels of courts, each of which has specific duties.

Reading Focus

1. What is the purpose of the U.S. district courts?
2. How are the U.S. courts of appeals different from the district courts?
3. What is the role of the U.S. Supreme Court?

Key Terms

jurisdiction, *p. 185*
district courts, *p. 186*
original jurisdiction, *p. 186*
courts of appeals, *p. 187*
appellate jurisdiction, *p. 187*
justices, *p. 188*

 **TAKING NOTES** As you read, take notes on how the U.S. federal court system is organized. Use a chart like this one to record your notes.

Bernie Ebbers, founder and former chief executive of WorldCom, exits a New York City court in July 2005 after being sentenced to 25 years in prison for his role in the company's accounting fraud case. Cases such as these are tried in the federal court system.

 Let's say that your favorite actor is arrested during a protest. She might agree to pay a fine, but she might also decide to take her case to court. Depending on the events surrounding the arrest, her lawyers might argue that her First Amendment right, her right to free speech, has been violated. If so, her case would be tried in a federal court.

U.S. District Courts

The U.S. Constitution, in Article III, Section 1, provides that "the judicial power of the United States shall be vested in one Supreme Court, and in such inferior [lower] courts as the Congress may from time to time ... establish." The First Congress used this constitutional power to set up a system of federal courts. There are three levels of federal courts.

Each level of the federal court system is given jurisdiction in several different kinds of cases. The **jurisdiction** of a court is the extent or scope of **authority** that court has to hear and decide a case that has properly been brought before it. There are two types of jurisdiction: original and appellate.

ACADEMIC VOCABULARY

authority: power, right to rule

U.S. Federal Districts

The lowest level of federal courts is the U.S. district courts. **District courts** are the trial courts, and they are courts of original jurisdiction. **Original jurisdiction** is the authority of a court to hear and decide a case for the first time. The district court is the only federal court in which jury trials are held. District courts cannot hear appeals from other courts.

Federal district courts are the "local" courts in the federal court system. There is at least one district court in each of the 50 states and in the District of Columbia. Some states are divided into as many as four federal court districts. There are 94 federal district courts in the United States.

U.S. District Judges

Judges, including federal judges, do not make law. That is the job of the legislature. Judges apply the relevant law to the case before them. In the federal court system, there may be one judge in a district court, or there may be as many as 28 judges, depending on the caseload of the court.

Federal district judges are trial judges. They conduct both civil and criminal trials, with and without juries. They also rule on court procedures and apply the relevant law to the facts of the case. If there is no jury, the judge also decides which side wins and sets the remedy for the winner. In a criminal case, the judge also decides the punishment.

All federal judges, except those in U.S. territories, are appointed for life by the president and must be approved by the Senate. Federal judges can be removed from office only by impeachment by Congress. Neither Congress nor the president can lower a judge's salary during his or her time in office. These guarantees were written into the Constitution to ensure that judges are not punished for their decisions in cases.

READING CHECK **Evaluating** Why are federal judges appointed for life at a fixed salary?

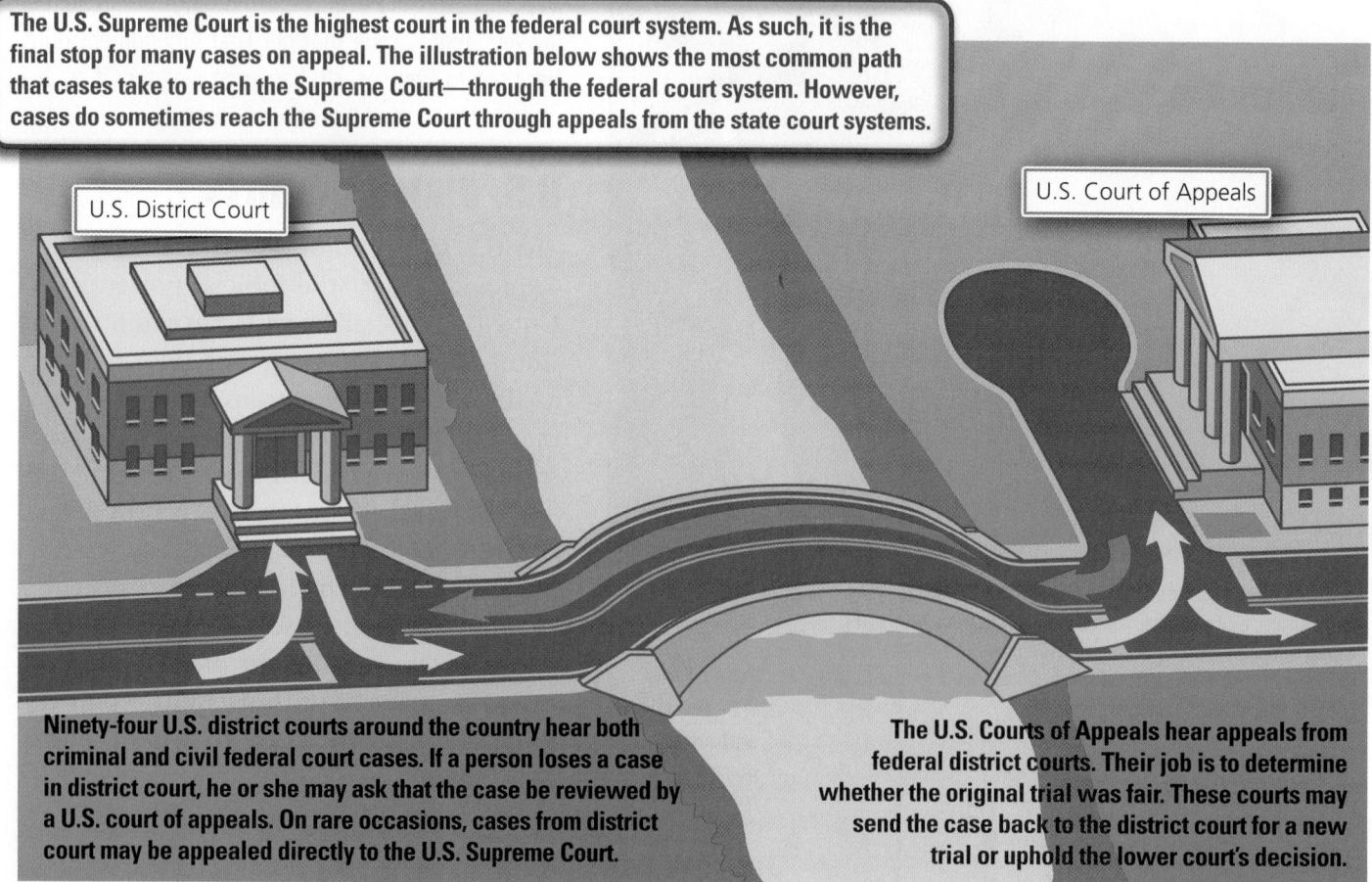

The U.S. Supreme Court is the highest court in the federal court system. As such, it is the final stop for many cases on appeal. The illustration below shows the most common path that cases take to reach the Supreme Court—through the federal court system. However, cases do sometimes reach the Supreme Court through appeals from the state court systems.

U.S. District Court

U.S. Court of Appeals

Ninety-four U.S. district courts around the country hear both criminal and civil federal court cases. If a person loses a case in district court, he or she may ask that the case be reviewed by a U.S. court of appeals. On rare occasions, cases from district court may be appealed directly to the U.S. Supreme Court.

The U.S. Courts of Appeals hear appeals from federal district courts. Their job is to determine whether the original trial was fair. These courts may send the case back to the district court for a new trial or uphold the lower court's decision.

U.S. Courts of Appeals

After a trial in a district court, the losing party may appeal to the next level of courts. The next level of courts in the federal court system consists of **courts of appeals**. These courts have what is called **appellate jurisdiction**. The term *appellate* means "relating to appeals," so a court with appellate jurisdiction has the power to review decisions made by lower courts.

The federal court system, with its 94 district courts, is divided into 12 judicial circuits. Each circuit has its own court of appeals. For example, if you live in West Virginia, Virginia, North Carolina, or South Carolina, you live in the 4th Judicial Circuit. The 12th circuit is the District of Columbia. Each court of appeals has between 6 and 28 judges. The judge of each circuit who has served the longest and is under 65 years of age serves as the senior judge. Again, like other federal judges, appellate court judges are appointed for life.

Courts of appeals do not hold trials. Instead, a panel of at least three judges makes a decision on the case. Appellate judges examine the records of the district court trial and hear arguments by the lawyers for both sides. The judges do not determine whether the accused person is guilty or innocent of the crime. Their job is to determine only whether the original trial was fair and if the law was interpreted correctly.

The judges reach their decision by majority vote. The court of appeals may send the case back to the district court for a new trial, or it may uphold the district court's decision. In most cases, the decision of the court of appeals is final. Sometimes, however, yet another appeal is made to the U.S. Supreme Court.

> **READING CHECK** **Identifying Cause and Effect**
> Why are cases sent to the court of appeals, and what are the possible results?

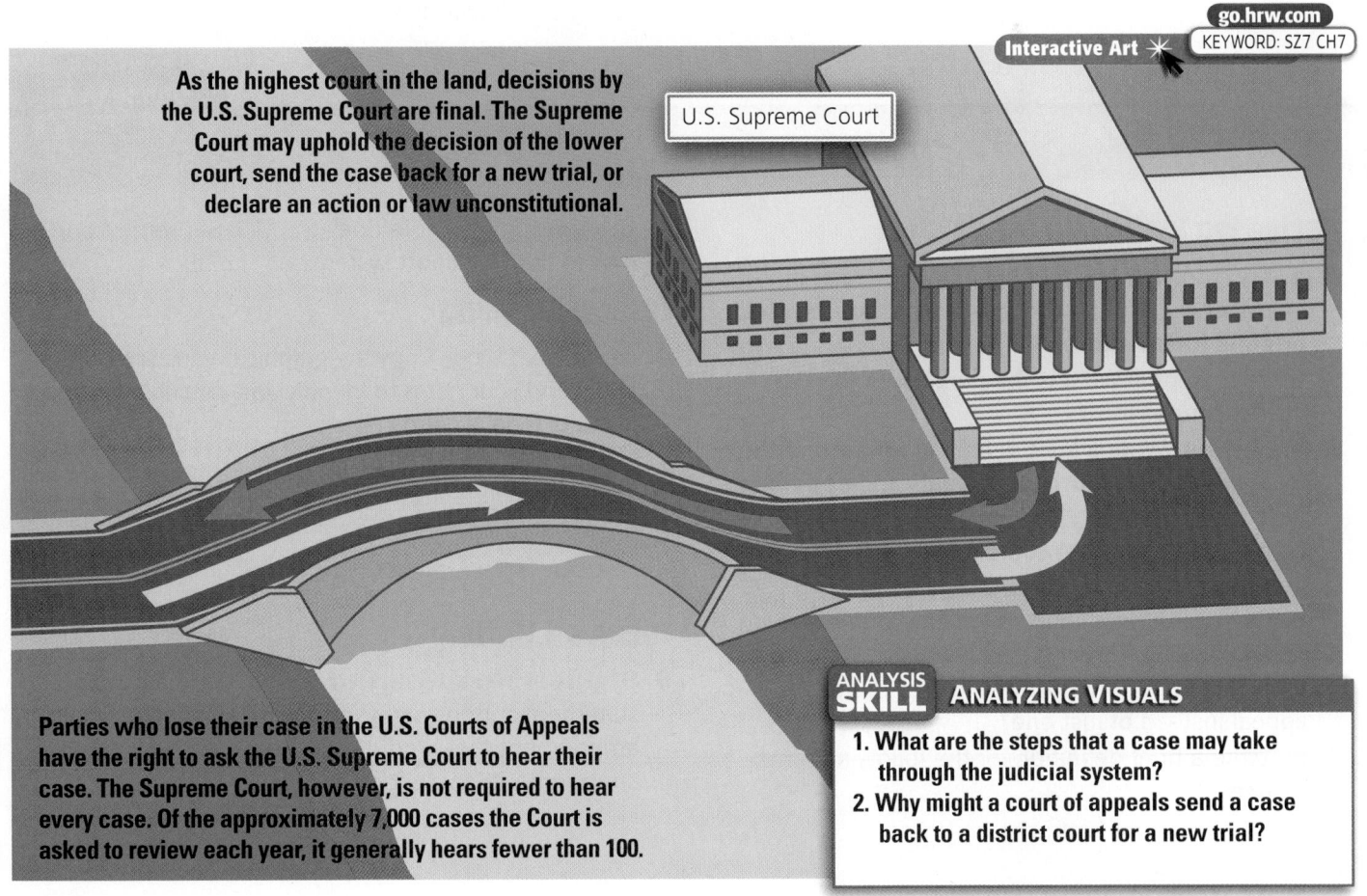

go.hrw.com
Interactive Art
KEYWORD: SZ7 CH7

As the highest court in the land, decisions by the U.S. Supreme Court are final. The Supreme Court may uphold the decision of the lower court, send the case back for a new trial, or declare an action or law unconstitutional.

U.S. Supreme Court

Parties who lose their case in the U.S. Courts of Appeals have the right to ask the U.S. Supreme Court to hear their case. The Supreme Court, however, is not required to hear every case. Of the approximately 7,000 cases the Court is asked to review each year, it generally hears fewer than 100.

ANALYSIS SKILL **ANALYZING VISUALS**

1. What are the steps that a case may take through the judicial system?
2. Why might a court of appeals send a case back to a district court for a new trial?

Makeup of the Supreme Court

The nine justices—a chief justice and eight associate justices—on the Supreme Court are appointed for life by the president, but the Senate must approve these appointments by majority vote.

- Chief Justice John G. Roberts Jr., appointed in 2005 by President George W. Bush
- John P. Stevens, appointed in 1975 by President Gerald R. Ford
- Antonin Scalia, appointed in1986 by President Ronald Reagan
- Anthony Kennedy, appointed in 1988 by President Ronald Reagan
- David H. Souter, appointed in 1990 by President George H. W. Bush
- Clarence Thomas, appointed in 1991 by President George H. W. Bush
- Ruth Bader Ginsberg, appointed in 1993 by President Bill Clinton
- Stephen G. Breyer, appointed in 1994 by President Bill Clinton
- Samuel A. Alito Jr., appointed in 2005 by President George W. Bush

ANALYSIS SKILL **ANALYZING INFORMATION**

Drawing Conclusions Why must the Senate approve the president's choices for the Supreme Court?

The U.S. Supreme Court

The highest court in the land is the U.S. Supreme Court, which meets in Washington, D.C. The Supreme Court is mainly an appeals court. It reviews cases that have been tried in lower federal courts and in state courts. The decisions of the Supreme Court's nine **justices**, or judges, cannot be appealed.

The Constitution does give the Supreme Court original jurisdiction in three types of cases. First, the Supreme Court tries cases involving diplomatic representatives of other countries. Second, the court has jurisdiction in cases between states. For example, the Supreme Court once settled a dispute between Arizona and California over the use of water from the Colorado River basin. The Court also hears cases involving a state and the federal government.

READING CHECK **Drawing Inferences and Conclusions** Why might the Supreme Court have been given original jurisdiction in the three areas mentioned above?

SECTION 2 ASSESSMENT

Reviewing Ideas and Terms

1. **a. Define** Write a brief definition for each of the following terms: **jurisdiction**, **district courts**, and **original jurisdiction**.

   b. Elaborate What is the purpose of the U.S. district courts?

2. **a. Define** Write a brief definition for each of the following terms: **courts of appeals** and **appellate jurisdiction**.

   b. Explain How are courts of appeals different from district courts?

   c. Evaluate In a court of appeals, a three-judge panel usually hears and decides cases. Why do you think it is important for three judges to hear an appeal instead of just one?

3. **a.** Write a brief definition for the following term: **justices**.

   b. Recall What role does the U.S. Supreme Court play in the U.S. court system?

Critical Thinking

4. **Summarizing** Copy the graphic organizer below. Use it and your notes to identify and describe the three levels of federal courts.

The Three Levels of Federal Courts

Focus on Writing

5. **Supporting a Point of View** Write a position statement supporting or opposing a constitutional amendment that would end the system of lifetime appointments for federal judges.

SECTION 3

The Supreme Court

The Main Idea

The Supreme Court hears appeals, reviews laws, and strongly influences American society.

Reading Focus

1. What is the power of judicial review?
2. What are the constitutional checks on the Supreme Court's powers?
3. How has the Supreme Court strengthened constitutional rights?

Key Terms

judicial review, *p. 189*
remand, *p. 190*
opinion, *p. 190*
concurring opinion, *p. 190*
dissenting opinion, *p. 191*

 As you read, take notes on how the Supreme Court can influence society. Use a graphic organizer like this one to record your notes.

The first eight chief justices of the Supreme Court were John Jay, John Rutledge, Oliver Ellsworth, John Marshall, Roger B. Taney, Salmon P. Chase, Morrison R. Waite, and Melville W. Fuller.

 What kinds of activities are protected by your right to free speech? What is cruel and unusual punishment? These are all constitutional questions, and many of them have been addressed by the courts. In fact, lower state and federal courts frequently deal with constitutional issues, but their rulings are not the final word. In our system of government, the Supreme Court has the final say about what is constitutional and what is not.

The Power of Judicial Review

Over the years, laws have been passed that have later been considered unconstitutional. Laws about segregation and discrimination are good examples. How can such laws be changed? The answers lie with a unique feature of the U.S. court system called the power of **judicial review**. This power allows courts to decide whether a law or a presidential action is in agreement with the Constitution. The Supreme Court holds the ultimate authority to make this decision. If a court decides that a law conflicts with the Constitution, that law is declared unconstitutional.

The Constitution does not **explicitly** give the judicial branch the power of judicial review. John Marshall established the power when he served as chief justice of the Supreme Court from 1801 to 1835. Marshall promoted the idea of judicial review for the first time in 1803 in the case of *Marbury* v. *Madison*.

The case involved William Marbury, who had been promised an appointment as a justice of the peace by outgoing president John Adams. President Thomas Jefferson ordered the new secretary of state, James Madison, to deny Marbury's appointment. Marbury claimed that the Judiciary Act of 1789 gave the Supreme Court the power to order Madison to give him the promised appointment. However, Chief Justice Marshall ruled that the act gave the Supreme Court powers that it had not been granted by the Constitution. Because the Constitution is the supreme law of the land, the Judiciary Act passed by Congress was declared unconstitutional. This was the first time the Supreme Court had declared an act of Congress unconstitutional and thus established the concept of judicial review.

Choosing Cases

More than 7,000 cases are filed with the Supreme Court each year. The Court may decide, with or without a formal written opinion, only about 130 to 150 of those cases. It accepts only those cases that generally deal with important constitutional or national questions. At least four of the nine justices must vote to hear a case. If the Supreme Court refuses to review a case, the decision of the lower court remains in effect. The Court may also **remand**, or return, a case to a lower court for a new trial.

Hearing and Deciding Cases

The Supreme Court hears cases by oral argument. Lawyers for the parties in a case each have 30 minutes to present their arguments. Then the justices spend their time reading written arguments and considering what was said in court. When they are ready to decide a case, they hold a private meeting to vote. Each justice has one vote, and decisions are reached by a simple majority.

After deliberation and voting, the Court delivers its opinion. An **opinion** explains the reasoning that led to the decision. The Court's opinion is binding on all lower courts. Sometimes a justice agrees with the decision of the majority, but for different reasons. In that case, the justice may decide to write a **concurring opinion**.

QUICK FACTS

Changing Court Opinions: Segregation

The Supreme Court has interpreted the Constitution differently at different times. For example, the Court ruled in *Scott* v. *Sandford* that African Americans were not considered U.S. citizens. Later, in *Plessy* v. *Ferguson*, the Court legalized "separate but equal" facilities for African Americans and whites. The Court put an end to legal segregation in 1954 in *Brown* v. *Board of Education*.

How were the rulings in Plessy *v.* Ferguson *and* Brown *v.* Board of Education *different?*

1857 *Scott* v. *Sandford*

Dred Scott's attempt to win his freedom was defeated when the Supreme Court ruled that slaves had no right to sue in federal courts because they were considered property, not citizens.

In many cases, one or more justices disagree with the majority opinion. These justices may file a dissenting opinion. The **dissenting opinion** explains why the justice believes the majority opinion is wrong. Although dissenting opinions have no effect on the law, they are still important. Many dissenting opinions have later become the law of the land when the beliefs of society and the opinions of the justices change. For example, in *Plessy* v. *Ferguson*, Justice John M. Harlan dissented, saying that the Constitution should not be interpreted in ways that recognize class or racial distinctions.

Supreme Court Justices

The size of the Supreme Court is determined by Congress. Since 1869, the number of justices has been set at nine. The Court has a chief justice, who is the principal judge, and eight associate justices. Supreme Court justices, like other federal judges, are appointed for life by the president and approved by the Senate. Justices can be removed only by impeachment. There are no special requirements to be a Supreme Court justice.

READING CHECK **Summarizing** How can the power of judicial review have an affect on the laws that are passed by Congress?

Checking the Court's Power

How do the other branches of government check the powers of the judicial branch? The executive branch—the president—has the power to appoint all federal judges, including Supreme Court justices. Of course, the Senate must confirm all nominees for federal judgeships, including Supreme Court justices. If a nominee cannot win the support of a majority of the senators, the nomination may be rejected and the president would have to appoint someone else.

If the Court rules that a law is unconstitutional, Congress can try to write a better law. Congress may change the law enough so that the Supreme Court can uphold the new law. Another way for Congress to check the Court's power is to amend the Constitution. For example, in 1895 the Supreme Court declared that an income tax law passed by Congress was unconstitutional. So in 1913 the states ratified the Sixteenth Amendment, which gave Congress the power to tax a person's income. The income tax then became legal and constitutional.

READING CHECK **Finding the Main Idea** What are two ways the legislative branch can check the power of the Supreme Court?

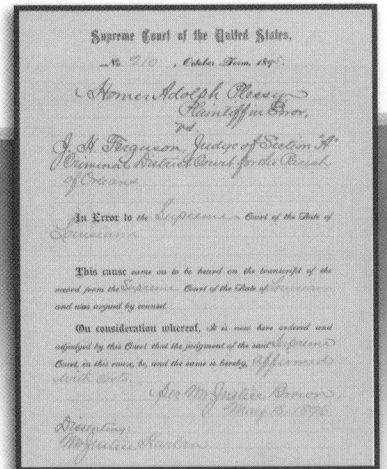

1896 *Plessy v. Ferguson*

African American Homer Plessy was arrested for riding in a "whites-only" railcar in Louisiana. The Court justified segregation by ruling that separate facilities for different races were legal as long as those facilities were equal to one another.

1954 *Brown v. Board of Education*

In a unanimous decision, the Supreme Court ruled that segregated schools were not equal and therefore violated the Fourteenth Amendment's guarantee of equal protection under the law.

FOCUS ON Thurgood Marshall
(1908—1993)

Thurgood Marshall was born in Baltimore, Maryland. He graduated first in his class from Howard Law School in 1933 and soon became a key legal council for the National Association for the Advancement of Colored People (NAACP). He helped the NAACP win several important civil rights cases. Perhaps his most famous victory was *Brown* v. *Board of Education*, which outlawed segregation in public schools.

Marshall was appointed to a federal court of appeals in 1961. He became the first African American justice on the Supreme Court in 1967, serving for more than 20 years. Marshall retired from the court in 1991. He left behind a legacy of defending individual rights and demanding equal justice for all Americans.

Explain How did Marshall contribute to the U.S. legal system?

Strengthening Rights

Supreme Court decisions have allowed the Constitution to meet the demands of changing times. For example, in 1954 the Court decided in the case of *Brown* v. *Board of Education* that the segregation of public schools was unconstitutional. By doing this the Court reversed an earlier opinion that said segregation was constitutional as long as there were separate-but-equal facilities for whites and African Americans. In *Brown*, the Court ruled that segregated schools were inherently unequal and therefore violated the Fourteenth Amendment. The Court ruled that public schools be desegregated "with all deliberate speed."

The 1954 *Brown* decision did not completely eliminate segregation. It took other cases and decisions to strike down other discriminatory laws.

Like the *Brown* decision, other Supreme Court opinions have made far-reaching changes in American life. For example, the Court has made several rulings on the rights of the accused and voting rights.

In the 1966 case of *Miranda* v. *Arizona*, the Court declared that the police must inform arrested suspects of their rights before questioning them.

The Court also made several decisions in the 1960s affecting voting rights and representation in Congress. These decisions were aimed at ensuring that each person's vote counts the same as any other person's vote.

READING CHECK **Analyzing Information** How has the Supreme Court made sure that the Constitution applies to all Americans?

go.hrw.com
Online Quiz
KEYWORD: SZ7 HP7

SECTION 3 ASSESSMENT

Reviewing Ideas and Terms

1. a. Define Write a brief definition for each of the following terms: **judicial review, remand, opinion, concurring opinion,** and **dissenting opinion.**

  b. Compare and Contrast What are the differences between a concurring opinion and a dissenting opinion?

2. a. Recall What can Congress do to check the power of the Supreme Court?

  b. Support a Point of View Does the Supreme Court have too much power? Why?

3. a. Summarize What are some issues Supreme Court cases have addressed?

  b. Elaborate What might happen if people did not have the rights established in *Miranda* v. *Arizona*? Explain your answer.

Critical Thinking

4. Sequencing Copy the graphic organizer. Use it to identify the steps a case goes through in the Supreme Court.

Focus on Writing

5. Identifying Points of View You are a senator considering a presidential nominee for Supreme Court justice. Write a letter to your colleagues explaining how you intend to vote for the nominee.

STUDENTS TAKE ACTION

Encouraging Safe Exercise

When Mexico, Missouri, bicyclists ride safely between Fairground and Lakeview Parks or on the Lakeview trail, they will have a local Project Citizen class to thank. These students supported the Lakeview trail proposal, wrote rules for the trail, and planned a bike-lane route to connect the two parks.

Community Connection Students in Ms. Diana Henage's class were concerned that their city did not provide any areas designated for bicycle riding. There were no bike trails and no bicycle lanes on city streets. When the students conducted community surveys, they found there was overwhelming public support for the creation of such bicycle lanes and trails.

Taking Action The class created a "Pedal to the Metal" proposal. They wanted to create bicycle lanes connecting two public parks. They also wanted to establish rules for cyclists, walkers, and people in wheelchairs on trails. They began by interviewing city officials about a park bicycle trail that was already being considered, as well as their new proposal. With student support, the park trail was approved, and the city council agreed to consider painting bike lanes. But the class did not stop there. The students gathered information on statewide bicycle programs and then sent lists of rules and regulations to the city manager and the city parks director for final approval. The students look forward to seeing their rules posted at the entrance of the new Lakeview Park Trail!

Designated bike lanes and bike trails make bicycling safer.

go.hrw.com
Project Citizen
KEYWORD: SZ7 CH7

SERVICE LEARNING

1. How were the students inspired to promote safe exercise in their community?
2. How did the students work with local officials to gain support for their ideas?

CHAPTER 7 REVIEW

Visual Summary

Use the visual summary to help you review the main ideas of the chapter.

There are three main levels of federal courts that lead to the U.S. Supreme Court, the court that has the final say on what is constitutional and what is not.

The Supreme Court

U.S. Court of Appeals

U.S. District Court

Reviewing Key Terms

For each term below, write a sentence explaining its significance to the judicial branch.

1. crime
2. criminal law
3. civil law
4. common law
5. precedent
6. constitutional law
7. appeal
8. jurisdiction
9. district courts
10. original jurisdiction
11. courts of appeals
12. appellate jurisdiction
13. justices
14. judicial review
15. remand
16. opinion
17. concurring opinion
18. dissenting opinion

Comprehension and Critical Thinking

SECTION 1 *(Pages 180–183)*

19. **a. Describe** What are the types of laws that exist in the United States?

    b. Explain What purposes do U.S. courts serve?

SECTION 2 *(Pages 185–188)*

20. **a. Recall** What two kinds of cases are tried in district courts?

    b. Sequence How is the federal court system organized?

SECTION 3 *(Pages 189–192)*

21. **a. Recall** How are appointments made to the Supreme Court, and how long do justices serve?

    b. Summarize How did John Marshall increase the Supreme Court's power?

    c. Elaborate How does the Supreme Court limit Congress's power?

Active Citizenship video program

Review the video to answer the closing question:
Why do Supreme Court decisions affect different groups of people all over the country?

Using the Internet

go.hrw.com
KEYWORD: SZ7 CH7

22. Visualizing the Judiciary With so many special courts and levels of responsibility, understanding the judicial branch of the U.S. government can be challenging. Enter the activity keyword to research the structure of the federal court system. Then create a mobile that displays your information. Focus on the jurisdictions of various courts and the cases that each court handles.

Civics Skills

Analyzing a News Article *Use the Civics Skills taught in this chapter to answer the question about the selection below.*

July 20, 2005
BUSH NOMINATES ROBERTS TO SUPREME COURT

Republicans praise nominee as Dems vow thorough review

WASHINGTON (CNN) -- President Bush on Tuesday chose as his first Supreme Court nominee U.S. Circuit Judge John Roberts Jr., a conservative whose selection pleased Republicans and prompted Democrats to vow a thorough review in the Senate.

If confirmed by the Senate, Roberts would replace retiring Justice Sandra Day O'Connor, who gained a reputation as a moderate swing voter in her 24 terms on the nation's highest court.

Bush called the selection of a nominee to the high court "one of the most consequential decisions a president makes."

Bush's announcement, televised nationally in prime time Tuesday from the White House, ended nearly three weeks of fervent speculation about who would take O'Connor's pivotal place on the court.

A senior administration official told CNN that Bush interviewed Roberts Friday at the White House and made his final decision Tuesday morning. He called Roberts about 12:30 p.m. to offer him the appointment.

With Roberts standing at his side, Bush said the nominee "has devoted his entire professional life to the cause of justice and is widely admired for his intellect, his sound judgment and personal decency."

In a brief statement, Roberts said, "It is both an honor and very humbling to be nominated to serve on the Supreme Court."

Source: CNN.com

23. Does this article seem to favor one side of the issue over another? Explain your answer.

Reading Skills

Distinguishing Between Fact and Opinion
Use the Reading Skill taught in this chapter to answer the question about the selection below.

The team created a "Pedal to the Metal" proposal. They wanted to create bicycle lanes connecting two public parks. They also wanted to establish rules for cyclists, walkers, and people in wheelchairs on trails. They began by interviewing city officials about a park bicycle trail that was already being considered, as well as their new proposal. With student support, the park trail was approved and the city council agreed to consider painting bike lanes. But the team did not stop there. The students gathered information on statewide bicycle programs and then sent lists of rules and regulations to the city manager and the city parks director for final approval. The students look forward to seeing their rules posted at the entrance of the new Lakeview Park Trail! (p. 193)

24. Which of the following statements from the passage is an opinion?

a. With student support, the park trail was approved.

b. The students look forward to seeing their rules posted at the entrance of the new Lakeview Park Trail!

c. The students gathered information on statewide bicycle programs.

d. The city council agreed to consider painting bike lanes.

FOCUS ON SPEAKING

25. Writing a Radio News Broadcast Review your notes on the process a court case takes, from the original trial all the way to the Supreme Court. Then, pick one of the Supreme Court cases discussed in your textbook. Using the library or an online resource, research the history of the case. Now write a radio news broadcast where you follow the case through the judicial system.

Judges for Life

Did the Supreme Court pull the plug on your music? In June 2005 the Supreme Court ruled that makers of file-sharing systems for the Internet could face criminal charges if people used their technology to illegally download copyrighted music. The technology involved in this case about copyrighted work had only been around for a few years. Some of the Supreme Court justices who decided the case were over age 70. Do you think age influenced the Court's decision?

Why it Matters Justices of the U.S. Supreme Court are appointed for life, as are all other federal judges. These people play an important role in interpreting the laws that govern our country and our lives. For instance, think about how the Court's decision on file-sharing technology might affect you. Federal judges decide many other issues that affect our daily lives and our futures. The public often debates whether it is fair for these decisions to be made by people who may sometimes be far removed from the younger generations their decisions affect the most.

But Article 2, Section 1, of the U.S. Constitution states that Supreme Court justices should be appointed for life. The framers wanted justices to be able to make decisions freely, without political influence or concerns about how their decisions might affect their chances of re-election. The justices can serve until they die or they choose to retire. William O. Douglas, the longest-serving Supreme Court justice, held his position for 36 years before retiring. The oldest justice, Oliver Wendell Holmes, served until he was 90. Many justices have served into their 80s.

Some people believe that there should be a required retirement age for Supreme Court justices. Others point out that Americans are now living longer, healthier lives. If older justices are able to do their jobs well, their age should not matter. And, they argue, the experience the justices gain with age will benefit the Court.

The nine justices of the U.S. Supreme Court in March 2006

ANALYSIS SKILL **EVALUATING THE LAW**

go.hrw.com
KEYWORD: SZ7 CH7

1. Do you think the age of Supreme Court justices affects their views on issues? Explain.
2. How might the role of justices and their decisions change if they were elected for set periods of time?

UNIT 3
STATE AND LOCAL GOVERNMENT

This Uncle Sam postcard celebrates the Fourth of July.

CHAPTER 8
STATE GOVERNMENT

NATIONAL STANDARDS®
FOR CIVICS AND GOVERNMENT

I. What are civic life, politics, and government?

   A. What purposes should government serve?

II. What are the foundations of the American political system?

   B. What are the distinctive characteristics of American society?

III. How does the government established by the Constitution embody the purposes, values, and principles of American democracy?

   C. How are state and local governments organized and what do they do?

   E. How does the American political system provide for choice and opportunities for participation?

Active Citizenship video program

Watch the video to learn how young citizens can work with state government to bring about change.

WHY CIVICS Matters

State governments provide many services to you and other citizens of your state, such as building highways and creating beautiful recreation areas. As an active citizen, you have a duty to be aware of how your state government spends your tax dollars.

STUDENTS TAKE ACTION

STOPPING DRUG SALES What if you learned that a gang was selling drugs down the street from your school or your church? What could you do to get your state government to solve the problem? As you read this chapter, think of actions you and your friends could take to make your street safe again.

FOCUS ON WRITING

BIOGRAPHICAL SKETCH In this chapter you will learn about the powers and the parts of state government. Read the chapter, and then write a two-page biographical sketch of someone important, either past or present, to your state's government.

Reading Skills

In this chapter you will read about the powers that the Tenth Amendment guarantees to state governments. You will learn what powers the states and federal government share. You will read about state lawmaking bodies and how they are organized. You will also learn how state laws are made, and how the executive branches of state governments enforce those laws. Finally, you will learn about the state court system and what kinds of cases it handles.

Using Primary Sources

FOCUS ON READING As you know from experience, second-hand information isn't always reliable. When you want to know what really happened, you need to talk to someone who was there. You need a primary source.

Primary Sources Primary sources can help you understand what a political candidate or government official said, did, or meant. A primary source is a document from someone who witnessed or took part in an event. Primary sources can be written documents, such as government records or letters. They can also be photographs, speeches, or even songs.

Identify the source's background. Understand who wrote the source and the conditions under which it was written. Ask yourself if the author is biased in some way.

Read the source. Read the source several times until you are confident you understand its meaning. Be sure to identify all facts. Note any statements that give you insight into the opinions of the author.

Draw conclusions. Use your careful reading of the source to draw conclusions about the topic or event discussed.

Helpful Hints for Identifying Primary Sources

1. To determine if something is a primary source, ask yourself when it was created. Primary sources are those that were created around the time of the event they describe.

2. Primary sources include speeches, diaries, letters, and photographs. They provide information about the event and give you glimpses of the attitudes, feelings, and concerns of the people involved.

You Try It!

The primary source on this page is part of North Carolina governor Michael F. Easley's 2001 State of the State address. Read the source and then answer the questions below.

> "I am proud to stand here before you tonight —at the beginning of a bright new age for North Carolina. We leave behind a decade that will long be remembered as one of the most rewarding in our history . . . The people of North Carolina rallied together like never before—for our schools, for our communities, for our families.
>
> I want to personally thank you for putting people first and putting party differences aside. Good government is not about Democrats and Republicans. It is about children, seniors and working families. You put them first . . .
>
> You are the first Legislature of the new century. You have a chance to be remembered as the group that brought sustained progress to North Carolina. You have a chance to make history and be remembered for it . . . Any state can make progress in good times. It's the great states that make progress in tough times."

After you have read the passage, answer the following questions.

1. Why might Easley's speech be a good source of information about the level of cooperation between Democrats and Republicans?

2. Imagine that in the week following the speech, you read a letter to the editor that contained the following comments:

   "Governor Easley's speech showed that he does not appreciate the hard work the legislature has done to improve our state."

   Is this primary source reliable and accurate? Why or why not?

As you read Chapter 8, notice what primary sources are used. Ask yourself if you think the text is a reliable secondary source.

KEY TERMS

Chapter 8

Academic Vocabulary

Success in school is related to knowing academic vocabulary—the words that are frequently used in school assignments and discussions. In this chapter, you will learn the following academic word:

develop *(p. 211)*

The States

The Main Idea

In the United States, all 50 independent states fit together to form one country. The federal system allows state governments to serve the needs of their citizens while cooperating as a united country.

Reading Focus

1. What powers do state governments have?
2. How do states work together with other states and with the national government in our federal system?

Key Terms

delegated powers, *p. 202*
reserved powers, *p. 202*
concurrent powers, *p. 203*
full faith and credit clause, *p. 205*
extradition, *p. 205*

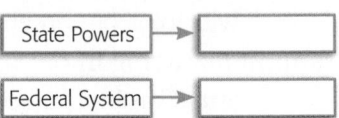 **TAKING NOTES** As you read, take notes on the powers of state governments and how state governments work in our federal system. Use a diagram like this one to record your notes.

State Powers →
Federal System →

 **CIVICS IN PRACTICE** For a few years after they won their independence, the 13 states acted like small, separate countries. Then they joined together under an agreement called the Constitution, which established the rules of the new country. Under the Constitution, the states set aside some of their own rights and powers for the good of the whole country. Those powers went to the new national government. The states, however, kept some of their powers.

State Government Powers

When the 13 states ratified the Constitution and agreed to come together as one country, they did not want to hand too much power over to the federal government. Instead, they chose a federal system that divides government powers between the federal and state governments. Some powers—**delegated powers**—were given to the federal government. Those powers include conducting foreign policy, printing money, maintaining a post office, and defending the country. Some powers were granted exclusively to the states, while other powers are shared by state and federal governments.

Powers Reserved to the States

The states kept control over more local concerns. The Tenth Amendment of the U.S. Constitution says any power not delegated to the federal government belongs to the people and the states. These powers are known as **reserved powers**.

Reserved powers allow state governments to establish rules for the health, safety, and welfare of the citizens of their states. For example, states are responsible for rules concerning marriage, driving laws, and traffic regulations. States also maintain education systems. The Constitution, however, requires that state laws meet appropriate federal standards and adhere to Supreme Court rulings.

Another reserved power of the state is to conduct all local, state, and national elections. States decide most of the qualifications for voting not otherwise specified in the U.S. Constitution. In addition, state governments have control over all governments within their boundaries—districts, cities, towns, townships, and counties. Local governments receive their powers from the states.

LAW 101

Schools and the Lottery

Education is expensive. Every day in school, you use many resources: computers, science equipment, and sports gear. Your school also employs many people, such as teachers, nurses, and maintenance staff. Where does the money to pay for everything come from?

Why it Matters Education is funded at many levels: the local, state, and federal. Most of the money used for school funding comes from taxes. Some states, though, have looked for other ways to raise money. One way used by many states is a lottery. People buy lottery tickets that give them a very small chance to win lots of money. People who support lottery funding say that everyone has to pay taxes, but playing the lottery is a choice. Other people think lotteries are not fair because people who earn less money are more likely to play the lottery. In 2005, 41 states, Washington, D.C., and Puerto Rico had lotteries, and at least 25 states used some of the money specifically for education. Some states also raise education money through slot machines.

In some states, like California, lottery money goes to help fund education.

ANALYSIS SKILL **EVALUATING THE LAW**

go.hrw.com
KEYWORD: SZ7 CH8

1. Is it fair that everyone should pay taxes to fund schools? Why or why not?
2. What is your opinion about using lotteries and slot machines to pay for education?

Concurrent Powers

Some government powers are shared by both state and federal governments. These shared powers are called **concurrent powers**. For example, taxation is a concurrent power. Both the federal government and the state governments can tax their citizens. The national government taxes U.S. citizens through federal income taxes. State governments may raise money with sales taxes, income taxes, and property taxes. The money raised through state taxes pays for state services such as education, highways, and health and safety programs.

Another important concurrent, or shared, power is making and enforcing laws. Similar to the national government, state governments have legislatures that propose and pass new laws. Most states also have a state police force that helps to enforce those laws and to keep the states safe.

Other concurrent powers used by the states are the establishment of state and local court systems and the power to borrow and spend money. Without these concurrent powers, states would be unable to carry out their day-to-day business.

Powers of the State

The U.S. Constitution established a federal system in which powers are divided between the national and state governments. Some powers are granted exclusively to the states, while others are shared with the national government.

Federal Powers — **Shared Powers** — **State Powers**

State Powers

- Establish and maintain schools
- Establish local governments
- Regulate business within the state
- Make marriage laws
- Provide for public safety
- Oversee elections
- Assume other powers not delegated to the national government nor prohibited to the states

Election Oversight

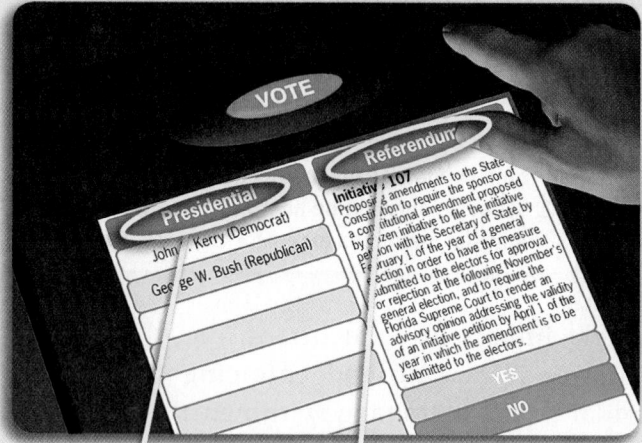

VOTE

Presidential
John F. Kerry (Democrat)
George W. Bush (Republican)

Referendum
Initiative 107
Proposes amendments to the State Constitution to require the sponsor of a constitutional amendment proposed by citizen initiative to file the initiative petition with the Secretary of State by February 1 of the year of a general election in order to have the measure submitted to the electors for approval or rejection at the following November's general election, and to require the Florida Supreme Court to render an advisory opinion addressing the validity of an initiative petition by April 1 of the year in which the amendment is to be submitted to the electors.

YES
NO

Federal elections, like the presidential election, are organized and monitored by the states, not the federal government.

States alone have the power to conduct elections. State election boards are responsible for organizing all federal and state elections.

Shared Powers

- Maintain law and order
- Levy taxes
- Borrow money
- Charter banks
- Establish courts
- Oversee public health and safety
- Enforce laws

Levy Taxes

Employee ID 5568292
Earnings Statement

Chuck's Burgers 'n Shakes
9874 Springhill Pond Road
Mistletoe, OH 45342-0000

Period Ending: 06/30/2005

2804

Advice Date:06/30/2005

Advice Number:647623

FEDERAL	STATE – OH	LOCAL
Marital Status: Single	Single	Single
Exemptions/Allowances: 1	1	1
Add'l Amount: 0	0	0
Add'l Percent: 0	0	0

Van Landingham, Anita C	Section 1 - Earnings	GROSS PAY
1742 Gayston Dr.	Rate 8.50	170.00
Mistletoe, OH 45342-0000	Hours 20	
	Current 170.00	
	YTD 680.00	

Section 2 - Tax Deductions					
	SocSec/Disability	Medicare	Federal Tax	State Tax	Total
Current	15.30	5.50	35.10	10.20	66.10
YTD	46.20	20.20	140.40	40.80	247.60

NET PAY 103.90

The federal government taxes individual incomes. Most workers have federal income and Social Security taxes deducted from their regular paychecks.

State governments can also levy taxes. State taxes include property taxes, sales tax, and income taxes. Not all states, however, have income taxes.

ANALYSIS SKILL **ANALYZING VISUALS**

Why do you think that some powers are granted exclusively to state governments?

State Constitutions

Each of the 50 states has its own constitution. These constitutions are the rules that organize the state government. Many state constitutions contain the following elements:

- a preamble that states the basic principles on which the state government is founded;
- a bill of rights that lists the rights guaranteed to all citizens of the state;
- an outline of the organization of the state's government, with the duties of each of the branches carefully spelled out;
- provisions for elections, including qualifications that citizens must meet for voting and rules for conducting elections;
- provisions for managing state affairs, such as education, law and order, transportation, and finance; and
- methods of amending the state constitution, as well as a list of any amendments that have been passed.

States have amended their constitutions as the powers and duties of state governments changed. Alabama, for example, has amended its constitution some 650 times since it was ratified in 1901.

READING CHECK **Finding Main Ideas** What powers are granted to state governments?

Our Federal System

As you have read, the U.S. Constitution establishes a federal system that divides power between the national government and the states. Some people see the federal system as two separate layers of government with different powers. In everyday practice, however, the separate layers of powers overlap and often mix. For example, the national, state, and even local governments make policies regarding education for the nation's students. States must work together on many other issues, and they must work with the national government if the needs of all the people are to be met.

States Work Together

By signing the U.S. Constitution, the states agreed to cooperate with each other. Article IV, Section 1 of the U.S. Constitution states "Full faith and credit [acceptance] shall be given in each State to the public acts, records, and judicial proceedings of every other State." This passage is known as the full faith and credit clause.

The **full faith and credit clause** ensures that each state will accept the decisions of civil courts in other states. An example of full faith and credit is the acceptance of a state's official records by the other states. For example, marriage certificates, birth certificates, wills, contracts, and property deeds issued by any one state are accepted by all other states.

States work together in other ways as well. A person who commits a crime cannot escape justice by fleeing to another state. For example, a person who steals a car in Utah and flees to Arizona can be returned to Utah for trial. This process of returning fugitives is called **extradition**.

States also cooperate on many projects. For example, a bridge that crosses a river bordering two states is built and maintained by the governments of both states. States may also join with other states in regional groups to work together to reduce water and air pollution.

States Work with the Federal Government

The states also work together with the federal government. Federal and state governments often work together to share the costs of providing a wide range of social services to the American people. For example, state and national governments cooperate to build highways, assist the unemployed, help people with low incomes, and conserve natural resources.

State and national governments also cooperate in times of crisis. After severe natural disasters, such as earthquakes, floods,

Hoover Dam

The Hoover Dam, which sits in Arizona and Nevada on the Colorado River, was built under the supervision of the federal government.

How is the Hoover Dam an example of the federal government and state governments working together?

Arizona

Las Vegas•

Lake Mead

Boulder City• •Hoover Dam

tornadoes, and hurricanes, federal and state governments often work together to provide aid to disaster victims. For example, after Hurricane Katrina devastated a large area of the U.S. Gulf Coast in 2005, President Bush announced that the federal government would work with state and local governments to help provide housing, job training, and medical aid to the victims of the hurricane.

The federal government also aids the states. For example, after the attacks of September 11, 2001, increasing security became an important issue. Because the cost of increasing security at airports and other facilitates was too expensive for individual states, the federal government took over the task.

READING CHECK **Drawing Inferences** Why do states cooperate with each other and the federal government?

go.hrw.com
Online Quiz
KEYWORD: SZ7 HP8

SECTION 1 ASSESSMENT

Reviewing Ideas and Terms

1. a. Define Write a brief definition for the terms **delegated powers**, **reserved powers**, and **concurrent powers**.

b. Analyze Why might states amend their constitutions?

c. Evaluate Is it important for state governments to retain control of affairs within their borders? Explain your answer.

2. a. Define Write a brief definition for the terms **full faith and credit clause** and **extradition**.

b. Draw Conclusions Why do states have to follow certain federal rules?

c. Predict How might our federal system be different if states did not work together with the national government?

Critical Thinking

3. Comparing and Contrasting Use your notes and a graphic organizer like this one to identify federal, state, and shared powers.

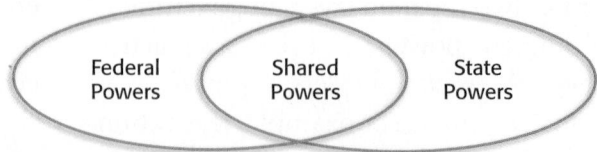

Federal Powers | Shared Powers | State Powers

Focus on Writing

4. Making Generalizations and Predictions Imagine that there is no full faith and credit clause and that your family intends to move to another state. In a short essay, explain how this might affect your family in your new residence.

206 CHAPTER 8

SECTION 2

State Legislatures

BEFORE YOU READ

The Main Idea

The process of passing state laws is similar to the process used in the U.S. Congress. In some states, citizens can take a direct role in making the state's laws.

Reading Focus

1. How are state legislatures organized to equally represent the citizens of their state?
2. How are state laws passed?
3. How do citizens participate in making state laws?

Key Terms

bicameral, *p. 207*
unicameral, *p. 207*
constituents, *p. 211*
initiative, *p. 211*
referendum, *p. 211*
recall, *p. 211*

TAKING NOTES As you read, take notes on state legislatures, passing laws, and how citizens can participate in state government. Use a diagram like this one to organize your notes.

State Legislature → Passing State Laws ← Citizens

Most state legislatures are modeled after the U.S. Congress.

California state Senator Dave Cogdill argues against a proposed bill as his fellow lawmakers contemplate its future.

CIVICS IN PRACTICE Your state legislature, or lawmaking body, is a smaller version of Congress. State representatives and senators introduce and pass bills in the same fashion as their national counterparts. Because you and your state legislators share many of the same concerns, you have a significant influence on your state government.

State Legislatures

Although it may go by a different name in some states, every state has a state legislature, or lawmaking body. Citizens elect state lawmakers—called legislators—to pass laws on their behalf. Like members of Congress, legislators are representatives of the citizens in the states' lawmaking bodies. These lawmaking bodies are organized to represent all citizens of the state equally.

Organization

All but one of the states have legislatures divided into two houses. These are known as **bicameral** legislatures. The larger of the two houses is usually called the House of Representatives. The smaller house is known as the Senate. Only Nebraska has a **unicameral**, or one-house, legislature, called the Senate.

POLITICAL CARTOON
Public Opinion about State Legislatures

Members of the public do not always agree with the actions of their state legislatures. Unpopular legislative action often prompts public criticism. This political cartoon shows one point of view regarding state legislatures.

In this cartoon, a state legislature is represented by figures usually associated with a circus.

ANALYSIS SKILL ANALYZING POLITICAL CARTOONS

What point about the public's opinion of state legislatures is this cartoon attempting to make?

State legislatures vary greatly in size. Alaska has the smallest legislature, with 40 representatives and 20 senators. New Hampshire's legislature is the largest in the United States. It has 400 representatives and 24 senators.

These state legislatures are organized to represent all citizens of the state equally. To ensure balanced representation, the state legislature divides the state into different legislative districts. Each member of the legislature represents the people who live in a particular district of that state. Citizens of those districts elect a representative and a senator to speak for that district in the state legislature.

In the 1964 case of *Reynolds* v. *Sims*, the U.S. Supreme Court ruled that state election districts must be equal in population—or as equal as possible. This ruling upheld the principle of "one person, one vote." The ruling attempted to establish equal representation for all citizens. Legislatures are now required to establish election districts that are almost equal in population.

Qualifications and Terms

Because state legislators have great responsibility, each state sets certain qualifications that candidates must meet. For example, most states require that members of the state legislature be U.S. citizens. In almost all states senators and representatives must live in the district that they represent. Generally, state senators must be at least 25 years of age to hold office. Most states require state representatives to be at least 21 years old. Some states, however, have lowered the age requirement to 18 for senators and representatives.

In most states senators are elected for four years, and representatives for two years. However, in a few states both senators and representatives are elected for four-year terms. In other states senators and representatives both serve two years. The senators who serve in Nebraska's one-house legislature are elected for four-year terms.

Sixteen states now limit the number of terms for state legislators. These laws limit the number of times a legislator may be elected to represent a district. For example, representatives in Arkansas can only serve three terms, a total of six years. Senators in Arkansas can serve only two terms, or eight years.

Compensation

The salaries and benefits received by state legislators vary widely from state to state. In Rhode Island, for example, legislators—who only serve part time—each receive $13,089 a year. New York's full-time legislators are among the highest paid in the country, each receiving an annual salary of $79,500, plus $138 a day for expenses.

Sessions and Leaders

Each state determines when its legislature meets. Most state legislatures meet in regular sessions every year. Other state legislatures meet once every two years. The California legislature has a two-year session that meets for that entire period. The North Carolina legislature holds a regular-length session in odd-numbered years and a shorter session in even-numbered years. In other states a session can last from 30 days to more than six months.

At the beginning of each session, members of the legislature choose the presiding officer and other leaders. In most states the lieutenant governor presides over the state Senate. In other states the Senate chooses its own presiding officer. Members of the lower house in all states choose their own presiding officer, usually called the speaker.

The presiding officer in each house appoints members of committees. As in the U.S. Congress, most of the work of the state legislatures is done in committees that specialize in certain areas, such as agriculture or education. The committees hold in-depth hearings on bills. These hearings allow legislators to gather information and debate bills before the bills are considered by the whole legislature.

READING CHECK **Contrasting** What are some of the different ways that state legislatures are organized?

Passing State Laws

States pass laws governing all areas within their responsibilty. In recent years, states also have become responsible for programs that had been run by the national government. As a result, state legislatures have passed bills to meet these responsibilities.

The lawmaking process in state legislatures is similar to the procedure followed in Congress. As in Congress, the process starts with a bill being introduced by a member of the legislature.

A Bill Is Introduced A member of either house may introduce a bill. Once introduced, the bill is assigned a number and is sent to the appropriate committee.

The Bill Is Sent to Committee In the next phase, the legislative committee decides whether or not to hold a hearing on the bill. If there is a hearing, witnesses testify

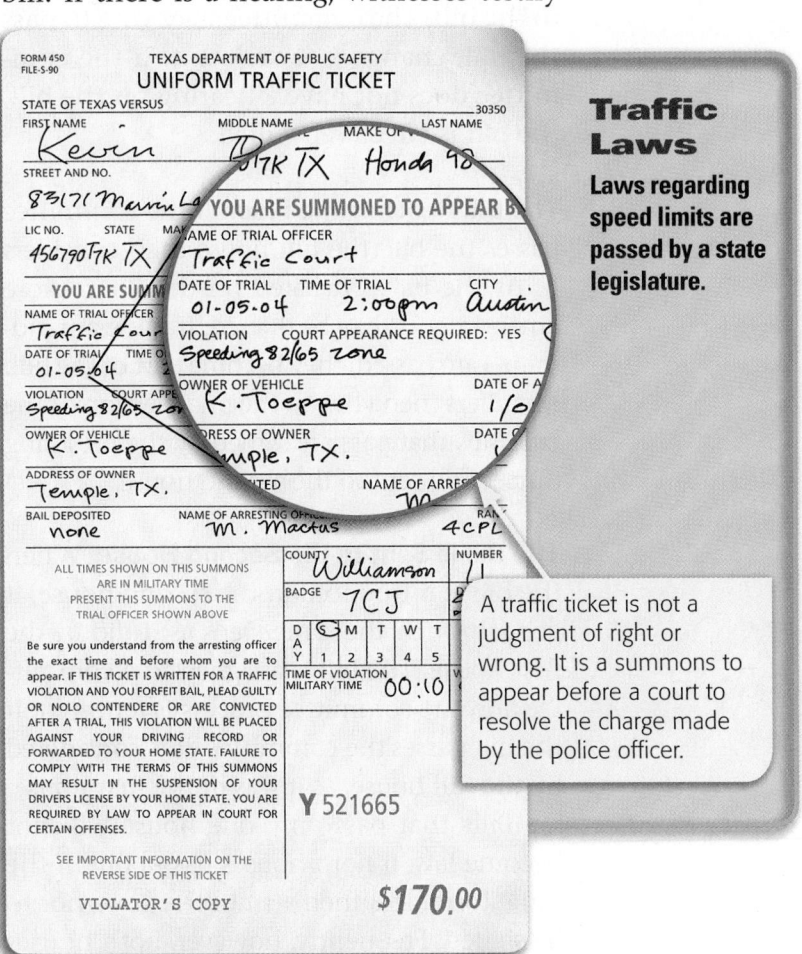

Traffic Laws

Laws regarding speed limits are passed by a state legislature.

A traffic ticket is not a judgment of right or wrong. It is a summons to appear before a court to resolve the charge made by the police officer.

about the bill. Amendments may be added to the bill. The committee may vote to pass the bill, change it, or reject it. If the committee does not have a hearing on the bill, the bill is effectively killed.

The Bill Reaches the Floor If the committee passes the bill, the full house then considers it. As the bill is debated on the floor, more amendments may be offered. If these amendments are passed, they become part of the bill. Members then vote on the final version of the bill. Bills that pass are signed by the presiding officer and sent to the second house.

The Bill Is Sent to the Second House When the bill is introduced in the second house, it goes through the same steps as it did in the first house. The bill is assigned to a committee and the committee process is repeated. If the bill passes the committee, it is considered by the full house, as it was in the first house.

Bills that pass only one house will not become law. If both houses pass a bill in the same form, it is then sent to the governor to be signed. Frequently, however, both houses

pass the bill, but in different forms. In this case, the bill is sent to a joint-conference committee to resolve the differences between the two bills.

The Bill Is Sent to a Joint Conference Committee Joint conference committees are made up of members from both houses. Committee members try to reach a compromise version of the bill that will be accepted by both houses. The two houses then vote on the compromise bill. Both houses usually accept this final version of the bill.

The Bill Is Sent to the Governor The final step in making a state law is to send the bill to the governor. If the governor signs the bill, it becomes a law. However, the governor may veto a bill he or she does not support. In most states the governor also has the power to veto only one part, or item, of an appropriation bill. This power is called an item veto. The legislature can pass a bill over the governor's veto by a two-thirds vote in each house.

READING CHECK **Analyzing Information** When in the legislative process can legislators amend bills?

How Citizens Participate in Lawmaking

Legislators and governors are not the only people who take part in lawmaking. There are many opportunities at the state level for citizens to participate in the lawmaking process. Legislators welcome input and information from the citizens they represent. These citizens are known as **constituents**.

Working with the Legislature

Constituents can help **develop** state laws. For example, if communities want more playgrounds, citizens may testify at a committee hearing to increase funding for parks. Other ways citizens can participate in the legislative process is to send letters or make phone calls.

The meetings and hearings of state legislatures are open to all citizens. Many state legislatures also broadcast meetings and hearings on television or over the Internet. Citizens can follow legislative activities through newspapers, televisions, and magazines.

Bypassing the Legislature

Some state constitutions allow the people to make laws themselves. Citizens are able to initiate, or start, new legislation through a process called the **initiative**. To begin an initiative, citizens write a petition describing the law they are proposing. This is called a proposition. A required number of voters—the number varies from state to state—must then sign the petition. If enough signatures are collected, then the proposition appears on the ballot at the next general election. If enough people vote for the bill, it becomes law.

Initiatives are often used to address major public policy issues that citizens think that the state government, especially the legislature, has overlooked or not adequately addressed.

In many states the voters must approve certain bills passed by the legislature before the bills can become laws. This method of referring potential laws directly to the people for approval is called a **referendum**.

Some states also allow voters to remove elected officials from office. This process, known as a **recall**, begins when a required number of voters signs a petition. A special election on the petition is then held. If a majority of voters favors the recall, the official is removed.

ACADEMIC VOCABULARY
develop: create

READING CHECK **Summarizing** What are three ways that citizens are able to have a direct role in making laws?

go.hrw.com
Online Quiz
KEYWORD: SZ7 HP8

SECTION 2 ASSESSMENT

Reviewing Ideas and Terms

1. a. Define Write a brief definition for the terms **bicameral** and **unicameral**.
   b. Predict How might unequal representation harm certain citizens or areas of a state?
2. Analyze What role do committees play in passing laws?
3. a. Define Write a brief definition for the terms **constituents**, **initiative**, **referendum**, and **recall**.
   b. Make Inferences Why are initiative, referendum, and recall important tools for citizens?

Critical Thinking

4. Summarizing Copy the graphic organizer. Use it and your notes to show the ways in which citizens can participate in state lawmaking.

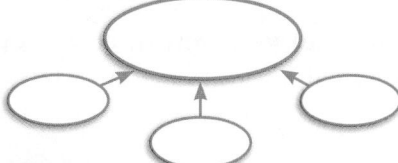

Focus on Writing

5. Supporting a Point of View Write a letter to a legislator encouraging him or her to pass legislation that would help you in your daily life.

Writing to Your Legislator

Learn

Let your legislator know what you are thinking—write him or her a letter. You can find the names of your legislators in the newspaper or by going online to official federal, state, county, or city Web sites. There are some basic rules to follow to make yours the kind of letter that receives an answer.

Practice

❶ Use the correct opening and closing. In the salutation, or greeting, use the person's correct title. For members of the U.S. House of Representatives, "Dear Representative (last name)," "Dear Congresswoman (last name)," or "Dear Congressman (last name)" are all acceptable. For members of the Senate, "Dear Senator (last name)" is the usual style. Titles of state officials vary. End your letter with the proper closing, such as "Respectfully yours" or "Sincerely yours." Then add your signature.

❷ Use your writing skills. Keep the body, or main part, of the letter as brief as possible. Clearly state your position or request in the first paragraph. Point out the relevant facts that will help your legislator understand your concerns.

❸ Be polite. Be sure to use respectful language in your letter—even if you disagree with your legislator's stand.

❹ Make sure that your return address is on the letter. This will allow your legislator to respond to you.

Apply

Use the letter below to help you answer the following questions.

❶ To whom is the letter addressed? What closing does the writer use?

❷ What issue is Aaron Campbell concerned about in his letter?

❸ Why might a letter be more convincing than a telephone call?

❹ Select a state or local issue that is important to you. Write a letter to one of your state legislators expressing your opinion, suggesting a solution, and asking for his or her support.

---

415 Sleepy Hollow
Roanoke, VA 24022
February 12, 2004

The Honorable Jane Doe
The State House
Richmond, VA 23218

Dear Representative Doe:

As you know, there is currently a bill before the legislature that would create 3,000 summer jobs for teenagers in our state. I strongly urge you to support this bill. Passage of Bill HR 1099 will give many teenagers the chance to earn money for school. It will also provide them with experience for future jobs. Finally, the state stands to benefit from all the work these teenagers will be doing in our parks, hospitals, and civic centers. I would appreciate knowing your position on this important issue.

Sincerely yours,

Aaron Campbell

Aaron Campbell

SECTION 3

The State Executive Branch

BEFORE YOU READ

The Main Idea

A state's executive branch carries out laws made by the state's legislative branch. Governors are the chief executives of state government.

Reading Focus

1. Who is the state's chief executive, and what are his or her powers and duties?
2. Who are the other officials of state executive branches?

Key Terms

governor, *p. 213*
patronage, *p. 215*
lieutenant governor, *p. 215*

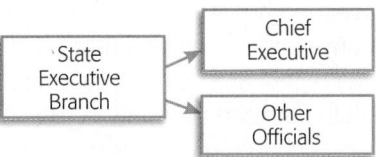
TAKING NOTES As you read, take notes on the state executive branch. Use a graphic organizer like this one to record your notes.

```
State
Executive    →    Chief Executive
Branch
             →    Other Officials
```

Democrat Kathleen Sebelius was elected governor of Kansas in 2002.

CIVICS IN PRACTICE What does the governor do? Once the legislature writes laws, the governor and his or her executive team put those laws into action. In this way, governors may affect your day-to-day affairs. Governors can also propose legislation or veto bills, just like the president.

The State's Chief Executive

The citizens of each state elect a governor to run the day-to-day affairs of their state. The **governor** is the chief executive in each state. The governor works for the people of his or her state. Governors lead the state government, set priorities, make government appointments, and implement laws to meet the needs of their states.

Qualifications and Terms of Governors

In each state, a constitution lists the qualifications for governor. In general, a candidate for governor must be a U.S. citizen and must have lived in the state for a certain number of years. Most states require a candidate for governor to be at least 30 years old. However, a few states, such as California and Ohio, allow persons as young as 18 years of age to run for governor.

In 2001 Ruth Ann Minner became Delaware's first female governor. Born and raised on a small farm, she left school at age 16 to help on her family's farm. Minner's husband died when she was 32. She had three sons to raise, but she returned to school, worked two jobs, and earned her G.E.D. After her second husband died, Minner began in politics by stuffing envelopes. She worked as an aide in the state legislature and as receptionist in the governor's office. She was elected to four terms in the state House of Representatives beginning in 1974, to three terms in the state Senate beginning in 1982, and to two terms as lieutenant governor in 1992 and 1996. Minner has also been honored in Delaware as Mother of the Year and Woman of the Year.

Draw Inferences Why might issues such as adult education and child welfare have been important to Governor Minner?

Most governors serve four-year terms. In some states, such as New Hampshire and Vermont, they serve for two years. About half of the states limit their governors to one or two terms in office.

The salaries of governors vary greatly from state to state. For example, the governor of New York receives $179,000 a year, and the governor of Nebraska receives $105,000 per year. To save their states money, the current governors of California and Tennessee—both wealthy men—donate their full salaries back to the state treasuries. The governor of New Jersey accepts only $1 annually. In addition, governors usually receive an allowance for expenses, such as travel. In most states governors and their families live in an official residence in the state capital.

Powers and Duties of Governors

A state governor is the highest-ranking official at the state level. He or she is responsible for "faithfully executing the laws" of the state. Like the president, a governor plays many roles. The three main roles are chief executive, chief legislator, and political party leader.

Chief Executive In most state constitutions, the governor is designated as the chief executive of the state. As chief executive, a governor may share executive powers with other "executives," such as the state treasurer, the attorney general, and the secretary of state, who are also elected officials. State governors usually have a number of executive powers.

- **Power of the Budget** One of the duties the governor in most states has is preparing a budget for one or two years. The governor submits this budget to the legislature. It sets priorities and offers solutions to state problems. Citizens of a state look to this budget as an indication of leadership.

- **Power to Make Appointments** A number of state agencies help the governor carry out the laws. Most states have executive departments that include agriculture, justice, labor, public safety (which includes the state police), public works, and transportation. Each state agency has a specific area of responsibility. For example, the state board of health enforces health laws and recommends measures to improve the health of state citizens. The department of human services supervises programs that help people who are disabled, poor, or unemployed. Other state agencies administer state laws on conservation and public utilities.

Although voters elect some of the heads of these agencies in some states, the governor usually has the power to appoint these state officials. Appointments typically require confirmation by the state Senate. An official who has been appointed by the governor can usually be removed or replaced by the governor.

- **Power to Supervise State Employees** In most states, many important state agencies are under the governor's control. By directing the operation of these agencies, the governor can have a major impact on state policies and state action. Overall, the 50 state governments employ more than 4.7 million people.

Most state government jobs are open to any qualified citizen who passes a state examination. However, some state jobs are filled through **patronage**. That is, the jobs are given to people recommended by political party leaders. Such jobs often go to people who provided valuable help during the election campaign.

Chief Legislator Only the state legislature can pass laws, but the governor plays an important part in proposing new laws. The governor usually appears before the state legislature at one of its early meetings. In some states this takes the form of a state of the state address to the legislature. At this meeting, the governor outlines laws he or she thinks should be passed. The governor may also submit legislation that he or she wants passed. He or she frequently talks to leaders of the legislature, urging them to pass specific bills and oppose others. State legislators know that if they pass a bill the governor opposes, the governor also has the power to veto legislation.

Political Party Leader The governor is the head of his or her political party in the state. State senators and representatives within the governor's party often model their opinions and policies after the governor's. The governor can help them during their campaigns for re-election.

Other Powers A governor has many other powers. Directors of many state agencies are appointed by the governor. The heads of the state police force and state militia report to the governor. In times of emergency, such as during floods or hurricanes, the governor may call out the National Guard to help keep order and assist with relief efforts. The governor also has the judicial power to pardon certain prisoners.

READING CHECK **Summarizing** What are three main roles of governors, and what responsibilities does each role entail?

Other State Executive Officials

Each state also has a number of other executive branch officials to help run the state government and enforce state laws. In most states voters elect these officials. In some states, however, the governor appoints these officials who are then a part of the governor's cabinet.

Lieutenant Governor

Most states have a **lieutenant governor**. The lieutenant governor becomes head of the state executive branch if the governor dies, resigns, or is removed from office. The lieutenant governor often serves as the presiding officer of the state senate. In some states it is possible for the lieutenant governor and the governor to belong to different political parties.

Governor Helps Out
Governor Haley Barbour of Mississippi helps unload water and other supplies as part of relief efforts for residents of Mississippi affected by Hurricane Katrina in 2005.

Secretary of State

The secretary of state keeps state records and carries out election laws. In states without a lieutenant governor, the secretary of state may take over as governor if the governor's office becomes vacant.

Attorney General

The attorney general is in charge of the state's legal business, or matters concerning the law. He or she provides state officials with advice about the meaning of laws. The attorney general or an assistant represents the state in court when the state is involved in a lawsuit. The attorney general may also assist local officials in the prosecution of criminals.

State Treasurer

In some states the state treasurer is in charge of handling all state funds. Sometimes this official supervises the collection of taxes and pays the state's bills as well.

State Auditor

The state auditor ensures that no public funds from the state treasury are used without authorization. The auditor also regularly examines the state's financial records to make sure that they are correct. The auditor is sometimes called the comptroller.

Superintendent of Public Instruction

The superintendent of public instruction carries out the policies of the state board of education. The state board makes regulations, under state law, that govern local school districts. The superintendent distributes state funds to local school systems according to state and federal laws. In some states this official is called the superintendent of public schools or the state commissioner of education.

READING CHECK **Supporting a Point of View** Which official do you think has the most important responsibilities, and why?

go.hrw.com
Online Quiz
KEYWORD: SZ7 HP8

SECTION 3 ASSESSMENT

Reviewing Ideas and Terms

1. a. Define Write a brief definition for the terms **governor** and **patronage**.

b. Summarize What are the primary powers and duties of most governors?

c. Draw Conclusions How does the governor's legislative power influence the types of bills legislators introduce?

d. Make Predictions What might happen if the governor and legislature do not agree on legislative priorities?

2. a. Define Write a brief definition for the term **lieutenant governor**.

b. Identify What state executive officials deal with state finances?

c. Compare and Contrast How are the duties and responsibilities of the lieutenant governor similar to those of the vice president of the United States? How are they different?

Critical Thinking

3. Categorizing Copy the graphic organizer. Use it and your notes to identify the role of each state official.

Position	Duties
Lieutenant Governor	
Secretary of State	
Attorney General	
State Treasurer	
State Auditor	
Superintendent of Public Instruction	

Focus on Writing

4. Problem Solving Imagine that you are part of the governor's executive team. You have been asked to put into action a bill that creates new after-school programs. Write out a plan for this program.

SECTION 4

State Courts

BEFORE YOU READ

The Main Idea

State court systems include lower courts, general trial courts, appeals courts, and state supreme courts.

Reading Focus

1 What kinds of cases do state courts handle?
2. How is the state court system organized?
3. How are state judges selected?

Key Terms

penal code, *p. 217*
Missouri Plan, *p. 220*

TAKING NOTES As you read, take notes on the state court system. Use a chart like this one to organize your notes.

State Court Cases	
State Court System	
Selection of State Judges	

The Louisiana Supreme Court building in New Orleans

CIVICS IN PRACTICE State legislatures write laws, and state executives put those laws into action. Then, state courts make sure everyone is following the rules. For example, a speeding ticket is usually handled in a low-level state court, such as a traffic court. Other cases are heard at different levels, all the way to the state supreme court.

State Court Cases

As a citizen, you are subject to two levels of law and two sets of judicial systems. Federal courts address violations of the United States Constitution and federal laws. State courts address violations of state constitutions and state laws. Each state is free to create its own court system to meet the state's needs. Each state is also free to determine the way in which judges for its courts are selected. But whatever the court system and however the judges are selected, the role of the state courts is the same: apply and enforce the criminal and civil laws of the state.

Each state creates its own penal code. A **penal code** is a set of criminal laws. State attorneys prosecute individuals who violate the penal code by committing a crime. These are called criminal cases. State judges hear these cases. If the criminal court finds

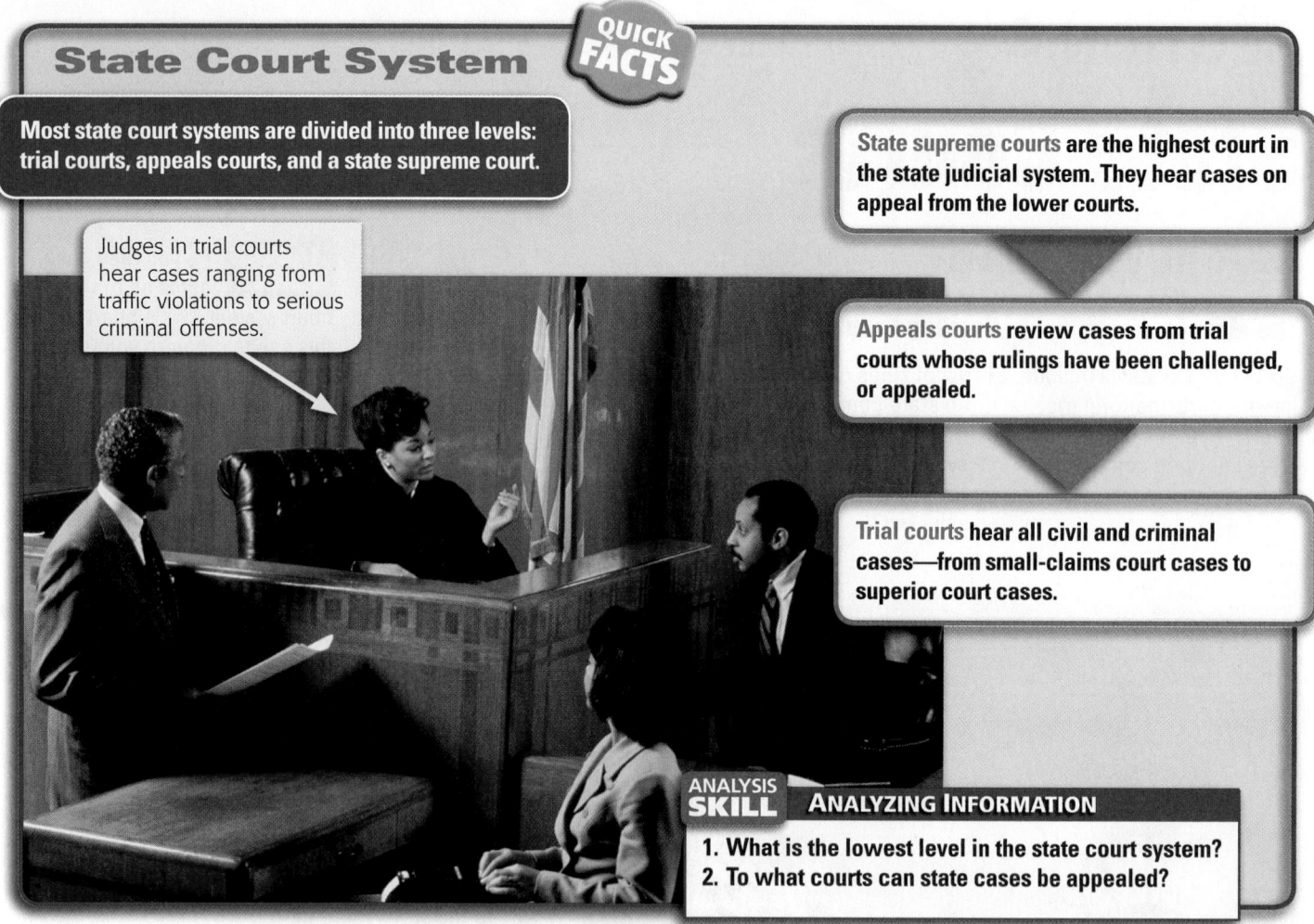

State Court System

Most state court systems are divided into three levels: trial courts, appeals courts, and a state supreme court.

Judges in trial courts hear cases ranging from traffic violations to serious criminal offenses.

State supreme courts are the highest court in the state judicial system. They hear cases on appeal from the lower courts.

Appeals courts review cases from trial courts whose rulings have been challenged, or appealed.

Trial courts hear all civil and criminal cases—from small-claims court cases to superior court cases.

ANALYSIS SKILL **ANALYZING INFORMATION**

1. What is the lowest level in the state court system?
2. To what courts can state cases be appealed?

a person guilty of a crime, it has the authority to punish that person.

State courts also hear civil law cases. Civil cases are disputes between individuals or businesses over property or money. They may also involve disputes between a business and the government, or between an individual and the government.

READING CHECK **Contrasting** How do criminal cases and civil cases differ?

State Court System

Like the federal judicial branch, state court systems are structured in levels. In state court systems, state judges perform most of the same duties that federal judges perform. Three types of courts are found in most states—general trial courts, appeals courts, and a state supreme court.

Trial Courts

Lower courts generally hear minor cases, including misdemeanor criminal cases and civil cases involving small amounts of money. Judges conduct hearings in these courts without a jury.

In many cities and towns, a justice of the peace hears cases. A justice of the peace can hand down fines or short jail sentences. These lower courts may also be called magistrate's courts or police courts. Their judges are usually elected. Many large cities have municipal courts, which may be divided into courts that handle specific types of cases. For example, traffic courts hear cases involving traffic violations, and family courts hear cases involving family disputes.

Most states have small-claims courts, which usually handle cases involving less than $5,000. No lawyers are needed. Each person in

Religious Displays on Public Property

In some circumstances, the U.S. government may recognize the role religion plays in the country. But it can be difficult to determine when the government's acknowledgement of religion is constitutional.

Two Supreme Court opinions issued on the same day in 2005 illustrate how complicated this issue is. In *Van Orden* v. *Perry*, the Court allowed Texas to keep a six-foot monument of the Ten Commandments on the grounds of the state capitol. Because the monument was one among 38 other markers commemorating Texas history, the Court concluded that the display was primarily historical and did not endorse religion.

However, in *McCreary County* v. *American Civil Liberties Union of Kentucky*, the Court found that displays of the Ten Commandments in two county courthouses in Kentucky were unconstitutional. These displays, the Court stated, specifically highlighted the religious foundation of American law and thus did endorse religion.

Why was a display of the Ten Commandments constitutional in one case and unconstitutional in the other? Explain in your own words.

the dispute explains his or her side of the argument, and the judge makes a decision. Major criminal and civil cases are handled in general trial courts. A jury hears most cases, and a judge presides. Some trial courts hear only civil cases, and others hear only criminal cases. In many states, voters elect these general trial court judges. Other names for trial courts in some states are superior courts and courts of common pleas.

Appeals Courts

Sometimes a person believes his or her case was not handled fairly in a trial court. That person may appeal the decision to an appeals court or an intermediate court of appeals. An appeal is a request for another court to consider the case. The usual basis for an appeal is that the person's guaranteed right to a fair trial was violated during the trial.

Appeals courts do not use juries. Instead, appeals court judges examine the trial record of the lower court and hear arguments from the lawyers on both sides. If the person is still not satisfied with the appeals court's decision, he or she can appeal again to the state supreme court.

State Supreme Court

The state supreme court is the highest court in most states. The judges who sit on the state supreme court hear cases on appeal in much the same way as the U.S. Supreme Court. Decisions on state law by the state supreme court are final.

READING CHECK **Finding the Main Idea** What roles do judges play in the different levels of state courts?

Selection of State Judges

In most states, citizens elect state supreme court judges. But in some states, the governor appoints supreme court judges. State law determines how judges are selected in each state and the length of each type of judge's term.

ECON 101

Small Claims Court

How much might you have to pay as a result of a judgment in a small-claims court? If you have ever seen judges deciding real cases on television, then you are already familiar with small claims courts. They decide cases such as unpaid personal debt, past-due rent, and reimbursement for goods and services. The maximum amount of money that can be involved in a small claims dispute is usually $5,000.

ANALYSIS SKILL **ANALYZING ECONOMICS**

Why are small claims courts an important part of the judicial system?

Election of Judges

People who support electing judges argue that elections make judges responsible to the people who will be affected by their decisions. Supporters of elected judges also argue that when the governor appoints judges, he or she is free to appoint political supporters or friends.

Those who oppose the election of judg-

es argue that judges should make decisions based on the facts and on the law that applies, not on what might please voters. Supporters of appointed judges believe that judges should be selected based on their abilities.

The Missouri Plan

Some states have adopted a method of selecting judges called the **Missouri Plan**. Under this plan, a committee of judges, lawyers, and ordinary citizens prepares a list of qualified judges. The governor appoints a judge from this list. The judge must then face the voters in the next election.

Terms of Service

State court judicial terms are set by state law. In most states, judges face the voters at the end of their term. Voters may elect the judge to a new term or may vote to replace the judge. Most states have methods for removing judges, usually by impeachment or recall.

READING CHECK **Making Inferences** Why might the Missouri Plan combine the best qualities of the election and appointment methods?

go.hrw.com
Online Quiz
KEYWORD: SZ7 HP8

SECTION 4 ASSESSMENT

Reviewing Ideas and Terms

1. **a. Define** Write a brief definition of the term **penal code**.
   b. Draw Conclusions Civil court cases often involve disputes over contracts and other types of business agreements. Why do you think it is important to read through contracts carefully before signing?
2. **a. Recall** What are the four levels of state court systems?
   b. Elaborate Why do most states have low-level courts such as small-claims courts and traffic courts?
   c. Compare and Contrast What are the differences between general trial courts and appeals courts?
3. **a. Define** Write a brief definition of the term **Missouri Plan**.

   b. Elaborate Do you think that electing judges is the best way to select state court judges? Why or why not?

Critical Thinking

4. **Sequencing** Copy the graphic organizer. Use it to identify the steps a civil case might go through in a state court system. Explain what happens at each stage.

   ⟶ ⟶

Focus on Writing

5. **Supporting a Point of View** In one or two paragraphs, explain why it is important for a state judicial system to have different levels and different kinds of courts.

PROJECT Citizen

Fighting Drug Dealers

In the Miami suburb of Hialeah, Florida, Jackie Viana's Project Citizen students watched as Governor Jeb Bush signed an important anti-drug bill. State Senate Bill 1588 outlawed the sale, manufacturing, or delivery of drugs within 1,000 feet of public parks, community centers, or recreational facilities. Dealing drugs was already illegal, but this law allowed for harsher punishments if a dealer was caught in these "drug-free" zones. This law would never have been introduced without the efforts of Ms. Viana's students.

Community Connection Students from Viana's class were concerned about drug use by young people their age. They saw drug dealing in public parks as an especially major problem. The students surveyed parents and students to get ideas and feedback on the problem and how the community could address it.

Taking Action The students put together a bill to combat drug dealing in public parks (and other public places popular with students) by making the punishment for selling drugs there very harsh. Then they presented their bill to the state legislature. Their task was not easy. The students spent two years lobbying to increase support from local and state officials. At one point they even arranged a meeting with the governor to get his help. They also contacted the media to spread the word about the bill. Finally, their efforts paid off. Some time after completing their Civics course, students saw the state legislature approve their bill and the governor sign it into law.

In Hialeah, Florida, students took action to get the state legislature to combat drug dealing in public parks.

go.hrw.com
Project Citizen
KEYWORD: SZ7 CH8

SERVICE LEARNING

1. How did Viana's students rally support for their bill?
2. What problems in your community could be addressed by changing a state law?

Visual Summary

Use the visual summary below to help you review the main ideas of the chapter.

The Constitution establishes two levels of government in the United States, the federal government and state governments. State governments have the same basic separation of powers as the federal government.

YOU

Local government

State government

Federal government

QUICK FACTS

Reviewing Key Terms

For each term or name below, write a sentence explaining its significance to state government.

1. delegated powers
2. reserved powers
3. concurrent powers
4. full faith and credit clause
5. extradition
6. bicameral
7. unicameral
8. constituents
9. initiative
10. referendum
11. recall
12. governor
13. patronage
14. lieutenant governor
15. penal code
16. Missouri Plan

Comprehension and Critical Thinking

SECTION 1 *(Pages 202–206)*

17. **a. Recall** What is the term for the powers granted to state governments, and what are two examples of some of those powers?

    b. Analyze Why is it necessary for states to work with other states? Give examples to support your answer.

    c. Elaborate What kinds of projects or programs are most likely to involve states working with the federal government? Give examples to support your answer.

SECTION 2 *(Pages 207–211)*

18. **a. Describe** How can citizens take direct action in legislation and state government?

    b. Evaluate Some states do not have provisions for citizen initiatives and recall. What arguments can you think of for not having initiative and recall?

Active Citizenship video program

Review the video to answer the closing question:
What are various ways that students can bring issues to the attention of their state legislators?

SECTION 3 *(Pages 213–216)*

19. a. Identify Who heads the state executive branch, and what are three roles he or she plays?

b. Analyze In what ways is the power of the state chief executive limited?

SECTION 4 *(Pages 217–220)*

20. a. Describe What types of courts exist in most states, and what does each do?

b. Evaluate Which method of selecting state court judges do you favor? Explain your reasoning.

Using the Internet

go.hrw.com
KEYWORD: SZ7 CH8

21. Meeting Your Executive Officials A state's legislative branch makes the laws for that state. Then the state executive branch carries out these laws. Enter the activity keyword and learn about the principal executive officials in your state. Then make a list of the officials in your state that contains their names, principal duties and responsibilities, salaries, and whether the officials were elected by the citizens or appointed by the governor.

Reading Skills

22. Using Primary Sources You have just been given a Civics assignment to compare and contrast the state legislatures in New Hampshire (called the General Court) and Nebraska (called the Unicameral). Which of these sources would you consult as a primary source? Choose as many as you think are applicable.

a. Your Civics textbook

b. The home page of the New Hampshire General Court on the Internet

c. An Internet Web site called "State and Local Government on the Net" that links you to specific state legislature home pages

d. A newspaper article written by a New Hampshire state legislator describing his experiences in the New Hampshire General Court

e. An interview with a Nebraska state legislator

Civics Skills

Writing to Your Legislator *Study the letter to a state legislator below. Then answer the questions that follow.*

The Honorable Jane Doe
The State House
Richmond, VA 23218

Dear Representative Doe:

As you know, there is currently a bill before the legislature that would create 3,000 summer jobs for teenagers in our state. I strongly urge you to support this bill. Passage of Bill HR 1099 will give many teenagers the chance to earn money for school. It will also provide them with experience for future jobs. Finally, the state stands to benefit from all the work these teenagers will be doing in our parks, hospitals, and civic centers. I would appreciate knowing your position on this important issue.

Sincerely yours,

Aaron Campbell

23. What is the author's stand regarding the proposed bill? What support does he provide?

24. What points might you address in a letter to the same state legislature if you opposed this bill?

25. Select an education issue that is important to you. Write a letter to one of your legislators explaining why you think the issue is important. Ask for the legislator's opinion on the issue. Remember to offer a solution to the issue and ask for his or her help in passing legislation that would solve the problem.

FOCUS ON WRITING

26. Writing Your Biographical Sketch Look over your notes about state government. Think about the three branches of state government. Do some research about an important governor, legislator, judge, or other state official in your state. Choose one of those people and write a brief biography about that person.

CHAPTER 9
LOCAL GOVERNMENT

SECTION 1
Units of Local Government

SECTION 2
Town, Township, and Village Governments

SECTION 3
City Government

SECTION 4
How Governments Work Together

NATIONAL STANDARDS®
FOR CIVICS AND GOVERNMENT

I. What are civic life, politics, and government?

    A. What purposes should government serve?

II. What are the foundations of the American political system?

    B. What are the distinctive characteristics of American society?

III. How does the government established by the Constitution embody the purposes, values, and principles of American democracy?

    A. How are power and responsibility distributed, shared, and limited in the government established by the United States Constitution?

    C. How are state and local governments organized and what do they do?

V. What are the roles of the citizen in American democracy?

    C. What are the responsibilities of citizens?

    E. How can citizens take part in civic life?

©1994, 2003 Center for Civic Education. All Rights Reserved.

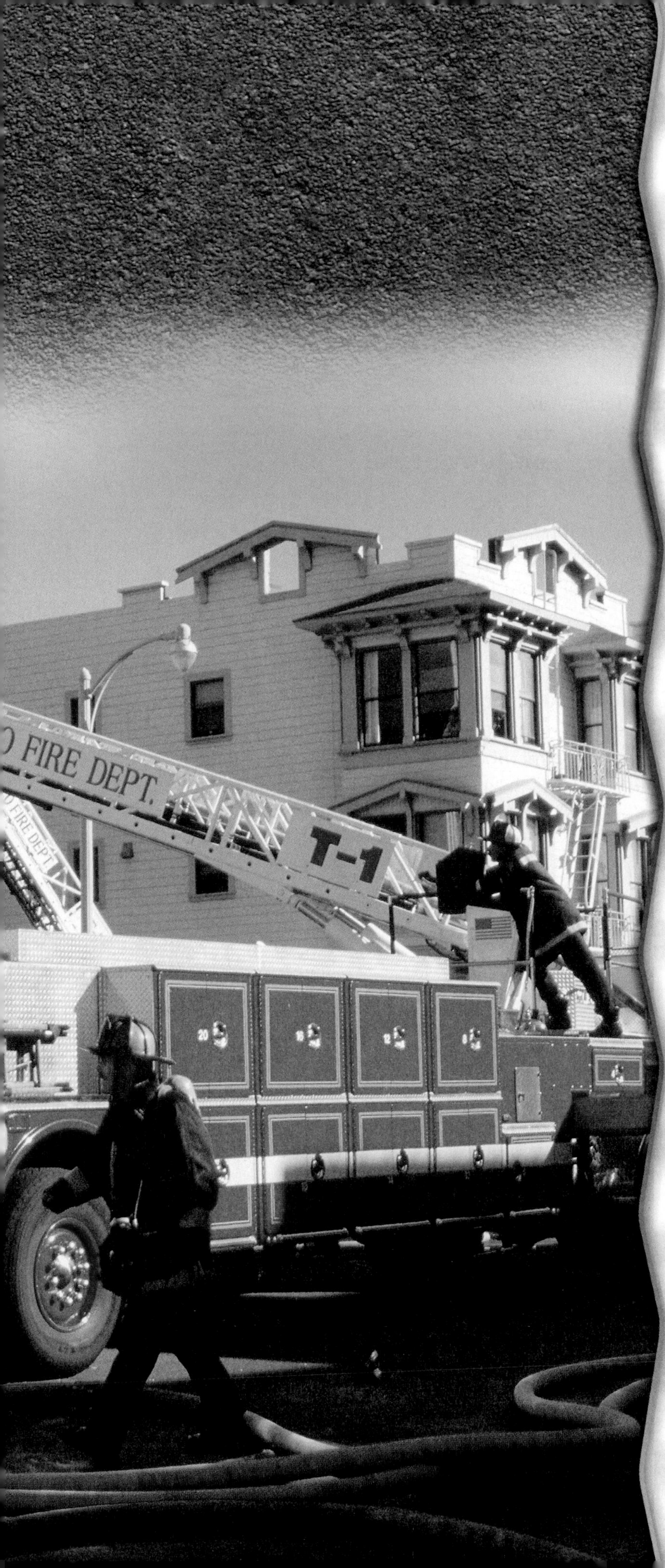

WHY CIVICS Matters

You live in a country, the United States of America. You live in one of the 50 states. You also live in a county and probably a city or a town. These local units of government have a direct impact on your life, like providing police and fire protection.

PROJECT Citizen

STUDENTS TAKE ACTION

CHANGING PARK RULES No bikes allowed in the park? If you can't ride your bike in the park, where can you go? A group of students in Pleasant Grove, Utah, were confused about local laws about bikes in city parks, so they went to their city government to solve the problem.

FOCUS ON WRITING

PERSUASIVE LETTER Your local newspaper is running a competition for students to answer the question, "How does your city or other local government affect your life? What would make this government better?" This chapter describes different levels and structures of local government and the different responsibilities these governments have. As you read, take notes on local governments and their powers.

In this chapter you will read about how local governments are established and about the many purposes they serve. You will also learn about how the many forms of government began and how they have changed over time.

Finally, you will learn how the federal, state, and local governments cooperate with each other and why they also sometimes compete with each other.

Understanding Political Cartoons

FOCUS ON READING Political cartoons frequently portray public opinion on different issues. Learning how to understand these cartoons will help you keep tabs on how some people feel about issues and events.

Political Cartoons Political cartoons use both words and images to convey their message. Political cartoonists often exaggerate particular aspects of events to make points about those events. They also use symbols to illustrate people's characteristics. For example, a member of the Democratic Party might be drawn as a donkey, while a Republican might be drawn as an elephant. Cartoonists also use titles, labels, and captions to get their message across.

Helpful Hints for Understanding Political Cartoons

1. Read any titles, labels, or captions to identify the cartoon's topic.

2. Identify the people and objects in the cartoon. Determine if they are exaggerated and, if so, why. Identify any symbols and analyze their meaning.

3. Draw conclusions about the message the cartoonist is trying to convey. Is the cartoonist portraying the subject in a positive or negative way?

"It's a red-letter day — she took her first step, and she received her first credit card application form."

1. What is the cartoon's topic?
Credit card applications being sent to young people

2. What is exaggerated? The age of the person receiving a credit card application—a baby

What is the cartoon's message?
Credit card companies are going to extremes by offering credit to younger and younger people. The cartoonist is portraying credit card companies in a negative way.

You Try It!

Look at the following cartoon and then answer the questions below.

After you have studied the cartoon, answer the following questions.

1. What is the general topic of the cartoon?

2. What is humorous about the boy's response to the father?

3. What attitude does the cartoonist have about using the Internet for schoolwork?

4. What is the message the cartoon conveys?

> **As you read Chapter 9,** think about what topics might make a good political cartoon.

Academic Vocabulary

Success in school is related to knowing academic vocabulary—the words that are frequently used in school assignments and discussions. In this chapter you will learn the following academic words:

primary *(p. 235)*
implement *(p. 241)*

Units of Local Government

BEFORE YOU READ

The Main Idea

Local governments have grown as the country has grown. As Americans settled in rural communities, towns, cities, and suburbs, they set up local governments.

Reading Focus

1. How are local governments established, and why are they needed?
2. How is county government organized, and what are the main purposes of each level of county government?
3. How do local and state governments work together?

Key Terms

municipality, *p. 228*
city, *p. 228*
county, *p. 229*
sheriff, *p. 229*
charter, *p. 230*
ordinances, *p. 230*

 **TAKING NOTES** As you read, take notes on establishing local governments, county governments, and how governments work together. Use a diagram like this one to record your notes.

 Have you lived through a flood, hurricane, or tornado? Did you lose electricity? Did you need to call the fire department or the police? Most of us do not think about basic services—at least until we do not have them. Your local government often provides all of these services.

Establishing Local Governments

What level of government is closest to you? As a student, you are most affected by the government of the city or town in which you live, and by the school district in which you are a student. In other words, you are most affected by local government.

Powers Come from the State

In the United States, the states have the right to establish local governments. States use their own constitutions to legalize and define their local governments. Local government is made up of municipalities. A **municipality** is a unit of local government that is incorporated by the state and that has a large degree of self-government. Munici-palities can include a state's cities, towns, villages, and boroughs.

The Need for Local Governments

Our local governments provide the conveniences and services that we have come to expect to make our daily lives easier. For example, we expect the roads to be in good repair and to allow us to get to and from work or school safely. Street cleaning and trash collection help keep our neighborhoods neat and disease-free. Electricity, running water, and sewage systems keep our homes, schools, and workplaces comfortable, efficient, and safe.

These services are often provided to us by local governments, such as city governments. A **city** is the largest type of municipality. Police and fire protection, water-conservation efforts, and snow removal are also provided by local governments. Local governments also provide education and keep records. Some governments supply their citizens with public transportation or recreation areas.

READING CHECK **Summarizing** What are some of the services local governments provide?

County Governments

The highest level of local government is the county. A **county** is a division of state government formed to carry out state laws, collect taxes, and supervise elections in a single small area. Louisiana calls its county-level government units parishes, while Alaska calls its counties boroughs.

County government is often the largest unit of local government. County employees provide services such as health care, police protection, welfare, corrections, recreational areas, and libraries. In some areas in a few states, county and city governments are combined into one legislative body.

At the head of county governments is a group of officials elected by the voters. This group may be called the county board, board of commissioners, county court, or board of county supervisors. These officials form the county's legislative body. They have the power to pass laws regulating health and safety throughout the county. They also may collect real estate taxes, sales taxes, and personal property taxes.

County governments also have an executive branch. However, unlike executive branches at other levels of government, county executive branches usually have no single leader. Instead, county voters elect several county officials, each with his or her own responsibilities. In some places, however, the traditional form of county government has been replaced with a county manager and county executive. The county executive is elected by the voters and the county manager is appointed by the county board to supervise county business and services.

One of these elected officials is the county **sheriff**, who usually commands several deputies and an office staff. The sheriff arrests lawbreakers and carries out the orders of county courts. In many states, the sheriff is responsible for law enforcement only in the areas of the county that are not part of a city.

PRIMARY SOURCE

POLITICAL CARTOON
Speed Trap

The sheriff is the top law enforcement official at the county level of government. One of the sheriff department's duties is enforcing traffic laws.

© 1998 John McPherson/Dist. by Universal Press Syndicate

CLANK!

The sheriff is operating the device to stop speeders.

E-MAIL:CLOSETOHOME@COMPUSERVE.COM

The Dortford County Sheriff's Department introduces its new electromagnetic speed-enforcement system.

ANALYSIS SKILL ANALYZING POLITICAL CARTOONS

Supporting a Point of View Why do you think the cartoonist chose to depict such an exaggerated method of stopping speeders?

Counties also have several other elected officials. The county clerk keeps a record of the actions and decisions of the county board. In addition, the clerk keeps birth records, marriage records, death records, and election results. County treasurers are responsible for the county's funds. County auditors also watch the money the county receives and the money it spends. County officials may also include a coroner, who investigates unnatural deaths, and a county prosecutor—also known as the district attorney—who represents the state in county trials.

READING CHECK **Summarizing** Describe the basic structure of county governments.

FOCUS ON
Antonio Villaraigosa
(1953 –)

In 2005 Antonio Villaraigosa became the first Hispanic mayor of Los Angeles, California, in 133 years. He was born and raised in the city by a single mother with four children.

Villaraigosa was elected to the California State Assembly in 1994 and four years later became assembly speaker. In this role, he sponsored legislation to modernize public schools, ban assault weapons, and provide health care for poor children.

After losing a bid for mayor in 2001, Villaraigosa focused on his research. For two years he studied and wrote about the future of American cities. In 2003, Antonio Villaraigosa won a seat on the Los Angeles city council, representing the city's northeast sector. During his term he became a leader in the council.

On a platform of progressive urban reform, Villaraigosa ran for mayor again in 2005. He defeated incumbent mayor James Hahn in a run-off election. When Mayor Villaraigosa was sworn in on July 1, many people in Los Angeles celebrated with a victory parade.

Making Inferences Why is it significant that Villaraigosa is the first Hispanic mayor of Los Angeles in 133 years?

Governments Work Together

The duties of local government officials are usually outlined in state-approved charters. A **charter** is a basic plan for a local government unit that defines its powers, responsibilities, and organization. Of course, a charter cannot violate state or federal laws.

It is the job of local governments to make communities better places to live. To accomplish this job, local lawmaking bodies have the power to pass **ordinances**, or regulations that govern a community. Ordinances also cannot conflict with state or federal laws. Local law enforcement groups, such as police departments, are responsible for enforcing both local ordinances and state laws.

Local governments also help the state by making sure election procedures follow state guidelines. Local officials both supervise the voting process and provide citizens with polling places—that is, places where people can cast their ballots. Without local assistance, state and federal elections could not happen.

READING CHECK **Summarizing** Why must states and local governments cooperate?

go.hrw.com
Online Quiz
KEYWORD: SZ7 HP9

SECTION 1 ASSESSMENT

Reviewing Ideas and Terms

1. a. Define Write a brief definition for each of the following terms: **municipality** and **city**.
b. Draw Conclusions Why can local governments provide some services more efficiently than state governments can?
2. a. Define Write a brief definition for each of the following terms: **county** and **sheriff**.
b. Explain Describe the organization of county government.
c. Compare and Evaluate What are some of the duties of county government?
3. a. Define Write a brief definition for each of the following terms: **charter** and **ordinances**.
b. Summarize In what ways do counties support state governments?

Critical Thinking

4. Summarizing Use your notes and a chart like this one to summarize the section.

County Board	
Sheriff	
County Clerk	
County Treasurer	
County Auditor	
District Attorney	

Focus on Writing

5. Supporting a Point of View Imagine that you live in a neighborhood in a rural county. Coyotes are beginning to come into the neighborhood and cause problems. Write a letter to the county board asking for assistance in handling the coyotes.

Town, Township, and Village Governments

BEFORE YOU READ

The Main Idea

Although counties are the largest unit of local government, they share the job of governing with other units of local government.

Reading Focus

1. Where did town government begin, and what is the purpose of the town meeting?
2. Why did townships and special districts develop, and how does each function?
3. Why are villages and boroughs created, and how do they operate?

Key Terms

town, *p. 231*
town meeting, *p. 231*
township, *p. 232*
special district, *p. 233*

TAKING NOTES As you read, take notes on the different kinds of local governments and the purpose of each. Use a chart like this one to record your notes.

Local Governments	
Kind	Purpose

Residents often vote on issues of importance to their community during a town meeting.

Many smaller communities in New England still hold town meetings to deal with local issues.

CIVICS IN PRACTICE When you vote in a class election, you participate in direct democracy. In some regions of the country that have small populations, direct democracy is still practiced at town meetings. When a town grows, elected representatives are needed to make the decisions.

Town Government

Towns first developed as New England colonists built homes and churches. A **town** is a unit of local government, usually larger than a village and smaller than a city. The colonial town included both the homes, churches, and other buildings and surrounding farmlands.

The people who lived in early New England towns created the town meeting, a simple yet powerful form of local government. In a **town meeting**, all citizens meet regularly to discuss town issues. After all opinions regarding an issue have been voiced, the people at the meeting vote on that issue. This means that each person has a direct voice in the government.

Finding Information on the Internet

Does your town have leash laws for pets? How many people live in your state? These questions can all be answered by using Web sites provided by your local government.

The Internet is also a great place to find practical information for daily life. Unfortunately, it can be hard to know if the Web sites you visit contain complete and accurate information. Many sites are sponsored by groups trying to sell a particular product or service.

Using a Web site sponsored and maintained by your local government can help you avoid these problems. These sites provide residents with useful information.

Illustrated example of a township Web site

Local government Web sites often provide useful links to public services, such as libraries.

TheDuchessTownship.gov
Duchess Township government online

Duchess Township Library System

go.hrw.com
KEYWORD: SZ7 CH9

ANALYSIS SKILL **MEDIA INVESTIGATION**

Evaluating How do you know you are on government Web sites?

Town meetings often are held in conjunction with town elections. At the elections, townspeople typically elect from three to five officials to manage the town's affairs between town meetings. The town meeting form of government can work well in areas that have small populations. Direct democracy is practical in such towns because it is easier for all the voters to gather in one central location at one time.

READING CHECK **Analyzing Information**
In what kind of community does a town meeting work well?

Townships and Special Districts

In some states, land is often divided into other smaller units. Two common subdivisions are townships and special districts. Townships are more common in certain states, but special districts are found in every state.

Townships

In colonial times, New England states used the town form of government. Other states, especially New York, New Jersey, and Penn-sylvania, used a form of government called a **township**. Townships in other parts of the country, especially the Midwest, have a different history. In the early 1800s, the United States expanded westward. Americans moved into new land where they had not previously settled. Congress divided this new land into perfectly square units, usually 6 miles (an hour's buggy ride) by 6 miles on a side. As people from the East moved in, they set up local governments they called civil townships.

Colonial townships were usually smaller than New England towns, while the Midwestern townships may have been larger than towns. But all townships perform many of the same governmental functions, such as building schools and roads, that towns perform. In general, a township is headed by an elected chairperson or supervisor. Voters also elect a board of commissioners or trustees to make township rules and regulations. An elected constable enforces the laws, and often an elected justice of the peace tries minor legal cases. Today, many township governments have decreased in importance as cities have taken over many of the governmental responsibilities.

Special Districts

People living in a certain area may have a special need. In such cases these people may go directly to the state legislature and ask for a charter to set up a special district. A **special district** is a unit of government formed to meet many different needs, including fire protection, libraries, parks and recreation centers, public transportation, and sewage disposal. A special district may include several cities. For example, a hospital district might serve several cities. Each city would have to pay taxes for the services it receives. The state legislature usually sets up a commission to handle the details of establishing and operating the special district. The commission members may be elected or appointed.

School districts are considered special districts by some researchers. These districts are created by states to provide funds for local schools. There are more than 13,000 school districts in the United States. Each district has its own governing body called a board of education. An executive, usually called a superintendent of schools, manages the district's day-to-day operations.

READING CHECK **Finding the Main Idea** Why do school districts qualify as special districts?

Village and Borough Governments

When rural communities grow to a population of 200 to 300, their residents often encounter problems that require them to work together. The residents may decide to establish a village or a borough and create their own local government.

A request to establish a village or borough must be approved by the state legislature. The legislature permits the village or borough to be a self-governing municipality. It then can collect taxes, set up fire and police departments, and provide other services that larger communities offer their residents.

A village or borough is often governed by a small council, or board of trustees. The voters also elect an executive or president of the board of trustees to carry out the laws.

If the population of a village or borough becomes large enough, the people may ask the state legislature to grant the community a city charter. When this happens its government would change accordingly.

READING CHECK **Analyzing Information** Why does an increase in population require the formation of a government?

SECTION 2 ASSESSMENT

Reviewing Ideas and Terms

1. **a. Define** Write a brief definition for each of the following terms: **town** and **town meeting**.
   b. Explain Why did town meetings develop?
2. **a. Define** Write a brief definition for each of the following terms: **township** and **special district**.
   b. Make Predictions What might happen if a local government did not make use of special districts?
3. **a. Recalling** What is the role of the state in the creation of villages and boroughs?
   b. Sequence When do rural areas become villages or boroughs?

Critical Thinking

4. **Comparing and Contrasting** Copy the graphic organizer. Use it and your notes to explain why townships and special districts develop, and how each is organized.

Townships
Why:
Organization:

Special Districts
Why:
Organization:

Focus on Writing

5. **Writing to Persuade** Write a letter from the perspective of a resident arguing why a rural area should or should not become a village.

SECTION 3
City Government

The Main Idea

A city is usually larger than a town or village. In many cities a large population is crowded into a relatively small area, which creates many challenges for city government.

Reading Focus

1. How are city governments organized under the home-rule system?
2. What are the different forms of city government?

Key Terms

home rule, *p. 234*
city council, *p. 235*
mayor, *p. 235*
commission, *p. 237*

TAKING NOTES As you read, take notes on the different forms of city government. Use a diagram like this one to record your notes.

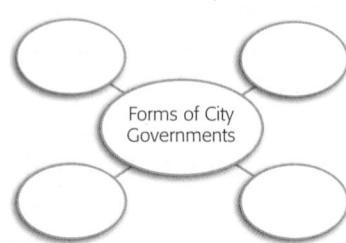

Forms of City Governments

A city may be small, like Jim Thorpe, Pennsylvania, or huge like New York City.

CIVICS IN PRACTICE City government can get very big. New York City, for example, has nearly 9,000 sanitation workers alone. The Los Angeles Police Department employs 12,500 people. These departments are the size of many small towns. To provide good service, a city must be organized in an efficient manner.

Home Rule Organization

A city is generally the largest kind of municipality. Cities vary greatly, however, in size. New York City, for example, has a population of more than 8 million. On the other hand, the city of Parker, Pennsylvania, has only 799 people.

Traditionally, cities received their charters and their authority from the state legislature. Increasingly, however, states have been granting to cities an authority called **home rule**. Under home rule, a city can write and amend its own municipal charter. This charter, usually written by a commission, must be approved by the voters.

READING CHECK **Making Predictions** Does home rule strengthen or weaken local governments? Explain your answer.

Community Meeting

The decisions of city governments can have a huge impact on citizens. City governments deal with a large number of issues, including building roads, providing police and fire production, regulating business and industry, and collecting taxes.

In order to get the public's feedback on important issues, city governments often hold community meetings. Citizens are given the opportunity to ask their elected officials questions and give their opinions on the issues facing the city.

Why is it important for citizens to attend community meetings?

City officials can explain various issues at community meetings.

Community meetings are a good forum for citizens to express their opinions.

Forms of City Government

Cities manage a variety of responsibilities, such as providing education, health, and safety to their residents. Transportation systems, sanitation, water supplies, and fire and police protection are also part of the daily business of city governments. A city government usually is organized in one of four ways. Depending on its charter, the city will have a mayor-council government, a strong-mayor government, a commission government, or a council-manager government.

Mayor-Council Government

The oldest and most common form of city government is the mayor-council government. In this kind of government, the **city council** is the legislative body, while the **mayor** is the city's chief executive officer.

In mayor-council governments, a city may be divided into several districts, often called wards. The people of each ward elect one person to represent them in a city council. In some cities, several council members at large are elected by all the voters in the city, rather than just the voters of one ward. Usually the mayor is also elected at large.

Weak-Mayor Plan During the country's early years, Americans remembered British governors who had abused their powers. For this reason, some cities developed the weak-mayor plan to limit the power of the mayor. Under the weak-mayor plan, the city council holds more power than the mayor. For example, the council appoints the city department heads, who report directly to the city council rather than to the mayor.

Strong-Mayor Plan Recently, many city governments using the mayor-council form of government have adopted a strong-mayor plan of city government. Under the strong-mayor plan, the mayor is the city's chief executive officer and has the **primary** responsibility for running the city's government. For example, the mayor appoints most of the city officials. He or she usually also prepares the city budget. In some cities, the mayor can also veto ordinances passed by the city council. Because executive power is concentrated in the mayor, many people think that the strong-mayor plan is more efficient than the weak-mayor form.

ACADEMIC VOCABULARY
primary: main, most important

4 Structures of Local Government

American city governments have four different structures. The weak-mayor system dates back to colonial days and, as cities grew, was mostly replaced by the strong-mayor system. The commission and council-manager plans are closely related.

Mayor-Council (Weak Mayor)

In the weak-mayor plan, the mayor has equal voting power with all the members of the council. A weak mayor's vote, however, may act as a tie breaker.

The weak-mayor plan was the earliest structure of American city government. The colonists brought the structure from England, where mayors, like the Lord Mayor of London (shown above), were more ceremonial figures than city leaders. It was favored in early America because it keeps one person from being too powerful.

Mayor-Council (Strong Mayor)

In the strong-mayor plan, the mayor has veto power on the decisions of the council. Mayors also appoint city officials and have power over the city budget.

Beginning in the 1800s, many cities changed from the weak-mayor to the strong-mayor plan. This change led to corruption in some places. New York City suffered under a corrupt city government, known as Tammany Hall, from the 1850s to the 1930s. Large cities, including New York, still have a strong mayor plan, but corruption is rare. Michael Bloomberg is currently the New York City mayor.

Commission

In the commission plan, each council member is in charge of a different city department. The mayor's vote carries the same weight as each of the commissioners' votes.

In 1900 Galveston, Texas, (shown above) suffered a devastating hurricane that killed one out of every six people living there. In response, the city formed the first city commission to make sure that responsibility for the many different jobs needed to rebuild the town would not fall just to the mayor.

Council-Manager

In cities with a council-manager plan, like Oklahoma City, Oklahoma, a city manager is appointed by the city council to run city departments. The mayor leads the city politically, and the manager directs the city's day-to-day operations.

The council-manager structure began in 1912 in Sumter, South Carolina. Sumter's mayor created it based on the city commission structure in Galveston, but he added a supervisory level—the city manager—to oversee the departments.

ANALYSIS SKILL **ANALYZING VISUALS**

1. **Identify** Describe the four structures of local government.
2. **Evaluate** Which structure of local government is most efficient? Explain.

Lord Mayor, The Granger Collection, New York

Commission Government

A new form of government was introduced in Galveston, Texas, around 1900. Under the **commission** form of government, a city is governed by a commission that usually consists of three to nine elected officials, or commissioners. The commission acts as the city's legislative body, passing laws for the community.

The commission also acts as the city's executive body, with each commissioner heading up a city department and enforcing laws relating to that department. For example, one commissioner usually heads the department of public safety, which includes the police and firefighters. Another commissioner oversees public works. This official sees that the city has an adequate supply of clean water and that the streets are kept in good repair. A third commissioner oversees the city's finances, including tax collection. Another commissioner might supervise the public welfare department, which helps the city's disadvantaged citizens. Still another commissioner might run the health department, which supervises hospitals, clinics, and health inspectors in the city.

The commission form of city government has certain disadvantages. For example, voters may find it difficult to elect officials who know how to run a department of the city's government. In addition, commissioners sometimes disagree about who should manage activities and budgets that fall under the jurisdiction of different departments.

Council-Manager Government

The council-manager plan of government is really a commission with a city manager added. Under the council-manager plan, voters elect a city council to act as the city's lawmaking body. The council then appoints a city manager as the city's chief executive. The city manager appoints the heads of the city departments. These officials report directly to the city manager, who may also remove them from office.

The council-manager government has several advantages. First, because the city manager is appointed and not elected, he or she is usually free from any political pressure. In addition, the council can fire the city manager if he or she does not do a good job.

However, there are disadvantages to this form of government. Some cities cannot afford to hire a good manager, and some critics argue that city officials should be directly accountable to the voters.

READING CHECK **Finding the Main Idea** What are the types of city government, and how are they different?

SECTION 3 ASSESSMENT

Reviewing Ideas and Terms

1. **a. Define** Write a brief definition for the term **home rule**.
   b. Draw Inferences and Conclusions How does home rule loosen the restrictions on a city?
2. **a. Define** Write a brief definition for the terms **city council, mayor,** and **commission**.
   b. Summarize How is a mayor-council government organized?
   c. Evaluate What are the strengths and weaknesses of the council-manager form of government?

Critical Thinking

3. **Evaluating** Use your notes and a chart like the one here to evaluate the advantages and disadvantages of each type of city government.

Types of City Government	Advantages	Disadvantages
Strong Mayor		
Weak Mayor		
Commission		
Council-Manager		

Focus on Writing

4. **Supporting** Imagine that you are part of a committee establishing a new city. Write a short speech explaining which of the four plans you believe is the most effective form of city government and why.

Analyzing an Editorial

Learn

Editorials are a special type of newspaper or magazine article. They express the opinion of the writer or of the editorial board of the publication. Oftentimes editorials take a stand on a recent event or policy. Most editorials use facts to support their point of view.

Today many newspapers dedicate a page or section to opinions and editorials. Use the tips below to learn how to analyze an editorial.

Practice

❶ **Determine the subject.** As you read an editorial, you should ask yourself what issue or event the article is addressing.

❷ **Identify the author's point of view.** What is the author's opinion? Look for words and phrases that indicate his or her point of view.

❸ **Locate the facts.** What facts does the author use to support his or her argument?

❹ **Decide where you stand on the issue.** Think carefully about the information presented in the editorial. Is there enough evidence to support the author's point of view? Do you agree or disagree with the author?

Apply

Read the editorial carefully. Use the tips for analyzing an editorial to help you answer the questions below.

1. How is this editorial framed—what issue, policy, or event does it address?

2. What is the author's point of view? How can you tell?

3. What facts and information does the author provide to support his or her opinion?

4. How would you frame a response to this editorial? What points would you make and how would you support them?

CONCERNS ABOUT TASERS

Police departments around the country are debating the use of Tasers, the electronic stunning devices widely used to subdue unruly suspects.

An influential police research group meeting in Houston last week recommended using the stun guns only on people violently resisting arrest because of the weapon's potential to kill. The Police Executive Research Forum also said suspects should be evaluated after one shock before being shocked again . . .

Although police departments, and the research forum, believe Tasers are important to police work, there is ample concern that more caution needs to be exercised when using them. Tasers shoot barbs that deliver 50,000 volts of electricity to the body and incapacitate the target they hit . . .

When it comes to the effectiveness of Tasers, much is still unknown. But in the past four years, more than 70 people have died in the United States after being stunned by Tasers, and that alone is cause for more study to help police officials develop proper training methods and use-of-force protocols . . .

There is widespread belief that Tasers have resulted in a decrease in lethal force when subduing suspects and in fewer injuries to officers. Although there is no doubt that a Taser is not as lethal as a gun, there is concern that officers are using Tasers indiscriminately or in routine confrontations . . . Police should have a clear protocol that directs officers to resort to Tasers only after other methods to subdue suspects fail.

Source: Austin American-Statesman

How Governments Work Together

BEFORE YOU READ

The Main Idea

You live under three levels of government— local, state, and federal. Without cooperation among these levels, everyday life would not run smoothly.

Reading Focus

1. How do the different levels of government work together?
2. How do governments cooperate to meet people's needs?
3. In what ways are different levels of government in competition?

Key Terms

grants-in-aid, *p. 241*
block grants, *p. 241*

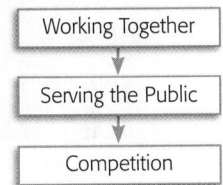 **TAKING NOTES** As you read, take notes on how governments work together and compete. Use a diagram like this one to record your notes.

> Working Together
> ↓
> Serving the Public
> ↓
> Competition

The "Big Dig" in Boston, Massachusetts, was an example of governments working together. From 1982 to 2006 the city of Boston worked with surrounding cities and the state to build new roads and interchanges.

 **CIVICS IN PRACTICE** If your heart, lungs, and brain did not work together, you could not function properly. The same is true of the three levels of government. If local, state, and federal government did not cooperate, life would be difficult.

Governments Work Together

As you read earlier in this chapter, most local units of government have their powers defined for them in charters written by the state legislatures. This outlines the duties and responsibilities of each level of government and ensures that all governmental bodies have the powers needed to do their jobs.

Under the U.S. federal system of government, the powers of each level of government are clearly defined and understood. At the top, the U.S. Constitution is the supreme law of the land. All levels of government must obey the Constitution. For example, no state or city can require public officials to do things that are prohibited by the U.S. Constitution. State constitutions set up rules that govern the people of each state.

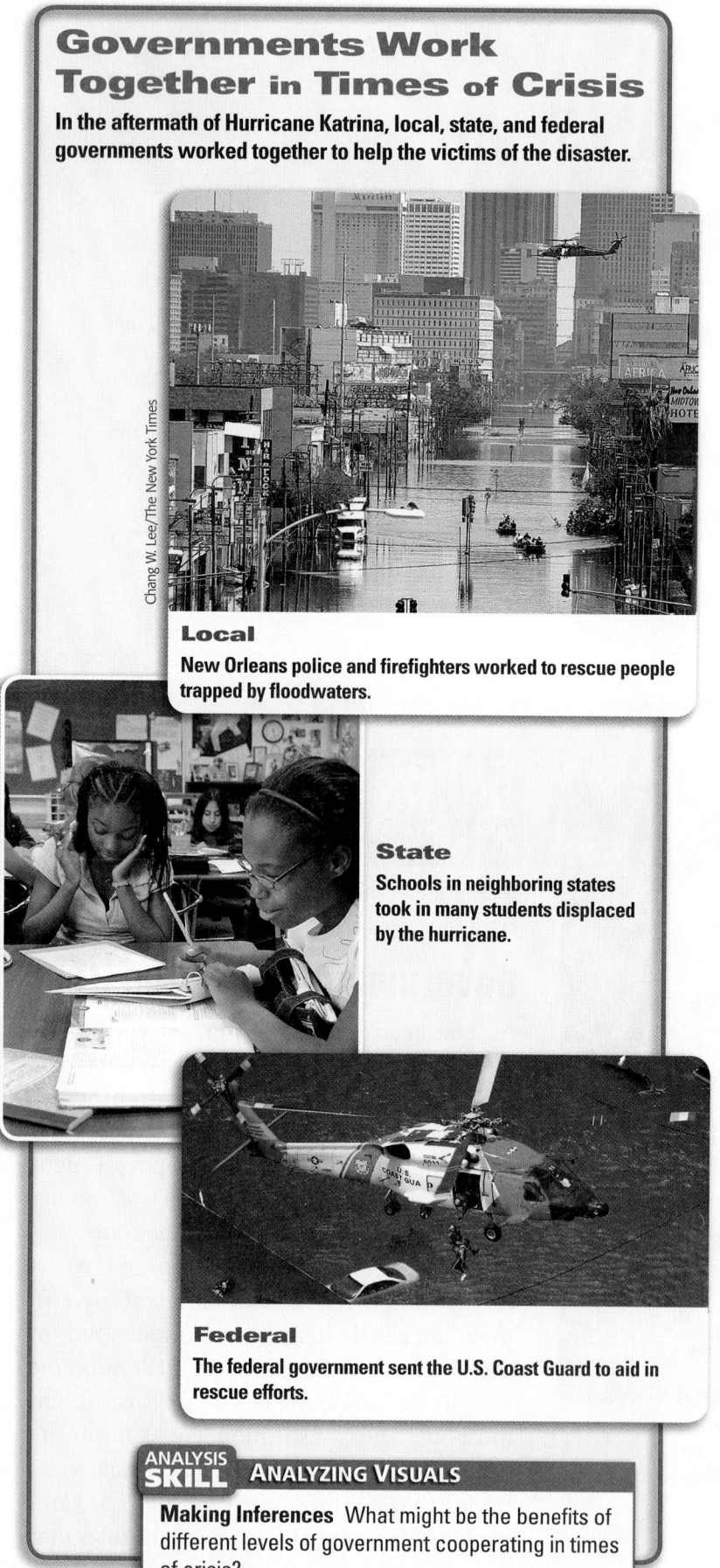

Governments Work Together in Times of Crisis

In the aftermath of Hurricane Katrina, local, state, and federal governments worked together to help the victims of the disaster.

Chang W. Lee/The New York Times

Local

New Orleans police and firefighters worked to rescue people trapped by floodwaters.

State

Schools in neighboring states took in many students displaced by the hurricane.

Federal

The federal government sent the U.S. Coast Guard to aid in rescue efforts.

ANALYSIS SKILL **ANALYZING VISUALS**

Making Inferences What might be the benefits of different levels of government cooperating in times of crisis?

Building Roads Together

Though each level has its defined roles, many issues call for cooperation among local, state, and federal governments. A good example can be seen in the nation's roads and highway systems. Today every state has a network of roads built with local, state, and federal funds.

In colonial days, building a road was a local project. If a town wanted a road, the townspeople built it. These early, primitive roads were cheap to build, and local governments could easily plan and pay for such roads. As the West opened up, the U.S. government did pay for the construction of some east-west roads. However, in general, road building remained a local responsibility.

In the late 1800s New Jersey became the first state to use state funds to help its counties improve their local roads. Massachusetts went a step further in 1893 when it established a state highway commission to build a statewide highway system. Other states soon established state highway departments to build main roads.

President Dwight D. Eisenhower was instrumental in the construction of the nation's interstate highway system. He recognized the importance of highway building in 1919 when he was a soldier and took part in the U.S. Army's first transcontinental motor convoy. The journey was a miserable two-month trip, slowed by poorly kept dirt roads and rickety old bridges. Then, during World War II, General Eisenhower saw the ease with which the German forces could travel through the countryside because of Germany's highway system. In 1956, partly as a result of his wartime experiences, President Eisenhower signed legislation that funded the creation of the U.S. interstate highway system.

Today more than 46,000 miles of interstate highways connect almost all parts of the country. The federal government pays 90 percent of the cost of building and maintaining the system and assists state and local governments in building and maintaining other highways.

City Governments Work Together

In the same way that the three levels of government work together, governments of different cities may work together to solve common problems. For example, all city governments are concerned about increasing funds for police departments, fire departments, and education. They look for ways to lessen air pollution and to safely dispose of trash. The U.S. Conference of Mayors meets regularly so that the country's mayors may compare problems and discuss possible solutions.

READING CHECK **Analyzing Information** How is the road system an example of cooperation between state and federal governments?

Governments Cooperate to Serve the Public

Public education is one of the most important areas in which governments cooperate to serve the public. State governments grant funds to their communities to help the communities operate their schools. State boards of education provide services for local school districts and see that they obey state laws. However, actual control of the schools is left to local boards of education. These local boards are more familiar with the needs of their communities and the students in their schools.

Federal Government Programs

The federal government ensures the cooperation of state and local governments by providing funds to help them **implement** important programs. For example, **grants-in-aid** are federal funds given to state and local governments for specific projects, such as airport construction or pollution control. The government receiving the funds must meet certain standards and conditions, and must often provide some money of its own for the project. Grant-in-aid projects are subject to supervision by the federal government.

Like grants-in-aid, **block grants** are funds given by the federal government to state and local governments. However, block grants are given for broadly defined purposes. State and local governments develop and carry out the programs on which the funds will be spent. However, they must establish a spending plan and report expenditures to the federal government.

ACADEMIC VOCABULARY
implement: to put in place

American Religious Liberties

The Role of Religion and Public Office

The inauguration of the president receives special attention in the Constitution, Article VI, which states that "no religious Test shall ever be required as a Qualification to any Office" of the United States. A candidate for president does not have to meet a religious test or belong to any religion to be elected.

In an additional effort to make sure that religion does not determine a public official's appointment, Article VI also says that all federal and state officials "shall be bound by Oath or Affirmation, to support this Constitution." The option to affirm rather than to swear an oath of office was specifically intended for Quakers, whose religion prohibits swearing oaths.

1. What evidence in the Constitution shows that the founding fathers did not want to impose any formal religious qualifications for public officials?

2. How might an elected official's religion influence his or her position? Give examples.

State and Local Governments

In the same way, states work with local governments to assure the quality of life in the United States. For example, stores and businesses must obey many state laws that require good business practices. State health regulations protect people eating at local restaurants. State education requirements ensure that all students in the state are offered the same education. For the same reason, workers in local factories and mines are protected by state inspectors who ensure that the industries obey all safety regulations. State bank inspectors help ensure that bank accounts are safe and that banks are following state and federal banking regulations.

State governments also establish state licensing boards. These boards administer examinations and issue licenses to accountants, dentists, doctors, engineers, lawyers, nurses, teachers, and other professionals. This service helps to ensure that communities have qualified professional workers and that these workers meet certain standards.

READING CHECK **Summarizing** What are some other ways that different levels of government cooperate?

Governments in Competition

While local, state, and federal governments often work together on many matters, all of these levels of government also compete with one another in several ways. For example, governments at all levels compete for citizens' tax dollars in the form of various income taxes, property taxes, and sales taxes.

States compete with each other to attract industry. State officials may offer tax breaks, a good supply of labor, efficient highway systems, and favorable laws to encourage industries to move to their state. Cities compete against each other for trade and industry in similar ways.

The combined system of federal, state, and local governments is complex. Conflicts among governments are to be expected at times. Only by working together can the country's three levels of government fulfill their duty to serve the American people.

READING CHECK **Analyzing Information** What are some of the areas in which governments compete?

go.hrw.com
Online Quiz
KEYWORD: SZ7 HP9

SECTION 4 ASSESSMENT

Reviewing Ideas and Terms

1. **a. Identify** What three levels of government provide services to the American people?
   b. Make Generalizations Government decisions at any level must not conflict with what national document?
2. **a. Define** Write a brief definition for each of the following terms: **grants-in-aid** and **block grants**.
   b. Make Generalizations Although all levels of government are involved in education, which government level actually controls the schools? Why?
3. **a. Summarize** In what areas might state and local governments compete for tax dollars?
   b. Recall What are some ways cities and states can attract new industry?

Critical Thinking

4. **Finding Main Ideas** Using your notes and a chart like the one below, write a main idea sentence for each element of how governments function.

Element	Main Idea
Working Together	
Serving the Public	
Competition	

Focus on Writing

5. **Analyzing Information** Imagine you have been invited by the local government to give a short speech titled "How Governmental Cooperation Serves Our Community." Write a speech that explains how the three levels of government work together to improve life in your community.

PROJECT Citizen

Changing Park Rules

When students in Pleasant Grove, Utah, rode their bicycles or skateboards to a park, they ran into a problem. Signs posted in the park said that no biking, skateboarding, or roller skating was allowed. The teens knew that if they wanted to change these rules, they would have to work with the city government.

Community Connection To find out the extent of the problem, the Project Citizen students in teacher Bill Spence's class talked to classmates and adults in the community. During these surveys, the students discovered that many people were confused about which activities were and were not allowed in the park. Some park signs further complicated the problem by giving conflicting information. For example, one park sign said both "No bikes" and "Park bikes in bike racks."

Taking Action The students decided to research local laws. They learned that one city law specifically allowed bicycles in parks and skateboards and roller skates in particular areas. Prepared with this information and their survey results, the students invited officials from the city's Leisure Services Division and the Parks and Recreation Department to a presentation at their school. The students presented their research and suggested a plan of action, which included replacing the confusing signs and making sure the park rules followed the city law. The officials agreed with the students' recommendation and posted new park signs. "The city's officials were very impressed with the students' research and presentation," said teacher Bill Spence.

Signs make it easier to know park rules.

go.hrw.com
Project Citizen
KEYWORD: SZ7 CH9

SERVICE LEARNING

1. Why was it useful for the students to interview others about their reactions to the park signs?
2. How did researching local laws help the students achieve their goal?

Visual Summary

Use this visual summary to help you review the main ideas of the chapter.

The actions of federal, state, and local governments have a huge impact on your life, but the government that usually has the most direct impact on your life is your local government.

YOU

Local government

State government

Federal government

QUICK FACTS

Reviewing Key Terms

Write a sentence explaining the significance to local government of each term or name below.

1. municipality
2. city
3. county
4. sheriff
5. charter
6. ordinances
7. town
8. town meeting
9. township
10. special district
11. home rule
12. city council
13. mayor
14. commission
15. grants-in-aid
16. block grants

Comprehension and Critical Thinking

SECTION 1 *(Pages 228–230)*

17. a. Explain How are local governments established?

   b. Describe How is county government generally organized, and what do counties do?

   c. Elaborate What purposes do local governments serve, and why do they cooperate with each other?

SECTION 2 *(Pages 231–233)*

18. a. Describe What is a town, and why are town meetings important to people in a town?

   b. Analyze What is the difference between a town or a village and a special district?

   c. Evaluate Do you think it is possible to have a "town meeting" at the state or national level? Why or why not?

Active Citizenship video program

Review the video to answer the closing question: *Name at least one argument in favor of and one argument against the power of eminent domain.*

SECTION 3 *(Pages 234–237)*

19. a. Recall What is the difference between a home-rule city and a city without home-rule power?

b. Evaluate Which of the forms of city government do you think offers the most effective system of checks and balances in local government?

SECTION 4 *(Pages 239–242)*

20. a. Recall In which areas do the three levels of government—local, state, and federal—cooperate?

b. Supporting a Point of View Explain why it is important that city, state, and national governments cooperate on such projects as road building.

Reading Skills

Understanding Political Cartoons *Use the Reading Skill taught in this chapter to complete the activity below.*

21. Create a political cartoon that is a visual representation of one aspect of the information below.

Level of Government	Source of Authority
Federal government	The people of the United States The Constitution
State governments	The people of the United States The Constitution State constitutions
Local governments	The people of the United States The Constitution State constitutions State charters

Using the Internet

go.hrw.com
KEYWORD: SZ7 CH9

22. Researching Local Government Your local government is the government closest to your daily life and you can see its work around you every day. Enter the activity keyword to research the organization, sources of revenue, and property tax rate for your county or city government. Then create a labeled diagram to illustrate your research.

Civics Skills

Analyzing an Editorial *Use the Civics Skill taught in this chapter to answer the question about the selection below.*

CONCERNS ABOUT TASERS

Police departments around the country are debating the use of Tasers, the electronic stunning devices widely used to subdue unruly suspects.

An influential police research group meeting in Houston last week recommended using the stun guns only on people violently resisting arrest because of the weapon's potential to kill. The Police Executive Research Forum also said suspects should be evaluated after one shock before being shocked again . . .

Although police departments, and the research forum, believe Tasers are important to police work, there is ample concern that more caution needs to be exercised when using them. Tasers shoot barbs that deliver 50,000 volts of electricity to the body and incapacitate the target they hit . . .

When it comes to the effectiveness of Tasers, much is still unknown. But in the past four years, more than 70 people have died in the United States after being stunned by Tasers, and that alone is cause for more study to help police officials develop proper training methods and use-of-force protocols . . .

There is widespread belief that Tasers have resulted in a decrease in lethal force when subduing suspects and in fewer injuries to officers. Although there is no doubt that a Taser is not as lethal as a gun, there is concern that officers are using Tasers indiscriminately or in routine confrontations . . . Police should have a clear protocol that directs officers to resort to Tasers only after other methods to subdue suspects fail.

Source: Austin American-Statesman

23. What point of view does this editorial express? What arguments might be used by people who oppose this point of view?

FOCUS ON WRITING

24. Writing Your Persuasive Letter You have described the levels of local government in your notes. Now think about issues in your community, your own local government, and how your government might address the problems. Then, write a two-paragraph persuasive letter to the newspaper arguing your position about how your local government might solve the problem and make your life better.

FOUNDATIONS®
of DEMOCRACY

Private Property for Public Use?

Suppose your town or county wants to build a new road—and officials decide that the best place for it is right through your home! Even if you object, the government can take control of your property, as long as you are paid a fair amount for it. This power to take private property is called "eminent domain." For years it has been used to create public roads, railroad tracks, military bases, and dams. But what if the government wants to take your land and sell it to a private company that might boost the local economy? Is that fair?

Why it Matters

The Fifth Amendment to the Constitution says that eminent domain applies only to land taken for "public use." But what is public use? Obviously a public roadway where anyone may travel is public use, but what about a sports arena where people must pay for tickets? What about a shopping mall, where companies benefit from people spending money?

In 2005 the Supreme Court ruled on an eminent domain case from New London, Connecticut. A private company proposed building a research facility on a large piece of unused land in New London. Hoping the new facility would revive the surrounding area's economy, the city planned a major renovation. The plan involved tearing down private homes to build a hotel, restaurants, shops, pedestrian areas, offices, and high-rise private apartments. The decision the Court had to make was whether these projects would qualify as public use. The Court held that, because it benefited the economic development of the community, the plan did indeed fit the definition of public use.

Many Americans believed that this decision gave local governments too much power to seize private property. In response to the ruling, some state and local governments have already begun considering new laws to limit the power of eminent domain.

This home in New London, Connecticut, was one of several condemned by the state to make room for a new hotel and other developments.

ANALYSIS
SKILL **EVALUATING THE LAW**

go.hrw.com
KEYWORD: SZ7 CH9

1. What kinds of projects might qualify as public use?
2. Do you think the government should be able to take private property to sell to a private business? Explain your answer.

UNIT 4
THE CITIZEN IN GOVERNMENT

I WANT YOU F.D.R.

STAY AND FINISH THE JOB!

INDEPENDENT VOTERS' COMMITTEE OF THE ARTS *and* SCIENCES *for* ROOSEVELT

In 1940, American voters elected Franklin D. Roosevelt to a third term as U.S. president.

247

CHAPTER 10

ELECTING LEADERS

NATIONAL STANDARDS
FOR CIVICS AND GOVERNMENT

I. What are civic life, politics, and government?

A. What is civic life, what is politics? What is government? Why are government and politics necessary? What purposes should government serve?

II. What are the foundations of the American political system?

C. What is American political culture?

III. How does the government established by the Constitution embody the purposes, values, and principles of American democracy?

E. How does the American political system provide for choice and opportunities for participation?

V. What are the roles of the citizen in American democracy?

C. What are the responsibilities of citizens? democracy?

E. How can citizens take part in civic life?

Active Citizenship video program
Watch the video to examine the role
of young voters.

WHY CIVICS Matters

Will you be ready to vote when you
turn 18? Voting is a responsibility
that all citizens should take seriously.
Study the U.S. political process
carefully. What you learn now will
help you become a well-informed
and intelligent voter later.

STUDENTS TAKE ACTION

**STUDENTS GET A NEW LIBRARY FOR
THEIR SCHOOL** What would you do if your
school did not have a library? How would you
approach the elected leaders on your school
board and convince them to establish a library?

FOCUS ON SPEAKING

CAMPAIGN PROMISES In this chapter you
will read about how we elect our leaders and
how candidates run for office. Then you will
create and present a list of campaign promises
that you would make if you were a politician
running for office. Serious problems face the
nation, and you must convince voters that you
should be the one to tackle those problems.

ELECTING LEADERS **249**

Reading Skills

In this chapter you will read about political parties and how the United States developed a strong two-party system. As you read, you will learn how political parties are organized and funded, and how they work to get candidates elected. You will read about the right to vote and the Voting Rights Act of 1965, which ensures the voting rights of all citizens. You will also read about presidential elections and how each party's candidates are chosen.

Identifying Bias

FOCUS ON READING Citizens often disagree about political and social issues. As you consider various viewpoints, you need to learn to recognize bias. Bias is a personal judgment not based on reason. People who see only one side of an issue or situation may become biased, or prejudiced against other points of view.

Recognizing Bias Bias is a negative attitude that keeps a person from being objective or fair. Bias sometimes leads people to see other viewpoints as completely wrong or bad without fully considering the issue. Recognizing a speaker or writer's bias will help you to evaluate how reliable their views are. For example, read the passage below. Do you think the author was biased?

Helpful Hints for Identifying Bias

1. Look at the words or images a writer uses. Do they present only one side? Are they emotionally charged?

2. Look at the writer's background to see if it would affect a particular point of view.

3. Look at the information. How much is opinion, and how much is fact?

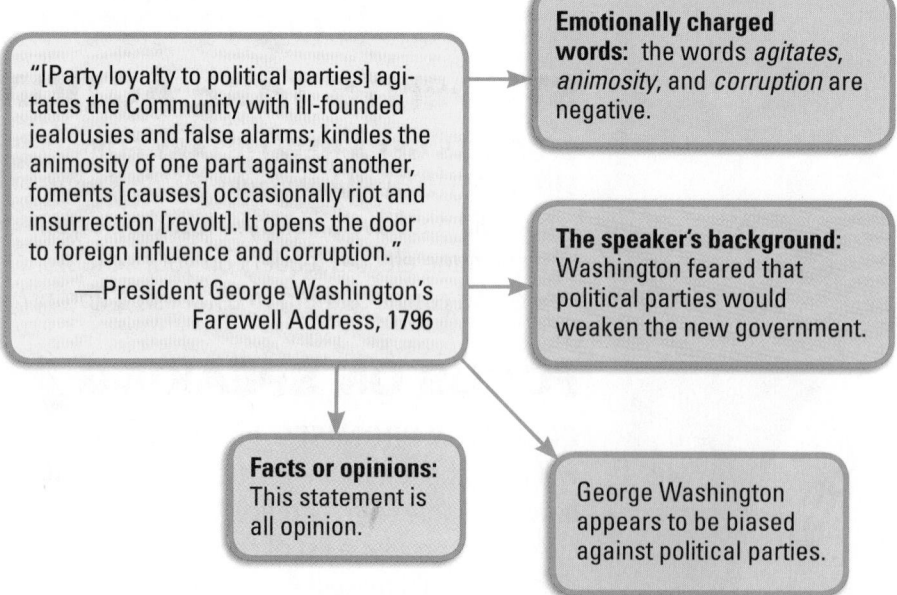

"[Party loyalty to political parties] agitates the Community with ill-founded jealousies and false alarms; kindles the animosity of one part against another, foments [causes] occasionally riot and insurrection [revolt]. It opens the door to foreign influence and corruption."

—President George Washington's Farewell Address, 1796

Emotionally charged words: the words *agitates*, *animosity*, and *corruption* are negative.

The speaker's background: Washington feared that political parties would weaken the new government.

Facts or opinions: This statement is all opinion.

George Washington appears to be biased against political parties.

You Try It!

The following passage is from the chapter you are about to read. Read it and then answer the questions below.

Political Party Finances

From Chapter 10, p. 257

The BCRA requires every political candidate in federal elections to report the name of each person who contributes $200 or more in a year. The law limits individual contributions to candidates to $2,100 for primary elections and another $2,100 for general elections. The Federal Election Commission enforces these laws. However, individuals and groups can still make unlimited contributions to activities, such as advertisements about issues, that are not part of a federal candidate's campaign. These are called "soft money" contributions.

After you have read the passage, answer the following questions.

1. You are the editor of your town's newspaper. You think the Federal Election Commission Act should be changed to prohibit contributions of soft money to political parties. You decide to write an editorial to express your opinion. Which of the phrases below would reveal your personal bias to your readers? Why? What words in each statement create bias?

   a. greedy politicians selling their votes

   b. ensuring equal opportunities for all candidates

   c. spineless Federal Election Commission

   d. concerned voters

2. If you were going to write the editorial described in question 1, how could you avoid biased statements? How do you think this might affect people's reactions to your writing?

As you read Chapter 10, think about how bias might creep into the campaign and election process.

Academic Vocabulary

Success in school is related to knowing academic vocabulary—the words that are frequently used in school assignments and discussions. In this chapter, you will learn the following academic words:

impact (p. 252)
process (p. 264)

SECTION 1

A Two-Party System

BEFORE YOU READ

The Main Idea

Political parties play an important role in the American democratic process. Party supporters put their political ideas to work at all levels of government.

Reading Focus

1. What is the role of political parties in the United States?
2. What are the differences between two-party and one-party political systems?
3. What impact have third parties had on the United States?

Key Terms

political party, *p. 252*
nominate, *p. 252*
candidate, *p. 252*
political spectrum, *p. 252*
two-party system, *p. 252*
multiparty system, *p. 253*
coalition, *p. 253*
one-party system, *p. 253*
third parties, *p. 254*

TAKING NOTES As you read, take notes on the role and development of political parties in the United States. Also take notes on the differences between the two main political parties. Use a chart like this one to record your notes.

Similarities	Differences
1.	1.
2.	2.

Do you consider yourself politically liberal or conservative? Are you conservative on some issues and liberal on other issues? Most of us fall somewhere in the middle. In any case, we can always change our minds. The strengths of our two-party system are that it offers choice and provides stability.

Political Parties

In democratic countries, citizens often join or support political parties. A **political party** is a group of citizens with similar views on public issues who work to put their ideas into effective government action. One job of political parties is to **nominate**, or select, candidates to run for political office. A **candidate** is a person who runs for government office.

ACADEMIC
VOCABULARY
impact: effect, result

The Role of Political Parties

Political parties try to convince voters to elect candidates who support the party's ideas. Most Americans who serve as public officials have been elected as candidates of a political party.

Political parties often take different positions on key issues. Some parties favor major changes to government policy, while others want few changes. Parties are often labeled as "liberal" or "conservative," and depending on their views, parties can be placed along a political spectrum. The term **political spectrum** refers to the range of differences in such political views between parties.

The Two-Party System

In the United States today, we have a **two-party system**, which means that we have two main political parties. In fact, the United States has hundreds of parties, but smaller political parties do not usually have a significant **impact** on national politics. The Democratic Party and the Republican Party are the two main parties. Generally, the Democratic Party is said to be more liberal. It favors a greater role for the federal government in providing social programs than the Republican Party does. In contrast, the Republican Party is said to be more conservative. It is more likely to support reducing the power of the federal government in operating social programs. Republicans generally, believe that social programs should be created and run by state and local governments and by nongovernmental organizations.

Advantages of the Two-Party System

Since the Civil War, the Democratic and Republican Parties have had almost equal strength, making the two-party system work remarkably well. Each party tries to attract as many voters as possible, so both parties tend to offer ideas and policies that are near the center of public opinion. Neither party wants to offer policies that might be considered too extreme because they know that if they fail to please a majority of voters, those voters may join the other party. This means that government policies are unlikely to change drastically in a short period of time.

Multiparty Systems

Several European countries have a **multiparty system**—one in which there are more than two strong political parties. If all the parties are of about equal strength, no one party can win a majority of votes. To run the government, two or more of the political parties must often agree to compromise and work together. This agreement between two or more political parties to work together is called a **coalition**. Coalition governments have worked well in some cases. However, this system has certain disadvantages. Often the political parties disagree and the coalition breaks apart, weakening both the government and the country.

One-Party Governments

In some countries voters have no choice between political parties. In countries with a **one-party system**, a single political party controls the government. In a one-party system, the law usually forbids the formation of all other political parties. Governments arising out of such a system are sometimes called dictatorships or totalitarian governments.

READING CHECK **Contrasting** What is the major difference between one-party and two-party systems?

Third-Party Candidates for President

Theodore Roosevelt
Election: 1912
Party: Progressive, or "Bull Moose"
Distinction: After serving as Republican president from 1901 to 1909, Roosevelt ran as a third-party candidate in 1912. He succeeded in taking votes from Republican William Taft, and Woodrow Wilson, the Democrat, won.

Lenora Fulani
Election: 1988, 1992
Party: New Alliance, Reform
Distinction: Fulani was the first woman and first African American person to appear on the ballot as a presidential candidate in all 50 states.

Ross Perot
Election: 1992, 1996
Party: United We Stand America, Reform
Distinction: Perot won 19 percent of vote in 1992—the highest of any third-party candidate since Roosevelt—and may have cost George H. W. Bush reelection. In 1996, he won 8 percent of the vote.

Ralph Nader
Election: 1996, 2000, 2004, 2008
Party: Green, Independent
Distinction: Many people believe that Nader split the liberal vote in the 2000 and 2004 elections, helping to ensure wins for George Bush.

ANALYSIS SKILL **ANALYZING INFORMATION**

How can third-party candidates affect presidential elections even if they do not win?

Third Parties

Although the Democrats and Republicans dominate the U.S. political system, a number of **third parties** do exist. At times, third parties have greatly influenced national politics, even though their candidate did not win the election.

In 1912, the Republican Party denied Theodore Roosevelt its presidential nomination. As a result, Roosevelt organized a third party called the Progressive Party and ran as the new party's presidential candidate. Roosevelt was not elected, but he took votes from Republican candidate William Taft. In this way, Roosevelt actually helped Democratic candidate Woodrow Wilson win the presidency.

In 1992 independent Ross Perot ran against Democrat Bill Clinton and Republican George Bush. Perot had the strongest showing of any third party or independent presidential candidate since Theodore Roosevelt. Although Bill Clinton won the presidential election, Perot won an impressive 19 percent of the vote. As in 1912, Perot's involvement in the election may have cost George Bush the election.

Third-party candidates have run for office throughout U.S. history, but few have done as well as Roosevelt and Perot. However, sometimes third parties have proposed important new ideas. For example, in the late 1800s, a group of citizens who favored several new ideas, such as a graduated income tax, an eight-hour workday, and immigration reform, formed the Populist Party. One of the Populist ideas was the election of U.S. senators directly by the voters. Democratic and Republican Party leaders favored the election of senators by the state legislatures as provided in the Constitution. Public support for the Populist proposal grew, however. As a result, the Seventeenth Amendment to the Constitution, which changed the method of electing U.S. senators, was adopted.

READING CHECK **Analyzing Information** How have third parties affected U.S. politics?

SECTION 1 ASSESSMENT

Reviewing Ideas and Terms

1. a. Define Write a brief definition of the terms **political party**, **nominate**, **candidate**, and **political spectrum**.

b. Elaborate How might a political party convince voters to vote for its candidate?

2. a. Define Write a brief definition of the terms **two-party system**, **multiparty system**, **coalition**, and **one-party system**.

b. Summarize What are the reasons that American citizens might reject a one-party system?

3. a. Define Write a brief definition of the term **third parties**.

b. Predict How might a third-party candidate win the presidency?

Critical Thinking

4. Comparing and Contrasting Copy the graphic organizer. Then compare and contrast a two-party political system, a multiparty political system, and a one-party political system.

	Two-Party	Multiparty	One-Party
Stability of Government			
Number of presidential candidates			
Response to public opinion			

Focus on Writing

5. Supporting a Point of View Imagine that you are a political expert advising citizens in a newly formed country on their country's future. Write a speech telling these citizens whether you think their country should have a two-party or a multiparty system, and where each party should fall on the political spectrum.

SECTION 2
Political Party Organization

BEFORE YOU READ

The Main Idea

Political parties have workers and committees at the local, state, and national levels. The party nominates candidates for office and campaigns to get those candidates elected.

Reading Focus

1. How are political parties organized?
2. How do political parties operate at the local level?
3. What are the two main sources of money for financing political campaigns?

Key Terms

precincts, *p. 256*
polling place, *p. 256*

 **TAKING NOTES** As you read, take notes on the responsibilities of party committees, political party finances, and the public financing of presidential elections. Use an organizer like this one to record your notes.

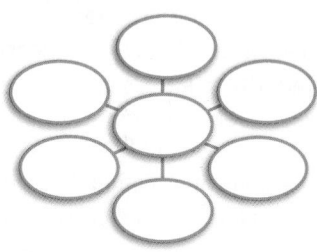

Young people often volunteer to work in political campaigns.

CIVICS IN PRACTICE If your class is planning to have a dance, a good first step would be to form a committee. A committee decides the theme, place, and other details for the dance. No one wants to get on the dance floor and discover there's no music. Effective action requires organization. This is especially true in politics. As a result, Republican and Democratic Parties are organized at the local, state, and national levels.

Party Organization

Political parties exist for one reason: to nominate and elect candidates to office. An effective party must be well organized. It must have leaders, committees, and workers able to carry out the party's program. The party must also be organized at the local, state, and national levels. It must be able to raise money to pay its expenses. The party must nominate its candidates for office and plan its campaign strategies to get these candidates elected.

FOCUS ON
Barack Obama
(1961-   )

In 2004, the people of Illinois elected Democrat Barack Obama to the U.S. Senate. He won a national reputation with his keynote address during the Democratic National Convention that year.

After graduating from law school, Obama worked in New York and Chicago as a civil rights lawyer and a community organizer. He was teaching constitutional law at the University of Chicago when he won a seat in the Illinois state Senate in 1997.

Obama ran his U.S. Senate race against former ambassador Alan Keyes. He won in a landslide. In 2008 Obama secured the Democratic Party's presidential nomination and then won the general election, the first African American to achieve either goal.

Analyzing Information How do you think Barack Obama's education and experience prepared him for public office?

Party Committees

Over the years, party members have established procedures for carrying out all of their activities. Today, both major parties—and many smaller parties—are organized in much the same way. The planning for each political party is done through a series of committees. Each political party has a national committee and a state central committee in each state. Each party also has local committees at the county, city, and sometimes township levels.

A chairperson heads each committee. Party supporters usually elect the committee members at election time. Sometimes, the members are chosen at special meetings of party leaders called caucuses.

ACADEMIC VOCABULARY
distribute: to divide among a group of people

National Committees

The largest party committee is the national committee. Members of the national committee may be elected by a state convention, elected by voters in a statewide election, or chosen by the state central committee. The party's presidential candidate often chooses the national committee chairperson.

The national committee selects the date, location, and rules for the party's national nominating convention. The party chooses its presidential and vice presidential candidates at this official party meeting.

State Committees

Each party has a state committee in each of the 50 states. This committee supervises the party organization in each state. It raises money and organizes campaigns to help candidates win elections. This committee's chairperson is a key party member in the state. He or she is often a member of the national committee.

READING CHECK **Categorizing** What are the functions of political party committees?

Local Organization

Perhaps the most important political party committees are those at the local level. These committees are responsible for conducting all local campaigns. They raise money for the party and party candidates. Party members elect local committee members. Committee members elect chairpersons and serve as local party leaders. For elections, all counties, cities, and wards are divided into voting districts called **precincts**. In each precinct, voters all vote at the same polling place. A **polling place** is where voting takes place. A rural precinct may cover large areas of countryside. A precinct in a city may cover just a few blocks. The precinct chair or captain is the party leader in the precinct.

Precinct leaders are busy at election time. For example, they organize volunteers to **distribute** campaign literature, arrange to have voters with disabilities driven to the polling place, and have party workers telephone voters and urge them to vote for party candidates.

READING CHECK **Finding the Main Idea** What role do parties play in the voting process at the local level?

Financing Campaigns

Running for political office is expensive. For example, the presidential candidates who ran in the 2004 election raised a total of more than $900 million for the campaigns.

Private Financing

Voters, business groups, labor unions, and many other organizations contribute money to the political party that they believe best represents their interests. However, people often worry that big contributors to a candidate will receive special favors if he or she wins. To limit political contributions, Congress passed the Federal Election Campaign Act (FECA) in 1972. In 2002, Congress passed the Bipartisan Campaign Reform Act (BCRA), which revised the contribution limits.

The BCRA requires every political candidate in federal elections to report the name of each person who contributes $200 or more in a year. The law limits individual contributions to candidates to $2,100 for primary elections and another $2,100 for general elections. The Federal Election Commission enforces these laws. However, individuals and groups can still make unlimited contributions to activities, such as advertisements about issues, that are not part of a federal candidate's campaign. These are called "soft money" contributions.

Public Financing

The FECA also created the Presidential Election Campaign Fund. By checking a box on their federal income tax forms, Americans can contribute $3 of their taxes to the election fund. This neither raises nor lowers the amount of tax a person pays.

The U.S. Treasury distributes the fund's money to the candidates. To be eligible, a presidential candidate trying to win a party's nomination for president must first raise at least $5,000 from private contributions in each of at least 20 states. The candidate then can receive up to a certain amount in matching public funds. To receive public funds, however, candidates must agree to limit their spending in nomination campaigns.

After winning the nomination of their party, presidential candidates who accept public financing cannot accept private contributions. Their campaigns must be paid for only with the public funds they receive.

READING CHECK **Finding the Main Idea** What are the two ways that presidential campaigns may be financed?

go.hrw.com
Online Quiz
KEYWORD: SZ7 HP10

SECTION 2 ASSESSMENT

Reviewing Ideas and Terms

1. a. Identify What are the three different levels of committees in political parties?
   b. Describe How does each level of party committees help elect candidates to office?
2. a. Define Write a brief description of the terms **precincts** and **polling places**.
   b. Summarize What are the functions of party committees?
3. a. Analyze Why did Congress pass the Federal Election Campaign Act in 1972?
   b. Evaluate What are the advantages and disadvantages of federal funding of presidential campaigns?

Critical Thinking

4. Summarizing Copy the graphic organizer. Use it to identify the levels of committees that run each of the major political parties and the functions of each committee.

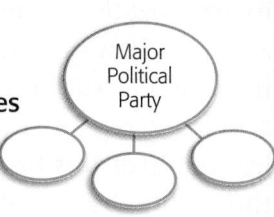

Focus On Writing

5. Supporting a Point of View Create a pamphlet explaining the guidelines you would suggest for federal financing of presidential campaigns.

STUDENTS TAKE ACTION

PROJECT Citizen

Creating a Library

Most schools in the United States have libraries for their students. What do you think you would do if your school did not have a library? A well-prepared proposal from student leaders in Rabat, Morocco, convinced the school's parent association to create and staff a school library.

Community Connection Although Morocco's Ministry of Education requires every school to have a library, it does not outline how those libraries should be organized or run. At one school in the city of Rabat, administrators just put textbooks on a few shelves in a classroom. There were no general interest books, and there was no space for students to sit and read.

Taking Action Project Citizen students in Mr. Mohammed Moussi's class wanted a real library, with space for books, a reading area, and a well-trained librarian. The teens studied their school and discovered that, although a library was included in the school's original architectural plan, it was never built. The students developed a proposal to build a new library, specifying its size, location, and cost. They identified partners to help sponsor the project, including parents, charity organizations, private donors, and local government. The students then submitted their plan to the school administration and parents' association. Parents soon began collecting books and equipment and searching for a librarian. The teens' leadership efforts have also expanded public awareness of the need to include libraries in other Moroccan schools.

School libraries are important for all students.

go.hrw.com
Project Citizen
KEYWORD: SZ7 CH10

SERVICE LEARNING

1. Why do you think students wanted a library in their school?
2. How do you think students decided which groups to contact to get support for their ideas?

SECTION 3

The Right to Vote

BEFORE YOU READ

The Main Idea

The right to vote is one of the most important rights held by U.S. citizens. It is the means through which citizens can most directly affect the actions of government.

Reading Focus

1. How do you become a voter in the United States?
2. What is the difference between primary elections and general elections?
3. How has the voting process changed over the years?

Key Terms

independent voters, *p. 259*
primary election, *p. 259*
general election, *p. 259*
closed primary, *p. 259*
open primary, *p. 259*
secret ballot, *p. 261*

 As you read, take notes on qualifications for voting, primary and general elections, and changes in the voting process. Use an organizer like this one to record your notes.

 Voting is key to democracy. If no one votes, democracy fails. If you don't vote, your voice is not heard.

Becoming a Voter

When they reach the age of 18, all U.S. citizens become eligible to vote in national, state, and local elections. The right to vote is one of the most important rights that you have.

Each state decides qualifications for registering to vote and voting. To register to vote, a person must be 18 by a set date before the next election. The Constitution forbids any state to deny a citizen the right to vote on the basis of race, color, or sex.

Most states require voters to register by giving their name, address, date of birth, and other information showing that they meet the voting qualifications. Their names are placed on a roll of eligible voters and they may be given cards showing that they are registered voters. Voter registration protects your vote. No one can vote more than once or claim to be you and cast your vote. When people register to vote, they may be asked to register as a member of the political party of their choice. They can change parties later by

registering again. Citizens may also register as **independent voters**, which means that they are not members of a political party.

READING CHECK **Finding the Main Idea** Why is voter registration important?

Elections

Most states hold two types of elections. The **primary election** takes place first and is usually held in the late spring or early summer. The primary election allows voters to choose the party candidates who will run in the later **general election**. The general election is where voters choose their leaders from the candidates offered by all the political parties.

Primary Elections

The two main types of primary elections are the closed primary and the open primary. In the **closed primary**, only those voters who are registered in a particular party can vote to choose the party's candidates. Most states use the closed primary. Those people who have registered as independent voters cannot vote in a closed primary. In the **open primary**, voters may vote for the candidates of either major party, whether or not the voters belong to that party.

FOUNDATIONS®
of DEMOCRACY

Early Primaries

In the months before a presidential election, people vote in primary elections (sometimes called caucuses) to choose which candidate will represent their party. Candidates try to gain momentum in the early primaries to help them win their party's nomination. Do people in your state have a fair voice in this process?

Why it Matters The attention given to the winners of the earliest primary elections often helps those candidates gain more support in the following primaries. This makes the first primaries very important—too important, some people think. Because lesser-known candidates may not win early primaries, they may have trouble raising money and getting noticed by the media later in the race. This system of giving the early primaries extra influence is called front-loading.

The first primary election in the country is always held by New Hampshire in late January. Should a state with a small population have so much influence? To increase their power in candidate selection, some other states have started holding their primaries early in the year too. In 2000, for example, 16 states held their primaries on "Super Tuesday" in March. In 2004, as many as 25 states held primaries before the end of March. Some people, however, oppose this shortened election season and are developing new ways to balance primaries.

Richard Gephardt dropped out of the presidential race in 2004 after a poor showing in the Iowa caucus.

ANALYSIS SKILL **EVALUATING THE LAW**

go.hrw.com
KEYWORD: SZ7 CH10

1. Do you think the primary election system is the best way to choose presidential candidates? Explain.
2. What changes, if any, would you make to the primary system?

In most states, whoever receives the most votes wins the primary election. In some states, however, the winner must receive a majority, or more than half, of the votes. If no candidate receives a majority, a runoff between the two leading candidates decides the winner.

In some states, political parties choose their candidates in a nominating convention. Various party committees select the delegates to this convention. The delegates then vote to choose candidates.

Independent Candidates

An independent candidate—one who does not belong to a political party—can have his or her name printed on the general election ballot if enough supporters sign a petition. Independent candidates usually receive only local grassroots support from individuals. Thus independent candidates are not elected as often as major-party candidates.

It is even possible to be elected without having your name on the ballot. Some states let voters write in the name of a candidate.

General Elections

Congress set the date for the general election of the president and Congress as the first Tuesday following the first Monday of November. Presidential elections take place every four years. Congressional elections occur every two years. Most general elections for state officials are also held in November. The president and members of Congress are elected in even-numbered years. State election dates are set by each state and can vary.

> **READING CHECK** **Contrasting** How do primary elections differ from general elections?

Voting

Voting methods have changed a great deal since the first elections were held in the United States. The responsibilities shared by voters, however, have remained the same.

Early Voting

During the first part of the 1800s, voting in the United States was usually by voice vote. Voters announced aloud to the election official their choice of candidate. This meant a person's vote was public knowledge.

In 1888, the United States adopted the secret ballot. A **secret ballot** is a paper ballot that lists the names of the candidates. A voter marks his or her ballot in private. Voting with ballots helps make elections fair and honest.

Voting Today

Today many states offer alternatives to the paper ballot, such as mechanical lever machines, punchcards, marksense, and direct recording electronic (DRE) systems. Voters using punchcards punch holes in paper to indicate their choices. The marksense or optical scan system requires voters to fill in little black circles or arrows with a pencil. The DRE system provides voters with the ballot on a special touch screen. Voters select their candidates by touching the person's name on the screen.

Polling places are usually open from early in the morning until evening on election day. In most states, the law requires that employers must give employees time off to vote.

Many voters vote a straight ticket—that is, they vote for all of the candidates of one party. Other voters vote a split ticket—choosing candidates of more than one political party.

However they vote, citizens should learn as much as possible about the candidates and issues. This allows voters to make informed choices that best reflect their views. Voting wisely is a key part of good citizenship.

> **READING CHECK** **Summarizing** How have voting methods changed during the past 200 years?

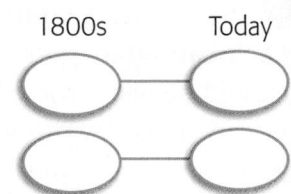

go.hrw.com
Online Quiz
KEYWORD: SZ7 HP10

SECTION 3 ASSESSMENT

Reviewing Ideas and Terms

1. **a. Define** Write a brief definition of the term **independent voters**.
   b. Summarize How does a person become a voter in the United States?
2. **a. Define** Write a brief definition of the terms **primary election**, **general election**, **closed primary**, and **open primary**.
   b. Contrast What are the differences between an open primary and a closed primary?
3. **a. Define** Write a brief definition of the term **secret ballot**.
   b. Interpret Why was the secret ballot method of voting developed?

Critical Thinking

4. **Contrasting** Copy the graphic organizer. Use it to show the ways that voting has changed since the first part of the 1800s.

1800s   Today

Focus On Writing

5. **Contrasting** Write a brief paragraph describing the different types of primary elections and the difference between primaries and general elections.

Reading an Election Map

Learn

Election maps often appear on the news to show the results of U.S. presidential elections. These maps show the votes that each candidate has—by state, county, or precinct. Usually, red indicates Republican states or counties, and blue represents Democratic areas. Third-party candidates show up on an election map if they receive enough votes.

Except for Maine and Nebraska each state gives all its electoral votes to the candidate who wins the most votes. The margin of victory in each state is not important. Similarly, the number of counties that a candidate wins is not as critical as the total number of votes he or she gets.

Practice

1 **Notice where "red" and "blue" areas are concentrated.** On a national election map, figure out which regions were won by the Democrats or the Republicans. On state election maps, look for how people voted in different counties.

2 **Determine whether a certain state had a close race.** Except in Maine and Nebraska, only one candidate can win all the electoral votes. But a close race can matter for future election campaigns.

3 **Pay attention to the total number of votes each candidate got.** In order to win the state, a candidate needs the majority of the state's votes, not the majority of the counties or precincts. By winning more populous counties, he or she may have a greater chance at winning the state.

Apply

The Arkansas election map below shows results from the 2004 presidential election. Use the map to answer the following questions.

1. Just by looking at the red and blue areas of the map, how close does the election in Arkansas appear to have been?

2. Look at the vote totals in the map key. What percentage of the vote did each candidate win?

3. What might explain the difference between the number of counties that each candidate won and the actual vote totals for each candidate?

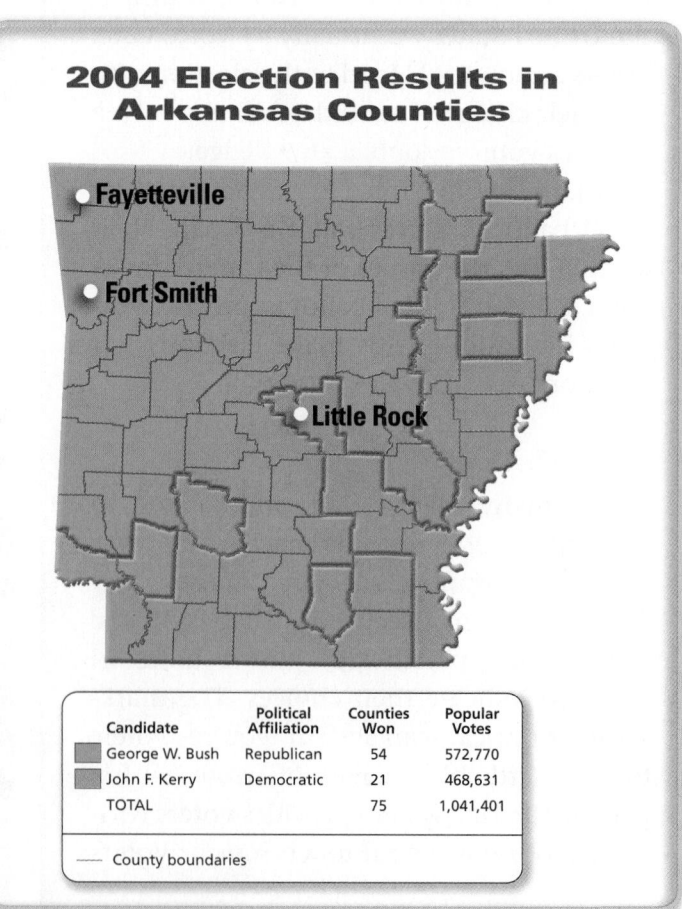

2004 Election Results in Arkansas Counties

Candidate	Political Affiliation	Counties Won	Popular Votes
George W. Bush	Republican	54	572,770
John F. Kerry	Democratic	21	468,631
TOTAL		75	1,041,401

— County boundaries

SECTION 4

Nominating and Electing Leaders

BEFORE YOU READ

The Main Idea

Every four years the United States elects a president. Citizens need to follow the presidential election campaign, stay informed about the candidates and the issues, and vote.

Reading Focus

1. What is the main purpose of the electoral college?
2. What is the nomination process at the national party conventions?

Key Terms

popular vote, *p. 263*
elector, *p. 263*
electoral college, *p. 263*
electoral votes, *p. 263*
platform, *p. 264*
plank, *p. 264*

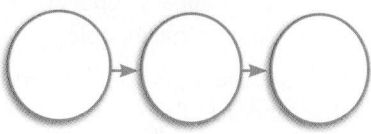 **TAKING NOTES** As you read, take notes on the electoral college. Use an organizer like this one to record your notes.

 **CIVICS IN PRACTICE** The United States is not a direct democracy. It is a representative democracy. We choose representatives to vote for us. This is true in presidential elections, too. Each of our individual votes helps to decide which political party's electors, or representatives, decide who becomes president.

The Electoral College

When you vote in a presidential election, your vote is part of the popular vote. The **popular vote** is the vote of the citizens of a country. Many people think that the candidate with the most popular votes becomes the president. That is not always true. Presidents are not elected by popular vote. That is, your vote does not count directly for the president. Your vote is actually for people called electors.

Voters Elect Electors

An **elector** is one of the people chosen from each state and the District of Columbia who formally select the president and vice president. The group of all the electors is called the **electoral college**.

There are 538 electors in the electoral college. Each state has a number of electors equal to the total number of senators and representatives that it has in Congress. In addition, the District of Columbia, which has no representatives in Congress, has three electoral votes. **Electoral votes** are votes cast by electors for president and vice president.

Before the presidential election, each political party in every state selects electors who promise to vote for the party's presidential candidate. Except in Maine and Nebraska, the party whose candidate received the most popular votes wins the state. For example, if the Democratic candidate wins a majority of the state's votes, the Democratic electors cast the state's electoral votes. The electors are not required by law to vote for their party's candidate. However, only rarely do electors cast their votes for a candidate who does not belong to their party.

Electors Elect the President

By adding up the electoral votes for each of the states won by each candidate, we can tell who will be officially elected as the next

Public Figures and the Press

If a newspaper, TV, or radio says untrue things about you, you can sue it for harming your reputation. But imagine how hard it would be to have a free press if publishers and producers had to worry about being sued every time they reported something negative about the president, the governor, or another public figure. In a democracy, we want the media to be able to critically report on political leaders and other people in the news.

In 1964, the Supreme Court ruled that, under the First Amendment, publishers and broadcasters cannot be sued for what they report about public officials unless they knew that statements were false or did not take the time to carefully check the facts. The Court later extended this protection to coverage about anyone who has become a "public figure." Public figures include anyone whose actions have generated media interest—politicians, celebrities, or even well-known criminals.

1. Why did the Supreme Court create a special rule for untrue statements about public figures?

2. How does the public-figure protection strike a balance between the interests of the press and the rights of individuals?

president. A few weeks after election day, electors in each state meet and cast their ballots. The results are then sent to and counted by Congress. The candidate who receives a majority—270 or more—of the electoral votes becomes the next president.

If no presidential candidate receives a majority of the electoral votes, the House of Representatives chooses the president from among the three leading candidates. If no candidate receives a majority of votes for vice president, the Senate chooses that official. Congress has had to choose the president only twice—in 1800 and 1824—and the vice president only once—in 1836.

READING CHECK Finding the Main Idea How does the electoral college work?

The Nomination Process

ACADEMIC VOCABULARY

process: a series of steps by which a task is accomplished

Winning the primaries is not the end of the **process** of becoming a presidential candidate. Before a candidate gets to the White House, he or she must win his or her party's nomination at a political convention.

In each state, members of each political party choose delegates to go to their party's convention to nominate candidates for president and vice president. A state's political party may send additional delegates to the convention if the party's candidate won in that state in the last presidential election.

Each party's national nominating convention is held during the summer of the presidential election year. Often, portions of the conventions are televised for voters to watch. As a result, party leaders use conventions to try to win the support of voters across the country for their platform and candidate. A party's **platform** is a statement of the party's views and policies on important issues. It sets out the party's program for actions to address the nation's problems. Each part of the platform is called a **plank**. For example, the platform may have a general statement that the party pledges to lower the crime rate. A plank related to that issue might call for increasing funding for police departments.

MEDIA INVESTIGATION

TELEVISION
Televised Debates

In September 1960 Republican nominee Richard M. Nixon faced-off against Democratic nominee John F. Kennedy in the first nationally televised presidential debate. Both candidates had a good understanding of the issues. However, Kennedy, who to many viewers seemed much more at ease before the camera, was commonly thought to have won the debate.

Televised debates allow voters to find out where the candidates stand on certain issues. At the same time, they create emotional reactions. Televised debates can help change a voter's mind about a candidate because of the candidate's television "personality." More often, though, the debates help to strengthen existing support for a candidate.

ANALYSIS SKILL **MEDIA LITERACY**

go.hrw.com
KEYWORD: SZ7 CH10

Drawing Conclusions What are some of the advantages and disadvantages of televised debates?

Presidential Candidates

The candidates for each party are usually determined after the primaries. However, candidates are officially chosen at the national nominating conventions. After all candidates are nominated, the balloting begins. To win the nomination, a candidate must receive a majority of the convention delegates' votes. The candidate who wins the majority of votes wins his or her party's nomination.

Vice Presidential Candidates

Next, the delegates nominate candidates for vice president. Vice presidential candidates are usually chosen for their ability to win votes. Generally, the nominee for president has the strongest voice in deciding who will be the vice presidential candidate.

READING CHECK **Summarizing** What takes place at nominating conventions?

go.hrw.com
Online Quiz
KEYWORD: SZ7 HP10

SECTION 4 ASSESSMENT

Reviewing Ideas and Terms

1. **a. Define** Write a brief definition of the terms **popular vote, elector, electoral college,** and **electoral votes**.
   b. Explain How does the electoral college elect the president?
2. **a. Define** Write a brief definition of the terms **platform** and **plank**.
   b. Analyze What is the main purpose of national nominating conventions?

Critical Thinking

3. **Summarizing** Copy the graphic organizer. Use it to show the process of nominating a candidate for president.

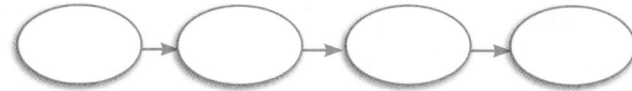

Focus On Writing

4. **Supporting a Point of View** Write an editorial arguing whether the president should be elected by the electoral college or by popular vote.

CHAPTER 10 REVIEW

Visual Summary

Use this visual summary to help you review the main ideas of the chapter.

Electing our leaders and representatives is a long and expensive process.

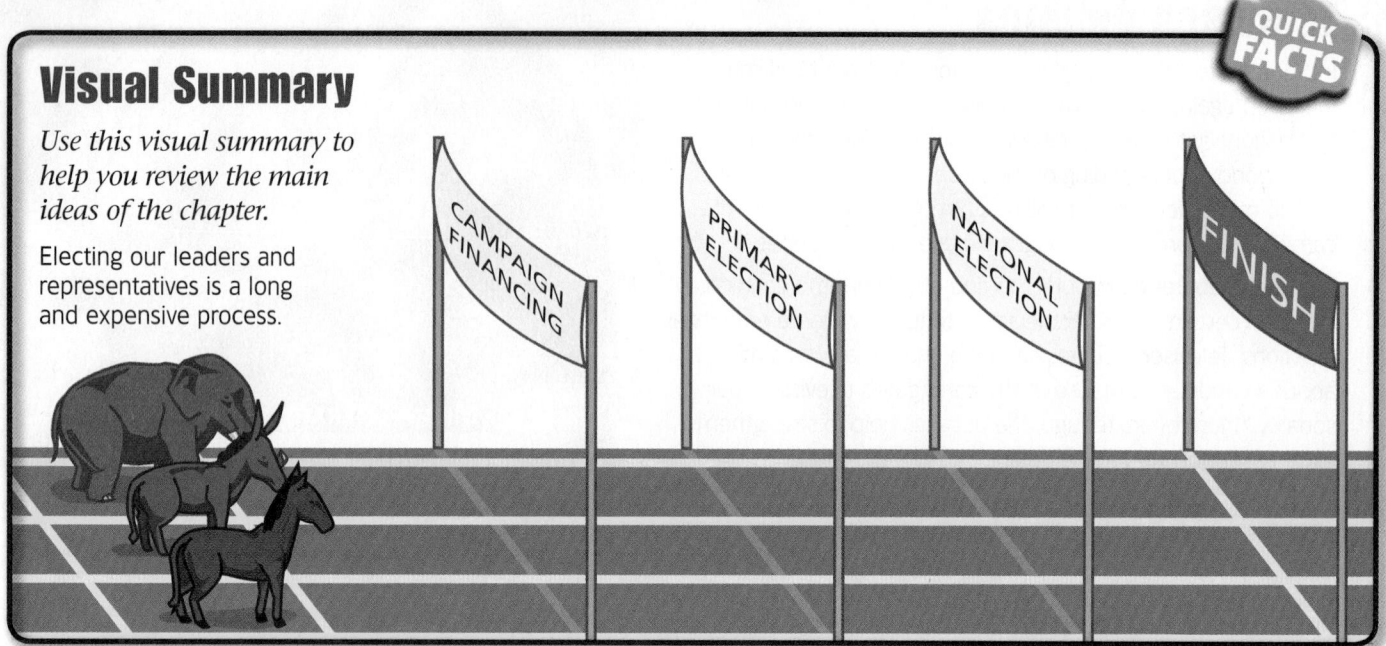

CAMPAIGN FINANCING

PRIMARY ELECTION

NATIONAL ELECTION

FINISH

Reviewing Key Terms

For each term below, write a sentence explaining its significance to electing leaders.

1. political party
2. nominate
3. candidate
4. political spectrum
5. two-party system
6. multiparty system
7. coalition
8. one-party system
9. third parties
10. precincts
11. polling place
12. independent voters
13. primary election
14. general election
15. closed primary
16. open primary
17. secret ballot
18. popular vote
19. elector
20. electoral college
21. electoral votes
22. platform
23. plank

Comprehension and Critical Thinking

SECTION 1 *(Pages 252–254)*

24. **a. Recall** What purposes do political parties serve?

   b. Draw Conclusions What are the advantages of a two-party system?

   c. Elaborate What are coalition governments, and why are they often unstable?

SECTION 2 *(Pages 255–257)*

25. **a. Describe** How are political parties organized on the national, state, and local levels?

   b. Explain How do political parties raise money, and how does Congress regulate fund-raising?

   c. Elaborate Do you think that federal money should be used to finance presidential campaigns? Why or why not?

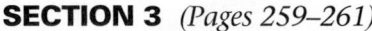

Active Citizenship video program

Review the video to answer the closing question:
*What qualities do people your age have that help
them become leaders in their school and community?*

SECTION 3 *(Pages 259–261)*

26. a. Recall What protections do voters receive
under the Constitution?

   b. Contrast What is the difference between a
   primary election and a general election?

   c. Predict How might new technology change
   the way people vote in the future?

SECTION 4 *(Pages 263–265)*

27. a. Describe How do the major political parties
select their presidential candidates?

   b. Explain What is the purpose of nominating
   conventions?

   c. Evaluate Do you think the electoral college is a fair method of choosing the president?
   Why or why not?

Civics Skills

Reading Maps *Use the Civics Skills taught in this
chapter to answer the question about the map below.*

28. Based on the information contained in the
map and key, in which part of the state would
you say most people lived?

2004 Election Results in Arkansas Counties

Fayetteville

Fort Smith

Little Rock

Candidate	Political Affiliation	Counties Won	Popular Votes
George W. Bush	Republican	54	572,770
John F. Kerry	Democratic	21	468,631
TOTAL		75	1,041,401

—— County boundaries

Reading Skills

Identifying Bias *Use the Reading Skills taught in
this chapter to answer the question about the reading
selection below.*

> " [Party loyalty] agitates the Community
> with ill-founded jealousies and false alarms;
> kindles the animosity of one part against
> another, foments [causes] occasionally riot
> and insurrection [revolt]. It opens the door
> to foreign influence and corruption..."
>
> —President George Washington's
> Farewell Address, 1796

29. Does Washington's speech show bias against
political parties? What words in this selection
support your answer?

Using the Internet

go.hrw.com
KEYWORD: SZ7 CH10

30. Reporting on Local Parties For almost 150
years, the dominant American political parties
have been the Democratic Party and the Republican Party. Enter the activity keyword to find
information about the local party structures
of the Republican or Democratic Party in your
community. Then create an oral report to present to your class. With your teacher's permission, you might want to invite local party leaders to class to answer questions you had during
your research.

FOCUS ON SPEAKING

31. Share Your Campaign Promises Review your
notes about possible campaign promises. Which
promises will be most helpful to getting you
elected? Look at your promises to see whether
they focus on issues important to voters. Then
write a speech including your campaign promises that you can deliver to your class.

CHAPTER 11

THE POLITICAL SYSTEM

SECTION 1
Shaping Public Opinion

SECTION 2
Interest Groups

SECTION 3
Taking Part
in Government

Express Yourself!
Speak Out!
Register to Vote!

ROCK
THE
VOTE

Active Citizenship Video Program
Watch the video to learn how young citizens are honoring America's past.

WHY CIVICS Matters

When you vote, you are part of the long tradition of American democracy. Your vote is important. To play your part, listen to and evaluate the political messages you get. Then it's your turn. Vote and send your own message.

STUDENTS TAKE ACTION

CREATE A HOLIDAY Few state or national holidays honor women's contributions to the nation. If you were to propose a new statewide holiday to honor a woman, what would you do to get the holiday created? As you read this chapter, think of actions you and your friends might take.

FOCUS ON WRITING

OUTLINE FOR A DOCUMENTARY FILM
Several filmmakers have made documentary films about politicians and our political system. There is always room for another good film. In this chapter you will read about the political system, shaping public opinion, and your part in our democratic system. Then you will create an outline for a documentary film to be used in your civics class.

Reading Skills

In this chapter you will read about how public opinion influences political decisions. You will learn how public opinion is measured and how groups try to shape public opinion in different ways. You will also learn how to recognize propaganda. You will discover how interest groups work to influence public opinion and what a lobbyist does. Finally, you will learn how all citizens can participate in their government and about the importance of voting.

Using Questions to Analyze Text

FOCUS ON READING When newspaper reporters want to get to the heart of a story, they ask certain questions: who, what, when, where, why, and how. When you are reading a textbook, you can use the same questions to get to the heart of the information you are reading.

Hypothetical Questions You can also use questions to dig deeper than what is in the text. You can ask hypothetical, or *what if*, questions, such as, What might have happened had the situation been different? Sometimes asking such questions can make the material come alive.

Helpful Hints for Using Questions to Analyze Text

1. Remember that the 5Ws and H questions are Who? What? Where? When? Why? and How?

2. See if you can answer the 5Ws and H questions about a passage.

3. Use What If? questions to help you think more about a passage.

Where?
United States

Who?
Political action committees

In the United States, political action committees (PACs) collect voluntary contributions from members and use this money to fund candidates that the committees favor. The number of PACs has risen dramatically in recent years – from 608 in 1974 to about 3,800 in 2000. PACs contributed nearly $260 million to candidates in the 2000 national election.

How?
Through voluntary contributions

Why?
To get candidates elected

What?
Gave $260 million to political candidates

What If? If PACs didn't exist, election campaigns would be more expensive for candidates.

You Try It!

The following passage is from the chapter you are about to read. Read it and then answer the questions below.

> Judy Heumann was born in New York City. When she was 1 1/2 years old, she contracted polio and was confined to a wheelchair. Because public schools could not meet the needs of disabled students, she was home-schooled until the fourth grade. After graduation, Heumann studied to become a teacher. However, New York would not certify her because of her physical disability. Heumann won a lawsuit against the state and later helped found Disabled in Action, a disabled-rights organization. She also served with the Centre for Independent Living, which helps integrate disabled individuals into local communities. In 2002 the World Bank appointed Heumann to the position of adviser for Disability and Development in the Human Development Network.
>
> *From Chapter 11, p. 281*

After you have read the passage, answer the following questions.

1. Who is this passage about?

2. What did she do?

3. When did she do this?

4. How do you think she accomplished it?

5. Why did she do it?

6. How do you think she got the money to begin the organization?

7. What if she had lost her fight? How might life for people with disabilities be different?

> **As you read Chapter 11,** ask the who, what, when, where, why, how, and what if questions to make sure you are getting to the heart of the material.

SECTION 1
Shaping Public Opinion

BEFORE YOU READ

The Main Idea

Political leaders and interest groups find many ways to shape public opinion and influence the beliefs of American citizens.

Reading Focus

1. What is public opinion, and how is it shaped?
2. What is propaganda, and what are six common propaganda techniques?
3. How is public opinion measured?

Key Terms

public opinion, *p. 273*
mass media, *p. 273*
propaganda, *p. 273*
poll, *p. 276*

TAKING NOTES As you read, take notes on public opinion. Use a chart like the one below to organize your notes.

Shaping Public Opinion	Propaganda	Measuring Public Opinion

President Clinton holds a baby at a political rally.

Political candidates try to shape public opinion through their words and actions.

CIVICS IN PRACTICE When you see or hear your favorite athlete or musician advertise a product, do want to buy that item? Many people do, judging by the money celebrities earn for product endorsements. Advertising must work, because companies spend a lot of money to sell their products. Remember that idea the next time you see a political advertisement. The same advertising methods that sell makeup, cars, and music also sell political issues and candidates. If you know how public opinion is shaped, you will be able to make informed choices.

Public Opinion and How It Is Shaped

What is your opinion? You have probably been asked this question many times. Your opinions can influence what others believe or how they act. In the United States, the opinions of the people—of the citizens—can influence the government. For example, an elected official who ignores the opinions of the people is not likely to be elected again.

We have all heard statements such as "Public opinion demands that something be

done." People sometimes think that public opinion is one opinion shared by all Americans. However, there are very few issues on which all Americans agree.

Public Opinion Is Many Opinions

On any particular issue, there may be many diverse opinions, each one held by a different group. Each group, therefore, makes up a "public." Because an issue may have many interested publics, **public opinion** is the total of the opinions held concerning a particular issue. Thus, the term *public opinion* really refers to many opinions.

Opinions are **influenced** or shaped by many factors. The first **factor** is usually the family. Because we share many of the same experiences with our family, we often have similar responses to issues. As we grow older, other people and experiences begin to influence what we believe. Friends, new ideas, teachers, and clubs can all play a major role in shaping our opinions.

Information and Public Opinion

Much of the information we need to make good decisions about public issues comes from the mass media. The **mass media** are forms of communication that transmit information to large numbers of people. Mass media include printed media such as books, magazines, and newspapers. Mass media also includes types of electronic media such as film, radio, television, and the Internet.

Today a lot of information is available on many issues. Simply having access to information, however, does not always mean you are well informed. Sometimes the information that you receive is inaccurate, misleading, or one-sided. A newspaper, for example, might give more favorable coverage to a political candidate it supports and less favorable coverage to a candidate it opposes. Web sites often present just one point of view.

Effective citizenship requires you to think critically about what you see, hear, and read. To participate fully in the democratic process, you must be well informed. You must learn to recognize the difference between fact and opinion. You should learn how to gather information from reliable sources.

Propaganda Shapes Public Opinion

Many of the ideas in the mass media are directed at us for a purpose. Someone or some group is urging us to do something—to buy something, to believe something, or to act in a certain way. Ideas that are spread to influence people are called **propaganda**. Communications satellites, computer networks, and television broadcasts all help spread propaganda farther and faster than ever before.

ACADEMIC VOCABULARY
influence: to change, or have an effect on
factor: a cause

Concealed Propaganda

Citizens must be alert to propaganda. They must be able to recognize it and be aware of the various methods used by propagandists. Sometimes propaganda is presented as fact and its sources are kept secret. This is called concealed propaganda. Concealed propaganda is used to fool people without letting them know that its purpose is to influence their views. Many political advertisements contain concealed propaganda.

Revealed Propaganda

Revealed propaganda is more common in the United States and in other democracies. Revealed propaganda makes readers or listeners aware that someone is trying to influence them. Television and radio commercials are direct appeals to the public to buy products. The commercials that political parties run to convince voters to support their candidates may contain concealed propaganda, but they also use revealed propaganda. For example, these commercials must be clearly labeled as paid advertisements. They also identify the organization that paid for the ad.

READING CHECK ▶ **Drawing Conclusions** How do concealed and revealed propaganda affect public opinion?

Propaganda Techniques

Whether you realize it or not, you are exposed to propaganda in many different ways. The Institute for Propaganda Analysis has identified several techniques that advertisers commonly use to influence people. Many of these techniques may seem familiar to you.

Testimonials

Political candidates and advertisers often seek endorsements from famous people. For example, advertisers know that people admire sports heroes. Therefore, advertisers pay famous athletes to say they use and like their products.

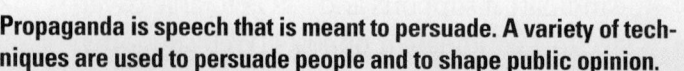

6 Propaganda Techniques

QUICK FACTS

Propaganda is speech that is meant to persuade. A variety of techniques are used to persuade people and to shape public opinion.

1 Testimonial

Bono of the rock band U2 tells about his work in Africa while lobbying the U.S. government to send aid to the continent.

2 Bandwagon

Organizations persuade young people to vote by showing celebrities, like Natalie Portman, who support their causes.

3 Name Calling

The Harry S. Truman campaign for president criticizes opponents.

The law requires that any endorsement by a celebrity must reflect the celebrity's honest experience or opinion. That is, if the celebrity says that he or she uses a product, the celebrity actually must use that product. An athlete in a commercial who says, "XYZ Shampoo makes my hair clean and shiny" must actually use XYZ Shampoo and must have the opinion that the shampoo makes his or her hair clean and shiny.

Bandwagon

People who write propaganda know that if you say something often enough and loud enough, people will believe it. If you can win some people over to your ideas, eventually more and more people will come over to your side. This is known as the bandwagon technique. "Everybody's doing it! Jump on the bandwagon!" This method appeals to people's desire to do what their friends and neighbors are doing. It takes advantage of the "peer pressure" factor.

Name Calling

A very common propaganda technique is name calling. Name calling is using an unpleasant label or description to harm a person, group, or product. For example, during an election campaign, both sides often use name-calling. You may hear that one candidate favors "reckless spending," or that another is "opposed to progress." You must ask yourself what proof is given of these charges and whether they are supported by any facts.

Glittering Generalities

Another technique used to influence people's thinking is the glittering generality. This technique uses words or vague statements that sound good but have little real meaning.

Political candidates often use glittering generalities because these statements tell voters nothing about what a candidate really believes. This type of propaganda often uses words such as *freedom* and *patriotism*.

go.hrw.com

Interactive Art ✳ KEYWORD: SZ7 CH11

4 Glittering Generalities

Former Attorney General John Ashcroft gives a speech on the Patriot Act that includes an emotional appeal to the ideal of liberty.

5 Plain-Folks Appeal

California Governor Arnold Schwarzenegger appeals for transportation funding by picking up a rake and helping workers fill potholes.

6 Card Stacking

One newspaper uses card stacking to show only one version of the disputed 2000 presidential election, which was undecided for weeks.

These words are chosen because they spark positive images with which most people in the country identify.

Plain-Folks Appeal

During election campaigns, many candidates describe themselves as being just plain, hardworking citizens. They stress that they understand the problems of average Americans. This plain-folks appeal is designed to show people that, as one of them, the candidate can best represent their interests.

Card Stacking

Another propaganda technique is card stacking. Card stacking uses facts that support only one side of a particular product, idea, or candidate. In other words, this technique stacks the cards against the truth. For example, newspapers may give front-page attention to the activities of the candidates they favor. The activities of the opposing party's candidates may be given less coverage or no coverage at all.

READING CHECK ▶ **Comparing and Contrasting** Explain how testimonials are similar to and different from plain-folks appeals.

Measuring Public Opinion

Government officials are responsible for carrying out the wishes of the people. How do government officials find out what the public wants? One important way of measuring public opinion is to conduct a public opinion **poll**, or survey.

Polls are used to find out what people think about specific issues and about politicians and their policies. A poll attempts to measure public opinion by asking the opinions of a sample, or portion, of the public.

Great care must be taken to choose a sample that is representative of the public. Unrepresentative samples can cause serious errors in a poll's results. Suppose your school conducted a poll to find out whether people wanted the cafeteria to remain open during the entire school day. A poll of teachers would have different results than a poll that included students. People who design opinion polls must be very careful to survey people who represent the general public.

READING CHECK ▶ **Summarizing** What do polls measure?

SECTION 1 ASSESSMENT

Reviewing Ideas and Terms

1. a. Define Write a brief definition of the following terms: **public opinion, mass media,** and **propaganda.**
   b. Recall How is public opinion shaped?
   c. Evaluate Which influence on public opinion is strongest? Explain your answer.
2. a. Recall What are six common propaganda techniques?
   b. Draw Conclusions Why might the plain-folks appeal persuade many voters?
   c. Elaborate With the spread of the Internet, will the use of propaganda become less common or more common? Give reasons for your answer.
3. a. Define Write a brief definition for the term **poll.**
   b. Explain How does a poll measure public opinion?

Critical Thinking

4. Evaluating Use your notes and a diagram like the one here to evaluate the effectiveness of the six common propaganda techniques.

Technique	Effectiveness

Focus on Writing

5. Identifying Bias Find an advertisement that uses some or all of the propaganda techniques covered in this section. Write a paragraph analyzing the message the advertisement promotes and explaining the techniques it uses.

Analyzing Public Opinion Polls

Learn

In the United States elected officials are supposed to represent and act on the views of the people who elected them. They frequently rely on polls—lists of questions or surveys—to help them understand what citizens think about different issues. People who do polling usually ask about 1,500 people to answer questions they have developed. By selecting the people carefully, pollsters can get an idea of how the American public as a whole feels about the issues.

Polls measure public opinion. However, polls often emphasize one finding over another. They present their findings in such a way as to mislead readers. For example, a poll might say that 98 percent of people polled plan to vote for a certain candidate. However, the poll might not mention that only a very small number of people were polled.

Analyzing polls is an important part of understanding the media. Follow the steps below to learn how to analyze a public opinion poll.

Practice

❶ **Identify the topic of the poll.** Understanding what the subject of the poll is can help you think critically about its findings.

❷ **Identify the people who were polled.** It is important to understand who was asked the poll questions. Was it a large, diverse group, or a small, select group? Consider how the people who answered the poll might affect its results.

❸ **Analyze the format of the poll.** Were people asked to answer yes or no, or were they given a variety of answers? The questions and answer choices might have a certain point of view.

❹ **Understand who sponsored or paid for the poll.** What kind of an organization sponsored the poll or developed the questions?

Apply

The graph below represents the results of a public opinion poll from 2008. The poll, sponsored by CNN, asked about 1,010 adults to identify the problem they believed to be the most important one facing the United States today. Use this graph and the steps for analyzing a poll to answer the questions below.

1. Who was polled? What are some points of view the pollsters brought to the poll? How do you know?

2. Who sponsored or paid for the poll? Do you think they influenced the outcome of the poll? Why or why not?

3. List the elements of this poll that make it neutral. Explain.

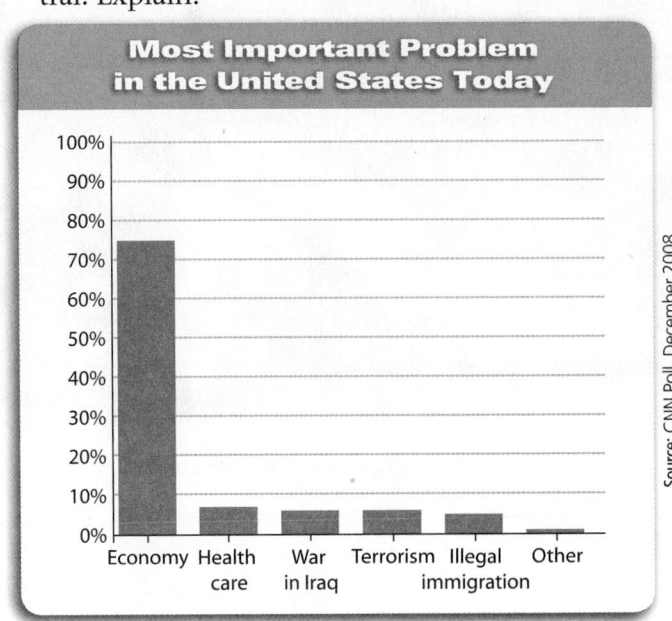

Most Important Problem in the United States Today

Source: CNN Poll, December 2008

SECTION 2
Interest Groups

BEFORE YOU READ

The Main Idea

Interest groups work to persuade the government to adopt particular policies and address specific issues.

Reading Focus

1. What are interest groups, and what are the different types of interest groups?
2. How do lobbyists try to influence government and public opinion?
3. Do interest groups have too much power?

Key Terms

interest groups, *p. 278*
lobby, *p. 278*
lobbyist, *p. 278*
public-interest groups, *p. 279*

TAKING NOTES As you read, take notes on interest groups. Use a diagram like this one to record your notes.

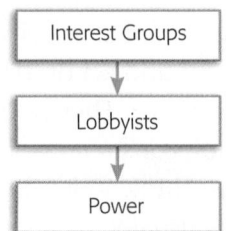

```
Interest Groups
      ↓
   Lobbyists
      ↓
    Power
```

Supporters of the rights of people with disabilities protest in front of the White House.

CIVICS IN PRACTICE Americans can express their opinions to government officials in many ways. One of the most effective ways to express an opinion is to join an interest group. Your legislator represents a district of about 640,000 people. One lone voice has only a small chance of being heard. By joining a group that shares your point of view, you can make your voice heard.

What Is an Interest Group?

Many Americans are members of one or more **interest groups**. These groups are organizations of people with a common interest that try to influence government policies and decisions. An interest group is also known as a pressure group, or **lobby**. A person who is paid by a lobby or interest group to represent that group's interests is called a **lobbyist**.

Interest groups are not the same as political parties. Both seek to influence government, but interest groups are more concerned with influencing public policies than in electing candidates.

LAW 101

The Motor Voter Act

Recent legislation now allows people in most states to register to vote while they apply for or renew their driver's license.

Why it Matters Voting is your opportunity to participate in our democratic system. Most states require you to register before you vote. The Motor Voter Act makes it easier for all citizens—especially young people—to register to vote. The law also allows you to register in other public offices or to mail in a form that is available on the Internet.

The Motor Voter Act has had a significant impact on voter registration. In 2001 and 2002, almost 20 million new voters registered. More than 70 percent of those were the result of provisions of the Motor Voter Act.

ANALYSIS SKILL **EVALUATING THE LAW**

go.hrw.com
KEYWORD: SZ7 CH11

Do you think linking voter registration to driver's license applications is a good idea? Why or why not?

Types of Interest Groups

The different kinds of interest groups include business associations, labor unions, farm organizations, veterans' organizations, teachers' associations, and consumer groups. Some interest groups represent the economic interests of their members. These groups include the National Association of Manufacturers, the United Mine Workers of America, and the American Farm Bureau Federation. Members of economic-interest groups seek to influence government policies that affect their industry or profession. For example, the American Farm Bureau Federation works to have bills passed that help farmers recover losses from natural disasters and falling crop prices.

Some interest groups are issue-oriented. That is, they focus on a specific issue or cause. For example, the National Association for the Advancement of Colored People (NAACP) works to promote racial equality. The National Organization for Women (NOW) is a special interest group that seeks to protect the rights of women.

Other groups, referred to as **public-interest groups**, promote the interests of the general public rather than just one part of it. These groups work to protect consumers, wildlife, and the environment.

Many interest groups hire lobbyists to represent them. Lobbyists work at all levels of government, although most are located in Washington, D.C. Some lobbyists are former members of the state legislatures or public agencies they now seek to influence. Other lobbyists are lawyers, public-relations experts, journalists, or specialists in particular fields.

READING CHECK **Finding Main Ideas** What are interest groups?

Lobbyists Influence Government

Many national, state, and local laws are the result of a struggle among various interest groups. One example is the minimum wage law. This law states that workers may not be paid less than a certain amount of money per hour. Labor groups often seek an increase in the minimum wage. Business groups generally oppose such an increase. Lobbyists for both interest groups present their arguments to Congress. After listening to both sides and considering all the facts, Congress makes its decision. The result is usually a compromise.

Lobbyists Work with Congress

Lobbyists use a variety of methods to promote the actions they seek. They argue in support of bills they favor and against bills they oppose. Sometimes lobbyists ask members of Congress to sponsor bills favored by members of the interest group. Lobbyists supply information for the bill and may help write the bill. Government officials often contact lobbyists to learn what interest groups think about certain issues affecting those groups.

Lobbyists Influence Public Opinion

Interest groups attempt to influence not only the government but public opinion as well. For example, interest groups place advertisements in the mass media in support of their positions. The groups often promise to help government officials in their next election campaigns by supplying workers and contributions. Sometimes lobbyists urge local groups and individuals to send letters and emails to public officials. They hope that public support will influence the lawmakers' decisions.

READING CHECK **Summarizing** How do lobbyists try to influence government and public opinion?

Interest Groups and Power

Interest groups may use any legal means to influence public officials and the public itself. To keep a record of groups, federal and state governments require lobbyists to register. They must indicate who they are working for and how much money they spend on their lobbying efforts. The Lobbying Disclosure Act of 1995 tightened regulations by closing many loopholes, or ways of evading the law.

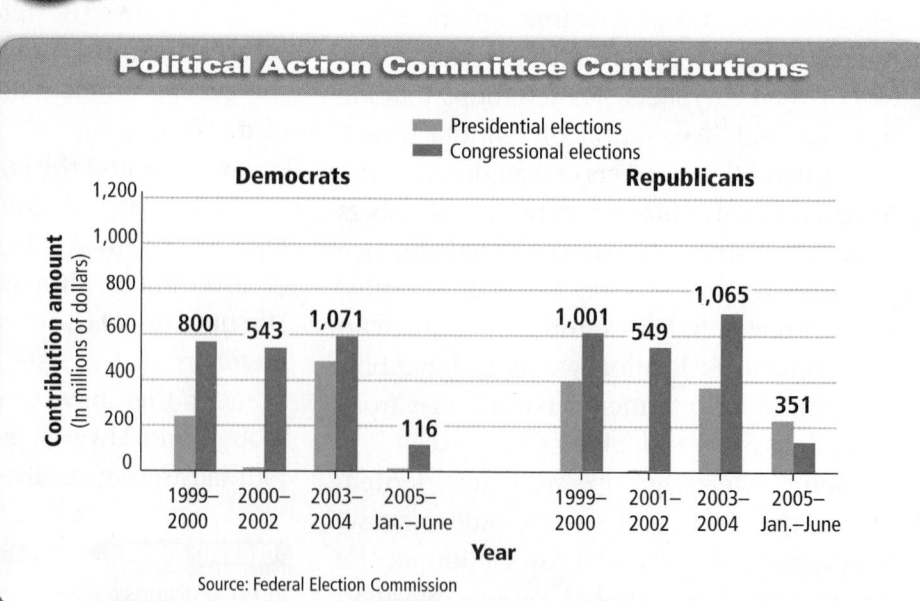

Special-Interest Groups

QUICK FACTS

Special-interest groups sometimes support candidates who share their views by donating money. Political action committees, a type of special-interest group, collect and distribute funds to candidates in local, state, and national elections. Contributions from special-interest groups are carefully monitored.

In what year did Republicans receive the most contributions from political action committees?

Political Action Committee Contributions

Presidential elections
Congressional elections

Democrats
Republicans

Contribution amount (In millions of dollars)

Democrats: 800 (1999–2000), 543 (2000–2002), 1,071 (2003–2004), 116 (2005–Jan.–June)

Republicans: 1,001 (1999–2000), 549 (2001–2002), 1,065 (2003–2004), 351 (2005–Jan.–June)

Year

Source: Federal Election Commission

Some people are critical of interest groups and their lobbyists. They believe these groups play too great a role in the lawmaking process. Critics charge that too much attention is paid to the interest group that is the most organized and best funded. As a result, some important interests—such as those of disadvantaged citizens—do not always receive equal attention from government officials.

Despite this criticism, interest groups do play an important role in the political process. Although you may not be aware of it, you probably belong to one or more interest groups. We the people—in our roles as students, consumers, workers, and veterans—make up interest groups. In a free society, citizens have the right to make their opinions known to government leaders. Interest groups are evidence of this political freedom.

READING CHECK ⟩ **Identifying Points of View**
Why do some critics feel that lobbyists are too powerful in American politics?

FOCUS ON
Judy Heumann
(1948–)

Judy Heumann was born in New York City. When she was 1 1/2 years old, she contracted polio and was confined to a wheelchair. Because public schools could not meet the needs of disabled students, she was home-schooled until the fourth grade. After graduation, Heumann studied to become a teacher. However, New York would not certify her because of her physical disability. Heumann won a lawsuit against the state and later helped found Disabled in Action, a disabled-rights organization. She also served with the Centre for Independent Living, which helps integrate disabled individuals into local communities. In 2002 the World Bank appointed Heumann to the position of adviser for Disability and Development in the Human Development Network.

Summarizing How has Heumann helped focus attention on the rights of the disabled?

go.hrw.com
Online Quiz
KEYWORD: SZ7 HP11

SECTION 2 ASSESSMENT

Reviewing Ideas and Terms

1. a. Define Write a brief definition for each of the following terms: **interest groups, lobby, lobbyist,** and **public-interest groups**.
b. Summarize Why are there so many kinds of interest groups?
c. Describe How does a public interest group differ from other kinds of interest groups? Use examples to support your answer.
2. a. Explain How do lobbyists play an important role in government?
b. Evaluate Lobbyists sometimes write legislation for Congress members to sponsor. In your opinion, is this practice good or bad for the country? Explain your answer.
3. a. Explain Do interest groups have too much influence on the government? Why or why not?
b. Evaluate How important do you think it is that interest groups be required to disclose all their sources of support? Explain your answer.

Critical Thinking

4. Categorizing Copy the graphic organizer. Use it and your notes to describe and give an example of each type of interest group.

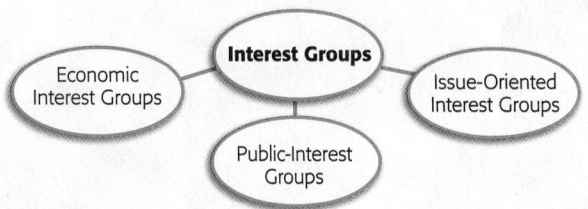

Focus on Writing

5. Supporting a Point of View Do you agree or disagree with the statement that "interest groups are evidence of political freedom"? Write a paragraph explaining your point of view. Be sure to include a suggestion for what might be done to better serve the interests of groups that lack money and representation.

SECTION 3
Taking Part in Government

BEFORE YOU READ

The Main Idea

Americans can participate in government by voting and speaking out on the issues that matter to them.

Reading Focus

1. What are the four ways that all citizens can participate in government?
2. Why is voting important, and why do so few U.S. citizens vote?
3. How do volunteers and interest groups help political campaigns?

Key Terms

volunteers, *p. 285*
political action committees (PACs), *p. 286*

 **TAKING NOTES** As you read, take notes on how citizens can participate in government, why voting is important, and how people can take part in political campaigns. Use a diagram like the one here to record your notes.

Voting is the right of every American citizen over the age of 18.

CIVICS IN PRACTICE Maybe you do not want to run for public office. Not everyone dreams of being president. However, you can still take part in government. Voting is a start. In fact, our government depends on the participation of citizens. If you do not pitch in, others will, and you might not be happy with the results. Remember, you have a voice in our political system. Being a good citizen means taking part and letting your voice be heard.

Four Ways Citizens Can Participate in Government

As a good citizen, it is your responsibility to participate in political activities. These activities are vital to the preservation of a democratic government. Any American can participate in government in at least four ways: speaking out on public issues, participating in a community action group, working on a political campaign, and—most importantly—voting.

Suppose the street corner near your home needs a traffic light. Or suppose you are opposed to a proposed 15-cent increase in your city's bus fare. Or perhaps the House of Representatives will vote soon on an issue that is important to you. How can you make your opinion on these issues known quickly?

Write letters to local officials or to your representative in Congress. Members of Congress receive a lot of mail. They welcome these letters as a way of learning what the people they represent think about the issues. Contact public officials by telephone, e-mail, or fax. Visit an official's office to express your opinions. Many officials have regular office hours for meetings with their constituents.

The quality of life in towns and cities depends largely on how well local governments serve their citizens. That is why it is important for all Americans to be active in their communities.

Community involvement is an important part of participating in government. In many cities, people work to improve their neighborhoods by forming block associations.

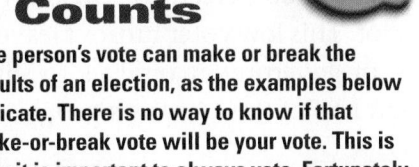

Every Vote Counts

QUICK FACTS

One person's vote can make or break the results of an election, as the examples below indicate. There is no way to know if that make-or-break vote will be your vote. This is why it is important to always vote. Fortunately, voting is easy to do. Just follow the simple steps to the right:

1. Pick up a voter registration form from a library, license bureau, grocery, etc.

2. Fill out the form and mail it in.

3. Educate yourself about the candidates and issues.

4. Use the Internet or newspaper to find your local polling place.

5. Cast your ballot on voting day.

City Commissioner Michele A. McFall-Conte
In 2001 Michele A. McFall-Conte was elected to the city commission of Deltona, Florida, after a coin toss settled a 565–565 tie.

Governor Christine Gregoire
In 2004 Christine Gregoire was elected governor of Washington by only 129 votes out of the 2.9 million cast.

President John F. Kennedy
In 1960 Kennedy won the popular vote against Richard M. Nixon by just under 120,000 votes out of 68,836,385 votes cast.

ANALYSIS SKILL **ANALYZING INFORMATION**

Why can even just one vote make a difference in an election?

The percentage of eligible voters aged 18 to 24 who voted in presidential elections dropped more than 10 percent between 1968 and 1980. However, early surveys indicate that younger voters turned out in much greater numbers in 2008 and may have exceeded 50 percent.

Why might fewer young voters take part in presidential elections?

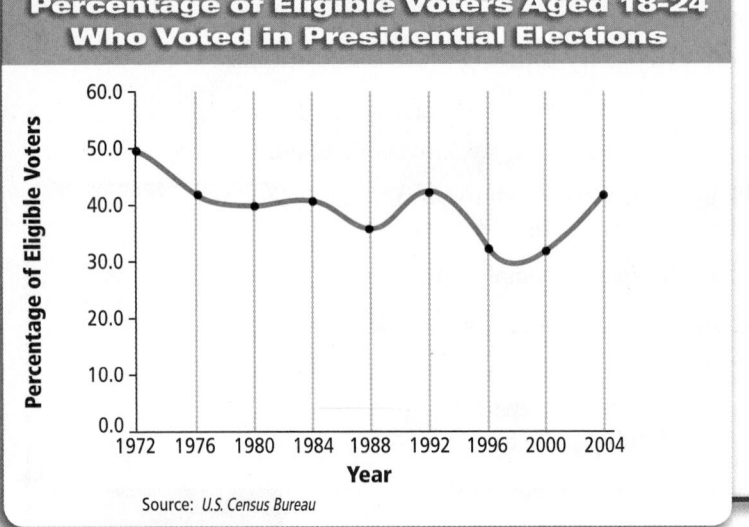

Percentage of Eligible Voters Aged 18-24 Who Voted in Presidential Elections

Source: *U.S. Census Bureau*

Residents of an apartment building might form a tenants' group to improve the condition of their building. Citizens in a town might organize to raise money for new library books or to repair the school's baseball field. Citizen involvement helps make democracy work.

READING CHECK ➤ **Identifying Cause and Effect** Why do people form community groups, and how do these groups make a difference?

Voting Is Important

When you are old enough, you can vote in local, state, and national elections. Voting is democracy in action. In fact, voting is probably the single most important opportunity for citizens to participate in government. It is also an important responsibility.

Because society relies on people performing a variety of duties, only a small percentage of citizens can serve in the government. Therefore, we elect officials to represent us. Every citizen can take part in selecting the various leaders who will represent and serve them.

Elections offer every citizen the chance to help determine what actions the government will take. You make your opinions on public issues known when you vote. When you choose candidates, you are expressing your opinions about their leadership abilities as well as their programs.

Voting is not only a right, it is an important responsibility. Yet millions of U.S. citizens do not vote. In fact, the United States has one of the lowest voter turnouts of any democratic country in the world. In recent presidential elections about 60 percent of eligible voters cast a ballot. This low voter turnout leaves the selection of government officials to slightly more than half of the country's people.

Why Do So Few People Vote?

According to a November 2004 survey by the United States Census Bureau, 64 percent of American citizens age 18 and over voted in the 2004 presidential election. This survey showed that of 197 million United States citizens 18 and older, 142 million, or 72 percent, reported they were registered to vote. And among those registered, 126 million, or 89 percent, said they voted. But that means that more than 50 million people who could register to vote did not register. Even among those who were registered to vote, there were millions of people who did not vote. Why do people not register? Why do people not vote?

Apathy, or a lack of interest or concern about the issues, discourages many people from voting. Some people do not register and thus are not eligible to vote. Others may not like any of the candidates running for office. Some people are ill and cannot reach the polling places on election day. Still others may be unexpectedly away from home and cannot reach the polling places where they are registered to vote. Others move and do not meet residency requirements for voting.

Every Vote Counts

Another reason for not voting is a person's belief that his or her vote does not count. Many people who do not vote think that their votes will not make a difference in the election's outcome. Of course, this is not true. The vote of every individual helps determine who wins or loses an election. By voting we influence the laws and policies that greatly affect our lives. The importance of every vote is demonstrated by the results of the 2000 presidential election.

On election day in 2000, as polls closed across the country, the news networks began to project results for several states. Americans began to realize that the outcome in Florida—and that state's 25 electoral votes—would decide the winner.

The Florida results were so close that Florida state law required recounts. Each campaign also challenged how votes in various parts of the state had been counted.

Eventually, the legal debate was heard before the Supreme Court. The Court ruled that using different standards for counting a vote in different counties violated the Constitution. Therefore, the hand recounts in several Florida counties were not valid. Florida's electoral votes went to George W. Bush, making him the winner with 271 electoral votes to Al Gore's 266. Nationwide, Gore won 50,999,897 popular votes, and Bush won 50,456,002 popular votes. Bush thus became the first president in more than 100 years who did not win the popular vote.

READING CHECK ▶ **Drawing Inferences and Conclusions** How do the results of the 2000 presidential election show the importance of voting?

Taking Part in Political Campaigns

Another way that you can influence political decisions is by participating in election campaigns. Although you must be 18 years old to vote, people of any age can work as volunteers in political campaigns. **Volunteers** are individuals who work without pay to help others.

American Civil Liberties

Campaign Advertising

Think back: How many political advertisements from the 2004 presidential election can you name? Do you remember any of them? You should—candidates George W. Bush and John Kerry spent approximately $2.5 billion to produce ads that were intended to sway public opinion.

Political speech like that found in advertising is strongly protected by the First Amendment. Politicians and their supporters can express their opinions on the issues. The U.S. Supreme Court has ruled that a candidate's own spending on these messages is central to political speech, so candidates can spend as much of their own money as they want on fliers, TV and radio advertisements,

Web sites, and other publicity.

But candidates are limited in how much they can collect from individual citizens like you. Your ability to contribute directly to campaigns has been limited by Congress. Because such individual contributions to political campaigns are one step removed from political speech—*your* contributions are being limited, not the candidate's—these limits are not seen as violating First Amendment rights.

1. Why are the restrictions on candidates' money and individual contributions different?

2. Present an argument for and against restricting political spending during campaigns.

ECON 101

Special-Interest Spending

In 2002, to make campaigns fairer, Congress passed a law to limit how much money groups and individuals can donate to candidates and parties. However, interest groups called 527s can still accept contributions of any amount, as long as they support *issues*, rather than candidates.

Many American voters who used to contribute directly to political parties now give money to 527s, which represent a variety of groups, including unions, human rights advocates, and the entertainment industry. From 2003–2004, 527s received almost $600 million. Much of this money went toward expensive "issue ads." None of these ads was endorsed by a candidate, but their messages of support were usually very clear. In the 2004 presidential election, interest groups in favor of one of the candidates spent more money on television ads than the candidate and his own party did!

The next time you see a political ad, listen to or read it carefully to learn if it was made by a candidate's party or by an interest group. Then evaluate its message.

ANALYSIS SKILL ANALYZING ECONOMICS

How might the spending power of 527 groups affect political campaigns? Give an example to support your answer.

Working as a campaign volunteer is an effective way to have a say in who represents you. You can also learn firsthand how the American political system works.

Interest groups often take part in political campaigns. They sometimes provide volunteers to help candidates who are sympathetic to their causes. They can also make financial contributions to election campaigns.

Although federal law prohibits interest groups from contributing money directly to candidates, they may contribute through **political action committees (PACs)**. PACs collect voluntary contributions from members and use this money to fund candidates that their committees favor. The number of PACs has risen dramatically in recent years—from 608 in 1974 to about 3,800 in 2000. PACs contributed nearly $260 million to candidates running in the 2000 national election, a figure that demonstrates their significance to the political process.

READING CHECK Finding the Main Idea How do interest groups take part in political campaigns?

go.hrw.com
Online Quiz
KEYWORD: SZ7 HP11

SECTION 3 ASSESSMENT

Reviewing Ideas and Terms

1. a. Recall What are four ways that a citizen can participate in government?

b. Elaborate What is meant by the statement that "citizen involvement helps make democracy work"? Give an example to support your answer.

2. a. Explain Why is voting considered such a fundamental right and responsibility?

b. Evaluate In your opinion, what could be done by political candidates to increase voter turnout and voter participation? Explain your answer.

3. a. Define Write a brief definition for each of the following terms: **volunteers** and **political action committees**.

b. Explain How can volunteers and interest groups participate in political campaigns?

Critical Thinking

4. Comparing and Contrasting Copy the graphic organizer. Use it to compare and contrast the ways that volunteers and interest groups help political campaigns.

Taking Part in Government

Focus on Writing

5. Problem Solving Imagine that the president of the United States has invited you to the White House to deliver a speech titled "How to Encourage Citizen Participation in Politics." Write a draft of the speech.

STUDENTS TAKE ACTION

Honoring a Hero

The United States has many holidays to honor people and events. We have holidays honoring George Washington, our country's independence, and Martin Luther King Jr. Did you know that none of these state or national holidays honors a woman? Project Citizen students in Dongola, Illinois, are hoping to change that.

Community Connection Students in Ms. Cindy Vines's social studies class had been learning about Jane Addams, who spent her life helping people. In 1889 Addams founded Hull House in Chicago, a place where women, children, immigrants, and others in need could come for aid. Addams's work led to changes all over the country in areas such as education and child labor. Students at Dongola want to create an Illinois holiday on the first Monday in March—Women's History Month—honoring this important woman.

Taking Action The teens have made dozens of phone calls to local officials and gave information to state legislators during Youth Democracy Day in Springfield, the state capital. One member of the Illinois General Assembly, Representative Brandon Phelps, has already promised the Dongola teens that he will introduce a bill asking for a statewide holiday to honor Jane Addams. Meanwhile, the students continue to work together in their community to raise awareness and support for Jane Addams Day. As student Jennifer Medlin explains, the proposed holiday "helps to recognize all women."

Students in Dongola, Illinois, speak out in favor of a state holiday honoring Jane Addams.

go.hrw.com
Project Citizen
KEYWORD: SZ7 CH11

SERVICE LEARNING

1. Why do the Dongola students believe that establishing a Jane Addams holiday is worth their efforts?
2. If you were to propose a new statewide holiday, who would you choose to honor? Why?

CHAPTER 11 REVIEW

Visual Summary

QUICK FACTS

Use the visual summary to help you review the main ideas of the chapter.

Public opinion and interest groups, as well as citizen participation, all help shape American politics.

MORE MONEY FOR SCHOOLS

NEWS 2

VOTE HERE TODAY

Polling Place

NO NEW TAXES

Re-elect Peña

Reviewing Key Terms

For each term or name below, write a sentence explaining its significance to the political system.

1. public opinion
2. mass media
3. propaganda
4. poll
5. interest groups
6. lobby
7. lobbyist
8. public-interest groups
9. volunteers
10. political action committees (PACs)

Comprehension and Critical Thinking

SECTION 1 *(Pages 272–276)*

11. a. Recall What is the relationship between public opinion and mass media?

b. Evaluate Which of the six propaganda techniques do you think is most effective? Give reasons to support your answer.

SECTION 2 *(Pages 278–281)*

12. a. Describe How do interest groups differ from political parties?

b. Elaborate How do lobbyists and interest groups try to influence public policy and public opinion?

SECTION 3 *(Pages 282–286)*

13. a. Identify What are four ways that a citizen can take part in the political system?

b. Analyze Why is voting such an important right and duty in a democratic society?

Active Citizenship Video Program
Review the video to answer the closing question:
Why are both new voters and young voters important to the election process?

Using the Internet

go.hrw.com
KEYWORD: SZ7 CH11

14. Lobbying for Understanding Interest groups play an important role in influencing government decisions and in shaping public opinion. They often hire lobbyists to promote the policies they favor. Enter the activity keyword to learn about selected interest groups and lobbyists. Then determine how and why these groups try to influence legislation and elections. Include both positive and negative viewpoints on their work. Then present a skit portraying a lobbyist activity.

Civics Skills

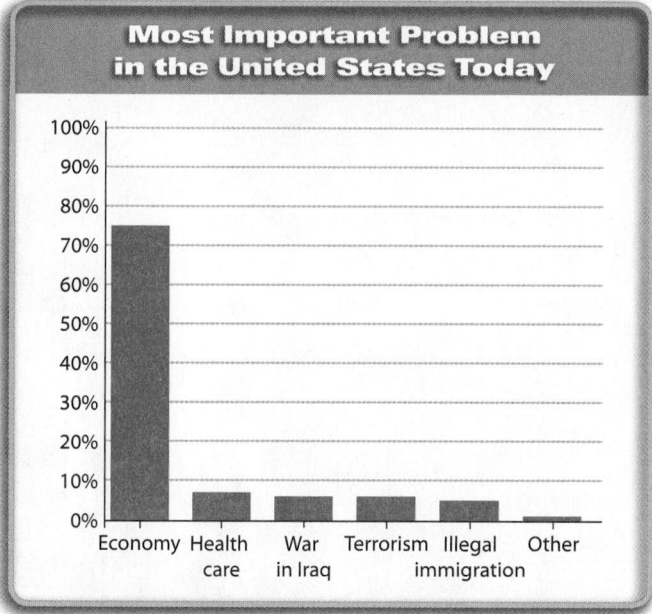

Most Important Problem in the United States Today

Analyzing Public Opinion Polls *Use the graph above to help you answer the questions below.*

15. What is the subject of this public opinion poll?

16. What did the majority of the group polled believe was the top problem in the United States at the time this poll was taken?

17. Suppose this poll had been sponsored by the Burgess High School Young Democrats Club. How might that affect the poll results?

Reading Skills

Using Questions to Analyze Text *Use the Reading Skills taught in this chapter to answer the question about the reading selection below.*

> According to a November 2004 survey by the United States Census Bureau, 64 percent of American citizens age 18 and over voted in the 2004 presidential election. This survey showed that of 197 million United States citizens 18 and older, 142 million, or 72 percent, reported they were registered to vote. And among those registered, 126 million, or 89 percent, said they voted. *(p. 284)*

18. Write three questions you have about the information in the passage above. Remember to use How? and the five Ws—Who? What? When? Where? and Why?

FOCUS ON WRITING

19. Writing an Outline for a Documentary Film Look back through your notes for the chapter. Choose one topic that you think would make a good 10-minute documentary film. Your outline should be organized by scene (no more than three scenes), in chronological order. For each scene, give the following information: main idea of scene, costumes and images to be used, audio to be used, and length of scene. As you plan, remember that your audience will be students your own age.

CHAPTER 12
PAYING FOR GOVERNMENT

SECTION 1
Raising Money

SECTION 2
Types of Taxes

SECTION 3
Managing the Country's Money

NATIONAL STANDARDS
FOR CIVICS AND GOVERNMENT

I. What are civic life, politics, and government?

  A. What purposes should government serve?

III. How does the government established by the Constitution embody the purposes, values, and principles of American democracy?

  A. How are power and responsibility distributed, shared, and limited in the government established by the United States Constitution?

  B. How is the national government organized and what does it do?

  C. How are state and local governments organized and what do they do?

V. What are the roles of the citizen in American democracy?

  C. What are the responsibilities of citizens?

Active Citizenship video program
Watch the video to learn how young citizens are working to improve their communities.

WHY CIVICS Matters

Taxes are one important way the government collects money. As a citizen, you should know how government collects and spends your tax money.

STUDENTS TAKE ACTION

HELPING TEENS IN NEED In some communities there are teens who are homeless. If you lived in one of these communities, what would you do to provide a place for homeless teens to do their homework and have access to other services? As you read this chapter, think of how you might change your community to help homeless teens.

FOCUS ON WRITING

WRITING A NEWSPAPER OR MAGAZINE ARTICLE For much of the country's history, newspapers and magazines have been an important way for citizens to learn about what their federal, state, and local governments are doing. In this chapter, you will read about how government is funded and how it manages and spends money. Then you will write a newspaper or magazine article about one aspect of government taxes or government spending.

Reading Skills

In this chapter you will read about how the government raises and spends money. You will also learn about the types of taxes that fund federal, state, and local governments. You will read about the various agencies that collect tax revenue and ensure that it is spent properly. You will discover how the federal budget is prepared and approved. Finally, you will study the national debt and why the government borrows money for the budget.

Problem Solving

FOCUS ON READING Governments often face problems. Officials and citizens usually work together to propose solutions to these problems. Understanding the problem-solving process will help you evaluate proposed solutions and deal with problems as they appear.

Solving Problems Problem solving involves several steps: asking questions, identifying and evaluating information, comparing and contrasting, and making judgments. It is a process for thinking through almost any situation.

Use the following steps to understand and solve problems.

1. **Identify the problem.** Ask questions to make sure you know exactly what the situation is and why it is a problem.
2. **Gather information.** Ask questions and conduct research to learn more about the problem.
3. **List options.** Identify possible options for solving the problem.
4. **Evaluate the options.** List the advantages and disadvantages of each possible solution.
5. **Choose and implement a solution.** Choose the solution that seems best and apply it.
6. **Evaluate the solution.** Once the solution has been tried, evaluate how effectively it solved the problem.

Helpful Hints for Problem Solving

1. Be sure to clearly identify the problem.

2. List as many options as possible when considering solutions.

3. Evaluate whether a solution worked or not. Understanding why a solution succeeded or failed can help you the next time you face a similar problem.

You Try It!

The following passage is from the chapter you are about to read. Read it and then answer the questions below.

Import Taxes

From Chapter 12, p. 303

The U.S. government collects taxes on many products imported from foreign countries. This import tax is called a tariff, or sometimes a customs duty. At one time customs duties were the main source of revenues for the federal government. For example, in 1850 about 90 percent of the federal budget came from customs duties.

Today the United States uses tariffs primarily to regulate foreign trade rather than to raise money. For example, tariffs can be used to raise the prices of imported goods. Tariffs make goods from other countries either as expensive or more expensive than American-made products. In this way tariffs can protect American industry from competition from foreign industry. On the other hand, tariffs can also hurt American consumers by raising the prices of certain products. Using tariffs as a way to control trade, rather than as a source of revenue, is often a difficult balancing act.

After you have read the passage, answer the following questions.

1. What problem is described in this passage?

2. What additional sources could you use to gather more information about the problem?

3. What are the advantages and disadvantages of using tariffs to control trade?

4. What other options for controlling foreign trade does the government have?

5. What solution would you propose? Give reasons to support your answer.

KEY TERMS

Chapter 12

Section 1

interest *(p. 295)*
national debt *(p. 295)*
revenue *(p. 296)*
fees *(p. 297)*
fine *(p. 297)*
bond *(p. 298)*

Section 2

income tax *(p. 299)*
progressive tax *(p. 300)*
profit *(p. 300)*
regressive tax *(p. 302)*
property tax *(p. 302)*
tariff *(p. 303)*

Section 3

balanced budget *(p. 307)*
surplus *(p. 307)*
deficit *(p. 307)*
audit *(p. 307)*

Academic Vocabulary

Success in school is related to knowing academic vocabulary—the words that are frequently used in school assignments and discussions. In this chapter, you will learn the following academic word:

primary *(p. 296)*

As you read Chapter 12, notice both the problems and solutions involved in the raising and spending of money by the government.

SECTION 1
Raising Money

BEFORE YOU READ

The Main Idea

Each year the local, state, and federal government provide Americans with services such as police, schools, highway construction, and defense. These services cost huge amounts of money. The government pays for these services with taxes collected from citizens.

Reading Focus

1. Why is the cost of government so high?
2. What guidelines do governments use when taxing citizens?
3. Other than taxes, what are two ways to pay for government?

Key Terms

interest, *p. 295*
national debt, *p. 295*
revenue, *p. 296*
fees, *p. 297*
fine, *p. 297*
bond, *p. 298*

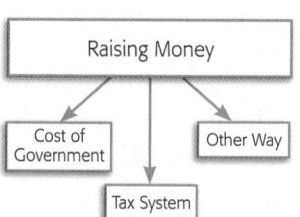

Many different kinds of taxes such as sales taxes on meals, pay for the goods and services you receive from government.

CIVICS IN PRACTICE Why should you pay taxes? One reason is that taxes help pay for the many services you receive. For example, imagine the United States without the Interstate Highway System. Taxes—money from people like you—helped pay for this huge highway network. As a citizen, it is up to you to pay a fair share for what you receive. At the same time, it is the right of citizens to question government spending and to make sure that taxes are spent wisely and fairly. You are entitled to know how and where your money goes.

The High Cost of Government

It costs an enormous amount of money today to run the government. One reason it costs so much is that the United States serves a larger population than ever before—more than 300 million people. As the population has grown, the cost of living has also risen. Today a dollar will not buy as much as in earlier years. Adding to the costs, the government provides many more programs and services today than in the past.

The Rising Cost of Government

Since 1960 the amount of money spent per capita by the federal government has more than doubled. The term *per capita* means "per individual" or "per person."

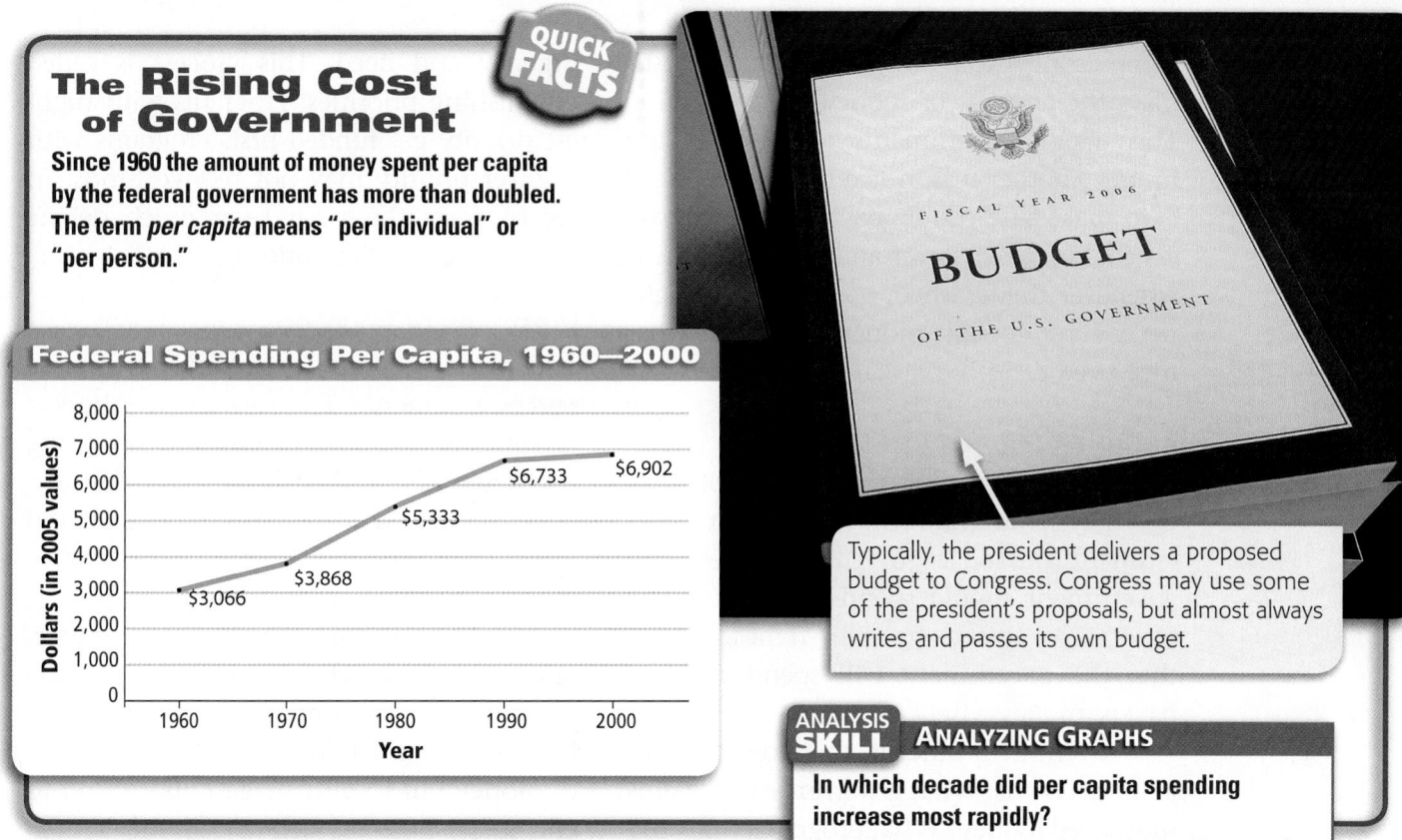

Federal Spending Per Capita, 1960–2000

Dollars (in 2005 values) — Year

$3,066 (1960)
$3,868 (1970)
$5,333 (1980)
$6,733 (1990)
$6,902 (2000)

FISCAL YEAR 2006
BUDGET
OF THE U.S. GOVERNMENT

Typically, the president delivers a proposed budget to Congress. Congress may use some of the president's proposals, but almost always writes and passes its own budget.

ANALYSIS SKILL **ANALYZING GRAPHS**

In which decade did per capita spending increase most rapidly?

The Federal Budget

Government programs and services are expensive. The single largest cost to the federal government is in benefit payments to people who are elderly, disabled, or living in poverty. For example, in 2007, total government spending was about $2.8 trillion. Of that amount, about $1.3 trillion, or about 45 percent, went to Social Security, Medicare, and Medicaid programs. The numbers of people who receive these benefits will continue to rise.

The government also spends a large amount of money on national defense. From 1990 to 2001, defense spending decreased. After 2001, however, defense costs began to rise. Following terrorist attacks in 2001, government leaders pushed for even greater increases. In December 2001 Congress approved a $318 billion defense bill. The 2003 invasion of Iraq and the ongoing war will cost about $200 billion. By 2007, defense spending accounted for about 17 percent of the federal budget. Defense spending will continue to account for a large portion of government spending.

Another large part of the budget is debt. Over the years, the government has spent more money than it has raised. To make up the difference, the government borrows money. Like any borrower, the government pays interest on this money. **Interest** is the payment made for the use of borrowed money. Interest is a certain percentage of the amount of money borrowed. When large amounts of money are borrowed, the amount of interest is also large. This interest plus the total amount of money that the U.S. government has borrowed is known as the **national debt**.

READING CHECK **Finding Main Ideas** What are the main expenses of the federal government?

The Tax System

Federal, state, and local governments all raise most of the money to pay for services and programs by collecting taxes. Taxes are compulsory—citizens and businesses are required to pay them. One reason taxes are compulsory is to allow governments to estimate the amount of money they will raise. This allows governments to plan for the future. Another reason taxes are compulsory is to make sure people pay them. If taxpayers could pay whatever amount suited them whenever they wished, governments might never have enough money to pay for what they need to do.

ACADEMIC
VOCABULARY
primary:
main, most
important

Establishing Priorities

Some people question the amount of taxes they pay. They think that the costs of government are too high. Others believe the government should spend more on public services. All citizens have the right to expect that the government will spend the taxpayers' money wisely.

Government officials, therefore, face difficult decisions. What government programs most need money? What programs will bring the greatest benefits to the most people?

Government officials must decide which activities need funding, in order of their urgency and need. This process is called establishing priorities. Programs with highest priority get funded first. Programs with a lower priority may not receive funds. In recent years there has been much debate over the country's priorities.

Purposes of Taxation

The **primary** purpose of taxes is to raise **revenue**, or money. This revenue pays the cost of running the government and providing public services. At the federal level, most revenue is collected in the form of personal and business income taxes. State and local governments also rely on taxes to raise money.

Another purpose of taxes is to regulate, or control, some activities. For example, taxes on imports are sometimes fixed at a high level. Their aim is not to raise large sums of money but to discourage imports and to encourage business activity in the United States. High taxes on cigarettes and alcoholic beverages are partly intended to discourage their use.

Linking to Today

Taxes, Then and Now

In the 1700s, before and after the Revolutionary War, government was funded with sales taxes collected on goods like tea and whiskey. Then, in the 1800s, the government found it needed to collect property and income taxes to cover things like the cost of war and building new roads.

In modern times, Americans pay taxes on where they live, what they buy, and the money they make from their jobs. However, we also have the right to elect officials whom we believe will spend that money in the best way possible.

ANALYSIS SKILL **DRAWING CONCLUSIONS**

Why do you think taxes are often an important issue in political campaigns?

Principles of Taxation

Governments try to follow certain principles, or rules, when they set up tax systems. These rules aim to raise the funds necessary to run the government without creating too great a burden for taxpayers.

Ability to Pay Taxes are set at different rates to make it possible for citizens at all income levels to pay. For example, taxes on people's earnings are lower for those with low incomes and higher for those with high incomes. People with very low incomes do not pay income taxes.

Equal Application The principle of equal application of taxes is an important part of the U.S. tax structure. Equal application means that taxes are applied at the same rate for similar taxable items. For example, a local tax on property is the same for all property worth the same amount of money. Sales taxes and other taxes collected on the goods we buy are the same for everyone purchasing goods of equal price.

Scheduled Payment Taxes are paid on a set schedule. Employers withhold a portion of taxes from their workers' paychecks. They send this tax revenue directly to the government on a regular schedule. People who are self-employed are responsible for withholding the necessary funds for their taxes. They also send this money directly to the government in installments during the tax year.

Imagine that all taxes had to be paid in one lump sum. Most Americans would find paying taxes in one lump sum very difficult. Instead, federal and state governments collect income taxes over the course of the year. People who owe more than the amount withheld from their paychecks must pay in full by an April 15 deadline. However, taxpayers can request to pay any taxes that they still owe in installments. These are payments made throughout the year on a set schedule. These late payments are charged interest and penalty fees.

READING CHECK **Drawing Inferences and Conclusions** Why are some taxes set at different rates?

Other Ways to Pay for Government

Although governments at all levels get most of their money from taxes of one kind or another, there are also other sources of revenue available. Governments may raise fees or fines and they may borrow money.

Fees and Fines

Fees are payments charged by governments for various licenses, such as hunting licenses and marriage licenses. The federal government raises billions of dollars annually by collecting a range of fees. The federal government receives fees for trademark registration, grazing rights on federal land, and entrance fees to national parks. State governments raise large sums of money from the fees paid by residents for driver's licenses and automobile license plates.

Money charged as a penalty for breaking certain laws is called a **fine**. Local governments in particular raise revenue from fines for actions such as illegal parking, speeding, and other traffic violations.

Governments also provide some special services that are paid for directly by the people or organizations who use these services. For example, the federal government sells timber from national forest reserves and electricity from certain federal dam projects. State governments collect payments from drivers who use certain toll roads and bridges. Many local governments install parking meters to collect payments from individuals who park their cars along city streets.

Government Borrowing

As you have read, governments raise most of their funds through taxes and other revenue. Occasionally, tax revenue is not enough to pay for government expenses. As a result, governments must borrow money to meet their expenses. Large projects, such as bridges or schools, cost a lot to build. State and local governments usually cannot pay for them in full out of the government's income for a single year. Therefore, state and local governments must borrow the additional money needed.

Governments borrow money by issuing bonds. A government **bond** is a certificate stating that the government has borrowed a certain sum of money from the owner of the bond. The government promises to repay the loan on a certain date and to pay interest on the amount borrowed. Bonds allow governments to raise money for public projects while giving investors an opportunity to make a profit.

When a government issues a bond, it is taking on debt that it must repay. For this reason, most local governments must have voter approval before they can issue a bond. Voters have a chance to support or oppose specific bond proposals in a bond election.

Government Bonds

Travis voters approve bonds

■ $185 million will be used for road and park projects, land purchases

By ALEX TAYLOR
American-Statesman Staff

State and local governments often use bonds to finance long-term projects, such as highway construction.

For example, bond elections often take place when school districts need to raise money to build or repair facilities. If a bond is not approved, officials have to find other ways to raise the money or to address that particular need.

READING CHECK ▶ **Analyzing Information** Why do governments borrow money?

go.hrw.com
Online Quiz
KEYWORD: SZ7 HP12

SECTION 1 ASSESSMENT

Reviewing Ideas and Terms

1. a. Define Write a brief definition of the terms **interest** and **national debt**.

b. Elaborate Why are businesses and citizens required to pay taxes?

2. a. Define Write a brief definition of the term **revenue**.

b. Explain What are the purposes of paying taxes?

c. Predict What might happen if the government did not collect any taxes?

3. a. Define Write a brief definition of the terms **fees**, **fine**, and **bond**.

b. Summarize What principles does the government use to set up taxes?

Critical Thinking

4. Analyzing Information Copy the graphic organizer. Use it and your notes to identify the three principles of taxation and to explain why each one is important.

Principle			
Importance			

Focus on Writing

5. Decision Making Write a proposal explaining what government programs and services you think should have the highest priority and why.

SECTION 2
Types of Taxes

BEFORE YOU READ

The Main Idea

Taxes are the main source of revenue for the local, state, and federal governments. The types of taxes each level of government uses to raise money vary.

Reading Focus

1. What are the two main kinds of income taxes?
2. What are the other major types of taxes?

Key Terms

income tax, *p. 299*
progressive tax, *p. 300*
profit, *p. 300*
regressive tax, *p. 302*
property tax, *p. 302*
tariff, *p. 303*

TAKING NOTES As you read, take notes on income taxes and other types of taxes used in the United States. Use a chart like this one to record your notes.

Income Taxes	Other Taxes

Taxpayers rush to post offices to mail their federal income tax returns by the April 15 deadline.

CIVICS IN PRACTICE Different levels of government rely on a variety of the taxes that you pay. For example, the federal government relies on income taxes. You are probably also familiar with sales taxes, which state and local governments depend on for their revenue. School districts rely on property taxes. Wherever you live and whatever job you have, you will pay taxes of one kind or another.

Income Taxes

The largest source of revenue collected by the federal government is the tax on the earnings—the income—of individual citizens and businesses. These taxes on earnings are called **income tax**. Americans filed more than 130 million individual federal tax returns in 2007. The federal government collected some $1.2 trillion in tax revenues from these returns. The amount any one citizen pays is calculated according to how much the person earns and other considerations set out in the U.S. tax code.

POLITICAL CARTOON
Social Security

For many Americans, income taxes are deducted directly from their paychecks. Federal and state income taxes as well as Social Security and Medicare taxes are deducted each time an employee is paid.

The Federal Insurance Contributions Act, or FICA, collects Social Security taxes from workers' paychecks.

ANALYSIS SKILL — ANALYZING PRIMARY SOURCES

Do you think having income taxes deducted from each paycheck is a good idea? Why or why not?

How Much Do We Pay?

The government permits all taxpayers to deduct, or subtract, a certain amount of money from their taxes for themselves and each dependent. A dependent is a person who relies on another person, usually a family member, for financial support. These amounts are called exemptions.

The individual income tax is a progressive tax. A **progressive tax** is a tax that takes a larger percentage of income from higher-income groups than from lower-income groups. Progressive taxes are based on a person's ability to pay.

How Do We Pay?

Most taxpayers do not pay all their income tax at the time they file their annual tax returns. Instead, their employers take income tax payments out of each paycheck throughout the year. Employers then forward the tax money on to the government. This system of making small tax payments each payday makes it easier for the government to collect the payments. This system also makes payment easier for most Americans to afford. Even so, it can take the federal government some time to accurately calculate the federal tax revenues for a single year. This is due in part to factors such as refunds and late payments.

Social Security Taxes

When an employer deducts income tax from an employee's paycheck, he or she also deducts Social Security tax. Money collected from this tax is used mainly to provide income to retired people and people with disabilities. You can read more about Social Security in another chapter.

State and Local Income Taxes

All but a few of the state governments and some city governments also collect an individual income tax. Each of these states and cities has its own income tax laws and rates. Such tax rates are much lower than those for the federal income tax.

Corporate Income Taxes

Like individual income taxes, corporate income taxes are an important source of revenue for both the federal and state governments. This tax is based on a corporation's profits. **Profit** is the income a business has left after paying its expenses. In 2007 the federal government collected more than $340 billion in corporate income taxes from over five million companies.

READING CHECK **Summarizing** What are the different types of income taxes?

Government Taxing and Spending

Each level of government collects taxes from many different sources and spends them on slightly different programs.

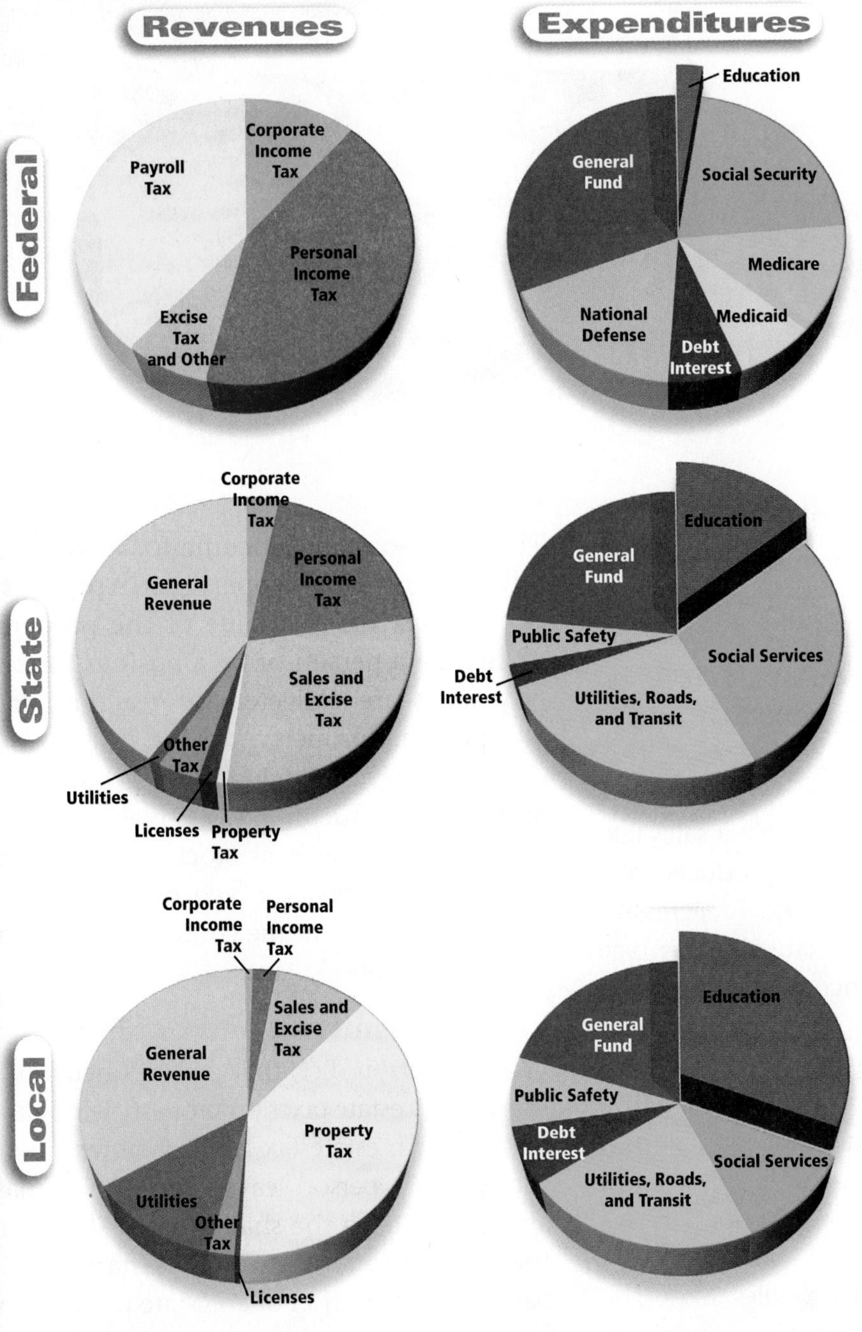

Revenues

Federal
- Corporate Income Tax
- Payroll Tax
- Personal Income Tax
- Excise Tax and Other

State
- Corporate Income Tax
- Personal Income Tax
- General Revenue
- Sales and Excise Tax
- Other Tax
- Utilities
- Licenses
- Property Tax

Local
- Corporate Income Tax
- Personal Income Tax
- Sales and Excise Tax
- General Revenue
- Property Tax
- Utilities
- Other Tax
- Licenses

Expenditures

Federal
- Education
- General Fund
- Social Security
- Medicare
- Medicaid
- Debt Interest
- National Defense

State
- Education
- General Fund
- Public Safety
- Social Services
- Debt Interest
- Utilities, Roads, and Transit

Local
- Education
- General Fund
- Public Safety
- Debt Interest
- Social Services
- Utilities, Roads, and Transit

This graph shows the percentage of revenues each level of government spends on education. One book equals one percent of total spending. As you can see, local governments spend a much larger percentage of their revenue on education.

Education Spending

Federal | State | Local

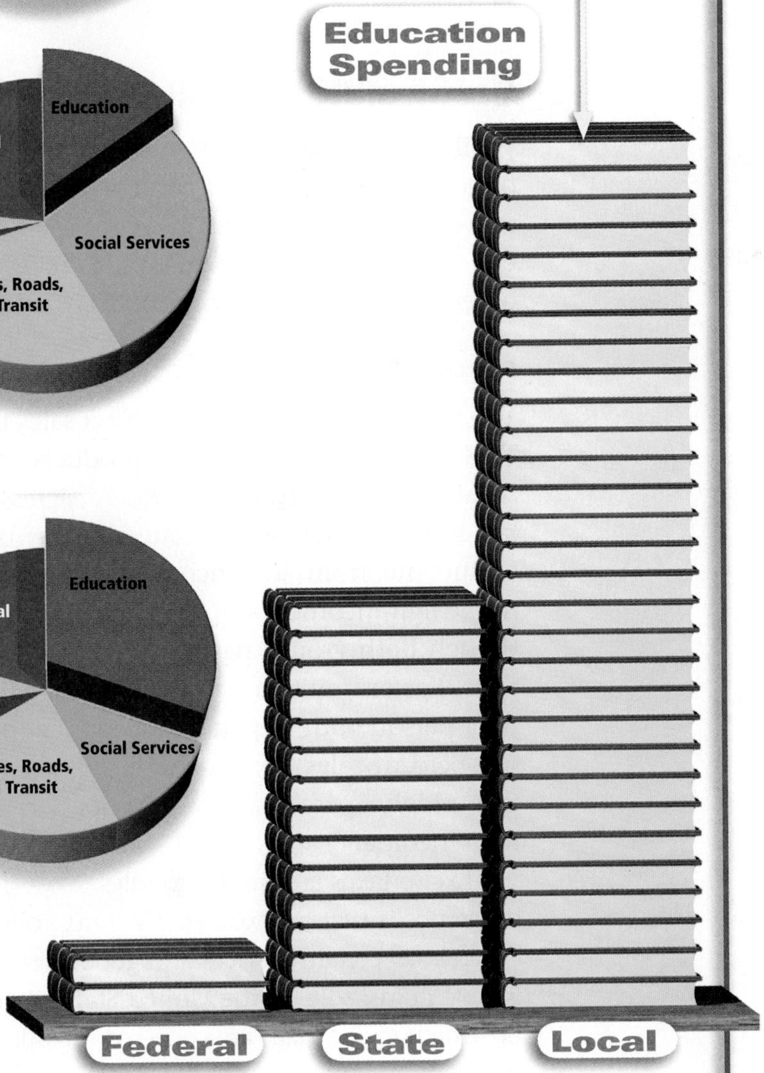

ANALYSIS SKILL — ANALYZING INFORMATION

1. Why do you think that local governments spend the largest portion of their revenue on education?
2. What are the largest forms of revenue for federal, state, and local governments?

QUICK FACTS

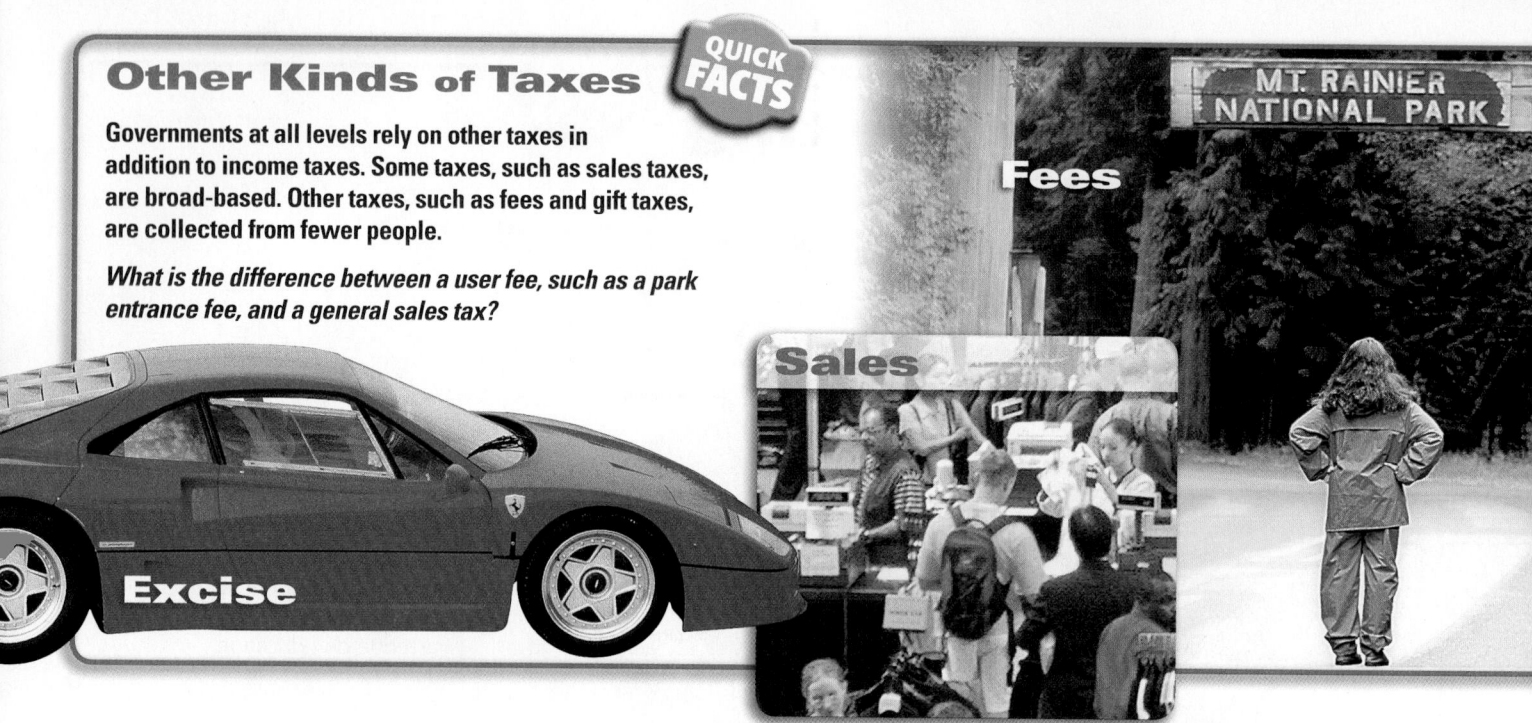

Other Kinds of Taxes **QUICK FACTS**

Governments at all levels rely on other taxes in addition to income taxes. Some taxes, such as sales taxes, are broad-based. Other taxes, such as fees and gift taxes, are collected from fewer people.

What is the difference between a user fee, such as a park entrance fee, and a general sales tax?

Excise

Sales

Fees

MT. RAINIER NATIONAL PARK

Other Major Taxes

While income taxes are important to all levels of government, state and local governments rely on a variety of other taxes for their revenue. The federal government also relies on other kinds of taxes for some of its revenue.

Sales and Excise Taxes

Most states and many cities have a sales tax. This tax is collected on most products sold. A sales tax is a **regressive tax**. A regressive tax is a tax that takes a larger percentage of income from low-income groups than from high-income groups. This is true even though both groups pay the same sales tax rates. For example, a wealthy person and a poor person both buy the same television. A five-percent sales tax on the television will take a higher percentage of the poor person's total income.

Excise taxes are similar to sales taxes. The difference is that an excise tax is a tax collected only on certain services and goods, usually luxury items, sold in the United States. Items on which excise taxes are collected include air travel and luxury automobiles.

Property Taxes

The chief source of income for most local governments is the property tax. A **property tax** is a tax on the value of the property owned by a person or by a business. Property taxes are collected on real property and personal property.

Real property includes land, buildings, and other structures. Personal property includes such items as stocks, bonds, jewelry, cars, and boats. Much of the funding for public schools in the United States comes from local property taxes.

Estate, Inheritance, and Gift Taxes

When a person dies, that person's heirs may have to pay estate taxes on property left by the deceased. An estate tax is a federal tax on all the wealth a person leaves. Individuals may also be taxed on the share of the estate that they inherit, or receive. The inheritance tax is based on the portion of an estate received by an individual after the estate is divided.

Even a gift of money may be subject to a tax by the federal government. Any person who gives a gift worth more than $12,000 must pay a gift tax.

Import

Estate

Import Taxes

The U.S. government collects taxes on many products imported from foreign countries. This import tax is called a **tariff**, or sometimes a customs duty. At one time customs duties were the main source of revenues for the federal government. For example, in 1850 about 90 percent of the federal budget came from customs duties.

Today the United States uses tariffs primarily to regulate foreign trade rather than to raise money. For example, tariffs can be used to raise the prices of imported goods. Tariffs make goods from other countries either as expensive or more expensive than American-made products. In this way tariffs can protect American industry from competition from foreign industry. On the other hand, tariffs can also hurt American consumers by raising the prices of certain products. Using tariffs as a way to control trade, rather than as a source of revenue, is often a difficult balancing act.

READING CHECK   **Analyzing Information** Why is it good for governments to rely on a wide variety of taxes?

go.hrw.com
Online Quiz
KEYWORD: SZ7 HP12

SECTION 2 ASSESSMENT

Reviewing Ideas and Terms

1. **a. Define** Write a brief definition of the terms **income tax**, **progressive tax**, and **profit**.
   b. Evaluate Do you think that a sales tax is a fair tax for all Americans?
2. **a. Define** Write a brief definition of the terms **regressive tax**, **property tax**, and **tariff**.
   b. Explain What is the difference between an estate tax and an inheritance tax?

Critical Thinking

3. **Categorizing** Copy the graphic organizer. Fill in each box with a type of tax and an example of something to which that tax could be applied.

Types of Taxes	

Focus on Writing

4. **Supporting a Point of View** Should all U.S. taxes be made progressive taxes? Why or why not?

Analyzing a Documentary

Learn

Not all films are works of fiction. Documentaries are non-fiction films or television programs that present information on a particular topic in a factual way. Documentaries might focus on the life of a particular person, like Abraham Lincoln, or they may concentrate on an important event, such as the first moon landing. In either case, a documentary uses a combination of original source documents, personal interviews, photographs, and film to convey information about a subject.

A good documentary should add to your knowledge of a subject. But documentaries, like other forms of media, are biased in that they are told from the perspective of their creators. When you watch a documentary, it is important that you evaluate it carefully. Use the tips below to help you analyze a documentary.

Practice

❶ **Identify the point of view.** Documentary films present a topic in a certain way. It is important to be aware of how the director is trying to shape your opinion.

❷ **Notice how the visuals and images make you feel.** Techniques like music, close-ups, slow-motion shots, or stills of a scene may be used to elicit emotional responses from the viewers. Notice how such techniques affect you emotionally. How do they affect the tone of the documentary?

❸ **Investigate the source.** Who produced and directed the documentary? Ask yourself if the filmmakers have a special interest in presenting a particular point of view.

❹ **Check the facts.** Be careful not to believe everything you see and hear. Use outside sources to confirm the information presented in the documentary.

Apply

Imagine that you have just watched a documentary about the artists that created the monument at Mount Rushmore. Use the image below and your knowledge of documentaries to answer the questions.

1. Who produced the film? How might that affect the point of view of the documentary?

2. What possible points of view might a documentary about Mount Rushmore present?

3. What sources might you use to verify the information presented in the documentary?

USA HOME VIDEO

THE CREATION OF
MOUNT RUSHMORE

DVD   NATIONAL TREASURES

SECTION 3

Managing the Country's Money

BEFORE YOU READ

The Main Idea

The federal, state and local governments collect and spend many billions of dollars each year. Each level of government has systems to manage public funds.

Reading Focus

1. How do governments collect public money?
2. What steps are involved in spending public money?
3. How do governments account for your money?

Key Terms

balanced budget, *p. 307*
surplus, *p. 307*
deficit, *p. 307*
audit, *p. 307*

 **TAKING NOTES** As you read, take notes on the steps involved in planning the federal budget. Use a chart like this one to record your notes.

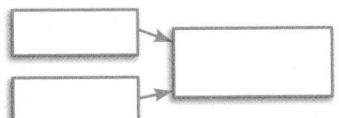

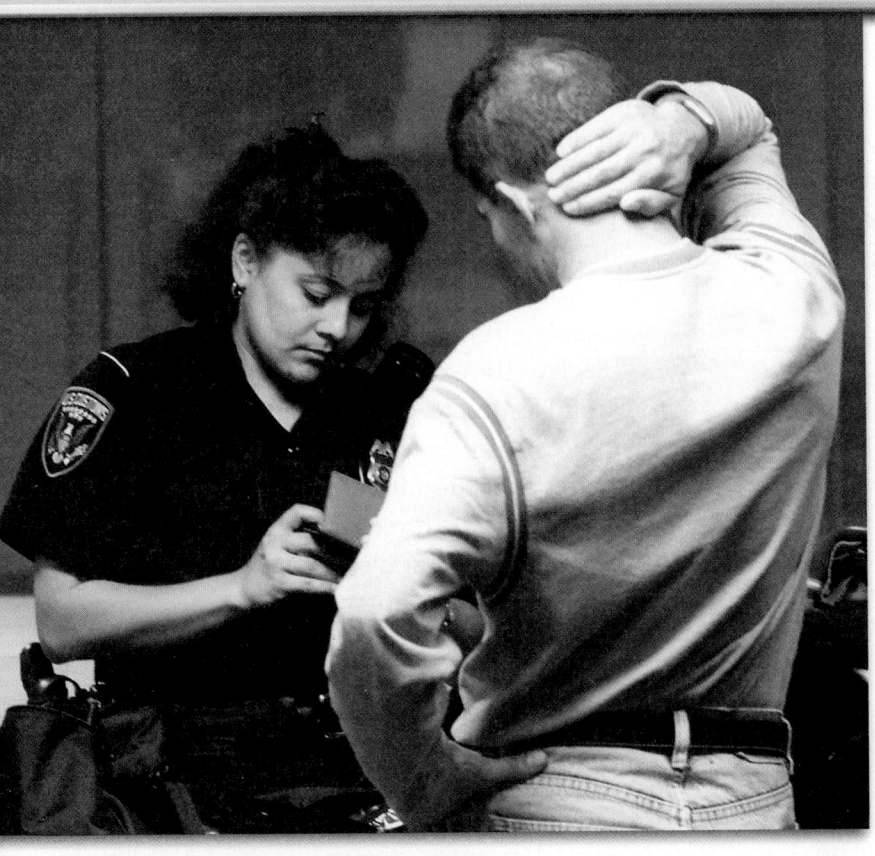

The U.S. Customs Service collects duties on goods brought into the United States.

 **CIVICS IN PRACTICE** You earn money. You spend money. Your goal is to spend less than you earn. This is called money management, or budgeting. Local, state, and national governments try to do the same. As a citizen you can contact your state representatives and members of Congress to let them know your concerns regarding government spending.

Collecting Public Money

Each level of government has a department whose responsibility it is to collect taxes. At the federal level, the collection of taxes is handled by the Internal Revenue Service (IRS). The IRS is an agency of the U.S. Department of the Treasury. Another agency of the federal government, the U.S. Customs Service, collects tariffs on imported goods.

State and local governments have established their own tax collection agencies. State tax collection agencies collect taxes such as state income taxes and inheritance taxes. Taxes collected by local tax collection agencies include local property taxes.

After tax money is collected, it is sent to the treasuries of the various governments. The U.S. Treasury Department spends federal tax dollars under the authorization of Congress.

In state and local governments the comptroller acts as the watchdog of the treasury. The comptroller is responsible for ensuring that public funds are spent only as authorized by the state legislature or city council.

> **READING CHECK** **Analyzing** Why is a state's comptroller of public accounts called a watchdog of the treasury?

Spending Public Money

As you have read, governments collect money to provide goods and services that taxpayers and other citizens want and need. Often, planning how to spend the money is the source of much political debate. As a citizen, you need to understand how governments at all levels plan to spend your money.

Planning Government Spending

All governments have budgets. As you know, a budget lists the amount and sources of expected revenue, or money income. A budget also specifies the proposed expenditures, or money to be spent, for various public purposes. A budget is usually written to pay for the government's operations for one year.

The management of public funds is divided between the executive and legislative branches of government. The chief executive, such as the president, governor, or mayor, is responsible for drawing up the budget. However, the legislative branch must pass a budget into law before any public money can be spent. Once the budget has been passed, the executive branch must spend the money according to the approved budget.

Preparing the Federal Budget

In the federal government the president prepares a budget that details how public funds should be raised and how they should be spent. Planning the federal budget is so complicated that the president needs the help of several government agencies.

The chief agency that helps the president prepare the budget is the Office of Management and Budget (OMB). The OMB forecasts the amount of tax income the government will receive in the coming year.

Each of the executive departments makes a careful estimate of how much money it plans to spend the following year. All these estimates are submitted to the OMB. The president and the director of the OMB study the many requests and establish priorities for the various departments' needs.

Congress and the Budget

Once the federal budget is prepared, the president sends it to Congress. Along with the budget, the president sends a message explaining the budget and urging that it be passed.

Congress makes its own study of the proposed budget. As you have learned, only Congress has the power to raise and spend money. The House of Representatives and the Senate debate the various items in the budget and make changes. Both houses of Congress must approve the final version of the federal budget. The budget is passed in the form of

FOCUS ON
Alexander Hamilton
(1757—1804)

Born on the West Indies island of Nevis in 1757, Alexander Hamilton moved to New York in 1772 for his formal education. Hamilton's abilities regarding finances revealed themselves at an early age.

In 1789 President George Washington appointed Hamilton as the first secretary of the treasury. As secretary of the treasury, Hamilton began a number of important proposals for the new nation, including a plan to collect import duties and excise taxes for raising revenue and for paying off the national debt. He also developed plans for a congressional charter for the first Bank of the United States.

Hamilton was fatally wounded during a duel on July 11, 1804. He died in New York City the following day.

Making Inferences Why were Hamilton's proposals to pay America's debts and create a national bank so important to the new nation?

appropriations bills. Appropriations bills are bills that authorize the spending of funds. If approved, these bills are sent to the president to be approved or vetoed. These bills become the laws under which your tax dollars will be spent for the coming year.

The National Debt

When a government has a **balanced budget**, its revenue equals its expenditures. That is, the amount of money the government collects equals the amount of money it spends. However, frequently a government budget is not balanced. When a government collects more money than it spends, it has a **surplus**, or an excess of money. When a government spends more money than it collects, it has a **deficit**, or a shortage of money. When it runs a deficit, the federal government must borrow money each year to make up the difference between income and expenses. Borrowing money contributes more to the national debt, which by 2005 had reached almost $8 trillion.

Part of the revenue collected each year must be used to pay the interest on the national debt. This portion of the budget cannot be used to fund programs and services for the people. The interest on the debt is so high that future generations will be repaying the money that is being borrowed now. In addition, the federal government borrows much of the money it needs to make up for the deficit by issuing government bonds. Increasingly, these bonds are being bought by foreign investors. This means public tax dollars are going overseas to pay interest on these bonds.

There is no constitutional limit on the size of the national debt. Congress establishes a limit above which the debt cannot go. However, it periodically raises this limit as the need for more spending arises.

READING CHECK **Categorizing** How are the budget responsibilities divided among the executive and legislative branches of government?

Calculating Using CPI

The Consumer Price Index (CPI) is a measure of the percentage change over time in the average cost of a market basket of goods and services purchased by consumers. The quantity and quality of the items in the basket are kept constant, so any changes in the cost of the basket are because of price changes and not because of changes to the items in the basket. An index number for each item in the basket and for the complete basket is given each year. You can calculate the percentage increase or decrease in prices by using these index numbers in this formula:

$$\left[\left(\frac{\text{Latest Index number}}{\text{Past Index number}}\right) \times 100\right] - 100 = \text{Percent Change}$$

Here are a few examples of CPI (1982–1984 = 100):

Year	CPI
1990	130.7
1995	152.4
2005	195.3

ANALYSIS SKILL **ANALYZING INFORMATION**

If a skateboard has an index number of 113 in 2006 and an index number of 89 in 1994, what has been the percentage increase in the price of the skateboard?

Accounting for Public Money

As a citizen, you have the right to know that your money is being handled properly. To ensure that funds are spent according to law, all levels of government provide for an audit of their accounts. An **audit** is a careful examination by trained accountants of every item of income and every expenditure.

Audits at Every Level

All governments must account for their revenues and expenditures. For example, in most states, local school districts must submit audit reports of their spending to the state department of education. At the federal level, the Government Accountability Office examines most federal expenditures.

MEDIA INVESTIGATION

INTERNET
Data and the Internet

What is the current national debt? If you use the Internet to search for an exact figure, you may be surprised to find many different answers. Finding reliable facts and figures on the Internet can be challenging, but certain clues will help you decide if an Internet source is reliable.

For example, reliable sources will provide the author's full name and contact information. They also should provide sources for their information. Be cautious of information you find on Web sites that do not provide this information.

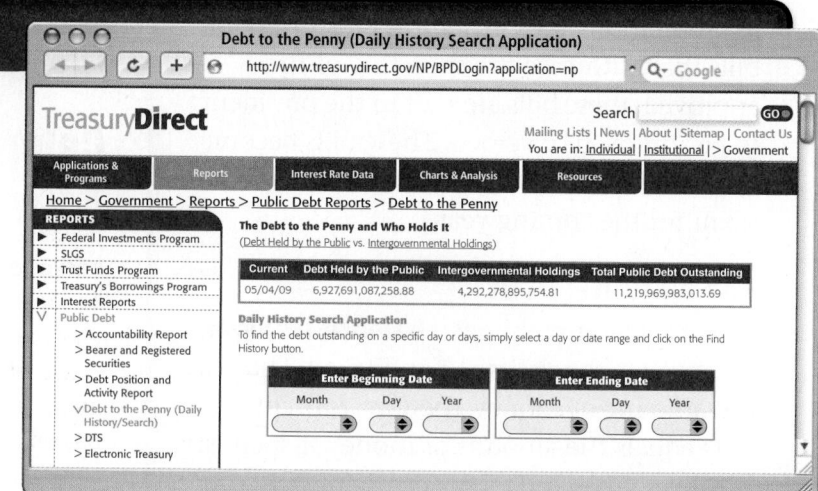

ANALYSIS SKILL MEDIA LITERACY

go.hrw.com KEYWORD: SZ7 CH12

What should you look for to determine if a Web site is reliable?

Citizen Responsibility

Even with audits and accountability, citizens must keep an eye on government revenue and spending. This means citizens must take an active role in the budgetary process. They must understand taxes, the use of public funds, and the national debt. When there is a problem or a question, citizens must make their voices heard and get an answer. They should also vote on the local and national level for politicians and policies that match their economic beliefs. After all, it is their money that is being spent.

READING CHECK ▶ **Finding the Main Idea** How do governments and citizens ensure that public funds are being spent properly?

---

go.hrw.com
Online Quiz
KEYWORD: SZ7 HP12

SECTION 3 ASSESSMENT

Reviewing Ideas and Terms

1 a. Recall What agencies collect revenue for the federal government?
b. Explain What is the purpose of a government budget?

2. a. Define Write a brief definition of the terms **balanced budget**, **surplus**, and **deficit**.
b. Contrast What are the differences between the budget responsibilities of the president and Congress?
c. Evaluate Do you think that the budget always reflects all of the needs of American citizens?

3. a. Define Write a brief definition of the term **audit**.
b. Predict In your opinion, how does a growing national debt affect future generations?

Critical Thinking

4. Categorizing Use the graphic organizer and your notes to identify the responsibilities of the two branches of government in creating the federal budget. Add rows to the organizer as necessary.

Executive Branch	Legislative Branch

Focus on Writing

5. Supporting a Point of View Write a letter to the president with your recommendations for keeping the federal budget balanced.

STUDENTS TAKE ACTION

Helping Homeless Teenagers

What would it be like to not have a home or anywhere to turn for help? For some teenagers, this question is a reality. Acting on a proposal by local students, the city of Newberg, Oregon, opened a drop-in center to help teenagers who do not have a place to live.

Community Connection Project Citizen students in Ms. Terry McElligott's class were concerned about the fate of homeless teenagers. In one year alone, more than 100 runaways were reported to police in Newberg. "As I got farther into the project I learned how many kids are on the streets," said team member Paula McKinney.

Taking Action The students contacted existing teen shelters to learn what sort of services would be needed to help the homeless. They also gathered input from local groups that helped teens. Students took on different roles in researching and preparing a proposal for the city to create a drop-in center where homeless teenagers could receive help and turn their lives around. They presented their proposal to the Newberg City Club and the School District Board of Directors. They also wrote to city leaders, contributed to articles in the local newspaper, published brochures sent out with the school newsletter, and interviewed citizens to build support for their plan. Finally, the city agreed to sponsor a drop-in center for teenagers in crisis. Officials used the careful research and reports the students had provided to apply for funding to pay for the new center.

YOUTH CENTER
support for homeless kids
DROP - IN CENTER

Communities around the country support youth centers to help homeless teenagers.

go.hrw.com
Project Citizen
KEYWORD: SZ7 CH12

SERVICE LEARNING

1. How did students in Newberg respond to the problem of teenage homelessness in their community?
2. What methods did the students use to gain support for their idea?

Visual Summary

Use the visual summary to help you review the main ideas of the chapter.

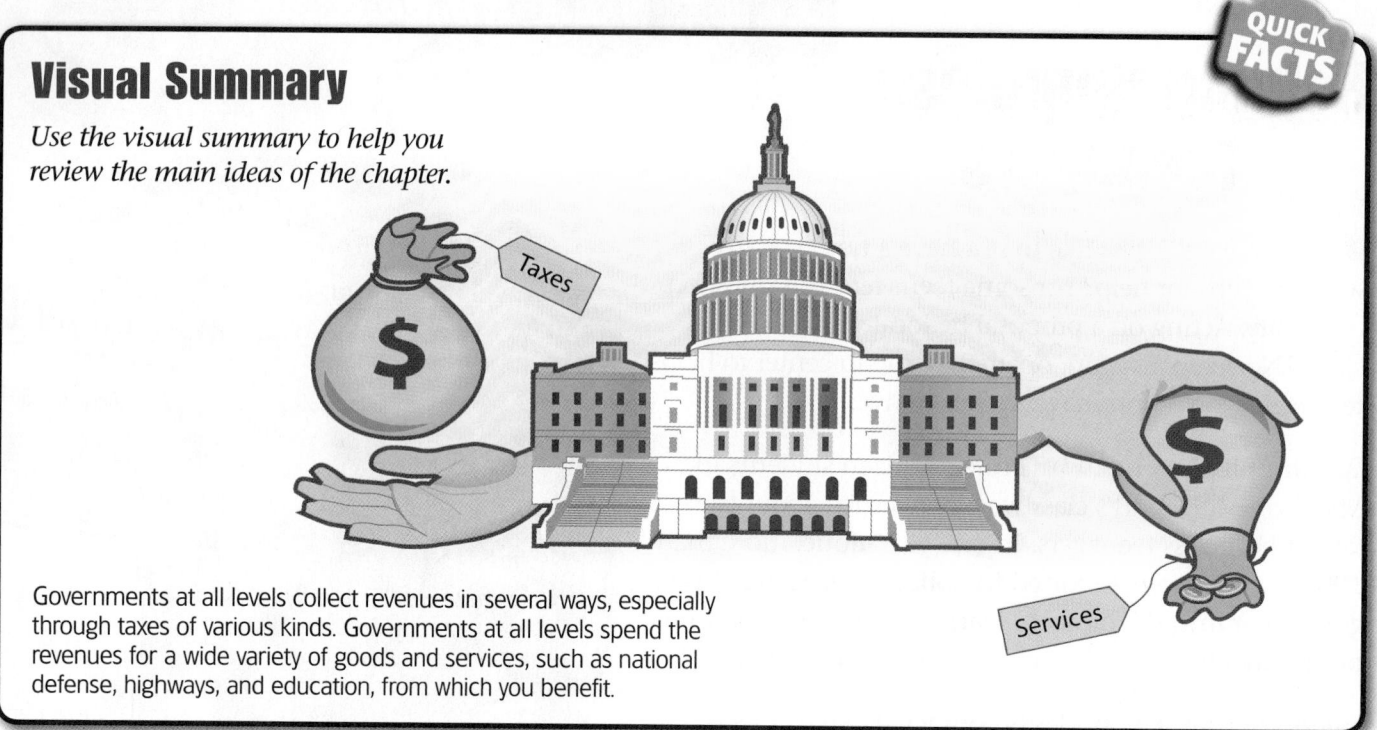

Taxes

Services

Governments at all levels collect revenues in several ways, especially through taxes of various kinds. Governments at all levels spend the revenues for a wide variety of goods and services, such as national defense, highways, and education, from which you benefit.

Reviewing Key Terms

For each term below, write a sentence explaining its significance.

1. interest
2. national debt
3. revenue
4. fees
5. fine
6. bond
7. income tax
8. progressive tax
9. profit
10. regressive tax
11. property tax
12. tariff
13. balanced budget
14. surplus
15. deficit
16. audit

Comprehension and Critical Thinking

SECTION 1 *(Pages 294–298)*

17. **a. Recall** What are three reasons for the high cost of government?

    b. Describe What are the purposes of taxation, and what principles does the government use to try to make taxation fair?

    c. Elaborate Explain one method governments use to finance large, long-term projects.

SECTION 2 *(Pages 299–303)*

18. **a. Recall** What are five main types of taxes that people have to pay?

    b. Explain How is individual income tax calculated, and how do citizens pay individual income taxes?

    c. Evaluate Do you think that the income tax should be a progressive tax? Why or why not?

Active Citizenship video program
Review the video to answer the closing question:
What are at least three benefits of working with others to improve your community?

SECTION 3 *(Pages 305–308)*

19. a. Recall What is the difference between a surplus and a deficit?

b. Elaborate How do the president and the Congress each play a role in the federal government budget process?

c. Identifying Points of View In recent years some federal officials and members of the public have sought a constitutional amendment to require a balanced federal budget each year. However, Congress and many citizens have strongly resisted such an action. What are the reasons for supporting or opposing a balanced budget amendment?

Civics Skills

Analyzing a Documentary *Use the steps for analyzing a documentary that you learned earlier in the chapter to answer the questions below.*

> **1** Identify the point of view.
>
> **2** Notice how the visuals and images make you feel.
>
> **3** Investigate the source.
>
> **4** Check the facts.

20. What types of information in a documentary might indicate the filmmaker's point of view?

21. Why might documentary filmmakers want to try to elicit some type of emotion from their viewers?

22. Why is it important to verify the information presented in a documentary?

Reading Skills

Problem Solving *Use the Reading Skills taught in this chapter to answer the questions about the reading selection below.*

> Government officials, therefore, face difficult decisions. What government programs most need money? What programs will bring the greatest benefits to the most people? Government officials must decide which activities need funding, in order of their urgency and need. This process is called establishing priorities. (p. 296)

23. What is the problem described in this passage?

24. List three standards you would use to determine which government programs received the highest priority for funding.

25. List several possible solutions to the problem described in the passage. What are the advantages and disadvantages of each?

Using the Internet

go.hrw.com
KEYWORD: SZ7 CH12

26. Exploring Government Finance Part of the responsibility of citizenship includes developing an understanding of how the government handles public funds and spending and then expressing concerns about how public funds are managed. Enter the activity keyword to build your understanding of the current federal budget and national debt. Then use the Holt Grapher to create a chart illustrating major expenditures in the current federal budget and a graph that illustrates the changes in the national debt from 1985 to the present.

FOCUS ON WRITING

27. Writing Your Article Review your notes from this chapter. Then choose the subject you think would make the best newspaper or magazine article. Write an attention-grabbing headline or title. Then write your article, giving both your opinion and as many facts as possible.

FOUNDATIONS®
of DEMOCRACY

Sales Tax on the Internet

When you go to a store and buy a new CD or book, in most states you pay an extra amount of 4 to 8 percent of the purchase price. This sales tax goes to the state or local government. If you buy the same item on the Internet, however, you will probably not pay sales tax. Some business owners say this system gives Internet retail companies an unfair advantage.

Why it Matters

People do have to pay taxes on goods purchased online from businesses in their own state. Out-of-state Internet sales, however, involve interstate commerce, which only Congress can regulate. In 1992 the Supreme Court ruled that cities and states cannot charge sales tax for any items purchased over the Internet from out-of-state companies. Since the time the Supreme Court made its ruling, however, Internet sales have exploded, cutting into the sales of many local stores—and the sales taxes they collect.

The Internet taxation issue trickles down even farther. The Internet shopping boom has hurt cities and states that rely on sales taxes to fund services. In the 1990s, some states responded by trying to pass special taxes on companies doing business over the Internet. Congress prohibited this practice in 1998 but encouraged states to begin working together to create a system that helps businesses easily calculate and pay any taxes they owe.

Since 2000 some 40 states have joined together to work toward this sales tax system. A number of Internet retailers have also started voluntarily collecting taxes on out-of-state sales. In addition, a California court ruling strengthened the effort to collect sales taxes by ordering a national music and book chain to pay taxes on Internet sales. Why? The court noted that, while customers purchased books online, they could return them at the company's local stores, which counted as local commerce.

Consumers, state governments, and retailers are working together to solve the issue of Internet sales taxes.

ANALYSIS SKILL — EVALUATING THE LAW

go.hrw.com
KEYWORD: SZ7 CH12

1. How does not paying sales tax on Internet purchases harm local businesses and city and state governments?
2. Do you think that people should pay sales tax on all Internet purchases? Why or why not?

UNIT 5
THE CITIZEN IN SOCIETY

In this 1942 poster Uncle Sam encourages Americans to support their community by helping the Red Cross.

YOUR RED CROSS NEEDS YOU!

CHAPTER 13

CITIZENSHIP AND THE FAMILY

SECTION 1
The Changing Family

SECTION 2
Law and the Family

SECTION 3
Your Family and You

NATIONAL STANDARDS®
FOR CIVICS AND GOVERNMENT

II. What are the foundations of the American political system?

B. What are the distinctive characteristics of American society?

V. What are the roles of the citizen in American democracy?

A. What is citizenship?

C. What are the responsibilities of citizens?

D. What civic dispositions or traits of private and public character are important to the preservation and improvement of American constitutional democracy?

©1994, 2003 Center for Civic Education. All Rights Reserved.

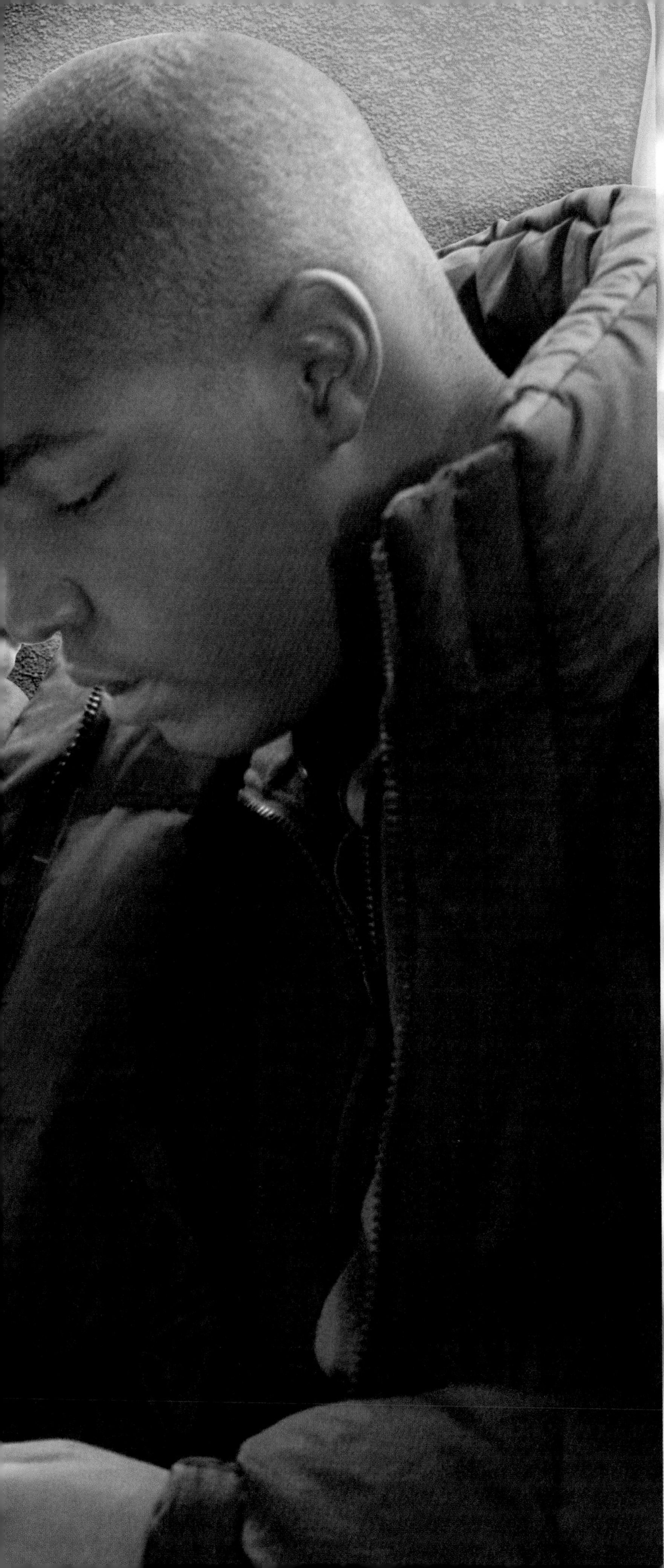

Active Citizenship Video Program
Watch the video to learn how young citizens can influence school policy.

WHY CIVICS Matters

Being a good citizen means more than just taking part in politics and government. Citizenship starts with the family. Families are the first place you learn some of the qualities of a good citizen, such as the ability to compromise, take responsibility for your actions, and participate in a positive way.

STUDENTS TAKE ACTION

TURNING BACK THE CLOCK Students in Anchorage, Alaska, wanted changes in their school calendar. The students made their case to the school board and were able to get the calendar changed. How could you bring about such a change in your school?

FOCUS ON WRITING

AN AUTOBIOGRAPHICAL SKETCH The American family has gone through many changes over the years. As you read this chapter, think about what family life was like during colonial times. Then you will write an autobiography of a fictional character, telling about his or her life. Your classmates are your audience.

Reading Skills

In this chapter you will read about how the American family has changed through the years. You will learn that there are many kinds of American families. You will read about how states pass laws to regulate marriage, divorce, and the rights of parents and children. You will also learn how the family performs important functions for its members and society. As you read, think about how your family is teaching you to be a good citizen.

Information and Propaganda

FOCUS ON READING Where do you get information about proposed laws or political issues? Many citizens rely on TV ads, newspaper editorials, or Internet blogs to get their information about important issues. These sources, however, often want to persuade people to act or think in a certain way. Their main purpose is not necessarily to provide a fair, objective look at an issue. Ideas that are spread to influence people are called propaganda.

Recognizing Propaganda Techniques To be an effective reader and an informed citizen, you should learn to recognize propaganda techniques. Then you will be able to separate propaganda from the facts.

Helpful Hints for Recognizing Propaganda

1. If the information wants you to believe something, buy something, or do something, it is propaganda.

2. If the information sounds like an advertisement, it may be propaganda.

3. If the information is one-sided, it may be propaganda.

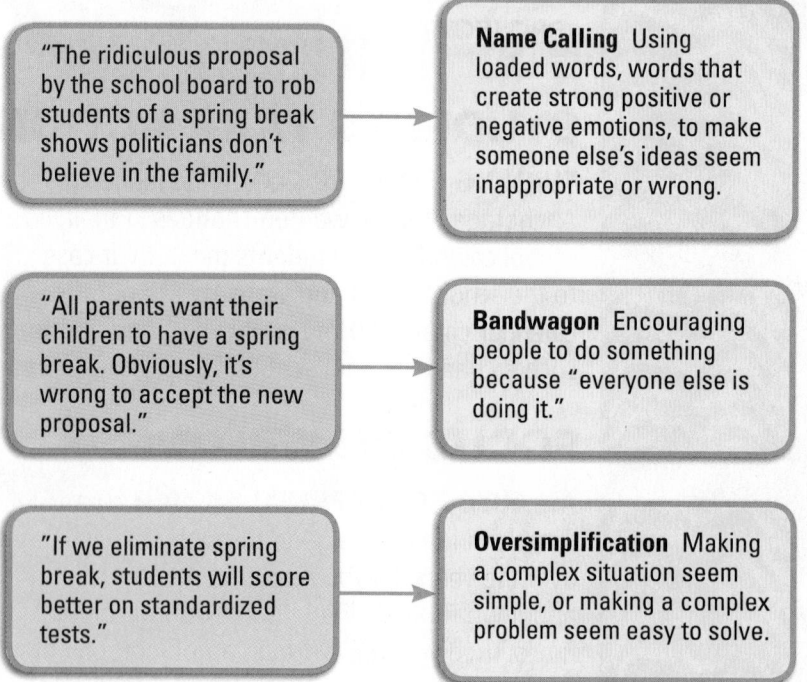

"The ridiculous proposal by the school board to rob students of a spring break shows politicians don't believe in the family."

→ **Name Calling** Using loaded words, words that create strong positive or negative emotions, to make someone else's ideas seem inappropriate or wrong.

"All parents want their children to have a spring break. Obviously, it's wrong to accept the new proposal."

→ **Bandwagon** Encouraging people to do something because "everyone else is doing it."

"If we eliminate spring break, students will score better on standardized tests."

→ **Oversimplification** Making a complex situation seem simple, or making a complex problem seem easy to solve.

You Try It!

Read the following passage and then answer the questions below.

> The school board is considering a proposal to remove spring break from the school calendar. Almost all students and parents strongly oppose the proposal. The school board should vote down the proposal.
>
> The proposal was brought in an effort to give students more class time and increase test scores. The idiot who came up with this proposal should apologize. Students and teachers deserve the spring break.
>
> If the school board wants to increase test scores, it should build new schools. Better classrooms would help students perform better.

After you have read the passage, answer the following questions.

1. Does this passage want readers to act or think in a certain way? If so, how?

2. What kind of propaganda technique is used in the second sentence?

3. Which sentence is an example of name calling?

4. Which sentence is an example of oversimplification?

As you read Chapter 13, notice ways in which you think the text tries to present facts objectively.

SECTION 1

The Changing Family

BEFORE YOU READ

The Main Idea

From colonial times to today, the American family has changed in many ways. However, the family still plays an important role in teaching young people the lessons that will stay with them for the rest of their lives.

Reading Focus

1. How has the American family changed since colonial times?
2. What are some new trends in marriage and family life?
3. Why is the number of two-income families increasing, and what additional stresses do single-parent families face?

Key Terms

delayed marriage, *p. 320*
remarriage, *p. 321*
blended families, *p. 321*
two-income families, *p. 321*
single-parent families, *p. 321*

TAKING NOTES As you read, take notes on the ways the American family and marriage trends have changed over time. Use a graphic organizer like this one to record your notes.

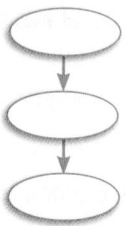

CIVICS IN PRACTICE Does your family look like the typical American family of 200 years ago? Not likely. Back then most people had big families and lived on farms. Today our families are smaller, and most of us live in or near big cities. Those aren't the only changes the American family has gone through. Families today range from small to large. Some might have children, some not. There's no such thing as a "typical" American family today.

American Families Have Changed

The family has always played an important economic and social role in the history of the United States. Although the American family has changed much since colonial times, the family remains the backbone of American life and culture.

The Colonial Family

How were colonial families different from families today? During colonial times, most families lived on farms. Because of this rural way of life, these families tended to be much larger than modern American families. Why? Colonial families needed many hands to do all the work required on a farm. Having many children helped these families to get their work done.

The colonial family produced most of what it needed to survive. Today factories and large farms produce most of the goods and food needed for survival.

The Move to Cities

During the 1800s a huge change began to happen in American life. Many people began moving to the cities. About 100 years ago 60 percent of all Americans lived on farms or in rural areas. Today only about 21 percent of Americans live in a rural area.

New inventions and improved **methods** of production, which led to the rise of factories, caused this shift from rural to urban living. People were needed to run the machines, so many families moved to urban areas seeking factory jobs.

ACADEMIC VOCABULARY

methods: ways of doing something

Three Centuries of the American Family

Families have made up the fabric of the United States since our founding. As our country has changed, families have changed, too. The largest change affecting the family is a transition from rural to urban life.

What motivated many farm families to move to the cities?

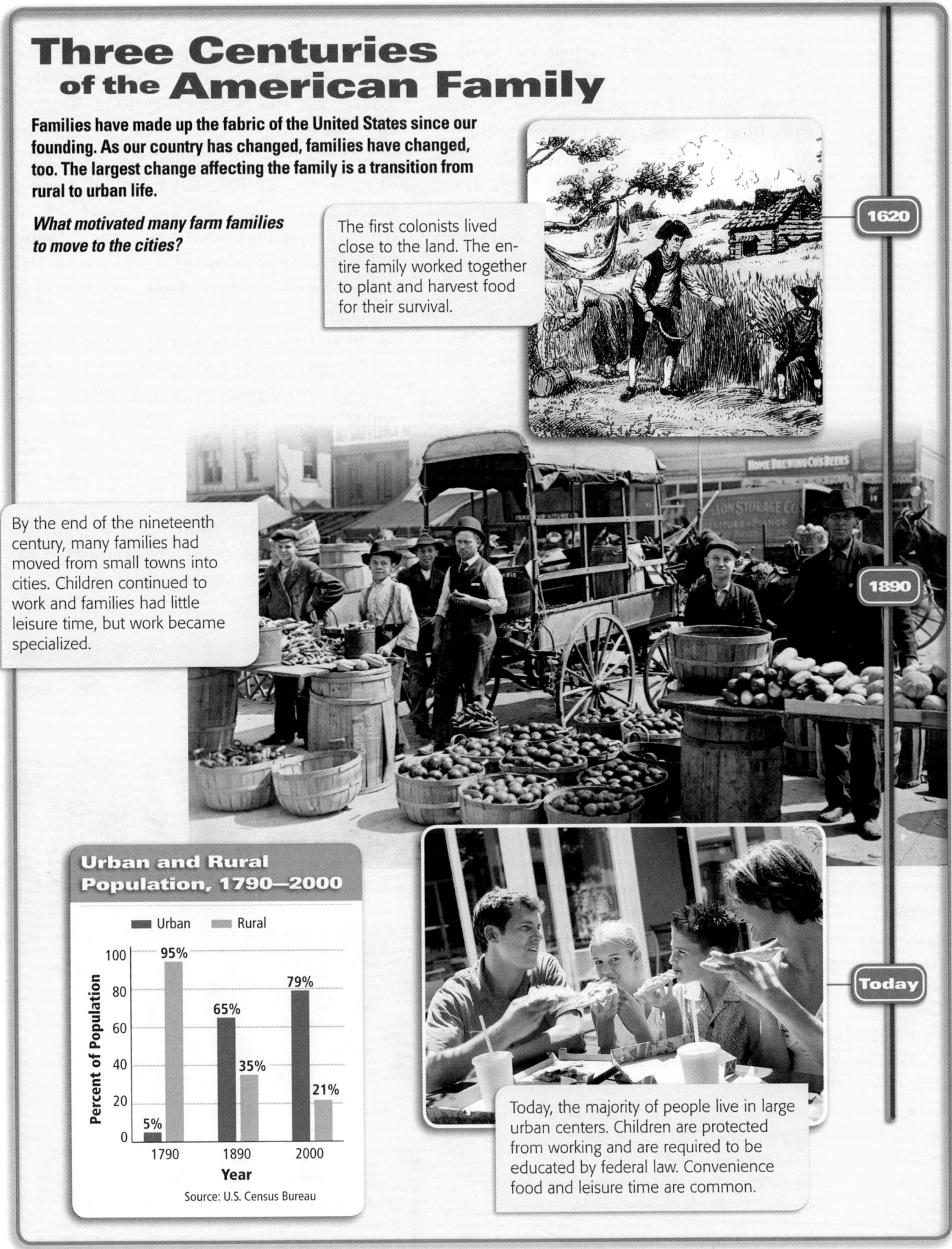

The first colonists lived close to the land. The entire family worked together to plant and harvest food for their survival.

1620

By the end of the nineteenth century, many families had moved from small towns into cities. Children continued to work and families had little leisure time, but work became specialized.

1890

Urban and Rural Population, 1790–2000

- Urban
- Rural

Percent of Population

Year	Urban	Rural
1790	5%	95%
1890	65%	35%
2000	79%	21%

Source: U.S. Census Bureau

Today

Today, the majority of people live in large urban centers. Children are protected from working and are required to be educated by federal law. Convenience food and leisure time are common.

The City Family

Imagine that you are part of a rural family that moved to the city during the late 1800s. Your father would probably work long hours in a factory to earn the money to buy things the family once produced on a farm. You and your siblings—even those who were very young—would most likely have to work in factories, too. Factory conditions, especially for children, were often difficult and dangerous.

READING CHECK **Contrasting** Describe how family life in the city was different from family life in rural areas.

Changing Marriage Trends

Family life changed a great deal when families moved to cities. Recently, family life has changed even more rapidly and there have been new marriage trends. These trends include delayed marriage and remarriage.

Delayed Marriage

In 2000 the average age at first marriage was 25.1 for women and 26.8 for men. This average age was much lower 40 or 50 years ago. For example, in 1960 the average age at first marriage for women was 20.3 years. The average age for men was 22.8. During the following decades, the average age at which people marry has risen steadily. Why did this change happen? There are several reasons for **delayed marriage**, or marrying at an older age.

In today's society remaining single has become more widely accepted. This has contributed to delayed marriages. Also, many young people choose to delay marriage to finish their education or start a career. This is especially true for women. As couples wait to get married, many also delay having children. Why? Today more couples want to wait until both spouses are established in their careers before having children.

MEDIA INVESTIGATION

TELEVISION
The Family Today

1950s

Today

1980s

When the television first appeared in American living rooms in the late 1940s, the country was still adjusting to the concepts of communism and the atomic bomb. Television shows tried to address Americans' need for an escape from daily life. Many shows, such as *Leave it to Beaver,* featured predominantly white, nuclear families living happily in the suburbs.

By the 1970s, television began to reflect changes taking place in society. Shows featuring single–parent and interracial families became more common, as did portrayal of life in cities. In the 1980s, one of the most popular shows of all time, *The Cosby Show,* focused on the life of a successful, wealthy African American family. For many viewers, it was the first time they had seen a black family portrayed on television without stereotypes.

Today, families of all varieties can be found on television. In *Hannah Montana,* Hannah's father and brother help the teenage girl balance her school life and her Hollywood life. Many shows focus on the challenges that American families face as well as the support family members lend one another.

ANALYSIS SKILL **MEDIA LITERACY** go.hrw.com KEYWORD: SZ7 CH13

What are some ways society is changed by television, and what are some ways television reflects society?

Blended Families

The United States has one of the highest divorce rates in the world. Despite this fact, Americans still strongly believe in marriage and the family—a belief that is demonstrated by the high number of remarriages. **Remarriage** means that one or both of the partners has been married before. In fact, more than 40 percent of the marriages taking place today are remarriages.

In some 65 percent of remarriages, one or both of the partners bring children from previous relationships into the new marriage. These new families are called **blended families**, or stepfamilies.

READING CHECK **Finding the Main Idea** How are blended families formed?

Two-Income and Single-Parent Families

In recent decades, the number of **two-income families**, or families in which both parents work, has increased. This increase is the result of the large number of married women who work outside the home. Over the past 50 years, the percentage of women with jobs outside the home has more than doubled.

Why have so many married women entered the workforce? One reason is economic need. It has become more difficult for many families to maintain the standard of living they desire when only one parent is working. Another reason is that women today have more career opportunities than ever before.

In recent years the number of single-parent families has increased significantly. **Single-parent families** are formed through divorce, the death of a spouse, single people adopting children, and births to unmarried women. About 30 percent of American families with children under the age of 18 are single-parent families.

Every family has its difficulties, but the single-parent family often has added stresses.

Not only is it difficult for one adult to be the sole caregiver for a child or several children, single-parent families often must make do with a smaller income than families with two working parents.

READING CHECK **Analyzing Information** What are some of the challenges that single-parent families face?

SECTION 1 ASSESSMENT

Reviewing Ideas and Terms

1. **a. Recall** Why were colonial families usually larger than families today?
   b. Summarize What caused many families to leave rural areas and move to the cities?
2. **a. Define** Write a brief definition for each of the following terms: **delayed marriage**, **remarriage**, and **blended families**.
   b. Summarize How are blended families formed?
3. **a. Define** Write a brief definition for each of the following terms: **two-income families** and **single-parent families**.
   b. Summarize What has led to the increase of two-income families?
   c. Compare What are some of the problems that single-parent families face that two-parent familes do not?

Critical Thinking

4. **Identifying Cause and Effect** Copy the graphic organizer. Use it and your notes to explain the reason American families began to change in the 1800s and the results of these changes.

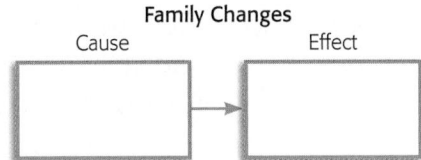

Family Changes

Cause → Effect

Focus on Writing

5. **Summarize** Imagine that you are a reporter assigned to investigate the increase in the average age at first marriage. Write a short article that explains the major reasons for this trend.

Using Television as a Resource

Learn

Most of our news and entertainment comes from television. In fact, in one year the average American watches 1,770 hours of television but spends only 109 hours reading books. Television is effectve as a media tool because it appeals to people's emotions through both sight and sound.

Consider how television programs are produced. A lot of people and money are involved, so producers plan very carefully. They decide what ideas the show will present. Then they make sure that their show delivers those ideas with an impact.

Practice

Before you turn on the TV, decide what you want from the programs you will watch. Do you want to be entertained or informed? Be ready to look at the meaning behind the message as well as the message itself.

1 **Separate fact from fluff.** Many television programs are based on real-life events—the evening news, documentaries, and reality shows. Documentaries give some facts and some opinion, all on one topic. Reality programs do not tell the "true story." They use what happened to build an entertaining story. Even news programs contain additional information besides "hard" news—the pressing news of the world. Hard news on a broadcast comes first, followed by human-interest stories, those that appeal to the emotions.

2 **Decide for yourself.** You do not have to agree with the ideas on television. Every show, even the news, is produced from a certain point of view. Ask yourself, "Do I agree with this show's point of view?"

3 **Make a viewing plan.** Television schedules are available in newspapers, online, and on your television set, if you have cable TV.

Apply

Study the schedule. Use it to answer the questions that follow.

1. Some of the programs on this schedule will be more factual than others. Make a list of the shows and write what you think each show might be about next to its title.

2. What would you watch if you were looking for fact-based shows? for entertainment?

3. Each of these shows is about a person or event. Which is most likely to present a "true story"? Which is least likely? What is your evidence that supports your conclusions?

Tuesday, December 11	6:00 P.M.	6:30 P.M.	7:00 P.M.
A&E (16) Arts & Entertainment	Biography: Jimmy Carter		U2 in Concert
NBC (17) National Broadcasting Co.	Local News	NBC Nightly News	Dateline: Running a Family Business
CNN (18)	News Night	Larry King Live: Bill, Hillary, and Chelsea Clinton	
DISC (19) Discovery	Extreme Surgery		Medical Miracles
PBS (20) Public Broadcasting Service	American Experience: Remember the Alamo		The News Hour with Jim Lehrer

SECTION 2

Law and the Family

BEFORE YOU READ

The Main Idea

U.S. law is set up to protect the well-being of children and families.

Reading Focus

1. What is the purpose of the various laws regulating marriage?
2. How do state laws work to protect children?
3. What types of decisions must be made by couples who are planning to divorce?

Key Terms

family law, *p. 323*
child abuse, *p. 325*
foster home, *p. 325*
guardian, *p. 325*
adopt, *p. 325*
divorce, *p. 325*
no-fault divorce, *p. 325*

TAKING NOTES As you read, take notes on the laws that regulate marriage and divorce and those that protect children. Use a chart like this one to record your notes.

Marriage	Divorce	Children

Marriage is a legal, social, and, often, religious institution.

CIVICS IN PRACTICE Although there are many different kinds of families in the United States, all families are subject to certain laws. These laws regulate marriage and divorce and protect the rights of children. Why are these laws necessary?

Laws Regulate Marriage

As an American you have certain rights, such as freedom of speech and freedom of religion. To protect these rights, the federal government has set up laws. People in families also have certain rights and responsibilities, which are protected by laws as well. Your state's legislature, rather than the federal legislature, makes these laws. Why? The needs and customs of families may differ in various areas of the country.

State legislatures can best make laws that fit the families in that region. **Family law** regulates marriage, divorce, and the responsibilities and the rights of adults and children in the family. All of the more than 2 million marriages that take place in the United States each year must follow the laws of the state in which they are performed.

Law and the Family

Each state has laws that affect the family by regulating marriage and divorce, and by protecting the well-being of family members. However, the strength of the family comes from the things that law has little or no power to control, like love, trust, tradition, wisdom, and security.

Family

Love · Security · Trust · Wisdom · Tradition

Families strive to protect and promote their members' well-being.

ANALYSIS SKILL INTERPRETING VISUALS

Of the family values listed in the pie chart, which one do you think is most important?

Most states require that people be at least 18 years old to marry without parental consent. In many states, however, boys and girls may marry at age 16 with the consent of their parents. Some states allow people to marry at even younger ages.

In an attempt to ensure that couples consider the seriousness of marriage before uniting, about half of all states require that couples wait for one to five days before a marriage license is issued. This waiting period allows couples time to "think it over." Some states also require that a man and woman applying for a marriage license have a medical examination. These exams check for certain diseases that can be passed on to another person.

Most states require that civil or religious officials perform marriages. Civil officials include a justice of the peace, judge, and mayor. Ministers, priests, and rabbis are some religious officials who often perform marriages. Witnesses must be present at the ceremony to testify that a legal marriage was performed.

READING CHECK Finding the Main Idea What is family law, and why is it needed?

Laws Protect Children

Most people who marry will eventually have children. The U.S. government believes that children have legal rights. If a child is not given proper care by parents, the authorities can step in to protect the child. Every state requires that doctors, teachers, and other people report suspected cases of child abuse. **Child abuse** is emotional abuse, physical injury, or sexual abuse inflicted on a child by another person.

An act that creates a risk of serious harm to a child or failing to act to protect a child are considered child abuse under the law. For example, leaving a very young child unattended for a long period of time is considered child abuse. The state may take children who are abused by their parents or other family members away from the family.

A child may be placed in a **foster home**, a home of people unrelated to the child who agree to take care of him or her. The state pays the foster parents to care for the child. Parents who abuse their children may face criminal charges.

If a child's parents die, a judge may appoint a relative or family friend to act as guardian. A **guardian** is a person appointed by a state court to care for a child or for an adult who is unable to care for him- or herself. Sometimes a guardian will **adopt** the child, which means the guardian has legally established the child as his or her own. If no one can be found to act as guardian, the state may put the child up for adoption.

> **READING CHECK** **Sequencing** What steps are typically taken to care for children whose parents die?

Divorce Means Decisions

Sometimes marriages fail. Legally ending a marriage is called **divorce**. Each state makes its own divorce laws. Sometimes people seeking divorce charge their partners with grounds such as desertion or abuse, but not always.

Often, couples simply state that their marriage has problems that cannot be resolved. This type of divorce is called **no-fault divorce**, because no specific charge is being made that places fault on either partner.

Getting a divorce is often a complicated process, so couples that divorce usually follow the advice of lawyers. The lawyers try to get the couple to resolve issues such as how their property should be divided, who gets custody of children, what visitation rights each parent will have with the children, and the amount of any spousal and child support payments. The case then goes before a judge. If the judge finds that the decisions presented in the case are fair, the divorce <u>agreement</u> is approved. If the couple cannot agree on these issues, the judge will decide the case.

FOCUS ON
Marian Wright Edelman
(1939-)

Marian Wright Edelman was born in Bennettsville, South Carolina. At an early age, she was encouraged to pursue her education and to use her abilities to help others. Her parents set the example for this by opening the Wright Home for the Aged. In addition, at various times during Edelman's childhood, her parents cared for 12 foster children.

When Edelman graduated from law school, she became active in the National Association for the Advancement of Colored People's struggle against segregation. In 1973 she founded the Children's Defense Fund, which helps children and tries to solve social issues concerning children by affecting public policy. The CDF has become the nation's strongest voice for children and families. Edelman has testified before Congress several times on children's issues. For her efforts, in 2000 Edelman received the Presidential Medal of Freedom, the nation's highest civilian award.

Summarize How have Edelman's efforts aided children?

Marriage

The majority of people in the United States over age 25 are married.

Up to 25 Years

8.6% are married

25 to 34 Years

52% are married

35 to 54 Years

66% are married

55 to 64 Years

69% are married

65 Years and Older

54% are married

> **ANALYSIS SKILL** **INTERPRETING VISUALS**
>
> Which age group has the smallest percentage of unmarried people?

The United States has one of the highest divorce rates in the world. More than 1 million marriages in this country end in divorce each year. These divorces affect more than 1 million children annually. Why do you think the United States has such a high divorce rate? There are several reasons. To begin with, the divorce process has become less complicated over the past few decades. American society in general has also become more tolerant and accepting of divorce.

READING CHECK **Contrasting** How does no-fault divorce differ from other divorces?

go.hrw.com
Online Quiz
KEYWORD: SZ7 HP13

SECTION 2 ASSESSMENT

Reviewing Ideas and Terms

1. a. Define Write a brief definition for the following term: **family law**.

b. Explain Why do many states have a waiting period before issuing a marriage license?

2. a. Define Write a brief definition for each of the following terms: **child abuse**, **foster home**, **guardian**, and **adopt**.

b. Summarize What legal measures do states put into place to protect children?

3. a. Define Write a brief definition for each of the following terms: **divorce** and **no-fault divorce**.

b. Summarize Why do couples considering divorce usually consult a lawyer?

Critical Thinking

4. Categorizing Use your notes and this diagram to identify the types of decisions that must be made by couples who are planning to divorce.

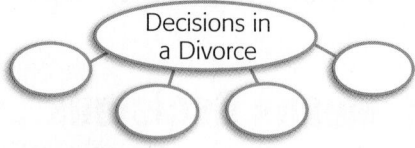

Decisions in a Divorce

Focus on Writing

5. Evaluating Imagine that you are part of a national committee attempting to reduce the high American divorce rate. List three of your suggestions and explain why you believe they will be successful.

STUDENTS TAKE ACTION

Turning Back the Clock

For many families with school-age children in Anchorage, Alaska, the 2006–2007 school year will always be remembered as the beginning of a whole new schedule. Before then, the school year had run from after Labor Day, in September, through June. Thanks to Project Citizen students in Mrs. Pam Collins's social studies class, school now begins in late August and ends before Memorial Day in May.

Community Connection The students had many reasons for wanting to change the school calendar. Students who were involved in activities such as football or cheerleading returned to practice in August, although school did not start for another several weeks. Also, because the first semester ended two weeks after the winter holiday break, students had to study for exams throughout their vacation and teachers often had to reteach material before finals. Through research and interviews, Mrs. Collins's students found that teachers also preferred the idea of starting in August and lining up the quarters with school breaks.

Taking Action After talking to community members and school officials, the students wrote and practiced presentations on changing the school calendar. Their careful preparation and presentation impressed the principal, the Parent Teacher Association, and the Anchorage School Board. One community member came to the school board meeting to oppose the proposed new calendar but changed his mind after hearing the students speak. The members of the school board themselves were so impressed that they agreed to vote on the students' proposal quickly. The proposal was passed unanimously, and the calendar was changed.

Students present their argument for changing the school calendar to the Anchorage School Board.

go.hrw.com
Project Citizen
KEYWORD: SZ7 CH13

SERVICE LEARNING

1. Why did the Anchorage students want to change the school calendar?
2. How did research and preparation play an important role in the students' success?

SECTION 3

Your Family and You

BEFORE YOU READ

The Main Idea

The family continues to be the most important group in American society. It performs many functions for its members and for the country.

Reading Focus

1. What are five ways the family serves the country?
2. Why is it important to respect the rights of other family members and for family members to compromise?
3. Why is it useful for a family to budget its money?

Key Terms

budget, *p. 330*
fixed expenses, *p. 330*

TAKING NOTES As you read, take notes about how families serve the country, the rights of family, and family budgets. Use a diagram like this one to organize your notes.

ACADEMIC VOCABULARY

influence: change, or have an effect on

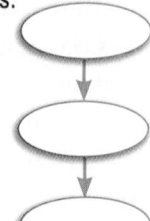

Much of what you need to know as a citizen, you will learn in your home from your family: how to get along with others; how to earn money and spend it wisely; what's right and what's wrong. Think of your family as a small nation with its own domestic, foreign, and economic policies.

Family Serves the Country

More than 70 million families live in the United States. The **influence** of these families on children is immense. We depend on families to teach children the skills they need to become responsible adults. In what ways does the family teach these skills?

Shaping the Country's Future The family helps keep the country strong when it provides a stable environment for children to learn and grow. In this way, families shape the country's future.

Families find security and fun together.

Education: A Family Decision

In colonial times, there were few education requirements. Children learned basic reading and writing, but there were no public schools. Children worked at home or learned a trade. Then in 1852, Massachusetts introduced a system of compulsory, or mandatory, education. Schools were free to residents, and children were required to attend. By 1918 nearly every state had created mandatory public elementary schools.

Years later, parents still play an active role in choosing where and how their children are educated. Some parents choose to send their children to private schools. For example, parents who wish for their children to receive a religious education may send their children to a religious, or parochial, school. These are an alternative to public schools and include religious instruction along with instruction in secular subjects.

In recent years, home schooling has become another option for parents who want more control over their children's education.

Why might some parents have been pleased when free public education was established? Why might other parents have been displeased?

Educating Its Members From their families, children learn many basic things that help them to survive. It is in the home that children learn to walk, talk, and dress themselves.

Teaching Good Behavior Your earliest ideas of right and wrong are taught in the home. Within the family, children learn how to behave in the world around them.

Helping Manage Money Members of the family earn and spend money to provide food, clothing, a place to live, and other necessities for its members. Some parents give their children an allowance, or a small sum of money, every week. This encourages children to learn how to manage money and to share financial responsibilities.

Teaching Good Citizenship The family must teach children to respect the rights of others and to fulfill their responsibilities as good citizens.

READING CHECK **Summarizing** What are some key ways that the family serves the country?

The Rights of the Family

When most Americans think of home, they picture a place where the family lives together in harmony. Of course, no family can live up to this ideal all the time. Disagreements are part of family life. The way families handle disagreements is important. Using self-restraint and considering other people's points of view can help prevent serious conflict. Each family member has rights. If a person's rights are respected, he or she is more likely to respect the rights of others.

Do you think arguments are good or bad? Although unpleasant, conflicts can often benefit a family. Arguments, if kept in hand, can teach you how to present your ideas effectively. They can also help you understand another person's point of view. By talking over ideas with members of your family, you learn to be understanding and patient.

READING CHECK **Finding the Main Idea** Why are respect and compromise important to family harmony?

ECON 101

The Importance of Saving

The amount of money that the average American family saves has decreased over the past decade. Some people say that a decline in savings will hurt our economy. Why?

The number of retirees increases every year. Many rely on government programs like Social Security, Medicare, and Medicaid for income and health care. More recipients of these benefits mean less money for each person. To combat this problem, economists insist that everyone must save money to ensure a safe retirement.

Investment also starts with saving. Think of our economy like a farm. The farmer does not sell some crops (saving) so that they can be planted next year (investing). From buying homes to buying stocks, our economy depends on investment.

ANALYSIS SKILL **ANALYZING ECONOMICS**

Information about savings accounts is available at bank locations and Web sites. Research several banks and write a paragraph comparing the different types of accounts the banks offer.

Families on a Budget

One issue that all families face is how to spend the family's money. Adults try to earn enough money to pay for all the things the family needs and wants. But there is only so much money to divide among the family members. People must compromise.

By deciding the best way to spend the family's money, each family member's needs can be provided for appropriately. A **budget** is a plan for using money. If a budget is carefully planned and followed, it can help reduce a family's worries about money.

So how does a family budget its money? The first step is to gather information about family expenses and income, and to make a plan based on these facts. The starting point in any budget is the total amount of money that is available to spend. Families must keep spending within this limit. First on a family's budget are regular expenses, or **fixed expenses**, that must be paid. These expenses may include rent or mortgage payments, the cost of food, and regular bills. The remaining money pays for health care, transportation, entertainment, and other items.

You can help your family stay within its budget. How? One important way is to help prevent waste in your home. Talk to your parents or guardian before you agree to activities that cost money.

READING CHECK **Analyzing Information** Why should families use a budget?

go.hrw.com
Online Quiz
KEYWORD: SZ7 HP13

SECTION 3 ASSESSMENT

Reviewing Ideas and Terms

1. **a. Recall** What are some ways that the family serves the country?
   b. Explain How can giving children an allowance encourage them to learn how to manage money?
2. **a. Summarize** How can arguments benefit a family?
   b. Elaborate How will learning to get along with family members help you in your adult life?
3. **a. Define** Write a brief definition for each of the following terms: **budget** and **fixed expenses**.
   b. Elaborate What are some ways that you can help your family stay within its budget plan?

Critical Thinking

4. **Summarizing** Copy the graphic organizer. Using your notes, explain the five important functions a family serves.

   Important Functions of the Family

Focus on Writing

5. **Evaluating** Write out a personal budget. First, list your weekly expenses. Next, list your weekly sources of income. Finally, write a paragraph evaluating your current use of money and setting goals for your future use of it.

Family and Medical Leave Act

Have you ever had to miss school or an after-school job because you were sick or had to help care for a sick family member? Did you worry about what would happen when you returned? Maybe you were nervous that you would be too far behind in your classes to catch up, or that your manager would give your job to someone else.

Until 1993, employees at full-time jobs also had to worry about these issues. Then Congress passed the Family and Medical Leave Act (FMLA).

Why it Matters

Family and work are both very important, and sometimes you may feel torn between your responsibilities to each. Under FMLA, if you have worked for a company of 50 or more employees for one year or longer, you are allowed to take up to 12 weeks of leave, or time off, if you or your parent, child, or spouse is sick. FMLA leave time may also be used when an employee, or an employee's spouse, gives birth to or adopts a child. Your employer does not have to pay you for the time you take off, but under most circumstances, you cannot lose your job for taking this leave. In addition, employers may not use FMLA leave as a reason to deny you a promotion or any benefits of your job.

People do not have to give up their medical privacy in order to take advantage of the FMLA. Employees are not required to give their employers medical records or other information about their medical condition or their family member's medical condition. However, employers may ask people taking FMLA leave to provide a doctor's statement confirming that a serious medical condition does exist. This ensures that employees do not use the law to take time off for other reasons.

The FMLA gives mothers and fathers time off of work to spend with their new babies.

ANALYSIS SKILL **EVALUATING THE LAW**

go.hrw.com
KEYWORD: SZ7 CH13

1. Why do you think that the FMLA does not apply to businesses that have fewer than 50 employees?
2. Would your opinion about FMLA leave differ if you ran your own business? What about if you were an employee of a small business?

CHAPTER 13 REVIEW

Visual Summary

Use the visual summary to help you review the main ideas of the chapter.

Five Functions of the Family
- Shaping the Country's Future
- Educating Its Members
- Teaching Good Behavior
- Helping Manage Money
- Teaching Good Citizenship

QUICK FACTS

Reviewing Key Terms

For each of the terms below, write a sentence explaining its significance to citizenship and the family.

1. delayed marriage
2. remarriage
3. blended families
4. two-income families
5. single-parent families
6. family law
7. child abuse
8. foster home
9. guardian
10. adopt
11. divorce
12. no-fault divorce
13. budget
14. fixed expenses

Comprehension and Critical Thinking

SECTION 1 *(Pages 318–321)*

15. **a. Recall** How did the move to cities bring changes to American families?

    b. Explain Why has the average age at first marriage increased in recent years?

    c. Predict Will the number of two-income families in the United States continue to increase? Why or why not?

SECTION 2 *(Pages 323–326)*

16. **a. Recall** Why do most states have a waiting period for couples applying for marriage licenses?

    b. Draw Conclusions How does having children affect the decisions that couples must make when considering a divorce?

    c. Support a Point of View Do you think that the government has the right to make and enforce laws that affect family life? Explain your answer.

Active Citizenship Video Program
Review the video to answer the closing question:
How can students be a powerful force in bringing about change in education?

SECTION 3 (Pages 328–330)

17. a. Identify What are five important functions of the family?

   b. Make Inferences How can a budget help a family manage its income and spending?

   c. Evaluate How might developing strong, respectful relationships with other family members benefit people in their lives outside the family?

Using the Internet

go.hrw.com
KEYWORD: SZ7 CH13

18. Researching the American Family The American family is vital to the strength of the nation. Enter the activity keyword and explore the ways in which the American family serves the country. Then create a collage to illustrate your research. Include a written description explaining how the photographs you chose for your collage represent the role of the family in citizenship and society.

Civics Skills

Using Television as a Resource *Study the television schedule below. Use the Civics Skills taught in this chapter to answer the question about the schedule below.*

6:00 P.M.	6:30 P.M.	7:00 P.M.
Biography: Jimmy Carter		U2 in Concert
Local News	NBC Nightly News	Dateline: Running a Family Business
News Night	Larry King Live: Bill, Hillary, and Chelsea Clinton	
Extreme Surgery		Medical Miracles
American Experience: Remember the Alamo		The News Hour with Jim Lehrer

19. Which of these shows would you expect to present an unbiased examination of its subject? Why?

Reading Skills

Information and Propaganda *Use the Reading Skills taught in this chapter to answer the question about the reading selection below.*

> The school board is considering a proposal to remove spring break from the school calendar. Almost all students and parents strongly oppose the proposal. The school board should vote down the proposal.
>
> The proposal was brought in an effort to give students more class time and increase test scores. The idiot who came up with this proposal should apologize. Students and teachers deserve the spring break.
>
> If the school board wants to increase test scores, it should build new schools. Better classrooms would help students perform better.

20. Which propaganda techniques are used in this passage?

   a. name calling

   b. bandwagon

   c. oversimplification

   d. all of the above

FOCUS ON WRITING

21. Writing Your Autobiography Review your notes about the importance of the American family. Then write your autobiography, being sure to mention the duties and responsibilities your character had within the family. How does your character feel about his or her life? What are your character's hopes and fears for the future? What are your character's opinions on his or her place in the family?

CHAPTER 14
CITIZENSHIP IN SCHOOL

SECTION 1
The U.S. School System

SECTION 2
The Best Education
for You

SECTION 3
Developing Your
Life Skills

NATIONAL STANDARDS®
FOR CIVICS AND GOVERNMENT

II. What are the foundations of the American
political system?

B. What are the distinctive characteristics of
American society?

V. What are the roles of the citizen in American
democracy?

C. What are the responsibilities of citizens?

D. What civic dispositions or traits of private
and public character are important to the
preservation and improvement of American
constitutional democracy?

©1994, 2003 Center for Civic Education. All Rights Reserved.

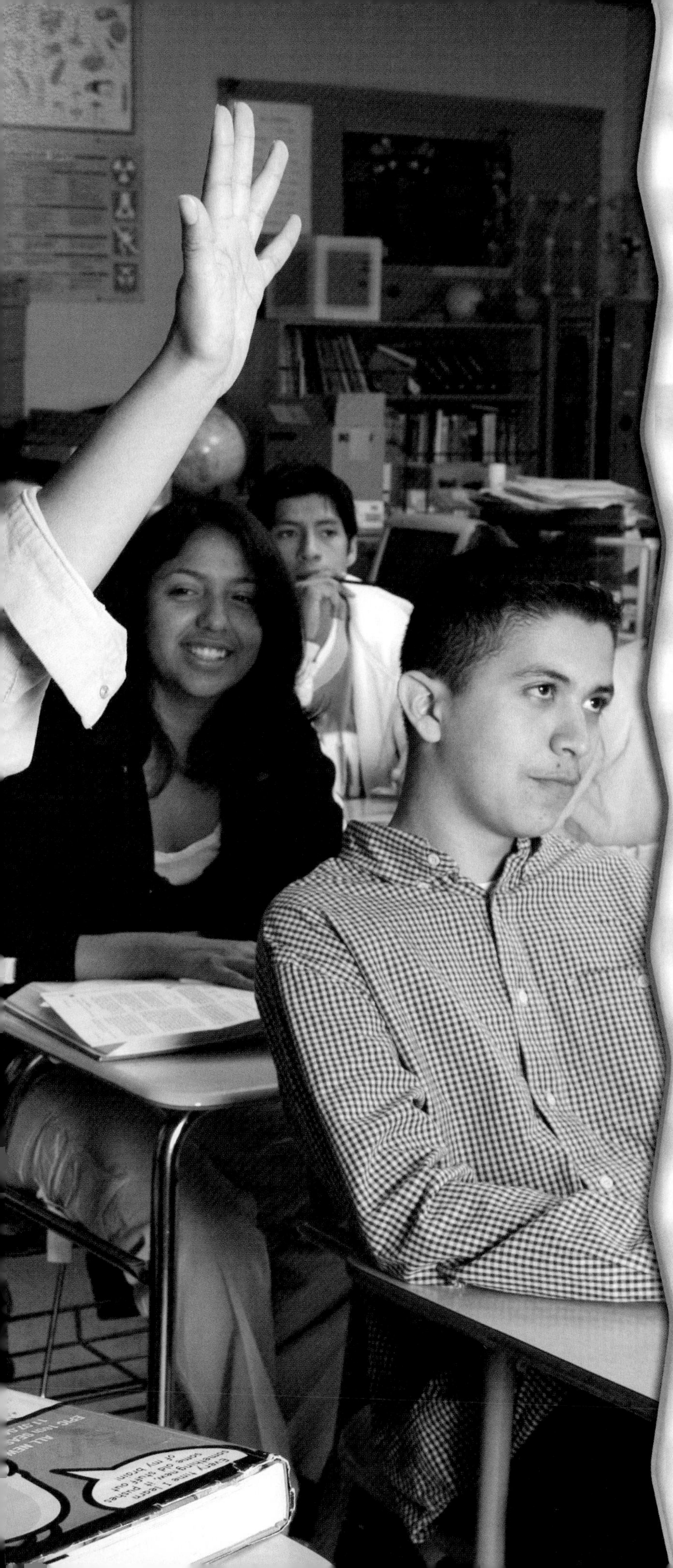

Active Citizenship video program
Watch the video to learn how young
citizens are promoting healthy lifestyles.

WHY CIVICS Matters

Have you thought about the kind of
work you want to do when you
become an adult? No matter what
future you choose for yourself, you will
profit by getting a good education.

PROJECT ★Citizen

STUDENTS TAKE ACTION

CREATING A HEALTHIER SCHOOL Is
childhood obesity a problem in your school?
Students in Allentown, Pennsylvania, were
worried about this problem, so they developed
a program to help their fellow students live
healthier lives. What can you do to teach people
at your school about the importance of exercise
and making better eating choices?

FOCUS ON WRITING

CREATING A WEB SITE Have you ever
designed your own Web site? If not, here is
your chance to create one. As you read this
chapter, you will gather information about the
importance of education. Then you will write
a description of how you would present this
same information on a Web site.

Reading Skills

In this chapter you will read about the U.S. educational system and the core values that guide it. You will also learn about the challenges that public education faces. You will read about the seven goals of education. You will also read about the importance of knowing how to learn and think clearly so that you can think for yourself and become a good citizen. Finally, you will learn how opinions are formed and how people are influenced by other people's thinking.

Summarizing Text

FOCUS ON READING Textbooks are full of information. Sometimes the sheer amount of information they contain can make processing what you read difficult. In those cases, it may be helpful to stop for a moment and summarize what you have read.

Writing a Summary A **summary** is a short restatement of the most important ideas in a text. The example below shows three steps used in writing a summary. First underline important details. Then write a short summary of each paragraph. Finally, combine these paragraph summaries into a short summary of the whole passage.

Helpful Hints for Summarizing Text

1. Ask yourself "What is the most important point of this paragraph?"

2. Try to restate the point in one sentence.

3. Focus on getting the big ideas, not the details.

The success you enjoy in school and the study and learning habits you develop may play a role in the person you will become. They will also influence the kind of job that you will have. What kinds of study and learning habits should you try to develop?

One of the first and most important study habits all students must learn is the wise use of time. A well-organized student finds time in his or her daily schedule for study, school activities, exercise, relaxation, and the proper amount of sleep.

Summary of Paragraph 1 Study and learning habits will influence the person you become and the kind of job you will have.

Summary of Paragraph 2 The most important study habit is learning to use time wisely by making and following a daily schedule.

Combined Summary Learning to use time wisely is an important study habit that can help you be successful in school and life.

You Try It!

The following passage is from the chapter you are about to read. As you read it, decide which facts you would include in a summary of the passage.

Extracurricular Activities Can Lead to Success

From Chapter 14, p. 348

School can be more than just classes, homework, tests, and projects. To get the most out of your education, you should get involved in the extracurricular activities that your school offers. Extracurricular activities are the groups, teams, and events that your school sponsors outside of the classroom.

So join a sport. Try out for the school play. Run for office in student government. Your effort will pay off. You may find a new hobby. You may improve your skills or learn new ones. Most likely, you will meet new people and make new friends.

There are benefits for the future, too. Extracurricular activities may help you get into the college of your choice or earn valuable scholarships. Of course, the most important reason to participate in school activities is because they are fun!

After you read the passage, answer the following questions.

1. Which of the following statements best summarizes the first paragraph of this passage?

   a. School is more fun with extracurricular activities.

   b. Extracurricular activities are an important part of your education.

2. Using the steps described on the previous page, write a summary of the second and third paragraphs of this passage.

3. Combine the summary statement you chose in question 1 with the summary statements you wrote in question 2 to create a single summary of this entire passage.

Academic Vocabulary

Success in school is related to knowing academic vocabulary—the words that are frequently used in school assignments and discussions. In this chapter, you will learn the following academic words:

As you read Chapter 14, decide which points you would include in a summary of the chapter.

The U.S. School System

BEFORE YOU READ

The Main Idea

Education is vital to American society and to American democracy. The U.S. school system helps prepare you to be a good citizen.

Reading Focus

1. Why is education important?
2. What are the levels of the U.S. school system?
3. What American values can be found in education, and what challenges face schools today?

Key Terms

university, *p. 341*

mainstreaming, *p. 342*

 As you read, take notes on the U.S. school system. Use the diagram below to take notes on the importance of education, the levels of the school system, and the values and challenges of education in the United States.

Many programs reward students for academic achievements. These students are the winners of college scholarships for academic excellence.

CIVICS IN PRACTICE Education is central to American society. As President Franklin D. Roosevelt said, "Democracy cannot succeed unless those who express their choice are prepared to choose wisely. The real safeguard of democracy, therefore, is education."

How does this affect you? Not only will a good education help you get a good job someday, but our country, our government, and our way of life will benefit from this as well. In this increasingly complex and technologically advanced world, the future of the United States depends on well-educated citizens. Society, as a whole, prospers when its citizens are educated.

Education Is Important

Maybe you have heard the expression, "Knowledge is power." Sir Francis Bacon, a sixteenth century British philosopher and inventor coined the phrase. Many Americans still believe in Bacon's idea. Today, there are more than 50 million students in grades K–12, and more than 3 million teachers. Education is important for two main reasons: Education helps individual citizens grow, and it builds a strong country.

Religious Clubs in Public Schools

Because public schools are funded by tax dollars, they must follow certain rules, which courts have established based on the Constitution. The First Amendment says that government cannot "establish" a religion—it must remain neutral. Courts have interpreted this neutrality to mean that public schools cannot start the school day with a prayer; this would be establishing a preference for religion. But what about allowing a Bible-study club to meet on school grounds after classes are over?

For a time, many public schools would not permit religious clubs to use school property because they did not want to show any preference for religious activities. But in 1990 the U.S. Supreme Court ruled that it is unconstitutional for a school to pick and choose among student-run clubs based on a club's purpose. A religious club must be treated the same as other student clubs.

What constitutional arguments do you think influenced the Supreme Court's decision?

Helping Individual Citizens Grow

Americans believe that all citizens should be able to make the most of their talents and abilities. Most agree that everyone should have the same opportunities to learn and succeed. That is why we strive to provide all citizens with equal access to education.

Building a Strong Country

Imagine if no one in our country ran for public office, or no one volunteered to help the homeless or clean up polluted parks. People are responsible for what goes on in their communities and neighborhoods. One purpose of education is to teach young citizens how to use their skills to help others and our nation.

READING CHECK **Finding the Main Idea** Why do Americans believe that education is important?

Levels of the School System

The American school system spans many different levels—from preschool through university. Each level provides important educational and social skills to American students.

The Educational Ladder

You and your friends will probably spend at least 14 years on the educational ladder—from preschool through high school. If you go on to college and graduate school, like medical school, you could spend as many as 12 more years getting your education!

Preschool Preschool is usually for children aged three through five. Children learn everything from the letters in the alphabet to cooperating with teachers and each other.

Kindergarten Kindergarten prepares children for first grade by teaching them basic academic skills. Children also start to learn thinking and social skills that will help them for the rest of their education.

Elementary School Children go to elementary school from first grade through fifth or sixth grade, depending on the school system. Students learn the building blocks of reading, writing, and mathematics. Many elementary schools also offer instruction in social studies, science, health, art, music, physical education, and citizenship.

Education and Earnings

Education is the key to success. In general, the more education someone has, the more money he or she earns. Of the millions of people who enter school at age 5 or 6, however, few stay in school long enough to earn that valuable college diploma.

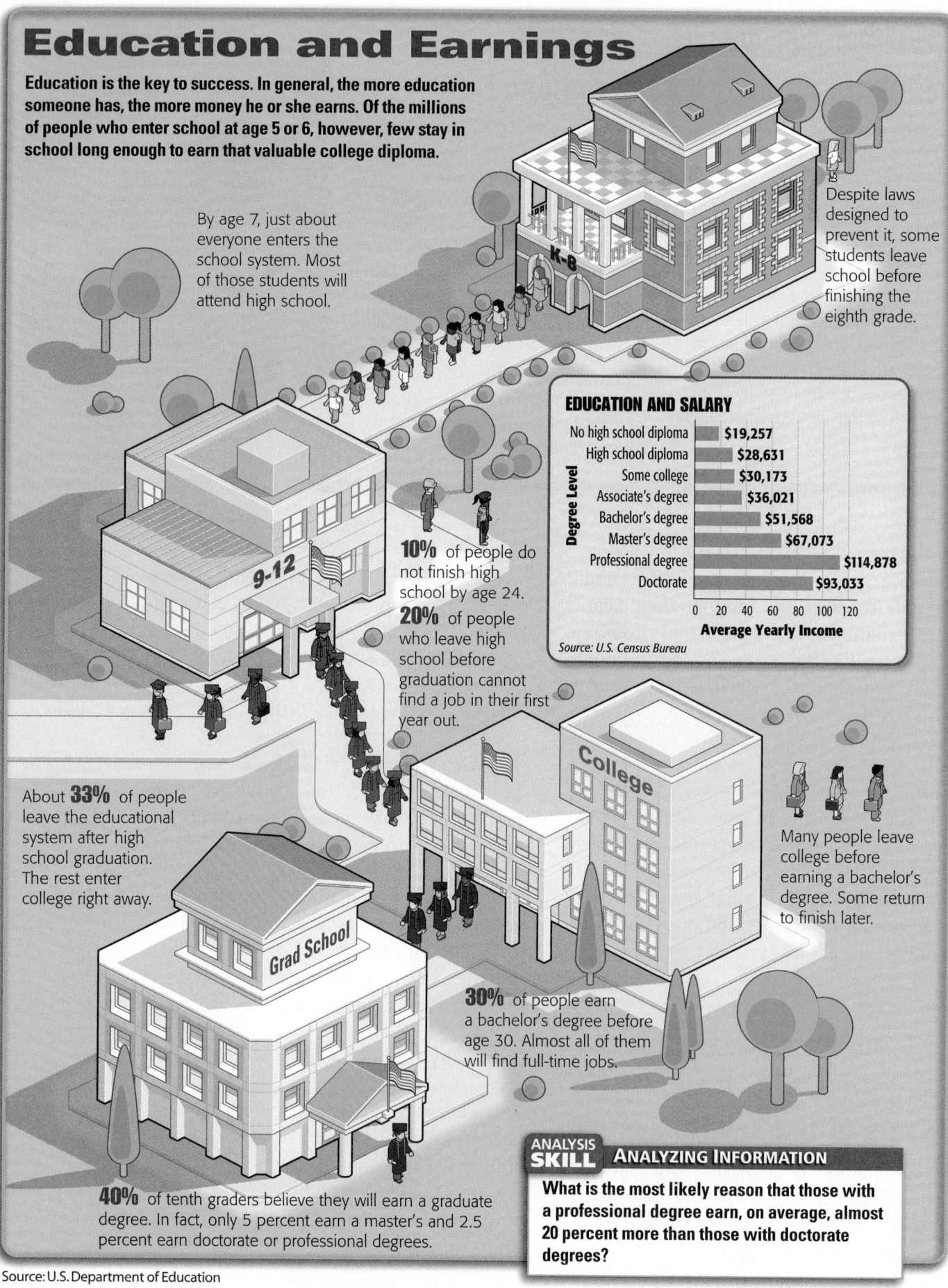

By age 7, just about everyone enters the school system. Most of those students will attend high school.

Despite laws designed to prevent it, some students leave school before finishing the eighth grade.

10% of people do not finish high school by age 24.

20% of people who leave high school before graduation cannot find a job in their first year out.

About **33%** of people leave the educational system after high school graduation. The rest enter college right away.

Many people leave college before earning a bachelor's degree. Some return to finish later.

30% of people earn a bachelor's degree before age 30. Almost all of them will find full-time jobs.

40% of tenth graders believe they will earn a graduate degree. In fact, only 5 percent earn a master's and 2.5 percent earn doctorate or professional degrees.

EDUCATION AND SALARY

Degree Level	Average Yearly Income
No high school diploma	$19,257
High school diploma	$28,631
Some college	$30,173
Associate's degree	$36,021
Bachelor's degree	$51,568
Master's degree	$67,073
Professional degree	$114,878
Doctorate	$93,033

Source: U.S. Census Bureau

ANALYSIS SKILL **ANALYZING INFORMATION**

What is the most likely reason that those with a professional degree earn, on average, almost 20 percent more than those with doctorate degrees?

Source: U.S. Department of Education

Junior High or Middle School Junior high schools usually range from seventh grade through ninth. Middle schools may range from grades four through eight. At this level, students are preparing for the last stage of their basic education—high school.

High School There are three kinds of high schools. Academic high schools prepare students for college. Technical or vocational high schools help students learn a specific trade or profession. Comprehensive high schools offer both educational options.

Higher Education

Many jobs in the United States today require more education and training than you receive in high school. There are two basic options for higher education.

Community Colleges Community or junior colleges are two-year institutions of higher education. Some courses of study provide enough training to go right into a profession, such as medical laboratory technician or computer technical support. Students at community colleges often transfer to four-year colleges to complete their studies.

Colleges and Universities A college is any four-year institution that offers degrees in a variety of fields. A college degree is called an undergraduate degree. A **university** includes one or more colleges. Universities grant undergraduate degrees, but they also provide advanced studies in most college courses. These advanced degrees are earned in graduate school. Some universities offer graduate studies in professional fields.

There are plenty of good reasons to go to college. The more education you have, the more career and life opportunities you will have. If you plan to enter a profession such as law or medicine you will need a higher degree.

READING CHECK **Summarizing** What are the levels of the U.S. school system?

Values and Challenges of Education

Today most schools offer a wide range of subjects and are filled with many different types of people. Students have opportunities to learn more than just academics. Modern schools have become the rich and varied environment they are because of some basic American **values** that are part of the U.S. education system.

Free Public Education All U.S. citizens can take advantage of free public education, usually from kindergarten through high school. Public education is not entirely free, though. It is paid for with taxes collected by local, state, and federal governments. For example, in 2002–2003, approximately $455 billion was spent to fund public education for grades prekindergarten through 12 and school construction, community services, and adult education programs.

ACADEMIC VOCABULARY

values: ideas that people hold dear and try to live by

FOCUS ON Margaret Spellings
(1957—   )

Margaret Spellings was born in Michigan in 1957, but she grew up in Houston, Texas. She studied political science at the University of Houston. Spellings is the mother of two school-age children. Spellings served as associate executive director for the Texas Association of School Boards and later became an education and political adviser to George W. Bush during his term as governor of Texas.

During Bush's first term in Washington, Spellings became an assistant to the president on domestic policy. She helped write the No Child Left Behind Act in 2001. The act helps to establish standards of accountability for America's schools. In 2005 Spellings became the eighth U.S. secretary of education.

Summarize What part of Spelling's life might have helped her to become secretary of education?

Equal Schooling, Open to All Schools cannot discriminate against anyone because of his or her race, gender, or religion. They also cannot discriminate against a person because of physical disabilities or financial status.

Free Education for Any Creed or Religion All Americans, no matter what their religious beliefs, can attend public schools. Schools cannot discriminate against a student because of his or her religious background.

Local Control Local communities operate their own public schools. Each school district decides how its schools can best serve its citizens.

Compulsory Attendance Each state sets its own attendance requirements. All states, however, require that young people go to school.

Enriching Environment In the United States, people expect schools to be more than just places that teach academics. Americans expect schools to help students develop to their full potential—in mind, body, and spirit.

Inclusive Instruction Most U.S. citizens believe in equal education opportunities for everyone, regardless of any special educational needs. The Handicapped Children's Act of 1975 requires that students with special needs be treated like everyone else and be taught in regular classrooms whenever possible. This practice is called **mainstreaming**, or inclusion.

Challenges Facing Our Schools

Our public school system faces a number of challenges today. These challenges include:

- paying for public schools,
- hiring and keeping good teachers,
- educational reform and student performance,
- violence in public schools.

These problems can affect the education that you receive. There are solutions to these problems. Everyone, including students themselves, must help to find those solutions so that schools can respond better to the needs of students.

READING CHECK **Summarizing** What are the principles that form the basis of the American education system?

SECTION 1 ASSESSMENT

Reviewing Ideas and Terms

1. a. Recall What are two main reasons that Americans think that education is important?

b. Make Inferences How can education make a person a better citizen?

2. a. Define Write a brief definition of the following term: **university**.

b. Sequence What are the levels of the U.S. school system?

3. a. Write a brief definition of the following term: **mainstreaming**.

b. Elaborating How does the inclusion of American values in the education system help schools make students better citizens?

Critical Thinking

4. Evaluating Review your notes on American values in education. Then create a graphic organizer that shows the top three values that you think are most important and why.

Most Important	Why

Focus on Writing

5. Problem Solving What solutions would you propose to the various challenges facing American schools today?

STUDENTS TAKE ACTION

Creating a Healthier School

How healthy is your school? Do students eat nutritious foods and get enough exercise? Do they study nutrition? One group of students in Allentown, Pennsylvania, felt that they could help younger students in their school live healthier lives.

Community Connection Since their school did not have a health education program, Project Citizen students in Mrs. Amy Weber's class decided to study nutrition and exercise so that they could teach others about these topics once a month. These "Health Helpers" were especially worried about childhood obesity, or kids who were facing medical problems due to their weight. The concerned students hoped that by sharing information about better eating choices and the importance of exercise, they could help with this problem.

Taking Action The Allentown students researched childhood obesity, surveyed and interviewed a variety of community members about the issue, and presented an action plan to school and district officials. With the support of the school principal and their teachers, the Health Helpers are on their way to making their program a reality. The school's physical education teacher has applied to the Pennsylvania Advocates for Nutrition and Activity (PANA), an organization created by the state government to help others learn about healthy choices, for money to support the students' education plan. Encouraged by the positive reactions they've received, the students are now getting ready to start their monthly program.

One of many changes Allentown students hope to make is improving food choices.

go.hrw.com
Project Citizen
KEYWORD: SZ7 CH14

SERVICE LEARNING

1. Why did the students from Allentown feel that it was important for their school to have a health education program?
2. Why do you think the students applied to a state organization for money to make the Health Helpers' plan become a reality?

The Best Education for You

BEFORE YOU READ

The Main Idea

You can be successful in school if you are aware of the opportunities that your school has to offer and if you are prepared to take advantage of those opportunities.

Reading Focus

1. How can being prepared for school help you be successful in school?
2. What are the seven goals of education?
3. How can extracurricular activities help you be successful in school?

Key Terms

extracurricular activities, *p. 348*

TAKING NOTES As you read, take notes on the best education for you. Use a chart like this one to record your notes.

Tips for Success	Goals for Education	Extracurricular Activities

Participating in drama can help prepare students for careers involving public speaking.

CIVICS IN PRACTICE

You probably know some students in your school who seem to be "lucky." They get good grades, they win awards, and they belong to successful teams or clubs. Maybe these students *are* lucky, but luck is only part of their success. Success comes from working hard and seizing opportunities. A "lucky" person is prepared for those opportunities and takes advantage of them.

Be Prepared, Be Successful

To get the most out of school, you have to make some effort. Are you making the most of your time in school? One of the most important skills you can learn is the smart use of your time.

Time management, or making and keeping a schedule, can help you in two ways. First, you will be able to make sure that everything you need to do—including having free time—gets done. Second, having a schedule helps to reduce your stress level. There are no surprises or last-minute projects that keep you up all night. Everything is planned and everything gets done.

To make a schedule, figure out how much time you need each day or week for your important activities—homework, after-school activities, eating, sleeping. Then calculate how much time is left for leisure. Write your schedule on a calendar. Stick to your schedule, and you have mastered a lifelong skill!

More Tips for Success

Having a schedule is an important first step toward success, but that is not all you need. Here are some more tips on studying and participating in class and in school activities.

Studying at Home Find a quiet, well-lighted place to study. Make sure you have all your materials that you will need nearby. Your bedroom or the local public library makes a good study place.

Know Your Textbook Here are some helpful hints for reading and using your textbooks.

- Use the study guides that are part of the book.
- Look over each chapter before you read. Read the chapter title, section headings, and other subheadings.
- Read the assigned text carefully, paying attention to topic sentences.
- Reread the chapter, but this time take notes on the important facts and ideas in the text.
- Answer the questions at the end of each section in a chapter as soon as you have finished reading.

Be Prepared to Participate Bring all of your supplies, including textbooks, pens or pencils, and notebooks. Make sure you have done the homework from the night before. Complete drills and do not be afraid to answer questions or offer your opinions.

Test-Taking Tips

When you take a test, look over the entire test before you begin. Find out how many questions there are and how long you will have to answer each question. Leave enough time, if possible, to review your answers when you finish. Take your time, and read each question carefully before you answer. If a question is too difficult at first, go on to other questions. But make sure to go back and answer anything you have skipped. Reread written answers and math solutions to look for mistakes. At the end, check to see that you have answered every question you can.

READING CHECK **Finding the Main Idea** What skills can help you do well in school?

Seven Goals of Education

American schools generally have seven goals they want their students to try to achieve. If you learn these skills from your school, you will be ready for most challenges in life.

Learn Basic Skills

The main goal of education is to teach students how to read, write, compute, and communicate. You should be able to listen to others, speak in front of a group, organize your thoughts, and express your ideas. You should know how to use a dictionary, conduct research, solve mathematical problems, support a point of view, and have basic knowledge of science. These are basic skills that you will use in college or on a job.

Learn to Work with Others

Schools teach students how to cooperate and collaborate, both in the classroom and in the community.

Build Good Health Habits

You cannot make the most of your education unless you are healthy. Nutrition, physical activity, and personal hygiene are important parts of a healthy life.

Train for Your Life's Work

College-educated workers generally make more money than high school graduates. The basic skills you learn in school prepare you for the specialized training that many jobs and careers require.

Success in School

Being successful in school is up to you. Your time, your health, your study habits, and your personal life will impact your academic experience positively or negatively—depending on your choices.

Excellence Is a Choice

To reach your goals in the future, set academic goals today.

Set personal goals to enrich your life with activities outside of school.

Set short-term goals, such as passing an upcoming test.

Set long-term goals, like graduating from high school or going to college.

Keep First Things First

Setting priorities is the best way to stay focused on your goals.

Managing your time well means setting and keeping a schedule for yourself.

Set aside time every week to get organized and stay organized.

Become an active participant in your own education by spending time studying every day.

A Good Attitude Is a Great Asset

The school supplies you need the most cannot be bought—a positive mental outlook and a belief in yourself.

Learn to work with others and to ask for help when you need it.

Make an effort to stay focused in class by being prepared and participating.

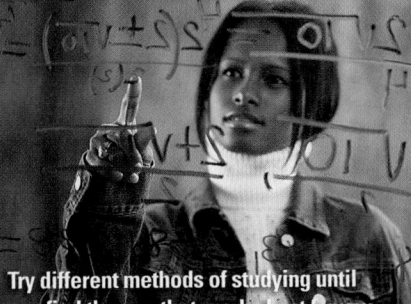

Try different methods of studying until you find the one that works best for you.

Take Care of Yourself

You must feel well to do well—in school and in life.

Teenagers need between 8 and 10 hours of sleep each night.

Fuel your mind and body with healthy food.

Exercise will help you feel better and learn better.

Become an Active Citizen

America is a democracy. That means that we, the citizens, run the country. Schools train students to be active citizens. School is a place where you and your classmates can practice the **principles** of our democracy—cooperation, participation, community service, and good judgment.

ACADEMIC VOCABULARY

principles: basic beliefs, rules, or laws

Develop Considerate Behavior

Respect is important to all of us. We want respect from our friends, families, teachers, employers, and neighbors. Respect is being considerate of others—believing in their right to live, grow, and be happy. In school you learn to listen to other points of view and value the privacy and property of others. You learn that when you respect others, they respect you.

Use Your Free Time Wisely

Your playtime is as important as your work time. Sometimes, the activities you do for fun develop skills and interests that can help you as an adult.

READING CHECK **Summarizing** What skills do schools try to teach students that will help them on the job?

Extracurricular Activities Can Lead to Success

School can be more than just classes, homework, tests, and projects. To get the most out of your education, you should get involved in the extracurricular activities that your school offers. **Extracurricular activities** are the groups, teams, and events that your school sponsors outside of the classroom.

So join a sport. Try out for the school play. Run for office in student government. Your effort will pay off. You may find a new hobby. You may improve your skills or learn new ones. Most likely, you will meet new people and make new friends.

There are benefits for the future, too. Extracurricular activities may help you get into the college of your choice or earn valuable scholarships. Of course, one of the most important reasons to participate in school activities is that they are fun!

READING CHECK **Drawing Inferences and Conclusions** What skills could you develop in your extracurricular activities that would help you succeed in your education?

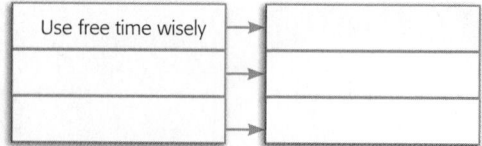

go.hrw.com
Online Quiz
KEYWORD: SZ7 HP14

SECTION 2 ASSESSMENT

Reviewing Ideas and Terms

1. a. Recall What are two ways in which making a schedule help you succeed in school?
b. Analyze How can making and keeping to a schedule reduce stress and anxiety?

2. a. Describe Why is learning to become an active citizen one goal of education?
b. Make Generalizations How can mastering the goals of education help you succeed in school and life?

3. a. Define Write a brief definition of the following term: **extracurricular activities**.
b. Analyze What skills might a student learn from extracurricular activities that he or she might not learn in the classroom?

Critical Thinking

4. Evaluating Review your notes on the seven goals of education. Then create a graphic organizer that shows three goals that you think are most important, and how reaching those goals will help you be more successful in school and in life.

Use free time wisely	→	
	→	
	→	

Focus on Writing

5. Supporting a Point of View Write a letter to the school board explaining what one new extracurricular program should be added to your school.

348 CHAPTER 14

Creating a Multimedia Presentation

Learn

Multimedia presentations are oral presentations that may use any or all of the following: text, audio, video, animation, graphic art, computer graphics, and many other types of media. Using many types of media engages your audience and encourages them to pay attention to the issues at hand.

Someone auditioning to be a recording artist might present a multimedia presentation that includes a written biography, a video of a concert, and a Web page with mp3 song samples to download. A student might give a presentation on Africa's wildlife by showing a video of animals on the savanna and playing audio of animal sounds.

Oftentimes in school or at work, you may be asked to give a presentation to a group of people. An engaging and exciting multimedia presentation will help your audience remember the information you presented. Follow the steps below to learn to create a multimedia presentation.

Practice

❶ **Know the equipment.** If you are using electronic equipment in your presentation, be sure you know how to operate it ahead of time.

❷ **Make a plan.** All presentations need a theme and a structure. Think about what you are trying to communicate and then decide the best way to share this message. Sketch out your ideas on a piece of paper or on note cards.

❸ **Identify content resources.** You may use content from a variety of sources—a page photocopied from a book, an image taken from the Internet, an mp3 file on a media player. Make sure that you credit your sources.

❹ **Practice, practice, practice.** An oral presentation is already challenging without a lot of equipment involved. Spend an hour the night before your presentation practicing. Follow up with 30 minutes of review before you are set to begin your presentation.

Apply

1. Look at the photo below. Is this a multimedia presentation? Why or why not?

2. Why is it important to be familiar with the equipment before giving a multimedia presentation?

3. You are running for student body president and decide to create a multimedia presentation for the school. What message would you like to share? What media elements will you use?

4. Create a schedule that you could use to create and prepare to deliver a multimedia presentation. Be sure to follow the steps you learned in the Practice section.

SECTION 3
Developing Your Life Skills

BEFORE YOU READ

The Main Idea

One of the key life skills you learn in school should be learning how to think. If you learn how to think critically, you will be able to solve many of the problems you face in school and in life.

Reading Focus

1. How are learning and experience related?
2. What are the steps involved in critical thinking?
3. Why should you learn to think for yourself?

Key Terms

experience, *p. 350*
conditioning, *p. 351*
habit, *p. 351*
motivation, *p. 351*
insight, *p. 352*
creativity, *p. 352*
critical thinking, *p. 352*
prejudice, *p. 354*

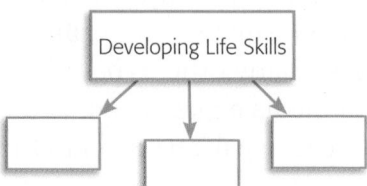

TAKING NOTES As you read, take notes on the learning experience, critical thinking, and thinking for yourself. Use a graphic organizer like this one to organize your notes.

Developing Life Skills

This student is creating a piece of pottery, a skill she has learned through study and experience.

CIVICS IN PRACTICE Have you ever thought "I'll never use this when I get out of school?" Most of us have. But there is one important skill you learn in school that you will definitely use every day of your life. That skill is the ability to reason—how to learn and how to think. While you may be able to reason now, school will help you improve upon that skill.

Learning Is an Experience

Maybe you have heard the expression, "We learn from experience." You have been learning from your experiences since you were a baby. Learning is gaining knowledge or skill through study or experience. **Experience** is observation of or participation in events.

Using Your Senses

The simplest kind of learning involves the experiences of your senses and muscles. You know from experience that ice is cold, fire is hot, and water is wet. For example, as a young child you probably learned that a stove is hot. You learned this because the first time you touched the stove, you felt the heat and immediately removed your hand.

POLITICAL CARTOON
Conditioning

Conditioning is a form of learning through experience. Scientists have performed experiments that show that even animals, like dogs and mice, can be conditioned to behave in certain ways.

The mice are trying to use conditioning to train a person to provide them with food.

"Remember, every time he gives you a pellet, reinforce that behavior by pulling the lever."

ANALYSIS SKILL **ANALYZING POLITICAL CARTOONS**

Make Inferences What point about conditioning is this political cartoon attempting to make?

Conditioning

You may have learned something else from this experience. When you touched the stove, an adult may have warned you, "Hot!" The next time you tried to touch the stove and heard that warning, you probably drew back your hand. Then you stayed away from the stove. This is a type of learning called **conditioning**.

Much of our behavior is learned by conditioning. If we are rewarded for our actions, then we are conditioned to repeat them. Some behaviors become habits. A **habit** is an action that we do automatically without thinking about it. We learn habits by repeating an action over and over again.

Imitation

We also learn by copying, or imitating, other people. As a child, you may have learned how to use a water fountain by copying someone else. Or perhaps you learned how to cook a meal by imitating a family member.

Observing

Much of what we learn comes through observation. We gain information through our senses—by looking, listening, touching, smelling, and tasting.

Learning Has No Limits

Everyone has the potential to learn, but how much you learn ultimately lies with you. You need to have the motivation to make the most of your experiences. **Motivation** is the internal drive to achieve your goals. Motivation is not something anyone else can teach you. You have to develop your own drive to succeed.

Learning in School

Schools today make good use of all of the ways in which human beings learn. They teach you where to look to find information on your own. They show you how to collect information from many sources and how to put facts together to reach your own conclusions. They

RADIO

War of the Worlds

On Sunday, October 30, 1938, millions of Americans sat listening to their radios. Listeners expecting to hear the broadcast of the Mercury Theater's weekly radio play received a shocking surprise. Invaders from Mars, it seemed, had landed in New Jersey and were heading for New York City!

In the early 1900s millions of Americans turned to radio broadcasts for entertainment. One popular program was Orson Welles's Mercury Theater on the Air, which dramatized well-known novels and plays. When the group decided to present H. G. Wells's science fiction novel, *The War of the Worlds,* they performed it as a real-life news program. So realistic was their presentation that thousands of listeners believed New York was under attack by aliens. Panicked listeners called police stations, hid in basements, and looked for ways to protect themselves.

Most listeners, however, knew there was no Martian invasion. *The War of the Worlds* taught many Americans to question and think critically about the media—and not to believe everything they hear.

This photo shows Orson Welles broadcasting *The War of the Worlds.*

go.hrw.com

ANALYSIS SKILL **MEDIA LITERACY** KEYWORD: SZ7 CH14

Drawing Conclusions What techniques might the presenters have used to convince people that the invasion was real?

---

allow you to work with others and make the most of your peers' skills and ideas.

READING CHECK **Finding the Main Idea** How do we learn from experience?

Learning to Think Critically

ACADEMIC VOCABULARY

complex: difficult, not simple

The most important skill we learn is how to think. Thinking is a **complex** process. It involves considering options, forming opinions, and making judgments.

How We Think

There are several ways to think. One way, called **insight**, is thinking that seems to come from your heart more than your mind. Sometimes you do not have direct experience with a problem, but you have the ability to see the details of a problem and understand it. Your insight comes from your experiences with other similar situations.

Another type of thinking is **creativity**. Creativity is the ability to find new ways to think about or do things. Everyone can think creatively. Whenever you solve a problem, you have used your creativity.

You have other thinking abilities as well. You can question and weigh information. You can draw conclusions and make predictions.

Critical Thinking

If someone told you that there is a car that drives itself, would you believe it? It seems possible, but you would probably want proof. Maybe you would like to read or hear more about it. Perhaps you would like to see this car for yourself, or better yet, take a ride in it before you decide whether it is real.

The thinking that we do to reach decisions and to solve problems is called **critical thinking**. Critical thinking involves several steps.

Defining the Issues The first step in critical thinking is identifying the issue, or problem at hand. Define the issue by looking for the main idea and turning it into a question.

Distinguishing Fact from Opinion Once you identify the issue, you need to find information to help you understand and judge the issue. Some information is fact and some is opinion. What are facts? Facts are pieces of information that can be proved by looking them up in resources like dictionaries or encyclopedias. Opinions are feelings or ideas that people have about the facts. Sometimes it is difficult to tell the difference between fact and opinion. Key phrases like "I think," "I believe," and "in my opinion" can alert you to statements of opinion. Be on the lookout for both facts and opinions when researching an issue.

Weighing the Evidence When you think about the information surrounding an issue, you are weighing the evidence. To weigh the evidence, look for all the information that can help you make a judgment about an issue. Use tables, charts, graphs, and other resources. Find facts that might be missing. After you have fully considered all the evidence, you are ready to make a decision.

Reaching a Conclusion The last and most important step in critical thinking is reaching a conclusion. This is the point where you say, "I think this because . . ." Reaching a conclusion can be difficult. Sometimes there is more than one solution to a problem. In that case, make a mental test of each solution to decide which is best. Some solutions work only under certain conditions. Imagine different outcomes. Then decide on the best possible solution. Keep an open mind when you make your final decision. New information may lead you to change your mind.

READING CHECK ⮞ **Summarizing** What are the steps involved in critical thinking?

MATH 101

Statistics and Polls

Since groups that conduct polls cannot ask everyone to answer their questions, they must choose a *sample* of the group of people they wish to poll. If this sample is not carefully chosen, poll results may be inaccurate. In the following poll, a sample of students were asked about their future plans. Here are the results:

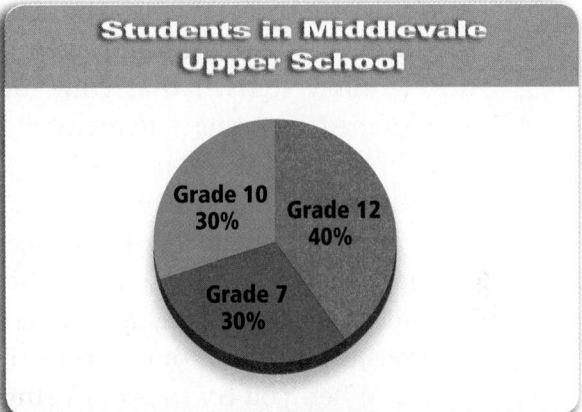

Students in Middlevale Upper School

- Grade 12 40%
- Grade 10 30%
- Grade 7 30%

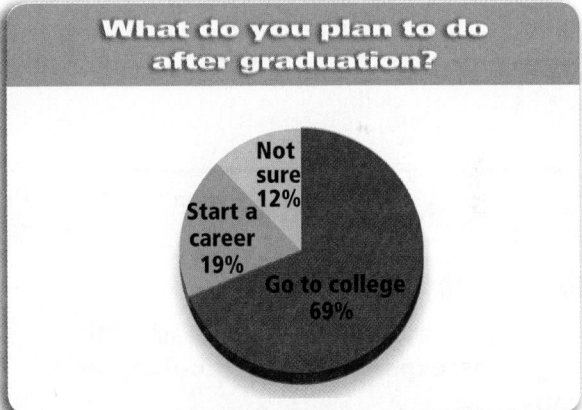

What do you plan to do after graduation?

- Go to college 69%
- Start a career 19%
- Not sure 12%

Using the poll results, you can learn more by estimating. To estimate how many of those polled were seventh graders who plan to go to college, multiply the percent of those expecting to go to college (69%) by the percent of seventh graders in the sample (30%). An estimated 21 percent of those polled were seventh graders who plan to go to college.

ANALYSIS SKILL **ANALYZING CHARTS**

Use the information above to estimate how many seventh graders plan to start a career.

Learn to Think for Yourself

We all like to think that our ideas are our own. No one tells us what to think. But have you ever changed your mind about a favorite song or video because someone told you they did not like it?

Influences on Your Thinking

We are all influenced by the opinions of others. Since you were small, the adults in your life have shaped your ideas about the world. Many of us are also influenced by the ideas of our friends and even celebrities. Remind yourself that your ideas are also shaped by others. Remember, when you think critically, you also look closely at your own opinions. Few of us are free from bias or prejudices. **Prejudice** is an opinion that is not based on the facts. Prejudices are common, and it is tough to avoid them, either our own or those of others. When you try to avoid being influenced by prejudice, though, you can judge an issue more fairly.

Thinking for Yourself

In Los Angeles, California, a group of students recently became angry about the number of large billboards advertising alcohol and tobacco products near their schools. They knew that companies should not be encouraging young people to drink and smoke. The students formed a group and succeeded in getting the billboards removed. In the end, the advertising companies put up antismoking signs that the students created themselves.

Thinking critically and forming your own opinions may be difficult. Sometimes a parent, teacher, or trusted adult, can help you learn to think for yourself. Learning to be a critical thinker takes practice and some effort. Often you have to look behind the stories you hear on TV. But the critical thinking skills you learn in school will help you be a responsible, active citizen.

READING CHECK **Draw Conclusions** Why is it important in a democracy for voters to think for themselves?

SECTION 3 ASSESSMENT

Reviewing Ideas and Terms

1. **a. Define** Write a brief definition of each of the following terms: **experience, conditioning, habit,** and **motivation**.
   b. Analyze What is the relationship between learning and experience?
2. **a. Define** Write a brief definition of each of the following terms: **insight, creativity,** and **critical thinking**.
   b. Sequence What are the steps involved in critical thinking? Which step, in your opinion, is most important and why?
3. **a. Define** Write a brief definition of the following term: **prejudice**.
   b. Draw Conclusions Why should you learn to think for yourself?

Critical Thinking

4. **Finding Main Ideas** Draw a graphic organizer like the one here on your own sheet of paper. Use the graphic organizer and your notes to write three sentences that identify the main ideas from this section.

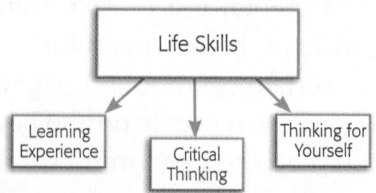

Focus on Writing

5. **Supporting a Position** Create a pamphlet that supports your position on creating an astronomy club as a school-sponsored activity.

FOUNDATIONS
of **DEMOCRACY**

Drug Testing in Schools

Is drug testing an issue in your school? Even if it is not, drug use by teenagers is a major concern in our society. In 2002 the U.S. Supreme Court upheld the rights of school districts to require random drug testing for all students who participate in extracurricular activities. Previously the Court had supported drug testing for student athletes, mainly for health reasons.

Why it Matters

For many years schools have been looking for ways to combat illegal drug use. Drug use can be tied to many problems that plague our schools, including poor student performance, violence, and the dropout rate. Because drugs can affect the health of students, many schools began requiring that student athletes be tested for drug use. Soon, some schools began to expand the number of students to be tested to include other extracurricular activities. Currently, several states require some level of student drug testing in all high schools.

Some people object to random drug testing, arguing that it is a violation of students' privacy. Others claim that drug testing is unnecessary if there is no reasonable suspicion that a student has used illegal drugs.

School administrators often argue that the fear of being caught by a drug test might prevent some students from trying drugs in the first place. The courts have sided with schools, saying that the needs of school districts to protect students come before student privacy rights.

High school athletes are often tested for drugs.

ANALYSIS SKILL **EVALUATING THE LAW**

go.hrw.com
KEYWORD: SZ7 CH14

1. Why do you think the courts have sided with school districts in supporting student drug testing?
2. Do you think random drug testing is a good way to prevent teens from using drugs? Why or why not?

Visual Summary

Use the visual summary to help you review the main ideas of the chapter.

Education is vital to American society. It teaches important values and provides us with many opportunities.

QUICK FACTS

Reviewing Vocabulary Terms

For each of the terms below, write a sentence explaining its significance to citizenship in school.

1. university
2. mainstreaming
3. extracurricular activities
4. experience
5. conditioning
6. habit
7. motivation
8. insight
9. creativity
10. critical thinking
11. prejudice

Comprehension and Critical Thinking

SECTION 1 *(Pages 338–342)*

12. **a. Recall** What are the two main reasons that Americans value education?

    b. Draw Conclusions Why does a college graduate have more career choices than a person who quits school after the sixth grade?

    c. Evaluate What are the advantages of mainstreaming students?

SECTION 2 *(Pages 344–348)*

13. **a. Describe** What approaches to learning and studying will make you more successful in school?

    b. Make Inferences Why is the wise use of time an important study habit?

    c. Predict How can participating in extracurricular activities improve your chances of getting a college scholarship?

Active Citizenship video program

Review the video to answer the closing question: *How can educating young people about healthy choices make a difference now and in the future?*

SECTION 3 *(Pages 350–354)*

14. a. Summarize What must a student do to develop and exercise critical thinking skills?

b. Explain What are the benefits of thinking through problems and issues for yourself?

c. Support a Point of View Which do you think is more important to the learning process—critical thinking or creative thinking? Explain your answer, using examples of each type of thinking.

Using the Internet

go.hrw.com
KEYWORD: SZ7 CH14

15. Preparing for Tests Part of the challenge of taking a test is preparing for it and developing the right skills to successfully approach it. Enter the activity keyword to research different ways of studying and preparing for tests. Then choose one method you found in your research and prepare a short report or oral presentation that describes the method and explains why you think it could be effective and useful.

Civics Skills

16. Creating a Multimedia Presentation Using the Civics Skills you learned in this chapter, create a multimedia presentation about the seven goals of education. In your presentation, use audio, video, animation, graphic art, computer graphics, or other media to illustrate each of the seven goals. You may use one medium or a combination of different media to present these concepts to your audience. Write a script for your presentation, including the text of your speech, a description of the media you are using, and an explanation of how the media is being used to illustrate each point. Finally, deliver your multimedia presentation to the class.

Reading Skills

Summarizing Text *Use the Reading Skills taught in this chapter to answer the question about the reading selection below.*

Today, most schools offer a wide range of subjects and are filled with many different types of people. Students have opportunities to learn more than just academics. Modern schools have become the rich and varied environment they are because of some basic American values that are part of the U.S. education system. *(p. 341)*

17. Which of the following is a good summary of the selection?

a. Schools today teach basic American values.

b. Today's schools provide opportunities to learn many things.

c. You can study what you want in today's schools.

d. A varied environment is a basic American value.

FOCUS ON WRITING

18. Designing Your Web Site Look back at your notes and how you have organized them. Have you included all important facts and details? Will people be able to find information easily? What will appear in menus or as hot links, and elsewhere on the page? What images will you include? Draw a rough diagram or sketch of your page. Be sure to label the parts of your page.

CHAPTER 15

CITIZENSHIP IN THE COMMUNITY

SECTION 1
Kinds of Communities

SECTION 2
Purposes of Communities

SECTION 3
Citizens Serve Communities

NATIONAL STANDARDS®
FOR CIVICS AND GOVERNMENT

II. What are the foundations of the American political system?

B. What are the distinctive characteristics of American society?

V. What are the roles of the citizen in American democracy?

A. What is citizenship?

C. What are the responsibilities of citizens?

D. What civic dispositions or traits of private and public character are important to the preservation and improvement of American constitutional democracy?

E. How can citizens take part in civic life?

©1994, 2003 Center for Civic Education. All Rights Reserved.

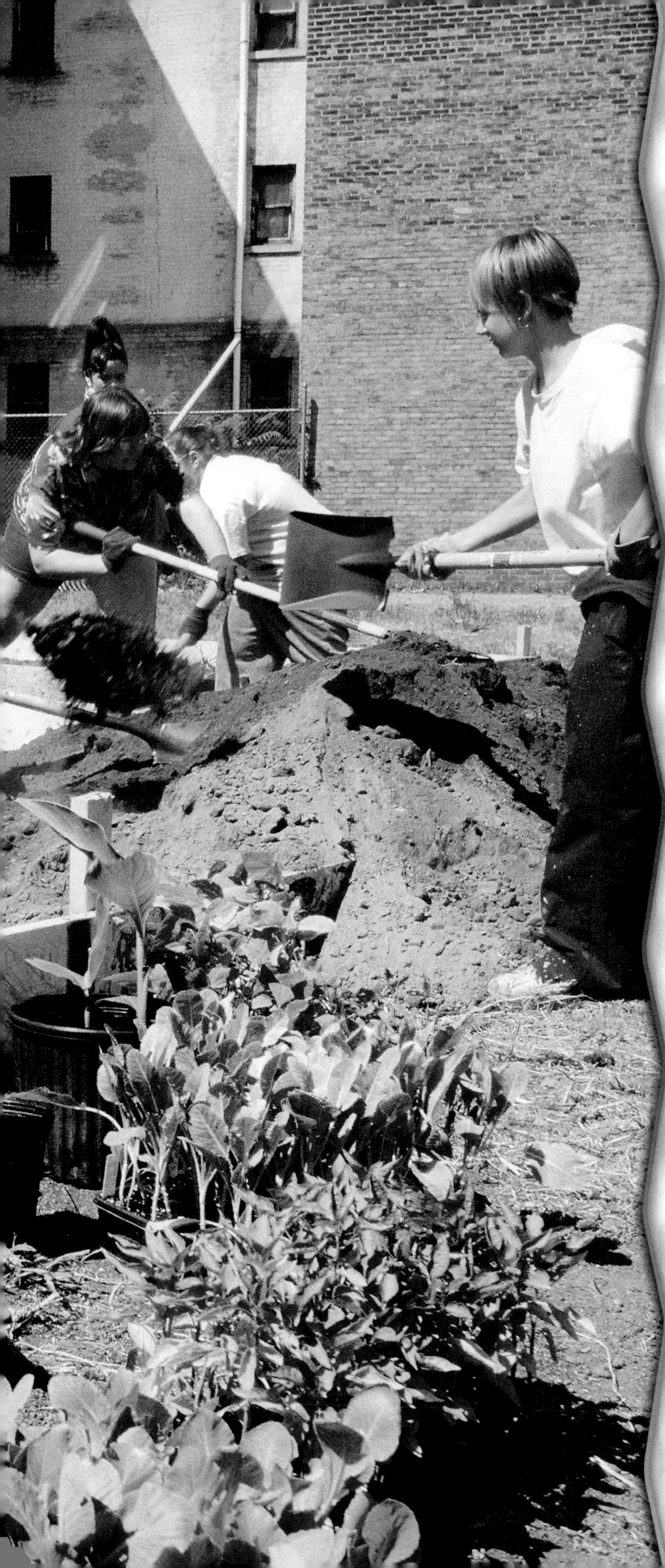

Active Citizenship video program
Watch the video to evaluate how government works to make everyday life accessible to people with disabilities.

WHY CIVICS Matters

A community is a group of people with common interests who live in the same area. Communities provide valuable goods and services for citizens. Citizens have a responsibility in return to make their community a good place to live.

STUDENTS TAKE ACTION

HELPING THE ELDERLY You may have a relative who lives in an assisted living facility (ALF). Wouldn't you want them to have the best care possible? Students in Hialeah, Florida, are working to improve the regulations governing ALFs. What could you do to improve the life of someone in your community?

FOCUS ON WRITING

WRITING A BROCHURE You've been hired to create a brochure called "Our Community." Your brochure will describe your community and the things it has to offer people who are considering moving to your city. As you read this chapter, think about all the ways that good citizenship can make a community a great place to live.

Reading Skills

In this chapter you will read about the kinds of communities in the United States. You will learn about the factors that influence the prosperity of different communities. You will read about the important purposes that communities serve for their citizens. You will read about how communities plan and carry out improvements. Finally, you will learn some ways that citizens can volunteer to improve and serve their communities.

Making Inferences

FOCUS ON READING An inference is a conclusion reached on the basis of evidence and reasoning. In other words, it is a result based on some knowledge or information.

Making Inferences About What You Read To make an inference, combine information from your reading with what you already know. Then make an educated guess about what it means. You may make more than one inference from your reading, and you may make a final inference from all the information you have.

Helpful Hints for Making Inferences

1. Ask a question.
2. Think about what you already know about the topic.
3. Think about what you are learning while you read about the topic.
4. Use both sets of information to make an educated guess, or inference.
5. You can draw more than one inference from the information you have. Sometimes there are several possible inferences you can draw.

Question: Why is my town growing so fast?

New Information	Information You know
• Climate and natural resources help communities to grow.	• My town has a mild climate and nice lakes.
• Communities often grow along major highways.	• A road to a city nearby has just been repaired.
• Rural areas are becoming more popular places to live or work.	• My town is definitely a suburb and not rural.
	• People keep moving to my town.

Inferences:

1. Good weather and natural resources are likely contributing to growth in my town.
2. The repaired road may be close enough to contribute to growth here.
3. My town may be rural enough to attract new citizens.

Final inference:

The most likely causes of growth in my town are the climate and natural resources. The highway factor may also be contributing to growth, but being a suburb probably is not.

You Try It!

The following passage is from the chapter you are about to read. Read it and then answer the questions below.

Types of Rural Communities

Chapter 15, p. 364

A rural area is a region of farms and small towns. Not all rural communities are agricultural. In general, there are two main types of rural communities.

Rural Farm Communities

The people who live and work on farms make up America's smallest kind of community—the rural farm community. Today there are about 2 million farms in the United States. They can be found in all regions of the country. Types of farms differ from region to region, though, because of climate differences.

Small Country Towns

Another kind of rural community is the small country town. Small country towns may have populations of less than 2,500 and are usually located near open farmland. These towns serve as places where farmers can buy supplies or sell their farm crops and animals.

After you have read the passage, answer the following questions.

1. Why might small country towns be located near open farmland?

2. Which of the following inferences can you draw from the information above?
   a. The two types of rural communities probably depend on each other.
   b. Farms in different climate regions may grow different crops.
   c. Most rural farm communities probably have fewer than 2,500 people.
   d. All of the above.

KEY TERMS

Chapter 15

Section 1
community *(p. 362)*
resources *(p. 362)*
climate *(p. 362)*
crossroads *(p. 364)*
megalopolis *(p. 365)*

Section 2
communication *(p. 367)*
public utility *(p. 369)*
recreation *(p. 369)*

Section 3
compulsory *(p. 372)*

Academic Vocabulary
Success in school is related to knowing academic vocabulary—the words that are frequently used in school assignments and discussions. In this chapter you will learn the following academic words:

factors *(p. 363)*
efficiently *(p. 367)*
purpose *(p. 374)*

As you read Chapter 15, use the information you find in the text to make inferences about your community.

Kinds of Communities

BEFORE YOU READ

The Main Idea

There are many kinds of communities. Some are located in transportation centers or farming regions. Others grow where there are jobs in factories or offices. Communities may be small or large, but all of them take advantage of their surroundings.

Reading Focus

1. What factors affect the location of communities?
2. What types of communities exist in rural areas?
3. What types of communities exist in urban areas?

Key Terms

community, *p. 362*
resources, *p. 362*
climate, *p. 362*
crossroads, *p. 364*
megalopolis, *p. 365*

TAKING NOTES As you read, take notes on the different kinds of communities found in the United States. Use an organizer like this one to record your notes.

Kinds of Communities

A neighborhood and the people who live there may be a community.

CIVICS IN PRACTICE Most of you usually live close to where your parents work. But why do they live there? Do they have family nearby? Was it a job that brought them there? Do they enjoy living in the city? These are some of the factors that determine where you may live one day.

Factors Affecting the Location of Communities

A **community** is a group of people who have common interests and live in the same area. Three **factors** affect where Americans build communities. The first factor is **resources**, or natural features of the land that people may use for living. The second factor is **climate**, or the weather. Plentiful resources and good weather tend to attract settlers. The third factor involves the convenience of local transportation. People want to live near where they work and the places they visit for recreation.

Communities

Communities form for different reasons. Amish communities, above left, share religious beliefs. Chinese communities, above right, reflect a shared culture.

What do the people who live in your community have in common?

The Importance of Resources

The greater the variety of resources in a region, the easier it is for the people who live there to become self-sufficient. On the other hand, a surplus of one or more key resources can bring enough wealth for a community to buy what it cannot produce for itself.

The United States has a rich supply of natural resources. For early American settlers, one of the most vital resources was land itself. Fertile soil helped farming prosper. Vast forests provided wood for fuel and construction. Rivers, lakes, and streams supplied fresh water. Eventually, mineral resources such as coal, iron, and petroleum helped fuel the Industrial Revolution. Yet the nation's growth has also brought with it the increasing challenge of how to manage the resources we have so that we continue to benefit from them.

Climate Matters

In some ways, the climate of an area can be seen as a resource. Successful farming depends on having enough rain and a long enough growing season. Weather can also create an environment that attracts tourists. Regular snowfall attracts people interested in winter sports, while many people flock to coastal areas with warm, sunny climates. The impact of climate has changed over time, however. Since fewer people are farmers, the suitability of local weather for raising crops also has less influence today on how people live.

Ease of Access

Abundant resources and an excellent climate are of little use if an area is too hard to reach. Communities often develop along convenient transportation routes. The first European colonists in North America settled along the eastern shore. The best seaports there became large cities that benefited from overseas trade, such as Boston, Charleston, New York, and Philadelphia. As settlers moved inland, they found travel by land to be difficult and slow. Water travel was much easier. So communities grew up along major rivers and lakes. For example, port towns along the Mississippi River—such as St. Louis and New Orleans—grew into major cities.

ACADEMIC VOCABULARY
factors:
causes

Communities also sprang up at places where two main roads met, called **crossroads**. When railroads began spreading across the country in the late 1840s, they created new crossroads and new settlements. Today automobiles are our major method of daily transportation, so the location of major highways has a huge impact on community growth.

Founding a community based on any of the three main factors has risks. A valuable resource may be used up over time, causing the community to suffer. Natural disasters like hurricanes and floods can strike towns and cities built along coastlines and rivers. Even ease of access can change if a new highway draws traffic away from a town or congestion slows down road travel. People are constantly weighing these changing factors when deciding where to live.

READING CHECK **Summarizing** How do resources, climate, and transportation influence the location of cities?

Types of Rural Communities

A rural area is a region of farms and small towns. Not all rural communities are agricultural. In general, there are two main types of rural communities.

Rural Farm Communities

The people who live and work on farms make up America's smallest kind of community— the rural farm community. Today there are about 2 million farms in the United States. They can be found in all regions of the country. Types of farms differ from region to region, though, because of climate differences.

Small Country Towns

Another kind of rural community is the small country town. Small country towns may have populations of less than 2,500 and are usually located near open farmland. These towns serve as places where farmers can buy supplies or sell their farm crops and animals.

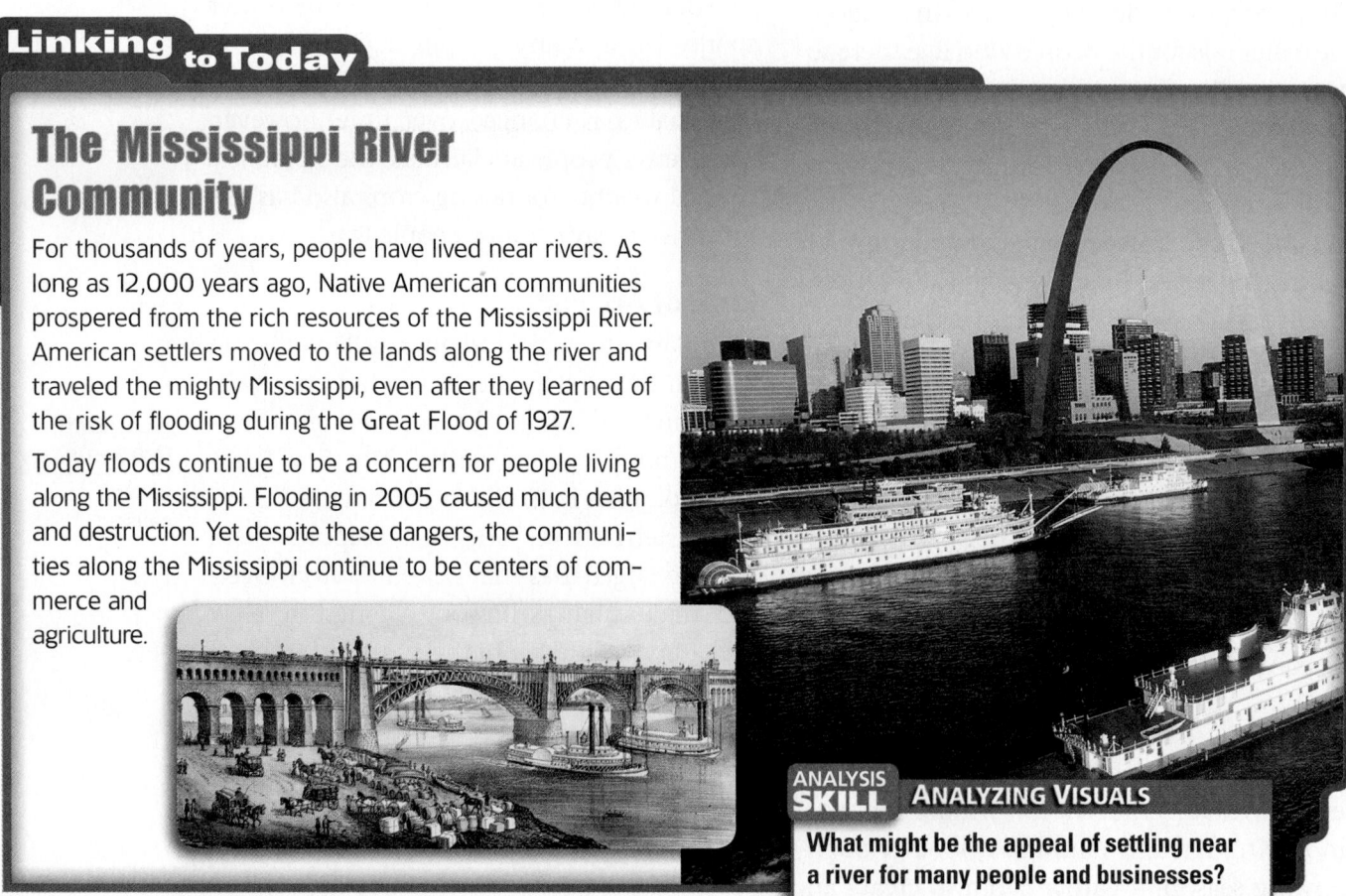

Linking to Today

The Mississippi River Community

For thousands of years, people have lived near rivers. As long as 12,000 years ago, Native American communities prospered from the rich resources of the Mississippi River. American settlers moved to the lands along the river and traveled the mighty Mississippi, even after they learned of the risk of flooding during the Great Flood of 1927.

Today floods continue to be a concern for people living along the Mississippi. Flooding in 2005 caused much death and destruction. Yet despite these dangers, the communities along the Mississippi continue to be centers of commerce and agriculture.

ANALYSIS SKILL **ANALYZING VISUALS**

What might be the appeal of settling near a river for many people and businesses?

As the country has grown, however, rural communities have been disappearing. Now less than 1 percent of the U.S. population is made up of farmers. Recently, some rural areas have begun to grow again. Small businesses sometimes move to rural areas, where land is often cheaper than in large cities.

> **READING CHECK** **Finding the Main Idea** What is the difference between the two types of communities you find in rural areas?

Types of Urban Communities

There are many different kinds of urban areas in the United States. Most urban areas also have nearby suburbs.

Urban Communities

The Census Bureau classifies areas as urban if they have a core of census blocks that have a population density of at least 1,000 people per square mile and surrounding census blocks that have an overall density of at least 500 people per square mile. Many Americans today live in urban areas. According to the 2000 census, 80 percent of all Americans live in urban communities. But recent data shows that 68 of the 251 largest U.S. cities lost population between 2000 and 2004. Today more than half of the nation's urban population lives outside the central cities, in areas called suburbs.

Suburbs

Suburbs have been growing ever since modern transportation allowed people to live away from where they work. A suburb is a town, village, or community located on the outskirts of a city. People who live in the suburbs often work in the city. Suburbs are very attractive to many people. They are smaller than cities, and some people prefer life in a smaller community. Suburbs have been growing so fast, though, that many suburban areas are now facing the same challenges as cities.

Metropolitan Areas

Some urban areas have become so large that it is hard to tell where these cities end and where the suburbs begin. A community like this—a large city and its surrounding towns and suburbs—is called a metropolitan area, or a metropolis. Some metropolitan areas have grown so large that they form a continuous urban chain. This type of giant urban area is called a **megalopolis**. The metropolitan areas of Boston, New York City, Philadelphia, Baltimore, and Washington, D.C., form a megalopolis along the Atlantic coast.

> **READING CHECK** **Summarizing** How are urban, suburban, and metropolitan areas different?

SECTION 1 ASSESSMENT

Reviewing Ideas and Terms

1. **a. Define** Write a brief definition for the terms **community**, **resources**, **climate**, and **crossroads**.
   b. Elaborate What types of businesses might do well in a community that lies along a major transportation route, like a rail line or a highway?
2. **a. Recall** What is a rural area?
   b. Predict Why might some rural communities try to attract small businesses?
3. **a. Define** Write a brief definition for the term **megalopolis**.
   b. Compare and Contrast How are an urban area and a metropolitan area similar and different?

Critical Thinking

4. **Contrasting** Copy the graphic organizer. Use it to identify the two types of communities that exist in rural America today and describe how they are different.

Country Town	Farm

Focus on Writing

5. **Evaluating** Write an editorial describing advantages and disadvantages of living in the suburbs compared to living in an urban area. Tell which area you would prefer to live in and why.

Purposes of Communities

BEFORE YOU READ

The Main Idea

People live together in communities for many reasons. Communities provide people with ways to communicate with one another and relax in their free time. Communities also provide services and local governments that help residents make the most of their resources and labor.

Reading Focus

1. What kinds of values do communities teach?
2. What types of services do communities provide?

Key Terms

communication, *p. 367*
public utility, *p. 369*
recreation, *p. 369*

TAKING NOTES As you read, take notes on the different purposes of communities. Use an organizer like this one to record your notes. Add more boxes if you need to.

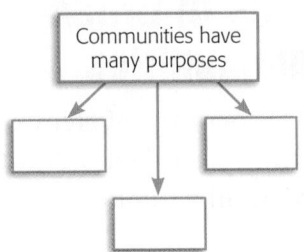

Communities have many purposes

Communities help teach people how to interact with others.

CIVICS IN PRACTICE

Could you clear a forest, build a house, farm the land, and make your own clothes and tools? Very few of us could. Life requires so many skills that one person would find it hard—if not impossible—to master all of them. So we rely on others to provide us with some things so that we can do other work. The necessity to cooperate led to the development of communities. Members of a community provide services for each other.

Communities Teach Values

People who live in any kind of community have to learn to get along with other people. No matter where you go, you will have to deal with other people. Two basic values—communicating with others and respect for laws—make getting along much easier.

Communication

You probably talk with your friends every day—and probably more than once a day! When you talk, you exchange all the latest news about other friends, your family, or the day's events. People want and need this kind of contact. The passing along of information, ideas, and beliefs from one person to another is known as **communication**.

Communication is an important reason people live in communities. Problems may seem less difficult when a person can talk them over with someone else. When you gather and share information, you are also adding to what you know about things around you. This knowledge makes it easier to reach good decisions and choices. Not only that, but knowing and understanding what is happening with your friends and neighbors will help you learn to respect them more.

Respect for Laws

Communities have governments in place to help citizens avoid conflict. In addition to providing basic services, local governments pass ordinances and laws to regulate everyday life. People who live together in a community need laws and regulations to keep order and live at peace with one another. Local courts, judges, and law enforcement officers help us follow the rules, so that everyone has the opportunity for a happy, successful life.

Local governments also provide citizens with a forum to discuss and address problems before they get out of hand. Local government is a way for you and your neighbors to participate in running your own community. By respecting each other and respecting the law, you and other members of your community can live together successfully.

READING CHECK **Finding the Main Idea** What do good communication and respecting the law have in common?

Community Services

We take many services in daily life for granted. When the electricity goes out in a thunderstorm, for example, we expect the electric company to repair the lines and restore power as quickly as possible. If there is a fire, the fire department will be there to fight the blaze within minutes.

FOCUS ON Given Kachepa
(1987—   )

Given Kachepa was an 11-year-old orphan in Zambia when he met an American who asked him to join a touring boys choir in the United States. The director promised that Kachepa would earn a salary and be educated, and that money would be sent to build schools in Zambia. Instead, Kachepa performed six or seven times a day for no money, with very little food, and no education.

After a year and a half of nonstop touring, American immigration officials discovered the scam and rescued the boys in the choir. Kachepa remained in the States. He then began appearing on national television and testifying to lawmakers about penalties for this type of crime.

In 2005 the Prudential Foundation recognized Kachepa as one of America's top ten youth volunteers and awarded him $5,000 for himself and $5,000 for the charity of his choice. Kachepa was honored in Congress and the Texas legislature. In 2005, Kachepa enrolled as a student at Stephen F. Austin State University in Texas.

Analyzing Information How did Kachepa contribute to his community?

Services like these are easier to provide in a community. People in a community can meet certain needs more **efficiently** by working together than by working separately. This is a major reason why people form communities. By pooling their resources and labor, members of villages and towns can improve the quality of life for everyone. Today communities provide a wide variety of services to their citizens.

ACADEMIC VOCABULARY
efficiently: productive and not wasteful

Safety

There are certain basic services that you and your neighbors expect from your community. You want to live in a community where you and your property are safe from violence and harm. In most communities, the police force and fire department help keep you and your neighbors safe.

The Planned Community

QUICK FACTS

Modern planned communities have roads, utilities, and housing for people. They may also have a bus or rail station so residents can travel easily to a nearby city. These communities also provide for social institutions, such as education, health care, recreation, religion, and civic organizations. Some communities also include small commercial centers, such as retail stores and small businesses. Often, these communities have housing for people with different income levels. Residents usually participate in governing the community.

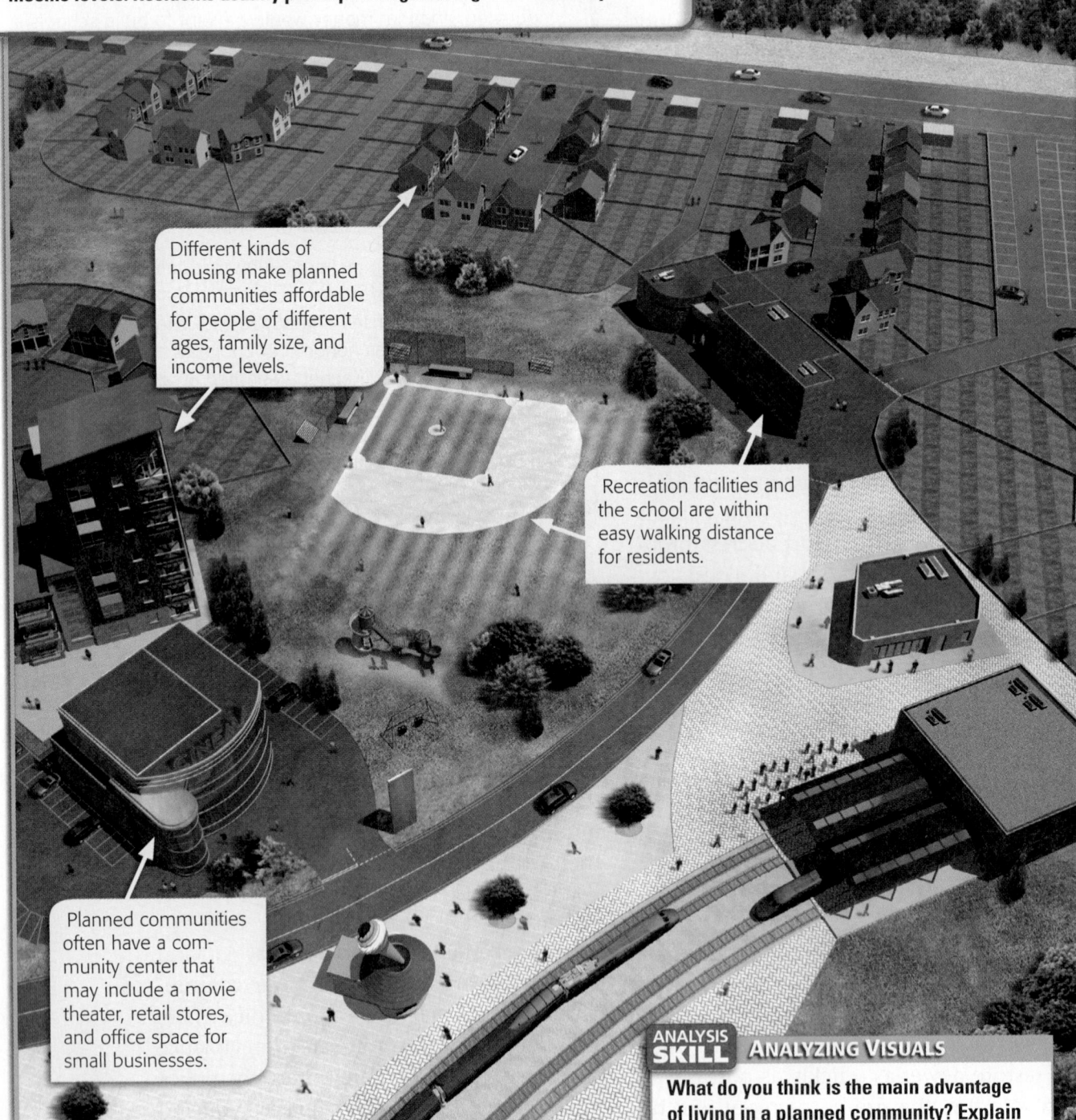

Different kinds of housing make planned communities affordable for people of different ages, family size, and income levels.

Recreation facilities and the school are within easy walking distance for residents.

Planned communities often have a community center that may include a movie theater, retail stores, and office space for small businesses.

ANALYSIS SKILL ANALYZING VISUALS

What do you think is the main advantage of living in a planned community? Explain your answer.

Education

Public schools provide an education to all of a community's young people. In many communities, some students attend private schools, and some students are home-schooled. In some communities, businesses and other local organizations provide tutoring and educational support for students who need extra help.

Public Utilities

Water, sewage, electricity, and trash collection are basic services. They are usually provided by public utilities. A **public utility** is one of a group of industries providing services, such as water, gas, and electricity, to both domestic and business customers. Public utilities are considered special industries. Everyone in a community needs their services. Utilities also need access to both public and private property to operate. Think of all the power and telephone lines you see in a typical neighborhood. Now consider all the pipelines that you cannot see, which carry gas, water, and sewage. Together these form a distribution network.

Sometimes local governments furnish these services. In other cases, private companies perform the necessary tasks. However these services are provided, citizens usually pay for them with some combination of fees and local taxes.

Recreation

Nearly all U.S. cities and towns have places of recreation, such as bowling alleys, movie theaters, parks, and skating rinks. **Recreation** is relaxation or amusement that comes from playing or doing something different from your usual activities. Sporting events and outdoor activities are popular forms of recreation.

A lot of recreational activities are free, like picnicking in parks or riding on a bicycle trail. However, it costs money to provide places where you may spend your leisure time. Many recreational facilities are maintained at public expense. Taxes support public playgrounds, athletic fields, picnic grounds, basketball courts, and golf courses.

In some communities, recreation is not just for local people. Unusually good climate or special geographical locations have helped certain communities attract tourists to their recreation destinations. Many lake communities and seaside towns offer boating, swimming, and water-skiing as special attractions. Rural communities promote hunting and fishing in their areas. Other communities have developed hiking, horseback riding, rock climbing, and skiing facilities.

READING CHECK **Analyzing Information** How do both basic services and recreational facilities contribute to the well-being of communities?

SECTION 2 ASSESSMENT

Reviewing Ideas and Terms

1. a. Define Write a brief definition of the term **communication**.
   b. Summarize What are two values that communities teach?
2. a. Define Write a brief definition of the terms **public utility** and **recreation**.
   b. Rank List the services that communities provide in order of importance, with number one being the service that you think is most important.

Critical Thinking

3. Summarizing Copy the graphic organizer. Use it to explain how communities help people enjoy their lives.

How communities bring enjoyment

Focus on Writing

4. Problem Solving Imagine that you have just been named to head the community services division of your local government. Write a recommendation to the mayor for ways to improve the existing services in your community.

Analyzing Talk Radio

Learn

Thousands of people every day turn on the radio, but not all of them listen to music. Talk radio programs are increasingly popular all around the nation. Talk radio is a format that focuses on discussion and often includes input from listeners. Today there are many different types of talk radio programs, from shows that discuss car repairs to gardening programs to political discussions.

Some of the most popular talk radio programs today deal with politics and current events. Many political talk radio programs represent balanced points of view. Often, however, political radio shows are one-sided. They may express liberal or conservative ideas, depending on the views of the host and the listeners. While listening to talk radio can be informative and entertaining, it is important to carefully analyze the views and ideas you hear.

Practice

❶ **Remember that talk radio is entertainment.** People tune in to talk radio to hear the latest news, funny commentary, and even extreme opinions. Even on political programs, the hosts try to grab listeners' attention by saying outrageous things.

❷ **Consider the views of callers carefully.** Many shows allow people to call in with questions or comments. Callers' ideas may not be factual or appropriate; on the other hand, some callers may present valid arguments against the host's opinions.

❸ **Look for political opinion.** The commentators on news shows may have political points of view. Learn to tell the difference between the news facts and the political opinions of hosts and commentators. Document evidence of the point of view.

Apply

Use the illustrated example of a talk radio program schedule shown below to answer the following questions.

1. Are there any shows in this station's weekly schedule that avoid political topics? Give evidence to explain your answer.

2. Explain which program you would select to hear the day's news.

3. What types of callers might you expect to hear on *Smith and Kelly*? Why?

	MON	TUE	WED	THU	FRI
6:00 AM	\multicolumn{5}{} **Breaking News Now** — The only one-hour talk news program that brings you the latest on all of today's headlines from around the nation and the world.				
7:00 AM	**The Shawn Michaels Report** — Two hours of political commentary from America's highest-rated talk radio host.				
8:00 AM					
9:00 AM	**Smith and Kelly** — The only show on talk radio today that brings you both political points of view. Conservative author Jim Smith and liberal journalist Bruce Kelly debate the issues and answer questions that all Americans need to hear.				
10:00 AM					
11:00 AM					
12:00 PM	**Talking Sports** — America's favorite sports talk host, Sal Peters, tackles the toughest issues in sports today and answers questions from listeners like you.				
1:00 PM					

SECTION 3

Citizens Serve Communities

BEFORE YOU READ

The Main Idea

Communities provide many benefits and services to their residents. But citizens also need to contribute their energy and efforts if they want their communities to remain welcoming and healthy. Communities depend on cooperation among people.

Reading Focus

1. How can citizens help their communities face challenges?
2. Why is volunteering important to help improve the communities in which we live?

Key Terms

compulsory, *p. 372*

TAKING NOTES As you read, take notes on how citizens can serve their communities. Use a concept web like this one to record your notes.

How Citizens Serve Communities

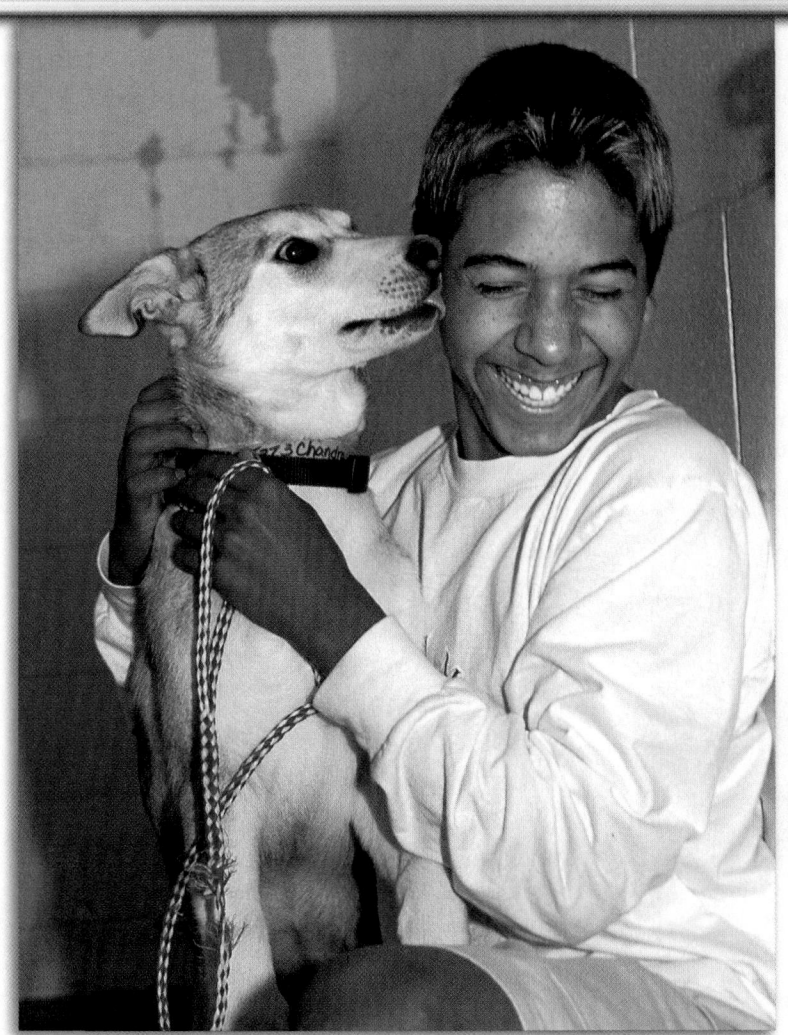
One way you could serve your community is to volunteer at a local animal shelter.

CIVICS IN PRACTICE "The more you give, the more you get." You've probably heard this expression. It is as true in a community as it is in other aspects of life. Citizens working together can help each other build a strong community. In turn, a strong community is more able to help its citizens.

Helping Your Community

Communities are people. People can make the community a good place to live or a place you want to get away from as quickly as possible. Communities depend on people to act in ways that help the community. Following rules that respect others in the community and volunteering are key ways citizens can help.

Good Citizens Make Good Communities

How do you define your community? Is it your neighborhood, your city or town, or your county? The smallest community to which you belong is your family. You are also a member of the largest community—the global community of people all over the world.

How You Can Get Involved

QUICK FACTS

One aspect of good citizenship is being involved with people or organizations in your community.

What are other ways for you to be involved with your community? Describe two ways you can think of.

① Volunteer at an organization that serves meals to people in need.

② Mentor or tutor a younger student.

③ Spend time with or assist an elderly person.

④ Help raise money for community charitable organizations.

⑤ Take part in community beautification activities.

You enjoy the benefits of your community. You attend its schools and enjoy its parks and recreation centers. Your police force and fire department protect you from harm. You depend on your community to provide you with services like electricity and clean running water. Someday you may work and raise a family in your community. It is up to you to contribute your fair share to help your community thrive. Without citizens helping out, your community would not be much more than a cluster of houses.

Communities depend on the cooperation of their members to make them work. In our families, we cooperate with and respect our family members. You want your little brother or sister to stay out of your room, but that means staying out of your sibling's space too. This kind of cooperation and respect should extend to the larger communities to which you belong. This is where being a good citizen becomes important.

Communities and Rules

To encourage cooperation and good citizenship, communities set certain standards that apply to all citizens. Some citizenship standards are **compulsory**, or required by law. For example, drivers have to obey traffic rules or pay the established penalty. Young people are required to go to school. Some communities have curfews in their parks, and some communities have requirements that all dogs must be on a leash when on public property. These kinds of rules are generally to protect the health and safety of the community's citizens.

Some communities have a different kind of compulsory standards. They have laws or rules about how tall the buildings in town can be, or how large a sign on a store can be. Some communities restrict the style of building that can be built. Restrictions such as these are generally enacted to preserve the nature and appearance of a community, such as the community's historic past.

LAW 101

Making Communities Accessible for Everyone

Imagine what life would be like if you could not get into public buildings, use public transportation, enter restaurants, read signs, or use the telephone. This is what daily life is like for many people with disabilities. In recent years, however, numerous laws have been passed to help these Americans gain better access to public services.

Why it Matters State and local laws requiring access to public facilities for people with disabilities vary throughout the country. That is why in 1990 the federal government set national standards by passing the Americans with Disabilities Act (ADA). This landmark law prohibits discrimination on the basis of a person's disability in employment, state and local government, transportation, and many other areas. For example, all new buildings—both public and commercial—must be made accessible for persons with physical limitations. This access might be by having wheelchair ramps or elevators. Many older buildings must also be renovated to meet the new requirements. Emergency services, such as 911, must be available to those with communication disabilities. The U.S. Supreme Court recently held that even a Norwegian cruise line that served American passengers and operated out of a U.S. port had to comply with the ADA.

Under the ADA, all new buildings must be wheelchair accessible.

ANALYSIS SKILL EVALUATING THE LAW

go.hrw.com
KEYWORD: SZ7 CH15

1. Why do you think the Supreme Court ruled that a foreign company had to obey a U.S. law?
2. Do you think it is fair to make business owners renovate their buildings to accommodate people with disabilities? Explain your opinion.

Improving Your Community

Communities also rely on people to respect the rights of others because it is the right thing to do. This is the voluntary part of good citizenship. There are things you can do on your own to help your community. Some do not require much effort at all, such as picking up litter or carrying groceries for a neighbor. You can be an active citizen and make your community a great place to live.

READING CHECK **Contrast** How are compulsory services different from voluntary services?

Volunteering Is Important

Every day, all around you, volunteers are working to improve your community. They help the sick, poor, elderly, and disabled. They collect money for charities. Volunteers may even put out fires and drive ambulances in your area. Many Americans do not even realize how much work volunteers do. Communities rely on the help of volunteers because no government knows all the needs of its citizens. Volunteers also help provide services a community might not be able to afford otherwise.

ACADEMIC
VOCABULARY

purpose:
the reason
something is
done

The United States has many different kinds of volunteer groups. Some are small local groups. A small group may be formed for a specific **purpose**, such as cleaning up the neighborhood. After the problem is solved, the group disbands. However, some communities have permanent neighborhood groups that meet regularly to discuss local needs.

Community Volunteer Groups

In many towns, cities, and counties, volunteers provide necessary services. Groups such as hospital volunteers, volunteer firefighters, and student-parent-teacher associations help make vital health, safety, and educational services available. In some communities, high school students take older citizens to doctor appointments. Retired people may spend a few hours each week helping in libraries, hospitals, and other community facilities. People of all ages can contribute their time to community centers.

Some groups require volunteers to take short courses to learn specific skills, such as providing first aid or operating special equipment. Whatever your skills or interests, you can probably find a way to volunteer in your community. People who participate in these programs perform valuable services for their community. And they learn useful new skills, too.

National Volunteer Groups

The amount of time and energy you devote to community groups is up to you. Throughout your life you have opportunities to be an active citizen. What you decide about community participation will be influenced by your interests, your values, your age, and other things going on in your life.

Volunteer at a community animal shelter. You may have heard of some of the large national volunteer groups, like the League of Women Voters, the United Way, the American Cancer Society, and Volunteers of America. These associations are supported by money from private contributors, but they depend on the work of local volunteers. Citizens who want to help often start local branches of these organizations. But there are many ways you can help. Your efforts can be large or small. You can support these groups with your time, ideas, or money.

READING CHECK **Summarizing** How do volunteer groups help improve communities?

go.hrw.com
Online Quiz
KEYWORD: SZ7 HP15

SECTION 3 ASSESSMENT

Reviewing Ideas and Terms

1. a. Define Write a brief definition of the term **compulsory**.
b. Evaluate In your opinion, does your community offer citizens opportunities to help improve the community? Explain your answer.
2. a. Recall What are some regular services that are provided by community volunteers?
b. Support a Point of View Do you think is it important for citizens to volunteer their services in their communities? Why or why not?

Critical Thinking

3. Categorizing Copy the graphic organizer. Use it to identify compulsory standards and voluntary services that people contribute to their communities. You may use services mentioned in the section or other examples from your own experiences.

Compulsory Standards	Volunteer Services
1.	1.
2.	2.

Focus on Writing

4. Decision Making Identify a variety of volunteer groups in your community. Write an application essay to the group that you are most interested in joining.

STUDENTS TAKE ACTION

Helping the Elderly

Do you have a grandparent or family friend who lives in an assisted living facility? Assisted living facilities, or ALFs, are centers where elderly or disabled adults receive housing, meals, and personal care. Jackie Viana's law studies class in Hialeah, Florida, has been studying the laws that affect residents at ALFs. These students are working to make sure that their neighbors receive the best care possible.

Community Connection The Project Citizen class of Hialeah students researched laws affecting ALFs in other states, such as California. They realized that their state's laws required less training for ALF staff and less frequent inspections. "It is a problem that all of us are going to have to face because we're all going to get old," said Kristal Otero, one of the students working on the project.

Students in a Project Citizen class in Hialeah, Florida, pose with Florida governor Jeb Bush.

Taking Action Armed with their research, the teens began work on a Florida law to increase the training hours for ALF administrators and guarantee inspections of ALFs every six months. The students want the new law to include drug-free zones around the facilities. In addition, students created brochures and diagrams to help them present their ideas to community leaders. Representative Rene Garcia was so impressed that he worked with the students to try to make the law a reality, helping them introduce it at the statehouse. "This teaches them by hard work and dedication that if they see something wrong in their community, they can change it," Garcia said of the students' impressive efforts.

go.hrw.com
Project Citizen
KEYWORD: SZ7 CH15

SERVICE LEARNING

1. Why do you think these young people were interested in working on a law to protect elderly and disabled adults?
2. Are there people in your community who need help? What is a law you would like to see passed to help those people?

QUICK
FACTS

Visual Summary

*Use the visual summary below to help
you review the main ideas of the chapter.*

Communities are more than
streets and buildings. People
make a community and support
community activities.

Reviewing Key Terms

*For each term below, write a sentence explaining its
significance to communities.*

1. community
2. resources
3. climate
4. crossroads
5. megalopolis
6. communication
7. public utility
8. recreation
9. compulsory

Comprehension and Critical Thinking

SECTION 1 *(Pages 362–365)*

10. a. Recall What are three factors that affect
where a community might locate?

b. Describe How are the two types of rural
communities different from each other? How
are they alike?

c. Evaluate How might living in a small
urban area, such as a village of 2,500 people, be
different from living in a large city of 500,000
people?

SECTION 2 *(Pages 366–369)*

11. a. Recall What are two important values that
communities help teach?

b. Summarize What are four basic services
that communities can provide?

c. Rank Which of the four basic services a
community might provide do you consider
most important? Which would you consider
least important? Give reasons for your answer.

SECTION 3 *(Pages 371–374)*

12. a. Explain What is the purpose of compulsory
community standards or rules?

b. Summarize Why do communities need
volunteers?

c. Predict As a community grows from a
small village or town into a larger city, do you
think the need for volunteer groups increases
or decreases? Explain your answer.

Active Citizenship video program
Review the video to answer the closing question:
Describe the challenges involved in making the United States accessible for every student.

Using the Internet

go.hrw.com
KEYWORD: SZ7 CH15

13. Making a Plan People in a community can meet certain needs more effectively by working together than by working separately. Volunteering is one way you can help in meeting those needs. Enter the activity keyword to find ideas on how you can volunteer in your community. Then work in a small group to come up with a plan that includes which people or groups in the community you could serve, how often you could volunteer, and the amount of time it would take to do the job at each visit.

Civics Skills

Analyzing Talk Radio *Use the Civics Skills taught in this chapter and study the illustrated example of a talk radio schedule below. Use the schedule to answer the questions that follow.*

	MON	TUE	WED	THU	FRI
6:00 AM	**Breaking News Now** The only one-hour talk news program that brings you the latest on all of today's headlines from around the nation and the world.				
7:00 AM 8:00 AM	**The Shawn Michaels Report** Two hours of political commentary from America's highest-rated talk radio host.				
9:00 AM 10:00 AM 11:00 AM	**Smith and Kelly** The only show on talk radio today that brings you both political points of view. Conservative author Jim Smith and liberal journalist Bruce Kelly debate the issues and answer questions that all Americans need to hear.				
12:00 PM 1:00 PM	**Talking Sports** America's favorite sports talk host, Sal Peters, tackles the toughest issues in sports today and answers questions from listeners like you.				

14. Which programs are likely to be mostly opinions? Explain your answer.

15. On which program can you be sure to hear listeners calling in? How do you know?

16. How would you rank these shows according to their entertainment value? Explain your answer.

Reading Skills

Making Inferences *Use the Reading Skills taught in this chapter and study the reading selection below. Then answer the questions that follow.*

> The United States has a rich supply of natural resources. For early American settlers, one of the most vital resources was land itself. Fertile soil helped farming prosper. Vast forests provided wood for fuel and construction. Rivers, lakes, and streams supplied fresh water. Eventually, mineral resources such as coal, iron, and petroleum helped fuel the Industrial Revolution. Yet the nation's growth has also brought with it the increasing challenge of how to manage the resources we have so that we continue to benefit from them. *(p. 363)*

17. According to the passage, what was the most important resource for early settlers?

18. Other than as a water supply, how might rivers and lakes have been used as a resource?

   a. As a source of food

   b. As a way for boats to take goods to markets

   c. To provide power for mills and factories

   d. All of the above

FOCUS ON WRITING

19. Writing Your Brochure You have gathered information about different kinds of communities, factors that influence where communities locate, the values that communities teach and the purposes communities serve, and how citizens can be active in making their communities better. Use that information to create a four-page brochure that explains to people either why your community is an attractive place to live or ways in which citizens could make your community a better place to live. Be sure to include examples.

CHAPTER 16

CITIZENSHIP AND THE LAW

SECTION 1
Crime in the United States

SECTION 2
The Criminal Justice System

SECTION 3
Juvenile Crime

NATIONAL STANDARDS
FOR CIVICS AND GOVERNMENT

II. What are the foundations of the American political system?

   D. What values and principles are basic to American constitutional democracy?

III. How does the government established by the Constitution embody the purposes, values, and principles of American democracy?

   D. What is the place of law in the American constitutional system?

V. What are the roles of the citizen in American democracy?

   B. What are the rights of citizens?

   C. What are the responsibilities of citizens?

   E. How can citizens take part in civic life?

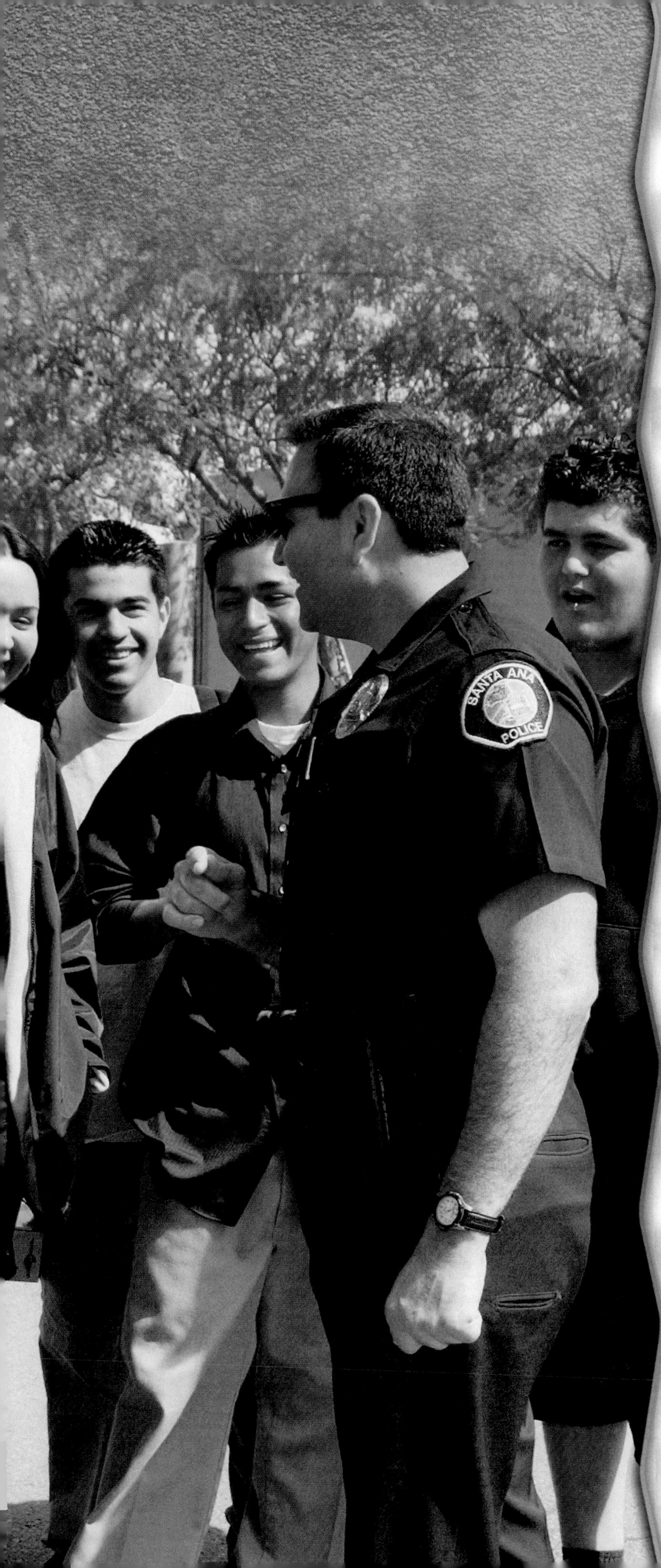

Active Citizenship video program
Watch the video to learn how young citizens
can participate in juvenile justice.

WHY CIVICS Matters

Laws exist to protect everybody.
Society, through the police force and
the judicial system, enforces its laws.
As a citizen, you have a duty to obey
the law and to uphold society's rules.

PROJECT Citizen

STUDENTS TAKE ACTION

MAKING CURFEW LAWS MORE EFFECTIVE
In order to curb juvenile crime, many cities have
curfew laws that limit how late young people
can be out by themselves. Does your city have
curfew laws? Do you think that those curfew
laws are fair? Think about what you can do to
improve your local curfew laws.

FOCUS ON SPEAKING

GIVING AN ORAL REPORT We rely on
a system of police, courts, and prisons to
guarantee our basic rights and freedoms and
protect us against those who break the law.
As you read this chapter, you will learn about
crime and law enforcement in the United
States. Then you will prepare and give an oral
report on how we can work toward being safe
in our homes, communities, and country.

Reading Skills

In this chapter you will read about how protection from crime is one of the services the government provides. You will learn about the types and causes of crime. You will read about the criminal justice system at the local, state, and national levels. You will also learn about the rights of citizens who are suspected of committing a crime. Finally, you will read about juvenile crime and how the judicial system has changed to handle young people accused of committing a crime.

Organizing Facts and Information

FOCUS ON READING Imagine trying to find a phone number in a phone book that did not have the listings arranged in alphabetical order. You probably would never be able to find the number if the phone book was not organized in some logical fashion. Information that is organized is much easier to read and understand than disorganized information.

Understanding Structural Patterns Writers often use four structural patterns to organize information effectively. By understanding the way a piece of writing is organized, you can better understand the information you are reading.

Helpful Hints for Understanding Structural Patterns

1. Look for the main idea of the passage.

2. Then look for clue words that signal a specific pattern.

3. Look for other important ideas and think about how the ideas connect. Is there an obvious pattern?

4. Use a graphic organizer to map the relationship among the facts and details.

Patterns of Organization

Pattern	Pattern	Graphic Organizer
• **Cause-effect** shows how one thing leads to another.	• As a result, therefore, because, this led to	Cause → Effect, Effect, Effect
• **Chronological Order** shows the sequence of events or actions.	• After, before, first, then, not long after, finally	First → Next → Next → Last
• **Compare-contrast** points out similarities and/or differences.	• although, but, however, on the other hand, similarly, also	Similarities: 1. 2. / Differences: 1. 2.
• **Listing** presents information in categories such as size, location, or importance.	• Also, most, important, for example, in fact	Category / Fact; Size / Large; Location / Here; Importance / Most important

You Try It!

The following passages are from the chapter you are about to read. As you read each set of sentences, ask yourself what structural pattern the writer used to organize the information.

(A) The problem is that gangs are often involved in serious crimes like murder and illegal drug and firearms trafficking. In 2000 the National Youth Gang Survey estimated that there were more than 772,000 active gang members in the United States.

From Chapter 16, p. 395

(B) After the jury has been selected, the trial begins. First, the prosecutor presents the case against the defendant. Next, the defense presents its case. During the trial, a defendant may choose whether or not to testify.

From Chapter 16, p. 391

(C) Imagine that you are seven years old again, and you have just stolen a loaf of bread from a local market. You got caught. If this had happened in the United States in the early 1800s, you would have been tried as an adult.

From Chapter 16, p. 396

After you have read the passage, answer the following questions.

1. What structural pattern did the writer use to organize passage A? How can you tell?

2. What structural pattern did the writer use to organize passage B? How can you tell?

3. What structural pattern did the writer use to organize passage C? How can you tell?

KEY TERMS

Chapter 16

Section 1
crime, *p. 382*
criminal, *p. 382*
felonies, *p. 382*
misdemeanors, *p. 382*
victimless crimes, *p. 384*
white-collar crimes, *p. 384*

Section 2
criminal justice system, *p. 388*
probable cause, *p. 388*
arrest warrant, *p. 388*
arraignment, *p. 389*
acquit, *p. 391*
plea bargain, *p. 391*

Section 3
juvenile, *p. 394*
delinquents, *p. 394*
probation, *p. 397*

Academic Vocabulary

Success in school is related to knowing academic vocabulary—the words that are frequently used in school assignments and discussions. In this chapter, you will learn the following academic words:

aspects *(p. 385)*
functions *(p. 388)*

As you read Chapter 16, think about the organization of the ideas. Ask yourself why the writer chose to organize the information in this way.

SECTION 1

Crime in the United States

BEFORE YOU READ

The Main Idea

When a person breaks a law, it is called a crime. There are several types of crimes and a variety of reasons why people commit crimes.

Reading Focus

1. What are five different types of crime?
2. What are four possible causes of crime?
3. How do we fight crime in the United States?

Key Terms

crime, *p. 382*
criminal, *p. 382*
felonies, *p. 382*
misdemeanors, *p. 382*
victimless crimes, *p. 384*
white-collar crimes, *p. 384*

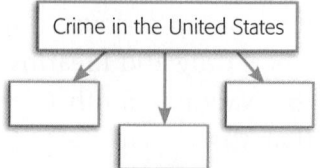 As you read, take notes on the types of crime, the causes of crime, and how we fight crime in the United States. Use a graphic organizer like this to record your notes.

Crime in the United States

 According to the FBI Uniform Crime Report, crime rates for all kinds of crime dropped from 2003 to 2005. Even so, the cost of crime is still huge. One economist's study reported that crime costs $1.7 trillion per year. That is about $5,800 per person. Crimes can range from shoplifting or disturbing the peace to murder, assault, or arson. And crime is a problem in small towns as well as cities. So what can you do about crime in your community? You might think you can do very little. But you might be surprised to learn that teenagers all across the country are taking action to fight crime and make their neighborhoods safer. There are many opportunities to protect yourself, your family, your friends, and your neighbors from crime.

Types of Crime

What is a crime? A **crime** is any act that breaks the law and for which there is a punishment. A **criminal** is a person who commits any type of crime. The Federal Bureau of Investigation (FBI) collects information on crime in the United States. The FBI identifies 29 types of crime. Serious crimes, such as murder and kidnapping, are called **felonies**. Less serious offenses, such as traffic viola-tions and disturbing the peace, are charged as **misdemeanors**.

The 29 types of crime can be categorized in other ways as well. Five main categories of crime are crimes against persons, crimes against property, victimless crimes, white-collar crimes, and organized crimes.

Crimes against Persons

Crimes against persons that include force or the threat of force are violent crimes. They include acts that harm a person, end a person's life, or threaten to end a life. From 2001 to 2007, more than 1.3 million violent crimes were reported each year. The most serious violent crime is homicide, or the kill-ing of one person by another. From 2001 to 2007, more than 16,000 homicides were committed in the United States each year.

The most common type of violent crime is aggravated assault. Aggravated assault is any kind of physical injury that is done inten-tionally to another person. Some aggravated assaults happen when a person robs someone else. More than 850,000 cases of aggravated assault occur each year.

Some crimes against persons are also hate crimes. Hate crimes are often violent crimes committed against people because of prejudice. Hate crimes include those committed against someone because of his or her race, religion, or other characteristics.

Another type of violent crime is the sexual violation of a person by force and against the person's will. The FBI calls this type of crime forcible rape. Between 2000 and 2004, more than 90,000 forcible rapes took place in the United States each year.

Crimes against Property

Most crimes committed in the United States are crimes against property. This type of crime involves stealing or destroying someone else's property. For example, burglary is the forcible or illegal entry into someone's home or other property with the intention to steal. In recent years, about 2 million burglaries were reported annually. Larceny is the theft of property without the use of force or violence against another person. Stealing from a cash register and shoplifting are examples of larceny.

Motor vehicle theft is a common crime against property and a serious national problem. About 1.2 million cars are reported stolen every year. Organized gangs often steal cars to resell them or to strip them and sell the parts. Sometimes people steal cars to use them in other crimes, like burglaries. In other cases, people steal the cars, drive them for awhile, and then abandon them.

Types of Crime

The FBI identifies 29 types of crime, which can be categorized into five main categories—crimes against persons, crimes against property, victimless crimes, white-collar crimes, and organized crimes. Depending on the offense, white-collar crimes may be considered either property crimes or victimless crimes. Organized crimes may fall into all three categories.

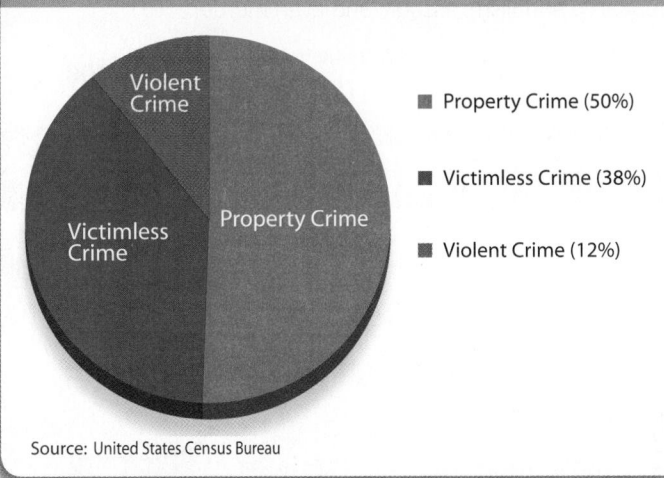

Arrests in the United States, 2003

- ■ Property Crime (50%)
- ■ Victimless Crime (38%)
- ■ Violent Crime (12%)

Source: United States Census Bureau

Violent

Crimes like murder, manslaughter, robbery, forcible rape, and aggravated assault are considered violent crimes.

Victimless

Gambling, drug abuse, breaking curfew, and running away are categorized as victimless crimes.

Property

Crimes against property include burglary, motor vehicle theft, shoplifting, and some white-collar crimes.

ANALYSIS SKILL **ANALYZING VISUALS**

What is the total percentage of arrests made for property crimes and victimless crimes?

Bicycle theft is a property crime. Many of these bikes were stolen and then abandoned.

MATH 101

Measuring Juvenile Crime

Law enforcement agencies carefully track crime statistics each year. Lately these statistics have shown that the juvenile arrest rate is decreasing, especially arrests for violent crimes. This drop in arrests is partially due to community curfews, mentoring programs, and changes in sentencing guidelines. However, minors are still arrested regularly for such crimes as burglary, vandalism, assault, and even murder.

$$\text{percent change} = \frac{\text{new value} - \text{original value}}{\text{original value}} \times 100$$

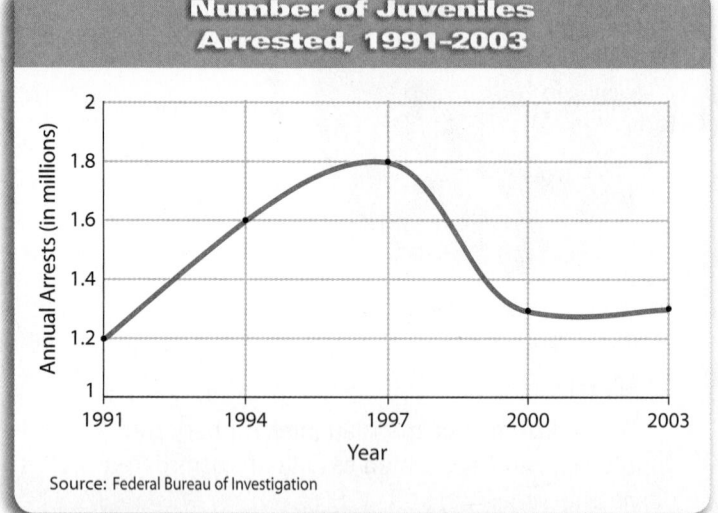

Number of Juveniles Arrested, 1991–2003

Source: Federal Bureau of Investigation

ANALYSIS SKILL — INTERPRETING GRAPHS

Use the formula for finding the percent change, shown above, to answer the following questions. What is the percent change in the arrest rate from 1997 to 2000? From 1994 to 1997?

Robbery is a crime that involves both property and people when committed. Many robberies involve taking something by threatening to hurt a person. In a mugging, for example, the robber may demand the person's property and back the threat with a weapon.

Other kinds of crime against property include vandalism and arson. Vandalism is the willful destruction of property, such as spray-painting the walls of a school. Arson is the destruction of property by setting fire to it.

Victimless Crimes

Some crimes, such as illegal gambling and the use of illegal drugs, are sometimes called **victimless crimes**. These crimes are considered victimless because the criminal does not violate another person's rights, but mainly harms himself or herself.

Nevertheless, victimless crimes are a problem for society. For example, the sale and possession of illegal drugs increases the death rate and often leads to other types of crime, like robbery. People who use drugs may hurt their family members or others if they become violent.

White-Collar Crimes

Some nonviolent crimes are called **white-collar crimes**. These crimes range from copyright violations to embezzlement and fraud. Embezzlement is the theft of money that has been entrusted to an individual's care. Fraud means cheating someone out of money or property. Embezzlement and fraud cost Americans millions of dollars each year.

White-collar crimes may involve computers in which essential and sensitive information is stored. This is called cybercrime. Some criminals, called hackers, break into computer systems to commit electronic theft, fraud, and embezzlement. Some hackers use computers to spread viruses that can damage computer systems worldwide.

Recently there has been an increase in identity theft. Identity theft occurs when someone uses your personal information—such as a Social Security number, date of birth, or address information—to commit fraud or other crimes. Criminals use this information to get credit cards in another person's name or to take money from bank accounts.

Experts estimate that the total cost to society of white-collar crimes may be billions of dollars. These costs are then passed along to consumers in the form of higher prices. Everyone in society ends up paying for white-collar crimes.

Organized Crime

Organized crime groups specialize in providing illegal goods and services. They operate in gambling, drug trafficking, prostitution, and lending money at extremely high interest rates. Crime syndicates often run legal businesses that serve as fronts, or covers, for illegal activities. Many times they use the threat of violence to keep people from going to the police.

READING CHECK Summarizing What are the main categories of crime?

Causes of Crime

Although no one really knows why people commit crimes, experts have a lot of theories. Poverty, illegal drug use, and other **aspects** of society are thought to contribute to crime.

- **Poverty** Poverty and unemployment are related to crime. When people cannot earn enough money to support themselves or their family, they may turn to crime to obtain things they don't have.
- **Illegal Drug Use** Many of the crimes committed each year are drug-related. People who commit these crimes may be stealing to support their drug habit, selling drugs, or acting under the influence of drugs.
- **Permissive Society** Some people believe that our permissive society contributes to crime. The idea is that many parents permit their children to do anything they want. Some children have not learned to act responsibly on their own or with others, so they commit crimes. Other people believe that judges often are too easy when sentencing criminals.
- **Urbanization** Some experts suggest that urbanization plays a role in crime. They offer a couple of reasons for this. More people live in cities, which means there are more potential victims for criminals. In addition, there are more young people in cities. People under the age of 25 account for almost half of the arrests in the United States.

- **Other Causes of Crime** Some people suggest that technological and social change may lead to crime as people fall behind the times. Without a good education, some people are unable to find jobs and may turn to crime. Others suggest that society's attitudes toward right and wrong have changed, or that violence in the media and in computer games inspire violent crimes. Still other people say that society does not spend enough money on law enforcement, which allows crime to grow.
- **No Single Cause** As you can see, a variety of aspects of today's society have been offered as causes of crime. Perhaps the one thing that experts do agree on is that today's crime problem probably cannot be blamed on any single cause.

ACADEMIC VOCABULARY

aspects: parts

READING CHECK Finding the Main Idea What are some of the main causes of crime?

FOCUS ON
Eric Holder
(1951–   )

When Eric Holder joined President Barack Obama's cabinet on February 2, 2009, he became the first African American attorney general of the United States. The attorney general is the "top cop" for the federal government and also heads up the Department of Justice.

Holder was born and raised in New York City, where he attended schools for gifted children. His early education prepared him for Columbia University, where he received his law degree in 1976. That same year, Holder joined the Department of Justice and began working his way through the ranks. In 1988 he was nominated by President Reagan as an associate judge of the Superior Court of the District of Columbia. Under President Clinton, Holder served as U.S. district attorney for the District of Columbia and then as deputy attorney general.

In 2007 Holder joined Obama's presidential campaign as a senior legal adviser. Holder also co-chaired the nominee's vice presidential–selection committee.

Making Inferences How might Holder's experience as a deputy attorney general help him perform his duties as attorney general?

Neighborhood Watch

Many communitites have formed Neighborhood Watch programs in which residents watch for criminal activity.

Fighting Crime

Whatever its causes, crime hurts everyone. Partly in response to the growing public outcry about crime, Congress passed a national crime bill in 1994. This bill illustrates some of the country's main strategies for reducing crime. One approach is to increase the number of police officers and expand the prison system. Another is to provide tougher legal penalties for criminals. For example, the 1994 crime bill increased the number of crimes eligible for the death penalty. It also introduced the so-called three-strikes rule. This federal law, which has been adopted by some states, gives life sentences to three-time violent offenders.

Other strategies focus on crime prevention. These include creating community-policing programs in neighborhoods to improve relationships between police and citizens. Schools can also provide crime prevention education.

These strategies have helped reduce crime rates, but there is no simple solution. Fighting crime effectively requires citizens to get involved. There are many things you can do to help your community. Report any crimes that you see. Take common-sense precautions to ensure your safety and that of others. Even small steps such as cleaning up graffiti in your neighborhood can help fight crime. Finally, try to support the police officers who work to protect your community.

READING CHECK **Analyzing Information** What can government and citizens do to fight crime?

go.hrw.com
Online Quiz
KEYWORD: SZ7 HP16

SECTION 1 ASSESSMENT

Reviewing Ideas and Terms

1. a. Define Write a brief definition for the terms **crime, criminal, felonies, misdemeanors, victimless crimes**, and **white-collar crimes**.

b. Defend a Point of View Some people argue that there is no such thing as a victimless crime. Do you agree? Why or why not?

2. a. Recall Describe at least four potential causes of crime.

b. Evaluate How might permissive courts contribute to crime?

3. a. Summarize What are two of the strategies for fighting crime that were included in the 1994 national crime bill?

b. Make Inferences Why do you think some citizens do not report crime?

Critical Thinking

4. Categorizing Use your notes and a chart like this one to fill in the boxes with different types of crime on the left and examples of each type of crime on the right.

Type of Crime	Examples

Focus on Writing

5. Problem Solving Imagine that you are a police commissioner for a city. Write a speech discussing how government and citizens can work to reduce crime.

STUDENTS TAKE ACTION

Making Curfew Laws More Effective

Many cities and towns have curfew laws that limit how late young people can be out by themselves. These laws are meant to prevent juvenile crime. In Plainfield, New Jersey, enforcing the 10 p.m. to 5:30 a.m. curfew was a major problem for police. The city council decided to temporarily suspend the city's curfew law in order to re-evaluate it. To help the council improve the curfew law, Project Citizen students in Ms. Brenda Noble's class shared their research and recommendations.

Community Connection The students wanted to know why enforcing the curfew was a problem. Was the law reasonable? The students surveyed friends and family members about their knowledge of and opinions about curfews. They then moved on to telephone interviews with a larger number of randomly chosen citizens, which yielded more representative data. The students also talked to local officials in Plainfield and in other communities to gather general information on curfew laws.

Taking Action The students' survey showed that most citizens and public officials believed that curfews helped reduce juvenile crime and protect young people from harm. However, the Plainfield police faced a major problem enforcing the curfew: Many parents and teen-agers in Plainfield were unaware of the law. Students explained to officials that they needed to teach the public about the curfew. The students also suggested that Plainfield's curfew needed more flexibility. For example, they recommended later curfew times on the weekends and for older teenagers who might be working. The students' recommendations won the support of the city council and the public.

PROHIBITED
IN THIS
BUSINESS DISTRICT

ROLLERBLADES / SKATEBOARDS
10.20.042(a) H.B.M.C.

RIDING BICYCLES ON SIDEWALK
10.84.160 H.B.M.C.

JUVENILE CURFEW
(10:00 P.M. – 6:00 A.M.)
9.68.020 H.B.M.C.

UNRESTRAINED DOGS
OC ORD. 4-1-45

STRICTLY ENFORCED

Many communities have curfews prohibiting young people from being out past certain hours.

go.hrw.com
Project Citizen
KEYWORD: SZ7 CH16

SERVICE LEARNING

1. How did the students adjust their research methods to get more accurate data?
2. What programs exist or could be started to reduce juvenile crime in your community?

SECTION 2
The Criminal Justice System

BEFORE YOU READ

The Main Idea

Police officers arrest people believed to be breaking the law. An accused person must be tried and, if found guilty, punished.

Reading Focus

1. What is the role of police officers in the criminal justice system?
2. What is the function of the courts after a suspect has been arrested?
3. How does our corrections system punish lawbreakers?

Key Terms

criminal justice system, *p. 388*
probable cause, *p. 388*
arrest warrant, *p. 388*
arraignment, *p. 389*
acquit, *p. 391*
plea bargain, *p. 391*

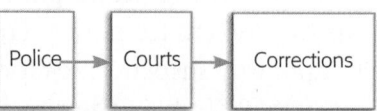 **TAKING NOTES** As you read, take notes on the three different parts of the criminal justice system in the United States. Use a graphic organizer like this one to record the role of the police, the courts, and the corrections system.

Police → Courts → Corrections

 Do you know what your rights are if you are arrested? Maybe you know from watching television. When suspects are arrested on TV, the police officers read them their Miranda rights: "You have the right to remain silent. Anything you say can and will be used against you in a court of law. You have the right to speak to an attorney, and to have an attorney present during any questioning. If you cannot afford a lawyer, one will be provided for you at government expense." These rights are guaranteed to all citizens by the Constitution.

The Role of the Police

The **criminal justice system** is the three-part system consisting of the police, courts, and corrections that is used to keep the peace and bring criminals to justice. Each part of the system has its own purpose and **functions**.

ACADEMIC VOCABULARY
functions: use or purpose

The Police

The police have a number of duties. These duties include protecting life and property, preventing crime, and arresting people who violate the law. They also include protecting the rights of individuals, maintaining peace and order, and controlling traffic.

Police Training

Today's police officers are usually carefully selected and trained. Candidates have their backgrounds fully investigated before they can be hired. They also complete difficult physical and psychological examinations. Most cities require police officers to be high school or even college graduates.

Police Arrests

Before he or she can arrest a suspect, a police officer must have probable cause. **Probable cause** means that the officer must have witnessed the crime or must have gathered enough evidence to make an arrest. If no one saw the suspect commit the crime, an **arrest warrant** may be necessary. An arrest warrant is an authorization by the court to make the arrest.

According to the Bill of Rights, all arrested suspects are entitled to due process. The police must inform suspects of their Miranda rights before questioning them. The Miranda warning lets suspects know what their rights are as protected by the Bill of Rights. If a suspect is not given this information before questioning, any statements he or she makes cannot be used as evidence in court.

Law Enforcement Training

Police officers receive training in many areas of law enforcement, including self-defense methods, fingerprinting, the law, and psychology.

P. ROBINSON

After the arrest, the suspect is taken to the police station for booking, when a record of the arrest is made. An officer writes down the name of the suspect, the time of the arrest, and the charges involved. If the person is suspected of a felony or a serious misdemeanor, he or she is usually fingerprinted and photographed. If a person is accused of a misdemeanor, a single fingerprint may be taken.

READING CHECK **Summarizing** What are the main functions of police officers?

The Courts: From Arrest to Sentencing

The second part of our U.S. criminal justice system is the court system. The courts are where suspects are tried for possible crimes and are found either guilty or innocent.

Preliminary Hearing

A preliminary hearing must be held soon after the accused's arrest. During this hearing, a judge must decide if there is enough evidence to send the case to trial. If there is not, the judge can dismiss, or drop, the charges. If the charges are not dropped, the judge must decide whether to set bail. Bail is the money a person—now called a defendant—posts as a guarantee that he or she will return for trial. The bail amount is usually related to the seriousness of the offense. For a minor offense, the judge may release the defendant on his or her own recognizance, or without bail. If the defendant being charged with a minor offense lives in the community and has a good reputation, the judge is more likely to release the defendant without bail. If the judge believes the defendant might try to flee, or if the crime is serious, he or she can order that the defendant be held in jail until the trial.

Grand Jury and Indictment

Before a defendant can be tried, a formal charge must be made. In some states a grand jury hears the evidence to decide whether to send the case to trial. If the grand jury finds probable cause, the defendant is indicted, or formally charged with the crime.

Arraignment

After he or she is charged, the defendant goes before a judge for arraignment. An **arraignment** is when the defendant enters a plea of guilty or not guilty to the charge. If he or she pleads guilty, no trial is necessary.

Stages in the Criminal Justice System

QUICK FACTS

1. Arrest

- A crime is committed
- Police investigate the crime
- An arrest is made

Crime
↓
Investigation
↓
Arrest
↓
Charged
↓
Hearing

2. Trial and Judgment

- The suspect is charged
- An arraignment hearing is held
- The suspect is held for trial or released on bail; or
- The case is dismissed and the suspect is free
- A trial is held or
- The suspect pleads guilty or enters a plea bargain
- If found innocent, charges are dismissed
- If found guilty or if a plea bargain is made, then the next stage is sentencing

Held for trial or bail   **Dismissed**

Plea   **Trial**

Guilty   **Not Guilty**

3. Sentence

If guilty, a judge or the jury decides on a punishment
- fine
- probation
- suspended sentence
- prison

Jail   **Probation**   **Fine**

ANALYSIS SKILL   **ANALYZING VISUALS**

What are the possible outcomes when a person is arrested for a crime?

Trial

If the defendant pleads not guilty to the charge, the case goes to trial. The defense represents the defendant. The prosecution represents the government's side of the case.

The defense and prosecution lawyers choose the jurors for the trial from a large group of people. In most states, both of these lawyers have the right to question prospective jurors. Each can reject people they believe might be prejudiced against his or her side of the case.

After the jury has been selected, the trial begins. First, the prosecutor presents the case against the defendant. Next, the defense presents its case. During the trial, a defendant may choose whether or not to testify. Under the U.S. Constitution, no defendant can be forced to testify against himself or herself. Witnesses may be called to testify by either side. Each attorney asks his or her witness questions, and then the attorney for the other side asks the same witness questions.

After both sides present their evidence, each lawyer makes a closing statement that summarizes his or her arguments. The judge then tells the jurors what they can and cannot consider under the law in reaching their verdict. Finally, the jury leaves the courtroom to deliberate, or discuss, the case.

Defendants are always presumed to be innocent until a verdict is delivered. It is the prosecution's job to prove that the defendant is guilty beyond a reasonable doubt. If there is reasonable doubt of guilt, the jury must **acquit** the defendant—that is, the jury must find him or her not guilty of the crime. If the jury cannot agree on a verdict, the case may be tried again before another jury.

Sentencing

If the defendant is found guilty, the judge decides on the punishment, or sentence. Some states have established mandatory sentences for certain crimes. That is, the law requires judges to give certain punishments for certain crimes.

Plea Bargaining

Most cases in the United States never go to trial. They are taken care of quickly by plea bargaining. In a **plea bargain** the defendant may plead guilty to a lesser offense than the original charge. Under a plea bargain agreement, the penalty is usually lighter than if a trial jury found the defendant guilty.

READING CHECK **Sequencing** What are the main steps in the court process, from arrest through sentencing?

Punishing Lawbreakers

If you break the law and are found guilty of a crime, you will be punished. The punishment is handled by the corrections system, the third part of the U.S. criminal justice system. Corrections can include imprisonment, parole, or capital punishment.

Imprisonment

Less serious crimes may be punished only with fines or with fines plus a suspended sentence and probation, in which a person is not imprisoned unless he or she violates the conditions imposed by the court's order. More serious crimes are typically punished with imprisonment. Most people agree that dangerous criminals should be removed from society for a period of time. Many American prisons face a serious overcrowding problem, however. Proposed solutions range from building more prisons to releasing inmates earlier, but no easy answers seem available.

Some people believe that society has the right to make the criminal pay for his or her crime. Other people view imprisonment as a deterrent to crime. That is, it discourages people from becoming criminals. A third view of imprisonment is that it serves as a means of rehabilitation. Some people believe that rehabilitated, or reformed, criminals can return to society as law-abiding citizens. Still other people view imprisonment as a means of social protection. People in prison cannot pose a threat to the lives or property of people in the community.

Parole

After serving a part of their sentences, many prisoners are eligible for parole, or early release. People are paroled on the condition that they obey certain rules and stay out of trouble. Parole is generally granted to prisoners who behave well and who show signs of rehabilitation. A parole board carefully reviews each application for parole and then accepts or denies the request. A paroled prisoner must report regularly to a parole officer. Parole usually lasts for the remaining length of a person's sentence.

Capital Punishment

The harshest punishment for crimes committed in the United States is capital punishment, or the death penalty. The issue of capital punishment is very controversial. Many people support the death penalty as a form of punishment for criminals. Others, however, question the procedures that determine how capital punishment is applied. It is a difficult topic that will continue to be debated for many years.

READING CHECK ▶ **Summarizing** What methods are used by the U.S. corrections system to punish criminals?

go.hrw.com
Online Quiz
KEYWORD: SZ7 HP16

SECTION 2 ASSESSMENT

Reviewing Ideas and Terms

1. a. Define Write a brief definition for the terms **criminal justice system**, **probable cause**, and **arrest warrant**.

b. Defend a Point of View Do you think it is important for police officers to issue the Miranda warning to suspects? Explain your answer.

2. a. Define Write a brief definition for the terms **arraignment**, **acquit**, and **plea bargain**.

b. Compare and Contrast What are some similarities and differences between the defense and prosecution sides in a case?

c. Evaluate Do you think that plea bargains should be allowed for all charges against an accused person? Explain your answer.

3. a. Summarize What are some of the purposes for imprisonment in the criminal justice system?

b. Elaborate Why do you think each state is allowed to establish its own capital punishment laws?

Critical Thinking

4. Sequencing Use your notes and a diagram like this one to describe the steps in the criminal justice system from arrest to sentencing. Add more circles as needed.

Focus on Writing

5. Supporting a Point of View Write a position statement for or against the parole of criminals.

Conducting Library Research

Learn

Libraries are a useful resource when you need to find books, periodicals, photographs, and audio-visual media. Most libraries now have computer-based catalogs, so you can search all the resources of the library on a computerized search engine. To do this, you have to identify keywords or subject headings relevant to your topic.

After getting a listing of all the relevant materials at a library, it is important to determine which materials are most useful. Resources intended for an academic or technical audience may not be suitable for a school research project. Also, materials that are not up-to-date may need to be excluded.

Practice

❶ **Figure out several keywords for your topic.** If your research topic is "juvenile crime," you can try those two terms. But using related words—adolescents, youth, courts, criminals—will help you get more results.

❷ **Select a variety of types of resources.** Using the help of the librarian, find books, magazines, journals, and videos. Focus on the most recent sources, if possible.

❸ **Go through materials before leaving the library.** Use the indexes in the books you have selected to find the pages relevant to your topic. Skim the magazine and journal articles and make sure they are not too technical or academic. If the materials still seem suitable, take some notes or photocopy the pages you need.

Apply

Use the illustrated example of a library keyword search shown in the visual below to answer the following questions.

1. Suppose you are researching white-collar crime. What are some keywords you would try in a keyword search?

2. Look at the search results for the topic of juvenile crime. Explain which resource you think would be the least useful for this research topic.

3. Look at the search results for the topic of juvenile crime. Predict which resource might be too specialized or technical for a school research project.

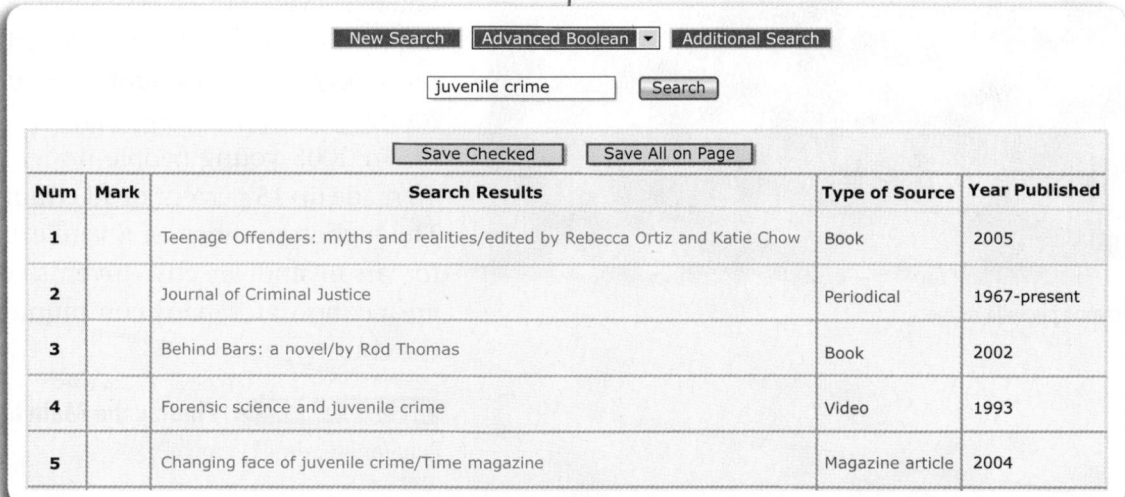

		New Search	Advanced Boolean ▾	Additional Search		
		juvenile crime	Search			
		Save Checked	Save All on Page			
Num	**Mark**	**Search Results**			**Type of Source**	**Year Published**
1		Teenage Offenders: myths and realities/edited by Rebecca Ortiz and Katie Chow			Book	2005
2		Journal of Criminal Justice			Periodical	1967-present
3		Behind Bars: a novel/by Rod Thomas			Book	2002
4		Forensic science and juvenile crime			Video	1993
5		Changing face of juvenile crime/Time magazine			Magazine article	2004

SECTION 3

Juvenile Crime

BEFORE YOU READ

The Main Idea

Most states prefer to handle juvenile, or young, criminals differently than adult criminals, but for some crimes this practice is changing.

Reading Focus

1. What is juvenile crime?
2. What are some possible causes of juvenile crime?
3. How does the judicial system handle juveniles who break the law?
4. What are some ways to avoid trouble with the law?

Key Terms

juvenile, *p. 394*
delinquents, *p. 394*
probation, *p. 397*

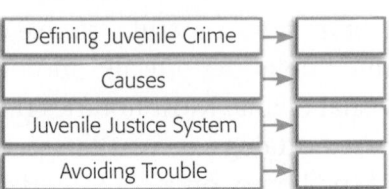 **TAKING NOTES** As you read, take notes on juvenile crime in the United States. Use a graphic organizer like this one to record your notes.

Defining Juvenile Crime	→	
Causes	→	
Juvenile Justice System	→	
Avoiding Trouble	→	

Graffiti is a common juvenile crime.

CIVICS IN PRACTICE What is the best way to handle kids who commit crimes? Not everyone agrees on the answer to this question. Some people believe young criminals should be punished in special detention centers. Others think that these offenders need help with self-esteem, drug treatment, or learning skills. There are also people who believe young offenders should be treated like adults and do adult time for adult crime.

Defining Juvenile Crime

The dictionary defines *juvenile* as "a young person." Most states define a **juvenile** as a person under the age of 18. Some states set the age as low as 16. But no matter where you live, every state has special laws for dealing with juveniles who commit crimes. Juveniles become **delinquents** when they are found guilty of breaking a law.

In 2005 young people under the age of 18 made up 15 percent of all criminal arrests. The highest numbers of juvenile arrests were for arson and larceny. Juvenile crime is a great concern for many communities around the country.

READING CHECK **Finding the Main Idea** What is juvenile crime?

Causes of Juvenile Crime

Why do some young people break the law? As with adult crime, there is no single answer. Experts who have studied the problem believe that there are a few main causes of juvenile crime.

Poor Home Conditions

Many juvenile offenders come from homes in which the parents do not or cannot take responsibility for their children. Sometimes parents are absent or rarely at home to help care for their children. Sometimes the parents are alcoholics, illegal drug users, or child abusers. Such parents often expose their children to criminal or violent behavior. It is not unusual for children in these situations to spend much of their time on the streets. Without responsible authority figures at home, neglected children may get into serious trouble.

Poor Neighborhood Conditions

The poorer areas of cities frequently have higher rates of crime than other areas. These neighborhoods typically do not offer the same educational and job opportunities as less poor communities. As a result, many young people in these areas feel hopeless and angry about their situations. Some young people see crime as their only way out of the poverty that surrounds them.

Gang Membership

Young people without stable homes may turn to gangs for support and a sense of belonging. In a sense the gang becomes a substitute family. The problem is that gangs are often involved in serious crimes like murder and illegal drug and firearms trafficking. In 2006, the National Youth Gang Survey estimated that there were approximately 785,000 active gang members in the United States. The problem of gang related crime has prompted many communities to look for ways to keep young people from joining gangs.

Dropping Out of School and Unemployment

It is not surprising that when young people have nothing to do, they may get into trouble. Juveniles who drop out of school often lack the education and skills to get a decent job. Dropouts are often unemployed and are often at greater risk of becoming involved in criminal activities.

Alcohol and Drugs

It is illegal to sell alcoholic beverages to minors. It is also illegal to sell habit-forming drugs to anyone who does not have a doctor's prescription. Yet many young people find ways to get alcohol and illegal drugs.

Drug and alcohol use can lead a person to do things that he or she might not do otherwise. People under the influence of drugs or alcohol may commit other crimes, like drunk driving or assault. In addition, addicts who need money to pay for their habits often turn to crime.

Peer Pressure

Some young people are pressured by their friends to commit crimes. Studies suggest that young people who socialize with delinquent peers are more likely to become involved in crime themselves.

READING CHECK **Summarizing** What are some of the explanations that experts offer as possible causes for juvenile crime?

The Juvenile Justice System

Imagine that you are seven years old again, and you have just stolen a loaf of bread from a local market. You got caught. If this had happened in the United States in the early 1800s, you would have been tried as an adult. Before the late 19th century, juveniles at least seven years old were held responsible for their crimes. They were tried in adult courts and sentenced to prison and even death.

Reform

During the 1870s, however, reformers began working to change the way the system treated young offenders. They believed that juveniles needed special understanding rather than punishment. Their reasoning was that young people are less able to understand their actions than adults.

As a result, many communities set up juvenile court systems. The purpose of the juvenile systems was not to punish children but to remove them from harmful environments. Reformers hoped to re-educate offenders by giving them care, discipline, supervision, and treatment. This would allow juvenile offenders to return to society as good citizens.

More changes to juvenile justice came about 40 years ago. In 1967 the Supreme Court issued a landmark ruling in a case called *In re Gault*. In the case, the Court said that juvenile offenders have the same rights of due process as adults. In the ruling, Justice Abe Fortas declared,

" In practically all jurisdictions, there are rights granted to adults which are withheld from juveniles … Under our Constitution, the condition of being a boy [or girl] does not justify a kangaroo court [an unfair trial]. "
—Associate Justice Abe Fortes, *In re Gault*, 1967

Today's Juvenile Justice System

The 1967 Supreme Court ruling changed the way young people are tried today. Juveniles, like adults, have the right to be informed of the charges brought against them and to be represented by a lawyer. They also have the right to question all witnesses in the case and can refuse to testify against themselves in court.

However, the Supreme Court later ruled that juveniles accused of crimes do not have the right to a jury trial. Instead of trials, juvenile courts hold hearings. Only parents or guardians and others directly involved in the case can attend. The purpose of the hearings is to determine the guilt or innocence of the accused young person.

Treatment or Punishment

During a juvenile hearing, a judge listens to evidence presented by both sides. At the end of the hearing, the judge must decide the guilt or innocence of the juvenile offender. If the judge finds the juvenile guilty, he or she may call for one or more of the following measures.

Foster Care If the judge decides that adult supervision where the juvenile lives is inadequate, the juvenile may be placed in a foster home. A foster home is a place where people other than the natural or adoptive parents raise a young person.

Minors and the Death Penalty

The Eight Amendment prohibits cruel and unusual punishments. But how do Americans define "cruel and unusual"? For years, the Supreme Court has struggled with this very question in terms of the death penalty.

When the Eighth Amendment was adopted, the death penalty was neither unusual nor considered excessively cruel by the framers of the Constitution. Over the years, however, many Americans began to feel differently, especially when it came to executing young criminals.

In two separate decisions in 1989, the Court ruled that a person with mental retardation, a 16-year-old boy, and a 17-year-old boy all could be executed for murders that they were convicted of committing. But in 2002, the Court overruled the first of those decisions, and in 2005, the Court reversed the second decision, ruling that no one could be executed for a crime they committed while under the age of 18.

In both of the later rulings, the Supreme Court looked to "the evolving [developing] standards of decency that mark the progress of a maturing society."

What does this mean? Recent changes in various state laws convinced the Court that American society now saw these two groups of people as less responsible for their actions and less able to make rational decisions than adults and individuals without mental handicaps. In society's eyes, and therefore the Court's view, executing these defendants now was "cruel and unusual" and therefore unconstitutional.

1. How did the Supreme Court's position on executing minors and persons with mental retardation change between 1989 and 2005?

2. What do the changes in the Supreme Court's interpretation of the Eighth Amendment say about the relationship between state and federal law?

Juvenile Corrections In serious cases the judge may send the youth to a juvenile corrections facility. Sometimes young people are held in juvenile detention centers, formal prisons for minors.

Another type of juvenile corrections facility is a training school, where young offenders may stay for a year. Juvenile offenders who have drug, alcohol, or mental health issues are often sent to residential treatment facilities. Some juvenile justice systems are also experimenting with the use of boot camps to rehabilitate young offenders. Like military boot camps, juvenile boot camps provide a highly disciplined, structured environment. However, recent research suggests that most of these corrections facilities have little effect on keeping juvenile delinquents from committing more crimes in the future.

Probation Another possible outcome for the juvenile offender is probation. **Probation** is a period of time during which offenders are given an opportunity to show that they can reform. Juveniles on probation must obey strict rules, like being home by a certain time each night and staying out of trouble. They also have to report regularly to a probation officer.

Counseling Many juvenile justice systems refer young offenders to counseling. They assign caseworkers to juveniles, who make sure that the young people get therapy and other social services they may need, like food stamps or job skills.

Juvenile Justice System

In many cases, juvenile court hearings are held in private. At those hearings, only the parents or guardians of the defendant, witnesses, and others directly involved in the case can attend. There is no jury—the judge alone decides the guilt or innocence of the accused. If the juvenile defendant is found guilty, the judge decides what punishment to issue.

Why are juvenile court hearings held in private?

The judge hears the case and rules whether the defendant is guilty or innocent.

Treating Juveniles as Adults

The number of serious crimes committed by juveniles has dropped since the 1990s. Still, some adults believe that juvenile offenders should be tried in adult criminal courts. Critics of the juvenile system point to serious crimes like murder as reasons for trying young people as adults.

For example, suppose a young person is convicted of murder. If sentenced as a juvenile, he or she may serve only a short sentence in a juvenile corrections facility. Despite the good intentions of corrections officers, that juvenile may commit further crimes after release. Some people also question the argument that young people who commit violent crimes are not as responsible for their actions as adults.

For these reasons, most states now certify juveniles for trial in adult criminal courts under certain circumstances. This usually happens when a youth is 14 or older and is accused of committing a felony. Young people who are found guilty—as an adult—of a crime in a criminal court are usually punished the way adults are punished. This means a young person convicted of a major felony is likely to get a longer sentence in a harsher facility.

As more young people have been tried as adults, more have been sentenced to adult prisons. But statistics show that sending juveniles into the adult judicial system does little to turn young offenders away from crime and may actually harm them. As a result, the debate over how best to handle juvenile offenders continues with no end in sight.

READING CHECK ▸ **Supporting a Point of View**
Do you support or oppose trying juveniles in adult criminal courts? Why?

Avoiding Trouble

Scientists who study crime and criminal behavior offer the following suggestions to young people who want to avoid trouble with the law. This advice is not always so easy to follow. However, choosing to take these steps will not only keep you out of trouble but will also help you achieve the goals that you set for yourself.

1. Do not use drugs. People who use drugs often end up in criminal courts and corrections facilities or jails. A criminal record can follow you for life.

2. Stay in school and get the best education possible. A good education will

provide you with important skills and increase your chances of getting a good job.

3. Have the courage to say no when friends ask you to do something illegal. Make sure that your friends and role models are a positive influence on you. Anyone can go along with the crowd, but it takes courage to stand up to one.

4. Try to live a full life, with plenty of physical activity and interesting hobbies. You might even discover a hidden talent. A person who is busy doing challenging things is less likely to become bored and turn to criminal activities as an outlet.

READING CHECK ▷ **Finding the Main Idea** How can a young person avoid trouble with the law?

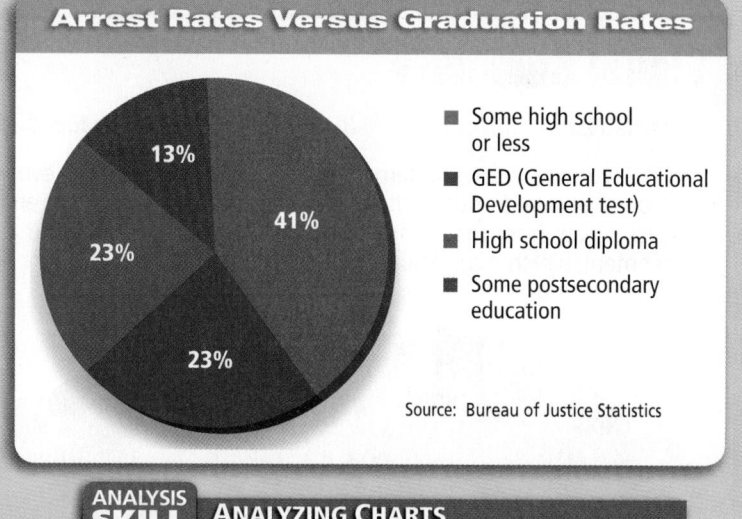

Juvenile Crime

The majority of inmates in state and federal prisons in the United States never finished high school. Less than half of the inmates have a high school diploma or a GED.

Arrest Rates Versus Graduation Rates

13%
41%
23%
23%

■ Some high school or less
■ GED (General Educational Development test)
■ High school diploma
■ Some postsecondary education

Source: Bureau of Justice Statistics

ANALYSIS SKILL ANALYZING CHARTS

What is the total percentage of prison inmates who have a high school diploma or additional education?

go.hrw.com
Online Quiz
KEYWORD: SZ7 HP16

SECTION 3 ASSESSMENT

Reviewing Ideas and Terms

1. a. Define Write a brief definition for the terms **juvenile** and **delinquents**.

b. Make Inferences Why do you think that states set different minimum ages for defining a person as a juvenile?

2. a. Recall What are three of the main reasons experts give for juvenile crime?

b. Analyze How could poor home conditions lead to some of the other causes of juvenile crime?

c. Make Evaluations What do you think is the most significant cause of juvenile crime? Explain your answer.

3. a. Define Write a brief definition for the term **probation**.

b. Summarize What are some of the punishments that a juvenile offender might face?

c. Compare and Contrast How are young people in the juvenile court system tried differently from adult offenders?

4. a. Make Generalizations In what ways might getting a good education help you stay out of trouble?

b. Draw Conclusions Why is it important to form a circle of friends who participate in positive, lawful behaviors?

Critical Thinking

5. Identifying Cause and Effect Copy the diagram below. Use your notes and the diagram to identify the causes of juvenile crime. Add more boxes as needed.

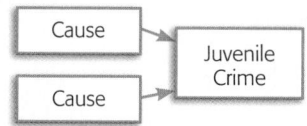

Cause → Juvenile Crime
Cause →

Focus on Writing

6. Supporting a Point of View Write a letter to your state legislature describing your position on whether juveniles should be tried as adults.

CHAPTER 16 REVIEW

Visual Summary

Use this visual summary to help you review the main ideas of the chapter.

The U.S. criminal justice system operates to protect everyone, even those who have been accused of committing criminal acts. All citizens are entitled to due process of law, from the moment of arrest, to trial, and—if found guilty—to punishment, which may include imprisonment.

Reviewing Key Terms

For each term below, write a sentence explaining its significance to citizenship and the law.

1. crime
2. criminal
3. felonies
4. misdemeanors
5. victimless crimes
6. white-collar crimes
7. criminal justice system
8. probable cause
9. arrest warrant
10. arraignment
11. acquit
12. plea bargain
13. juvenile
14. delinquents
15. probation

Comprehension and Critical Thinking

SECTION 1 *(Pages 382–386)*

16. **a. Identify** Name and describe specific examples of the five categories of crime.

    b. Compare and Contrast What is the difference between a crime against a person and a crime against property?

    c. Elaborate What are some causes of crime?

SECTION 2 *(Pages 388–392)*

17. **a. Recall** What are the punishments that a convicted criminal faces?

    b. Sequence What steps does a criminal suspect go through from the time of arrest to the time of sentencing?

    c. Evaluate Some people believe that prisons should focus on rehabilitating criminals and helping them rejoin society. Others argue that prisons are intended to punish criminals and protect the rest of society. What do you think the role of prisons should be?

Active Citizenship video program
Review the video to answer the closing question:
*How might the impact of a teen court ruling differ
from that of an actual judge's decision?*

SECTION 3 *(Pages 394–399)*

18. a. Describe What are the possible causes of juvenile delinquency?

b. Compare and Contrast How are juvenile offenders treated differently than adult offenders?

c. Support a Point of View Should juveniles who commit serious crimes such as murder be tried in adult courts, and should those convicted of these crimes face the same punishments as adult offenders? Explain your answers.

Using the Internet

go.hrw.com
KEYWORD: SZ7 CH16

19. Writing on Teen Court Enforcement of the law is not always limited to adults. Enter the activity keyword. Then research teen court in different states. Write a paper about how teen court is organized, who it benefits, and what the roles of teen jurors, bailiffs, and attorneys are. Include a paragraph discussing whether or not you would like to participate in a teen court.

Civics Skills

Conducting Library Research *Use the Civics Skill taught in this chapter to complete the activity below.*

20. Look at the search results for the topic of juvenile crime. Predict which resource might be too specialized or technical for a school research project.

21. Research the subject of plea bargaining. Then write a report about whether you think criminals should be allowed to plea bargain, and in what circumstances.

Reading Skills

Organizing Facts and Information *Use the Reading Skill taught in this chapter to complete the activity below.*

22. Study the chart on page 390. Then, using the cause-effect pattern of organization, write a paragraph describing the stages in the criminal justice system.

FOCUS ON WRITING

23. Giving an Oral Report Review your notes about crime and law enforcement in the United States. Pay special attention to juvenile crime and its causes. Now write your oral report on how you and your classmates can curb juvenile crime in your community. If time permits, you may give your report to the class.

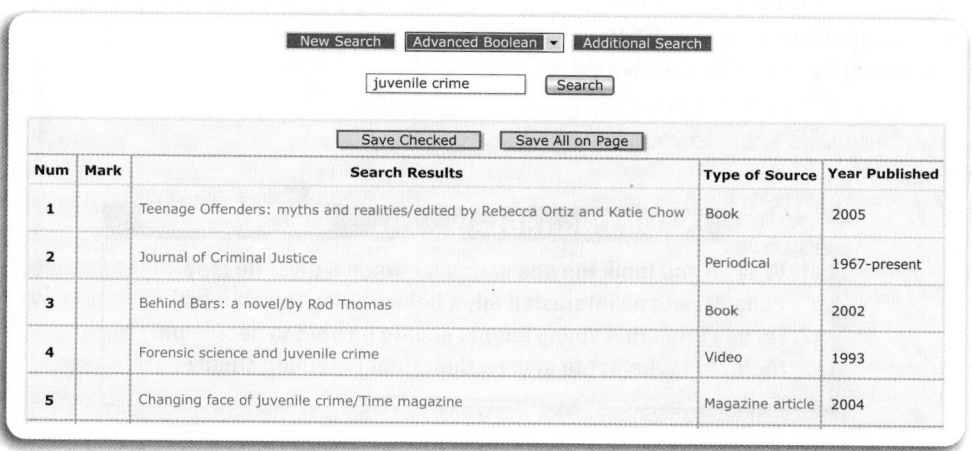

New Search	Advanced Boolean ▼	Additional Search

juvenile crime | Search

Save Checked | Save All on Page

Num	Mark	Search Results	Type of Source	Year Published
1		Teenage Offenders: myths and realities/edited by Rebecca Ortiz and Katie Chow	Book	2005
2		Journal of Criminal Justice	Periodical	1967-present
3		Behind Bars: a novel/by Rod Thomas	Book	2002
4		Forensic science and juvenile crime	Video	1993
5		Changing face of juvenile crime/Time magazine	Magazine article	2004

Miranda Warnings and Juveniles

While watching movies or the news, you may have heard people say that they will "take the Fifth" when asked to testify at a trial, before Congress, or at a grand jury hearing. They are talking about the Fifth Amendment of the U.S. Constitution, which protects people from being forced to provide information that may lead to their prosecution for a crime. In 1966, this protection was made even stronger. The U.S. Supreme Court ruled in Miranda v. Arizona *that people must be informed of their right to remain silent or have a lawyer present when being questioned by the police. This information is known as a Miranda warning.*

Why it Matters

How does the Miranda decision apply to young people? One aspect of Miranda warnings is that people can choose to give up their right to remain silent and talk to police freely, even confessing to crimes. Some people have expressed concerns that juveniles questioned by police might be easily frightened into giving up their rights without understanding the consequences. These advocates for juveniles argue that young people need special protection during police questioning. However, although the Supreme Court has ruled that juveniles should receive Miranda warnings, the Court has also ruled that as long as these young people understand their rights, they can give them up voluntarily—just like adults.

Some states' laws do require that minors be allowed to consult with an interested adult, someone who will look out for their best interests, before being questioned. Usually this interested adult is a parent, but in some cases—such as when a juvenile might be questioned about crimes committed by his or her parents—another trusted adult may be consulted. In some states these laws apply to young people under the age of 14. In other states they apply to those under the age of 18.

The Supreme Court has ruled that juveniles must receive Miranda warnings when being questioned by police.

ANALYSIS SKILL **EVALUATING THE LAW**

go.hrw.com
KEYWORD: SZ7 CH16

1. **Why do you think the age varies for when a juvenile may consult with an interested adult before being questioned?**
2. **Do you think that young people should be able to decide on their own whether to give up their right to remain silent?**

CRIMINAL JUSTICE SYSTEM HANDBOOK

Learn the basics about the American court system.

HOLT McDOUGAL

CRIMINAL JUSTICE SYSTEM

The American criminal justice system can be a complicated process. Everyone involved in the process—from the police to lawyers to ordinary citizens—has specific duties to fulfill and certain procedures to follow. To better understand these duties and procedures, let's follow a case from the investigation through the trial and its outcome.

From Arrest to Trial

It had been a good vacation, but everyone was ready to be home. The Citizen family had spent a week at the beach, sunbathing and splashing in the ocean, but now they just wanted to curl up in their own beds and get some sleep. In the back seat, twins Sandy and Sally perked up as the car turned into their neighborhood. However, their excitement changed to shock when they pulled into the driveway and discovered that their house had been robbed! The Citizens could see through a broken window that most of their possessions were gone. Quickly, Mom pulled out her cell phone and called the police.

The Investigation

Detective Kenneth Kopp arrived at the Citizens' house about an hour after they got home. He immediately got to work, checking inside and outside the house for clues. He dusted the house for fingerprints, and found one set on the sill of the broken window. Informing the Citizens that he would send the prints to a lab for identification, he decided to ask the Citizens' neighbors if they had seen anything.

The first three neighbors Detective Kopp checked with knew nothing about the crime. However, the woman who lived next door, Ms. Nadia Naybor, told the curious officer that she had seen an unfamiliar blue car drive past the Citizens' house several times the previous day. Suspicious, she had written down the car's license plate number, which she gave to the grateful Detective Kopp. When asked, she described the driver of the car as a young woman with short brown hair.

Before long, Officer Kopp heard back from the crime lab. The fingerprints he had found belonged to a young woman named Betty Burgle, who, it turned out, also drove a light blue car. A quick check on a police database matched the license plate number Ms. Naybor had reported to her car. Officer Kopp had a <u>suspect</u>. He and his partner hurried to Burgle's apartment to arrest her.

VOCABULARY

suspect a person the police believe may have committed a particular crime

The Arraignment

After Burgle had been arrested and brought to jail, she contacted a lawyer to handle her case. The lawyer she chose was Douglas Doubt, a well-known and very successful defense attorney. Doubt and Burgle sat down to discuss the details of her case.

The next morning, Burgle was brought before Judge Joy Justice for her arraignment. With her lawyer she listened as the judge explained the crimes with which she had been charged—burglary, or breaking into a private building, and larceny, or theft—and declared that, if found guilty, Burgle could be sentenced to several years in jail. The judge then set a date for a preliminary hearing to be held in two weeks. The purpose for this hearing, she explained, was for the prosecution to prove that it had enough evidence to support a case against Burgle. With the hearing date set, the judge set Burgle's <u>bail</u> and ended the arraignment proceedings.

The arraignment completed, Burgle paid her bail and set out for home after promising to return for her hearing in two weeks.

VOCABULARY

bail money paid to a court in exchange for the temporary release of a prisoner before his or her trial; bail is returned to the payer when the prisoner returns to court

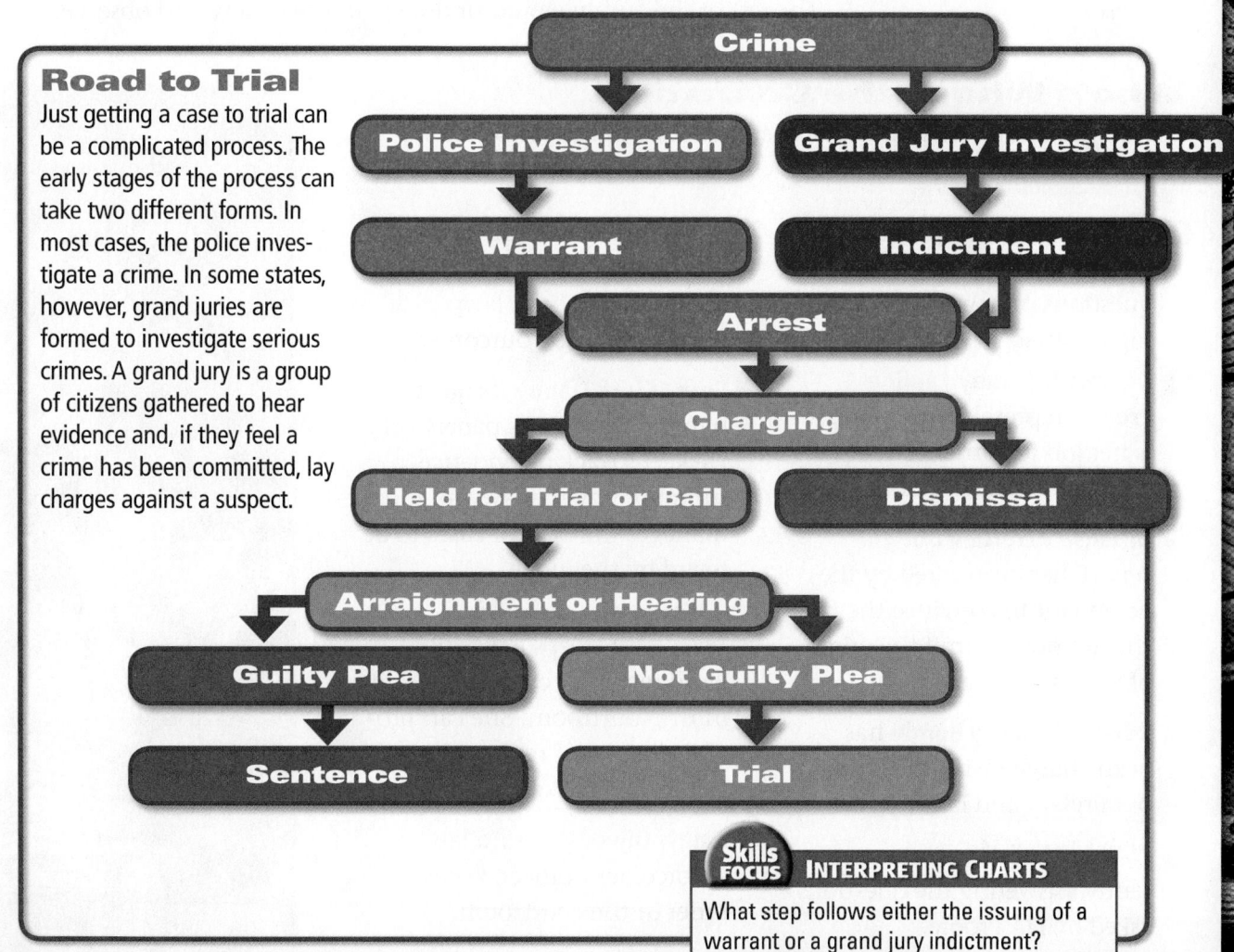

Road to Trial

Just getting a case to trial can be a complicated process. The early stages of the process can take two different forms. In most cases, the police investigate a crime. In some states, however, grand juries are formed to investigate serious crimes. A grand jury is a group of citizens gathered to hear evidence and, if they feel a crime has been committed, lay charges against a suspect.

Skills FOCUS **INTERPRETING CHARTS**

What step follows either the issuing of a warrant or a grand jury indictment?

The Preliminary Hearing

The two weeks passed quickly, and Burgle once again entered the courtroom. This time, in addition to the judge and her own lawyer, the prosecuting attorney, District Attorney (DA) Pauline Proofe was present. When the hearing had begun, DA Proofe stood up and explained the case against Burgle. She described how the police had found fingerprints matching Burgle's at the crime scene and how neighbors had seen someone matching her description in the neighborhood the day of the crime. Once the DA had finished, Judge Justice decided that the state had enough evidence to try Burgle after all. The trial was set to begin in three weeks.

Trial Proceedings

On the morning of Betty Burgle's trial, Sandy and Sally Citizen woke up early. They were going to the courthouse with their parents to watch the trial. Their father, who had received a subpoena the week before, was going to testify as a witness, so his presence was required. The rest of the family would sit quietly in the gallery and observe.

VOCABULARY

subpoena a legal document requiring someone to appear in court, usually as a defendant or a witness

Who's Who in the Courtroom

Because cameras are not allowed into most courtrooms, the images we see of trials are usually created by sketch artists. The sketch shows key players:

❶ **Judge Joy Justice** presides over the courtroom. She answers all questions of law that arise during the trial.

❷ **District Attorney Pauline Proofe** represents the state. It is her job to convince the jury of the defendant's guilt.

❸ **Defense Attorney Douglas Doubt** has been hired by the defendant to convince the jury she did not commit the crime of which she is accused.

❹ **Defendant Betty Burgle** has been charged with the crimes of burglary and larceny.

❺ **Witness Nadia Naybor** is currently answering the questions asked by DA Proofe.

❻ **The jury** listens to the testimony of all witnesses and the arguments of both lawyers to decide the case's outcome.

❼ **Court Clerk Donny Dockett** handles the court's paperwork. He keeps track of evidence submitted by the lawyers and manages the flow of cases to be heard by the judge.

❽ **Court Reporter Tracy Transcript** keeps a word-by-word record of everything said in the courtroom. She can provide an instant replay of any testimony if asked.

❾ **Bailiff Oliver Order,** a law enforcement officer, keeps order in the courtroom.

Shortly after the Citizens found seats in the gallery, the trial began. The bailiff asked everyone to stand as the judge entered the room and called the court to order. Court Clerk Donny Dockett then announced the case, *People* v. *Burgle*.

Opening Arguments

Once everyone was seated, DA Proofe stood for her opening argument. "Ladies and gentlemen of the jury," she began, "what would you do if someone stole all of your worldly possessions?" She explained to the jury that she would attempt to prove, through evidence and witness <u>testimony</u>, that Betty Burgle had broken into the Citizens' home while they were away and robbed it. She said the evidence against the <u>defendant</u> was so overwhelming that the outcome would be clear.

As the DA sat down, Defense Attorney Doubt took the floor. Though it was sad that the Citizens had been robbed, he said, there was no proof that his client had been the one to rob them. He argued that the evidence was not strong enough to convict Burgle.

VOCABULARY

testimony a firsthand account of an event
defendant in a trial, the person accused of a crime

Presentation of Evidence

With the opening statements complete, it was time to begin the heart of the trial—the presentation of evidence. The ultimate outcome of the trial would be based on what was said and seen here.

The Prosecution Calls Witnesses

The prosecution began by calling its first witness: Mr. Citizen. Before his testimony began, he had to swear an <u>oath</u> to tell "the truth, the whole truth, and nothing but the truth." Then, DA Proofe began her questioning. She asked Mr. Citizen to describe the scene at his house when he returned from vacation. In response, Mr. Citizen described his broken window and missing belongings. Once he had finished, DA Proofe declared that she had no more questions. The defense now had a chance to <u>cross-examine</u> the witness, but Doubt had no questions for Mr. Citizen.

Proofe next called Officer Kopp to the stand to describe his investigation. She asked him about the fingerprints found at the scene,

VOCABULARY

oath a promise to tell the truth
cross-examine to examine a witness who has already testified for the purpose of checking or discrediting his or her testimony

Trial Stages and Key Players

Although each court case is different, all of them involve certain key stages, which are outlined to the right. Each court also features people performing the same tasks, whose roles are described in the boxes below.

Opening

- The case is officially announced and the trial is begun.
- The charges against the defendant are read aloud.

Opening Statements

- Prosecution attempts to clarify the charges laid against the defendant.
- Both attorneys preview the evidence they will present.

Judge, Joy Justice

- Presides over the courtroom
- Answers all questions about law
- Issues sentence

District Attorney, Pauline Proofe

- Represents the people
- Attempts to prove the defendant's guilt beyond any reasonable doubt

Defense Attorney, Douglas Doubt

- Represents the defendant
- Attempts to prove the defendant's innocence by showing weakness in the prosecution's case

which had been admitted to the court as evidence. Was he certain they belonged to the defendant? Officer Kopp was indeed certain.

Doubt then stood to cross-examine. He asked where at the Citizens' house the police had found the fingerprints. Kopp responded that they had been found outside on a broken window. In that case, Doubt asked, wasn't it possible that Miss Burgle had simply been walking by and touched a window? Officer Kopp conceded that this was a possibility, though it seemed unlikely to him.

The next witness was Ms. Nadia Naybor, who lived next to the Citizens. She reported seeing a light blue car driven by a woman with brown hair pass the Citizens' house the day of the robbery. The DA then asked if Ms. Naybor thought Burgle looked interested in the house, but Doubt called out an objection. He pointed out that it had not been proved that his client was in the car, so the DA should not imply that she was. The judge agreed, and Proofe withdrew her question. Later, during his cross-examination, Doubt asked if Ms. Naybor had seen the driver's face when the car passed. She had not.

Presentation of Evidence	Closing Statements	Deliberating and Sentencing
• Attorneys question witnesses . • Each attorney has a chance to cross-examine witnesses called by his or her opponent. • Attorneys present physical evidence that supports their case.	• Attorneys summarize the cases they have presented and point out possible weaknesses in their opponents' cases.	• The jury retires to discuss its decision. • Once the jury has deliberated, the verdict is announced to the court. • In the case of a guilty verdict, the judge determines the defendant's punishment.

Witness, Nadia Naybor

• Answers questions posed by the attorneys
• Provides truthful and complete answers to all questions

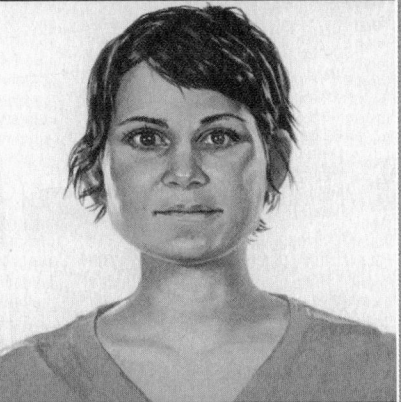

Defendant, Betty Burgle

• Attempts to prove innocence
• Cannot be required to provide evidence that will incriminate himself or herself

Jury Member, Pedro Peer

• Listens to all evidence presented by both sides
• Debates evidence with other jurors to determine the final verdict

The Defense Calls Witnesses

After Ms. Naybor's testimony, the prosecution announced that it had no more witnesses to call. As a result, the defense now had a chance to call witnesses of its own. Attorney Doubt called only one witness: Betty Burgle herself. In her testimony, Burgle said that she was at home watching television when the Citizens' house was robbed.

When the defense had finished its questioning, DA Proofe had a chance to cross-examine. She asked what program Burgle had been watching on the evening in question. Burgle answered with the name of a popular game show. In response, Proofe pulled out a newspaper from the day of the robbery. Turning to the television listings, she noted that the show in question had not actually been aired that night. Proofe also asked Burgle if anyone else could verify that she had been at home that night. Upon learning that no one could, Proofe ended her questioning as well.

In many states, registering to vote or registering for a driver's license also registers a person for jury duty. Potential jurors are selected at random and sent summonses like the one at right.

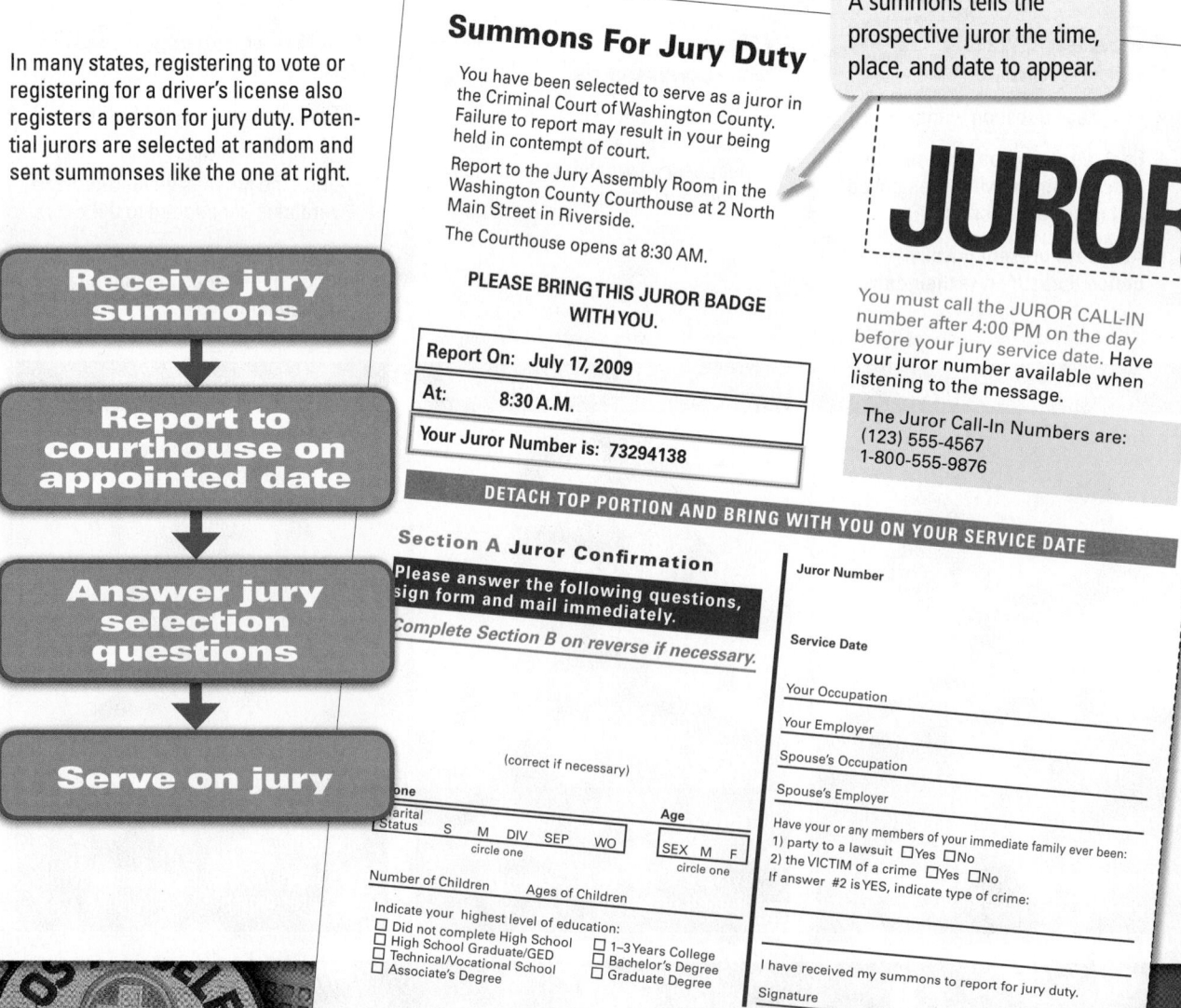

Summons For Jury Duty

You have been selected to serve as a juror in the Criminal Court of Washington County. Failure to report may result in your being held in contempt of court.

Report to the Jury Assembly Room in the Washington County Courthouse at 2 North Main Street in Riverside.

The Courthouse opens at 8:30 AM.

PLEASE BRING THIS JUROR BADGE WITH YOU.

Report On:	July 17, 2009
At:	8:30 A.M.
Your Juror Number is:	73294138

A summons tells the prospective juror the time, place, and date to appear.

JUROR

You must call the JUROR CALL-IN number after 4:00 PM on the day before your jury service date. Have your juror number available when listening to the message.

The Juror Call-In Numbers are:
(123) 555-4567
1-800-555-9876

DETACH TOP PORTION AND BRING WITH YOU ON YOUR SERVICE DATE

Section A Juror Confirmation

Please answer the following questions, sign form and mail immediately.

Complete Section B on reverse if necessary.

Juror Number

Service Date

Your Occupation

Your Employer

Spouse's Occupation

Spouse's Employer

(correct if necessary)

one

Marital Status   S   M   DIV   SEP   WO   Age
circle one

SEX   M   F
circle one

Number of Children   Ages of Children

Indicate your highest level of education:
☐ Did not complete High School
☐ High School Graduate/GED   ☐ 1–3 Years College
☐ Technical/Vocational School   ☐ Bachelor's Degree
☐ Associate's Degree   ☐ Graduate Degree

Have your or any members of your immediate family ever been:
1) party to a lawsuit ☐Yes ☐No
2) the VICTIM of a crime ☐Yes ☐No
If answer #2 is YES, indicate type of crime:

I have received my summons to report for jury duty.
Signature   Date

Receive jury summons

Report to courthouse on appointed date

Answer jury selection questions

Serve on jury

Closing Arguments

With all of the witnesses' testimony complete, it was time for the lawyers' closing arguments. Again speaking first, DA Proofe reminded the judge and the jury of the evidence against Miss Burgle, especially the fingerprints and the presence of her car in the neighborhood. In his closing, in contrast, Attorney Doubt argued that none of this evidence was convincing. All of the evidence that the prosecution had presented could be explained by pure coincidence; thus; his client should be found not guilty.

The arguments were complete, and so the jury now had to decide the outcome of the case. As the bailiff escorted the jury out of the room to deliberate in private, Sandy and Sally Citizen wished that they could hear what was happening in the jury room.

The Jury

The first juror to leave the room was Pedro Peer. As he led the other jurors down a hallway to the jury room, he thought back over how he had become part of the jury.

The Summons and Selection

About a month before the trial, Mr. Peer had received a letter in the mail saying that he had been selected for jury duty. The letter, called a summons, asked him to complete and return a form with information about himself and to appear at the courthouse on a certain date. When that day arrived, Mr. Peer and other potential jurors were escorted to a large room where they were introduced to the lawyers involved in the case.

The potential jurors were called one at a time to answer questions asked by the lawyers, a process called voir dire. These questions were designed to find out which potential jurors could act fairly and impartially during the trial. Among the questions asked were whether the potential jurors had ever been accused of a crime, whether their homes had ever been robbed, and how they felt about long jail sentences. Those who answered in ways the lawyers did not like were dismissed from the room.

Neither lawyer objected to Mr. Peer's answers, so he was deemed acceptable as a juror. As it turned out, he was the first person actually selected to serve on the jury, which made him its foreperson, or official spokesperson.

How to Behave on a Jury

1. Always be on time.

2. Pay careful attention to all testimony. If necessary, ask to have a statement repeated.

3. Do not let your reactions to testimony show during the trial. Do not make faces or exclamations that might reveal your emotions.

4. Make no judgments until all testimony has been delivered.

5. Do not speculate or guess about anything related to the trial.

6. Do not discuss the trial with anyone outside of the courtroom. Do not read newspapers or watch television reports about the trial or investigate the trial on your own time. Doing so could unfairly influence your opinion. Your decision must be based only on what is said in the courtroom.

VOCABULARY

summons a legal order to appear in court, usually as a witness or juror

voir dire a questioning process designed to determine the suitability of a juror or witness

Trial and Deliberation

Mr. Peer and his fellow jurors arrived in the jury room to make their decision. Without delay, the jurors decided to take a vote to see where they stood. The voting revealed that 10 jurors thought the defendant was guilty and two thought she was not. However, the rules of the court stated that the jury's decision had to be <u>unanimous</u>, so the outcome was not yet determined.

For the next two hours, the jurors discussed the trial. They debated statements made by the witnesses, discussed evidence presented by the lawyers, and argued over their interpretations of the facts. Finally, though, they took another vote, and this time the results were unanimous. As foreperson, Mr. Peer informed the bailiff that they had reached a <u>verdict</u>.

The Sentence

Sandy and Sally Citizen sat up straight as the doors at the rear of the courtroom opened and the jury filed back in. From her seat behind the bench, Judge Justice asked if the jury had reached a decision. Mr. Peer, acting as the foreperson, stated that they had. On behalf of his fellow jurors, he announced that they had found the defendant guilty of both burglary and larceny. As this announcement was made, Miss Burgle slumped in her chair, obviously upset.

With the jury's verdict announced, Judge Justice now had to decide on a fair <u>sentence</u> under the law. Looking straight at Betty Burgle, the judge announced that Burgle would be sentenced to spend time in jail, punctuating her statement by pounding her gavel on the bench. Miss Burgle was led out of the room by the bailiff, the audience gathered in the gallery dispersed, and the trial ended.

VOCABULARY

unanimous in full agreement, with no dissenting votes
verdict the decision or judgment of a jury
sentence the punishment imposed on a criminal after a trial

Once a jury has finished its deliberations and decided on a guilty verdict, the judge must decide on the most appropriate sentence, or punishment, for the defendant.

Assessment

1. Sequence What are the major stages in a criminal trial? What happens during each stage?

2. Draw Conclusions Why do you think the jury in this case found Betty Burgle guilty of burglary and larceny?

3. Apply Conduct research using news sources in the library or on the Internet to learn more about a particular trial. Write a short report about the trial, identifying the key players in it, including the defendant, the judge, and the lawyers. Also include in your report a brief summary of the trial proceedings, the final verdict, and the sentence, if any.

THE WORLD ALMANAC®

go.hrw.com

World Almanac Online

KEYWORD: SS World Almanac

 HOLT McDOUGAL

United States

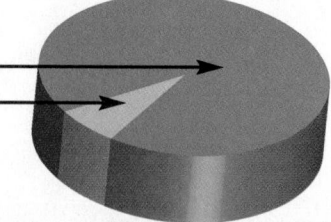

FACTS &FIGURES

AREA 50 states and Washington, D.C.

LAND	3,537,437	square miles
WATER	181,272	square miles
TOTAL	3,718,709	square miles

POPULATION (MID-2005):
295,734,134

CAPITAL:
Washington, D.C.

LARGEST, HIGHEST, AND OTHER STATISTICS

Sears Tower

Largest state:	Alaska (663,267 square miles)
Smallest state:	Rhode Island (1,545 square miles)
Northernmost city:	Barrow, Alaska (71°17' north latitude)
Southernmost city:	Hilo, Hawaii (19°44' north latitude)
Easternmost city:	Eastport, Maine (66°59'05" west longitude)
Westernmost city:	Atka, Alaska (174°12' west longitude)
Highest settlement:	Climax, Colorado (11,360 feet)
Lowest settlement:	Calipatria, California (184 feet below sea level)
Oldest national park:	Yellowstone National Park (Idaho, Montana, Wyoming), 2,219,791 acres, established 1872
Largest national park:	Wrangell-St. Elias, Alaska (8,323,148 acres)
Longest river system:	Mississippi-Missouri-Red Rock (3,710 miles)
Deepest lake:	Crater Lake, Oregon (1,932 feet)
Highest mountain:	Mount McKinley, Alaska (20,320 feet)
Lowest point:	Death Valley, California (282 feet below sea level)
Tallest building:	Sears Tower, Chicago, Illinois (1,450 feet)
Tallest structure:	TV tower, Blanchard, North Dakota (2,063 feet)
Longest bridge span:	Verrazano-Narrows Bridge, New York (4,260 feet)
Highest bridge:	Royal Gorge, Colorado (1,053 feet above water)

INTERNATIONAL BOUNDARY LINES OF THE U.S.

U.S.-Canadian border........ 3,987 miles
(excluding Alaska)
Alaska-Canadian border ..... 1,538 miles
U.S.-Mexican border .... 1,933 miles
(Gulf of Mexico to Pacific Ocean)

Atlantic coast.............. 2,069 miles
Gulf of Mexico coast .... 1,631 miles
Pacific coast .... 7,623 miles
Arctic coast, Alaska .... 1,060 miles

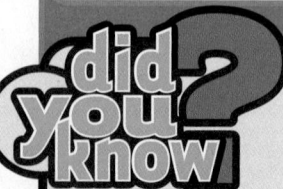

MAPMAKING ODDITY *On many maps, the top of Maine looks like the northernmost point in the U.S. outside of Alaska. But that's an optical illusion. No part of the lower 48 states is above 49 degrees of latitude except a "bubble" on the Minnesota/Canada border. That's the Northwest Angle, a 130-square mile peninsula that juts out eastward from the Canadian province of Manitoba into a lake. It's surrounded by Canadian territory, and belongs to the U.S. because of an error by mapmakers.*

SYMBOLS of the United States

The Great Seal

The Great Seal of the United States shows an American bald eagle with a ribbon in its mouth bearing the Latin words *e pluribus unum* (out of many, one). In its talons are the arrows of war and an olive branch of peace. On the back of the Great Seal is an unfinished pyramid with an eye (the eye of Providence) above it. The seal was approved by Congress on June 20, 1782.

THE FLAG

1777

1795

1818

The flag of the United States has 50 stars (one for each state) and 13 stripes (one for each of the original 13 states). It is unofficially called the "Stars and Stripes."

The first U.S. flag was commissioned by the Second Continental Congress in 1777 but did not exist until 1783, after the American Revolution. Historians are not certain who designed the Stars and Stripes. Many different flags are believed to have been used during the American Revolution.

The flag of 1777 was used until 1795. In that year Congress passed an act ordering that a new flag have 15 stripes, alternate red and white, and 15 stars on a blue field. In 1818, Congress directed that the flag have 13 stripes and that a new star be added for each new state of the Union. The last star was added in 1960 for the state of Hawaii.

There are many customs for flying the flag and treating it with respect. For example, it should not touch the floor and no other flag should be flown above it, except for the UN flag at UN head-quarters. When the flag is raised or lowered, or passes in a parade, or during the Pledge of Allegiance, people should face it and stand at attention. Those in military uniform should salute. Others should put their right hand over their heart. The flag is flown at half staff as a sign of mourning.

Pledge of Allegiance to the Flag

"I pledge allegiance to the flag of the United States of America and to the republic for which it stands, one nation under God, indivisible, with liberty and justice for all."

THE NATIONAL ANTHEM

"The Star-Spangled Banner" was a poem written in 1814 by Francis Scott Key as he watched British ships bombard Fort McHenry, Maryland, during the War of 1812. It became the National Anthem by an act of Congress in 1931. The music to "The Star-Spangled Banner" was originally a tune called "Anacreon in Heaven."

THE U.S. CONSTITUTION

The Foundation of American Government

The Constitution is the document that created the present government of the United States. It was written in 1787 and went into effect in 1789. It establishes the three branches of the U.S. government — the executive (headed by the president), the legislative (Congress), and the judicial (the Supreme Court and other federal courts). The first 10 amendments to the Constitution (the **Bill of Rights**) explain the basic rights of all American citizens.

You can find the constitution on-line at:

WEBSITE http://www.house.gov/Constitution/Constitution.html

The Preamble to the Constitution

The Constitution begins with a short statement called the Preamble. The Preamble states that the government of the United States was established by the people.

"We the people of the United States, in order to form a more perfect union, establish justice, insure domestic tranquility, provide for the common defense, promote the general welfare, and secure the blessings of liberty to ourselves and our posterity, do ordain and establish this Constitution for the United States of America."

THE ARTICLES

The original Constitution contained seven articles. The first three articles of the Constitution establish the three branches of the U.S. government.

Article 1, Legislative Branch Creates the Senate and House of Representatives and describes their functions and powers.

Article 2, Executive Branch Creates the office of the President and the Electoral College and lists their powers and responsibilities.

Article 3, Judicial Branch Creates the Supreme Court and gives Congress the power to create lower courts. The powers of the courts and certain crimes are defined.

Article 4, The States Discusses the relationship of the states to one another and to the citizens. Defines the states' powers.

Article 5, Amending the Constitution Describes how the Constitution can be amended (changed).

Article 6, Federal Law Makes the Constitution the supreme law of the land over state laws and constitutions.

Article 7, Ratifying the Constitution Establishes how to ratify (approve) the Constitution.

Amendments *to the* Constitution

The writers of the Constitution understood that it might need to be amended, or changed, in the future, but they wanted to be careful and made it hard to change. Article 5 describes how the Constitution can be amended.

In order to take effect, an amendment must be approved by a two-thirds majority in both the House of Representatives and the Senate. It must then be approved (ratified) by three-fourths of the states (38 states). So far, there have been 27 amendments. One of them (the 18th, ratified in 1919) banned the manufacture or sale of liquor. It was canceled by the 21st Amendment, in 1933.

The Bill of Rights: *The First Ten Amendments*

The first ten amendments were adopted in 1791 and contain the basic freedoms Americans enjoy as a people. These amendments are known as the Bill of Rights.

1 Guarantees freedom of religion, speech, and the press.

2 Guarantees the right to have firearms.

3 Guarantees that soldiers cannot be lodged in private homes unless the owner agrees.

4 Protects people from being searched or having property searched or taken away by the government without reason.

5 Protects rights of people on trial for crimes.

6 Guarantees people accused of crimes the right to a speedy public trial by jury.

7 Guarantees the right to a trial by jury for other kinds of cases.

8 Prohibits "cruel and unusual punishments."

9 Says specific rights listed in the Constitution do not take away rights that may not be listed.

10 Establishes that any powers not given specifically to the federal government belong to states or the people.

Other Important Amendments

13 (1865): Ends slavery in the United States.

14 (1868): Bars states from denying rights to citizens; guarantees equal protection under the law for all citizens.

15 (1870): Guarantees that a person cannot be denied the right to vote because of race or color.

19 (1920): Gives women the right to vote.

22 (1951): Limits the president to two four-year terms of office.

24 (1964): Outlaws the poll tax (a tax people had to pay before they could vote) in federal elections. (The poll tax had been used to keep African Americans in the South from voting.)

25 (1967): Specifies presidential succession; also gives the president the power to appoint a new vice president, if one dies or leaves office in the middle of a term.

26 (1971): Lowers the voting age to 18 from 21.

The Executive Branch

The **executive branch** of the federal government is headed by the president, who enforces the laws passed by Congress and is commander in chief of the U.S. armed forces. It also includes the vice president, people who work for the president or vice president, the major departments of the government, and special agencies. The **cabinet** is made up of the vice president, heads of major departments, and other officials. It meets when the president chooses. The chart at right shows cabinet departments in the order in which they were created. The Department of Homeland Security was created by a law signed in November 2002.

PRESIDENT

VICE PRESIDENT

CABINET DEPARTMENTS

1. State
2. Treasury
3. Defense
4. Justice
5. Interior
6. Agriculture
7. Commerce
8. Labor
9. Housing and Urban Development
10. Transportation
11. Energy
12. Education
13. Health and Human Services
14. Veterans Affairs
15. Homeland Security

HOW LONG DOES THE PRESIDENT SERVE?

The president serves a four-year term, starting on January 20. No president can be elected more than twice, or more than once if he or she had served two years as president filling out the term of a president who left office.

WHAT HAPPENS IF THE PRESIDENT DIES?

If the president dies in office or cannot complete the term, the vice president becomes president. If the president is unable to perform his or her duties, the vice president can become acting president. The next person to become president after the vice president would be the Speaker of the House of Representatives.

The White House has an address on the World Wide Web especially for kids. It is:
WEB SITE http://www.whitehousekids.gov

You can send e-mail to the president at:
EMAIL president@whitehouse.gov

The White House, home of the U.S. president

PRESIDENTS AND VICE PRESIDENTS OF THE UNITED STATES

PRESIDENT / VICE PRESIDENT	YEARS IN OFFICE
❶ **George Washington**	**1789–1797**
John Adams	1789–1797
❷ **John Adams**	**1797–1801**
Thomas Jefferson	1797–1801
❸ **Thomas Jefferson**	**1801–1809**
Aaron Burr	1801–1805
George Clinton	1805–1809
❹ **James Madison**	**1809–1817**
George Clinton	1809–1812
Elbridge Gerry	1813–1814
❺ **James Monroe**	**1817–1825**
Daniel D. Tompkins	1817–1825
❻ **John Quincy Adams**	**1825–1829**
John C. Calhoun	1825–1829
❼ **Andrew Jackson**	**1829–1837**
John C. Calhoun	1829–1832
Martin Van Buren	1833–1837
❽ **Martin Van Buren**	**1837–1841**
Richard M. Johnson	1837–1841
❾ **William H. Harrison**	**1841**
John Tyler	1841
❿ **John Tyler**	**1841–1845**
No Vice President	
⓫ **James Knox Polk**	**1845–1849**
George M. Dallas	1845–1849
⓬ **Zachary Taylor**	**1849–1850**
Millard Fillmore	1849–1850
⓭ **Millard Fillmore**	**1850–1853**
No Vice President	
⓮ **Franklin Pierce**	**1853–1857**
William R. King	1853
⓯ **James Buchanan**	**1857–1861**
John C. Breckinridge	1857–1861
⓰ **Abraham Lincoln**	**1861–1865**
Hannibal Hamlin	1861–1865
Andrew Johnson	1865
⓱ **Andrew Johnson**	**1865–1869**
No Vice President	
⓲ **Ulysses S. Grant**	**1869–1877**
Schuyler Colfax	1869–1873
Henry Wilson	1873–1875
⓳ **Rutherford B. Hayes**	**1877–1881**
William A. Wheeler	1877–1881
⓴ **James A. Garfield**	**1881**
Chester A. Arthur	1881
㉑ **Chester A. Arthur**	**1881–1885**
No Vice President	
㉒ **Grover Cleveland**	**1885–1889**
Thomas A. Hendricks	1885
㉓ **Benjamin Harrison**	**1889–1893**
Levi P. Morton	1889–1893
㉔ **Grover Cleveland**	**1893–1897**
Adlai E. Stevenson	1893–1897
㉕ **William McKinley**	**1897–1901**
Garret A. Hobart	1897–1899
Theodore Roosevelt	1901
㉖ **Theodore Roosevelt**	**1901–1909**
Charles W. Fairbanks	1905–1909
㉗ **William Howard Taft**	**1909–1913**
James S. Sherman	1909–1912
㉘ **Woodrow Wilson**	**1913–1921**
Thomas R. Marshall	1913–1921
㉙ **Warren G. Harding**	**1921–1923**
Calvin Coolidge	1921–1923
㉚ **Calvin Coolidge**	**1923–1929**
Charles G. Dawes	1925–1929
㉛ **Herbert Hoover**	**1929–1933**
Charles Curtis	1929–1933
㉜ **Franklin D. Roosevelt**	**1933–1945**
John Nance Garner	1933–1941
Henry A. Wallace	1941–1945
Harry S. Truman	1945
㉝ **Harry S. Truman**	**1945–1953**
Alben W. Barkley	1949–1953
㉞ **Dwight D. Eisenhower**	**1953–1961**
Richard M. Nixon	1953–1961
㉟ **John F. Kennedy**	**1961–1963**
Lyndon B. Johnson	1961–1963
㊱ **Lyndon B. Johnson**	**1963–1969**
Hubert H. Humphrey	1965–1969
㊲ **Richard M. Nixon**	**1969–1974**
Spiro T. Agnew	1969–1973
Gerald R. Ford	1973–1974
㊳ **Gerald R. Ford**	**1974–1977**
Nelson A. Rockefeller	1974–1977
㊴ **Jimmy Carter**	**1977–1981**
Walter F. Mondale	1977–1981
㊵ **Ronald Reagan**	**1981–1989**
George H. W. Bush	1981–1989
㊶ **George H. W. Bush**	**1989–1993**
Dan Quayle	1989–1993
㊷ **Bill Clinton**	**1993–2001**
Al Gore	1993–2001
㊸ **George W. Bush**	**2001–2009**
Richard B. Cheney	2001–2009
㊹ **Barack Obama**	**2009–**
Joe Biden	2009–

The Legislative Branch

CONGRESS

The Congress of the United States is the legislative branch of the federal government. Congress's major responsibility is to pass the laws that govern the country and determine how money collected in taxes is spent. It is the president's responsibility to enforce the laws. Congress consists of two parts—the Senate and the House of Representatives.

▲ The Senate

THE SENATE

The Senate has 100 members, two from each state. The Constitution says that the Senate will have equal representation (the same number of representatives) from each state. Thus, small states have the same number of senators as large states. Senators are elected for six-year terms. There is no limit on the number of terms a senator can serve.

The Senate also has the responsibility of approving people the president appoints for certain jobs: for example, cabinet members and Supreme Court justices. The Senate must approve all treaties by at least a two-thirds vote. It also has the responsibility under the Constitution of putting on trial high-ranking federal officials who have been impeached by the House of Representatives.

WEB SITE www.senate.gov

THE HOUSE OF REPRESENTATIVES

▼ The Capitol, where Congress meets

The number of members of the House of Representatives for each state depends on its population according to a recent census. But each state has at least one representative, no matter how small its population. A term lasts two years.

The first House of Representatives in 1789 had 65 members. As the country's population grew, the number of representatives increased. Since the 1910 census, however, the total membership has been kept at 435. After the results of Census 2000 were added up, 8 states gained seats and 10 states lost seats.

WEB SITE www.house.gov

THE HOUSE OF REPRESENTATIVES, BY STATE

Here are the numbers of representatives each state had in 2007, compared with earlier times:

	2007	1995	1975		2007	1995	1975
Alabama	7	7	7	Montana	1	1	2
Alaska	1	1	1	Nebraska	3	3	3
Arizona	8	6	4	Nevada	3	2	1
Arkansas	4	4	4	New Hampshire	2	2	2
California	53	52	43	New Jersey	13	13	15
Colorado	7	6	5	New Mexico	3	3	2
Connecticut	5	6	6	New York	29	31	39
Delaware	1	1	1	North Carolina	13	12	11
Florida	25	23	15	North Dakota	1	1	1
Georgia	13	11	10	Ohio	18	19	23
Hawaii	2	2	2	Oklahoma	5	6	6
Idaho	2	2	2	Oregon	5	5	4
Illinois	19	20	24	Pennsylvania	19	21	25
Indiana	9	10	11	Rhode Island	2	2	2
Iowa	5	5	6	South Carolina	6	6	6
Kansas	4	4	5	South Dakota	1	1	2
Kentucky	6	6	7	Tennessee	9	9	9
Louisiana	7	7	8	Texas	32	30	24
Maine	2	2	2	Utah	3	3	2
Maryland	8	8	8	Vermont	1	1	1
Massachusetts	10	10	12	Virginia	11	11	10
Michigan	15	16	19	Washington	9	9	7
Minnesota	8	8	8	West Virginia	3	3	4
Mississippi	4	5	5	Wisconsin	8	9	9
Missouri	9	9	10	Wyoming	1	1	1

Washington, D.C., Puerto Rico, American Samoa, Guam, and the Virgin Islands each have one nonvoting member of the House of Representatives.

Women in Congress

▶ As of January 2007, there were 87 women in Congress (71 in the U.S. House of Representatives and 16 in the U.S. Senate). This is more than ever before.

▶ The first woman elected to the House was Jeannette Rankin (Montana) in 1916. In 1932, Hattie Caraway (Arkansas) was the first woman to be elected to the Senate. Margaret Chase Smith, of Maine, was the first woman elected to both houses of Congress (House in 1940, Senate in 1948).

▶ New York's Shirley Chisholm became the first African-American woman in Congress after being elected to the House in 1968. In 1992, Carol Moseley Braun of Illinois became the first African-American woman elected to the Senate.

▶ As of January 2007, California Representative Nancy Pelosi is the Speaker of the House, the highest position in Congress ever held by a woman.

Nancy Pelosi ➤

THE JUDICIAL BRANCH

The Supreme Court

The highest court in the United States is the Supreme Court. It has nine justices who are appointed for life by the president with the approval of the Senate. Eight of the nine members are called associate justices. The ninth is the Chief Justice, who presides over the Court's meetings.

What Does the Supreme Court Do?

The Supreme Court's major responsibilities are to judge cases that involve reviewing federal laws, actions of the president, treaties of the United States, and laws passed by state governments to be sure they do not conflict with the U.S. Constitution. If the Supreme Court finds that a law or action violates the Constitution, the law is struck down.

The Supreme Court's Decision Is Final.

Most cases must go through other state courts or federal courts before they reach the Supreme Court. The Supreme Court is the final court for a case, and the justices decide which cases they will review. After the Supreme Court hears a case, it may agree or disagree with the decision by a lower court. Each justice has one vote, and the majority rules. When the Supreme Court makes a ruling, its decision is final, so each of the justices has a very important job.

Below are the nine justices who were on the Supreme Court in May 2007. **Back row** (from left to right): Stephen Breyer, Clarence Thomas, Ruth Bader Ginsburg, Samuel Alito. **Front row** (from left to right): Anthony M. Kennedy, John Paul Stevens, Chief Justice John G. Roberts, Antonin Scalia, David H. Souter.

HOW A **BILL** BECOMES A **LAW** ⭐

STEP 1 SENATORS AND REPRESENTATIVES PROPOSE BILL.

A proposed law is called a **bill**. Any member of Congress may propose (introduce) a bill. A bill is introduced in each house of Congress. The House of Representatives and the Senate consider a bill separately. A member of Congress who introduces a bill is known as the bill's **sponsor**. Bills to raise money always begin in the House of Representatives.

STEP 2 HOUSE AND SENATE COMMITTEES CONSIDER THE BILL.

The bill is then sent to appropriate committees for consideration. A bill relating to agriculture, for example, would be sent to the agriculture committees in the House and in the Senate. A committee is made up of a small number of members of the House or Senate. Whichever party has a majority in the House or Senate has a majority on each committee. When committees are considering a bill, they hold **hearings** at which people can speak for or against it.

STEP 3 COMMITTEES VOTE ON THE BILL.

The committees can change the bill as they see fit. Then they vote on it.

STEP 4 THE BILL IS DEBATED IN THE HOUSE AND SENATE.

If the committees vote in favor of the bill, it goes to the full House and Senate, where it is debated and may be changed further. The House and Senate can then vote on it.

STEP 5 FROM HOUSE AND SENATE TO CONFERENCE COMMITTEE.

If the House and the Senate pass different versions of the same bill, the bill must go to a **conference committee,** where differences between the two versions must be worked out. A conference committee is a special committee made up of both Senate and House members.

STEP 6 FINAL VOTE IN THE HOUSE AND SENATE.

The House and the Senate then vote on the conference committee version. In order for this version to become a law, it must be approved by a majority of members of both houses of Congress and signed by the president.

STEP 7 THE PRESIDENT SIGNS THE BILL INTO LAW.

If the bill passes both houses of Congress, it goes to the president for his signature. Once the president signs a bill, it becomes law.

STEP 8 WHAT IF THE PRESIDENT DOESN'T SIGN IT?

Sometimes the president does not approve of a bill and decides not to sign it. This is called **vetoing** it. A bill that has been vetoed goes back to Congress, where the members can vote again. If the House and the Senate pass the bill with a two-thirds majority vote, it becomes law. This is called **overriding** the veto.

THE ★★★★★★★ PRESIDENTS OF THE UNITED STATES

1

GEORGE WASHINGTON Federalist Party   1789–1797
Born: Feb. 22, 1732, at Wakefield, Westmoreland County, Virginia
Married: Martha Dandridge Custis (1731-1802); no children
Died: Dec. 14, 1799; buried at Mount Vernon, Fairfax County, Virginia
Early Career: Soldier; head of the Virginia militia; commander of the
    Continental Army; chairman of Constitutional Convention (1787)

2

JOHN ADAMS Federalist Party   1797–1801
Born: Oct. 30, 1735, in Braintree (now Quincy), Massachusetts
Married: Abigail Smith (1744-1818); 3 sons, 2 daughters
Died: July 4, 1826; buried in Quincy, Massachusetts
Early Career: Lawyer; delegate to Continental Congress; signer of
    the Declaration of Independence; first vice president

3

THOMAS JEFFERSON Democratic-Republican Party   1801–1809
Born: Apr. 13, 1743, at Shadwell, Albemarle County, Virginia
Married: Martha Wayles Skelton (1748-1782); 1 son, 5 daughters
Died: July 4, 1826; buried at Monticello, Albemarle County, Virginia
Early Career: Lawyer; member of the Continental Congress; author of the
    Declaration of Independence; governor of Virginia; first secretary of
    state; author of the Virginia Statute on Religious Freedom

4

JAMES MADISON Democratic-Republican Party   1809-1817
Born: Mar. 16, 1751, at Port Conway, King George County, Virginia
Married: Dolley Payne Todd (1768-1849); no children
Died: June 28, 1836; buried at Montpelier Station, Virginia
Early Career: Member of the Virginia Constitutional Convention (1776);
    member of the Continental Congress; major contributor to the U.S.
    Constitution; writer of the *Federalist Papers*; secretary of state

5

JAMES MONROE Democratic-Republican Party   1817–1825
Born: Apr. 28, 1758, in Westmoreland County, Virginia
Married: Elizabeth Kortright (1768-1830); 1 son, 2 daughters
Died: July 4, 1831; buried in Richmond, Virginia
Early Career: Soldier; lawyer; U.S. senator; governor of Virginia;
    secretary of state

6

JOHN QUINCY ADAMS Democratic-Republican Party   1825–1829
Born: July 11, 1767, in Braintree (now Quincy), Massachusetts
Married: Louisa Catherine Johnson (1775-1852); 3 sons, 1 daughter
Died: Feb. 23, 1848; buried in Quincy, Massachusetts
Early Career: Diplomat; U.S. senator; secretary of state

7 ANDREW JACKSON Democratic Party   1829–1837
  Born: Mar. 15, 1767, in Waxhaw, South Carolina
  Married: Rachel Donelson Robards (1767-1828); 1 son (adopted)
  Died: June 8, 1845; buried in Nashville, Tennessee
  Early Career: Lawyer; U.S. representative and senator; U.S. Army
    general

8 MARTIN VAN BUREN Democratic Party   1837–1841
  Born: Dec. 5, 1782, at Kinderhook, New York
  Married: Hannah Hoes (1783-1819); 4 sons
  Died: July 24, 1862; buried at Kinderhook, New York
  Early Career: Governor of New York; secretary of state; vice president

9 WILLIAM HENRY HARRISON Whig Party   1841
  Born: Feb. 9, 1773, at Berkeley, Charles City County, Virginia
  Married: Anna Symmes (1775-1864); 6 sons, 4 daughters
  Died: Apr. 4, 1841; buried in North Bend, Ohio
  Early Career: First governor of Indiana Territory; superintendent of
    Indian affairs; U.S. representative and senator

10 JOHN TYLER Whig Party   1841–1845
  Born: Mar. 29, 1790, in Greenway, Charles City County, Virginia
  Married: Letitia Christian (1790-1842); 3 sons, 5 daughters
    Julia Gardiner (1820-1889); 5 sons, 2 daughters
  Died: Jan. 18, 1862; buried in Richmond, Virginia
  Early Career: U.S. representative and senator; vice president

11 JAMES KNOX POLK Democratic Party   1845–1849
  Born: Nov. 2, 1795, in Mecklenburg County, North Carolina
  Married: Sarah Childress (1803-1891); no children
  Died: June 15, 1849; buried in Nashville, Tennessee
  Early Career: U.S. representative; Speaker of the House; governor
    of Tennessee

12 ZACHARY TAYLOR Whig Party   1849–1850
  Born: Nov. 24, 1784, in Orange County, Virginia
  Married: Margaret Smith (1788-1852); 1 son, 5 daughters
  Died: July 9, 1850; buried in Louisville, Kentucky
  Early Career: General in the U.S. Army

13 MILLARD FILLMORE Whig Party   1850–1853
  Born: Jan. 7, 1800, in Cayuga County, New York
  Married: Abigail Powers (1798-1853); 1 son, 1 daughter
    Caroline Carmichael McIntosh (1813-1881); no children
  Died: Mar. 8, 1874; buried in Buffalo, New York
  Early Career: Farmer; lawyer; U.S. representative; vice president

14 **FRANKLIN PIERCE** Democratic Party   1853–1857
Born: Nov. 23, 1804, in Hillsboro, New Hampshire
Married: Jane Means Appleton (1806-1863); 3 sons
Died: Oct. 8, 1869; buried in Concord, New Hampshire
Early Career: U.S. representative, senator

15 **JAMES BUCHANAN** Democratic Party   1857–1861
Born: Apr. 23, 1791, Cove Gap, near Mercersburg, Pennsylvania
Married: Never
Died: June 1, 1868, buried in Lancaster, Pennsylvania
Early Career: U.S. representative; secretary of state

16 **ABRAHAM LINCOLN** Republican Party   **1861-1865**
Born: Feb. 12, 1809, in Hardin County, Kentucky
Married: Mary Todd (1818-1882); 4 sons
Died: Apr. 15, 1865; buried in Springfield, Illinois
Early Career: Lawyer; U.S. representative

17 **ANDREW JOHNSON** Democratic Party   1865–1869
Born: Dec. 29, 1808, in Raleigh, North Carolina
Married: Eliza McCardle (1810-1876); 3 sons, 2 daughters
Died: July 31, 1875; buried in Greeneville, Tennessee
Early Career: Tailor; member of state legislature; U.S. representative; governor of Tennessee; U.S. senator; vice president

18 **ULYSSES S. GRANT** Republican Party   1869–1877
Born: Apr. 27, 1822, in Point Pleasant, Ohio
Married: Julia Dent (1826-1902); 3 sons, 1 daughter
Died: July 23, 1885; buried in New York City
Early Career: Army officer; commander of Union forces during Civil War

19 **RUTHERFORD B. HAYES** Republican Party   1877–1881
Born: Oct. 4, 1822, in Delaware, Ohio
Married: Lucy Ware Webb (1831-1889); 7 sons, 1 daughter
Died: Jan. 17, 1893; buried in Fremont, Ohio
Early Career: Lawyer; general in Union Army; U.S. representative; governor of Ohio

20 **JAMES A. GARFIELD** Republican Party   1881
Born: Nov. 19, 1831, in Orange, Cuyahoga County, Ohio
Married: Lucretia Rudolph (1832-1918); 5 sons, 2 daughters
Died: Sept. 19, 1881; buried in Cleveland, Ohio
Early Career: Teacher; Ohio state senator; general in Union Army; U.S. representative

21 CHESTER A. ARTHUR Republican Party   1881–1885
Born: Oct. 5, 1829, in Fairfield, Vermont
Married: Ellen Lewis Herndon (1837-1880); 2 sons, 1 daughter
Died: Nov. 18, 1886; buried in Albany, New York
Early Career: Teacher; lawyer; vice president

22 GROVER CLEVELAND Democratic Party   1885–1889
Born: Mar. 18, 1837, in Caldwell, New Jersey
Married: Frances Folsom (1864-1947); 2 sons, 3 daughters
Died: June 24, 1908; buried in Princeton, New Jersey
Early Career: Lawyer; mayor of Buffalo; governor of New York

23 BENJAMIN HARRISON Republican Party   1889-1893
Born: Aug. 20, 1833, in North Bend, Ohio
Married: Caroline Lavinia Scott (1832-1892); 1 son, 1 daughter
    Mary Scott Lord Dimmick (1858-1948); 1 daughter
Died: Mar. 13, 1901; buried in Indianapolis, Indiana
Early Career: Lawyer; general in Union Army; U.S. senator

24 GROVER CLEVELAND   1893–1897
See 22, above

25 WILLIAM MCKINLEY Republican Party   1897–1901
Born: Jan. 29, 1843, in Niles, Ohio
Married: Ida Saxton (1847-1907); 2 daughters
Died: Sept. 14, 1901; buried in Canton, Ohio
Early Career: Lawyer; U.S. representative; governor of Ohio

26 THEODORE ROOSEVELT Republican Party   1901–1909
Born: Oct. 27, 1858, in New York City
Married: Alice Hathaway Lee (1861-1884); 1 daughter
    Edith Kermit Carow (1861-1948); 4 sons, 1 daughter
Died: Jan. 6, 1919; buried in Oyster Bay, New York
Early Career: Assistant secretary of the Navy; cavalry leader in
    Spanish-American War; governor of New York; vice president

27 WILLIAM HOWARD TAFT Republican Party   1909–1913
Born: Sept. 15, 1857, in Cincinnati, Ohio
Married: Helen Herron (1861-1943); 2 sons, 1 daughter
Died: Mar. 8, 1930; buried in Arlington National Cemetery, Virginia
Early Career: Reporter; lawyer; judge; secretary of war

28 WOODROW WILSON Democratic Party   1913–1921
Born: Dec. 28, 1856, in Staunton, Virginia
Married: Ellen Louise Axson (1860-1914); 3 daughters
    Edith Bolling Galt (1872-1961); no children
Died: Feb. 3, 1924; buried in Washington, D.C.
Early Career: College professor and president; governor of New Jersey

29 **WARREN G. HARDING** Republican Party 1921–1923
Born: Nov. 2, 1865, near Corsica (now Blooming Grove), Ohio
Married: Florence Kling De Wolfe (1860-1924); 1 daughter
Died: Aug. 2, 1923; buried in Marion, Ohio
Early Career: Ohio state senator; U.S. senator

30 **CALVIN COOLIDGE** Republican Party 1923–1929
Born: July 4, 1872, in Plymouth, Vermont
Married: Grace Anna Goodhue (1879-1957); 2 sons
Died: Jan. 5, 1933; buried in Plymouth, Vermont
Early Career: Massachusetts state legislator; lieutenant governor and governor; vice president

31 **HERBERT HOOVER** Republican Party 1929–1933
Born: Aug. 10, 1874, in West Branch, Iowa
Married: Lou Henry (1875-1944); 2 sons
Died: Oct. 20, 1964; buried in West Branch, Iowa
Early Career: Mining engineer; secretary of commerce

32 **FRANKLIN DELANO ROOSEVELT** Democratic Party 1933–1945
Born: Jan. 30, 1882, in Hyde Park, New York
Married: Anna Eleanor Roosevelt (1884-1962); 4 sons, 1 daughter
Died: Apr. 12, 1945; buried in Hyde Park, New York
Early Career: Lawyer; New York state senator; assistant secretary of the Navy; governor of New York

33 **HARRY S. TRUMAN** Democratic Party 1945–1953
Born: May 8, 1884, in Lamar, Missouri
Married: Elizabeth Virginia "Bess" Wallace (1885-1982); 1 daughter
Died: Dec. 26, 1972; buried in Independence, Missouri
Early Career: Farmer; haberdasher (ran men's clothing store); judge; U.S. senator; vice president

34 **DWIGHT D. EISENHOWER** Republican Party 1953–1961
Born: Oct. 14, 1890, in Denison, Texas
Married: Mary "Mamie" Geneva Doud (1896-1979); 2 sons
Died: Mar. 28, 1969; buried in Abilene, Kansas
Early Career: General, U.S. Army, Supreme Allied Commander in Europe during World War II; president of Columbia University

35 **JOHN FITZGERALD KENNEDY** Democratic Party 1961–1963
Born: May 29, 1917, in Brookline, Massachusetts
Married: Jacqueline Lee Bouvier (1929-1994); 2 sons, 1 daughter
Died: Nov. 22, 1963; buried in Arlington National Cemetery, Virginia
Early Career: U.S. Naval officer; U.S. representative and senator

36 **LYNDON BAINES JOHNSON** Democratic Party 1963–1969
Born: Aug. 27, 1908, near Stonewall, Texas
Married: Claudia "Lady Bird" Alta Taylor (1912-2007); 2 daughters
Died: Jan. 22, 1973; buried in Johnson City, Texas
Early Career: U.S. representative and senator; vice president

37 RICHARD MILHOUS NIXON Republican Party 1969–1974
Born: Jan. 9, 1913, in Yorba Linda, California
Married: Thelma "Pat" Ryan (1912-1993); 2 daughters
Died: Apr. 22, 1994; buried in Yorba Linda, California
Early Career: Lawyer; U.S. representative and senator; vice president

38 GERALD R. FORD Republican Party 1974–1977
Born: July 14, 1913, in Omaha, Nebraska
Married: Elizabeth "Betty" Bloomer (b. 1918); 3 sons, 1 daughter
Died: December 26, 2006; buried in Grand Rapids, Michigan
Early Career: Lawyer; U.S. representative; vice president

39 JIMMY (JAMES EARL) CARTER Democratic Party 1977–1981
Born: Oct. 1, 1924, in Plains, Georgia
Married: Rosalynn Smith (b. 1927); 3 sons, 1 daughter
Early Career: Peanut farmer; Georgia state senator; governor
of Georgia

40 RONALD REAGAN Republican Party 1981–1989
Born: Feb. 6, 1911, in Tampico, Illinois
Married: Jane Wyman (b. 1914); 1 son, 1 daughter
Nancy Davis (b. 1923); 1 son, 1 daughter
Died: June 5, 2004; buried in Simi Valley, California
Early Career: Film and television actor; governor of California

41 GEORGE H.W. BUSH Republican Party 1989–1993
Born: June 12, 1924, in Milton, Massachusetts
Married: Barbara Pierce (b. 1925); 4 sons, 2 daughters
Early Career: U.S. Navy pilot; businessman; U.S. representative; U.S.
ambassador to the UN; CIA director, vice president

42 BILL (WILLIAM JEFFERSON) CLINTON Democratic Party 1993–2001
Born: Aug. 19, 1946, in Hope, Arkansas
Married: Hillary Rodham (b. 1947); 1 daughter
Early Career: College professor; Arkansas state attorney general;
governor of Arkansas

43 GEORGE W. BUSH Republican Party 2001–2009
Born: July 6, 1946, in New Haven, Connecticut
Married: Laura Welch (b. 1946); 2 daughters
Early Career: Political adviser; businessman; governor of Texas

44 BARACK OBAMA Democratic Party 2009–
Born: Aug. 4, 1961, in Honolulu, Hawaii
Married: Michelle Robinson (b. 1964); 2 daughters
Early Career: Lawyer; Illinois state legislator, 1997–2004;
U.S. senator, 2005–09

FACTS About the STATES

After every state name is the postal abbreviation. The Area includes both land and water; it is given in square miles (sq. mi.) and square kilometers (sq. km.). Numbers in parentheses after Population, Area, and Entered Union show the state's rank compared with other states. City populations are for mid-2005.

ALABAMA (AL) Heart of Dixie, Camellia State

POPULATION (2006): 4,599,030 (23rd) **AREA:** 52,419 sq. mi. (30th) (135,765 sq. km.) 🌼 Camellia 🐦 Yellowhammer 🌲 Southern longleaf pine 🎵 "Alabama" **ENTERED UNION:** December 14, 1819 (22nd) ⭐ Montgomery **LARGEST CITIES (WITH POP.):** Birmingham, 231,483; Montgomery, 200,127; Mobile, 191,544; Huntsville, 166,313

⚙️ clothing and textiles, metal products, transportation equipment, paper, industrial machinery, food products, lumber, coal, oil, natural gas, livestock, peanuts, cotton

did you know? *Montgomery was the capital of the Confederacy during the early months of the Civil War between February 18 and May 21, 1861. The Confederate capital then moved to Richmond, Virginia.*

ALASKA (AK) The Last Frontier

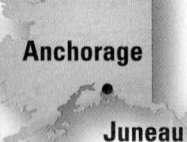

POPULATION (2006): 670,053 (47th) **AREA:** 663,267 sq. mi. (1st) (1,717,854 sq. km.) 🌼 Forget-me-not 🐦 Willow ptarmigan 🌲 Sitka spruce 🎵 "Alaska's Flag" **ENTERED UNION:** January 3, 1959 (49th) ⭐ Juneau **LARGEST CITIES (WITH POP.):** Anchorage, 275,043; Fairbanks, 31,324; Juneau, 30,987; Sitka, 8,986

⚙️ oil, natural gas, fish, food products, lumber and wood products, fur

did you know? *In 1867, the U.S. purchased Alaska from Russia for $7.2 million, or about 2 cents per acre. When Alaska was admitted to the Union as the 49th state in 1959, it increased the area of the U.S. by 20%.*

ARIZONA (AZ) Grand Canyon State

POPULATION (2006): 6,166,318 (16th) **AREA:** 113,998 sq. mi. (6th) (295,253 sq. km.) 🌼 Blossom of the Saguaro cactus 🐦 Cactus wren 🌲 Paloverde 🎵 "Arizona" **ENTERED UNION:** February 14, 1912 (48th) ⭐ Phoenix **LARGEST CITIES (WITH POP.):** Phoenix, 1,461,575; Tucson, 515,526; Mesa, 442,780; Glendale, 239,435; Chandler, 234,939; Scottsdale, 226,013

⚙️ electronic equipment, transportation and industrial equipment, instruments, printing and publishing, copper and other metals

did you know? *You can find London Bridge in Lake Havasu City, AZ. Built in London, England, in the 1830s, the bridge was taken down and sold to Robert P. McCulloch in 1968. He re-assembled it on Lake Havasu in 1971.*

WAforKids.com Go to *www.WAforKids.com* for even more U.S. facts.

ARKANSAS (AR) Natural State, Razorback State

Little Rock

POPULATION (2006): 2,810,872 (32nd) **AREA:** 53,179 sq. mi. (29th) (137,733 sq. km.) ⚙️Apple blossom 🐦Mockingbird 🌲Pine 🎵"Arkansas" **ENTERED UNION:** June 15, 1836 (25th) ⭐Little Rock **LARGEST CITIES (WITH POP.):** Little Rock, 184,564; Fort Smith, 82,481; Fayetteville, 66,655; Springdale, 60,096

⚙️ food products, paper, electronic equipment, industrial machinery, metal products, lumber and wood products, livestock, soybeans, rice, cotton, natural gas

did you know? *The only working diamond mine in the U.S. is located in Murfreesboro, AR, at Crater of Diamonds State Park. It is also the only diamond-producing site in the world that is open to the public. Visitors can keep whatever diamonds they find.*

CALIFORNIA (CA) Golden State

POPULATION (2006): 36,457,549 (1st) **AREA:** 163,696 sq. mi. (3rd) (423,971 sq. km.) ⚙️Golden poppy 🐦California valley quail 🌲California redwood 🎵"I Love You, California" **ENTERED UNION:** September 9, 1850 (31st) ⭐Sacramento **LARGEST CITIES (WITH POP.):** Los Angeles, 3,844,829; San Diego, 1,255,540; San Jose, 912,332; San Francisco, 739,426; Long Beach, 474,014; Fresno, 461,116; Sacramento, 456,441; Oakland, 395,274

Sacramento
San Francisco
Los Angeles
San Diego

⚙️ transportation and industrial equipment, electronic equipment, oil, natural gas, motion pictures, milk, cattle, fruit, vegetables

did you know? *In Death Valley, the hottest and driest place in the U.S., the summer temperatures soar above 115° F. It also has the lowest elevation in the U.S. at 282 feet below sea level.*

COLORADO (CO) Centennial State

Denver
Colorado Springs

POPULATION (2006): 4,753,377 (22nd) **AREA:** 104,094 sq. mi. (8th) (269,602 sq. km.) ⚙️Rocky Mountain columbine 🐦Lark bunting 🌲Colorado blue spruce 🎵"Where the Columbines Grow" **ENTERED UNION:** August 1, 1876 (38th) ⭐Denver **LARGEST CITIES (WITH POP.):** Denver, 557,917; Colorado Springs, 369,815; Aurora, 297,235; Lakewood, 140,671; Fort Collins, 128,026

⚙️ instruments and industrial machinery, food products, printing and publishing, metal products, electronic equipment, oil, coal, cattle

did you know? *The Anasazi Indians built entire cities into cliffsides across the American southwest. The settlements built between 1100 and 1300 at Mesa Verde in southwestern Colorado are the largest and best preserved.*

Key: ⚙️Flower 🐦Bird 🌲Tree 🎵Song ⭐Capital ⚙️Important Products

293

CONNECTICUT (CT) Constitution State, Nutmeg State

Hartford

POPULATION (2006): 3,504,809 (29th) **AREA:** 5,543 sq. mi. (48th) (14,356 sq. km.) ✿Mountain laurel ♪American robin ♣White oak ♪"Yankee Doodle" **ENTERED UNION:** January 9, 1788 (5th) ★ Hartford **LARGEST CITIES (WITH POP.):** Bridgeport, 139,008; New Haven, 124,791; Hartford, 124,397; Stamford, 120,045; Waterbury, 107,902

⚙ aircraft parts, helicopters, industrial machinery, metals and metal products, electronic equipment, printing and publishing, medical instruments, chemicals, dairy products, stone

did you know? The Hartford Courant *is the country's oldest newspaper in continuous publication. It started as a weekly in 1764. George Washington once placed an ad in the paper to rent out some of his land in Mount Vernon, VA.*

DELAWARE (DE) First State, Diamond State

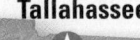
Dover
★

POPULATION (2006): 853,476 (45th) **AREA:** 2,489 sq. mi. (49th) (6,446 sq. km.) ✿Peach blossom ♪Blue hen chicken ♣American holly ♪"Our Delaware" **ENTERED UNION:** December 7, 1787 (1st) ★Dover **LARGEST CITIES (WITH POP.):** Wilmington, 72,786; Dover, 34,288; Newark, 30,060

⚙ chemicals, transportation equipment, food products, chickens

did you know? The Mason-Dixon line is an L-shaped border that separates Delaware, Pennsylvania, and Maryland. Charles Mason and Jeremiah Dixon drew it in the 1760s to settle a dispute between the colonies. The border is marked to this day with stones about every 1,000 feet.

FLORIDA (FL) Sunshine State

Tallahassee
★
Jacksonville

Miami ●

POPULATION (2006): 18,089,888 (4th) **AREA:** 65,755 sq. mi. (22nd) (170,305 sq. km.) ✿Orange blossom ♪Mockingbird ♣Sabal palmetto palm ♪"Old Folks at Home" **ENTERED UNION:** March 3, 1845 (27th) ★Tallahassee (population, 155,171) **LARGEST CITIES (WITH POP.):** Jacksonville, 782,623; Miami, 386,417; Tampa, 325,989; St. Petersburg, 249,079; Hialeah, 220,485; Orlando, 213,223; Ft. Lauderdale, 167,380

⚙ electronic and transportation equipment, industrial machinery, printing and publishing, food products, citrus fruits, vegetables, livestock, phosphates, fish

did you know? *NASA's main launch site, the Kennedy Space Center, is located on Cape Canaveral on the state's eastern coast. Since 1962, many famous spaceflights have launched there, including the Apollo missions to the Moon and more than 117 space shuttle flights.*

WAforKids.com   Go to *www.WAforKids.com* for even more U.S. facts.

430   294

GEORGIA (GA) Empire State of the South, Peach State

POPULATION (2006): 9,363,941 (9th) **AREA:** 59,425 sq. mi. (24th) (153,910 sq. km.) Cherokee rose 🐦Brown thrasher 🌲Live oak 🎵"Georgia on My Mind" **ENTERED UNION:** January 2, 1788 (4th) ⭐Atlanta **LARGEST CITIES (WITH POP.):** Atlanta, 470,688; Augusta, 190,782; Columbus, 185,271; Savannah, 128,453; Athens, 103,238

⚙️ clothing and textiles, transportation equipment, food products, paper, chickens, peanuts, peaches, clay

did you know? Blackbeard Island Wildlife Refuge, just off the coast of Georgia, is named for Blackbeard the pirate (real name Edward Teach). Blackbeard used the island as a hideout sometime around 1716. No buried treasure has been found there.

⭐ **Atlanta**

HAWAII (HI) Aloha State

POPULATION (2006): 1,285,498 (42nd) **AREA:** 10,931 sq. mi. (43rd) (28,311 sq. km.) 🌺Yellow hibiscus 🐦Hawaiian goose 🌲Kukui 🎵"Hawaii Ponoi" **ENTERED UNION:** August 21, 1959 (50th) ⭐Honolulu **LARGEST CITIES (WITH POP.):** Honolulu, 377,379; Hilo, 40,759; Kailua, 36,513; Kaneohe, 34,970

⚙️ food products, pineapples, sugar, printing and publishing, fish, flowers

⭐ **Honolulu**

did you know? The most massive volcano in the world, Mauna Loa ("Long Mountain"), is located on the island of Hawaii, the "Big" island. About four-fifths of the volcano lies underwater, but its peak reaches 13,681 feet above sea level.

IDAHO (ID) Gem State

POPULATION (2006): 1,466,465 (39th) **AREA:** 83,570 sq. mi. (14th) (216,445 sq. km.) 🌸Syringa 🐦Mountain bluebird 🌲White pine 🎵"Here We Have Idaho" **ENTERED UNION:** July 3, 1890 (43rd) ⭐Boise **LARGEST CITIES (WITH POP.):** Boise, 193,161; Nampa, 71,713; Pocatello, 53,372; Idaho Falls, 52,338

⚙️ potatoes, hay, wheat, cattle, milk, lumber and wood products, food products

⭐ **Boise**

did you know? In 1951, an experimental nuclear reactor built near Arco, ID became the first to produce electricity that was usable in homes and buildings. In 1955, Arco became the world's first town to have all of its power generated by a nuclear reactor.

Key: 🌸Flower 🐦Bird 🌲Tree 🎵Song ⭐Capital ⚙️Important Products

ILLINOIS (IL) Prairie State

POPULATION (2006): 12,831,970 (5th) **AREA:** 57,914 sq. mi. (25th) (149,997 sq. km.) 🌸Native violet 🐦Cardinal 🌳White oak 🎵"Illinois" **ENTERED UNION:** December 3, 1818 (21st) ⭐Springfield **LARGEST CITIES (WITH POP.):** Chicago, 2,842,518; Aurora, 168,181; Rockford, 152,916; Naperville, 141,579; Joliet, 136,208; Springfield, 115,668; Peoria, 112,685

⚙ industrial machinery, metals and metal products, printing and publishing, electronic equipment, food products, corn, soybeans, hogs

did you know? *The Chicago River, which today flows away from Lake Michigan, used to flow in the opposite direction. Between 1898 and 1900, engineers dug what became known as the Sanitary and Ship Canal, or Main Canal, connecting the Chicago River to the Mississippi River. This caused the water to reverse its flow.*

INDIANA (IN) Hoosier State

POPULATION (2006): 6,313,520 (15th) **AREA:** 36,418 sq. mi. (38th) (94,322 sq. km.) 🌸Peony 🐦Cardinal 🌳Tulip poplar 🎵"On the Banks of the Wabash, Far Away" **ENTERED UNION:** December 11, 1816 (19th) ⭐Indianapolis **LARGEST CITIES (WITH POP.):** Indianapolis, 784,118; Fort Wayne, 223,341; Evansville, 115,918; South Bend, 105,262; Gary, 98,715

⚙ transportation equipment, electronic equipment, industrial machinery, iron and steel, metal products, corn, soybeans, livestock, coal

did you know? *True to its motto, "Crossroads of America," Indiana has more miles of interstate highway per square mile than any other state.*

IOWA (IA) Hawkeye State

POPULATION (2006): 2,982,085 (30th) **AREA:** 56,272 sq. mi. (26th) (145,744 sq. km.) 🌸Wild rose 🐦Eastern goldfinch 🌳Oak 🎵"The Song of Iowa" **ENTERED UNION:** December 28, 1846 (29th) ⭐Des Moines **LARGEST CITIES (WITH POP.):** Des Moines, 194,163; Cedar Rapids, 123,119; Davenport, 98,845; Sioux City, 83,148

⚙ corn, soybeans, hogs, cattle, industrial machinery, food products

The only member of the Lewis and Clark expedition to die was Sgt. Charles Floyd. He died from peritonitis near present-day Sioux City, IA. A monument stands where he was buried.

●WAforKids.com Go to *www.WAforKids.com* for even more U.S. facts.

432

296

KANSAS (KS) Sunflower State

POPULATION (2006): 2,764,075 (33rd) **AREA:** 82,277 sq. mi. (15th) (213,096 sq. km.) ✿Native sunflower 🦅Western meadowlark 🌲Cottonwood 🎵"Home on the Range" **ENTERED UNION:** January 29, 1861 (34th) ⭐Topeka **LARGEST CITIES (WITH POP.):** Wichita, 354,865; Overland Park, 164,811; Kansas City, 144,210; Topeka, 121,946

⚙ cattle, aircraft and other transportation equipment, industrial machinery, food products, wheat, corn, hay, oil, natural gas

The Chisholm Trail, used by cowboys to drive cattle from Texas through Indian Territory (now Oklahoma), ended in Abilene, KS. Wyatt Earp, marshall of Dodge City, was among the legendary lawmen who kept peace in the rowdy frontier towns along the way.

KENTUCKY (KY) Bluegrass State

POPULATION (2006): 4,206,074 (26th) **AREA:** 40,409 sq. mi. (37th) (104,659 sq. km.) ✿Goldenrod 🦅Cardinal 🌲Tulip poplar 🎵"My Old Kentucky Home" **ENTERED UNION:** June 1, 1792 (15th) ⭐Frankfort (population, 27,660) **LARGEST CITIES (WITH POP.):** Louisville, 556,429; Lexington, 268,080; Owensboro, 55,459; Bowling Green, 52,272

⚙ coal, industrial machinery, electronic equipment, transportation equipment, metals, tobacco, cattle

More than 360 miles of natural caves and underground passageways have been mapped under Mammoth Cave National Park. It's the largest network of natural tunnels in the world and extends up to 1,000 miles.

LOUISIANA (LA) Pelican State

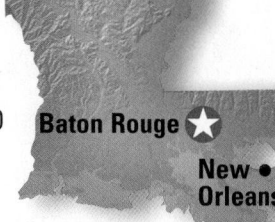

POPULATION (2006): 4,287,768 (25th) **AREA:** 51,840 sq. mi. (31st) (134,265 sq. km.) ✿Magnolia 🦅Eastern brown pelican 🌲Cypress 🎵"Give Me Louisiana" **ENTERED UNION:** April 30, 1812 (18th) ⭐Baton Rouge **LARGEST CITIES (WITH POP.):** New Orleans, 454,863; Baton Rouge, 222,064; Shreveport, 198,874; Lafayette, 112,030

⚙ natural gas, oil, chemicals, transportation equipment, paper, food products, cotton, fish

Louisiana is the only state whose legal system comes from Napoleonic Code, the system put into place in France by Napoleon Bonaparte. This is because Louisiana used to belong to France. The law codes of the other 49 states are based on English common law, which was practiced in England. The differences are minor.

Key:  ✿Flower 🦅Bird 🌲Tree 🎵Song ⭐Capital ⚙Important Products

MAINE (ME) Pine Tree State

POPULATION (2006): 1,321,574 (40th) **AREA:** 35,385 sq. mi. (39th) (91,647 sq. km.) ⚙White pine cone and tassel 🐦Chickadee 🌲Eastern white pine 🎵"State of Maine Song" **ENTERED UNION:** March 15, 1820 (23rd) ⭐Augusta (population, 18,551) **LARGEST CITIES (WITH POP.):** Portland, 63,889; Lewiston, 36,050; Bangor, 31,074

⚙ paper, transportation equipment, wood and wood products, electronic equipment, footwear, clothing, potatoes, milk, eggs, fish, seafood

Augusta ⭐

did you know? Maine is nearly as big as the five other New England states (Connecticut, Massachusetts, New Hampshire, Rhose Island, Vermont) combined. About 90% of all U.S. lobsters and 30% of all U.S. blueberries are harvested there.

MARYLAND (MD) Old Line State, Free State

Baltimore •

Annapolis ⭐

Washington, D.C. ⭐

POPULATION (2006): 5,615,727 (19th) **AREA:** 12,407 sq. mi. (42nd) (32,134 sq. km.) ⚙Black-eyed susan 🐦Baltimore oriole 🌲White oak 🎵"Maryland, My Maryland" **ENTERED UNION:** April 28, 1788 (7th) ⭐Annapolis (population, 36,196) **LARGEST CITIES (WITH POP.):** Baltimore, 635,815; Frederick, 57,907; Gaithersburg, 57,698; Rockville, 57,402; Bowie, 53,878

⚙ printing and publishing, food products, transportation equipment, electronic equipment, chickens, soybeans, corn, stone

did you know? Maryland's official state sport is jousting. Competitors on horseback ride through a course and use their lances to collect rings. Competitors are called either "knights" or "maids."

MASSACHUSETTS (MA) Bay State, Old Colony

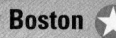

Boston ⭐

POPULATION (2006): 6,437,193 (13th) **AREA:** 10,555 sq. mi. (44th) (27,337 sq. km.) ⚙Mayflower 🐦Chickadee 🌲American elm 🎵"All Hail to Massachusetts" **ENTERED UNION:** February 6, 1788 (6th) ⭐Boston **LARGEST CITIES (WITH POP.):** Boston, 559,034; Worcester, 175,898; Springfield, 151,732; Lowell, 103,111; Cambridge, 100,135

⚙ industrial machinery, electronic equipment, instruments, printing and publishing, metal products, fish, flowers and shrubs, cranberries

did you know? The chocolate chip cookie was invented in Whitman, MA, in the 1930s by Ruth Wakefield.

WAforKids.com Go to *www.WAforKids.com* for even more U.S. facts.

MICHIGAN (MI) Great Lakes State, Wolverine State

POPULATION (2006): 10,095,643 (8th) **AREA:** 96,716 sq. mi. (11th) (250,493 sq. km.) ⚙️Apple blossom 🐦Robin 🌲White pine 🎵"Michigan, My Michigan"
ENTERED UNION: January 26, 1837 (26th) ⭐Lansing
LARGEST CITIES (WITH POP.): Detroit, 886,671; Grand Rapids, 193,780; Warren, 135,311; Sterling Heights, 128,034; Flint, 118,551; Lansing, 115,518; Ann Arbor, 113,271

⚙️ automobiles, industrial machinery, metal products, office furniture, plastic products, chemicals, food products, milk, corn, natural gas, iron ore, blueberries

Battle Creek, the headquarters for Kellogg's, Ralston Foods, and the Post Cereal division of Kraft Foods, is known as the Cereal Capital of the World.

MINNESOTA (MN) North Star State, Gopher State

POPULATION (2006): 5,167,101 (21st) **AREA:** 86,939 sq. mi. (12th) (225,171 sq. km.) ⚙️Pink and white lady slipper 🐦Common loon 🌲Red pine 🎵"Hail! Minnesota" **ENTERED UNION:** May 11, 1858 (32nd) ⭐St. Paul **LARGEST CITIES (WITH POP.):** Minneapolis, 372,811; St. Paul, 275,150; Rochester, 94,950; Duluth, 84,896; Bloomington, 81,164

⚙️ industrial machinery, printing and publishing, computers, food products, scientific and medical instruments, milk, hogs, cattle, corn, soybeans, iron ore

The "Land of 10,000 Lakes" has 11,842 lakes bigger than 10 acres within its borders. One out of every six Minnesotans owns a boat, the highest rate of any state.

MISSISSIPPI (MS) Magnolia State

POPULATION (2006): 2,910,540 (31st) **AREA:** 48,430 sq. mi. (32nd) (125,433 sq. km.) ⚙️Magnolia 🐦Mockingbird 🌲Magnolia 🎵"Go, Mississippi!"
ENTERED UNION: December 10, 1817 (20th) ⭐Jackson **LARGEST CITIES (WITH POP.):** Jackson, 177,977; Gulfport, 72,464; Biloxi, 50,209

⚙️ transportation equipment, furniture, electrical machinery, lumber and wood products, cotton, rice, chickens, cattle

In 1902, President Theodore "Teddy" Roosevelt went bear hunting in Mississippi. He refused to shoot a bear that had been tied to a tree by his companions. The story inspired some toy makers to create a stuffed toy bear, which they called "Teddy's Bear." That's how the teddy bear was born.

Key: Flower Bird Tree Song Capital Important Products

MISSOURI

(MO) Show Me State

POPULATION (2006): 5,842,713 (18th) **AREA:** 69,704 sq. mi. (21st) (180,533 sq. km.) 🌼Hawthorn 🐦Bluebird 🌲Dogwood 🎵"Missouri Waltz" **ENTERED UNION:** August 10, 1821 (24th) ⭐Jefferson City (population, 39,079) **LARGEST CITIES (WITH POP.):** Kansas City, 444,965; St. Louis, 344,362; Springfield, 150,298; Independence, 110,208

⚙ transportation equipment, electrical and electronic equipment, printing and publishing, food products, cattle, hogs, milk, soybeans, corn, hay, lead

did you know? The Gateway Arch in St. Louis, which honors the spirit of the western pioneers, is the tallest monument (630 feet high) in the U.S.

MONTANA

(MT) Treasure State

POPULATION (2006): 944,632 (44th) **AREA:** 147,042 sq. mi. (4th) (380,837 sq. km.) 🌼Bitterroot 🐦Western meadowlark 🌲Ponderosa pine 🎵"Montana" **ENTERED UNION:** November 8, 1889 (41st) ⭐Helena (population, 26,353) **LARGEST CITIES (WITH POP.):** Billings, 98,721; Missoula, 62,923; Great Falls, 56,338; Bozeman, 33,535

⚙ cattle, copper, gold, wheat, barley, wood and paper products

did you know? Montanan Jeanette Rankin in 1917 became the first woman to serve in the U.S. House of Representatives. She was the only member of Congress to vote against the U.S. taking part in both World War I and World War II.

NEBRASKA

(NE) Cornhusker State

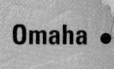

POPULATION (2006): 1,768,331 (38th) **AREA:** 77,354 sq. mi. (16th) (200,346 sq. km.) 🌼Goldenrod 🐦Western meadowlark 🌲Cottonwood 🎵"Beautiful Nebraska" **ENTERED UNION:** March 1, 1867 (37th) ⭐Lincoln **LARGEST CITIES (WITH POP.):** Omaha, 414,521; Lincoln, 239,213; Bellevue, 47,334; Grand Island, 44,546

⚙ cattle, hogs, milk, corn, soybeans, hay, wheat, sorghum, food products, industrial machinery

did you know? Nebraska has the only unicameral (one house) state legislature in the U.S. Called the Nebraska Unicameral, its members are called Senators and they serve four-year terms. The head of their legislature is called the Speaker.

●WAforKids.com Go to *www.WAforKids.com* for even more U.S. facts.

NEVADA (NV) Sagebrush State, Battle Born State, Silver State

POPULATION (2006): 2,495,529 (35th) **AREA:** 110,561 sq. mi. (7th) (286,352 sq. km.) Sagebrush Mountain bluebird Single-leaf piñon, bristlecone pine "Home Means Nevada" **ENTERED UNION:** October 31, 1864 (36th) Carson City (population, 54,311) **LARGEST CITIES (WITH POP.):** Las Vegas, 545,147; Henderson, 232,146; Reno, 203,550; North Las Vegas, 176,635

gold, silver, cattle, hay, food products, plastics, chemicals

did you know? Extending for about 110 miles, Lake Mead is the largest artificial lake in the U.S. It provides water for Nevada, Arizona, California, and northern Mexico. It was formed on the Colorado River when the Hoover Dam was built in 1936.

NEW HAMPSHIRE (NH) Granite State

POPULATION (2006): 1,314,895 (41st) **AREA:** 9,350 sq. mi. (46th) (24,216 sq. km.) Purple lilac Purple finch White birch "Old New Hampshire" **ENTERED UNION:** June 21, 1788 (9th) Concord **LARGEST CITIES (WITH POP.):** Manchester, 109,691; Nashua, 87,321; Concord, 42,336

industrial machinery, electric and electronic equipment, metal products, plastic products, dairy products, maple syrup and maple sugar

did you know? New Hampshire was the first colony to declare its independence from England and start its own government in 1776—six months before the Declaration of Independence was signed.

NEW JERSEY (NJ) Garden State

POPULATION (2006): 8,724,560 (11th) **AREA:** 8,721 sq. mi. (47th) (22,587 sq. km.) Purple violet Eastern goldfinch Red oak none **ENTERED UNION:** December 18, 1787 (3rd) Trenton **LARGEST CITIES (WITH POP.):** Newark, 280,666; Jersey City, 239,614; Paterson, 149,843; Elizabeth, 125,809; Trenton, 84,639

chemicals, pharmaceuticals/drugs, electronic equipment, nursery and greenhouse products, food products, tomatoes, blueberries, and peaches

did you know? The city of Paterson is one of the birthplaces of the Industrial Revolution in America. In the 1790s, the Society for Establishing Useful Manufacturers built a factory on the Passaic River. Until the early 20th century, Paterson produced many types of goods, including large amounts of silk fabric, inspiring the nickname "Silk City."

Key: Flower Bird Tree Song Capital 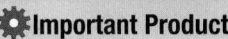Important Products

NEW MEXICO (NM) Land of Enchantment

Santa Fe

Albuquerque

POPULATION (2006): 1,954,599 (36th) **AREA:** 121,589 sq. mi. (5th) (314,914 sq. km.) Yucca Roadrunner Piñon "O, Fair New Mexico" **ENTERED UNION:** January 6, 1912 (47th) Santa Fe **LARGEST CITIES (WITH POP.):** Albuquerque, 494,236; Las Cruces, 82,671; Santa Fe, 70,631; Rio Rancho, 66,599

electronic equipment, foods, machinery, clothing, lumber, transportation equipment, hay, onions, chiles

Carlsbad Caverns National Park contains Lechuguilla Cave, the deepest cave in the U.S. It is more than 1,570 feet deep. Hundreds of thousands of bats swarm out of the caverns every night to feed on insects.

NEW YORK (NY) Empire State

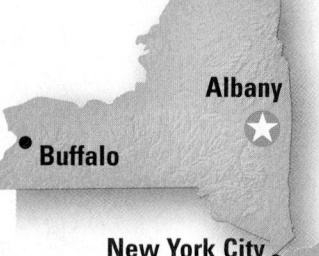

Albany

Buffalo

New York City

POPULATION (2006): 19,306,183 (3rd) **AREA:** 54,556 sq. mi. (27th) (141,299 sq. km.) Rose Bluebird Sugar maple "I Love New York" **ENTERED UNION:** July 26, 1788 (11th) Albany (population, 93,779) **LARGEST CITIES (WITH POP.):** New York, 8,143,197; Buffalo, 279,745; Rochester, 211,091; Yonkers, 196,425; Syracuse, 141,683

books and magazines, automobile and aircraft parts, toys and sporting goods, electronic equipment, machinery, clothing and textiles, metal products, milk, cattle, hay, apples

New York City is the largest city in the U.S. and was the nation's first capital. It was also the home of another major first in American history—the first pizza restaurant in the U.S. opened there in 1895.

NORTH CAROLINA (NC) Tar Heel State, Old North State

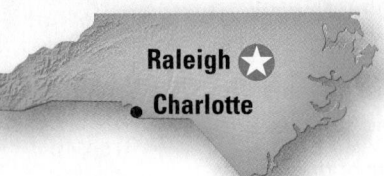

Raleigh

Charlotte

POPULATION (2006): 8,856,505 (10th) **AREA:** 53,819 sq. mi. (28th) (139,391 sq. km.) Dogwood Cardinal Pine "The Old North State" **ENTERED UNION:** November 21, 1789 (12th) Raleigh **LARGEST CITIES (WITH POP.):** Charlotte, 610,949; Raleigh, 341,530; Greensboro, 231,962; Durham, 204,845; Winston-Salem, 193,755; Fayetteville 129,928

clothing and textiles, tobacco and tobacco products, industrial machinery, electronic equipment, furniture, cotton, soybeans, peanuts

English settlers established a colony on North Carolina's Roanoke Island in 1585, but abandoned it a year later. A second colony was founded in 1587, but had mysteriously disappeared by 1590.

WAforKids.com Go to *www.WAforKids.com* for even more U.S. facts.

NORTH DAKOTA (ND) Peace Garden State

POPULATION (2006): 635,867 (48th) **AREA:** 70,700 sq. mi. (19th) (183,112 sq. km.) Wild prairie rose Western meadowlark American elm "North Dakota Hymn" **ENTERED UNION:** November 2, 1889 (39th) Bismarck **LARGEST CITIES (WITH POP.):** Fargo, 90,672; Bismarck, 57,377; Grand Forks, 49,792; Minot, 34,984

⚙ wheat, barley, hay, sunflowers, sugar beets, cattle, sand and gravel, food products, farm equipment, high-tech electronics

did you know? *The state's nickname is taken from the International Peace Garden, which straddles the boundary between North Dakota and Manitoba in Canada.*

OHIO (OH) Buckeye State

POPULATION (2006): 11,478,006 (7th) **AREA:** 44,825 sq. mi. (34th) (116,096 sq. km.) Scarlet carnation Cardinal Buckeye "Beautiful Ohio" **ENTERED UNION:** March 1, 1803 (17th) Columbus **LARGEST CITIES (WITH POP.):** Columbus, 730,657; Cleveland, 452,208; Cincinnati, 308,728; Toledo, 301,285; Akron, 210,795; Dayton, 158,873

Cleveland
Columbus
Cincinnati

⚙ metal and metal products, transportation equipment, industrial machinery, rubber and plastic products, electronic equipment, printing and publishing, chemicals, food products, corn, soybeans, livestock, milk

did you know? *Though it was admitted to the Union in 1803, Ohio didn't technically become a state until 1953. Because of an oversight, Congress didn't formally vote on the resolution to admit Ohio as a state until August 7, 1953, when it made Ohio's statehood official, retroactive to 1803.*

OKLAHOMA (OK) Sooner State

POPULATION (2006): 3,579,212 (28th) **AREA:** 69,898 sq. mi. (20th) (181,035 sq. km.) Mistletoe Scissor-tailed flycatcher Redbud "Oklahoma!" **ENTERED UNION:** November 16, 1907 (46th) Oklahoma City **LARGEST CITIES (WITH POP.):** Oklahoma City, 531,324; Tulsa, 382,457; Norman, 101,719; Lawton, 90,234; Broken Arrow, 86,228

Tulsa
Oklahoma City

⚙ natural gas, oil, cattle, nonelectrical machinery, transportation equipment, metal products, wheat, hay

did you know? *The American Indian nations called the Five Civilized Tribes (Cherokee, Chickasaw, Choctaw, Creek, and Seminole) were resettled in eastern Oklahoma by the federal government between 1817 and 1842.*

Key: ⚙Flower 🐦Bird 🌲Tree 🎵Song ⭐Capital ⚙Important Products

OREGON (OR) Beaver State

- Portland
- ★ Salem

POPULATION (2006): 3,700,758 (27th) **AREA:** 98,381 sq. mi. (9th) (254,806 sq. km.) ⚙Oregon grape 🐦Western meadowlark 🌲Douglas fir 🎵"Oregon, My Oregon" **ENTERED UNION:** February 14, 1859 (33rd) ★Salem **LARGEST CITIES (WITH POP.):** Portland, 533,427; Salem, 148,751; Eugene, 144,515; Gresham, 96,072

⚙ lumber and wood products, electronics and semiconductors, food products, paper, cattle, hay, vegetables, Christmas trees

did you know? *Oregon's natural features have some real depth to them. Hells Canyon, 7,900 feet deep at its maximum, is one of the deepest canyons in the world. Crater Lake, which gets as deep as 1,932 feet, is the deepest lake in the U.S.*

PENNSYLVANIA (PA) Keystone State

Harrisburg
- Pittsburgh ★
Philadelphia ●

POPULATION (2006): 12,440,621 (6th) **AREA:** 46,055 sq. mi. (33rd) (119,282 sq. km.) ⚙Mountain laurel 🐦Ruffed grouse 🌲Hemlock 🎵"Pennsylvania" **ENTERED UNION:** December 12, 1787 (2nd) ★Harrisburg (population, 48,540) **LARGEST CITIES (WITH POP.):** Philadelphia, 1,463,281; Pittsburgh, 316,718; Allentown, 106,992; Erie, 102,612

⚙ iron and steel, coal, industrial machinery, printing and publishing, food products, electronic equipment, transportation equipment, stone, clay and glass products

did you know? *An enormous fire has been burning since 1962 in the coal mines below the town of Centralia. Fewer than 20 people remain in the town. Surface temperatures have been measured at over 700°F.*

RHODE ISLAND (RI) Little Rhody, Ocean State

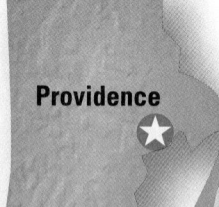

Providence ★

POPULATION (2006): 1,067,610 (43rd) **AREA:** 1,545 sq. mi. (50th) (4,002 sq. km.) ⚙Violet 🐦Rhode Island red 🌲Red maple 🎵"Rhode Island" **ENTERED UNION:** May 29, 1790 (13th) ★ Providence **LARGEST CITIES (WITH POP.):** Providence, 176,862; Warwick, 87,233; Cranston, 81,614; Pawtucket, 73,742

⚙ costume jewelry, toys, textiles, machinery, electronic equipment, fish

did you know? *Rhode Island is the smallest state in the U.S. It was the last of the original 13 colonies to ratify the Constitution (in 1790).*

WAforKids.com   Go to *www.WAforKids.com* for even more U.S. facts.

SOUTH CAROLINA (SC) Palmetto State

POPULATION (2006): 4,321,249 (24th) **AREA:** 32,020 sq. mi. (40th) (82,931 sq. km.) ⚙️Yellow jessamine 🐦Carolina wren 🌲Palmetto 🎵"Carolina" **ENTERED UNION:** May 23, 1788 (8th) ⭐Columbia **LARGEST CITIES (WITH POP.):** Columbia, 117,088; Charleston, 106,712; North Charleston, 86,313; Rock Hill, 59,554

⚙️ clothing and textiles, chemicals, industrial machinery, metal products, livestock, tobacco, Portland cement

Columbia ⭐

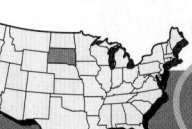

More battles of the American Revolution were fought in South Carolina than in any other colony. The first shots of the Civil War were fired on Fort Sumter in Charleston harbor, in April, 1861.

SOUTH DAKOTA (SD) Mt. Rushmore State, Coyote State

POPULATION (2006): 781,919 (46th) **AREA:** 77,116 sq. mi. (17th) (199,730 sq. km.) ⚙️Pasqueflower 🐦Chinese ring-necked pheasant 🌲Black Hills spruce 🎵"Hail, South Dakota" **ENTERED UNION:** November 2, 1889 (40th) ⭐Pierre (population, 14,012) **LARGEST CITIES (WITH POP.):** Sioux Falls, 139,517; Rapid City, 62,167; Aberdeen, 24,098

⭐ Pierre

⚙️ food and food products, machinery, electric and electronic equipment, corn, soybeans

The Corn Palace in Mitchell is redecorated every year with themed murals made from corn, grains, and grasses by local artisans. When winter comes, birds and squirrels munch away the exterior.

TENNESSEE (TN) Volunteer State

⭐ **Nashville**

Memphis ●

POPULATION (2006): 6,038,803 (17th) **AREA:** 42,143 sq. mi. (36th) (109,150 sq. km.) ⚙️Iris 🐦Mockingbird 🌲Tulip poplar 🎵"My Homeland, Tennessee"; "When It's Iris Time in Tennessee"; "My Tennessee"; "Tennessee Waltz"; "Rocky Top" **ENTERED UNION:** June 1, 1796 (16th) ⭐Nashville **LARGEST CITIES (WITH POP.):** Memphis, 672,277; Nashville, 549,110; Knoxville, 180,130; Chattanooga, 154,762

⚙️ chemicals, machinery, vehicles, food products, metal products, publishing, electronic equipment, paper products, rubber and plastic products, tobacco

The Grand Ole Opry, the world's longest-running live radio program, was first broadcast from Nashville in 1925. It was originally called the WSM Barn Dance, but the name changed to the Grand Ole Opry in 1927.

Key: **Flower** **Bird** **Tree** **Song** **Capital** **Important Products**

TEXAS (TX) Lone Star State

Dallas •
• El Paso
Austin ★ Houston •
San Antonio •

POPULATION (2006): 23,507,783 (2nd) **AREA:** 268,581 sq. mi. (2nd) (695,622 sq. km.) ✿Bluebonnet ♫Mockingbird 🌲Pecan ♪"Texas, Our Texas" **ENTERED UNION:** December 29, 1845 (28th) ★Austin **LARGEST CITIES (WITH POP.):** Houston, 2,016,582; San Antonio, 1,256,509; Dallas, 1,213,825; Austin, 690,252; Fort Worth, 624,067; El Paso, 598,590; Arlington, 362,805; Corpus Christi, 283,474; Plano, 250,096

⚙ oil, natural gas, cattle, milk, eggs, transportation equipment, chemicals, clothing, industrial machinery, electrical and electronic equipment, cotton, grains

did you know? *Before it became a state in 1845, Texas had been an independent republic for about nine years. It had declared its independence after Texans defeated Mexican General Antonio López de Santa Anna on April 21, 1836. Sam Houston was its first president.*

UTAH (UT) Beehive State

★
Salt Lake City

POPULATION (2006): 2,550,063 (34th) **AREA:** 84,899 sq. mi. (13th) (219,887 sq. km.) ✿Sego lily ♫Seagull 🌲Blue spruce ♪"Utah, This is the Place" **ENTERED UNION:** January 4, 1896 (45th) ★Salt Lake City **LARGEST CITIES (WITH POP.):** Salt Lake City, 178,097; Provo, 113,459; West Valley City, 113,300; West Jordan, 91,444

⚙ transportation equipment, medical instruments, electronic parts, food products, steel, copper, cattle, corn, hay, wheat, barley

did you know? *Early white settlers in Utah were saved from starvation by seagulls, the state bird. In 1848, hordes of locusts came into the Salt Lake Valley and began devouring the settlers' crops. All seemed lost before a flock of seagulls flew in and ate the locusts, saving the crops.*

VERMONT (VT) Green Mountain State

Montpelier
★

POPULATION (2006): 623,908 (49th) **AREA:** 9,614 sq. mi. (45th) (24,900 sq. km.) ✿Red clover ♫Hermit thrush 🍁Sugar maple ♪"These Green Mountains" **ENTERED UNION:** March 4, 1791 (14th) ★Montpelier (population, 8,026) **LARGEST CITIES (WITH POP.):** Burlington, 38,531; Essex Junction, 19,146; Colchester, 17,165; Rutland, 17,046

⚙ machine tools, furniture, scales, books, computer parts, foods, dairy products, apples, maple syrup

did you know? *The Green Mountain Boys who famously fought against the British during the American Revolution were originally formed in 1770 to fight off New York settlers. When the revolution broke out, the Vermonters and New Yorkers set aside their differences and united against the British.*

●WAforKids.com Go to www.WAforKids.com for even more U.S. facts.

VIRGINIA (VA) Old Dominion

POPULATION (2006): 7,642,884 (12th) **AREA:** 42,774 sq. mi. (35th) (110,784 sq. km.) Dogwood Cardinal Dogwood "Carry Me Back to Old Virginia" **ENTERED UNION:** June 25, 1788 (10th) Richmond **LARGEST CITIES (WITH POP.):** Virginia Beach, 438,415; Norfolk, 231,954; Chesapeake, 218,968; Arlington, 195,965; Richmond, 193,777; Newport News, 179,899

transportation equipment, textiles, chemicals, printing, machinery, electronic equipment, food products, coal, livestock, tobacco, wood products, furniture

Nancy Langhorne Astor in 1919 became the first woman to serve in the British House of Commons. She was born and raised in Virginia.

Alexandria
Richmond
Norfolk

WASHINGTON (WA) Evergreen State

POPULATION (2006): 6,395,798 (14th)
AREA: 71,300 sq. mi. (18th) (184,666 sq. km.) Western rhododendron Willow goldfinch Western hemlock "Washington, My Home" **ENTERED UNION:** November 11, 1889 (42nd) Olympia (population, 43,519) **LARGEST CITIES (WITH POP.):** Seattle, 573,911; Spokane, 196,818; Tacoma, 195,898; Vancouver, 157,493; Bellevue, 117,137

aircraft, lumber, pulp and paper, machinery, electronics, computer software, aluminum, processed fruits and vegetables

Seattle
Olympia

Mount Rainier is the tallest volcano in the lower 48 states. It hasn't erupted in centuries. However, another volcano in Washington, Mount St. Helens, had a huge eruption on May 18, 1980. It lasted 9 hours and destroyed 230 square miles of woods. It is still active today.

WEST VIRGINIA (WV) Mountain State

POPULATION (2006): 1,818,470 (37th) **AREA:** 24,230 sq. mi. (41st) (62,755 sq. km.) Big rhododendron Cardinal Sugar maple "The West Virginia Hills"; "This Is My West Virginia"; "West Virginia, My Home Sweet Home" **ENTERED UNION:** June 20, 1863 (35th) Charleston **LARGEST CITIES (WITH POP.):** Charleston, 51,176; Huntington, 49,198; Parkersburg, 32,020; Wheeling, 29,639

coal, natural gas, fabricated metal products, chemicals, automobile parts, aluminum, steel, machinery, cattle, hay, apples, peaches, tobacco

Charleston

On October 16, 1859, abolitionist leader John Brown and 18 others seized the federal arsenal in Harpers Ferry in an attempt to end slavery by force. Federal troops captured him and he was put to death in Charlestown later that year.

Key: Flower Bird Tree Song Capital Important Products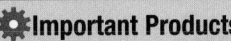

WISCONSIN (WI) Badger State

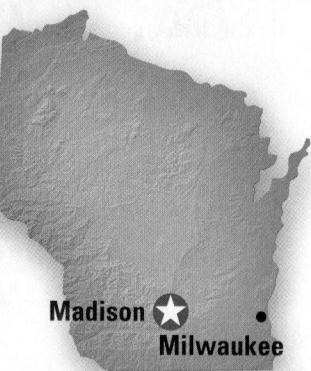

POPULATION (2006): 5,556,506 (20th) **AREA:** 65,498 sq. mi. (23rd) (169,639 sq. km.) ⚙Wood violet ♫Robin 🌲Sugar maple 🎵"On, Wisconsin!" **ENTERED UNION:** May 29, 1848 (30th) ⭐Madison **LARGEST CITIES (WITH POP.):** Milwaukee, 578,887; Madison, 221,551; Green Bay, 101,203; Kenosha, 95,240; Racine, 79,392

⚙ paper products, printing, milk, butter, cheese, foods, food products, motor vehicles and equipment, medical instruments and supplies, plastics, corn, hay, vegetables

Madison ⭐
• Milwaukee

did you know? The first ever ice cream sundaes were served in the towns of Manitowoe and Two Rivers in 1851.

WYOMING (WY) Cowboy State

POPULATION (2006): 515,004 (50th) **AREA:** 97,814 sq. mi. (10th) (253,337 sq. km.) ⚙Indian paintbrush ♫Western meadowlark 🌲Plains cottonwood 🎵"Wyoming" **ENTERED UNION:** July 10, 1890 (44th) ⭐Cheyenne **LARGEST CITIES (WITH POP.):** Cheyenne, 55,731; Casper, 51,738; Laramie, 26,050

⚙ oil, natural gas, petroleum (oil) products, cattle, wheat, beans

Cheyenne ⭐

did you know? Wyoming is also known as the Equality State and has many firsts for women in America: Women were first given the right to vote while it was still a territory in 1869. Eliza Stewart was the first woman to be part of a grand jury in 1870. Nellie Tayloe Ross became the first female governor in 1925.

COMMONWEALTH OF PUERTO RICO (PR)

⭐
San Juan

HISTORY: Christopher Columbus landed in Puerto Rico in 1493. Puerto Rico was a Spanish colony for centuries, then was ceded (given) to the United States in 1898 after the Spanish-American War. In 1952, still associated with the United States, Puerto Rico became a commonwealth with its own constitution. **POPULATION (2006):** 3,927,776 **AREA:** 5,324 sq. mi. (13,789 sq. km.) ⚙Maga ♫Reinita 🌲Ceiba **NATIONAL ANTHEM:** "La Borinqueña" ⭐San Juan **LARGEST CITIES (WITH POP.):** San Juan, 428,591; Bayamón, 222,195; Carolina, 187,472; Ponce, 182,387; Caguas, 142,378

⚙ chemicals, food products, electronic equipment, clothing and textiles, industrial machinery, coffee, sugarcane, fruit, hogs

did you know? Puerto Ricans have most of the same rights as other Americans, but they cannot vote in U.S. presidential elections and they have no voting representatives in the federal government. They don't have to pay federal taxes.

WAforKids.com Go to *www.WAforKids.com* for even more U.S. facts.

444 308

UNIT 6
THE AMERICAN ECONOMY

UNCLE SAM WANTS *your* IDEAS!

PUT 'EM IN THE SUGGESTION BOX!

HOW TO PRODUCE MORE
HOW TO BUILD BETTER

KEEP 'EM FIRING!

The government encouraged Americans to suggest improvements to the American economy with this World War II–era poster.

CHAPTER 17

THE ECONOMIC SYSTEM

SECTION 1
The Economic System at Work

SECTION 2
Business Organizations

SECTION 3
Making Business Decisions

NATIONAL STANDARDS®
FOR CIVICS AND GOVERNMENT

I. What are civic life, politics, and government?
   A. What purposes should government serve?

II. What are the foundations of the American political system?
   B. What are the distinctive characteristics of American society?
   D. What values and principles are basic to American constitutional democracy?

III. How does the government established by the Constitution embody the purposes, values, and principles of American democracy?

V. What are the roles of the citizen in American democracy?
   B. What are the rights of citizens?

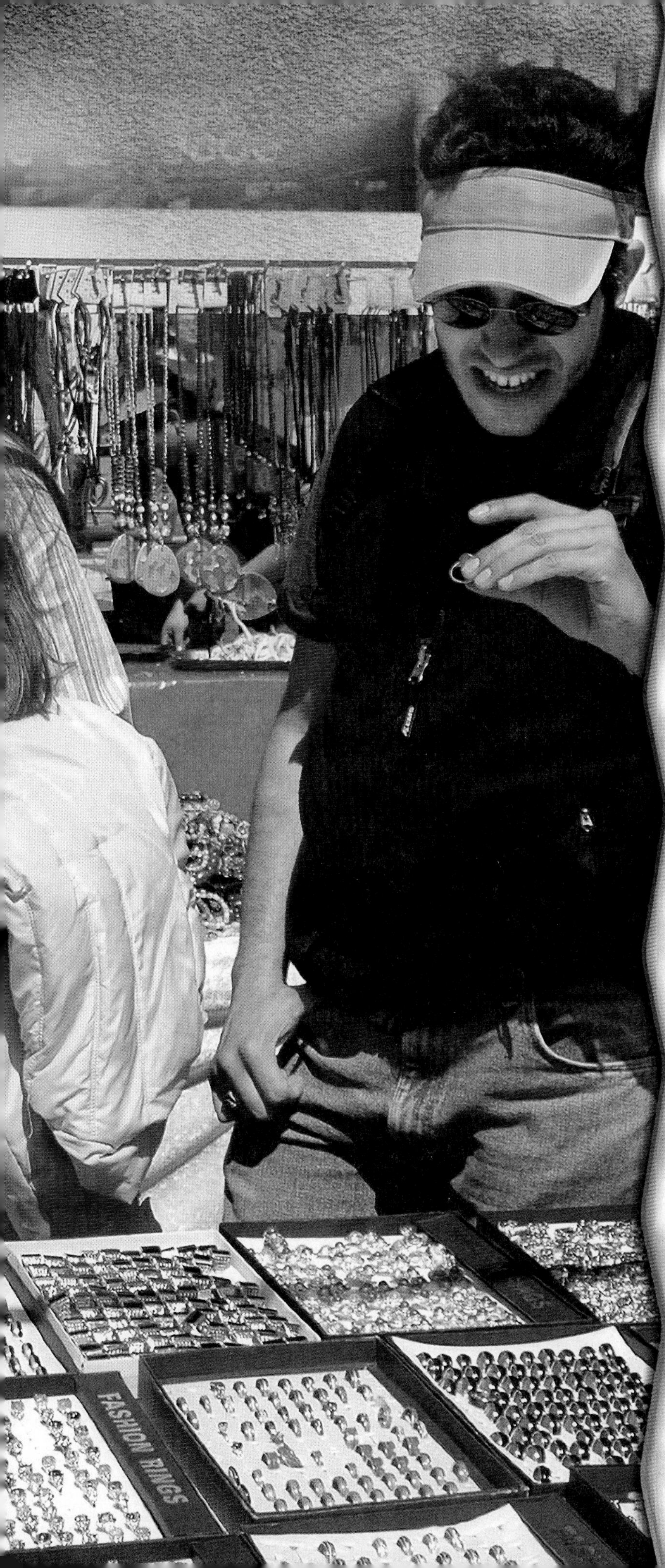

WHY CIVICS Matters

Some of your rights as an American citizen are economic rights. For example, you have the right to own property, to start a business, and to make a profit. Rights such as these are the foundation of our economic system in the United States.

STUDENTS TAKE ACTION

PROVIDING EMERGENCY HEALTH CARE
Many people in the United States live in communities that do not have a hospital to provide emergency health care. If you lived in one of these areas, what could you do to build support for a critical care facility? As you read this chapter, think about the steps you might take.

FOCUS ON WRITING

NEWSPAPER ADVERTISEMENT Going into business for yourself is one of the economic freedoms that you enjoy in this country. Imagine you own a business that sells an innovative new lighting system. Write a newspaper advertisement that highlights the features of your product and persuades people to buy your new lighting system.

Reading Skills

In this chapter you will learn about economics. You will study the U.S. economy and the role that the government plays in the economic system. You will also discover the many different ways that American businesses can be organized, including how corporations are set up and run. Lastly, you will learn about how business success depends on decisions regarding the four factors of production.

Interpreting Basic Indicators of Economic Performance

FOCUS ON READING The government uses some key indicators to judge the overall health of the economy. These indicators can help the government, businesses, and consumers make financial decisions.

Economic Indicators The Consumer Price Index (CPI) measures how much it would cost to buy a typical basket of goods and services. The higher the number, the more things cost. The unemployment rate measures how many people who do not have a job are looking for work. When the rate drops, fewer people are out of work. The prime interest rate shows how much interest, or money, banks charge people to borrow money. The higher the rate, the more it costs to borrow.

Helpful Hints for Interpreting Economic Indicators

1. Look for trends. For example, are the numbers mostly going up or going down?

2. Compare information from several months or years to determine if the change is a big one or small one.

3. Make sure you understand the data. Look for information that explains what the data means.

Consumer Price Index

The basic cost of the basket of goods used in the CPI was set at $100 for the base years 1982–1984. The base years are used as a benchmark. At the end of each year, the price of the basket of goods—compared to $100—is given. Then the government compares how much the price has changed from the year before. The higher the change, the more prices are increasing. That means things cost you more.

Year	Consumer Price Index	Change from previous year
2000	$172.20	3.4%
2001	$177.10	2.8%
2002	$179.90	1.6%
2003	$184.00	2.3%
2004	$188.90	2.7%

Interpreting the CPI: As you can see from the chart, prices have been rising since the year 2000. However, some years the prices have risen faster than others. The biggest change came in 2000, when prices changed 3.4 percent. The smallest change came in 2002, when prices went up just 1.6 percent.

You Try It!

The following charts track the U.S. unemployment rate over several years. Study these charts and then answer the questions that follow.

U.S. Unemployment Rate, 2004—2008

	Jan	Feb	Mar	Apr	May	Jun	Jul	Aug	Sep	Oct	Nov	Dec
2004	5.7	5.6	5.7	5.5	5.6	5.6	5.5	5.4	5.4	5.5	5.4	5.4
2005	5.2	5.4	5.2	5.2	5.1	5.1	5.0	4.9	5.0	5.0	5.0	4.8
2006	4.7	4.8	4.7	4.7	4.7	4.6	4.7	4.7	4.5	4.4	4.5	4.4
2007	4.6	4.5	4.4	4.5	4.5	4.6	4.7	4.7	4.7	4.8	4.7	4.9
2008	4.9	4.8	5.1	5.0	5.5	5.6	5.8	6.2	6.2	6.6	6.8	7.2

Annual Unemployment Rate	
2004	5.5
2005	5.1
2006	4.6
2007	4.6
2008	5.8

After you have studied the tables, answer the following questions.

1. Which month in 2008 had the highest unemployment?

2. Which month in 2005 had the lowest unemployment?

3. Which year had the highest unemployment rate?

4. Which years had the lowest unemployment rate?

5. What general trend did the unemployment rate show during this period?

As you read Chapter 17, look for ways that economic indicators can help businesses make decisions.

Academic Vocabulary

Success in school is related to knowing academic vocabulary—the words that are frequently used in school assignments and discussions. In this chapter, you will learn the following academic word:

structure (p. 463)

SECTION 1

The Economic System at Work

BEFORE YOU READ

The Main Idea

Countries form many types of economic systems to meet their citizens' needs and wants. The United States has a market economy.

Reading Focus

1. How do different economic systems help satisfy people's needs?
2. What factors shape life in a market economy?
3. What is the U.S. economic system like?

Key Terms

market economy, *p. 452*
free market, *p. 452*
profit, *p. 453*
scarcity, *p. 453*
law of supply, *p. 453*
law of demand, *p. 453*
free enterprise, *p. 455*
capitalism, *p. 455*
monopoly, *p. 456*

 As you read, take notes on economic systems, life in a market economy, and the U.S. economic system. Use a chart like this one to record your notes.

 Our society is based on principles of individual freedom. Those same principles of freedom apply to the U.S. economic system. We have what is called a free market economy. This means that if you want to start a business, you can. Your success will be determined by your business ability and the market, not by a government agency.

Economic Systems

Suppose you wanted to make a sandwich but you discovered that you had no bread. How could you get more? Would you have to grind wheat into flour so that you could bake a new loaf? Might you have to stand in a long line for hours before someone gave you a few slices? Of course you wouldn't. With a quick trip to the store, you could buy as many loaves of bread as you wanted.

In other parts of the world, however, getting items like bread is not as simple. How people get the things they want is determined by a country's economic system. The nature of economic systems varies widely from place to place. However, they all help people create and obtain the goods and services they need.

The Need for Economic Systems

All around the world, people need certain things to survive. People cannot live without food and water, shelter, and clothing. These basic materials that people cannot live without are called needs.

In addition to their needs, there are many items that people want in order to make their lives more comfortable. These items are not necessary for survival, but they can have great value to people. For example, you may want a television, a cell phone, or a car. You do not really need any of these things in order to live, but they can make your life easier, more comfortable, or more enjoyable. These types of items are called wants. Different people have different wants. In addition, a person's wants can change over time.

People satisfy their wants by obtaining goods and services. For example, if you want fun, you can buy a new game. The process of obtaining goods and services to satisfy your wants is called the want-satisfaction chain. How people obtain goods and services is what distinguishes different economic systems from each other.

The Want-Satisfaction Chain

To satisfy your need for food, you may want a sandwich on a bun. This want-satisfaction chain shows the steps involved in helping you satisfy that want.

❶ Grain becomes Flour

Farmers harvest grain and send it to mills where it is ground into flour.

❷ Flour becomes Bread

Bakers use flour to make all kinds of bread products, including sandwich buns.

❸ Bread is Delivered

Kitchens, restaurants, and cafeterias receive bread from bakeries.

❹ Lunch is Served

The final step in the want-satisfaction chain is a tasty sandwich on a bun.

ANALYSIS SKILL **ANALYZING VISUALS**

What different industries are involved in the want-satisfaction chain?

Types of Economic Systems

There are three basic economic systems in the world: traditional, command, and market economies. Most countries today use a mix of these systems to satisfy their citizens' wants and needs.

In a traditional economy, economic decisions are based on how economic activity has been carried out in the past. People may grow their own food and make their own goods. They might grow and make everything they need to survive, or they might trade to obtain things that they cannot make themselves. If they do trade, they may or may not use money. They may use a barter system in which they trade goods for other goods.

A second type of economic system is called a command economy. In this kind of system, the government makes all economic decisions. In addition, the government owns or controls all capital, tools, and production equipment. It tells managers and workers on farms and in factories what they can produce, how much of it to produce, and how much they can charge for it. Historically, many Communist countries have tried to set up command economies. Most of these economies have collapsed, but North Korea and Cuba still have command economies.

The third type of economy is the one found in most countries, including the United States. It is called a market economy. A **market economy** is one in which economic decisions are made by individuals looking out for their own and their families' best interests. People can start businesses to make and sell any legal products they choose. Based on the market, they can also set their own prices for these products. In other words, the government does not tell people what to produce or buy. In this way, a market economy is the opposite of a command economy.

A market economy is based on freedom. People are free to own property, to create companies, and to buy products as they choose. The right to buy and sell goods as you want is called a **free market**. Companies also need to be free to compete with each other. In a free market, competition among sellers—not any government policy—is the main factor in setting prices. Sellers try to price their goods lower than their competitors so that people will buy them. At the same time, they have to be careful not to set their prices so low that they lose money.

READING CHECK **Explaining** Why do countries need economic systems?

QUICK FACTS

American Economic Freedoms

Among the basic rights we have as Americans are certain economic freedoms. These economic freedoms are the foundation of our free market economy.

How do these freedoms affect our everyday lives?

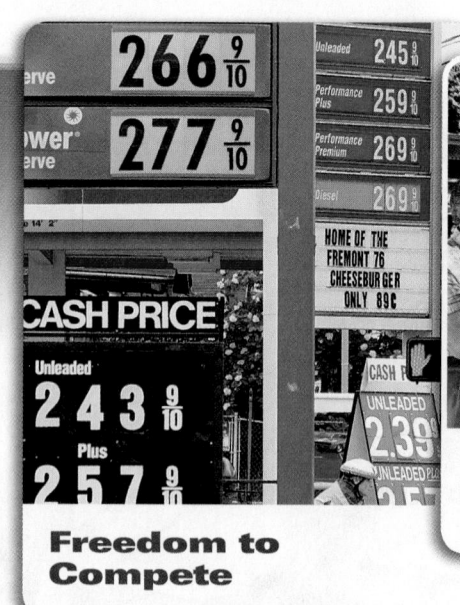

Freedom to Compete

Freedom to Own Property

Life in a Market Economy

In a market economy, people are free to start a business and pursue profit. **Profit** is the money a business has left after it has paid its expenses. The profit motive, or the desire to make a profit, is essential to a successful market economy. If people do not want profit, they will not start businesses and people will have no way to obtain goods and services.

Competition for Resources

In order to make a profit, people need to provide a good or service. In order to provide a good or service, they need resources. As you know, however, resources are not unlimited. As a result, businesses and individuals must compete for the resources they need. This competition eventually affects everyone, not just business owners. In time, it affects the prices we pay for the goods we want.

One result of the competition for these resources is scarcity. **Scarcity** is the lack of a particular resource. When a resource becomes scarce, it is harder for producers to obtain. Products made with that resource also become more difficult to obtain. As a result, the prices for these items usually rise.

Supply and Demand

Changes in prices are usually the result of the laws of supply and demand. These laws are among the most basic of all economic principles. The **law of supply** states that businesses will produce more products when they can sell them at higher prices. They will produce fewer products when prices are low. The **law of demand**, on the other hand, states that buyers will demand, or want, a greater quantity of a good when its price is low. Likewise, as prices rise, the quantity demanded falls. That is, when the price of a good goes up, people buy less of that good.

Although you may not realize it, you are probably already familiar with the principles of supply and demand. Imagine, for example, that you are paid $100 by each of your neighbors to mow their lawns. You will probably want to mow quite a few lawns, because that is a good price for your service. Imagine, however, that your neighbors only wanted to pay you $1 per lawn. Would you still want to mow as many? Most people would not, because that price is too low. That is what the law of supply states—people are more eager to provide a good or service for a high price than for a low one.

Freedom to Buy and Sell

Freedom of Workers to Compete for Jobs

Freedom to Earn Profits

LAW 101

FOUNDATIONS® of DEMOCRACY

File-Sharing and Copyright Law

In June 2005 the U.S. Supreme Court ruled that a popular Web site was responsible for violating copyright laws. The company itself did not download illegal material. However, its file-sharing technology helped individuals share copyrighted materials, such as movies and music, without paying for them.

Why it Matters Article I, Section 8 of the Constitution gives Congress the power to make copyright laws. Copyright laws give artists such as writers, painters, and performers lifetime ownership of their work. People who wish to use a copyrighted work must receive the owner's permission and often pay a fee. For example, whenever you buy a CD, the copyright holder gets paid.

But how would the copyright holder get paid if you did not pay for the CD? People are often tempted to download music files without paying. This is illegal—it violates the artist's copyright. For some artists, the lost income from illegally downloaded works may threaten their ability to continue working. Other artists, however, offer free, legal downloads of their music on the Internet to attract more listeners.

Downloading music from the Internet without paying for it may violate copyright laws.

go.hrw.com KEYWORD: SZ7 CH17

ANALYSIS SKILL **EVALUATING THE LAW**

1. Why do you think the framers of the Constitution wanted to protect artists' rights to their works?
2. What do you think can be done to discourage people from illegally obtaining copyrighted music and movies?

The law of demand works in the same way. If you went to a CD store and found that CDs were priced at $2 each, how many would you buy? At that price, you might buy quite a few of them. How many would you buy, though, if they cost $25 each? You would probably buy fewer, because the price is so much higher. That is the basic idea behind the law of demand.

What business owners hope is that the supply of and demand for a product will balance each other. Because they want to find a price at which consumers will continue to buy a product, the price cannot be too high. At the same time, however, business owners need to make a profit. Therefore, the price cannot be too low either.

To understand this balance, imagine that you are selling lemonade. You need to figure out a good price to charge for your product. First you think that you would like to charge $10 per glass. That way you will make a large profit on each glass that you sell. Unfortunately, however, people do not want to pay that much for it, and you are left with lots of unsold lemonade.

To try to sell more, you decide to drop your price. Now you will sell lemonade for a nickel a glass. Lots of people are willing to buy it now. However, you quickly learn that it costs you more to make the lemonade than you earn by selling it. Obviously, you will need to raise your prices if you want to stay in business for long.

In response, you raise your prices to $2 per glass. You now have fewer customers than you did before, but your business is still steady. You are also making less profit per glass than you did when you charged $10, but you are not losing money. In other words, you have managed to achieve a balance between supply and demand.

Free Enterprise

In a market economy, no one orders business owners how to run their businesses. Of course, if owners do not follow the laws of supply and demand, their businesses fail. Still, business owners may operate however they see fit, with little direction or interference by government. This principle is called **free enterprise**.

The free-enterprise system offers enterprising businesspeople the opportunity to make huge profits. For example, Bill Gates and Steve Jobs are two Americans who used their economic freedom to start successful companies. With no intervention from the government, they turned their companies—Microsoft and Apple Computer—into hugely successful operations.

Most companies are not as successful as Microsoft and Apple, though. By accepting the opportunity to make profits, business owners also open themselves to the possibility of huge losses if their companies do not perform well. They might create a product only to learn that there is no demand for it, or they might find that they have to charge more than people are willing to pay for their goods. Mistakes like these can cost business owners. Some even end up losing their companies. This is the main risk that people face in a free-enterprise system.

Competition is vital to the free-enterprise system. As you have already learned, competition between companies is the main factor in setting prices. In addition, competition drives companies to improve their products. Each company wants the products it creates to be the best so that people will buy them.

The constant desire to improve products means that innovation is also important in free enterprise. Clever thinkers are always looking for new products they can create or for ways to improve existing products. They hope that their innovations will help them make huge profits from their products.

Innovative people do not want others to steal their ideas. They want ways to protect what they have created so that no one else can take credit for it or make money from it. In the United States, there are two ways to protect ideas. A patent gives you the exclusive right to make and sell your invention for a certain number of years. A copyright is the exclusive right to publish or sell a piece of writing, music, or art.

Capitalism

The main driving force behind the American economy today is capitalism. **Capitalism** is an economic system in which the productive resources—farms, factories, machines, and so on—are owned by private citizens.

Capitalism is closely linked to a market economy. People are free to buy and sell as they please. Capitalism also encourages people to invest their money so that they will be successful financially. If they are successful, they will be able to improve their quality of life. Anyone with a little extra money has the opportunity to invest it, either in a company of their own or in someone else's company.

If a company is successful, it can make huge profits, and not only for its owners. All the people who invested in the company can also make profits. By encouraging investment, innovation, and the production of quality goods, the capitalist system benefits the American people as a whole.

Monopolies

Since competition is an essential part of the free-enterprise system, business practices that limit competition are frowned upon. Such practices disrupt the free market and weaken a market economy.

POLITICAL CARTOON
Monopolies

Because monopolies limit competition, they harm our free-enterprise system. As a result, they are outlawed in the United States.

© Cartoon Stock

"'Freddie, the Little Merger Mogul, didn't expect to have a monopoly right away. He planned to start small by rigging markets, restraining trade, and suppressing competition—<u>then</u> . . . '"

ANALYSIS SKILL ANALYZING PRIMARY SOURCES

What is the artist's point of view regarding monopolies? How can you tell?

As a result, most countries that have market economies have banned companies from creating monopolies. A company is said to have a **monopoly** if it is the only one selling a product or providing a service. A company that holds a monopoly can set any price it wants. This can cause many problems, especially if the item in question is a necessity.

In the United States, monopolies—except for certain public utilities—are illegal. The U.S. government watches businesses to see that no new monopolies are formed and that consumers are protected.

READING CHECK Finding the Main Idea How are supply, demand, and free enterprise key to a market economy?

The U.S. Economic System

As you have already learned, the United States has a market economy. For the most part, people are free to produce and buy any goods they wish in any way that they wish.

In a few instances, however, the U.S. government does impose some regulations on businesses, much like you would find in a command economy. In this way, our market economy also includes a mix of elements of other economic systems.

A Mixed Economy

An economy that mixes elements of different economic systems is called a mixed economy. In most mixed economies, businesses are largely free to operate as they please. Their operations, however, must fall within certain regulations set up and monitored by the government. The U.S. economic system is a mixed economy.

Many of our government's regulations on business are intended to protect people. For example, federal and state governments have established laws, such as minimum wage laws, to help protect workers. Some laws guarantee workers' safety and protect people from discrimination. Other government regulations are intended to protect the natural environment. For example, the government sets limits on how many chemicals companies can release into the air or water. These regulations sometimes cost companies money, which results in higher prices for consumers. At the same time, however, the regulations result in cleaner air and water and less pollution.

The federal government may sometimes intervene in business to help control prices. One way the government does this is by subsidizing, or giving money to, certain industries. For example, to make sure that people can buy flour, cereal, and other wheat products cheaply, the government might give subsidies to wheat farmers. Because they are receiving money from the government, the farmers do not have to charge high prices for their crops. As a result, prices for wheat products stay low.

American Business

Think about the companies that made some of the products you own. What do you know about these companies? Most of the products you own were probably made by large companies. Many of the businesses we deal with in the United States today are huge. They employ millions of people and do business all around the world. This has not always been the case, however.

In the early days of the United States, most businesses were small. They served only local needs. Few people ever needed to do business with people who lived far away. For example, a farmer who needed a new piece of equipment probably only had to travel a few miles to purchase it.

In the late 1800s, however, larger businesses began to develop in the United States. Improvements in transportation allowed big companies to sell to customers who lived far away. As businesses became more successful, they gained more money. By reinvesting this money in their businesses, they were able to grow even larger.

Today, big businesses are essential to the American economy. Many of the goods and services we use every day could not be produced by small companies. For example, to produce steel, electricity, automobiles, and ships requires large and expensive machines. Only large companies have the resources and the tools to produce these goods efficiently. Economists refer to this ability of large companies to produce many goods efficiently as the economy of scale.

In the last few decades of the 1900s, companies began to grow even larger. Businesses began to join together to form huge organizations called conglomerates. A conglomerate is formed by the merger of businesses that produce, supply, or sell a number

Comparing
Economic Systems
Command, market, and traditional economies differ in the way goods are produced and sold. Most countries use a mix of two more of these systems.

This sign explains to customers that they are limited to only 113 grams of bread per person.

Command

Market

Traditional

ANALYSIS SKILL ANALYZING VISUALS

How is the United States a mix of different economic systems?

PRESS CONFERENCES
Understanding Publicity

In 1997 the federal government charged the Microsoft corporation with violating antitrust laws. To announce the trial and its results, both the government and Microsoft used a powerful tool—the press conference.

During a press conference reporters gather to hear statements from an individual or an organization. They generally report the information to the public in newspapers, on radio and television, or on the Internet.

Often people hold press conferences to express their point of view. Press conferences are good publicity tools because they give people control over the way in which information is presented. They are an opportunity for photographs to be taken with a background and presentation.

An attorney for the U.S. Justice Department holds a press conference during the Microsoft antitrust trial.

ANALYSIS SKILL   **MEDIA INVESTIGATION**   go.hrw.com   KEYWORD: SZ7 CH17

What steps would one have to take to hold a press conference?

---

of unrelated goods. For example, a single conglomerate might control communication systems, insurance companies, hotel chains, and many other businesses. The government monitors conglomerates closely to be sure that economic competition is not harmed.

Of course, small businesses have never disappeared in the United States. Even as big companies get bigger, many small companies continue to thrive. It is largely because of the mix of large and small businesses that the U.S. economy remains powerful today.

READING CHECK   **Summarizing** What is the U.S. economy like today?

go.hrw.com
Online Quiz
KEYWORD: SZ7 HP17

SECTION 1 ASSESSMENT

Reviewing Ideas and Terms

1. a. Define Write a definition for the terms **market economy, free market, profit, scarcity, law of supply,** and **law of demand.**
   b. Analyze Information How are scarcity and the laws of supply and demand connected?
2. a. Define Write a definition for the terms **free enterprise, capitalism,** and **monopoly.**
   b. Draw Conclusions How do monopolies harm free enterprise?
3. a. Summarize Why is the United States described as a mixed economy?
   b. Analyze How is capitalism linked to a market economy?

Critical Thinking

4. Summarizing Use your notes and a graphic organizer like this one to identify the five economic freedoms that Americans enjoy.

Economic Freedoms

Focus on Writing

5. Contrasting Explain how the U.S. economic system differs from the economic system in Cuba.

STUDENTS TAKE ACTION

Providing Emergency Care

In 2005 officials in Iron County, Missouri, opened a 24-hour critical care facility to treat emergency patients. The center provides sorely needed services in a county whose only hospital had closed several years earlier. The new emergency care center was made possible in part by the efforts of local students who convinced a nonprofit foundation to make a sound business decision based on local need.

Community Connection Like many other people in their community, students participating in the Project Citizen program in Mr. Don Barzowski's government class were concerned about the lack of a hospital in their area. "The lack of emergency care in Iron County affects everyone," said one student. The students decided to work on getting support for a new critical care facility.

Taking Action Working with other groups, students contacted local, county, state, and federal government officials to gain support for funding a new facility. The students also gathered data to see how the absence of a hospital affected the area. When the state's largest foundation for hospital funding held public forums to discuss a new facility, the students attended, prepared with a detailed presentation. The teens noted that Iron County had the fourth highest accident rate in Missouri. With no local ambulance service or urgent care facility, it took between 32 and 50 minutes to travel to the nearest hospital. When the foundation agreed to give $900,000 to help fund a new facility, it cited the presentation by Mr. Barzowski's students as a major influence on its decision.

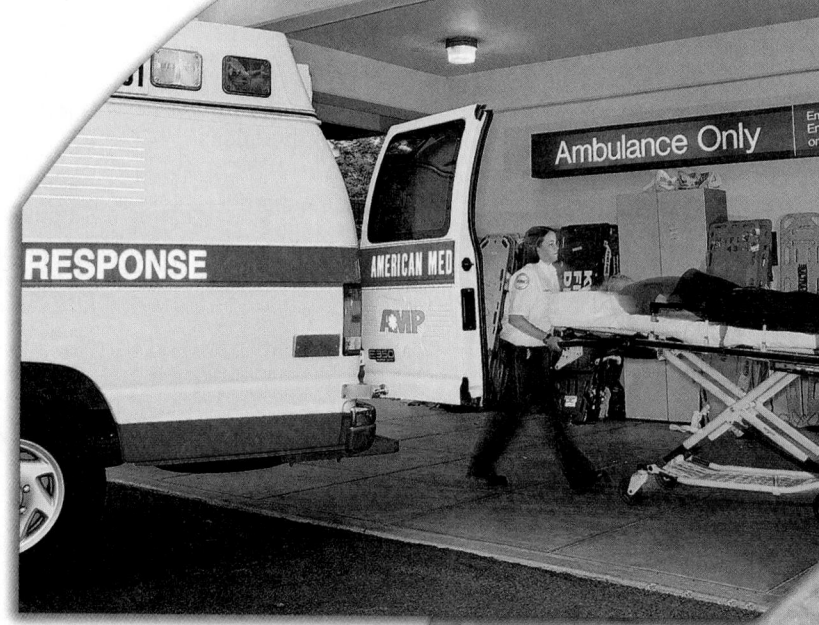

Students in Iron County, Missouri, helped bring a critical care facility like this one to their community.

go.hrw.com
Project Citizen
KEYWORD: SZ7 CH17

SERVICE LEARNING

1. What steps did the students take to gather support for their idea?
2. Why do you think the Iron County students were able to convince the foundation to help fund a new critical care facility?

SECTION 2

Business Organizations

BEFORE YOU READ

The Main Idea

American businesses may be organized as sole proprietorships, partnerships, corporations, or nonprofit organizations.

Reading Focus

1. What are the different types of business organizations?
2. How do corporations function?
3. What is a nonprofit organization?

Key Terms

sole proprietorship, *p. 460*
partnership, *p. 461*
corporation, *p. 461*
stock, *p. 463*
stockholders, *p. 463*
dividends, *p. 463*
nonprofit organizations, *p. 464*

As you read, take notes on the different ways in which businesses in the United States can be organized. Use a graphic organizer like this one to record your notes.

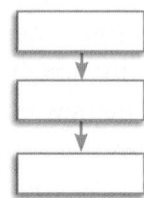

If you make and sell handmade bamboo fly rods, your business will be small. In fact, you may be the only employee. If you mass produce plumbing fixtures, your business may grow large. You may have dozens, or even hundreds, of employees. You may form a corporation. Businesses come in all sizes. The type of business organization you select is often related to the size or complexity of the business, but there are other reasons you might choose one form of business over another.

Business Organizations

If you want to start your own business, one of the first decisions you will have to make is how your business will be owned. In the United States, there are three basic types of business ownership or business organization: the sole proprietorship, the partnership, and the corporation. Each type of organization has advantages and disadvantages.

Sole Proprietorships

There are more than 23.5 million business firms in the United States today. Of these, more than 18 million are small businesses owned by one person. These businesses include game stores, record stores, grocery stores, hair salons, and other businesses that serve people who live nearby. A small business owned by one person is called a **sole proprietorship**.

There are many advantages to going into business for yourself. For example, sole proprietors are their own bosses. They decide the hours the businesses will be open and how their business will operate. In addition, the owners take all the profits the business produces.

Yet there are disadvantages to being a sole proprietor. Owners must have or borrow all the money they need to rent or buy buildings or office space and equipment. If a sole proprietor hires help, he or she must be able to pay the employees. He or she is also personally liable for taxes. Although an owner may hire others to help, the owner is responsible for the success or failure of the business. For example, if the business fails, the proprietor must face the losses. In that case, a proprietor may have to sell his or her personal belongings to pay business debts.

Different Kinds of Businesses

In the United States, businesses come in all types and sizes. Our economic freedoms allow each person to be a part of the type of business he or she chooses.

How are sole proprietorships different from corporations?

Law Offices of Jack Riordan
ESTATE PLANNING • TRUSTS • WILLS

KERRY RIORDAN SYKES — Attorney At Law

MAUREEN S. McFADDEN — Attorney At Law

JACK GREALISH — Tax Preparation

Partnership

Sole Proprietor

Corporation

Partnership

The owner of a small business sometimes seeks another person to become a partner in the business. A business in which two or more people share the responsibilities, costs, profits, and losses is known as a **partnership**. This form of ownership gives businesses more capital and a better chance of success.

The advantages and disadvantages of a partnership are similar to those of a sole proprietorship. The greatest difference is that in a partnership there is more than one person to provide capital, share responsibility, furnish ideas, and do the work. The partners also share the risks. If the business fails, the partners share responsibility for the debts.

Partnerships also have disadvantages. Partners can lose their personal belongings if their business fails, just like sole proprietors. Partnerships have another unique weakness. If the partners disagree strongly about how to run the business, serious problems can result. The company may lose efficiency or be unable to act at all. For this reason it is a good idea to have a written partnership agreement in place. This document sets out what responsibilities each partner has for running the business. It also establishes how the partners will be paid if the business earns profits. These guidelines will not prevent disagreements from happening, but may help minimize their effects and keep the business running.

Corporations

The third basic form of business organization is the corporation. A **corporation** is a type of business that is recognized as a separate legal entity. Most of the country's large businesses—and many smaller companies—are corporations. The corporation is a permanent organization, unlike proprietorships and partnerships, which end when their owners die. Corporations play a vital role in the U.S. economy.

READING CHECK **Categorizing** What are three ways that businesses are organized?

How a Corporation is Created and Organized

QUICK FACTS

Corporations can be very large or very small. Individuals, small businesses, and multinational companies can all become corporations.

❶ Start Small

Many businesses start out with a sole proprietor, which means just one owner. Some small businesses incorporate, and some do not.

❷ Grow

To increase staffing and production, a small business needs money. To get money it may ask a small number of people to invest in the business.

❸ Incorporate

If a business needs to raise money from more than 35 people, it must incorporate.

❹ Trade Publicly

A corporation can issue public stock, or shares of ownership. The people who buy stock are called stockholders.

Organization and Control in a Typical Corporation

Stockholders are the owners of a corporation.

Stockholders

Every corporation must have a **board of directors** that answers to the stockholders.

Board of Directors

The board of directors appoints **company officers**, such as the chief executive officer (CEO) and the chief financial officer (CFO), to run the corporation.

Corporate Officers

The CEO hires **managers** to run different areas of the business.

Managers

The **employees** carry out the orders of the management.

Employees

Corporations often hold annual meetings that their stockholders can attend.

ANALYSIS SKILL ANALYZING VISUALS

Based on the illustration, under what circumstance must a business incorporate?

How Corporations Function

A sole proprietor is personally responsible for the business he or she owns. Partners are also personally responsible for the partnership's success or failure. A corporation, however, is different. A corporation is a type of business organization that is recognized by law as a separate legal entity from the people who own it. It is treated as if it were a person.

Raising Money

Corporations raise money by selling **stock**, or shares of ownership. Each share of stock represents part of the corporation. The people who buy corporate stocks are called **stockholders**.

Suppose that a new corporation needs $1 million to set up business. The corporation could sell 10,000 shares of its stock at $100 a share. Each purchaser of one share of stock would then own one ten-thousandth of the company. The new corporation would have $1 million in capital to begin work.

If the corporation has profits to distribute, each owner of a single share of stock would receive one ten-thousandth of the total. Corporate profits paid to stockholders are called **dividends**. Each stockholder receives a portion of the profits based on the number of shares he or she owns.

Another way corporations can raise money is by selling bonds. Bonds are loans. People who buy bonds are lending money to the company. The company must pay the interest on its bonds before paying its stockholders. This interest is due whether or not the company earns any profits for the year. The company must pay back the original amount of the loan when the bond expires.

Rights to Operate

State governments grant corporations the right to operate. Each state has laws on how to incorporate a business. After incorporation, the company has the right to conduct business, to sell stock, and to receive the protection of state laws.

In return for these benefits, corporations must obey state regulations in regard to their organization. They must file reports that make public certain financial information and must pay whatever taxes they owe. They may not sell their stock in ways that are fraudulent or deceptive.

Elected Directors

The stockholders elect the directors of the corporation. Every corporation is required by law to hold at least one meeting of its stockholders each year. All stockholders have the right to attend and address the meeting—even if they own only one share.

At this annual meeting, stockholders elect a board of directors. They may also vote on changes in the corporation's business **structure**. Each share of stock entitles its owner to one vote. The board of directors, representing the stockholders, meets during the year to make decisions about the corporation.

Choosing Executives

The board of directors chooses corporate officers, or the people who will manage the affairs of the corporation. The officers include the company's president and any vice presidents, the secretary, and the treasurer. The president usually chooses the other major assistants. Together, these officials oversee the daily operations of the corporation.

Debt Responsibility

If the corporation's business fails, neither the stockholders nor the corporation's executives are responsible for the corporation's debts. This is the advantage the corporation has in gathering large amounts of capital. If a corporation goes out of business, its assets, including its property, buildings, and other valuables, are sold. The money raised is then used to pay off the corporation's debts.

> **ACADEMIC VOCABULARY**
> **structure:** the way something is set up or organized

READING CHECK **Finding the Main Idea** What advantages do corporations have when raising money or dealing with debts?

FOCUS ON
Meg Whitman
(1957–   )

As the chief executive officer of eBay, Incorporated, Margaret "Meg" Whitman is one of the most powerful businesspeople in the United States. She attended college at Princeton University, where she first pursued a career in medicine. After working one summer selling advertising for a school publication, she decided to become an economics major. After earning a master of business administration degree at Harvard University, Whitman went to work for Proctor & Gamble. Whitman later moved on to lead in such companies as Walt Disney, Stride Rite Shoes, and the toy company Hasbro.

In 1998 Whitman became president and CEO of eBay, which had fewer than 100 employees at the time. She helped turn the company into a household name that operates worldwide and employs some 13,000 people. The online auction site now greets seven million Web-surfers each day as a result of Whitman's efforts and talent.

Drawing Conclusions What qualities have made Meg Whitman a successful business leader?

Nonprofit Organizations

Some business organizations provide goods and services without seeking to earn a profit for stockholders. These organizations are known as **nonprofit organizations**. They include charities, scientific research associations, and organizations dedicated to cultural and educational programs. Because they do not make a profit, these organizations are not taxed by the government. They are also not allowed to contribute to political campaigns. Most nonprofits use donations from individuals and businesses to operate.

Larger nonprofit organizations are often corporations. They take this step for the same reasons regular businesses do—to help raise money and protect the assets of their members. Among the many nonprofit corporations in the United States are the American Red Cross, the American Heart Association, the United Way, Boy Scouts, and Girl Scouts.

READING CHECK **Summarizing** What are the characteristics of a nonprofit organization?

go.hrw.com
Online Quiz
KEYWORD: SZ7 HP17

SECTION 2 ASSESSMENT

Reviewing Ideas and Terms

1. a. Define Write a definition for the terms **sole proprietorship**, **partnership**, and **corporation**.
b. Summarize What are the advantages and disadvantages of operating a sole proprietorship?
2. a. Define Write a definition for the terms **stock**, **stockholders**, and **dividends**.
b. Analyzing Information How do corporations raise money, and how are the debts of a corporation paid if the corporation fails?
3. a. Define Write a definition for the term **nonprofit organizations**.
b. Defend a Point of View Do you think that nonprofit organizations should be required to pay taxes? Why or why not?

Critical Thinking

4. Categorizing Use your notes and a graphic organizer like this one to describe the four types of U.S. businesses.

Business	Characteristics

Focus on Writing

5. Decision Making If you were to start a business of your own, would you organize it as a sole proprietorship, a partnership, a corporation, or a nonprofit organization? Explain your answer.

Evaluating Primary Sources

Learn

Primary sources are documents created at the time of a historical event. They may be photographs, legal agreements, letters, or other materials. You may have learned about history by reading textbooks or novels or by viewing movies set in historical times. These are secondary sources; they are different from primary sources because they were created after the historical events took place.

A benefit of using primary sources to learn about history is that you can form your own interpretation of the event from the available materials. Primary sources can also be difficult to use since you need to evaluate many sources to get a complete picture.

Practice

❶ **Figure out how the source was originally used.** Inspect the source material and figure out its purpose. Is it a document that was displayed in public or something people used in their homes? Think of how the material was used in another historical time.

❷ **Consider the historical changes represented in the source.** An advertisement from a magazine, like the one shown here, can seem like a minor piece of information. But you can find out about things that turn out to be major changes in how people live or how the economy works.

❸ **Look for clues about values or cultural norms.** Primary sources can help you see what people thought was more or less important at a certain time in history. Look for clues in the wording or in the pictures.

Apply

The advertisement shown below is from a 1926 issue of a U.S. women's magazine. Answer the questions below using this primary source.

1. Who was this item intended for, and how would they have used it?

2. What change in American culture could this primary source be evidence of?

3. What does this advertisement show you about values that were important at the time to people reading this magazine?

SECTION 3

Making Business Decisions

BEFORE YOU READ

The Main Idea

Business owners must make decisions about their use of natural resources, capital, labor, and entrepreneurship. Business owners are free to make these decisions with little interference from the government.

Reading Focus

1. What are the four factors of production?
2. What is the government's role in the economy?

Key Terms

natural resources, *p. 466*
capital, *p. 467*
labor, *p. 467*
entrepreneur, *p. 468*

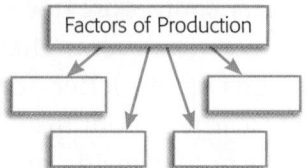 **TAKING NOTES** As you read, take notes on the different factors of production. Use a graphic organizer like this one to take notes on each factor and its significance.

Factors of Production

 If you decide to go into business for yourself, you will have to make many business decisions. Most of these decisions will be about the four factors of production. For example, suppose that you want to design and market new computer games. You will have to decide where to have your offices and how many people to hire, and that's just the beginning. You will have to make a business plan that takes into account all of the factors of production.

Factors of Production

You have, at one time or another, had to make a decision about how to spend your money. Sometimes, there may be only one thing that you want. That makes the decision easy. If you want more than one thing—a new game and some new clothes—and your funds are limited, you have to make a choice.

Countries make similar choices about production. Every country must ask "What are we going to produce?" "How are we going to produce it?" and "For whom are we producing it?" The answers to these questions help us decide how to use the four factors of production: natural resources, capital, labor, and entrepreneurship.

Natural Resources

Items provided by nature without human intervention that can be used to produce goods and to provide services are called natural resources. **Natural resources** can be found on or in the Earth or in Earth's atmosphere. The raw materials needed to produce goods of all kinds come from the oceans, rivers, mines, fields, and forests that help make up the world's natural resources.

Many natural resources in our country are limited, however. A natural resource is considered a factor of production only when some payment is necessary for its use. For example, the air you breathe on the beach is not a factor of production because you do not have to pay to use it.

For example, consider the resource of land. Every business needs a place to locate. People starting a business have several key decisions to make when choosing where they will set up shop. They must consider what locations will best benefit their business. Companies that provide services need to be in a location that is convenient for potential customers to reach. Manufacturers want to be in areas with good transportation so they can ship their goods.

Cost also plays a role when choosing a location. Crowded downtown areas are often more expensive to build or rent office space in than places on the edge of town. Yet their access to customers may be worth the higher price. Business owners must also decide whether to build or rent their facilities. Rent is money paid to use property owned by someone else. Building may be more expensive up front but less expensive than renting in the long run. As you can see, business owners have to consider many such issues when deciding where to locate.

Capital

Suppose you have opened a bakery. In addition to land, you will also need equipment such as mixers and ovens. This equipment is called capital. **Capital** is the manufactured goods used to make other goods and services. Capital includes tools, trucks, machines of all sorts, and office equipment, such as computers. These tools, machines, and other items are often called capital goods to distinguish them from financial capital. Financial capital is the money that is used to buy the tools and equipment—the capital goods—used in production.

Where will you get financial capital? If you have a good business plan and you have good credit, you might take out a loan from a bank. You might also apply for a loan from the Small Business Administration (SBA). The SBA is an agency of the federal government whose mission is to provide a variety of assistance programs for small businesses.

Perhaps you will decide instead to seek one or more other people who are willing to invest in your bakery business. You also may decide to set up your business as a corporation and sell stock to raise capital. As you make these decisions, you must weigh the opportunity costs and analyze costs and benefits of each plan.

Labor

All human effort, skills, and abilities used to produce goods and services are called **labor**.

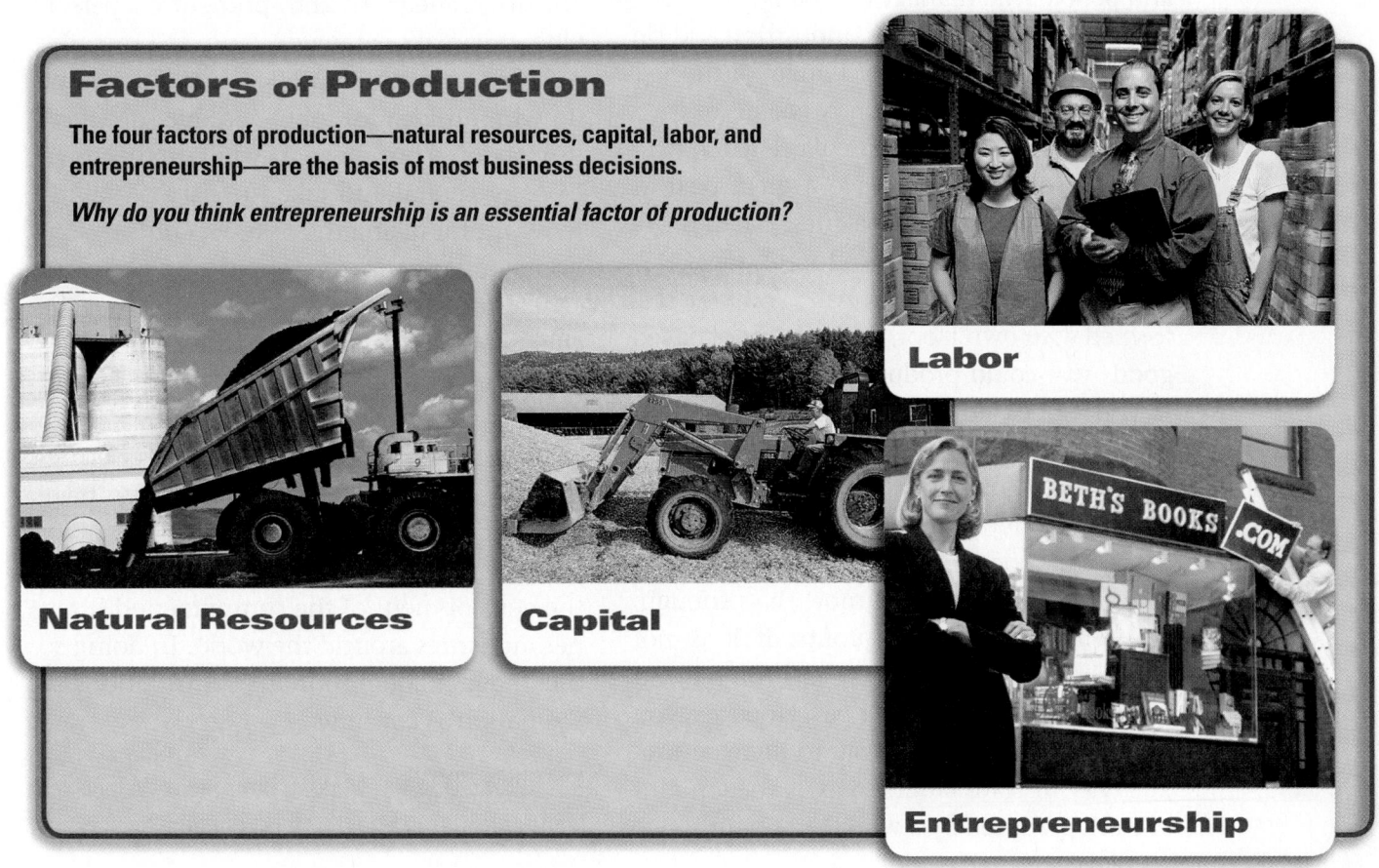

Factors of Production

The four factors of production—natural resources, capital, labor, and entrepreneurship—are the basis of most business decisions.

Why do you think entrepreneurship is an essential factor of production?

Natural Resources

Capital

Labor

Entrepreneurship

Our Career Choices

There is an old saying that in the United States anyone can grow up to be president. In fact, anyone can grow up to be anything—there are no rules that require you to take a certain job or that keep you from your chosen career.

In 1897 New York State tried to limit bakery employees to working a maximum of 10 hours a day. In *Lochner v. New York* (1905), the U.S. Supreme Court overturned this state law, ruling that the Fourteenth Amendment gives citizens the freedom to choose where, when, and how long they work.

Lochner is no longer the law today. State governments often do pass legislation that protects employees, such as minimum-wage laws, overtime laws, and occupational safety regulations. However, the basic idea that individuals have the right to choose their own jobs and negotiate their own employment agreements is still in effect.

1. Who do you think would have argued against enforcement of New York's 10-hour workday—employees or employers?

2. Why do you think state governments pass laws to regulate working conditions and the amount of hours people can work?

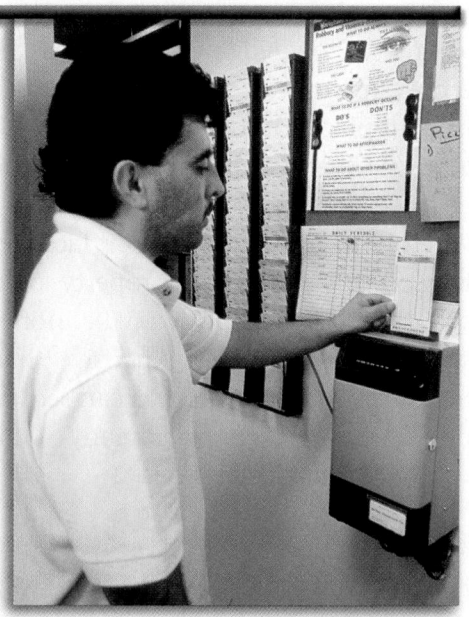

Workers often keep track of the hours they work by punching time cards.

However, the word *labor* is often used to refer specifically to workers as opposed to owners and people who manage companies.

Workers in businesses, industries, and on farms sell their labor in exchange for money. Some workers are paid hourly wages for their labor. Other workers, particularly those who manage companies or have a great deal of responsibility, are paid salaries. Salaries are fixed earnings , rather than hourly wages.

Imagine you owned a bakery. If you performed your own labor, the amount of baked goods you could produce would be limited. If you hired more labor, your production would increase but you would have to pay higher labor costs.

The money you received for selling the additional goods needs to be at least enough to cover all your costs. If it is more than enough, you will increase your profits. If it is not enough to pay the workers, you will have to lay them off, or lower their pay. However, you might be able to find a way to increase productivity instead. Productivity is the amount of work produced by a worker per hour.

Entrepreneurship

If you start your own business, you may be an entrepreneur. An **entrepreneur** is a person who organizes, manages, and assumes the risks of a business. Entrepreneurs often come up with an idea for a new product or a new way of doing business. They put up their own labor or capital and take the risks of failure. In return for taking the risks, an entrepreneur hopes to make a substantial profit. In our capitalist system, many people think that the efforts of entrepreneurs—starting businesses and creating jobs—are an important part of creating society's wealth.

For example, Bill Gates and other entrepreneurs in the computer industry have provided people with innovative computer software. Entrepreneurs have also shaped the development of the computer and Internet industries around the world. In doing so they have made important contributions to the nation's economy.

READING CHECK **Making Inferences** Why is labor considered a factor of production?

The Government's Role

Although the U.S. government does not tell business owners what products to make or how much to charge, it does influence business in many ways. For example, government ensures that big corporations do not destroy competition from small businesses. The government also protects a person's rights to own private property and to buy and sell in a free market. In addition, the federal government taxes business income. Changes in the tax code can affect business plans.

Many agencies of the federal government help businesses. For example, the Small Business Administration helps small businesses as they compete in the economy. The government plays many other roles in business. It helps business by providing information that managers can use in planning their production levels, sales, and costs. It sometimes provides loans and other types of assistance to businesses. The government also tries to keep the economy running smoothly.

The government protects workers' health and safety, prevents pollution of the environment, and protects buyers from dis-honest practices and harmful products. The government also ensures that employers cannot discriminate against workers or job applicants. Congress has also established a federal minimum wage law. This law requires a minimum hourly wage for employees who are not exempt.

Some people believe that the government has gone too far in doing its job as overseer. For example, tens of thousands of pages are needed to print all the business regulations issued by the federal government. On the one hand, some regulations are necessary. Others, however, are criticized for adding to the cost of doing business without providing much benefit to people. These higher business costs can be passed on to consumers as higher prices.

Achieving the correct level of government involvement is difficult. How much regulation is needed is a subject of great debate. As a citizen in a free economy, you will help decide this issue with your vote and your voice.

READING CHECK **Finding the Main Idea** Why does the government need to regulate businesses in the United States, and how does it do so?

SECTION 3 ASSESSMENT

Reviewing Ideas and Terms

1. a. Define Write a brief definition for each of the following terms: **natural resources**, **labor**, **capital** and **entrepreneur**.

b. Analyze Information What are three ways people get capital for their businesses?

c. Draw Inferences and Conclusions Why do businesses need labor, and how are they affected by productivity?

2. a. Elaborate What are some of the ways in which the government regulates business?

b. Defend a Point of View Do you think the government should regulate business? Why or why not?

Critical Thinking

3. Summarizing Copy the graphic organizer. Use it and your notes to identify the four factors necessary for a business to be successful.

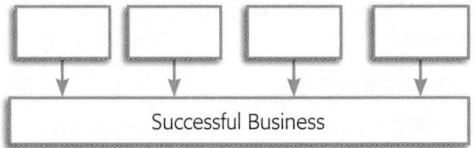

Successful Business

Focus on Writing

4. Making Decisions Imagine that you are planning to open a small business in your community. Make a list of the decisions that you must make before you can open your store.

Visual Summary

Use this visual summary to help you review the main ideas of the chapter.

The U.S. free market economic system is based on principles of economic freedom. The laws of supply and demand and the factors of production influence the economic decisions of the various business organizations in the United States.

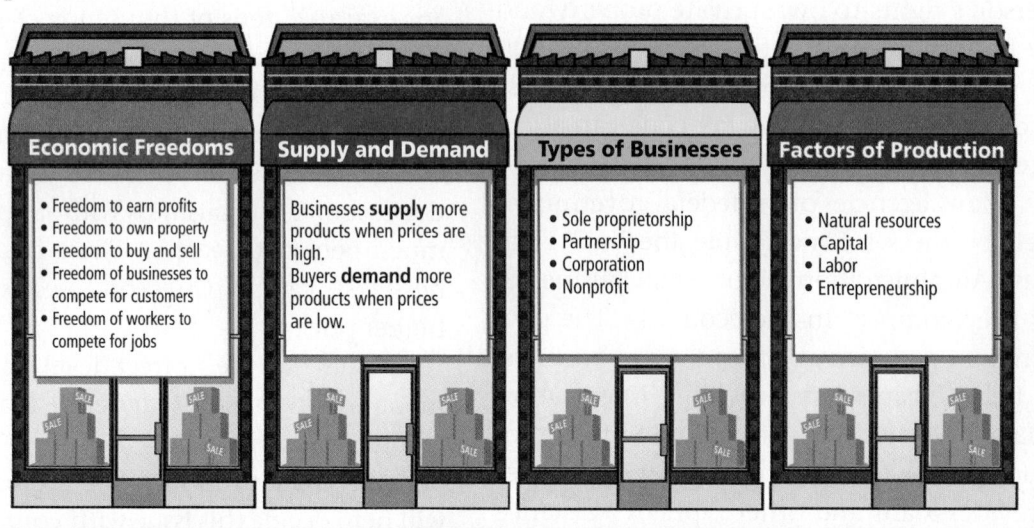

Economic Freedoms

- Freedom to earn profits
- Freedom to own property
- Freedom to buy and sell
- Freedom of businesses to compete for customers
- Freedom of workers to compete for jobs

Supply and Demand

Businesses **supply** more products when prices are high.
Buyers **demand** more products when prices are low.

Types of Businesses

- Sole proprietorship
- Partnership
- Corporation
- Nonprofit

Factors of Production

- Natural resources
- Capital
- Labor
- Entrepreneurship

Reviewing Key Terms

For each term below, write a sentence explaining its significance to the American economy.

1. market economy
2. free market
3. profit
4. scarcity
5. law of supply
6. law of demand
7. free enterprise
8. capitalism
9. monopoly
10. sole proprietorship
11. partnership
12. corporation
13. stock
14. stockholders
15. dividends
16. nonprofit organizations
17. natural resources
18. capital
19. labor
20. entrepreneur

Comprehension and Critical Thinking

SECTION 1 *(pp. 450–458)*

21. a. Describe Name and describe the three main economic systems.

  b. Analyze What role does competition play in the free enterprise system?

  c. Elaborate Do you agree that monopolies weaken a market economy? Explain your answer.

SECTION 2 *(pp. 460–464)*

22. a. Identify What is a nonprofit organization?

  b. Compare and Contrast In what ways are sole proprietorships, partnerships, and corporations similar and different?

  c. Elaborate Which of the different business organizations would you most want to be a part of? Why?

SECTION 3 *(Pages 466–469)*

23. a. Recall What are the four factors of production? Why is each important to a business?

b. Draw Inferences and Conclusions Why must the factors of production be considered when starting a new business?

c. Predict What might happen if governments did not regulate some business operations?

Civics Skills

Evaluating Primary Sources *The primary source below is a 1926 advertisement from a women's magazine. Use the source to answer the questions that follow.*

24. What is the subject of this primary source? How do you think it was originally used?

25. What does this primary source tell you about the period from which it was produced?

Reading Skills

Interpreting Basic Indicators of Economic Performance *Use the Reading Skills taught in this chapter and the chart below to answer the questions that follow.*

Year	Consumer Price Index	Change from previous year
2000	$172.20	3.4%
2001	$177.10	2.8%
2002	$179.90	1.6%
2003	$184.00	2.3%
2004	$188.90	2.7%

26. Between what two years did the Consumer Price Index change the most?

27. What overall trend does the chart indicate?

Using the Internet

go.hrw.com
KEYWORD: SZ7 CH17

28. Access the Internet through the HRW Go site to research stock and stock markets. Then imagine you are a corporate officer about to issue stock to raise money for your company. Create a company profile that explains what you produce, why you are issuing the stock at this time, what kind of stock will be issued, how much each share will be, and your projections on how your stock will do in the market.

FOCUS ON WRITING

29. Writing a Newspaper Advertisement Use your notes about economic systems to help you plan your newspaper advertisement. Develop a list of information about your lighting system that consumers might want to know. Then design your advertisement, making sure to include both text and interesting visuals. Remember to explain what makes your product different from the competition. Use your advertisement to persuade people to purchase your product.

CHAPTER 18

GOODS AND SERVICES

SECTION 1
American Production

SECTION 2
Distributing Goods

SECTION 3
You the Consumer

NATIONAL STANDARDS
FOR CIVICS AND GOVERNMENT

IV. What is the relationship of the United States to other nations and to world affairs?

B. How do the domestic politics and constitutional principles of the United States affect its relations with the world?

D. What is the place of law in the American constitutional system?

V. What are the roles of the citizen in American democracy?

C. What are the responsibilities of citizens?

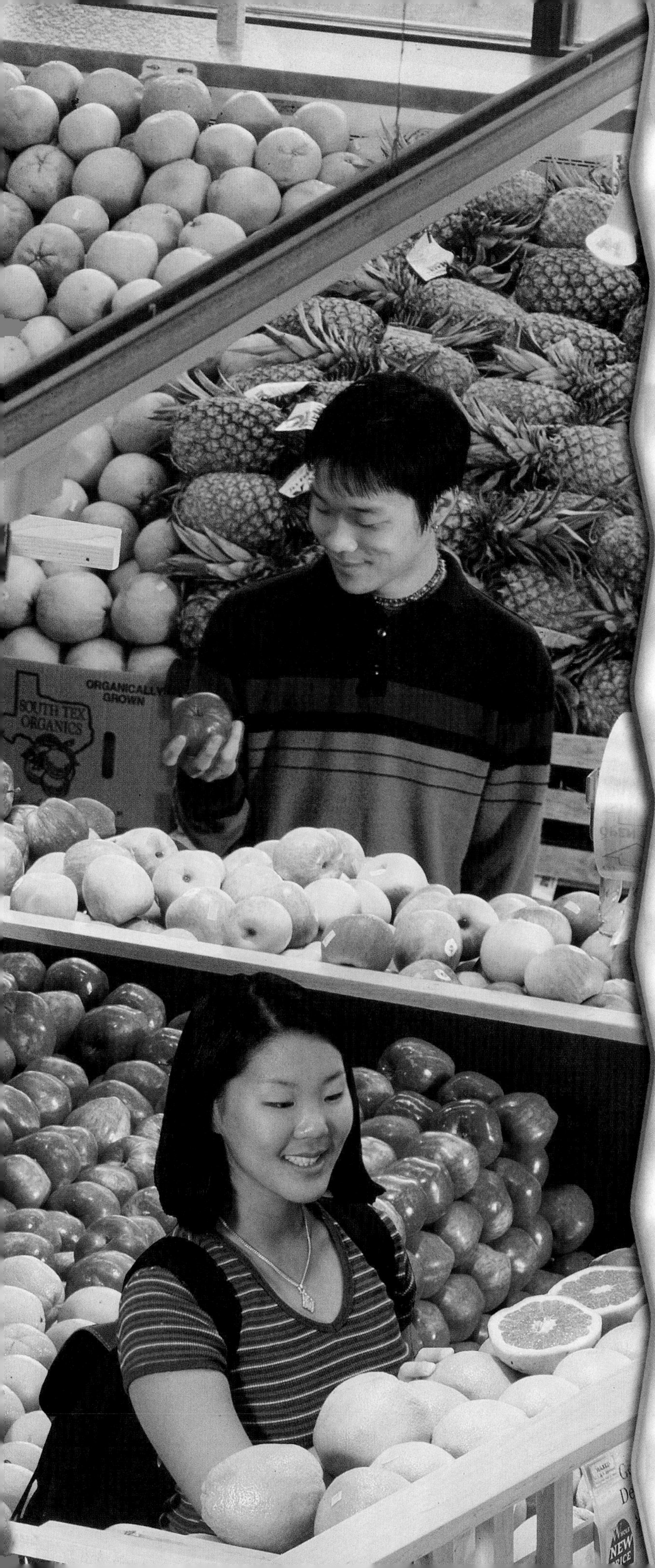

WHY CIVICS Matters

Many of the things that you buy, from cereal to compact discs, are made in the United States. How the United States makes and distributes goods and services has contributed to the country's economic success.

STUDENTS TAKE ACTION

ESTABLISHING SMOKE-FREE ZONES
Concerned about the health problems caused by secondhand smoke, students in Mexico, Missouri, set out to make all of the restaurants in their city smoke-free. Is smoking allowed in public places in your community? What can you do to inform people about the risks of secondhand smoke?

FOCUS ON WRITING

AN INFOMERCIAL Each year, the United States produces more than $6 trillion worth of goods and services. As you read this chapter, take notes on how the United States makes and distributes its products throughout the world. Then write an infomercial to teach citizens about America's free-enterprise economy.

Reading Skills

In this chapter you will read about the goods and services that the United States produces annually. You will learn what mass production is and how it allows the United States to produce more goods than any other country.

You will also read about how American goods are shipped to consumers around the world and how marketing helps to sell these products. Finally, you will learn how to be a wise consumer and find out about the resources available to help you make smart purchases.

Interpreting a Table

FOCUS ON READING A table condenses data into a format that is easy to read and understand. However, tables show information without analysis or interpretation. It is up to readers to interpret the table and draw their own conclusions.

Reading Tables To read a table, first look at the title to understand the table's subject and purpose. Then study the headings for each vertical column or horizontal row. Analyze the information to draw conclusions about the data. Look for trends by looking down each column and along each row.

Title This table is about how people traveled between cities.

Mode of Transportation of People Traveling between Cities

Year	By Railroad	By Airline
1950	6%	2%
2000	1%	19%

Headings These headings tell you that the data will show the year and kind of transportation used.

Conclusions By studying the information, you can see that there was a big jump in the use of airlines and a drop in the railroads. You would conclude that airlines have become more widely used than railroads for passenger travel.

Helpful Hints for Interpreting Tables

1. To locate specific facts on a table, look down a column and across a row.

2. Where the column and row intersect, or meet, is where you will find the data you need.

3. Analyze the information by looking for how the numbers change. Is there a pattern that suggests a trend?

You Try It!

Study the table below. Then answer the questions that follow.

U.S. Balance of Trade, 1995–2000 (in billions of dollars)			
Year	Exports	Imports	Balance
2000	1,065	1,441	-376
1999	957	1,219	-262
1998	932	1,099	-167
1997	937	1,047	-110
1996	851	959	-108
1995	795	895	-100

After you have studied the table, answer the following questions.

1. What years are included in the table?

2. What is the meaning of the minus signs (-) in the "Balance" column?

3. What was the U.S. balance of trade in 1995? In 2000?

4. Do you see a trend in the value of U.S. exports included in the table? Do you see a trend in the value of goods the United States imports? Describe both trends.

5. How did the U.S. balance of trade change during the years included in the table?

> **As you read Chapter 18,** think about what facts and figures might be put into a table format.

Academic Vocabulary

Success in school is related to knowing academic vocabulary—the words that are frequently used in school assignments and discussions. In this chapter, you will learn the following academic word:

features *(p. 487)*

American Production

BEFORE YOU READ

The Main Idea

American systems of mass production have made it possible to produce goods more efficiently, which raises the U.S. standard of living. The American economic system has made our economy one of the most successful in the world.

Reading Focus

1. What are goods and services, and why are they important in the economy?
2. What are the main features of modern mass production?
3. What is the service sector of the economy?
4. How are profit, risk, and innovation related?

Key Terms

goods, *p. 476*
services, *p. 476*
gross domestic product (GDP), *p. 477*
mass production, *p. 477*
profit, *p. 480*

TAKING NOTES As you read, take notes about American production. Use a web diagram like this one to record your notes.

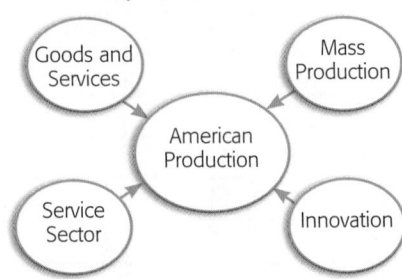

Mass production assembly lines, such as the one shown here, make goods more affordable.

These workers are responsible for just a few parts instead of having to build the entire vehicle.

CIVICS IN PRACTICE Did you ever make a model car or sew a dress from a pattern? What if you had to make hundreds or thousands of them to sell? What would you need to charge for each item to make a living? How much would the public be willing to pay for your products? Mass production is the key to producing affordable goods for millions of Americans and people all over the world.

What Are Goods and Services?

Goods and services are all the things that are produced by a country's economy. Physical products that you can see or touch are called goods. **Goods** are things that are manufactured, or made, and that consumers can buy and own. Examples of goods include food, cars, CD players, buildings, and airplanes. Products that are not physical objects are called **services**. Services are things that people do. Consumers get the benefit of the services but do not own anything as a result. Examples of people who provide services include doctors, tax return preparers, translators, painters, and auto mechanics.

Modern Mass Production

In 1913, inspired by the conveyor belts in grain mills, Henry Ford sped up the 12-year-old assembly line process. He paired humans with machines to divide the assembly of his Model T cars into 84 quick steps. Suddenly, it was possible to produce more automobiles at a much lower cost.

In 1961 a robot named *Unimate* was put to work on a General Motors assembly line as a welder. Since then, industrial robots have become important players in mass production, often performing tasks in conditions too dangerous for humans.

ANALYSIS SKILL **ANALYZING VISUALS**

How did the capability to produce more goods in less time help lower costs?

Some products are a combination of goods and services. For example, a house painter delivers a service —the painting—but also provides a good —the paint itself. A restaurant provides food preparation, ambiance, and cleaning up, but it also provides the food.

The market value of all goods and services produced annually in the United States is called the **gross domestic product (GDP)**. Economists use the GDP as one measure of how well the U.S. economy is performing. Other measures of economic well-being include the unemployment rate, the business failure rate, and the amount of tax revenue that American businesses and citizens produce.

> **READING CHECK** **Finding the Main Idea** How is the GDP related to goods and services?

Mass Production of Goods

American's production of goods depends heavily on the process of **mass production**, or the rapid production by machine of large numbers of identical objects. The key to mass production is to develop machine tools that produce exactly identical parts. Each worker can then be responsible for

monitoring only one machine instead of having to make the whole product. Specialized workers can work faster and more efficiently. Because all the parts are interchangeable, a single worker can do the final assembly of the finished product. Later, if a part wears out, it can easily be replaced by a new identical part.

Power for Mass Production

In the early 1800s, manufacturers learned to move beyond the force of falling water, or water power, as the main source of power to operate their machines. Once Scottish engineer James Watt invented an efficient steam engine, steam power became the leading source of industrial power.

In the late 1800s, the internal combustion engine was developed. This engine used the power released by exploding gasoline. It was often used to run small machines and, later, automobiles as well.

The source of power that contributed most to modern mass production, however, was electricity. In the late 1800s, Thomas Edison made the widespread use of electricity practical and affordable.

LAW 101

Teens and Labor Laws

Suppose you are 14 years old and your parents have given you permission to get your first job. You might ask yourself, "What kind of job would I like?" The first questions you should ask, however, are, "What kinds of jobs am I legally allowed to have, and how many hours am I allowed to work?"

Why it Matters For many years in this country, children as young as 5 or 6 sometimes worked to help support their families. Children as young as 8 could work in coal mines and factories. Many people believed that working long and difficult hours was not a healthy way to spend a childhood. For this reason, Congress outlawed child labor in 1938.

Today the federal government limits the hours that children can work and the types of jobs they can hold. The laws vary, depending on how old you are. For example, children 13 and younger can only work at certain jobs, such as babysitting, delivering newspapers, or acting in theatrical, motion picture, and broadcast productions. If you are 14 or 15, you can work only three hours on a school day and not more than 18 hours during a school week. You can, however, work full time during the summer. Teens aged 16 or 17 can work more hours during the school year, but there are certain jobs that are off limits for anyone under 18. These prohibited jobs involve dangerous work, such as mining and operating heavy equipment.

During the early 1900s, young children often worked long hours in dangerous factory jobs.

ANALYSIS SKILL **EVALUATING THE LAW** go.hrw.com KEYWORD: SZ7 CH18

1. Why do you think the government limits the hours and types of jobs that teens can have?
2. Do you think the laws affecting teen labor are fair? Explain.

Modern Mass Production

Today, mass production is an essential part of all large-scale production. Whether you visit an automobile manufacturing plant or a large bakery, you will see some of the same production processes in operation. Each worker is highly skilled at a specialized job. Instead of having the workers move around, a moving track called an assembly line moves the product through stages of production until it is completed. Workers are positioned along the line and add parts or make adjustments as the product moves past them.

Mass Production Worldwide

Mass production was first developed in the United States but has since spread around the world. Some countries can produce goods as rapidly and efficiently as the United States. Other countries have had less success.

Cuba, for example, uses mass production methods but has not achieved the same level of productivity. One reason is that in Cuba the government controls the economy. Property is not privately owned, and private enterprise is allowed only on a limited basis.

The government generally decides what prices to charge and the amount of goods and services to produce. As a result, most goods like cooking oil and other foods, and even shirts and shoes, can be difficult to buy. Many Cubans buy these goods on the black market—an illegal market that the Cuban government does not regulate.

A command economy like Cuba's does not have the same incentives, or motives, as a free economy. The lack of a profit motive in particular discourages people from increasing productivity. In turn, lower productivity means that there is less money available for modernizing factories and paying workers.

> **READING CHECK** ▶ **Identifying Points of View**
> Why is mass production less effective in some foreign countries than in other countries?

The Service Sector

Our economy is sometimes called a service economy. In earlier times, most of the country's economic effort went into producing goods. As the economy has matured, however, fewer and fewer workers are involved in the manufacture of products. At the same time, people have developed a need for many types of services. Today, a significant portion of the U.S. workforce is dedicated to the production and delivery of these services.

Personal Services

One type of services, called personal services, is performed directly on consumers. You are probably familiar with many of these services. Personal services include medical care, haircutting and makeup services, and physical training services such as personal fitness, yoga, and golf lessons.

Repair Services

Another type of service is performed on goods that you own, usually to repair them, keep them in good working condition, or improve them. These include heater and air conditioner maintenance and auto repair.

Growth of the Service Sector

The U.S. Bureau of Labor Statistics predicts that in the 10 years leading up to 2012, 21.6 million new jobs will be created. Of those, 20.8 million will be in the service sector. For example, one in four of the jobs will be in health or education.

Advances in technology and an increasing number of service jobs mean that education is more important than ever for U.S. workers. Of the 50 highest paying jobs, 49 require an undergraduate degree or higher.

The Department of Labor's *Occupational Outlook Handbook* can be found on the Internet. Use it to compare the skills and education needed for three different jobs. You can also use this chart to hypothesize about how the changing job market might affect agricultural imports and the cost of manufacturing things in the United States.

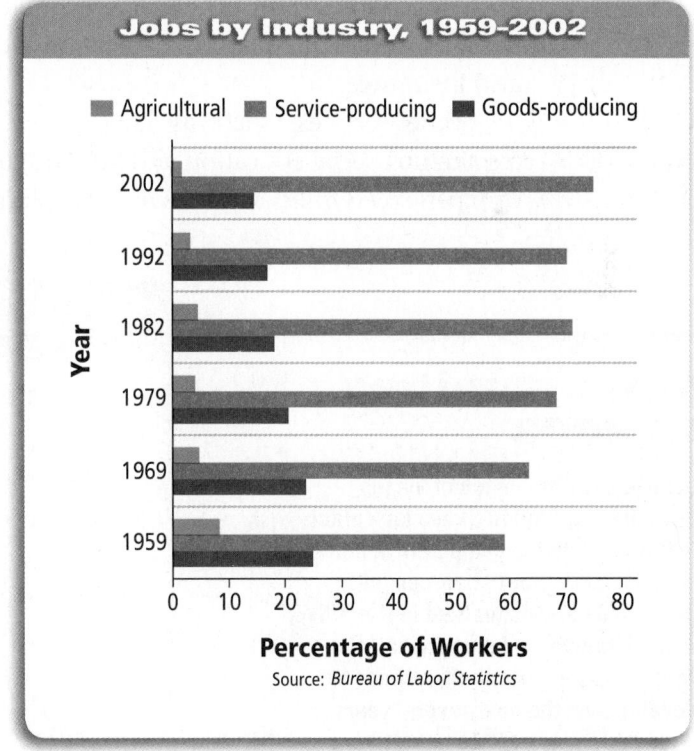

Jobs by Industry, 1959–2002

Source: *Bureau of Labor Statistics*

ANALYSIS SKILL **ANALYZING ECONOMICS**

Which industries show an increase in jobs between 1959 and 2002, and which show a decrease in the same time period?

Predicted Fastest-Growing Jobs (2004–2014)

1 Home health aides

2 Network systems and data communication analysts

3 Medical assistants

4 Physician assistants

5 Computer software engineers, applications

6 Physical therapist assistants

7 Dental hygienists

8 Computer software engineers, systems software

9 Dental assistants

10 Personal and home care aides

Source: Bureau of Labor Statistics, *Monthly Labor Review,* November 2005

Other Services

You are probably familiar with retail services, such as malls and online sellers, and entertainment services, such as movies, music, and videogames. Still other services include banking, financial planning, legal services, and insurance.

Some services, such as lawn mowing, require no special education and little training or experience. Others, like auto repair or plumb-ing, need some study and perhaps on-the-job training, including a formal apprenticeship, or period of supervised training. Some services, such as legal or medical services, require considerable advanced training beyond college and usually some practical supervision as well.

READING CHECK **Identifying Points of View** Why are services becoming a larger and larger part of the U.S. economy?

Profit, Risk, and Innovation

A free-market economy encourages people to take risks by offering them the possibility of a reward, such as making a profit, for taking the risk. **Profit** is the difference between the total cost of production and the total revenues received from buyers. In a market economy such as ours, businesses make decisions about what to produce and how much to produce based on how much profit they think they can make.

A businessperson who can earn a large profit for taking a large business risk, such as offering a new product or service, may be motivated to take that risk.

Opportunities in 2008

In the early 2000s much of the job growth in the United States took place in fields related to computers or health care. By 2008 about 11 percent of employed persons worked in executive, administrative, and managerial jobs. Forecasters expect similar trends to develop over the next several years.

Job Opportunities

■ Professional and technical   ■ Administrative support and clerical
■ Services   ■ Operators, fabricators, and laborers
■ Executive, administrative, and managerial   ■ Marketing and sales
■ Precision production, craft and repair   ■ Agriculture, fishing, and forestry

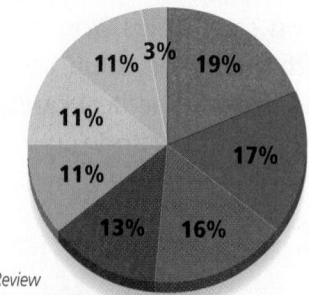

11% 3% 19%

11%

11%

17%

13% 16%

Source: *Monthly Labor Review*
*Figures are rounded to the nearest percent.

ANALYSIS SKILL **ANALYZING CHARTS**

What percentage of U.S. jobs involved marketing, sales, and services in 2008?

For example, when Michael Dell was in college, he was bothered by the high cost of personal computers and the lack of technical support offered by their makers. In 1984 Dell took a risk and launched his own computer business. He used direct advertising and, later, the Internet to sell made-to-order computers directly to customers. This lowered his costs, which allowed Dell to offer his customers lower prices and better service. Dell Computers now does about $50 billion of business a year.

Dell's idea was an innovation in production methods. An innovation is the development of a new product, system, or process that has wide-ranging effects on the economy. If one company begins to use a successful innovation, its competitors have to copy the innovation if they are going to remain competitive. When Dell Computers was successful with its direct retail approach, other companies followed with their own direct-to-consumers marketing.

READING CHECK ▶ **Summarizing** How did Michael Dell change the computer industry?

SECTION 1 ASSESSMENT

Reviewing Ideas and Terms

1. a. Define Write a brief definition for the terms **goods**, **services**, and **gross domestic product (GDP)**.
   b. Explain How can a person or a business offer both a good and a service at the same time? Give an example.

2. a. Define Write a brief definition for the term **mass production**.
   b. Identify Why did the introduction of electrical power have such an impact on the U.S. economy?

3. a. Summarize Why is the U.S. economy sometimes called a service economy?
   b. Draw Conclusions Why has the U.S. economy moved away from producing goods and focused more on providing services?

4. a. Define Write a brief definition for the term **profit**.

   b. Elaborate What is the relationship between innovation, taking risks, and earning profits?

Critical Thinking

5. Comparing and Contrasting Use your notes and a diagram like this one to identify the similarities and differences between goods and services.

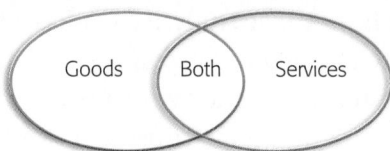

Goods   Both   Services

Focus on Writing

6. Summarizing Imagine that you are the president of an automobile manufacturer. Write a paragraph explaining how your factory uses assembly lines and mass production to build cars.

Establishing Smoke-Free Zones

In Mexico, Missouri, teacher Diana Henage's Project Citizen students are thinking ahead. They know that secondhand cigarette smoke can cause many health problems. Because they don't want people in their community to get sick, these students are working to make all restaurants in the city smoke-free.

Community Connection While researching the effects of secondhand smoke, students learned that it can cause serious health problems. The students also learned that smoke-free restaurants pay less in maintenance and cleaning costs and that chain restaurants that become smoke-free do not lose business. This was good marketing news for the restaurant managers with whom students spoke.

Taking Action The students next partnered with the Audrain County Team, a group that works against substance abuse, to help get their message out to the community. In a brochure that they wrote and distributed to medical offices, they included some of these facts, such as, "If you sit in a restaurant for two hours that allows smoking, you have smoked two cigarettes!" and information about cancer risks. In addition to their brochure, the students recorded radio announcements, wrote articles for the local newspaper, created anti-smoking stickers for restaurants to put on customers' bills, and visited smoke-free restaurants to award "thank you" certificates. The students' work continues; they hope that the City Council will pass a law banning smoking in all city restaurants. As they work toward that goal, the teens are collecting signatures in support of the law, drafting a sample law for the council, and informing local company owners that smoking may be bad for business.

Students in Mexico, Missouri, are fighting secondhand smoke.

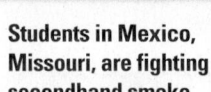

go.hrw.com
Project Citizen
KEYWORD: SZ7 CH18

SERVICE LEARNING

1. How did students work with business owners to achieve their goals? Why was this cooperation important?
2. Is smoking allowed in public places in your community? How do you feel about this?

SECTION 2
Distributing Goods

BEFORE YOU READ

The Main Idea

Producing goods is only the first step in filling consumers' needs. Getting goods to consumers involves a complex transportation system that makes it possible for American businesses to sell their goods throughout the country and the world.

Reading Focus

1. How are goods transported from manufacturers to consumers?
2. How are services delivered to consumers in the United States?
3. How are goods and services marketed to consumers?

Key Terms

marketing, *p. 486*
mass marketing, *p. 486*

 **TAKING NOTES** As you read, take notes on how goods and services are transported, delivered and marketed. Use an organizer like this one to record your notes.

Transporting	Delivering	Marketing

Cargo containers carrying American goods are loaded onto ships to be transported to customers around the world.

 How can supermarkets stock fruit and vegetables in winter? If we only had local farmers to provide for us, we would eat only the food that was in season. When you go into an electronics store at the mall to buy the latest game, do you ever think about how the game gets into your hands?

Transporting Goods

In the early days of our country, goods were usually delivered by horse-drawn wagon or by boat, if there was a river flowing the right way. These were slow and often unreliable methods of transportation. The development of the railroad sped things up somewhat, but a truly efficient national economy needed faster and more effective ways of getting products from the manufacturer to the consumers.

Today, goods in our economy are still shipped by rail and by water, similar to the ways goods were shipped 150 years ago. But today we also use trucks and other motor vehicles to carry much of our freight. Airplanes carry freight that must move quickly from one place to another.

Railroads

Railroads are an important part of the country's transportation system. They carry bulk cargo, such as coal and grain. Railroads helped create a single, large market for products. Long freight trains rolled from coast to coast carrying raw materials and finished products. The railroads brought new goods to every American city, to most towns, and within reach of many farms. The railroads gave businesspeople a means of rapid travel and communication. For about a century, starting around 1850, railroads were the country's chief method of transportation. After that, railroads were challenged by other competing means of transportation—trucks, buses, automobiles, and airplanes. In the 1960s and 1970s, many railroads went out of business.

Railroads today carry a much smaller percentage of freight than they did in the late 1800s. Measured by dollar value, only about 4 percent of goods in the United States are transported by rail. When the goods are measured by weight, trains carry about 16 percent of our goods. However, when the goods are measured by both weight and number of miles hauled, trains carry about 40 percent of the goods.

Airlines

Airlines are also important in transporting freight. For example, planes now carry all first-class mail between U.S. cities located over a certain distance apart. Airlines can carry all kinds of freight—from small packages to large industrial machinery and automobiles—with great speed. However, airlines carry only a small percentage—about 3 percent by value—of the freight shipped throughout the United States. It is much cheaper to ship items by rail or by truck.

Transportation of goods by air also has its problems. Airplanes can carry heavy cargo, but not much of it at any one time. Also, large cargo planes cannot land at small airports. Cargo must be delivered to large airports and then transported by some other means. Airlines also face higher prices for aviation fuel, so the cost of delivering goods by airplane may become more expensive. Finally, air cargo companies have had to increase security as a result of the September 11, 2001, terrorist attacks. These increased security measures have been expensive. If more measures are necessary, transporting goods by air may become even more costly.

Distribution of Goods and Services

QUICK FACTS

Goods go through several steps from the factory to your home. Some goods are assembled by people and some are assembled by machines. However they are assembled, all goods must eventually be delivered to a customer. This system is called the distribution chain.

How does each step of the distribution chain add to the price the consumer pays for a product?

❶ Manufacturing
Workers assemble the parts needed to build a television set.

Highways

The motor vehicle is the leading means of transportation in the United States. Individual Americans and their families do about 85 percent of their traveling in personal vehicles (cars, light trucks, and SUVs). Motor vehicles, especially trucks, are also the leading means of transporting goods in this country. Trucks carry about three-fourths of all goods by dollar value and about two-thirds of all goods by weight.

Rapid highway transportation depends on good roads. To speed motor traffic, the country maintains a vast interstate highway system. The United States now has about 4 million miles (6.5 million km) of roads. Together these roads form an interconnected highway system that reaches every part of the country.

Highway transportation also depends on a steady supply of fuel. Even though currently there may be no shortage of gasoline or diesel fuel, prices for these fuels continue to increase because of global political conflict and supply uncertainty. As fuel prices rise, the cost of delivering goods over the highways increases. Consumers eventually end up paying more for these goods.

Rivers

Transportation of goods by water—rivers, canals, and oceans—continues to be an important means of transportation. Although relatively little—only about 1 percent by value; about 6 percent by weight—of our goods are shipped by water, there are some advantages to this method.

For those manufacturers and consumers located close to major rivers, barge or boat transportation of goods can be fast and inexpensive. The development of modern container shipping, where goods are packed in large container boxes that can be carried on the back of a truck or loaded onto a barge, has made it easier to use a combination of land and water transportation to deliver goods.

Transportation by water does have some disadvantages. For example, river transportation is subject to the weather. During 2003, for example, lack of rain led to low water levels in the Mississippi River that delayed river shipments.

READING CHECK **Comparing and Contrasting** What are the advantages and disadvantages of shipping goods by highways and by rivers?

❷ Packing
Completed television sets are packaged for safe and efficient shipping.

❸ Warehousing
Factories often sell goods in large quantities to a wholesaler, who stores goods in a warehouse and later sells them to retailers.

❹ Buying/Selling
Retailers offer a variety of goods for sale to their customers.

Delivering Services

The growing service sector includes a wide variety of businesses, such as tourism, restaurants, personal care, retail, and entertainment (including the record industry, the music industry, radio, television, computer games, and movies.) Services also include the news media, the leisure industry (such as amusement parks and resorts), education, health care, consulting, investment, and legal advice and services. All these services need to be delivered.

Services can be delivered in a wide variety of ways, such as in person, over the Internet, through the mail, at retail stores (including places like restaurants or travel agencies), and by telephone. Each service provider finds the best way to deliver the service offered.

As services have become a larger and larger part of the economy, service providers have put more effort into finding the best ways to market and deliver their products. But service providers face some problems that manufacturers of goods do not face. For example, services are not something you can hold or touch, like a cell phone or a car. It may be difficult for consumers to know—in terms of freshness, training, skill level, accuracy, or other measure of quality—exactly what they are getting when they ask for a certain service. How do you know which insurance agent or travel agent to pick?

How can you tell which agent is honest, careful, accurate, and experienced? It may be difficult to know. Consumers may also have difficulty choosing one provider over others for certain services. Most restaurants offer similar food choices, and many shops offer similar haircuts or beauty services. How do you decide which store to shop in or which restaurant to eat in? Service providers must find ways to convince you to choose them for the service that you want.

READING CHECK ▶ **Analyzing** What are two problems that consumers face when selecting a service provider?

Types of Services

The service sector has become the fastest growing part of the U.S. economy. Services include health care, personal care, education, and information services.

Health Service

Marketing Goods and Services

Once goods are made and shipped, or once services are ready to be offered, the goods or services must be made available to the consumer. At the same time, consumers have to be made aware that the goods and services are available. Consumers must also be convinced to buy a particular product or service.

The process of making goods and services available to consumers and convincing them to buy the product is called **marketing**. Even if you develop the most exciting new product, your business will not survive unless you have a way of telling people what you have created and then convincing them your product is something they want to own. Today, most selling is done on a large scale, reaching out to thousands or even millions of people.

Mass Marketing

Selling goods in large quantities often requires mass marketing. **Mass marketing** is the process of selling a good or a service in which the same

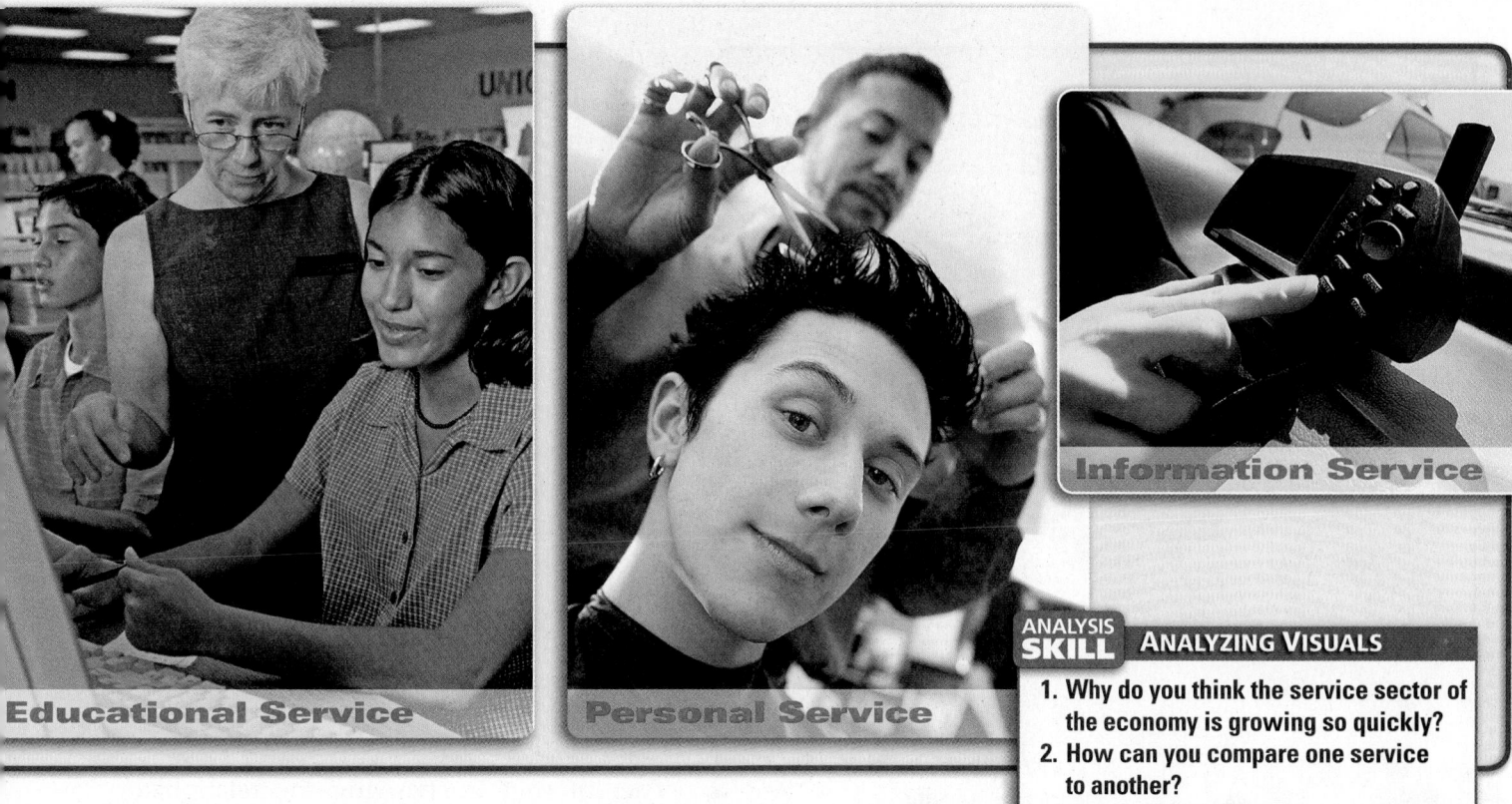

Educational Service

Personal Service

Information Service

product, price, promotion, and distribution is used for all consumers in a particular market. Mass marketing involves preparing products that are the same wherever they are sold. You can go into any drug store to buy your favorite brand of toothpaste and know you will get the product you want. Three important **features** of mass marketing are the one-price system, self-service, and standard packaging.

One-price system In the one-price system, prices are stamped or bar-coded onto products. A bar code, also known as the Universal Product Code (UPC), is the pattern of lines and spaces and the numerals usually printed on a label that is found on most commercial goods. The code, which can be read by a computer, contains information about the product and allows cashiers to ring up items quickly.

Self-service Most modern stores use a type of marketing and delivery called self-service. Self-service is an efficient and inexpensive way to sell goods because it saves time and labor. In self-service stores like supermarkets and department stores, customers typically push carts up and down the aisles, selecting items and serving themselves. Some stores now even allow customers to check out by themselves by passing their purchases through a scanner that reads the bar code.

Standard packaging Standard packaging also adds to the efficiency of the self-service system. Goods come from factories already wrapped. Crackers, for example, are wrapped and sold in boxes. Sugar comes in boxes or bags of different weights. New technology continues to provide new uses for the bar codes you see on packages. For example, bar codes help a store track inventory and reorder products that are selling out. Bar codes are also used to keep track of products during shipping and can carry various information about the product.

Many stores are now in constant communication with their suppliers to keep their shelves stocked without having to store a lot of extra product. Using this "just-in-time" supply keeps stores from running out of popular products while keeping costs down.

ACADEMIC VOCABULARY
features
characteristics

Types of Advertising

Competitive

Competitive advertising tries to persuade consumers that a product is better than or easier to use than its competitors.

Informative

Informative advertising gives consumers information about a product, such as its price, its quality, its history, and its special features. Informative ads may be combined with competitive ads.

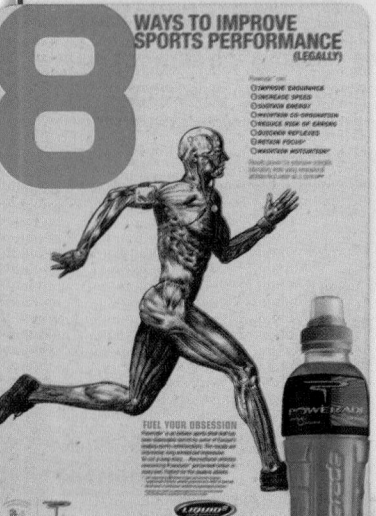

Emotional

Some advertisers use words or pictures that attempt to appeal to a consumer's emotions. Advertisers may also appeal to fear, happiness, or a consumer's sense of well-being.

ANALYSIS SKILL ANALYZING VISUALS

What do you think helps make an advertisement interesting or informative?

Wholesalers and Retailers

Products may pass through several hands when moving from the factory to you. A factory or manufacturer often sells goods in large quantities to a wholesaler—a businessperson who owns a large warehouse where goods are stored. The wholesaler then sells the goods to retailers. Retailers, or retail stores, sell the goods directly to the public. Wholesalers, also called distributors, perform the service of linking the factory and the retailer. In the end, of course, the customer pays for this service. Today, retailers may be a single store that offers only one type of good or service, or you may buy your goods and services at a shopping mall or at a large "big-box" store.

Internet Sellers

The Internet is changing the relationship between retailers and the public. Purchasers can often shop online, viewing goods and some services on their computers and purchasing items electronically. Goods are then sent to the purchaser using the postal service or a private delivery service. This service has become especially popular for books or clothing but is also used for furniture, rugs, and other large and expensive items. Internet retailers do not need as many stores or local warehouses if they can ship to customers from a central point. Services, such as insurance quotes, may be delivered by e-mail to the customer.

Advertising

Marketing goods and services would not be possible without advertising. Advertising informs people about products and tries to persuade consumers to buy the products. When producers of similar products compete, advertising may make the difference between the success and failure of a particular product.

The goal of an advertiser is to give a consumer a reason to buy the advertised product. Some advertising is designed to increase people's recognition of a product's name. A brand-name product is a widely advertised and distributed product. People often buy brand-name products they have heard about most favorably or most often. Other advertising tries to convince consumers that one company's product is better, more effective, longer lasting, or less expensive than another company's product.

Some people believe that some forms of advertising do not accurately represent products and can be misleading. They also think that advertising encourages people to buy products that they do not really need. Others argue that competition among mass producers, marketers, and advertisers helps keep the quality of products high and prices low. Finally, some people think that advertising can be a good way to inform consumers about new—or improved—goods or services that are coming to the market.

READING CHECK **Analyzing Information** How is advertising part of the marketing chain of delivering goods and services to consumers?

go.hrw.com
Online Quiz
KEYWORD: SZ7 HP18

SECTION 2 ASSESSMENT

Reviewing Ideas and Terms

1. a. Identify What are the four main ways that goods are transported to consumers?

b. Compare and Contrast If you want to ship a large quantity of sand from one part of the United States to another, would you ship by truck or by rail? Explain your answer.

2. a. Explain Why can services be delivered to consumers in so many different ways?

b. Evaluate Many services are offered on the Internet. Is information offered by Internet sellers likely to be more or less accurate than information in a national magazine? Explain your answer.

3. a. Define Write a brief definition for the terms **marketing** and **mass marketing**.

b. Analyze How does mass marketing help the U.S. economy?

Critical Thinking

4. Summarizing Copy the graphic organizer. Use it and your notes to summarize the process of manufacturing, transporting, and marketing goods to consumers in the United States.

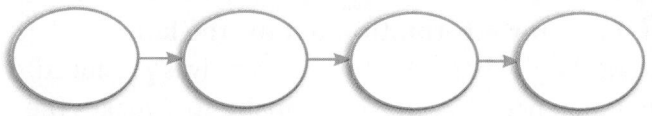

Focus on Writing

5. Identifying Points of View Imagine that you are a newspaper reporter covering a debate on the role of advertising in the U.S. economy. Write a newspaper article outlining the debate.

Reading Labels

Learn

Different types of products have different labeling regulations. Milk, meat, clothing, and computers all must carry labels, but what those labels have to say is different. That is one reason why it is important to read labels carefully.

At the same time, companies are *not* required to disclose everything about a product on its label. Milk companies, for example, do not have to address their use of any drugs on the cows that produce the milk. Beef packages do not tell whether a cow lived its life outside or inside.

Practice

❶ Determine what type of information you need. Fat content, price, and expiration date are all required labels on a carton of milk. It is up to you to decide what information you want and need.

❷ Well-known brands are not always best. Brand names are not always a good indicator of the quality or value of a product. For example, the "Local Dairy" milk brand shown here is most likely the same as nationally known brands.

❸ Look for information left off the label. To find out where or when an item was produced, you may need to call the company that makes the product. Often, the company's phone number will be on the package.

Apply

Use the two milk carton labels shown below to answer the following questions.

1. Which milk is lower in fat? Explain how you know.

2. What additional information would help you to choose between the two products?

3. If the price of the Local Dairy milk were $1.99 and the price of the Happy Cows Farm milk were $2.59, which product would be a better value? Explain your choice.

REDUCED FAT MILK
2% Milkfat

Nutrition Facts	
Serving Size 1 cup (236ml)	
Servings Per Container 1	
Amounts Per Serving	
Calories 120	Calories from Fat 45
	% Daily Value*
Total Fat 5g	8%
Saturated Fat 3g	15%
Cholesterol 200mg	7%
Sodium 120mg	5%
Total Carbohydrate 11mg	4%
Dietary Fiber 0g	0%
Sugars 11g	
Protein 9g	17%
Vitamin A 10% • Vitamin C 4%	
Calcium 30% • Iron 0% • Vitamin D 25%	
* Percent Daily Values are based on a 2,000 calorie diet. Your daily values may be higher or lower depending on your calorie needs.	

CHOCOLATE NONFAT MILK

Nutrition Facts	
Serving Size 1 cup (236ml)	
Servings Per Container 1	
Amounts Per Serving	
Calories 80	Calories from Fat 0
	% Daily Value*
Total Fat 0g	0%
Saturated Fat 0g	0%
Cholesterol Less than 5mg	0%
Sodium 120mg	5%
Total Carbohydrate 11mg	4%
Dietary Fiber 0g	0%
Sugars 11g	
Protein 9g	17%
Vitamin A 10% • Vitamin C 4%	
Calcium 30% • Iron 0% • Vitamin D 25%	
* Percent Daily Values are based on a 2,000 calorie diet. Your daily values may be higher or lower depending on your calorie needs.	

SECTION 3
You the Consumer

BEFORE YOU READ

The Main Idea

As consumers, we learn about the products we buy so that we can make the best choices. Some independent and governmental organizations help protect consumers' interests.

Reading Focus

1. What are the keys to becoming a wise consumer?
2. What should a consumer consider in deciding to buy on credit?
3. What do independent organizations and the government do to protect consumers?

Key Terms

consumer, *p. 492*
brand, *p. 492*
generic product, *p. 492*
debit card, *p. 494*
charge account, *p. 495*
credit cards, *p. 495*

TAKING NOTES As you read, take notes about what it takes to be a wise consumer. Use an organizer like this one to record your notes.

Being a Wise Consumer	
Buying on Credit	
Consumer Protection	

When shopping, you should try to be a wise consumer.

CIVICS IN PRACTICE Think of your favorite commercial or magazine ad. How much information does the ad really give you? Have you ever been disappointed after buying a product because you thought you would be getting something more? The purpose of advertising is to sell products, not necessarily to educate consumers. For the kind of information you need to make wise choices, you have to look elsewhere.

Keys to Wise Consuming

Each year businesses spend billions of dollars encouraging us to buy their products. They run advertisements in newspapers and magazines, on the Internet, on billboards, on the radio, and on television. Businesses create slogans they hope we will remember. They know that some of us will buy the product whose slogan appeals to us most. Often, however, a product's slogan has little to do with its quality or usefulness. There are steps that you can take to make sure that you spend your money wisely.

Feature versus Price

When buying expensive items, like appliances or a car, it is wise to compare the features being offered. The overall price may be affected by what is offered—or not offered—in the package.

MSRP: $26,095*
6-speed Sport AT automatic transmission w/paddle shifters

INTERIOR TRIM PACKAGE $3,600

- Aluminum & leather shift
- Aluminum pedals
- Glass rear window with defogger
- Air conditioning
- Cruise control
- Power windows, door locks, and mirrors
- Power door locks with remote keyless entry

> Look carefully at the options list and the amount charged for them. Often a consumer can negotiate the price of an option, or can purchase a vehicle on which several options are offered as a package at a lower overall price.

PREMIUM PACKAGE $1,600

- Xenon HID headlights
- Dynamic Stability Control w/Traction Control
- Limited-slip differential (MT only)
- Advanced Keyless Entry & Start System
- Anti-theft alarm

DESTINATION FEE $560

Illustrated example of an auto price sticker

Learn When and Where to Buy

First of all, learn when to buy a product and the best place to buy it. Each of us is a consumer. A **consumer** is a person who buys or uses goods and services. As consumers, we play an important part in the American free-enterprise system. However, we must also learn to be responsible shoppers.

Some shoppers, called impulse buyers, make a quick decision to buy a product based on the product's slogan, a display in the store, or television advertising. A wise shopper spends more time thinking about what to buy.

Consumers can get the most for their limited shopping dollars in a number of ways. For example, wise food shoppers study advertisements in the newspaper to find out which stores are having sales. Using coupons can also help shoppers save money.

By watching for sales, you can buy clothing, books, furniture, hardware, and other items at reduced prices. Some people never pay the full price for an item. They stock up when the price is low. A low-price item is not always a bargain, however. An item is not a bargain if it is something you cannot really use or if it is poorly made.

Brand Names and Generic Products

Wise shoppers choose goods and services at the price and quality that best suit their needs. Some consumers buy only brand-name products. A **brand** is a name given by the maker to a product or range of products. Brands are what companies advertise. Many people buy brand-name items because they believe, from past experience or for other reasons, that a brand name must be of good quality.

Other consumers buy generic products. A **generic product** is a product that does not have a manufacturer's name or brand. Generic goods are often plainly packaged. They may not offer guarantees of quality. Generic products are often less expensive than brand-name products. Many consumers buy generic products that meet their needs and their tastes.

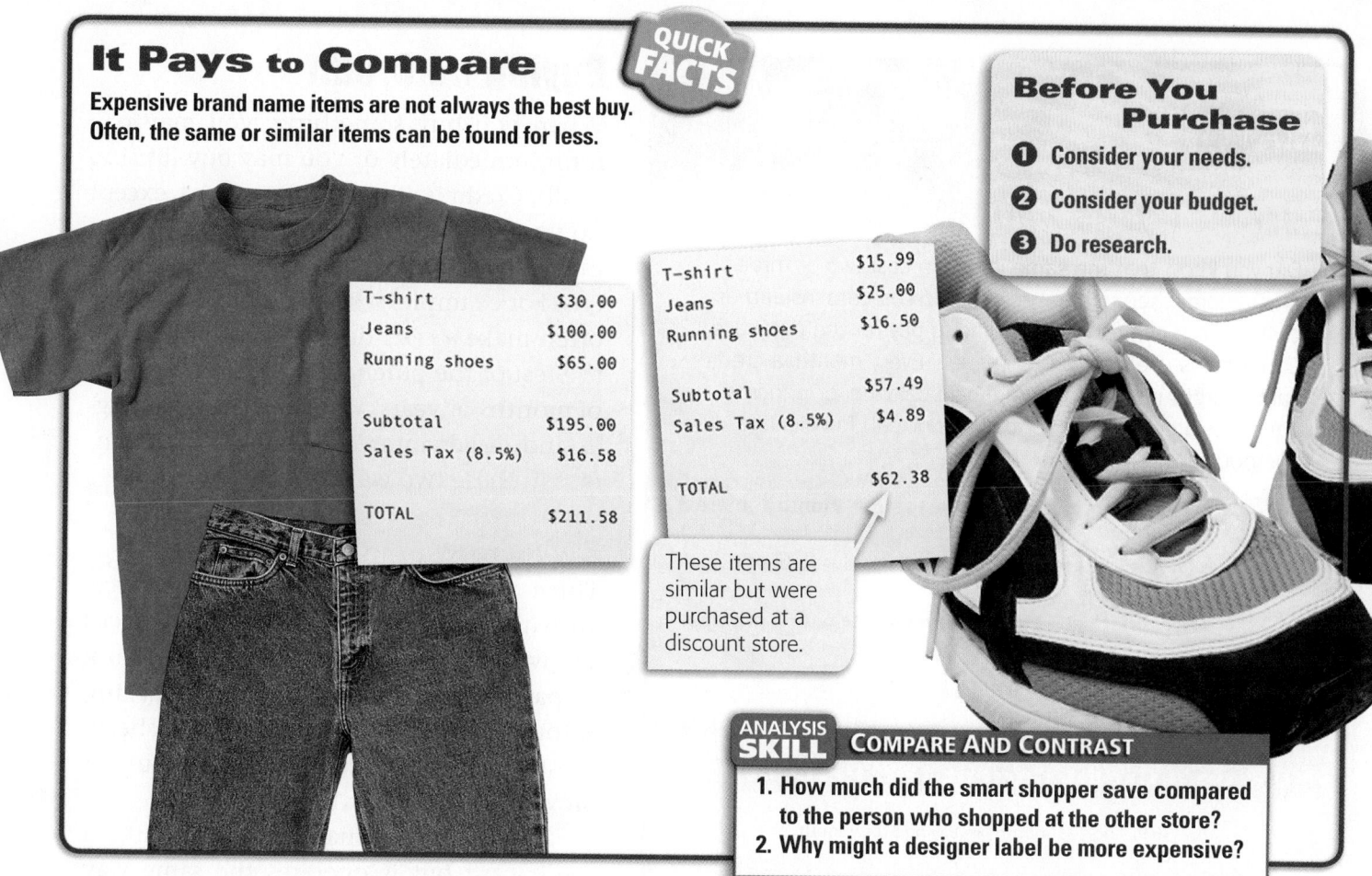

It Pays to Compare

QUICK FACTS

Expensive brand name items are not always the best buy. Often, the same or similar items can be found for less.

T-shirt	$30.00
Jeans	$100.00
Running shoes	$65.00
Subtotal	$195.00
Sales Tax (8.5%)	$16.58
TOTAL	$211.58

T-shirt	$15.99
Jeans	$25.00
Running shoes	$16.50
Subtotal	$57.49
Sales Tax (8.5%)	$4.89
TOTAL	$62.38

These items are similar but were purchased at a discount store.

Before You Purchase
1. Consider your needs.
2. Consider your budget.
3. Do research.

ANALYSIS SKILL COMPARE AND CONTRAST

1. How much did the smart shopper save compared to the person who shopped at the other store?
2. Why might a designer label be more expensive?

Study Labels

Labels are placed on foods, clothing, and other items to protect consumers. The government requires that certain information be included on these labels to help consumers judge product quality. There are a number of federal laws regarding labeling. The Fair Packaging and Labeling Act requires businesses to supply certain information, including manufacturer information, package contents, and the weight or quantity of the items in the package.

The Nutrition Labeling and Education Act of 1990, amended in 1994, requires that food companies, in addition to listing serving sizes, show the fat, cholesterol, sodium, fiber, and nutrient totals contained in each serving. The figures are given as a percentage of a person's daily dietary allowance.

In addition to weight and content information, meat packages must have instructions for safe handling and cooking.

The labels must also warn consumers that improper handling or cooking of meat may lead to illness. Even though the meat has passed government inspection, it must still have a warning label.

The packages of many products, including milk and cheese, must include the date by which the product must be sold or used. Dating a product ensures that it will be fresh when purchased by consumers.

Some laws also require unit pricing. The price tag must show price per unit of the product—per ounce or gram, for example. Larger sizes are often a better bargain because they have a lower price per unit. This is not always true, however. You must read labels carefully to get the best bargain.

READING CHECK **Finding the Main Idea** What are three steps you can take to become a wise consumer?

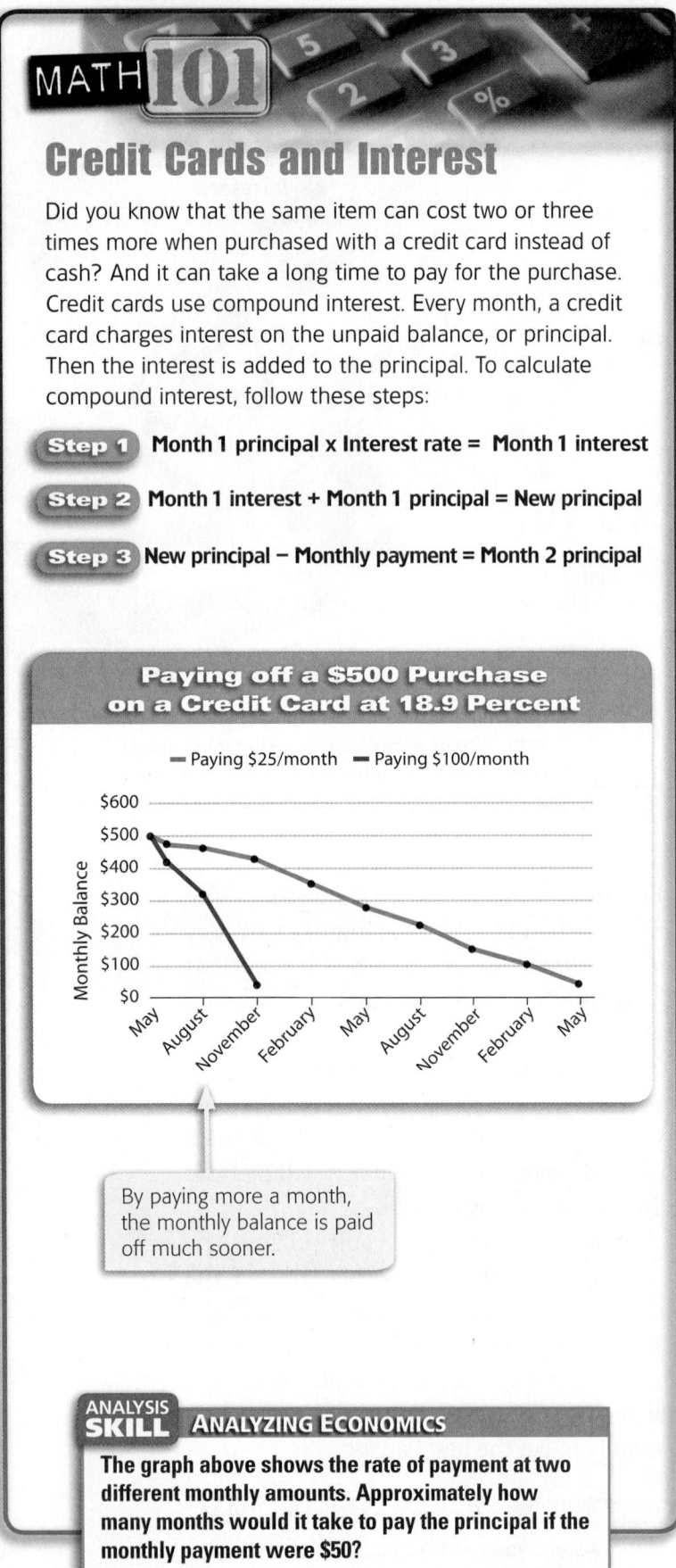

MATH 101

Credit Cards and Interest

Did you know that the same item can cost two or three times more when purchased with a credit card instead of cash? And it can take a long time to pay for the purchase. Credit cards use compound interest. Every month, a credit card charges interest on the unpaid balance, or principal. Then the interest is added to the principal. To calculate compound interest, follow these steps:

Step 1 Month 1 principal x Interest rate = Month 1 interest

Step 2 Month 1 interest + Month 1 principal = New principal

Step 3 New principal − Monthly payment = Month 2 principal

Paying off a $500 Purchase on a Credit Card at 18.9 Percent

— Paying $25/month — Paying $100/month

By paying more a month, the monthly balance is paid off much sooner.

ANALYSIS SKILL ANALYZING ECONOMICS

The graph above shows the rate of payment at two different monthly amounts. Approximately how many months would it take to pay the principal if the monthly payment were $50?

Buying on Credit

When you buy something, you may pay for it immediately or you may buy it using credit. Credit is all money borrowed, except home financing. For some purchases, you may use a combination of the two methods. For example, when you buy a car, you often make a cash down payment but pay the rest of the purchase price over a period of months or years. What are the advantages and disadvantages of buying merchandise in these two ways?

Paying Now

Three ways of paying now for products are with cash, checks, or debit cards. Checks are written and signed orders to a bank to pay a sum of money from a checking account to the party named on the check. Most sellers will accept checks if you can provide proper identification.

A **debit card** usually looks just like a credit card but it operates the same way that a check does. When you use the card, money is deducted directly from your bank account. Paying with either a check or a debit card usually means that you will be charged the amount of your purchase within a few days at most. Once you have spent the cash, it is gone.

The advantage to paying now for your purchase is that you will probably think more carefully about spending your money. Once you make the purchase, the money immediately comes out of your pocket or your bank account. You do not have to borrow money or pay interest that adds to the overall purchase price of the item.

One disadvantage to paying now is that you may not have enough cash to buy what you need or want. You may have to put off buying the product until you have had time to save more money. Or you may have to adjust your budget and go without some other things so that you can afford to buy the product you want now.

Paying Later

Suppose you find a bargain on something you want now, but you do not have the cash on hand to pay for it. Buying the item with a charge account or credit card provides you with the ability to purchase the item immediately.

A **charge account** is a form of credit that stores grant to many of their customers. Most large retail chains offer charge accounts that are good at all of the company's stores across the nation. **Credit cards** are similar to the charge cards provided for charge accounts but are issued by banks and other lending institutions. Unlike charge cards, which can only be used at specific stores, credit cards can be used at thousands of stores and other businesses around the world.

These forms of credit allow customers to buy goods and services without paying until they receive a bill from the store or bank. A good credit rating—which means that you pay your bills on time—is important for buying a car or gaining a bank loan.

Installment Plans

Installment plans also allow consumers to buy goods without paying the full amount in cash when they make their purchases. Under an installment plan, the buyer uses cash to pay part of the purchase price. This money is called a down payment. The rest of what the buyer owes is called the balance. The balance is paid in equal payments, or installments, over a period of weeks, months, or years.

In addition to the regular price, a service charge and interest on the unpaid balance are included in the installment payments. An installment plan allows a buyer to use a product while paying for it. However, until the final payment is made, the product still belongs to the seller. If the buyer misses payments, the seller can charge extra fees or repossess, or take back, the item. When this happens, the buyer loses the item and the amount of money that has already been paid on the item. Buying an item on an install-ment plan increases the consumer's cost of that item. In addition to the regular price, a service charge and interest on the unpaid balance are included in the installment payments. When you buy an item under an installment plan, you may find it cheaper to take out a bank loan for a purchase. The interest and loan fee paid to the bank may be less than the service charge and interest under an installment plan. It is wise to make as large a down payment as possible. It is also wise to pay off the balance as quickly as possible to reduce the item's total cost to you.

Dangers of Credit

Charge accounts, credit cards, and installment plans can make shopping more convenient. They can also help you build a good credit rating, which is important for getting loans in the future. However, customers must be careful not to make foolish purchases or run up credit card debt. The interest rates paid on unpaid balances can be very high, making the debt harder to pay. Also, if you miss a payment, there can be penalties and a new higher interest rate on the unpaid balance. Some cards also have an annual fee that holders must pay just for the use of the card.

If you decide to apply for a credit card, be sure that you know the fees that are associated with the card. You should be careful using credit cards by phone or on the Internet so your credit card information does not get stolen. In some cases, you can be held responsible for paying the charges that have been made on your stolen credit card.

Charge accounts and credit cards can be used for a wide variety of goods and services, from small, inexpensive items to automobiles and other large purchases. Installment plans are usually used to purchase expensive items. Buying a house is done on a particular type of installment plan called a mortgage.

READING CHECK **Summarizing** What are some of the alternatives to paying for an item immediately?

Consumer Protection

Sometimes you may find that a product has been falsely labeled or advertised, or that you have purchased something that is defective. If you believe you have been misled by an unfair business practice, or if the item is defective, you should first make a complaint to the business that sold you the product or service. Most of the time, the seller will try to solve the problem with you. However, if that does not happen, there are organizations and agencies that offer protection and assistance to consumers.

Private Consumer Organizations

If you are not satisfied with a good or a service you have purchased, you should contact the local Better Business Bureau. There is a bureau in or near most communities. This organization gives advice and assistance to people who believe they have been cheated or treated unfairly by a company.

A number of private organizations help consumers as well. Among these is Consumers Union, which tests and rates nearly every product the public buys. Consumers Union publishes the results of its tests in magazines and special reports. An examination of these and other publications will help you compare various brands of the same product.

Government Consumer Protection

The federal government also protects consumers through its agencies, such as the Federal Trade Commission (FTC). The FTC has the power to bring to court any company anywhere in the United States that uses false or misleading advertising or false labeling.

The Department of Agriculture sets nationwide standards for—and inspects and grades—meat, poultry, and certain other foods sold in interstate commerce. The U.S. Postal Service makes sure that businesses and individuals do not cheat the public through the mail. The Consumer Product Safety Commission (CPSC) monitors product safety nationwide to make sure that products in the marketplace do not cause injuries.

Most states and many cities also have consumer protection offices. These offices publish advice for consumers and issue warnings to businesses that violate consumer laws. The businesses can be brought

---

MEDIA INVESTIGATION

Product Warnings

Advertisements often include valuable warning information about a product.

"Warning: Contents are flammable." "Caution: Keep out of reach of children." More and more, companies are using product warnings in their advertisements. The ad shown here lists side effects related to medicine.

Why do advertisers include these warnings? Many products, such as tobacco, prescription medicines, and movies, are required by law to include warnings to potential consumers. Other advertisers choose to feature warnings to help their customers. When you examine advertisements, pay careful attention to such warnings.

This warning label includes an alert to consumers about possible allergic reactions.

go.hrw.com

ANALYSIS SKILL **MEDIA INVESTIGATION** KEYWORD: SZ7 CH18

Making Decisions Would a product warning in an advertisement discourage you from purchasing the product? Why or why not?

to court if they continue to cheat or mislead consumers.

Problems Caused by Consumers

Consumers often accuse businesses of misleading advertising, poor service, and inferior products. However, some people cause problems for businesses. Shoplifting, or stealing an item displayed in stores, costs businesses in the United States billions of dollars each year. Sometimes people break or damage a store owner's property. Sometimes they demand refunds for merchandise they have already used or abused. Items in motels, hotels, and restaurants are often stolen or damaged. Sometimes people fail to pay for purchases obtained on credit.

Such thefts add to the costs of doing business. Businesses pass on these costs to consumers—that is to say, you—in the form of higher prices.

READING CHECK ▶ **Finding the Main Idea** What can consumers do if they are dissatisfied with a product or service?

FOCUS ON
Florence Kelley
(1859–1932)

Florence Kelley was raised to believe in her own abilities. Upon graduating from Cornell University in 1882, Kelley discovered that women had few opportunities to make use of their talents. She set her mind on reforming those circumstances.

Settling in Chicago in 1891, Kelley joined up with Jane Addams's settlement house movement. There Kelley drafted a report on the conditions faced by child workers in area sweatshops. In 1899 she helped found the National Consumers' League (NCL), often considered the most effective lobbying group for the interests of women and children. For years the NCL's white label certified products that were made without child labor. Kelley continued as head of the NCL until her death in 1932. The League continues its work to this day.

Summarizing How did the NCL's white-label program provide information to consumers?

go.hrw.com
Online Quiz
KEYWORD: SZ7 HP18

SECTION 3 ASSESSMENT

Reviewing Ideas and Terms

1. a. Define Write a brief definition for the terms **consumer**, **brand**, and **generic product**.
b. Explain Why is it important to be a wise consumer?
c. Evaluate If an item, such as paper towels or tomato sauce, is on sale at a low price, is it a good idea to rush out and buy 24 rolls of paper towels or 24 cans of tomato sauce? Why or why not?

2. a. Define Write a brief definition for the terms **debit card**, **charge account**, and **credit cards**.
b. Analyze How can a consumer use credit cards and installment plans and still be a wise consumer?

3. a. Recall What is the first step you should take if you think that you have been misled about a product or that the product you purchased is defective?
b. Make Inferences Why is it important that the federal government have the power to protect consumers?

Critical Thinking

4. Comparing and Contrasting Copy the graphic organizer. Use it and your notes to show the advantages and disadvantages of the different ways that a consumer can pay for a product.

Payment Method	Advantages	Disadvantages

Focus on Writing

5. Decision Making A friend wants to buy a new computer and asks you for advice on choosing one. Write a list of five recommendations for your friend for finding the highest-quality product for the lowest possible price. Explain why you think those recommendations are important.

CHAPTER 18 REVIEW

Visual Summary

Use the visual summary to help you review the main ideas of the chapter.

In order to move goods from the producer to the consumer, a system of distribution is necessary.

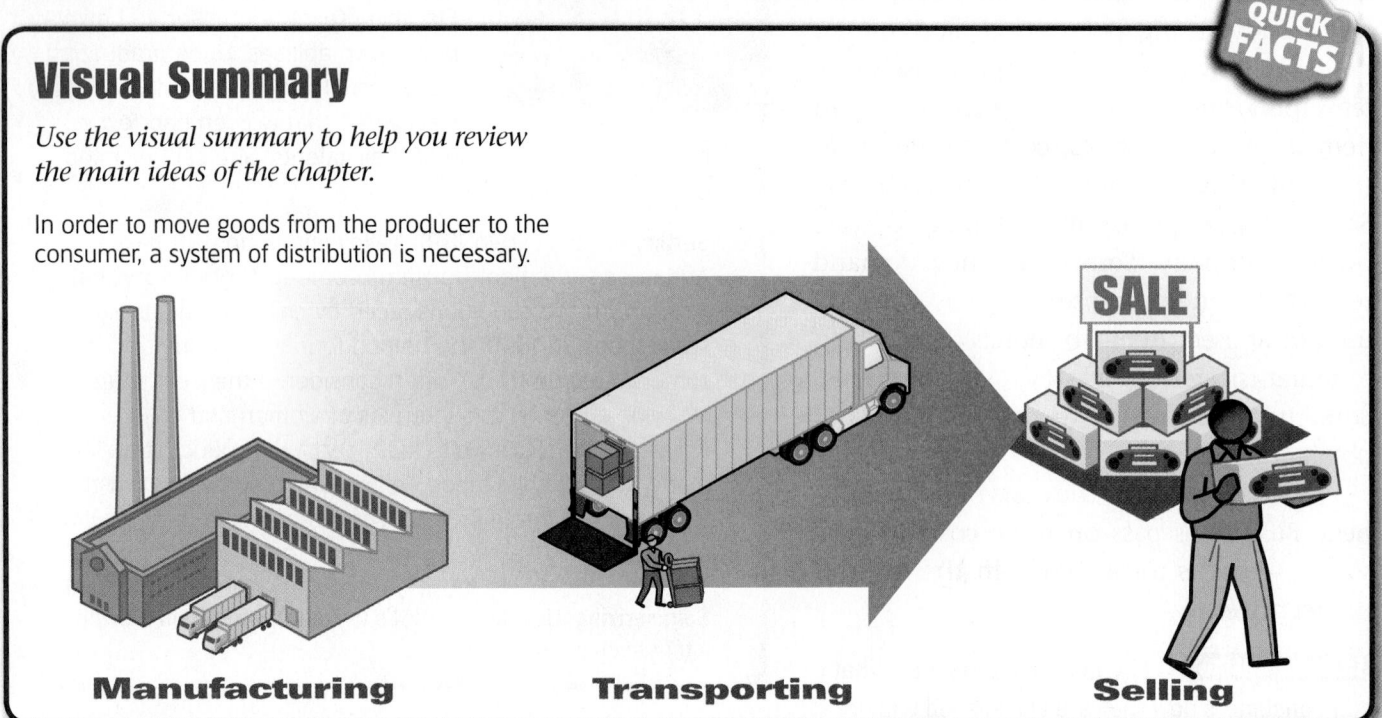

Manufacturing   **Transporting**   **Selling**

Reviewing Key Terms

For each term below, write a sentence explaining its significance to the economy.

1. goods
2. services
3. gross domestic product (GDP)
4. mass production
5. profit
6. marketing
7. mass marketing
8. consumer
9. brand
10. generic product
11. debit card
12. charge account
13. credit cards

Comprehension and Critical Thinking

SECTION 1 *(Pages 476–481)*

14. a. Recall What are the three main features of mass production?

   b. Explain What incentive is a key part of mass production, and why is it important?

SECTION 2 *(Pages 483–489)*

15. a. Describe Why does the U.S. economy depend on the transportation and marketing of goods?

   b. Sequence How are products distributed from the manufacturer to the customer?

SECTION 3 *(Pages 491–497)*

16. a. Identify What choices are available to help consumers make smart purchases?

   b. Compare and Contrast What are the advantages and disadvantages of using charge accounts, credit cards, and installment plans?

Active Citizenship video program
Review the video to answer the closing question:
How might Americans and our government help improve working conditions in foreign countries?

Using the Internet

go.hrw.com
KEYWORD: SZ7 CH18

17. Reporting on Production Have you ever wondered what goes on behind the scenes at a manufacturing facility? Enter the activity keyword and investigate how some well-known products are manufactured. Then write a newspaper or magazine article describing all the materials it takes to manufacture a product from one of the selected companies, the steps involved in production, and how the product is marketed.

Civics Skills

Reading Labels *Use the Civics Skills taught in the chapter and study the labels below. Then answer the question that follows.*

REDUCED FAT MILK
2% Milkfat

Nutrition Facts

Serving Size 1 cup (236ml)
Servings Per Container 1

Amounts Per Serving

Calories 120   Calories from Fat 45

% Daily Value*

Total Fat 5g	8%
Saturated Fat 3g	15%
Cholesterol 200mg	7%
Sodium 120mg	5%
Total Carbohydrate 11mg	4%
Dietary Fiber 0g	0%
Sugars 11g	
Protein 9g	17%

Vitamin A 10%   •   Vitamin C 4%

Calcium 30% • Iron 0% • Vitamin D 25%

* Percent Daily Values are based on a 2,000 calorie diet. Your daily values may be higher or lower depending on your calorie needs.

CHOCOLATE NONFAT MILK

Nutrition Facts

Serving Size 1 cup (236ml)
Servings Per Container 1

Amounts Per Serving

Calories 80   Calories from Fat 0

% Daily Value*

Total Fat 0g	0%
Saturated Fat 0g	0%
Cholesterol Less than 5mg	0%
Sodium 120mg	5%
Total Carbohydrate 11mg	4%
Dietary Fiber 0g	0%
Sugars 11g	
Protein 9g	17%

Vitamin A 10%   •   Vitamin C 4%

Calcium 30% • Iron 0% • Vitamin D 25%

* Percent Daily Values are based on a 2,000 calorie diet. Your daily values may be higher or lower depending on your calorie needs.

18. Which milk has more calories?

19. Which milk has less fat?

Reading Skills

Interpreting a Table *Use the Reading Skills taught in this chapter and study the table below. Then answer the questions that follow.*

U.S. Balance of Trade, 1995–2000 (in billions of dollars)			
Year	**Exports**	**Imports**	**Balance**
2000	1,065	1,441	-376
1999	957	1,219	-262
1998	932	1,099	-167
1997	937	1,047	-110
1996	851	959	-108
1995	795	895	-100

20. Which of the following correctly identifies a trend apparent in the data from the table?

a. The value of U.S. exports fell dramatically between 1995 and 2000.

b. The value of U.S. exports far exceeds the value of imports to the United States.

c. The value of imports to the United States exceeds the value of U.S. exports.

d. Until 1998 the United States maintained a positive trade balance.

21. Between 1997 and 1998, what happened to the value of U.S. exports?

22. By what amount did the value of U.S. imports increase between 1995 and 2000?

FOCUS ON WRITING

23. Writing Your Infomercial Review your notes about the U.S. economy. Pay special attention to the process in which goods and services are created and how they are distributed throughout the country and the rest of the world. Now write an infomercial in which you outline this process and explain its effect on the world economy. Then devise some visual aids and deliver your infomercial to the class.

PERSONAL FINANCES

NATIONAL STANDARDS®
FOR CIVICS AND GOVERNMENT

I. What are civic life, politics, and government?

 B. What are the essential characteristics of limited and unlimited government?

 7. What is the relationship of limited government to political and economic freedom?

V. What are the roles of the citizen in American democracy?

 C. What are the responsibilities of citizens?

 D. What civic dispositions or traits of private and public character are important to the preservation and improvement of American constitutional democracy?

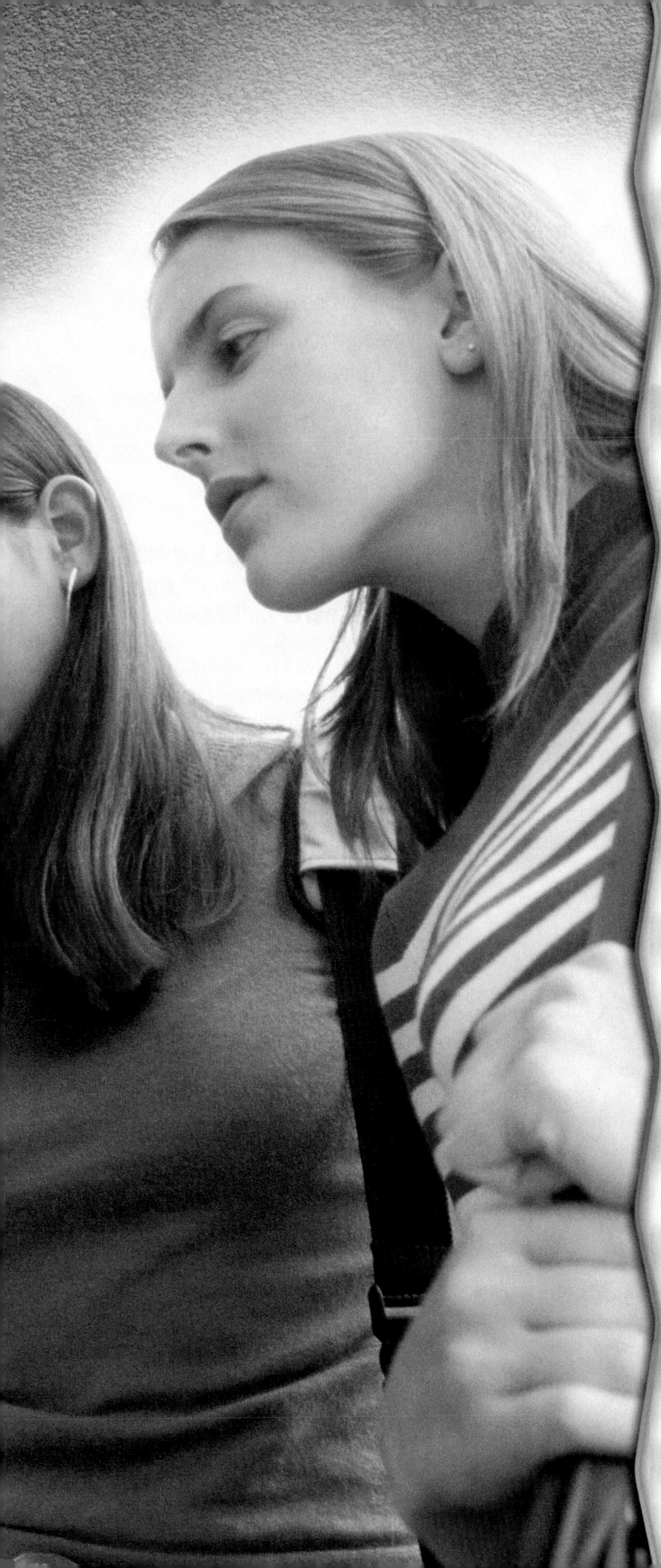

WHY CIVICS Matters

Imagine life without money. If you couldn't trade for the goods you wanted, you would be out of luck. Fortunately, we have a system in which you can exchange money for what you need. Understanding personal finances is an important part of being a good citizen.

PROJECT Citizen

STUDENTS TAKE ACTION

GAINING ACCESS TO LIBRARIES What if you had to pay to use the public library, even for materials you needed for school? Think about steps you could take to convince people that you should have access to a public library at no charge.

FOCUS ON WRITING

WRITING A LETTER OF RECOMMENDATION Your friend has applied for a job at a local bank and has asked you to write her a letter of recommendation. After you read this chapter about personal finance, you will write a letter to convince the bank that your friend is the perfect candidate for the job.

Reading Skills

In this chapter you will read about the basic characteristics of currency. You will learn why people and businesses accept checks as payment instead of cash. You will also learn about the role credit plays in the economy. You will discover about how the Federal Reserve System regulates the amount of money in circulation. You will learn about the importance of saving money and the different ways people invest their money. Finally, you will read about private insurance and Social Security.

Making and Understanding Charts and Graphs

FOCUS ON READING When writers want to communicate complex information in a simple way, they often use visuals such as charts and graphs. Charts show how the parts of something relate to the whole thing. Graphs show changes or trends over time.

Making Charts and Graphs To create a visual, first decide whether a chart or graph is better. One common chart is a pie chart. It shows the sizes of the different parts, or slices, of the whole. Pie charts often use percentages instead of specific numbers. In a graph, the horizontal line, called an axis, often represents points in time such as hours, days, or years. The vertical axis often shows quantities or amounts.

Helpful Hints for Making and Understanding Charts and Graphs

1. Read the title to determine the subject of the chart or graph.

2. Study the labels. A pie chart will label the slices, or main categories. A graph will have labels on each axis.

3. Analyze the data. What does the information mean?

4. Draw conclusions about the subject.

Title Create a title that identifies the subject of the chart.

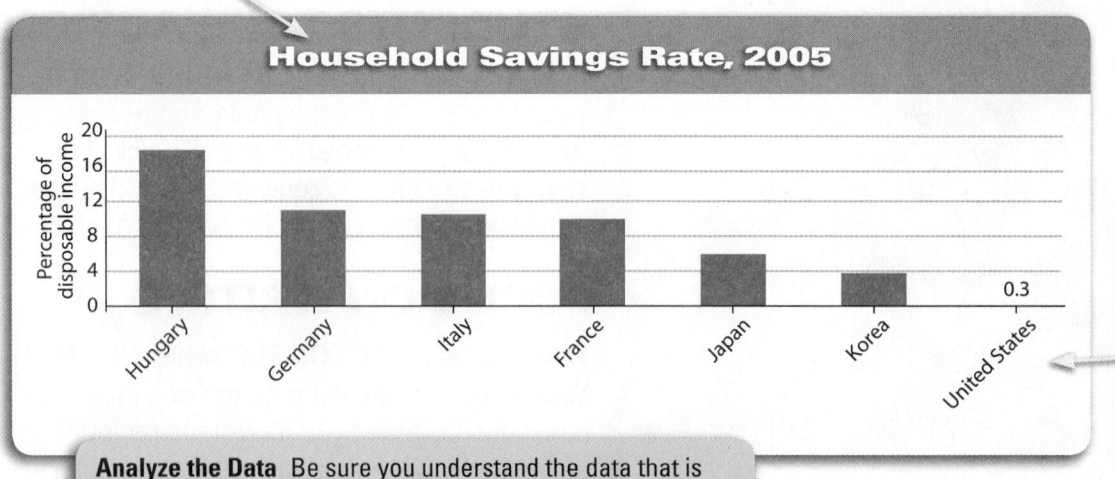

Labels Use labels to show the main categories or pieces of data that the chart or graph represents.

Analyze the Data Be sure you understand the data that is presented. Read the title and any labels to identify the subject of the chart or graph. This bar graph, for example, illustrates the percentage of disposable income that households in several countries put into savings in 2005.

You Try It!

Study the line graph below and then answer the questions that follow.

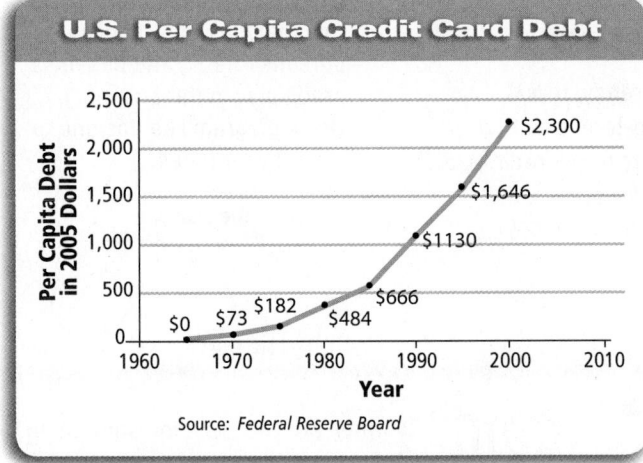

U.S. Per Capita Credit Card Debt

Per Capita Debt in 2005 Dollars

$0 $73 $182 $484 $666 $1130 $1,646 $2,300

Year: 1960   1970   1980   1990   2000   2010

Source: *Federal Reserve Board*

After you have studied the graph, answer the following questions.

1. What is the subject of this graph?

2. What time period does the graph cover?

3. What is the lowest amount of per capita credit card debt on the graph? In approximately what year did that amount occur?

4. What is the highest amount of per capita credit card debt? When did that amount occur?

5. What general trend does this graph indicate?

As you read Chapter 19, notice what information could be illustrated as a chart or graph.

SECTION 1
Money and Credit

BEFORE YOU READ

The Main Idea

In addition to using dollar bills and coins, individuals and businesses use checks, debit cards, and credit to pay for their purchases.

Reading Focus

1. What are three basic characteristics of currency?
2. Why do people and businesses accept checks as payment?
3. How is credit important to individuals and families?
4. How is business credit useful to the economy as a whole?

Key Terms

currency, *p. 504*
long-term credit, *p. 507*
short-term credit, *p. 507*
bankruptcy, *p. 508*
creditors, *p. 508*

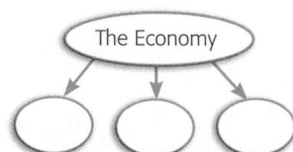 **TAKING NOTES** As you read, take notes on the role that currency, checks, personal credit, and business credit play in the economy. Use a diagram like this one to record your notes.

The Economy

One way you pay for what you buy is with currency, or coins and paper money. Other times you might borrow money or use a credit card.

CIVICS IN PRACTICE How do you pay for something? If an item is inexpensive, you may use cash, or currency. If goods and services are more costly, however, it may become inconvenient to carry around enough cash to buy what you want. As a result, you are more likely to write checks or use credit or debit cards. For expensive purchases, like cars and houses, people usually arrange loans.

Characteristics of Currency

Every country in the world has an official form of currency. The word **currency** is another term for coins and paper money. Whatever it is called, all currencies share at least three common features:

1. Currency must be easy to carry. It must be small and light so people can carry it with them for everyday use.

2. Currency must be durable, or last a long time. It should not wear out too quickly or fall apart.

3. Currency must be made in a standard form and must be considered legal tender by the government that issues it. In this way, people can be certain that their coins and bills will be accepted in exchange for goods and services.

A History of Cash

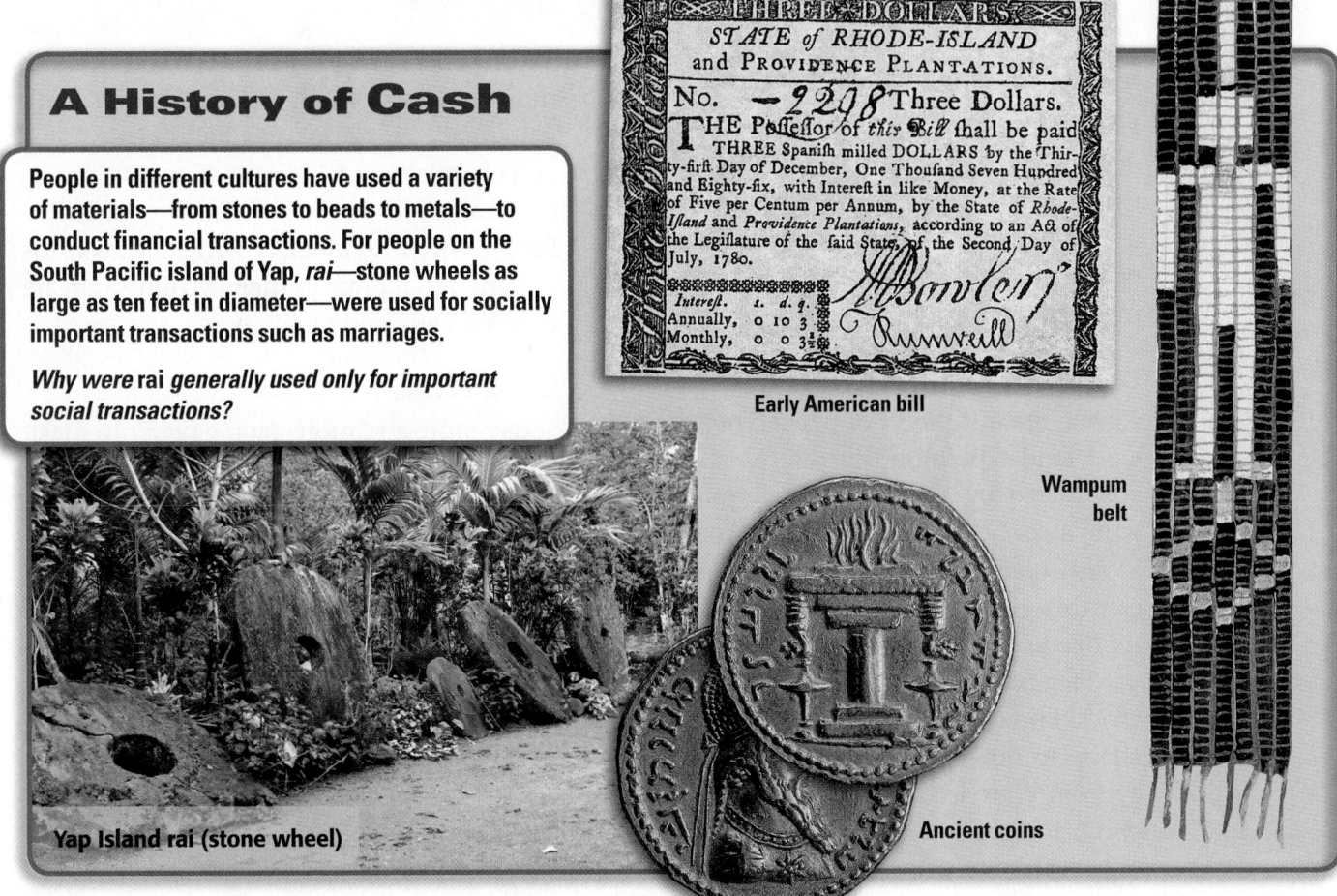

People in different cultures have used a variety of materials—from stones to beads to metals—to conduct financial transactions. For people on the South Pacific island of Yap, *rai*—stone wheels as large as ten feet in diameter—were used for socially important transactions such as marriages.

Why were rai *generally used only for important social transactions?*

Early American bill

Wampum belt

Yap Island rai (stone wheel)

Ancient coins

Earlier in our history, one of the weaknesses under the Articles of Confederation was the lack of a standard currency. Each state issued its own money. The different values and exchange rates for these currencies made trade among the states very difficult. The Constitution solved this problem by granting Congress the sole right to coin money and to regulate its value.

Today, the currency used by Americans is issued by the federal government. Two mints—plants where coins are made—now make most coins for general circulation. The two mints, located in Philadelphia, Pennsylvania, and Denver, Colorado, produce more than 65 million coins a day.

In the United States, six coins are used: pennies, nickels, dimes, quarters, half-dollars, and dollar coins. For many years the value of a coin was equal to the value of the metal that it contained. A silver dollar, for example, yielded about a dollar's worth of silver when melted down. In the past,

many Americans would only accept coins. They believed coins were more valuable and reliable than paper money.

Most money issued today is paper money, printed in Washington, D.C., at the Treasury Department's Bureau of Engraving and Printing. Bills are printed in denominations of $1, $2, $5, $10, $20, $50, and $100. The $5, $10, $20, $50, and $100 bills have been redesigned in recent years to make them more difficult to counterfeit.

All U.S. paper money and coins are legal tender. This means that by law people must accept this money as payment for goods and services in the United States. This system has worked for many years. Thus, everyone knows that these same dollars and coins will be accepted without hesitation when they are presented at stores, banks, or elsewhere.

READING CHECK **Summarizing** What are the three common characteristics of all currencies?

Checks and Debit Cards

Paper money and coins were important in developing a strong financial system in the United States. Today most buyers do not use coins or paper money for the majority of their purchases. Instead, Americans often make payments by check or debit card.

Checks

Checks are just pieces of paper. They are not legal tender because they are not issued or guaranteed by the federal government. To write a check for a purchase, you must have a particular kind of bank account—usually called a checking account—and enough money in that account to cover the check.

Merchants and others who receive the check know that the bank will honor the check. In other words, banks will take money from your account in the amount of the check and issue that money to the person or organization to whom the check was written.

Today, paper checks and debit cards account for almost 50 percent of U.S. consumer purchases. Cash still accounts for about one third of all purchases.

If people write checks for more money than they have in their account, the bank will usually charge an overdraft penalty. This penalty might be $25 or more, so it is important to watch your bank balance carefully. People who intentionally write checks without enough money in their accounts may be charged with a crime.

Debit Cards

Today more and more people prefer to make payments from their checking accounts with debit cards instead of writing checks. Debit cards are like electronic checks. Instead of writing out a check in the store, you can give the cashier your debit card. The money will be deducted from your account just like with a check. Debit cards offer an increasingly popular alternative to carrying cash or a checkbook.

READING CHECK **Drawing Inferences and Conclusions** Why are people more likely to use a check or debit card than cash to make a purchase?

Credit and the Economy

Sometimes a consumer may want to make a purchase but does not have enough cash in his or her wallet or bank account. When this happens that person needs access to credit. Buying something on credit means that a person is able to buy something now with the promise to pay for it later. Credit is a loan of money that is repaid plus interest. Interest is a payment charged for borrowed money.

Charge and Credit Cards

Some stores issue charge cards to many of their customers. A charge card is a form of borrowing. Customers can buy items without paying for them immediately because the store lends them the money for the purchase.

The amount of the purchase is added to the customer's account balance and billed to the customer each month. The customer then sends the store a payment for some or all of the amount due. A minimum payment is

America's Credit Card Debt

The first general-purpose credit card was introduced in 1958, when the BankAmericard was sent to 60,000 potential customers. By 1970, two major credit cards were available, but only about half of the people who received cards were using them. The average credit card debt was $185.

Credit card companies have changed a lot since those early days. Today there are over 20,000 different types of credit cards available. Companies now research the financial background of potential customers. To make more money, they also charge penalty fees and offer people higher credit lines and lower minimum payments. The average household today has an average of $8,000 in credit card debt, up from about $3,000 15 years ago.

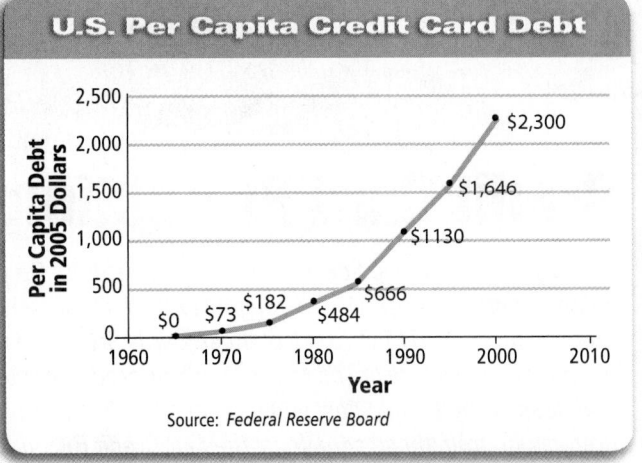

U.S. Per Capita Credit Card Debt

Per Capita Debt in 2005 Dollars

$0, $73, $182, $484, $666, $1130, $1,646, $2,300

Year: 1960, 1970, 1980, 1990, 2000, 2010

Source: *Federal Reserve Board*

ANALYSIS SKILL — **DRAWING CONCLUSIONS**

Why do you think Americans are more likely to charge expenses today than they were 30 years ago?

---

typically required. Usually there is no interest charge if the customer pays the full balance by the due date. If the customer only pays part of the balance, the store usually charges interest on the remaining amount.

Credit cards, while similar to charge cards, are much more common. They are issued by banks and other lending institutions. Unlike a charge card, which can only be used in the store or chain of stores that issued it, a credit card can be used almost anywhere. You present the credit card when making a purchase and the store charges the credit card company for the amount of the purchase. The credit card company pays the store and sends you a monthly bill for the total amount of all your purchases.

As with charge cards, the customer pays all or part of the credit card bill once a month. Most customers send credit card companies checks, but many people now use the Internet to transfer funds directly from their bank account to pay their credit card bills. Interest charges, which can be quite high, are added to the unpaid portion of the monthly bill.

Credit and the Family

If used wisely, credit can help the average American family. For example, few young families have saved enough money to **acquire** a house. Borrowing from a bank or mortgage company will give them the extra money they need for that purchase. They can then pay the loan off gradually—often over as long as 30 years—from money they earn. Of course, they also have to pay interest on the loan.

Loans payable over long periods are also called **long-term credit**. Most American families use long-term credit to buy cars, and many use it for other expensive purchases such as major appliances and furniture. If a family plans to pay for an item within just a few weeks or months, it needs only **short-term credit**. This type of credit can be especially helpful for emergency purchases, such as replacing a broken furnace or refrigerator.

If used unwisely, credit can cause serious financial problems. A person might buy so much on credit that he or she cannot afford to make the payments on time. Often the lender has the right to charge a penalty and to raise the interest rate after missed payments.

ACADEMIC VOCABULARY
acquire: to get, purchase or buy

FOUNDATIONS®
of DEMOCRACY

Credit Card Protection

When you buy a movie ticket, how do you pay for it? Do you use a debit or credit card? Maybe you pay with cash that you withdrew using your ATM card. All of these cards are convenient, but because they are linked to your bank or credit account, their loss or theft could cost you a great deal. Two laws help protect you from these situations: the Fair Credit Billing Act (FCBA) and the Electronic Fund Transfer Act (EFTA).

Why it Matters The FCBA and the EFTA offer protection if you report your lost or stolen card immediately. Under the FCBA, if you report a credit card missing before someone uses it, you will not pay for any unauthorized purchases, although you may be charged a fee up to $50. For debit and ATM cards, the EFTA protects you from charges if you file a report before the card is used. However, if the card is used after two days, you can be charged $50, and later, up to $500. After 60 days, you may have to pay for all the unauthorized charges.

Protect yourself. Always know where your cards are and keep a list of your account numbers and the phone numbers of your banks and card companies in a safe place. Save your receipts and check them against your account statements. If you see charges you did not make, report them immediately.

If you have a credit card, check your monthly statement carefully.

ANALYSIS SKILL EVALUATING THE LAW

go.hrw.com
KEYWORD: SZ7 CH19

1. Is it more dangerous to lose a credit or debit card? Explain your answer.
2. What impact do you think the FCBA has on credit card companies and their responsibilities? Explain your answer.

This makes the balance even harder to pay off. Stores may repossess, or take back, purchases that have not been fully paid for.

A credit card holder may be sued for the outstanding balance, and in the worst case may have to declare bankruptcy. **Bankruptcy** is a legal declaration that a person or business cannot pay debts owed. If a bankruptcy judge agrees, the person may be excused from the debt or be allowed to pay a reduced amount. In some cases, one may have to sell most of the things he or she owns to satisfy the **creditors**, those people who are owed money. Declaring bankruptcy can hurt a person's credit rating for years. This makes it more difficult to borrow money for a car, home, or other needed items. In 2005 Congress passed strict new bankruptcy laws. It is now more difficult to declare bankruptcy, and the amount of debt that can be excused has been reduced.

READING CHECK **Analyzing Information** What are the positive and negative aspects of credit?

Business Credit and the Economy

Businesses often use credit rather than currency in most sales involving large amounts of goods. Credit helps merchants by allowing them to buy more goods at one time, which means they have more merchandise to sell to their customers.

Imagine that you are the owner of a snowboard shop and you need to stock 50 snowboards for the next season. If the boards cost you $200 each, then you would need $10,000 to pay for the shipment. But you may not have that money until you can sell all the boards. The snowboard manufacturer may agree to deliver the boards on credit, allowing you some period of time to pay for the boards. Alternatively, you may arrange to borrow the money from a bank to pay for the shipment. Then you would repay the bank as the boards are sold.

Credit is important to the purchase and sale of goods and services in a free market. It is therefore very important to the successful operation of the U.S. economy as a whole.

The wise use of credit by individuals and families lets them buy and use things before they have saved enough money to pay cash for them. For example, instead of renting a house for years while saving up their money, a family might buy a house and begin living in it now. They can do this by borrowing the money they need from a bank.

When consumers buy goods sooner, the economy grows faster. The builder gets paid for building a house now rather than years from now, as do the people who supply the wood or the brick, or who sell the furnace or the air conditioning system. Consumer spending is an important force in the economy.

Similarly, careful use of credit allows businesses to produce and sell more goods and services than they could afford to by using only cash. This also helps the economy grow—businesses will buy more raw materials, rent more production space, hire more employees, and so on.

READING CHECK **Finding the Main Idea** How does credit help keep the economy in balance?

SECTION 1 ASSESSMENT

Reviewing Ideas and Terms

1. a. Define Write a brief definition for the term **currency**.

b. Summarize What three common features do all currencies have?

2. a. Summarize Why are checks not considered legal tender, and why do businesses accept them anyway?

b. Compare and Contrast How are charge cards and credit cards similar and different?

c. Defend a Point of View Would you prefer to use cash or checks when shopping? Explain.

3. a. Define Write a brief definition for the terms **long-term credit, short-term credit, bankruptcy,** and **creditors**.

b. Summarize How can individual credit be both helpful and harmful?

4. a. Recall Why do businesses often use credit for purchases rather than cash?

b. Elaborate How does the use of business credit allow the economy to grow?

Critical Thinking

5. Categorizing Copy the graphic organizer. Use it and your notes to show how credit can be used to help balance the economy.

Credit

High Production

Low Production

Focus on Writing

6. Analyzing Information Imagine that you are the editor of a financial magazine. Write an article explaining what families should consider when they purchase goods on credit.

Analyzing TV News

Learn

One of the most powerful forms of media today is television news. Since the television boom in the 1950s, news programs have been broadcast on television across the nation and the world. Most major television networks broadcast national and international news programs every night. In addition, most local stations have nightly news programs that focus on local news.

In the last 20 years, 24-hour news channels have changed television news. Such networks can show live coverage of events around the world as they happen, because they broadcast throughout the day. Because television news is one of the major sources of information about local, national, and world events, it is important to watch the news with a critical eye. Use the strategies below to help you analyze television news.

Practice

❶ **Pay attention to the stories.** What types of stories does a news program cover? Whether they focus on politics, international relations, or financial issues, the choice of stories can tell you about the priorities of the news station. Also pay attention to the order in which stories appear—it might indicate which stories the news directors feel are most important.

❷ **Identify the point of view.** Ideally, news stories are supposed to be balanced. That is, they offer both sides of an issue or event. Often, however, some stories can present only one point of view. Pay careful attention to the words and phrases the reporter uses, as they can indicate a particular point of view.

❸ **Analyze the visual information.** Often, news stories are intended only to provide viewers with information about an event. They may also serve other purposes. Examine the visual information—what is the background of the screen, the dress of the reporter, or the visual information used to present the story? How does it affect the story?

❹ **Notice the balance of stories on international and domestic topics.** News programs usually cover both events happening in the United States, and those happening abroad. Often the relevance to Americans—in terms of economics or national security—is stressed in international stories.

Apply

Use the photo below to help you answer the following questions.

1. What is likely the subject of the news story pictured below? How can you tell?

2. What does this television news program use to capture the audience's attention?

3. Is this news story likely intended for a local, national, or international audience? Explain.

SECTION 2

Banks and Banking

BEFORE YOU READ

The Main Idea

Banks provide a safe place to keep money and help businesses and individuals by making loans.

Reading Focus

1. How and why were the first banks established?
2. What is the purpose of banks and the banking system?
3. How and why does the U.S. Federal Reserve System regulate the amount of money in circulation?
4. How does a person get a bank loan?

Key Terms

collateral, *p. 512*
savings and loan associations, *p. 513*
credit unions, *p. 514*
Federal Reserve System, *p. 514*
discount rate, *p. 515*
discounting, *p. 516*

TAKING NOTES As you read, take notes on the origins of banking, the banking system, the Federal Reserve System, and getting a bank loan. Use a diagram like this one to organize your notes.

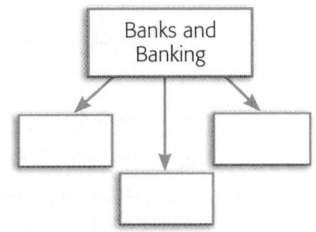

CIVICS IN PRACTICE Not all banks are the same, although many of them offer the same services. They protect your money in a checking or savings account. They lend money to businesses. If you start your own business, you might apply to a bank for a small business loan. Banks also lend money to individuals. One day, you may buy a car or a house with money from a bank loan.

Banks are secure locations where people can safely deposit their money.

The Origins of Banking

Money presented problems for many people 1,000 years ago just as it does today. People had difficulty finding a safe place to keep their riches. Carrying money made people the targets of thieves. Hiding it in their homes did not guarantee its safety either.

In most communities there were goldsmiths who kept a supply of gold to work on in their business. Because gold was so valuable, the goldsmiths kept it in heavy safes. In time, the townspeople began to bring their money to the goldsmiths for safekeeping. Before long, local goldsmiths had entered the money-keeping business, charging a small fee for the service.

Eventually, goldsmiths began providing money-lending services as well. Townspeople who needed money came to the goldsmiths for loans. In return for the loans, they signed a paper promising to repay the money by a certain date and to pay interest for using the money. The first banks were born.

Borrowers guaranteed their loans by promising to give up their property to the money lender if the loans were not repaid on time. Property used to guarantee repayment of a loan is called **collateral**. Over time, these money-lending practices developed into the banking system we know today.

READING CHECK ▶ **Finding the Main Idea** Why did banks first become necessary?

The Banking System

Our modern banking system is much more complicated than that of the early money lenders. Banks today handle billions of dollars' worth of deposits and withdrawals. Businesses and individuals rely upon the services and security of banks to help them protect and manage their money.

Types of Bank Accounts

Most people rely on banks for checking and savings accounts. Although you usually do not earn interest on regular checking accounts, you can easily access the money

in these accounts. Money in a checking account is called a demand deposit. That is, the bank must give you your money when you request, or demand, it by coming to the bank in person to withdraw it or by writing checks. Many banks also will issue automated teller machine (ATM) cards. These cards allow you to withdraw cash from your accounts at various locations at any time of day, even when the bank is closed. Another popular option for withdrawing money is the debit card, which acts as an electronic check.

You can also deposit your money in a savings account, where it earns interest. If the bank requires you to keep the money in your savings account for a minimum period of time, then the account is called a time deposit. The amount of interest you are paid depends on the type of account. Longer time deposit accounts are usually called certificates of deposit, or CDs. With these accounts you receive a certificate recording the deposit, the time period, and the interest rate. Another type of savings account is

Types of Banks QUICK FACTS

Today businesses and individuals have a variety of different types of banks to choose from. While the basic services of each type of bank are similar, they offer different services to their customers.

Commercial Banks
Commercial banks offer a full range of financial services to businesses and individuals.

Savings and Loan
Savings and loan associations are institutions that help people save and obtain home mortgages.

Credit Union
Credit unions are member-owned institutions that provide the same services as banks and savings and loans.

called a money market deposit account, or money market account. As long as a minimum balance is maintained, this account typically earns a higher rate of interest than a standard account. There are limits on how often you may take money out of this type of account.

Another popular type of bank account combines checking and savings. This is the negotiable order of withdrawal (NOW) account. With a NOW account, you can write checks and receive interest on the money in the account. Most banks require that you maintain a certain minimum balance in your NOW account.

Types of Banks

There are four main types of banks in the United States—commercial banks, savings and loan associations, savings banks, and credit unions. Although the differences among these banks have blurred in recent years, some important distinctions remain.

Commercial Banks Most of the banks in the United States are commercial banks. Commercial banks offer a full range of services. They offer checking, savings, and NOW accounts. They also make loans to individuals and businesses. Many commercial banks even issue credit cards and manage retirement accounts. They have departments that help customers manage property and invest money.

Accounts in commercial banks are insured by a government agency called the Federal Deposit Insurance Corporation (FDIC). In 2009 each depositor was insured up to $250,000. If for some reason a bank is unable to give its depositors their money, the FDIC will refund their deposits up to this limit.

Savings and Loan Associations Banks known as **savings and loan associations**, or S&Ls, were created in the mid-1800s to help people purchase homes. They still account for a large percentage of home mortgage loans.

PRIMARY SOURCE

POLITICAL CARTOON
Savings and Loans

Savings and loan associations were popular places for many families to save money and to take out loans to buy homes.

From 1980 to 1982, some 118 U.S. savings and loan institutions, with assets worth $43 billion, failed. In the 45 years before 1980, only 143 savings and loans, with a total of $4.5 billion in assets, had failed. Clearly, there was a crisis in the savings and loan industry.

This cartoon was published in 1989. By then, some 565 savings and loan associations had failed.

THE GOOD NEWS IS WE'VE BEEN SAVING FOR YOUR COLLEGE EDUCATION SINCE YOU WERE BORN... THE BAD NEWS IS IT WAS IN A SAVINGS & LOAN.

ANALYSIS SKILL ANALYZING POLITICAL CARTOONS

How does this cartoon reflect the impact of the savings and loan crisis of the 1980s on the ordinary family?

During the 1980s federal legislation allowed S&Ls to expand their services to offer many of the same services as commercial banks. Customers can obtain loans, open checking, savings, and NOW accounts, and apply for credit cards. When this deregulation first began, many S&Ls made risky loans and other bad investments. As a result, hundreds of S&Ls throughout the country failed in what became known as the S&L crisis.

Until 1989 the Federal Savings and Loan Insurance Corporation (FSLIC) insured S&L deposits. Faced with paying the costs of the failed S&Ls, the FSLIC ran out of money. The government then formed the Resolution Trust Corporation (RTC) to sort out the savings and loan crisis. Administered by the FDIC, the RTC took over the FSLIC's insurance obligations.

By August 1994 the RTC had saved more than 730 savings and loans. The total cost to taxpayers was estimated at nearly $165 billion.

Savings Banks Savings banks began in the early 1800s to encourage people who could make only very small deposits to save. Today these banks offer a variety of services, including home loans. As with commercial banks, deposits in savings banks are insured by the FDIC.

Credit Unions Most **credit unions** are established by people who work for a single company or belong to a single organization. Credit unions are owned and operated by their members.

FOCUS ON
Anna Escobedo Cabral
(1959–   )

In 2004, President George W. Bush nominated Anna Escobedo Cabral to be the forty-second treasurer of the United States. During her tenure as treasurer, Cabral's signature appeared on each new piece of currency to make the bill official.

Cabral, who grew up in California, studied political science at the University of California, Davis. She later earned a master of public administration degree at Harvard University. In the 1990s Cabral became deputy staff director of the Senate Judiciary Committee, and she served as executive staff director of the Senate Republican Conference Task Force on Hispanic Affairs, leading 25 senators on a mission to respond to Hispanic communities. Afterwards, she became president and chief executive officer of the Hispanic Association on Corporate Responsibility and the director of the Smithsonian Institution's Center for Latino Initiatives.

As treasurer, Cabral was in charge of collecting taxes through the Internal Revenue Service. She also oversaw the printing and minting of American currency, and served as a spokesperson on financial education.

Evaluating What are the duties of the United States treasurer? Why is this position important?

When members make deposits, they buy interest-paying shares in the credit union. These deposits are pooled in order to make low-interest loans available to members. Depositors may also write checks, which are called share drafts.

Deposits in credit unions are insured by a government agency called the National Credit Union Association (NCUA). Each depositor is insured up to $100,000.

READING CHECK **Comparing** How are the different types of banks similar?

The Federal Reserve System

At one time, banks were allowed to conduct business with few rules. As a result, they sometimes lent money to high-risk customers and did not get enough collateral in return for loans. Some banks lent too much money and did not keep enough in reserve. Under these conditions, some banks failed.

Rumors occasionally spread that a particular bank was shaky. Depositors might then start a run on the bank—rushing to the bank to withdraw all their money in case the bank did fail. If too many depositors withdrew their money at once, the bank would have no funds left. People with money still in the bank would have lost their savings.

To prevent such bank failures and to give people more confidence in the safety of banks, the federal government created a plan to regulate the U.S. banking system. In 1913 Congress set up the **Federal Reserve System**, sometimes called the Fed. The Fed regulates banks by requiring that they keep a certain amount of money in reserve.

Federal Reserve Banks

The Federal Reserve System divides the United States into 12 federal districts. A Federal Reserve bank is located in each district. Federal Reserve banks do not do business directly with individuals or companies. Instead, they act as bankers for the federal government and for other banks.

Federal Reserve banks serve two main purposes. First, they handle the banking needs of the federal government. For example, Federal Reserve banks handle the sale of bonds issued by the government. In addition, most U.S. currency is put into circulation through the Federal Reserve System. From these banks, the money spreads out into the economy for use by businesses and consumers.

Second, the 12 Federal Reserve banks provide various services to state and national banks, and control the banking system. For example, a member bank can go to the Federal Reserve bank in its district and borrow money. Doing so allows the member bank to meet a high demand for cash from its customers.

The member bank must pay interest on the loans it receives from the Fed, just like individuals or businesses. The rate of interest charged to member banks by the Federal Reserve is called the **discount rate**. This rate often influences the amount of money available to banks for making loans.

The Board of Governors

The Federal Reserve System is managed from Washington, D.C., by a seven-member board of governors. Each member is appointed by the president, with the consent of the Senate, and serves for a single 14-year term.

Through its influence over the banking system, the Fed tries to keep the right amount of currency in circulation. When the economy is growing and more goods and services are being produced, more currency is needed in circulation. The additional currency allows businesses and individuals to take part in a growing economy.

When the currency supply grows faster than the supply of goods, prices tend to rise. To prevent this, the Fed may try to slow the growth of the money supply or even take money out of circulation.

READING CHECK > **Analyzing Information** How does the Federal Reserve regulate the economy?

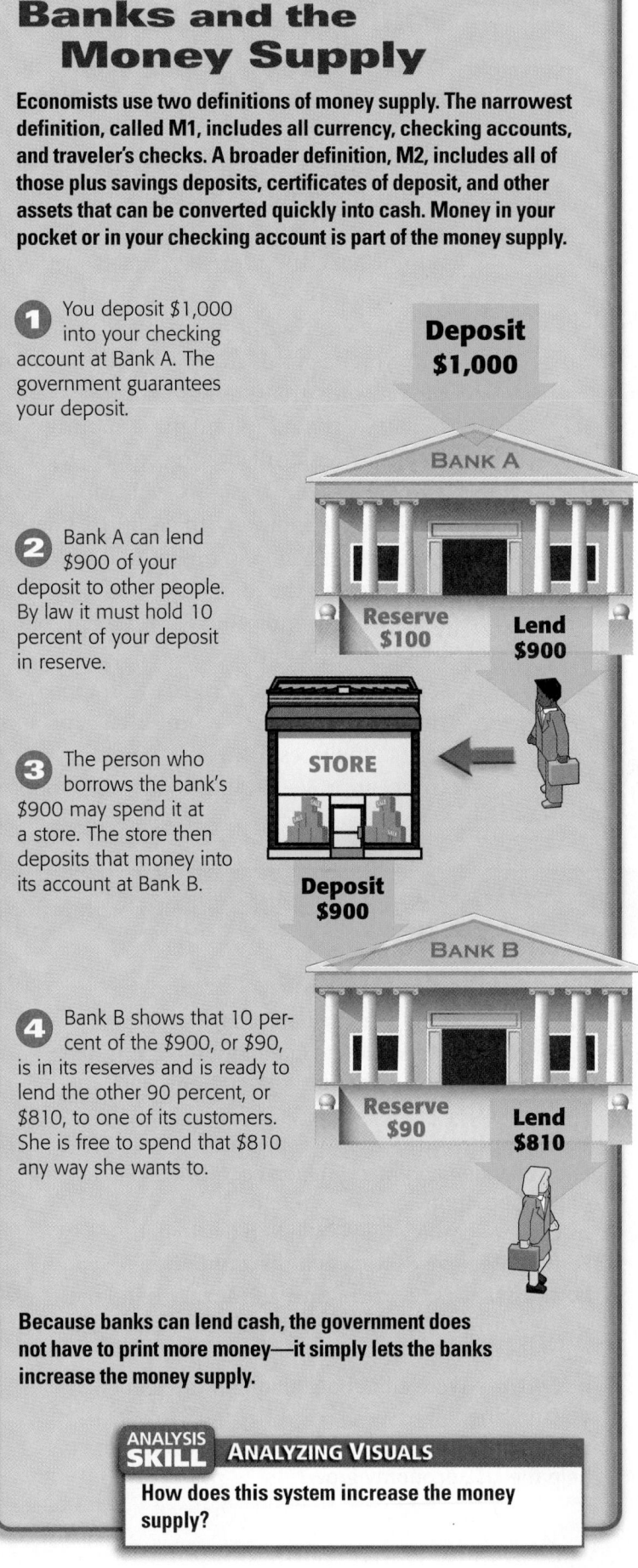

Banks and the Money Supply

Economists use two definitions of money supply. The narrowest definition, called M1, includes all currency, checking accounts, and traveler's checks. A broader definition, M2, includes all of those plus savings deposits, certificates of deposit, and other assets that can be converted quickly into cash. Money in your pocket or in your checking account is part of the money supply.

1 You deposit $1,000 into your checking account at Bank A. The government guarantees your deposit.

Deposit $1,000

BANK A

Reserve $100 **Lend $900**

2 Bank A can lend $900 of your deposit to other people. By law it must hold 10 percent of your deposit in reserve.

STORE

3 The person who borrows the bank's $900 may spend it at a store. The store then deposits that money into its account at Bank B.

Deposit $900

BANK B

Reserve $90 **Lend $810**

4 Bank B shows that 10 percent of the $900, or $90, is in its reserves and is ready to lend the other 90 percent, or $810, to one of its customers. She is free to spend that $810 any way she wants to.

Because banks can lend cash, the government does not have to print more money—it simply lets the banks increase the money supply.

ANALYSIS SKILL **ANALYZING VISUALS**
How does this system increase the money supply?

Getting a Bank Loan

What happens when you borrow money from a bank? Imagine that you own and operate a small computer repair service company. You need $5,000 to buy some new equipment in order to service the latest generation of computers. Because you do not have the money yourself, you apply for a loan.

You meet with a loan officer to explain why you need this money. You bring in business records that show that you have been making a profit. You might also bring financial analyses, called projections, that estimate how your business will improve with the added equipment. In addition, you want to convince the loan officer that you will be able to repay the loan. So you also point out that you have no other debts except for a car loan, which you have always paid on time.

The loan officer needs the approval of the bank's lending committee for larger loans. She does, however, have the authority to approve smaller loans like yours on her own. You receive a short-term loan of $5,000, which you must repay in 90 days. You do not receive the full $5,000, however. The bank deducts a small amount in advance as the interest it is charging for the loan. It deposits the remainder as a credit in your checking account at the bank. Deducting the interest on a loan in advance is known as **discounting**.

After you receive the loan, you buy the new equipment. This starts a chain of events into action. You can now offer better service to your customers, which should help you make more money. The bank also makes money on the loan. The equipment company uses the money it got from you and other customers to pay its employees and suppliers. Perhaps it will even be able to expand its business as well. In this way, your loan and other forms of credit circulate throughout the U.S. economy.

READING CHECK **Identifying Cause and Effect** What factors might cause a bank to agree to lend money?

go.hrw.com
Online Quiz
KEYWORD: SZ7 HP19

SECTION 2 ASSESSMENT

Reviewing Ideas and Terms

1. **Explain** How did the first banks originate?
2. **a. Define** Write a brief definition for the terms **collateral, savings and loan associations,** and **credit unions.**
   b. Compare and Contrast What is the difference between a demand deposit account and a time deposit account?
3. **a. Define** Write a brief definition for the terms **Federal Reserve System** and **discount rate.**
   b. Identifying Cause and Effect Why did the U.S. government decide to regulate banks, and how did it do this?
4. **a. Define** Write a brief definition for the term **discounting.**
   b. Analyze Information How do business loans help the U.S. economy grow?

Critical Thinking

5. **Summarizing** Use your notes and a chart like the one here to summarize the different types of banks that operate in the United States.

Commercial Banks	Savings and Loans	Savings Banks	Credit Unions

Focus on Writing

6. **Summarizing** Imagine that you are an economics professor teaching a course to future bankers. Write a brief lesson explaining the purpose of the Federal Reserve banks.

SECTION 3

Saving and Investing

BEFORE YOU READ

The Main Idea

There are many ways to save money. Saving helps the economy by providing banks with money to make loans to others.

Reading Focus

1. Why is it important to save money?
2. What are some ways people save and invest their money?
3. How does saving money help the U.S. economy?
4. How does the government protect savings and investments?

Key Terms

certificates of deposit (CDs), p. 518
brokers, p. 518
stock exchange, p. 518
mutual funds, p. 518
money market funds, p. 519

TAKING NOTES As you read, take notes on saving and investing. Use a chart like this one to organize your notes.

Saving is Important	
Ways to Invest	
Saving Helps the Economy	
Protecting Savings and Investments	

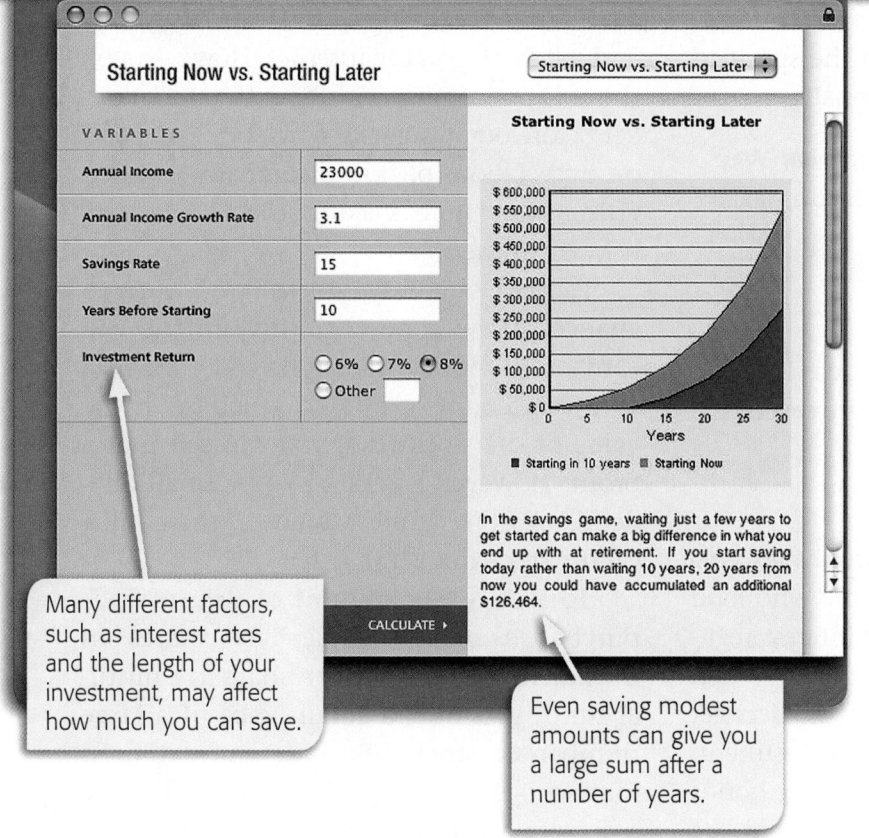

Starting Now vs. Starting Later

VARIABLES

Annual Income	23000
Annual Income Growth Rate	3.1
Savings Rate	15
Years Before Starting	10
Investment Return	○6% ○7% ●8% ○Other

Starting Now vs. Starting Later

In the savings game, waiting just a few years to get started can make a big difference in what you end up with at retirement. If you start saving today rather than waiting 10 years, 20 years from now you could have accumulated an additional $126,464.

CALCULATE ▶

Many different factors, such as interest rates and the length of your investment, may affect how much you can save.

Even saving modest amounts can give you a large sum after a number of years.

CIVICS IN PRACTICE Many people put aside part of what they earn to meet unexpected expenses, to pay for an expensive item, or to live more comfortably when they retire. You will, too, someday. Money can be kept in a savings account, or it can be invested in stocks and bonds. A savings account is probably safer. Stock market investments are riskier but might be more rewarding. Savings and investment both make your money available to others and help the economy grow.

Saving Is Important

There are many different ways to save your money. You can hide your money under a mattress, put it in a cookie jar, or keep it in a piggy bank, but these places are not very safe and do not pay interest.

Saving Accounts

Many Americans set aside a regular amount in a savings account each week or each month. The bank pays interest on all money deposited in a savings account. In this way, your money earns more money for you. If you save money on a regular basis, you can build a large sum over time. The money can be withdrawn when it is needed.

Regular savings accounts usually require you to keep only a small minimum balance. However, some banks charge a service fee if your account falls below the minimum balance or if you exceed a specified number of transactions within a certain time period.

Certificates of Deposit

Banks and other financial institutions also offer **certificates of deposit (CDs)**. Savers who use CDs invest a certain amount of money for a specified period of time. Most CDs are issued in units of $1,000 or more. The interest to be paid when the CD matures is set at the time of purchase and usually remains constant.

CDs can have terms lasting weeks, months, or even years. Usually, the longer the money is invested, the higher the interest paid on the CD. However, if you withdraw your money before the end of the specified term, you may have to pay a penalty.

READING CHECK ▸ **Analyzing Information** Why might banks require a minimum balance be maintained in a savings account?

Ways to Invest

Another way to save for the future is to invest your money. Bonds and stocks are two of the most popular investments.

Buying Bonds

Bonds are certificates of debt issued by governments and corporations to people who lend them money. Most bonds pay interest regularly, such as every calendar quarter. When the bond reaches maturity, bond holders get back the amount of their original investment. U.S. government bonds, as well as the bonds of most states, localities, and corporations, are a relatively safe form of investment.

One form of bond, the U.S. savings bond, does not pay interest until the bond matures and you cash it in. For example, a savings bond bought for $100 might earn $100 in interest over 12 years. If you paid $100 for one of these bonds, you would receive $200 when you cashed it in. Meanwhile, your money is safe because the federal government can be counted on to repays its debt. However, the interest rate for savings bonds is usually lower than for many other kinds of investments.

Buying Stocks

Business organizations known as brokerage houses buy and sell various stocks for their customers. The people employed by brokerage houses are known as **brokers**. Each brokerage house is a member of one or more stock exchanges. Millions of shares of stock are bought and sold every working day at a **stock exchange**. One of the most influential stock exchanges in the world is the New York Stock Exchange in New York City.

Anyone can buy stocks through a brokerage house. In addition, you can easily buy and sell stocks via the Internet. However, you should know a great deal about the stock market before buying stocks. Stock prices depend on expectations of how a company will perform in the future, making stocks a relatively risky investment.

People who buy stocks are taking a chance. They hope their investment will earn more money than it would earn in a savings account or a bond purchase. If the value of the stock rises, you can sell it at a profit. However, stocks may pay small dividends or none at all. Moreover, their value on the stock market may fall.

To reduce the amount of risk in stock purchases, many people buy shares in **mutual funds**. By buying a share in a mutual fund, you own a small piece of a large number of stocks. Because mutual fund managers buy many different stocks, the risk from any one stock is not great. Before buying shares in a mutual fund, however, you should research the fund. You should determine what stocks the fund holds, its performance over time, and its management. A mutual fund that is poorly managed can be risky.

Money market funds are mutual funds that buy short-term bonds. Most short-term bonds have stable values, so you can be fairly confident that a dollar invested will still be worth a dollar when you take it out. You can withdraw your money at any time. Money market funds do not guarantee a specified amount of interest, but often can pay a slightly higher rate than most banks. However, the rate of interest may rise or fall. Also, this form of saving is not insured by the government, which means it can be a risky investment.

READING CHECK **Evaluating** What should a person take into consideration before investing?

Saving Helps the Economy

What happens to the money that Americans have in savings accounts, bonds, stocks, and other forms of saving? That money is used to help expand the U.S. economy. How does saving promote such growth?

Economic growth occurs when factories and other means of production increase their production. However, expanding production normally requires money to pay for a variety of needs. These needs can include more employees, new factories, machine tools, and other capital goods. Some of the money will come from the company's profits that it saves to fund expansion. Much of the rest will come from other people's savings that banks lend to the company.

Businesses can use a combination of saving and borrowing to finance expansion. Most corporations put aside a portion of their profits before paying dividends to their stockholders. This money is reinvested in the business in the form of new capital. The new capital might be in the form of new machines or larger factories. It helps businesses establish new branches or add new lines of products or services to what the company already produces.

READING CHECK **Finding the Main Idea** How does saving contribute to economic growth?

Protecting Savings and Investments

When people deposit money in a bank account, they want to know that their money will be safe. They also want to know that they will be able to get their money back when they ask for it. Likewise, when people buy stocks or bonds, they want to be sure that they are not taking unnecessary risks with their money.

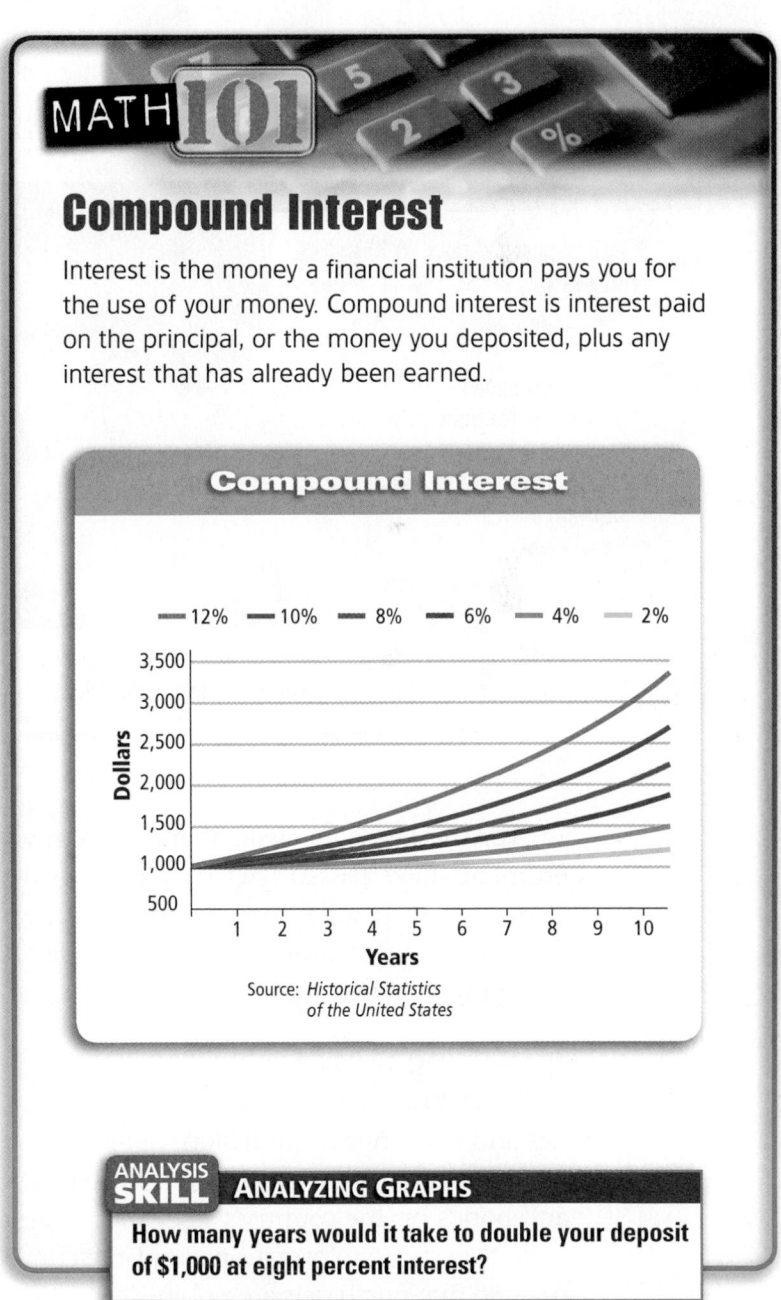

MATH 101

Compound Interest

Interest is the money a financial institution pays you for the use of your money. Compound interest is interest paid on the principal, or the money you deposited, plus any interest that has already been earned.

Compound Interest

— 12% — 10% — 8% — 6% — 4% — 2%

Source: *Historical Statistics of the United States*

ANALYSIS SKILL **ANALYZING GRAPHS**
How many years would it take to double your deposit of $1,000 at eight percent interest?

National Savings Rates

Saving is important to the national economy because the money set aside can be lent to other people to invest or spend. For example, businesses may borrow the funds and invest in new equipment or hire more workers. The economy as a whole benefits when you save.

Disposable income is the money income you have left after you have paid all taxes. Disposable means that you can spend the money.

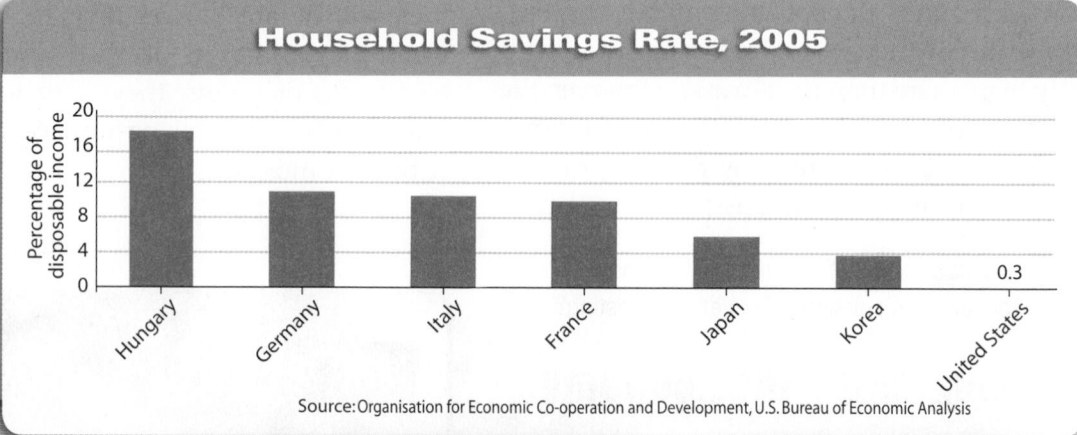

Household Savings Rate, 2005

Source: Organisation for Economic Co-operation and Development, U.S. Bureau of Economic Analysis

Things You Might Want to Save For

- New video game
- Clothes
- Living expenses (such as telephone bills)
- New cell phone
- Car and automotive expenses
- College education
- Apartment

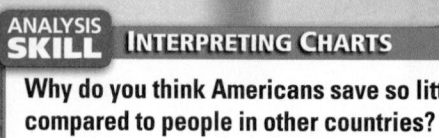

ANALYSIS SKILL **INTERPRETING CHARTS**

Why do you think Americans save so little compared to people in other countries?

For these reasons, federal and state governments have passed laws regulating institutions that handle money. All financial institutions must receive a state or federal charter to operate.

Regulating Stock Exchanges

In the 1930s Congress established the Securities and Exchange Commission, or SEC. This organization ensures that all offerings of stocks and bonds on the country's stock exchanges include accurate information about the company so that purchasers are not misled.

In years past, people sometimes sold watered-down stock. This stock did not fully represent the value claimed for it. There were also many other types of stock fraud and deception by which dishonest people and firms cheated the American public.

The regulations of the Securities and Exchange Commission were established to stop such practices. The SEC constantly monitors the practices of the country's stock exchanges and the brokers who buy and sell stock. This does not mean, however, that all stocks are safe investments.

Regulating Savings Organizations

All of the country's savings organizations come under state or federal government supervision. Like banks, savings and loan associations are also regulated by laws. Even company credit unions must allow government accountants to examine their records regularly to determine if they have enough capital and are operating properly.

As you have read, money in savings and loan accounts is insured against loss. Deposit insurance is administered by the Federal Deposit Insurance Corporation. In 2009 deposits were insured up to $250,000. The insurance covers savings accounts, certificates of deposit, and money market accounts. Credit union accounts are similarly insured by the National Credit Union Share Insurance Fund.

Saving is important to the prosperity of the United States and its citizens. Because of this, it is essential that individual savings be protected.

READING CHECK **Summarizing** How does the government protect the savings of individuals?

MEDIA INVESTIGATION

NEWSPAPER HEADLINES
The 1929 Stock Market Crash

Headlines are designed to sell newspapers. They use active language that makes people want to read the article. A well-written headline will tell what the article is about without exaggeration.

Some writers try so hard to get a reader's attention that their headlines are misleading. Such headlines often point up the most violent or sensational aspect of an event, regardless of whether it fairly represents the whole story.

In October 1929, when the U.S. stock market crashed, many people first learned of the collapse from newspapers. Investors were very worried—even panicked—about losing their money. Some headlines reflected that panic, but it is also possible that they contributed to creating it, too.

ANALYSIS SKILL **MEDIA INVESTIGATION** | go.hrw.com KEYWORD: SZ7 CH19

What page of the newspaper is likely to have the most sensational headlines? Why?

---

go.hrw.com
Online Quiz
KEYWORD: SZ7 HP19

SECTION 3 ASSESSMENT

Reviewing Ideas and Terms

1. a. Define Write a brief definition for the term **certificates of deposit (CDs)**.
   b. Summarize What are some ways that people can save money?
2. a. Define Write a definition for the terms **brokers**, **stock exchange**, **mutual funds**, and **money market funds**.
   b. Compare and Contrast What is the difference between saving and financial investments?
3. a. Summarize How does the U.S. economy benefit when people deposit money in savings accounts, bonds, or stocks?
   b. Draw Inferences and Conclusions Why do businesses often invest much of their profit in expanding their companies?

4. Summarize What are some of the ways the government protects your savings and investments?

Critical Thinking

5. Summarizing Copy the graphic organizer at right. Use it and your notes to show the different ways people save and invest their money.

Focus on Writing

6. Decision Making Write a paragraph telling how you might invest $1,000 and why you would choose such a form or forms of investment.

SECTION 4

Insurance against Hardship

BEFORE YOU READ

The Main Idea

Insurance companies offer policies to protect people from possible financial hardships. The federal government also has several programs to help protect people from risks and uncertainties.

Reading Focus

1 How are insurance companies able to protect you?
2. What are some forms of insurance provided by the government?

Key Terms

insurance, *p. 522*
premium, *p. 522*
private insurance, *p. 523*
beneficiary, *p. 523*
social insurance, *p. 524*
Social Security, *p. 524*
Medicare, *p. 526*
Medicaid, *p. 526*

TAKING NOTES As you read, take notes on the different types of insurance. Use a graphic organizer like this one to list the different types of insurance and their purpose.

Private Insurance	Government Insurance

Homeowners can buy insurance against damage from wind, water, floods, and fires.

The concept of insurance is at least 4,000 years old. Babylonian merchants traveling in caravans to East Asia protected themselves by contributing to a collective fund to cover losses to bandits. Over the centuries, the idea has become increasingly popular. What was once common only for businesses and wealthy individuals is available today for many Americans. Risk and uncertainty are a part of life, but insurance provides a way to protect yourself and your family.

Insurance Protects You

Insurance is a system of spreading risks over large numbers of people. These people each pay a small amount to an insurance company to avoid the risk of a large loss. For example, if you own a $20,000 car, it could be ruined in an accident. You might be willing to pay a much smaller sum—perhaps $750 each year—to protect yourself against the risk of an accident.

The amount you pay for this protection is called a **premium**. Premiums may be paid yearly or more often. The contract that gives this kind of protection is called an insurance policy.

Types of Insurance

Families may need a variety of types of insurance to protect themselves from unexpected losses.

Life

Auto

Health

Property

ANALYSIS SKILL COMPARING AND CONTRASTING

If you were a college student, unmarried in your early 20s, which types of insurance might you buy? Explain your answer.

How can insurance companies take small amounts of money from people, yet pay them a large sum if a hardship occurs? The reason is simple—not everyone has a hardship. You may pay premiums on accident insurance all your life and never collect a cent because you never have an accident.

A large insurance company has millions of policyholders who pay their premiums regularly. Part of this money goes into a reserve fund. State laws specify how large a reserve fund a company must maintain. Claims are paid from the reserve fund. As long as the insurance company collects more in premiums than it has to pay out in claims, it can make a profit. Major natural disasters can cause a problem for insurance companies, however.

The voluntary insurance that individuals and companies pay to cover unexpected losses is called **private insurance**. There are many different kinds of losses that private insurance covers, from life insurance to health insurance to property insurance.

Life Insurance

The main purpose of life insurance is to provide the policyholder's family with money in the event that the policyholder dies. In this way, the family is protected from financial hardship. The person named in the policy to receive the money when the policyholder dies is called the **beneficiary**.

The two kinds of life insurance are term insurance and whole-life insurance. Term insurance covers only a specified period of time. Because it expires at the end of the specified term, it is relatively inexpensive. Whole-life insurance covers the policyholder throughout his or her life, and is more expensive.

Disability and Health Insurance

Other insurance policies cover policyholders if they are injured in an accident or suffer an illness. Disability income insurance, for example, provides payments to replace lost wages when the policyholder cannot work due to a total or partial disability.

Health insurance covers medical or hospital expenses. Major medical expense insurance pays a large portion of the medical costs resulting from a serious illness or injury. Premiums for these kinds of insurance are often paid in part by you and in part by your employer.

Property and Liability Insurance

Some types of insurance protect your personal property from events such as fires, hurricanes, vandalism, and theft. The most widely purchased form of property and liability insurance is automobile insurance. This type of insurance protects you against liability for injuring another person or damaging another car in an automobile accident. It also provides coverage if your car is stolen, vandalized, or damaged in an accident.

READING CHECK **Analyzing Information** How do insurance companies stay profitable while still paying policyholders for their claims?

Insurance Provided by the Government

During the Great Depression of the 1930s, many businesses and factories closed, and millions of men and women lost their jobs. Banks failed, and thousands of people lost their life savings. In response, President Franklin D. Roosevelt recommended and Congress passed a series of laws called the New Deal. Some of the new laws brought immediate assistance to needy people. Other laws were intended to protect people against severe economic risks and hardships in case of future recessions.

Government programs like these that are meant to protect individuals from future hardship are called **social insurance**. The Social Security Act of 1935 set up a system of social insurance known as **Social Security**. It has three major parts—old-age and survivors insurance, disability insurance, and unemployment insurance.

Old-Age, Survivors, and Disability Insurance

The basic idea behind this type of insurance is simple. People pay a percentage of their salary each month while they work in order to receive cash benefits later, when they retire. During the years when workers earn money, they and their employers contribute to a fund. After workers retire, or if they become disabled and are no longer earning money, they receive payments from the fund.

By law monthly contributions made under the Social Security Act are shared equally by workers and by employers. These contributions are actually a tax because they are compulsory, or required.

If workers die before reaching retirement age, their families receive survivors' payments. A payment is made for each child under 18 and for the surviving spouse. When children reach the age of 18, payments to them stop.

Unemployment Compensation

When the Social Security Act was passed in 1935, unemployment was a serious problem. Millions of Americans had lost their jobs during the Great Depression. The Social Security Act contained a plan to help workers who lost their jobs due to circumstances beyond their control. This plan is called the unemployment compensation program.

To receive benefits, workers who become unemployed must first register with a state employment office. Then they report periodically to the office to see if it can help them find jobs. If the job search is unsuccessful, unemployed workers receive weekly benefits based on their average earnings over a certain period of time. The amount paid varies from state to state, but most states provide benefits for up to 26 weeks.

Workers' Compensation

Federal and state workers' compensation programs help people who have job-related injuries or illnesses resulting from working conditions. These programs pay the medical expenses

The Social Security System

The Social Security Act was passed in 1935 to provide economic assistance to retired workers. Since then, the system has grown and changed to aid more people.

Employees

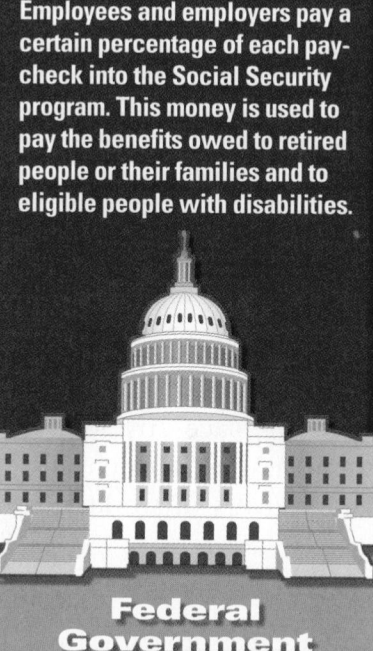

Employees and employers pay a certain percentage of each paycheck into the Social Security program. This money is used to pay the benefits owed to retired people or their families and to eligible people with disabilities.

Federal Government

Employer

$

Employees put **7.5** percent of their earnings into the Social Security system.

$

Employers match the **7.5** percent for each employee.

Social Security Trust Fund

The Social Security trust fund pays benefits to eligible retirees, survivors, and disabled people.

$

$

General Fund

The general fund makes payments to those eligible for supplemental income.

The Future

The Social Security system faces a possible problem because eventually it may not have enough money to pay full benefits to everyone entitled to them. The system is expected to be able to make payments easily until 2014. After that it will have to take money from its savings fund. Some experts predict that in 2041 the system will no longer have enough money to pay full benefits to everyone in the system. How to solve this problem is a matter of national debate.

TODAY
Full benefits paid

2014
Full benefits paid, but using savings fund

2041
Full benefits cannot be paid

ANALYSIS SKILL **ANALYZING VISUALS**

If you were in Congress, what solution might you provide to avoid the problem in 2041?

People today live longer and healthier lives. However, many elderly people need Medicare or Medicaid to help pay for health care.

of the workers and help replace any lost income. Workers' compensation also pays death benefits to the survivors of workers killed while on the job.

Medicare and Medicaid

The federal government also has programs to help poor and older citizens pay their medical expenses. In 1965 Congress passed the health insurance program called **Medicare** to help U.S. citizens who are 65 and older pay for hospital care and for some nursing home care. Medicare includes a voluntary medical insurance plan that helps many older citizens pay their medical bills. People with disabilities who are unable to work are also eligible for Medicare benefits. In 2003 Congress added a prescription medicine benefit to Medicare.

Congress also passed the **Medicaid** health insurance program in 1965. This program provides money to the states to help pay the medical costs of people with low incomes. For example, it helps some people pay for treatments they might not otherwise be able to afford.

In recent years the cost of Social Security has become a major concern. As more Americans live longer, retire, and collect benefits, the expense of the program grows. Attempts to reform the program have caused national debate that has yet to be settled.

READING CHECK **Finding the Main Idea** What is the main purpose of social insurance?

go.hrw.com
Online Quiz
KEYWORD: SZ7 HP19

SECTION 4 ASSESSMENT

Reviewing Ideas and Terms

1. a. Define Write a brief definition for the terms **insurance, premium, private insurance,** and **beneficiary.**

b. Summarize How can insurance companies cover large risks in return for relatively small premiums?

2. a. Define Write a brief definition for the terms **social insurance, Social Security, Medicare,** and **Medicaid.**

b. Compare and Contrast What is the difference between unemployment compensation and workers' compensation?

c. Summarize What do the Medicare and Medicaid programs provide?

Critical Thinking

3. Summarizing Copy the graphic organizer below. Using your notes, list the different kinds of insurance you have read about and what each kind covers. Add boxes if you need to.

Insurance	
Type	What it Covers

Focus on Writing

4. Supporting a Point of View Do you think Social Security has encouraged Americans to become too dependent on the state and federal governments for support in times of need? Write a paragraph explaining your answer.

PROJECT Citizen

Lobbying for Library Access

In the city of Newberg, Oregon, many students in the Newberg Public School District lived outside the city's public library district. These students had to pay a fee to use the library's resources, including books and other educational materials. Because some families could not afford to pay, many students could not use the public library.

Community Connection Project Citizen students in Ms. Terry McElligott's social studies class decided that all local public school students should have access to the library. However, the teens found from their research that most local residents outside of the library district opposed expanding its boundaries. Being included in the library district would increase some homeowners' property taxes, costing them more than the current library usage fee.

Taking Action The teens focused on two goals: increasing public support for expanding the library district boundaries and funding library access for young people. With support from a city council member and a local librarian, the students lobbied citizens and public officials both in person and through the media. They explained how extending the library district's boundaries would benefit all students and increased awareness of the issue of library access. They also raised more than $400 for a private fund to pay for out-of-district cards for students in need.

Local libraries are a valuable asset for many students.

go.hrw.com
Project Citizen
KEYWORD: SZ7 CH19

SERVICE LEARNING

1. How did the students take into account the economic concerns of different groups in the community when developing their action plan?
2. What compromises might help win more support for the students' plan to extend district boundaries?

QUICK FACTS

Visual Summary

Use this visual summary to help you review the main ideas of the chapter.

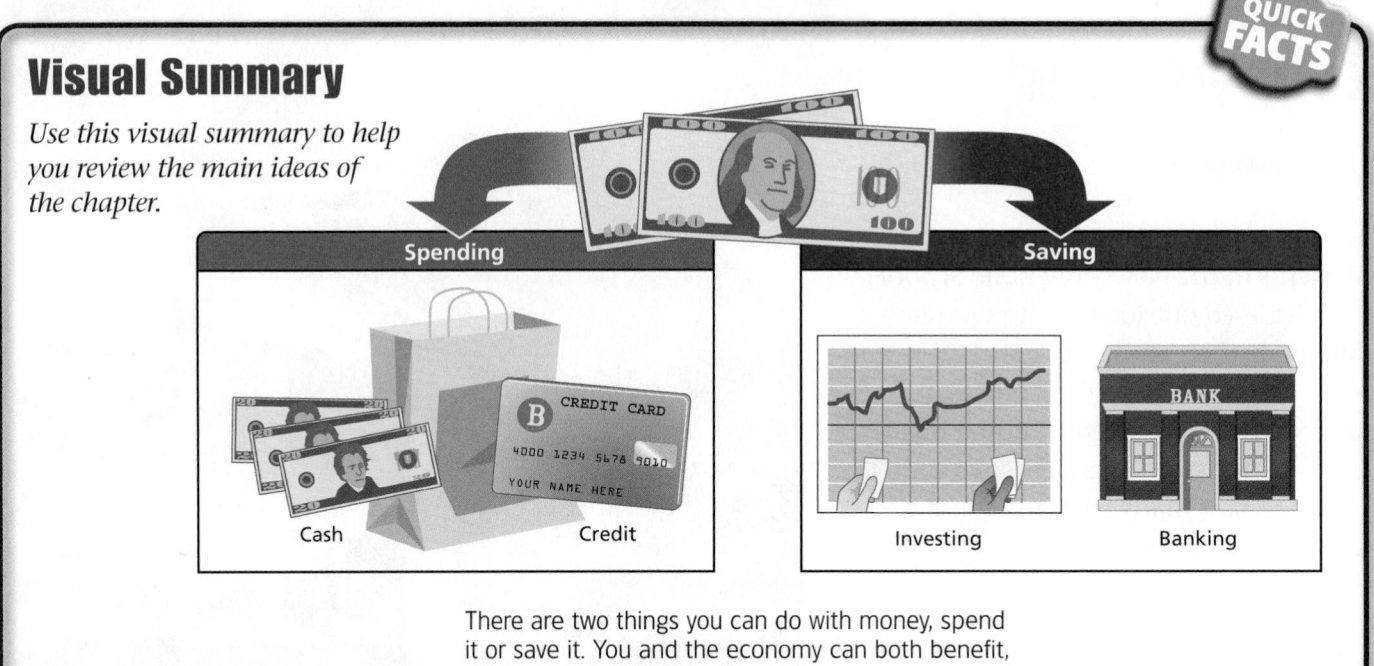

Spending	Saving

Cash   Credit

CREDIT CARD
B
4000 1234 5678 9010
YOUR NAME HERE

Investing   Banking

BANK

There are two things you can do with money, spend it or save it. You and the economy can both benefit, whatever you decide to do.

Reviewing Key Terms

For each term below, write a sentence explaining its significance to personal finances.

1. currency
2. long-term credit
3. short-term credit
4. bankruptcy
5. creditors
6. collateral
7. savings and loan associations
8. credit unions
9. Federal Reserve System
10. discount rate
11. discounting
12. certificates of deposit
13. brokers
14. stock exchange
15. mutual funds
16. money market funds
17. insurance
18. premium
19. private insurance
20. beneficiary
21. social insurance
22. Social Security
23. Medicare
24. Medicaid

Comprehension and Critical Thinking

SECTION 1 *(Pages 504–509)*

25. a. **Recall** Why are checks not considered legal tender, and why do people accept them for payment even though they are not legal tender?

b. **Elaborate** How do charge cards differ from credit cards?

c. **Supporting a Point of View** Periodically in the United States there is debate about abolishing the penny. Do you think the penny should be abolished? How might this affect the economy?

SECTION 2 *(Pages 511–516)*

26. a. **Describe** What are the four main types of financial institutions?

b. **Compare and Contrast** What are the different types of bank accounts? How are they similar and different?

c. **Predict** How might our financial system be different without the Federal Reserve System?

Active Citizenship video program
Review the video to answer the closing question:
In your opinion, is it the government's responsibility to protect citizens from identity theft?

SECTION 3 *(Pages 517–521)*

27 a. Recall How does saving money help the economy grow?

   b. Summarize What different opportunities do people have to save and invest?

   c. Evaluate Do you think Americans should save more money? Give reasons for your answer.

SECTION 4 *(Pages 522–526)*

28. a. Explain What enables insurance companies to stay in business while still charging the premiums that they do?

   b. Compare and Contrast What are the similarities and differences between private insurance and social insurance?

   c. Evaluate In your opinion, should the federal government continue the Social Security system? Why or why not?

Civics Skills

Analyzing TV News *Use the Civics Skills taught in this chapter to answer the questions about the photo below.*

29. What type of news program might this photo show?

30. What clues might indicate if a news story is biased?

Reading Skills

Making and Understanding Charts and Graphs *Use the Reading Skills taught in this chapter to answer the question about the line graph below.*

31. What is the subject of this line graph? What labels does the graph use?

32. What was the per capita debt in 1970? 2000?

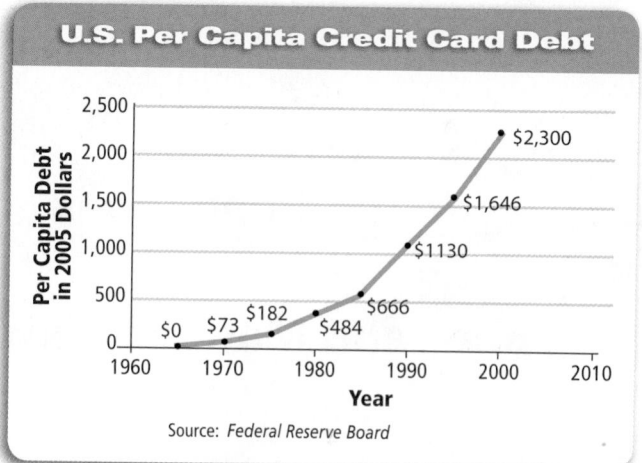

U.S. Per Capita Credit Card Debt

Source: *Federal Reserve Board*

Using the Internet

go.hrw.com
KEYWORD: SZ7 CH19

33. Managing Money Whether you are making it, spending it, or saving it, money is an integral part of life in the United States. Enter the activity keyword. Using the links provided, conduct research on money, loans, and credit. Then create a skit to explain the importance of money, loans, and credit in terms of the national economy. Make sure you use correct terminology and explain the role of money, loans, and credit in your skit.

FOCUS ON WRITING

34. Writing a Letter of Recommendation Review your notes on personal finance. Then write a two- to three-paragraph letter to the bank to which your friend has applied for a job. Explain to the bank why you think it should hire your friend.

ECONOMIC CHALLENGES

NATIONAL STANDARDS®
FOR CIVICS AND GOVERNMENT

I. What are civic life, politics, and government?

B. What are the essential characteristics of limited and unlimited government?

7. What is the relationship of limited government to political and economic freedom?

V. What are the roles of the citizen in American democracy?

C. What are the responsibilities of citizens?

D. What civic dispositions or traits of private and public character are important to the preservation and improvement of American constitutional democracy?

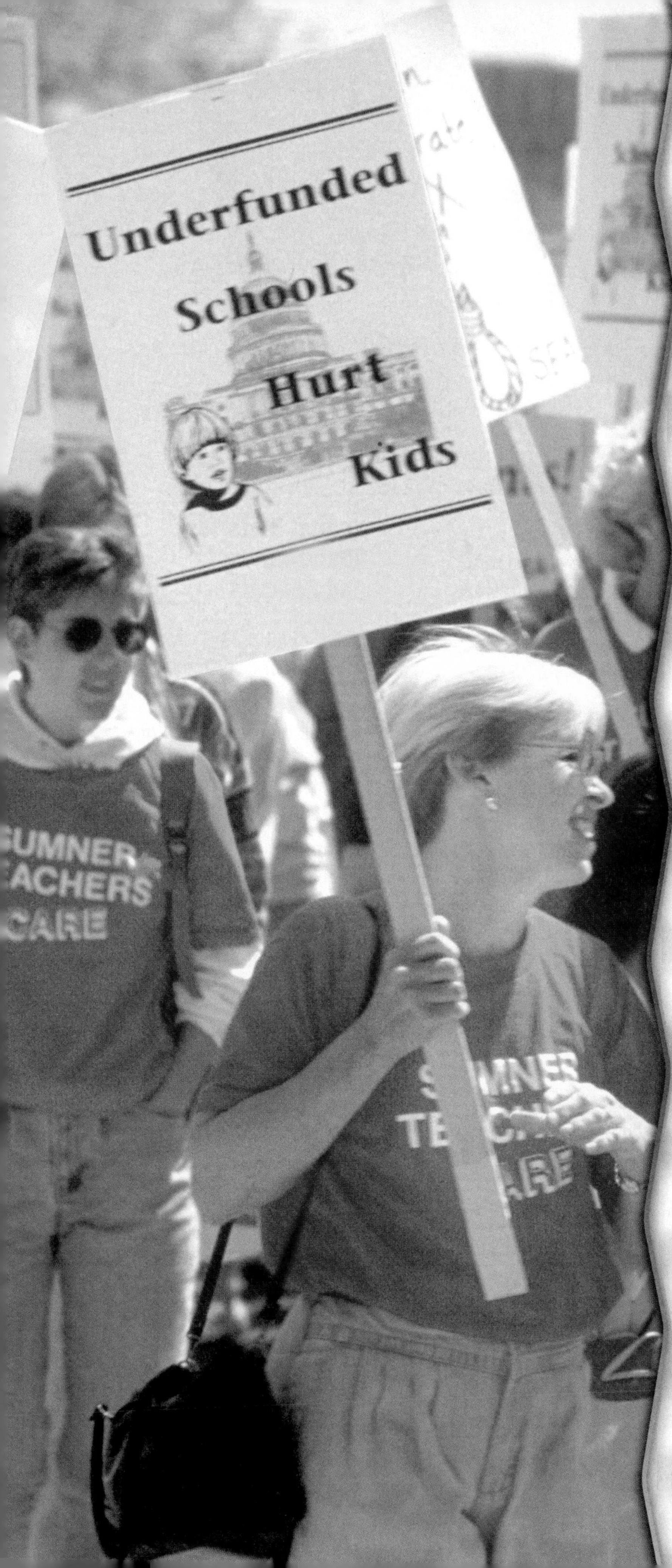

Active Citizenship Video Program

Watch the video to learn how students can organize to protect school resources.

WHY CIVICS Matters

Did you know that you play a role in the U.S. economy? Every time you make a purchase, deposit money in the bank, or perform work, you are contributing to the economy. The economy changes over time. Its ups and downs cause problems that affect all Americans.

 **PROJECT** ★ Citizen

RESTORING SCHOOL RECESS When the school board in Madison, Wisconsin, decided to abolish the morning recess break, students went into action. What would you do if you did not agree with a change in your school's policies?

FOCUS ON WRITING ✏

A MEMO You are a writer at a television network with an idea for a financial news segment. Draft a memo to your boss telling her about your idea. As you read this chapter, gather information about the economic challenges the country has faced in the past and may experience again. Then write your memo about these challenges, how they were met, and how they may be dealt with in the future.

Reading Skills

In this chapter you will read about the business cycle of a free-market economy. You will learn about the Great Depression and how the government became more involved in regulating the country's economy. You will read about the challenges the national economy faces. You will learn about the policies the government uses to respond to those challenges. You will read about the ways workers and employers negotiate with one another.

Conducting Cost-Benefit Analyses

FOCUS ON READING Everything you do has both costs and benefits connected to it. Benefits are things that you gain from something. Costs are what you give up to obtain benefits. The ability to analyze costs and benefits is a valuable life skill for you as a student and as a citizen. Weighing an action's benefits against its costs can help you and society make good decisions.

For example, if you buy a video game, the benefit of your action to you is the enjoyment you get from playing the game. The clearest cost is what you pay for the game. Other costs may not involve money, such as the time you spend playing the game. This time is a cost because you give up something else, such as doing your homework or watching a TV show, when you choose to play the game.

Costs and Benefits Another example is a conflict between business owners and workers. To force business owners to bargain with them, labor unions can decide to strike. In a strike, union members walk off the job. Production stops, and the company loses money. As a worker, you might analyze the decision to strike by comparing the benefits and costs.

Helpful Hints for Analyzing Costs and Benefits

1. First determine what the action or decision is trying to accomplish.

2. Look for the positive or successful results of the action or decision. These are the benefits.

3. Consider the negative or unsuccessful effects of the action or decision. Also think about what positive things would have happened if it had not occurred.

4. Compare the benefits to the costs and evaluate the action.

Benefits of a Strike	Costs of a Strike
• May cause business owners to bargain with workers • Could obtain higher wages and better benefits • Workers feel they have bargaining power	• Workers lose salary while on strike • Production stops and business loses money • Workers could be replaced by new employees and lose their jobs

You Try It!

The following passage is from the chapter you are about to read. Read it and then answer the questions below.

> In 2002 the shippers association started a lockout that kept dockworkers out of 29 West Coast ports for 10 days. When a strike or lockout happens, both sides may suffer. Workers do not get paid, and their companies lose sales. Other people also are hurt by strikes . . . During the shipping lockout, cargo piled up on ships and some manufacturers had to shut down because they could not get raw materials.
>
> *From Chapter 20, p. 547*

After you have read the passage, answer the following questions.

1. Imagine that you are a member of the shipper's association. What might be the benefits to you of shutting down your business and locking workers out?

2. What are the business costs of a long dispute with the workers?

3. Chapter 19 made the following point: *"In a healthy economy when business is doing well, there must be plenty of money available to consumers. Otherwise, the goods being produced cannot be sold. This would slow production. Slowing production could cut into profits and possibly result in layoffs of workers. Free-flowing money in the form of credit makes it possible for consumers to buy whenever there are goods to be sold."* Based on this passage, what are the benefits to the national economy when you borrow money to buy a stereo?

As you read Chapter 20, look for situations in which doing a cost-benefit analysis could help the country make economic decisions.

KEY TERMS

Chapter 20

Section 1

business cycle *(p. 534)*
expansion *(p. 534)*
inflation *(p. 535)*
costs of production *(p. 535)*
peak *(p. 535)*
contraction *(p. 535)*
recession *(p. 535)*
trough *(p. 535)*
depression *(p. 535)*

Section 2

fiscal policy *(p. 541)*
monetary policy *(p. 541)*

Section 3

labor unions *(p. 544)*
collective bargaining *(p. 544)*
strike *(p. 545)*
picketing *(p. 545)*
job action *(p. 545)*
mediation *(p. 547)*
arbitration *(p. 547)*

Academic Vocabulary

Success in school is related to knowing academic vocabulary—the words that are frequently used in school assignments and discussions. In this chapter you will learn the following academic words:

policy *(p. 541)*
contract *(p. 545)*

The Business Cycle

BEFORE YOU READ

The Main Idea

The economy has periods of uneven growth called business cycles. Sometimes the economy grows quickly, but other times it may grow very slowly or even shrink. The worst point in the business cycle in the United States was the Great Depression.

Reading Focus

1. What are the different parts of the business cycle?
2. What was the Great Depression?
3. What was the government's response to the Great Depression?

Key Terms

business cycle, *p. 534*
expansion, *p. 534*
inflation, *p. 535*
costs of production, *p. 535*
peak, *p. 535*
contraction, *p. 535*
recession, *p. 535*
trough, *p. 535*
depression, *p. 535*

TAKING NOTES As you read, take notes on the business cycle, the Great Depression, and the government's response. Use a graphic organizer like this one to record your notes.

The Business Cycle	
Great Depression	
Government's Response	

People who make a living selling stocks and bonds may be greatly affected by changes in the business cycle.

CIVICS IN PRACTICE Do you know anyone who has lost a job in a business downturn? The job market can change quickly, with little warning. When business thrives, factories hire more people. However, when business falters, factories lay off people.

The Business Cycle

This shifting of the economy from good times to bad and then back to good times again is called the **business cycle**. The business cycle is a common feature in free-market economies.

When the economy is booming, the gross domestic product (GDP) increases. As you have learned, the GDP is the total amount of goods and services produced by the country in one year. Such a period of growth is called **expansion** because the economy is growing larger.

The expansion of the economy during a boom period is generally good for the country—most people have jobs and businesses are doing well. However, expansion can also cause economic problems. One problem that often accompanies a boom is inflation.

The Business Cycle

The U.S. economy goes through business cycles of expansion and contraction. As the economy expands, more workers are needed to meet the demand for more goods. When the economy begins to contract, people may lose their jobs because fewer goods are demanded and manufacturers must cut back.

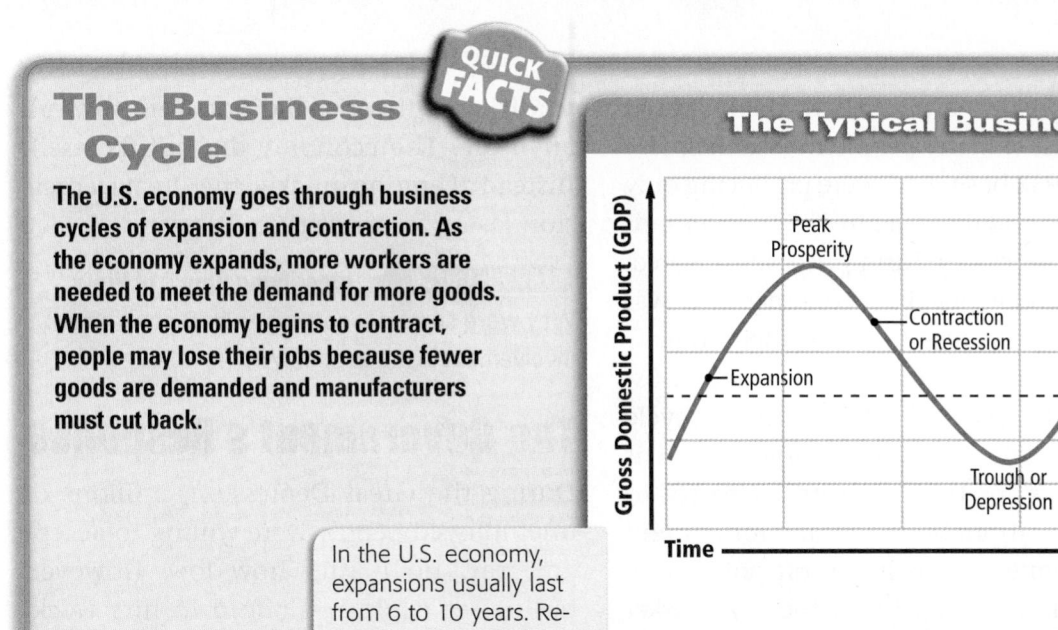

The Typical Business Cycle

In the U.S. economy, expansions usually last from 6 to 10 years. Recessions generally last about six months to two years.

ANALYSIS SKILL **ANALYZING CHARTS**

How does consumer spending affect the business cycle?

Inflation refers to a general increase in the price level of goods and services. During periods of prosperity, people have more income to spend, causing the demand for goods and services to increase. Prices inflate, or rise, as customers compete with each other to buy goods and services. Sometimes, prices rise faster than wages. People have to spend more but do not get more for their money.

The costs of doing business also increase during a period of economic expansion. Increased competition forces businesses to pay higher prices for raw materials and transportation. Because jobs are more plentiful, businesses may also have to increase wages to keep their workers. Wages, payments for raw materials, transportation, rent, and interest on money borrowed are all part of the **costs of production**. When inflation makes these costs rise, businesses may have to increase the prices of their products to make a profit.

At some point, the expansion of the economy and the inflation that goes with it stop. When this happens, the business cycle has reached a **peak**, or high point. After the economy peaks, business activity begins to slow. This economic slowdown is called a **contraction**. If the contraction becomes severe enough, a **recession** may occur. During a recession, businesses fail, people lose their jobs, and profits fall.

When the economy reaches its lowest point, it is said to be in a **trough**. When the trough is particularly low, economists say the economy is in a **depression**. During a depression, unemployment is very high. Unemployed people cannot buy many goods and services, so businesses suffer or close. Usually troughs are not so low as to throw the economy into a depression.

READING CHECK **Sequencing** List the stages of the business cycle in the correct order.

The Great Depression

The worst depression in the country's history took place during the 1930s. This period is known as the Great Depression. The first sign of trouble came in October 1929.

Prices of stocks on the New York Stock Exchange fell sharply. Then many banks failed, causing many people to lose their savings. By 1932 businesses were producing only half as much as they had in 1929. Thousands of businesses closed. Farm prices plummeted. By 1933 about one in four Americans was unemployed. Many people lost their homes.

Before the Great Depression, most economists believed the business cycle should be left alone. They argued that it was unwise for the government to try to control inflation, boost production, or end unemployment. This hands-off philosophy was based on the idea that the free market was self-correcting. Economists believed that the problems that came with the business cycle would solve themselves. If prices rose too high, people would stop buying goods and services until prices fell again.

Many economists also thought that recessions could not last long. Workers who lost their jobs would soon be willing to accept lower wages. Businesses would then be able to hire people for lower pay. Other costs of production would also be lower than before.

Then came the Great Depression. The **traditional** theories did not seem to work anymore. The economy did not fix itself. Instead of ending quickly, the Great Depression lasted for more than 10 years.

READING CHECK **Identifying Points of View** Why were some economists against government involvement in the economy?

The Government's Response

During the Great Depression, millions of unemployed people were willing to accept any pay, no matter how low. However, businesses could not afford to hire workers, even at low wages.

Those businesses that did survive during the Depression did not expand. After all, there was no point in producing more goods when few people had enough money to buy them.

Finally, many people were willing to allow the government to take steps to improve the economy. President Franklin D. Roosevelt established a program called the New Deal that included many approaches to improving the economy.

The Great Depression

During the Great Depression of the 1930s, many people lost their jobs and their homes because they could not pay their mortgages. Some lived in shanty towns called Hoovervilles, such as the one shown here. Hoovervilles were named after President Hoover, who was blamed for the Depression.

In what ways do you think life changed for people who lost their jobs, savings, and homes?

One approach was to have the government create more jobs. Many people were hired to do civic construction projects, such as building parks and schools.

The government created the Federal Deposit Insurance Corporation (FDIC) to insure bank deposits and increase people's confidence in the banking system. The Securities and Exchange Commission (SEC) was established to oversee the buying and selling of stocks and bonds. The goal of the SEC was to prevent the stock market fraud that had contributed to the depression.

Another important part of the New Deal program was the creation of the Social Security system. This system was established to give regular payments to retired citizens and to help others in need. Unemployment compensation was created to provide workers with some money when they had lost their jobs.

READING CHECK ▶ **Finding the Main Idea** Why did many Americans begin to support government intervention in the economy?

PRIMARY SOURCE

POLITICAL CARTOON
WPA and the New Deal

The New Deal was a variety of different programs designed to end the Great Depression and strengthen the U.S. economy. The Works Project Administration (WPA) was a "make work" program that provided jobs to unemployed Americans during the Depression.

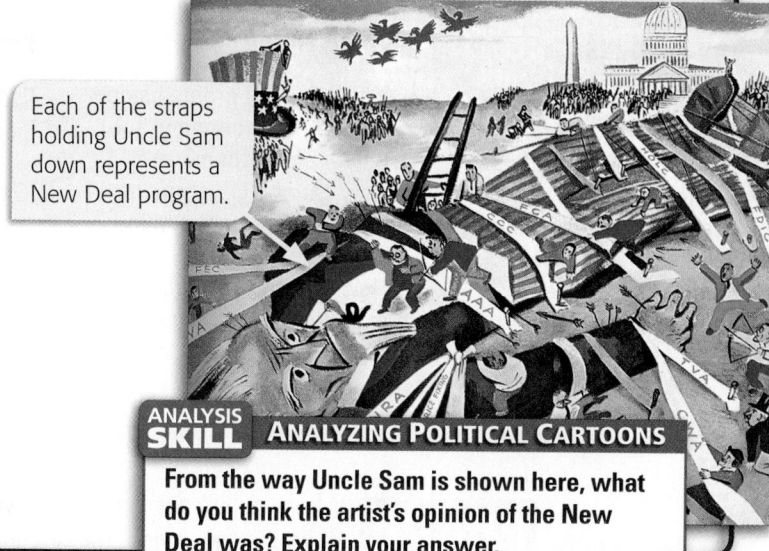

Each of the straps holding Uncle Sam down represents a New Deal program.

ANALYSIS SKILL **ANALYZING POLITICAL CARTOONS**

From the way Uncle Sam is shown here, what do you think the artist's opinion of the New Deal was? Explain your answer.

go.hrw.com
Online Quiz
KEYWORD: SZ7 HP20

SECTION 1 ASSESSMENT

Reviewing Ideas and Terms

1. a. Define Write a brief definition for the terms **business cycle**, **expansion**, **inflation**, **costs of production**, **peak**, **contraction**, **recession**, **trough**, and **depression**.

   b. Draw Conclusions What are the economic effects of a recession?

2. a. Recall What were some of the problems businesses faced during the Great Depression?

   b. Draw Conclusions Why did the Great Depression cause economists to rethink their theories about the business cycle?

3. a. Summarize What changes did the government make to try to improve the economy during the Great Depression?

   b. Make Evaluations Are government agencies like the FDIC and the SEC still needed today? Why or why not?

Critical Thinking

4. Summarize Use your notes and a chart like the one here to identify the programs created by the New Deal and explain how they addressed economic problems.

The New Deal	
Problem	Solution
bank problems	
stock market fraud	
unemployment	
economic hardship	

Focus on Writing

5. Contrasting Write a paragraph explaining how contractions, recessions, and depressions are different.

SECTION 2

Coping with Economic Challenges

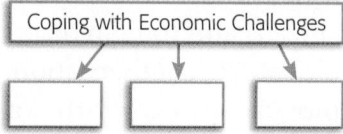
 When you are not feeling well, you go to a doctor. When the economy is unhealthy, the government and the Federal Reserve make changes to control inflation and unemployment. Balance is the goal. The ups and downs of the business cycle are normal, but an economic depression is not.

Causes of Economic Problems

During times of economic growth, the economy often experiences inflation. Inflation harms workers whose wages are not rising as fast as the inflation rate. Even though workers may have the same wages, they cannot buy as much with their money. As a result, their standard of living goes down.

On the other hand, an economy that is not growing supports fewer jobs and leads to higher unemployment. Unemployment grows during periods of recession. Because businesses are producing less, they need fewer workers.

Unemployment hurts the individual unemployed workers and also harms the overall economy. Unemployed workers cannot pay bills or taxes. They buy fewer goods and services, which hurts American businesses. Sometimes unemployed people must seek government assistance, which costs taxpayers money.

As you can see, inflation, unemployment, and recession pose serious challenges for the economy. What contributes to these economic difficulties? Economists point to many different reasons, including the money supply, government spending, and productivity.

The Money Supply

One major cause of inflation is having too much money in circulation. As people spend this additional money, they cause prices to rise. As a result, the Federal Reserve tries to control the amount of money circulating in the U.S. economy.

Inflation may also be caused when financial institutions make too many loans.

Teens and Minimum Wage

Do you have a plan to get an after-school job? How much do you hope to earn? Years ago, some employers took advantage of young workers. They paid them extremely low wages for working long hours at sometimes dangerous jobs. Today, even teenagers working their first job are guaranteed a minimum wage.

Why it Matters The first national minimum wage of 25 cents per hour was created in 1938 by the Fair Labor Standards Act. The law also said that workers who worked more than 44 hours per week had to be paid at a higher rate for the extra time. Today, many workers who work more than 40 hours per week are paid an "overtime" rate.

Since 1938 Congress has increased the minimum wage many times. The minimum wage has been $5.15 per hour since 1997. There are some exceptions, however. For example, workers who rely heavily on tips, such as waiters, can be paid a lower hourly rate. For workers under 20, the minimum wage is $4.25 per hour during their first 90 days of employment.

Most teens' first jobs, such as working at a mall store, will pay minimum wage.

ANALYSIS SKILL **EVALUATING THE LAW**

go.hrw.com
KEYWORD: SZ7 CH20

1. Do you think the current minimum wage is fair? Why or why not?
2. Why do you think that people under the age of 20 may be paid less than the minimum wage for a short time?

People and businesses who borrow money then spend that money on goods and services. Thus, loaning money is the same as putting more money into the economy, contributing to inflation. Businesses that borrow and expand too rapidly may produce more goods than they can sell. These businesses must then slow their production, which contributes to economic recession.

Government Spending

The government spends many billions of dollars each year. Much of the money spent by the government comes from taxes paid by individuals and business firms. The government also borrows some of the money it spends. Government borrowing and spending may contribute to inflation because it puts more money into the economy.

Productivity

The amount that a worker produces per hour is called productivity. Rising productivity usually leads to higher wages, higher profits, and lower prices. However, in recent years worker productivity in the United States has lagged behind that of some other countries. This makes many foreign products less expensive than American-made goods.

READING CHECK **Finding the Main Idea** What are the most serious challenges to the economy?

Government Response to the Business Cycle

QUICK FACTS

By using fiscal and monetary policy, the government can influence fluctuations in the business cycle to soften the impact on the American public.

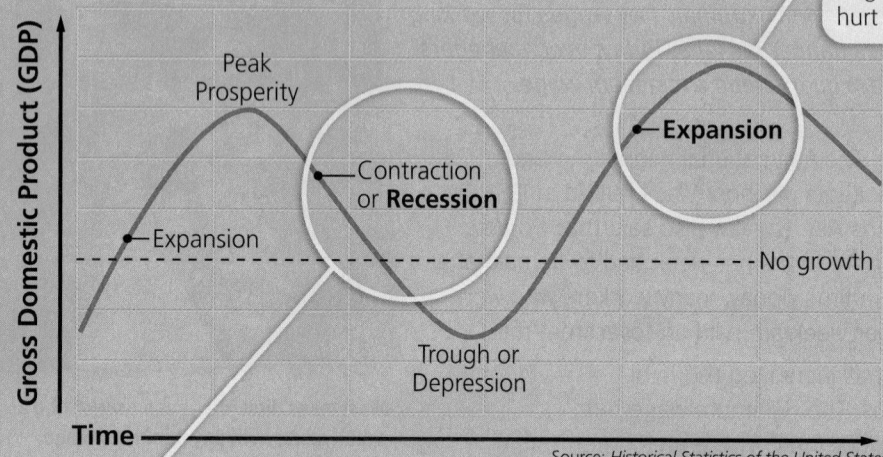

The Typical Business Cycle

During economic **expansion**, inflation—the rise in the price of goods and services—can hurt consumers.

Gross Domestic Product (GDP)

Peak Prosperity

Expansion

Contraction or **Recession**

Expansion

No growth

Trough or Depression

Time

Source: *Historical Statistics of the United States*

During a **recession** or contraction, business activity slows. Businesses may fail, people lose jobs, and profits fall.

Fiscal Policy

Fiscal policy is how the government collects and spends its money. Fiscal policy is decided by the president and Congress.

Recession Government fiscal policy may include reducing taxes and increasing government spending. Either step will put more money into the economy and promote economic expansion.

Expansion To slow inflation and to prolong expansion, government fiscal policy might include tax increases and spending cuts.

Monetary Policy

The Federal Reserve System (the Fed) uses monetary policy to influence financial conditions in the economy. The Fed's main tool is its control of short-term interest rates.

Recession The Federal Reserve may reduce interest rates so that people and businesses would borrow and spend more money.

Expansion The Federal Reserve can raise interest rates. When interest rates rise, people borrow less and spend less, thus slowing economic expansion.

ANALYSIS SKILL **INTERPRETING CHARTS**

What actions would you recommend to the president and the Fed to try to move the economy from a recession into a period of growth?

Government's Response to Economic Problems

The government can respond to challenges facing the U.S. economy in a number of ways. The federal government can change its **fiscal policy**, or its <u>policy</u> of taxing and spending, to aid the ailing economy.

If the economy is entering a recession, the government may reduce the amount of taxes that individuals pay and also may increase its own spending. In response to the deep recession the country entered in 2008, President Barack Obama passed a huge stimulus bill that attempted to do both. The bill cut taxes for the middle class. It also invested billions of dollars in the nation's infrastructure, including health care, education, and energy programs. The bill was designed to create new jobs—both in government and in the private sector—and relieve those most affected by the recession.

During a recession, the economy may also be aided by changes in **monetary policy**, or a change in the money supply. The Federal Reserve System (the Fed) is the country's central bank and works to control the amount of money in the economy.

In a recession, the Fed may increase the money supply by buying government bonds back from banks or lowering the reserve requirements for member banks. It may also invest money in the banks to aid the flow of credit to consumers. If inflation becomes too high, the Fed may take money out of the economy by raising interest rates or the reserve requirement.

> **READING CHECK** **Analyzing Information** How might the government respond to a recession?

ACADEMIC VOCABULARY
policy: rule, course of action

Other Ways to Help the Economy

Fiscal and monetary policies do not always ensure a healthy economy. What more can be done to improve the economy?

Reduce Government Spending The government can reduce wasteful spending and halt unnecessary government programs.

Increase Saving Consumers can help the economy by reducing their spending and saving more of their income.

Buy American-Made Products When consumers buy products made in the United States, they help American businesses.

Increase Productivity Business managers and workers can try to improve their efficiency.

> **READING CHECK** **Summarizing** How can consumers help to improve the economy?

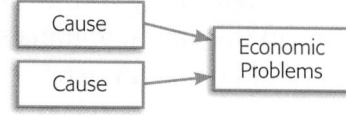

SECTION 2 ASSESSMENT

Reviewing Ideas and Terms

1. a. Recall What are some problems that have a negative impact on the economy?

  b. Compare and Contrast How can government and consumer spending affect the economy?

2. a. Define Write a brief definition for the terms **fiscal policy** and **monetary policy**.

  b. Explain How does the federal government try to solve economic problems?

3. a. Summarize What are some ways that the government can reduce spending?

Critical Thinking

4. Identifying Causes Use your notes and a diagram like this one to identify the causes of economic problems.

Cause	
Cause	→ Economic Problems

Focus on Writing

5. Support a Point of View Do you think Americans should buy only American-made products? Explain your answer.

Analyzing Line Graphs

Learn

Line graphs visually represent the relationship between two variables. For instance, a line graph could represent the connection between percentage of employees in a union and hourly wages. In a line graph, the areas between known data points are connected, so it is possible to determine patterns. If the graph shows a clear pattern, it may even be possible to draw a conclusion about data not shown on the graph.

Practice

❶ Find out the two variables. You can use the labeling on the x-axis and the y-axis to determine the two variables. Be sure to check the units used. In the line graph "Retail Gasoline Prices" the unit for price is U.S. dollars. If time is one of the variables shown on a line graph, it is usually on the horizontal axis, or the x-axis. The variable that changes over time would then be shown on the y-axis.

❷ Determine the trends shown in the graph. Is there a clear correlation between the two variables? You can try to figure out how one variable affects the other, and also why there may be parts of the graph that do not follow the same trend.

❸ Decide whether you can extrapolate based on the graph. If there is a clear pattern in the graph, you can infer what would happen outside of the data shown in the graph. However, if there is no pattern in the graph, you may not be able to predict what would happen next.

Apply

Use the line graph titled "Retail Gasoline Prices" to answer the following questions:

1. What was the average price per gallon of gasoline in 2005?

2. Based on this graph, what trend in the price of gasoline can you detect?

3. Considering the economic challenges the country faced in 2008, how might the price of gas have affected many American consumers?

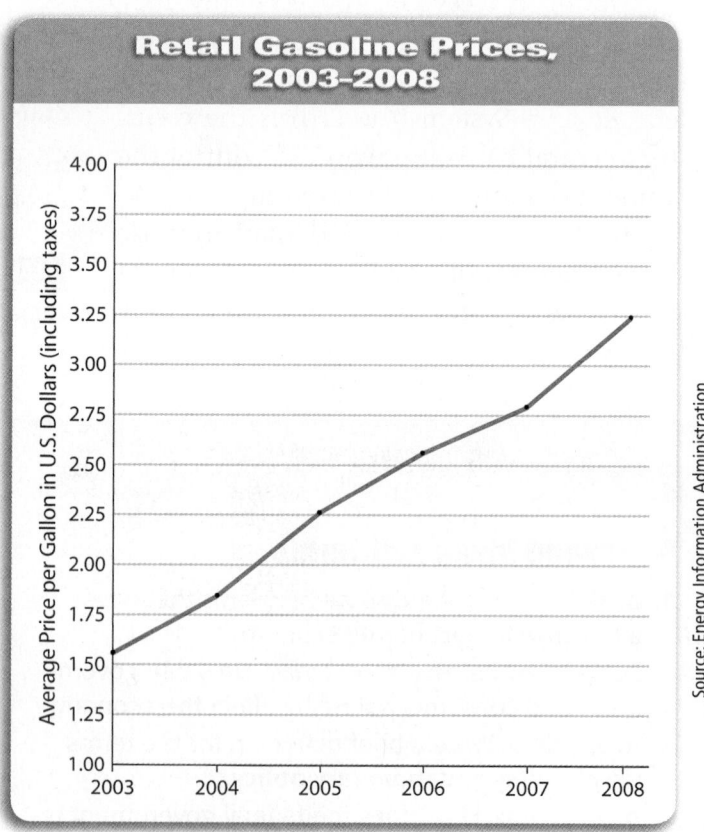

Retail Gasoline Prices, 2003–2008

Source: Energy Information Administration

Labor and Management

BEFORE YOU READ

The Main Idea

Workers formed labor unions to force employers to improve working conditions and wages. Businesses and unions have had conflicts over the years, so the federal government passed laws dealing with labor relations.

Reading Focus

1. What led to the rise of factories in the 1800s?
2. What are labor unions?
3. What laws have been passed to ease relations between labor and management?
4. What is the status of labor unions and labor relations today?

Key Terms

labor unions, *p. 544*
collective bargaining, *p. 544*
strike, *p. 545*
picketing, *p. 545*
job action, *p. 545*
mediation, *p. 547*
arbitration, *p. 547*

 **TAKING NOTES** As you read, take notes on the origins of factories, the rise of labor unions, labor laws, and labor today. Use a diagram like this one to organize your notes.

Labor and Management

In the early 1900s, boys as young as 8 years old worked underground in coal mines.

 **CIVICS IN PRACTICE** As an employee, you want the best wages for your labor. As an employer, you want to control costs. One of your costs will be the cost of employee wages. How can labor and management both get what they want?

The Rise of Factories

In the early days of the United States, many Americans worked for themselves on small farms or in their own workshops or stores. With the start of the Industrial Revolution between about 1790 and 1850, however, work began to change. Inventors created machines to manufacture a range of products faster and more cheaply than they could be made by hand. This machinery quickly grew too large to fit inside a home or workshop. As a result, business owners built large factories to house their machinery and workers.

Now instead of working for themselves, thousands of workers took factory jobs for wages. Factory owners often hired hundreds of workers, including men, women, and many young children. Often, entire families worked in the factories.

Conditions in these early factories were often very difficult. The workweek typically lasted six days. The working day was also longer than we are used to, ranging from 12 to as many as 16 hours long. For greater efficiency, jobs were broken down into many small tasks. Workers performed the same routine task over and over throughout the day. This type of work was a great contrast to craftwork done at home or in small shops, where one person might work on an item from start to finish.

In addition, because there were no safety laws, many factories were dangerous places. Early machinery ran using exposed belts and gears that could catch hair or loose clothing. Serious injuries and deaths were common. Dust often filled the air and damaged workers' lungs. Many factories had poor lighting, heating, and cooling. If workers were hurt on the job or got sick, they had no insurance or sick days. Workers' wages were typically low, so saving money was difficult.

READING CHECK ▶ **Contrasting** How was factory work different from the work done by many Americans before the Industrial Revolution?

The Rise of Labor Unions

As American industry expanded, growing numbers of workers became dissatisfied with their labor conditions. Men and women began to organize into groups to demand better conditions from their employers. These organizations of workers became known as **labor unions**.

Collective Bargaining

Typical labor union demands included better wages, safer working conditions, and shorter workdays. To achieve these goals, union leaders needed the right to bargain with employers.

This form of negotiation between labor and management is called **collective bargaining**. Under collective bargaining, representatives from a labor union meet with representatives of an employer. Each side argues for the changes it wants or does not want. Usually some sort of compromise is necessary. For example, employers may argue that meeting union wage demands will harm the company's profits. Union leaders might agree to a lower wage increase if some pieces of old and dangerous equipment are replaced.

TIME LINE

QUICK FACTS

The Labor Movement

In 1850, most people worked at home or in small shops. Then, the Industrial Revolution began in the mid-1800s, and people began to work in factories.

On March 25, 1911, the Triangle Shirtwaist factory fire killed 146 workers in New York City.

1850

1894

1903

1911

On May 11, 1894, Pullman workers went on strike in Chicago.

In July 1903, Mother Jones led a protest march to draw attention to child labor.

When an agreement is reached, its terms are put into a written <u>contract</u>. The employer and the officers of the union sign this labor contract. Most contracts expire after a certain time period. Then the process of collective bargaining begins all over again.

Methods Used by Labor

Collective bargaining only works if both sides are willing to sit down and talk to each other. When employers refused to recognize or deal with unions, labor leaders often responded with a **strike**. In a strike, union members walk off the job if employers do not agree to labor's demands.

If a company tries to hire other workers during a strike, the strikers try to prevent this by **picketing**. Picketing strikers walk back and forth, often carrying signs, in front of company buildings. They discourage other workers from entering and taking over their jobs.

A later variation on the traditional strike was the sit-down strike. In a sit-down strike workers actually occupy the factory in which they work. This prevents the company from bringing in replacement workers and can cost employers a great deal of money. How-

ever, the strikers can be charged with trespassing on company property. Instead of striking, workers sometimes stay on the job but work much more slowly than usual. This union action is called a slowdown. Any kind of slowdown, or action short of a strike, is called a **job action**.

Methods Used by Employers

Business owners often viewed union workers as troublemakers. To fight the unions, employers sometimes locked workers out so they could not work. Employers also sent lists of names of workers who were active in the unions to other companies and asked them not to hire anyone named on the list.

In addition, business owners often hired armed guards to protect their property from striking workers. Sometimes these company men attacked union members. Also, in several major strikes, employers asked government officials for help. In some cases, the government ordered strikers back to work and used police and state militias to end the strikes.

> **READING CHECK** **Summarizing** Why did labor unions develop, and what methods have they used?

ACADEMIC
VOCABULARY
contract:
a binding legal
agreement

In 2005 one-third of the AFL-CIO membership left the organization to form a new group.

1955	1962
In 1955 the AFL, which was formed in 1886, merged with the CIO, which had been formed in 1935.	César Chávez formed the National Farm Workers Association in 1962.

ANALYSIS SKILL **READING TIME LINES**

Evaluating As the number of U.S. manufacturing jobs declines, do you think that labor unions still serve a purpose?

FOCUS ON
César Chávez
(1927-1993)

César Chávez was born in Arizona, but he lived in dozens of towns as his family moved in search of farm work. His early experiences led him to help form unions for migrant workers. Chávez viewed union work as a part of a larger fight for human rights—a goal he called *La Causa*, or "The Cause." His successes included the formation of the United Farm Workers and a nationally publicized hunger strike against grape growers that led to a better labor contract for farmworkers.

Chávez's patience and dedication to the cause of human rights inspired many people and won him many supporters. He helped make migrant farmworkers' rights a national issue. Before his death in 1993, Chávez insisted, "It's not me who counts, it's the movement."

Elaborate How did Chávez's youth influence his goals in *La Causa* later in his life?

Labor Laws

In the late 1800s conflicts between labor and management grew more violent. National strikes in the coal, railroad, and steel industries threatened the country's economy. These problems worried political leaders, who then attempted to bring labor and employers together. In 1902, President Theodore Roosevelt even helped end a national coal strike, marking the first time a president had supported labor unions.

Congress Acts

Few gains were made on a national level, however, until the Great Depression. With the economy struggling, millions of people out of work, and the public demanding answers, Congress passed a number of labor laws. These and later laws regulate union organizing, labor negotiations, and strikes. One reason for these laws is to protect the public from violence between unions and management. They also reduce the likelihood of strikes in industries vital to the national economy.

Congress also has passed several laws to prevent employers from using unfair practices in dealing with workers and to make unions act fairly in their disputes with employers. Congress has tried to stop dishonest actions by some union leaders and to ensure that unions are run democratically.

National Labor Relations Act

The National Labor Relations Act (NLRA), sometimes called the Wagner Act, was passed by Congress in 1935. It guarantees the right of workers to organize and bargain collectively through representatives. The law also provides specific ways of settling disputes between labor unions and employers.

In addition, this act set up an independent government agency, the National Labor Relations Board (NLRB). The board judges the fairness of the activities of unions and employers toward each other.

Labor-Management Relations Act

The Labor-Management Relations Act, often referred to as the Taft-Hartley Act, was passed in 1947. It served to revise the Wagner Act in several ways. The Taft-Hartley Act allows the president to order any union to delay a strike for 80 days if such a strike would threaten the national welfare. During this "cooling-off" period, a fact-finding commission may meet and recommend a settlement. At the end of the 80 days, the union may go ahead with its strike if no settlement is reached.

Landrum-Griffin Act

The Landrum-Griffin Act was passed in 1959 to prevent certain abuses by union officials. It prohibits convicted criminals from serving as union officials for a period of five years after being released from prison. In addition, the law requires unions to file reports of their finances with the secretary of labor each year. Finally, it guarantees union members the right to a secret ballot in union elections and to freedom of speech in meetings.

READING CHECK **Summarizing** What do the major pieces of labor legislation provide?

Labor Today

Today violent conflicts between unions and employers are rare in the United States. Many Americans, including union members, enjoy much better working conditions than they did in the past. Still, there are disputes between unions and employers. Major issues of concern include employer-provided health insurance, retirement plans, and preserving jobs in the United States.

Settling Disputes

Unions and employers today generally prefer to settle their differences through collective bargaining, with representatives of the two sides negotiating directly. However, if they are unable to reach an agreement, they may call for help.

For example, the National Hockey League went on strike during the 2004–05 season. In 2002 the shippers association started a lockout that kept dockworkers out of 29 West Coast ports for 10 days. When a strike or lockout happens, both sides may suffer. Workers do not get paid, and their companies lose sales. Other people also are hurt by strikes. For example, during the season-long hockey strike, small businesses located near the hockey arenas lost business. During the shipping lockout, cargo piled up on ships and some manufacturers had to shut down because they could not get raw materials. Some economists estimated that the U.S. economy lost about one billion dollars a day from this dispute.

Sometimes, to resolve a dispute, an expert on relations between labor and management may be asked to examine the issue and recommend a solution. This method is called **mediation**. The recommendations of the mediator are not legally binding on either the union or the employer. They are simply suggestions for a solution to the issues at hand.

Sometimes another method, called **arbitration**, is used instead. In these cases the decision of the expert arbitrator is binding on both sides.

Linking to Today

Craft Unions

Unions have been a part of U.S. labor history since colonial times. As emigrants from Europe established businesses, they brought with them centuries' worth of experience with craft guilds. These associations were made up of three levels of workers: apprentices, journeymen, and masters. It could take years for an apprentice to train to be a journeyman, and many more years to become a master. But these strict training guidelines helped guilds maintain high workmanship standards—and sometimes a monopoly. Early Americans used this approach to start local craft unions.

The spike in manufacturing in the mid-1800s and then the early 1900s changed the outlook for unions. Many local craft unions were absorbed into national industrial unions, which accepted skilled and unskilled workers as members. However, several craft-based unions still exist today. Many of these groups, such as those for plumbers and carpenters, continue to follow the apprentice–journeyman–master training approach.

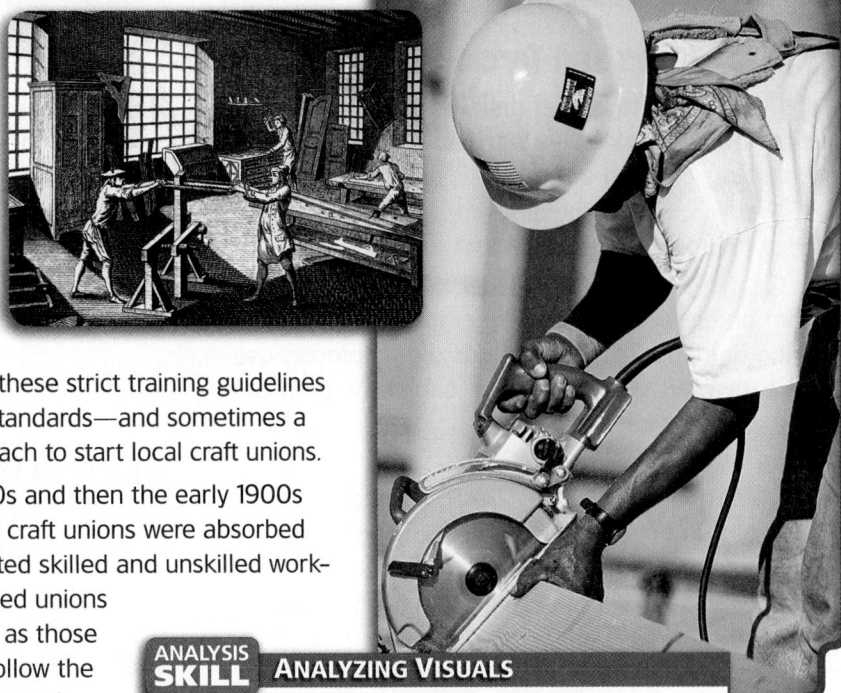

ANALYSIS SKILL **ANALYZING VISUALS**

Drawing Conclusions How would the appeal of a craft union differ from that of a larger industrial union?

Labor Struggles

In recent years labor unions have struggled. One problem has been the gradual loss of American manufacturing jobs to overseas competition. These jobs formed the core of the union movement. In addition, many states have right to work laws that ban the closed shop. A closed shop is a workplace where all employees are required to belong to a union.

The right to work is a legal principle that means that all employees who are qualified for their job are entitled to work at unionized workplaces, whether they join the union or not. Right to work does not mean that every person is entitled to a job.

Labor leaders have been divided on how to rebuild union strength. Some union officials want to put union money into political campaigns, typically supporting Democrats. They hope to influence labor laws by helping elect supportive congressional and presidential candidates. However, many other union members disagree with this approach.

In 2005 conflict among labor leaders led to a split in the nation's largest association of unions, the AFL-CIO. Five unions representing more than one-third of the AFL-CIO's membership broke away and banded together in a new coalition called the Change to Win Federation. Its leaders claimed that many AFL-CIO policies had weakened the labor movement in the United States and led to reduced union membership. They also believed that AFL-CIO leaders spent too much time dealing with politics and too little trying to improve the lives of workers.

The effects of the split in the labor movement remain to be seen. Some feel that conflict between groups will lead to dissatisfaction and a further decline in union membership. Others, however, believe that the existence of a new large labor organization will re-energize the movement and lead to major improvements for American workers.

READING CHECK **Finding the Main Idea** How are most labor disputes settled today?

go.hrw.com
Online Quiz
KEYWORD: SZ7 HP20

SECTION 3 ASSESSMENT

Reviewing Ideas and Terms

1. **a. Define** Write a brief definition for the terms **labor unions, collective bargaining, strike, picketing,** and **job action**.
   b. Summarize Why did American workers form labor unions during the 1800s?
   c. Compare and Contrast What methods do labor unions use to persuade employers to agree to union demands? What methods did employers use in the early years of labor unions to fight the unions?
2. **a. Explain** What is the purpose of the Labor-Management Relations Act?
   b. Defend a Point of View Should the government get involved in disputes between labor and management? Why or why not?
3. **a. Define** Write a brief definition for the terms **mediation** and **arbitration**.
   b. Predict Which method of increasing union influence do you think will have the most success? Can either option work? Explain your answer.

Critical Thinking

4. **Contrasting** Use your notes and a chart like this one to identify the different methods used by labor and employers in collective bargaining.

Labor's Methods	Employer's Methods

Focus on Writing

5. **Decision Making** Imagine that you head the nurses' union in a large hospital. You and the other nurses are unhappy with the level of your pay. How do you think the union should address its problems with its employer?

STUDENTS TAKE ACTION

Restoring School Recess

Traditionally, students in Madison, Wisconsin, had two recess periods. Then in order to save money—about $650,000 per year—the Madison Metropolitan School District decided to replace morning recess with a shorter indoor break. The school board did not anticipate students' reactions, however.

Community Connection At one of the schools in the district, a Project Citizen class of 36 students believed that the lack of exercise during the morning made students restless before lunchtime. Some parents and teachers agreed. In order to get recess restored, however, the students needed to convince the school board to change its policy, without losing money.

Taking Action The students contacted members of the media, and several newspapers and television stations came out in favor of the "Recess Rebels." The students also created a public service announcement for radio and put up posters in the community. They surveyed school and community members about the recess cut and graphed the results. After the students appealed to the school board and state officials, the board decided to let the teachers' union vote on the issue. Partly because of the disruption the change would have caused in the middle of the school year, most teachers voted against it. Despite this setback, the students realized that they could make a difference and decided to continue their campaign. One student said, "Before … I thought a citizen was someone who flew a flag and voted. I now know that I am a citizen and I have a voice."

Students can have a voice and take action to try to change school policies.

go.hrw.com
Project Citizen
KEYWORD: SZ7 CH20

SERVICE LEARNING

1. How did the students go about getting support for their campaign? Were they successful?
2. What do you think the students might do differently next time?

Visual Summary

QUICK FACTS

Use this visual summary to help you review the main ideas of the chapter.

The U.S. economy goes through cycles. The government has tools to respond to or make changes in the economy. Decisions by labor and management can also have an effect on the economy.

Fiscal and Monetary Policy

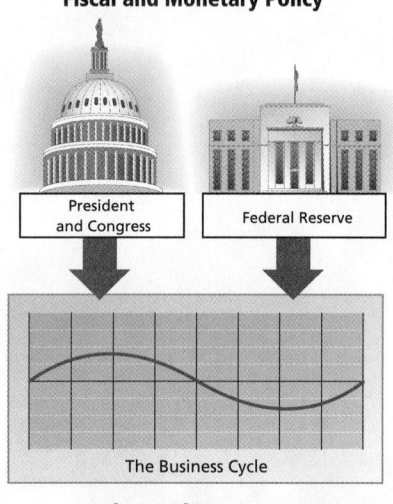

President and Congress

Federal Reserve

The Business Cycle

Labor and Management

BETTER WORKING CONDITIONS!

HEALTH CARE!

FAIR WAGES!

Reviewing Key Terms

For each term below, write a sentence explaining its significance to facing economic challenges.

1. business cycle
2. expansion
3. inflation
4. costs of production
5. peak
6. contraction
7. recession
8. trough
9. depression
10. fiscal policy
11. monetary policy
12. labor unions
13. collective bargaining
14. strike
15. picketing
16. job action
17. mediation
18. arbitration

Comprehension and Critical Thinking

SECTION 1 *(Pages 534–537)*

19. **a. Recall** What is the business cycle?

   b. Describe What was government's response to the Great Depression?

   c. Elaborate How did the government's role in the economy change during the Great Depression?

SECTION 2 *(Pages 538–541)*

20. **a. Explain** What is the difference between fiscal policy and monetary policy?

   b. Describe What measures does the Federal Reserve take to control the amount of money in the economy, and why does it do so?

   c. Evaluate How important are the actions of consumers in affecting the economy? Explain your answer.

SECTION 3 *(Pages 543–548)*

21. **a. Recall** What first caused workers in the United States to form labor unions?

   b. Describe What methods do unions and employers use to try to achieve their goals?

   c. Evaluate Why is it important for workers and management to compromise?

Using the Internet

go.hrw.com
KEYWORD: SZ7 CH20

22. **Contributing to the Economy** Citizens play an important role in developing and maintaining a healthy economic climate in the country. Enter the activity keyword and explore some of the ways you can contribute to working toward a healthy economy. Then make up a crossword puzzle and answer key using economic terms that are important for students to know.

Active Citizenship video program
Review the video to answer the closing question:
What are some creative ways you can make your voice heard in the school community?

Civics Skills

Line Graphs *Use the Civics Skills taught in this chapter to answer the question about the line graph below.*

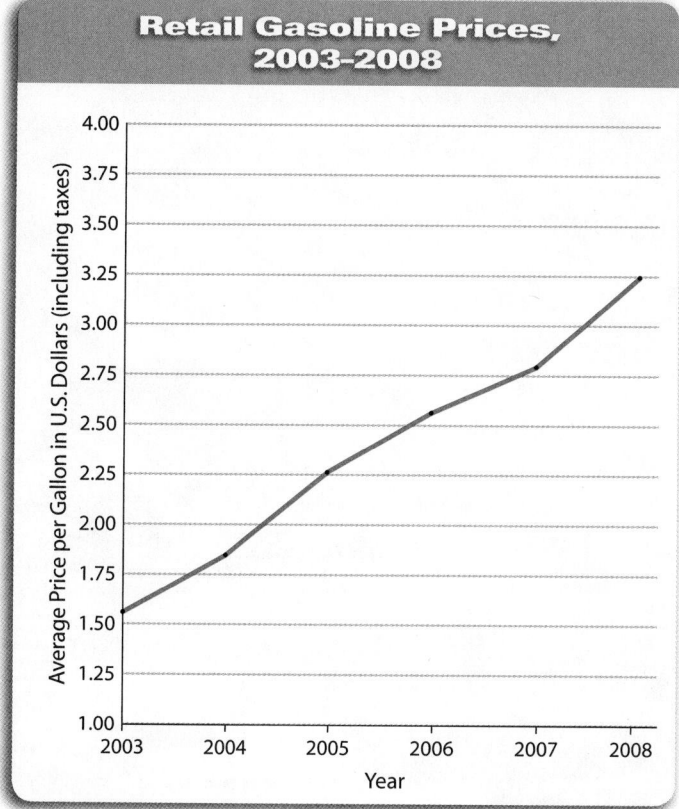

Retail Gasoline Prices, 2003–2008

Average Price per Gallon in U.S. Dollars (including taxes)

Year

Source: Energy Information Administration

23. During which year was the price of gasoline highest?

a. 2007

b. 2006

c. 2008

d. 2003

24. Between which years did the price of gasoline rise most sharply?

a. 2007–2008

b. 2003–2004

c. 2005–2006

d. 2004–2005

Reading Skills

Conducting Cost–Benefit Analyses *Use the Reading Skills taught in this chapter to answer the question about the reading selection below.*

In 2002 the shippers association started a lockout that kept dockworkers out of 29 West Coast ports for 10 days. When a strike or lockout happens, both sides may suffer. Workers do not get paid, and their companies lose sales. Other people also are hurt by strikes . . . During the shipping lockout, cargo piled up on ships and some manufacturers had to shut down because they could not get raw materials. *(p. 549)*

25. Food products, electronic goods, and toys are often delivered by ships. Knowing this, predict how the lockout might have been harmful to U.S. consumers in general.

FOCUS ON WRITING

26. Writing Your Memo Look back over your notes about economic challenges the country has experienced and what was done to solve the problems. Decide which of these problems you will include in your first financial news segment. Then draft a one- to two-paragraph memo to your boss briefly describing the segment. Remember to explain the problem and show how it was solved.

CHAPTER 21

THE U.S. ECONOMY AND THE WORLD

NATIONAL STANDARDS®
FOR CIVICS AND GOVERNMENT

III. How does the government established by the Constitution embody the purposes, values, and principles of American democracy?

A. How are power and responsibility distributed, shared, and limited in the government established by the United States Constitution?

IV. What is the relationship of the United States to other nations and to world affairs?

B. How do the domestic politics and constitutional principles of the United States affect its relations with the world?

C. How has the United States influenced other nations, and how have other nations influenced American politics and society?

©1994, 2003 Center for Civic Education. All Rights Reserved.

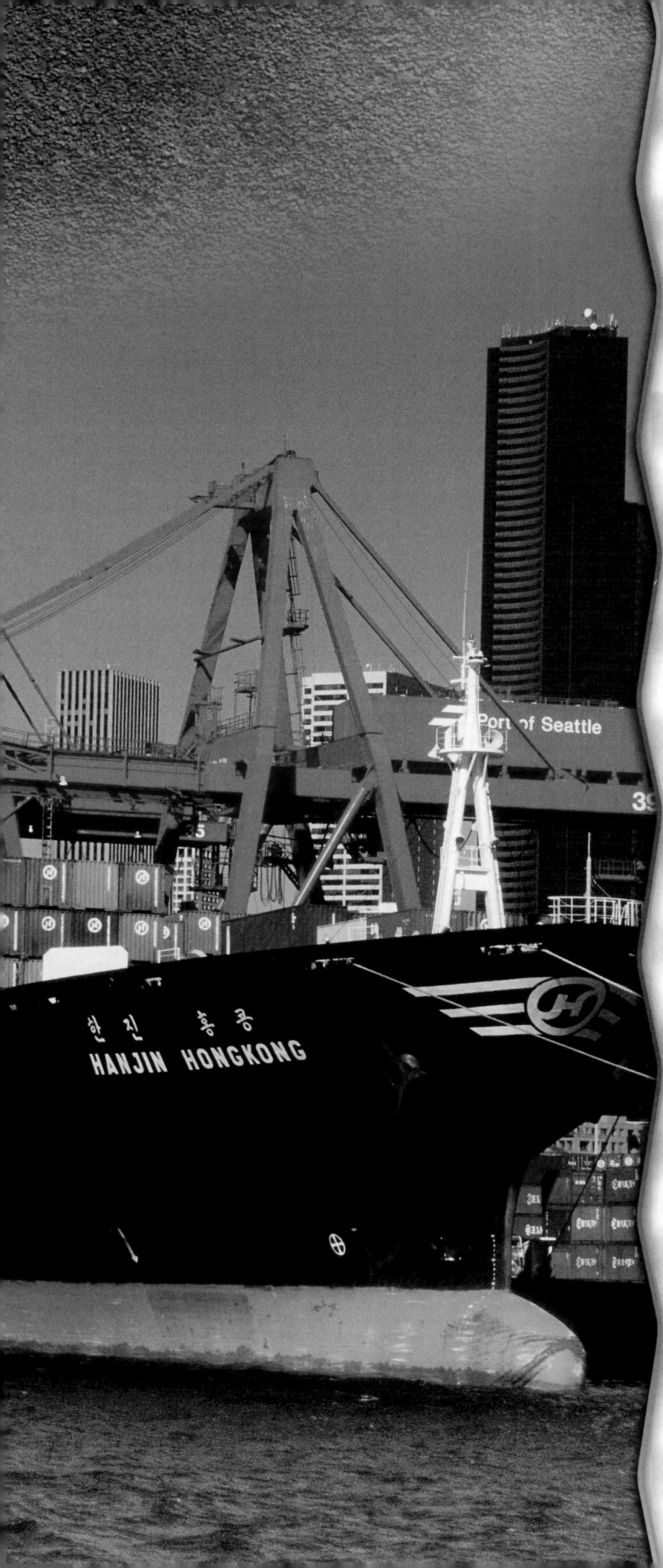

WHY CIVICS Matters

Whenever you buy a new game or new clothes, chances are high that what you are buying came— at least in part—from another country. The U.S. economy is the largest and strongest in the world, but it is also a part of global business and global trade.

PROJECT ★ Citizen

STUDENTS TAKE ACTION

EDUCATING THE PUBLIC Some students are proud of their schools. What if you learned that your favorite school was no longer necessary and was going to be torn down? What could you do to save it? As you read this chapter, think about steps you could take to convince the authorities to save your school.

FOCUS ON WRITING

A JOB DESCRIPTION You run a small company that makes computer games and wants to expand. You need to hire a new employee to help sell your computer games internationally. Read this chapter and then use what you learn to write a job description that would allow you to find good candidates for this job.

Reading Skills

In this chapter you will read about how goods and services flow through the U.S. economy. You will learn how the marketplace affects the price of goods, about the business cycle, and about factors that affect the national economy.

You will also learn how and why the government influences the economy. Finally, you will read about how international trade affects the U.S. economy and creates interdependence among the world's countries.

Analyzing Essential Information

FOCUS ON READING To be informed about important U.S. economic policies, you will need to read many facts, statistics, terms, and descriptions. You do not want to become distracted by unimportant details.

Identifying Relevant and Essential Information Whether you are reading a textbook, an editorial, or political campaign literature, the information should be relevant. It should also be verifiable and essential to understanding the subject. Anything else distracts from the material you are reading.

> The September 11 attacks, which happened on a beautiful morning, hurt several industries. Many Americans were afraid to travel by airplane, causing airlines to lose business. Many businesses reported that their sales dropped in the weeks after September 11. Today, people remember where they were when they heard the news about the attacks. As a result, the unexpected tragedy of September 11 weakened the U.S. economy. With better security, the attacks never would have happened. As Americans began to feel more confident, economists predicted that the economy would again be on the upswing.

→ **The weather on September 11 is not essential information.**

→ **How people remember September 11 is not relevant to the topic of the impact of the attacks on the economy.**

→ **This is an opinion that cannot be proved or verified. It is also not relevant to discussing the economic impact.**

Helpful Hints for Analyzing Essential Information

1. Look out for opinions that cannot be proven.

2. Make sure the facts and information support the main idea. Anything else is not relevant.

3. Draw your own conclusions by focusing only on the essential and relevant information.

You Try It!

The following passage is adapted from the chapter you are about to read. As you read, look for irrelevant, nonessential, or unverifiable information.

Discount Rate

adapted from Chapter 21, p. 568

The Fed also uses a tool called the discount rate, which is the interest rate the Fed charges banks to borrow money. When the Fed changes this rate, it signals commercial banks that the Fed wants to loosen or tighten the money supply. There are thousands of banks across the country. For example, when the Fed lowers the discount rate, banks may borrow and loan more money. The money supply increases, and the economy expands. That helps the economy grow. Canada and Mexico have different economic problems. Raising the discount rate has the opposite effect. If the Fed wants to slow economic growth, it may raise the discount rate. Recently, the Fed raised the discount rate too quickly. The money supply contracts, and the economy may not grow as quickly. Economists love to argue about whether the Fed is doing a good job regulating the economy.

After you have read the passage, answer the following questions.

1. Which sentence in this passage is unverifiable and should be cut?

2. Find two sentences in this passage that are irrelevant to the discussion of the discount rate. What makes those sentences irrelevant?

3. Look at the last sentence of the passage. Do you think this sentence is essential to the discussion? Why or why not?

As you read Chapter 21, ask yourself what makes the information you are reading essential to a study of the U.S. economy.

Academic Vocabulary

Success in school is related to knowing academic vocabulary—the words that are frequently used in school assignments and discussions. In this chapter, you will learn the following academic words:

development *(p. 560)*
agreement *(p. 572)*

SECTION 1
Overview of the U.S. Economy

BEFORE YOU READ

The Main Idea

In a market economy, buyers and sellers interact in the marketplace and respond to changes in prices by changing the amounts demanded and the amounts supplied.

Reading Focus

1. What are four basic economic systems?
2. What is the free-enterprise economic system?
3. What are three ways to invest in the economy?

Key Terms

consumer, *p. 557*
producer, *p. 557*
circular-flow model, *p. 558*
competition, *p. 558*

TAKING NOTES As you read, take notes on the U.S. economy. Use a graphic organizer like this one to record your notes.

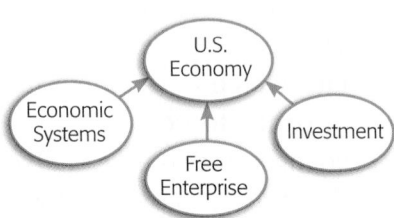

Money is exchanged from the consumer to the producer.

The forces of supply and demand affect every business transaction.

CIVICS IN PRACTICE Economics is about choices. Whenever you buy something, you are making a choice about the product and the price. Your choice, plus the choices of other consumers, helps determine what sellers will produce and what they will charge for it. Why do some brands of jeans cost more than others? Why can't you get a summer job that pays $100 an hour? Economics helps answer these questions. By studying your choices and those of others, you can see how all of those choices together combine to form an economy.

Basic Economic Systems

There are four basic types of economic systems. They are the traditional economy, command economy, market economy, and mixed economy. At least one of these systems is found in every country in the world. What are the characteristics of each type of economic system?

Traditional Economy In a traditional economy, economic decisions, such as what to produce, are based on customs and traditions. Goods and services are also distributed according to custom. It is hard to find a true traditional economy in today's world.

Command Economy In a command economy, government officials decide what goods will be made and how. They also decide who can own these goods. A command economy is highly centralized because a small number of people control the economy. This centralization tends to be inefficient.

Market Economy In a market economy, basic economic questions, such as what to produce, depend on the interaction of producers and consumers. Producers supply goods, services, and resources. Consumers demand goods, services, and resources.

Mixed Economy Most economies today—including the U.S. economy—are mixed economies. A mixed economy can include elements of traditional, command, and market economies. Countries with mixed economies that are closely related to the pure market model are called capitalist. The United States, which has some government involvement in the economy, is a capitalist country.

READING CHECK **Summarizing** What are the main features of traditional, command, market, and mixed economies?

The Free-Enterprise System

The U.S. economic system is also referred to as a free-enterprise system. Under a free-enterprise system, individuals have the right to own private property and to make individual choices about how to use that property and their own creativity to make money.

There are two major groups that make decisions affecting the free enterprise economy. A person who buys goods or services is called a **consumer**. A person or company that provides goods or services is called a **producer**. Many people act as both consumers and producers. For example, when you buy food, clothing, or music, you are a consumer. When you work after school or mow a neighbor's lawn, you are a producer providing a service.

QUICK FACTS

Supply and Demand

In a free-market economy, the laws of supply and demand determine prices and the amount of goods available. In this illustration, the arrows represent the rise and fall of demand.

As demand for goods and services increases, prices rise. At higher prices, producers will produce more.

The laws of supply and demand work together to keep prices at a balanced point where consumers are willing to buy and producers can make a profit.

If demand for goods and services decreases, prices fall. At lower prices, producers will produce less.

ANALYSIS SKILL **ANALYZING VISUALS**
1. How does demand for a good affect the price of that good?
2. How does the supply of a good affect the price of that good?

Circular-Flow Model

In a free-enterprise economy, different groups interact with each other to acquire goods, services, and resources through markets. Among these groups are households, businesses, government, financial institutions, and charities. The interaction of groups in the economy can be illustrated by the **circular-flow model**. Here is a description of how three of these groups—households, businesses, and government—interact in the marketplace.

Households sell resources to businesses and the government. In return, households receive payment, called income, for those resources. For example, when households sell labor to businesses or the government, they receive wages in payment. Wages are one form of income.

Businesses sell goods and services to households and the government. In return, businesses receive payment, called revenue, for the goods and services sold.

The government receives tax revenue from businesses and households. It uses this tax money to provide government goods and services, as well as financial support for citizens with limited income.

The circular flow consists of goods, services, and resources moving in one direction, with money moving in the opposite direction. This makes sense because we use money as payment for goods, services, and resources.

Prices and Supply and Demand

In a free-enterprise system, consumers and producers are free to act in their own interests. Consumers want low prices while producers prefer higher prices. Supply and demand affect prices. In economics, the quantity demanded is the amount of a good or a service that a consumer is willing and able to buy at various possible prices during a given time period.

The connection between quantity demanded for a good or service and its price is described by the law of demand. When prices go up, quantity demanded drops. When prices go down, quantity demanded often increases.

Supply is the quantity of goods and services that producers are willing to offer at various possible prices during a given time period. Prices and quantity supplied are related. According to the law of supply, producers supply more goods and services when they can sell them at higher prices. When prices are lower, producers supply fewer goods and services. The interaction of supply and demand in the marketplace establishes a price at which consumers are willing to buy all of the goods that producers are willing to make.

Competition

Another factor that affects prices is competition. **Competition** is the economic rivalry among businesses selling similar products. Producers compete to satisfy the wants of consumers. Producers may invent new products or improve existing products to get ahead of their business rivals.

READING CHECK **Evaluating** What are the most important elements of a free-enterprise system?

FOCUS ON
Adam Smith
(1723–1790)

Adam Smith was born in a small village in Scotland. His mother raised him until he entered the University of Glasgow at age 14.

In 1776 Smith published his book on economic theory, *The Wealth of Nations*. Smith's book explains how rational self-interest—people making reasoned decisions about what to buy and sell—leads to economic well-being.

One of Smith's theories is that the free market, while appearing unregulated, is actually guided to produce the right amount of goods. For example, if there is a shortage of some good, its price will rise because people will pay more to get it. This increased price is incentive for others to enter the market, which will eventually cure the shortage.

Make Inferences How does the U.S. economic system reflect Smith's theories?

The Circular Flow of Resources and Money

This chart illustrates the exchange of resources, products, and money payments in the U.S. economy.

To Business

To Federal Government

To Federal Government

To Individuals

Federal Government

The government buys products from businesses, and collects taxes from businesses and individuals. The government also provides services to businesses and individuals.

To Business

To Individuals

Business

Businesses produce goods and services that are purchased by households. Businesses also pay wages to individuals and taxes to the government.

Households

Households buy goods and services from businesses and the government. Individuals also provide businesses with labor and the government with labor and taxes.

ANALYSIS SKILL ANALYZING CHARTS

1. What is the government's role according to the circular-flow model?
2. How can a household be both a consumer and a producer? Explain.

Investment and the Economy

In the United States you are free to spend your money on whatever you want. You are also free to save your money or to invest it.

There are many ways to invest your money. One popular method is to invest in stocks. Stock represents partial ownership of a business. For example, if a company issues 100,000 shares of stock, and you own 100 shares, you own 1/1,000th of the company. If the company does well, this entitles you to a share of its profits based on the amount of stock you own. You can also purchase bonds. A bond is a loan from you to the business issuing the bond. When you buy the bond you receive a certificate from the corporation promising to pay you back. In addition, the corporation promises to pay you interest for the use of your money. Governments also issue bonds to raise funds.

Venture Capital

You can also invest directly in starting a new business. Money invested by outsiders to help new businesses grow is called venture capital. Venture capital helps entrepreneurs develop an idea into a new product. Venture capital might be used to finish developing a marketable product, build or improve production facilities or to pay for product distribution.

Investment and Technology

ACADEMIC
VOCABULARY
development:
creation

Venture capital is just one of the ways in which investment can bring about new technology. Many companies use their own money to invest in technological research and **development**. If they are successful, they will be able to bring new products to market based on the new technology. They can also license their technology to other companies. News that a company is close to an important technology breakthrough also encourages individuals to buy that company's stock. This flow of money for investment helps promote continued technological development. That technology in turn helps the economy grow.

Risk and Return

Most financial investment involves some level of risk. When businesses are profitable, demand for their stock tends to rise. This higher demand increases the stock price. That means a greater return on investment for those who hold the stock. However, if a business is not profitable, its stock value typically falls. Investing in property such as real estate holds a similar risk that prices will fall. Investors then lose money.

Careful investors always research whatever investments they are planning to make. Their goal is to be able to judge its prospects for success. If all goes well, both individual investors and the economy as a whole will profit from wise investments.

READING CHECK **Drawing Inferences and Conclusions** How might investment help the economy?

go.hrw.com
Online Quiz
KEYWORD: SZ7 HP21

SECTION 1 ASSESSMENT

Reviewing Ideas and Terms

1. a. Recall What are the differences between a command economy and a market economy?
b. Analyze Why is the ownership of private property so important to a market economy?
2. a. Define Write a definition for the terms **consumer, producer, circular-flow model**, and **competition**.
b. Explain Why are consumers and producers both important to a free-enterprise economic system?
c. Evaluate In your opinion, how important is the government's role in the U.S. economy? Explain your reasoning.
3. a. Summarize How does investment help the economy?
b. Predict What might happen to new technology products if investors decided to invest only in safe, risk-free businesses? Explain your answer.

Critical Thinking

4. Analyzing Information Copy the graphic organizer. Use it to describe the flow of goods and services among consumers, producers, and the government in the U.S. economy.

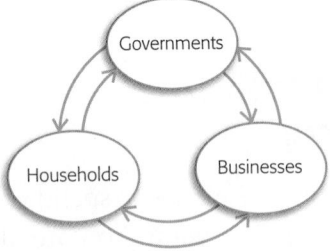

Focus on Writing

5. Summarizing Write a short paragraph that explains how various factors work together to influence prices. Be sure to consider the role of supply and demand.

SECTION 2

Factors Affecting the U.S. Economy

BEFORE YOU READ

The Main Idea

Sometimes the economy performs well. Sometimes economic activity is not as strong. Many factors affect the performance of the economy. Economists try to understand how the economy is doing and predict its direction in order to advise businesses and the government.

Reading Focus

1. What is the business cycle?
2. Why are human and capital resources important to the economy?
3. How do current events affect the economy?

Key Terms

leading indicators, *p. 563*
coincident indicators, *p. 563*
lagging indicators, *p. 563*

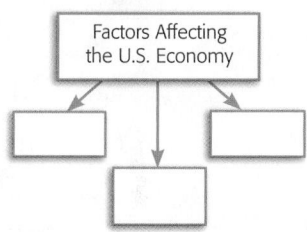 **TAKING NOTES** As you read, take notes on the business cycle, human and capital resources, and current events and the economy. Use a diagram like this one to organize your notes.

Factors Affecting the U.S. Economy

Changes in the economy can have a direct effect on you. For example, when the economy is slow, you may have trouble finding a job.

 **CIVICS IN PRACTICE** Goods and services are constantly flowing through the U.S. economy. Prices increase and prices fall. At times, your choices of available goods and services increase. At other times, you have fewer choices. The number of jobs available may also vary from year to year. Sometimes you may feel like all the news about the economy is just too much noise. You should try to understand what is happening because how much you pay for a gallon of gasoline or the latest computer game depends on so many different factors—even the weather!

The Business Cycle

As you have learned, free-enterprise economies go through something called the business cycle. The business cycle is the repeated series of periods of growth, or expansion, and contraction through which an economy goes. It reflects the changes in economic activity.

Sending Jobs Overseas

Several U.S. companies have moved their call support centers to India in order to cut labor costs.

How can a company save money by sending jobs overseas?

Stages of the Business Cycle

Economists generally divide the business cycle into four stages. The first stage is called expansion. During the expansion phase, the economy grows. Eventually, the economy reaches a peak, or a high point. In this stage, the economy—including production and employment—is at its strongest.

After the economy peaks, it enters a period of business slowdown. This third phase is called a contraction, or a recession. A lengthy period of contraction is called a depression. The final stage in the business cycle is the trough, when demand, production, and employment are at their lowest levels. After the economy bottoms out, the business cycle usually starts over.

Influences on the Business Cycle

Many factors influence the business cycle. These factors include the level of business investment, the availability of money and credit, public expectations about the future, and external factors.

Business Investment Businesses invest in capital goods such as new production facilities and new machinery. Business investment promotes economic expansion in three ways. First, by purchasing new capital goods, businesses contribute to the demand for such goods. Second, businesses can invest in new equipment to improve efficiency, which can lead to growth. Third, investment can support research into new technologies that increase production and lower costs.

Money and Credit The availability of money and credit also affects the business cycle. Individuals and businesses generally borrow more money when interest rates are low.

Public Opinion Public expectations about the future of the economy also play a role in the business cycle. For example, if consumers believe the economic future looks good, they are more willing to spend, which promotes economic growth. The expectations of business owners also affect the economy. If the owners believe that the economy will be strong, they are more willing to make investments.

International Events World events can also affect business. For example, the terrorist attacks of September 11, 2001, led to declines in private investments as Americans were left uncertain about the future. The subsequent war in Iraq led to a reduction in oil production and higher oil prices, leaving companies less money for corporate investment.

Predicting the Business Cycle

Predicting changes to the business cycle is a critical job for economists. Economists typically use three types of indicators, or sets of information, to study the economy. These are called leading, coincident, and lagging indicators. Indicators determine what phase the business cycle is in to determine if the economy is likely to expand or contract.

Leading Indicators Economists make predictions about future economic growth with the help of **leading indicators**. They come before, or lead, major changes in the business cycle. An example of a leading indicator is the number of building permits issued. An increase in building permits usually means that more buildings will be built, which means that more jobs will be created.

Coincident Indicators The second group of indicators is called **coincident indicators**, which are signs that show economists how the economy is doing at the present time. Coincident indicators tell economists if an upturn or downturn has begun. For example, if people's incomes have increased, the economy may have entered an upturn.

Lagging Indicators The final group of indicators is called **lagging indicators**, which are economic signs that lag behind, or follow, major changes in the business cycle. They help economists determine how long the current phase of the business cycle may last. For example, if the economy is expanding, more people may decide to start new businesses. It takes several months before they can get these businesses started, so an increase in new businesses comes after, or lags behind, the trend.

READING CHECK **Summarizing** What are the stages of the business cycle?

Human and Capital Resources

The availability of resources also plays a key role in the U.S. economy. Human resources, that is labor, and capital resources often come from different locations. The location and movement of these resources can affect the economy in a number of ways.

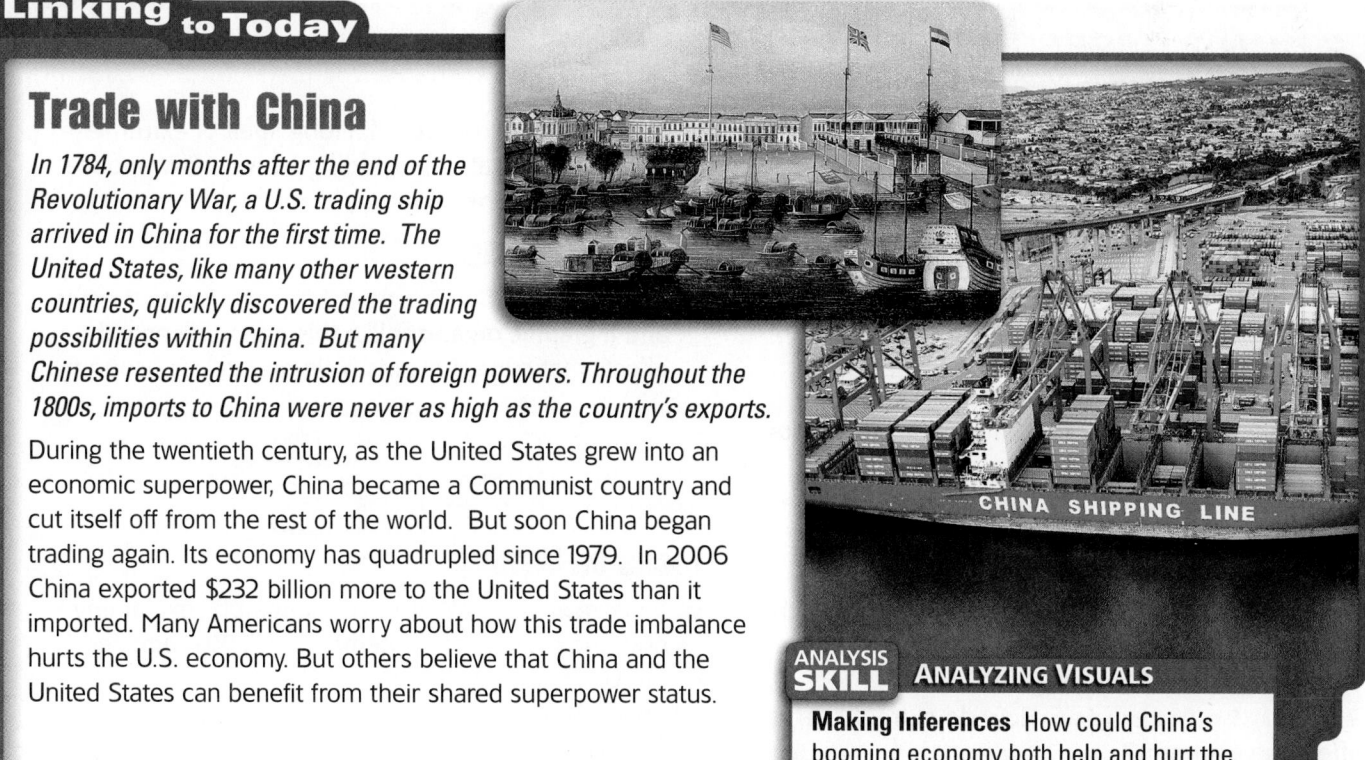

Linking to Today

Trade with China

In 1784, only months after the end of the Revolutionary War, a U.S. trading ship arrived in China for the first time. The United States, like many other western countries, quickly discovered the trading possibilities within China. But many Chinese resented the intrusion of foreign powers. Throughout the 1800s, imports to China were never as high as the country's exports.

During the twentieth century, as the United States grew into an economic superpower, China became a Communist country and cut itself off from the rest of the world. But soon China began trading again. Its economy has quadrupled since 1979. In 2006 China exported $232 billion more to the United States than it imported. Many Americans worry about how this trade imbalance hurts the U.S. economy. But others believe that China and the United States can benefit from their shared superpower status.

CHINA SHIPPING LINE

ANALYSIS SKILL **ANALYZING VISUALS**

Making Inferences How could China's booming economy both help and hurt the American economy?

For example, in recent years, the desire for labor at a lower cost has led some American companies to open factories in foreign countries. Workers in some countries are willing to work for much less than the common American wage. As a result, some American computer and Internet-related companies have also begun to use foreign labor. Some American companies have set up customer-service call centers in foreign countries like India where labor costs are lower.

> **READING CHECK** **Analyzing Information** In what ways does the movement of resources affect the U.S. economy?

Current Events and the Economy

Economists and government officials use economic indicators to plan changes to make the economy perform well. However, there are some events for which economists cannot prepare. At times, current events can affect the economy in ways no one expected.

For example, the terrorist attacks of September 11, 2001, affected many businesses in New York City and caused the New York Stock Exchange to close for several days. The attacks also hurt the airline industry, because many Americans were afraid to fly after the hijackings. The overall U.S. economy was weakened. As Americans began to feel more confident, however, spending increased and businesses returned to normal.

Even weather may affect the economy. For example, in 2005 Hurricane Katrina struck New Orleans, Louisiana, and many other cities along the Gulf of Mexico. From Louisiana to Florida, the hurricane disrupted port facilities and highways. Imports and exports were almost halted. Oil and gas refineries were shut down. As a result of Katrina's devastation, consumers had to pay higher prices for gasoline and petroleum-based products ranging from tires to paint.

> **READING CHECK** **Analyzing** How can a major storm in one area affect the entire U.S. economy?

go.hrw.com
Online Quiz
KEYWORD: SZ7 HP21

SECTION 2 ASSESSMENT

Reviewing Ideas and Terms

1. a. Define Write a definition for the terms **leading indicators**, **coincident indicators**, and **lagging indicators**.
  b. Explain What tools do economists use to explain the business cycle?
  c. Predict What would you predict for the economic cycle if leading economic indicators were negative and coincident economic indicators were positive? Explain your reasoning.
2. a. Analyze Why would a computer manufacturer consider moving its 24-hour a day technical support center to a foreign country?
  b. Support a Point of View Do you think that U.S. companies should move jobs overseas in order to save money? Why or why not?
3. a. Find the Main Idea How do current events affect the economy?

b. Predict How would a long spell of extremely cold winter weather, including heavy snow and ice storms, affect the economy? Explain your answer.

Critical Thinking

4. Identifying Cause and Effect Use your notes and a graphic organizer like this one to identify the effects that current events have on the U.S. economy.

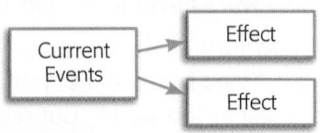

Focus on Writing

5. Summarizing Write two paragraphs explaining how the tragedy of September 11, 2001, affected the U.S. economy.

SECTION 3

Government's Role in the U.S. Economy

BEFORE YOU READ

The Main Idea

The government affects the economy through regulation and policy, the Fed through fiscal monetary policy. Proper use of these tools helps keep the economy functioning more smoothly and effectively.

Reading Focus

1. What are the goals of government regulation?
2. How is fiscal policy used to influence the economy?
3. How does the Federal Reserve use monetary policy to influence the economy?

Key Terms

tax incentives, *p. 567*
easy-money policy, *p. 568*
tight-money policy, *p. 568*
open-market operations, *p. 568*
reserve requirement, *p. 568*

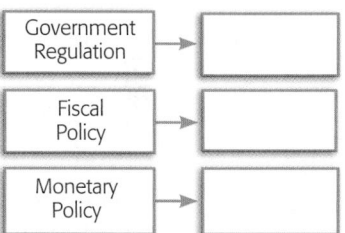 **TAKING NOTES** As you read, take notes on the government's use of regulation and fiscal and monetary policy to influence the U.S. economy. Use an organizer like this one for your notes.

Government Regulation	→	
Fiscal Policy	→	
Monetary Policy	→	

The federal Environmental Protection Agency inspects toxic-waste sites to protect citizens from negative effects.

 **CIVICS IN PRACTICE** Government plays several important roles in the U.S. economy. As you know from reading about the circular-flow model, the government creates millions of jobs and buys many goods and services. The government also affects the economy by collecting taxes and providing services to the people. In addition, the government regulates the growth of the economy directly in a variety of ways. The money that the government spends is really your money, from your taxes, so it is a good idea for you to know how government policies on regulation, taxing, and spending work.

Government Regulation

In the United States, all levels of governments—federal, state, and local—regulate business. Government regulation has five main goals: to protect workers, to protect consumers, to limit negative effects, to encourage competition, and to regulate property.

Protecting Workers

Government tries to prevent businesses from using workers in ways that are unsafe or unfair. For example, the Equal Employment Opportunity Commission (EEOC) makes and enforces rules that prohibit businesses from discriminating against people when hiring and promoting workers. The government also sets standards for safe working conditions. The Occupational Safety and Health Administration (OSHA) makes certain that employees work under safe conditions.

Protecting Consumers

The second goal of government regulation is to protect consumers. For example, the Food and Drug Administration (FDA) protects people from unsafe medicines and foods. The Consumer Product Safety Commission (CPSC) makes certain that items such as toys are not dangerous. The federal government also insures people's savings and checking accounts.

Limiting Negative Effects

The third goal of government regulation is to limit the negative side effects of some economic activities. For example, the Environmental Protection Agency (EPA) has rules that limit negative effects of industry such as air and water pollution.

Encouraging Competition

Encouraging competition is the final goal of government regulation. The U.S. Department of Justice and the Federal Trade Commission (FTC) supervise some corporate behavior, such as mergers, to make certain that companies compete fairly with one another. Many states also regulate competition.

Government Regulation of Private Property

Generally, in a free-enterprise system property owners may use their property in any way that they wish. However, government does have the power to regulate the use of property in some cases.

MEDIA INVESTIGATION

PHOTOJOURNALISM
Understanding Photographs and Video

The media helps to keep us informed about our government. Because so much of our news and information comes from photographs, it is important to understand how and why they are used.

Photographs are used to illustrate and tell news stories because they can convey a great deal of information in one glance. They are also an effective way to communicate concepts that are new or difficult to describe by words alone. Dramatic photos have the power to leave lasting impressions on the public. Some images may be too shocking for a particular audience, so news editors must select photos and video footage carefully.

Study photographs and videos to see if they are informative and truthful. Ask yourself: Why was this picture or video chosen? What story does it tell? Is the subject posing or is the shot candid? Does any part of the video seem rehearsed?

The Coast Guard patrols a cargo ship as part of increased homeland security efforts.

ANALYSIS SKILL **MEDIA INVESTIGATION** go.hrw.com KEYWORD: SZ7 CH21

What does the picture above say about the Coast Guard's role in homeland security?

A main way that local governments regulate property is by controlling land use. Zoning laws limit certain types of economic activities to specific areas. For example, a zoning law may allow a factory to be built in an industrial area while banning it in a residential neighborhood.

READING CHECK > **Finding the Main Idea** How does the government try to regulate the U.S. economy?

Fiscal Policy

Fiscal policy—government taxing, spending, and making payments—is one tool that the government uses to influence the economy. For example, in 2003 the federal, state, and local governments employed about 23 million people. Governments may also loan money to small businesses, which helps the economy to grow.

Taxes

The federal government can change tax rates to affect the nation's economy. If taxes are raised, consumers have less money to spend. They buy fewer goods and services. When spending slows, the economy slows. On the other hand, lower taxes mean that people give less money to government and have more in their pockets. With more money to spend, many people buy more goods and services. Businesses sell more, and they hire new employees, so the economy speeds up. The government can also offer **tax incentives**. These are special tax reductions that help lower a company's tax bill if it follows certain policies the government favors.

Government Spending

The federal government can also affect the economy by adjusting its own spending. When the government buys more goods and services, it puts more money into circulation. This stimulates the economy. When the government purchases fewer goods and services, the result may be that the economy slows.

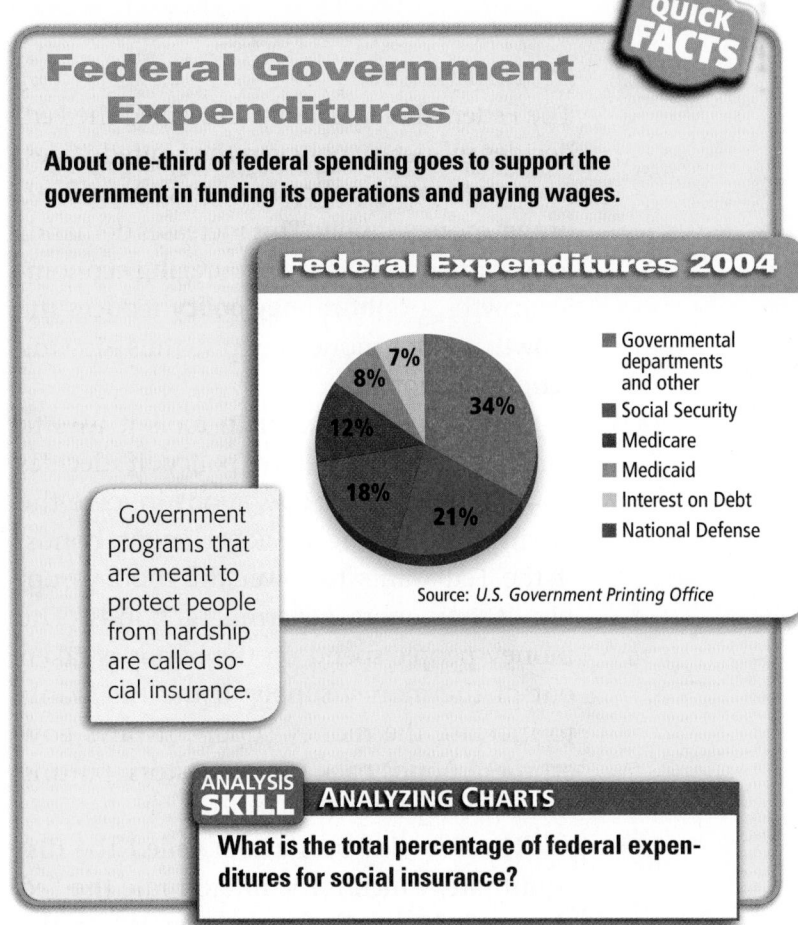

QUICK FACTS

Federal Government Expenditures

About one-third of federal spending goes to support the government in funding its operations and paying wages.

Federal Expenditures 2004

7%
8%
34%
12%
18%
21%

- Governmental departments and other
- Social Security
- Medicare
- Medicaid
- Interest on Debt
- National Defense

Source: *U.S. Government Printing Office*

Government programs that are meant to protect people from hardship are called social insurance.

ANALYSIS SKILL **ANALYZING CHARTS**
What is the total percentage of federal expenditures for social insurance?

Public Transfer Payments

Another tool of fiscal policy is public transfer payments. For example, governments provide tax dollars to people who are not working by offering unemployment compensation. By providing assistance to unemployed workers, governments make certain that these workers can still buy goods and services.

READING CHECK > **Analyzing Information** What are some ways fiscal policy can affect the U.S. economy?

Monetary Policy

The Federal Reserve System uses monetary policy to promote economic stability. Monetary policy controls the amount of money in the economy. By controlling the money supply, the Fed can promote or slow economic growth.

The Federal Reserve and Monetary Policy

The Federal Reserve Bank, also called the Fed, decides monetary policy in the United States. An **easy-money policy** increases the growth of the money supply. This increases demands for goods and services, encouraging economic growth. A **tight-money policy** reduces the growth of the money supply, thus slowing economic growth.

The Fed has three main tools it uses to carry out the monetary policy it decides upon. **Open-market operations** involve the buying and selling of government bonds. If the Fed wants to lower the money supply, it sells more government bonds. The money people spend on the bonds is taken out of the money supply. If the Fed wants to increase the money supply, it buys government bonds back from investors, putting more money into circulation.

The Fed also uses a tool called the discount rate, which is the interest rate the Fed charges banks to borrow money. When the Fed changes this rate, it signals commercial banks that the Fed wants to loosen or tighten the money supply. For example, when the Fed lowers the discount rate, banks may borrow and loan more money. That helps the economy grow. Raising the discount rate has the opposite effect.

Finally, the Fed makes use of the **reserve requirement**. This reserve is the amount of money banks must have available at all times. By lowering the reserve requirement, the Fed frees up banks to loan more money. By raising the reserve requirement, the Fed forces banks to keep more of their money.

Timing is important to monetary policy. First, the Fed must determine the current state of the economy. Second, Fed members must decide the best way to use monetary policy at that time. Finally, it takes time for businesses and investors to adjust to changes in monetary policy. This is why the economy usually does not react instantly to the Fed's policy changes.

READING CHECK **Summarizing** What are the goals of monetary policy, and how quickly does monetary policy affect the economy?

SECTION 3 ASSESSMENT

Reviewing Ideas and Terms

1. a. Recall What are the four main goals of government regulation of the economy?

b. Explain Why is it necessary for the government to regulate the safety of drugs and medicine?

2. a. Define Write a definition for the term **tax incentives**.

b. Evaluate Which government policy might be better for the economy in the long term, a policy that pays unemployment benefits to people who are not working or a policy that trains people for jobs and helps them find work? Explain your reasoning.

3. a. Define Write a definition of the terms **easy-money policy**, **tight-money policy**, **open-market operations**, and **reserve requirement**.

b. Predict During a period of inflation, how might a change in the Federal Reserve's policy, from easy money to tight money, affect consumer confidence?

Critical Thinking

4. Analyzing Information Use your notes and a graphic organizer like this one to identify the different ways in which the government regulates the economy.

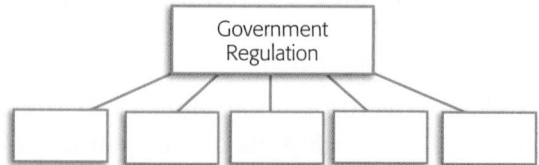

Focus on Writing

5. Summarizing Compare and contrast fiscal policy and monetary policy.

Analyzing Music Videos

Learn

What was the last music video you saw? Did it have a message behind it, or was it created purely for entertainment? While some music videos are just plain entertainment, many music videos today have a lesson behind them. They make viewers think and react to important issues. For example, a music video may show touching images of soldiers returning from war or of families struggling to make ends meet. Videos like these send messages to their viewers. An important part of understanding today's mass media is being able to understand music videos. Use the tips below to help you analyze a music video.

Practice

❶ **Notice how the song lyrics connect to the images.** The meaning of the lyrics will probably be clearer if you look at how they fit with the video images. The images may help you better understand the words to the song. They often make the message of the video clearer.

❷ **Pay attention to how the artist or band appears.** Are the performers simply shown singing the song? Are they acting out some other storyline as they sing the song? Maybe the song is only playing in the background of the video.

❸ **Take note of any surprising images.** Watching a music video, you may see images you would not expect to go with the music. In your analysis, consider why these images were chosen and whether you think they are appropriate or not.

❹ **Identify the video's message.** Use the information you have collected to identify the message of the video. What do you think the artist or band is trying to say?

Apply

Copy the graphic organizer below on your own paper. Think of a video that you have seen recently, then analyze that video by completing the graphic organizer. Use the information to answer the questions that follow.

1. How do you think the images in the video connect with the song lyrics? Why do you think the makers of the video chose the images they did?

2. Does the artist or band appear in the video? If so, in what role?

3. What do you think is the purpose of this video? Does it succeed? Why or why not?

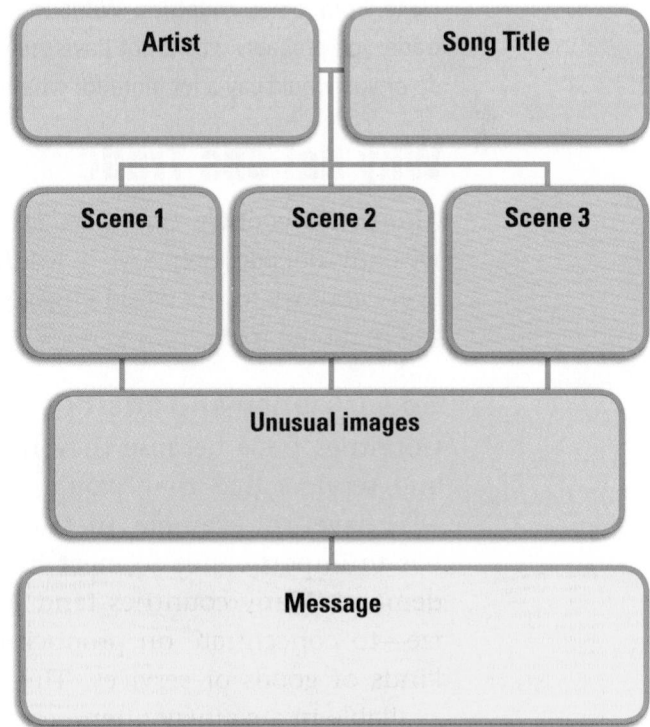

Living in a World Economy

BEFORE YOU READ

The Main Idea

International trade allows countries to specialize in producing the goods and services where they are most efficient. Trade gives people access to more goods and services. Trade also makes countries interdependent.

Reading Focus

1. Why do countries trade with one another?
2. What are the differences between free trade and protectionism?
3. How does international trade affect jobs and consumers?

Key Terms

absolute advantage, *p. 570*
comparative advantage, *p. 570*
opportunity cost, *p. 570*
trade barrier, *p. 572*
balance of payments, *p. 574*
trade surplus, *p. 574*
trade deficit, *p. 574*

TAKING NOTES As you read, take notes on why nations trade, free trade versus protectionism, and international trade. Use a graphic organizer like this one to record your notes.

Living in a World Economy	
Why Nations Trade	
Free Trade vs. Protectionism	
International Trade	

Make a list of all the goods you use in a week, from clothing to electronic equipment to food. Then consider how many of these goods came from other countries. Without international trade, you probably would not have the choices you do or you would pay a lot more for what you buy.

Why Nations Trade

Almost no country can meet all its needs without outside help. As a result, almost every country in the world engages in some international trade.

Specialization and Interdependence

Countries trade because they need goods and services that they would not otherwise have. For example, the United States has to import coffee to meet its domestic demand. Many countries tend to specialize—to concentrate on producing certain kinds of goods or services. The resources available in a country often determine the kinds of goods it produces.

Countries that specialize in production and then engage in trade with each other are interdependent. Interdependence means that peoples depend on each other for different goods and services.

Trade and Comparative Advantage

Countries decide what goods and services to provide by examining their absolute and comparative advantages. A nation has an **absolute advantage** when it can produce more of a given product than another country can. Even if a country has an absolute advantage in several goods and services, it will usually specialize and produce goods and services in which it has a comparative advantage. A country has a **comparative advantage** when it can provide a product more efficiently—at a lower opportunity cost— than another country can. **Opportunity cost** is the value of the next best alternative that is given up when a country specializes. Why specialize? Countries specialize and trade because they can get more goods overall.

READING CHECK **Drawing Inferences and Conclusions** How does a country determine which goods and services it should produce and which it should import?

The Global Economy

Manufacturing today is a global process. Products we think of as American are actually designed and built all over the world. An mp3 player, for example, may be made of parts from a dozen different countries.

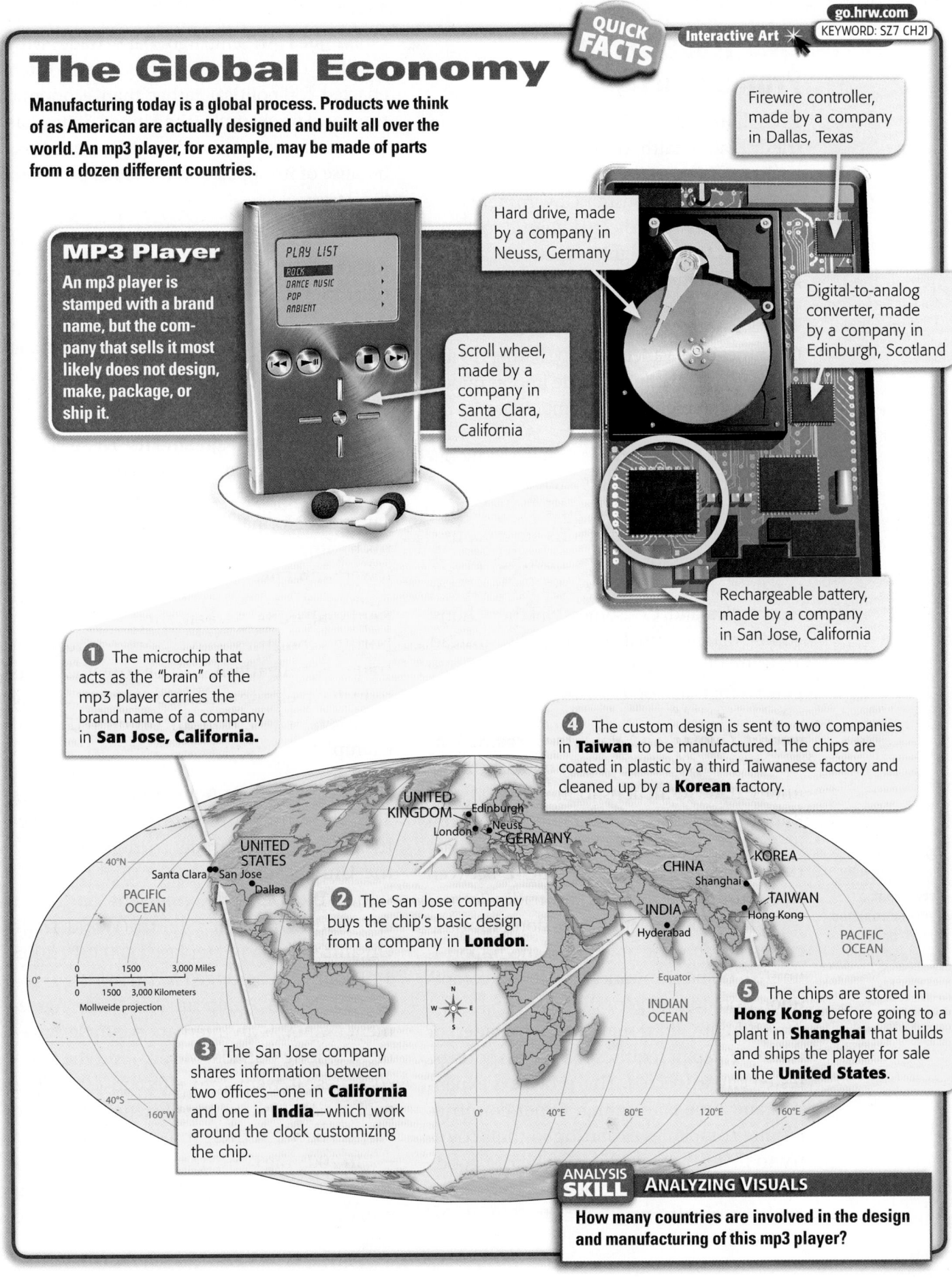

MP3 Player

An mp3 player is stamped with a brand name, but the company that sells it most likely does not design, make, package, or ship it.

PLAY LIST
ROCK
DANCE MUSIC
POP
AMBIENT

Firewire controller, made by a company in Dallas, Texas

Hard drive, made by a company in Neuss, Germany

Digital-to-analog converter, made by a company in Edinburgh, Scotland

Scroll wheel, made by a company in Santa Clara, California

Rechargeable battery, made by a company in San Jose, California

1 The microchip that acts as the "brain" of the mp3 player carries the brand name of a company in **San Jose, California.**

4 The custom design is sent to two companies in **Taiwan** to be manufactured. The chips are coated in plastic by a third Taiwanese factory and cleaned up by a **Korean** factory.

2 The San Jose company buys the chip's basic design from a company in **London**.

3 The San Jose company shares information between two offices—one in **California** and one in **India**—which work around the clock customizing the chip.

5 The chips are stored in **Hong Kong** before going to a plant in **Shanghai** that builds and ships the player for sale in the **United States**.

UNITED KINGDOM • Edinburgh
London • • Neuss
GERMANY
KOREA
CHINA
Shanghai •
TAIWAN
INDIA
Hyderabad •
Hong Kong
UNITED STATES
Santa Clara • • San Jose
• Dallas
40°N
PACIFIC OCEAN
PACIFIC OCEAN
INDIAN OCEAN
Equator
0°
40°S
160°W
0°
40°E
80°E
120°E
160°E

0   1500   3,000 Miles
0 1500 3,000 Kilometers
Mollweide projection

N
W   E
S

ANALYSIS SKILL **ANALYZING VISUALS**

How many countries are involved in the design and manufacturing of this mp3 player?

Free Trade Versus Protectionism

Even though international trade allows countries to gain wealth, countries often limit the exchange of goods across their borders. This is called protectionism. Governments use trade barriers to protect domestic jobs and industries from foreign competition. A **trade barrier** is a limit on the exchange of goods.

Trade Barriers

Countries use a variety of trade barriers to limit trade. Trade barriers include import quotas, voluntary restrictions, and embargoes.

Tariffs Goods and services purchased by one country from another are called imports. A tax on imports is called a tariff. There are two kinds of tariffs. Revenue tariffs are a tax used to raise money for a government. A protective tariff makes foreign goods cost more and reduces demand. Consumers will then choose goods manufactured domestically instead. The United States has used such protectionist policies for much of its history.

Import Quotas and Voluntary Restrictions Governments also use import quotas and voluntary trade restrictions to limit imports. An import quota is a law that limits the amount of a particular imported good. A voluntary trade restriction is an **agreement** between two countries to limit certain trade. Both of these forms of regulation help domestic businesses. Because the amount of the import is limited, domestic businesses face less competition from foreign goods.

There are additional barriers to trade. For example, Japan requires that all imports be tested and inspected. This process is expensive and time-consuming. Other countries require companies exporting to their country to first get special licenses before goods can be imported. These licenses can be difficult to obtain, which limits imports to such countries.

ACADEMIC VOCABULARY

agreement: a decision reached by two or more people or groups

Embargoes An embargo bans trade with specific countries. Embargoes are often enacted for political rather than economic reasons. For example, the United States has had a trade embargo against Cuba since 1960 because of its opposition to Cuban president Fidel Castro.

International Cooperation

Although many countries enact trade barriers, they still support international trade. Some examples of trade cooperation are reciprocal trade agreements, regional trade organizations, and international trade agreements.

Reciprocal Trade Agreements These agreements between countries usually reduce protective tariffs. For example, the U.S. Congress can grant Normal Trade Relations (NTR) status to other countries, which may give them lower tariff rates.

Regional Trade Agreements Many neighboring countries have formed regional trade organizations. These organizations reduce or eliminate trade barriers among members. The European Union (EU) is an example.

International Trade Agreements Countries also enter into international trade agreements to reduce trade barriers. In 1947 the United States and 22 other countries signed the General Agreement on Tariffs and Trade (GATT). In 1995 the World Trade Organization (WTO) replaced GATT. In 2005 149 countries belonged to the WTO.

The North American Free Trade Agreement (NAFTA) is an international trade agreement among Canada, Mexico, and the United States. It went into effect in 1994. The goal of NAFTA is to gradually remove all trade barriers between these three countries.

In 2005 the United States signed a similar agreement with five Central American countries called CAFTA, the Central American Free Trade Agreement.

Counterfeiting and Consumer Protection

Have you ever bought a high-fashion handbag or a fancy watch at a price too good to believe? Chances are the item is a cheap imitation of the real thing. If you know this ahead of time, you might decide that buying the item is not a big deal. But how would you feel if you paid full price and later learned you had bought a fake, or counterfeit, product?

Why it Matters Counterfeiting goods is against the law, and can cause legitimate businesses to lose sales and profits. The U.S. government issues patents and trademarks to companies to make sure that they can control who manufactures them.

U.S manufacturers must follow consumer protection laws to ensure the safety and quality of their products. But counterfeiters often try to pass off shoddy products, produced at a fraction of the cost, as the real thing. This can be dangerous, as well as illegal—counterfeit cosmetics or car parts made from inferior materials could endanger people's lives.

Counterfeit merchandise can also contribute to other illegal activity. Gangs and terrorists sometimes fund their activities by selling counterfeit merchandise. One job of the U.S. Customs Service is to protect Americans by preventing the importation of counterfeit goods.

Counterfeiters often copy well-known brand names and logos.

ANALYSIS SKILL   EVALUATING THE LAW

go.hrw.com
KEYWORD: SZ7 CH21

1. Why is it illegal to counterfeit goods?
2. Who do you think is hurt the most by counterfeiting? Explain.

Free Trade and Protectionism

The goal of NAFTA and other agreements is to promote free trade. Not everyone supports free trade, however. Some people support protectionism for a variety of reasons. These reasons include protecting industries and jobs, maintaining high wages, and national security. Some opponents of free trade argue that other countries are not as concerned as the United States about worker safety and environmental protection.

Protectionist policies may, however, harm the economy. Protectionism may lead to price increases and trade wars, which could mean that consumers would pay higher prices for their goods and services. Few governments have a trade policy that is completely protectionist or completely based on free trade. Most countries' policies are a mixture of the two.

READING CHECK **Summarizing** How can trade agreements help international trade?

International Trade, Jobs, and Consumers

Countries must carefully watch how international trade affects their economies. A country's **balance of payments** is the difference between the value of its exports and its imports. If a country sells more than it buys, it has a **trade surplus**. If it buys more than it sells, it has a **trade deficit**.

The United States typically buys much more from other countries than it sells. For example, in 2005 the United States bought more than $1.99 trillion in goods from other countries while its exports totaled around $1.27 trillion. That means the U.S. trade deficit was more than $725 billion.

Effects on Jobs

International trade can both create jobs and reduce the number of available jobs. As a country trades, it finds new markets for its goods. Consequently, demand for its goods increases. Producers then build new factories, buy more equipment, and hire new workers. Therefore, international trade can benefit workers.

Under NAFTA, many U.S. businesses took advantage of the new free-trade environment to move their factories to Mexico where labor costs are lower than in the United States. Debate continues on the actual effects of these moves.

Effects on Consumers

International trade allows consumers access to goods that are scarce in their own country. It also increases competition. As a result, prices drop, and consumers can buy goods at lower prices. With the savings, they can purchase more goods or services, causing their standard of living to rise. International trade also gives consumers more choices. If you could only buy goods made in the United States, your choices would be limited. There are some things that the United States cannot produce. For example, coffee does not grow well here. Coffee plants require a different climate. International trade allows Americans to enjoy coffee and other goods that would otherwise be unavailable.

READING CHECK **Summarizing** What are three ways international trade benefits consumers?

go.hrw.com
Online Quiz
KEYWORD: SZ7 HP21

SECTION 4 ASSESSMENT

Reviewing Ideas and Terms

1. a. Define Write a definition for the terms **absolute advantage**, **comparative advantage**, and **opportunity cost**.

b. Explain Under what circumstances might a country continue to produce a good that it could purchase for less money from another country?

2. a. Define Write a definition for the term **trade barrier**.

b. Summarize What is NAFTA, and how does it benefit the United States?

c. Elaborate Why do some countries use tests and inspections as trade barriers instead of tariffs and quotas?

3. a. Define Write a definition for the terms **balance of payments**, **trade surplus**, and **trade deficit**.

b. Predict What might be the various effects on the U.S. economy if an advanced cell phone became available from China at a new, low price?

Critical Thinking

4. Analyzing Information Use your notes and a graphic organizer like this one to identify the ways that international trade affects jobs and consumers.

```
                         ┌──────────────┐
                    ┌──→ │  Consumers   │
┌──────────────┐    │    └──────────────┘
│ International │────┤
│    Trade      │    │    ┌──────────────┐
└──────────────┘    └──→ │     Jobs     │
                         └──────────────┘
```

Focus on Writing

5. Making Comparisons Suppose that you are a journalist writing a story on trade issues. Compare and contrast free trade and protectionism for your readers.

STUDENTS TAKE ACTION

Educating the Public

Byrd Community Academy was located in an old building in a poor area of Chicago. Because the school had no lunchroom, students ate in the hallways. Its many problems included a leaky roof, missing doors in the bathrooms, and a broken heating system. Project Citizen students in teacher Brian Schultz's class decided it was time to act.

Community Connection The students discovered that several years earlier the local school board had promised to build the school an entirely new campus. However, the funds earmarked for Byrd were used to rebuild a different worn-out school.

Ralph Nader visits with students at the Byrd Community Academy in Chicago.

Taking Action The students wanted the school board to fulfill its promise. They researched and developed an 11-point action plan for achieving their goal. To generate public support, they took pictures of the building, produced a documentary video showing its problems, and wrote to government officials. The vice president of the United States, a U.S. senator, a U.S. representative, and an independent presidential candidate all expressed support for the plan. Donations poured in from private citizens. However, the school had low enrollment, and district resources were scarce. The school board made an economic choice to use the money it would cost to rebuild the school for other uses benefiting more students. Byrd Academy closed, and its students were moved to another school. Although the students did not achieve their goal, they attracted national attention to the issue of how a school's physical environment can affect student learning.

go.hrw.com
Project Citizen
KEYWORD: SZ7 CH21

SERVICE LEARNING

1. What inspired the Byrd students to follow up on the school board's past plan to rebuild the school?
2. How was the students' project successful, even though their school eventually closed?

Visual Summary

QUICK FACTS

Use the visual summary to help you review the main ideas of the chapter.

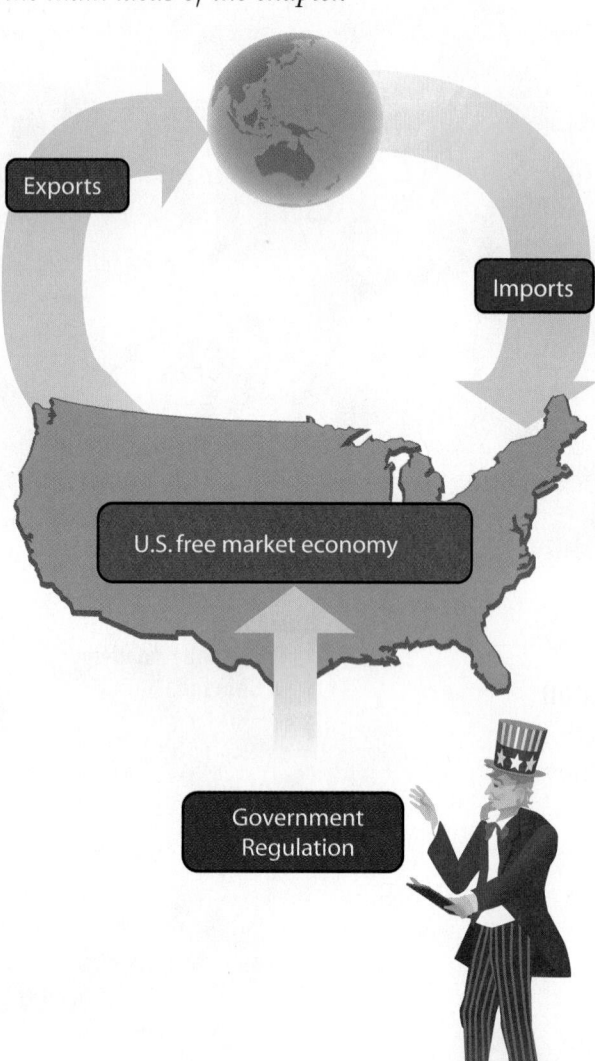

Exports

Imports

U.S. free market economy

Government Regulation

The U.S. economy is based on a free-enterprise system in which good and services are exchanged between producers, consumers, and the government. The system also allows the United States to trade goods and services around the world.

Reviewing Key Terms

For each term below, write a sentence explaining its significance to the U.S. economy and the world.

1. consumer
2. producer
3. circular-flow model
4. competition
5. leading indicators
6. coincident indicators
7. lagging indicators
8. tax incentives
9. easy-money policy
10. tight-money policy
11. open-market operations
12. reserve requirement
13. absolute advantage
14. comparative advantage
15. opportunity cost
16. trade barrier
17. balance of payments
18. trade surplus
19. trade deficit

Comprehension and Critical Thinking

SECTION 1 *(Pages 556–560)*

20. **a. Define** What is the circular flow model?

    b. Compare and Contrast How do traditional economies differ from market economies?

    c. Elaborate Why is investment important in a free-enterprise system?

SECTION 2 *(Pages 561–564)*

21. **a. Describe** How does the location of capital and human resources affect the U.S. economy?

    b. Sequence What are the stages of the business cycle?

    c. Predict What are some possible ways that current events can affect a country's economy? Explain.

Active Citizenship video program
Review the video to answer the closing question:
Why are students often the best people to identify problems with their school?

SECTION 3 *(Pages 565–568)*

22. a. Identify What are the goals of government regulation?

   b. Explain What is the role of the Federal Reserve System in the U.S. economy?

   c. Evaluate Is there a place for government regulation in the free-enterprise system? Explain.

SECTION 4 *(Pages 570–574)*

23. a. Recall Why do countries have tariffs?

   b. Make Generalizations What industries do protectionists believe should be protected from foreign competition? Why?

   c. Support a Point of View Free trade brings many benefits to the U.S. economy. Should the United States end protectionism and eliminate all trade barriers? Why or why not?

Civics Skills

Analyzing Music Videos *Use the Civics Skill taught in this chapter to complete the activity below.*

24. Watch two or three music videos by different bands or artists. Then write a paragraph about each video analyzing its content. Consider:

- Does the video have a message?
- If so, what is that message?
- How do the images in the video connect with the lyrics of the song?

Using the Internet

go.hrw.com
KEYWORD: SZ7 CH21

25. Influencing the Economy By controlling the supply of money, the government can promote or slow economic growth. The Federal Reserve System decides monetary policy in the United States. Enter the activity keyword and research the Federal Reserve System. Create a poster that explains the role of the Federal Reserve System in the economy and government. Include in your poster facts and statistics on recent actions by the Federal Reserve Board.

Reading Skills

Analyzing Essential Information *Using the Reading Skill taught in this chapter, read the following passage and answer the question below.*

> Adam Smith was born in a small village in Scotland. His mother raised him until he entered the University of Glasgow at age 14.
>
> In 1776 Smith published his book on economic theory, *The Wealth of Nations*. Smith's book explains how rational self-interest—people making reasoned decisions about what to buy and sell—leads to economic well-being.
>
> One of Smith's theories is that the free market, while appearing unregulated, is actually guided to produce the right amount of goods. For example, if there is a shortage of some good, its price will rise because people will pay more to get it. This increased price is incentive for others to enter the market, which will eventually cure the shortage. *(p. 558)*

26. Which sentence or sentences in this passage are irrelevant to the discussion of Smith's economic theories?

FOCUS ON WRITING

27. A Job Description Review your notes about the U.S. economy and the world. Pay special attention to international trade. Now write a job description for a salesperson that will help your company sell its computer games in other countries. Focus on the skills and knowledge this person will need to have for the position.

CHAPTER 22
CAREER CHOICES

SECTION 1
The Challenge of a Career

SECTION 2
The World of Work

SECTION 3
Unlimited Opportunities

SECTION 4
Learning More about Careers

SECTION 5
Learning More about Yourself

NATIONAL STANDARDS
FOR CIVICS AND GOVERNMENT

II. What are the foundations of the American political system?

B. What are the distinctive characteristics of American society?

D. What is the place of law in the American constitutional system?

V. What are the roles of the citizen in American democracy?

B. What are the rights of citizens?

C. What are the responsibilities of citizens?

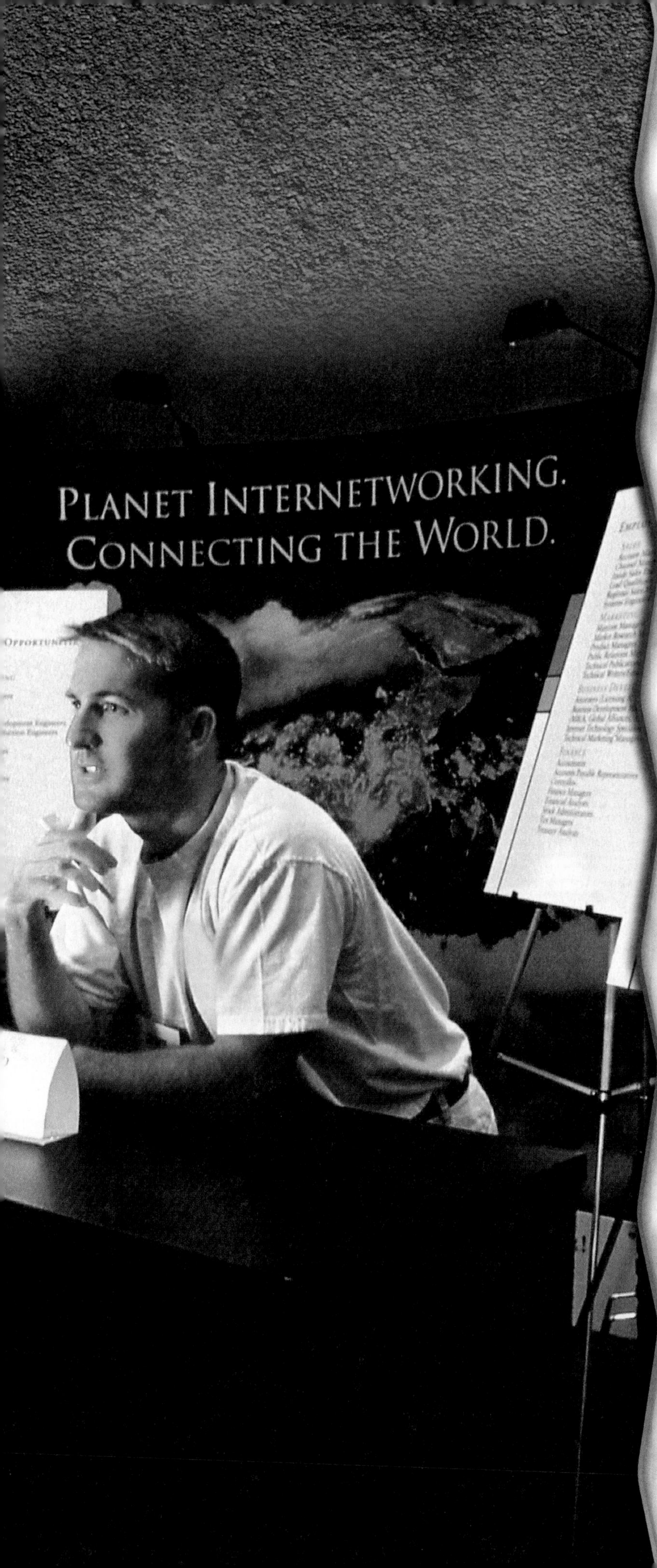

WHY CIVICS Matters

"What do you want to be when you grow up?" You have undoubtedly been asked that question since you were a toddler. You probably have begun to ask yourself that question recently. Career opportunities are available in hundreds of fields. You will want to choose a career in which you can do your best.

STUDENTS TAKE ACTION

REFORESTING LAND New trees will be planted in Jamestown, Rhode Island, because some students wanted to improve the area around their schools. What can you do to make your community more beautiful?

FOCUS ON WRITING

JOB HISTORY One of the first things that a potential employer will want to know about you is what jobs you have had in the past. As you read this chapter, think about how to best present your work history to a potential employer.

PLANET INTERNETWORKING.
CONNECTING THE WORLD.

Reading Skills

In this chapter you will learn about the freedom you have in choosing a career that best suits you. You will also discover the four main categories of workers so that you can familiarize yourself with a variety of career fields. You will learn about career fields that are on the rise and about laws that keep employers from discriminating against job applicants. Finally, you will also discover how to learn more about yourself and how to choose a career that uses your interests and skills.

Drawing Conclusions

FOCUS ON READING You have probably heard the phrase, "Put two and two together." When people say that, they don't mean "2 + 2 = 4." They mean, "Put the information together."

Drawing Conclusions A conclusion is a judgment you make by combing information. You put information from what you are reading together with what you already know.

Helpful Hints for Drawing Conclusions

1. Gather information from the passage as you read.

2. Think about what you already know about the topic from books, TV, movies, or your own experience.

3. Put your background knowledge together with what the passage says to draw a conclusion.

The U.S. Department of Labor constantly studies jobs and job opportunities throughout the country. Each year it reports where people are working and what jobs they are performing. It also attempts to predict which jobs will need more workers in the coming years. The department has predicted that the health care and computer fields in particular will need many more workers in years to come.

Information you learned from the passage: Health care and computer fields will need more workers in the future.

+

What you already know about the topic: My cousin is studying computers in vocational school.

Conclusion: My cousin should not have a hard time finding a job when she finishes school.

You Try It!

The following passage is from the chapter you are about to read. Read it carefully and then answer the questions below.

> The country's largest employer is the U.S. government. More than 2.7 million Americans work for the federal government, not including the men and women who serve in the armed forces. Federal employees hold a wide range of jobs.
>
> Some federal employees deliver the mail, care for war veterans, or protect against counterfeiting. Others run the national parks, forecast the weather, or inspect food and medicines to ensure that they are not contaminated. Many thousands of clerks, word processors, and secretaries are also needed to carry out the everyday business of the federal government.

From Chapter 22, p. 590

Use information from the passage and what you already know to draw conclusions about what you have read.

1. Imagine that you have an older sister who has just graduated and is starting a job search. From this passage, what could you conclude about employers she should consider?

2. Based on what you have read in previous chapters, what can you conclude about why the federal government is the country's largest employer?

3. Based on this passage, what can you conclude about the types of jobs available in the U.S. government?

As you read Chapter 22, think about what you already know about careers and draw conclusions to expand your knowledge.

Academic Vocabulary

Success in school is related to knowing academic vocabulary—the words that are frequently used in school assignments and discussions. In this chapter, you will learn the following academic words:

incentive *(p. 583)*
execute *(p. 586)*
logical *(p. 599)*

SECTION 1

The Challenge of a Career

The Main Idea

You will spend most of your adult life in one or more jobs. You may even have more than one career. Education and self-knowledge are important in finding a career that best suits you.

Reading Focus

1. What influences a person's career choice?
2. What do employers look for in a job candidate?

Key Terms

personal values, *p. 582*
qualifications, *p. 582*

TAKING NOTES As you read, take notes on the challenges of selecting a career. Use a graphic organizer like this one to record your notes.

Choosing Your Career	What Employers Want

One half of your life will be spent working at a job. Do you have an idea of what you want to do? Dreams can change, but a good education will prepare you to take advantage of more opportunities.

Choosing Your Career

Americans have the freedom to apply for whichever jobs they like. No government official tells them where, when, and how they may work. You will learn how important this freedom of choice is as you decide on a career. You are free to pursue any kind of work that suits your interests, intelligence, and abilities.

The freedom to decide which job to take is sometimes limited by economic conditions, though. During times of high unemployment, people may have to settle for less than their first choice. Yet they are still free to succeed in the jobs they have, or to change jobs when the chance comes.

With so many choices and opportunities, it may be hard to decide which career you would like to pursue. A good first step

is to decide what is important to you in a career, and whether you have what it takes to succeed in that line of work.

Personal Values

How people choose a career often depends on their personal values. **Personal values** are the things that people believe to be most important in their lives.

Someone whose main purpose is to earn as much money as possible will seek an occupation that pays well. Someone else may consider helping others to be a more important aim and only feel happy in a service career. Such a person may become a teacher, health-care worker, or a social worker. Personal values play a strong role in determining a person's career choice.

What Is Best for You

Before making a decision about a career, you should take a good, hard look at your own qualifications. **Qualifications** are the skills and knowledge that you possess.

With your abilities, talents, interests, and skills, there are probably many different careers you can pursue. Learning about

Nursing in the United States

During the Civil War a severe shortage of medical personnel led to the explosion of the nursing profession, especially for women. Over the years, nursing has expanded from a job with simple on-site training to a career requiring specialized training and certification.

Today, as the U.S. population ages and preventative medicine grows in demand, there is a pressing need for more nurses. In particular, there is a shortage of male nurses. After World Wars I and II, the government encouraged women, rather than men, to go to nursing school. Accordingly, as of 2003, men made up only 5.3 percent of all nurses.

Many organizations today recruit both men and women to go into nursing. The Bureau of Labor Statistics predicts that more new jobs will be created for registered nurses that in any other occupation for many years to come.

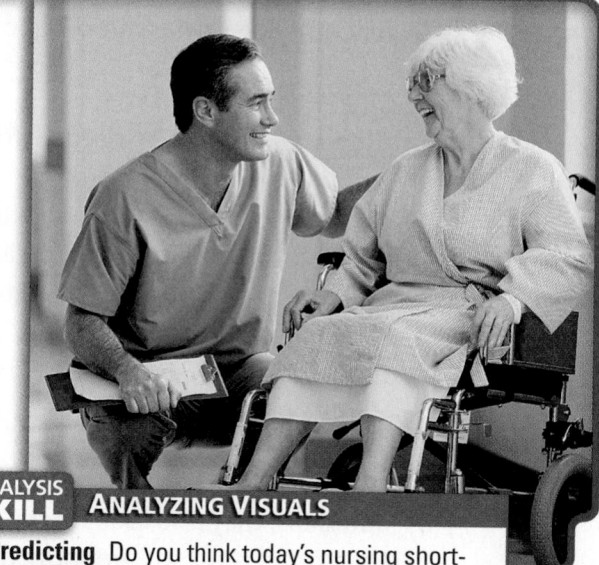

ANALYSIS SKILL   ANALYZING VISUALS

Predicting Do you think today's nursing shortage will affect the male-female ratio in the nursing profession? Explain.

careers can help you narrow your choices to occupations that have a special appeal for you. Do not narrow your choices too soon, however. You may discover new and rewarding opportunities as you learn more about careers that interest you.

READING CHECK ▶ **Finding the Main Idea** What two factors can influence a person's career choice?

What Do Employers Want?

Employers look for many things in a potential employee, including dedication and reliability. One of the most important qualifications, however, is a good education. One reason is that educated people are usually able to meet the challenges of new situations.

Education Is the Key

To succeed in today's rapidly changing world, you will need the best education you can get. Most employers want men and women who have been trained well. In some jobs, this means being able to read well, write clearly, and solve problems. In other jobs, it may mean having special skills, like using tools and operating machinery. Still other jobs may require special training.

On average, the more education you have, the higher your income. Education does not guarantee success, but it does improve your chances for earning a higher income during your lifetime. That should be a good **incentive** for getting a good education. Educated people have demonstrated that they are able to learn and can meet the challenges of new situations.

Some students find education difficult and drop out of school. They may believe that quitting school and going to work will give them a head start in earning money. However, leaving school is the worst thing to do if you want to earn a good income.

Dropouts may begin to earn money sooner than students who remain in school, but most dropouts earn low wages. They do not have the education, training, and skills needed for most occupations that provide a higher income. Also, dropouts often find themselves without work. With every year that passes, a person who does not finish high school will find it more difficult to earn a living.

ACADEMIC VOCABULARY

incentive: something that leads people to follow a certain course of action

Also, many tasks that were once done by less-skilled workers are now done by machines or workers in other countries.

On-the-Job Training

If special training is needed for a position, employers sometimes provide it on the job. For example, someone hired as a secretary needs to have organizational and computer skills. He or she is not expected to know much about the company's procedures. That information can be learned on the job.

The Right Attitude

Not only do employers look for education and skills, they also look for the right attitude. Employers want to hire individuals who will make their business more successful. To that end, they want employees who are dedicated, enthusiastic, and flexible.

READING CHECK **Summarizing** Why is education the key to success in obtaining employment?

There are many careers available for you to choose from. All require hard work, a basic education, and some sort of training in order to succeed.

go.hrw.com
Online Quiz
KEYWORD: SZ7 HP22

SECTION 1 ASSESSMENT

Reviewing Ideas and Terms

1. a. Define Write a brief definition for the terms **personal values** and **qualifications**.

  b. Make Generalizations What are some motivations that drive a person's career choice?

  c. Evaluate In your opinion, which is more important—finding a career that pays well or finding a career that you enjoy?

2. a. Summarize How does education benefit job seekers, and how might a lack of education put them at a disadvantage?

  b. Analyze What skills do most employers expect workers to have, and what training do some employers provide for workers once they are hired?

  c. Predict In the future, will it be easier or more difficult to find a good job without a college education? Explain your answer.

Critical Thinking

3. Finding Main Ideas Use your notes and a graphic organizer like the one here to identify the different elements in choosing a career.

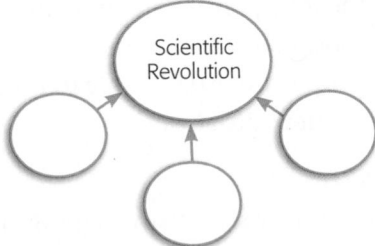

Focus on Writing

4. Summarizing Imagine that you are beginning your job search. Make a list of your strengths and weaknesses, interests, skills, personal values, and accomplishments. Based on the list, write a summary of your accomplishments and professional goals for a job that interests you.

Reading Help-Wanted Ads

Learn

Help-wanted ads are placed by companies or organizations that are seeking new employees. These ads provide information about available positions, such as salary, hours, and benefits. They also list the requirements of the job, such as educational background, prior experience, and weekend availability.

Help-wanted ads often appear in the classified section of most newspapers. It is also possible to find help-wanted ads in other sources, such as magazines, or special job Web sites. Understanding help-wanted ads can help you find a job that you want to apply for.

Practice

❶ **Understand the organization of help-wanted sections.** Usually the help-wanted ads are divided by profession, such as education, medical, and office/clerical. Some help-wanted sections even divide each profession into sub-categories. Look at the ads listed under professions that most appeal to you.

❷ **Read the ads carefully.** The type of job is usually listed at the top of each ad to help you spot job possibilities. Note what training or experience is required. What is the salary? Are there benefits, such as paid vacation or health insurance, associated with the position? Who should you contact to apply for the job?

❸ **Learn about the abbreviations used in ads.** To save space, employers usually use abbreviations. FT and PT stand for full-time and part-time. 37k means $37,000. BA means Bachelor of Arts. Other abbreviations may be specific to the type of job advertised.

Apply

Use the help-wanted ads shown below to answer the following questions.

1. Under what headings would you expect to find the two help-wanted ads shown, if you saw them in a newspaper?

2. Would a recent high-school graduate qualify for either of the jobs shown? Explain your answer.

3. Based on the information provided in one of these two ads, what is one question you want to ask the employer about the job?

An illustrated example of two help-wanted advertisements

RN/LPN

Maple Lane Retirement Community
Westchester County, NY
Job Term: Full-time
$40-52K
Excellent opportunity for a focused professional who is a quick learner to join a terrific facility. Nurturing and supportive community enjoying the very best in long- and short-term nursing care, rehabilitative services, and living options. RNs will administer nursing to all patients through assessing, planning, implementing, and evaluating the patient's needs. LPNs will assist RNs in working with adult clients to oversee medical systems, distribute meds, and maintain patient charts. RN requirements: Licensed Registered Nurse. Bachelor's in nursing from accredited school. 1 year hospital or long-term care experience. LPN requirements: LPN license. Assoc. degree in nursing from accredited school. 1 year hospital or long-term care experience. All general nursing positions require a license and current registration as an RN or LPN in New York State. Experience required in specialty areas. New graduates are accepted in non-specialty services. Please email resume to: Norma Brenes, nbrenes@maplelane.com
NO PHONE CALLS PLEASE

CNA/CHHA

Hillbrook Nursing Home, Edgewater, NJ. Job Term: Temporary. Salary: $9.00 per hour. Requirements: Nursing assistant or home health aid certification. Job description: Upscale assisted-living facility in Edgewater, NJ is seeking experienced CNAs or CHHAs for on-going assignments. This is a brand new residential facility for highly functional senior citizens. Please fax or email resume to: The Nightingale Agency, 101 Madison Avenue, 4th Floor New York, NY 10017
temps@nightingaleagency.com
212-407-9222 (Phone)
212-409-9364 (Fax)

BEFORE YOU READ

The Main Idea

When considering your future career, you should learn about a variety of career fields.

Reading Focus

1. What are white-collar professions?
2. What are blue-collar jobs?
3. What careers are available in the agricultural and service fields?

Key Terms

white-collar workers, *p. 586*
professionals, *p. 586*
technicians, *p. 586*
blue-collar workers, *p. 587*
apprenticeship, *p. 587*
operators, *p. 587*
automation, *p. 587*
laborers, *p. 588*
agribusinesses, *p. 588*
service industries, *p. 588*

TAKING NOTES As you read, take notes on the different groups of workers and the types of work they do. Use a graphic organizer like this one to record your notes.

Workers	Types of work

 Learning what people in your community do for a living can give you an idea of what you might want to do. New technologies create new jobs every day.

White-Collar Workers

White-collar workers make up the largest and fastest-growing group of workers in the country today. **White-collar workers** are those who work in a professional, technical, managerial, administrative, or sales job.

ACADEMIC VOCABULARY

execute:
to perform, carry out

Professionals

Jobs that require many years of education and training, and in which the work tends to be mental rather than physical, are referred to as professions. Examples of **professionals** include doctors, nurses, lawyers, and architects. As the economy has changed and grown, the demand for professional workers has increased. Among today's fastest-growing career fields are those in the computer and health-care professions.

Technicians

People who perform jobs that require some specialized skill in addition to a solid, basic education are called **technicians**. Among these skilled workers are laboratory technicians, medical X-ray technicians, physical therapists, and dental hygienists. Other technicians are employed in radio and television, the film industry, manufacturing, and computer industries.

Managers and Administrators

The people in charge of businesses and corporations are managers and administrators. Because they **execute** the operations of a business, they are also known as executives.

Today U.S. businesses are experiencing stiff competition from other countries around the world. To remain competitive in the global economy, American businesses must continue to attract experienced, well-educated, and well-trained managers and executives. Businesses build on the ideas and skills of these individuals.

Support and Sales Workers

People who sell goods and services are sales workers. Sales workers may be clerks in retail stores or door-to-door salespeople. They also may sell to other businesses, institutions, or governments.

Bookkeepers, secretaries, office clerks, and word processors are examples of administrative support workers. They do much of the paperwork required to keep American businesses and industries operating smoothly.

READING CHECK ▶ **Summarizing** What types of jobs do white-collar workers do?

Blue-Collar Workers

Workers who perform jobs that require manual labor are known as **blue-collar workers**. They work in construction, manufacturing, mining, petroleum, steel, transportation, and many other industries.

Trades and Crafts

People who work in trades or crafts include electricians, plumbers, auto mechanics, artists, painters, and others who make things by hand. An important requirement for these workers is manual ability.

To train for a craft, a new worker may serve an **apprenticeship**, or fixed period of on-the-job training. The amount of training varies according to the job. Some industries and labor unions reduce apprenticeship time by giving credit for job-training courses from high school or trade school.

Operators

People who operate machines or equipment in factories, mills, industrial plants, gas stations, mines, and laundries are known as **operators**. Other factory workers, such as those who inspect, assemble, and package goods, are included in this group. Truck and bus drivers are also operators. The number of machine operators in American industry has declined. Factories have come to rely on **automation**, or the use of machines, instead of workers.

World of Work in Film

Jobs of all types can be found in almost any field. For example, the film industry requires white collar, blue collar, and service workers.

What educational background might be necessary for jobs in the film industry?

Director
A film director is a white-collar worker, and is responsible for the way that a film looks and sounds.

Make-up Artist
A make-up artist is a service worker who creates the look and feel appropriate for the actors and the script.

Crew
Film crew members are often blue-collar workers who are skilled carpenters, electricians, and lighting experts.

Laborers

There are and probably always will be jobs that call for little or no training. Workers without special skills are often employed to mix cement, carry bricks, dig ditches, and handle freight. Workers who perform this type of heavy physical work are called **laborers**.

READING CHECK ▶ **Finding Main Ideas** What are some of the jobs of blue-collar workers?

Agriculture and Service Industries

When this nation was founded, most people worked as farmers. In the past 100 years, the need for agricultural workers has decreased greatly. However, the service industry is one of the fastest-growing industries in the country.

Agricultural Workers

People who operate, manage, or work on farms are called agricultural workers. Today many small farms have been replaced by large farms known as **agribusinesses**. Agribusinesses are owned by corporations and rely heavily on mechanized equipment. They are able to produce larger yields using fewer workers. To compete, many small farmers have turned to organic farming and other specialty crops.

Service Workers

Today one in every six employed Americans is a service worker. Service workers provide the public with some type of assistance. Firefighters, police officers, teachers, paramedics, dental assistants, nurses, and many other professionals are considered service workers.

Businesses that sell services rather than products are called **service industries**. They include hospitals, security companies, hotels, restaurants, dry cleaners, auto repair, and hair salons. Some service industry jobs require a college education or training courses. In other industries, workers learn the needed skills on the job.

READING CHECK ▶ **Contrasting** How does the work performed by service workers and agricultural workers differ?

go.hrw.com
Online Quiz
KEYWORD: SZ7 HP22

SECTION 2 ASSESSMENT

Reviewing Ideas and Terms

1. a. Define Write a brief definition for the terms **white-collar workers**, **professionals**, and **technicians**.
   b. Make Inferences Why are professional jobs called white-collar jobs?
2. a. Define Write a brief definition for the terms **blue-collar workers**, **apprenticeship**, **operators**, **automation**, and **laborers**.
   b. Draw Conclusions Why do some industries give apprentices credit for job-training courses they take in school?
3. a. Define Write a brief definition for the terms **agribusinesses** and **service industries**.
   b. Elaborate In which type of job would you most want to work? Why?

Critical Thinking

4. Categorizing Use your notes and a chart like this one to list occupations that require mostly mental work, mostly physical work, or both mental and physical work. Then provide examples of each type of job.

Types of work	Examples of jobs

Focus on Writing

5. Drawing Inferences and Conclusions Imagine that you are an analyst of business and the global economy. Write a two-paragraph article explaining why businesses need a well-educated, well-trained workforce to operate effectively and remain competitive in the global marketplace.

STUDENTS TAKE ACTION

PROJECT ★ Citizen

Reforesting Land

On the island of Jamestown, Rhode Island, officials have begun replanting trees in a large area between two local schools. The land had once been covered with trees, but the trees became diseased and had to be cut down. Thanks to the efforts of a Project Citizen class, trees will grow there once again.

Community Connection Students at Jamestown's Lawn Avenue School noticed that when the diseased trees near their school were removed, no new trees were planted. The students researched city statutes and discovered that local laws require that any trees that are cut down must be replaced. The town council even appoints a tree warden whose job includes helping to ensure compliance with this law.

Students worked with the local tree warden and the town council to get new trees planted at their school.

Taking Action The students decided that, according to the law, the trees that had been near their school should be replanted. "Students did a wonderful job utilizing community resources to address the problem," said teacher Maureen McGuirl. The students contacted the tree warden, town workers, and staff members at their school. One problem facing the group was how to pay for the new trees. The problem was solved when the tree warden applied for and received a grant to pay most of the costs. The local school board also agreed to contribute. Volunteers from the community helped city workers prepare the land for replanting. Soon these new trees will cover the area.

go.hrw.com
Project Citizen
KEYWORD: SZ7 CH22

SERVICE LEARNING

1. What environmental and legal problems did students identify in their community?
2. How did the students work with town employees to help the project succeed?

SECTION 3
Unlimited Opportunities

BEFORE YOU READ

The Main Idea

By law, employers cannot discriminate against job applicants because of their sex, age, race, skin color, religion, or ethnic background.

Reading Focus

1. What types of qualifications are necessary for careers in the government?
2. What industries are expected to see job growth?
3. What does it mean to be an equal opportunity employer?

Key Terms

equal opportunity employer, p. 592

 **TAKING NOTES** As you read, take notes on careers in government, growing industries, and equal employment opportunities. Use a graphic organizer like this one to record your notes.

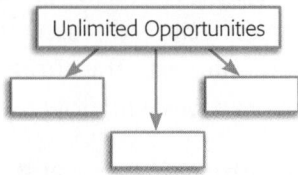

 When looking for a job, do not forget about local, state, or federal government. Not everyone in government is an elected official. In fact, most are not.

Careers in Government

The country's largest employer is the U.S. government. More than 2.7 million Americans work for the federal government, not including the men and women who serve in the armed forces. Federal employees hold a wide range of jobs.

Federal, State, and Local Government

Some federal employees deliver the mail, care for war veterans, or protect against counterfeiting. Others run the national parks, forecast the weather, or inspect food and medicines to ensure that they are not contaminated. Many thousands of clerks, word processors, and secretaries are also needed to carry out the everyday business of the federal government.

Applicants typically submit a résumé or an application form that includes a detailed history of their background and education.

Some government agencies also require a written test for certain positions. As with any job, government agencies interview candidates and choose the best qualified candidate for the job. Before a candidate is offered a job, he or she may be subject to an extensive background check.

Like the federal government, state and local governments employ many different kinds of workers. The process for hiring in a state or local government agency is similar to that of the federal government.

Armed Forces

There are many opportunities for employment in the armed forces. A high school diploma is required for most jobs in the armed forces. Training in the military is available for jobs such as electronics technician, radar operator and technician, motor mechanic, and surveyor. In addition, some combat positions on aircraft and ships are open to both men and women in the armed forces.

READING CHECK **Drawing Conclusions** Why might some government jobs require a written test?

Growing Industries

The U.S. Department of Labor constantly studies jobs and job opportunities throughout the country. It also attempts to predict which jobs will need more workers in coming years.

Workers in Demand

The Department of Labor has predicted that the health care and computer fields in particular will need many more workers. Of course, some kinds of workers are always in demand. For example, law enforcement officers and teachers are always needed. Keep in mind that the need for a particular type of worker may be greater in some parts of the country than in others. For example, some areas have more openings for manufacturing or high-tech jobs than do others.

Also remember that in all industries and fields there is a degree of turnover because of promotions, job changes, and retirements. These and other circumstances almost always create job openings for new employees. The well-prepared job seeker should be ready to seize employment opportunities when they happen.

Unemployment

There are times when the U.S. economy experiences a recession or depression. During such times many people are without work. People who are working may not have been able to find jobs in their chosen fields or are working only part-time.

As you are considering possible careers, you should remember that there will be periods of high unemployment in the future. It is wise to have multiple interests and, if possible, to develop skills in more than one area of work. It is also vital that you continue to develop and expand your skills in your chosen area of work in order to remain competitive.

READING CHECK **Analyzing Information** How can employment seekers make the most of opportunities in the job world?

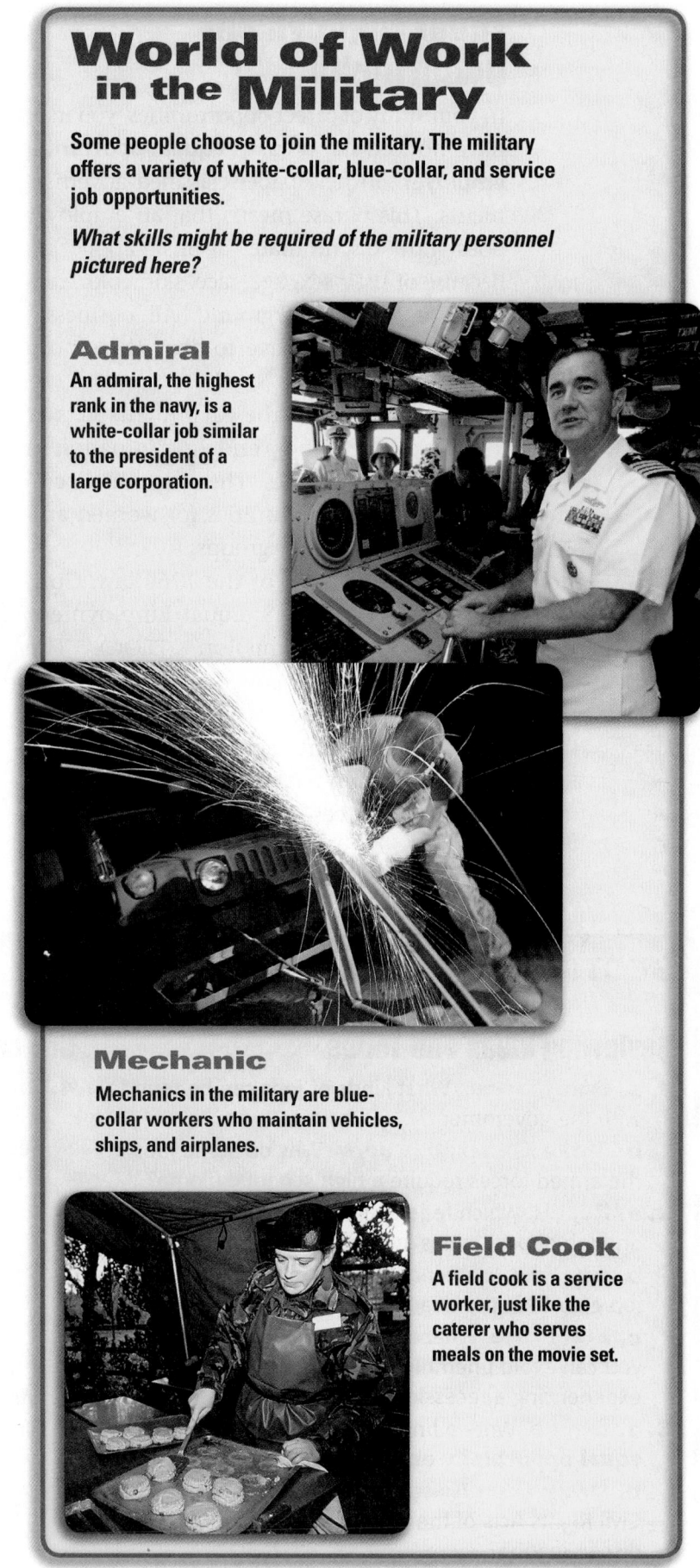

World of Work in the Military

Some people choose to join the military. The military offers a variety of white-collar, blue-collar, and service job opportunities.

What skills might be required of the military personnel pictured here?

Admiral
An admiral, the highest rank in the navy, is a white-collar job similar to the president of a large corporation.

Mechanic
Mechanics in the military are blue-collar workers who maintain vehicles, ships, and airplanes.

Field Cook
A field cook is a service worker, just like the caterer who serves meals on the movie set.

Equal Employment Opportunity

In your study of career opportunities, you may have noticed the phrase "**equal opportunity employer**" in newspaper classified advertisements. This phrase means that an employer does not discriminate against applicants because of their sex, age, race, skin color, religion, or ethnic background. All businesses over a certain size have to obey these non-discrimination laws.

Congress passed the Civil Rights Acts of 1964 and 1968 to help end discrimination in hiring and wage rates. These acts have created new job opportunities for women and members of minority groups.

To enforce parts of the 1964 law, Congress created the U.S. Equal Employment Opportunity Commission (EEOC). The EEOC's jurisdiction covers all government employers at all levels, private employers and employment agencies, educational institutions, and labor unions. The commission enforces laws that require equal pay for equal work and that prohibit employment discrimination under the Americans with Disabilities Act. The commissioners and the chief legal counsel of the EEOC are appointed by the president. Most states have similar commissions.

Partly as a result of civil rights legislation of the 1960s, women's struggle for equal rights has opened doors to careers previously unavailable to women. The EEOC is an important part of enforcing laws against gender discrimination. Today women are members of Congress, judges, doctors, scientists, engineers, pilots, cab drivers, police officers, and astronauts. Most jobs in the military are also now open to women.

The same laws that have opened doors for women have also opened doors for people of different races, religions, ethnicities, and national origins. And with the passage of the Americans with Disabilities Act in 1990, job discrimination against people with disabilities was also made illegal.

READING CHECK **Finding the Main Idea** What two acts passed by Congress influenced the rights of employees, and what effect did they have?

go.hrw.com
Online Quiz
KEYWORD: SZ7 HP22

SECTION 3 ASSESSMENT

Reviewing Ideas and Terms

1. **a. Summarize** What kinds of jobs can be found with the government?
   b. Make Generalizations Why do some jobs in the armed forces require a high school diploma?
2. **a. Recall** Which federal agency studies job trends and job opportunities in the United States?
   b. Analyze What industries are expected to see job growth in the near future? Why?
   c. Elaborate What are some possible ways that you can avoid unemployment when the economy is experiencing a recession or depression?
3. **a. Define** Write a brief definition of the term **equal opportunity employer**.
   b. Draw Conclusions In what ways did the Civil Rights Acts of the 1960s help end job discrimination?

Critical Thinking

4. **Summarizing** Copy the graphic organizer. Use it and your notes to summarize the qualifications needed to work in government or military jobs.

	Qualifications
Government	
Military	

Focus on Writing

5. **Making Generalizations and Predictions** Write a speech for Congress explaining what fields will be growing in the next 10 years and how the country can ensure that there are enough workers in these professions.

SECTION 4

Learning More about Careers

BEFORE YOU READ

The Main Idea

Before making your career choice, learn more about what particular jobs involve and how they will benefit you and your future.

Reading Focus

1. How can job seekers find information about careers?
2. What questions should you ask yourself when considering a career?

Key Terms

career fair, p. 593

 **TAKING NOTES** As you read, take notes on how to learn about careers. Use a graphic organizer like this one to record your notes.

Ways to Learn about Careers	Questions to Ask Yourself

Your school counselor can give you information about careers.

CIVICS IN PRACTICE Now is the best time to learn about careers. You have the time to read and learn about various jobs. Summer vacation is a good time to try a job in a field that interests you. Working all day at a job can help you decide if it is right for you.

Ways to Learn about Careers

You probably are discovering that you already know a great deal about the careers and jobs that will be available to you someday. However, no single source can give you all the information you need about various jobs. You may have to spend time looking in many places to find the facts you need to choose a career.

Career Fairs

One way to learn more about careers is to attend a career fair. A **career fair** is an event where representatives from one or more companies are on hand to discuss job opportunities. Representatives from government agencies or the military may also be there. Career fairs are often held in schools, at libraries, in convention centers, at hotels, and sometimes at a company's office.

Ways to Learn More about a Career

There are several ways to learn more about careers. One way is to talk to someone you know about his or her job. You can also find information on the Internet about almost any career you can think of. Today many schools and libraries have career centers where you can learn more about different careers.

Why is the Internet a useful tool in learning more about careers?

Career fairs are good ways to learn more about what companies do, what type of jobs are available, and the skills and qualifications companies look for in a job candidate. At some job fairs, employers conduct job interviews and may even offer positions. Some employers may not be hiring but are looking for candidates for the future. Either way, it is a good idea to have a résumé that you can give to a company representative at a career fair.

Read about Careers

One of the best ways you can learn about careers is to read about them. The Internet is a good source of career information, as are the many books, magazines, and pamphlets available on the subject. Explore your library or a local bookstore.

Your local or state employment office has information about careers in your community, including free booklets. Because large businesses are always looking for good employees, many of them publish brochures that contain useful job information about their industry.

Another helpful source of information about jobs is the Department of Labor. It publishes the *Occupational Outlook Handbook*,

a very important reference for job seekers. Also helpful is the *Encyclopedia of Careers and Vocational Guidance*.

Watch Others at Work

You can learn about careers by investigating job opportunities in your community. Through school-sponsored trips, you might find out about the jobs available in nearby factories, offices, and stores. Also, someone in your family may be able to arrange for you to visit his or her place of employment. You can even learn about jobs as you go about your daily affairs. Observe the work of bus drivers, police officers, teachers, salespeople, office workers, and others you meet each day.

Learn by Working

Another good way to discover more about careers is to work at a job. For many students, responsibilities at home make having a job impossible. Some students, however, have enough time to work at part-time or summer jobs. You can learn from any job.

Baby-sitting, for example, may lead you to think about a future job in child care. Part-time and summer jobs help teach you why being prompt, responsible, and dependable are important in any job. Working as a newspaper carrier, clerk, gasoline station attendant, or movie usher is another way in which you can learn about a career.

> **READING CHECK** **Summarizing** What are some resources you can use to find career information?

Questions to Ask Yourself

As you consider your future career, ask yourself the following questions. Your answers will help you learn if you are making a wise choice.

1. *What kind of work will I do in this job?*
2. *What personal qualities does the job require?*
3. *How much education and training does the job require?*
4. *What different job opportunities are available in this field?*
5. *What salary does the job pay?*
6. *Where will I have to live and work for this kind of job?*
7. *How do I feel about this job?*

By answering these questions, you will get an idea of whether or not a job is right for you. For example, a job may require that you be available to move to a different part

FOCUS ON
Mary T. Washington
(1906–2005)

Mary T. Washington was the first African American woman to become a certified public accountant. In the 1920s Washington started working at Binga State Bank, one of the largest African American–owned banks in the country. She assisted a vice president of the bank, which began her career path to becoming an accountant. In 1939, while still in college, Washington started her own accounting firm.

In 1941 Washington graduated from Northwestern University with a business degree. In 1968 she founded the accounting firm Washington, Pittman, and McKeever. She retired in 1985 and lived in Chicago to the age of 99.

Evaluate How did Washington's experience in the Binga State Bank influence her career choice?

of the country or to travel a great deal. These requirements may not be right for you. By asking yourself these questions you can better understand what you want out of a career.

> **READING CHECK** **Summarizing** What basic information should you consider regarding a future career?

go.hrw.com
Online Quiz
KEYWORD: SZ7 HP22

SECTION 4 ASSESSMENT

Reviewing Ideas and Terms

1. **a. Define** Write a brief definition of the term **career fair**.
   b. Make Inferences How can you learn about careers from observing other people at work?
   c. Elaborate How can part-time jobs help you learn more about possible careers?
2. **a. Summarize** What questions should you ask yourself when you are considering a future career?
   b. Elaborate Of the questions that you should ask yourself when considering a career, which do you think is most important? Why?

Critical Thinking

3. **Summarizing** Use your notes and a graphic organizer like this one to summarize the different ways you can learn more about careers.

   Learning about Careers

Focus on Writing

4. **Analyzing Information** It is time to begin exploring your career path. Create an action plan listing different ways of finding out about various fields and careers.

Learning More about Yourself

BEFORE YOU READ

The Main Idea

Learning more about your strengths and your weaknesses can help you decide on a career.

Reading Focus

1. How should you prepare to apply for a job?
2. What do employers want to know about you?
3. How can tests help you understand yourself and your abilities?

Key Terms

motor skills, *p. 598*
perceptual skills, *p. 598*
interpersonal skills, *p. 599*
aptitude tests, *p. 599*

 **TAKING NOTES** As you read, take notes on how to prepare to apply for a job, what employers want to know, and how tests can help you learn more about your abilities. Use a diagram like this one to record your notes.

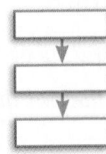 **CIVICS IN PRACTICE** What do you need to know about yourself to choose the right job? Taking a good look at your interests and skills can help you select a career. Once you have found a job that interests you, you must be prepared to tell a potential employer why that job interests you and why you are the best candidate for the job.

Preparing to Apply for a Job

When you look for your first job, you will probably have to fill out a job application. An application is a printed form on which you are asked to supply information about yourself and your qualifications for the job. Your job application helps the employer decide if you are the right person for the position.

Many businesses and corporations have human resources workers whose job it is to hire or recommend new employees. Human resources workers examine job applications and interview people to determine the best-qualified applicant for an available job.

You will find it helpful to practice filling out a job application. Then when you apply for a job, you will know what type of information you may be asked to supply.

You can practice completing job applications in several ways. You may want to fill out an actual application used by a local business. You can also find sample job applications on the Internet. You may want to prepare a resume, or outline of important facts about yourself. Many students prefer to write short autobiographies that include the chief facts about their lives.

 **READING CHECK** **Summarizing** In what ways can you prepare to apply for a job?

What Employers Want to Know

Employers want to know about job applicants. Be prepared to give them information about your school history, health record, activities, and special interests.

School History

School records tell employers a lot about you. List the subjects you have taken in the last two years and the grades you received. Then look at the reasons for these grades.

What do grades mean? Perhaps you have high marks in English because you enjoy

Telling Employers What They Want to Know

A one-page resume usually gives an employer all the information he or she needs.

Why is it important to adjust a resume to the employer who will be reading it?

Volunteering (or interning) in a field of interest shows dedication both to the career and to the community.

Leadership shows willingness to take on responsibilities and the ability to inspire and direct people.

Employers are people, too. Information about outside interests, even if they are just hobbies, shows that Allison might be an interesting and fun person to have at work.

ALLISON DAVIS
143 Great Cove Circle
Pflugerville, Texas 78660
(555) 585-1012

OBJECTIVE: To obtain a full-time position as a veterinary assistant while I study part-time at the University of Texas toward a degree in veterinary medicine

EXPERIENCE:
Barton Creek Humane Society   Austin, TX, 2003-2005
Volunteer
  • Walked, fed and watered, and petted cats, dogs, and other animals
  • Assisted with animal intake, including answering phones and filing forms

Travis County 4-H   Austin, TX, 1999-2005
Local, county, and state participant
  • Raised and showed Longhorn bulls at livestock shows up to state level
  • Best Handler, Texas 4-H Dog Show, 2001

Travis High School Biology Club   Austin, TX, 2004-2005
President
  • Arranged trips to zoos, rescue shelters, and laboratories
  • Initiated guest speaker program for speakers including Dr. Emil Layton, Chair of Microbiology, Cornell University, and Bill Nye the Science Guy

EDUCATION:
Accepted, University of Texas   2005
High school graduate, Travis High School GPA 3.75   2005
Certificate of completion, Pre-Veterinarian's Assistant Program   2005
  • Coursework includes: College Biology I, II; College Chemistry I, II; Organic Chemistry I, II; Human Anatomy I
  • Courses in junior and senior year taken at Austin Community College

INTERESTS:
Astronomy, tennis, and swing dancing

REFERENCES:
Mr. Chuck Warner, Head of the science department, Travis
Miss Leigh Tripp, 4-H Club president, Travis County 4-H
Mrs. Sandra Krouch, Director, Barton Creek Human Society

Working hard in school is a signal to employers that Allison will work hard on the job, too. GPA and other academic achievements should always be included on a resume when they show above-average performance.

expressing yourself through writing. This may show that you should consider an occupation in which you can use your writing skills. In contrast, you may have poor grades in mathematics. Does this mean you should not consider a job that requires mathematical ability? Not necessarily.

Low grades in a subject are not necessarily a sign that the student cannot learn that subject. Some students who have received low marks in mathematics may be late in discovering their ability in this subject. With added effort and support, they may be able to catch up in their studies. They are then on their way to mastering math and earning higher grades.

Health Record

Good health is an important qualification for any job. Some occupations even require that workers have special physical qualifications and pass physical examinations.

You should examine your health record and review your fitness routine. On the other hand, having a disability should not prevent you from holding a job. There are many job opportunities for people who have a disability. The Americans with Disabilities Act has made it illegal for employers to discriminate against people with disabilities.

Extracurricular Activities

Make a list of your extracurricular activities. This should include your hobbies, school offices that you have held, sports in which you take part, school organizations to which you belong, and jobs you have had.

After you have completed this list, take another look at it. Does it show many different activities? What part of each activity did you like best? This review can tell you and an employer a great deal about your job skills.

Exploring Special Interests

You may have a special interest, such as cooking, that could become a career.

What are three ways you could develop a special interest into a job or a career?

Special Interests

The things that interest you now may also point the way to your future. List any special interests that might help you make a career choice. Consider the subjects you like best in school. Determine whether your interests have helped you do well in these subjects. Finally, review your hobbies and your part-time jobs to find which interests they emphasize. You may find, for example, that your love of drawing is suited for a career as a graphic designer.

A future employer will know and understand you better if he or she is aware of your special interests. For example, these interests tell employers whether you prefer working alone or with others. They might also indicate if you are more of a leader or a follower.

READING CHECK ▶ **Finding the Main Idea** What do employers want to know about a job applicant?

Tests that Help You Focus

Tests are another means of helping you understand yourself and your abilities. Every test you take in school measures certain skills. Various tests show how well you study, how accurately you remember what you read, and how well you express yourself. Here are some of the strengths such tests seek to measure.

Motor Skills

Certain tests are used to determine how well people can use their hands—their **motor skills**. The tests measure how quickly and precisely individuals can do things with their hands. Certain other tests determine how well people can handle and arrange small objects. Such skills are useful to a watchmaker or a worker assembling electronic equipment, for example.

Number Skills

One of the most common tests measures a person's ability to work quickly and accurately with numbers. Such number skills are essential to bookkeepers, carpenters, and accountants.

Perceptual Skills

How well can you picture things—that is, see them in your mind? To read a blueprint, for example, you must be able to picture how a building will look when it is finished. **Perceptual skills** allow you to visualize depth and width from a flat drawing. Such skills are necessary for architects, designers, and artists.

Language Skills

Teachers explaining an idea to students, salespeople talking to customers, and parents describing to children how to do something are all using language skills. Many tests focus on your language skills. Are you a skilled writer or speaker? Editors, television and newspaper reporters, lawyers, and translators must all be skilled in using written language.

Special Talents

Some tests try to discover whether you have artistic and creative talent. There are also tests that measure your ability to organize and present facts in a **logical** fashion. Special talents like these are useful in many kinds of jobs.

Interpersonal Skills

Some tests check how well you handle personal relationships or get along with others. These **interpersonal skills** are important in teaching, sales, and many other jobs that require you to interact with the public.

Interests and Aptitudes

Certain tests can help you to know yourself better. These are called interest tests, or **aptitude tests**. Some schools offer aptitude tests to their students. Private organizations also offer aptitude tests and scoring for a fee. The tests are easy and often fun to take. They can reveal things about you that might otherwise be overlooked. Your teacher or counselor can explain the results of these tests.

Such tests probably will not tell you the exact job you should seek. No test can map out the future for you. What they can do is help you discover your abilities and interests, strengths and weaknesses. It is up to you to match what you have discovered about yourself with what you have learned about various career opportunities.

By now you probably have made a good start in getting to know yourself better. As you study careers, compare your opportunities with your abilities. Your present goal should be to choose a general field of work—that is, a type of work rather than a specific job. Leave the door open so that you can enter another field of work if necessary. Remember, your first job choice may not be the final one.

READING CHECK **Evaluating** How can tests help measure a person's skills and talents, and why are they beneficial?

ACADEMIC VOCABULARY

logical: reasoned, well thought out

go.hrw.com
Online Quiz
KEYWORD: SZ7 HP22

SECTION 5 ASSESSMENT

Reviewing Ideas and Terms

1. a. Summarize What is the purpose of a job application?

b. Make Inferences Why is filling out a job application useful for preparing for employment?

2. a. Summarize What information should you be prepared to supply to a potential employer?

b. Draw Conclusions Why might an employer want to know about your school history and special interests?

3. a. Define Write a brief definition for each of the following terms: **motor skills**, **perceptual skills**, **interpersonal skills**, and **aptitude tests**.

b. Compare and Contrast How are motor skills and perceptual skills different? How are they alike?

c. Make Inferences Why do you think some jobs might require good interpersonal skills?

Critical Thinking

4. Evaluating Using your notes and a chart like this one, list the different things employers want to know about job applicants. Then evaluate your own qualifications.

Qualifications	Evaluation

Focus on Writing

5. Solving Problems Make an outline of your skills and assess yourself honestly on each one. Identify your strengths and weaknesses and explain why you think they are such. Suggest how you can improve your level of skill in each area in which you are weak.

CHAPTER 22 REVIEW

Visual Summary

Use the visual summary to help you review the main ideas of the chapter.

Each person has his or her own combination of education, goals, skills, and interests that can lead to a job or career. Generally, education is key to obtaining a better job.

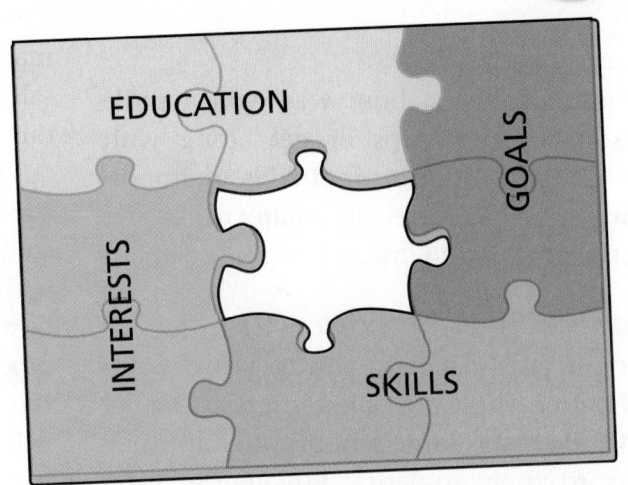

REVIEWING KEY TERMS

For each term below, write a sentence explaining its significance to career choices.

1. personal values
2. qualifications
3. white-collar workers
4. professionals
5. technicians
6. blue-collar workers
7. apprenticeship
8. operators
9. automation
10. laborers
11. agribusinesses
12. service industries
13. equal opportunity employer
14. career fair
15. motor skills
16. perceptual skills
17. interpersonal skills
18. aptitude tests

Comprehension and Critical Thinking

SECTION 1 *(Pages 582–584)*

19. a. Make Inferences What is the relationship between personal values and career choice?

   b. Explain What is the importance of education in seeking a career?

SECTION 2 *(Pages 586–588)*

20. a. Describe What types of labor do white-collar, blue-collar, service, and agricultural workers mostly perform in their jobs?

   b. Analyze Why is the need for agricultural workers and laborers decreasing in the United States?

SECTION 3 *(Pages 590–592)*

21. a. Recall What types of jobs are available in the military?

   b. Explain How do job applicants know they are protected from employer discrimination?

Active Citizenship Video Program
Review the video to answer the closing question:
Why is it important for citizens to actively work to preserve and protect the environment?

SECTION 4 *(Pages 593–595)*

22. a. Explain What is the best way to learn about occupations and careers?

b. Elaborate What can you learn by asking yourself questions and examining your hobbies and activities?

SECTION 5 *(Pages 596–599)*

23. a. Describe What is a good way to prepare for applying for jobs?

b. Summarize What information about a job applicant might be of interest to an employer, and why?

Civics Skills

Reading Help-Wanted Ads
Use the Civics Skills you learned in this chapter to answer the question that follows.

> **CNA/CHHA**
> Hillbrook Nursing Home, Edgewater, NJ. Job Term: Temporary. Salary: $9.00 per hour. Requirements: Nursing assistant or home health aid certification. Job description: Upscale assisted-living facility in Edgewater, NJ is seeking experienced CNAs or CHHAs for on-going assignments. This is a brand new residential facility for highly functional senior citizens. Please fax or email resume to: The Nightingale Agency. 101 Madison Avenue, 4th Floor New York, NY 10017
> temps@nightingaleagency.com
> 212-407-9222 (Phone)
> 212-409-9364 (Fax)

24. What amount of training and education is required for this job?

go.hrw.com

Using the Internet

KEYWORD: SZ7 CH22

25. Making Career Choices There are so many options and opportunities that trying to decide what career is right for you can be overwhelming. Enter the activity keyword. Then research information that can help you identify your interests and abilities and guide you toward a career in an area that you might enjoy. Make a poster about your interests and a career possibility that would be well suited for you. Be creative!

Reading Skills

Drawing Conclusions *Use the Reading Skills taught in this chapter to answer the questions about the reading selection below.*

> "The service-producing sector will continue to be the dominant employment generator in the economy, adding 20.5 million jobs by 2010. Within the goods-producing sector, construction and durable manufacturing will contribute relatively modest employment gains... Health services, business services, social services, and engineering, management, and related services ... account for a large share of the fastest-growing industries... Employment in all seven education or training categories that generally require a college degree or other post secondary award is projected to grow faster than the average across all occupations."
>
> —Bureau of Labor Statistics

26. What connections does the source make between education and job growth?

FOCUS ON WRITING

27. Writing a Job History Review your notes about what employers look for in a job applicant. Make a list of your jobs (including chores), skills, and interests that might interest an employer. Write a two-paragraph job history that convinces the employer that he or she should hire you.

FOUNDATIONS of DEMOCRACY

Preventing Discrimination in Employment

Every American should have an equal opportunity to work and succeed based on his or her abilities, although some jobs require special skills or certain levels of education. But what if someone decided that you did not qualify for a job simply because of your race, gender, or age? Would this be fair?

Why it Matters For many years job discrimination was common in the United States. For example, by law, African Americans and women could not hold certain jobs. Then Congress began to pass laws against such discrimination. The most important anti-discrimination employment law is Title VII of the Civil Rights Act of 1964, which prohibits job discrimination based on race, color, religion, sex, or national origin. Since then, other federal laws have been passed to protect people from being discriminated against because they are over 40 years of age or because they have a physical disability that is not related to the skill requirements of the job. Most of these laws apply to companies that have more than 15 employees and take part in interstate commerce, which covers most businesses.

The federal government also established the Equal Employment Opportunity Commission (EEOC) to investigate suspected discrimination. The EEOC determines if discrimination took place and tries to get individuals or companies to follow the law. If necessary, the EEOC will sue employers who repeatedly break the law. Job discrimination is often hard to prove unless there is a pattern that can be shown over time, such as a company that never hires or promotes African American employees even though many qualified African Americans have applied for positions. If you ever think you are the victim of job discrimination, you can contact the EEOC for help.

President Lyndon B. Johnson shakes hands with civil rights leader Martin Luther King Jr. after signing the Civil Rights Act of 1964.

ANALYSIS SKILL **EVALUATING THE LAW**

go.hrw.com
KEYWORD: SZ7 CH22

1. Why it is important to prevent job discrimination based on race, religion, gender, age, or disability?
2. What might be evidence that an employer is practicing job discrimination?

PERSONAL FINANCE HANDBOOK

Learn the basics about earning, saving, and investing your money and discover how to make the best choices for managing your finances.

go.hrw.com
KEYWORD: SS PERSONAL FINANCE

HOLT McDOUGAL

Income

You deal with money every day. You make it, spend it, save it, and invest it. But how much do you really know about your money? Are you making the best decisions about how to use your money? Do you know how to make your money work for you? This Personal Finance Handbook was written to help you learn more about the basics of managing your money. You will also learn how to use tools such as checking accounts, budgets, and portfolios to make the most of the money you have.

Why Money Matters

Imagine that you had never seen money. Wouldn't you wonder why people are interested in little green pieces of paper? After all, you can't eat money, wear it, or use it for shelter from the elements. When looked at that way, money doesn't seem very important at all. After some examination, however, you would probably realize that money is not important for what it is but for what it does.

Money is a medium of exchange. In other words, it allows people to trade one thing—money—for other items that they need or want. Imagine living in a world without money. What would life be like? If you wanted food, you couldn't run to a store or restaurant and purchase some. Instead, you would either have to grow or find your own or trade with someone who had food. If you didn't have anything that he or she wanted, then life could get very difficult.

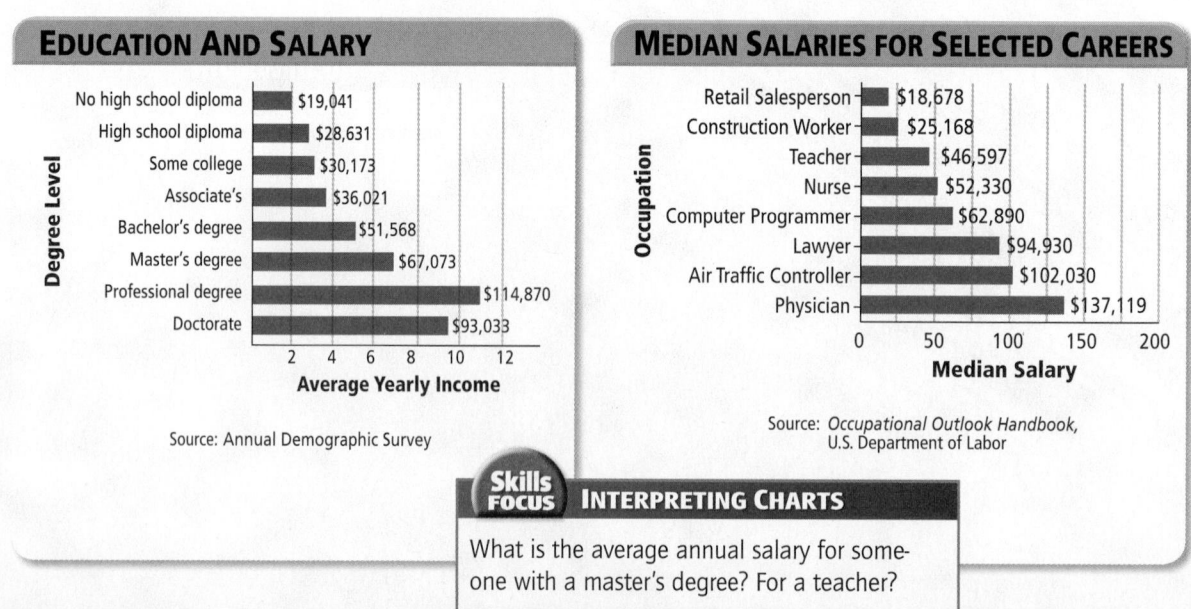

EDUCATION AND SALARY

Degree Level	Average Yearly Income
No high school diploma	$19,041
High school diploma	$28,631
Some college	$30,173
Associate's	$36,021
Bachelor's degree	$51,568
Master's degree	$67,073
Professional degree	$114,870
Doctorate	$93,033

Source: Annual Demographic Survey

MEDIAN SALARIES FOR SELECTED CAREERS

Occupation	Median Salary
Retail Salesperson	$18,678
Construction Worker	$25,168
Teacher	$46,597
Nurse	$52,330
Computer Programmer	$62,890
Lawyer	$94,930
Air Traffic Controller	$102,030
Physician	$137,119

Source: *Occupational Outlook Handbook,* U.S. Department of Labor

Skills Focus INTERPRETING CHARTS

What is the average annual salary for someone with a master's degree? For a teacher?

Sources of Income

Because we all need certain goods and services, we each need a source of income, or a way to make money. For most people the primary source of income is a job. The types of jobs people have vary widely, from after-school positions as sales clerks, to full-time jobs as doctors that require years of training. As a result the amount of income that people earn also varies.

Though there are exceptions, jobs that require extensive education or training or that create high amounts of stress are generally the highest paid. This trend is illustrated by the graphs on the previous page. The first graph shows that a person's income can vary greatly depending on his or her education and career choice.

Not everyone, however, wants to work for another person. Some, called entrepreneurs, choose instead to create their own businesses. Entrepreneurs open businesses for many reasons. Some think that they can make more money or find more satisfaction by running a business than by working for someone else. Others have ideas for new types of businesses that do not currently exist.

Whatever the reason for starting a business, doing so can be a risky move. Many new businesses fail in their first few years of operation. Even those that succeed may not turn a substantial profit for several years. However, the right business can achieve great success and lead to wealth. Some of the largest businesses in the country today began as small companies.

Although most people depend on their jobs for income, jobs are not the only way in which people make money. In fact, most people earn at least some income from other sources during their lives. Among these other possible sources of income are

- interest on money saved or invested in accounts.
- gifts or inheritances from friends and relatives.
- winnings from games or contests.
- rent collected on property used by others.
- profit from selling possessions, such as a house.

Most people earn their income through jobs, whether working for large companies or starting businesses of their own.

Factors Affecting Income

Imagine that you have obtained a part-time job working after school in a local restaurant. The job pays $7 per hour, and you will be working 10 hours each week. You should make $70 each week from the job, right? Yes and no. Although $70 will be your total weekly income, or gross pay, your take-home pay will actually be less.

VOCABULARY

entrepreneur an individual who begins and runs his or her own business

profit the money one has earned from a business or transaction after all expenses have been paid

gross pay the total amount a worker earns before any deductions have been calculated

Several factors affect how much money from your gross pay you get to keep. From that total your employer is required to make a number of deductions, which are listed on the stub of your paycheck. The money that is left after all these deductions is called your net pay, the amount of your paycheck that you get to take home.

The money deducted from your paycheck covers a variety of expenses. Part of it goes to the government in the form of taxes and contributions to programs like Social Security. Other deductions may be taken to pay for employer-sponsored programs, such as insurance benefits or charitable donations. In some jobs, union dues may also be deducted from your paycheck. Of these deductions, only the taxes and federal contributions are mandatory. All other deductions are optional and require your written permission before any money can be taken from your paycheck. The following types of deductions are often taken from payroll checks.

Federal and State Income Tax

Everyone is required to pay federal income tax, which is calculated as a percentage of your total income. In most cases your employer will deduct a certain percentage of your earnings to send to the government as your income tax. Then, when you file your income taxes each year, you will compare how much you owe to what you have already paid and reconcile the difference. In states that levy a state income tax, money will also be deducted from your paycheck for that tax.

VOCABULARY

net pay the money remaining from a paycheck after deductions
tax money collected by a government to pay for public programs or projects
income tax a form of tax based on the total income of an individual or business

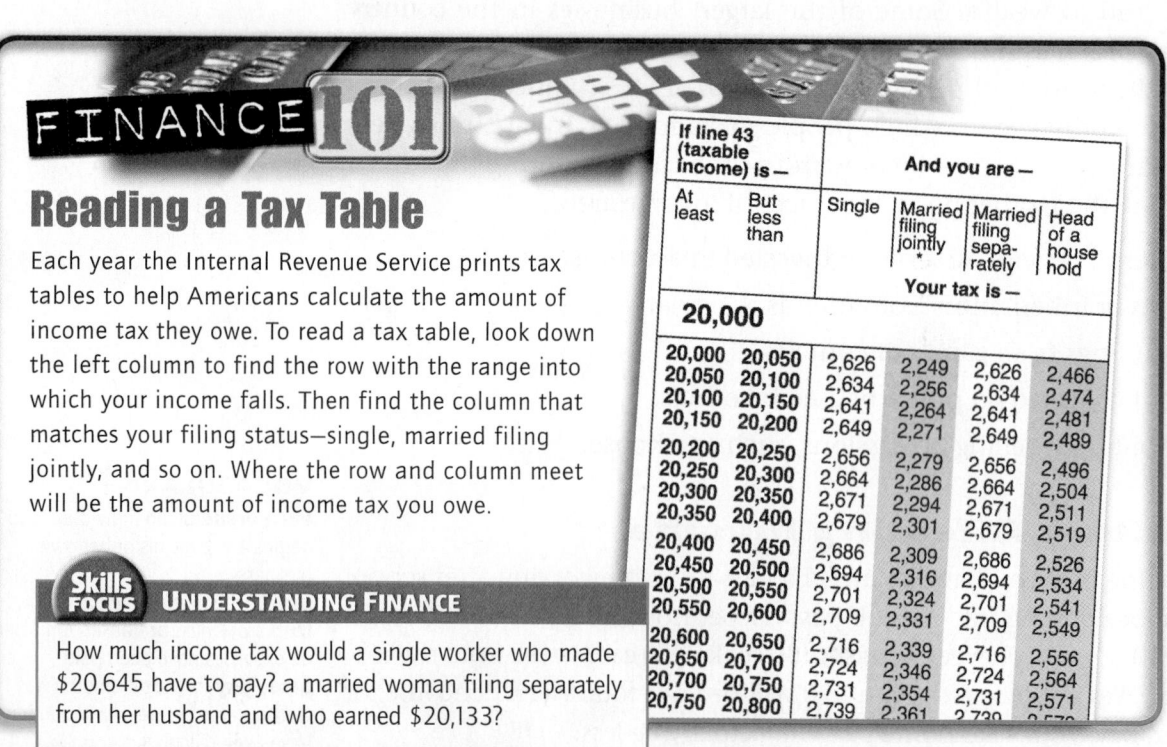

FINANCE 101

Reading a Tax Table

Each year the Internal Revenue Service prints tax tables to help Americans calculate the amount of income tax they owe. To read a tax table, look down the left column to find the row with the range into which your income falls. Then find the column that matches your filing status—single, married filing jointly, and so on. Where the row and column meet will be the amount of income tax you owe.

Skills FOCUS **UNDERSTANDING FINANCE**

How much income tax would a single worker who made $20,645 have to pay? a married woman filing separately from her husband and who earned $20,133?

If line 43 (taxable income) is —		And you are —			
At least	But less than	Single	Married filing jointly *	Married filing separately	Head of a household
		Your tax is —			
20,000					
20,000	20,050	2,626	2,249	2,626	2,466
20,050	20,100	2,634	2,256	2,634	2,474
20,100	20,150	2,641	2,264	2,641	2,481
20,150	20,200	2,649	2,271	2,649	2,489
20,200	20,250	2,656	2,279	2,656	2,496
20,250	20,300	2,664	2,286	2,664	2,504
20,300	20,350	2,671	2,294	2,671	2,511
20,350	20,400	2,679	2,301	2,679	2,519
20,400	20,450	2,686	2,309	2,686	2,526
20,450	20,500	2,694	2,316	2,694	2,534
20,500	20,550	2,701	2,324	2,701	2,541
20,550	20,600	2,709	2,331	2,709	2,549
20,600	20,650	2,716	2,339	2,716	2,556
20,650	20,700	2,724	2,346	2,724	2,564
20,700	20,750	2,731	2,354	2,731	2,571
20,750	20,800	2,739	2,361	2,739	2,579

Barney's Burger Barn

Barney's Burger Barn

Employee Earnings Statement
Week Ending April 28, 2007

EMPLOYEE: Timothy Taxpayer
SSN: 000-00-0000

	Taxes/Deductions	
Regular Earnings: $376.00	Federal Taxes	$54.40
Overtime Earnings: $0	FICA	$28.76
	State Tax	$9.52
Gross Earnings: $376.00	Insurance	$17.60
	Retirement	$8.30
	NET PAY	**$257.42**

Detach and retain top portion for your records

> Employers take deductions from employees' paychecks for federal and state taxes. In addition, many employees opt to have the cost of benefits deducted from their checks.

> The money that remains after all deductions have been made is called your net or take-home pay.

FICA

The Federal Insurance Contribution Act (FICA) requires that money be deducted from paychecks to help fund two programs that help support retired Americans: Social Security and Medicare. Between 7 and 8 percent of your gross income will usually be deducted for FICA. Full-time students may be exempt from paying FICA expenses.

Benefit Costs

Many companies offer their employees certain benefits, such as subsidized life and medical insurance. In this case the company pays for a portion of the cost of the insurance, and the employee pays only what remains.

Retirement Funds

In addition to offering insurance benefits, many companies also offer their employees the chance to create a retirement fund, such as a 401K account. A 401K is a special savings account that sets aside money for an employee to use after retiring. As an added benefit, some companies even contribute additional funds to their employees' retirement accounts. Contributions to a 401K account are deducted from each paycheck before taxes are calculated.

Charitable Donations

Some companies offer their employees a chance to donate part of each paycheck—either a set amount or a percentage of the total check—to charitable organizations. In such cases these donations would also appear as deductions.

Union Dues

Many members of labor unions have their membership dues deducted from their paychecks.

Other Deductions

Your employer may offer other programs that will lead to payroll deductions. You will learn about such programs when you are hired.

Inflation and Purchasing Power

On average, people today make considerably more money than people did in the past. It would seem, then, that people could afford to buy more than people in the past, wouldn't it? In reality, however, that is not necessarily the case. While wages were increasing, prices increased as well. For example, in 1960 the average price of a gallon of gasoline was about 25 cents. In 2007 that price rose to just over $3. Economists call the trend of prices rising over time <u>inflation</u>.

If prices rise faster than salaries, then people can afford less with the same amount of money. Look at the graph on this page for an example. It shows an increase in the price of certain foods between 1997 and 2006. If a person's income did not increase during this period, then he or she would not be able to purchase as much food each month. The measurement of how much people are able to buy with their income is called <u>purchasing power</u>. Simply put, if prices increase while salaries stay level, purchasing power decreases. If prices drop and salaries stay level, purchasing power increases.

VOCABULARY

inflation a rise in general price levels over time

purchasing power a measure of how much people can buy with their income

AVERAGE PRICE OF SELECT GOODS OVER TIME

Source: U.S. Department of Labor, Bureau of Labor Statistics

Skills Focus **INTERPRETING CHARTS**

During which period did the average price of these goods decrease slightly?

Calculating Discretionary Income

Your discretionary income is the amount of money you have left to spend after you have paid for all necessary expenses, such as housing, food, utilities, and so on. To calculate this figure, simply subtract your total expenses from your total income during the period. For example, suppose you earn $2,000 each month and your expenses total $1,500. To calculate, perform this simple operation:

$$\$2,000 - \$1,500 = \$500$$

Your discretionary income would total $500.

Skills FOCUS UNDERSTANDING FINANCE

Suppose your monthly income was $1,250. What would your discretionary income be if your expenses totaled $925? if your expenses totaled $575?

Discretionary Income

When economists talk about incomes, they look at two different figures. One is disposable income, which is the amount of money people have left after all deductions have been taken from their paychecks. In other words, disposable income is the same as net pay.

However, just because you take a certain amount of money home each month does not mean you can spend it on whatever you would like. People have certain monetary obligations that they have to meet each month, such as paying a mortgage or rent, buying food, and paying bills. The money you have left after all of these expenses are calculated is called your discretionary income. Being aware of your discretionary income allows you to plan your purchases wisely and avoid financial troubles.

VOCABULARY

disposable income another name for net pay; the money remaining from a paycheck after deductions

discretionary income the money that remains after one's expenses have all been paid

Assessment

1. **Describe** Why do people need money? How do they get that money?

2. **Explain** Why do employers make deductions from employees' paychecks? How do these deductions affect the employees' net pay?

3. **Apply** Make a list of five jobs that you might be interested in having during your lifetime. For each job on your list, write down what you think the educational requirements and average salary are. Then use the library or other sources to conduct research into the actual requirements and salary. What factors might influence that salary?

Money Management

Once you have money in your pocket, what do you do with it? Do you immediately rush out to buy all the latest CDs and movies? Do you set the money aside to pay for future needs or bills? Do you give some of it to charity? Do you deposit it in a bank account to collect interest in the meantime? All of these choices are valid options, each with its own benefits and drawbacks. As a consumer, though, you must decide which option is the best for you. In other words, it is your responsibility to manage your money.

Making Financial Choices

Personal finance is largely a matter of choices. As consumers, we are constantly faced with ways to spend money. You must decide how to use your money to satisfy your wants and needs.

To many people, getting a first job is an exciting experience. When they receive their first paycheck, they may go on shopping sprees and spend their cash on various items. This kind of impulse shopping can be quite fun in the short term. However, it is generally better to consider a longer-term approach to financial decisions.

For example, suppose that you have just received your first paycheck from a part-time job. While out with some friends, you see a shirt that you love and want to buy. Since you now have cash from your job, buying the shirt should be no problem, right?

Suppose that you have also decided that you want to purchase a new computer. You don't currently have enough money, but if you wait a few more weeks and save the money from your paychecks, you will. Any money you spend on other items (like the shirt you want) will mean a longer wait for the computer. Now you are faced with a tougher choice—buy the shirt or save for the computer.

The choice becomes even tougher when you look at longer-term goals. In the future you might like to buy a car, which will require substantial savings. You may want to attend college, which is also very expensive. The more money you spend on clothes, CDs, and other such items now, the less you will have to fulfill your goals later. You have to decide which is more important to you: satisfying your immediate wants or working toward fulfilling your long-term goals. Setting priorities like these is the kind of decision you face when planning how to spend your money.

Financial Planning

One of the best ways to make good financial decisions is to make a budget, or a plan for how you will spend your money. A budget lists your total income over a period of time and your anticipated expenses for the same period. By comparing how much money you will make with how much you will have to spend, a good budget can help you make better use of your money.

A budget is not hard to prepare, but it does take some careful thought. First, you must decide how long a period you want your budget to cover. Most people prefer to create monthly budgets, because many of the most common expenses in their lives—rents and mortgages, automobile payments, utility bills, and so on—are charged once each month. Other people prefer weekly or yearly budgets.

Next, you must decide how to record your budget. Some people like handwritten records. Other people prefer to keep track of their budgets on their home computers. A basic spreadsheet program can easily keep track of the numbers involved in a budget. In addition, many companies make special software that makes keeping track of your personal budget easier than ever.

Once you have decided how you will keep track of your budget, you must gather information for it. Collect all of your financial records together—paycheck stubs, receipts, bills, and so forth—and prepare to organize your financial goals.

VOCABULARY

budget a spending plan based on an individual or family's income

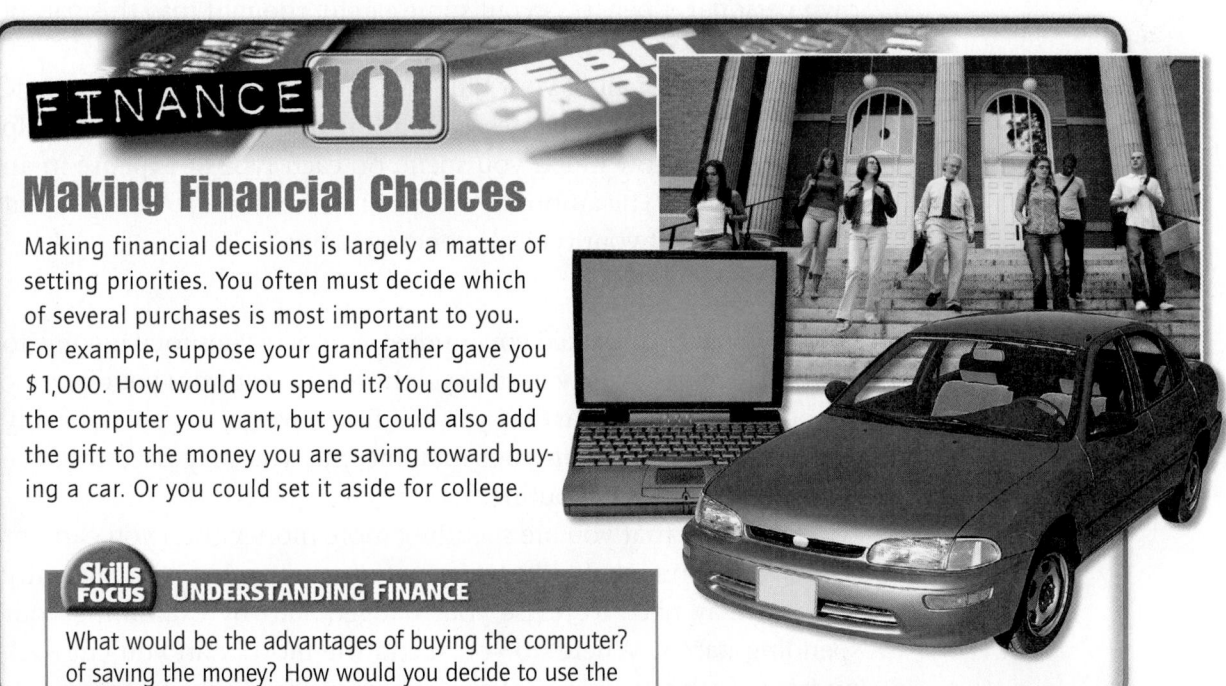

FINANCE 101

Making Financial Choices

Making financial decisions is largely a matter of setting priorities. You often must decide which of several purchases is most important to you. For example, suppose your grandfather gave you $1,000. How would you spend it? You could buy the computer you want, but you could also add the gift to the money you are saving toward buying a car. Or you could set it aside for college.

Skills FOCUS **UNDERSTANDING FINANCE**

What would be the advantages of buying the computer? of saving the money? How would you decide to use the money? Give reasons to support your answer.

Calculate Income

The first step in preparing your budget is to estimate your total income. Remember that your income includes your salary as well as any other money that you receive as well. Look at the sample household budget on the next page for an example. In addition to the $7,000 that the members of the family brought home in their paychecks, they earned money as interest during this month.

Calculate Expenditures

Once you have calculated your total income, you must estimate your total expenditures. Start by totaling all of your fixed expenditures, or those that do not change over time. Mortgage and rent payments, for example, are generally the same from month to month, as are payments on a car loan or student loan. Record your total fixed expenses on your budget sheet.

Now comes the trickier part: calculating your monthly living expenses. These expenses include everything that you have not already recorded, from food to gasoline to entertainment. Living expenses can be difficult to estimate, because some vary from month to month. For example, gasoline costs vary based on the price of gas and on how much you drive during a given period.

Look at the sample budget on the next page to see what kinds of costs are included as living expenses. Not all of these categories will apply to every budget. Some people may have other regular expenses that do not fit into these categories. Your budget should reflect your own personal expenses, so put some careful thought into this part of the budgeting process.

Save copies of all of your bills and store receipts to help estimate your monthly living expenses. Examining these documents can help you figure out how much you spend on each type of expense in an average month. The amounts you fill in do not have to be exact, but they must reflect your typical spending habits.

Figure Your Budget

Once you have completed your budget, compare your total income to your total expenses. Any money you have left over from your income is yours to spend or save as you see fit. However, if your monthly expenses are higher than your total income, you may need to make some changes in your routine.

If you find that you are spending more money than you earn, or if you think you would like to save more money than you currently are, you may need to revise your budget. Start by examining your spending habits. Where do you spend the most? Can you cut back on how much you spend? If so, by how much? Each reduction you make to your spending will yield greater savings in the end.

VOCABULARY

expenditures money that you have spent

Preparing a Budget

Preparing a budget is the best way to keep track of your spending. By detailing how much money you have and how you spend it, you can often find ways to improve your spending habits.

The total income you record on your budget should include paychecks and any other money you make during the period.

Fixed payments are those that you cannot change, such as rent or loan payments.

Living expenses may vary from month to month, so it is important that you carefully estimate how much you spend in each category.

Skills FOCUS UNDERSTANDING FINANCE

Imagine this was your budget. What adjustments would you make to increase your discretionary income by $200?

Household Budget Plan
April, 2007

INCOME	
Salaries/Wages/Tips	$7,000
Social Security/Retirement	
Interest	$10
Other Income	
Total Take Home Income	**$7,010**

MONTHLY FIXED PAYMENTS	
Mortgate/Rent	$1,250
Student Loans	$323
Auto Loans/Leases	$568
Other Debts	$200
Other Loans	
Total Fixed Payments	**$2,341**

MONTHLY LIVING EXPENSES	
Auto Gas and Repair	$200
Auto Insurance	$150
Cable TV/Satellite Fees	$65
Charitable Contributions	$25
Child Care	$300
Childrens' Activities	$150
Clothing	$300
Credit Card Bills	$400
Electric Bill	$150
Dining and Entertainment	$400
Gas and Oil Bills	$100
Groceries	$500
Internet	$65
Insurance	$125
Medical Expenses	$90
Subscriptions	$30
Telephone (Home, Cell, Pager)	$75
Trash Disposal	$10
Tuition and School Supplies	$300
Water Bill	$45
Other Expenses	$100
Total Monthly Living Expenses	**$3,580**

SUMMARY	
Total Take Home (Income)	$7,010
Total Fixed Payments (-)	$2,341
Total Monthly Living Expenses (-)	$3,580
Discretionary Income **	**$1,089**

As an example, look back at the sample household budget on the previous page. Suppose that the family who created this budget decided that they wanted to save additional money to pay for a family vacation. Where could they cut back on their expenses? In examining their budget, they see that their largest single expense is their mortgage, but that is a fixed expense. They will have to look for other opportunities to save.

In the end, the family decides to cut back on several expenses. They agree to dine out less often, which should cut their dining expenses in half. Dad decides to bicycle to work rather than take a car, which will save about $50 in gasoline money. In addition, the family agrees to conserve electricity and hopes to cut their electric bill by $25 a month. By following this new budget, the family should save an extra $275 each month toward their vacation.

Determining Net Worth

A family's possessions, such as their home, car, and clothing, factor into their net worth. Other factors that shape net worth include savings and investments.

Following a budget is not always easy. Cutting back on your spending sometimes means passing up things that you really want. In the end, however, staying within a budget can be a key step in becoming a responsible financial citizen.

Calculating Net Worth

Following a budget can help you increase your savings. In turn, increased savings will improve your <u>net worth</u>, or financial standing. To calculate your net worth, you first need to add up the value of all your <u>assets</u>, including your savings, investments, and property. From that total you then subtract your <u>liabilities</u>, or money you owe.

Knowing your net worth can be important when you want to borrow money from a bank or credit card company. These institutions look at applicants' net worth as part of their process for deciding to whom they will lend money.

To better understand how to calculate net worth, let's look at a hypothetical couple, George and Martha Jackson. As a couple, the Jacksons have the following assets:

- bank accounts totaling $14,235
- stocks and bonds totaling $5,332
- two cars worth a total of $38,985
- a house valued at $165,000
- the contents of their house, valued at $5,877

The Jacksons' liabilities include the following:

- a remaining balance on their mortgage of $84,938
- a remaining balance on a car loan of $6,873
- other loans totaling $4,083
- credit card debt totaling $2,945

Adding up these figures, we learn that the Jacksons' assets total $229,429, and their liabilities total $98,839. By subtracting their liabilities from their assets, we find that the Jackson's net worth is currently $130,590.

Risk Management

No matter how carefully you plan your finances, the chance always exists that unforeseen circumstances will cause financial hardship. For example, a member of your family might become ill or injured, your car might be wrecked in an accident, or your house might catch fire. Good financial planning involves preparing for the unexpected. Among the best steps you can take in this preparation are purchasing <u>insurance</u> and understanding <u>warranties</u>.

VOCABULARY

net worth a person's overall financial standing, equal to assets minus liabilities
assets the total value of all your money and possessions
liabilities the total amount of money you owe

VOCABULARY

insurance a system of protection in which smaller periodic payments are used to ensure compensation for future losses
warranty a written guarantee of a product's quality and the manufacturer's responsibilities to the buyer

Types of Insurance

Health insurance helps cover the cost of medical bills in case of illness or accidents.

Home insurance helps pay for the repair of damage to your home or its contents.

Car insurance helps pay for the repair of damages to your automobile.

Pet insurance helps pay veterinary bills should a family pet become ill.

Insurance

An insurance policy reduces the costs you have to pay in case of an accident. In return for a relatively low cost, you are protected from having to pay the full cost of repairing or replacing your most valuable possessions. For example, you may pay $150 every month for car insurance, but that is a low cost compared to the $20,000 you might have to pay if your car were destroyed in a wreck. Similarly, health insurance can save you from having to pay hundreds or even thousands of dollars in unexpected medical bills in case of an accident. Life insurance is designed to help families who have lost loved ones. Life insurance policies provide cash to the families of the insured person after his or her death.

Warranties

Like insurance policies, warranties are a form of risk management available to consumers. A warranty is a written guarantee issued by a manufacturer that its products will stay in working condition. Most companies are required by law to provide warranties to protect customers from shoddy workmanship and substandard products. As a result, a warranty should include information about the product, its properties, and its life span; the manufacturer's obligations to the consumer; and the manufacturer's plan to assure proper product performance. For example, a warranty may include an agreement to replace or repair a product that breaks.

To take full advantage of a warranty, you must always read it carefully and thoroughly. Many warranties have restrictions that limit the manufacturer's responsibilities. For example, the warranty may be voided if the consumer tries to repair a product at home or if damage was caused by negligence. In addition, many warranties do not cover all parts of a product. A television warranty might cover only the electronic components of the set and not its external casing. Always read warranties carefully.

Assessment

1. **Identify** What are some key factors that influence the financial decisions people make?

2. **Explain** Why do people buy insurance and take advantage of warranties? Why are insurance policies and warranties considered forms of risk management for consumers?

3. **Apply** Prepare a monthly budget for yourself. If you have a part-time job or allowance, use that figure for your total income. If you do not, choose a reasonable figure to represent your income. Carefully estimate your monthly expenses and add those figures into your budget. Once you have prepared your budget, look over it to see how you could make adjustments to save money each month.

Spending and Credit

You've worked hard to earn your money and fol-low a budget, and now it's time to spend some of your hard-earned cash. Spending may seem like the easiest part of personal finance, but it's not as easy as it may seem. Careful spending requires thought. By putting a little time and energy into your shopping, you can save yourself a lot of money in the long run.

Your Spending Decisions

Smart shoppers plan ahead. Before setting out for the grocery store or heading to the mall, you should think about how you can complete your trip efficiently and affordably. First, think about exactly what you need. If you're going to the grocery store, make a list so you don't end up with a lot of <u>impulse buys</u>. If you are preparing for a larger purchase, decide in advance which features you will need. For exam-ple, if you are buying a new cell phone, know whether you want your phone to take pictures, browse the Internet, and so on.

Second, set a price limit for yourself. Check your budget to see how much money you have to spend. You don't want to cause prob-lems for yourself later by spending too much money at one time.

VOCABULARY

impulse buy an unplanned purchase, usually of something unnecessary or frivolous

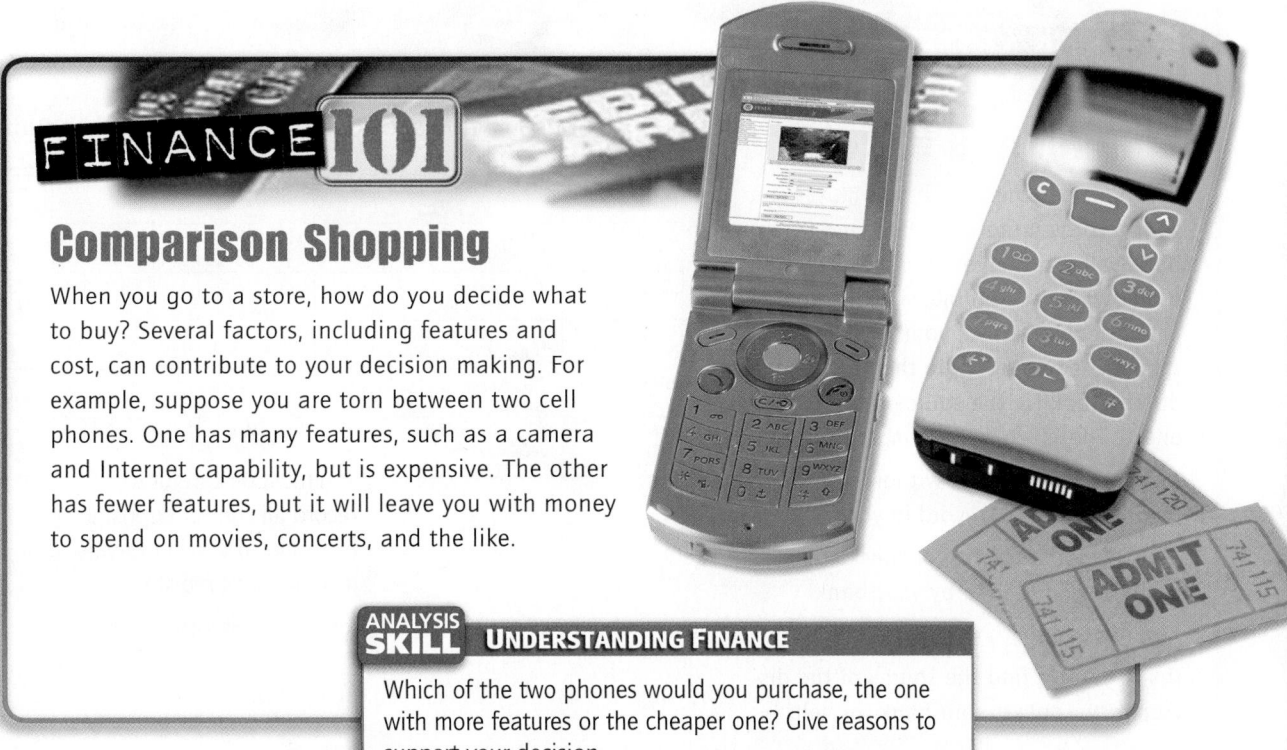

FINANCE 101

Comparison Shopping

When you go to a store, how do you decide what to buy? Several factors, including features and cost, can contribute to your decision making. For example, suppose you are torn between two cell phones. One has many features, such as a camera and Internet capability, but is expensive. The other has fewer features, but it will leave you with money to spend on movies, concerts, and the like.

ANALYSIS SKILL **UNDERSTANDING FINANCE**

Which of the two phones would you purchase, the one with more features or the cheaper one? Give reasons to support your decision.

Choosing the Right Checking Account

Banks offer many types of checking accounts, each with its own features. To choose the right account for you, ask:

- Does this account include monthly fees?

- Do I have to pay for each check I write?

- Am I limited to a certain number of checks each month?

- Will I earn interest on my account balance?

- Can more than one person write checks from this account?

Third, do your research. Consult consumer magazines and other sources to read reviews of various products. This research is especially valuable when making major purchases. You do not want to throw your money away on substandard merchandise that will break or need to be replaced soon. Also, research prices. Check various stores or advertisements to find the best deal. Remember that certain products can be cheaper at certain times of the year as well. For example, cars are often cheaper to buy in the spring and summer when dealers are trying to make room for new models.

Payment Methods

Once you have gone to the store and made your selections of items to purchase, you have another important decision to make. How will you pay for your items? Your method of payment can make a significant difference in the long run.

Cash

Cash is the simplest payment method. You hand over your money, the merchant hands you your products, and everything is done. You have no more steps to complete. However, paying with cash is not always possible, so other options are necessary.

FINANCE 101

Balancing a Checkbook

If you have a checkbook, you must keep your records up to date. Each month your bank will provide you with a statement, either written or online, showing your account activity. Check your records against the bank's to make sure they agree. If they do not, look for the source of any differences. These are some common sources:

- checks, deposits, or withdrawals that you have forgotten to record in your checkbook.

- outstanding checks, or checks that have not yet been cashed by your bank.

- bank fees you have not accounted for.

If you cannot find the source of the discrepancy, contact your bank for help.

RECORD ALL TRANSACTIONS THAT AFFECT YOUR ACCOUNT

NUMBER	DATE	DESCRIPTION OF TRANSACTION	PAYMENT/DEBIT (-)	FEE (IF ANY) (-)	DEPOSIT/CREDIT (-)	BALANCE	
						237	15
513	3/18	Bud's Music and Movies DVDs	21.73			−21 215	73 42
ATM	3/19	Atm widthdrawal	20.00			−20 195	00 42
Dep	3/24	PAycheck			132.28	+132 327	28 70
514	4/1	Office World School Supplies	9.45			−9 318	45 25
515	4/4	Fashion Attack Shirt	53.72			−53 264	72 53
debit	4/7	Pizza Palace Dinner	19.76			−19 243	76 77

You must be careful to record all checks, deposits, fees, and ATM withdrawals in your check register.

Checks

Checking accounts offer the convenience of paying for goods and services without having to keep cash on hand. By filling in a few blanks, you can turn a small piece of paper into payment. However, if you do not have enough money in your checking account to cover the check's amount, you could get into trouble.

To stay safe when writing checks, you must balance your checkbook regularly. Balancing a checkbook means comparing your records to the bank's records to make sure they are the same. The first step in keeping a balanced checkbook is to record all withdrawals that you make from your account—checks, ATM withdrawals, debit card purchases, and so on. You also need to record all deposits and fees.

Every month your bank will send you a statement that details all of your account activity for that month. When you receive the statement, carefully check your records against it. If you find any inconsistencies, go back through your records to verify that you have recorded everything correctly. If you have double checked all of your records and you still find an inconsistency, you should contact your bank immediately for assistance.

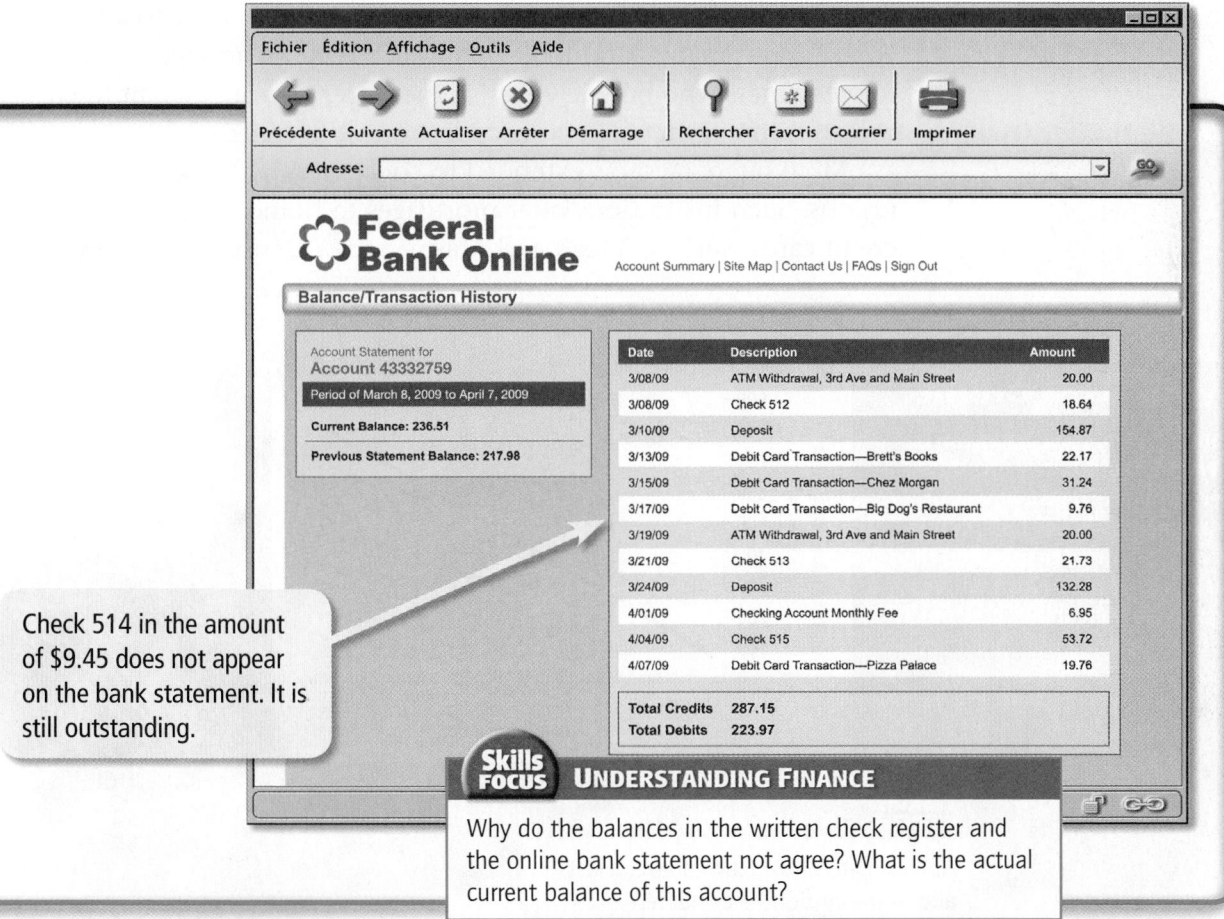

Check 514 in the amount of $9.45 does not appear on the bank statement. It is still outstanding.

Federal Bank Online

Account Summary | Site Map | Contact Us | FAQs | Sign Out

Balance/Transaction History

Account Statement for
Account 43332759

Period of March 8, 2009 to April 7, 2009

Current Balance: 236.51

Previous Statement Balance: 217.98

Date	Description	Amount
3/08/09	ATM Withdrawal, 3rd Ave and Main Street	20.00
3/08/09	Check 512	18.64
3/10/09	Deposit	154.87
3/13/09	Debit Card Transaction—Brett's Books	22.17
3/15/09	Debit Card Transaction—Chez Morgan	31.24
3/17/09	Debit Card Transaction—Big Dog's Restaurant	9.76
3/19/09	ATM Withdrawal, 3rd Ave and Main Street	20.00
3/21/09	Check 513	21.73
3/24/09	Deposit	132.28
4/01/09	Checking Account Monthly Fee	6.95
4/04/09	Check 515	53.72
4/07/09	Debit Card Transaction—Pizza Palace	19.76

| Total Credits | 287.15 |
| Total Debits | 223.97 |

Skills FOCUS UNDERSTANDING FINANCE

Why do the balances in the written check register and the online bank statement not agree? What is the actual current balance of this account?

Buying on Credit

Sometimes you need to purchase expensive items for which we may not have enough cash on hand or in a checking account. In these cases you may wish to pay with credit. Credit allows you to make a purchase now and pay for it over time in installments. As a result, many people use credit to make large purchases such as houses, cars, and appliances.

In return for the opportunity to spread payments out, however, you have to pay <u>interest</u>. Most of the time this interest is equal to a percentage of your outstanding balance, calculated monthly. By law, a <u>creditor</u>—the person or company that extends credit to you—is required to notify you in writing of the interest rate you will have to pay, as well as any finance charges you may incur.

Because interest costs can add up quickly, buying an item on credit often results in your paying more than if you had paid for the same item with cash. See the graph below for an example of this increased cost.

Getting Credit

A buyer can be offered credit by one of two types of sources. In some cases the vendor selling a product offers to extend credit to a buyer. For example, many automobile manufacturers will arrange financing for customers who buy new cars. Some stores also offer credit to customers in the form of charge accounts or credit cards.

More often, credit is extended to consumers by banks and credit unions. Such institutions offer mortgages to home buyers as well as credit cards, such as Visa® and Mastercard®. Consumers who wish

VOCABULARY

interest payment for the use of loaned money

creditor any person or company that extends a loan in the form of credit to a consumer

Paying with Credit

Although paying with credit can be convenient, it ultimately results in higher prices. Each installment of your payment is lower, but interest costs result in greater spending than if you had paid for an item with cash. The graph at right shows how much a $750 laptop computer could actually cost when bought on credit.

THE COST OF INTEREST

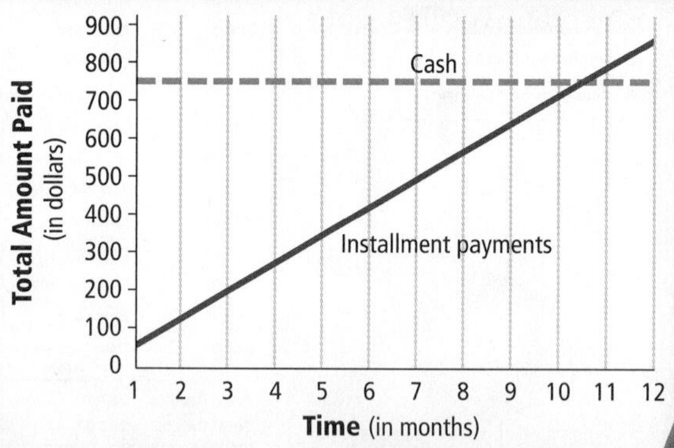

Skills Focus INTERPRETING CHARTS

Approximately how much does interest add to the cost of the computer?

to obtain these cards fill out applications with information such as place of employment, annual income, and outstanding debts. If the application is approved, then the bank will send the customer a credit card. Most new cards have set credit limits, which indicate the maximum amount the customer is allowed to spend using credit on that card. The exact limit will be determined by several factors, including an applicant's income and previous credit record, when he or she first applies for the card.

Credit Ratings

If you ever apply for credit, either from a store or a bank, one factor that will help determine whether your application is approved is your credit rating. Calculated by companies called credit bureaus, this rating is a number, usually between 300 and 850, that represents the probability that you will pay back any loans made to you. A higher number indicates a higher chance of repayment. Your credit rating is determined by several factors, including your income, your monthly expenditures, and your credit spending history.

Even after you have been approved for credit, your credit rating can change. If you misuse your credit or are late making payments on an account, lenders report this information to credit bureaus, who reduce your credit rating accordingly. If your credit rating drops too low, you may find it very difficult or even impossible to obtain credit in the future.

Credit Card Safety

Credit cards can be a great convenience. However, they can also be a source of great heartache if they are lost or stolen. Thieves can use a stolen credit card to run up enormous expenses for which you might be held responsible. Even if you do not have to pay the bills generated in your name, clearing your bill and your credit rating can take much time and energy. To help protect yourself and your credit, follow these simple rules.

- Keep track of your credit card at all times. Never leave your credit cards unattended.

- Make a list of all your credit card numbers and the banks that issued them. If a card is ever lost or stolen, call the issuing bank immediately to cancel it.

- Never give your credit card number to strangers or read it aloud where strangers can overhear. Also, never e-mail your card number or use it to make purchases from nonsecure Web sites.

Use these rules and some common sense to save yourself both time and expense.

VOCABULARY

credit rating a number that represents the probability that an individual will pay back any loans made to him or her

FINANCE 101

Understanding Credit Card Offers

Consumers receive credit card offers in the mail every day. Before you accept any such offer, you should read it very carefully. For example, check the offered interest rate, which is often expressed in the form of an annual percentage rate, or APR. Offered APRs vary widely, and what appears to be a generous offer can sometimes hide a high interest rate and costly fees. Though the dense language in which credit card offers are written can be difficult to understand, you should not agree to accept any credit card without fully understanding the terms to which you would be agreeing. As an example, read the credit card offer at right. Then try to rephrase what you have read in your own words.

Start saving with a 0% intro APR until October 1, 2010, on balance transfers.

Keep saving after October 1, 2010, with a low 9.99% fixed APR. Your APRs may increase if you default under any agreement you have with us for any of the following reasons: We do not receive, for any payment that is owed on this account or any other account with us, at least the minimum payment due by the date and time due; you exceed your credit line on this account; or you make a payment that is not authorized by your bank. Your APR may increase on the first day of the billing cycle in which the default occurs.

Skills FOCUS   UNDERSTANDING FINANCE

What interest rate is offered for purchases made with this credit card offer? What could change that rate?

Credit Debt and Bankruptcy

Many people, when they receive their first credit card, immediately rush out and buy many things. Because they do not have to spend any cash at the time of the purchase, they feel as though they are getting their purchases for nothing! This feeling, however, is entirely misleading. Reckless credit card spending can lead quickly to massive debt and serious financial problems.

Over time, some people fall so deeply into debt that they cannot hope to ever pay off their bills. In most cases this debt is the result of a crisis, such as the loss of a job or sudden serious illness. If the debt reaches too great a level, the person may have no choice but to declare bankruptcy.

Bankruptcy is a serious step not to be taken lightly. It will affect a person's finances for many years. By declaring bankruptcy, a person is cleared from most—though not all—debts. In some cases, most of his or her possessions are repossessed and sold, with any money earned passed on to creditors. The creditors are then legally barred from contacting the person in search of further payment. However, that person's credit rating falls drastically. Because bankruptcy records remain on a credit rating for 10 years, that person could find it difficult to make major purchases for a long time.

VOCABULARY

bankruptcy a legal declaration that a person or business cannot pay his, her, or its debts

To avoid credit debt, always use credit cards wisely. Don't apply for several cards just to have them; keep a few cards, but use them sparingly. Also, pay all of your credit card bills on time. In addition, it is always best to pay off your credit card balances in full each month. If you cannot, pay as much as you are able to afford. To save money, you should avoid making only the minimum required payment each month whenever possible. Making only a minimum payment can drag your debt out over months or even years. For example, consider a shopper who charges $1,000 on a credit card that charges 18 percent interest. Her minimum payment each month is 2 percent of her balance. Paying only that amount, she will not have the debt paid off until more than 19 years have passed! By the time she has finished paying, she will have been charged more than $1,900 in interest on a debt that started at about half that amount.

Assessment

1. Describe What are some advantages to paying for transactions with cash?

2. Identify Cause and Effect Why do many people make large purchases with credit? What effect does credit have on the total amount they pay?

3. Apply Choose one type of product that you might consider buying in the future, such as a television or computer. Research three different models or brands of that item and make a list of the advantages and disadvantages of buying each one. Then decide which you would buy if you had the choice and explain why.

The Effects of Bankruptcy

- You could lose most of your possessions.

- Your credit report will show a record of your bankruptcy for 10 years. This record could negatively affect your ability to borrow money, establish credit, or make large purchases.

- Any credit you are offered after bankruptcy will likely have very high interest rates.

- You will still owe any unpaid taxes, child support, or student loans. Bankruptcy does not cancel any of these debts.

Consumer Rights and Responsibilities

As a consumer, you have the right to

- have accurate and detailed information about products.

- have a variety of goods from which to choose.

- be safe from injury or illness caused by dangerous products.

- speak up about consumer issues.

- learn more about the marketplace and your role in it.

- receive quality service.

As a consumer, you have the responsibility to

- research products to make the best choices for your needs and wants.

- compare prices to find the best deals.

- speak out in favor of fairness and report questionable business practices.

- behave in an ethical manner.

- limit waste.

Saving and Investing

What if someone told you that you could give him $10 and after a few weeks, he would give you back your money plus an additional $5? Would you wonder what the catch was? This is the basic idea behind saving and investing your money. By either depositing your money with a bank or investing it, you hope to earn profit over time.

To Save or to Invest?

People save money so that they will have it to spend in the future. They may have money earmarked for future purchases, such as a car or college, or they may set money aside to support themselves after they retire. Saving guarantees that consumers will have money when they need it later and earn interest at the same time.

Investors, however, are not content to let their money sit still. They want to use what they have to make more money. They may buy shares of <u>stock</u> in a company, hoping to score big when the company's profits rise. They may buy <u>bonds</u>, which are loans to companies that are paid back with interest. In any case, investors hope to end up with more money than they had before investing.

The choice between saving and investing is a personal one. Your decision should be based on your goals, needs, and lifestyle. In general, saving is less risky: You will not lose any money, but you do not stand to make as much either. Investments are riskier, but you might make more money. Many people choose to put money into a range of savings and investments. Before making any decisions, consider all your options. You may also wish to seek professional advice.

VOCABULARY

stock a share of ownership in a corporation

bond a certificate of debt issued by a government or company to people from whom it has borrowed money

Knowing Your Options

Consumers today have hundreds of options for saving and investing their money. Some of the major options are listed in the table on the following page.

As you can see, some options, such as treasury bills, are backed by the U.S. government. In general, these investments are the safest, though they offer the lowest potential returns. Bank investments, such as certificates of deposit and money market accounts, have more restrictions but offer higher interest rates.

RETURNS ON $100

Legend: Invested, Kept at Home, Saved

Skills FOCUS INTERPRETING CHARTS

What does this graph suggest about the risks and rewards of investing money?

Comparing Investment Options

Consumers who want to save or invest money have a wide range of options open to them today, from low-risk savings bonds to risky but potentially profitable stocks and bonds. The table below lists a few of the more common saving and investing options, along with some advantages and disadvantages of each.

Type of Investment	Issuer	Level of Risk	Advantages	Disadvantages
Treasury Bill	U. S. Government	Low	• No risk of loss if bill is held to maturity • Short term	• Low return on investment • No chance for high return
Savings Bond	U. S. Government	Low	• No risk of loss if bill is held to maturity • Replacement if lost or stolen	• Low return on investment • Long holding period before maturity
Certificate of Deposit	Bank or other lending institution	Low	• Higher interest rates than savings accounts • Deposit insured by FDIC	• Money unavailable for withdrawal during deposit period
Money Market Account	Bank or other lending institution	Low	• Interest rates increase as total savings increase • Money available for withdrawal at any time	• Lower interest rates for people with smaller investments
Stocks	Corporation	High	• If prices rise, profits can be huge • Can pay annual dividends	• If prices drop, losses can be substantial • Activity difficult to predict
Corporate Bonds	Corporation	High	• Fixed income level • Less risky than stocks	• If issuing company goes bankrupt, bonds lose all value
Mutual Funds	Investment Company	High	• Diversified holdings reduce chance of major losses • Costs of investment shared with others • Professional account management	• Chance for losses on investment • Investment companies charge fees to manage accounts

FINANCE 101

Reading a Stock Table

In order to make the most out of your stock holdings, you need up-to-date information about how your stocks are performing. A good source of such information is a newspaper's financial section, which usually includes a chart like the one shown here. For each company listed, the chart lists a three-letter code by which the stock is identified. It also lists the highest and lowest prices for which a share of stock sold that day, the closing price, and the overall change in price since the previous day (net change). Stocks that show a positive change have made money, and those with a negative change have lost money.

Stock	Ticker	High	Low	Close	Net Change
Pratt Manuf	PRT	68.33	66.12	67.95	-1.30
Prazite Mining	PRZ	96.21	96.15	96.20	-0.05
Premium Imp	PMM	13.67	13.21	13.57	-0.02
Prescott Ind	PCT	78.94	75.67	78.94	+1.62
Prevention Insur	PVI	10.38	9.98	10.05	+.12
Price Cutters	PCU	8.04	7.63	7.63	0
Pride-Walker Inc	PWI	38.32	34.64	37.68	+.01
Princess Co	PRN	4.87	4.26	4.44	-.04

Skills FOCUS INTERPRETING CHARTS

Which company's stock showed the highest net change on the day this chart was created? Which dropped the most? Which remained even?

VOCABULARY

portfolio a list of all the investments held by an individual
diversify to increase variety
mutual fund a type of investment designed to reduce risk by pooling shareholders' resources into a mutual account and investing in many different stocks

Corporate stocks and bonds are the riskiest, but potentially most profitable, investment opportunities. Stock- and bondholders can make—or lose—huge amounts of money based on their portfolios, or holdings. To minimize investors' risk, many investment counselors recommend diversifying, or investing in both stocks and bonds issued by many companies. By diversifying, you protect yourself in case one company performs poorly; the other companies' performance could be good enough to still earn a profit. Diversity is the principle behind mutual funds. In such funds, a pool of investors gives money to a financial specialist, who uses the money to buy a diverse portfolio. By sharing the costs and risks of investing, investors in a mutual fund stand less risk of losing money than individual investors do. At the same time, they have less chance to make huge profits.

Assessment

1. **Define** What are stocks, bonds, and mutual funds?

2. **Compare and Contrast** How are saving and investing similar? How are they different?

3. **Apply** Find the financial section of a local or national newspaper and choose one stock. Imagine that you own 100 shares of this stock and follow its progress for a week. At the end of the week, would you have gained or lost money?

UNIT 7
THE UNITED STATES AND THE WORLD

This 1944 army recruitment poster reminds Americans about the importance of military defense.

FOREIGN POLICY

NATIONAL STANDARDS®
FOR CIVICS AND GOVERNMENT

I.   What are civic life, politics, and government?

A. What is government? Why are government and politics necessary? What purposes should government serve?

IV. What is the relationship of the United States to other nations and to world affairs?

A. How is the world organized politically?

B. How do the domestic politics and constitutional principles of the United States affect its relations with the world?

C. How has the United States influenced other nations, and how have other nations influenced American politics and society?

©1994, 2003 Center for Civic Education. All Rights Reserved.

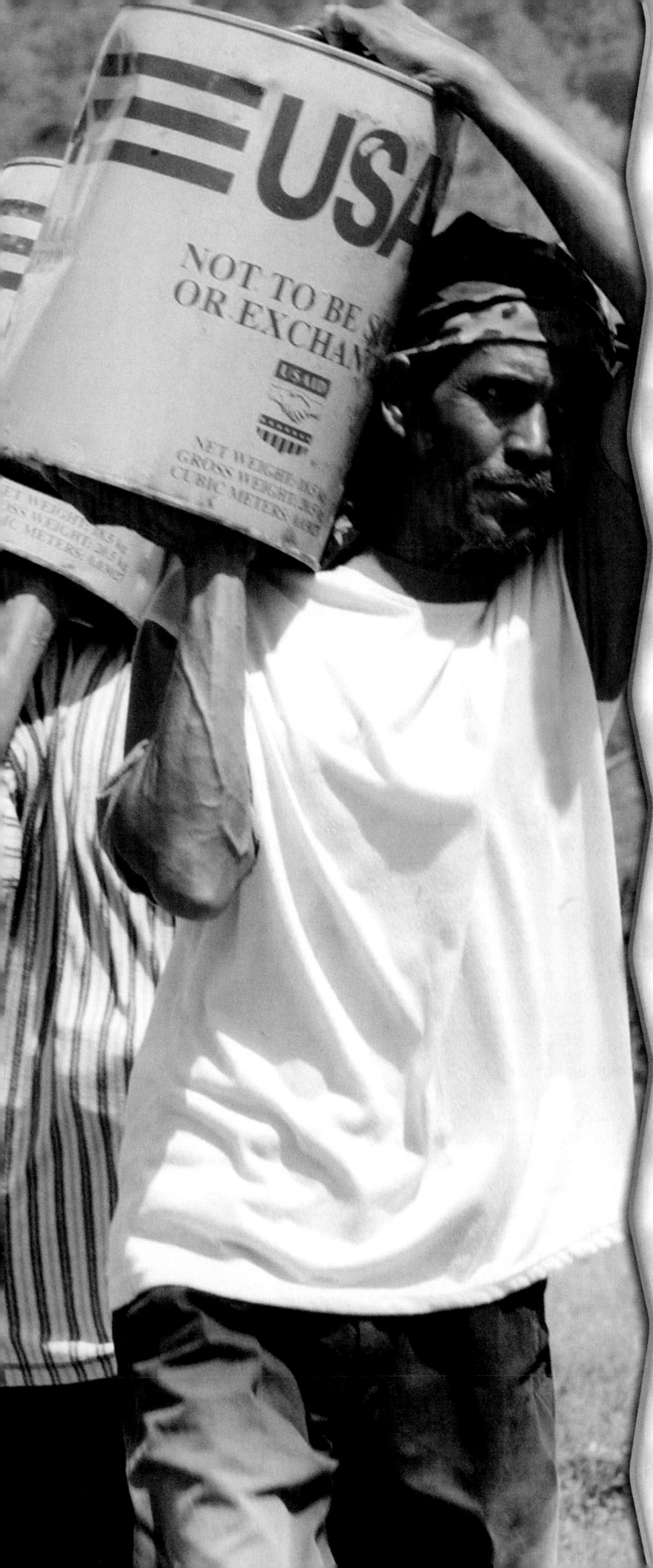

Active Citizenship video program
Watch the video to learn how young citizens are actively involved in the global community.

WHY CIVICS Matters

Following the tsunami that hit countries along the Indian Ocean in 2004, the United States sent aid in the form of food, clothing, medical supplies, and other items to regions affected by the disaster.

PROJECT Citizen

STUDENTS TAKE ACTION

INSPIRING A VILLAGE In the United States, most people can get to a pharmacy to obtain essential medicines. In other countries, though, small villages and towns may have no access to medicine or other medical supplies. If you lived in such a village and someone in your family needed a regular supply of medicine, what would you do?

FOCUS ON WRITING

A LIST OF PROS AND CONS AND A RECOMMENDATION As you read this chapter, you will study the ways in which the United States conducts its foreign policy. In order to analyze the advantages and disadvantages of America's relationships with other nations, you will need to create a list of the pros and cons of U.S involvement with those other nations.

Reading Skills

In this chapter you will read about the purpose of foreign policy. You learn what powers the president has concerning foreign relations. You will also read about the powers that Congress has to balance the president's authority. You will learn about the alliances that the United States has made to promote world peace. You will also read about the role of foreign aid and foreign trade. Finally, you will read about how the United Nations serves the world.

Online Research

FOCUS ON READING The World Wide Web contains huge amounts of information. To find what you need, you can use a search engine, keywords, or a directory. When you use a search engine, you look for Web sites by doing a keyword search. A keyword search lets you look for Web sites that contain specific words or phrases. A directory is an organized list of Web sites. Directories organize sites into categories, such as sports. Each category is broken down into smaller and smaller categories, helping you narrow your search.

Refining a Key Word Search Sometimes your keyword search will list too many Web sites to look at, or sometimes it may not find any sites at all. When this happens, you need to narrow your keyword search. Try the strategies below to narrow your searches.

Strategy	Example
Use specific terms.	To find information on foreign trade, enter "World Trade Organization" or "balance of trade" instead of "international trade."
Put words that go together as a phrase in quotation marks.	Type in "U.S. foreign ambassadors" to find the names of current ambassadors instead of information on foreign countries or ambassadors from other countries.
Use AND and NOT	Type in "Franklin Roosevelt" AND "Winston Churchill" to find sites on both world leaders. To find sites about diplomatic summits, but not mountain summits, type "summit NOT mountain."

Helpful Hints for Researching Online

1. Remember that not all Web sites are equal or necessarily accurate.

2. Choose Web sites from universities, government agencies, major newspapers, and broadcast networks.

3. If you are not sure where to start, try using a directory, which lists categories. The categories may help you narrow your search.

You Try It!

The following passage is from the chapter you are about to read. Read it and then answer the questions below.

> . . . in 2001 more than 160 countries met to discuss environmental policy. The main topic was the voluntary reduction of carbon dioxide and other gases believed to be responsible for the gradual warming of the Earth. However, countries have often struggled to agree on the exact terms of treaties and how they will be enforced. . . . Negotiations for international treaties have continued. As the global economy expands, environmental diplomacy will undoubtedly remain an important part of foreign policy.
>
> *(Chapter 23, p. 620)*

After you have read the passage, answer the following questions.

1. To look up more information online on the 2001 meeting on global warming, what keywords could you use?

2. To learn about specific treaties on environmental issues, what keywords would you use?

3. What general category would you look under in a directory to find information about environmental diplomacy?

> **As you read Chapter 23,** think about what topics you might enjoy reading more information about online.

KEY TERMS

Chapter 23

Section 1
alliance *(p. 609)*
executive agreement *(p. 610)*
diplomatic recognition *(p. 610)*
diplomatic corps *(p. 611)*

Section 2
diplomacy *(p. 614)*
summit *(p. 614)*
foreign aid *(p. 616)*
balance of trade *(p. 617)*

Section 3
United Nations *(p. 622)*
General Assembly *(p. 623)*
Security Council *(p. 623)*
International Court of Justice *(p. 623)*

Academic Vocabulary

Success in school is related to knowing academic vocabulary—the words that are frequently used in school assignments and discussions. In this chapter, you will learn the following academic word:

aspects *(p. 610)*

Conducting Foreign Relations

BEFORE YOU READ

The Main Idea

The United States has relationships with many foreign countries. Both the president and Congress play roles in conducting foreign policy.

Reading Focus

1. What are the goals of U.S. foreign policy?
2. What are the president's military and diplomatic powers?
3. What other governmental agencies help the president and Congress conduct foreign policy?
4. How do the powers of Congress balance the president's powers?

Key Terms

alliance, p. 609
executive agreement, p. 610
diplomatic recognition, p. 610
diplomatic corps, p. 611

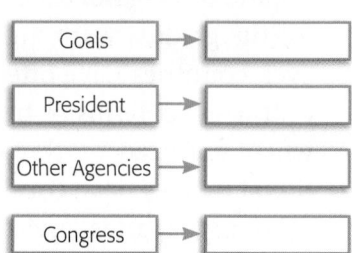

TAKING NOTES As you read, take notes about how the U.S. government conducts foreign policy. Use a diagram like this one to record your notes.

Goals	→	
President	→	
Other Agencies	→	
Congress	→	

Many Americans volunteer to help in other countries during times of crisis, like this doctor who traveled to Sri Lanka to help treat victims of the 2004 Indian Ocean tsunami.

CIVICS IN PRACTICE Why should you care about foreign relations? The simple answer is because foreign relations may have domestic effects. You live in a world where things are happening. It is important that you be aware that some of those events will touch your life.

Goals of U.S. Foreign Policy

As a result of advances in communication, trade, and travel, the world seems to be smaller these days. The nations of the world have become more interdependent, or reliant on each other. And because events in one country can quickly have dramatic effects in other countries, these interdependent nations must cooperate.

The plan that a country follows for interacting with other countries is called foreign policy. The success of a country's foreign policy affects its foreign relations, or the way

PHOTOGRAPH
Diplomatic Relations

In order to foster diplomatic relations with other nations, the president must meet with leaders of other countries. These meetings take place at the White House, in the leaders' home countries, in neutral locations, and in other places. In the first year of his presidency, President Barack Obama traveled to Europe and Latin America to take part in meetings with other leaders. He also visited Turkey in an effort to build better relations with Muslim nations. Here, Obama is shown meeting with Canada's prime minister, Stephen Harper.

ANALYSIS SKILL **ANALYZING PRIMARY SOURCES**

Why is it important for the president to maintain good diplomatic relations with other leaders?

it interacts with other countries. Every country's foreign policy has certain goals. The goals of U.S. foreign policy include maintaining national security, supporting democracy, promoting world peace, and providing aid to people in need. Since the 1930s, establishing open trade has become another goal of U.S. foreign policy.

Forming U.S. foreign policy is a complex process. The government must strike a balance between cooperation and competition with other countries. The process requires the work of many government officials.

READING CHECK **Summarizing** What are the goals of U.S. foreign policy?

The President's Powers

President Harry S. Truman once said, "I make American foreign policy." He meant that the president is responsible for major foreign policy decisions. Article II, Section 2, of the Constitution gives the president authority to conduct the nation's foreign relations. The president's powers include military, treaty-making, and diplomatic powers. The president decides when and how to use each power.

Military Powers

In general, the president makes recommendations to Congress about the operation of the U.S. military. As commander in chief, the president can order the military into action. However, under the War Powers Act, troops sent abroad must be recalled within 60 to 90 days unless Congress approves the action. Only Congress can declare war.

Treaty-Making Powers

Treaties are written agreements between countries. They are an important part of U.S. foreign relations. With the advice and consent of the Senate, the president has the power to make three types of treaties.

Peace treaties are agreements to end wars. They spell out the terms for ending the fighting and bringing about peace.

Alliance treaties are agreements between countries to help each other for defense, economic, scientific, or other reasons. The United States has established such alliances with many countries of the world. An **alliance** is an agreement in which two or more countries commit to help each other.

Commercial treaties are economic agreements between two or more countries to trade with each other on favorable terms. All treaties must be approved by a two-thirds vote of the Senate.

ACADEMIC VOCABULARY
aspects: parts

Executive Agreements

Agreements between countries do not always require treaties. The Constitution does recognize a distinction between treaties and agreements, so the president may enter into agreements with other countries. The president and the leader of a foreign government may meet and establish a mutual understanding, or **executive agreement**. Executive agreements have been used often in recent years. For example, on October 2, 2002, President Bush signed a Status of Forces Agreement (SOFA) with the nation of East Timor. SOFAs define the rights and responsibilities of soldiers from one country who are based in another country.

Diplomatic Powers

The president appoints ambassadors to represent the United States in foreign countries. The president also receives ambassadors from other countries.

The president has the power of **diplomatic recognition**. That is, the president may recognize, or establish official relations with, a foreign government. Sending a U.S. ambassador to that country and receiving that country's ambassador means that official recognition has taken place.

The president may refuse to recognize a government whose foreign policies are considered unfriendly or dangerous to the United States or its allies. For many years, the United States refused to recognize the Communist government of China. When recognition was granted in the 1970s, the two countries exchanged ambassadors.

READING CHECK **Finding the Main Idea** What are some of the president's diplomatic powers?

Other Foreign Policy Agencies

Many departments in the executive branch help keep the president informed about the different **aspects** of foreign policy. Most important are the Department of State and the Department of Defense.

Department of State

The principal organization for carrying out U.S. foreign policy as established by the president is the Department of State. It acts as the "eyes and ears" of the president, obtaining information from around the world on which U.S. foreign relations are based.

The secretary of state heads the Department of State and is appointed by the president. The president's nominee must be approved by the Senate. The secretary of state, assisted by a large staff, reports directly to the president.

The secretary of state advises the president and supervises the activities of U.S. ambassadors, ministers, and consuls.

4 Goals of Foreign Policy

The president determines foreign policy and sets the tone for relations with other countries. However, Congress must fund and approve the president's policies before the policies can be implemented.

Promote World Peace

Maintain National Security

Support Democracy

Provide Aid

Presidential Powers

- Commit armed forces to war
- Threaten to wage war unless certain conditions are met
- Nominate ambassadors to foreign countries and to the United Nations
- Advocate for democratic elections in foreign countries
- Advocate for peaceful resolutions to conflicts
- Meet with foreign leaders to encourage or broker peaceful resolutions to conflicts

Congressional Powers

- Approve declaration of act of war
- Provide funding for waging war
- Approve or reject nominees for ambassador
- Approve sanctions against other countries
- Ratify or reject treaties
- Approve funding for foreign aid

One of the constitutional powers of the president is to appoint ambassadors. These officials and their assistants are members of the **diplomatic corps**.

Department of Defense

An important source of military information for the president is the Department of Defense. The secretary of defense heads the department. The secretary of defense advises the president on troop movements, placement of military bases, and weapons development.

The secretary of defense and the president receive advice on military matters from the Joint Chiefs of Staff. The Joint Chiefs include a chairperson, a vice chairperson, and the highest ranking military officer of the army, navy, air force, and marines.

Other Sources of Assistance

Other executive departments assist with foreign policy in various ways. For example, the secretary of agriculture keeps the president informed of available surplus foods that may be sent to needy countries.

Congress has also created a number of specialized agencies to help establish and carry out the country's foreign policy. The Central Intelligence Agency (CIA) is responsible for gathering information about military and political trends and developments in various countries.

Freedom of the Press and Embedded Reporters

In 1735, New York publisher John Peter Zenger wrote articles critical of the governor and his colleagues. The governor charged Zenger with "seditious libel" (a falsehood against the government). The case went to trial, and Zenger's victory in court was the beginning of a strong free-press sentiment that was written into the Bill of Rights 50 years later. Thanks to the First Amendment, the American media is free to report whatever it learns and can be critical of the government.

Today, we have come to enjoy the benefits of a free press. During the second U.S. war in Iraq, the American government invited some reporters to live with military units in Iraq (such as the one shown at right). Many people believe that this "embedded reporter" program gives the public access to more accurate reporting on the war. Critics claim, however, that the government controls what the reporters can experience, subtly reducing journalistic objectivity—one of the most important features of a free press.

1. What role did the Zenger trial play in promoting freedom of the press?
2. How might embedding reporters affect freedom of the press?

The National Security Council (NSC), in the Executive Office of the President, was created to help coordinate U.S. military and foreign policy. Another agency that assists in foreign relations is the Agency for International Development (AID). It provides billions of dollars' worth of food, fuel, medical supplies, and loans to help the world's peoples.

READING CHECK **Summarizing** In addition to the Departments of State and Defense, what other agencies assist with foreign policy, and what are their duties?

Congress Provides a Balance

The president leads the country in dealing with world affairs, but the president must work closely with Congress when deciding foreign-policy issues. The Senate Foreign Relations Committee and the House Committee on International Relations make foreign-policy recommendations to Congress and the president.

Approval Powers

As you know, the Senate must approve all treaties between the United States and other countries by a two-thirds vote. For example, after World War I, President Woodrow Wilson wanted the United States to join the League of Nations. A provision for joining this peacekeeping organization was included as a part of the Treaty of Versailles that ended World War I. However, a powerful group of senators opposed U.S. membership in the League of Nations.

They eventually succeeded in preventing a two-thirds majority vote of the Senate in favor of the treaty. As a result, the United States did not approve the Treaty of Versailles or join the League of Nations.

By a majority vote in both houses, Congress may also pass legislation authorizing the president to enter into an executive agreement with one or more foreign countries. These agreements have the same effect as treaties.

The Power to Declare War

Under the U.S. Constitution, only Congress can declare war. Yet over the years, presidents have sent troops to foreign countries without a declaration of war. For example, Presidents John F. Kennedy, Lyndon B. Johnson, and Richard M. Nixon sent a total of more than 2 million American troops to Vietnam during the 1960s and early 1970s. In 1973, seeking to avoid "another Vietnam," Congress passed the War Powers Act to reaffirm its constitutional right to declare war. This act limits the president's power to send troops abroad without the approval of Congress.

Financial Powers

As you have read, both houses of Congress must approve all expenditures of public funds. This power also allows Congress to influence foreign affairs. For example, Congress must approve all spending for national defense. The president may recommend new military spending. However, these policies cannot be carried out unless Congress votes for the necessary money.

READING CHECK ▶ **Finding the Main Idea** Why did Congress reject the Treaty of Versailles?

League of Nations MARCH

David Lloyd George   Georges Clemenceau

Woodrow Wilson

Vittorio Orlando   Baron Makino

BY
William T. Pierson
Composer of "Sons of America" "Carry On" and "Just A Song of Home"
Published for Band and Orchestra   Price 50 Cents

League of Nations

After World War I, a group of powerful U.S. senators wanted the United States to stay out of European affairs. As a result, the United States did not join the League of Nations. The League of Nations was replaced by the United Nations after World War II.

How does the failure of the United States to join the League of Nations show Congress's power to shape foreign policy?

go.hrw.com
Online Quiz
KEYWORD: SZ7 HP23

SECTION 1 ASSESSMENT

Reviewing Ideas and Terms

1. a. Recall What are five goals of U.S. foreign policy?
  b. Explain How does today's rapid access to information affect U.S. relations with other countries?

2. a. Define Write a brief definition for the terms **alliances**, **executive agreement**, and **diplomatic recognition**.
  b. Explain What powers are granted to the president in the area of conducting foreign policy?

3. a. Define Write a brief definition for the term **diplomatic corps**.
  b. Compare and Contrast How do the Department of State and the Department of Defense keep the president informed in matters of foreign policy?

4. a. Summarize How can Congress balance the president's foreign-policy powers?
  b. Evaluate Should Congress have the power to approve all treaties? Why or why not?

Critical Thinking

5. Categorizing Copy the graphic organizer. Use it to identify the diplomatic and military powers of the president.

President

Military Powers   Diplomatic Powers

Focus on Writing

6. Supporting a Point of View Should citizens be kept informed of all foreign-policy decisions? Explain your reasoning.

SECTION 2

Working for Peace

BEFORE YOU READ

The Main Idea

To promote peace and stability, the United States engages in diplomacy with other nations. These alliances with other countries serve mutual defense, economic, and other needs.

Reading Focus

1. Why is diplomacy important; and what alliances has the United States made with other countries to promote mutual defense?
2. What forms can U.S. foreign aid take?
3. What organizations exist to promote international trade and economic stability, and what does each one do?

Key Terms

diplomacy, *p. 614*
summit, *p. 614*
foreign aid, *p. 616*
balance of trade, *p. 617*

TAKING NOTES As you read, take notes about how the United States works for peace. Use a chart like this one to record your notes.

Effort	Outcome
Diplomacy	
Alliances	
Foreign Aid	
Foreign Trade	

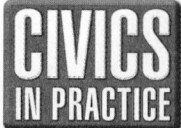

CIVICS IN PRACTICE One way that you feel safe is to be with a group of friends. Friends listen to each other and try to solve problems they have. Sometimes friends lend each other money or stand up for each other in a dispute. Nations are like that, too. They form alliances for many of the same reasons you have a group of friends.

Diplomacy and Alliances

The process of conducting relations between countries is called **diplomacy**. Diplomacy is used to prevent war, negotiate an end to conflicts, solve problems, and establish communication between countries. The president is the country's chief diplomat.

To carry out this role, presidents often use personal diplomacy. They travel to other countries to meet with foreign leaders. They also consult with foreign officials in the United States. One such example of personal diplomacy is a summit. A **summit** is a meeting between the leaders of two or more countries to discuss issues that concern those countries.

Other government officials also engage in diplomacy. For example, State Department officials often represent the president in trying to settle conflicts between other countries. In recent years, U.S. diplomats have traveled back and forth between different countries so often that this kind of peace seeking has become known as "shuttle diplomacy."

Alliances for Defense

One of the main goals of U.S. foreign policy is to promote peace and stability. One way to promote peace is to form alliances for defense. The United States has defense alliances with many countries, including Japan, South Korea, and the Philippines.

The United States and most countries in Latin America formed the Organization of American States (OAS) in 1948. The goal of the OAS is mutual defense and the peaceful settlement of disputes among member countries. In 1951 Australia, New Zealand, and the United States formed an alliance called ANZUS. The purpose of ANZUS is to provide mutual defense in case of attack.

3 Kinds of Alliances

The United States has many goals to accomplish around the world. To achieve them we rely on relationships with other countries. Political, economic, and military goals are best achieved through diplomatic means—treaties, pacts, and agreements with other nations.

Political

The United States forms political alliances with other countries to provide for mutual defense and a peaceful way to settle disputes.

Military

The United States forms military alliances with other countries to protect the members from aggression by other countries. One example is NATO, which includes the United States and many Western European countries.

Economic

The United States forms economic alliances with other countries to create mutual well being through trade.

Former president Jimmy Carter oversees elections in Haiti.

Secretary of State Condoleezza Rice meets with a U.S. general before a meeting of NATO leaders.

New cars imported from Europe await transport to dealers around the United States.

ANALYSIS SKILL DRAWING CONCLUSIONS

1. In what ways does the United States benefit from its alliances with other countries?
2. How can all three kinds of alliances be used together in relations with another country?

NATO

Perhaps the most important security alliance of which the United States is a member is the North Atlantic Treaty Organization (NATO). The United States and its allies formed NATO in 1949 to establish a united front against aggression by the Soviet Union and its communist allies. Most Western European countries belong to this alliance.

During the 1990s, NATO's focus changed as several Eastern European countries overturned their Communist governments and the Soviet Union dissolved. In fact, Russia and many of its former allies have either joined NATO or assist the organization in military exercises and peacekeeping operations. In 2003, NATO, in its first action outside of Europe, took command of the international forces in Afghanistan.

READING CHECK **Drawing Inferences and Conclusions** How are defense alliances part of the nation's diplomacy?

Forms of Foreign Aid

Another important part of U.S. foreign policy is foreign aid. **Foreign aid** is any government program that provides economic or military assistance to another country. For example, the United States first gave large amounts of foreign aid during and after World War II. After the war's devastation, the people of Western Europe needed food, clothing, and housing.

In 1947 U.S. Secretary of State George Marshall proposed a plan to help the war-torn countries of Europe rebuild. Under the Marshall Plan, Congress granted more than $13 billion in aid to these countries. By 1952 the economies of Western Europe had recovered to a remarkable degree. Marshall Plan aid, having accomplished its goal, ended.

The United States continues humanitarian aid efforts. It pledged $350 million in assistance to the countries devastated by the tsunami in the Indian Ocean in 2004.

READING CHECK **Summarizing** Why does the United States give aid to foreign countries?

Diplomatic Gifts

The United States has received many famous gifts from other nations. The Statue of Liberty was a gift from France and was presented to the United States in 1884. In 1972 the People's Republic of China sent two giant pandas to the Washington National Zoo.

Drawing Inferences Why might other nations present the United States with a gift?

POLITICAL CARTOON
The Debate over Foreign Aid

Each year the United States gives billions of dollars of economic and humanitarian aid to countries around the world. Yet some Americans believe that this generosity could be improved. As the chart below shows, when the numbers are broken down per citizen, U.S. foreign aid is much less than that given by other countries. However, other Americans argue that as the third-most populous country in the world, the United States needs to concentrate more on providing aid to its own citizens.

How has the cartoonist chosen to represent the United States? How does this person's appearance and dress help to highlight the cartoon's message?

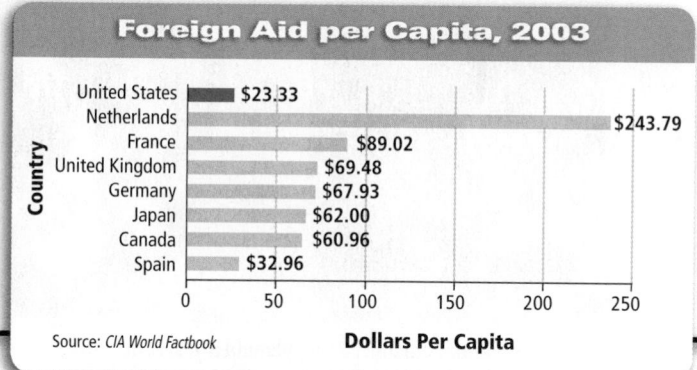

Foreign Aid per Capita, 2003

Country	Dollars Per Capita
United States	$23.33
Netherlands	$243.79
France	$89.02
United Kingdom	$69.48
Germany	$67.93
Japan	$62.00
Canada	$60.96
Spain	$32.96

Source: *CIA World Factbook*

ANALYSIS SKILL **ANALYZING POLITICAL CARTOONS**

Drawing Inferences How does the information in the graph illustrate the message in the cartoon?

Organizations Promote Foreign Trade

The U.S. government frequently deals with economic challenges facing this country. The United States has long held a position of strength in the global economy. However, in recent decades foreign competition and economic alliances in other parts of the world have challenged its economic position. Thus, foreign trade is a central focus of U.S. foreign policy.

Foreign Trade and the Balance of Trade

The countries of the Pacific Rim, for example, compete with the United States in producing and selling goods. These countries include, among others, Australia, China, Indonesia, Japan, Malaysia, New Zealand, the Philippines, Singapore, South Korea, and Taiwan.

Pacific Rim countries have the ability to produce high-quality, low-priced goods such as automobiles, computers, and electronic equipment. There is a high demand for these goods in the United States and many other countries around the world.

The success of the Pacific Rim countries has had a significant effect on the U.S. balance of trade. The **balance of trade** is the difference in the value between a country's exports and imports over a period of time. Exports are those goods and services that the United States sells to other countries. Imports are those goods and services that the United States buys from other countries.

In recent years the United States has suffered serious trade deficits. The country spends more money buying foreign goods (imports) than it earns from selling American-made goods (exports) to other countries. Trade agreements help address this imbalance.

LAW 101

FOUNDATIONS of DEMOCRACY

The Draft

Why is it important for the United States to have a military? Do you think every person, male and female, should be required to serve some time in the military—even when the country is not at war?

Why it Matters Most countries need a military for self-defense. Many countries draft citizens, or require them to serve several years in the military. In Israel, for example, young men and women must do two to three years of military service. The United States, though, has drafted only men and only at times of crisis. The first U.S. draft was issued during the Civil War, followed by another during World War I. The United States has also instituted peacetime drafts, before World War II and during the Cold War. Since 1973, however, the United States has had an all-volunteer military, despite recent proposals to issue a new draft since the invasion of Iraq in 2003.

Although there is no draft today, the Selective Service System (the federal agency that runs the draft) requires that all men between the ages of 18 and 26 be registered in case of a future draft. Despite their expanded roles in the military, American women are not required to register with the Selective Service System.

Young men from western Pennsylvania are sworn in to the Army after being drafted for service in the Vietnam War in 1967.

ANALYSIS SKILL **EVALUATING THE LAW**

go.hrw.com
KEYWORD: SZ7 CH23

1. Do you think the United States should have a draft today? Why or why not?
2. Should both men and women be required to register with the Selective Service System? Explain your opinion.

Economic alliances among other countries also challenge the U.S. position in the global economy. For example, the European Union (EU) is an alliance of 25 European countries. One of its goals is the free movement of goods, workers, and capital among member countries. In 2002 the EU launched a single currency, the euro, which is intended to simplify trade between member nations. If the EU is successful in its plans, member countries will share an economic relationship that will make the EU a very powerful force in the global economy.

Meeting Global Economic Challenges

Foreign competition has led the United States to seek ways to improve its position in the global economy. For example, the United States signed the North American Free Trade Agreement (NAFTA) in 1993. This agreement allows free trade among the United States, Canada, and Mexico. By eliminating trade barriers, NAFTA members have opened new markets, created jobs, and encouraged growth in member economies.

In August 2005 the United States signed the Central American Free Trade Agreement.

Like NAFTA, the agreement is designed to increase trade between the United States and the Central American countries of Costa Rica, the Dominican Republic, El Salvador, Guatemala, Honduras, and Nicaragua.

The United States also hopes to better its economic position through its membership in the Asia-Pacific Economic Cooperation group (APEC). APEC is made up of the United States, Canada, Chile, Mexico, and 17 other countries of the Pacific Rim. Its goal is to promote cooperation among Asia-Pacific countries. In its association with APEC, the United States hopes to encourage the Pacific Rim countries, particularly Japan, to lower restrictions on U.S. exports and to expand trade in the region. In 2003 the United States urged APEC to intensify the efforts to fight global terrorism. The alliance adopted tougher security measures at its 2003 meeting.

Supervising International Trade

As the number of exports grew, many countries proposed the formation of an organization to set rules for international trade. In 1995, 128 countries joined together to form the World Trade Organization (WTO) to supervise international trade. By July 2008, the number of WTO members had risen to 153.

The United Nations World Bank offers another way for countries to cooperate on economic issues. The International Monetary Fund (IMF), another UN agency, also lends money to countries in need. As international trade has grown, the IMF has raised the amount and number of loans it makes. The IMF has loaned money to Russia and a number of countries in Eastern Europe. This money may help these countries change from communism to free-market economies.

Debating Free Trade

The WTO, NAFTA, and CAFTA are expected to help American consumers and producers in the long run. However, not all Americans support such measures. Opponents of the trade agreements fear that American jobs will

ECON 101

The North American Free Trade Agreement (NAFTA)

The North American Free Trade Agreement, or NAFTA, connects Canada, Mexico, and the United States in a free-trade zone. This means that tariffs on many categories of goods—such as cars, computers, fruits, and vegetables—were completely removed in 2008.

The effect of NAFTA remains controversial in all three countries. Americans are concerned about free trade with Mexico, which does not regulate environmental protection as strictly as the United States. Mexicans have noted that poverty and unemployment have gone up since NAFTA began. It is difficult, however, to separate NAFTA as the single cause of problems as complex as poverty and environmental pollution.

When President Clinton signed NAFTA in 1993, he said, "When you live in a time of change, the only way to recover your security and to broaden your horizons is to adapt to the change, to embrace it, and to move forward."

ANALYSIS SKILL — ANALYZING ECONOMICS

1. In response to what changes do you think NAFTA was enacted?

2. Ask a store owner, factory worker, car salesperson, or other professional affected by NAFTA what he or she thinks of the trade agreement.

be lost because U.S. corporations will relocate their factories and other manufacturing operations to other countries, where labor costs are lower and raw materials are cheaper. Some opponents of free trade believe that tariffs are needed to protect American industries and jobs from foreign competition. They maintain that raising the prices of foreign goods through tariffs will encourage American consumers to buy American-made goods. This approach would protect American jobs.

In contrast, supporters of free trade believe that opening the United States to foreign trade will help the country gain greater access to foreign markets. Greater access to foreign markets will lead to increased growth in the U.S. economy. This growth will then improve the country's position in the global economy.

U.S. Imports

Regulating trade and the environment are important elements of U.S. foreign policy. Imports play a large role in that policy.

The United States receives a variety of goods from foreign countries.

U.S. Imports, 2005

Vehicles
Oil
Media hardware
Clothing
Shoes
Media software

0 5 10 15 20 25 30
Amount
(in billions of dollars)

Source: *American Manufacturing Trade Action Coalition*

ANALYSIS SKILL ANALYZING GRAPHS

What was the total dollar amount of imports to the United States in 2005?

Environmental Diplomacy

As concerns about the environment become issues of international importance, environmental policy is influencing foreign relations. The United Nations and other international organizations have served as vehicles for establishing agreements on environmental standards.

For example, in 2001 more than 160 countries met to discuss environmental policy. The main topic was the voluntary reduction of carbon dioxide and other gases believed to be responsible for the gradual warming of the Earth. However, countries have often struggled to agree on the exact terms of treaties and how they will be enforced. The cost of implementing environmental protections and the debate over different methods and strategies to reduce emissions and pollution have also prevented many nations from coming to an agreement on the treaties.

Environmental issues facing nations today include air and water pollution; the possibility of global warming and its effects on climate and weather; finding alternative energy sources; and protecting endangered species and their habitats.

Negotiations for international treaties have continued. As the global economy expands, environmental diplomacy will undoubtedly remain an important part of foreign policy.

READING CHECK **Contrasting** What are some of the advantages and disadvantages of international environmental agreements?

go.hrw.com
Online Quiz
KEYWORD: SZ7 HP23

SECTION 2 ASSESSMENT

Reviewing Ideas and Terms

1. a. Define Write a brief definition for each of the following terms: **diplomacy** and **summit**.

b. Explain Why does the United States form defense alliances with other countries?

2. a. Define Write a brief definition for the term **foreign aid**.

b. Elaborate Why is providing humanitarian aid to foreign countries a useful part of U.S. foreign policy?

3. a. Define Write a brief definition for the term **balance of trade**.

b. Predict What might happen to American manufacturing jobs if Pacific Rim countries continue

to make high-quality, low-cost products that are in high demand in the United States?

Critical Thinking

4. Categorizing Copy the graphic organizer. Use it to list organizations around the world that work for peace. Include the purpose of each organization.

Organization	Purpose

Focus on Writing

5. Decision Making Imagine that you are a member of Congress considering trade policy. Should the United States place high taxes on imported goods?

Analyzing Bar Graphs and Pie Charts

Learn

Bar graphs and pie charts provide information in a visual format. They help people picture relationships among and between related items. Publications such as textbooks, reference materials, and news sources use them to present figures and numbers.

A bar graph shows changes in quantity over time and helps people recognize patterns and trends. Double bar graphs make it easy to compare amounts within a category. Pie charts have a similar function, helping a person see how the sizes of the "pieces" of the larger set compare.

Practice

The following guidelines will help you interpret data that is presented in a bar graph or a pie chart.

1 **Read all titles and labels.** The titles and labels tell you what information the graphic contains. A bar graph is labeled with the categories and the numerical scale. Each piece in a pie chart is labeled with a category as well as its percentage of the whole.

2 **Analyze the details.** Look for relationships in the data. In a pie chart, the pieces are relative in size to each other. In a bar graph, note any increases or decreases. Use the results to form generalizations and draw conclusions about the information.

3 **Be aware of misleading graphs or charts.** Sometimes publications will try to manipulate viewers by presenting misleading graphics. The scale on bar graphs can be inappropriately drawn, making the difference between the bars appear smaller or larger. Pie charts can be drawn so that one piece stands out, making it look larger.

Apply

Use the graphs to answer the following questions.

1. What is the subject of the pie chart?

2. Which chart would you use to find out what country receives the most U.S. exports? What answer would you find?

3. Keep track of your grades in a particular class. Then create a bar graph that displays your grades for each assignment.

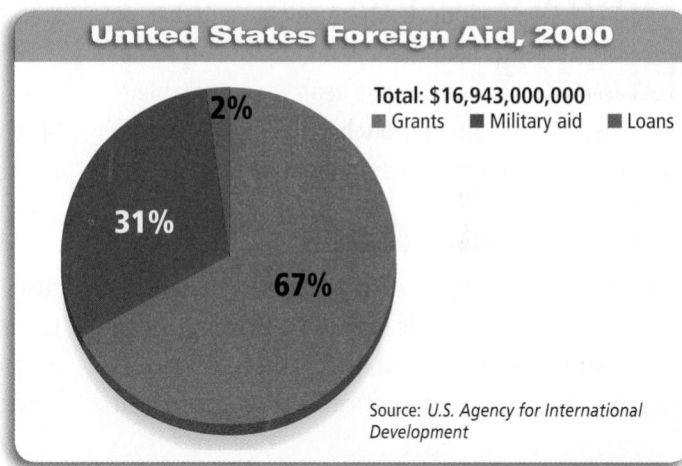

United States Foreign Aid, 2000

Total: $16,943,000,000
■ Grants ■ Military aid ■ Loans

2%
31%
67%

Source: *U.S. Agency for International Development*

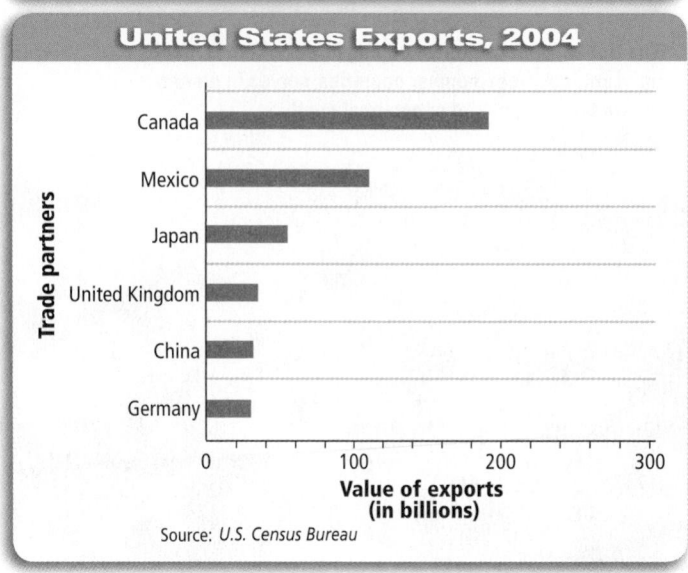

United States Exports, 2004

Trade partners: Canada, Mexico, Japan, United Kingdom, China, Germany

Value of exports (in billions): 0, 100, 200, 300

Source: *U.S. Census Bureau*

SECTION 3

The United Nations

TAKING NOTES — As you read, take notes about the history of the United Nations, its organization, and its role in the modern world. Use a chart like this one to record your notes.

History | Organization | Role

BEFORE YOU READ

The Main Idea

The United Nations provides a forum in which countries may discuss serious problems and work toward solutions.

Reading Focus

1. What is the United Nations and how is it organized?
2. What is the role of the United Nations in the modern world?

Key Terms

United Nations, *p. 622*
General Assembly, *p. 623*
Security Council, *p. 623*
International Court of Justice, *p. 623*

CIVICS IN PRACTICE — If two of your teammates argue, your team may get together to help them find a solution. If someone on the team has a problem, the rest of the team may pitch in to help. Nations in an alliance help each other in times of crisis, too.

The United Nations

In 1941, during World War II, President Franklin D. Roosevelt met with British prime minister Winston Churchill. The two leaders agreed that all people should have the right to choose their own government and live free from war, fear, or want.

After the war, in 1945, representatives from 50 countries met to form the **United Nations** (UN), an organization that promotes peaceful coexistence and worldwide cooperation.

According to the UN charter, or constitution, countries pledge to save future generations from war. They promise to live in peace as good neighbors and agree to work toward protecting basic human rights.

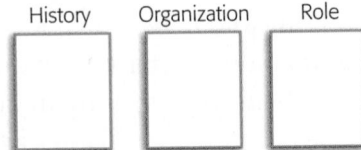

The United Nations peacekeeping force, which is made up of soldiers from member countries, serves in places where there is conflict or potential conflict.

Organization of the UN

Today the United Nations is an international organization with 192 permanent members. The UN headquarters is located in New York City. The United Nations has six main divisions, which are described below.

General Assembly The body that discusses, debates, and recommends solutions to problems is called the **General Assembly**. Each member country has one vote in the General Assembly. A two-thirds majority of the Assembly is needed to decide all important issues. The Assembly meets annually. If necessary, it may be called into emergency session. The Assembly elects its own president and makes its own rules of procedure.

Security Council The UN body that is mainly responsible for peacekeeping is the **Security Council**. It has 15 members, including 5 permanent members: China, France, the United Kingdom, Russia, and the United States. Ten temporary members are chosen by the General Assembly for two-year terms. Each country on the Security Council has one delegate.

All measures that come before the Security Council must receive a vote of 9 out of 15 members to pass. However, if one of the permanent members of the council votes against it, the measure is automatically defeated.

To prevent war, the Security Council may call on quarreling countries to work out a peaceful settlement. If diplomatic measures fail, the Security Council may recommend that UN member countries use military force against an aggressor country.

International Court of Justice Member countries may take international legal disputes to the UN law court—the **International Court of Justice**. This court is also known as the World Court.

The court consists of 15 judges from various countries who are elected by the General Assembly and the Security Council. Judges serve nine-year terms, and decisions are made by majority vote. Court headquarters are located at The Hague, in the Netherlands. The court decides matters such as boundary disputes and debt payments.

Economic and Social Council The Economic and Social Council is dedicated to improving the lives of the world's people. It conducts studies in areas such as health, human rights, education, narcotics, and world population. It then makes recommendations to the General Assembly.

Trusteeship Council The United Nations created the Trusteeship Council to help various non-self-governing colonies, called trust territories, at the end of World War II. These areas were called trust territories. The Trusteeship Council suspended operations in 1994 when the last trust territory became independent.

Secretariat The Secretariat manages the day-to-day activities of the United Nations and provides services to other UN divisions. The secretary-general is in charge of the Secretariat and also serves as the chief administrator of the United Nations. The secretary-general, who serves a five-year term, is nominated by the Security Council and appointed by the General Assembly. All five permanent members of the Security Council must agree on the nomination, and appointment is decided by majority vote.

Specialized Agencies

Much of the work of the United Nations is carried out through its many specialized agencies. Each agency is independent of the main UN body. The Economic and Social Council ensures that the United Nations and the specialized agencies work together. These agencies work to improve the lives of people around the world.

READING CHECK **Contrasting** How is the UN General Assembly different from the Security Council?

The UN in the Modern World

The United Nations provides a forum, or place, where the world's countries can express their views about problems that threaten peace. In its quest for peace, the organization largely depends on the cooperation of its members to settle their disputes diplomatically. This expectation of peaceful cooperation has met with great success.

Disputes between countries, however, cannot always be settled through diplomatic channels. Therefore, the United Nations has organized what is known as a peacekeeping force. The United Nations has no permanent armed forces of its own. The main purpose of the peacekeepers is to monitor conflicts, oversee territorial agreements and cease-fires, and help stabilize political situations. UN peacekeepers are allowed to use their weapons only in self-defense.

Some Americans are critical of the United Nations. They believe that the United States pays too much of the organization's operating costs. They point out that powerful nations can be outvoted in the General Assembly.

United Nations Agencies

- **FAO** The Food and Agriculture Organization
- **UNESCO** The United Nations Educational, Scientific and Cultural Organization
- **WMO** The World Meteorological Organization
- **World Bank** The World Bank
- **ITU** The International Telecommunication Union

They argue that the lack of a permanent UN army prevents the United Nations from ending military disputes.

In contrast, some Americans believe that the United Nations is the world's best hope for peace. They note that it has frequently succeeded in bringing quarreling countries to the conference table. These supporters do not believe the lack of a permanent UN army is a problem. UN supporters claim that creating a forum where all countries can be heard encourages world peace.

READING CHECK **Making Generalizations and Predictions** What might the world be like today without the United Nations?

---

go.hrw.com
Online Quiz
KEYWORD: SZ7 HP23

SECTION 3 ASSESSMENT

Reviewing Ideas and Terms

1. a. Define Write a brief definition for each of the following terms: **United Nations, General Assembly, Security Council,** and **International Court of Justice.**

b. Explain What led to the creation of the United Nations, and what do member countries pledge to do?

c. Evaluate Which UN body, the General Assembly or the Security Council, do you think has the most power? Give reasons for your answer.

2. a. Recall In the UN's quest for peace, upon what does the organization largely depend to settle disputes among members?

b. Evaluate In your opinion, does the United Nations have a role to play in today's modern world? Why or why not?

Critical Thinking

3. Categorizing Copy the graphic organizer. Use it to list four main divisions of the United Nations and their functions.

Name	Purpose

Focus on Writing

4. Supporting a Point of View Should the United Nations establish a permanent army to enforce its decisions? Why or why not?

STUDENTS TAKE ACTION

Inspiring a Village

In San Miguel Arcángel, Argentina, students wanted to do more than just a regular class project: They wanted to help community members live healthier lives. Through their participation in Project Citizen, the students helped their village gain essential medicine and showed the community that diplomatically working with local government can bring about positive change.

Community Connection In the small village of San Miguel, there is a first-aid station but no pharmacy where residents can buy necessary medicines. Students at the Instituto Senderos worked together on a plan to supply pharmacy items to the community. First, they would need to ask everyone in the community to help them prepare a fully stocked first-aid kit. Then the students would ask their local government to replace items in the kit as they ran out.

Taking Action The students requested an interview with a local government official, who liked their idea. Together with health workers and other local authorities, students put the plan into action. The government even formed a committee to oversee the project. Now, when the first-aid kit is empty, government officials purchase replacements and make sure that these items get to San Miguel.

Since this successful project, there have been larger changes in San Miguel. In the past, residents did not approach local government officials with ideas to help the village. Now, says teacher Mabel Oliva Ruppel, "some groups of the community are . . . thinking about proposals to be made to the local authorities regarding other problems."

Students in San Miguel Arcángel, Argentina, worked with officials to ensure that people in their small village had access to important medicine and a complete first-aid kit.

go.hrw.com
Project Citizen
KEYWORD: SZ7 CH23

SERVICE LEARNING

1. Why did the project for the first-aid kit need to involve both community members and government officials?
2. What are some important ways that these students have helped to improve life in their village?
3. How can one person's attempt to change his or her community affect others?

QUICK FACTS

Visual Summary

Use the visual summary to help you review the main ideas of the chapter.

The United States uses diplomacy and alliances to promote peace throughout the world.

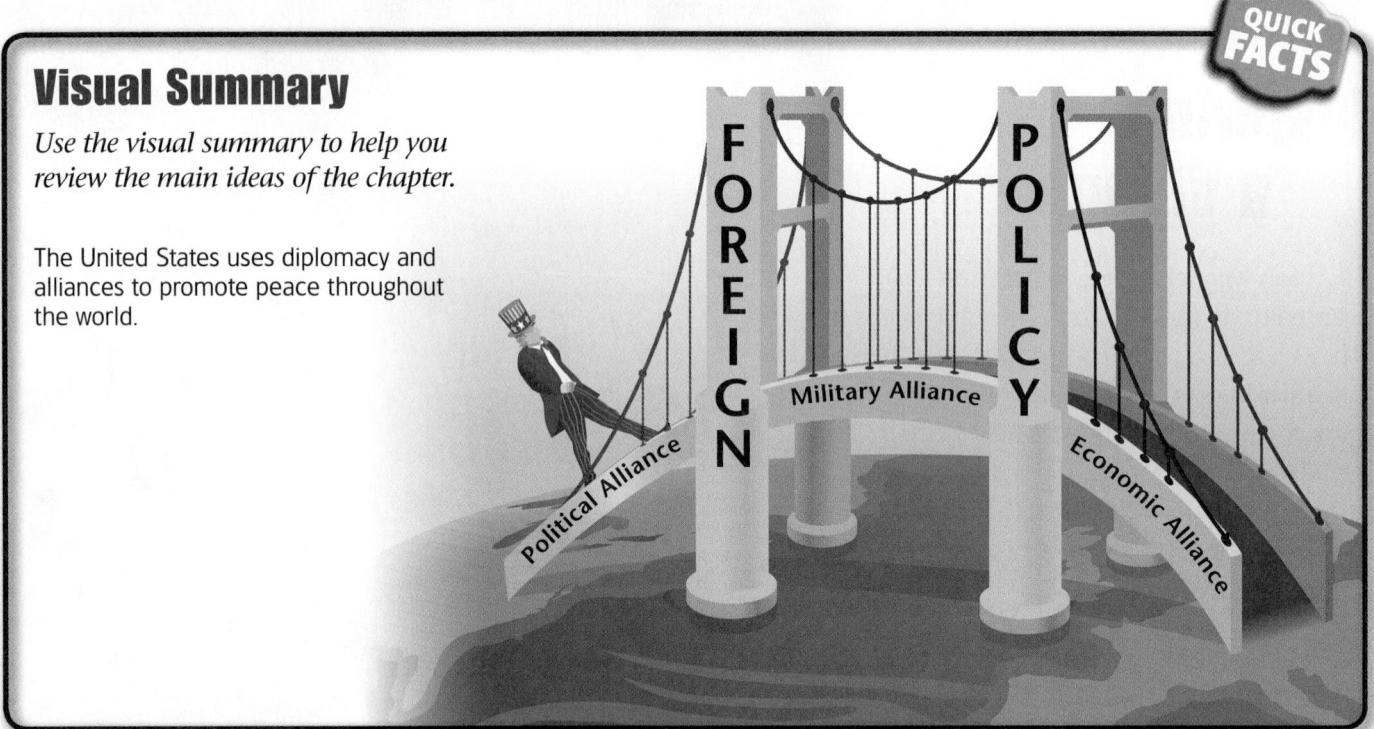

Reviewing Key Terms

Identify the correct term from the chapter that best fits each of the following descriptions.

1. The process of conducting relations between countries

2. An organization that promotes international cooperation and peaceful coexistence

3. The ambassadors, ministers, and consuls whose activities are supervised by the secretary of state

4. Agreements between countries to help each other for defense or other purposes

5. A meeting between the leaders of two or more countries to discuss issues of concern to the countries

6. The UN law court, also known as the World Court

7. When the president establishes official relations with a foreign government

8. The UN body that discusses and debates problems and recommends solutions to them

9. A government program that provides economic or military assistance to another country

10. UN body mainly responsible for peacekeeping

11. The difference in value over time between a country's imports and a country's exports

12. An agreement of mutual understanding established between the president and leaders of one or more foreign countries

Comprehension and Critical Thinking

SECTION 1 *(Pages 608–613)*

13. **a. Explain** What are four main goals of American foreign policy?

    b. Analyze What roles do the president and Congress play in the creation and execution of American foreign policy?

    c. Support a Point of View The United States faces many economic challenges, both at home and abroad. Which do you think should be the main concern of the president—the U.S. economy or the global economy? Explain your answer.

Active Citizenship video program
Review the video to answer the closing question:
How can young people have a positive impact even in countries far from where they live?

SECTION 2 *(Pages 614–620)*

14. a. Explain Why was NATO created?

b. Analyze Why does the United States give foreign aid to other countries, and what forms does it take?

c. Analyze Information While the goals of U.S. foreign policy have remained fairly constant, global challenges have changed greatly over the years. What do you think is the greatest foreign-policy challenge facing the United States today?

SECTION 3 *(Pages 622–624)*

15. a. Identify What is the purpose of the United Nations, and what are its six main divisions?

b. Explain What are the arguments for and against a permanent UN army?

c. Draw Inferences and Conclusions Ambassadors who live in foreign countries have diplomatic immunity. This means they cannot be arrested, even if they break the law. Why do you think such a rule exists, and how might the lifting of this rule affect diplomatic relations?

Civics Skills

Analyzing Bar Graphs and Pie Charts *Use the Civics Skills taught in this chapter to answer the question about the graphic below.*

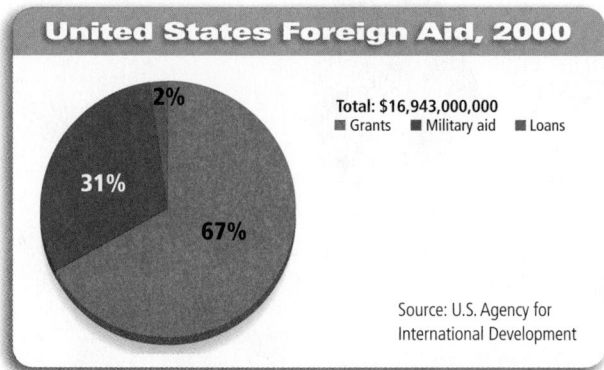

United States Foreign Aid, 2000

2%
31%
67%

Total: $16,943,000,000
■ Grants ■ Military aid ■ Loans

Source: U.S. Agency for International Development

16. What is the approximate value of U.S. military aid?

a. $200 billion

b. $200 million

c. $110 billion

d. $5.3 billion

Reading Skills

Online Research *Use the Reading Skill taught in this chapter to answer the question below.*

17. Which of the following would be the best Web site to find official policy information about current U.S. relations with China?

a. a Chinese history Web page

b. a Web page of a group that promotes understanding and cooperation between the United States and greater China

c. a State Department international information Web page

d. an official Chinese government information Web page

Using the Internet

go.hrw.com
KEYWORD: SZ7 CH23

18. Promoting World Peace Imagine you are a news reporter doing a piece on foreign policy for the evening news. Enter the activity keyword and visit some of the government departments and agencies that work to maintain peace in the world. Make a presentation or videotape about the importance of clearly defined foreign policy and how one of the departments you researched works to achieve the goal of world peace.

FOCUS ON WRITING

19. Writing Your List of Pros and Cons Review the notes you have made from this chapter. Choose the pros and cons about American foreign relations to include in your final list. Decide whether you want to include only facts, only opinions, or some of each. When you have finished your list, use it as the basis for a paragraph to make a recommendation to the president either that the United States continue to involve itself in foreign relations or that it pull back from such involvement.

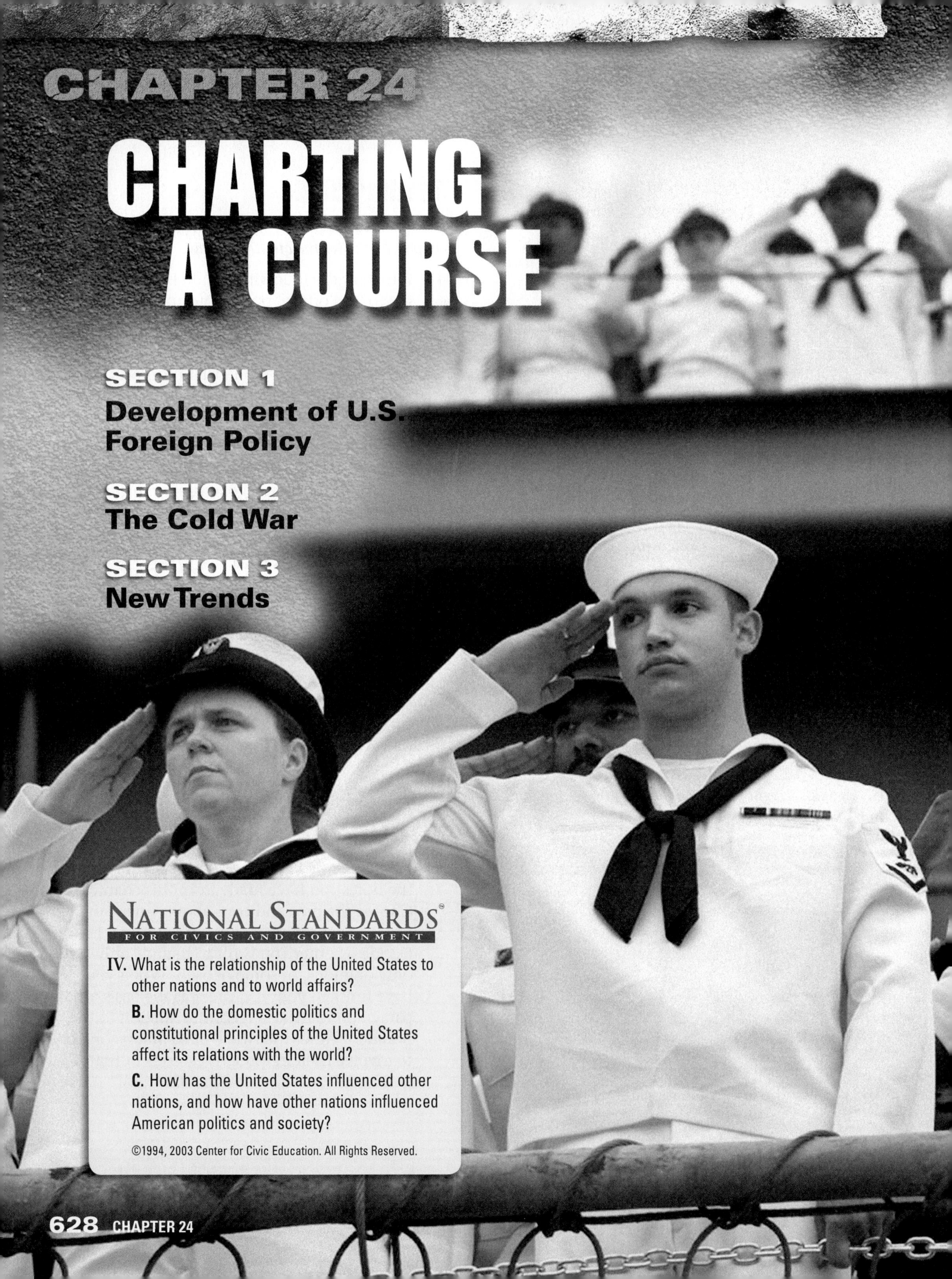

CHAPTER 24

CHARTING A COURSE

SECTION 1
Development of U.S. Foreign Policy

SECTION 2
The Cold War

SECTION 3
New Trends

NATIONAL STANDARDS®
FOR CIVICS AND GOVERNMENT

IV. What is the relationship of the United States to other nations and to world affairs?

B. How do the domestic politics and constitutional principles of the United States affect its relations with the world?

C. How has the United States influenced other nations, and how have other nations influenced American politics and society?

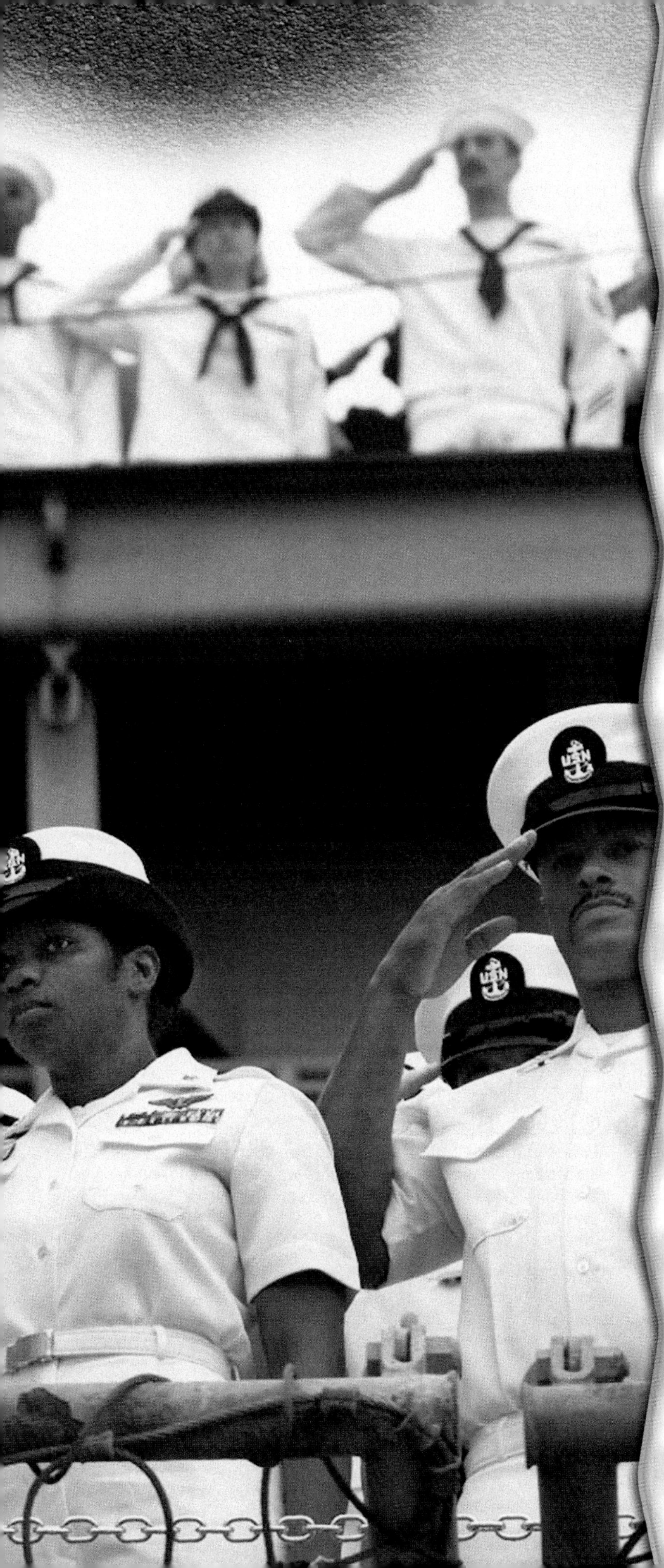

Active Citizenship video program
Watch the video to investigate how
international laws can impact U.S. citizens.

WHY CIVICS Matters

The United States has become a
leader in global politics. Why? Because
Americans understand that the world's
future depends on people committed
to the goals of peace and freedom for
all people.

STUDENTS TAKE ACTION

PROTECTING MONUMENTS What if
beautiful historic monuments in your city were
being damaged by skateboarders? What action
could you and your friends take to help preserve
the monuments?

FOCUS ON WRITING ✏

A NOBEL NOMINATION Every year a few
people are nominated for a Nobel Prize for
their work to improve the world. As you read
this chapter, take notes on the development
of American foreign policy and the goals of
U.S. foreign policy today. Then choose a leader,
either one mentioned in this chapter or one
currently in the news, and write a Nobel Prize
nomination for him or her.

Reading Skills

In this chapter you will read about how the foreign policy of the United States has changed over the centuries. You will learn about how the two world wars in the 1900s moved the United States into deeper involvement in foreign policy. You will read about the Cold War and how the United States worked to stop the spread of communism. Finally, you will learn about the new foreign policy challenges the United States has faced since the Cold War ended.

Comparing Texts

FOCUS ON READING A good way to learn about American foreign policy is to read what U.S. presidents have written. By comparing writings by different presidents during different time periods, you can learn a great deal about how the United States views involvement with other countries.

How to Compare Texts When you compare texts, you should consider several things: who wrote the documents and what the intent of each of the documents was (what the documents were meant to achieve), and what the writers' main point or points are.

Helpful Hints for Comparing Texts

1. Read the texts carefully. Make sure you understand the main points.

2. Ask yourself if the writers are basically agreeing with or disagreeing with each other.

3. Think about how the time period influenced the writer's thinking.

> " [It is] a principle in which the rights and interests of the United States are involved, that the American continents, by the free and independent condition which they have assumed and maintain, are henceforth not to be considered as subjects for future colonization by any European powers. "
>
> — President James Monroe, State of the Union Address, 1823

> " The world order which we seek is the cooperation of free countries, working together in a friendly, civilized society. "
>
> — President Franklin D. Roosevelt State of the Union Address, 1941

1st Document	2nd Document
Writer: President Monroe	**Writer:** President Roosevelt
Date: 1823	**Date:** 1941
Intent: To describe U.S. foreign policy	**Intent:** To describe U.S. foreign policy
Main Point: The United States would not allow another country to take over any country in the Americas.	**Main Point:** The United States wants to work for and with free countries.

You Try It!

Read the following passages, both of which were made by U.S. presidents. As you read, look for the main point each president makes.

> *"Freedom means the supremacy of human rights everywhere. Our support goes to those who struggle to gain those rights or keep them. Our strength is in our unity of purpose. To that high concept there can be no end save victory."*
>
> — President Franklin D. Roosevelt,
> State of the Union Address, 1941

> *"We have suffered great loss. And in our grief and anger we have found our mission and our moment. Freedom and fear are at war. The advance of human freedom ... now depends on us ... We will not tire, ... and we will not fail."*
>
> — President George W. Bush,
> after the September 11, 2001, terrorist attacks

After you read the passages, answer the following questions.

1. What was the main point Roosevelt made about freedom?

2. What was the main point Bush made about freedom?

3. How can a comparison of Roosevelt's and Bush's addresses help you understand the values that shape U.S. foreign policy?

As you read Chapter 24, compare statements made by U.S. leaders about foreign policy.

Section 1
isolationism *(p. 632)*
doctrine *(p. 634)*
corollary *(p. 634)*
dollar diplomacy *(p. 635)*
neutrality *(p. 635)*

Section 2
communism *(p. 638)*
satellite nations *(p. 639)*
containment *(p. 639)*
balance of power *(p. 640)*
limited war *(p. 641)*
détente *(p. 642)*

Section 3
terrorists *(p. 644)*
War on Drugs *(p. 646)*
embargo *(p. 647)*
World Trade Center *(p. 647)*
Pentagon *(p. 647)*
Northern Alliance *(p. 648)*

Academic Vocabulary
Success in school is related to knowing academic vocabulary—the words that are frequently used in school assignments and discussions. In this chapter, you will learn the following academic words:

consequences *(p. 633)*
strategies *(p. 639)*
facilitate *(p. 644)*

Development of U.S. Foreign Policy

BEFORE YOU READ

The Main Idea

For many years, U.S. leaders shaped foreign policy to avoid involvement in the affairs of other countries. As times changed and the United States became more closely tied to other countries, the nation became more involved in world affairs.

Reading Focus

1. Why did the United States find it difficult to maintain a policy of isolationism in its early years?
2. What impact did the Monroe Doctrine and the Good Neighbor policy have on U.S. international relations?
3. How did World War I and World War II end U.S. isolationism?

Key Terms

isolationism, *p. 632*
doctrine, *p. 634*
corollary, *p. 634*
dollar diplomacy, *p. 635*
neutrality, *p. 635*

TAKING NOTES As you read, take notes on the War of 1812, the Monroe Doctrine, the Good Neighbor Policy, and the events that led to the end of isolationism. Use a chart like this one to record your notes.

Events	Outcomes
Independence and Isolationism	
The U.S. and International Relations	
Wars End Isolationism	

This painting shows Commodore Perry of the U.S. Navy during the War of 1812. Perry is transferring his colors (the flag) to another ship during the Battle of Lake Erie on Sept. 10, 1813.

CIVICS IN PRACTICE Life is always easier if we maintain good relationships with our neighbors, but sometimes this is not easy. This is also true of foreign policy. American foreign policy shapes our nation's relationships with other countries. Out of necessity, our foreign policy has changed several times since the United States became a nation.

Independence and Isolationism

When the United States won its independence after the Revolutionary War, the country was deeply in debt and struggling to build its economy. It was busy seeking solutions to many domestic problems. Most government leaders strongly believed that the United States should concentrate on its own development and growth, and stay out of foreign politics. This belief that the United States should avoid involvement in all foreign affairs is known as **isolationism**.

HISTORICAL DOCUMENT
Washington's Farewell Address

On September 19, 1796, President George Washington's Farewell Address first appeared in a Philadelphia newspaper. In it, Washington offered advice about the nation's foreign policy.

"It is our true policy to steer clear of permanent alliances with any portion of the foreign world ...There can be no greater error than to expect, or calculate [plan] upon real favors from nation to nation. It is an illusion, which experience must cure, which a just pride ought to discard.

The duty of holding a neutral conduct may be inferred ...from the obligation which justice and humanity impose on every nation ...to maintain inviolate [unchanging] the relations of peace and amity [friendship] towards other nations."

ANALYSIS SKILL **ANALYZING PRIMARY SOURCES**
1. What do you think Washington meant when he wrote: "There can be no greater error than to expect, or calculate upon real favors from nation to nation"?
2. Why did Washington suggest neutrality as a foreign policy?

Avoiding Alliances

The French Revolution, inspired in part by the American Revolution, began in 1789. Soon, Britain and France were at war. Many Americans supported one side or the other. In 1793, President Washington issued his Neutrality Proclamation, which said that the United States would not take sides with any European country that was at war. The Proclamation was a statement of U.S. policy. Other countries had their own foreign policies, which often involved the United States against its will.

At no time in U.S. history has the policy of isolationism been an easy one to follow. In the late 1700s, President George Washington was faced with a troubled border situation with the British colony of Canada. To the south and west lay Spanish territory, which blocked U.S. expansion westward and threatened trade on the Mississippi River. When U.S. ships ventured east into the Atlantic seeking trade, British or French navy ships often seized them.

The War of 1812

Problems with Britain intensified in the early 1800s. British ships were interfering with American trade at sea and capturing American sailors and forcing them to serve on British ships. Also, Americans claimed that the British were arming American Indians and encouraging them to attack outposts on the western borders.

Despite the fact that Britain's large navy gave it an advantage at sea, American forces held their own against the British. On land, the U.S. army was able to stop British offenses in the East and South. Although the War of 1812 ended in a stalemate—neither side won a clear-cut victory—the conflict had several positive **consequences** for the United States. The war produced intense feelings of patriotism among many Americans for having stood up to the powerful British. Most importantly, the War of 1812 won the United States a newly found respect among the nations of Europe. The treaty that ended the war eventually led to improved relations with Britain. For nearly 100 years afterward, the United States avoided becoming involved in European conflicts.

ACADEMIC VOCABULARY
consequences: the effects of a particular event or events

READING CHECK **Finding the Main Idea** What early foreign policy challenges did the United States face?

Foreign Policy 1793-1945

President George Washington issued his Neutrality Proclamation in 1793.

1793

1895

President Monroe's foreign policy doctrine eventually led to war against Spain in 1895.

The Germans sank the ocean liner *Lusitania*, killing 1,201 passengers. Americans were outraged. In 1917 the United States entered WWI.

1915

THE NEW YORK HERALD.

THE LUSITANIA IS SUNK; 1,000 PROBABLY ARE LOST

The United States and International Relations

After the War of 1812, the United States worried that Europe might interfere in the Western Hemisphere. U.S. leaders developed two policies to address U.S. relations with Europe, Latin America, and Canada—the Monroe Doctrine and the Good Neighbor Policy.

The Monroe Doctrine

Most of the countries of Latin America won their independence from Spain in the early 1800s. However, President James Monroe worried that other European powers might try to take control of the newly independent Latin American countries. In 1823 President Monroe declared that the United States would consider any European interference in the affairs of any country in the Western Hemisphere an unfriendly act.

Monroe's policy came to be called the Monroe Doctrine. A foreign-policy **doctrine** is a statement of policy that sets forth a way of interacting with other countries.

The Monroe Doctrine set the course of U.S. relations with both Latin America and Europe for many years.

The United States and Latin America

At first the countries of Latin America welcomed the support of the United States. For example, the United States helped settle a boundary dispute between Venezuela and Great Britain. Later on, some European countries threatened to use force to collect debts owed by Latin American countries. The United States prevented the interference. After Cuba rebelled against Spain in 1895, the United States declared war on Spain in 1898 and defeated the Spanish fleet.

President Theodore Roosevelt strengthened the Monroe Doctrine in 1904. He announced that the United States would police the Western Hemisphere. If Latin American countries could not manage their own affairs, the United States would become involved. This policy became known as the Roosevelt Corollary to the Monroe Doctrine. A **corollary** is a statement that follows as a natural or logical result.

go.hrw.com

Interactive Art ✳ KEYWORD: SZ7 CH24

On December 7, 1941, the Japanese military attacked Americans at Pearl Harbor, Hawaii. The next day, the United States entered World War II.

1933

1941

1945

Franklin Roosevelt's Good Neighbor policy reversed the Monroe Doctrine.

After World War II, the United States joined the United Nations.

ANALYSIS SKILL **READING TIME LINES**

Making Generalizations Based on this time line, what conclusions could you draw about American foreign policy?

After the Roosevelt Corollary, many Americans began to invest money in Latin American companies. When internal disorder threatened these investments, the United States sometimes sent troops to maintain peace. U.S. foreign policy in Latin America thus became known as **dollar diplomacy**.

The Good Neighbor Policy

Although U.S. actions helped Latin American countries, they also created bad feelings. Latin American leaders believed that the United States had turned from protector to oppressor. As a result, the United States took steps to improve its relations with Latin America.

In the 1930s the United States stated that the Monroe Doctrine would no longer be used to justify U.S. involvement in Latin America. In 1933 President Franklin D. Roosevelt announced the Good Neighbor Policy. This policy opposed armed intervention by the United States in Latin American affairs. It emphasized friendly agreements.

READING CHECK **Making Generalizations** Why do you think the United States became more involved in Latin American affairs?

Wars End Isolationism

In 1914, when World War I broke out in Europe, the United States attempted to stay out of the conflict. President Woodrow Wilson announced a policy of **neutrality**. That is, the United States would not assist or favor either side.

Neutrality was difficult to maintain. In 1915, a German submarine sank the ocean liner *Lusitania*. The United States protested, but Germany continued its submarine warfare. When German submarines sank U.S. merchant ships without warning, remaining neutral became impossible. Congress declared war on Germany in 1917.

President Wilson declared that the United States had entered the war to help "make the world safe for democracy." The victory of the United States and its allies brought hope for lasting peace. Wilson centered his hopes on a new international organization called the League of Nations. The League promised to solve disputes in a friendly fashion and to go to war only as a last resort.

A provision for joining the League of Nations was submitted to the U.S. Senate. However, many Americans, including some powerful senators, opposed membership in the League. The spirit of isolationism remained strong. As a result, the United States never joined the League of Nations.

The beginning of World War II found the United States in a neutral position once again. However, the bombing of Pearl Harbor by the Japanese on December 7, 1941, changed that. The attack shocked the American people, who realized that isolationism in a worldwide conflict was impossible. The United States declared war on Japan and the Axis powers. Even during the war, plans to establish a postwar peacekeeping organization were already underway. In 1945 the United States joined with many other countries to form the United Nations.

READING CHECK ▶ **Identifying Points of View** Why did many Americans fear the end of isolationism?

Peace with Japan

On September 2, 1945, the Japanese government surrendered aboard the battleship USS *Missouri,* bringing an end to World War II.

How was American foreign policy different in 1945 from what it was in 1793?

Online Quiz
KEYWORD: SZ7 HP24

SECTION 1 ASSESSMENT

Reviewing Ideas and Terms

1. **a. Define** Write a brief definition for the following term: **isolationism**.
   b. Analyze Information Why was it difficult for the United States to follow a policy of isolationism?
   c. Evaluate How did the War of 1812 change U.S. international relations?
2. **a. Define** Write a brief definition for each of the following terms: **doctrine, corollary,** and **dollar diplomacy**.
   b. Analyze Information Why did President Roosevelt replace the Monroe Doctrine with the Good Neighbor Policy?
   c. Support a Point of View Defend or criticize President Monroe's position on Latin America.
3. **a. Define** Write a brief definition for the following term: **neutrality**.
   b. Summarize Why did President Wilson decide to enter World War I?

Critical Thinking

4. **Identifying Cause and Effect** Copy the graphic organizer and use it to show why the United States entered World Wars I and II, and the results of U.S. actions.

Focus on Writing

5. **Identifying Points of View** Imagine that you are reporting on a debate about the pros and cons of isolationism. In a three-paragraph article, describe the arguments of the debate in detail. Include examples used to support each opinion; then indicate whose point of view won and why.

636 CHAPTER 24

Civics Skills

MEDIA
LITERACY

CRITICAL
THINKING

PARTICIPATION

Analyzing Photographs

Learn

Since the first cameras were developed, photographers, journalists, and regular people have been recording the events around them. Like a piece of writing, photographs have the ability to tell a story. Photographers take pictures to show a moment in time as well as to provide a visual interpretation of an event.

You can see photographs in different ways. On a literal level, the image tells you about a specific time, place, person, or event. On an emotional level, a photograph makes you feel a certain way about what you are viewing.

Practice

1 **Determine the subject.** A photographer has a choice of what to capture. To help figure out when and where the photograph was taken, study the details, such as what clothing people are wearing and what objects are in the background.

2 **Determine the point of view.** A photograph records the way a specific event affected the photographer. Clues within the photograph, such as where the camera is focused, help reveal the photographer's attitude toward the subject.

3 **Explore your emotions.** Most photographers want to make viewers feel a certain way or think about the subject of the photograph more carefully. They work to create a mood using lighting and framing.

4 **Use outside knowledge.** What do you know about what is happening around the world that can help you interpret the photograph you are studying?

Apply

Study the photograph and then answer the questions that follow.

1. What seems to be the photographer's point of view toward this scene?

2. How does this photograph make you feel? Why?

3. What details in the photograph itself help you determine its subject? Using those details, write a caption for this photograph.

SECTION 2

The Cold War

BEFORE YOU READ

The Main Idea

The United States and the Soviet Union worked together during World War II, but the two nations became rivals soon after the war ended. Their political rivalry turned into a competition for global power that became known as the Cold War.

Reading Focus

1. What were the causes of the Cold War?
2. How did the United States use its containment policy to respond to the Berlin blockade, the Cuban missile crisis, the Korean War, and the Vietnam War?
3. What events marked the end of the Cold War?

Key Terms

communism, *p. 638*
satellite nations, *p. 639*
containment, *p. 639*
balance of power, *p. 640*
limited war, *p. 641*
détente, *p. 642*

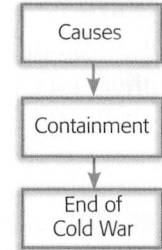 **TAKING NOTES** As you read, take notes on the causes of the Cold War, the policy of containment, and the end of the Cold War. Use a graphic organizer like this one to record your notes.

Causes
↓
Containment
↓
End of Cold War

 For more than 40 years, the Cold War had a profound effect on the lives of American citizens. During the Cold War, Americans lived in fear of a nuclear attack. Some Americans even built bomb shelters for protection. The Cold War dominated U.S. foreign policy from the end of World War II until the 1990s, when communism in Eastern Europe fell and the Soviet Union collapsed.

Causes of the Cold War

During World War II, the United States and the Soviet Union were allied in fighting Nazi Germany. After the war ended, however, the two countries became rivals. The roots of the conflict lay in the two countries' different economic systems and forms of government. The United States is a representative democracy. The Soviet Union was a Communist country.

Roots of Communism

German writer Karl Marx is credited with the ideas that led to the economic and political system known as communism. Under **communism**, the government owns the means of production—land, capital, and labor—and decides what products will be made. Marx believed that capitalists were getting rich by treating workers unfairly. He argued that the working class, called the proletariat, would take over all factories and businesses. The proletariat would set up governments, in the name of the workers, to run nations and their economies.

In 1917 Communists in Russia staged a revolution and seized control of the government, becoming the first country to adopt a Communist system. Russia was renamed the Union of Soviet Socialist Republics (USSR), or the Soviet Union. For decades, the Communist Party of the Soviet Union maintained the center of government power. The Soviet government made all economic decisions. It owned and managed all of the country's industries and farms. It also controlled most aspects of citizens' lives and punished those who spoke out against the government.

Berlin Airlift

German children wave to U.S. planes bringing in food supplies during the Berlin airlift.

How was the Berlin airlift part of the American policy of containment of communism?

The Cold War Begins

Soon after World War II, the Soviet Union had established Communist governments in Albania, Bulgaria, Czechoslovakia, East Germany, Hungary, Romania, and Poland. The Soviet Union had turned the countries along its borders into **satellite nations**—countries controlled by another country.

With the nations of Eastern Europe under its control, the Soviet Union tried to increase its power elsewhere. The United States saw this expansion of Soviet power and communism as a serious threat to U.S. national security and to world peace.

The resulting competition for global power and influence became known as the Cold War. On one side was the Soviet Union and its satellites. The United States and other noncommunist countries stood on the other side. Both sides used propaganda, spying, alliances, foreign aid, and other **strategies** to "win" the war.

> **READING CHECK** **Summarizing** How did the Cold War begin?

The Policy of Containment

Even as World War II was ending in 1945, President Harry S. Truman was worried that the Soviet Union would become a danger to the United States and the free world. Then, in March 1947 President Truman announced that the United States would give economic aid to help countries fighting communism. This policy became known as the Truman Doctrine. The idea behind Truman's policy came to be called **containment**. The United States wanted to prevent Soviet communism from spreading and keep the Soviet Union "contained" to the area it had occupied up to 1947. However, U.S. policy makers expected that the Soviet Union would test the containment policy.

The Berlin Blockade

The first real test of containment came in 1948 in Berlin, Germany. At the end of World War II, Germany was divided into separate zones. The Soviet Union occupied the eastern zone. France, Great Britain, and the United States jointly occupied the western zone.

ACADEMIC VOCABULARY
strategies: plans for fighting a battle or a war

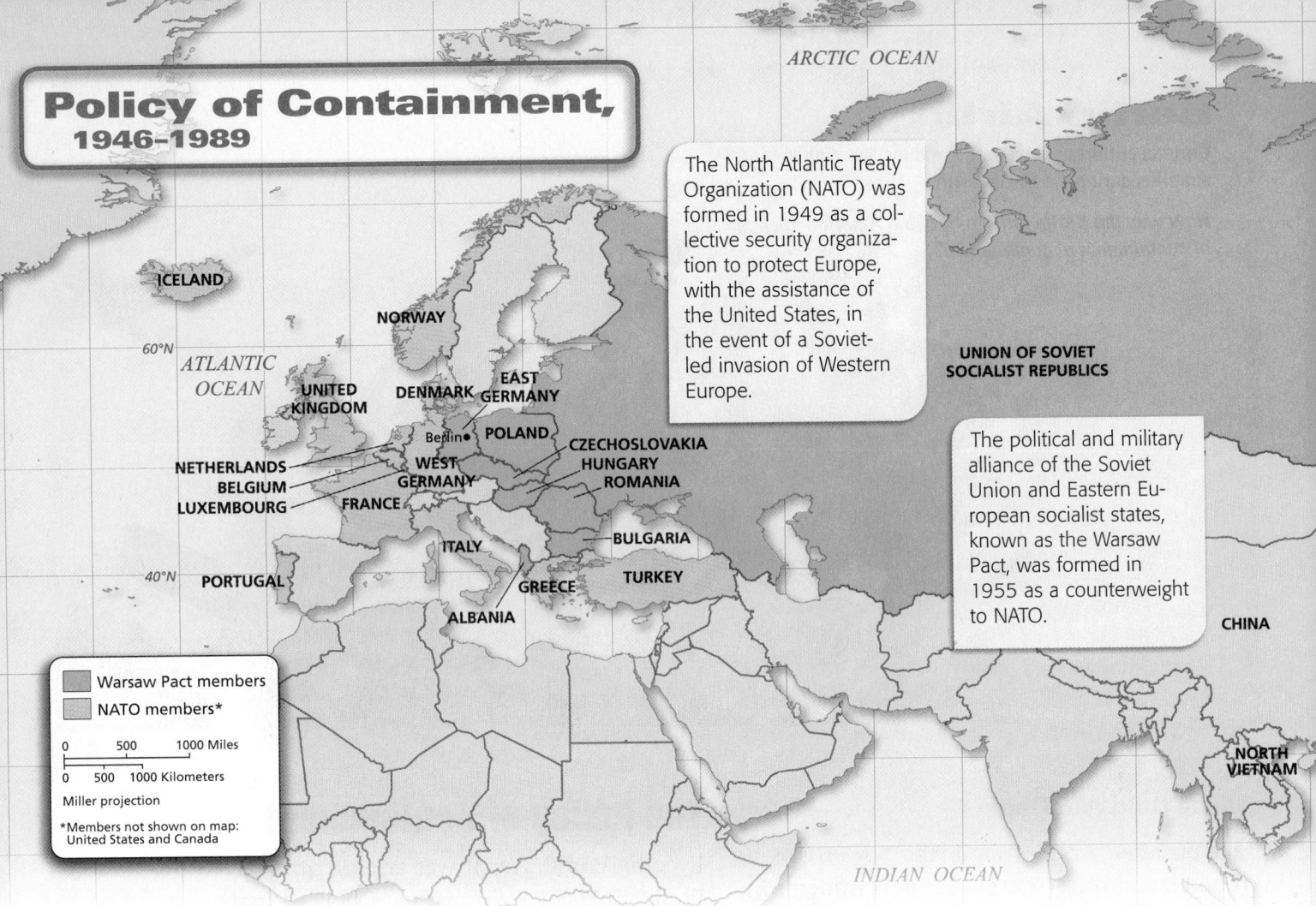

Policy of Containment, 1946–1989

ARCTIC OCEAN

The North Atlantic Treaty Organization (NATO) was formed in 1949 as a collective security organization to protect Europe, with the assistance of the United States, in the event of a Soviet-led invasion of Western Europe.

The political and military alliance of the Soviet Union and Eastern European socialist states, known as the Warsaw Pact, was formed in 1955 as a counterweight to NATO.

ICELAND

NORWAY

60°N
ATLANTIC OCEAN

UNITED KINGDOM

DENMARK   EAST GERMANY

Berlin•   POLAND

NETHERLANDS   WEST   CZECHOSLOVAKIA
BELGIUM   GERMANY   HUNGARY
LUXEMBOURG   FRANCE   ROMANIA

ITALY   BULGARIA

40°N   PORTUGAL   GREECE   TURKEY

ALBANIA

UNION OF SOVIET SOCIALIST REPUBLICS

CHINA

NORTH VIETNAM

INDIAN OCEAN

Warsaw Pact members
NATO members*

0   500   1000 Miles
0   500   1000 Kilometers
Miller projection

*Members not shown on map:
United States and Canada

Berlin, the capital, was located in the Soviet-occupied zone, but it was divided among France, Great Britain, the Soviet Union, and the United States. Each country controlled a part of the city.

In June 1948 the Soviet Union tried to force the democratic occupation troops in West Berlin to leave the city. The Soviets blockaded Berlin by closing all western land routes to the city. Residents of West Berlin were cut off from food and supplies. The United States and Great Britain began a massive airlift of fuel, food, clothing, and other essential items. More than 272,000 flights brought 2.3 million tons of needed supplies to West Berlin. The Soviets finally agreed to lift the blockade in 1949.

Communism in China

After World War II, a full-scale civil war broke out in China. In 1949 Chinese Communists defeated the government led by Chiang Kai-shek. Chiang's forces fled to the island of Taiwan, off the southeastern coast of China. There they set up a government in exile, called Nationalist China, or the Republic of China. The Communists held the mainland—known as the People's Republic of China (PRC). The first head of the People's Republic of China was Mao Zedong. China remains Communist today. Tensions still exist between Taiwan and the PRC, which maintains that Taiwan is still its territory.

The Cuban Missile Crisis

In 1949 the Soviet Union demonstrated to the world that it also had developed nuclear weapons. A **balance of power**, or a situation in which countries are about equal in strength, developed between the Soviet Union and the United States. Each country began testing the other for weaknesses.

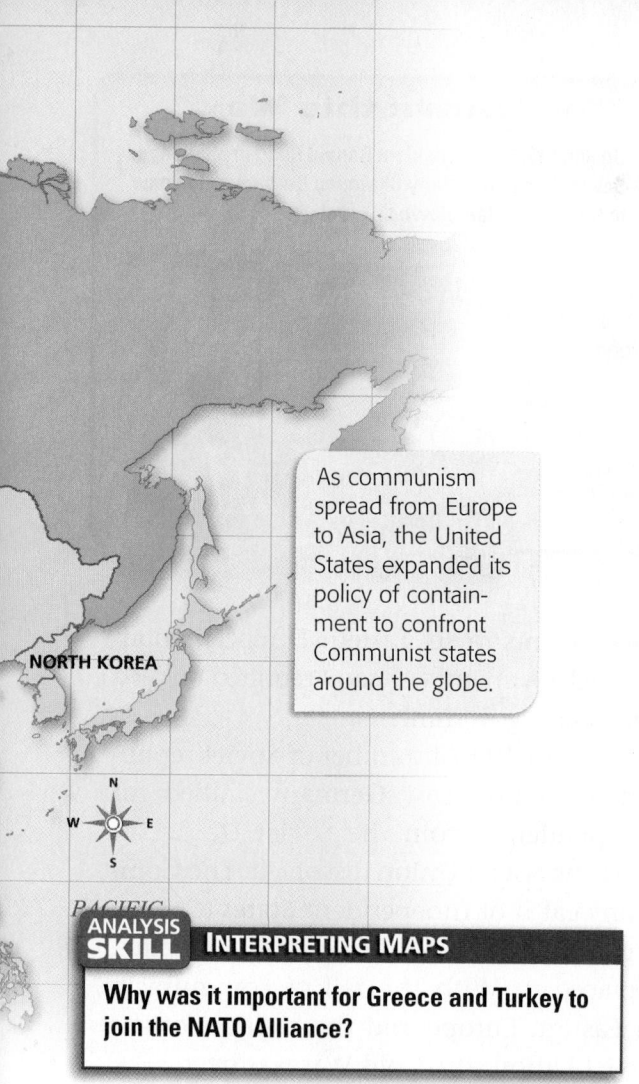

As communism spread from Europe to Asia, the United States expanded its policy of containment to confront Communist states around the globe.

NORTH KOREA

N
W   E
S

PACIFIC

ANALYSIS SKILL **INTERPRETING MAPS**

Why was it important for Greece and Turkey to join the NATO Alliance?

The most dangerous of these confrontations took place in October 1962, when President John F. Kennedy was informed that the Soviets were building secret missile bases in Cuba. Fidel Castro had set up a Communist government on the island in 1959.

Kennedy knew that these missile bases could threaten the United States, so he demanded that the Soviet Union remove its missiles from Cuba. Kennedy declared that the United States was ready to take military action if necessary. The U.S. Navy and Air Force were used to search foreign ships bound for Cuba, and Army troops were put on alert. As a result of this show of military strength and determination, the Soviet Union backed down and agreed to remove its missiles from Cuba.

The Korean War

During the Cold War, the United States also became involved in military conflicts that were limited in scope. A **limited war** is fought without using a country's full power, particularly nuclear weapons.

As a result of an agreement reached after World War II, the Asian country of Korea was divided into Communist North Korea and noncommunist South Korea. In June 1950, North Korea invaded South Korea in an attempt to reunite the country under a Communist government. North Korea was equipped with Soviet weapons. Chinese troops also began helping the North Koreans.

The U.S. government called on the United Nations to halt the invasion. Troops from the United States and 15 other members of the United Nations helped defend South Korea. By July 1953, the conflict had reached a stalemate. The two sides agreed that Korea would remain divided into Communist North Korea and noncommunist South Korea. Tensions remain high between the two Korean countries today.

The Vietnam War

In 1954 several French colonies in Southeast Asia—Vietnam, Laos, and Cambodia—became independent. Vietnam, like Korea, was divided into a Communist northern half and a noncommunist southern half. The agreements called for elections to be held throughout Vietnam in 1956 to reunite the country. When the elections did not take place, Communist guerillas revolted. Troops and supplies from North Vietnam supported guerilla forces in the south. The North Vietnamese received military supplies from the Soviet Union and China.

U.S. officials feared that if South Vietnam fell to the Communists, other countries in Southeast Asia might also fall. The United States sent economic aid and military advisers to South Vietnam and eventually combat troops were sent into action. By 1969 some 540,000 Americans were fighting in Vietnam.

In January 1973 a peace agreement was announced and the war came to an end for the United States. The war had lasted more than eight years, killed some 58,000 Americans, and wounded more than 300,000. It cost nearly $140 billion. Despite the peace agreement, fighting continued in Vietnam. By 1975 the Communist government controlled all of Vietnam.

READING CHECK **Analyzing Information** Why did the United States become involved in the Vietnam War?

The End of the Cold War

The Soviet Union suffered from the costs of the Cold War. In 1985, Mikhail Gorbachev became leader of the Soviet Union. Faced with a failing economy, citizen unrest, and a stifling political system, Gorbachev began a series of reforms. Gorbachev's reform policies included efforts at **détente**, or a lessening of tensions, between the United States and the Soviet Union.

Social changes throughout Eastern Europe caused a number of citizens in several Soviet satellite nations to overturn their Communist governments. By 1990 the Communist

"Tear Down this Wall"

On June 12, 1987, President Ronald Reagan challenged Soviet Communist Party Chairman Gorbachev to come to Berlin and "tear down this wall."

The sign behind President Reagan is a warning that you are now leaving West Berlin.

governments in six Eastern European countries fell. Germany was soon reunited under a democratic government.

Also in 1990 a number of Soviet republics, including East Germany, rallied for independence from the Soviet Union. In 1991 the Soviet Union dissolved. The Commonwealth of Independent States (CIS), an organization of former Soviet republics, replaced it. With the fall of communism in Eastern Europe and the collapse of the Soviet Union, the Cold War was over.

READING CHECK **Summarizing** How did the Cold War end?

go.hrw.com
Online Quiz
KEYWORD: SZ7 HP24

SECTION 2 ASSESSMENT

Reviewing Ideas and Terms

1. a. Define Write a brief definition for each of the following terms: **communism** and **satellite nations**.
b. Analyze Information In what ways is communism both an economic and a political system?

2. a. Define Write a brief definition for each of the following terms: **containment, balance of power,** and **limited war**.
b. Compare and Contrast How did the U.S. response to the Berlin blockade and the Cuban missile crisis differ?

3. a. Define Write a brief definition for the following term: **détente**.
b. Summarize In what ways did the reforms introduced by Mikhail Gorbachev help end the Cold War?

Critical Thinking

4. Sequencing Copy the time line. Use it to list some of the important events of the Cold War in their proper order.

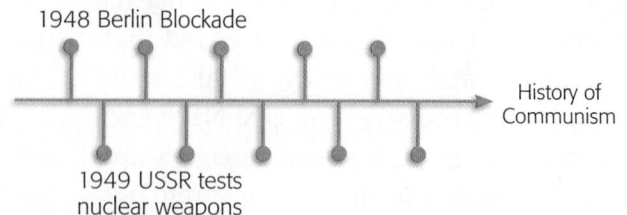

1948 Berlin Blockade

History of Communism

1949 USSR tests nuclear weapons

Focus on Writing

5. Problem Solving Write a newspaper article describing the end of the Cold War.

SECTION 3
New Trends

BEFORE YOU READ

The Main Idea

A primary goal of U.S. foreign policy has been to promote peace, trade, and friendship throughout the world. In the face of terrorism, war, and ongoing conflict in the Middle East, the United States and other governments have had to take a more aggressive approach to foreign policy in recent years.

Reading Focus

1. What global conflicts has the United States faced since the end of the Cold War?
2. What global political problems and trade issues has the United States faced since the end of the Cold War?
3. What impact has terrorism had on the United States and the rest of the world since the September 11, 2001, attacks?

Key Terms

terrorists, *p. 644*
War on Drugs, *p. 646*
embargo, *p. 647*
World Trade Center, *p. 647*
Pentagon, *p. 647*
Northern Alliance, *p. 648*

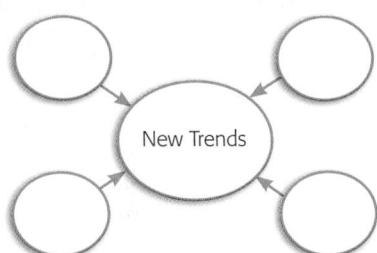 **TAKING NOTES** As you read, take notes on global conflicts, global politics and trade issues, and the impact of terrorism on the United States and the world. Place your notes on each issue in a graphic organizer like this one.

New Trends

American soldiers hunt for al Qaeda terrorists in Afghanistan in 2002.

 **CIVICS IN PRACTICE** Much of the world breathed a sigh of relief following the end of the Cold War. However, other pressing international issues took the place of the Cold War on the world stage. Today, American foreign policy addresses political and social problems in Eastern Europe, the Middle East, Asia, South America, and Africa. And a new threat, an increase in global terrorism, has become the United States's top foreign policy priority.

Global Conflicts

With the collapse of the Soviet Union in the 1990s, the United States became the world's only superpower. Since then, the U.S. government has played a greater peacekeeping role in world affairs.

Russia and Eastern Europe

Since the end of the Cold War, Russia has struggled to make the transition to a free-market economy. Large amounts of money are needed to modernize outdated factories and equipment, stimulate entrepreneurship, and encourage foreign investment.

POLITICAL CARTOON
The Iraq War

In March 2003 the United States and its allies moved into Iraq and removed dictator Saddam Hussein from power. Since that time, representatives from both the United States and its allies and from Iraq have worked to establish a democratic government for the country. The democratic process has faced many challenges along the way.

The runner's arm says, "U.S. Public Support." What might this mean?

The runner is only on mile 3 of 26.

THE MARATHON RUNNER

ANALYSIS SKILL **ANALYZING PRIMARY SOURCES**

How does the cartoonist use the runner to illustrate establishing democracy in Iraq?

ACADEMIC VOCABULARY
facilitate: to bring about

In 1995 Russia joined NATO's Partnership for Peace program. Russia now joins NATO in military exercises, peacekeeping operations, and other activities as preparation for possible future membership in NATO. In 2002 NATO accepted Russia as a limited partner. Like the United States, Russia has been the victim of terrorist attacks. **Terrorists** use violence against civilians to achieve political goals. In 2002 and 2004, Chechen terrorists launched attacks on a Russian theater and school.

In other former Communist countries, U.S. foreign policy has focused on resolving conflicts. After the collapse of the Soviet Union, ethnic groups in parts of Eastern Europe have turned to violence. For example, ethnic conflict and war have devastated the southeastern European region of the former Yugoslavia throughout the 1990s. The United States and other members of NATO worked to promote stability by helping the groups involved negotiate peace agreements in 1995 and 1999.

Iraq

In 1990 Iraqi tanks and ground troops invaded Kuwait. Iraqi leader Saddam Hussein claimed that Kuwait was legally Iraqi territory. In 1991 the United States led an international coalition in an assault on Iraq and freed Kuwait from Iraqi control. However, Saddam remained in power and failed to keep some of the cease-fire terms.

Saddam continued to refuse UN demands for open arms inspections. In March 2003, the United States and allied forces moved into Iraq and removed Hussein from power. U.S. and allied forces remain in Iraq to rebuild the country and maintain security. In January 2005, Iraqis elected delegates for their first national assembly, which convened later that year to draft a new constitution, approved in October. The next month Iraqis went to the polls once more to select their first leaders under the new constitution. As a result of this election, Nouri al-Maliki became the first prime minister of liberated Iraq.

Israel

The ongoing conflict between Israel and the Palestinians continues to challenge international relations in the Middle East. Palestine, a small eastern Mediterranean region, was controlled by Great Britain after World War I, until the United Nations partitioned it into a Jewish and an Arab state. Israel was created in 1948, but Arab leaders rejected partition and attacked Israel.

Israel won the war. Jordan and Egypt took over the West Bank and Gaza, land assigned for an Arab state. The Palestine Liberation Organization (PLO) formed in 1964 and launched a terrorism campaign against Israel, demanding that Israel be replaced by an Arab Palestinian state. During another war in 1967, Israel captured the West Bank and Gaza. Since the 1960s, PLO attacks have killed hundreds of Jews, and Israel has retaliated.

To help bring stability to the region, the United States has **facilitated** peace agreements between Israel and Egypt (1979) and Israel and Jordan (1994). In 1993 President Bill Clinton hosted the signing of a historic agreement between Israeli prime minister Yitzhak Rabin and Palestinian leader Yasser Arafat. However, violence by Palestinians and Israeli reprisals continued. After Arafat died in 2005, Mahmoud Abbas became the Palestinian authority chair. That same year, Israeli prime minister Ariel Sharon and Mahmoud Abbas declared a truce. To ease tensions, Israel removed settlers and Israeli troops from the Gaza Strip—a coastal region controlled by Israel but inhabited mostly by Palestinians—in 2005. However, violence continued. Thousands of Israelis and Palestinians have been killed in attacks and retaliatory actions since the withdrawal.

India and Pakistan

India and Pakistan have fought three wars since the two countries became independent in 1947. The possibility of conflict between India and Pakistan again became

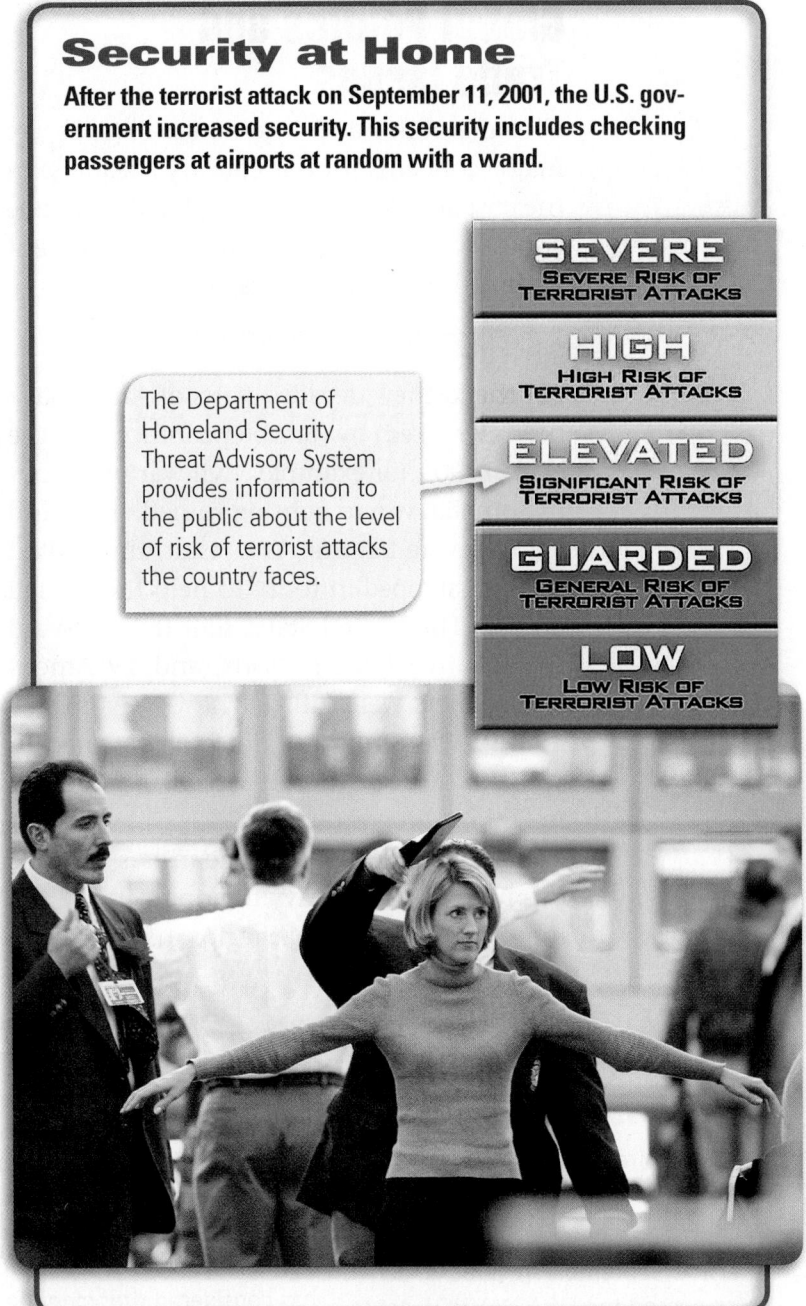

Security at Home

After the terrorist attack on September 11, 2001, the U.S. government increased security. This security includes checking passengers at airports at random with a wand.

SEVERE
SEVERE RISK OF TERRORIST ATTACKS

HIGH
HIGH RISK OF TERRORIST ATTACKS

ELEVATED
SIGNIFICANT RISK OF TERRORIST ATTACKS

GUARDED
GENERAL RISK OF TERRORIST ATTACKS

LOW
LOW RISK OF TERRORIST ATTACKS

The Department of Homeland Security Threat Advisory System provides information to the public about the level of risk of terrorist attacks the country faces.

an international issue when both countries tested nuclear weapons in 1998.

At first, the United States responded to these hostilities by imposing economic sanctions on India and Pakistan. However, recent diplomatic efforts have shifted to promoting better communication and easing tensions between the two countries.

READING CHECK **Analyzing Information** How has the United States reacted to various conflicts in the Middle East and Asia?

Global Politics and Trade Issues

Global politics and international trade are major concerns for our country's leaders. In the past decade, for example, global and trade issues have shaped American involvement with Africa, Latin America, and Canada.

Africa

For the last few decades, parts of Africa have been wracked by terrible conflict. In the early 1990s, for example, civil war broke out in Somalia, where fighting ruined crops and led to severe famine. As a result, the United Nations stepped in to try to help the Somali people. The United States sent troops to aid the UN in its relief efforts, and 19 American soldiers were killed. The UN withdrew in 1995, but order has not been restored in Somalia. A new wave of violence broke out in 2006, killing thousands.

The Darfur region of Sudan has likewise been the scene of heavy fighting. Since 2003 intense fighting in that region has had devastating effects on the population. Tens of thousands of residents have been killed, and more than 2 million more have fled their homes as refugees. Led by the UN, many countries have sought ways to aid the victims of this conflict.

Latin America and Canada

The main goal of U.S. foreign policy in Latin America today is to expand trade and open new markets. The North American Free Trade Agreement (NAFTA) and other trade issues continue to shape relations between Canada, Mexico, and the United States. A similar agreement with Central and South American countries was approved in 1995.

Fighting drug trafficking has also shaped U.S. policy in Latin America. The **War on Drugs**—an organized effort to end the trade and use of illegal drugs—began in the 1970s. It has become an important part of U.S.-Latin American relations. U.S. aid to some Latin American countries has been earmarked for fighting drug production and trafficking.

American Civil Liberties

Freedom versus Security

How much freedom do you think Americans are willing to give up in the interest of national security?

After the September 11 attacks, Congress passed the USA PATRIOT Act to help law enforcement catch terrorists by tracking their communications and finances. But since its passage in 2001, this piece of legislation has been criticized for allowing government officials too much access to private affairs, perhaps in violation of the Constitution. For example, under the act, officials can get secret authorization to search people's homes and to monitor their phone calls without a warrant—even if those people are not suspected terrorists.

The PATRIOT Act also lets officials access library and bookstore records to track which books a person has checked out or purchased. Congress has considered dropping the power to access library and bookstore records from the law.

1. What do you think is the most important purpose of the Patriot Act?
2. Why might people object to the government knowing what they are reading?

Attorney General John Ashcroft strongly supported the PATRIOT Act.

Cuba is the only Communist country in Latin America. The United States had put into place an **embargo**, or government order forbidding trade, against Cuba. However, the U.S. government now allows the donation of humanitarian supplies, such as medicine, food, and clothing. The U.S. government continues to work to encourage Cuba to adopt a more democratic form of government.

READING CHECK > **Summarizing** What are some of the ways that the United States has responded to political and trade issues throughout the world?

September 11th

Terrorism has been a problem throughout the world for many years. However, it took on a different meaning for Americans early in the 21st century. Terrorist attacks on U.S. soil have changed the resolve of the American people and reshaped U.S. foreign policy.

On September 11, 2001, terrorists hijacked four U.S. commercial airliners after they took off from different airports. The terrorists crashed two planes into the **World Trade Center**, a business complex in New York City. The twin towers of the center collapsed as a result. The third plane hit the **Pentagon**, the headquarters of the U.S. military leadership. The fourth plane crashed in rural Pennsylvania. Thousands of people were killed in the attacks.

In a national address, President George W. Bush called the terrorist attacks an act of war. He promised that the United States would bring those responsible to justice and wage war on terrorist organizations and the national governments that supported terrorism.

President Bush appointed Governor Tom Ridge of Pennsylvania as head of the Office of Homeland Security (now the Department of Homeland Security), a new cabinet-level position. This office was created to coordinate the domestic national security efforts of various government agencies. Key goals included improving airport security and protecting vital systems such as transportation

FOCUS ON
Eric Shinseki
(1942 -)

General Eric Shinseki was the chief of staff of the Army from 1999 to 2003. He is the first Japanese American to reach this top position. The chief of staff of the Army is the top military adviser to the president.

Shinseki served as artillery forward observer and commander during the Vietnam War, where he was injured by a land mine. He served as commander of the NATO Stabilization Force during the Bosnian conflict. He served as vice chief of staff during Operation Enduring Freedom in Afghanistan, and he was chief of staff when the Iraq war began in 2003.

One of Shinseki's most notable achievements in the military is his creation of Stryker Brigade Combat Teams, which are eight-wheeled, armored combat vehicles manned by four soldiers. Shinseki designed the Strykers to make the Army lighter, faster, and ready to respond quickly to conflict. Strykers are designed to take a four-soldier team anywhere in the world in only 96 hours.

Drawing Conclusions Why would Shinseki want combat teams to be able to respond anywhere within 96 hours?

and power networks from attack. Political leaders such as U.S. Attorney General John Ashcroft also called for expanded law-enforcement powers to combat terrorism.

A prime suspect in the attacks surfaced almost immediately—Osama bin Laden. This wealthy Saudi Arabian exile, a supporter of an extreme form of Islamic fundamentalism, was already wanted for his suspected role in earlier terrorist attacks against U.S. forces overseas. Bin Laden's global terrorism network is known as al Qaeda, or "the Base." Officials later produced evidence that linked bin Laden to the attacks.

U.S. officials then singled out the Taliban regime of Afghanistan as a key sponsor of terrorism. Osama bin Laden was in Afghanistan when the terrorist attacks occurred. President Bush called for the Taliban to turn over bin Laden to U.S. officials or face retaliation. The Taliban refused to comply with U.S. demands.

Fighting Terrorism

Secretary of State Colin Powell led U.S. efforts to build an international coalition against terrorism. Great Britain and Russia pledged their support. On October 7, 2001, the United States and Great Britain began air strikes against al Qaeda and Taliban targets in Afghanistan. The **Northern Alliance**, an Afghan group that had fought against the Taliban since the early 1990s, provided ground support. American and British ground troops soon followed. As the troops advanced, they slowly drove out the Taliban and captured members of al Qaeda. On December 17, 2001, the American flag was raised at the U.S. embassy in Kabul for the first time since 1989.

Meanwhile, the international community worked with the Afghan people to help establish a new government. Hamid Karzai, an Afghan tribal chief and political leader, was sworn in as leader of the interim government. Karzai welcomed international peacekeeping forces to maintain peace and stability in Afghanistan. In December 2003 Afghanistan adopted a constitution that included equal rights for men and women. Elections were held in 2004, and Karzai was elected president.

Since the September 11 terrorist attacks, fighting terrorism has become a central part of U.S. foreign policy. In 2003 U.S. forces attacked Iraq as part of U.S. efforts to combat threats to world peace. (See page 644.) Secretary of State Condoleezza Rice continued to foster the main goals of U.S. foreign policy—promoting peace, democracy, and trade—while fighting terrorism around the world. New situations and new problems will continue to challenge U.S. foreign policy makers.

Fighting terrorism also means protecting citizens here at home from another attack like the one in 2001. The goals of the Department of Homeland Security (DHS) are to protect the nation from a terrorist attack and to reduce the country's vulnerability to such attacks.

READING CHECK **Analyzing Information** How did the United States respond to the September 11 terrorist attacks?

go.hrw.com
Online Quiz
KEYWORD: SZ7 HP24

SECTION 3 ASSESSMENT

Reviewing Ideas and Terms

1. a. Define Write a brief definition of the following term: **terrorists**.

b. Recall How has the end of the Cold War changed the way the United States conducts foreign policy?

2. a. Define Write a brief definition of the following terms: **War on Drugs** and **embargo**.

b. Draw Conclusions Why is trade the main goal of U.S. foreign policy in Latin America?

3. a. Define Write a brief definition for each of the following terms: **World Trade Center**, **Pentagon**, and **Northern Alliance**.

b. Summarize How did the terrorists attack the United States on September 11, 2001?

c. Elaborate Why do you think that it was important for the United States to build an international coalition against terrorism?

Critical Thinking

4. Categorizing Copy the graphic organizer. Use it to list the issues that have shaped U.S. foreign policy since the end of the Cold War.

Country/Region	Issue

Focus on Writing

5. Making Generalizations and Predictions Imagine that you are a foreign-policy adviser to the president. Write a memo to the president explaining what foreign-policy issues will be important in the future. Be sure to explain your choices.

STUDENTS TAKE ACTION

Preserving History

The city of Vladivostok, Russia, recently announced plans to build a public skateboarding area. This decision would never have been made without the efforts of students from Ms. Irina Palachshenko's class. This Project Citizen class—from a former Soviet country with little experience with democracy—got involved in changing their community.

Community Connection In Vladivostok, skateboarding was very popular among teenagers. Popular places to skateboard included the marble of public monuments. However, wear and tear from skateboarding was damaging some of the monuments. The students in Irina Palachshenko's class were concerned about this destruction, but they did not feel that laws against skateboarding would be very effective. Instead, they wanted the government to create a positive alternative.

Taking Action The students started by contacting people who worked with the monuments and asking about the damage and the cost of repairs. Soon, museum leaders and officials from local agencies that supported sports like skateboarding agreed to work with the students. The students wrote letters to the mayor and members of the Duma (a Russian legislature) supporting a public skateboarding area. The teens then had a meeting with the mayor, who liked their idea but had no extra money in that year's city budget. The members of the Duma, however, promised to consider including funds for the project in the next year's budget. City officials soon started looking for a location for the park. By the end of the year, the city had a plan to begin building a public skateboarding park.

> Our Problem
>
> A blasphemous attitude toward monuments
>
> НАША ПРОБЛЕМА
>
> КОШУНСТВЕННОЕ ОТНОШЕНИЕ К ПАМЯТНИКАМ
>
> Alternative ways

Students in Vladivostok took action to protect historic public monuments.

go.hrw.com
Project Citizen
KEYWORD: SZ7 CH24

SERVICE LEARNING

1. What problem did Ms. Palachshenko's students identify in their community?
2. How did the students go about getting support for their idea?

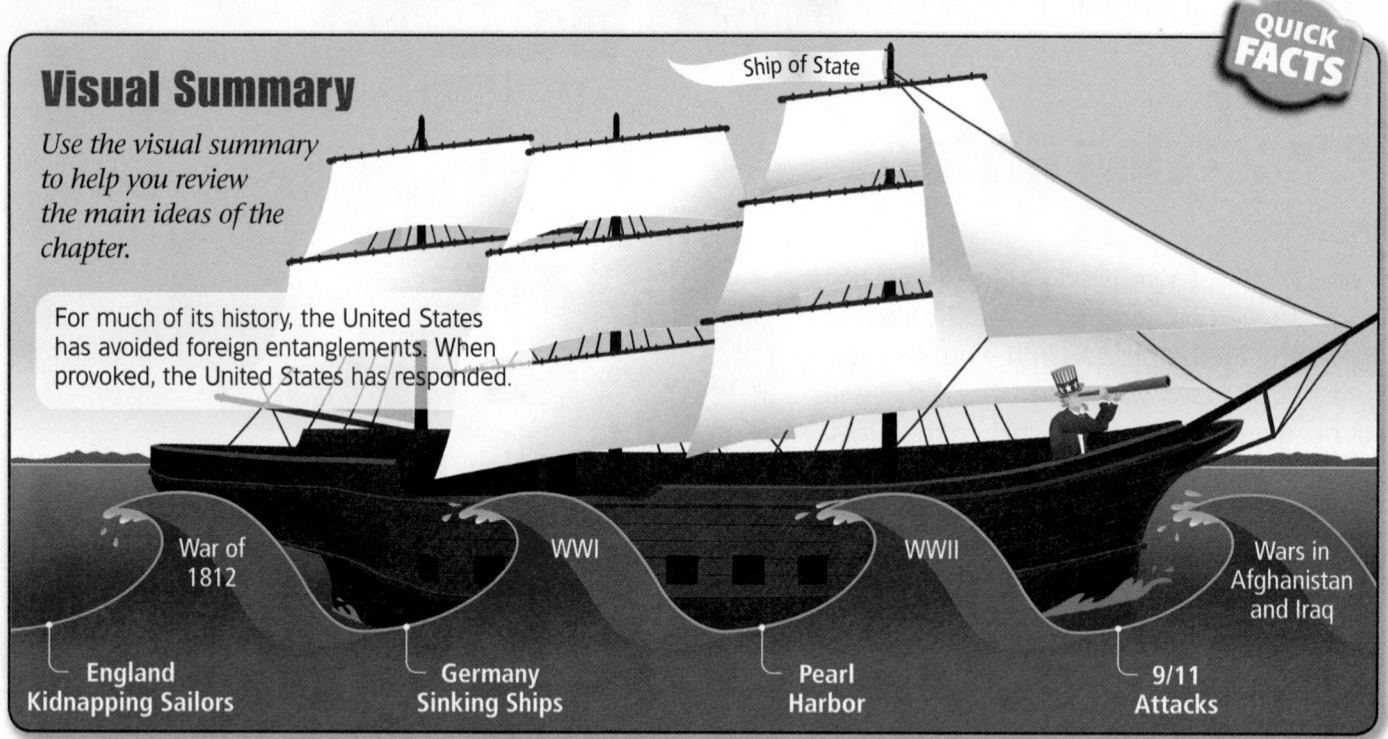

QUICK FACTS

Visual Summary

Use the visual summary to help you review the main ideas of the chapter.

For much of its history, the United States has avoided foreign entanglements. When provoked, the United States has responded.

Ship of State

War of 1812

WWI

WWII

Wars in Afghanistan and Iraq

England Kidnapping Sailors

Germany Sinking Ships

Pearl Harbor

9/11 Attacks

Reviewing Key Terms

For each term below, write a sentence explaining its significance to U.S. foreign policy.

1. isolationism
2. doctrine
3. corollary
4. dollar diplomacy
5. neutrality
6. communism
7. satellite nations
8. containment
9. balance of power
10. limited war
11. détente
12. terrorists
13. War on Drugs
14. embargo
15. World Trade Center
16. Pentagon
17. Northern Alliance

Comprehension and Critical Thinking

SECTION 1 *(Pages 632–636)*

18. **a. Summarize** Why did many U.S. officials favor isolationism, and why was this policy difficult to follow?

    b. Explain What caused the United States to lose neutrality in the world wars?

SECTION 2 *(Pages 638–642)*

19. **a. Recall** Why did the United States pursue a policy of containment during the Cold War?

    b. Identify Cause and Effect What was the U.S. response to the Berlin blockade and the Cuban missile crisis?

SECTION 3 *(Pages 643–648)*

20. **a. Describe** What new foreign policy challenges have emerged since the Cold War ended?

    b. Explain What actions did the U.S. government take after the terrorist attacks of September 11, 2001?

Active Citizenship video program

Review the video to answer the closing question:
Do you think a country's laws are a reflection of its values? Explain.

Using the Internet

go.hrw.com
KEYWORD: SZ7 CH24

21. Ending the Cold War By the 1980s, the Cold War had been going on for decades. But times were changing, communism was falling apart, and the world would never be the same again. Enter the activity keyword and use the links provided to research the causes and effects of the decline of communism in the world. Then create a pamphlet that explains the reasons for the decline of communism, the global effects, and the struggle of former communist countries to rebuild their societies.

Civics Skills

Analyzing Photographs *Study the photograph below. Then answer the questions that follow.*

22. Which of the following best represents the photographer's point of view?

a. He wants to show how unprepared the United States was for the attack on Pearl Harbor.

b. He wants to show living conditions at the military bases at Pearl Harbor.

c. He wants American citizens to respond to the attack on Pearl Harbor.

d. Both a and c are correct.

23. What impact does showing the sailor in the foreground of the photo have on the viewer?

Reading Skills

Comparing Texts *Use the Reading Skills taught in this chapter to answer the questions about the excerpts from two different speeches.*

"The first caution was that we must continue to respect our Constitution and protect our civil liberties in the wake of the attacks . . . Yet we must examine every item that is proposed in response to these events to be sure we are not rewarding these terrorists and weakening ourselves by giving up the cherished freedoms that they seek to destroy."

—Senator Russell Feingold, October 12, 2001

"Like all Americans, I cherish our civil liberties. They are at the very heart of what it means to live in freedom. I am committed to preserving them in everything we do at the Department of Justice. That's why I've tried to keep an open mind in this dialogue. I have been willing to listen to those who have ideas they believe will clarify or strengthen the PATRIOT Act. But what I cannot nor will not accept are changes to our laws that would leave Americans less safe from terrorism and crime."

—Attorney General Alberto Gonzales, June 5, 2005

24. Make a table comparing the two excerpts. Include the name of the speaker, the date of the speech, the speaker's intent, and the speaker's main point. Using your table, identify which speaker you think is in favor of the PATRIOT Act.

25. Based on your comparison and your analysis, with which speaker do you think most Americans would agree? Explain your answer.

FOCUS ON WRITING

26. Writing a Nobel Nomination Begin your nomination with a sentence that identifies the person you are nominating. Then give at least three reasons for your nomination, including specific achievements or contributions of this person. Be persuasive.

FOUNDATIONS *of* DEMOCRACY

Following the Law in Foreign Countries

In 2005 U.S. actress Hilary Swank was fined $163 for bringing an apple and an orange into New Zealand, which forbids imported fruit. If Swank had known the laws of New Zealand before visiting the country, she could have saved herself a fine and a lot of trouble. Visiting a foreign country can be exciting, fun, and educational. But it is important to be familiar with and respect the laws of the countries you visit.

Why it Matters As a U.S. citizen, you are protected by state and federal laws when you are in this country. But when you visit another country, you are expected to follow its laws, just as visitors to the United States are expected to follow our laws. Other countries may have very different rules about things you would never think of, and not knowing the law can get you into trouble. For example, the British drive on the left side of the road. If you are driving in London on the right, you will be stopped and given a ticket.

Other offenses can be much more serious, and many countries have fewer protections for individual rights than in the United States. Prisons in most other countries are very different from those in the United States. Many are severely overcrowded, with unsanitary conditions. Also, penalties in some countries may be very severe for offenses that in the United States are relatively minor.

When you travel abroad, be sure to obey the laws of your host country. Not knowing the law is almost never an excuse, and it will not help you avoid arrest. Do not expect special treatment because you are an American. If you are in trouble with the law, your one right as an American is to speak with a U.S. consular officer. This person can be contacted at the U.S. embassy or consulate in the country you are visiting.

The American embassy may be able to assist you if you are in legal trouble in a foreign country.

ANALYSIS SKILL **EVALUATING THE LAW**

go.hrw.com
KEYWORD: SZ7 CH24

1. Why is it important to know the laws of foreign countries you visit?
2. What would you do if you were arrested in a foreign country?

REFERENCES

Magna Carta

England's King John angered many people with high taxes. In 1215, a group of English nobles joined the Archbishop of Canterbury to force the king to agree to sign Magna Carta. This document stated that the king was subject to the rule of law, just as other citizens of England were. It also presented the ideas of a fair and speedy trial and the due process of law. These principles are still a part of the U.S. Bill of Rights.

1. In the first place have granted to God, and by this our present charter confirmed for us and our heirs for ever that the English church shall be free, and shall have its rights undiminished and its liberties unimpaired . . . We have also granted to all free men of our kingdom, for ourselves and our heirs for ever, all the liberties written below, to be had and held by them and their heirs of us and our heirs.

2. If any of our earls or barons or others holding of us in chief by knight service dies, and at his death his heir be of full age and owe relief he shall have his inheritance on payment of the old relief, namely the heir or heirs of an earl 100 for a whole earl's barony, the heir or heirs of a baron 100 for a whole barony, the heir or heirs of a knight 100s, at most, for a whole knight's fee; and he who owes less shall give less according to the ancient usage of fiefs.

3. If, however, the heir of any such be under age and a ward, he shall have his inheritance when he comes of age without paying relief and without making fine.

40. To no one will we sell, to no one will we refuse or delay right or justice.

41. All merchants shall be able to go out of and come into England safely and securely and stay and travel throughout England, as well by land as by water, for buying and selling by the ancient and right customs free from all evil tolls, except in time of war and if they are of the land that is at war with us. . .

42. It shall be lawful in future for anyone, without prejudicing the allegiance due to us, to leave our kingdom and return safely and securely by land and water, save, in the public interest, for a short period in time of war—except for those imprisoned or outlawed in accordance with the law of the kingdom and natives of a land that is at war with us and merchants (who shall be treated as aforesaid).

62. And we have fully remitted and pardoned to everyone all the ill-will, indignation and rancour that have arisen between us and our men, clergy and laity, from the time of the quarrel. Furthermore, we have fully remitted to all, clergy and laity, and as far as pertains to us have completely forgiven, all trespasses occasioned by the same quarrel between Easter in the sixteenth year of our reign and the restoration of peace. And, besides, we have caused to be made for them letters testimonial patent of the lord Stephen archbishop of Canterbury, of the lord Henry archbishop of Dublin and of the aforementioned bishops and of master Pandulf about this security and the aforementioned concessions.

63. An oath, moreover, has been taken, as well on our part as on the part of the barons, that all these things aforesaid shall be observed in good faith and without evil disposition. Witness the above-mentioned and many others. Given by our hand in the meadow which is called Runnymede between Windsor and Staines on the fifteenth day of June, in the seventeenth year of our reign.

From "English Bill of Rights." Britannica Online . Vers. 99.1. 1994-1999. Encyclopedia Britannica. Copyright © 1994-1999 Encyclopedia Britannica, Inc. <http://search.eb.com/bol/topic?xref=7314>

The Mayflower Compact

In November 1620, the Pilgrim leaders aboard the Mayflower drafted the Mayflower Compact, the first guidelines for self-government in the English colonies. This excerpt describes the principles of the colony's government.

"We whose names are underwritten . . . do by these presents [this document] solemnly and mutually in the presence of God, and one of another, covenant [promise] and combine ourselves together into a body politic [government] for our better ordering and preservation and furtherance of the ends aforesaid; and by virtue hereof, to enact, constitute, and frame such just and equal laws, ordinances, acts, constitutions, and offices . . . as shall be thought most meet [fitting] and convenient for the general good of the colony unto which we promise all due submission and obedience."

From "The Mayflower Compact" reprinted by The Avalon Project: Mayflower Compact 1620 . Copyright ©1997 The Avalon Project. September 14, 1999. <http://www.yale.edu/lawweb/avalon/ mayflowr.htm>

The Virginia Declaration of Rights

Thomas Jefferson drew upon Virginia's Declaration of Rights for the opening paragraphs of the Declaration of Independence. It was widely copied by the other colonies and became the basis of the Bill of Rights. Written by George Mason, it was adopted by the Virginia Constitutional Convention on June 12, 1776.

A Declaration of Rights made by the representatives of the good people of Virginia, assembled in full and free convention which rights do pertain to them and their posterity, as the basis and foundation of government.

Section 1. That all men are by nature equally free and independent and have certain inherent rights, of which, when they enter into a state of society, they cannot, by any compact, deprive or divest their posterity; namely, the enjoyment of life and liberty, with the means of acquiring and possessing property, and pursuing and obtaining happiness and safety.

Section 2. That all power is vested in, and consequently derived from, the people; that magistrates are their trustees and servants and at all times amenable to them.

Section 3. That government is, or ought to be, instituted for the common benefit, protection, and security of the people, nation, or community; of all the various modes and forms of government, that is best which is capable of producing the greatest degree of happiness and safety and is most effectually secured against the danger of maladministration. And that, when any government shall be found inadequate or contrary to these purposes, a majority of the community has an indubitable, inalienable, and indefeasible right to reform, alter, or abolish it, in such manner as shall be judged most conducive to the public weal.

http://www.archives.gov/national-archives-experience/charters/virginia_declaration_of_rights. html

Virginia Statute for Religious Freedom

In Virginia, after the American Revolution, many people believed that the new state should continue to tax its citizens to pay support to recognized churches. Other people believed that public support of churches was a way of imposing religion on people. Thomas Jefferson and James Madison argued that religious beliefs were matters of individual conscience only and that there should be no interference by the state. Jefferson believed that a high wall should always separate church and state. The statute was adopted by the Virginia legislature in 1786.

Be it enacted by the General Assembly, That no man shall be compelled to frequent or support any religious worship, place, or ministry whatsoever, nor shall be enforced, restrained, molested, or burthened [loaded down] in his body or goods, nor shall otherwise suffer on account of his religious opinions or belief; but that all men shall be free to profess, and by argument to maintain, their opinion in matters of religion, and that the same shall in no wise diminish enlarge, or affect their civil capacities.

From W.W. Hening, ed., Statutes at Large of Virginia, vol. 12 (1823): 84-86. http://usinfo.state.gov/usa/infousa/facts/democrac/42.htm

Articles of Confederation

After winning the Revolutionary War in 1777, the newly formed United States of America created a government under the Articles of Confederation. This government allowed the states to have more power than the central government, a situation that would lead to problems later.

Articles of Confederation and perpetual Union between the states of New Hampshire, Massachusetts-bay Rhode Island and Providence Plantations, Connecticut, New York, New Jersey, Pennsylvania, Delaware, Maryland, Virginia, North Carolina, South Carolina and Georgia.

I. The Stile of this Confederacy shall be "The United States of America".

II. Each state retains its sovereignty, freedom, and independence, and every power, jurisdiction, and right, which is not by this Confederation expressly delegated to the United States, in Congress assembled.

III. The said States hereby severally enter into a firm league of friendship with each other, for their common defense, the security of their liberties, and their mutual and general welfare, binding themselves to assist each other, against all force offered to, or attacks made upon them, or any of them, on account of religion, sovereignty, trade, or any other pretense whatever.

VI. No State, without the consent of the United States in Congress assembled, shall send any embassy to, or receive any embassy from, or enter into any conference, agreement, alliance or treaty with any King, Prince or State; nor shall any person holding any office of profit or trust under the United States, or any of them, accept any present, emolument, office or title of any kind whatever from any King, Prince or foreign State; nor shall the United States in Congress assembled, or any of them, grant any title of nobility.

VIII. All charges of war, and all other expenses that shall be incurred for the common defense or general welfare, and allowed by the United States in Congress assembled, shall be defrayed out of a common treasury, which shall be supplied by the several States in proportion to the value of all land within each State, granted or surveyed for any person, as such land and the buildings and improvements thereon shall be estimated according to such mode as the United States in Congress assembled, shall from time to time direct and appoint.

IX. The taxes for paying that proportion shall be laid and levied by the authority and direction of the legislatures of the several States within the time agreed upon by the United States in Congress assembled.

From the National Archives : http://www.ourdocuments.gov/doc.php?flash=true&doc=3&page=transcript

Federalist Paper Number 51

In 1788 the newly written Constitution faced opponents who believed it gave too much power to the federal government. James Madison, Alexander Hamilton, and John Jay anonymously wrote a collection of essays that became known as the Federalist Papers. *The following essay, written by James Madison, outlines reasons why the division of power written into the Constitution would keep the government from harming citizens.*

In order to lay a due foundation for that separate and distinct exercise of the different powers of government, which to a certain extent is admitted on all hands to be essential to the preservation of liberty, it is evident that each department should have a will of its own; and consequently should be so constituted that the members of each should have as little agency as possible in the appointment of the members of the others. Were this principle rigorously adhered to, it would require that all the appointments for the supreme executive, legislative, and judiciary magistracies should be drawn from the same fountain of authority, the people, through channels having no communication whatever with one another. Perhaps such a plan of constructing the several departments would be less difficult in practice than it may in contemplation appear. Some difficulties, however, and some additional expense would attend the execution of it. Some deviations, therefore, from the principle must be admitted. In the constitution of the judiciary department in particular, it might be inexpedient to insist rigorously on the principle: first, because peculiar qualifications being essential in the members, the primary consideration ought to be to select that mode of choice which best secures these qualifications; secondly, because the permanent tenure by which the appointments are held in that department, must soon destroy all sense of dependence on the authority conferring them.

It is equally evident, that the members of each department should be as little dependent as possible on those of the others, for the emoluments annexed to their offices. Were the executive magistrate, or the judges, not independent of the legislature in this particular, their independence in every other would be merely nominal.

But the great security against a gradual concentration of the several powers in the same department, consists in giving to those who administer each department the necessary constitutional means and personal motives to resist encroachments of the others. The provision for defense must in this, as in all other cases, be made commensurate to the danger of attack. Ambition must be made to counteract ambition. The interest of the man must be connected with the constitutional rights of the place. It may be a reflection on human nature, that such devices should be necessary to control the abuses of government. But what is government itself, but the greatest of all reflections on human nature? If men were angels, no government would be necessary. If angels were to govern men, neither external nor internal controls on government would be necessary. In framing a government which is to be administered by men over men, the great difficulty lies in this: you must first enable the government to control the governed; and in the next place oblige it to control itself. A dependence on the people is, no doubt, the primary control on the government; but experience has taught mankind the necessity of auxiliary precautions.

Washington's Farewell Address

On September 19, 1796, President George Washington's Farewell Address first appeared in a Philadelphia newspaper. In it, he wrote about the potential dangers posed by political parties.

"Friends and Fellow-Citizens . .

"Let me . . . warn you in the most solemn manner against the baneful effects of the Spirit of Party, generally . . . This spirit, unfortunately, is inseparable from our nature, having its root in the strongest passions of the human mind. It exists under different shapes in all governments . . . [Party loyalty] agitates the Community with ill-founded jealousies and false alarms; kindles the animosity of one part against another, foments [causes] occasionally riot and insurrection [revolt]. It opens the door to foreign influence and corruption, which find . . . access to the government itself through the channels of party passions. . . There is an opinion, that parties in free countries are useful checks upon the administration of the Government, and serve to keep alive the spirit of Liberty. This within certain limits is probably true. . . [But] there [is a] constant danger of excess."

From Annals of Congress, 4th Congress, pp. 2869–2880. American Memory Library of Congress. 1999. <http://memory.loc.gov/cgibin/ampage?collId=llac2&fileName=006/llac006.db&recNum=677>Address

The Monroe Doctrine

The Monroe Doctrine is not a law passed by Congress. It is a statement of foreign policy made by President James Monroe in a State of the Union Address to Congress December 2, 1823. The Monroe Doctrine is one of the most important documents in the country's history. It has influenced U.S. foreign policy to the present time. The Monroe Doctrine asserts the country's dedication to freedom. It warns foreign countries that the Americas—North, South, and Central—are closed to colonization.

"[It is] a principle in which the rights and interests of the United States are involved, that the American continents, by the free and independent condition which they have assumed and maintain, are henceforth not to be considered as subjects for future colonization by any European powers. . .

We owe it, therefore, to candor and to the amicable [friendly] relations existing between the United States and those powers to declare that we should consider any attempt on their part to extend their system to any portion of this hemisphere as dangerous to our peace and safety. With the existing colonies or dependencies of any European power, we have not interfered and shall not interfere. But with the Governments who have declared their independence and maintained it, and whose independence we have, on great consideration and on just principles, acknowledged, we could not view any interposition [interference] for the purpose of oppressing them, or controlling in any other manner their destiny, by any European power in any other light than as the manifestation [evidence] of an unfriendly disposition toward the United States."

From "The Monroe Doctrine" by James Monroe reprinted in The Annals of America: Volume 5, 1821-1832. Copyright © 1976 by Encyclopedia Britannica.

Seneca Falls Declaration of Sentiments

One of the first documents to express the desire for equal rights for women is the Declaration of Sentiments, issued in 1848 at the Seneca Falls Convention in Seneca Falls, New York. Led by Elizabeth Cady Stanton and Lucretia Mott, the convention delegates adopted a set of resolutions modeled on the Declaration of Independence.

"When, in the course of human events, it becomes necessary for one portion of the family of man to assume among the peoples of the earth a position different from that which they have hitherto occupied, but one to which the laws of nature and of nature's God entitle them, a decent respect to the opinions of mankind requires that they should declare the causes that impel them to such a course.

We hold these truths to be self-evident: that all men and women are created equal; that they are endowed by their Creator with certain inalienable rights; that among these are life, liberty, and the pursuit of happiness; that to secure these rights governments are instituted, deriving their just powers from the consent of the governed. . .

The history of mankind is a history of repeated injuries and usurpations [seizures] on the part of man toward woman, having in direct object the establishment of an absolute tyranny [unjust rule] over her. To prove this, let facts be submitted to a candid [fair] world.

He has never permitted her to exercise her inalienable right to . . . [the vote]. . .

He has taken from her all right in property, even to the wages she earns. . .

He has monopolized nearly all the profitable employments, and from those she is permitted to follow, she receives but a scanty remuneration [payment]. He closes to her all the avenues to wealth and distinction. . .

He has denied her the facilities for obtaining a thorough education, all colleges being closed against her. . .

He has endeavored, in every way that he could, to destroy her confidence in her own powers, to lessen her self-respect, and to make her willing to lead a dependent and abject [hopeless] life.

Resolved, That all laws which prevent woman from occupying such a station in society as her conscience shall dictate, or which place her in a position inferior to that of man, are contrary to the great precept [example] of nature, and therefore, of no force of authority.

Resolved, That woman is man's equal—was intended to be so by the Creator, and the highest good of the race demands that she should be recognized as such. . .

Resolved, That it is the duty of the women of this country to secure to themselves their sacred right to the elective franchise [the vote]. . ."

From "Seneca Falls Declaration on Women's Rights" reprinted in The Annals of America: Volume 7, 1841-1849. Copyright © 1976 by Encyclopedia Britannica.

The Emancipation Proclamation

When the Union Army won the Battle of Antietam, President Lincoln decided to issue the Emancipation Proclamation, which freed all enslaved people in states under Confederate control. The proclamation, which went into effect on January 1, 1863, was a step toward the Thirteenth Amendment (1865), which ended slavery in the United States.

"Whereas on the twenty-second day of September, a.d. 1862, a proclamation was issued by the President of the United States, containing, among other things, the following, to wit:

"That on the first day of January, a.d. 1863, all persons held as slaves within any state or designated part of a state, the people whereof shall then be in rebellion against the United States, shall be then, thenceforward, and forever free; and the executive government of the United States, including the military and naval authority thereof, will recognize and maintain the freedom of such persons and will do no act or acts to repress such persons or any of them, in any efforts they may make for their actual freedom.

"That the Executive will on the first day of January aforesaid, by proclamation, designate the states and parts of states, if any, in which the people thereof, respectively, shall then be in rebellion against the United States; and the fact that any state or the people thereof shall on that day be in good faith represented in the Congress of the United States by members chosen thereto at elections wherein a majority of the qualified voters of such states shall have participated shall, in the absence of strong countervailing [opposing] testimony, be deemed conclusive evidence that such state and the people thereof are not then in rebellion against the United States . . ."

From "Emancipation Proclamation" by Abraham Lincoln. Reprinted in The Annals of America: Volume 9, 1858-1865. Copyright © 1776 by Encyclopedia Britannica, Inc.

The Gettysburg Address

On November 19, 1863, Abraham Lincoln addressed a crowd gathered to dedicate a cemetery at the Gettysburg battlefield. His short speech reiterates American ideals.

"Fourscore and seven years ago our fathers brought forth on this continent a new nation, conceived in liberty, and dedicated to the proposition that all men are created equal. Now we are engaged in a great civil war, testing whether that nation, or any nation so conceived and so dedicated can long endure. We are met on a great battlefield of that war. We have come to dedicate a portion of that field as a final resting place for those who here gave their lives that that nation might live. It is altogether fitting and proper that we do this.

But, in a larger sense, we cannot dedicate—we cannot consecrate—we cannot hallow—this ground. The brave men, living and dead, who struggled here, have consecrated it far above our poor power to add or detract. The world will little note nor long remember what we say here, but it can never forget what they did here. It is for us, the living, rather, to be dedicated here to the unfinished work which they who fought here have thus far so nobly advanced. It is rather for us to be here dedicated to the great task remaining before us—that from these honored dead we take increased devotion to the cause for which they gave the last full measure of devotion; that we here highly resolve that these dead shall not have died in vain; that this nation, under God, shall have a new birth of freedom; and that government of the people, by the people, for the people, shall not perish from the earth."

From "The Gettysburg Address" by Abraham Lincoln. Reprinted in The Annals of America: Volume 9, 1858-1865. Copyright © 1776 by Encyclopedia Britannica, Inc.

Andrew Carnegie's "Gospel of Wealth"

The following is from an article written by Andrew Carnegie in 1889. Later called "The Gospel of Wealth," it explains his views on capitalism.

"Individualism, private property, and the law of accumulation [collection] of wealth, and the law of competition . . . these are the highest results of human experience, the soil in which society so far has produced the best fruit. Unequally or unjustly, perhaps, as these laws sometimes operate, and imperfect as they appear to the idealist, they are, nevertheless . . . the best and most valuable of all that humanity has yet accomplished."

From Andrew Carnegie, "Wealth," North American Review, 148, no. 391 (June 1889): 653, 65762. at: http://www.fordham.edu/halsall/mod/1889carnegie.html

The American's Creed

William Tyler Page wrote the American's Creed during World War I. The House of Representatives adopted it in 1918 as "the best summary of the political faith of America."

"I believe in the United States of America as a government of the people, by the people, for the people; whose just powers are derived from the consent of the governed;

a democracy in a Republic;

a sovereign nation of many sovereign States;

a perfect Union, one and inseparable;

established upon those principles of freedom, equality, justice, and humanity for which American patriots sacrificed their lives and fortunes.

I therefore believe it is my duty to my country to love it;

to support its Constitution;

to obey its laws;

to respect its flag;

and to defend it against all enemies."

From http://www.ushistory.org/documents/creed.htm

Franklin D. Roosevelt's Inaugural Address

President Franklin D. Roosevelt's first inaugural address was broadcast on the radio. He tried to encourage Americans struggling during the depression.

"This great nation will endure as it has endured, will revive and will prosper. So, first of all, let me assert [state] my firm belief that the only thing we have to fear is fear itself. . . . Our greatest primary task is to put people to work. This is no unsolvable problem if we face it wisely and courageously. It can be accomplished in part by direct recruiting by the government itself, treating the task as we would treat the emergency of a war."

From Inaugural Addresses of the Presidents of the United States. 1989. Bartleby Library. <http://www.bartleby.com/124/pres49.html>

Franklin D. Roosevelt's Four Freedoms

President Franklin D. Roosevelt gave a State of the Union Address before Congress in January 1941. In the address Roosevelt stated four freedoms to which the United States was firmly committed. These freedoms inspired Americans during World War II and remain at the heart of the country's domestic and foreign policies.

"I address you, the members of this new Congress, at a moment unprecedented in the history of the Union. I use the word "unprecedented," because at no previous time has American security been as seriously threatened from without [outside] as it is today. . .

I suppose that every realist knows that the democratic way of life is at this moment being directly assailed in every part of the world—assailed either by arms or by secret spreading of poisonous propaganda by those who seek to destroy unity and promote discord in nations that are still at peace.

During sixteen long months this assault has blotted out the whole pattern of democratic life in an appalling number of independent nations, great and small. And the assailants [attackers] are still on the march, threatening other nations, great and small.

In the future days, which we seek to make secure, we look forward to a world founded upon four essential freedoms.

The first is freedom of speech and freedom of expression—everywhere in the world.

The second is freedom of every person to worship God in his own way—everywhere in the world.

The third is freedom from want—which, translated into world terms, means economic understandings which will secure to every nation healthy peacetime life for its inhabitants—everywhere in the world.

The fourth is freedom from fear—which, translated into world terms, means a worldwide reduction of armaments to such a point and in such a thorough fashion that no nation will be in a position to commit an act of physical aggression against any neighbor—anywhere in the world. That is no vision of a distant millennium. It is a definite basis for a kind of world attainable in our own time and generation. That kind of world is the very antithesis of the so-called "new order" of tyranny which the dictators seek to create with the crash of a bomb.

To that new order we oppose the greater conception—the moral order. A good society is able to face schemes of world domination and foreign revolutions alike without fear. Since the beginning of our American history we have been engaged in change, in a perpetual, peaceful revolution, a revolution which goes on steadily, quietly, adjusting itself to changing conditions without the concentration camp or the quicklime in the ditch. The world order which we seek is the cooperation of free countries, working together in a friendly, civilized society.

This nation has placed its destiny in the hands and heads and hearts of its millions of free men and women; and its faith in freedom under the guidance of God. Freedom means the supremacy of human rights everywhere. Our support goes to those who struggle to gain those rights or keep them. Our strength is in our unity of purpose.

To that high concept there can be no end save victory."

From "The Four Freedoms"-- President Franklin Delano Roosevelt, State of the Union Address (January 6, 1941), 87 Cong. Rec. 44

Kennedy's Inaugural Address

John F. Kennedy, at age 43, was the youngest person ever elected president. His inaugural address of January 20, 1961, inspired many Americans.

"Let the word go forth from this time and place, to friend and foe alike, that the torch has been passed to a new generation of Americans-born in this century, tempered by war, disciplined by a hard and bitter peace, proud of our ancient heritage-and unwilling to witness or permit the slow undoing of those human rights to which this nation has always been committed, and to which we are committed today at home and around the world.

Let every nation know, whether it wishes us well or ill, that we shall pay any price, bear any burden, meet any hardship, support any friend, oppose any foe in order to ensure the survival and the success of liberty. This much we pledge—and more . . .

And so, my fellow Americans: Ask not what your country can do for you—ask what you can do for your country."

From Inaugural Addresses of the Presidents of the United States. 1989. Bartleby Library. <http://www.bartleby.com/124/pres56.html>

Martin Luther King, Jr.'s, "I Have a Dream"

In 1963 civil rights leader Martin Luther King, Jr., addressed more than 250,000 Americans at the civil rights rally known as the March on Washington. His speech, made to the huge crowd assembled before the Lincoln Memorial, sets forth his dream of a country where all Americans are truly equal and free.

"I say to you today, my friends, that in spite of the difficulties and frustrations of the moment I still have a dream. It is a dream deeply rooted in the American Dream.

I have a dream that one day this nation will rise up and live out the true meaning of its creed: 'We hold these truths to be self-evident: that all men are created equal . . .'

I have a dream that my four little children will one day live in a nation where they will not be judged by the color of their skin but by the content of their character . . .

I have a dream today . . .

This is our hope. This is the faith with which I return to the South. With this faith we will be able to cut out of the mountain of despair a stone of hope. With this faith we will be able to change the jangling discords of our nation into a beautiful symphony of brotherhood. With this faith we will be able to work together, to pray together, to struggle together, to go to jail together, to stand up for freedom together, knowing that we will be free some day.

This will be the day when all of God's children will be able to sing with new meaning 'My country 'tis of thee, sweet land of liberty, of thee I sing. Land where my fathers died, land of the pilgrim's pride, from every mountainside, let freedom ring.' And if America is to be a great nation, this must become true. . . From every mountainside, let freedom ring.

(continued next page)

HISTORIC DOCUMENTS

When we let freedom ring, when we let it ring from every village and every hamlet, from every state and every city, we will be able to speed up that day when all of God's children, black people and white people, Jews, Protestants, and Catholics, will be able to join hands and sing in the words of the old Negro spiritual, 'Free at last! Free at last, thank God almighty we are free at last!'"

"I Have a Dream" by Martin Luther King, Jr. Copyright © 1963 by the Estate of Martin Luther King, Jr.; copyright renewed © 1991 by Coretta Scott King. Reprinted by permission of Intellectual Properties Management, Atlanta, Georgia, as exclusive licensor of the King Estate.

Civil Rights Act of 1964

The Civil Rights Act of 1964 prohibits discrimination on the basis of race, color, religion, or national origin. Under the terms of this act, discrimination is outlawed in the exercise of voting rights, and in public places, public education, and employment practices.

Voting Rights
No person acting under color of law shall—in determining whether any individual is qualified under State law or laws to vote in any election, apply any standard, practice, or procedure different from the standards, practices, or procedures applied under such law or laws to other individuals within the same county, parish, or similar political subdivision who have been found by State officials to be qualified to vote. . .

Discrimination in Places of Public Accommodation
All persons shall be entitled to the full and equal enjoyment of the goods, services, facilities, privileges, advantages, and accommodations of any place of public accommodation, as defined in this section, without discrimination or segregation on the ground of race, color, religion, or national origin. . .

Equal Employment Opportunity
It shall be an unlawful employment practice for an employer—to fail or refuse to hire or to discharge any individual, or otherwise to discriminate against any individual with respect to his compensation, terms, conditions, or privileges of employment, because of such individual's race, color, religion, sex, or national origin; or to limit, segregate, or classify his employees in any way . . . because of such individual's race, color, religion, sex, or national origin.

Voting Rights Act of 1965

The Voting Rights Act of 1965 banned voting discrimination based on race or color in federal, state, and local elections. The act also made practices such as literacy tests for voters illegal.

"To assure that the right of citizens of the United States is not denied or abridged on account of race or color, no citizen shall be denied the right to vote in any Federal, State, or local election because of his failure to comply with any test or device in any State . . .

The phrase "test or device" shall mean any requirement that a person as a prerequisite for voting or registration for voting (1) demonstrate the ability to read, write, understand, or interpret any matter, (2) demonstrate any educational achievement or his knowledge of any particular subject, (3) possess good moral character, or (4) prove his qualifications by the voucher of registered voters or members of any other class."

President Bush's Address to the Nation

On the morning of September 11, 2001, terrorists attacked the United States. That evening, President George W. Bush addressed the citizens of the nation in the following televised speech.

Good evening. Today, our fellow citizens, our way of life, our very freedom came under attack in a series of deliberate and deadly terrorist acts. The victims were in airplanes, or in their offices; secretaries, businessmen and women, military and federal workers; moms and dads, friends and neighbors. Thousands of lives were suddenly ended by evil, despicable acts of terror.

The pictures of airplanes flying into buildings, fires burning, huge structures collapsing, have filled us with disbelief, terrible sadness, and a quiet, unyielding anger. These acts of mass murder were intended to frighten our nation into chaos and retreat. But they have failed; our country is strong.

A great people has been moved to defend a great nation. Terrorist attacks can shake the foundations of our biggest buildings, but they cannot touch the foundation of America. These acts shattered steel, but they cannot dent the steel of American resolve. America was targeted for attack because we're the brightest beacon for freedom and opportunity in the world. And no one will keep that light from shining.

Today, our nation saw evil, the very worst of human nature. And we responded with the best of America—with the daring of our rescue workers, with the caring for strangers and neighbors who came to give blood and help in any way they could.

Immediately following the first attack, I implemented our government's emergency response plans. Our military is powerful, and it's prepared. Our emergency teams are working in New York City and Washington, D.C. to help with local rescue efforts. Our first priority is to get help to those who have been injured, and to take every precaution to protect our citizens at home and around the world from further attacks . . .

The search is underway for those who are behind these evil acts. I've directed the full resources of our intelligence and law enforcement communities to find those responsible and to bring them to justice. We will make no distinction between the terrorists who committed these acts and those who harbor them.

I appreciate so very much the members of Congress who have joined me in strongly condemning these attacks. And on behalf of the American people, I thank the many world leaders who have called to offer their condolences and assistance.

America and our friends and allies join with all those who want peace and security in the world, and we stand together to win the war against terrorism. Tonight, I ask for your prayers for all those who grieve, for the children whose worlds have been shattered, for all whose sense of safety and security has been threatened. And I pray they will be comforted by a power greater than any of us, spoken through the ages in Psalm 23: "Even though I walk through the valley of the shadow of death, I fear no evil, for You are with me."

This is a day when all Americans from every walk of life unite in our resolve for justice and peace. America has stood down enemies before, and we will do so this time. None of us will ever forget this day. Yet, we go forward to defend freedom and all that is good and just in our world.

Thank you. Good night, and God bless America.

From http://www.whitehouse.gov/news/releases/2001/09/20010911-16.html

Supreme Court Decisions

Marbury v. Madison (1803)

Significance: This ruling established the Supreme Court's power of judicial review, by which the Court decides whether laws passed by Congress are constitutional. This decision greatly increased the prestige of the Court and gave the judiciary branch a powerful check against the legislative and executive branches.

Background: William Marbury and others were commissioned as judges by Federalist president John Adams during his last days in office. This act angered the new Democratic-Republican president, Thomas Jefferson. Jefferson ordered his secretary of state, James Madison, not to deliver the commissions. Marbury took advantage of a section in the Judiciary Act of 1789 that allowed him to take his case directly to the Supreme Court. He sued Madison, demanding the commission and the judgeship.

Decision: This case was decided on February 24, 1803, by a vote of 5 to 0. Chief Justice John Marshall spoke for the Court, which decided against Marbury. The court ruled that although Marbury's commission had been unfairly withheld, he could not lawfully take his case to the Supreme Court without first trying it in a lower court. Marshall said that the section of the Judiciary Act that Marbury had used was actually unconstitutional, and that the Constitution must take priority over laws passed by Congress.

McCulloch v. Maryland (1819)

Significance: This ruling established that Congress had the constitutional power to charter a national bank. It also established the principle of national supremacy, which states that the Constitution and other laws of the federal government take priority over state laws. The ruling also reinforced the loose construction interpretation of the Constitution favored by many Federalists.

Background: In 1816 the federal government set up the Second Bank of the United States to stabilize the economy following the War of 1812. Many states were opposed to the competition provided by the new national bank. Some of these states passed heavy taxes on the Bank. The national bank refused to pay the taxes. This led the state of Maryland to sue James McCulloch, the cashier of the Baltimore, Maryland, branch of the national bank.

Decision: This case was decided on March 6, 1819, by a vote of 7 to 0. Chief Justice John Marshall spoke for the unanimous Court, which ruled that the national bank was constitutional because it helped the federal government carry out other powers granted to it by the Constitution. The Court declared that any attempt by the states to interfere with the duties of the federal government could not be permitted.

Gibbons v. Ogden (1824)

Significance: This ruling was the first to deal with the clause of the Constitution that allows Congress to regulate interstate and foreign commerce. It was important because it reinforced both the authority of the federal government over the states and the division of powers between the federal government and the state governments.

Background: Steamboat operators who wanted to travel on New York waters had to obtain a state license. Thomas Gibbons had a federal license to travel along the coast, but not a state license for New York. He wanted to compete with state-licensed Aaron Ogden for steam travel between New Jersey and the New York island of Manhattan.

Decision: This case was decided on March 2, 1824, by a vote of 6 to 0. Chief Justice John Marshall spoke for the Court, which ruled in favor of Gibbons. The Court stated that the congressional statute (Gibbons's federal license) took priority over the state statute (Ogden's state-monopoly license). The ruling also defined commerce as more than simply the exchange of goods, broadening it to include the transportation of people and the use of new inventions (such as the steamboat).

Worcester v. Georgia (1832)

Significance: This ruling made Georgia's removal of the Cherokee illegal. However, Georgia, with President Andrew Jackson's support, defied the Court's decision. By not enforcing the Court's ruling, Jackson violated his constitutional oath as president. As a result, the Cherokee and other American Indian tribes continued to be forced off of lands protected by treaties.

Background: The state of Georgia wanted to remove Cherokee Indians from lands they held by treaty. Samuel Worcester, a missionary who worked with the Cherokee Nation, was arrested for failing to take an oath of allegiance to the state and to obey a Georgia militia order to leave the Cherokee's lands. Worcester sued, charging that Georgia had no legal authority on Cherokee lands.

Decision: This case was decided on March 3, 1832, by a vote of 5 to 1 in favor of Worcester. Chief Justice John Marshall spoke for the Supreme Court, which ruled that the Cherokee were an independent political community. The Court decided that only the federal government, not the state of Georgia, had authority over legal matters involving the Cherokee people.

Scott v. Sandford (1857)

Significance: This ruling denied enslaved African Americans U.S. citizenship and the right to sue in federal court. The decision also invalidated the Missouri Compromise, which had prevented slavery in territories north of the 36° 30′ line of latitude. The ruling increased the controversy over the expansion of slavery in new states and territories.

Background: John Emerson, an army doctor, took his slave Dred Scott with him to live in Illinois and then Wisconsin Territory, both of which had banned slavery. In 1842 the two moved to Missouri, a slave state. Four years later, Scott sued for his freedom according to a Missouri legal principle of "once free, always free." The principle meant that a slave was entitled to freedom if he or she had once lived in a free state or territory.

Decision: This case was decided March 6–7, 1857, by a vote of 7 to 2. Chief Justice Roger B. Taney spoke for the Court, which ruled that slaves did not have the right to sue in federal courts because they were considered property, not citizens. In addition, the Court ruled that Congress did not have the power to abolish slavery in territories because that power was not strictly defined in the Constitution. Furthermore, the Court overturned the once-free, always-free principle.

Civil Rights Cases (1883)

Significance: This ruling struck down the Civil Rights Act of 1875. It allowed private businesses to discriminate based on race or color. The Court ruled that Congress could only make laws preventing states, not private individuals or companies, from discriminating.

Background: Five separate cases were combined under this one decision. After the Civil Rights Act of 1875 was passed, individuals and private businesses continued to discriminate against former slaves and other African Americans. In the five separate cases, African Americans were denied the same accommodations that whites were provided.

Decision: The case was decided on October 15, 1883, by a vote of 8 to 1. Justice Joseph P. Bradley wrote the opinion, which said of the Fourteenth Amendment, "Individual invasion of individual rights is not the subject-matter of the amendment." Justice John Marshall Harlan was the lone dissenter, claiming that the Thirteenth Amendment gave Congress the right to make the law. "The letter of the law is the body," he said. "[T]he sense and reason of the law is the soul."

Wabash, St. Louis & Pacific Railroad v. Illinois (1886)

Significance: This ruling reversed an earlier decision in Munn v. Illinois and removed the power from the states to regulate railroad rates. It reasserted the authority of Congress over interstate commerce and led to the creation of the Interstate Commerce Commission.

Background: The state of Illinois passed a law attempting to regulate the shipping rates of railroads that passed through the state, including the Wabash, St. Louis & Pacific line. In an attempt to operate without regulation, the railroad company sued the state.

Decision: The Court struck down the Illinois law, saying that the state was able to regulate businesses that operated only within its boundaries. Businesses that operated between states were subject to regulation by the national government.

United States v. E.C. Knight Co. (1895)

Significance: The ruling effectively put most monopolies out of the reach of the Sherman Antitrust Act of 1890. It declared that local manufacturing was out of the scope of the interstate commerce regulatory power of Congress.

Background: The E.C. Knight Company enjoyed a virtual monopoly of sugar refining within the United States. The federal government sued the company under the Sherman Antitrust Act in an attempt to break this monopoly and allow other companies to refine sugar.

Decision: The court ruled that although the act was legal, it did not apply to manufacturing. Justice Melville Fuller said that manufacturing was not interstate commerce and could therefore not be regulated by Congress.

In Re Debs (1895)

Significance: The Court upheld the right of the federal government to halt strikes organized by union workers. After losing, Debs ran for president from his jail cell.

Background: Railway union official Eugene V. Debs had organized a strike of union workers. The government petitioned him to halt the strike, and a court held him in contempt when he refused. Debs fought his conviction.

Decision: In a unanimous decision, the Court declared that the federal government did have the power to order Debs to halt the strike. Justice Brewer wrote the opinion of the Court, which stated the U.S. government "acts directly upon each citizen."

Plessy v. Ferguson (1896)

Significance: This case upheld the constitutionality of racial segregation by ruling that separate facilities for different races were legal as long as those facilities were equal to one another. This case provided a legal justification for racial segregation for nearly 60 years until it was overturned by Brown v. Board of Education in 1954.

Background: An 1890 Louisiana law required that all railway companies in the state use "separate-but-equal" railcars for white and African American passengers. A group of citizens in New Orleans banded together to challenge the law and chose Homer Plessy to test the law in 1892. Plessy took a seat in a whites-only coach, and when he refused to move, he was arrested. Plessy eventually sought review by the U.S. Supreme Court, claiming that the Louisiana law violated his Fourteenth Amendment right to equal protection.

Decision: This case was decided on May 18, 1896, by a vote of 7 to 1. Justice Henry Billings Brown spoke for the Court, which upheld the constitutionality of the Louisiana law that segregated railcars. Justice John M. Harlan dissented, arguing that the Constitution should not be interpreted in ways that recognize class or racial distinctions.

Northern Securities Co. v. United States (1904)

Significance: In this ruling the Court declared that the federal government had the right to break up companies if their formation was illegal, whether or not dissolving the company would have a harmful impact on the business community.

Background: The Northern Securities Company held stock in several major railroads. Although President Theodore Roosevelt claimed the company was a trust and therefore illegal under the Sherman Antitrust Act, some disagreed that the idea of trusts extended into the realm of owning stocks.

Decision: In a 5 to 4 decision, the Court ruled that the formation of the company was illegal, and that the federal government had the power to disband it. Writing for the majority, Justice John Marshal Harlan said, "every corporation created by a state is necessarily subject to the supreme law of the land," meaning the federal government.

Lochner v. New York (1905)

Significance: This decision established the Supreme Court's role in overseeing state regulations. For more than 30 years Lochner was often used as a precedent in striking down state laws such as minimum-wage laws, child labor laws, and regulations placed on the banking and transportation industries.

Background: In 1895 the state of New York passed a labor law limiting bakers to working no more than 10 hours per day or 60 hours per week. The purpose of the law was to protect the health of bakers, who worked in hot and damp conditions and breathed in large quantities of flour dust. In 1902 Joseph Lochner, the owner of a small bakery in New York, claimed that the state law violated his Fourteenth Amendment rights by unfairly depriving him of the liberty to make contracts with employees. This case went to the U.S. Supreme Court.

Decision: This case was decided on April 17, 1905, by a vote of 5 to 4 in favor of Lochner. The Supreme Court judged that the Fourteenth Amendment protected the right to sell and buy labor, and that any state law restricting that right was unconstitutional. The Court rejected the argument that the limited workday and workweek were necessary to protect the health of bakery workers.

Muller v. *Oregon* (1908)

Significance: A landmark for cases involving social reform, this decision established the Court's recognition of social and economic conditions (in this case, women's health) as a factor in making laws.

Background: In 1903 Oregon passed a law limiting workdays to 10 hours for female workers in laundries and factories. In 1905 Curt Muller's Grand Laundry was found guilty of breaking this law. Muller appealed, claiming that the state law violated his freedom of contract (the Supreme Court had upheld a similar claim that year in Lochner v. New York). When this case came to the Court, the National Consumers' League hired lawyer Louis D. Brandeis to present Oregon's argument. Brandeis argued that the Court had already defended the state's police power to protect its citizens' health, safety, and welfare.

Decision: This case was decided on February 24, 1908, by a vote of 9 to 0 upholding the Oregon law. The Court agreed that women's well-being was in the state's public interest and that the 10-hour law was a valid way to protect their well-being.

Schenck v. *United States* (1919)

Significance: The Supreme Court ruling in Schenck v. United States established the "clear-and-present danger" test to decide what limits could be set on speech without violating individual freedom. The ruling states that speech that jeopardizes national security or the personal safety of others is not protected by the Constitution.

Background: Charles Schenck, a Socialist Party member, objected to the U.S. entry into World War I. He mailed pamphlets to those who had been drafted urging them not to participate in the fighting. The government charged Schenck with violating the Espionage Act of 1917, which made obstructing the draft illegal. Schenck was found guilty, and he appealed the verdict, claiming that the Espionage Act was unconstitutional because it limited the First Amendment right to freedom of speech.

Decision: The case was argued on January 9–10, 1919, and decided on March 3, 1919, by a vote of 9 to 0. Justice Oliver Wendell Holmes spoke for the unanimous Court, which upheld the government's conviction of Schenck. The Court judged that the protection of free speech under the First Amendment had limits and that Schenck's actions had gone beyond those limits.

Schechter Poultry Corp. v. *United States* (1935)

Significance: This ruling declared that the United States could not regulate businesses that operated only within one state. It dealt a severe blow to President Franklin Roosevelt's New Deal.

Background: In an attempt to lessen the effects of the Great Depression, Roosevelt encouraged Congress to pass a Recovery Act that set a minimum wage and restricted working hours. The Schechter Poultry Corporation, which operated only within New York City, maintained that the federal government did not have a constitutional right to regulate its businesses practices.

Decision: In a unanimous decision, the Court upheld the Schechter Corporation's claim. Chief Justice Charles Evans Hughes wrote the opinion, which stated that the transactions in the case—wages, salaries, and working hours—were a local concern outside of the scope of federal regulation.

Korematsu v. *United States* (1944)

Significance: This case addressed the question of whether government action that treats a racial group differently from other people violates the Equal Protection Clause of the Fourteenth Amendment. The ruling in the case held that distinctions based on race are "inherently suspect," and that laws and rules based on race must withstand "strict scrutiny" by the courts.

Background: When the United States declared war on Japan in 1941, about 112,000 Japanese-Americans lived on the West Coast. About 70,000 of these Japanese-Americans were citizens. In 1942, the U.S. military was afraid that these people could not be trusted in wartime. They ordered most of the Japanese-Americans to move to special camps far from their homes. Fred Korematsu, a Japanese-American and an American citizen, did not go to the camps as ordered. He stayed in California and was arrested. He was sent to a camp in Utah. Korematsu then sued, claiming that the government acted illegally when it sent people of Japanese descent to camps.

Decision: By a 6-3 margin, the Supreme Court said the orders moving the Japanese-Americans into the camps were constitutional. Justice Hugo Black wrote the opinion for the Court. He said that the unusual demands of wartime security justified the orders. However, he made it clear that distinctions based on race are "inherently suspect," and that laws based on race must withstand "strict scrutiny" by the courts. Justice Robert H. Jackson dissented; he wrote that Korematsu was "convicted of an act not commonly a crime ... being present in the state [where] he is a citizen, near where he was born, and where all his life he has lived." Justice Frank Murphy, another dissenter, said the military order was based on racial prejudice. Though the case went against the Japanese, the Court still applies the "strict scrutiny" standard today to cases involving race and other groups.

Brown v. Board of Education (1954)

Significance: This ruling reversed the Supreme Court's earlier position on segregation set by Plessy v. Ferguson (1896). The decision also inspired Congress and the federal courts to help carry out further civil rights reforms for African Americans.

Background: Beginning in the 1930s, the National Association for the Advancement of Colored People (NAACP) began using the courts to challenge racial segregation in public education. In 1952 the NAACP took a number of school segregation cases to the Supreme Court. These included the Brown family's suit against the school board of Topeka, Kansas, over its "separate-but-equal" policy.

Decision: This case was decided on May 17, 1954, by a vote of 9 to 0. Chief Justice Earl Warren spoke for the unanimous Court, which ruled that segregation in public education created inequality. The Court held that racial segregation in public schools was by nature unequal, even if the school facilities were equal. The Court noted that such segregation created feelings of inferiority that could not be undone. Therefore, enforced separation of the races in public education is unconstitutional.

Watkins v. United States (1957)

Significance: The decision limited the inquiry powers of Congress. It was expected not to engage in law enforcement (an executive function), nor to act as a trial agency (a judicial function), but to inquire only as far as was necessary for the functioning of Congress.

Background: Watkins was a labor union officer who appeared before the House Un-American Activities Committee. Although he was willing to answer personal questions about himself and others whom he knew to be members of the Communist party, he would not answer questions about past members of the Communist party. He was held in contempt of Congress.

Decision: In a vote of 6 to 1 handed down on June 17, 1957, the Court threw out the charge of contempt against Watkins. Congress, it said, did not have the right to invade the private lives of individuals.

Mapp v. Ohio (1961)

Significance: In this ruling the Court declared that evidence discovered in the process of an illegal search could not be used in state courts.

Background: While searching for a bombing suspect, police found evidence of a separate crime in the house of Dollree Mapp. The police did not have permission to enter the home, nor did they have a search warrant. Upon conviction for the separate crime, Mapp appealed her case to the Supreme Court.

Decision: In a 5 to 3 decision, the Court stated that convictions based on illegally obtained evidence must be overturned. Justice Tom Clark wrote for the majority, "all evidence obtained by searches and seizures in violation of the Constitution is... inadmissible in a state court."

Baker v. Carr (1962)

Significance: Through this decision, the Court ruled that the judiciary branch may involve itself in hearing cases about political matters.

Background: Voters from Tennessee sued their state in federal court, arguing that the way the state drew the boundary lines between representative districts created unequal representation within the legislature, and therefore unequal protection under the laws of the state. Tennessee argued that the federal court did not have the jurisdiction to hear the case.

Decision: By a 6 to 2 margin, the Court decided that the federal court did have the right to hear the case, and that the voters had the right to sue over the issue. Writing for the majority, Justice William Brennan said that the voters "are entitled to a trial and a decision" on whether they were denied equal protection.

Engel v. Vitale (1962)

Significance: The case deals with the specific issue of organized prayer in schools and the broader issue of the proper relationship between government and religion under the First Amendment. The question in the case was whether a state violates the First Amendment when it composes a prayer that students must say at the beginning of each school day. This decision was--and still is--very controversial. Many people felt it was against religion. Attempts have been made to change the Constitution to permit prayer, but none have been successful.

Background: The state of New York recommended that public schools in the state begin the day by having students recite a prayer. In fact, the state wrote the prayer for students to say. A group of parents sued to stop the official prayer, saying that it was contrary to their beliefs and their children's beliefs. They said the law was unconstitutional.

The parents argued that the state prayer amounted to "establishing" (officially supporting) religion. Though students were permitted to remain silent, the parents claimed that there would always be pressure on students to pray. New York replied that no one was forced to pray, and that it didn't involve spending any tax dollars and it didn't establish religion.

Decision: By a 6-1 margin (two justices did not take part in the case), the Court agreed with the parents. It struck down the state law. Justice Hugo Black wrote for the majority. He pointed out that the prayer was clearly religious. He said that under the First Amendment, "it is no part of the business of government to compose official prayers for any group of American people to recite as part of a religious program carried on by government."

Black, referring to Jefferson and Madison, said "These men knew that the First Amendment, which tried to put an end to governmental control of religion and prayer, was not written to destroy either."

Gideon v. Wainwright (1963)

Significance: This ruling was one of several key Supreme Court decisions establishing free legal help for those who cannot otherwise afford representation in court.

Background: Clarence Earl Gideon was accused of robbery in Florida. Gideon could not afford a lawyer for his trial, and the judge refused to supply him with one for free. Gideon tried to defend himself and was found guilty. He eventually appealed to the U.S. Supreme Court, claiming that the lower court's denial of a court-appointed lawyer violated his Sixth and Fourteenth Amendment rights.

Decision: This case was decided on March 18, 1963, by a vote of 9 to 0 in favor of Gideon. The Court agreed that the Sixth Amendment (which protects a citizen's right to have a lawyer for his or her defense) applied to the states because it fell under the due process clause of the Fourteenth Amendment. Thus, the states are required to provide legal aid to those defendants in criminal cases who cannot afford to pay for legal representation.

Heart of Atlanta Motel v. United States (1964)

Significance: The ruling upheld the public accommodations clause of the Civil Rights Act of 1964. It enforced the right of African Americans to receive access to the same accommodations as whites and gave Congress judicial backing for passing more civil rights legislation.

Background: The owner of the Heart of Atlanta Motel routinely discriminated against African Americans. He claimed that his business was not an interstate business and therefore not subject to regulation by Congressional acts.

Decision: In a unanimous decision, the Court declared that as a business that served people from across state boundaries, the Heart of Atlanta Motel was in fact an interstate business, and that therefore Congressional acts did apply.

Reynolds v. Sims (1964)

Significance: This ruling upheld the principle of "one person, one vote." It firmly established that representation in state legislatures must be based mainly on population so that each citizen's vote has as equal a value as possible. The ruling led to widespread changes in state voting districts throughout the country.

Background: Residents of Jefferson County, Alabama, filed a complaint challenging the apportionment of the Alabama state legislature. This apportionment was based on the 1900 federal census, making it extremely out of date with changes in state population. The residents argued that Alabama's unequal apportionment system violated the Equal Protection Clause of the Fourteenth Amendment.

Decision: This case was argued on November 13, 1963, and decided on June 15, 1964, by a vote of 8 to 1. Chief Justice Earl Warren spoke for the majority, "the achievement of fair and effective representation for all citizens is concededly the basic aim of legislative apportionment." The Court ruled that the state of Alabama had established a system that did not fairly represent a large number of its citizens.

Miranda v. Arizona (1966)

Significance: This decision ruled that an accused person's Fifth Amendment rights begin at the time of arrest. The ruling caused controversy because it made the questioning of suspects and collecting evidence more difficult for law enforcement officers.

Background: In 1963 Ernesto Miranda was arrested in Arizona for a kidnapping. Miranda signed a confession and was later found guilty of the crime. The arresting police officers, however, admitted that they had not told Miranda of his right to talk with an attorney before his confession. Miranda appealed his conviction on the grounds that by not informing him of his legal rights the police had violated his Fifth Amendment right against self-incrimination.

Decision: This case was decided on June 13, 1966, by a vote of 5 to 4. Chief Justice Earl Warren spoke for the Court, which ruled in Miranda's favor. The Court decided that an accused person must be given four warnings after being taken into police custody: (1) the suspect has the right to remain silent, (2) anything the suspect says can and will be used against him or her, (3) the suspect has the right to consult with an attorney and to have

an attorney present during questioning, and (4) if the suspect cannot afford a lawyer, one will be provided before questioning begins.

Tinker v. Des Moines Independent Community School District (1969)

Significance: This ruling established the extent to which American public school students can take part in political protests in their schools. The question the case raised is whether, under the First Amendment, school officials can prohibit students from wearing armbands to symbolize political protest.

Background: Some students in Des Moines, Iowa, decided to wear black armbands to protest the Vietnam War. Two days before the protest, the school board created a new policy. The policy stated that any student who wore an armband to school and refused to remove it would be suspended. Three students wore armbands and were suspended. They said that their First Amendment right to freedom of speech had been violated. In 1969 the U.S. Supreme Court decided their case.

Decision: By a 7-2 margin, the Court agreed with the students. Justice Abe Fortas wrote for the majority. He said that students do not "shed their constitutional rights to freedom of speech . . . at the schoolhouse gate." Fortas admitted that school officials had the right to set rules. However, their rules must be consistent with the First Amendment. In this case, Des Moines school officials thought their rule was justified. They feared that the protest would disrupt learning. Fortas's opinion held that wearing an armband symbolizing political protest was a form of speech called symbolic speech. Symbolic speech is conduct that expresses an idea. Even though the protest did not involve spoken words, called pure speech, it did express an opinion. This expression is protected the same as pure speech is. Fortas wrote that student symbolic speech could be punished, but only if it really disrupts education. Fortas also noted that school officials allowed other political symbols, such as campaign buttons, to be worn in school.

Reed v. Reed (1971)

Significance: This ruling was the first in a century of Fourteenth Amendment decisions to say that gender discrimination violated the equal protection clause. This case was later used to strike down other statutes that discriminated against women.

Background: Cecil and Sally Reed were separated. When their son died without a will, the law gave preference to Cecil to be appointed the administrator of the son's estate. Sally sued Cecil for the right to administer the estate, challenging the gender preference in the law.

Decision: This case was decided on November 22, 1971, by a vote of 7 to 0. Chief Justice Warren Burger spoke for the unanimous Supreme Court. Although the Court had upheld laws based on gender preference in the past, in this case it reversed its position. The Court declared that gender discrimination violated the equal protection clause of the Fourteenth Amendment and therefore could not be the basis for a law.

New York Times v. United States (1971)

Significance: In this ruling the Court dismissed the idea of "prior restraint," or attempting to stop an action before it happens, by the government as unconstitutional. The ruling allowed the *New York Times* to continue publishing documents that were critical of the government's handling of the Vietnam War.

Background: The *New York Times* began publishing a series of papers called the Pentagon Papers that were critical of the government. The government attempted to stop publication of the papers with a court order, citing national security. Because of the national importance of the case, the Supreme Court agreed to hear the case quickly.

Decision: In a 6 to 3 decision, the Court declared that the government could not stop publication of the Pentagon Papers. Although the government did have the right to stop publication if it could prove the danger to national security, the Court said that in this case the government had not met the burden of proof.

Roe v. Wade (1973)

Significance: This ruling made abortions available to women during their first trimester of pregnancy, even when their health was not in danger.

Background: The case was brought in the name of Jane Roe against the restrictive abortion laws of Texas. Until this case, states had widely varying laws about the availability of abortions, some restricting them altogether.

Decision: With a 7 to 2 decision, the Court said that elective abortions must be available to any woman in her first three months of pregnancy. Because of the variety of moral opinions about when life begins, the court ruled that a fetus does not have the same rights as an infant.

United States v. Nixon (1974)

Significance: This ruling forced President Nixon to turn over tapes of White House conversations to the congressional committee investigating his wrongdoing in the Watergate break-in. Nixon resigned shortly after.

Background: Nixon had been secretly taping every conversation that took place in the Oval Office. After the president was implicated in the cover-up of the Watergate Hotel break in, Congress wanted to hear these tapes. Nixon refused to hand them over, claiming "executive privilege" to keep some information secret.

Decision: In a unanimous decision, the Court ruled that Nixon must turn the tapes over to the prosecution as requested. Writing for the Court, Chief Justice Warren Burger stated that finding the truth requires that courts have all the evidence they need, even if it includes presidential communication.

New Jersey v. TLO (1985)

Significance: In this ruling, the Court declared that searches of juveniles on school grounds are not subject to the same standards of "reasonableness" and "probable cause" that protect other citizens.

Background: T. L. O. was a 14-year-old who was caught smoking in the girls' bathroom of her school. A principal at the school questioned the girl and searched her purse, finding marijuana and other drug paraphernalia.

Decision: In a 7 to 2 decision, the Court ruled that the suspension of the rules of "reasonable" search and seizure as defined by the Fourth Amendment and later court rulings applied only to school officials and not to law enforcement officers.

Texas v. Johnson (1989)

Significance: This ruling answered the question of whether the First Amendment protects burning the U.S. flag as a form of symbolic speech. It deals with the limits of symbolic speech. This case is particularly important because it involves burning the flag, one of our national symbols.

Background: At the 1984 Republican National Convention in Texas, Gregory Lee Johnson doused a U.S. flag with kerosene. He did this during a demonstration as a form of protest. Johnson was convicted of violating a Texas law that made it a crime to desecrate [treat disrespectfully] the national flag. He was sentenced to one year in prison and fined $2,000. The Texas Court of Criminal Appeals reversed the conviction because, it said, Johnson's burning of the flag was a form of symbolic speech protected by the First Amendment. Texas then appealed to the U.S. Supreme Court.

Decision: The Court ruled for Johnson, five to four. Justice William Brennan wrote for the majority. He said that Johnson was within his constitutional rights when he burned the U.S. flag in protest. As in *Tinker* v. *Des Moines Independent Community School District* (1969), the Court looked at the First Amendment and "symbolic speech." Brennan concluded that Johnson's burning the flag was a form of symbolic speech—like the students wearing armbands in Des Moines—and is protected by the First Amendment. According to Brennan, "Government may not prohibit the expression of an idea [because it is] offensive." Chief Justice Rehnquist dissented. He said the flag is "the visible symbol embodying our Nation. It does not represent the views of any particular political party, and it does not represent any particular political philosophy. The flag is not simply another 'idea' or 'point of view' competing for recognition in the marketplace of ideas." Since this decision, several amendments banning flag burning have been proposed in Congress, but so far all have failed.

Cruzan v. Director, Missouri Department of Health (1990)

Significance: This ruling helped define who may refuse medical treatment. Although the issue is still undecided, this case began a series of efforts to provide legislative and judicial guidelines for the "right to die."

Background: The parents of comatose patient Nancy Cruzan wanted to remove her life support system. The Department of Health ruled that Cruzan had not previously made clear her desire to refuse medical treatment in the event of brain damage.

Decision: By a 5 to 4 margin, the Court ruled that Cruzan's parents could not remove her from life support because she had not clearly expressed her desires previously. Writing for the majority, Chief Justice William Rehnquist stated that it was Nancy's demand to be removed from life support, not her parents, that the state must respect in such cases.

Planned Parenthood of Southeastern Pennsylvania, et al. v. Casey (1992)

Significance: In this ruling the Court upheld its decision in *Roe* v. *Wade* of the right to elective abortion but allowed the state of Pennsylvania to impose restrictions of notification and consent upon minors.

Background: In 1988 and 1989, Pennsylvania revised its abortion control laws to require that minors receive consent from a parent and that married women notify their husbands. The laws were challenged by several abortion clinics and physicians.

Decision: In a 5 to 4 decision, the Court upheld its previous ruling of *Roe* v. *Wade* that women have the right to an abortion in the first trimester of pregnancy, but provided that a state may allow that minors must have the consent of one parent 24 hours before the procedure. The Court struck down the part of the Pennsylvania laws that required married women to notify their husbands, saying that it could be an "undue burden" upon the woman.

Vernonia School District v. Acton (1995)

Significance: The ruling allowed random drug testing of minors on school property as a safety measure.

Background: James Acton, a student athlete in the Vernonia School District, refused to participate in drug testing, stating that the policy invaded his right to privacy and was an illegal search and seizure.

Decision: In a 6 to 3 decision, the Court ruled that while on school property, students are subject to greater control of personal rights than free adults. Furthermore, concern over the safety of minors under governmental supervision outweighs the minimal intrusion into a student's privacy.

Bush v. Gore (2000)

Significance: In effect, the Supreme Court picked which candidate was the next president of the United States. The question before the court was whether ballots that could not be read by voting machines should be recounted by hand. The broader issues were whether the Supreme Court can overrule state court decisions on state laws and whether an appointed judiciary can affect the result of democratic elections.

Background: The 2000 presidential election between Democrat Gore and Republican Bush was very close. Who would be president would be determined by votes in the state of Florida. People in Florida voted by punching a hole in a ballot card. The votes were counted by a machine that detected these holes. According to that count, Bush won the state of Florida by a few hundred votes. Florida's Election Commission declared that Bush had won Florida. However, about 60,000 ballots were not counted because the machines could not detect a hole in the ballot. Gore argued in the Florida Supreme Court that these votes should be recounted by hand. The Florida Supreme Court ordered counties to recount all those votes. Bush appealed to the U.S. Supreme Court, which issued an order to stop the recounts while it made a decision.

Decision: On December 12, 2000, the Supreme Court voted 5-4 to end the hand recount of votes ordered by the Florida Supreme Court. The majority said that the Florida Supreme Court had ordered a recount without setting standards for what was a valid vote. Different vote-counters might use different standards. The Court said that this inconsistency meant that votes were treated arbitrarily (based on a person's choice rather than on standards). This arbitrariness, said the Court, violated the due process clause and the equal protection clause of the Constitution. Also, the justices said that Florida law required the vote count to be finalized by December 12. The justices said that rules for recounts could not be made by that date, so they ordered election officials to stop recounting votes.

Gratz v. Bollinger and Grutter v. Bollinger (2003)

Significance: These cases considered whether a university violates the Constitution by using race as a factor for admitting students to its undergraduate school and its law school. The ruling affects use of affirmative action programs in higher education. The decisions gave colleges guidelines as to what is permitted and what is not. The decisions were limited to higher education and may not apply to other affirmative action programs such as getting a job or a government contract.

Background: Jennifer Gratz and Barbara Grutter are both white. They challenged the University of Michigan's affirmative action admissions policies. Gratz said that the university violated the Constitution by considering race as a factor in its undergraduate admissions programs. Grutter claimed that the University of Michigan Law School also did so.

Decisions: In Gratz, the Court ruled 6-3 that the undergraduate program—which gave each minority applicant an automatic 20 points toward admission—was unconstitutional. Chief Justice Rehnquist's opinion held that the policy violated the equal protection clause because it did not consider each applicant individually. "The ... automatic distribution of 20 points has the effect of making 'the factor of race ... decisive' for virtually every minimally qualified underrepresented minority applicant." It was almost an automatic preference based on the minority status of the applicant. The result was different when the Court turned to the affirmative action policy of Michigan's Law School, which used race as one factor for admission. In Grutter, by a 5-4 margin, the Court held that this policy did not violate the Equal Protection Clause. Justice O'Connor wrote for the majority. "Truly individualized consideration demands that race be used in a flexible, non-mechanical way . . . Universities can . . . consider race or ethnicity . . . as a 'plus' factor [when individually considering] each and every applicant." Thus, the law school policy was constitutional.

United States v. American Library Association (2003)

Significance: This case deals with the constitutionality of a federal law called the Children's Internet Protection Act (CIPA). The law was designed to protect children from being exposed to pornographic Web sites while using computers in public libraries. The question before the Court was: Does a public library violate the First Amendment by installing Internet filtering software on its public computers?

Background: The law, CIPA, applies to public libraries that accept federal money to help pay for Internet access. These libraries must install filtering software to block pornographic images. Some library associations sued to block these filtering requirements. They argued that by linking money and filters, the law required public libraries to violate the First Amendment's guarantees of free speech. The libraries argued that filters block some nonpornographic sites along with pornographic ones. That, they said, violates library patrons' First Amendment rights. CIPA does allow anyone to ask a librarian to unblock a specific Web site. It also allows adults to ask that the filter be turned off altogether. But, the libraries argued, people using the library would find these remedies embarrassing and impractical.

Decision: In this case, Chief Justice Rehnquist authored a plurality opinion. He explained that the law does not require any library to accept federal money. A library can choose to do without federal money. If the library makes that choice, they do not have to install Internet filters. Rehnquist also did not think that filtering software's tendency to overblock nonpornographic sites was a constitutional problem. Adult patrons could simply ask a librarian to unblock a blocked site or have the filter disabled entirely.

The Dissents: Justice Stevens viewed CIPA "as a blunt nationwide restraint on adult access to an enormous amount" of valuable and often constitutionally protected speech. Justice Souter noted that he would have joined the plurality if the First Amendment interests raised in this case were those of children rather than those of adults.

Hamdi v. Rumsfeld and Rasul v. Bush (2004)

Significance: These cases addressed the balance between the government's powers to fight terrorism and the Constitution's promise of due process. Each case raised a slightly different question:

1. Can the government hold American citizens for an indefinite period as "enemy combatants" and not permit them to access to American courts, and

2. Whether foreigners captured overseas and jailed at Guantanamo Bay, Cuba, have the right to ask American courts to decide if they are being held legally?

Background
Detaining American Citizens: In *Hamdi* v. *Rumsfeld*, Yaser Hamdi, an American citizen, was captured in Afghanistan in 2001. The U.S. military said Hamdi was an enemy combatant and claimed that "it has the authority to hold ... enemy combatants captured on the battlefield ... to prevent them from returning to the battle." Hamdi's attorney said that Hamdi deserved the due process rights that other Americans have, including a hearing in court to argue that he was not an enemy combatant.

Detaining Foreigners at Guantanamo Bay: The prisoners in *Rasul* v. *Bush* also claimed they were wrongly imprisoned. They wanted a court hearing, but Guantanamo Bay Naval Base is on Cuban soil. Cuba leases the base to the U.S. In an earlier case, the Court had ruled that "if an alien is outside the country's sovereign territory, then ... the alien is not permitted access to the courts of the United States to enforce the Constitution."

Decisions: In *Hamdi*, the Court ruled 6-3 that Hamdi had a right to a hearing. Justice O'Connor wrote that the Court has "made clear that a state of war is not a blank check for the president when it comes to the rights of the nation's citizens." The government decided not to prosecute Hamdi. In *Rasul*, also decided 6-3, Justice Stevens wrote that the prisoners had been held for more than two years in territory that the United States controls. Thus, even though the prisoners are not on U.S. soil, they can ask U.S. courts if their detention is legal.

The North Pole

0   200   400 Miles
0   200   400 Kilometers

Projection:
Polar Azimuthal Equidistant

EUROPE

Barents Sea

Kara Sea

Norwegian Sea

Laptev Sea

ASIA

ARCTIC OCEAN

Greenland Sea

Arctic Circle

Greenland (DENMARK)

ATLANTIC OCEAN

North Pole

International Date Line

POLAR ICE PACK

North Magnetic Pole +

Baffin Bay

Beaufort Sea

Bering Sea

NORTH AMERICA

90°E
120°E
150°E
150°N
80°N
70°N
60°N
50°N
180°
30°E
30°W
60°W

The South Pole

International Date Line

PACIFIC OCEAN

SOUTH AMERICA

Antarctic Circle

Amundsen Sea

Bellingshausen Sea

Antarctic Peninsula

POLAR ICE PACK

Ross Sea

Marie Byrd Land

Vinson Massif 16,067 ft (4,897 m) ▲

Ellsworth Land

Ross Ice Shelf

Ronne Ice Shelf

Weddell Sea

POLAR ICE PACK

▲ Mount Markham over 14,275 ft (over 4,351 m)

+ South Pole

Edith Ronne Land

Filchner Ice Shelf

Adelie Land

South + Magnetic Pole

WILKES LAND

ANTARCTICA

ICE CAP

Coats Land

ATLANTIC OCEAN

QUEEN MAUD LAND

Shackleton Ice Shelf

American Highland

Enderby Land

INDIAN OCEAN

0   250   500 Miles
0   250   500 Kilometers

Projection:
Polar Azimuthal Equidistant

180°
150°W
120°W
90°W
60°W
150°E
120°E
90°E
60°E
30°E
0°
30°W
70°S
80°S
60°S
50°S

United States: Physical

PACIFIC OCEAN

Strait of Juan de Fuca

Mount Rainier
14,410 ft
(4,392 m)

Puget Sound

Franklin D. Roosevelt Lake

Flathead Lake

Lewis Range

Milk River

Missouri River

Fort Peck Lake

Lake Sakakawea

COAST RANGES

CASCADE RANGE

Columbia River

Pend Oreille River

Bitterroot Range

Salmon River

Salmon River Mts.

CONTINENTAL

ROCKY

Yellowstone River

Bighorn Mts

Bighorn River

Powder River

Lake Oahe

G R E A T

Cape Mendocino

Klamath River

Goose Lake

Columbia Plateau

Sawtooth Mts.

Snake River

Grand Tetons

Yellowstone River

Wind River Range

Cheyenne River

White River

Black Hills

James River

Shasta Lake

Pyramid Lake

Gannett Peak
13,804 ft
(4,207 m)

M O U N T A I N S

Niobrara River

I N T E R

San Francisco Bay

Sacramento River

Central Valley

Lake Tahoe

GREAT SALT LAKE

Wasatch Range

Uinta Mts.

Green River

Front Range

North Platte River

DIVIDE

SIERRA NEVADA

Great Basin

Great Salt Lake

Utah Lake

Colorado River

South Platte River

P L A I N S

San Joaquin River

Coast Ranges

Mount Whitney
14,494 ft
(4,419 m)

Death Valley

Mojave Desert

Lake Mead

Grand Canyon

COLORADO

Lake Powell

San Juan River

Mount Elbert
14,433 ft
(4,400 m)

Pikes Peak
14,110 ft
(4,301 m)

Republican River

Smoky Hill River

Monterey Bay

Channel Islands

Salton Sea

Imperial Valley

Colorado River

PLATEAU

Painted Desert

Rio Grande

San Luis Valley

DIVIDE

Sangre De Cristo Mts.

Canadian River

PACIFIC OCEAN

Gila River

Sonoran Desert

CONTINENTAL

Pecos River

Colorado Riv.

Amistad Reservoir

Rio Grande

Nueces River

Gulf of California

MEXICO

Pac. Isla

To understand the relative locations of Alaska and Hawaii, as well as the vast distances separating them from the rest of the United States, see the world map.

HAWAII

Kauai
Niihau
Oahu
Molokai
Lanai
Maui
Kahoolawe

PACIFIC OCEAN

Mauna Kea
13,796 ft
(4,206 m)

Hawaii

22°N
155°W
19°N

0   75   150 Miles
0   75   150 Kilometers
Projection: Mercator

ARCTIC OCEAN

RUSSIA

Arctic Circle

Bering Strait

BROOKS RANGE

Yukon River

CANADA

St. Lawrence Island
St. Matthew Island

Nunivak Island

Kuskokwim River

Tanana River

ALASKA RANGE

Mount McKinley
20,320 ft
(6,194 m)

Bering Sea

Gulf of Alaska

Kodiak Island

Alexander Archipelago

ALEUTIAN ISLANDS

Attu Island

PACIFIC OCEAN

0   250   500 Miles
0   250   500 Kilometers
Projection: Albers Equal Area

50°N
55°N
170°E
180°
160°W
150°W
140°W

45°N
40°N
35°N
30°N
125°W
120°W

CANADA

Isle Royale

Mesabi Range

Lake Superior

Minnesota River

Mississippi River

Wisconsin River

Lake Michigan

Lake Huron

Des Moines River

Illinois River

St. Lawrence River

St. Lawrence Seaway

Lake Champlain

Adirondack Mts.

Green Mts.

White Mts.

Longfellow Mts.

Penobscot River

St. John River

Lake Ontario

Lake Erie

PLATEAU

Catskill Mts.

Allegheny R.

Susquehanna River

APPALACHIAN MOUNTAINS

Cape Cod

Long Island Sound

Long Island

40°N

Missouri River

Arkansas R.

Kansas R.

P L A I N S

Lake of the Ozarks

OZARK PLATEAU

Keystone Lake

Wabash River

Scioto River

Ohio River

ALLEGHENY

Monongahela R.

Potomac River

Kanawha R.

James River

Roanoke River

Delaware River

Delaware Bay

Chesapeake Bay

ATLANTIC OCEAN

70°W

Cumberland Plateau

Lake Barkley

Cumberland River

Great Smoky Mts.

BLUE RIDGE MOUNTAINS

Pamlico Sound

Cape Hatteras

35°N

Faula Lake

Ouachita Mts.

Lake Texoma

White River

Kentucky Lake

Tennessee River

P I E D M O N T

Coosa River

Oconee River

Savannah River

Trinity River

Saline River

Red River

Arkansas River

Tombigbee River

Alabama R.

Pearl River

Chattahoochee River

Altamaha River

Sea Islands

Toledo Bend Reservoir

C O A S T A L

P L A I N

Chandeleur Islands

Mississippi Delta

Okefenokee Swamp

FLORIDA PENINSULA

Cape Canaveral

80°W

GULF

85°W

90°W

95°W

N E S W

Gulf of Mexico

Lake Okeechobee

The Everglades

Cape Sable

Florida Keys

Straits of Florida

BAHAMAS

25°N

75°W

ELEVATION

Feet | Meters
13,120 | 4,000
6,560 | 2,000
1,640 | 500
656 | 200
(Sea level) 0 | 0 (Sea level)
Below sea level | Below sea level

0 100 200 Miles
0 100 200 Kilometers

Projection: Albers Equal Area

ATLAS

ATLAS R27

ATLAS

ARCTIC 80°N OCEAN

Greenland

Beaufort Sea

Victoria Island

Baffin Bay

Baffin Island

Iceland

Denmark Strait

Bering Strait

Great Bear Lake

Davis Strait

Mackenzie River

Yukon River

Great Slave Lake

60°N

Bering Sea

Gulf of Alaska

Lake Winnipeg

Hudson Bay

Aleutian Islands

Vancouver Island

ROCKY MOUNTAINS

Missouri River

Great Lakes

St. Lawrence River

40°N

NORTH AMERICA

Colorado River

Mississippi River

APPALACHIAN MTS.

ATLANTIC OCEAN

Strait of Gibraltar

SIERRA MADRE

Rio Grande

Gulf of Mexico

Bahamas

Tropic of Cancer

Hawaiian Islands

20°N

Greater Antilles

Caribbean Sea

Lesser Antilles

Niger

PACIFIC OCEAN

Isthmus of Panama

GUIANA HIGHLANDS

N

W   E

S

0° Equator

ANDES MOUNTAINS

Amazon River

SOUTH AMERICA

BRAZILIAN HIGHLANDS

20°S

Tropic of Capricorn

River

Paraná

ATLANTIC OCEAN

40°S

ANDES MOUNTAINS

Strait of Magellan

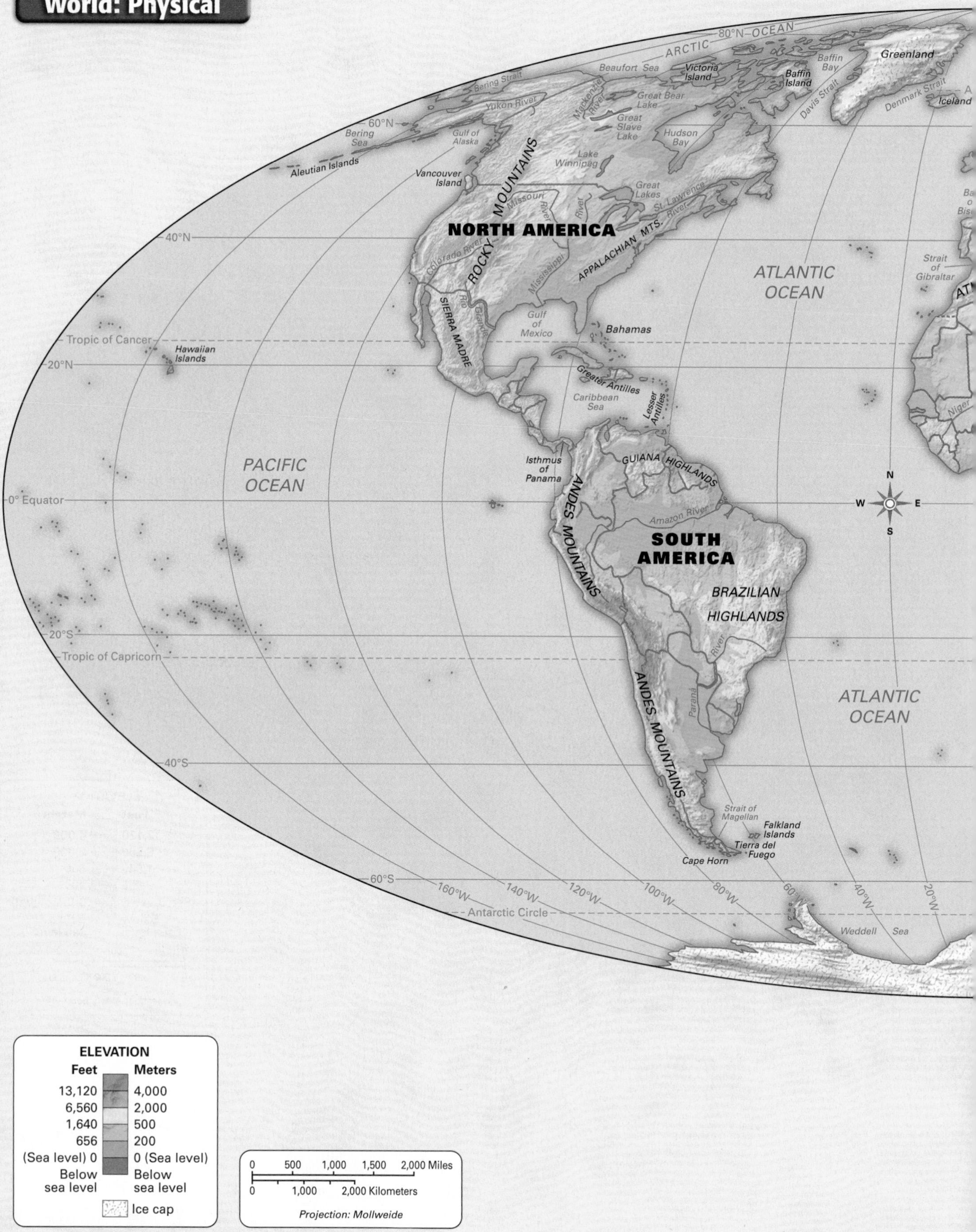

Falkland Islands

Tierra del Fuego

Cape Horn

60°S

160°W   140°W   120°W   100°W   80°W   60°W   40°W   20°W

Antarctic Circle

Weddell Sea

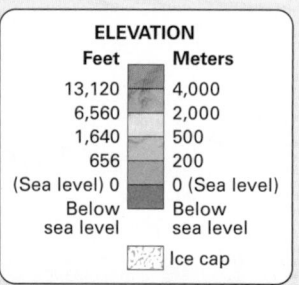

ELEVATION

Feet		Meters
13,120		4,000
6,560		2,000
1,640		500
656		200
(Sea level) 0		0 (Sea level)
Below sea level		Below sea level

Ice cap

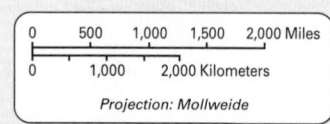

0   500   1,000   1,500   2,000 Miles

0   1,000   2,000 Kilometers

Projection: Mollweide

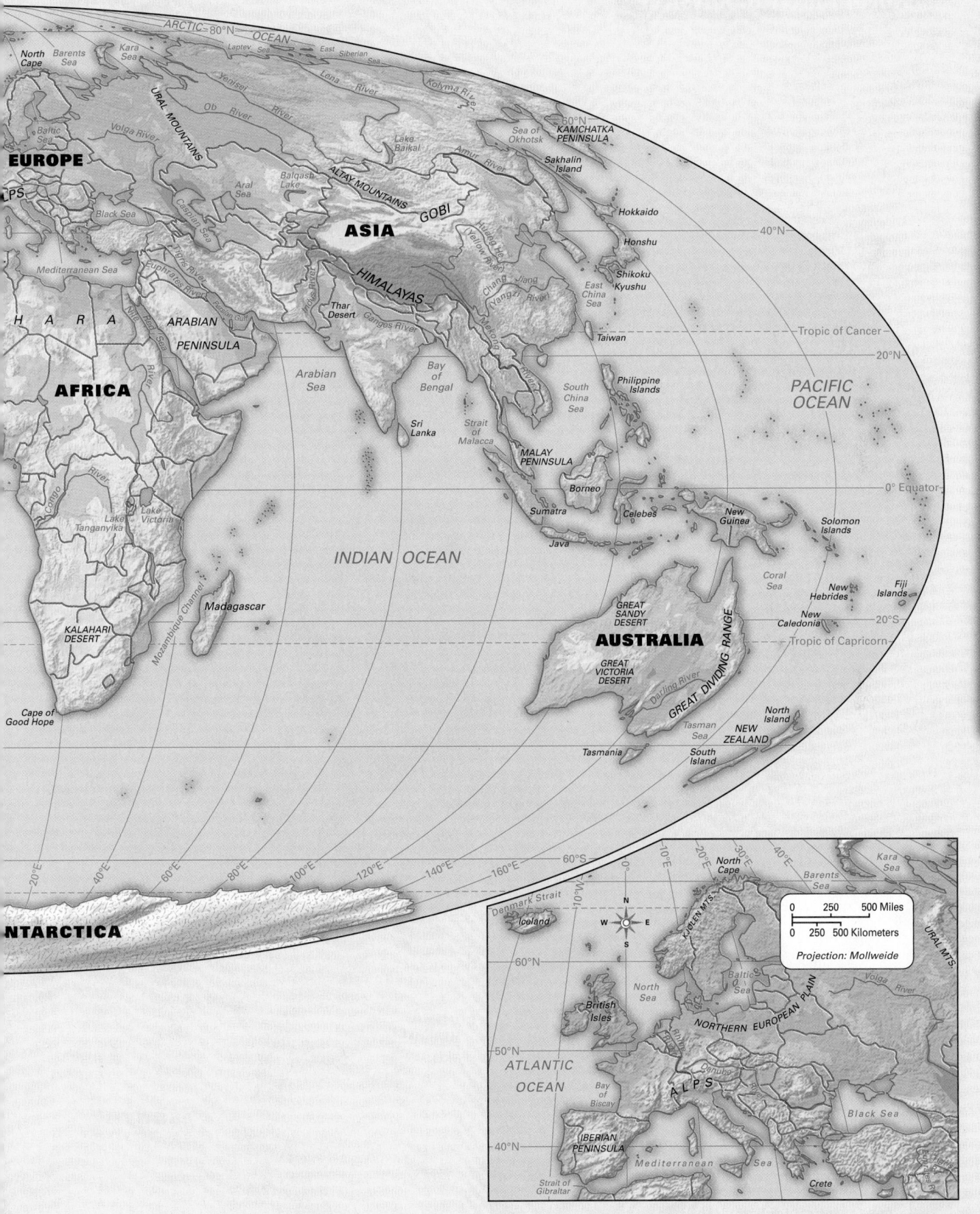

ARCTIC 80°N OCEAN

North Cape
Barents Sea
Kara Sea
Laptev Sea
East Siberian Sea

EUROPE

Baltic Sea
ALPS

URAL MOUNTAINS

Ob River
Yenisei River
Lena River
Kolyma River

60°N
KAMCHATKA PENINSULA
Sea of Okhotsk

Volga River

Black Sea
Caspian Sea
Aral Sea
Balqash Lake
Lake Baikal

ALTAY MOUNTAINS

Sakhalin Island

Mediterranean Sea

ASIA
GOBI

Amur River

Hokkaido

40°N

Tigris River
Euphrates River
Persian Gulf

ARABIAN PENINSULA

HIMALAYAS

Thar Desert
Ganges River

Indus River

Huang He (Yellow River)

Chang Jiang (Yangzi River)

Honshu

East China Sea

Shikoku
Kyushu

S A H A R A

AFRICA

Red Sea

Niger River

Arabian Sea

Bay of Bengal

Mekong River

Taiwan

Tropic of Cancer

20°N

Sri Lanka

Strait of Malacca

South China Sea

Philippine Islands

PACIFIC OCEAN

Congo River

MALAY PENINSULA

Lake Tanganyika
Lake Victoria

Sumatra

Borneo

Celebes

New Guinea

0° Equator

Solomon Islands

INDIAN OCEAN

Java

Madagascar

Coral Sea

New Hebrides

Fiji Islands

KALAHARI DESERT

GREAT SANDY DESERT

New Caledonia

20°S

Tropic of Capricorn

Mozambique Channel

AUSTRALIA

GREAT VICTORIA DESERT

GREAT DIVIDING RANGE

Darling River

North Island

Cape of Good Hope

NEW ZEALAND

Tasman Sea

Tasmania

South Island

60°S

20°E 40°E 60°E 80°E 100°E 120°E 140°E 160°E

NTARCTICA

ATLAS

Denmark Strait
North Cape
Barents Sea
Kara Sea

Iceland

KJØLEN MTS.

N
W E
S

British Isles

North Sea

Baltic Sea

URAL MTS.

Volga River

NORTHERN EUROPEAN PLAIN

ATLANTIC OCEAN

60°N

50°N

Bay of Biscay

Danube

ALPS

0 250 500 Miles
0 250 500 Kilometers

Projection: Mollweide

40°N

IBERIAN PENINSULA

Mediterranean Sea

Black Sea

Strait of Gibraltar

Crete

-10°E -20°E -30°E -40°E

-20°W -10°W 0° 10°E 20°E 30°E

ASIA

EUROPE

ATLAS

ARCTIC OCEAN

+North Pole

POLAR ICE PACK

St. Lawrence Island

Bering Strait

Nunivak Island

Bering Sea

Kodiak Island

Gulf of Alaska

Alexander Archipelago

Queen Charlotte Islands

Vancouver Island

BROOKS RANGE

ALASKA RANGE

Mt. McKinley 20,320 ft (6,194 m)

Yukon River

YUKON PLATEAU

Mackenzie River

Great Bear Lake

Great Slave Lake

Lake Athabasca

Peace River

Athabasca River

Saskatchewan River

Nelson River

Lake Winnipeg

ROCKY

GREAT

MOUNTAINS

Mount Rainier 14,410 ft (4,392 m)

CASCADE RANGE

COAST RANGES

Columbia

Snake River

SIERRA NEVADA

CENTRAL VALLEY

GREAT BASIN

DEATH VALLEY

Mount Whitney 14,494 ft (4,419 m)

COLORADO PLATEAU

BLACK HILLS

Great Salt Lake

Colorado River

PLAINS

Platte River

Missouri River

INTERIOR PLAINS

OZARK PLATEAU

Arkansas River

Red River

Mississippi River

Ohio

Cumberland R.

Tennessee River

APPALACHIAN MOUNTAINS

PIEDMONT

ATLANTIC COASTAL PLAIN

GULF COASTAL PLAIN

Rio Grande

Brazos River

BAJA CALIFORNIA

Gulf of California

SIERRA MADRE OCCIDENTAL

SIERRA MADRE ORIENTAL

Popocatépetl 17,887 ft (5,452 m)

SIERRA MADRE DEL SUR

YUCATÁN PENINSULA

Gulf of Mexico

Florida Keys

FLORIDA PENINSULA

Cape Canaveral

Straits of Florida

Bahamas

Cuba

Greater Antilles

Jamaica

Hispaniola

Puerto Rico

Lesser Antilles

Trinidad

Caribbean Sea

Lake Nicaragua

CENTRAL AMERICA

ISTHMUS OF PANAMA

Victoria Island

Banks Island

Beaufort Sea

Queen Elizabeth Islands

Ellesmere Island

Greenland

Baffin Bay

Baffin Island

Southampton Island

Coats Island

Mansel Island

Hudson Strait

Hudson Bay

CANADIAN

SHIELD

Labrador Sea

Davis Strait

Denmark Strait

Cape Farewell

Arctic Circle

Anticosti Island

Newfoundland

St. Lawrence River

Gulf of St. Lawrence

Prince Edward Island

Cape Breton Island

Lake Superior

Lake Michigan

Lake Huron

Lake Erie

Lake Ontario

Cape Cod

Long Island

Cape Hatteras

Bermuda

ATLANTIC OCEAN

PACIFIC OCEAN

Cape Mendocino

Guadalupe Island

SOUTH AMERICA

Tropic of Cancer

Equator

ELEVATION

Feet		Meters
13,120		4,000
6,560		2,000
1,640		500
656		200
(Sea level) 0		0 (Sea level)
Below sea level		Below sea level

Ice cap

0 300 600 Miles

0 300 600 Kilometers

Projection: Azimuthal Equal Area

North America: Political

ASIA

EUROPE

North Pole

160°E
170°E
180°
170°W
160°W
150°W
140°W
130°W
120°W
110°W
100°W
90°W
80°W
70°W
60°W
50°W
40°W
30°W
20°W
10°W
0°
10°E

ICELAND

Arctic Circle

St. Lawrence Island
Bering Sea
Nunivak Island
Bering Strait

Point Barrow
Beaufort Sea

Banks Island

Queen Elizabeth Islands
Ellesmere Island

Greenland (DENMARK)

Denmark Strait

ALASKA (U.S.)

Victoria Island

Baffin Bay

Baffin Island

Cape Farewell

Anchorage

Gulf of Alaska

Great Bear Lake

Davis Strait

Kodiak Island

Labrador Sea

Juneau

Alexander Archipelago

Great Slave Lake

Southampton Island

Hudson Strait

Queen Charlotte Islands

Coats Island
Mansel Island

Anticosti Island

Newfoundland

PACIFIC OCEAN

Vancouver Island

Edmonton

CANADA

Hudson Bay

St. Pierre and Miquelon (FRANCE)

Calgary

Lake Winnipeg

Prince Edward Island
Gulf of St. Lawrence
Cape Breton Island

Seattle
Vancouver

Winnipeg

Lake Superior

Quebec
Montreal

Portland

Lake Huron

Ottawa
Toronto

Boston
Cape Cod

San Francisco

Minneapolis

Lake Michigan
Lake Ontario
Lake Erie

New York City

ATLANTIC OCEAN

San Jose

Salt Lake City
Great Salt Lake

Milwaukee
Chicago

Detroit
Cleveland

Philadelphia
Baltimore

Denver
Kansas City

Indianapolis
St. Louis

Columbus
Washington, D.C.

Los Angeles
San Diego
Tijuana

UNITED STATES

Memphis

Norfolk

Phoenix

Birmingham
Atlanta

Bermuda (U.K.)

Dallas

Jacksonville

Tropic of Cancer

Austin
San Antonio

Houston

New Orleans

Florida Keys

Miami
BAHAMAS

Turks and Caicos Islands (U.K.)

Puerto Rico (U.S.)

ST. KITTS & NEVIS

Monterrey

Gulf of Mexico

Nassau

DOMINICAN REPUBLIC

San Juan

ANTIGUA & BARBUDA
Guadeloupe (FRANCE)

MEXICO

Havana

Straits of Florida

CUBA

Santo Domingo
Virgin Is. (U.S., U.K.)

DOMINICA
BARBADOS

Guadalajara
Mexico City

Mérida

Cayman Is. (U.K.)

HAITI

Martinique (FRANCE)

Puebla

Kingston
JAMAICA

Port-au-Prince

ST. LUCIA
ST. VINCENT AND THE GRENADINES

Netherlands Antilles (NETHERLANDS)

GRENADA

Belmopan
BELIZE

Caribbean Sea

GUATEMALA
Guatemala City

HONDURAS

Aruba (NETHERLANDS)

TRINIDAD AND TOBAGO

San Salvador
EL SALVADOR

Tegucigalpa
NICARAGUA
Managua

Panama Canal

San José

Panama City

COSTA RICA

PANAMA

SOUTH AMERICA

0° Equator

Legend

⊛ National capital
● Other city

0   300   600 Miles

0   300   600 Kilometers

Projection: Azimuthal Equal-Area

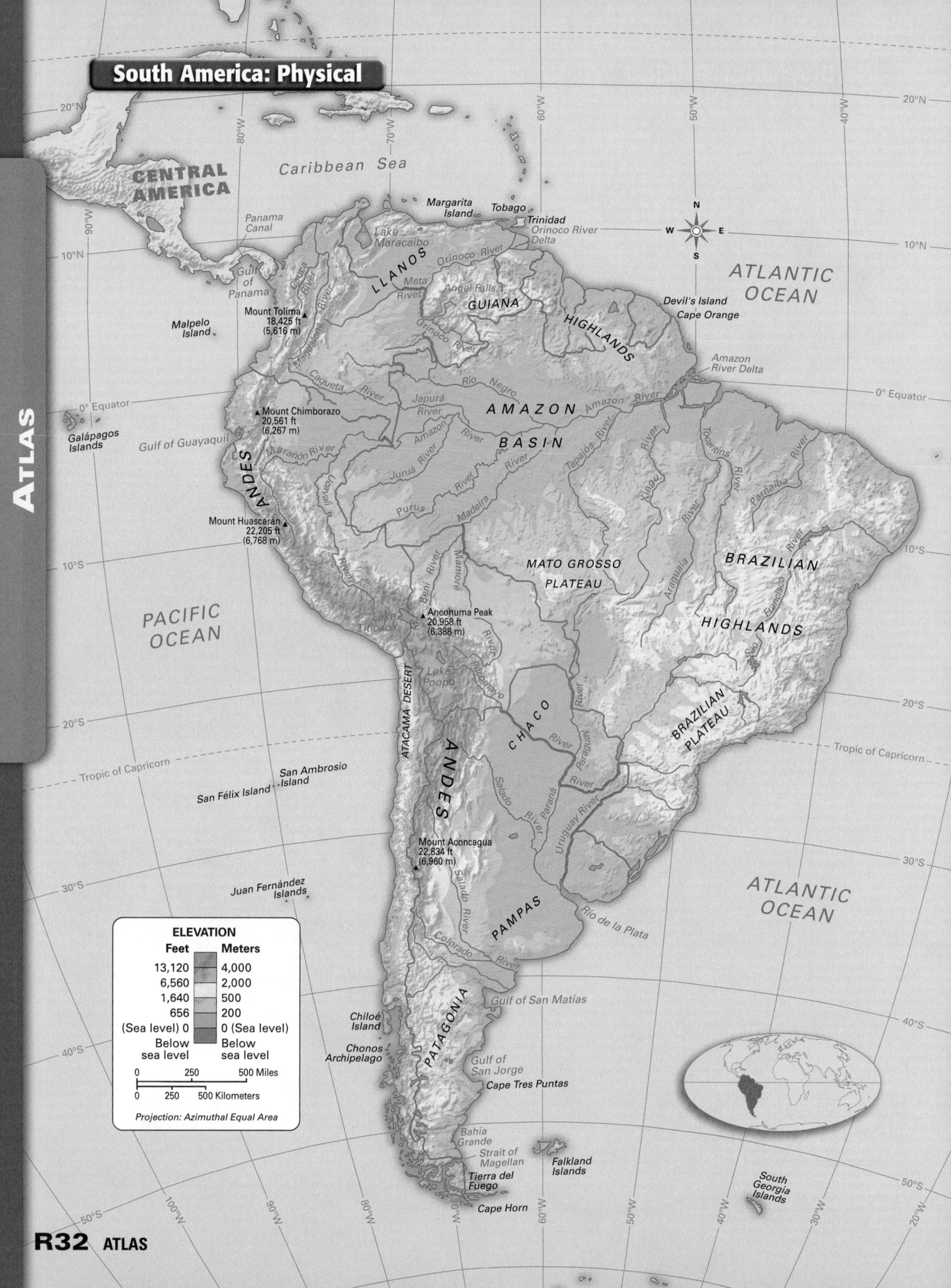

South America: Physical

CENTRAL AMERICA

Caribbean Sea

Panama Canal

Gulf of Panama

Malpelo Island

Margarita Island
Tobago
Trinidad
Orinoco River Delta

Lake Maracaibo

LLANOS

Meta River

Orinoco River

Cauca River

Mount Tolima
18,425 ft
(5,616 m)

Magdalena River

Angel Falls

GUIANA

HIGHLANDS

Devil's Island
Cape Orange

ATLANTIC OCEAN

Amazon River Delta

Caquetá River

Japurá River

Rio Negro

AMAZON BASIN

Amazon River

Mount Chimborazo
20,561 ft
(6,267 m)

Galápagos Islands

Gulf of Guayaquil

ANDES

Marañón River

Ucayali River

Amazon River

Juruá River

Purus

River

Madeira

Tapajós River

River

Tocantins

Xingu

River

River

Parnaíba

River

BRAZILIAN

Mount Huascarán
22,205 ft
(6,768 m)

Beni River

Mamoré

MATO GROSSO PLATEAU

São Francisco River

HIGHLANDS

Araguaia

PACIFIC OCEAN

Ancohuma Peak
20,958 ft
(6,388 m)

Lake Titicaca

River

Pilcomayo

Lake Poopó

ATACAMA DESERT

ANDES

CHACO

River

Paraguay

River

BRAZILIAN PLATEAU

San Félix Island

San Ambrosio Island

Salado

River

Paraná

River

Tropic of Capricorn

Uruguay River

Juan Fernández Islands

Mount Aconcagua
22,834 ft
(6,960 m)

Salado River

Rio de la Plata

ATLANTIC OCEAN

PAMPAS

Colorado

River

Gulf of San Matías

Chiloé Island

Chonos Archipelago

PATAGONIA

Gulf of San Jorge

Cape Tres Puntas

Falkland Islands

South Georgia Islands

Bahía Grande

Strait of Magellan

Tierra del Fuego

Cape Horn

N
W   E
S

ELEVATION

Feet	Meters
13,120	4,000
6,560	2,000
1,640	500
656	200
(Sea level) 0	0 (Sea level)
Below sea level	Below sea level

0   250   500 Miles
0   250   500 Kilometers

Projection: Azimuthal Equal Area

ATLAS

South America: Political

CENTRAL AMERICA

Caribbean Sea

Barranquilla
Cartagena
Caracas
VENEZUELA
Lake Maracaibo

Medellín
Bogotá
COLOMBIA
Cali

Georgetown
Paramaribo
GUYANA
Cayenne
SURINAME
French Guiana (FRANCE)

ATLANTIC OCEAN

Malpelo Island (COLOMBIA)

Quito
ECUADOR
Guayaquil

Galápagos Islands (ECUADOR)

0° Equator

Belém

PERU

Trujillo

BRAZIL

Recife

Callao
Lima

PACIFIC OCEAN

Arequipa

Lake Titicaca
La Paz
Lake Poopó
BOLIVIA
Sucre

Brasília

Salvador

Belo Horizonte

Campinas
São Paulo

PARAGUAY
Asunción

Rio de Janeiro

Curitiba

San Félix Island (CHILE)
San Ambrosio Island (CHILE)

CHILE

Pôrto Alegre

Juan Fernández Islands (CHILE)

Córdoba

Rosario

URUGUAY

ATLANTIC OCEAN

Valparaíso
Santiago

Buenos Aires
Montevideo

ARGENTINA

- ⊛ National capital
- • Other city

| 0 | 250 | 500 Miles |
| 0 | 250 | 500 Kilometers |

Projection: Azimuthal Equal-Area

Strait of Magellan

Falkland Islands (U.K.)

South Georgia Island (U.K.)

Tierra del Fuego

N
W E
S

20°N
10°N
0° Equator
10°S
20°S Tropic of Capricorn
30°S
40°S
50°S

Tropic of Capricorn

ASIA

URAL MOUNTAINS

Caspian Sea

Mt. Elbrus (5,642 m) 18,510 ft

CAUCASUS MTS.

SOUTHWEST ASIA

River

Pechora River

Kama River

Volga River

Don River

CRIMEAN PENINSULA

Black Sea

KOLA PENINSULA

White Sea

Barents Sea

North Cape

Lake Onega

Lake Ladoga

Rybinsk Reservoir

Dnister River

Dnipro River

Sea of Azov

Sea of Marmara

Aegean Sea

Rhodes

Crete

N O R T H E R N   E U R O P E A N   P L A I N

CENTRAL RUSSIAN PLAINS

Volga River

Daugava R.

Western Dvina River

ARCTIC OCEAN

Gulf of Finland

B A L T I C   P L A I N

Vistula River

CARPATHIAN MTS.

TRANSYLVANIAN ALPS

BALKAN PENINSULA

Danube River

DINARIC ALPS

Adriatic Sea

Sea

KJÖLEN MOUNTAINS

Gulf of Bothnia

Baltic Sea

Lake Vänern

Lake Vättern

Oder River

Elbe River

Danube River

Rhine River

A L P S

APENNINES

Tiber River

Tyrrhenian Sea

Sicily

Malta

North Cape

Skagerrak

Kattegat

Iceland

Norwegian Sea

Faeroe Islands

Shetland Islands

Orkney Islands

Hebrides

British Isles

Irish Sea

PENNINES

North Sea

Thames River

English Channel

Seine River

Loire River

Garonne River

Rhine River

Rhône River

Lake Geneva

Mont Blanc 15,781 ft (4,810 m)

PYRENEES

Corsica

Sardinia

Balearic Islands

Mediterranean Sea

Bay of Biscay

Po River

ATLANTIC OCEAN

Cape Finisterre

IBERIAN PENINSULA

Douro River

Duero River

Tagus River

Guadiana River

Guadalquivir River

Ebro River

Strait of Gibraltar

AFRICA

N E W S (compass rose)

Arctic Circle

Europe: Physical

ELEVATION

Feet	Meters
13,120	4,000
6,560	2,000
1,640	500
656	200
0 (Sea level)	0 (Sea level)
Below sea level	Below sea level

Ice cap

300 Miles

0   150   300 Kilometers

0   150   300 Miles

Projection: Azimuthal Equal Area

Europe: Political

ASIA

URAL MOUNTAINS

RUSSIA

Nizhny Novgorod

Moscow

Caspian Sea

SOUTHWEST ASIA

Barents Sea

White Sea

North Cape

St. Petersburg

Black Sea

ARCTIC OCEAN

FINLAND

Helsinki

Gulf of Bothnia

ESTONIA
Tallinn

LATVIA
Riga

LITHUANIA
Vilnius

RUSSIA

BELARUS
Minsk

UKRAINE
Kiev

MOLDOVA
Chișinău

ROMANIA
Bucharest

BULGARIA
Sofia

Aegean Sea

Rhodes

Crete

SWEDEN

Stockholm

Göteborg

Baltic Sea

POLAND
Warsaw

Kraków

SLOVAKIA
Bratislava

HUNGARY
Budapest

CROATIA
Zagreb

SERBIA
Belgrade

BOSNIA AND HERZEGOVINA
Sarajevo

MONTENEGRO
Podgorica

MACEDONIA
Skopje

Tirana
ALBANIA

GREECE
Athens

Sea

NORWAY

Oslo

Bergen

DENMARK
Copenhagen

Hamburg

GERMANY
Berlin

Dresden

Prague
CZECH REPUBLIC

Vienna
AUSTRIA

SLOVENIA
Ljubljana

Milan

San Marino
SAN MARINO

Adriatic Sea

ITALY
Rome

VATICAN CITY

Naples

Sicily

MALTA
Valletta

North Sea

Amsterdam
THE NETHERLANDS

Cologne
Bonn

Luxembourg
LUXEMBOURG

Brussels
BELGIUM

Munich

LIECHTENSTEIN
Vaduz

Bern
SWITZERLAND

Lake Geneva

ALPS

Monaco
MONACO

Corsica (FRANCE)

Sardinia (ITALY)

Mediterranean Sea

SCOTLAND
Edinburgh

Liverpool

UNITED KINGDOM

ENGLAND
London

WALES

NORTHERN IRELAND
Belfast

IRELAND
Dublin

British Isles

Channel Islands (U.K.)

English Channel

Paris

FRANCE

Lyon

Marseille

PYRENEES

ANDORRA
Andorra la Vella

Barcelona

Balearic Islands (SPAIN)

Bay of Biscay

SPAIN
Madrid

Valencia

Seville

Gibraltar (U.K.)

Strait of Gibraltar

PORTUGAL
Lisbon

ICELAND
Reykjavik

Faeroe Islands (DENMARK)

Shetland Islands

Arctic Circle

ATLANTIC OCEAN

AFRICA

70°N

60°N

50°N

40°N

30°W

20°W

10°W

0°

10°E

20°E

30°E

40°E

50°E

70°N

ATLAS R35

Legend

- ✪ National capital
- • Other city

300 Miles
150

300 Kilometers
150

Projection: Azimuthal Equal-Area

Asia: Physical

ELEVATION

Feet	Meters
13,120	4,000
6,560	2,000
1,640	500
656	200
0 (Sea level)	0 (Sea level)
Below sea level	Below sea level

Ice cap

750 Miles
0   250   500   750 Kilometers

Projection: Two-Point Equidistant

EUROPE

AFRICA

AUSTRALIA

PACIFIC OCEAN

INDIAN OCEAN

North Pole

Aleutian Islands

KAMCHATKA PENINSULA

Bering Sea

Sea of Okhotsk

Wrangel Island

New Siberian Islands

Sakhalin Island

Kuril Islands

Hokkaido

Honshu

Shikoku

Kyushu

Sea of Japan (East Sea)

Korea Strait

East China Sea

Yellow Sea

Okinawa

Ryukyu Islands

Taiwan

Luzon Strait

Luzon

Philippines

Mindanao

New Guinea

MAOKE MOUNTAINS

Molucca's

Banda Sea

Arafura Sea

Celebes Sea

Celebes

Borneo

Java Sea

Java

Bangka

Sumatra

MALAY PENINSULA

Mentawai Islands

INDOCHINA PENINSULA

Gulf of Thailand

Gulf of Tonkin

Hainan

South China Sea

Chao Phraya River

Mekong River

Hong River (Red River)

Chang Jiang (Yangtze) River

Huang He (Yellow River)

NORTH CHINA PLAIN

BOHEA HILLS

QIN LING

GREATER KHINGAN RANGE

MONGOLIAN PLATEAU

GOBI

Amur River

STANOVOY MOUNTAINS

YABLONOV RANGE

Shilka River

Lake Baykal

Lena River

Aldan River

CHERSKY RANGE

VERKHOYANSKIY RANGE

KOLYMA MTS.

CENTRAL RANGE

CENTRAL SIBERIAN PLATEAU

TAYMYR PENINSULA

North Land

Franz Josef Land

Novaya Zemlya

Barents Sea

Kara Sea

Laptev Sea

Lower Tunguska River

Angara River

Yenisey River

S I B E R I A

WEST SIBERIAN PLAIN

Ob River

Irtysh River

URAL MOUNTAINS

SAYAN MOUNTAINS

ALTAY MOUNTAINS

TIAN SHAN

TARIM BASIN

TAKLIMAKAN DESERT

KUNLUN MOUNTAINS

PLATEAU OF TIBET

Mount Everest 29,035 ft (8,850 m)

H I M A L A Y A S

Nu River

Brahmaputra River

Ganges River

INDO-GANGETIC PLAIN

THAR DESERT

DECCAN PLATEAU

EASTERN GHATS

WESTERN GHATS

Godavari River

Sri Lanka

Bay of Bengal

Andaman Islands

Nicobar Islands

Andaman Sea

Irrawaddy River

Salween River

Indus River

HINDU KUSH

Syr Darya

Amu Darya

KYZYL KUM

KARA KUM

TURAN LOWLAND

USTYURT PLATEAU

Aral Sea

Balqash Lake

KAZAKH UPLANDS

Ishim River

Ural River

GREAT SALT DESERT

Caspian Sea

ZAGROS MTS.

Persian Gulf

Gulf of Oman

Strait of Hormuz

RUB' AL-KHALI

AN-NAFUD

SYRIAN DESERT

Euphrates River

Tigris River

ANATOLIAN PLATEAU

Mount Ararat 16,945 ft (5,165 m)

CAUCASUS MTS.

Black Sea

Bosporus

Cyprus

SINAI PENINSULA

Red Sea

Gulf of Aden

Socotra Island

Arabian Sea

Lakshadweep Islands

Maldives

INDIAN OCEAN

Mediterranean Sea

Arctic Circle

Tropic of Cancer

Equator

National capitals
• **Other cities**

750 Miles
500   750 Kilometers
250
0

Projection: Two-Point Equidistant

EUROPE

RUSSIA

AFRICA

AUSTRALIA

RUSSIA

Moscow

Yekaterinburg
Chelyabinsk
Omsk
Novosibirsk
Astana

URAL MOUNTAINS

KAZAKHSTAN

Aral Sea

Lake Balkhash

Almaty
Bishkek
KYRGYZSTAN

Tashkent
UZBEKISTAN
TURKMENISTAN
Ashgabat

Dushanbe
TAJIKISTAN

Caspian Sea

GEORGIA
Tbilisi
ARMENIA
Yerevan
Baku
AZERBAIJAN

Istanbul
Ankara
TURKEY
Izmir

CYPRUS
Nicosia
LEBANON
Beirut
SYRIA
Damascus
ISRAEL
Tel Aviv
Jerusalem
Amman
JORDAN

Black Sea

Mediterranean Sea

Mosul
Baghdad
IRAQ
Basra
KUWAIT
Kuwait City

IRAN
Tehran
Shiraz

SAUDI ARABIA
Riyadh
Mecca
Jidda

Red Sea

Gulf of Aden

Socotra (YEMEN)

YEMEN
Sanaa

QATAR
Doha
BAHRAIN
Manama
Abu Dhabi
UNITED ARAB EMIRATES
OMAN
Masqat (Muscat)

Persian Gulf

Arabian Sea

AFGHANISTAN
Kabul

PAKISTAN
Islamabad
Lahore
Karachi

INDIA
New Delhi
Delhi
Jaipur
Ahmadabad
Mumbai (Bombay)
Bangalore
Chennai (Madras)

Lakshadweep Islands (INDIA)

MALDIVES
Male

Colombo
SRI LANKA

INDIAN OCEAN

NEPAL
Kathmandu
BHUTAN
Thimphu
BANGLADESH
Dhaka
Kolkata (Calcutta)

Bay of Bengal

Andaman Islands (INDIA)

Nicobar Islands (INDIA)

MYANMAR (BURMA)
Mandalay
Yangon (Rangoon)

Andaman Sea

MONGOLIA
Ulaanbaatar

Lake Baykal

Irkutsk

Yakutsk

CHINA

Beijing
Fushun
Harbin
Dalian
Qingdao
Nanjing
Shanghai
Wuhan
Chongqing
Chengdu
Guangzhou
Macao
Hong Kong
Hainan (CHINA)

Yellow Sea

East China Sea

Tropic of Cancer

NORTH KOREA
Pyongyang
SOUTH KOREA
Seoul
Pusan

Vladivostok

Sea of Okhotsk

Sakhalin Island

Kuril Islands (RUSSIA)

Sapporo

JAPAN
Tokyo
Yokohama
Kyoto
Osaka
Hiroshima
Nagasaki

Ryukyu Islands (JAPAN)

TAIWAN
Taipei

Aleutian Islands

Bering Sea

North Pole

Arctic Circle

Kara Sea

Barents Sea

Kara Sea

LAOS
Vientiane
THAILAND
Bangkok
VIETNAM
Hanoi
CAMBODIA
Phnom Penh
Ho Chi Minh City

Gulf of Thailand

South China Sea

PHILIPPINES
Manila

Luzon Strait

MALAYSIA
Kuala Lumpur
BRUNEI
Bandar Seri Begawan
SINGAPORE
Singapore
Medan

INDONESIA
Jakarta
Bandung
Surabaya
Ujung Pandang

Celebes Sea

Java Sea

EAST TIMOR
Dili

Arafura Sea

New Guinea

PACIFIC OCEAN

Equator

ATLAS

ATLAS **R37**

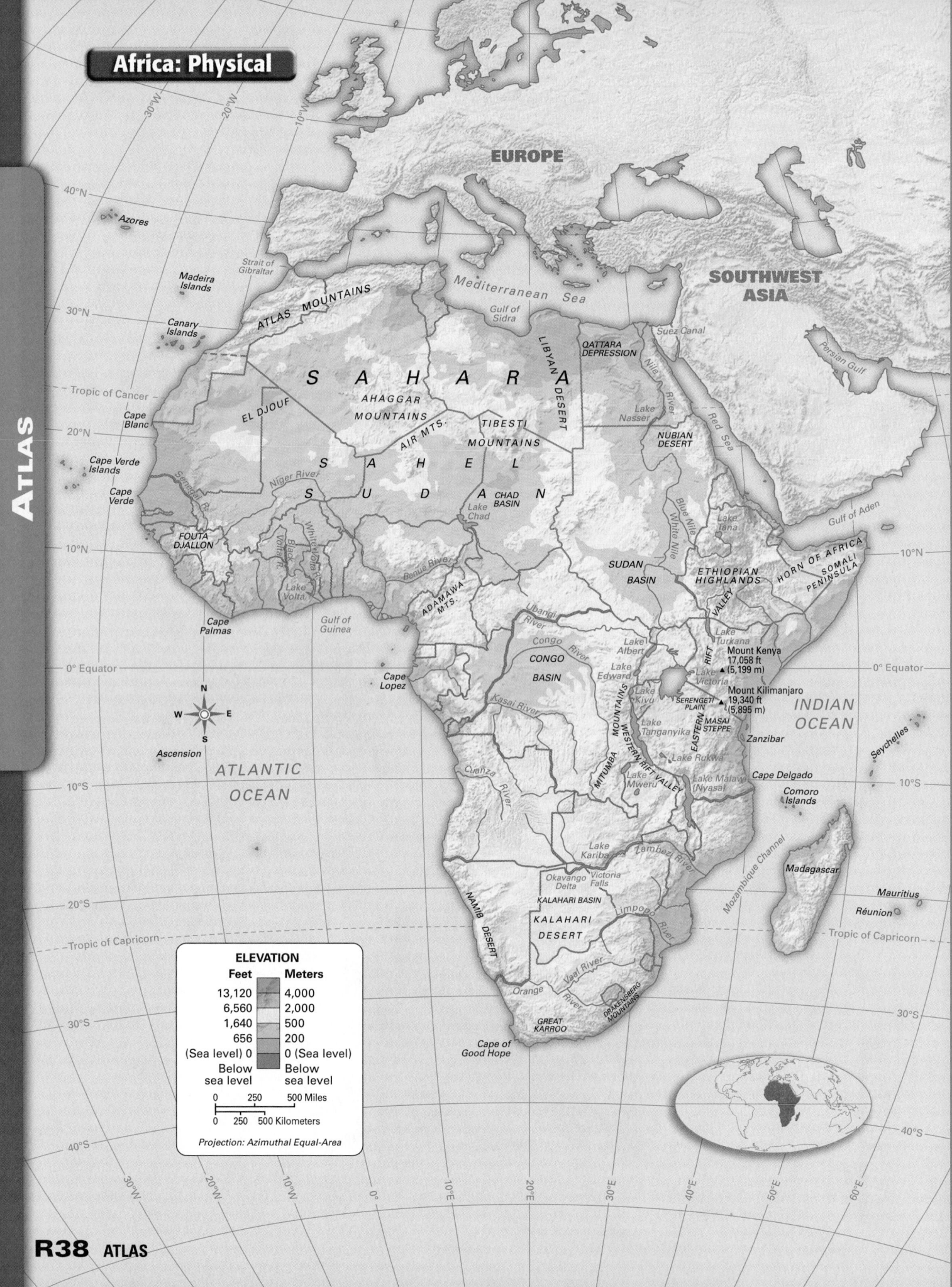

ATLAS

EUROPE

SOUTHWEST ASIA

Azores

Madeira Islands

Strait of Gibraltar

Mediterranean Sea

Gulf of Sidra

Suez Canal

Persian Gulf

Canary Islands

Tropic of Cancer

Cape Blanc

ATLAS MOUNTAINS

QATTARA DEPRESSION

S A H A R A

EL DJOUF

AHAGGAR MOUNTAINS

AIR MTS.

LIBYAN DESERT

Nile River

Lake Nasser

Red Sea

NUBIAN DESERT

Cape Verde Islands

Cape Verde

TIBESTI MOUNTAINS

S A H E L

Niger River

S U D A N

Lake Chad

CHAD BASIN

Blue Nile

White Nile

Lake Tana

Gulf of Aden

HORN OF AFRICA

FOUTA DJALLON

Black Volta R.

White Volta R.

Senegal R.

Benue River

Lake Volta

SUDAN BASIN

ETHIOPIAN HIGHLANDS

SOMALI PENINSULA

Cape Palmas

Gulf of Guinea

ADAMAWA MTS.

Ubangi River

Congo River

Lake Albert

Lake Turkana

Mount Kenya
17,058 ft
(5,199 m)

Cape Lopez

CONGO BASIN

Kasai River

Lake Edward

Lake Kivu

Lake Victoria

SERENGETI PLAIN

MASAI STEPPE

Mount Kilimanjaro
19,340 ft
(5,895 m)

Zanzibar

0° Equator

N W E S

RIFT VALLEY

EASTERN

WESTERN RIFT VALLEY

MITUMBA MOUNTAINS

Lake Tanganyika

Lake Rukwa

INDIAN OCEAN

Ascension

ATLANTIC OCEAN

Cuanza River

Lake Mweru

Lake Malawi (Nyasa)

Cape Delgado

Comoro Islands

Seychelles

Zambezi River

Lake Kariba

Mozambique Channel

Madagascar

Mauritius

NAMIB DESERT

Okavango Delta

Victoria Falls

KALAHARI BASIN

KALAHARI DESERT

Impopo River

Réunion

Tropic of Capricorn

Vaal River

Orange River

GREAT KARROO

DRAKENSBERG MOUNTAINS

Cape of Good Hope

ELEVATION

Feet	Meters
13,120	4,000
6,560	2,000
1,640	500
656	200
(Sea level) 0	0 (Sea level)
Below sea level	Below sea level

0   250   500 Miles

0   250   500 Kilometers

Projection: Azimuthal Equal-Area

Africa: Political

EUROPE

SOUTHWEST ASIA

Mediterranean Sea

Strait of Gibraltar

Azores (PORTUGAL)

Madeira (PORTUGAL)

Casablanca · Rabat

Algiers · Tunis

MOROCCO

TUNISIA

Tripoli

Canary Islands (SPAIN)

El Aaiún ·

WESTERN SAHARA (Claimed by Morocco)

ALGERIA

LIBYA

Alexandria

Giza · Cairo

EGYPT

Red Sea

Tropic of Cancer

MAURITANIA

Nouakchott

MALI

NIGER

CHAD

Khartoum

SUDAN

Lake Chad

ERITREA

Asmara

Gulf of Aden

DJIBOUTI

Djibouti

CAPE VERDE

· Praia

SENEGAL

Dakar

GAMBIA

Banjul

Bamako

Niamey

BURKINA FASO

Ouagadougou

N'Djamena

ETHIOPIA

Addis Ababa

Bissau

GUINEA-BISSAU

GUINEA

Conakry

Freetown

SIERRA LEONE

Monrovia

LIBERIA

CÔTE D'IVOIRE

Yamoussoukro

Abidjan

GHANA

Lomé

Accra

BENIN

TOGO

Porto-Novo

NIGERIA

· Abuja

Lagos

CENTRAL AFRICAN REPUBLIC

Bangui

SOMALIA

Mogadishu

CAMEROON

Malabo

Yaoundé

EQUATORIAL GUINEA

SÃO TOMÉ AND PRÍNCIPE

São Tomé

Gulf of Guinea

REPUBLIC OF THE CONGO

GABON

Libreville

Kisangani ·

UGANDA

Kampala

KENYA

Nairobi

RWANDA

Kigali

INDIAN OCEAN

Equator

DEMOCRATIC REPUBLIC OF THE CONGO

Brazzaville

Kinshasa

CABINDA (ANGOLA)

Bujumbura

BURUNDI

Lake Victoria

TANZANIA

Dodoma

Mombasa ·

Pemba

Zanzibar

Dar es Salaam

Lake Tanganyika

Victoria ·

SEYCHELLES

Luanda

ATLANTIC OCEAN

St. Helena (U.K.)

ANGOLA

Lubumbashi ·

ZAMBIA

Lusaka

Lake Malawi (Nyasa)

MALAWI

Lilongwe

COMOROS

Moroni

Harare

ZIMBABWE

Bulawayo

MOZAMBIQUE

MADAGASCAR

Antananarivo

MAURITIUS

Port Louis

Réunion (FRANCE)

NAMIBIA

Windhoek

BOTSWANA

Gaborone

Pretoria

Johannesburg

Bloemfontein

Maputo

Mbabane

SWAZILAND

Maseru

LESOTHO

Tropic of Capricorn

SOUTH AFRICA

Cape Town

Legend

✪ National capital

● Other city

0   250   500 Miles

0   250   500 Kilometers

Projection: Azimuthal Equal-Area

The Pacific: Political

ASIA

NORTH AMERICA

National capital
Other city

1,000 Miles
1,000 Kilometers
500
500

Projection: Azimuthal Equal-Area

NORTH PACIFIC OCEAN

SOUTH PACIFIC OCEAN

Tropic of Cancer

0° Equator

Tropic of Capricorn

International Date Line

Philippine Sea

South China Sea

Bonin Islands (JAPAN)

Volcano Islands (JAPAN)

Northern Marianas (U.S.)

Guam (U.S.) · Agana

PALAU · Koror

FEDERATED STATES OF MICRONESIA

Palikir

Truk Is.

MICRONESIA

MARSHALL ISLANDS

Eniwetok I.

Kwajalein Island

Majuro

Wake Island (U.S.)

Gilbert Islands

Tarawa

NAURU

SOLOMON ISLANDS

Honiara

Guadalcanal I.

Bismarck Archipelago

PAPUA NEW GUINEA

Port Moresby

New Guinea

Arafura Sea

Timor Sea

Darwin

Coral Sea

MELANESIA

VANUATU

Espiritu Santo I.

Malekula I.

Port-Vila

New Caledonia (FRANCE)

Noumea

Loyalty Islands (FRANCE)

Norfolk Island (AUSTRALIA)

Kingman Reef

Palmyra Island (U.S.)

Washington Island (U.S.)

Fanning Island

Howland I. (U.S.)

Baker I. (U.S.)

Jarvis I. (U.S.)

McKean I.

Gardner

Phoenix Islands

KIRIBATI

Starbuck Island

Manihiki Island

Tokelau (N.Z.)

SAMOA

Apia

American Samoa

Pago Pago

Cook Islands (NEW ZEALAND)

Rarotonga Island

Niue (N.Z.)

TONGA

Nuku'alofa

Wallis & Futuna (FR.)

TUVALU

Funafuti

FIJI

Suva

Kermadec Islands (N.Z.)

Marquesas Islands (FRANCE)

Tuamotu Archipelago (FRANCE)

French Polynesia

Society Islands (FRANCE)

Papeete

Tahiti (FRANCE)

Tubuai Islands (FRANCE)

Rapa Island (FRANCE)

POLYNESIA

Pitcairn (U.K.)

Pitcairn Island

Ducie Island

Easter Island (CHILE)

Hawaiian Islands

Hawaii (U.S.)

Midway Island (U.S.)

Johnston Island (U.S.)

Christmas Island (AUSTRALIA)

AUSTRALIA

Perth

Adelaide

Melbourne

Hobart

Sydney

Canberra

Brisbane

Tasman Sea

INDIAN OCEAN

NEW ZEALAND

North Island

South Island

Auckland

Wellington

Christchurch

Chatham Islands (N.Z.)

Bounty Islands (N.Z.)

Auckland Islands (NEW ZEALAND)

N E W

E

N

S

W

English and Spanish Glossary

A

absolute advantage Situation that exists when a country can produce a good better than its trading partners can. (p. 570)
ventaja absoluta Situación que existe cuando un país puede producir bienes de forma mejor que sus socios comerciales. (pág. 570)

acquit To find a defendant not guilty. (p. 391)
exonerar Hallar que un acusado no es culpable. (pág. 391)

act A law. (p. 148)
ley Legislación. (pág. 148)

adopt To legally establish a child as one's own. (p. 325)
adoptar Establecer legalmente que un niño es hijo de uno. (pág. 325)

agribusinesses Large farms that are owned by corporations and that rely heavily on mechanized equipment. (p. 588)
agroindustrias Grandes granjas que pertenec en a corporaciones y que dependen en gran parte de la maquinaria mecanizada. (pág. 588)

aliens People who live in a nation but are not citizens of that nation. (p. 14)
extranjeros Personas que viven en un país sin ser ciudadanos del mismo. (pág. 14)

alliance Agreement in which two or more countries commit to helping each other for defense, economic, scientific, or other reasons. (p. 609)
alianza Acuerdo entre dos o más países para ayudarse mutuamente en la defensa, el desarrollo económico o científico, o en otros temas. (pág. 609)

ambassadors The highest-ranking officials representing a government in a foreign country. (p. 169)
embajadores Los funcionarios de más alto rango que representan a un gobierno en otro país. (pág. 169)

amendment A written change to the Constitution. (p. 100)
enmienda Cambio escrito en la Constitución. (pág. 100)

Antifederalists Opponents of the Constitution who urged its rejection. (p. 47)
antifederalistas Oponentes de la constitución que exigieron que fuera rechazada. (pág. 47)

appeal The right of a convicted person to ask a higher court to review his or her case. (p. 183)
apelación Derecho de una persona condenada de cometer un delito a que su caso sea revisado por una corte superior. (pág. 183)

appellate jurisdiction The authority of some courts to review decisions made by lower courts. (p. 187)
jurisdicción apelativa Autoridad de algunas cortes para revisar las decisiones tomadas en cortes inferiores. (pág. 187)

apportioned To be distributed, as in the seats in the House of Representatives. (p. 136)
distribuido Repartido, como los puestos en la Cámara de representantes. (pág. 136)

apprenticeship A fixed period of on-the-job training. (p. 587)
aprendizaje Periodo de entrenamiento para un trabajo. (pág. 587)

appropriation bill A bill approving the spending of extra public money. (p. 148)
proyecto de ley de asignación de fondos Proyecto de ley que aprueba un aumento del gasto público. (pág. 148)

aptitude tests Tests that help people determine their interests and talents. (p. 599)
pruebas de aptitud Pruebas que ayudan a las personas a determinar sus intereses y talentos. (pág. 599)

arbitration A method of settling differences between labor unions and employers in which a third party's decision must be accepted by both sides. (p. 547)
arbitraje Método de resolución de diferencias entre sindicatos y empleados en el que la decision de un tercero debe ser aceptada por las dos partes. (pág. 547)

arraignment Process during which an accused person appears before a court to enter a plea of guilty or not guilty. (p. 389)
comparecencia ante el juez Proceso en el que una persona acusada se presenta ante la corte para declararse culpable o inocente. (pág. 389)

arrest warrant An authorization by a court to make an arrest. (p. 388)
orden de arresto Autorización de una corte para arrestar a alguien. (pág. 388)

ENGLISH AND SPANISH GLOSSARY

attorney general The chief legal officer of the nation or of a state. (p. 169)
secretario de justicia Encargado legal principal de una nación o estado. (pág. 169)

audit An examination by an accountant of a government's or business's income and expenditures. (p. 307)
auditoría Análisis que un contador hace de los ingresos y gastos del gobierno o de una empresa. (pág. 307)

automation The use of machines instead of workers to provide goods and services. (p. 587)
automatización Uso de máquinas en lugar de trabajadores para proporcionar bienes o servicios. (pág. 587)

B

bail Money or property an accused person gives a court to hold as a guarantee that he or she will appear for trial. (p. 116)
fianza Dinero o propiedades que una persona acusada le da a una corte para garantizar que se presentará al juicio. (pág. 116)

balanced budget A budget in which revenue equals expenditures. (p. 307)
presupuesto equilibrado Presupuesto en el que los ingresos son iguales a los gastos. (pág. 307)

balance of power A situation in which countries or groups of countries have equal levels of strength. (p. 640)
equilibrio de poder Situación en la que distintos países o grupos de países tienen el mismo poder. (pág. 640)

balance of payments The difference in value between a country's imports and exports. (p. 574)
balanza de pagos Diferencia de valor entre las importaciones y las exportaciones de un país. (pág. 574)

bankruptcy A legal declaration that a person or business cannot pay his or her or its debts. (p. 508)
bancarrota Declaración legal de que una persona o empresa no puede pagar sus deudas. (pág. 508)

beneficiary The person named in an insurance policy to receive the amount of the policy when the policyholder dies. (p. 523)
beneficiario Persona nombrada en una póliza de seguros para recibir la cantidad de la póliza cuando el asegurado muere. (pág. 523)

bicameral Consisting of two houses, as in a lawmaking body. (p. 136, 207)
bicameral De dos cámaras; por ejemplo, en los grupos que crean leyes. (pág. 136, 207)

bill Proposed law being considered by a lawmaking body. (p. 148)
proyectos de ley Ley que es considerada por un grupo que crea leyes. (pág. 148)

Bill of Rights The first 10 amendments to the U.S. Constitution, which set forth basic rights guaranteed to all Americans. (p. 110)
Carta de Derechos Primeras 10 enmiendas hechas a la Constitución de Estados Unidos, que enumeran los derechos básicos garantizados a todos los estadounidenses. (pág. 110)

birthrate The annual number of live births per 1,000 members of a population. (p. 19)
tasa de natalidad Número de nacimientos vivos anuales por cada 1,000 habitantes. (pág. 19)

blended families Families in which one or both partners brings children from a previous marriage into the new marriage. (p. 321)
familias combinadas Familias en las que uno o ambos miembros de la pareja traen al nuevo matrimonio hijos de un matrimonio anterior. (pág. 321)

block grants Federal funds given to state and local governments for broad purposes. (p. 241)
subsidios en bloque Fondos federales otorgados a los gobiernos estatales y locales con objetivos amplios. (pág. 241)

blue-collar workers People who perform jobs requiring manual labor. (p. 587)
obreros Personas que realizan labores manuales en su trabajo. (pág. 587)

bond A certificate of debt issued by governments and corporations to persons from whom they have borrowed money. (p. 298)
bono Certificado de deuda emitido por gobiernos y corporaciones a las personas que les prestan dinero. (pág. 298)

brand A name given by the maker to a product or a range of products. (p. 492)
marca de fábrica Un nombre dado por el fabricante a un producto un rango de productos. (pág. 492)

brokers Brokerage house employees who buy and sell stock. (p. 518)
corredores de bolsa Empleados de agencias de bolsa que compran y venden acciones. (pág. 518)

budget A plan of income and spending. (p. 330)
presupuesto Plan de ingresos y gastos. (pág. 330)

bureaucracy The many departments and agencies at all levels of government. (p. 173)
burocracia Los muchos departamentos y agencias de todos los niveles del gobierno. (pág. 173)

business cycle Economic patterns in which a free-market economy goes through periods of prosperity and depression. (p. 534)
ciclo comercial Patrones económicos de prosperidad y depresión de las economías de libre mercado. (pág. 534)

C

cabinet The leaders of the executive departments, who also act as advisers to the president. (p. 101)
gabinete Líderes de los departamentos ejecutivos, que también son consejeros del presidente. (pág. 101)

candidate A person who runs for election to public office. (p. 252)
candidato Persona que se postula para ser elegida a un cargo público. (pág. 252)

capital Money invested in business; also, property and equipment used to produce goods or services. (p. 467)
capital Dinero invertido en un negocio; también, propiedad y equipo usados para producir bienes o servicios. (pág. 467)

capitalism An economic system based on private ownership of the means of production. (p. 455)
capitalismo Sistema económico basado en la propiedad privada de los medios de producción. (pág. 455)

career fair An event where representatives from one or more companies are on hand to discuss job opportunities with their firms. (p. 593)
feria de profesiones Evento en el que hay representantes de una o más compañías para hablar de las oportunidades de trabajo que ofrecen sus empresas. (pág. 593)

caucuses Meetings of party leaders to determine party policy or to choose the party's candidates for public office. (p. 141)
caucus Reuniones de los líderes de los partidos para determinar las políticas del partido o seleccionar a sus candidatos a los cargos públicos. (pág. 141)

censure The formal disapproval of the actions of a member of Congress by the other members. (p. 139)
censura Desaprobación formal de las acciones del congreso por parte de sus integrantes. (pág. 139)

census An official count of the number of people in a country. (p. 17)
censo Conteo oficial de la cantidad de habitantes de un país. (pág. 17)

certificates of deposit (CDs) Investments in which an amount of money invested for a specified period of time earns a guaranteed rate of interest. (p. 518)
certificados de depósito Inversiones en las que una cantidad de dinero se invierte durante un período específico de tiempo para ganar una tasa garantizada de interés. (pág. 518)

charge account A form of credit that stores grant to customers to buy goods now and pay for them later. (p. 495)
cuenta de crédito Forma de crédito que las tiendas ofrecen a los clientes para que compren productos ahora y los paguen más adelante. (pág. 495)

charter A basic plan of government granted by state legislatures to local governments. (p. 230)
fuero Plan básico de gobierno otorgado por las asambleas legislativas estatales a los gobiernos locales. (pág. 230)

ENGLISH AND SPANISH GLOSSARY

checks and balances A system in which the powers of government are balanced among different branches so that each branch can check, or limit, the power of the other branches. (p. 96)
equilibrio de poderes Sistema mediante el cual el poder de un gobierno está distribuido entre las distintas ramas, de manera que cada rama pueda limitar el poder de las demás. (pág. 96)

child abuse The mental, physical, or sexual mistreatment of a child. (p. 325)
abuso de menores Maltrato mental, físico o sexual de un niño o niña. (pág. 325)

circular-flow model An economic model that displays how households, businesses, and the government interact in the U.S. economy. (p. 558)
modelo de flujo circular Modelo económico que muestra la interacción entre los hogares, los comercios y el gobierno en la economía de Estados Unidos. (pág. 558)

citizen A legal member of a country. (p. 6)
ciudadano Miembro legal de un país. (pág. 6)

city The largest type of municipality. (p. 228)
ciudad El tipo de municipalidad más grande. (pág. 228)

city council The lawmaking body of a city. (p. 235)
concejo municipal Cuerpo de una ciudad que crea leyes. (pág. 235)

civics The study of what it means to be a U.S. citizen. (p. 6)
civismo Estudio de lo que significa ser un ciudadano de Estados Unidos. (pág. 6)

civil law The body of law that governs relationships among individuals and that defines people's legal rights. (p. 181)
derecho civil Grupo de leyes que regulan las relaciones entre los individuos y que definen los derechos legales de las personas. (pág. 181)

civil rights The rights guaranteed to all U.S. citizens. (p. 118)
derechos civiles Derechos garantizados a todos los ciudadanos de Estados Unidos. (pág. 118)

climate The average weather conditions in an area. (p. 362)
clima Condiciones promedio del tiempo en una zona. (pág. 362)

closed primary A primary election in which only voters who are members of the party can vote for the party's candidates. (p. 259)
primarias cerradas Elecciones primarias en las que sólo los votantes que son miembros del partido pueden votar para elegir a sus candidatos. (pág. 259)

cloture A limit on the debate of a bill in the Senate. (p. 150)
límite del debate Restricción sobre el debate de un proyecto de ley en el Senado. (pág. 150)

coalition An agreement between two or more political parties to work together to run a government. (p. 253)
coalición Acuerdo entre dos o más partidos políticos para trabajar juntos en la administración de un gobierno. (pág. 253)

coincident indicators Economic signs that help economists determine how the economy is doing at the present time. (p. 563)
indicadores coincidentes Señales económicas usadas por los economistas para determinar el estado de la economía. (pág. 563)

collateral Property used to guarantee that a loan will be repaid. (p. 512)
collateral Propiedad usada para garantizar el pago de un préstamo. (pág. 512)

collective bargaining A process in which representatives of a labor union and an employer work to reach an agreement about wages and working conditions. (p. 544)
negociación colectiva Proceso por el cual los representantes de un sindicato laboral y un empleador trabajan por llegar a acuerdos en cuanto a los salarios y las condiciones de trabajo. (pág. 544)

commission A local government body that has both legislative and executive powers. (p. 237)
comisión Cuerpo local de gobierno que tiene poderes legislativos y ejecutivos. (pág. 237)

common law Customary law that develops from judges' decisions and is followed in situations not covered by statutory law. (p. 182)
derecho consuetudinario Ley basada en costumbres que se desarrolla a partir de las decisiones de los jueces y que se aplica en situaciones no incluidas en las leyes formales. (pág. 182)

communication The passing along of ideas, information, and beliefs from one person to another. (p. 367)

comunicación Transmisión de ideas, información y creencias de una persona a otra. (pág. 367)

communism An economic system based on the theories of Karl Marx and in which the means of production are owned by government and the government decides what will be produced. (p. 638)

comunismo Sistema económico basado en las teorías de Karl Marx, donde los medios de producción son propiedad del gobierno y el gobierno decide lo que se produce. (pág. 638)

community A group of people who have common interests and live in the same area. (p. 362)

comunidad Un grupo de la gente que tiene intereses comunes y vive en la misma área. (pág. 362)

commutation The act of making a convicted person's sentence less severe. (p. 166)

conmutación Acto de hacer menos severa la sentencia de una persona condenada. (pág. 166)

comparative advantage Method of determining which products or services offer a nation the greatest absolute advantage. (p. 570)

ventaja comparativa Método que permite a una nación determinar qué productos o servicios le ofrecen la mayor ventaja absoluta posible. (pág. 570)

competition The economic rivalry among businesses selling products. (p. 558)

competencia Rivalidad económica entre empresas que venden productos. (pág. 558)

compromise An agreement in which each side gives up part of its demands. (p. 46)

compromiso Acuerdo en el que cada lado cede una parte de sus exigencias. (pág. 46)

compulsory Required by law. (p. 372)

obligatorio Requerido por ley. (pág. 372)

concurrent powers Powers shared by the federal government and the states. (pp. 91, 203)

poderes concurrentes Poderes compartidos por el gobierno federal y los estados. (pág. 91, 203)

concurring opinion A statement written by a Supreme Court justice who agrees with the majority's decision but for different reasons. (p. 190)

opinión concurrente Acuerdo redactado por un juez de la Corte Suprema que concuerda con la decisión mayoritaria, pero con razones diferentes. (pág. 190)

conditioning Learning that is the result of experience involving the motor nerves. (p. 351)

condicionamiento Aprendizaje que resulta de experiencias con los nervios motores. (pág. 351)

confederation A loose association of states. (p. 36)

confederación Asociación flexible de estados. (pág. 36)

constituents People represented by members of a lawmaking body. (p. 211)

electores Personas representadas por los miembros de un cuerpo que crea leyes. (pág. 211)

constitution A written plan of government. (p. 32)

constitución Plan escrito de gobierno. (pág. 32)

constitutional law Law based on the U.S. Constitution and Supreme Court decisions. (p. 183)

derecho constitucional Leyes basadas en la Constitución de Estados Unidos y en las decisiones de la Corte Suprema. (pág. 183)

consul An official who works to promote U.S. commercial interests in a foreign country. (p. 169)

cónsul Representante que promueve los intereses comerciales de Estados Unidos en otro país. (pág. 169)

consulate The office of a consul. (p. 169)

consulado Oficina de un cónsul. (pág. 169)

consumer A person who buys or uses products and services. (pp. 492, 557)

consumidor Persona que compra o usa bienes y servicios. (pág. 492, 557)

containment The U.S. foreign policy of preventing the spread of communism. (p. 639)

contención Política exterior estadounidense de prevenir la expansión del comunismo. (pág. 639)

contraction A period in a business cycle during which the economy is slowing. (p. 535)

contracción Período de un ciclo comercial en el que la economía disminuye su ritmo. (pág. 535)

corollary A statement that follows as a natural or logical result. (p. 634)

corolario Afirmación que sigue como resultado natural o lógico. (pág. 634)

corporation A business organization chartered by a state government and given power to conduct business, sell stock, and receive protection of state laws. (p. 461)

corporación Organización comercial reconocida por el gobierno estatal y autorizada para realizar operaciones comerciales, vender acciones y recibir la protección de las leyes estatales. (pág. 461)

costs of production Business costs, such as wages, payments for raw materials, transportation, rent, and interest on borrowed money. (p. 535)

costos de producción Costos comerciales, como salarios, compra de materias primas, gastos de transporte, alquiler e intereses sobre los préstamos. (pág. 535)

county A subdivision of state government formed to carry out state laws, collect taxes, and supervise elections. (p. 229)

condado Subdivisión del gobierno estatal formada para aplicar leyes estatales, recaudar impuestos y supervisar elecciones. (pág. 229)

courts of appeals Federal courts that review decisions appealed from district courts. (p. 187)

cortes de apelaciones Cortes federales que revisan las decisiones de las cortes del distrito que se han apelado. (pág. 187)

creativity The ability to find new ways of thinking and doing things. (p. 352)

creatividad Habilidad de econtrar nuevas formas de pensar y de hacer las cosas. (pág. 352)

credit cards A form of credit issued by banks and other major lending institutions and accepted by most businesses worldwide. (p. 495)

tarjeta de crédito Forma de crédito emitida por bancos y otras instituciones prestamistas importantes aceptada en la mayor parte de los comercios de todo el mundo. (pág. 495)

creditors People who are owed money. (p. 508)

acreedores Personas a quienes se les debe dinero. (pág. 508)

credit unions Banks that are owned by their members to create a pool of money for low-interest loans. (p. 514)

cooperativas de crédito Bancos que pertenecen a sus miembros creados con el fin de crear un fondo de dinero que les proporcione préstamos con bajo interés. (pág. 514)

crime Any act that breaks the law and for which a punishment has been established. (pp. 181, 382)

delito Cualquier acción que desobedece las leyes y que está sujeta a un castigo establecido. (pág. 181, 382)

criminal A person who commits any type of crime. (p. 382)

delincuente Persona que comete un delito de cualquier tipo. (pág. 382)

criminal justice system The system of police, courts, and corrections used to bring criminals to justice. (p. 388)

sistema penal de justicia Sistema de la policía, las cortes y el sistema penitenciario usado para aplicar justicia a los delincuentes. (pág. 388)

criminal law The body of law that regulates the conduct of individuals as members of the state. (p. 181)

derecho penal Grupo de leyes que regulan la conducta de los individuos como miembros del estado. (pág. 181)

critical thinking A type of thinking one does to reach decisions and solve problems. (p. 352)

razonamiento crítico Tipo de pensamiento que conduce a la toma de decisiones y la resolución de problemas. (pág. 352)

crossroads A location where two roads meet. (p. 364)

encrucijada Punto de encuentro de dos caminos. (pág. 364)

currency Coins and paper money. (p. 504)

moneda Monedas y dinero en papel. (pág. 504)

death rate The annual number of deaths per 1,000 members of a population. (p. 19)

tasa de mortalidad Número de muertes anuales por cada 1,000 habitantes. (pág. 19)

debit card A small card similar to a credit card that operates the way that checks do, deducting money directly from a bank account. (p. 494)

tarjeta de débito Tarjeta pequeña parecida a la tarjeta de crédito que funciona de la misma forma que los cheques, deduciendo dinero directamente de una cuenta de banco. (pág. 494)

deficit The amount by which expenditures exceed income. (p. 307)

déficit Cantidad en la que los gastos superan a los ingresos. (pág. 307)

delayed marriage The tendency to marry at older ages. (p. 320)

matrimonio tardío Tendencia a casarse a una edad mayor. (pág. 320)

delegated powers Powers given to the federal government by the Constitution. (pp. 90, 202)

poderes delegados Poderes otorgados por la Constitución al gobierno federal. (pág. 90, 202)

delinquents Juveniles who break the law. (p. 394)

jóvenes delincuentes Jóvenes que desobedecen la ley. (pág. 394)

democracy A form of government in which the people of a country either rule directly or through elected representatives. (p. 31)

democracia Forma de gobierno en la que los habitantes del país gobiernan directamente o a través de representantes electos. (pág. 31)

demographics The study of the characteristics of human populations. (p. 18)

demografía Estudio de las características de las poblaciones humanas. (pág. 18)

Department of Homeland Security Executive department of the federal government established after the terrorist attacks of September 11, 2001, to protect the United States against future terrorist attacks. (p. 170)

Departamento de Seguridad Nacional Departamento ejecutivo del gobierno federal creado después de los ataques terroristas del 11 de septiembre de 2001 para proteger a Estados Unidos de futuros ataques terroristas. (pág. 170)

depression A sharp decline in a country's business activity, during which many workers lose their jobs and many businesses close down. (p. 535)

depresión Importante reducción de las actividades comerciales de un país, durante la que muchos trabajadores pierden sus empleos y muchos negocios cierran. (pág. 535)

détente A lessening of tensions. (p. 642)

distensión Reducción de tensiones. (pág. 642)

dictator A person who rules with complete and absolute power. (p. 30)

dictador Persona que gobierna con poder total y absoluto. (pág. 30)

diplomacy The art of dealing with foreign governments. (pp. 166, 614)

diplomacia Arte de tratar con gobiernos extranjeros. (pág. 166, 614)

diplomatic corps The ambassadors and other representatives of a nation serving in foreign countries. (p. 611)

cuerpo diplomático Embajadores y otros representantes de una nación que prestan servicio en otros países. (pág. 611)

diplomatic recognition The power of the president to decide whether to establish official relations with a foreign government. (p. 610)

reconocimiento diplomático Poder del presidente para decidir si debe o no establecer relaciones diplomáticas con un país. (pág. 610)

direct democracy A form of government in which all the people meet together at one place to make laws and decide what actions to take. (p. 31)

democracia directa Forma de gobierno en la que los habitantes de un país se reúnen para crear leyes y tomar decisiones sobre lo que van a hacer. (pág. 31)

discounting The practice of deducting interest on a loan before money is given to the borrower. (p. 516)

descontar Práctica de reducir los intereses de un préstamo antes de que el dinero se entregue a la persona que lo toma prestado. (pág. 516)

discount rate The rate of interest charged by Federal Reserve banks on loans to member banks. (p. 515)

tasa de descuento Tasa de interés que cobra la Reserva Federal por los préstamos que otorga a sus bancos afiliados. (pág. 515)

dissenting opinion A statement written by a Supreme Court justice who disagrees with the majority's decision. (p. 191)

opinion disidente Escrito de un juez de la Corte Suprema que está en desacuerdo con la decisión mayoritaria. (pág. 191)

district courts Lower federal courts that have original jurisdiction in most cases involving federal laws. (p. 186)

cortes de distrito Cortes federales inferiores que tienen la primera jurisdicción en la mayoría de los juicios relacionados con las leyes federales. (pág. 186)

dividends Profits paid to corporate stockholders. (p. 463)

dividendos Ganancias que reciben los accionistas de una corporación. (pág. 463)

divorce A legal ending of a marriage. (p. 325)
  divorcio Fin legal de un matrimonio. (pág. 325)

doctrine A statement that sets forth a new government policy with respect to other countries. (p. 634)
  doctrina Declaración que expresa una nueva política del gobierno en relación con otros países. (pág. 634)

dollar diplomacy The practice of sending U.S. troops to other countries to protect U.S. investments. (p. 635)
  diplomacia del dólar Práctica de enviar tropas estadounidenses a otros países para proteger las inversiones de Estados Unidos. (pág. 635)

draft A policy requiring men to serve in the military. (p. 125)
  reclutamiento obligatorio Política que requiere a los hombres que sirvan en las fuerzas militares. (pág. 125)

due process of law The fair application of the law to one's case. (p. 115)
  debido proceso legal Aplicación justa de la ley al caso de uno. (pág. 115)

E

easy-money policy An economic policy that increases the amount of money in the money supply. (p. 568)
  política de dinero fácil Política económica que aumenta la cantidad de dinero circulante. (pág. 568)

elastic clause Article 1, Section 8 of the U.S. Constitution; known also as the "necessary and proper" clause that allows Congress to extend its delegated powers. (p. 144)
  cláusula elástica Artículo 1, Sección 8 de la Constitución de Estados Unidos; también conocida como la cláusula "necesaria y apropiada" que permite al Congreso ampliar sus poderes delegados. (pág. 144)

elector A person elected by the voters in a presidential election to be a member of the electoral college. (p. 263)
  elector Persona elegida por los votantes de las elecciones presidenciales para formar parte del colegio electoral. (pág. 263)

electoral college The group of electors that casts the official votes that elect the president and vice president. (p. 263)
  colegio electoral Grupo de personas que votan oficialmente para elegir al presidente y vicepresidente. (pág. 263)

electoral votes The votes cast by the electoral college for president and vice president. (p. 263)
  votos electorales Votos del colegio electoral en las elecciones del presidente y vicepresidente. (pág. 263)

embargo Measure that bans imports from specific countries. (p. 647)
  embargo Medida que prohíbe la importación de productos de ciertos países. (pág. 647)

embassy The official residence of an ambassador in a foreign country. (p. 169)
  embajada Residencia oficial de un embajador en otro país. (pág. 169)

eminent domain The power of the government to take private property for public use. (p. 115)
  derecho de expropiación Poder del gobierno de tomar el control de la propiedad privada para el uso público. (pág. 115)

entrepreneur A business owner. (p. 468)
  empresario Dueño de un negocio. (pág. 468)

equal opportunity employer An employer who does not discriminate against job applicants because of their sex, age, race, skin color, religion, or ethnic background. (p. 592)
  empleador con igualdad de oportunidades Empleador que no discrimina entre los candidatos a un trabajo por su sexo, edad, raza, color de piel, religión u origen étnico. (pág. 592)

executive agreement A mutual understanding between the president of the United States and the leader of a foreign government. (p. 610)
  acuerdo ejecutivo Acuerdo mutuo entre el presidente de Estados Unidos y el líder de otra nación. (pág. 610)

executive branch The branch of government that carries out the laws. (p. 94)
  poder ejecutivo Rama del gobierno que hace cumplir las leyes. (pág. 94)

expansion A period in a business cycle during which the economy is growing. (p. 534)
  expansion Período de crecimiento económico en un ciclo comercial. (pág. 534)

experience Direct observation or participation in events. (p. 350)
experiencia Observación o participación directa en los sucesos. (pág. 350)

expulsion The removal of a person from an institution, such as Congress, for serious misconduct. (p. 139)
expulsión Despido de una persona de una institución, como el Congreso, por mala conducta. (pág. 139)

extracurricular activities Activities that students participate in outside of the classroom. (p. 348)
actividades extracurriculares Actividades en las que participan los estudiantes fuera del salón de clases. (pág. 348)

extradition A legal process for returning criminals to the place from which they fled. (p. 205)
extradición Proceso legal para regresar a un criminal al lugar de donde huyó. (pág. 205)

F

family law The legal regulation of marriage, divorce, and the duties of parents and children. (p. 323)
ley de familia Reglamentación legal del matrimonio, el divorcio y de las obligaciones de los padres y los hijos. (pág. 323)

federalism A system of government in which the powers of government are divided between the national government, which governs the whole country, and the state governments, which govern the people of each state. (p. 46)
federalismo Sistema de gobierno en el que los poderes del gobierno se dividen entre el gobierno federal, que gobierna a la nación, y los gobiernos estatales, que gobiernan a los habitantes de cada estado. (pág. 46)

Federalists Supporters of the U.S. Constitution who urged its adoption. (p. 47)
federalistas Personas que apoyaban la Constitución de Estados Unidos y pedían su adopción. (pág. 47)

Federal Reserve System The U.S. banking system that handles the banking needs of the federal government and regulates the money supply. (p. 514)
Sistema de la Reserva Federal Sistema bancario estadounidense que administra las necesidades bancarias del gobierno federal y regula el dinero circulante. (pág. 514)

fees Government charges for a service or license. (p. 297)
derechos Cobros del gobierno por un servicio o permiso. (pág. 297)

felonies Serious crimes, such as homicide and kidnapping. (p. 382)
delitos graves Delitos serios como el homicidio y el secuestro. (pág. 382)

filibuster A method of delaying action on a bill in the Senate by making long speeches. (p. 150)
obstruccionismo Método para retrasar las decisiones sobre un proyecto de ley en el Senado presentando discursos largos. (pág. 150)

fine Money paid as a penalty for breaking certain laws. (p. 297)
multa Dinero que una persona paga como castigo cuando desobedece ciertas leyes. (pág. 297)

fiscal policy A government's policy of taxation and spending. (p. 541)
política fiscal Política de gastos y recaudación de impuestos de un gobierno. (pág. 541)

fixed expenses Expenses that occur regularly. (p. 330)
gastos fijos Gastos que ocurren de forma regular. (pág. 330)

foreign aid A government program that provides economic and military assistance to other countries. (p. 616)
ayuda exterior Programa del gobierno que ofrece ayuda económica y militar a otros países. (pág. 616)

foreign policy A country's plan for dealing with other countries of the world. (p. 165)
política exterior Plan de un país para tratar con otros países del mundo. (pág. 165)

foster home A home of people who are unrelated to a child but who agree to act as the child's caregivers. (p. 325)
hogar de acogida Hogar de personas que no son parientes de un niño pero que aceptan actuar como tutores del niño. (pág. 325)

free enterprise Principle that business owners in a free market are allowed to run their businesses in any way they see fit, with little government interference. (p. 455)

libre empresa Principio en el que los dueños de negocios en un mercado libre son libres de dirigir sus negocios como mejor les parezca, con interferencia mínima por parte del gobierno. (pág. 455)

free market An economic system in which buyers and sellers are free to exchange goods and services as they choose. (p. 452)

mercado libre Sistema económico en el que los compradores y los vendedores tienen la libertad de intercambiar los bienes y servicios como prefieran. (pág. 452)

full faith and credit clause The provision in the U.S. Constitution ensuring that each state will accept the decisions of civil courts in other states. (p. 205)

cláusula de plena fe y crédito Disposición de la Constitución de Estados Unidos que establece que cada estado debe respetar las decisiones de las cortes civiles de otros estados. (pág. 205)

General Assembly The body within the United Nations that discusses, debates, and recommends solutions to problems. (p. 623)

Asamblea General Cuerpo de las Naciones Unidas que discute, debate y recomienda soluciones a los problemas. (pág. 623)

general election An election in which the voters elect their leaders. (p. 259)

elecciones generales Elecciones en la que los votantes eligen a sus líderes. (pág. 259)

generic product A product that does not have a manufacturer's name or brand on the package. Generic products are often less expensive than brand-name products. (p. 492)

producto genérico Producto que no tiene el nombre o la marca del fabricante en el paquete o envase. Por lo general, los productos genéricos son menos costosos que los productos de marca. (pág. 492)

gerrymandering The process of drawing congressional district lines to favor a political party. (p. 137)

manipulación de distritos Proceso de demarcar las líneas divisorias de los distritos de manera que favorezcan a un partido político. (pág. 137)

goods Products that are manufactured and that consumers can buy and own. (p. 476)

bienes Productos manufacturados que los consumidores pueden comprar y poseer. (pág. 476)

government Organizations, institutions, and individuals that exercise political authority on behalf of a group of people. (p. 7)

gobierno Organizaciones, instituciones e individuos que ejercen autoridad política a nombre de un grupo de personas. (pág. 7)

governor The chief executive of a state government. (p. 213)

gobernador Jefe ejecutivo de un gobierno estatal. (pág. 213)

grants-in-aid Federal funds given to state and local governments for specific projects. (p. 241)

subsidios Fondos federales otorgados a los gobiernos estatales y locales para desarrollar proyectos específicos. (pág. 241)

gross domestic product (GDP) The value of all goods and services produced in a country each year. (p. 477)

producto interno bruto (PIB) Valor de todos los bienes y servicios producidos en un país cada año. (pág. 477)

guardian A person appointed by a state court to look after an individual who is not an adult or who is unable to care for himself or herself. (p. 325)

tutor Persona asignada por una corte estatal para cuidar a una persona que no es un adulto o que no puede cuidar de sí mismo. (pág. 325)

habit An action performed automatically. (p. 351)

hábito Acción realizada de manera automática. (pág. 351)

home rule The power of a city to write its own municipal charter and to manage its own affairs. (p. 234)

autogobierno Poder de una ciudad para crear su propio fuero municipal y administrar sus propios asuntos. (pág. 234)

human rights The basic rights to which all people are entitled as human beings. (p. 34)
derechos humanos Derechos básicos que les corresponden a todas las personas por ser seres humanos. (pág. 34)

immigrants People who come to a country to settle as permanent residents. (p. 12)
inmigrantes Personas que llegan a un país para quedarse como residentes permanentes. (pág. 12)

immunity Legal protection. (p. 138)
inmunidad Protección legal. (pág. 138)

impeach To charge a government official with misconduct. (p. 144)
acusación política Acusación formal en contra de un funcionario del gobierno. (pág. 144)

implied powers Powers not specifically granted to Congress by the U.S. Constitution that are suggested to be necessary to carry out the powers delegated to Congress under the Constitution. (p. 144)
poderes implícitos Poderes que la Constitución de Estados Unidos no otorga específicamente al Congreso, pero que se sugiere que son necesarios para poder aplicar los poderes delegados al Congreso en la Constitución. (pág. 144)

income tax A tax on the income that individuals and companies earn. (p. 299)
impuesto sobre la renta Impuesto sobre los ingresos que ganan los individuos y las compañías. (pág. 299)

independent agencies Agencies in the executive branch of the federal government formed by Congress to help enforce laws and regulations not covered by the executive departments. (p. 171)
agencias independientes Agencias del poder ejecutivo federal creadas por el Congreso para supervisar la aplicación de las leyes y reglamentos que no se incluyen en los departamentos ejecutivos. (pág. 171)

independent voters Voters who are not members of a political party. (p. 259)
votantes independientes Votantes que no pertenecen a ningún partido político. (pág. 259)

inflation A rise in the costs of goods and services. (p. 535)
inflación Aumento del costo de los bienes y servicios. (pág. 535)

initiative A process by which citizens of a state may propose a law by collecting signatures on a petition. (p. 211)
iniciativa Proceso por el cual los ciudadanos de un estado pueden proponer una ley recopilando firmas para una petición. (pág. 211)

insight A process by which people unconsciously take what they know about a subject and apply it to a problem or question in order to find an answer. (p. 352)
percepción Proceso inconsciente en el que las personas usan lo que saben de un tema y lo aplican a un problema o una pregunta para encontrar una respuesta. (pág. 352)

insurance A system of protection in which people pay small sums periodically to avoid the risk of a large loss. (p. 522)
seguro Sistema de protección en el que se las personas pagan pequeñas cantidades de dinero periódicamente para evitar el riesgo de una gran pérdida. (pág. 522)

interest Payment for the use of loaned money. (p. 295)
interés Pago por el uso del dinero prestado. (pág. 295)

interest groups Organizations of people with common interests who try to influence government policies and decisions. (p. 278)
grupos de interés Organizaciones con intereses comunes que intentan influir en las decisiones y políticas del gobierno. (pág. 278)

International Court of Justice The international legal court of the United Nations, also known as the World Court. (p. 623)
Corte Internacional de Justicia Corte legal internacional de las Naciones Unidas, también conocida como el Tribunal Mundial. (pág. 623)

interpersonal skills Skills involving an individual's ability to interact with others. (p. 599)
destrezas interpersonales Habilidades relacionadas con la capacidad de una persona para relacionarse con los demás. (pág. 599)

ENGLISH AND SPANISH GLOSSARY

isolationism A policy of avoiding involvement in foreign affairs. (p. 632)

aislacionismo Política de evitar la participación en los asuntos exteriores. (pág. 632)

J

job action Any kind of slowdown or action short of a strike. (p. 545)

acción laboral Cualquier tipo de disminución en el ritmo laboral u otra acción que no llega a la huelga. (pág. 545)

Joint Chiefs of Staff The group made up of the highest-ranking officers from the army, navy, and air force that advises the president on military affairs. (p. 169)

Jefes del Estado Mayor Grupo formado por los oficiales de mayor rango del ejército, la armada y la fuerza aérea que aconseja al presidente sobre temas militares. (pág. 169)

judicial branch The branch of government that interprets the laws and punishes lawbreakers. (p. 94)

poder judicial Rama del gobierno que interpreta las leyes y castiga a quienes las desobedecen. (pág. 94)

judicial review The power of the U.S. Supreme Court to determine if a law passed by Congress or a presidential action is in accord with the Constitution. (p. 189)

recurso de inconstitucionalidad Poder de la Corte Suprema de Estados Unidos de determinar si una ley aprobada por el Congreso o una acción presidencial se adapta a la Constitución. (pág. 189)

jurisdiction The authority to interpret and administer the law; also, the range of that authority. (p. 185)

jurisdicción Autoridad para interpretar y aplicar la ley; también, el alcance de esa autoridad. (pág. 185)

jury duty Serving on a jury. (p. 125)

turno de jurado Participación en un jurado. (pág. 125)

justices Judges of the Supreme Court. (p. 188)

magistrados Jueces de la Corte Suprema. (pág. 188)

juvenile In most states, a person under the age of 18. (p. 394)

menor En la mayoría de los estados, una persona menor de 18 años. (pág. 394)

L

labor Human effort used to make goods and services. (p. 467)

mano de obra Esfuerzo humano usado para producir bienes y servicios. (pág. 467)

laborers People who perform unskilled or heavy physical labor. (p. 588)

obreros Personas que realizan tareas no especializadas o que requieren trabajo físico. (pág. 588)

labor unions Organizations of workers formed to bargain for higher wages and improved working conditions and to protect workers' rights. (p. 544)

sindicatos laborales Organizaciones de trabajadores creadas para negociar mejores salarios y condiciones de trabajo y para proteger los derechos de los trabajadores. (pág. 544)

lagging indicators Economic signs that help economists determine how long the current economic situation will last. (p. 563)

indicadores retrasados Señales económicas que permiten a los economistas determinar cuánto durará la situación actual de la economía. (pág. 563)

law of demand An economic rule that states that buyers will demand more products when they can buy them at lower prices and fewer products when they must buy them at higher prices. (p. 453)

ley de la demanda Regla económica que afirma que los consumidores exigirán más productos cuando pueden comprarlos a precios más bajos, y menos productos cuando los precios son más altos. (pág. 453)

law of supply An economic rule that states that businesses will provide more products when they can sell them at higher prices and fewer products when they must sell them at lower prices. (p. 453)

ley de la oferta Regla económica que afirma que las compañías ofrecerán más productos cuando pueden venderlos a precios más altos, y menos productos cuando tengan que venderlos a precios más bajos. (pág. 453)

leading indicators Economic signs that help economists make predictions about future economic growth. (p. 563)

indicadores líderes Señales económicas que ayudan a los economistas a predecir el crecimiento futuro de la economía. (pág. 563)

legislative branch The lawmaking branch of government. (p. 94)

poder legislativo Rama del gobierno que crea leyes. (pág. 94)

lieutenant governor The official who succeeds the governor if the governor dies, resigns, or is removed from office. (p. 215)

lugarteniente del gobernador Persona que reemplaza al gobernador en caso de que éste fallezca, renuncie o sea destituido de su cargo. (pág. 215)

limited government A system in which government powers are carefully spelled out to prevent government from becoming too powerful. (p. 88)

gobierno limitado Sistema en el que los poderes del gobierno están claramente definidos para evitar que el gobierno adquiera demasiada autoridad. (pág. 88)

limited war A war fought without using a country's full power, particularly nuclear weapons. (p. 641)

guerra limitada Guerra que se lucha sin utilizar la máxima capacidad de un país, en especial las armas nucleares. (pág. 641)

lobby An interest group. (p. 278)

lobby Grupo de interés. (pág. 278)

lobbyist A person paid to represent an interest group's viewpoint. (p. 278)

miembro de un lobby Persona que recibe un pago por representar la opinión de un grupo de interés. (pág. 278)

long-term credit An advance of money to be repaid in installments over a long period of time. (p. 507)

crédito a largo plazo Suma de dinero que se obtiene por anticipado y se paga en cuotas parciales durante un período largo de tiempo. (pág. 507)

M

mainstreaming The practice of placing students with special needs in regular schools and classes. (p. 342)

regularizar Práctica de colocar a los estudiantes con necesidades especiales en escuelas y clases regulares. (pág. 342)

majority rule A system in which the decision of more than half the people is accepted by all. (p. 88)

gobierno de mayoría Sistema en el que las decisiones hechas por más de la mitad de la población son aceptadas por todos. (pág. 88)

market economy An economic system in which individuals are free to compete, to earn a living, to earn a profit, and to own property. (p. 452)

economía de mercado Sistema económico en el que los individuos son libres de elegir cualquier oficio o método de obtener ganancias y de poseer propiedades. (pág. 452)

marketing The process of making goods and services available to consumers and convincing them to buy the product or service. (p. 486)

marketing Proceso de lograr que los bienes y servicios estén disponibles para los consumidores y convencerlos de comprar el producto o servicio. (pág. 486)

mass marketing The process of selling goods in large quantities. (p. 486)

marketing masivo Proceso de vender productos en grandes cantidades. (pág. 486)

mass media Forms of communication that transmit information to large numbers of people. (p. 273)

medios de comunicación masiva Formas de comunicación que transmiten información a grandes cantidades de personas. (pág. 273)

mass production The rapid production by machine of large numbers of identical objects. (p. 477)
producción en serie Fabricación rápida de grandes cantidades de objetos idénticos con máquinas. (pág. 477)

mayor The chief executive of a city government. (p. 235)
alcalde Jefe del poder ejecutivo del gobierno de una ciudad. (pág. 235)

mediation A method of settling disputes between labor unions and employers through the use of a third party who offers a nonbinding solution. (p. 547)
mediación Método de resolución de disputas entre sindicatos y empleadores en el que un tercero ofrece una solución no vinculante. (pág. 547)

Medicaid A federal program that helps the states pay the medical costs of low-income people. (p. 526)
Medicaid Programa federal que ayuda a los estados a pagar los gastos médicos de las personas de pocos recursos. (pág. 526)

Medicare A federal program of health insurance for people age 65 and older. (p. 526)
Medicare Programa federal de seguro médico para personas de 65 años o más. (pág. 526)

megalopolis A continuous, giant urban area that includes many cities. (p. 365)
megalópolis Gran zona urbana continua que incluye muchas ciudades. (pág. 365)

migration The movement of people from region to region. (p. 20)
migración Movimiento de personas de una región a otra. (pág. 20)

misdemeanors Less serious crimes, such as traffic violations or disorderly conduct. (p. 382)
delitos menores Faltas menores, como infracciones de tráfico o alteraciones del orden público. (pág. 382)

Missouri Plan A method of selecting state judges in which a state committee prepares a list of qualified candidates, and the governor appoints a judge from this list. (p. 220)
Plan de Missouri Método para la selección de jueces estatales según el cual un comité estatal prepara una lista de candidatos calificados y el gobernador elige de entre ellos a un juez. (pág. 220)

monarch King or queen. (p. 30)
monarca Rey o reina. (pág. 30)

monetary policy A government's policy of regulating the amount of money in the economy. (p. 541)
política monetaria Política del gobierno para regular la cantidad de dinero que hay en su economía. (pág. 541)

money market funds Investments that are similar to a mutual fund but do not guarantee a specified amount of interest and are not insured by the government. (p. 519)
fondos del mercado monetario Inversiones parecidas a los fondos de inversión, pero que no garantizan una cantidad específica de intereses y no están aseguradas por el gobierno. (pág. 519)

monopoly A company that controls all production of a good or service. (p. 456)
monopolio Compañía que controla toda la producción de un bien o servicio. (pág. 456)

motivation An internal drive that stirs people and directs their behavior. (p. 351)
motivación Empuje interno que anima a las personas y guía su conducta. (pág. 351)

motor skills How well people can perform tasks with their hands. (p. 598)
destrezas motoras Capacidad de las personas para realizar tareas con las manos. (pág. 598)

multiparty system A political system in which many political parties play a role in government. (p. 253)
sistema multipartidista Sistema político en el que muchos partidos políticos participan en el gobierno. (pág. 253)

municipality A unit of local government that is incorporated by the state and has a large degree of self-government. (p. 228)
municipalidades Unidades locales de gobierno incorporadas a los estados, pero que cuentan con suficiente autonomía. (pág. 228)

mutual funds Investments that reduce risk to shareholders by investing in many different stocks. (p. 518)
fondos de inversión Inversiones que reducen el riesgo de los accionistas al distribuirse entre muchas acciones distintas. (pág. 518)

national debt The total amount of money owed by the U.S. government plus the interest that must be paid on this borrowed money. (p. 295)
deuda nacional Cantidad total de dinero que debe el gobierno de Estados Unidos, más los intereses que debe pagar por ese dinero presta- do. (pág. 295)

native-born citizen A person who has citizenship based on birth in the United States or its ter- ritories. (p. 15)
ciudadano de nacimiento Persona que tiene la ciudadanía por haber nacido en Estados Unidos. (pág. 15)

naturalization A legal process by which aliens become citizens. (p. 15)
naturalización Proceso legal por el cual los extranjeros se convierten en ciudadanos. (pág. 15)

natural resources Any natural materials that are used by humans, such as water, petroleum, minerals, forests, and animals. (p. 466)
recursos naturales Materiales naturales utiliza- dos por los seres humanos, como agua, petróleo, minerales, bosques y animales. (pág. 466)

neutrality A policy of not favoring one side or the other in a conflict. (p. 635)
neutralidad Política de no favorecer a ninguna de las partes de un conflicto. (pág. 635)

no-fault divorce A divorce in which a couple states the marriage has problems that cannot be resolved but does not assign blame to either party. (p. 325)
divorcio por consentimiento mutuo Divorcio en el cual una pareja declara que el matrimonio tiene problemas que no se pueden resolver pero no culpa a ninguna de las dos partes. (pág. 325)

nominate To select candidates to run for public office. (p. 252)
nominar Seleccionar candidatos para postularse a cargos públicos. (pág. 252)

nonprofit organizations Business organizations that provide goods and services without seeking to earn a profit. (p. 464)
organizaciones sin fines de lucro Instituciones comerciales que ofrecen bienes y servicios sin la intención de obtener ganancias. (pág. 464)

Northern Alliance A rebel group in Afghanistan that opposed the Taliban regime. (p. 648)
Alianza del Norte Grupo rebelde en Afganistán que se opuso al régimen Talibán. (pág. 648)

one-party system A political system in which a single political party controls the government, and all other parties are banned. (p. 253)
sistema unipartidista Sistema político en el que un solo partido político controla el gobierno, y los demás partidos están prohibidos. (pág. 253)

open-market operations The buying and selling of government securities. (p. 568)
operaciones de mercado abierto Compra y venta de bonos del gobierno. (pág. 568)

open primary A primary election in which voters may vote for the candidates of any party. (p. 259)
primarias abiertas Elecciones primarias en las que los votantes pueden votar por los candida- tos de cualquier partido. (pág. 259)

operators People who operate machinery, who inspect, assemble, and pack goods in a factory, or who drive a truck, bus, or automobile. (p. 587)
operarios Personas que operan maquinaria, que inspeccionan, ensamblan y empacan productos en una fábrica, o que manejan un camión, auto- bús o automóvil. (pág. 587)

opinion A written statement by the U.S. Supreme Court explaining its reasoning behind a decision. (p. 190)
opinión Declaración escrita de la Corte Suprema de Estados Unidos en la que se explican las razones en las que basa una decisión. (pág. 190)

opportunity cost The value of an alternative good or service that a company or country has chosen not to produce in order to specialize in something else. (p. 570)
costo de oportunidad Valor de un bien o ser- vicio alternativo que una compañía o país ha decidido no producir para especializarse en otra cosa. (pág. 570)

ordinances Regulations that govern a local govern- mental unit. (p. 230)
ordenanzas Reglamentos que rigen una unidad de gobierno local. (pág. 230)

original jurisdiction The authority of a court to be the first court to hold trials in certain kinds of cases. (p. 186)
jurisdicción de primera instancia Autoridad de una corte para ser la primera corte en ver cierto tipo de casos. (pág. 186)

P

pardon An official act by the president or by a governor forgiving a person convicted of a crime and freeing that person from serving out his or her sentence. (p. 166)
indulto Acción oficial por parte del presidente o de un gobernador en la que se perdona a una persona condenada por un delito, y se libera a esa persona de tener que cumplir el resto de su sentencia. (pág. 166)

Parliament The lawmaking body of British government. (p. 44)
Parlamento Cuerpo del gobierno británico que crea leyes. (pág. 44)

partnership A business organization in which two or more persons share responsibilities, costs, profits, and losses. (p. 461)
sociedades Organizaciones comerciales en las que dos o más personas comparten responsabilidades, costos, ganancias y pérdidas. (pág. 461)

party whip The assistant to the floor leader in each house of Congress who tries to persuade party members to vote for bills the party supports. (p. 142)
portavoz auxiliar Asistente del portavoz de cada cámara del Congreso, que intenta persuadir a los miembros de su partido de votar por los proyectos de ley que el partido apoya. (pág. 142)

passports Formal documents that allow U.S. citizens to travel abroad. (p. 169)
pasaportes Documentos formales que permiten a los ciudadanos estadounidenses viajar a otros países. (pág. 169)

patronage A system in which government jobs are given to people recommended by political party leaders and officeholders. (p. 215)
tráfico de influencias Sistema en el que los empleos del gobierno se otorgan a personas recomendadas por los líderes de los partidos políticos y los cargos públicos. (pág. 215)

peak A high point in a business cycle. (p. 535)
pico Punto alto de un ciclo comercial. (pág. 535)

penal code A set of criminal laws. (p. 217)
código penal Conjunto de leyes penales. (pág. 217)

Pentagon The headquarters of the U.S. military leadership. (p. 647)
Pentágono Cuartel general de los líderes de las fuerzas armadas de Estados Unidos. (pág. 647)

perceptual skills Skills involving an individual's ability to visualize objects in their mind. (p. 598)
destrezas de percepción Habilidades relacionadas con la capacidad de una persona de visualizar objetos en la mente. (pág. 598)

personal values Things that people believe are most important in their lives. (p. 582)
valores personales Las cosas a las que las personas les dan más importancia en su vida. (pág. 582)

picketing Marching in front of one's workplace, often with signs urging others not to work for the company or buy its goods and services. (p. 545)
piquetear Marchar frente al lugar de trabajo de uno, frecuentemente con carteles que piden a los demás que no trabajen para esa compañía ni compren sus bienes y servicios. (pág. 545)

plank A political party's specific proposal for legislation or a statement of a short-term goal regarding a single issue. Planks are the components of a party platform. (p. 264)
punto de programa Propuesta específica de un partido político para la legislación, o declaración de una meta a corto plazo relacionada con un asunto específico. Los puntos de programa son los elementos que forman la plataforma de un partido. (pág. 264)

platform A written statement outlining a political party's views on issues and describing the programs it proposes. (p. 264)
plataforma Declaración escrita en la que se enumeran las opiniones de un partido político sobre distintos temas y se describen los programas que propone. (pág. 264)

plea bargain An agreement between the prosecutor and the defense in which an accused person pleads guilty to a reduced charge. (p. 391)

alegación preacordada Acuerdo entre la acusación y la defensa, en el que el acusado se declara culpable de cargos menores. (pág. 391)

pocket veto A means by which the president can reject a bill, when Congress is not in session, by not signing it. (p. 152)

veto indirecto Manera en que el presidente puede rechazar un proyecto de ley al no firmarlo en un momento en que el Congreso no esté en sesión. (pág. 152)

political action committees (PACs) The political arms of an interest group that collect voluntary contributions from members to fund political candidates and parties the interest group favors. (p. 286)

comités de acción política Brazos políticos de un grupo de interés que reúnen donaciones voluntarias de sus miembros para financiar a los candidatos y partidos politicos que el grupo de interés favorece. (pág. 286)

political party An organization of citizens who have similar views on issues and who work to put their ideas into effect through government action. (p. 252)

partido politico Organización de ciudadanos con puntos de vista similares que trabajan en conjunto para aplicar sus ideas mediante acciones del gobierno. (pág. 252)

political spectrum The differences in political views held by the different political parties. (p. 252)

espectro político Diferencias entre las ideas políticas de los distintos partidos políticos. (p. 252)

poll A survey taken to measure public opinion. (p. 276)

encuesta Sondeo realizado para conocer la opinión pública. (pág. 276)

polling place A place where citizens go to vote. (p. 256)

centro electoral Lugar al que los ciudadanos acuden a votar. (pág. 256)

poll tax A special tax that had to be paid in order to vote. (p. 122)

impuesto electoral Impuesto especial que tenía que pagarse para poder votar. (pág. 122)

popular sovereignty Government by consent of the governed. (p. 87)

soberanía popular Gobierno que actúa con el consentimiento de los gobernados. (pág. 87)

popular vote The votes cast by citizens in a presidential election. (p. 263)

voto popular Votos de los ciudadanos en las elecciones presidenciales. (pág. 263)

Preamble The beginning of the U.S. Constitution, which describes its purposes. (p. 87)

preámbulo Comienzo de la Constitución de Estados Unidos, en el que se describe el propósito de la misma. (pág. 87)

precedent An earlier court decision that guides judges' decisions in later cases. (p. 183)

precedente Decisión previa de una corte que guía las decisiones de los jueces en casos posteriores. (pág. 183)

precincts Local voting districts in a county, city, or ward. (p. 256)

distritos electorales Distritos locales de votación en un condado, ciudad o subdivisión. (pág. 256)

prejudice An opinion not based on careful and reasonable investigation of the facts. (p. 354)

prejuicio Opinión que no se basa en una investigación cuidadosa y razonable de los hechos. (pág. 354)

premium A payment made for insurance protection. (p. 522)

prima Pago realizado para recibir la protección de un seguro. (pág. 522)

presidential succession The order in which the office of president is to be filled if it becomes vacant. (p. 162)

sucesión presidencial Orden en que el puesto de presidente debe ocuparse si se encuentra vacante. (pág. 162)

president pro tempore The official who presides over the Senate in the vice president's absence. (p. 141)

presidente pro tempore Funcionario que preside el senado en ausencia del vicepresidente. (pág. 141)

primary election An election in which the voters of various parties choose candidates to run for office in a general election. (p. 259)

elecciones primarias Elecciones en la que votantes de diferentes partidos eligen a los candidatos que se postularán al cargo en las elecciones generales. (pág. 259)

private insurance Insurance individuals and companies voluntarily pay to cover unexpected losses. (p. 523)
  seguros privados Seguros que los individuos y las compañías pagan voluntariamente para cubrir pérdidas inesperadas. (pág. 523)

probable cause The reason for an arrest, based on the knowledge of a crime and the available evidence. (p. 388)
  causa probable Razón de un arresto, basada en el conocimiento del delito y la evidencia disponible. (pág. 388)

probation A period of time during which a person guilty of an offense does not go to prison but instead must follow certain rules and report to a probation officer. (p. 397)
  libertad condicional Período de tiempo en el que una persona declarada culpable de un delito no es enviada a prisión, sino que debe seguir ciertas reglas y presentarse de manera regular ante un supervisor. (pág. 397)

producer A person or company who provides a good or service that satisfies consumers' needs. (p. 557)
  productor Persona o compañía que proporciona un bien o servicio para satisfacer ciertas necesidades de los consumidores. (pág. 557)

professionals People whose jobs require many years of education and training and who perform mostly mental, rather than physical, work. (p. 586)
  profesionales Personas cuyo trabajo requiere de muchos años de educación y capacitación para realizar un trabajo que es mayormente mental y no físico. (pág. 586)

profit The income a business has left after paying its expenses. (pp. 300, 453, 480)
  ganancias Ingresos de un negocio después de pagar sus gastos. (pág. 300, 453, 480)

progressive tax A tax that takes a larger percentage of income from high-income groups than from low-income groups. (p. 300)
  impuesto progresivo Impuesto calculado en mayor porcentaje para los grupos que ganan más dinero y en menor porcentaje para quienes ganan menos. (pág. 300)

propaganda Ideas used to influence people's thinking or behavior. (p. 273)
  propaganda Ideas usadas para influir en las ideas o en la conducta de las personas. (pág. 273)

property tax A local or state tax collected on real property or personal property. (p. 302)
  impuesto sobre la propiedad Impuesto local o estatal aplicado a las propiedades inmuebles o personales. (pág. 302)

public-interest groups Groups seeking to promote the interests of the general public rather than just one part of it. (p. 279)
  grupos de interés público Grupos que promueven los intereses del público en general y no los de solo una parte. (pág. 279)

public opinion The total of the opinions held concerning a particular issue. (p. 273)
  opinión pública Total de las opiniones sobre un tema específico. (pág. 273)

public utility A legal monopoly that provides essential services to the public. (p. 369)
  servicio público Monopolio legal que ofrece servicios básicos al público. (pág. 369)

Q

qualifications The skills and knowledge possessed by an individual. (p. 582)
  preparación Destrezas y conocimientos de un individuo. (pág. 582)

quota Set number, such as for immigrants who may enter a country in a year. (p. 14)
  cuota Número máximo fijo, como en el caso de los inmigrantes que pueden entrar en un país cada año. (pág. 14)

R

ratification Approval by a formal vote. (p. 47)
  ratificación Aprobación por voto formal. (pág. 47)

rationed Limited by law to a certain amount per household. (p. 125)
  racionado Limitado por ley a una cantidad determinada por familia. (pág. 125)

recall A process by which voters may remove an elected official from office. (p. 211)
  destitución Proceso por el cual los votantes pueden retirar a un funcionario electo de su cargo. (pág. 211)

recession A severe contraction in a business cycle. (p. 535)

recesión Contracción severa de un ciclo comercial. (pág. 535)

recreation Relaxation or amusement. (p. 369)

recreación Relajación o diversión. (pág. 369)

referendum A method of referring a bill to the voters for approval before the bill can become law. (p. 211)

referéndum Método que permite pedir a los votantes su aprobación de un proyecto de ley antes de que sea aprobado. (pág. 211)

regressive tax A tax that takes a larger percentage of income from low-income groups than from high-income groups. (p. 302)

impuesto regresivo Impuesto recaudado en mayor porcentaje de los grupos de menores ingresos y en menor porcentaje de los grupos de mayores ingresos. (pág. 302)

regulatory commissions Independent agencies created by Congress that can make rules concerning certain activities and bring violators to court. (p. 172)

comisiones reguladoras Agencias independientes fundadas por el Congreso para crear leyes relacionadas con actividades específicas y enjuiciar a quienes violan la ley. (pág. 172)

remand To return an appealed case to a lower court for a new trial. (p. 190)

remisión Devolución de una apelación a una corte inferior para iniciar un nuevo juicio. (pág. 190)

remarriage A marriage in which one or both of the partners has been married before. (p. 321)

nuevo matrimonio Matrimonio en el que uno o ambos esposos ha estado casado antes. (pág. 321)

repeal Cancel. (p. 100)

revocar Cancelar. (pág. 100)

representative democracy A form of government in which the people elect representatives to carry on the work of government for them. (p. 31)

democracia representativa Forma de gobierno en la que el pueblo elige a representantes para que lleven a cabo del trabajo del gobierno en su nombre. (pág. 31)

reprieve A postponement in the carrying out of a prison sentence. (p. 166)

conmutación Retraso en el cumplimiento de una sentencia de cárcel. (pág. 166)

republic A form of government in which the people elect representatives to carry on the work of government for them. (p. 31)

república Forma de gobierno en la que el pueblo elige a representantes para que lleven a cabo del trabajo del gobierno en su nombre. (pág. 31)

reserved powers Powers set aside by the U.S. Constitution for the states or for the people. (pp. 91, 202)

poderes reservados Poderes asignados por la Constitución de Estados Unidos a los estados o al pueblo. (pág. 91, 202)

reserve requirement The amount of money that banks must have on hand. (p. 568)

requisito de reserva Cantidad de dinero que los bancos tienen que tener disponible. (pág. 568)

resources The natural features of the land that people may use for living. (p. 362)

recursos Características naturales de la tierra que las personas pueden utilizar para vivir. (pág. 362)

revenue Income. (p. 296)

ingresos Entrada de dinero. (pág. 296)

S

satellite nations Countries that are controlled by other countries. (p. 639)

naciones satélite Países controlados por otros países. (pág. 639)

savings and loan associations Banks originally established to help people buy homes. (p. 513)

sociedades de ahorro y préstamos Bancos creados inicialmente para ayudar a las personas a comprar viviendas. (pág. 513)

scarcity The problem of limited resources. (p. 453)

escasez Problema de recursos limitados. (pág. 453)

secretary An official who heads an executive department in the federal government. (p. 168)

secretario Funcionario que dirige un departamento ejecutivo del gobierno federal. (pág. 168)

secret ballot Method of voting in which a voter marks a ballot in secret. (p. 261)

boleta secretas Método de votación en el que las personas marcan en secreto su boleta. (pág. 261)

Security Council The United Nations body mainly responsible for peacekeeping. It has 15 members, including 5 permanent members (China, France, Great Britain, Russia, and the United States), and 10 temporary members who serve on a rotating basis. (p. 623)

Consejo de Seguridad Organismo de las Naciones Unidas que se ocupa principalmente de mantener la paz. Tiene 15 miembros, 5 de ellos permanentes (China, Francia, Gran Bretaña, Rusia y Estados Unidos), y 10 temporales que participan siguiendo un proceso de rotación. (pág. 623)

self-incrimination Testifying against oneself. (p. 115)

autoincriminarse Testificar en contra de uno mismo. (pág. 115)

separation of church and state The division between religion and government. (p. 112)

separación entre iglesia y estado División entre la religión y el gobierno. (pág. 112)

separation of powers The distribution of political power among the branches of government, giving each branch a particular set of responsibilities. (p. 93)

separación de poderes Distribución del poder político que da a cada poder del gobierno un conjunto particular de responsabilidades. (pág. 93)

service industries Businesses that sell services rather than products. (p. 588)

industrias de servicios Negocios que venden servicios en lugar de productos. (pág. 588)

services Work that does not produce an actual product, but which consumers can buy. (p. 476)

servicios Trabajo que no genera un producto real, pero que los consumidores pueden comprar. (pág. 476)

sessions Meetings of Congress. (p. 140)

sesiones Reuniones del Congreso. (pág. 140)

sheriff The chief law-enforcement official in some county governments. (p. 229)

sheriff Principal agente de la ley de algunos gobiernos de condados. (pág. 229)

short-term credit An advance of money to be repaid within a short period of time. (p. 507)

crédito a corto plazo Anticipo de dinero que debe pagarse en poco tiempo. (pág. 507)

single-parent families Families with only one parent, typically formed through divorce, widowhood, adoption by single people, and births to single women. (p. 321)

familias monoparentales Familias que sólo cuentan con un padre o una madre, por lo general a causa de divorcio, viudez, adopción de madre o padre soltero, o hijos nacidos de madres solteras. (pág. 321)

social insurance Government programs that are meant to protect individuals from future hardship and that individuals and businesses are required to pay for by state and federal laws. (p. 524)

protección social Programas del gobierno creados con el fin de proteger a los individuos de las posibles dificultades en el futuro y que los individuos y negocios tienen obligación de pagar, en cumplimiento de las leyes estatales y federales. (pág. 524)

Social Security A system of government insurance that provides benefits for retired people, people with disabilities, unemployed people, and people with job-related injuries or illnesses. (p. 524)

Seguro Social Sistema de seguro del gobierno que proporciona beneficios a los retirados, discapacitados, desempleados, y a las personas con lesiones o enfermedades producidas en el trabajo. (pág. 524)

sole proprietorships Business organizations owned by one person. (p. 460)

sociedades unipersonales Organizaciones comerciales que pertenecen a una sola persona. (pág. 460)

sovereignty A government's absolute power or authority. (p. 36)

soberanía Poder o autoridad absoluta de un gobierno. (pág. 36)

Speaker of the House The presiding officer of the House of Representatives. (p. 142)

presidente de la Cámara Persona que preside la Cámara de Representantes. (pág. 142)

special district A unit of local government set up to provide a specific service. (p. 233)

distrito especial Unidad de gobierno local creada para proporcionar un servicio específico. (pág. 233)

State of the Union Address A yearly report by the president to Congress describing the nation's condition and recommending programs and policies. (p. 164)

informe del Estado de la Unión Informe presentado cada año por el presidente dirigido al Congreso en el que describe el estado del país y recomienda programas y políticas. (pág. 164)

stock A share of ownership in a corporation. (p. 463)

acción Participación en la propiedad de una corporación. (pág. 463)

stock exchange A market where stocks are bought and sold. (p. 518)

bolsa de valores Mercado en el que se compran y venden acciones. (pág. 518)

stockholders People who own corporate stock. (p. 463)

accionistas Personas que poseen acciones corporativas. (pág. 463)

strike A situation in which workers walk off the job and refuse to work until labor issues are settled. (p. 545)

huelga Situación en la que los trabajadores se van de su trabajo y se niegan a trabajar hasta que se resuelvan temas laborales. (pág. 545)

suffrage The right to vote. (p. 119)

sufragio Derecho al voto. (pág. 119)

summit A meeting among the leaders of two or more nations. (p. 614)

cumbre Reunión entre los líderes de dos o más naciones. (pág. 614)

surplus An amount by which income exceeds expenditures. (p. 307)

excedente Cantidad en la que los ingresos superan a los gastos. (pág. 307)

T

tariff A tax on products imported from other countries. (p. 303)

arancel Impuesto aplicado a los productos importados de otros países. (pág. 303)

tax incentives Special tax breaks for businesses to encourage investment. (p. 567)

incentivos fiscales Reducciones especiales de impuestos para las compañías con el fin de fomentar las inversiones. (pág. 567)

technicians Skilled workers who handle complex instruments or machinery. (p. 586)

técnicos Trabajadores especializados que operan instrumentos o maquinarias complejas. (pág. 586)

terrorists Individuals who use violence against civilians to achieve political goals. (p. 644)

terroristas Individuos que usan la violencia en contra de civiles para lograr objetivos políticos. (pág. 644)

third parties Minor political parties in a two-party system. (p. 254)

terceros partidos Partidos políticos de menor importancia en un sistema bipartidista. (pág. 254)

tight-money policy Economic policy that involves raising interest rates to decrease the amount of money borrowed and reduce inflation. (p. 568)

política de alza de intereses Política económica de aumentar las tasas de interés para reducir la cantidad de dinero prestado y reducir la inflación. (pág. 568)

town A unit of local government, usually larger than a village and smaller than a city. (p. 231)

pueblo Unidad de gobierno local que suele ser más grande que un poblado, pero más pequeña que una ciudad. (pág. 231)

town meeting A form of government in which all citizens meet regularly to discuss town issues. (p. 231)

reunión del pueblo Forma de gobierno en que los ciudadanos se reúnen regularmente para analizar temas del pueblo. (pág. 231)

township A unit of local government that maintains local roads and rural schools within counties. (p. 232)

municipalidades Unidades de gobierno local que dan mantenimiento a las carreteras locales y escuelas rurales del condado. (pág. 232)

trade barrier A government action that limits the exchange of goods. (p. 572)

barrera comercial Acción del gobierno que limita el intercambio de bienes. (pág. 572)

trade deficit Situation in which a nation buys more goods than it sells. (p. 574)

déficit comercial Situación en la que un país compra más bienes de los que vende. (pág. 574)

trade surplus Situation in which a nation buys fewer goods than it sells. (p. 574)
　excedente comercial Situación en la que un país compra menos bienes de los que vende. (pág. 574)

treason An act that betrays and endangers one's country. (p. 145)
　traición Acción que defrauda y pone en peligro al propio país. (pág. 145)

treaties Written agreements between nations. (p. 166)
　tratados Acuerdos escritos entre naciones. (pág. 166)

trough A low point in a business cycle. (p. 535)
　depresión Punto bajo en un ciclo comercial. (pág. 535)

two-income families Families in which both partners work. (p. 321)
　familias de dos ingresos Familias en las que los dos miembros de la pareja trabajan. (pág. 321)

two-party system A political system with two strong political parties. (p. 252)
　sistema bipartidista Sistema político con dos partidos políticos fuertes. (pág. 252)

U

unicameral Consisting of one house, as in a lawmaking body. (p. 207)
　unicameral De una sola cámara, como los cuerpos legisladores. (pág. 207)

union See labor unions
　sindicato Ver sindicatos laborales

United Nations An international organization that promotes peaceful coexistence and global cooperation. (p. 622)
　Naciones Unidas Organización internacional que promueve la coexistencia pacífica y la cooperación global. (pág. 622)

university An institution of higher learning that includes one or more colleges as well as graduate programs. (p. 341)
　universidad Institución de enseñanza superior que incluye uno o más *colleges* y programas de posgrado. (pág. 341)

V

veto A refusal by the president or a governor to sign a bill. (pp. 96, 152)
　veto Negativa de firmar un proyecto de ley por parte del presidente o de un gobernador. (pág. 96, 152)

victimless crimes Crimes in which there is no victim whose rights are invaded by another person. (p. 384)
　delitos sin víctimas Delitos en los que no hay víctimas cuyos derechos hayan sido violados por otra persona. (pág. 384)

visas Documents that allow people from one country to visit another country. (p. 169)
　visas Documentos que permiten a las personas de un país visitar otro país. (pág. 169)

volunteers People who work without pay to help others. (p. 285)
　voluntarios Personas que trabajan sin que se les pague para ayudar a otras. (pág. 285)

W

War on Drugs Organized effort to end the trade and use of illegal drugs. (p. 646)
　Guerra contra las Drogas Esfuerzo organizado para acabar con el comercio y el consumo de drogas. (pág. 646)

white-collar crimes Crimes committed by people in the course of their work. (p. 384)
　delitos de cuello blanco Delitos cometidos por las personas en su trabajo. (pág. 384)

white-collar workers People in a profession or who perform technical, managerial, sales, or administrative support work. (p. 586)
　trabajadores de cuello blanco Profesionales o personas que realizan tareas técnicas, gerenciales, de ventas o administrativas. (pág. 586)

World Trade Center A business complex in New York City that was destroyed by terrorist attack on September 11, 2001. (p. 647)
　World Trade Center Complejo comercial en la ciudad de Nueva York que fue destruido en un ataque terrorista el 11 de septiembre del 2001. (pág. 647)

Index

CDF (Children's Defense Fund), 325
censure, (def.) 139
census, (def.) 17; diversity of population and, 20; migration and, 20; population growth and, 17–19, *g*18; representation and, 136
Census Bureau (U.S.), 18, 284
Center for Civic Education: Law 101: accessible communities, *g*373; Constitution and presidency, *g*165; Constitution Day, *g*149; counterfeiting and consumer protection, *g*573; credit card protection, *g*508; draft, *g*618; drug testing in schools, *g*355; early primaries, *g*260; educating the public, *g*575; Family and Medical Leave Act, *g*331; file sharing and copyright, *g*454; Fourth Amendment and electronic world, *g*52; judges for life, *g*196; laws in foreign countries, *g*656; learning English, *g*20; Miranda warnings, *g*402; Motor Voter Act, *g*279; private property and public use, *g*246; sales tax and the Internet, *g*312; school records, *g*130; schools and the lottery, *g*203; state seat belt laws, *g*90; teens and labor laws, *g*478; teens and minimum wage, *g*539
Center for Civic Education: Students Take Action: assisted living facilities, 375; bullying law, 153; cigarette ads, 23; community health, 98; curfew laws, 387; drug-free zones, 221; educating the public, 575; emergency care, 459; health care, 625; healthy schools, 343; homeless teens, 309; new holiday, 287; new library, 258; park rules, 243; recycling, 163; reforestation, 589; safe exercise, 193; school calendar, 327; school safety, 123; skateboarding park, 647; smoke-free zones, 482; student safety, 49
Center for Security and Arms Control, 610
Central America, 13, 572, 618–19
Central American Free Trade Agreement (CAFTA), 572, 618–19
Central Intelligence Agency (CIA), 611
CEO (Chief Executive Officer), *g*462
certificate of deposit (CD), (def.) 518
CFO (Chief Financial Officer), *g*462
charge account, (def.) 495, 506
charter, (def.) 230
Chase, Salmon P., *p*189
Chavez, Cesar, *g*544–45, *p*545; biography, 546, *p*546
Chechnya, 644
checks, 506, *p*506
checks and balances, (def.) 96; congressional, 612–13; judicial, 97, 166; as principle of limited government, 89, 94, *g*95, 96, *g*96; as strength of the Constitution, *g*46
Cheney, Richard, 162
Chicago, Illinois, 256, 287, *p*287, *g*546–47
Chief Executive Officer (CEO), *g*462
Chief Financial Officer (CFO), *g*462
child abuse, (def.) 325
child labor, *g*478, *p*478, 497, 543, *p*543
Children's Defense Fund (CDF), 325

Chili, 619
China. *See* People's Republic of China
Chinese Exclusion Act of 1882, 14
Chisholm, Shirley, 419
CIA (Central Intelligence Agency), 611
cigarettes, 23, 296, 354, 482
circular-flow model, (def.) 558, *g*559
CIS (Commonwealth of Independent States), 642
citizens, (def.) 6; community involvement, *p*358–59, 371–74, *p*372; diversity of, 11–12; fighting crime, 386, *p*386; government taxing and spending and, 308; participating in government, 283–86; voting and, 10, *g*101, *p*101, 261, *p*268–69. *See also* citizenship; Project Citizen
citizenship, 7–8, *p*11; duties and responsibilities, 9–10, 124–27, *p*126, 282–84, 308; gaining, 14–15, *g*15; laws and, 182, *p*472–73; requirements for, *g*15. *See also* citizens
city, (def.) 228. *See also* communities; local government; metropolitan areas; *names of individual cities*
city council, (def.) 235, *g*236
civics, (def.) 6
Civics Skills: advertisements, 147; bar graphs and pie charts, 621; documentaries, 304; editorials, 238; election maps, 262; fine art, 42; flowcharts, 103; help-wanted ads, 585; Internet research, 22; Internet resources, 167; labels, 490; letter to legislator, 212; library research, 393; line graphs, 542; multimedia presentations, 349; music videos, 569; news articles, 184; oral presentations, 117; photographs, 641; primary sources, 465; public opinion polls, 277; talk radio, 370; television, 322; television news, 510
civil case, 218, *g*218
civil law, (def.) 181, 218, *g*218
civil liberties, *g*90, 192
civil rights, (def.) 118, *g*119, 120, 192, 592
Civil Rights Act of 1964, *g*602, *p*602, R12
Civil War, *g*100, 118, 120, 162
Claghorn, Edward J., *g*90
clear and present danger rule, 112
climate, (def.) 362
Clinton, Bill, *g*145, *p*145, 254, *p*272, *p*611, *g*619, 645
closed primary, (def.) 259
cloture, (def.) 150
coalition, (def.) 253
coast guard (U.S.), *g*240, *p*240
coincident indicators, (def.) 563
coins. *See* currency; money
Cold War, 638–39, *m*640–41
collateral, (def.) 512
collective bargaining, (def.) 544
college, 341; basic skills and, 345; community, 341; earnings and, *g*340; extracurricular activities and, 348; police training and, 388; statistics and polls, 353; university, 341
colonies, American: family in, 318, *p*319; flag of, 413, government of, 235, *g*236, 240; original thirteen, 36,

*g*36, *m*36, *g*43; Second Amendment and, 114, *g*114
Colorado: congressional representation, *m*137, *g*419; facts about, 429
Colorado River basin, 188
Columbus, Christopher, *g*12, 13
command economy, 452, *g*457, *p*457, (def.) 458, 479, 556–57
commander in chief, *p*42, 165, 609
Commerce, Department of, *g*169, *g*416
commercial banks, *g*512, *p*512, 513
commercial treaty, 610
commission, *g*236, (def.) 237
committees: bills in, 150, *g*151, *g*421; structure of, *g*141, 142; political, 256
common law, (def.) 182
Commonwealth of Independent States (CIS), 642
communication, (def.) 367
communism, 452, 610, 616, (def.) 638, 640–41, 647
communities, (def.) 362; Amish, *p*363; citizens and, *p*358–59, 371–74, *p*372; crime prevention and, 386; location of, 362–63; planned, *g*368, *p*368; purposes of, 366–69; river, *g*364, *p*364; rural, 364–65, 369; services, 367; urban, 365; volunteers and, 373–74. *See also* local government
community college, 341
community involvement, 127, 283–84, *p*358–59
commutation, (def.) 166
comparative advantage, (def.) 570
comparison shopping, *g*493, *p*493
competition, *g*452–53, *p*452–53, 455, 481, 535, (def.) 558; foreign, 572, 619
complex, (def.) 352
compound interest, *g*494, *g*519
compromise, (def.) 46
compulsory, (def.) 372
compulsory education, *g*329
computers: careers and, 341, *g*480, 584, 586; foreign trade and, 564, *g*619; Fourth Amendment and, 52; games, 385; industry, 468, 481, 586; as innovation, 481, *g*481; Internet and, 167, 312, *p*312; multimedia presentations and, 349; propaganda and, 273; white-collar crime and, 384. *See also* technology
conclusions, drawing, 580
concurrent powers, (def.) 91, (def.) 203
concurring opinion, (def.) 190
conditioning, *g*351, *g*351
confederate states, 119, 120
confederation, (def.) 36
Conference of Mayors, U.S., 241
conglomerates, 457–58
congressional districts, 137
Congressional Record, 149
congressional representation, 136–37, *m*137
Congress (U.S.), *p*93; about, 418–19; bills in, 148–52, *g*151, *g*421; checks and balances, *g*95, 96, *g*96, 191; committee structure, 142; creation of under U.S. Constitution, 46; electoral college and, 263; establishment of under Articles of Confederation, 36; flag and, 413; foreign policy and,

Credits and Acknowledgments

For permission to reproduce copyrighted material, grateful acknowledgment is made to the following sources:

Austin American-Statesman: From "Concerns about Tasers" from *Austin American-Statesman* Web site, accessed November 7, 2005, at http://www.statesman.com/opinion/content/editorial/stories/10/23tasers_edit.html. Copyright 2001–2005 by Cox Texas Newspapers, L.P. All rights reserved.

Cable News Network LP, LLLP: From "Bush nominates Roberts to Supreme Court" from *CNN* Web site, accessed November 7, 2005, at www.cnn.com/2005/POLITICS/07/19/scotus.main/. Copyright © 2005 by Cable News Network LP, LLLP.

PHOTOGRAPHY CREDITS

Cover: (U.S. Capitol), Joseph Sohm; Visions of America/Corbis; (flag), Royalty Free/Corbis.

Frontmatter: Page iv(t), Paul J.Richards/AFP/Getty Images; iv(b), ©2001 Jay Mallin; v(t), Tony Freeman/PhotoEdit, Inc.; v(c), Chuck Savage/CORBIS; vi(t), Eric Draper/Handout/Reuters/CORBIS; vi(b), James Earle Fraser/CORBIS; vii(t), George Hall/CORBIS; vii(b), Tim Sloan/AFP/Getty Images; viii(t), Ryan McVay/Getty Images; ix(t), Spencer Grant/PhotoEdit, Inc.; ix(c), Jeff Greenberg/PhotoEdit, Inc.; ix(b), David Young Wolff/PhotoEdit, Inc.; x(t), Andresen Ross/Getty Images; x(b), Brand X PicturesAlamy; xi(t), Photo by Staff Sgt. Bill Lisbon/DOD/ZUMA Press. ©Copyright 2004 by US DOD Photo; xi(b), Patrick Olear/PhotoEdit, Inc.; xii(t), Jose Henao/Getty Images; xii(b), Jordon R. Beesley/US Navy/NewsCom; xiv(tr) Courtesy Massachusets Historical Society; xiv(tl), The Granger Collection, New York, xiv(br), Joseph Sohm/Chromosohm Inc./CORBIS, xv, Daryl Cagle, Cagle Cartoons; xvi, Philip James Corwin/CORBIS; xviii, Colin Young-Wolff/PhotoEdit, Inc ; xix, Stephanie Maze/CORBIS, xxx, Brand X Pictures; xxxi, EyeWire.

Unit One: 1, David Pollack/K.J. Historical/CORBIS.

Chapter One: 2–3, Joseph Sohm; ChromoSohm Inc./CORBIS; 6, Joseph Sohm; Visions of America/CORBIS; 7(b), News & Observer, Corey Lowenstein/AP/Wide World Photos; 7(c), Chuck Savage/CORBIS; 7(tr), AP/Wide World Photos; 8, Bettmann/CORBIS; 9, John A. Rizzo/Getty Images; 11(tl), © Ron Sachs/CNP/CORBIS; 11(bc), Chuck Pefley/Stock Boston, LLC; 12(l), National Anthropological Museum Mexico/Dagli

Orti/The Art Archive; 12(r), "The First Landing of Christopher Columbus (1450–1506) in America," 1862 (oil on canvas), Puebla Tolin, Dioscoro Teofilo de la (1832–1901)/ Ayuntamiento de Coruna, Spain/ Bridgeman Art Library; 13(tr), Royalty Free/CORBIS; 13(bl), Col. Ernest Swanson Papers, Swenson Swedish Immigration Research Center, Augustana College, Rock Island, IL; 13(bc), National Archives (NARA); 13(br), Lester Lefkowitz/Getty Images; 15(bl), Paul J. Richards/AFP/Getty Images; 15(tr), Khue Bui/AP/Wide World Photos; 17, Time & Life Pictures/Getty Images; 18, Richard Laird/Getty Images; 20, Spencer Grant/PhotoEdit, Inc.; 23, Dale Newton, Project Citizen teacher.

Chapter Two: 26–27, Chris Minerva/Index Stock Imagery, Inc.; 31, © 2003 Mike Keefe/The Denver Post; 32(t), Courtesy of CNN/ZUMA Press; 32(b), Jeff Klein/ZUMA Press; 35, Archive Photos/Getty Images; 39, the Granger Collection, New York; 42, The Granger Collection, New York; 43, The Granger Collection, New York; 44 (detail), Réunion des Musées Nationaux/Art Resource, NY; 45(ship, tr), Bettmann/CORBIS; 45(br), "White House Historical Association (White House Collection)" (55); 45(l), Joseph Sohm/Chromosohm Inc./CORBIS; 47 (detail), "The Trial of the Seven Bishops in the House of Commons during the Reign of James II," John Rogers Herbert (1810–90)/ Private Collection © Agnew's, London, UK/ Bridgeman Art Library; 48, The Granger Collection, New York; 49, David Lucas/Reuters/CORBIS; 51, The Granger Collection, New York; 52, Masterfile Royalty Free; 53; Randy Santos/SuperStock; 58(l), Dennis Cook/AP/Wide World Photos; 59(l), Mark Wilson/Getty Images; 59(r), Brooks Kraft/CORBIS; 60, Royalty Free/CORBIS; 70(l), Yang Liu/CORBIS; 70(r), Norm Detlaff, Las Cruces Sun-News/AP/Wide World Photos; 71(l), ©Alex Webb/Magnum Photos; 71(c), David Young-Wolff/PhotoEdit, Inc.; 71(r), Bettmann/CORBIS; 75, Library of Congress/PRC Archive; 77, Library of Congress; 79(l), Bettmann/CORBIS; 79(r), Oscar White/CORBIS; 80(tl), Dr. Hector P. Garcia Papers, Special Collections & Archives, Texas A&M University–Corpus Christi, Bell Library; 80(bl), Texas State Library & Archives Commission; 80(tr), ©1978 Matt Herron/TakeStock.

Chapter Three: 82–83, Alex Wong/Getty Images; 86, Bettmann/CORBIS; 88–89, Joseph Sohm; ChromoSohm Inc./CORBIS; 90, Myrleen Ferguson Cate/PhotoEdit, Inc.; 92, H. Armstrong Roberts; 93, Mark Wilson/Getty Images; 96, © 2007 Mike Lane - All Rights Reserved; 98, Courtesy of Debbie Clinebell; 99, Joseph Sohm; ChromoSohm Inc./CORBIS; 100, Library of Congress; 101(tr), David Young-Wolff/PhotoEdit, Inc.; 101(bl), Library of Congress; 101(br), Tony Freeman/PhotoEdit, Inc.; 102; National Gallery of Art, Washington D.C./SuperStock.

Chapter Four: 106–107, Jeff Greenberg/PhotoEdit, Inc.; 111(document), The Granger Collection, New York, 111(pray), Yang Liu/CORBIS; 111(student), Norm Detlaff, Las Cruces Sun-News/AP/Wide World Photos; 111(megaphone), David Young-Wolff/PhotoEdit, Inc.; 111(liberty), Bettmann/CORBIS; 111(Nixon), Bettmann/CORBIS; 112, © 2006 M.E. Cohen - All Rights Reserved; 113, American Media, Inc.; 114(detail), The Granger Collection, New York; 117, Charles Gupton/CORBIS; 118, North Wind Picture Archives; 120, North Wind Picture Archives; 121, Chuck Savage/CORBIS; 123, Courtesy of Martin Leal; 124, Getty Images; 125, Victoria Smith/HRW; 126, Ariel Skelley/CORBIS; 130, Barry Rosenthal/Getty Images.

Unit Two: 131, MPI/Getty Images.

Chapter Five: 132–133, Stephanie Maze/CORBIS; 138, George Danby/Bangor Daily News; 140, © AP Photo/Ron Edmonds; 142, KRT/NewsCom; 143, Paul Conklin/PhotoEdit, Inc.; 144, Lester Lefkowitz/CORBIS; 145(l), David J. & Janice L. Frent Collection/CORBIS; 145(r), Wally McNamee/CORBIS; 147, Fisher/Thatcher/Getty Images; 149, Evan Vucci/AP/Wide World Photos; 153, Syracuse Newspapers/David Lassman/The Image Works; 155, Fisher/Thatcher/Getty Images.

Chapter Six: 156–157, © Michael Reynolds/epa/CORBIS; 160, © Joe Raedle/Getty Images; 161, © AP Photo/Frank Augstein; 162, The Granger Collection, New York; 163, Erin Stevens/Quabbin Regional Middle School, Barre, MA; 165, Courtesy Everett Collection; 167, HRW; 171, AFP/CORBIS; 172, Steve Brenn/Copley News Service/NewsCom.

Chapter Seven: 176–177, James Earle Fraser/CORBIS; 180, Tracy Woodward-Pool/Getty Images; 182, Michael Kelley/Getty Images; 185, Spencer Platt/Getty Images; 189, Courtesy of the Library of Congress; 190, The Granger Collection,

New York; 191(l), National Archives; 191(r), Bettmann/CORBIS; 192, © Robert Trippett/Pool/CNP/CORBIS; 193, David Stoecklein/CORBIS; 196, Paul J. Richards/AFP/Getty Images/ News Com.

Unit Three: 197, K.J. Historical/CORBIS.

Chapter Eight: 198–199, Bob Pardue/ Alamy; 203, Justin Sullivan/Getty Images; 206, Jim Winkley/Ecoscene/ CORBIS; 207, Rich Pedroncelli/ AP/World Wide Photos; 208, SARGENT © 1997 Austin American-Statesman. Reprinted with permission of UNIVERSAL PRESS SYNDICATE. All rights reserved; 210, David McNew/Getty Images; 213, Charlie Riedel/AP/Wide World Photos; 214, Pat Crowe II/AP/Wide World Photos; 215, Suzi Altman/ZUMA Press; 217, Steve Hamblin/Alamy; 218, © Jose Luis Pelaez, Inc./CORBIS; 219, Jana Birchum/ Getty Images; 221, Joe Sohm/The Image Works.

Chapter Nine: 224–225, George Hall/ CORBIS; 226, © Etta Hulme, Fort Worth Star-Telegram; 227, Bruce Beattie, © 2001 Daytona Beach News-Journal, Copley News Service; 229, CLOSE TO HOME © 1998 John McPherson. Reprinted with permission of UNIVERSAL PRESS SYNDICATE. All rights reserved; 230, Robyn Beck/ AFP/Getty Images; 231, © Kevin Fleming/CORBIS; 234(t), James Marshall/CORBIS; 234(b), Alan Schein/ zefa/CORBIS; 235(t), Jeff Greenberg/ The Image Works; 235(b), Mitch Wojnarowicz/The Image Works; 236(l), The Granger Collection, New York; 236(cl), Craig Warga-Pool/Getty Images; 236(cr), Underwood & Underwood/ CORBIS; 236(r), Royalty Free/CORBIS; 239, Ed Quinn/CORBIS; 240(t), Chang W. Lee/The New York Times; 240(c), Bob Daemmrich/The Image Works; 240(b), David J. Phillip/AP/Wide World Photos; 241, Bill Greenblatt/Liaison/ Getty Images; 243, Clayton Sharrard/ PhotoEdit, Inc.; 246, Spencer Platt/ Getty Images.

Unit Four: 247, The Granger Collection, New York.

Chapter Ten: 248–249, Ramin Talaie/ CORBIS; 253(tl), Bettmann/CORBIS; 253(tr), Michael Smith/Getty Images; 253(bl), William Coupon/CORBIS; 253(br), Catherine Karnow/CORBIS; 255, Lou Dematteis/Reuters/CORBIS; 256, Lionel Hahn/KRT/Newscom; 258, Tony Freeman/PhotoEdit, Inc.; 260, Spencer Platt/Getty Images; 264, INF Star Max, Inc./NewsCom; 265, Paul Schutzer/Time Life Pictures/Getty Images.

Chapter Eleven: 268–269, Photo courtesy of Rock the Vote Education Fund; 272, Peter Turnley/CORBIS; 274(l), Hyungwon Kang/Reuters/ CORBIS; 274(c), Marc Serota/Reuters/ CORBIS; 274(r), David J. & Janice L. Frent/CORBIS; 275(l), Luke Frazza/AFP/ Getty Images; 275(c), Paul Sakuma/ AP/Wide World Photos; 275(r), Henry Ray Abrams/AFP/Getty Images; 278, Manny Ceneta/AFP/Getty Images; 279, Novastock/PhotoEdit, Inc.; 281, Simone McCourtie/The World Bank; 282, Fred Prouser/Reuters/CORBIS; 283(l), Courtesy of Commissioner Michele A. McFall-Conte; 283(c), Courtesy the Office of Governor Christine Gregoire; 283(r), Courtesy National Archives, photo no. (194255); 285, Photographers Showcase/ NewsCom; 287, Photo courtesy of Cindy Vines.

Chapter Twelve: 290–291, Jeff Greenberg/Index Stock; 294, AP/ Wide World Photos; 295, Kevin Lamarque/Reuters/CORBIS; 296(tl), Andy Manis/AP/Wide World Photos; 296(br), The Granger Collection, New York; 298(l), Wes Thompson/CORBIS; 298(r), Sam Dudgeon, Courtesy Austin American-Statesman; 299, Tim Boyle/Newsmakers/Getty Images; 300, LUCKY COW © 2003 Mark Pett Dist. By UNIVERSAL PRESS SYNDICATE. Reprinted with permission. All rights reserved; 302(l), Martyn Goddard/Getty Images; 302(c), Tina Fineberg/AP/Wide World Photos; 302(r), Joe Devenney/Alamy; 303(l), AP/Wide World Photos; 303(r), Kevin Fleming/CORBIS; 305, Colin Braley/ Reuters/CORBIS; 306, Stock Montage/ Getty Images; 308, Bureau of the Public Debt/United States Department of the Treasury; 309, Rachel Epstein/ PhotoEdit, Inc.; 312, Colin Young-Wolff/PhotoEdit, Inc.

Unit Five: 313, James Montgomery Flagg/CORBIS.

Chapter Thirteen: 314–315, Skjold Photographs/PhotoEdit, Inc.; 319(t), The Granger Collection, New York; 319(c); Lewis Wickes Hine/CORBIS; 319(b), Banana Stock/Fotosearch; 320(tl), Courtesy Everett Collection; 320(tr), © AP Photo/Amanda Parks; 320(bl), Jacques M. Chenet/CORBIS; 323, Ryan McVay/Getty Images; 324, Randy Faris/CORBIS; 325; Bob Burgess/ AP/Wide World Photos; 327, Courtesy of Pam Collins, Goldenview Middle School; 328, Ronnie Kaufman/CORBIS; 329; Robin Sachs/PhotoEdit, Inc.; 331, Barros & Barros/Getty Images.

Chapter Fourteen: 334–335, Michael Newman/PhotoEdit, Inc.; 338, China Photos/Getty Images; 339, Bob Daemmrich/The Image Works; 341, AP/ Wide World Photos; 343, Burke/ Triolo Productions/FoodPix/ JupiterImages; 344, Dana White/ PhotoEdit, Inc.; 346(tl), Charles Gupton/CORBIS; 346(tr), Randy Faris/CORBIS; 346(bc), E. Klawitter/ zefa/CORBIS; 346(others), Royalty Free/CORBIS; 347(tl), Tom McCarthy/ PhotoEdit, Inc.; 347(tc), Steve Prezant/ CORBIS; 347(tr), Michael Newman/ PhotoEdit, Inc.; 347(bl, bc), Royalty Free/CORBIS; 347(br), Richard Gross/ CORBIS; 349, Michael Newman/ PhotoEdit, Inc; 350, Richard Hutchings/ PhotoEdit, Inc.; 351, © 2005 Joe Dator from cartoonbank.com. All Rights Reserved; 352, Bettmann/ CORBIS; 355, Dennis MacDonald/ PhotoEdit, Inc.

Chapter Fifteen: 358–359, Jim West/ The Image Works; 362, Patrick Molnar/ Getty Images; 363(l), Ian Adams; 363(r), Bob Krist/CORBIS; 364(l), Library of Congress; 364(r), Annie Griffiths Belt/CORBIS; 366, Jeff Greenberg/PhotoEdit, Inc.; 367, Photograph by Madden Photography, courtesy of Sandy Shepherd; 371, Mary Steinbache/PhotoEdit, Inc.; 372(meals), Michael Newman/PhotoEdit, Inc.; 372(read), Eastcott-Momatiuk/The Image Works; 372(walk), James Shaffer/PhotoEdit, Inc.; 372(trash), Jeff Greenberg/PhotoEdit, Inc.; 372(carwash), Yellow Dog Productions/ Getty Images; 373, Michael Newman/ PhotoEdit, Inc.; 375, Courtesy of Jackie Viana/Hialeah Middle School.

Chapter Sixteen: 378–379, Spencer Grant/Photo Researchers, Inc..; 383, David De Lossy/Photodisc Green/ Getty Images; 385, White House/AP/ Wide World Photos; 386, Michael Newman/PhotoEdit, Inc.; 387, Jeff Greenberg/Alamy; 389(l), Philadelphia Daily News/Jim MacMillan/The Image Works; 389(c), Thinkstock/Getty Images; 389(r), Bob Daemmrich/The Image Works; 390(t), Zigy Kaluzny/ Getty Images; 390(c), Art Lien/AFP/ Getty Images; 390(b), A. Ramey/ PhotoEdit, Inc.; 391, Daryl Cagle, Cagle Cartoons; 394, Jay Nubile/The Image Works; 395, Christopher Ruppel/ Getty Images; 397, Alex Wong/Getty Images; 398, Richard Hutchings/ PhotoEdit, Inc.; 402, Paul Conklin/ PhotoEdit, Inc.

Criminal Justice System Handbook: Page 402a, ©2009 Radius Images/Jupiter Images; 402b-410 (border-patches), © David Frazier/CORBIS; (border-Sup Ct.), © Alan Schein/zefa/CORBIS; (border-badge), © Marv Lyons/CORBIS.

Unit Six: 445, Courtesy National Archives, photo no. (534244),